PEARSON CUSTOM
ANTHROPOLOGY

ANTH 100: Introduction to Anthropology
Anthropology 13/e by Ember, Ember and Peregrine
Purdue University Edition - Dr. Richard Blanton

Managing Editor
Jeffrey H. Cohen
Ohio State University

Associate Editor
Douglas E. Crews
Ohio State University

Contributing Editors–Cultural Anthropology
Randal Allison
Blinn College

Lee Cronk
Rutgers (New Brunswick)

Donald C. Wood
Akita University Medical School

Contributing Editors–Biological/Physical Anthropology
Susan Kirkpatrick-Smith
Kennesaw State University

James Stewart
Columbus State Community College

PEARSON

Senior Vice President, Editorial: Patrick F. Boles
Editor: Ana Díaz-Caneja
Development Editor: Megan Tully
Operations Manager: Eric M. Kenney
Production Manager: Jennifer Berry
Rights Manager: Michael E. Mushlitz
Art Director: Renée Sartell
Cover Designer: Kristen Kiley

Cover Art: Art Wolfe, "Karo Tribesman and Child" Courtesy of Corbis Photography/Veer Incorporated. "Tattooed Man Holding Baby" Courtesy of Art Wolfe/Veer Incorporated. "Cheering Fans" Courtesy of Corbis Photography/ Veer Incorporated. "Alaska Native Eskimo Woman in Fur Parka" Courtesy of Canopy Photography/Veer Incorporated. "Portrait of an Asian woman holding up the palm of her hand which has henna patterns on it." Courtesy of Alloy Photography/Veer Incorporated. J. Rufenach, "Close up of man's face with lip ring" Courtesy of J. Rufenach/Veer Incorporated. Malcolm S. Kirk, "Mendi woman, New Guinea" Courtesy of Malcolm S. Kirk/Veer Incorporated. Grant Faint, "Karo tribe woman, portrait, close up" Courtesy of Grant Faint/Getty Images, Inc. Evolution of Man, Courtesy of James W. Porter/Corbis. Doctor treating boy in Ghana, Courtesy of Mika/Corbis. Tunichil Muknai, Belize (photo of skull), courtesy of Steven Alvarez/Getty Images. Girl with chimpanzee, portrait, Courtesy of Megan Lorenz/Getty Images.

Printed in the United States of America.

Please visit our website at *www.pearsonlearningsolutions.com.*

Attention Bookstores: For permission to return any unsold stock, contact *us at pe-uscustomreturns@pearson.com.*

Pearson Learning Solutions, 501 Boylston Street, Suite 900, Boston, MA 02116
A Pearson Education Company
www.pearsoned.com

ISBN 10: 1-256-55833-8
ISBN 13: 978-1-256-55833-0

Table of Contents

What Is Anthropology?

What Is Anthropology?

nthropology, by definition, is a discipline of infinite curiosity about human beings. The term comes from the Greek *anthropos* for "man, human" and *logos* for "study." Anthropologists seek answers to an enormous variety of questions about humans. They are interested in both universals and differences in human populations. They want to discover when, where, and why humans appeared on the earth, how and why they have changed since then, and how and why modern human populations vary in their biological and cultural features. Anthropology has a practical side too. Applied and practicing anthropologists put anthropological methods, information, and results to use, in efforts to solve practical problems.

Defining anthropology as the study of human beings is not complete, however, for such a definition would appear to incorporate a whole catalog of disciplines: sociology, psychology, political science, economics, history, human biology, and perhaps even the humanistic disciplines of philosophy and literature. Needless to say, practitioners of the many other disciplines concerned with humans would not be happy to be regarded as being in subbranches of anthropology. After all, most of those disciplines have existed longer than anthropology, and each is somewhat distinctive. There must, then, be something unique about anthropology—a reason for its having developed as a separate discipline and for its having retained a separate identity over the last 100 years.

● ○ ●

THE SCOPE OF ANTHROPOLOGY

Anthropologists are generally thought of as individuals who travel to little-known corners of the world to study exotic peoples or who dig deep into the earth to uncover the fossil remains or the tools and pots of people who lived long ago. These views, though clearly stereotyped, do indicate how anthropology differs from other disciplines concerned with humans. Anthropology is broader in scope, both geographically and historically. Anthropology is concerned explicitly and directly with all varieties of people throughout the world, not just those close at hand or within a limited area. Anthropologists are also interested in people of all periods. Beginning with the immediate ancestors of humans, who lived a few million years ago, anthropology traces the development of humans until the present. Every part of the world that has ever contained a human population is of interest to anthropologists.

Anthropologists have not always been as global and comprehensive in their concerns as they are today. Traditionally, they concentrated on non-Western cultures and left the study of Western civilization and similarly complex societies, with their recorded histories, to other disciplines. In recent years, however, this division of labor among the disciplines has begun to disappear. Now anthropologists work in their own and other complex societies.

What induces anthropologists to choose so broad a subject for study? In part, they are motivated by the belief that any suggested generalization about human beings, any possible explanation of some characteristic of human culture or biology, should be shown to apply to many times and places of human existence. If a generalization or explanation does not prove to apply widely, anthropologists are entitled or even obliged to be skeptical about it.

The skeptical attitude, in the absence of persuasive evidence, is our best protection against accepting invalid ideas about humans.

For example, when American educators discovered in the 1960s that African American schoolchildren rarely drank milk, they assumed that lack of money or education was the cause. But evidence from anthropology suggested a different explanation. Anthropologists had known for years that people do not drink fresh milk in many parts of the world where milking animals are kept; rather, they sour it before they drink it, or they make it into cheese. Why they do so is now clear. Many people lack the enzyme lactase that is necessary for breaking down lactose, the sugar in milk. When such people drink regular milk, it actually interferes with digestion. Not only is the lactose in milk not digested, but other nutrients are less likely to be digested as well; in many cases, drinking milk will cause cramps, stomach gas, diarrhea, and nausea. Studies indicate that milk intolerance is found in many parts of the world.[1] The condition is common in adulthood among Asians, southern Europeans, Arabs and Jews, West Africans, Inuit (Eskimos), and North and South American native peoples, as well as African Americans. Because anthropologists are acquainted with human life in an enormous variety of geographic and historical settings, they are often able to correct mistaken beliefs about different groups of people.

THE HOLISTIC APPROACH

In addition to the worldwide as well as historical scope of anthropology, another distinguishing feature of the discipline is its **holistic,** or multifaceted, approach to the study of human beings. Anthropologists study not only all varieties of people but many aspects of human experience as well. For example, when describing a group of people, an anthropologist might discuss the history of the area in which the people live, the physical environment, the organization of family life, the general features of their language, the group's settlement patterns, political and economic systems, religion, and styles of art and dress. The goal is not just to understand these aspects separately, but to understand the connections between different aspects of physical and social life.

In the past, individual anthropologists tried to cover as many subjects as possible. Today, as in many other disciplines, so much information has been accumulated that anthropologists tend to specialize in one topic or area. Thus, one anthropologist may investigate the physical characteristics of some of our prehistoric ancestors. Another may study the biological effect of the environment on a human population over time. Still another will concentrate on many customs of a particular group of people. Despite this specialization, however, the discipline of anthropology retains its holistic orientation in that its many different specialties, taken together, describe many aspects of human existence, both past and present.

THE ANTHROPOLOGICAL CURIOSITY

Thus far, we have described anthropology as being broader in scope, both historically and geographically, and more holistic in approach than other disciplines concerned with human beings. But this statement again implies that anthropology is the all-inclusive human science. How, then, is anthropology really different from the other disciplines? We suggest that anthropology's distinctiveness lies principally in the kind of curiosity it arouses.

In studying a human population, anthropologists tend to focus on *typical* characteristics (traits, customs) of that population: People in many societies depend on agriculture. Why? And where and when did people first start to farm? Why do some populations have lighter skin than others? Why do some languages contain more terms for color than others? Why do some societies have more political participation than others? Individuals may provide information to anthropologists, but the anthropological curiosity mostly focuses on the typical characteristics of human groups and how to understand and explain them. For example, whereas economists take a monetary system for granted and study how it operates, anthropologists would ask how frequently monetary systems are found, why they vary, and why only some societies during the last few thousand years used money. This is not to imply that anthropologists are not interested in variation within human groups. In understanding a political system, anthropologists might want to know why certain people tend to be leaders, or why rural communities operate differently than urban ones. Or, variation in a physical trait might be related to susceptibility to a particular disease. Rather, a focus on typical characteristics of human groups—how and why populations and their characteristics have varied around the globe and throughout the ages—is what mainly distinguishes anthropology from other disciplines.

FIELDS OF ANTHROPOLOGY

Different anthropologists concentrate on different characteristics of societies. Some are concerned primarily with *biological* or *physical characteristics* of human populations; others are interested principally in what we call *cultural characteristics.* Hence, there are two broad classifications of subject matter in anthropology: **biological (physical) anthropology** and **cultural anthropology.** Biological anthropology is one major field of anthropology. Cultural anthropology is divided into three major subfields—archaeology, linguistics, and ethnology. Ethnology, the study of recent cultures, is now usually referred to by the parent name, cultural anthropology (see Figure 1). Crosscutting these four fields is a fifth, **applied** or **practicing anthropology.**

Biological Anthropology

Biological (physical) anthropology seeks to answer two distinct sets of questions. The first set includes questions

FIGURE 1 The Subdivisions of Anthropology
The four major subdisciplines of anthropology (in bold letters) may be classified according to subject matter (biological or cultural) and according to the period with which each is concerned (distant past versus recent past and present). There are applications of anthropology in all four subdisciplines.

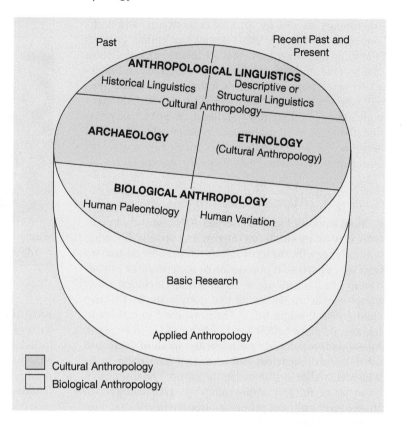

about the emergence of humans and their later evolution (this focus is called **human paleontology** or **paleoanthropology**). The second set includes questions about how and why contemporary human populations vary biologically (this focus is called **human variation**).

To reconstruct human evolution, human paleontologists search for and study the buried, hardened remains or impressions—known as **fossils**—of humans, prehumans, and related animals. Paleontologists working in East Africa, for instance, have excavated the fossil remains of humanlike beings that lived more than 4 million years ago. These findings have suggested the approximate dates when our ancestors began to develop two-legged walking, very flexible hands, and a larger brain.

In attempting to clarify evolutionary relationships, human paleontologists may use not only the fossil record but also geological information on the succession of climates, environments, and plant and animal populations. Moreover, when reconstructing the past of humans, paleontologists are also interested in the behavior and evolution of our closest relatives among the mammals—the prosimians, monkeys, and apes, which, like ourselves, are members of the order of **Primates.** Anthropologists, psychologists, and biologists who specialize in the study of primates are called **primatologists.** The various species of primates are observed in the wild and in the laboratory. One especially popular subject of study is the chimpanzee, which bears a close resemblance to humans in behavior and physical appearance, has a similar blood chemistry, and is susceptible to many of the same diseases. It now appears that chimpanzees share 99 percent of their genes with humans.[2]

Birute Galdikas works with two orangutans in Borneo.

From primate studies, biological anthropologists try to discover characteristics that are distinctly human, as opposed to those that might be part of the primate heritage. With this information, they may be able to infer what our prehistoric ancestors were like. The inferences from primate studies are checked against the fossil record. The evidence from the earth, collected in bits and pieces, is correlated with scientific observations of our closest living relatives. In short, biological anthropologists piece together bits of information obtained from different sources. They construct theories that explain the changes observed in the fossil record and then attempt to evaluate their theories by checking one kind of evidence against another. Human paleontology thus overlaps disciplines such as geology, general vertebrate (and particularly primate) paleontology, comparative anatomy, and the study of comparative primate behavior.

The second major focus of biological anthropology, the study of human variation, investigates how and why contemporary human populations differ in biological or physical characteristics. All living people belong to one species, **Homo sapiens,** for all can successfully interbreed. Yet, much varies among human populations. Investigators of human variation ask such questions as: Why are some peoples taller than others? How have human populations adapted physically to their environmental conditions? Are some peoples, such as Inuit (Eskimos), better equipped than other peoples to endure cold? Does darker skin pigmentation offer special protection against the tropical sun?

To understand better the biological variations observable among contemporary human populations, biological

5

anthropologists use the principles, concepts, and techniques of at least three other disciplines: human genetics (the study of human traits that are inherited), population biology (the study of environmental effects on, and interaction with, population characteristics), and epidemiology (the study of how and why diseases affect different populations in different ways). Research on human variation, therefore, overlaps research in other fields. Biological anthropologists, however, are concerned most with human populations and how they vary biologically.

Cultural Anthropology

Cultural anthropology is concerned with how and why cultures vary or are similar in the past and present. But what is culture? Briefly, the term *culture* refers to the customary ways that a particular population or society thinks and behaves. The culture of a social group includes many things—from the language that people speak, the way children are brought up, the roles assigned to males and females, religious beliefs and practices, and preferences in music. Anthropologists are interested in all of these and other learned behaviors and ideas that have come to be widely shared or customary in the group. The three main branches of cultural anthropology are **archaeology** (the study of past cultures, primarily through their material remains), **anthropological linguistics** (the anthropological study of languages), and **ethnology** (the study of existing and recent cultures), now usually referred to by the parent name, *cultural anthropology*.

Archaeology Archaeologists seek not only to reconstruct the daily life and customs of peoples who lived in the past but also to trace cultural changes and to offer possible explanations for those changes. This concern is similar to that of historians, but archaeologists reach much farther back in time. Historians deal only with societies that left written records and are therefore limited to the last 5,000 years of human history. Human societies, however, have existed for more than a million years, and only a small proportion in the last 5,000 years had writing. For all those past societies lacking a written record, archaeologists serve as historians. Lacking written records for study, archaeologists must try to reconstruct history from the remains of human cultures. Some of these remains are as grand as the Mayan temples discovered at Chichén Itzá in Yucatán, Mexico. More often, they are as ordinary as bits of broken pottery, stone tools, and garbage heaps.

Most archaeologists deal with **prehistory,** the time before written records. But a specialty within archaeology, called **historical archaeology,** studies the remains of recent peoples who left written records. This specialty, as its name implies, employs the methods of both archaeologists and historians to study recent societies for which there is both archaeological and historical information.

In trying to understand how and why ways of life have changed through time in different parts of the world, archaeologists collect materials from sites of human

In urban areas before new construction begins, archaeologists may be called upon to excavate and record information on historical sites, as here in New York City.

Robert Brenner/PhotoEdit Inc.

occupation. Usually, these sites must be unearthed. On the basis of materials they have excavated and otherwise collected, they then ask various questions: Where, when, and why did the distinctive human characteristic of toolmaking first emerge? Where, when, and why did agriculture first develop? Where, when, and why did people first begin to live in cities?

To collect the data they need to suggest answers to these and other questions, archaeologists use techniques and findings borrowed from other disciplines, as well as what they can infer from anthropological studies of recent and contemporary cultures. For example, to guess where to dig for evidence of early toolmaking, archaeologists rely on geology to tell them where sites of early human occupation are likely to be found, because of erosion and uplifting, near the surface of the earth. To infer when agriculture first developed, archaeologists date the relevant excavated materials by a process originally developed by chemical scientists. To try to understand why cities first emerged, archaeologists may use information from historians, geographers, and others about how recent and contemporary cities are related economically and politically to their hinterlands. If we can discover what recent and contemporary cities have in common, we can speculate on why cities developed originally. Thus, archaeologists use information from the present and recent past in trying to understand the distant past.

Anthropological Linguistics Anthropological linguistics is another branch of cultural anthropology. Linguistics, or the study of languages, is a somewhat older discipline than anthropology, but the early linguists concentrated on the study of languages that had been written for a long time—languages such as English that had been written for nearly a thousand years. Anthropological linguists began to do fieldwork in places where the language was not yet written. This meant that anthropologists could not consult a dictionary or grammar to help them learn the language. Instead, they first had to construct a dictionary and grammar. Then they could study the structure and history of the language.

new perspectives on gender

Researcher at Work: Elizabeth M. Brumfiel

Now a professor of anthropology at Northwestern University, Elizabeth M. Brumfiel became interested in the origins of social inequality when she was an undergraduate. Archaeologists had known for some time that substantial wealth differences between families developed only recently (archaeologically speaking), that is, only after about 6,000 years ago. The archaeological indicators of inequality are fairly clear—elaborate burials with valuable goods for some families and large differences in houses and possessions. However, why the transformation occurred was not so clear. When she was in graduate school at the University of Michigan, Brumfiel says, she didn't accept the then-current explanation that inequality provided benefits to the society (e.g., the standard of living of most people improved as the leaders got richer). Consequently, for her PhD research in central Mexico, she began to test the "benefit" explanation in an area that had been independent politically at first and then became part of the Aztec Empire. She studied the surface material remains in the area and historical documents written by Europeans and Aztec nobility. Her findings contradicted the benefit explanation of social inequality; she found little improvement in the standard of living of the local people after the Aztec Empire had absorbed them.

Another important part of her research agenda was understanding the lives of women. How were they affected by the expansion of the Aztec Empire? Did their work change? How were women portrayed in art? In the Aztec capital of

Dona Maria (right) interpreting during the meeting of Cortez and Montezuma II in 1519. Women like Dona Maria apparently held high status in Aztec culture.

The Granger Collection, New York

Tenochtitlán, images of militarism and masculinity became increasingly important with the growth of the empire, and sculptures showed women in positions of work (e.g., kneeling). However, the images of women in the area of Brumfiel's fieldwork did not change. For example, most of the sculptures after the Aztecs had taken over still showed women standing, not kneeling.

Like many anthropologists, Brumfiel asked herself how she could contribute to the community in which she did her fieldwork. She decided to design an exhibit to display the successes of the people who had lived in the area for 1,200 years. The exhibit tells the people of Xaltocan what she found out from her studies.

As she continues to explore issues about the origins of inequality and the position of women, Brumfiel is quite comfortable with knowing that someone will think that she has "gotten it wrong, and will set out on a lifetime of archaeological research to find her own answers."

Source: Brumfiel 2009.

Like biological anthropologists, linguists study changes that have taken place over time, as well as contemporary variation. Some anthropological linguists are concerned with the emergence of language and also with the divergence of languages over thousands of years. The study of how languages change over time and how they may be related is known as **historical linguistics.** Anthropological linguists are also interested in how contemporary languages differ, especially in their construction. This focus of linguistics is generally called **descriptive** or **structural linguistics.** The study of how language is used in social contexts is called **sociolinguistics.**

In contrast with human paleontologists and archaeologists, who have physical remains to help them reconstruct change over time, historical linguists deal only with languages—and usually unwritten ones at that. (Remember

current research and issues

Researcher at Work: Terence E. Hays

Books and articles often report research in a straightforward manner: here's the problem, here's the answer—that kind of thing. However, many researchers know from experience that knowledge does not always come in a straightforward manner. A professor at Rhode Island College, Terence E. Hays has reflected on the twists and turns in his fieldwork among the Ndumba in the Eastern Highlands province of Papua New Guinea. He first started studying whether different types of people (e.g., women and men) had different types of plant knowledge and whether they classified plants differently. (The interest in plant and animal classification, *ethnobiology*, is closely connected with linguistic research.) In the course of his first fieldwork, in 1972, he witnessed an initiation ceremony for 10- to 12-year-old males—a dramatic and traumatic rite of passage ceremony that included the physical trauma of nosebleeding as well as the social traumas of "attacks" by women and seclusion in the forest. The ceremony was full of symbolism of why the sexes needed to avoid each other. Although he collected stories and myths about plants for his research on ethnobiology, he kept uncovering themes in the stories about the danger of men associating with women.

Hays's curiosity was aroused about these ceremonies and myths. How

Terence Hays during fieldwork in New Guinea.

important are myths in perpetuating cultural themes? Do other societies that have separate men's houses have similar myths? He realized when he returned home from the field that many societies have similar stories. Are these stories generally linked to initiation rites and to physical segregation of the sexes? Answering these questions required comparison, so he embarked on collecting myths and folktales from colleagues who worked in other New Guinea Highland societies. In the course of collecting these comparative materials, he realized he didn't have all

the ethnographic information he needed, so he went back to the field to get it. As Hays remarked, "As an ethnographer I was continually faced with the question, How do you know it's true? But even when I could reach a (hard-won) conviction that something was true for the Ndumba, the second question awaited: How do you know it's generally true, which you can't know without comparison?"

Source: Hays 2009.

that writing is only about 5,000 years old, and most languages since then have not been written.) Because unwritten languages must be heard to be studied, they do not leave any trace once speakers have died. Linguists interested in reconstructing the history of unwritten languages must begin in the present, with comparisons of contemporary languages. On the basis of these comparisons, they draw inferences about the kinds of change in language that may have occurred in the past and that may account for similarities and differences observed in the present. Historical linguists typically ask such questions as these: Did two or more contemporary languages diverge from a common ancestral language? If they are related, how far back in time did they begin to differ?

Unlike historical linguists, the descriptive (or structural) linguists are typically concerned with discovering and recording the principles that determine how sounds and words are put together in speech. For example, a structural description of a particular language might tell us that the sounds *t* and *k* are interchangeable in a word without causing a difference in meaning. In American Samoa, one could say *Tutuila* or *Kukuila* as the name of the largest island, and everyone, except perhaps newly arrived anthropologists who know little about the Samoan language yet, would understand that the same island was being mentioned.

Sociolinguists are interested in the social aspects of language, including what people speak about and how they interact conversationally, their attitudes toward speakers of other dialects or languages, and how people speak differently in different social contexts. In English, for example, we do not address everyone we meet in the same way. "Hi, Sandy" may be the customary way a person greets a friend. But we would probably feel uncomfortable addressing a doctor by a first name; instead, we would probably say, "Good morning, Dr. Brown." Such variations in language use, which are determined by the social status of the people being addressed, are significant for sociolinguists.

Ethnology (Cultural Anthropology) Ethnologists, or cultural anthropologists, try to understand how and why peoples today and in the recent past differ or are similar in their customary ways of thinking and acting. Also, how and why do cultures develop and change? How does one aspect of culture affect others? Cultural anthropologists ask questions such as: Why is the custom of marriage nearly universal in all cultures? What explains why families live with or near their kin in some societies, but not in other societies? What changes result from the introduction of money to a previously noncommercial economy? When family members move far away to work, what are the impacts on social relationships? What happens when a society is severely stressed because of natural disasters or violent conflicts? The aim of ethnologists is largely the same as that of archaeologists. However, ethnologists generally use data collected through observation and interviews of living peoples. Archaeologists, on the other hand, must work with fragmentary remains of past cultures, on the basis of which they can only make inferences about the customs of prehistoric peoples.

One type of ethnologist, **ethnographers,** usually spend a year or so living with, talking to, and observing the people whose customs they are studying. This fieldwork provides the data for a detailed description (an **ethnography**) of customary behavior and thought. Ethnographers vary in the degree to which they strive for completeness in their coverage of cultural and social life. Earlier ethnographers tended to strive for holistic coverage; more recent ethnographers have tended to specialize or focus on narrower realms such as ritual healing or curing, interaction with the environment, effects of modernization or globalization, or gender issues. Ethnographies often go beyond description; they may address current anthropological issues or try to explain some aspect of culture.

Many cultures have undergone extensive change in the recent past so trying to understand what life was like in earlier times is important. Ethnographers can ask older people what life was like when they were young, and information about the past may be contained in historical documents usually not written by anthropologists. An **ethnohistorian** studies how the ways of life of a particular group of people have changed over time. Ethnohistorians investigate written documents such as missionary accounts, reports by traders and explorers, and government records, to try to establish the cultural changes that have occurred. Unlike ethnographers, who rely mostly on their own observations and interviewing, ethnohistorians rely on the reports of others. Often, they must attempt to piece together and make sense of widely scattered, and even apparently contradictory, information. Thus, the ethnohistorian's research is very much like that of a historian, except that ethnohistorians are usually concerned with the history of a people who did not themselves leave written records. Ethnohistorians try to reconstruct the recent history of a people and may also suggest why certain changes in their way of life took place.

Ethnographic and ethnohistorical research is very time-consuming, and it is a rare for one person to study more than a few cultures. The **cross-cultural researcher** (who may be a cultural anthropologist or some other kind of social scientist,) is interested in discovering general patterns about cultural traits—what is universal, what is variable, why traits vary, and what the consequences of the variability might be. Why, for example, is there more gender inequality in some societies than in others? Is family violence related to aggression in other areas of life? What are the effects of living in a very unpredictable environment? In testing possible answers to such questions, cross-cultural researchers use data from samples of cultures (usually described initially by ethnographers) to try to arrive at explanations or relationships that hold across cultures. Archaeologists may find the results of cross-cultural research useful for making inferences about the past, particularly if they can discover material indicators of cultural variation.

Because ethnologists may be interested in many aspects of customary behavior and thought—from economic behavior to political behavior to styles of art, music, and religion—ethnology overlaps with disciplines that concentrate on some particular aspect of human existence, such as sociology, psychology, economics, political science, art, music, and comparative religion. But the distinctive feature of cultural anthropology is its interest in how all these aspects of human existence vary from society to society, in all historical periods, and in all parts of the world.

Applied Anthropology

All knowledge may turn out to be useful. In the physical and biological sciences, it is well understood that technological breakthroughs like DNA splicing, spacecraft docking in outer space, and the development of miniscule computer chips could not have taken place without an enormous amount of basic research to uncover the laws of nature in the physical and biological worlds. If we did not understand fundamental principles, the technological achievements we are so proud of would not be possible. Researchers are often simply driven by curiosity, with no thought to where the research might lead, which is why such research is sometimes called *basic research*. The same is true of the social sciences. If a researcher finds out that societies with combative sports tend to have more wars, it may lead to other inquiries about the relationships between one kind of aggression and another. The knowledge acquired may ultimately lead to discovering ways to correct social problems, such as family violence and war.

applied anthropology

Getting Development Programs to Notice Women's Contributions to Agriculture

When Anita Spring first did fieldwork in Zambia in the 1970s, she was not particularly interested in agriculture. Rather, medical anthropology was her interest. Her work focused on customary healing practices, particularly involving women and children. She was surprised at the end of the year when a delegation of women came to tell her that she didn't understand what it meant to be a woman. "To be a woman is to be a farmer," they said. She admits that it took her a while to pay attention to women as farmers, but then she began to participate in efforts to provide technical assistance to them. Like many others interested in women in development, Spring realized that all too often development agents downplay women's contributions to agriculture.

How does one bring about change in male-centered attitudes and practices? One way is to document how much women actually contribute to agriculture. Beginning with the influential writing of Ester Boserup in *Woman's Role in Economic Development* (1970), scholars began to report that in Africa south of the Sahara, in the Caribbean, and in parts of Southeast Asia, women were the principal farmers or agricultural laborers. Moreover, as agriculture became more complex, it required more work time in the fields, so the women's contribution to agriculture increased. In addition, men increasingly went away to work, so women had to do much of what used to be men's work on the farms.

In the 1980s, Spring designed and directed the Women in Agricultural Development Project in Malawi, funded by the Office of Women in the U.S. Agency for International Development. Rather than focusing just on women, the project aimed to collect data on both female and male agriculturalists and how development agents treated them. The project did more than collect information; mini-projects were set up and evaluated so that successful training techniques could be passed on to development agents in other regions. Spring points out that the success of the program was due not just to the design of the project. Much of the success depended on the interest and willingness of Malawi itself to change. It didn't hurt that the United Nations and other donor organizations increasingly focused attention on women. It takes the efforts of many to bring about change. Increasingly, applied anthropologists like Anita Spring are involved in these efforts from beginning to end, from the design stage to implementation and evaluation.

Source: Spring 1995; 2000b.

Whereas basic research may ultimately help to solve practical problems, applied research is more explicit in its practical goals. Today, more than half of all professional anthropologists are applied, or practicing, anthropologists.[3] Applied or practicing anthropology is explicit in its concern with making anthropological knowledge useful.[4] Applied anthropologists may be trained in any or all of the subfields of anthropology. In contrast to basic researchers, who are almost always employed in colleges, universities, and museums, applied anthropologists are commonly employed in settings outside traditional academia, including government agencies, international development agencies, private consulting firms, businesses, public health organizations, medical schools, law offices, community development agencies, and charitable foundations.

Biological anthropologists may be called upon to give forensic evidence in court, or they may work in public health, or design clothes and equipment to fit human anatomy. Archaeologists may be involved in preserving and exhibiting artifacts for museums and in doing contract work to find and preserve cultural sites that might be damaged by construction or excavation. Linguists may work in bilingual educational training programs or may work on ways to improve communication. Ethnologists may work in a wide variety of applied projects ranging from community development, urban planning, health care, and agricultural improvement to personnel and organizational management and assessment of the impact of change programs on people's lives.[5]

SPECIALIZATION

As disciplines grow, they tend to develop more and more specialties. This trend is probably inevitable because, as knowledge accumulates and methods become more advanced, there is a limit to what any one person can reasonably keep track of. So, in addition to the general divisions we have outlined already, particular anthropologists tend to identify themselves with a variety of specializations. Anthropologists commonly have a geographic specialty, which may be as broad as Old World or New World or as narrow as the southwestern United States. Those who study the past (archaeologists or human paleontologists) may also specialize in different time periods. Ethnologists often specialize in more specific subject

© Christopher J. Morris/Corbis

Forensic anthropology is one kind of applied anthropology. Kathy Reichs is a forensic anthropologist working in a medical examiner's office.

matters in addition to one or two cultural areas. Some ethnologists identify themselves as *economic anthropologists, political anthropologists,* or *psychological anthropologists.* Others may identify themselves by theoretical orientations, such as *cultural ecologists,* who are concerned with the relationship between culture and the physical and social environments. These specialties are not mutually exclusive, however. A cultural ecologist, for example, might be interested in the effects of the environment on economic behavior, political behavior, or how people bring up their children.

Does specialization isolate an anthropologist from other kinds of research? Not necessarily. Some specialties have to draw on information from several fields, inside and outside anthropology. For example, *medical anthropologists* study the cultural and biological contexts of human health and illness. Thus, they need to understand the economy, diet, and patterns of social interaction, as well as attitudes and beliefs regarding illness and health. In addition, they may need to draw on research in human genetics, public health, and medicine.

THE RELEVANCE OF ANTHROPOLOGY

Anthropology is a comparatively young discipline. Anthropologists only began to go to live with people in faraway places in the late 1800s. Compared to our knowledge of the physical laws of nature, we know much less about people, about how and why they behave as they do. That anthropology and other sciences dealing with humans began to develop only relatively recently is not in itself a sufficient reason for our knowing less than in the physical sciences. Why, in our quest for knowledge of all kinds, did we wait so long to study ourselves? Leslie White suggests that those phenomena most remote from us and least significant as determinants of human behavior were the first to be studied. The reason, he surmises, is that humans like to think of themselves as citadels of free will, subject to no

laws of nature. Hence, there is no need to see ourselves as objects to be explained.[6]

The idea that it is impossible to account for human behavior scientifically, either because our actions and beliefs are too individualistic and complex or because human beings are understandable only in otherworldly terms, is a self-fulfilling notion. We cannot discover principles explaining human behavior if we neither believe such principles exist nor bother to look for them. The result is assured from the beginning. People who do not believe in principles of human behavior will be reinforced by their finding none. If we are to increase our understanding of human beings, we first have to believe it is possible to do so.

If we aim to understand humans, it is essential that we study humans in all times and places. We must study ancient humans and modern humans. We must study their cultures and their biology. How else can we understand what is true of humans generally or how they are capable of varying? If we study just our own society, we may come up only with explanations that are culture-bound, not general or applicable to most or all humans. Anthropology is useful, then, to the degree that it contributes to our understanding of human beings everywhere.

In addition, anthropology is relevant because it helps us avoid misunderstandings between peoples. If we can understand why other groups are different from ourselves, we might have less reason to condemn them for behavior that appears strange to us. We may then come to realize that many differences between peoples are products of physical and cultural adaptations to different environments. For example, someone who first finds out about the !Kung as they lived in the Kalahari Desert of southern Africa in the 1950s might assume that the !Kung were "backward." (The exclamation point in the name *!Kung* signifies one of the clicking sounds made with the tongue by speakers of the !Kung language.) The !Kung wore little clothing, had few possessions, lived in meager shelters, and enjoyed none of our technological niceties like radio and computers. But let us reflect on how a typical North American community might react if it awoke to find itself in an environment similar to that in which the !Kung lived. The people would find that the arid land makes both agriculture and animal husbandry impossible, and they might have to think about adopting a nomadic existence. They might then discard many of their material possessions so that they could travel easily, to take advantage of changing water and food supplies. Because of the extreme heat and the lack of extra water for laundry, they might find it more practical to be almost naked than to wear clothes. They would undoubtedly find it impossible to build elaborate homes. For social security, they might start to share the food brought into the group. Thus, if they survived at all, they might end up looking and acting far more like the !Kung looked than like typical North Americans.

Physical differences, too, may be seen as results of adaptations to the environment. For example, in our society, we admire people who are tall and slim. If these same

A large number of emigrants from the former Soviet Union, particularly from Black Sea cities and towns such as Odessa, live in the Brighton Beach neighborhood of Brooklyn. Migrant and immigrant communities, such as "Little Odessa," are an increasing focus of anthropological study.

individuals were forced to live above the Arctic Circle, however, they might wish they could trade their tall, slim bodies for short, compact ones, because stocky physiques conserve body heat more effectively and may therefore be more adaptive in cold climates.

Exposure to anthropology might help to alleviate some of the misunderstandings that arise between people of different cultural groups from subtle causes operating below the level of consciousness. For example, different cultures have different conceptions of the gestures and interpersonal distances that are appropriate under various circumstances. Arabs consider it proper to stand close enough to other people to smell them.[7] On the basis of the popularity of deodorants in our culture, we can deduce that Americans prefer to keep the olfactory dimension out of interpersonal relations. We may feel that a person who comes too close is being too intimate. We should remember, however, that this person may only be acting according to a culturally conditioned conception of what is proper in a given situation. If our intolerance for others results in part from a lack of understanding of why peoples vary, then the knowledge that anthropologists accumulate may help lessen that intolerance.

As the world becomes increasingly interconnected or globalized, the importance of understanding and trying to respect cultural and physical differences becomes more and more important. Minor misunderstandings can escalate quickly into more serious problems. Even when powerful countries think they are being helpful, they may convey that other countries are inferior. They may also unknowingly promote behaviors that are not in the best interest of the people they are trying to help. At the extreme, misunderstandings can lead to violent confrontations. In today's world, going to war with modern weapons of mass destruction can kill more people than ever before.

Is understanding and respecting cultural and biological differences enough? Although education is undoubtedly useful, many anthropologists think that more explicit attention has to be paid toward solving real world problems at both the global and local levels. At the global level, we have to deal with many types of violent conflict, the degradation of the environment, the growing inequality between rich and poor countries, and major threats to health. At the local level, we have to grapple with whether particular development plans are advantageous and how to improve nutrition and health of particular societies. One solution does not necessarily fit all—what's good for some may not be good for others in different circumstances. To find out if some change will be advantageous requires careful study. Many ethical issues arise. Is it ethical to try to interfere with other people's lives? Is it ethical not to, if they are suffering or ask for help?

Knowledge of our past may bring both a feeling of humility and a sense of accomplishment. If we are to attempt to deal with the problems of our world, we must be aware of our vulnerability so that we do not think that problems will solve themselves. But we also have to think enough of our accomplishments to believe that we can find solutions to problems. Much of the trouble we get into may be a result of feelings of self-importance and invulnerability—in short, our lack of humility. Knowing something about our evolutionary past may help us to understand and accept our place in the biological world. Just as for any other form of life, there is no guarantee that any particular human population, or even the entire human species, will perpetuate itself indefinitely. The earth changes, the environment changes, and humanity itself changes. What survives and flourishes in the present might not do so in the future.

Yet, our vulnerability should not make us feel powerless. We have many reasons to feel confident about the future. Consider what we have accomplished so far. By means of tools and weapons fashioned from sticks and stones, we were able to hunt animals larger and more powerful than ourselves. We discovered how to make fire, and we learned to use it to keep ourselves warm and to cook our food. As we domesticated plants and animals, we gained greater control over our food supply and were able to establish more permanent settlements. We mined and smelted ores to fashion more durable tools. We built cities and irrigation systems, monuments and ships. We made it possible to travel from one continent to another in a single day. We conquered some illnesses and prolonged human life.

In short, human beings and their cultures have changed considerably over the course of history. Human populations have often been able to adapt to changing circumstances. Let us hope that humans continue to adapt to the challenges of the present and future.

SUMMARY ● ○ ○

1. Anthropology is literally the study of human beings. It differs from other disciplines concerned with people in that it is broader in scope. It is concerned with humans in all places of the world (not simply those places close to us), and it traces human evolution and cultural development from millions of years ago to the present day.

2. Another distinguishing feature of anthropology is its holistic approach to the study of human beings. Anthropologists study not only all varieties of people but also all aspects of those peoples' experiences and how different aspects of life relate to each other.

3. Anthropologists are commonly concerned with identifying and explaining typical characteristics (traits and customs) of particular human populations.

4. Biological or physical anthropology is one of the major fields of the discipline. Biological anthropology studies the emergence of humans and their later physical evolution (the focus called human paleontology). It also studies how and why contemporary human populations vary biologically (the focus called human variation).

5. Another broad area of concern to anthropology is cultural anthropology. Its three subfields—archaeology, anthropological linguistics, and ethnology (now usually referred to by the parent name, *cultural anthropology*)—all deal with aspects of human culture, that is, with the customary ways of thinking and behaving of particular societies.

6. Archaeologists seek not only to reconstruct the daily life and customs of prehistoric peoples but also to trace cultural changes and offer possible explanations for those changes. Therefore, archaeologists try to reconstruct history from the remains of human cultures.

7. Anthropological linguists are concerned with the emergence of language and with the divergence of languages over time (a subject known as historical linguistics). They also study how contemporary languages differ, both in construction (descriptive or structural linguistics) and in actual speech (sociolinguistics).

8. Ethnologists (now often called simply cultural anthropologists) seek to understand how and why peoples of today and the recent past differ or are similar in their customary ways of thinking and acting. One type of ethnologist, the ethnographer, usually spends a year or so living with and talking to a particular population and observing their customs. Later, ethnographers may prepare a detailed description (an ethnography) of many or some aspects of cultural and social life. Another type of ethnologist, the ethnohistorian, investigates written documents to determine how the ways of life of a particular group of people have changed over time. A third type of ethnologist, the cross-cultural researcher, studies data collected by ethnographers and ethnohistorians for a sample of cultures and attempts to discover which explanations of particular customs may be generally applicable.

9. In all four major subdisciplines of anthropology are applied anthropologists, people who apply anthropological knowledge to achieve more practical goals, usually in the service of an agency outside the traditional academic setting.

10. Anthropology may help people to be more tolerant. Anthropological studies can show us why other people are the way they are, both culturally and physically. Customs or actions that appear improper or offensive to us may be other peoples' adaptations to particular environmental and social conditions.

11. Anthropology is also valuable in that knowledge of our past may bring us both a feeling of humility and a sense of accomplishment. Like any other form of life, we have no guarantee that any particular human population will perpetuate itself indefinitely. Yet, knowledge of our achievements in the past may give us confidence in our ability to solve the problems of the future.

GLOSSARY TERMS ○ ● ○

anthropological linguistics
anthropology
applied (practicing) anthropology
archaeology
biological (physical) anthropology
cross-cultural researcher
cultural anthropology
descriptive (structural) linguistics
ethnographer
ethnography
ethnohistorian
ethnology
fossils
historical archaeology
historical linguistics
holistic
Homo sapiens
human paleontology
human variation
paleoanthropology
prehistory
Primates
primatologists
sociolinguistics

CRITICAL QUESTIONS ○ ○ ●

1. Why study anthropology? What are its goals, and how is it useful?

2. How does anthropology differ from other fields of study you've encountered that deal with humans? (Compare with psychology, sociology, political science, history, or biology, among others.)

3. What do you think about the suggestion that anthropology is the fundamental discipline studying humans?

PEARSON myanthrolab

Read the chapter by Terence E. Hays, "From Ethnographer to Comparativist and Back Again," on MyAnthroLab, and answer the following questions:

1. Many researchers find that their interests change when they go to the field. What did Hays start out studying? What did he get more interested in?

2. Explain why Hays thinks that you need both ethnography and comparison.

NOTES ● ○ ○

1. Harrison 1975; Durham 1991, 228–37.
2. Chimpanzee Sequencing and Analysis Consortium 2005.
3. Nolan 2003, 2.
4. Van Willigen 2002, 7.
5. Kedia and van Willigen 2005; Miracle 2009.
6. White 1968.
7. Hall 1966, 144–53.

Genetics and Evolution

Genetics and Evolution

Astronomers estimate that the universe has been in existence for some 15 billion years, plus or minus a few billion. To make this awesome history more understandable, Carl Sagan devised a calendar that condenses this span into a single year.[1] Using 24 days for every billion years and 1 second for every 475 years as a scale, Sagan moves from the "big bang" or beginning of the universe on January 1, to the origin of the Milky Way on May 1. In this system, September 9 marks the beginning of our solar system, and September 25 the origin of life on earth. At 10:30 in the evening of December 31, the first humanlike primates appear. Sagan's compression of history provides us with a manageable way to compare the short span of human existence with the total time span of the universe. Humanlike beings have been around for only about 90 minutes out of a 12-month period.

Some 55 million to 65 million years ago, the first primates appeared. They were ancestral to all living primates, including monkeys, apes, and humans. The early primates may or may not have lived in trees, but they had flexible digits and could grasp things. Later, about 35 million years ago, the first monkeys and apes appeared. About 15 million years ago, some 20 million years after the appearance of monkeys and apes, the immediate apelike ancestors of humans probably emerged. About 4 million years ago, the first humanlike beings appeared. Modern-looking humans evolved only about 100,000 years ago.

How do we account for the biological and cultural evolution of humans? In this chapter, we focus on how the modern theory of evolution developed and how it accounts for change over time. ● ○ ●

THE PRINCIPLES OF NATURAL SELECTION

Charles Darwin developed the evolutionary theory. Darwin was not the first person to view the creation of new species in evolutionary terms, but he was the first to provide a comprehensive, well-documented explanation—natural selection—for the way evolution had occurred. **Natural selection** is the main process that increases the frequency of adaptive traits through time. The operation of natural selection involves three conditions or principles.[2] The first is *variation:* Every species is composed of a great variety of individuals, some of which are better adapted to their environment than others. The existence of variety is important. Without it, natural selection has nothing on which to operate; without variation, one kind of characteristic could not be favored over another. The second principle of natural selection is *heritability:* Offspring inherit traits from their parents, at least to some degree and in some way. The third principle of natural selection is *differential reproductive success:* Because better-adapted individuals generally produce more offspring over the generations than poorer-adapted individuals, the frequency of adaptive traits gradually increases in subsequent generations. A new species emerges when changes in traits or geographic barriers result in the reproductive isolation of the population.

When we say that certain traits are **adaptive** or advantageous, we mean that they result in greater reproductive success in a particular environment. The phrase "particular environment" is very important. Even though a species may become more adapted to a particular environment over time, we cannot say that one species adapted to its environment is "better" than another species adapted to a different environment. For example, we may like to think of ourselves as "better" than other animals, but humans are clearly less adapted than fish for living underwater, than bats for catching flying insects, or than raccoons for living on suburban garbage.

Although the theory of natural selection suggests that disadvantageous or **maladaptive** traits will generally decline in frequency or even disappear eventually, it does not necessarily follow that all such traits will do so. After all, species derive from prior forms that have certain structures. This means that not all changes are possible; it also means that some traits are linked to others that might have advantages that outweigh the disadvantages. Choking may be very maladaptive for any animal, yet all vertebrates are capable of choking because their digestive and respiratory systems cross in the throat. This trait is a genetic legacy, probably from the time when the respiratory system developed from tissue in the digestive system of some ancestral organism. Apparently, the propensity to choke has not been correctable evolutionarily.[3]

Changes in a species can be expected to occur as the environment changes or as some members of the species move into a new environment. With environmental change, different traits become adaptive. The forms of the species that possess the more adaptive traits will become more frequent, whereas those forms whose characteristics make continued existence more difficult or impossible in the modified environment will eventually become extinct.

Consider how the theory of natural selection would explain why giraffes became long-necked. Originally, the necks of giraffes varied in length, as happens with virtually any physical characteristic in a population. During a period when food was scarce, those giraffes with longer necks, who could reach higher tree leaves, might be better able to survive and suckle their offspring, and thus they would leave more offspring than shorter-necked giraffes. Because of heredity, the offspring of long-necked giraffes are more likely to have long necks. Eventually, the shorter-necked giraffes would diminish in number and the longer-necked giraffes would increase. The resultant population of giraffes would still have variation in neck length but on the average would be longer-necked than earlier forms.

Natural selection does not account for all variation in the frequencies of traits. In particular, it does not account for variation in the frequencies of neutral traits—that is, those traits that do not seem to confer any advantages or disadvantages on their carriers. Changes in the frequencies of neutral traits may result rather from random processes that affect gene frequencies in isolated populations—*genetic drift*—or from matings between populations—*gene flow*. We discuss these other processes later in the chapter.

Observed Examples of Natural Selection

Natural selection is a process we can see at work in the world today. It is a process that has been studied in both the laboratory and in nature, and it is a process that most scientists would argue is very well understood. However, as in all scientific endeavors, understanding grows and changes as new information is obtained. The understanding of natural selection we have today is quite different from that originally put forward by Darwin. A century and a half of research has added tremendously to the information Darwin had to work with, and entirely new fields, like population genetics, have emerged. With this new information, we know that Darwin was unaware of some things. For example, it seems clear that natural selection is not always a uniform process, but can act in jumps and starts. The fact that the ideas put forward by Darwin have changed, and are changing as new research is done, does not mean they were wrong. Darwin's ideas were simply incomplete. As we add to our knowledge base each day, we move closer to an even more complete understanding of natural selection. Because the process of natural selection may involve nearly imperceptible gradations over generations, it is often difficult to observe directly. Nevertheless, because some life forms reproduce rapidly, some examples of natural selection have been observed over relatively short periods in changing environments.

For example, scientists think they have observed natural selection in action in British moths. In 1850, an almost black moth was spotted for the first time in Manchester. That was quite unusual, for most of the moths were speckled gray. A century later, 95 percent of the moths in industrial parts of Britain were black; only in the rural areas were the moths mostly gray. How is this to be explained? It seems that, in the rural areas, the gray-speckled moth is hard to spot by bird predators against the lichen growing on the bark of trees. But in industrial areas, lichen is killed by pollution. The gray-speckled moths, formerly well adapted to blend into their environment, became clearly visible against the darker background of the lichen-free trees and were easier prey for birds. In contrast, the black moths, which previously would have had a disadvantage against the lighter bark, were now better adapted for survival. Their dark color was an advantage, and subsequently the darker moths became the predominant variety in industrial regions.

How can we be sure that natural selection was the mechanism accounting for the change? Consistent evidence comes from a series of experiments performed by H. B. D. Kettlewell. He deliberately released specially marked moths, black and gray, into two areas of England—one urban industrial and one rural—and then set light traps to recapture them subsequently. The proportions of the two kinds of moths recovered tell us about differential survival. Kettlewell found that proportionately more black moths compared with gray moths were recovered in the urban industrial area. Just the reverse happened in the rural area; proportionately more gray-speckled moths were recovered.[4] Questions have been raised recently about whether the Kettlewell experiments were properly conducted.[5] However, the basic conclusion has been replicated by subsequent research.[6] The same transformation—the switch to darker color—has occurred in 70 other species of moth, as well as in a beetle and a millipede. And the transformation did not just occur in Britain; it also happened in other highly polluted areas, including the Ruhr area of Germany and the Pittsburgh area of the United States. Moreover, in the Pittsburgh area, antipollution measures in the last 50 years have apparently caused the black moth to dwindle in number once again.[7]

The type of natural selection in the moth example is called **directional selection** because a particular trait seems to be positively favored and the average value shifts over time toward the adaptive trait. But there can also be **normalizing selection.** In this type of selection, the average value does not change, but natural selection removes the extremes. An example is the birth weight of babies. Both very low birth weights and very high birth weights are disadvantageous and would be selected against. Directional and normalizing selection both assume that natural selection will either favor or disfavor genes, but there is a third possibility—balancing selection. **Balancing selection** occurs when a *heterozygous* (varied) combination of *alleles* (genes) is positively favored, even though a *homozygous* (genes in the pairs are the same) combination is disfavored. There is a trait that apparently involves balancing selection—sickle-cell anemia—which is found in people of West African ancestry, among other populations.

Another well-known example of observed natural selection is the acquired resistance of houseflies to the insecticide DDT. When DDT was first used to kill insects, beginning in the 1940s, several new, DDT-resistant strains of housefly evolved. In the early DDT environment, many houseflies were killed, but the few that survived were the ones that reproduced, and their resistant characteristics became common to the housefly populations. To the chagrin of medical practitioners, similar resistances develop in bacteria. A particular antibiotic may lose its effectiveness after it comes into wide use because new, resistant bacterial strains emerge. These new strains will become more frequent than the original ones because of natural selection. In the United States now, a few strains are resistant to all antibiotics on the market, a fact that worries medical practitioners. One possible way to deal with the problem is to stop using antibiotics for a few years, so resistance to those antibiotics might not develop or develop only slowly.

The theory of natural selection answered many questions, but it also raised at least one whose answer eluded Darwin and others. The appearance of a beneficial trait may assist the survival of an organism, but what happens when the organism reproduces by mating with members that do not possess this new variation? Will not the new adaptive trait eventually disappear if subsequent generations mate with individuals that lack this trait? Darwin knew variations were transmitted through heredity, but he did not have a clear model of the mode of inheritance.

Gregor Mendel's pioneering studies in the science of genetics provided the foundation for such a model, but his discoveries did not become widely known until 1900.

HEREDITY
Gregor Mendel's Experiments

Mendel (1822–1884), a monk and amateur botanist who lived in what is now the Czech Republic, bred several varieties of pea plants and made detailed observations of their offspring. He chose as breeding partners plants that differed by only one observable trait. Tall plants were crossed with short ones, and yellow ones with green, for example.

When the pollen from a yellow pea plant was transferred to a green pea plant, Mendel observed a curious phenomenon: All of the first-generation offspring bore yellow peas. It seemed that the green trait had disappeared. But when seeds from this first generation were crossed, they produced both yellow and green pea plants in a ratio of three yellow to one green pea plant (see Figure 1). Apparently, Mendel reasoned, the green trait had not been lost or altered; the yellow trait was simply **dominant** and the green trait was **recessive.** Mendel observed similar results with other traits. Tallness dominated

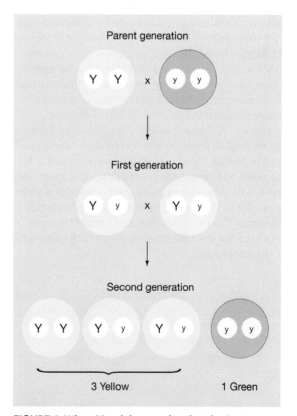

FIGURE 1 When Mendel crossed a plant having two genes for yellow peas (YY) with a plant having two genes for green peas (yy), each offspring pea was yellow but carried one gene for yellow and one gene for green (Yy). The peas were yellow because the gene for yellow is dominant over the recessive gene for green. Crossing the first generation yielded three yellow pea plants for each green pea plant.

shortness, and the factor for smooth-skinned peas dominated the factor for wrinkled ones. In each cross, the three-to-one ratio appeared in the second generation. Self-fertilization, however, produced different results. Green pea plants always yielded green pea plants, and short plants always produced short plants.

From his numerical results, Mendel concluded that some yellow pea plants were pure (*homozygous*) for that trait, whereas others also possessed a green factor (the plants were *heterozygous*). That is, although two plants might both have yellow peas, one of them might produce offspring with green peas. In such cases, the genetic makeup, the **genotype,** differed from the observable appearance, or **phenotype.**

Genes: The Conveyors of Inherited Traits

Mendel's units of heredity were what we now call **genes.** He concluded that these units occurred in pairs for each trait and that offspring inherited one unit of the pair from each parent. Each member of a gene pair or group is called an **allele.** If the two genes, or alleles, for a trait are the same, the organism is **homozygous** for that trait; if the two genes for a characteristic differ, the organism is **heterozygous** for that trait. A pea plant that contains a pair of genes for yellow is homozygous for the trait. A yellow pea plant with a dominant gene for yellow and a recessive gene for green, although phenotypically yellow, has a heterozygous genotype. As Mendel demonstrated, the recessive green gene can reappear in subsequent generations. But Mendel knew nothing of the composition of genes or the processes that transmit them from parent to offspring. Many years of scientific research have yielded much of the missing information.

The genes of higher organisms (not including bacteria and primitive plants such as blue-green algae) are located on ropelike bodies called **chromosomes** within the nucleus of every one of the organism's cells. Chromosomes, like genes, usually occur in pairs. Each allele for a given trait is carried in the identical position on corresponding chromosomes. The two genes that determined the color of Mendel's peas, for example, were opposite each other on a pair of chromosomes.

Mitosis and Meiosis The body cells of every plant or animal carry chromosome pairs in a number appropriate for its species. Humans have 23 pairs, or a total of 46 chromosomes, each carrying many times that number of genes. Each new body cell receives this number of chromosomes during cellular reproduction, or **mitosis,** as each pair of chromosomes duplicates itself.

But what happens when a sperm cell and an egg cell unite to form a new organism? What prevents the human baby from receiving twice the number of chromosomes characteristic of its species—23 pairs from the sperm and 23 pairs from the egg? The process by which the reproductive cells are formed, **meiosis,** ensures that this will not happen (see Figure 2). Each reproductive cell contains half the number of chromosomes appropriate for the species. Only one member of each chromosome pair is carried in every egg or sperm. At fertilization, the human embryo normally receives 23 separate chromosomes from its mother and the same number from its father, which add up to the 23 pairs.

DNA As we have said, genes are located on chromosomes. Each gene carries a set of instructions encoded in its chemical structure. It is from this coded information carried in genes that a cell makes all the rest of its structural parts and chemical machinery. It appears that, in most living organisms, heredity is controlled by the same chemical substance, **DNA**—deoxyribonucleic acid. An enormous amount of research has been directed toward understanding DNA—what its structure is, how it duplicates itself in reproduction, and how it conveys or instructs the formation of a complete organism.

One of the most important keys to understanding human development and genetics is the structure and function of DNA. In 1953, American biologist James Watson, with British molecular biologist Francis Crick, proposed that DNA is a long, two-stranded molecule shaped like a double helix (see Figure 3). Genetic information is stored in the linear sequences of the bases; different species have different sequences, and every individual is slightly different from every other individual. Notice that each base in the DNA molecule always has the same opposite base; adenine and thymine are paired, as are cy-

Meiosis in a plant cell. The left image shows the metaphase stage. Note how the chromosomes (stained dark red) lie against and even on top of one another. The right image shows the anaphase stage, when the chromosomes separate and the cell is ready to divide.

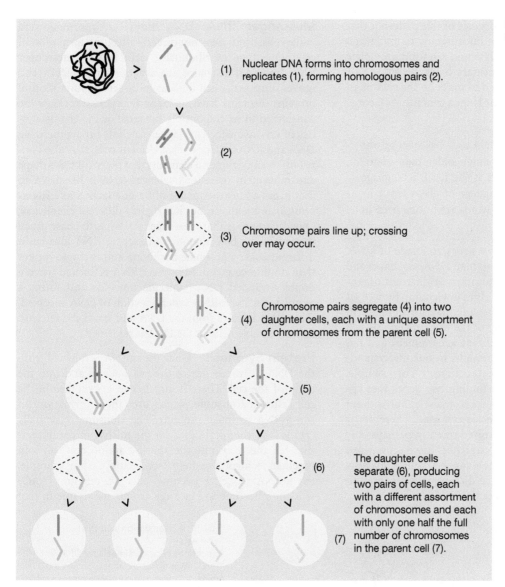

FIGURE 2 Meiosis (sex cells)

(1) Nuclear DNA forms into chromosomes and replicates (1), forming homologous pairs (2).

(2)

(3) Chromosome pairs line up; crossing over may occur.

(4) Chromosome pairs segregate (4) into two daughter cells, each with a unique assortment of chromosomes from the parent cell (5).

(5)

(6) The daughter cells separate (6), producing two pairs of cells, each with a different assortment of chromosomes and each with only one half the full number of chromosomes in the parent cell (7).

(7)

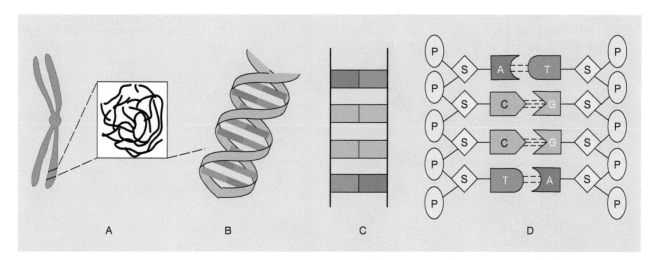

A   B   C   D

FIGURE 3 DNA
Chromosomes are built of DNA (A), which consists of two spiral sugar-phosphate strands (B) linked by the nitrogenous bases adenine, guanine, thymine, and cytosine (C). When the DNA molecule reproduces, the bases separate and the spiral strands unwind (D). Because adenine can only bond to thymine, and cytosine can only bond to guanine, each original strand serves as a mold along which a new complementary chain is formed.

tosine and guanine. The importance of this pattern is that the two strands carry the same information, so that, when the double helix unwinds, each strand can form a template for a new strand of complementary bases. Because DNA stores the information required to make up the cells of an organism, it has been called the language of life. As George and Muriel Beadle put it,

the deciphering of the DNA code has revealed our possession of a language much older than hieroglyphics, a language as old as life itself, a language that is the most living language of all—even if its letters are invisible and its words are buried deep in the cells of our bodies.[8]

Once it was understood that genes are made of DNA, concerted efforts were begun to map DNA sequences and their locations on the chromosomes of different organisms. A project known as the Human Genome Project set out to assemble a complete genetic map for humans. In July 2000, the initial mapping of the human genome was completed.[9] This was a significant achievement and has already led to several breakthroughs in our understanding of how the genetic code functions.[10] For example, researchers recently reported finding two genes that appear to provide partial resistance to malaria, but without the damaging effects of the sickle-cell gene. These newly found genes appear to have evolved recently, perhaps only a few thousand years ago. If researchers can discover how these genes help to defend their carriers against malaria, that may help medical science discover how to prevent or treat this devastating disease.[11]

Messenger RNA DNA stores the information to make cells, but it does not directly affect the formation of cells. One type of ribonucleic acid (RNA), **messenger RNA (mRNA),** is copied from a portion of DNA and moves outside the cell nucleus to direct the formation of proteins. Proteins have so many functions that they are considered to be responsible for most of the characteristics of an organism. They act as catalysts for synthesizing DNA and RNA and for the activities of cells; they also contribute many structural elements that determine the shape and movement of cells. Messenger RNA is like DNA in that it has a linear sequence of bases attached to a sugar-phosphate backbone, but it is slightly different chemically. One difference is that messenger RNA has the base uracil instead of the base thymine. Messenger RNA also has a different sugar-phosphate backbone and is single- rather than double-stranded. Messenger RNA is formed when a double-stranded DNA molecule unwinds and forms a template for the mRNA. After a section of DNA is copied, the mRNA releases from the DNA and leaves the nucleus, and the double helix of the DNA is reformed.

Protein Synthesis Once the mRNA is released from the DNA, it travels out of the cell nucleus and into the body of the cell. There it attaches to a structure in the cell called a **ribosome,** which uses the information on the mRNA to make proteins. The ribosome essentially "reads" the chemical bases on the mRNA in commands that tell the ribosome the specific amino acids to join together to form a protein (see Figure 4). For example, the mRNA sequence adenine, adenine, guanine (AAG) tells the ribosome to place the amino acid lysine in that

FIGURE 4 Translation and Protein Synthesis
The mRNA copy of the cellular DNA is "read" by a ribosome that attaches the amino acid with the corresponding transfer RNA (tRNA) to a growing chain of amino acids (called a polypeptide chain because the amino acids are linked together by peptide bonds). A chain more than 100 amino acids long is called a protein.

applied anthropology

Who Owns Your DNA?

In this chapter, we have shown that your DNA is a blueprint for the proteins that form your body. In some ways, then, your DNA *is* you. What happens to your DNA when you give blood or have a biopsy? Does it stop being you or a blueprint for you? Have you given away a part of you, or do you always retain control of your DNA, because it is the essence of you? These questions have become increasingly important ethically, as DNA is now more easily extracted and sequenced from blood and body cells, and particularly because medical research has found some DNA sources valuable as experimental tools and structures for the design of new drugs.

Consider the case of Henrietta Lacks, who died of cervical cancer in 1951. Mrs. Lacks's cancer was particularly virulent; indeed, the cells grew more quickly than any human cells the Johns Hopkins University doctors had previously seen. Samples of her cancer were cultured and, because of their ability to reproduce so rapidly, were sent to researchers at other institutions where they became the targets of decades of medical research and the development of treatments. More than half a century after her death, the cells Henrietta Lacks

provided are still alive, growing in labs on every continent, and interacting daily with thousands of scientists. Are these cells Henrietta Lacks? Has she gained a type of immortality? Or are they simply samples of highly virulent cancer tissue? It is important to note that Mrs. Lacks did not give permission for her cells to be used in this way, nor did she need to. In 1951, as today, cells obtained through surgery or medical treatment are considered the property of the doctor or facility that obtained them.

For anthropologist Margaret Everett, the question of who controls an individual's DNA came to the forefront of her research when her infant son Jack was diagnosed with, and later died from, a genetic disorder. Samples of Jack's DNA were taken as part of his autopsy. Dr. Everett later learned these samples were being used in labs in England and Italy, and that several research papers had been published on them. As she relates about one of these publications, "I soon found myself combing through the article, looking for Jack in a handful of samples described in a series of tables." But was Jack there? From research conducted to explore the impact of an Oregon law that makes genetic

information the property of the individuals from which it is derived, Dr. Everett learned that her questions and concerns were widely held. Oregonians, she discovered, wanted to control access to their own DNA, and felt that privacy and consent needed to be assured when samples were taken.

In non-Western cultures, the situation may become even more complex. In the United States, we view the individual as autonomous and self-defining. We create ourselves through our work and contributions to our communities. Who you are is defined by kinship and social class as well as by your work and activity. In many cultures, who you are may be mostly defined by others, not by you. In such situations, assuring privacy and consent may mean keeping private the location or identity of whole communities, or of gaining consent from kin group leaders in addition to individuals. As Dr. Everett puts it, "Property is never a thing—it is a bundle of rights, embedded in social relations." This is nowhere more true than when dealing with genetic property.

Sources: Everett 2007; Landecker 2000.

---

location, whereas the sequence adenine, adenine, cytosine (AAC) calls for the amino acid histidine. There are also mRNA commands that tell the ribosome when to begin and when to stop constructing a protein. Thus, the DNA code copied onto mRNA provides all the information necessary for ribosomes to build the proteins that make up the structures of organisms and drive the processes of life.

SOURCES OF VARIABILITY

Natural selection proceeds only when individuals within a population vary. There are two genetic sources of new variation: genetic recombination and mutation. There are also two processes through which variations are shuffled through populations: gene flow and genetic drift. Scholars have recently begun to consider one other potential source of variability: hybridization.

Genetic Recombination

The distribution of traits from parents to children varies from one offspring to another. Brothers and sisters, after all, do not look exactly alike, nor does each child resemble 50 percent of the mother and 50 percent of the father. This variation occurs because, when a sperm cell or an egg is formed, the single member of each chromosome pair it receives is a matter of chance. Each reproductive cell, then, carries a random assortment of chromosomes and their respective genes. At fertilization, the egg and sperm that unite are different from every other egg carried by the mother and every other sperm carried by the father. A unique offspring is thus produced by a shuffling of the parents' genes. One cause of this shuffling is the random **segregation,** or sorting, of chromosomes in meiosis. Conceivably, an individual could get any of the possible assortments of the paternal and maternal chromosomes. Another cause of the shuffling of parental genes is

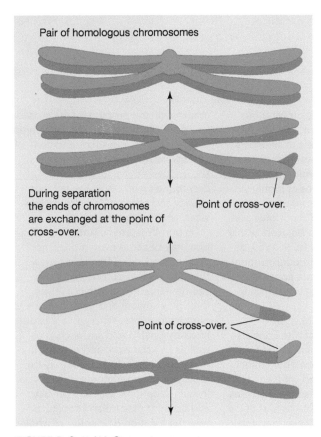

Pair of homologous chromosomes

During separation the ends of chromosomes are exchanged at the point of cross-over.

Point of cross-over.

Point of cross-over.

FIGURE 5 Crossing-Over

Source: From Boaz and Almquist 1997.
Boaz, Noel T.; Almquist, Alan J., *Biological Anthropology: A Synthetic Approach To Human Evolution*, 1st, © 1997. Electronically reproduced by permission of Pearson Education, Inc., Upper Saddle River, New Jersey.

crossing-over, the exchange of sections of chromosomes between one chromosome and another (see Figure 5). Thus, after meiosis, the egg and sperm do not receive just a random mixture of complete paternal and maternal chromosomes; because of crossing-over, they also receive chromosomes in which some of the sections may have been replaced.

The traits displayed by each organism are not simply the result of combinations of dominant and recessive genes, as Mendel had hypothesized. In humans, most traits are influenced by the activity of many genes. Skin color, for example, is the result of several inherited characteristics. A brownish shade results from the presence of a pigment known as *melanin;* the degree of darkness in the hue depends largely on the amount of melanin present and how it is distributed in the layers of the skin. Another factor contributing to the color of all human skin is the blood that flows in blood vessels located in the outer layers of the skin. Humans carry at least five different genes for the manufacture of melanin and many other genes for the other components of skin hue. In fact, almost all physical characteristics in humans are the result of the concerted action of many genes. Some traits are sex-linked. The X chromosome, which together with the presence or absence of a Y chromosome determines sex, may also carry the gene for hemophilia or the gene for color blindness. The expression of these two characteristics depends on the sex of the organism.

Genetic recombination produces variety, which is essential for the operation of natural selection. Ultimately, however, the major source of variability is mutation. This is because mutation replenishes the supply of variability, which is constantly being reduced by the selective elimination of less fit variants. Mutation also produces variety in organisms that reproduce asexually.

Mutation

A **mutation** is a change in the DNA sequence. Such a change produces an altered gene. The majority of mutations are thought to occur because of occasional mismating of the chemical bases that make up DNA. Just as a typist will make errors in copying a manuscript, so will DNA, in duplicating itself, occasionally change its code. A mutation will result from such an error. Some mutations have more drastic consequences than others. Suppose the error is in one base on a DNA strand. The effect depends on what that portion of the DNA controls. The effect may be minimal if the product hardly affects the organism. On the other hand, if the change occurs at a place where the DNA regulates the production of many proteins, the effect on the organism can be serious.

Although it is very difficult to estimate the proportions of mutations that are harmful, neutral, or beneficial, there is no doubt that some mutations have lethal consequences. We can discuss the relative merits or disadvantages of a mutant gene only in terms of the physical, cultural, and genetic environment of that gene. Galactosemia, for example, is caused by a recessive mutant gene and usually results in

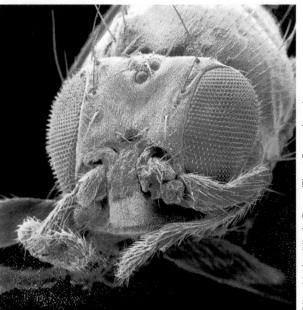

A mutation in a fruit fly causes legs to grow where antennae should be. Although most mutations are either neutral or harmful (like this one), some can be adaptive and spread rapidly through a population.

Oliver Meckes/Nicole Ottawa/Photo Researchers, Inc.

mental retardation and blindness. But it can be prevented by dietary restrictions begun at an early age. In this instance, the intervention of human culture counteracts the mutant gene and allows the afflicted individual to lead a normal life. Thus, some cultural factors can modify the effects of natural selection by helping to perpetuate a harmful mutant gene. People with the galactosemia trait who are enabled to function normally can reproduce and pass on one of the recessive genes to their children. Without cultural interference, natural selection would prevent such reproduction. Usually, natural selection acts to retain only those mutations that aid survival.

Even though most mutations may not be adaptive, those that are will multiply in a population relatively quickly, by natural selection. As Theodosius Dobzhansky has suggested:

> Consistently useful mutants are like needles in a haystack of harmful ones. A needle in a haystack is hard to find, even though one may be sure it is there. But if the needle is valuable, the task of finding it is facilitated by setting the haystack on fire and looking for the needle among the ashes. The role of the fire in this parable is played in biological evolution by natural selection.[12]

The black moth that was spotted in Manchester in 1850, probably resulted from a mutation. If the tree trunks had been light-colored, that moth or its offspring probably would have died out. But as industrialization increased and the tree trunks became darker, a trait that was once maladaptive became adaptive.

Genetic recombination and mutation are the sources of new variations, but evolutionary biologists have identified two other processes that are important in distributing those variations through populations: genetic drift and gene flow.

Genetic Drift

The term **genetic drift** refers to various random processes that affect gene frequencies in small, relatively isolated populations. Genetic drift is also known as the *Wright effect,* after geneticist Sewall Wright, who first directed attention to this process. Over time in a small population, genetic drift may result in a neutral or nearly neutral gene becoming more or less frequent just by chance.

One variety of genetic drift, called the *founder effect,* occurs when a small group of organisms recently derived from a larger population migrates to a relatively isolated location. If a particular gene is absent just by chance in the migrant group, the descendants are also likely to lack that gene, assuming that the group remains isolated. Similarly, if all members of the original migrant group just by chance carried a particular gene, their descendants would also be likely to share that gene. Isolation can occur for physical reasons, such as when a group moves to a previously uninhabited place and does not return. The populations that traveled over land when the Bering land bridge connected Asia to North America could not readily return when the sea level rose. This may explain why Native Americans have a higher proportion of individuals with type O blood than other populations—the first migrants may have had, by chance, a predominance of individuals with type O blood.

Isolation can also occur for social reasons. A religious sect of Anabaptists called "Dunkers" emigrated from Germany to the United States in the early 1700s. The fact that the 50 original families kept to themselves probably explains why some of their gene frequencies differ from what is found in both the German and general U.S. populations.[13]

Gene Flow

Gene flow is the process whereby genes pass from one population to another through mating and reproduction. Unlike the other processes of natural selection and genetic drift, which generally increase the differences between populations in different environments, gene flow tends to work in the opposite direction—it *decreases* differences between populations. Two populations at opposite ends of a region may have different frequencies of a particular gene, but the populations located between them have an intermediate gene frequency because of gene flow between them. The variation in gene frequency from one end of the region to the other is called a **cline.** In Europe, for example, there is a cline in the distribution of type B blood, which gradually diminishes in frequency from east to west.[14]

Most genetically determined characteristics in humans have gradually or clinally varying frequencies as one moves from one area to another. Neighboring regions have more similar gene frequencies than regions widely separated. But these clines do not always coincide, which makes the concept of "race" as applied to humans not very useful for understanding human biological variation.[15]

Gene flow may occur between distant as well as close populations. Long-range movements of people, to trade or raid or settle, may result in gene flow. But they do not always do so.

Hybridization

A **species** is a population that consists of organisms able to interbreed and produce fertile and viable offspring. In general, individuals from one species do not successfully mate with members of a different species because of genetic and behavioral differences. If members of different species do mate, fertilization usually does not occur and, if it does, the embryo does not survive. In the cases where offspring are born, they are usually infertile. However, recent studies have suggested that **hybridization,** the creation of a viable offspring from two different species, may be more possible than once thought. Hybridization may be an important source of new variation in some populations.

current research and issues

Is Evolution Slow and Steady or Fast and Abrupt?

Darwin's evolutionary theory suggested that new species emerge gradually over time. Through the process of natural selection, frequencies of traits would slowly change, and eventually a new species would appear. But Darwin did not explain why so much speciation has occurred. If trait frequencies change only gradually over time, wouldn't descendant populations retain their ability to interbreed and wouldn't they, therefore, continue to belong to the same species?

In the 1930s and 1940s, biologists and geneticists advanced what came to be called the "modern synthesis" in evolutionary theory, adding what was known from genetics about heredity. Mutation and the recombination of genes now provided for genetic variety. The driving force of change was still adaptation to environments through natural selection; gene frequencies of a population presumably changed slowly as adaptive traits (because of existing genes or mutations) increased in prevalence and maladaptive traits decreased. As for speciation, the development and divergence of different species, the modern synthesis postulated that it would occur

when subpopulations became isolated by geographic barriers or when different subpopulations encountered different climatic conditions or moved into new ecological niches; those environmental isolating processes would eventually result in the development of reproductive isolation and therefore new species.

Niles Eldredge and Stephen Jay Gould challenged this gradualist view of evolution in 1972. Their alternative model of evolution is referred to as "punctuated equilibrium." They still assume that natural selection is the primary mechanism of evolutionary change, but they see the pace of evolution quite differently. In their view, new species evolve quickly; but once a successful species emerges, its characteristics are likely to change very little over long periods of time. Thus, in contrast to the modern synthesis, Eldredge and Gould do not think it is common for the world's species to change gradually into descendant species. Rather, species are born more or less abruptly, they have lifetimes during which they do not change much, and they become extinct. As examples, Eldredge and Gould cite

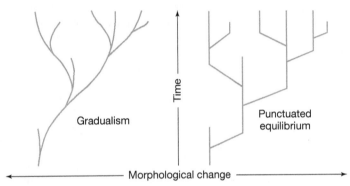

FIGURE 6 A Graphical Depiction of Gradual Versus Punctuated Evolutionary Change

Hybridization is an important source of variation in some plant species, such as these South African Gazanias.

The finches of the Galápagos Islands that Darwin used as evidence for natural selection and that we refer to in the box "Is Evolution Slow and Steady or Fast and Abrupt?" also provide an example of hybridization in action. Many female cactus finches (*Geospiza scandens*) died during a period of severe drought, leaving an abundance of males. High competition for mates led some female ground finches (*Geospiza fortis*) to mate with the abundant male cactus finches, something that would not normally occur. The result was hybrid offspring with unique characteristics. These hybrids, both male and female, went on to mate only with cactus finches, because they imprinted on the male cactus finch song as infants. The end result was a one-time influx of ground finch genes into the cactus finch population, adding new variations upon which natural selection could work.[16]

THE ORIGIN OF SPECIES

One of the most controversial aspects of Darwin's theory was the suggestion that one species could, over time, evolve into another. How could one species evolve into the history of North American trilobites and Bermudan land snails. In both groups of animals, it looks as if the different species did not change for a long period of time—millions of years for some species—but then certain species seem to have been quickly replaced by related species from nearby areas. In short, Eldredge and Gould believe that the succession of one species after another involves replacement from outside more often than gradual change over time.

Evolution may or may not occur as the model of punctuated equilibrium specifies, but most evolutionists today agree that change could occur relatively quickly. Recent research suggests that some relatively quick climate changes in the earth's history helped bring about massive extinctions of species and families of species and exponential increases in the subsequent number of new families. For example, there is considerable evidence that a large meteorite collided with the earth at the end of the Cretaceous geological period, about 65 million years ago. Louis Alvarez and his colleagues proposed that so much dust was sent into the atmosphere by the collision that the earth was shrouded in darkness for months, if not longer. Some investigators now think that the meteorite impact may have also triggered a great deal of volcanic activity, even on the opposite side of the world, which would also have reduced solar radiation to the earth's surface. Not only the dinosaurs disappeared about 65 million years ago, so also did many sea animals and plants. Afterward, the earth saw the proliferation of many other kinds of animals, such as fish, lizards, birds, and mammals, as well as flowering trees. Our own biological order, the Primates, is believed to have emerged around that time.

Peter Grant recently studied the same finches on the Galápagos Islands that partially inspired Darwin's theory. But, unlike Darwin, Grant had the chance to see natural selection in action. It was surprisingly quick. Central to the project was the attachment of colored bands to each individual bird, which allowed each bird to be identified at a distance. In the midst of the project, in 1977, when half the birds had been banded, there was a serious drought. Of the two main species of finch on one island, the cactus finch (*Geospiza scandens*) and the medium ground finch (*Geospiza fortis*), only the cactus finches were able to breed, but they had no surviving offspring. During the next 18 months, 85 percent of the adult medium ground finches disappeared. Those finches that survived tended to be larger and to have larger beaks than the ones that died. Why larger beaks? Both species of finch eat seeds, but small seeds produced by grasses and herbs are scarce in a drought; bigger seeds are more available. So it seems that natural selection under conditions of drought favored finches with bigger beaks, which are better at cracking the husks of large seeds.

If it were not for the fact that wet years, which favor smaller finches, occur between years of drought, we might see the quick evolution of new finch species. An estimated 20 drought episodes would be sufficient to produce a new species of finch. Galápagos finches do not really provide an example of punctuated equilibrium (no replacement from outside occurred), but they do suggest that evolutionary change could be a lot quicker than Darwin imagined.

Controversy continues over whether evolution is slow and steady or fast and abrupt. But many scholars, including Gould, point out that there is no need to pit one model against the other. Both may be correct in different instances. In any case, much more investigation of evolutionary sequences is needed to help us evaluate the competing theoretical models.

Sources: Devillers and Chaline 1993; Grant 1991, 82–87; Tattersall 2009; Weiner 1994.

another? What is the explanation for this differentiation? How does one group of organisms become so unlike another group with the same ancestry that it forms a totally new species? **Speciation,** or the development of a new species, may occur if one subgroup of a species finds itself in a radically different environment. In adapting to their separate environments, the two populations may undergo enough genetic changes to prevent them from interbreeding, should they renew contact. Numerous factors can prevent the exchange of genes. Two species living in the same area may breed at different times of the year, or their behavior during breeding—their courtship rituals—may be distinct. The difference in body structure of closely related forms may in itself bar interbreeding. Geographic barriers may be the most common barriers to interbreeding.

Do new species diverge quickly or slowly from their ancestors? Paleontologists disagree about the pace of speciation. The traditional view is that evolution occurs very slowly over time; new species emerge gradually. Others who espouse what's called "punctuated equilibrium" believe that species are very stable over long periods of time, but when divergence occurs it is quick (see the box titled "Is Evolution Slow and Steady or Fast and Abrupt?")

Speciation Versus Creation

But some people, particularly those who call themselves "scientific creationists," argue that, although natural selection can produce variation within species (often referred to as *microevolution*), it cannot produce new species (often referred to as *macroevolution*). Creationists argue that God created all living things, and that evolution has only changed those living things in minor ways and has not created new kinds of living things. The major problem with the creationist view is that there is solid empirical evidence for speciation. For example, William Rice and George Salt demonstrated that, if they sorted fruit flies by their environmental preferences (such as light intensity and temperature) and then bred the sorted groups separately, they could produce flies incapable of interbreeding—separate species—in as little as 35 generations.[17] The fossil record contains numerous examples of speciation and even the development of entirely new kinds of creatures. For example, the evolution of birds from terrestrial creatures is clearly evidenced in the fossil record.[18] Although many creationists downplay the evidence for speciation, the evidence is plentiful, and can be seen by the public in museums all over the world.

With the abundant evidence for speciation found in both the fossil record and in experimental observations, creationists have recently developed a new argument to discount the role of natural selection in the process of speciation. The new argument is that life in general, and species in particular, are so complex that a random, undirected process like natural selection could never have created them. The complexity of life, these creationists argue, must stem from "intelligent design." This new appeal to intelligent design in the origin of species is actually an old, and widely discredited, one. In his 1802 book *Natural Theology*, William Paley wrote, "Suppose I had found a watch upon the ground, and it should be enquired how the watch happened to be in that place . . . the inference, we think, is inevitable; that the watch must have had a maker. . . ."[19] By this, Paley implied that if we find a complex mechanism at work in the world, like a watch, we must conclude that a maker exists. Paley extended the argument to the complexity of life, and concluded that life must stem from an intelligent designer—God.

Darwin wrote *On the Origin of Species* in part as a response to Paley, and Darwinists have been responding ever since. But in recent years, the "intelligent design" movement, or as proponents call it, the "wedge," has brought Paley's ideas back with force. Indeed, the force is an active political one, with the explicit purpose "to reverse the stifling dominance of the materialist world view, and to replace it with a science consonant with Christian and theistic convictions."[20] Intelligent design is, at the core, a political movement. The problem, however, is that intelligent design cannot explain speciation in a scientific way. The central argument made by proponents of intelligent design is simply that what we see in the world is too complex to be accounted for by natural selection, but they offer no alternative natural mechanism. They argue that, if natural selection may not account for all cases of speciation, then the only alternative is divine intervention. Clearly, this reasoning is flawed. Just because we do not understand something today does not mean we should toss out all we do know. Rather, the scientific approach is to continue to examine unexplained phenomena to learn more about them.

Intelligent design proponents also fail to answer critics who point out that natural selection can and has accounted for even the most complex of features—such as wings and eyes—and hence that intelligent design arguments lack a basis in fact. The key facts that intelligent design and other creationist scholars appeal to are biblical ones. But it is important to point out that most biblical scholars do not agree with creationist arguments. As theologian Ernan McMullin suggests, the Bible "ought to be understood as conveying fundamental theological truths about dependence of the natural and human worlds on their Creator, rather than explaining how exactly these worlds first took shape."[21] On the other hand, there is nothing in science that can absolutely rule out supernatural intervention in the natural world, because supernatural activities are beyond the realm of scientific explanation. For example, although we now know that people with a condition called hypertrichosis grow hair all over their faces because of a single mutation on the X chromosome, science cannot rule out the possibility that the mutation was caused by the "curse of the werewolf" or a divine punishment for sin.[22] Science cannot rule out such possibilities because they cannot be observed, measured, or experimentally tested. Science and religion should be regarded as different ways of understanding the world, the former relying on evidence, the latter relying on faith.

NATURAL SELECTION OF BEHAVIORAL TRAITS

Until now, we have discussed how natural selection might operate to change a population's physical traits, such as the color of moths or the neck length of giraffes. But natural selection can also operate on the behavioral characteristics of populations. Although this idea is not new, it is now receiving more attention. The approaches called **sociobiology**,[23] behavioral ecology,[24] evolutionary psychology,[25] and dual-inheritance theory[26] involve the application of evolutionary principles to the behavior of animals and humans. Behavioral ecology looks at how all kinds of behavior related to the environment; sociobiology looks at social organization and social behavior; evolutionary psychology looks at how evolution may have produced lasting variation in the way humans behave, interact, and perceive the world; and dual-inheritance theory looks at how beneficial cultural traits might be selected for and transmitted. The typical behaviors of a species are assumed to be adaptive and to have evolved by natural selection. For example, why do related species exhibit different social behaviors even though they derive from a common ancestral species?

Consider the lion, as compared with other cats. Although members of the cat family are normally solitary creatures, lions live in social groups called *prides*. Why? George Schaller has suggested that lion social groups may have evolved primarily because group hunting is a more successful way to catch large mammals in open terrain. He has observed that not only are several lions more successful in catching prey than are solitary lions, but several lions are more likely to catch and kill large and dangerous prey such as giraffes. Then, too, cubs are generally safer from predators when in a social group than when alone with their mothers. Thus, the social behavior of lions may have evolved primarily because it provided selective advantages in the lions' open-country environment.[27]

It is important to remember that natural selection operates on expressed characteristics, or the phenotype, of an individual. In the moth example, the color of the moth is part of its *phenotype,* subject to natural selection. Behavior is also an expressed characteristic. If hunting in groups, a behavioral trait, gets you more food, then individuals who hunt in groups will do better. But we must also remember that natural selection requires traits to be heritable. Can the concept of heritability be applied to learned behavior, not just genetically transmitted behavior? And, even more controversially, if the concept of heritability can include learning, can it also include cultural learning? Recent research on domesticated dogs suggests it may. Domesticated dogs appear to inherently understand social cues used by humans, such as pointing, whereas wolves do not. These findings suggest that some aspects of cultural learning in animals may be heritable.[28]

Early theorizing in sociobiology and behavioral ecology appeared to emphasize the genetic component of behavior. For example, Edward O. Wilson, in his book *Sociobiology,* defined sociobiology as "the systematic study of the biological causes of behavior."[29] But Bobbi Low points out that, although the term *biological* may have been interpreted to mean "genetic," most biologists understand that expressed or observable characteristics are the results of genes, environment, and life history, all interacting. Behavior is a product of all three. If we say that some behavior is heritable, we mean that the child's behavior is more likely to resemble the parents' behavior than the behavior of others.[30] Learning from a parent could be an important part of why the offspring is like the parent. If the child is more like the parent than like others, then the likeness is heritable, even if it is entirely learned from the parent.

The sociobiological approach has aroused considerable controversy in anthropology, probably because of its apparent emphasis on genes, rather than experience and learning, as determinants of human behavior. Anthropologists have argued that the customs of a society may be more or less adaptive because cultural behaviors also have reproductive consequences. It is not just an individual's behavior that may have reproductive consequences. So, does natural selection also operate in the evolution of culture? Many biologists think not. They say there are substantial differences between biological and cultural evolution. How do cultural evolution and biological evolution compare? To answer this question, we must remember that the operation of natural selection requires three conditions, as we already noted: variation, heritability or mechanisms that duplicate traits in offspring, and differential reproduction because of heritable differences. Do these three requirements apply to cultural behavior?

In biological evolution, variability comes from genetic recombination and mutation. In cultural evolution, it comes from recombination of learned behaviors and from invention.[31] Cultures are not closed or reproductively isolated, as species are. A species cannot borrow genetic traits from another species, but a culture can borrow new things and behaviors from other cultures. The custom of growing corn, which has spread from the New World to many other areas, is an example of this phenomenon. As for the requirement of heritability, although learned traits obviously are not passed to offspring through purely genetic inheritance, parents who exhibit adaptive behavioral traits are more likely to "reproduce" those traits in their children, who may learn them by imitation or by parental instruction. Children and adults may also copy adaptive traits they see in people outside the family. Finally, as for the requirement of differential reproduction, it does not matter whether the trait in question is genetic or learned or both. As Henry Nissen emphasized, "behavioral incompetence leads to extinction as surely as does morphological disproportion or deficiency in any vital organ. Behavior is subject to selection as much as bodily size or resistance to disease."[32]

Many theorists are comfortable with the idea of applying the theory of natural selection to cultural evolution, but others prefer to use different terminology when dealing with traits that do not depend on purely genetic transmission from one generation to the next. For example, Robert Boyd and Peter Richerson discuss human behavior as involving "dual inheritance." They distinguish cultural transmission, by learning and imitation, from genetic transmission, but they emphasize the importance of understanding both and the interaction between them.[33] William Durham also deals separately with cultural

Tim Ridley © Dorling Kindersley.

Domesticated dogs have evolved the ability to understand human social cues far better than wolves.

transmission, using the term *meme* (analogous to the term *gene*) for the unit of cultural transmission. He directs our attention to the interaction between genes and culture, calling that interaction "coevolution," and provides examples of how genetic evolution and cultural evolution may lead to changes in each other, how they may enhance each other, and how they may even oppose each other.[34]

So biological and cultural evolution in humans may not be completely separate processes. Some of the most important biological features of humans—such as our relatively large brains—may have been favored by natural selection because our ancestors made tools, a cultural trait. Conversely, the cultural trait of informal and formal education may have been favored by natural selection because humans have a long period of immaturity, a biological trait.

As long as the human species continues to exist and the social and physical environment continues to change, there is reason to think that natural selection of biological and cultural traits will also continue. However, as humans learn more about genetic structure, they will become more capable of curing genetically caused disorders and even altering the way evolution proceeds. Today, genetic researchers are capable of diagnosing genetic defects in developing fetuses, and parents can and do decide often whether to terminate a pregnancy. Soon, genetic engineering will probably allow humans to fix defects and even try to "improve" the genetic code of a growing fetus. Whether and to what extent humans should alter genes will undoubtedly be the subject of continuing debate. Whatever the decisions we eventually make about genetic engineering, they will affect the course of human biological and cultural evolution.

SUMMARY ● ○ ○

1. Charles Darwin and Alfred Wallace proposed the mechanism of natural selection to account for the evolution of species. Basic principles of the theory of natural selection are that (1) every species is composed of a great variety of individuals, some of which are better adapted to their environment than others; (2) offspring inherit traits from their parents at least to some degree and in some way; and (3) because better-adapted individuals generally produce more offspring over the generations than the poorer-adapted individuals, the frequency of adaptive traits increases in subsequent generations. In this way, natural selection results in increasing proportions of individuals with advantageous traits.

2. Mendel's and subsequent research in genetics and our understanding of the structure and function of DNA

and mRNA help us to understand the biological mechanisms by which traits may be passed from one generation to the next.

3. Natural selection depends on variation within a population. The primary sources of biological variation are genetic recombination, mutation, genetic drift, gene flow, and hybridization.

4. Speciation, the development of a new species, may occur if one subgroup becomes separated from other subgroups. In adapting to different environments, these subpopulations may undergo enough genetic changes to prevent interbreeding, even if they reestablish contact. Once species differentiation occurs, it is believed that the evolutionary process cannot be reversed.

5. So-called "creation scientists" and proponents of "intelligent design" theory argue that the origin of species cannot be accounted for through natural selection. This argument ignores the enormous body of evidence—experimental, fossil, and field data—that demonstrates how natural selection works to create new species.

6. Natural selection can also operate on the behavioral characteristics of populations. The approaches such as sociobiology and behavioral ecology involve the application of evolutionary principles to the behavior of animals. Much controversy surrounds the degree to which the theory of natural selection can be applied to human behavior, particularly cultural behavior. There is more agreement that biological and cultural evolution in humans may influence each other.

GLOSSARY TERMS ○ ● ○

adaptive	maladaptive
allele	meiosis
balancing	messenger RNA
selection	(mRNA)
chromosome	mitosis
cline	mutation
crossing-over	natural selection
directional selection	normalizing
DNA	selection
dominant	phenotype
genes	recessive
gene flow	ribosome
genetic drift	segregation
genotype	sociobiology
heterozygous	speciation
homozygous	species
hybridization	

CRITICAL QUESTIONS ○ ○ ●

1. Do you think the theory of natural selection is compatible with religious beliefs? Explain your reasoning.

2. How might the discovery of genetic cures and the use of genetic engineering affect the future of evolution?

3. Why do you think humans have remained one species?

PEARSON
myanthrolab

Read the chapter by Jonathan Marks titled "Genes, Bodies, and Species" on MyAnthroLab. Answer the following questions:

1. Compare Marks's discussion of the "Hardy-Weinberg Law" and Figure 1, which displays the distribution of genotypes in pea plants identified by Mendel. Explain how the Hardy-Weinberg Law relates to Mendel's discovery.

2. Marks argues that speciation requires a gene pool to be divided into isolated groups. Explain why this is the case. Given the enormous gene flow in human populations, is it likely (or even possible) that a new species of human will evolve under current conditions?

3. Marks concludes his essay by stating that genetic mutation is more complex than we had previously thought. In what ways does Marks's discussion of mutation and its effects differ from that we present in this text? Does Marks's discussion appear to make the process of mutation more complex than ours?

NOTES ● ○ ○

1. Sagan 1975.
2. R. N. Brandon 1990, 6–7.
3. G. Williams 1992, 7.
4. J. M. Smith 1989, 42–45.
5. Hooper 2002.
6. Grant 2002.
7. Devillers and Chaline 1993, 22–23.
8. Beadle and Beadle 1966, 216.
9. Golden et al. 2000; Hayden 2000; Marshall 2000; Pennisi 2000; Travis 2000.
10. Daiger 2005.
11. Olsen 2002.
12. Dobzhansky 1962, 138–40.
13. Relethford 1990, 94.
14. G. A. Harrison et al. 1988, 198–200.
15. Brace 1996.
16. Grant and Grant 2002.
17. Rennie 2002, 83.
18. Chatterjee 1997.
19. Paley 1810.
20. Center for Renewal of Science and Culture, "The Wedge Strategy," cited in Forrest 2001, 16.
21. McMullin 2001, 174.
22. Rennie 2002.
23. Barash 1977.
24. Krebs and Davies 1984; 1987.
25. Badcock 2000.
26. Boyd and Richerson 2005.
27. Schaller 1972.
28. Hare et al. 2002.
29. E. O. Wilson 1975.
30. B. Low 2009.
31. D. Campbell 1965.
32. Nissen 1958.
33. Boyd and Richerson 1985/1996.
34. Durham 1991.

Human Variation and Adaptation

From Chapter 5 of *Anthropology*, 13/e. Carol R. Ember. Melvin Ember. Peter N. Peregrine. Copyright © 2011 by Pearson Education. Published by Prentice Hall. All rights reserved.

Human Variation and Adaptation

In any given human population, individuals vary in external features such as skin color or height and in internal features such as blood type or susceptibility to a disease. If you measure the frequencies of such features in different populations, you will typically find differences on average from one population to another. So, for example, some populations are typically darker in skin color than other populations.

Why do these physical differences exist? They may be largely the product of differences in genes. They may be largely due to growing up in a particular environment, physical and cultural. They are perhaps the result of an interaction between environmental factors and genes.

We turn first to the processes that may singly or jointly produce the varying frequencies of physical traits in different human populations. Then we discuss specific differences in external and internal characteristics and how they might be explained. Finally, we close with a critical examination of racial classification and whether it helps or hinders the study of human variation.

● ○ ●

PROCESSES IN HUMAN VARIATION AND ADAPTATION

Mutations—changes in the structure of a gene—are the ultimate source of all genetic variation. Because different genes make for greater or lesser chances of survival and reproduction, natural selection results in more favorable genes becoming more frequent in a population over time. We call this process **adaptation.** Adaptations are genetic changes that give their carriers a better chance to survive and reproduce than individuals without the genetic change who live in the same environment. It is the environment, of course, that favors the reproductive success of some traits rather than others.

How adaptive a gene or trait is depends on the specific environment; what is adaptive in one environment may not be adaptive in another. For example, the advantage that dark moths had over light moths when certain areas of England became industrialized. Predators could not easily see the darker moths against the newly darkened trees, and these moths soon outnumbered the lighter variety. Similarly, human populations live in a great variety of environments, so we would expect natural selection to favor different genes and traits in those different environments. As we shall see, variations in skin color and body build are among the many features that may be at least partly explainable by how natural selection works in different environments.

Adaptation through natural selection does not account for variation in frequencies of neutral traits—that is, traits that do not confer any advantages or disadvantages on their carriers. The sometimes different and sometimes similar frequencies of neutral traits in human populations may result, then, from genetic drift or gene flow. Genetic drift refers to variations in a population that appear because of random processes such as isolation (the "founder effect"), mating patterns, and the random segregation of chromosomes during meiosis. Gene flow involves the exchange of genes between populations. Neither genetic drift nor gene flow is an adaptive

process. Genetic drift may increase the differences between populations. Gene flow tends to work in the opposite direction—it tends to decrease differences between populations.

Acclimatization

Natural selection may favor certain genes because of certain physical environmental conditions, as in the case of the moths in England. But the physical environment can sometimes produce variation even in the absence of genetic change. As we shall see, climate may influence the way the human body grows and develops, and therefore some kinds of human variation may be explainable largely as a function of environmental variation. We call this process *acclimatization*. **Acclimatization** involves physiological adjustments to environmental conditions in individuals. Acclimatizations may have underlying genetic factors, but they are not themselves genetic. Individuals develop them during their lifetimes, rather than being born with them.

Many acclimatizations are simple physiological changes in the body that appear and disappear as the environment changes. For example, when we are chilled, our bodies attempt to create heat by making our muscles work, a physiological response to the environment that we experience as shivering. Longer exposure to cold weather leads our bodies to increase our metabolic rates so that we generate more internal heat. Both these physiological changes are acclimatizations, one short-term (shivering), one longer-term (increased metabolic rate).

As we discuss later in this chapter, some long-term acclimatizations are difficult to distinguish from adaptations because they become established as normal operating processes, and they may persist even after the individual moves into an environment that is different from the one that originally fostered the acclimatization. It also appears that some acclimatizations are closely related to genetic adaptations. For example, tanning, an acclimatization among light-skinned people when exposed to high levels of solar radiation, is likely in people where light skin color is adapted to environments with typically low solar radiation.

Influence of the Cultural Environment

Humans are not only influenced by their environments through adaptations and acclimatizations, but, humans can also dramatically affect their environments. Culture allows humans to modify their environments, and such modifications may lessen the likelihood of genetic adaptations and physiological acclimitizations. For example, the effects of cold may be modified by the culture traits of living in houses, harnessing energy to create heat, and clothing the body to insulate it. In these cultural ways, we alter our "microenvironments." Iron deficiency may be overcome by the culture trait of cooking in iron pots. If a physical environment lacks certain nutrients, people may get them by the culture trait of trading for them; trading

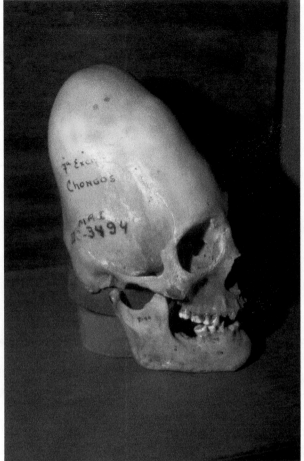

A cranium from the prehistoric Paracas culture of Peru, showing the effects of head binding.

for salt has been common in world history. Culture can also influence the direction of natural selection. As we shall see, the culture of dairying seems to have increased the frequency of genes that allow adults to digest milk.[1]

In addition, individual cultures sometimes practice behaviors that lead to physical variations between their members and between members of one culture and another. For example, elites in many highland Andean societies (the Inca, for example) practiced head binding. The heads of elite children were tightly bound with cloth. As the children grew, the binding forced the skull to take on an elongated, almost conical shape. This cultural practice, then, created physical variations among individuals that were intended to identify members of elite groups.[2] Many cultures have practices that are intended to create physical variations that distinguish members of their culture from members of other cultures. The Hebrew Bible, for example, tells the story of how Abraham was instructed by God to circumcise himself and all his male descendants as a sign of the covenant between them.[3] Thus, male descendants of Abraham traditionally share a culturally induced physical variation (lack of a foreskin) to identify themselves as a group.

In the next section, we discuss some aspects of human (physical) variation for which we have explanations that involve one or more of the processes just described.

PHYSICAL VARIATION IN HUMAN POPULATIONS

The most noticeable physical variations among populations are those that are external, on the surface—body build, facial features, skin color, and height. No less important are those variations that are internal, such as variation in susceptibility to different diseases and differences in the ability to produce certain enzymes.

We begin our survey with some physical features that appear to be strongly linked to variation in climate, particularly variation in temperature, sunlight, and altitude.

Body Build and Facial Construction

Scientists have suggested that the body build of many birds and mammals may vary according to the temperature of the environment in which they live. Bergmann and Allen, two 19th century-naturalists, suggested some general rules for animals, but researchers did not begin to examine whether these rules applied to human populations until the 1950s.[4] **Bergmann's rule** describes what seems to be a general relationship between body size and temperature: The slenderer populations of a species inhabit the warmer parts of its geographic range, and the more robust populations inhabit the cooler areas.

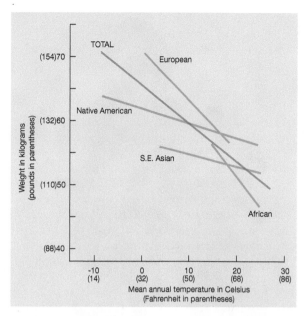

FIGURE 1 Relationship Between Body Weight of Males and Average Annual Temperature for Four Major Population Groups

Source: From Roberts 1953.
From D. F. Roberts, "Body Weight, Race, and Climate," *American Journal of Physical Anthropology*, 11 (1953), Reprinted with permission of John Wiley & Sons, Inc.

D. F. Roberts's studies of variation in mean body weight of human populations in regions with widely differing temperatures have provided support for Bergmann's rule.[5] Roberts discovered that the lowest body weights were found among residents of areas with the highest mean annual temperatures, and vice versa. Figure 1 shows the relationship between body weight of males and average annual temperature for four different geographic populations. Although the slope of the relationship is slightly different for each group, the trend is the same—with colder temperatures, weight is greater. Looking at the general trend across populations (see the "Total" line), we see that, where the mean annual temperatures are about freezing (32°F; 0°C), the average weight for males is about 143 pounds (65 kilograms); where the mean annual temperatures are about 77°F (25°C), men weigh, on the average, about 110 pounds (50 kilograms).

Allen's rule refers to another kind of variation in body build among birds and mammals: Protruding body parts (e.g., limbs) are relatively shorter in the cooler areas of a species' range than in the warmer areas. Research comparing human populations tends to support Allen's rule.[6]

The rationale behind these theories is that the long-limbed, lean body type often found in equatorial regions provides more surface area in relation to body mass and thus facilitates the dissipation of body heat. In contrast, the chunkier, shorter-limbed body type found among residents of cold regions promotes retention of body heat because the amount of surface area relative to body mass is lessened. The build of the Inuit (Eskimo) appears to exemplify Bergmann's and Allen's rules. The relatively large bodies and short legs of the Inuit may be adapted to the cold temperatures in which they live.

It is not clear whether differences in body build among populations are due solely to natural selection of different

These Samburu people from Kenya illustrate Bergmann's rule. They have the long-limbed, lean body type that is often found in equatorial regions. Such a body type provides more surface area in relation to body mass and thus may facilitate the dissipation of body heat.

Tim Davis/Corbis RF

Human skin color varies dramatically, and Gloger's rule explains this variation as an adaptation to climate. In humans, the intensity of sunlight is a key factor in skin color variation.

This Inuit father and son illustrate Allen's rule. Both have relatively large bodies and short limbs, which help them maintain body heat in the cold climate they inhabit.

genes under different conditions of cold or heat. Some of the variations may be acclimatizations induced during the life span of individuals.[7] Alphonse Riesenfeld provided experimental evidence that extreme cold can affect body proportions during growth and development. Rats raised under conditions of extreme cold generally showed changes that resemble characteristics of humans in cold environments. These cold-related changes included shortening of the long bones, consistent with Allen's rule.[8]

Like body build, facial structure may also be affected by environment. Riesenfeld found experimentally that the facial width of rats increased in cold temperatures and their nasal openings grew smaller.[9] Because the rats raised in cold environments were genetically similar to those raised in warmer environments, we can confidently conclude that the environment, not genes, brought about these changes in the rats. How much the environment directly affects variation in the human face is not clear. We do know that variation in climate is associated with facial variation. For example, people living in the humid tropics tend to have broad, short, flat noses, whereas people living in climates with low humidity (with cold or hot temperatures) tend to have long, thin noses. A narrow nose may be a more efficient humidifier of drier air than a broad nose.[10]

Skin Color

Human populations obviously differ in average skin color. Many people consider skin color the most important indicator of "race," and they sometimes treat others differently solely on this basis. But anthropologists, in addition to

being critical of prejudice, also note that skin color is not a good indicator of ancestry. For example, dark skin is commonly found in sub-Saharan Africa. However, natives of southern India have skin as dark or darker than that of many Africans. Yet, these people are not closely related to Africans, either genetically or historically.

How can we explain the wide range of skin colors among the peoples of the world? The color of a person's skin depends on both the amount of dark pigment, or melanin, in the skin and the amount of blood in the small blood vessels of the skin.[11] Despite the fact that there is still much to understand about the genetics of skin color, we can explain much of the variation.

The amount of melanin in the skin seems to be related to the climate in which a person lives. **Gloger's rule** states that populations of birds and mammals living in warmer climates have more melanin and, therefore, darker skin, fur, or feathers, than do populations of the same species living in cooler areas. On the whole, this association with climate holds true for people as well as for other mammals and birds.

The populations of darker-skinned humans do live mostly in warm climates, particularly sunny climates (see Figure 2). Dark pigmentation seems to have at least one specific advantage in sunny climates. Melanin protects the sensitive inner layers of the skin from the sun's damaging ultraviolet rays; therefore, dark-skinned people living in sunny areas are safer from sunburn and skin cancers than are light-skinned people. Dark skin may also confer other important biological advantages in tropical environments, such as greater resistance to tropical diseases.[12]

What, then, might be the advantages of light-colored skin? Presumably, there must be some benefits in some environments; otherwise, all human populations would tend to have relatively dark skin. Although light-skinned people are more susceptible to sunburn and skin cancers, the ultraviolet radiation that light skin absorbs also facilitates the body's production of vitamin D. Vitamin D helps the body incorporate calcium and thus is necessary for the proper growth and maintenance of bones. Too much vitamin D,

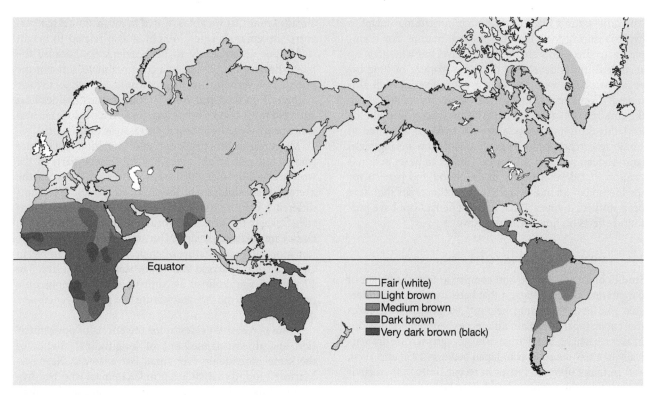

Equator

Fair (white)
Light brown
Medium brown
Dark brown
Very dark brown (black)

FIGURE 2 Variation in Skin Color

Source: From Robins 1991.
From *Biological Perspectives on Human Pigmentation* by Ashley H. Robins. Copyright © by Cambridge University Press. Reprinted by permission of Cambridge University Press.

however, can cause illness. Thus, the light-colored skin of people in temperate latitudes maximizes ultraviolet penetration, perhaps ensuring production of sufficient amounts of vitamin D for good health, whereas the darker skin of people in tropical latitudes minimizes ultraviolet penetration, perhaps preventing illness from too much vitamin D.[13] Light skin may also confer another advantage in colder environments: It is less likely to be damaged by frostbite.[14]

We now have direct evidence that confirms the connection between solar radiation and skin pigmentation. Anthropologists Nina Jablonski and George Chaplin used data from NASA satellites to determine the average amount of ultraviolet radiation people were exposed to in different parts of the world. They compared these average radiation amounts to data on skin reflectance (the lighter one's skin, the more light it reflects) and found that dark skin is more prevalent where ultraviolet radiation is more intense. Interestingly, there seems to be one notable exception—Native Americans tend to be lighter-skinned than expected. Jablonski and Chaplin suggest that this is because they are recent migrants to the New World, and their skin colors have not adapted to the varying levels of ultraviolet radiation they encountered in the Americas, just as the skin colors of European colonizers have not.[15]

Adaptation to High Altitude

Oxygen constitutes 21 percent of the air we breathe at sea level. At high altitudes, the percentage of oxygen in the air is the same, but because the barometric pressure is lower, we take in less oxygen with each breath.[16] We breathe more rapidly, our hearts beat faster, and all activity is more

difficult. The net effects are discomfort and a condition known as **hypoxia,** or oxygen deficiency.

If high altitude presents such difficulties for many human beings, how is it that populations numbering in the millions can live out their lives, healthy and productive, at altitudes of 6,000, 12,000, or even 17,000 feet? Populations in the Himalayas and the Andes have adapted to their environments and do not display the symptoms that low-altitude dwellers suffer when they are exposed to high altitudes. Moreover, high-altitude dwellers have come to terms physiologically with extreme cold, deficient nutrition, strong winds, rough countryside, and intense solar radiation.[17]

Early studies of Andean high-altitude dwellers found that they differed in certain physical ways from low-altitude dwellers. Compared with low-altitude dwellers, high-altitude Andean Indians had larger chests and greater lung capacity, as well as more surface area in the capillaries of the lungs (which was believed to facilitate the transfer of oxygen to the blood).[18] Early researchers thought that genetic changes had allowed the Andeans to maximize their ability to take in oxygen at the lower barometric pressure of their high-altitude environment. Recent research, however, has cast some doubt on this conclusion. It appears now that other populations living at high altitudes do not show the Andean pattern of physical differences. In the Himalayas, for example, low-altitude dwellers and high-altitude dwellers do not differ in chest size or lung size, even though both groups show adequate lung functioning.[19]

Thus, current research does not suggest that high-altitude living requires biological adaptations that are purely genetic. In fact, some evidence suggests that humans

39

who grow up in a high-altitude environment may adapt to hypoxia during their lifetimes, as they mature. For example, Peruvians who were born at sea level but who grew up at high altitudes developed the same amount of lung capacity as people who spent their entire lives at high altitudes.[20] Consistent with a presumed environmental effect, the children of high-altitude Peruvians who grow up in the lowlands do not develop larger chests. What appeared to earlier researchers to be a genetic adaptation among highland Andean populations appears in fact to be an acclimatization that develops early in childhood and persists for the lifetime of an individual. As with other traits that have been studied, it appears that life experiences can have profound effects on how the body grows.

Height

Studies of identical twins and comparisons of the height of parents and children suggest that heredity plays a considerable role in determining height,[21] so genetic differences must at least partly explain differences between populations in average height. But if average height can increase dramatically in a few decades, as in Japan between 1950 and 1980, and in many other countries in recent times,[22] then environmental influences are also likely to be important.

The considerable variation in average height among human populations may be partly explained by temperature differences. The Dutch, in Europe, are among the tallest populations in the world on average, and the Mbuti of Zaire, in central Africa, are among the shortest.[23] We

In recent times, there has been a dramatic increase in average height, which may be due to one or more environmental factors. Here we see a Chinese American girl who is taller than her mother and almost as tall as her father.

© Ken Huang/Image Bank/Getty Images, Inc.

already know that weight is related to mean annual temperature (Bergmann's rule). Weight is also related to height (taller people are likely to be heavier). So, because the taller (heavier) Dutch live in a cooler climate, some of the population variation in height would appear to involve adaptation to heat and cold.[24] Other factors besides heat and cold must also be operating, however, because tall and short peoples can be found in most areas of the world.

Many researchers think that poor nutrition and disease lead to reduced height and weight. In many parts of the world, children in higher social classes are taller on the average than children in lower social classes,[25] and this difference is more marked in economically poorer countries,[26] where the wealth and health differences between the classes are particularly large. During times of war and poor nutrition, children's stature often decreases. For example, in Germany during World War II, the stature of children 7 to 17 years of age declined as compared with previous time periods, despite the fact that stature had generally increased over time.[27]

More persuasive evidence for the effects of poor nutrition and disease comes out of longitudinal studies of the same individuals over time. For example, Reynaldo Martorell found that children in Guatemala who had frequent bouts of diarrhea were on the average over an inch shorter at age 7 than children without frequent diarrhea.[28] Although malnourished or diseased children can catch up in their growth, follow-up research on Guatemalan children suggests that, if stunting occurs before 3 years of age, stature at age 18 will still be reduced.[29]

A controversial set of studies links a very different environmental factor to variation in height in human populations. The factor at issue is stress, physical and emotional, in infancy.[30] Contrary to the view that any kind of stress is harmful, it appears that some presumably stressful experiences in infancy are associated with greater height and weight. Experimental studies with rats provided the original stimulus for the studies investigating the possible effect of stress on height. The experiments showed that rats that were physically handled ("petted") by the experimenters grew to be longer and heavier than rats not petted. Researchers originally thought that this was because the petted rats had received "tender loving care." But someone noticed that the petted rats seemed terrified (they urinated and defecated) when petted by humans, which suggested that the petting might have been stressful. It turned out in subsequent studies that even more obviously stressful experiences such as electric shock, vibration, and temperature extremes also produced rats with longer skeletons as compared with unstressed rats.

Thomas Landauer and John Whiting thought that stress in human infants might similarly produce greater adult height. Many cultures have customs for treating infants that could be physically stressful, including circumcision, branding of the skin with sharp objects, piercing the nose, ears, or lips for the insertion of ornaments, molding and stretching the head and limbs for cosmetic purposes, and vaccination. In addition, Shulamith Gunders and John Whiting suggested that separating the baby from its mother right after birth is another kind of stress.

In cross-cultural comparisons by Whiting and his colleagues,[31] it seems that *both* physical stress and mother-infant separation, *if practiced before 2 years of age*, predict greater adult height; males are on the average 2 inches taller in such societies. (It is important to note that the stresses being discussed are short in duration, often a one-time occurrence, and do not constitute prolonged stress or abuse, which can have opposite effects.)

Because the cross-cultural evidence is associational, not experimental, it is possible that the results are due to some factor confounded with infant stress. Perhaps societies with infant stress have better nutrition or have climates that favor tallness. Recently, using new cross-cultural comparisons, J. Patrick Gray and Linda Wolfe attempted to assess different possible predictors of height variation between populations. The predictors compared were nutrition, climate, geography, physical stress, and mother-infant separation. Gray and Wolfe's analysis indicated which of those factors predicted adult height independently of the others. It turned out that geographic region, climatic zone, and customs of infant stress were all significant independent predictors of height.[32] So the results now available clearly show that the effect of infant stress cannot be discounted.

Persuasive evidence for the stress hypothesis also comes from an experimental study conducted in Kenya.[33] Landauer and Whiting arranged for a randomly selected sample of children to be vaccinated before they were 2 years old. Other children were vaccinated soon after they were 2. A few years later, the two groups were compared with respect to height. Consistent with the cross-cultural evidence on the possible effect of stress on height, the children vaccinated before the age of 2 were significantly taller than the children vaccinated later. The children vaccinated before the age of 2 were selected randomly for early vaccination, so it is unlikely that nutritional or other differences between the two groups account for their difference in height.

migrants and immigrants

Physical Differences between Natives and Immigrants

Physical anthropologists in the late 19th century were fascinated with the concept of "race." Physical anthropologists focused their careers on identifying and describing the particular characteristics that distinguished one "race" of humans from another. There was no debate about the biological reality of human "races," as there is today; rather, the idea that "races" existed seemed obviously true to anyone with eyes. People differed, and those differences could be identified, measured, and compared to show that specific variations were more common among one group of people than another. Some of the greatest scientists of the 19th century—Louis Agassiz, Paul Broca, Francis Galton, Karl Pearson—actively contributed to the identification and description of human "races."

There was a problem, however. The stability of identified so-called "racial" characteristics was untested. It was simply assumed that features used to classify "races," features such as the width of the face and roundness of the head—were stable over long periods of time and under different environmental conditions. If they were not, the characteristics of the supposed "races" might be only short-lived constellations of traits, and not fixed characteristics of

human groups created when modern humans spread around the earth.

Franz Boas, the founder of anthropology in the United States, saw an opportunity to test the stability of "racial" characteristics using data on the massive influx of immigrants into the United States at the close of the 19th century. Boas convinced the U.S. Immigration Commission that a large-scale study of immigrants and their children would help the federal government better serve these new citizens. He received funding to conduct a thorough physical study of several thousand immigrant families, and, over the course of several years, collected data on nearly 18,000 individuals.

Boas's results were surprising. He found that immigrants and their children differed in small but statistically significant ways. In particular, he found that cranial shape was not immutable, as physical anthropologists had assumed at the time, but rather could change in a single generation. And the direction of change was not always the same. The heads of first-generation offspring born in the United States of relatively long-headed Italians and relatively round-headed Eastern European Jews were more like one another than either was like their parents. What was going on?

Boas provided no clear answer, although he suggested that the similar environment of New York where all these children grew up might have played a role. Boas's study of immigrants proved to be very controversial. At the time, it questioned the assumption that "racial" characteristics were stable and unchanging and, in doing so, questioned the entire notion of "race" that had guided physical anthropology for a half century. Interestingly, Boas's study still remains somewhat controversial. In 2003, two groups of scholars published contradictory reanalyses of Boas's original data. One group claimed Boas got it wrong—that Boas overstated his findings and that, in reality, "racial" features were remarkably stable; the other group claimed that Boas basically got it right, despite the comparatively limited statistical analyses available to him. Both agree, however, with Boas that supposedly stable "racial" characteristics can change within a generation.

Sources: Brace 2005; Gravlee, Bernard, and Leonard 2003; Sparks and Jantz 2003

As we noted earlier, people have been getting taller in several areas of the world. What accounts for this recent trend toward greater height? Several factors may be involved. Some researchers think that it may be the result of improved nutrition and lower incidence of infectious diseases.[34] But it might also be that infant stress has increased as a result of giving birth in hospitals, which usually separate babies from mothers and also subject the newborns to medical tests, including taking blood. Various kinds of vaccinations have also become more common in infancy.[35]

In short, differences in human size seem to be the result of both adaptations and acclimatizations, with both of these, in turn, affected by cultural factors such as nutrition and stress.

Susceptibility to Infectious Diseases

Certain populations seem to have developed inherited resistances to particular infectious diseases. That is, populations repeatedly decimated by certain diseases in the past now have a high frequency of genetic characteristics that ameliorate the effects of these diseases. As Arno Motulsky pointed out, if there are genes that protect people from dying when they are infected by one of the diseases prevalent in their area, these genes will tend to become more common in succeeding generations.[36]

A field study of the infectious disease myxomatosis in rabbits supports this theory. When the virus responsible for the disease was first introduced into the Australian rabbit population, more than 95 percent of the infected animals died. But among the offspring of animals exposed to successive epidemics of myxomatosis, the percentage of animals that died from the disease decreased from year to year. The more epidemics the animals' ancestors had lived through, the smaller the percentage of current animals that died of the disease. Thus, the data suggested that the rabbits had developed a genetic resistance to myxomatosis.[37]

Infectious diseases seem to follow a similar pattern among human populations. When tuberculosis first strikes a population that has had no previous contact with it, the disease is usually fatal. But some populations seem to have inherited a resistance to death from tuberculosis. For example, the Ashkenazi Jews in America (those whose ancestors came from central and eastern Europe) are one of several populations whose ancestors survived many years of exposure to tuberculosis in the crowded European ghettos where they had previously lived. Although the rate of tuberculosis infection is identical among American Jews and non-Jews, the rate of tuberculosis mortality is significantly lower among Jews than among non-Jews in the United States.[38] After reviewing other data on this subject, Motulsky thought it likely "that the present relatively high resistance of Western populations to tuberculosis is genetically conditioned through natural selection during long contact with the disease."[39]

We tend to think of measles as a childhood disease that kills virtually no one, and we now have a vaccine against it. But when first introduced into populations, the measles virus can kill large numbers of people. In 1949, the Tupari Indians of Brazil numbered about 200 people. By 1955, two-thirds of the Tupari had died of measles introduced into the tribe by rubber gatherers in the area.[40] Large numbers of people died of measles in epidemics in the Faeroe Islands in 1846, in Hawaii in 1848, in the Fiji Islands in 1874, and among the Canadian Inuit very recently. It is possible that, where mortality rates from measles are low, populations have acquired a genetic resistance to death from this disease.[41]

Why is a population susceptible to a disease in the first place? Epidemiologist Francis Black suggests that lack of genes for resistance is not the whole answer. A high degree of genetic homogeneity in the population may also increase

Permanent settlements and high population densities allow diseases to spread rapidly and produce epidemics. Shown here is Banda Aceh's Peunayong Market in Indonesia. Close contact between chickens and humans in markets like this one provided the opportunity for the deadly H5N1 strain of bird flu to evolve.

susceptibility.[42] A virus grown in one host is preadapted to a genetically similar new host and is therefore likely to be more virulent in the new host. For example, the measles virus adapts to a host individual; when it replicates, the viral forms that the host cannot kill are those most likely to survive and continue replicating. When the virus passes to a new host with similar genes, the preadapted virus is likely to kill the new host. On the other hand, if the next host is very different genetically, the adaptation process starts over again; the virus is not so virulent at first because the host can kill it.

Populations that recently came to an area, and that had a small group of founders (as was probably true for the first Native Americans and the Polynesian seafarers who first settled many islands in the Pacific), tended to have a high degree of genetic homogeneity. Therefore, epidemic diseases introduced by Europeans (such as measles) would be likely to kill many of the natives within the first few years after contact. Up to an estimated 56 million people died in the New World after contact with Europeans, mostly because of introduced diseases such as smallpox and measles. Similarly caused depopulation occurred widely in the Pacific.[43]

Some researchers suggest that nongenetic factors may also partly explain differential resistance to infectious disease. For example, cultural practices may partly explain the epidemics of measles among the Yanomamö Indians of Venezuela and Brazil. The Yanomamö frequently visit other villages, and that, together with the non-isolation of sick individuals, promoted a very rapid spread of the disease. Because many individuals were sick at the same time, there were not enough healthy people to feed and care for the sick; mothers down with measles could not even nurse their babies. Thus, cultural factors may increase exposure to a disease and worsen its effect on a population.[44]

Epidemics of infectious disease may occur only if many people live near each other. Hunter-gatherers, who usually live in small dispersed bands, do not have enough people in and near the community to keep an epidemic going. Without enough people to infect, short-lived microorganisms that cause or carry diseases die out. In contrast, among agriculturalists, there are larger numbers of people in and around the community to whom a disease can spread. Permanent settlements, particularly urban settlements, also are likely to have poor sanitation and contaminated water.[45] Tuberculosis is an example of an infectious disease that, although very old, began to kill large numbers of people only after the emergence of sedentary, larger communities.[46]

Sickle-Cell Anemia

Another biological variation is an abnormality of the red blood cells known as **sickle-cell anemia,** or **sicklemia.** This is a condition in which normal, disk-shaped red blood cells assume a crescent (sickle) shape when deprived of oxygen. The sickle-shaped red blood cells do not move through the body as readily as normal cells, and thus cause more oxygen deficiency and damage to the heart, lungs, brain, and other vital organs. In addition, the red blood

cells tend to "die" more rapidly, and the anemia worsens still more.[47]

Sickle-cell anemia is caused by a variant form of the genetic instructions for hemoglobin, the protein that carries oxygen in the red blood cells.[48] Individuals who have sickle-cell anemia have inherited the same allele (Hb^S) from both parents and are therefore homozygous for that gene. Individuals who receive this allele from only one parent are heterozygous; they have one Hb^S allele and one allele for normal hemoglobin (Hb^A). Heterozygotes generally will not show the full-blown symptoms of sickle-cell disease, although a heterozygous individual may have a mild case of anemia in some cases. A heterozygous person has a 50 percent chance of passing on the sickle-cell allele to a child. And if the child later mates with another person who is also a carrier of the sickle-cell allele, the statistical probability is that 25 percent of their children will develop sickle-cell anemia. Without advanced medical care, most individuals with two Hb^S alleles are unlikely to live more than a few years.[49]

Why has the allele for sickle-cell persisted in various populations? If people with sickle-cell anemia do not usually live to reproduce, we would expect a reduction in the frequency of Hb^S to near zero through the process of *normalizing selection.* But the sickle-cell allele occurs fairly often in some parts of the world, particularly in the wet tropical belt of Africa, where frequencies may be between 20 percent and 30 percent, and in Greece, Sicily, and southern India.[50]

Because the sickle-cell gene occurs in these places much more often than expected, researchers in the 1940s and the 1950s began to suspect that heterozygous individuals (who carry one Hb^S allele) might have a reproductive advantage in a malarial environment.[51] If the heterozygotes were more resistant to attacks of malaria than the homozygotes for normal hemoglobin (who get the Hb^A allele from both parents), the heterozygotes would be more likely to survive and reproduce, and therefore the recessive Hb^S allele would persist at a higher-than-expected frequency in the population. This kind of outcome is an example of *balancing selection.*[52]

A number of pieces of evidence support the "malaria theory." First, geographic comparisons show that the sickle-cell allele tends to be found where the incidence of malaria is high (see Figure 3). Second, as land in the tropics is opened to yam and rice agriculture, the incidence of the sickle-cell allele also increases. Indeed, recent studies suggest malaria may have evolved alongside agriculture in these regions.[53] The reason seems to be that malaria, carried principally by the *Anopheles gambiae* mosquito, becomes more prevalent as tropical forest gives way to more open land where mosquitoes can thrive in warm, sunlit ponds. Indeed, even among peoples of similar cultural backgrounds, the incidence of the sickle-cell allele increases with greater rainfall and surpluses of water. Third, children who are heterozygous for the sickle-cell trait tend to have fewer malarial parasites in their bodies than do homozygous normal individuals, and they are more likely to survive.[54] The sickling trait does not necessarily keep people from contracting malaria, but it greatly

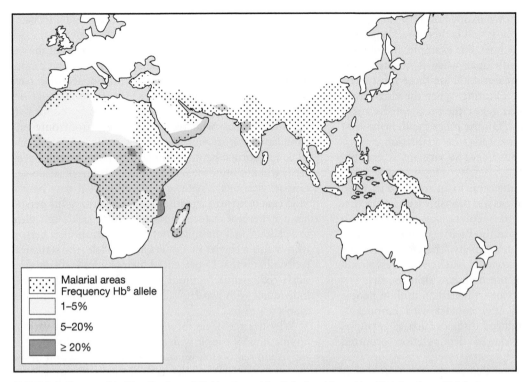

FIGURE 3 Geographic Distribution of Sicklemia and Its Relationship to the Distribution of Malaria

decreases the rate of mortality from malaria—and in evolutionary terms, the overall effect is the same.[55] Fourth, if there is no balancing selection because malaria is no longer present, we should find a rapid decline in the incidence of the sickle-cell allele. Indeed, we find such a decline in populations with African ancestry. Those who live in malaria-free zones of the New World have a much lower incidence of sicklemia than do those who live in malarial regions of the New World.[56]

Hb[S] is not the only abnormal hemoglobin to have a distribution related to malaria. It seems that a number of abnormal hemoglobins may be widespread because of the advantage that heterozygotes have against the disease. For example, another abnormal hemoglobin, Hb[E], occurs in populations from India through Southeast Asia and New Guinea where malaria occurs, but Hb[S] is not that common. Why should Hb[E] heterozygotes have resistance to malaria? One possibility is that malarial parasites are less able to survive in an individual's blood with some normal and some abnormal hemoglobin. Abnormal hemoglobin cells are more delicate and live less long, so they may not readily support malarial parasites.[57]

Lactase Deficiency

When American educators discovered that African American schoolchildren very often did not drink milk, they assumed that lack of money or education was the reason. These assumptions provided the impetus for establishing the school milk programs prevalent around the country. However, it now appears that, after infancy, many people lack the enzyme lactase, which is necessary for breaking down the sugar in milk—lactose—into simpler sugars that can be absorbed into the bloodstream.[58] Thus, a person without lactase cannot digest milk properly, and drinking it may cause bloating, cramps, stomach gas, and diarrhea. A study conducted in Baltimore among 312 African American and 221 European American children in grades 1 through 6 in two elementary schools indicated that 85 percent of the African American children and 17 percent of the European American children were milk-intolerant.[59]

More recent studies indicate that lactose intolerance occurs frequently in adults in many parts of the world.[60] The condition is common in Southeast and East Asia, India, the Mediterranean and the Near East, sub-Saharan Africa, and among Native North and South Americans. The widespread incidence of lactose intolerance should not be surprising. After infancy, mammals normally stop producing lactase.[61]

If lactose intolerance in adulthood in mammals is normal, we need to understand why only some human populations have the ability to make lactase in adulthood and digest lactose. Why would selection favor this genetic ability in some populations but not in others? In the late 1960s, F. J. Simoons and Robert McCracken noted a relationship between lactose absorption and dairying (raising cows for milk). They suggested that, with the advent of dairying, individuals with the genetic ability to produce lactase in adulthood would have greater reproductive success; hence, dairying populations would come to have a high proportion of individuals with the ability to break down lactose.[62]

(Top) Milking a cow in Barnstable, Massachusetts. Natural selection may favor production of the enzyme lactase, a genetic way of making milk digestible in dairying populations far from the equator. (Bottom) A Masai woman milking a cow in Kenya. Natural selection may favor the souring of milk, a cultural way of making it digestible in dairying populations close to the equator.

But people in some dairying societies do not produce lactase in adulthood. Rather, they seem to have developed a cultural solution to the problem of lactase deficiency; they transform their milk into cheese, yogurt, sour cream, and other milk products that are low in lactose. To make these low-lactose products, people separate the lactose-rich whey from the curds or treat the milk with a bacterium (*Lactobacillus*) that breaks down the lactose, thus making the milk product digestible by a lactase-deficient person.[63]

So, why did natural selection favor a biological solution (the production of the enzyme lactase in adulthood) in some dairying societies rather than the cultural solution? William Durham has collected evidence that natural selection may favor the biological solution in dairying societies farther from the equator. The theory is that lactose behaves biochemically like vitamin D, facilitating the absorption of calcium—but only in people who produce lactase so that they can absorb the lactose. Because people in more temperate latitudes are not exposed to that much sunlight, particularly in the winter, and therefore make less vitamin D in their skin, natural selection may have favored the lactase way of absorbing dietary calcium.[64] In other words, natural selection may favor lactase production in adulthood, as well as lighter skin, at higher latitudes (where there is less sunlight).

This is an example of how culture may influence the way natural selection favors some genes over others. Without dairying, natural selection may not have favored the genetic propensity to produce lactase. This propensity is yet another example of the complex ways in which genes, environment, and culture interact to create human variation.

RACE AND RACISM

Fortunately, internal variations such as lactase deficiency have never been associated with intergroup tensions—perhaps because such differences are not immediately obvious. Unfortunately, the same cannot be said for some of the more obvious external human differences such as skin color.

For as long as any of us can remember, countless aggressive actions—from fistfights to large-scale riots and civil wars—have stemmed from tensions and misunderstandings between various groups commonly referred to by many as "races." *Race* has become such a common term that most of us take the concept for granted, not bothering to consider what it does and does not mean. We may talk about the "human race," which means that all humans belong to the same breeding population. Yet we are often asked to check a box to identify our particular "race." We discuss first how biologists sometimes use the term *race*; then we turn to why most biological anthropologists now conclude that the concept of race does not apply usefully to humans. We discuss how racial classifications are largely social constructions that have been used to justify discrimination, exploitation, and even the extermination of certain categories of people.

Race as a Construct in Biology

Biological variation is not uniformly distributed in any species. Although all members of a species can potentially interbreed with others, most matings take place within smaller groups or breeding populations. Through the processes of natural selection and genetic drift, populations inhabiting different geographic regions will come to exhibit some differences in biological traits. When differences within a species become sufficiently noticeable, biologists may classify different populations into different *varieties,* or *races.* If the term **race** is understood to be just a shorthand or classificatory way that biologists describe slight population variants within a species, the concept of race would probably not be controversial. Unfortunately, as applied to humans, racial classifications have often been confounded with **racism,** the belief that some "races" are innately inferior to others.

applied anthropology

The Use of Race in Forensic Anthropology

In this chapter, we have made the point that human "races" are not valid biological entities. There is more genetic variation within alleged "races" than between them, and the characteristics used to define "races" are primarily visual—skin color, hair form, eye form, and the like. Most anthropologists (over 70 percent according to a recent survey) disagree with the statement "There are biological races in the species *Homo sapiens*." Given this fact, it seems odd that many forensic anthropologists still employ "race" as one of the categories for identifying skeletal remains.

Diana Smay and George Armelagos argue that forensic anthropologists still employ the concept of "race" for three primary reasons. First, they suggest that some forensic anthropologists genuinely believe that "race" is a useful analytical tool. For these anthropologists, the fact that it is easy for anyone to categorize others into "races" must mean something is genuine about the concept. Indeed, some forensic anthropologists suggest that they can determine "race" with 80 percent accuracy from skeletal remains (although others argue that, without

clear information about the specific geographical location where the remains were found, accuracy drops to less than 20 percent). This leads to a second reason (according to Smay and Armelagos) that may lead forensic anthropologists to employ the "race" concept—it works for them. Within local areas, at least, a well-trained forensic anthropologist can determine whether a skeleton comes from one of the major "race" groups. But as forensic anthropologist Madeleine Hinkes explains: "sometimes it is only the anthropologist's experience that tells him there is an undefinable 'something' about the skeleton that suggests one race over another"—not a very convincing argument for the analytical utility of "race."

A third reason Smay and Armelagos give for why many forensic anthropologists continue to employ the concept of "race" is that they asked to do so. As Stanley Rhine points out, "The forensic anthropologist who can tell officials that an unknown skull is, for instance, Hispanic, provides a datum useful in narrowing search parameters. By contrast, the forensic anthropologist who delivers a

philosophical lecture to the sheriff on the non-existence of human races is unlikely to be consulted again." But is this a good reason to employ the concept of "race"? Might there be a better way to provide information to police and other officials to help them identify a set of human remains? Alice Brues thinks so. She argues that forensic anthropologists should focus on local, geographic variations among populations that we know do exist and avoid the large "race" categories that we know do not. In Alaska, for example, forensic anthropologists might be able to distinguish between Inuit and Aleut remains, or between Chinese, Japanese, and Polynesian in California. Brues argues that, by lumping the real variation that is present in these local populations into predefined "racial" categories, forensic anthropologists limit their ability to use the full range of variation to identify unique, local variations that might be useful in identifying human remains.

Sources: Brues 1992; Hinkes 1993, 51; Lieberman et al. 2003; Rhine 1993, 55; Smay and Armelagos 2000.

The misuse and misunderstanding of the term *race* and its association with racist thinking is one reason why many biological anthropologists and others have suggested that the term should not be applied to human biological differences.

A second reason for not applying racial classification to humans is that humans have exhibited so much interbreeding that different populations are not clearly classifiable into discrete groups that can be defined in terms of the presence or absence of particular biological traits.[65] Therefore, many argue that "race" is not scientifically useful for describing human biological variation. The difficulty in employing racial classification is evident by comparing the number of "races" that classifiers come up with. The number of "racial" categories in humans has varied from as few as 3 to more than 37.[66]

How can human groups be clearly divided into "races" if most adaptive biological traits show clines or gradual differences from one region to another?[67] Skin color is a

good example of clinal variation. In the area around Egypt, there is a gradient of skin color as one moves from north to south in the Nile Valley. Skin generally becomes darker closer to the equator (south) and lighter closer to the Mediterranean. But other adaptive traits may not have north-south clines, because the environmental predictors may be distributed differently. Nose shape varies with humidity, but clines in humidity do not particularly correspond to variation in latitude. So the gradient for skin color would not be the same as the gradient for nose shape. Because adaptive traits tend to be clinally distributed, there is no line you could draw on a world map that would separate "white" from "black" people or "whites" from "Asians."[68] Only traits that are neutral in terms of natural selection will tend (because of genetic drift) to cluster in regions.[69]

Racial classification is problematic also because there is sometimes more physical, physiological, and genetic diversity *within* a single geographic group that might be called a "race" (e.g., Africans) than there is *between* supposed "racial" groups. Africans vary more among themselves than they do in comparison with people elsewhere.[70] Analyses of all human populations have demonstrated that between 93 percent and 95 percent of genetic variation is due to individual differences within populations, whereas only 3 percent to 5 percent of genetic variation is due to differences between major human population groups.[71] "Race," when applied to humans, is a social category, not a scientific one.

Race and Civilization

Many people hold the racist viewpoint that the biological inferiority of certain groups, which they call "races," is reflected in the supposedly "primitive" quality of their cultures. They will argue that the "developed" nations are "white" and the "underdeveloped" nations are not. (We put terms like "white," which are used as racial categories, in quotes to indicate the problematic nature of the categories.) But to make such an argument ignores much of history. Many of today's so-called underdeveloped nations—primarily in Asia, Africa, and South America—had developed complex and sophisticated civilizations long before European nations expanded and acquired considerable power. The advanced societies of the Shang dynasty in China, the Mayans in Mesoamerica, and the

African empire of Ghana were all founded and developed by "nonwhites."

Between 1523 and 1028 B.C., China had a complex form of government, armies, metal tools and weapons, and production and storage facilities for large quantities of grain. The early Chinese civilization also had writing and elaborate religious rituals.[72] From A.D. 300 to 900, the Mayans were a large population with a thriving economy. They built many large and beautiful cities in which were centered great pyramids and luxurious palaces.[73] According to legend, the West African civilization of Ghana was founded during the 2nd century A.D. By A.D. 770, the time of the Sonniki rulers, Ghana had developed two capital cities—one Muslim and the other non-Muslim—each with its own ruler and both supported largely by Ghana's lucrative gold market.[74]

Considering how recently northern Europeans developed cities and central governments, it seems odd that some "whites" should label Africans, Native Americans, and others backward in terms of historical achievement, or biologically inferior in terms of capacity for civilization. But racists, both "white" and "nonwhite," choose to ignore the fact that many populations have achieved remarkable advances in civilization. Most significant, racists refuse to believe that they can acknowledge the achievements of another group without in any way downgrading the achievements of their own.

Race, Conquest, and the Role of Infectious Disease

There are those who would argue that Europeans' superiority accounted for their ability to colonize much of the world during the last few hundred years. But it now appears that Europeans were able to dominate at least partly because many native peoples were susceptible to diseases they introduced.[75] Earlier, we discussed how continued exposure to epidemics of infectious diseases, such as tuberculosis and measles, can cause succeeding generations to acquire a genetic resistance to death from such diseases. Smallpox had a long history in Europe and Africa; genetic resistance eventually made it mostly a survivable childhood disease. But in the New World, it was quite another story. Cortez and the conquistadores were inadvertently aided by smallpox in their attempt to defeat the Aztecs of Mexico. In 1520, a member of Cortez's army unwittingly transmitted smallpox to the natives. The disease spread rapidly, killing at least 50 percent of the population, and so the Aztecs were at a considerable disadvantage in their battling with the Spanish.[76]

Outbreaks of smallpox repeatedly decimated many Native American populations in North America a century or two later. In the early 19th century, the Massachusett and Narragansett Indians, with populations of 30,000 and 9,000, respectively, were reduced by smallpox to a few hundred members. Extremely high mortality rates were also noted among the Crow, the Blackfoot, and other

African metal workers created magnificent works of art like this golden head from Ghana long before Europeans arrived.

The conquest of the Aztecs was aided by smallpox contracted from the Spanish, which killed at least half the population.

Native American groups during the 19th century. The germ theory alone may not completely explain these epidemics; Europeans may have deliberately encouraged the spread of one new disease, smallpox, by purposely distributing infected blankets to the natives. Motulsky calls the spread of smallpox "one of the first examples of biological warfare."[77]

Race and Behavior

As an outgrowth of earlier attempts to show that inferior "races" have "primitive" cultures, some scholars have attempted to demonstrate behavioral differences between "races." One of the most active has been psychologist J. Philippe Rushton, whose 1995 book *Race, Evolution, and Behavior* purports to demonstrate behavioral differences between the "Negroid," "Caucasoid," and "Mongoloid" "races" in terms of sexual practices, parenting, social deviance, and family structure, among others.

Rushton argues that these behaviors have a genetic basis rooted in adaptations to particular environments. He suggests that "Negroids" are adapted to the warm environments of East Africa, where humans first evolved, through a reproductive strategy in which individuals have many offspring but put little energy into their children's upbringing and care. This strategy is known in evolutionary theory as *r-selected,* and is well documented among creatures such as fish, reptiles, and even some mammals (rabbits, for example).[78] Rushton further suggests that, as humans left Africa they adapted to the "colder" climates of Asia by adopting a more *K-selected* reproductive strategy, which involves having few offspring but putting lots of energy into their upbringing and care. K-selected strategies are also well documented in the animal world, and it is interesting to note that apes (and humans) are often presented as examples of highly K-selected species.[79]

The data Rushton uses to support his argument come almost entirely from modern nations, many with a history of racial discrimination (such as South Africa, Japan, and the United States). But if genetic differences in behavior do exist among these three "races," differences that have their origins in the exodus of modern humans from Africa more than 100,000 years ago, then those differences should be apparent both between and among all the cultures of the world. That is, "Negroid" cultures should all share behaviors that are clearly different from those of "Caucasoid" cultures; "Caucasoid" cultures should all share behaviors that are different from those of "Mongoloid" cultures; and so on. Do such differences exist?

The authors of this text used information about the 186 cultures composing the Standard Cross-Cultural Sample to test whether Rushton's ideas hold up.[80] We examined 26 separate behaviors that Rushton predicted would differ among the "races." Contrary to Rushton's predictions, most of the behaviors showed no differences between the supposed "racial" groups. Only one of them showed the differences that Rushton predicted, and five of them demonstrated a pattern that was the *opposite* of what Rushton predicted. So Rushton's gross division of humans into three "races" does not generally predict variation in human behavior. His ideas appear plainly wrong and do not support the belief that it is scientifically useful to distinguish human "races."[81]

Race and Intelligence

Attempts to document differences in intelligence among the so-called races have a fairly long history. In the 19th century, European white supremacists tried to find scientific justification for what they felt was the genetically inherited mental inferiority of "blacks." They did this by measuring skulls. It was believed that the larger the skull, the greater the cranial capacity and the bigger (hence, also better) the brain. Although the skull-measuring mania quickly disappeared and is no longer considered seriously as a way to measure intelligence, other "facts" may be used to demonstrate the presumed intellectual superiority of "white" people—namely, statistics from intelligence tests.

The first large-scale intelligence testing in the United States began with the nation's entry into World War I, in 1917. Thousands of draftees were given the so-called alpha and beta IQ tests to determine military assignments. Later, psychologists arranged the test results according to the "racial" categories of "white" and "black" and found what they had expected—"blacks" scored consistently lower than "whites." This result was viewed as scientific proof of the innate intellectual inferiority of "blacks" and was used to justify further discrimination against them, both in and out of the army.[82]

Otto Klineberg's subsequent statistical analyses of IQ test results demonstrated that "blacks" from northern states scored higher than "blacks" from the South. Although dedicated racists explained that this difference was due to the northward migration of innately intelligent "blacks," most academics attributed the result to the influence of superior education and more stimulating environments in the North. When further studies showed that northern "blacks" scored higher than southern "whites," the better-education-in-the-North theory gained support, but again racists insisted such results were due to northward migration by more intelligent "whites."

As a further test of his conclusions, Klineberg gave IQ tests to "black" schoolgirls born and partly raised in the South who had spent varying lengths of time in New York City. He found that the longer the girls had been in the North, the higher their average IQ. In addition to providing support for the belief that "blacks" are not inherently inferior to "whites," these findings suggested that cultural factors can and do influence IQ scores, and that IQ is not a fixed quantity.

The controversy about race and intelligence was fueled again in 1969 by Arthur Jensen.[83] He suggested that, although the IQ scores of American "blacks" overlapped considerably with the IQ scores of "whites," the average score for "blacks" was 15 points lower than the average for "whites." IQ scores presumably have a large genetic component, so the lower average score for "blacks" implied to Jensen that "blacks" were genetically inferior to "whites." Jensen's arguments were further developed by Richard Herrnstein and Charles Murray in their 1994 book, *The Bell Curve*. Herrnstein and Murray purported to show that the intelligence of an individual was largely inherited and unchangeable throughout the life span, that an individual's success was largely based on intelligence, and that African Americans were likely to remain at the bottom of society because they had less intelligence than European Americans.[84] Herrnstein and Murray appealed to a lot of studies to buttress their argument. But their argument was still faulty.

If you look at the average scores on many standard intelligence tests, you might conclude, as racists have, that African Americans are less intelligent than European Americans. The averages are different between the two groups; African Americans typically have lower scores. But what does this average difference mean? Herrnstein and Murray, like Jensen and others before them, fail to distinguish between a measure, such as a particular IQ test, and what is supposedly being measured, intelligence. If a test only imperfectly measures what it purports to measure, lower average IQ scores merely mean lower scores on that particular IQ test; they do not necessarily reflect lower intelligence.[85] There are many reasons why some smart people might not do well on particular kinds of IQ tests. For example, the way the tests are administered may affect performance, as may lack of familiarity with the format or the experiences and objects referred to. The test might also not measure particular kinds of intelligence such as social "smarts" and creativity.

If African Americans were really less intelligent, more than their average IQ scores would be lower. The whole frequency distribution of their individual scores should also be lower—they should have fewer geniuses and more retarded individuals. That is, the bell-shaped curve showing how their scores are distributed should range lower than the curve for other Americans, and African Americans should also have proportionately fewer scores at the very high end of the scale. But neither expectation is confirmed.[86] Critics have pointed to many other problems with the evidence presented in *The Bell Curve*. But the fundamental problem is the same as with all attempts to use differences in average IQ scores to make judgments about the capability of different groups. IQ tests may not adequately measure what they purport to measure.

First, there is widespread recognition now that IQ tests are probably not accurate measures of "intelligence" because they are probably biased in favor of the subculture of those who construct the tests. That is, many of the questions on the test refer to things that "white," middle-class children are familiar with, thus giving such children an advantage.[87] So far, no one has come up with a "culture-fair," or bias-free, test. There is more agreement that, although the IQ test may not measure "intelligence" well, it may predict scholastic success or how well a child will do in the primarily "white"-oriented school system.[88]

A second major problem with a purely genetic interpretation of the IQ difference is that many studies show that IQ scores can be influenced by the social environment. Economically deprived children, whether "black" or "white," will generally score lower than affluent "white" or "black" children. And training of children with low IQ scores clearly improves their test scores.[89] More dramatic evidence is provided by Sandra Scarr and her colleagues. "Black" children adopted by well-off "white" families have IQ scores above the average for "whites." And those "blacks" with more European ancestry do not have higher IQ scores.[90] So the average difference between "blacks" and "whites" in IQ cannot be attributed to a presumed genetic difference. For all we know, the 15-point average difference may be due completely to differences in environment or to test bias. New studies show very subtle effects of the social environment on test and school performance. Simply reminding "blacks" of their "race" before a test causes them to do worse. The difference on the Graduate Record Exam between "blacks" and "whites" disappeared after President Obama's election. These and other results strongly suggest that the pervasive stereotype of "blacks" not performing as well as "whites" (particularly potent prior to Obama's election) caused worse performance among "blacks."[91]

Geneticist Theodosius Dobzhansky reminded us that conclusions about the causes of different levels of achievement on IQ tests cannot be drawn until all people have equal opportunities to develop their potentials. He stressed the need for an open society operating under the democratic ideal, where all people are given an equal opportunity to develop whatever gifts or aptitudes they possess and choose to develop.[92]

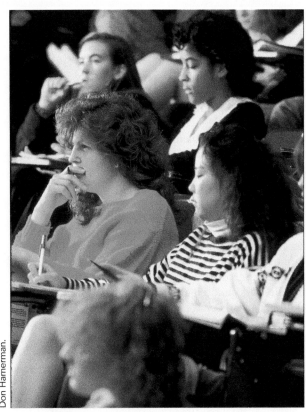

Don Hamerman.

Until all people have an equal education and opportunities to achieve, there is no way we can be sure that some people are smarter than others.

THE FUTURE OF HUMAN VARIATION

Laboratory fertilization, subsequent transplantation of the embryo, and successful birth have been accomplished with humans and nonhumans. *Cloning*—the exact reproduction of an individual from cellular tissue—has been achieved with frogs, sheep, and other animals. *Genetic engineering*—the substitution of some genes for others—is increasingly practiced in nonhuman organisms. And *stem cells*, which can be induced to grow into any tissue type, are in clinical trials for human use. What are the implications of such practices for the genetic future of humans? Will it really be possible someday to control the genetic makeup of our species? If so, will the effects be positive or negative?

It is interesting to speculate on the development of a "perfect human." Aside from the serious ethical question of who would decide what the perfect human should be like, there is the serious biological question of whether such a development might in the long run be detrimental to the human species, for what is perfectly suited to one physical or social environment may be totally unsuited to another. The collection of physical, emotional, and intellectual attributes that might be "perfect" in the early 21st century might be inappropriate in the 22nd century.[93] Even defects such as the sickle-cell trait may confer advantages under certain conditions, as we have seen.

In the long run, the perpetuation of genetic variability is probably more advantageous than the creation of a "perfect" and invariable human being. In the event of dramatic changes in the world environment, absolute uniformity in the human species might be an evolutionary dead end. Such uniformity might lead to the extinction of the human species if new conditions favored genetic or cultural variations that were no longer present in the species. Perhaps our best hope for maximizing our chances of survival is to tolerate, and even encourage, the persistence of many aspects of human variation, both biological and cultural.[94]

SUMMARY ● ○ ○

1. Physical variation—variation in the frequencies of physical traits—from one human population to another is the result of one or more of the following factors: adaptation, acclimatization, and the influence of the social or cultural environment.

2. Some physical variations in human populations involve genetic variation; other variations, including body build, facial construction, and skin color, may be adapted to variation in climate. Still other variations, such as the ability to make lactase, may be adapted partially to variation in cultural environment.

3. Most biological anthropologists today agree that "race" is not a useful way of referring to human biological variation because human populations do not unambiguously fall into discrete groups defined by a particular set of biological traits. Physical traits that are adaptive vary clinally, which makes it meaningless to divide humans into discrete "racial" entities. Rather, it is suggested that "racial" classifications are mostly social categories that are presumed to have a biological basis.

4. Perhaps the most controversial aspect of racial discrimination is the relationship supposed between "racial" categories and intelligence. Attempts have been made to show, by IQ tests and other means, the innate intellectual superiority of one "racial" category over another. But there is doubt that IQ tests measure intelligence fairly. Because evidence indicates that IQ scores are influenced by both genes and environment, conclusions about the causes of differences in IQ scores cannot be drawn until all the people being compared have equal opportunities to develop their potentials.

GLOSSARY TERMS ○ ● ○

acclimatization	hypoxia
adaptation	race
Allen's rule	racism
Bergmann's rule	sickle-cell anemia
Gloger's rule	(sicklemia)

CRITICAL QUESTIONS ○ ○ ●

1. Why is skin color used more often than hair or eye color or body proportions in "racial" classifications?

2. If Europeans had been more susceptible to New World and Pacific diseases, would the world be different today?

3. How might studies of natural selection help increase tolerance of other populations?

PEARSON
myanthrolab

Read the chapter by C. Loring Brace titled "The Concept of Race in Physical Anthropology" on MyAnthroLab. Answer the following questions:

1. What does Brace mean when he states that "'race' is whatever people think it should be"?

2. How do geographic populations (or clines) differ from biological races?

3. How might the concept of "race" limit our ability to understand human variation?

NOTES ● ○ ○

1. See Durham 1991, 154–225, for an extensive discussion of the relationship between genes and culture.
2. Stewart 1950.
3. *Genesis* 17: 9–15.
4. Hanna, Little, and Austin 1989, 133–36; G. A. Harrison et al. 1988, 504–07.
5. D. F. Roberts 1953. Cited in Garn 1971, 73. See also Roberts 1978.
6. D. F. Roberts 1953.
7. G. A. Harrison et al. 1988, 505.
8. Riesenfeld 1973, 427–59.
9. Riesenfeld 1973, 452–53.
10. J. S. Weiner 1954, 615–18; Steegman 1975. See also Larsen 2009.
11. G. A. Harrison et al. 1988, 308–10.
12. Polednak 1974, 49–57. See also Branda and Eaton 1978.
13. Loomis 1967.
14. Post, Daniels, and Binford 1975, 65–80.
15. Holden 2000; Jablonski and Chaplin 2000.
16. Stini 1975, 53.
17. Mazess 1975.
18. Greksa and Beall 1989, 223.
19. Greksa and Beall 1989, 226.
20. Frisancho and Greksa 1989, 204.
21. Eveleth and Tanner 1990, 176–79.
22. Eveleth and Tanner 1990, 205–06.
23. Bogin 1988, 105–106.
24. G. A. Harrison et al. 1988, 300.
25. G. A. Harrison et al. 1988, 198.
26. Huss-Ashmore and Johnston 1985, 482–83.
27. G. A. Harrison et al. 1988, 385–86.
28. Martorell 1980, 81–106.
29. Martorell et al. 1991.
30. Landauer and Whiting 1964; 1981; Gunders and Whiting 1968; Gray and Wolfe 1980.
31. Landauer and Whiting 1964; 1981; Gunders and Whiting 1968.
32. Gray and Wolfe 2009.
33. Landauer and Whiting 1981.
34. Eveleth and Tanner 1990, 205.
35. Landauer 1973.
36. Motulsky 1971, 223.
37. Motulsky 1971, 226.
38. Motulsky 1971, 229.
39. Motulsky 1971, 230.
40. Motulsky 1971, 233.
41. Ibid.
42. Black 1992.
43. An examination of the epidemic diseases spread by Europeans can be found in Chapter 11 of J. Diamond 1997a.
44. Neel et al. 1970; Patrick Tierney in his *Darkness in El Dorado* (New York: Norton, 2000) accused the Neel research team of fueling a measles outbreak among the Yanomamö by administering a harmful measles vaccine. However, the scientific evidence indicates that Tierney is wrong. The vaccine Neel and associates used was widely pretested and there was no way that the vaccine could have caused the epidemic. Measles was already spreading in the Amazon, which was why the vaccination program was initiated. See Gregor and Gross 2004.
45. Relethford 1990, 425–27.
46. Merbs 1992.
47. Durham 1991, 105–07.
48. Ibid.
49. Ibid.
50. G. A. Harrison et al. 1988, 231.
51. For a review of the early research, see Durham 1991, 123–27. The particular form of malaria that is discussed is caused by the species *Plasmodium falciparum*.
52. See Madigral 1989 for a report of her own research and a review of earlier studies.
53. Pennisi 2001a.
54. Durham 1991, 124–45.
55. Motulsky 1971, 238.
56. J. Diamond 1993.
57. Molnar 1998, 158; Pennisi 2001b.
58. Durham 1991, 230.
59. Brodey 1971.
60. Durham 1991, 233–35.
61. Relethford 1990, 127.
62. McCracken 1971; see also references to the work of F. J. Simoons as referred to in Durham 1991, 240–41.
63. McCracken 1971; Huang 2002.
64. Durham 1991, 263–69.
65. Marks 1994; Shanklin 1993, 15–17.
66. Molnar 1998, 19.
67. Brace et al. 1993.
68. Brooks et al. 1993.
69. Brace et al. 1993.
70. Brooks et al. 1993.
71. M. King and Motulsky 2002.
72. Goodrich 1959, 7–15.
73. Coe 1966, 74–76.
74. Thompson 1966, 89.
75. McNeill 1976.
76. Motulsky 1971, 232.
77. Ibid.
78. MacArthur and Wilson 1967.

79. Johanson and Edey 1981.
80. Peregrine et al. 2000; 2003.
81. Lieberman 1999.
82. Klineberg 1935; 1944.
83. Jensen 1969.
84. Herrnstein and Murray 1994.
85. Kamin 1995.
86. Grubb 1987.
87. M. W. Smith 1974.
88. Dobzhansky 1973, 11.
89. Dobzhansky 1973, 14–15.
90. Research by Sandra Scarr and others reported in Boyd and Richerson 1985: 56.
91. Nisbett 2009.
92. Dobzhansky 1962, 243.
93. Haldane 1963.
94. Simpson 1971, 297–308.

The Living Primates

From Chapter 6 of *Anthropology*, 13/e. Carol R. Ember. Melvin Ember. Peter N. Peregrine. Copyright © 2011 by Pearson Education. Published by Prentice Hall. All rights reserved.

The Living Primates

he goal of **primatology**, the study of primates, is to understand how different primates have adapted anatomically and behaviorally to their environments. The results of such studies may help us to understand the behavior and evolution of the human primate.

But how can living primates such as chimpanzees tell us anything about humans or the primates that were our ancestors? After all, each living primate species has its own history of evolutionary divergence from the earliest primate forms. All living primates, including humans, evolved from earlier primates that are now extinct. Nonetheless, by observing how humans and other primates differ from and resemble each other, we may be able to infer how and why humans diverged from the other primates.

In conjunction with fossil evidence, anatomical and behavioral comparisons of living primates may help us reconstruct what early primates were like. For example, if we know that modern primates that swing through the trees have a particular kind of shoulder bone structure, we can infer that similar fossil bones probably belonged to an animal that also swung through the trees. Differing adaptations of living primates may also suggest why certain divergences occurred in primate evolution. If we know what traits belong to humans, and to humans alone, this knowledge may suggest why the line of primates that led to humans branched away from the line leading to chimpanzees and gorillas.

In this chapter, we first examine the common features of the living primates. Next we introduce the different animals that belong to the order Primates, focusing on the distinctive characteristics of each major type. Then we discuss the traits that make humans different from all other primates. We close with a look at possible explanations of some of the varying adaptations exhibited by the different primate species. The purpose of this chapter is to help us understand more about humans. Therefore, we emphasize the features of primate anatomy and behavior that perhaps have the greatest bearing on human evolution.

● ○ ●

COMMON PRIMATE TRAITS

All primates belong to the class Mammalia, and they share all the common features of mammals. Except for humans, the bodies of primates are covered with dense hair or fur, which provides insulation. Even humans have hair in various places, though perhaps not always for insulation. Mammals are *warm-blooded*; that is, their body temperature is more or less constantly warm and usually higher than that of the air around them. Almost all mammals give birth to live young that develop to a considerable size within the mother and are nourished by suckling from the mother's mammary glands. The young have a relatively long period of dependence on adults after birth. This period is also a time of learning, for a great deal of adult mammal behavior is learned rather than instinctive. Play is a learning technique common to mammal young and is especially important to primates, as we shall see later in this chapter.

The primates have a number of physical and social traits that set them apart from other mammals.

Physical Features

No one of the primates' physical features is unique to primates; animals from other orders share one or more of the following described characteristics. But the complex of all these physical traits is unique to primates.[1]

Many skeletal features of the primates reflect an **arboreal** (tree-living) existence. All primate hind limbs are structured principally to provide support, but the "feet" in most primates can also grasp things (see Figure 1). Some primates—orangutans, for instance—can suspend themselves from their hind limbs. The forelimbs are especially flexible, built to withstand both pushing and pulling forces. Each of the hind limbs and forelimbs has one bone in the upper portion and two bones in the lower portion (with the exception of the tarsier). This feature has changed little since the time of the earliest primate ancestors. It has remained in modern primates (although many other mammals have lost it) because the double bones give great mobility for rotating arms and legs.

Another characteristic structure of primates is the clavicle, or collarbone. The clavicle also gives primates great freedom of movement, allowing them to move the shoulders both up and down and back and forth. Although humans obviously do not use this flexibility for arboreal activity, they do use it for other activities. Without a clavicle, we could not throw a spear or a ball; we could not make any fine tools or turn doorknobs if we did not have rotatable forearms.

Primates generally are **omnivorous;** that is, they eat all kinds of food, including insects and small animals, as well as fruits, seeds, leaves, and roots. The teeth of primates reflect this omnivorous diet. The chewing teeth—the **molars** and **premolars**—are unspecialized, particularly in comparison with those of other groups of animals, such as the grazers. The front teeth—the **incisors** and **canines**—are often very specialized, principally in the lower primates. For example, the slender, tightly packed lower incisors and canines in many prosimians form a "dental comb" that the animals use in grooming or for scraping hardened tree gum (which is a food for them) from tree trunks.[2]

Primate hands are extremely flexible. All primates have prehensile—grasping—hands, which can be wrapped around an object. Primates have five digits on both hands and feet (in some cases, one digit may be reduced to a stub), and their nails, with few exceptions, are broad and flat, not clawlike. This structure allows them to grip

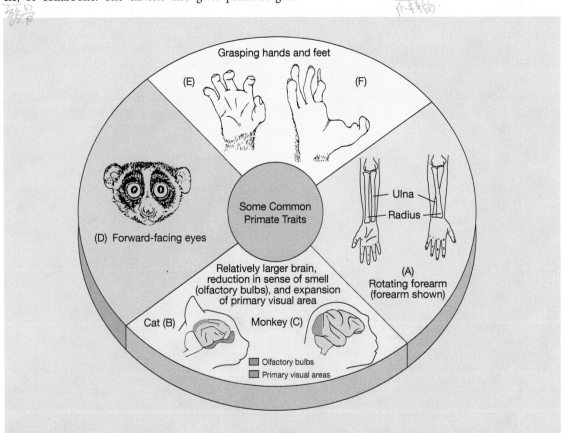

FIGURE 1 Some Common Primate Traits

Source: (A) From Wolff 1991, 255. Reprinted with permission of D.C. Heath; (B, C) from Deacon 1992, 110; (D) from Cartmill 1992b, 25; and (E, F) from Cartmill 1992b, 24.

(A) From Ronald G. Wolff, Functional Chordate Anatomy (Lexington, MA: D.C. Heath and Company, 1991), p. 255. Reprinted with permission of Lilia C. Koo, (B and C) From Terrence Deacon, "Primate Brains and Senses," in Stephen Jones, Robert Martin, and David Pilbeam, eds., *The Cambridge Encyclopedia of Human Evolution* (New York: Cambridge University Press, 1992), p. 110. Reprinted with the permission of Cambridge University Press, (D) From Matt Cartmill, "Non-Human Primates," in Stephen Jones, Robert Martin, and David Pilbeam, eds., *The Cambridge Encyclopedia of Human Evolution* (New York: Cambridge University Press, 1992), p. 25. Reprinted with the permission of Cambridge University Press, (E and F) From Matt Cartmill, Non-Human Primates," in Stephen Jones, Robert Martin, and David Pilbeam, eds., *The Cambridge Encyclopedia of Human Evolution* (New York: Cambridge University Press, 1992), p. 24. Reprinted with the permission of Cambridge University Press.

objects; the hairless, sensitive pads on their fingers, toes, heels, and palms also help them to grip. Most primates have **opposable thumbs,** a feature that allows an even more precise and powerful grip.

Vision is very important to primate life. Compared with other mammals, primates have a relatively larger portion of the brain devoted to vision rather than smell. Primates are characterized by stereoscopic, or depth, vision. Their eyes are directed forward rather than sideways, as in other animals—a trait that allows them to focus on an object (insects or other food or a distant branch) with both eyes at once. Most primates also have color vision, perhaps to recognize when plant foods are ready to eat.

Another important primate feature is a large brain relative to body size. That is, primates generally have larger brains than animals of similar size, perhaps because their survival depends on an enormous amount of learning, as we discuss later. In general, animals with large brains seem to mature more slowly and to live longer than animals with small brains.[3] The more slowly an animal matures and the longer it lives, the more it can learn.

Finally, the primate reproductive system sets this order of animals apart from other mammals. Males of most primate species have a pendulous penis that is not attached to the abdomen by skin, a trait shared by a few other animals, including bats and bears. Females of most primate species have two nipples on the chest (a few prosimians have more than two nipples). The uterus is usually constructed to hold a single fetus (only the marmosets and tamarins typically give birth to twins), not a litter, as with most other animals. This reproductive system can be seen as emphasizing quality over quantity—an adaptation possibly related to the dangers of life in the trees, particularly the risk of falls.[4] Primate infants tend to be relatively well developed at birth, although humans, apes, and some monkeys have helpless infants. Most infant primates, except humans, can cling to their mothers from birth. Primates typically take a long time to mature. For example, the rhesus monkey is not sexually mature until about 3 years of age, and the chimpanzee is not until about age 9.

Social Features

For the most part, primates are social animals. Just as physical traits such as grasping hands and stereoscopic vision may have developed as adaptations to the environment, so may have many patterns of social behavior. For most primates, particularly those that are **diurnal**—that is, active during the day—group life may be crucial to survival, as we will see later in this chapter.

Dependency and Development in a Social Context
Social relationships begin with the mother and other adults during the fairly long dependency period of primates. (For the dependency period of primates, the

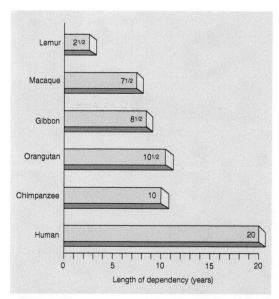

FIGURE 2 A Comparison of the Dependency Periods of Primate Offspring

Source: Data from Jolly 1985, 292.

infancy and juvenile phases, see Figure 2.) The prolonged dependency of infant monkeys and apes probably offers an evolutionary advantage in that it allows infants more time to observe and learn the complex behaviors essential to survival while enjoying the care and protection of mature adults.

Primates without a warm, social relationship with a mother or another individual do not appear to develop appropriate patterns of social interaction. In a series of classic experiments with rhesus monkeys, Harry Harlow investigated the effects of maternal neglect and isolation on offspring.[5] He found that, as a result of either inadequate mothering or isolation from other infants, some monkeys are unable to lead normal social lives. They develop aberrant sexual activities and may even become juvenile delinquents. Harlow mated socially deprived female monkeys with well-adjusted males. When these females gave birth, their behavior was not at all motherly, and they often rejected their babies entirely. Their abnormal behavior was offered as evidence that mothering is more than instinctive. Harlow's experiments underline the importance of maternal care and attention for monkeys and, as a corollary, for humans.

In many primate groups, the mother is not the only individual providing care to the dependent young. Among gray langur monkeys, the birth and subsequent rearing of a baby absorb the attention of most female members of the troop.[6] And in some primate species, the father may spend as much time caring for infants as the mother.[7]

Primates at Play Harlow's investigations have provided other information about social learning in young primates. The experiments that showed the importance of maternal care to baby rhesus monkeys also revealed that

Martin Rogers/Woodfin Camp & Associates, Inc.

A baby macaque clings to its (wire-and-cloth) "surrogate mother" during the Harry Harlow experiment. Harlow demonstrated that social interaction was necessary for primates to develop normally.

Learning from Others We know that primates, nonhuman and human alike, learn many things in social groups. Among humans, children often imitate others, and adults often deliberately teach the young. In English we say, "Isn't it cute how Tommy 'apes' his father?" But do apes (and monkeys) imitate others, or do they just learn to do similar things whether or not observing a model? There is controversy among researchers as to how much imitation versus independent learning occurs in nonhuman primates. Even more arguable is whether deliberate teaching occurs among nonhuman primates.[11]

Some fieldworkers have suggested that chimpanzees may learn by imitation to use tools. For example, Jane Goodall cited an occasion when a female with diarrhea picked up a handful of leaves to wipe her bottom. Her 2-year-old infant watched closely, and then twice picked up leaves to wipe its own, clean behind.[12] Termite "fishing," using a grass stalk to withdraw termites from a termite mound, is probably the best-known example of chimpanzee tool use. Immature chimpanzees in the wild have been observed to watch attentively and pick up stalks while others are "fishing." Mothers also let their infants hold on to the stalks while the mothers "fish." But some observers do not think these reports provide clear evidence of imitation or teaching. Even though the mother lets the infant hold on to the "fishing" stalk, the infant is doing the activity with her, not watching it and then independently repeating it soon after.[13]

CLASSIFICATION OF PRIMATES

Classification provides a useful way to refer to groups of species that are similar in biologically important ways. Sometimes classification schemes vary because the classifiers emphasize somewhat different aspects of similarity and difference. For instance, one type of classification stresses the evolutionary branching that led to the primates of today, another the quantity of shared features. A third approach considers the evolutionary lines as well as similarity and difference of features, but not all features are equally weighted. More "advanced" and specialized features that develop in an evolutionary line are emphasized.[14] Figure 3 gives a classification scheme that follows this last approach.[15]

Despite the different ways to classify, there is generally little disagreement about how the various primates should be classified. Most of the disagreement, as we shall see when we discuss the various primates, revolves around the classification of tarsiers and humans.

The order Primates is often divided into two suborders: the *prosimians*—literally, premonkeys—and the *anthropoids.* The prosimians include lemurs, lorises, and tarsiers. The anthropoid suborder includes New World monkeys, Old World monkeys, the lesser apes (gibbons, siamangs), the great apes (orangutans, gorillas, and chimpanzees), and humans.

play is another crucial ingredient of normal development during the dependency period. Just as monkeys raised without mothers showed abnormal behavior as adults, so did monkeys raised with mothers but with no peers to play with. In fact, when some of the monkeys raised without mothers were allowed a regular playtime with peers, many of them behaved more normally. Subsequent work has supported Harlow's findings.[8]

Play is important for learning.[9] It provides practice for the physical skills necessary or useful in adulthood. For example, young monkeys racing through the trees at top speed are gaining coordination that may save their lives if predators chase them later on. Play is also a way of learning social skills, particularly in interacting and communicating with other members of the group. Some dominance relationships seem to be established partly through the rough-and-tumble games that older juveniles play, where winning depends on such factors as size, strength, and agility. These qualities, or the lack of them, may influence an individual's status throughout adult life. (Other factors also help determine an individual's status. For instance, the mother's status has been shown to be very important in some primates.[10])

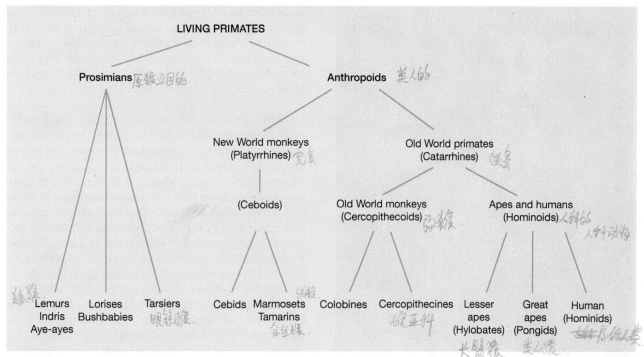

FIGURE 3 A Simplified Classification of the Living Primates

THE VARIOUS PRIMATES

Now that we have discussed their common features, let us focus on some of the ways in which the primates living in the world today vary. (A major division exists between those living in Europe, Asia, and Africa versus those living in the Americas.)

Prosimians

The **prosimians** resemble other mammals more than the anthropoid primates do. For example, the prosimians depend much more on smell for information than do anthropoids. Also in contrast with the anthropoids, they typically have more mobile ears, whiskers, longer snouts, and relatively fixed facial expressions. The prosimians also exhibit many traits shared by all primates, including grasping hands, stereoscopic vision, and enlarged visual centers in the brain.

Lemurlike Forms   Lemurs and their relatives, the indris and the aye-ayes, are found only on two island areas off the southeastern coast of Africa, Madagascar, and the Comoro Islands. These primates range in size from the mouse lemur to the 4-foot-long indri. Members of the lemur group

© Kevin Schafer/Image Bank/Getty Images, Inc.

A ring-tailed lemur mother and its baby holding on. Prosimians such as ring-tailed lemurs depend much more on smell than do anthropoids. Prosimians also have more mobile ears, whiskers, longer snouts, and relatively fixed facial expressions.

The bush baby is a small arboreal prosimian that eats both fruit and insects. It is an energetic nocturnal animal that moves by vertical clinging and leaping.

usually produce single offspring, although twins and even triplets are common in some species. Many of the species in this group are **quadrupeds**—animals that move on all fours; they walk on all fours in the trees as well as on the ground. Some species, such as the indris, use their hind limbs alone to push off from one vertical position to another in a mode of locomotion called **vertical clinging and leaping.** Lemurs are mostly vegetarians, eating fruit, leaves, bark, and flowers. Lemur species vary greatly in their group size. Many lemur species, particularly those that are **nocturnal** (active during the night), are solitary during

their active hours. Others are much more social, living in groups ranging in size from a small family to as many as 60 members.[16] An unusual feature of the lemurlike primates is that females often dominate males, particularly over access to food. In most primates, and in most other mammals, female dominance is rarely observed.[17]

Lorislike Forms Members of the loris group, found in both Southeast Asia and sub-Saharan Africa, are all nocturnal and arboreal. They eat fruit, tree gum, and insects, and usually give birth to single infants.[18] There are two major subfamilies, the lorises and the bush babies (galagos), and they show wide behavioral differences. Bush babies are quick, active animals that hop between branches and tree trunks in the vertical-clinging-and-leaping pattern. On the ground, they often resort to a kangaroo-like hop. Lorises are much slower, walking sedately along branches hand over hand in the quadrupedal fashion.

With the use of searchlights and technical aids such as radio tracking, field researchers have learned a good deal about these nocturnal primates. For example, we know that among bush babies, females, particularly mothers and young adult daughters, stay together in small groups, whereas the males disperse. Newborns are born in nests or hollows of trees (which related females may share), and mothers return to nurse them regularly. A few days after birth, a mother may carry her infant in her mouth to nearby trees, "parking" it while she eats.[19]

Tarsiers The nocturnal, tree-living tarsiers, found now only on the islands of the Philippines and Indonesia, are the only primates that depend completely on animal foods. They are usually insect eaters, but they sometimes capture and eat other small animals. They are well equipped for night vision, possessing enormous eyes, extraordinary eyesight, and enlarged visual centers in the brain. The tarsiers get their name from their elongated tarsal bones (the bones of the ankle), which give them tremendous leverage for their long jumps. Tarsiers are very skilled at vertical

Nocturnal tree-living tarsiers, like this one in the Philippines, are the only primates that depend completely on animal foods. Their enormous eyes equip them to find insects and other prey in the night. Their elongated anklebones (tarsals) make them very good at vertical clinging and leaping.

clinging and leaping. They live in family groups composed of a mated pair and their offspring. Like some higher primates, male and female tarsiers sing together each evening to advertise their territories.[20]

The classification of tarsiers is somewhat controversial. Instead of placing them with the suborder prosimians, as we have done here, some classifiers group tarsiers with anthropoids. In this other classification scheme, the suborders of primates are labeled *strepsirhines* (which includes lemurs and lorises) and *haplorhines* (which includes tarsiers and anthropoids). Tarsiers have chromosomes similar to those of other prosimians; they also have claws for grooming on some of their toes, more than two nipples, and a uterus shaped like that of other prosimians (two-horned). Like bush babies, tarsiers move about through vertical clinging and leaping. In other respects, tarsiers are more like the anthropoids. They have a reduced dependence on smell; not only are their noses smaller, but they lack the wet, doglike snout of lemurs. In common with the anthropoids, their eyes are closer together and are protected by bony orbits. Reproductively, the tarsier, like anthropoids, has a placenta that allows contact between the mother's blood and that of the fetus.[21]

Anthropoids

The anthropoid suborder includes humans, apes, and monkeys. Most **anthropoids** share several traits in varying degrees. They have rounded braincases; reduced, nonmobile outer ears; and relatively small, flat faces instead of muzzles. They have highly efficient reproductive systems. They also have highly dextrous hands.[22] The anthropoid order is divided into two main groups: **platyrrhines** and **catarrhines** (see Figure 4). These groups take their names from the nose shape of the different anthropoids, but they differ in other features as well, as we shall see. Platyrrhines have broad, flat-bridged noses, with nostrils facing outward; these monkeys are found only in the New World, in Central and South America. Catarrhines have narrow noses with nostrils facing downward. Catarrhines include monkeys of the Old World (Africa, Asia, and Europe), as well as apes and humans.

New World Monkeys   Besides the shape of the nose and the position of the nostrils, other anatomical features distinguish the New World monkeys (platyrrhines) from the catarrhine anthropoids. The New World species have three premolars, whereas the Old World species have two. Some New World monkeys have a **prehensile** (grasping) tail; no Old World monkeys do. All the New World monkeys are completely arboreal; they vary a lot in the size of their groups; and their food ranges from insects to nectar and sap to fruits and leaves.[23]

Two main families of New World monkeys have traditionally been defined. One family, the *callitrichids,* contains marmosets and tamarins; the other family, the *cebids,* contains all the other New World monkeys. Although scholars recognize some problems with this division, it is a

FIGURE 4 Features of Platyrrhines and Catarrhines

Source: Boaz and Almquist 1999.
From Noel Boaz and Alan J. Almquist, *Biological Anthropology.* © 1997. Reprinted by permission of Pearson Education.

The squirrel monkey, like all platyrrhines, almost never leaves the trees. It is well suited to an arboreal lifestyle; note how it uses both hands and feet to grasp branches.

MICHAEL & PATRICIA FOGDEN/Minden Pictures

useful one for gaining a basic understanding of the New World monkeys. The callitrichids are very small, have claws instead of fingernails, and give birth to twins who mature in about two years. Perhaps because twinning is so common and the infants have to be carried, callitrichid mothers cannot take care of them alone. Fathers and older siblings have often been observed carrying infants. Indeed, males may do more carrying than females. Callitrichid groups may contain a mated pair (monogamy) or a female mated to more than one male (polyandry). The callitrichids eat a lot of fruit and tree sap, but like other very small primates, they obtain a large portion of their protein requirements from insects.[24]

Cebids are generally larger than callitrichids, take about twice as long to mature, and tend to bear only one offspring at a time.[25] The cebids vary widely in size, group composition, and diet. For example, squirrel monkeys weigh about 2 pounds, whereas woolly spider monkeys weigh more than 16 pounds. Some cebids have small groups with one male-female pair; others have groups of up to 50 individuals. Some of the smallest cebids have a diet of leaves, insects, flowers, and fruits, whereas others are mostly fruit eaters with lesser dependence on seeds, leaves, or insects.[26]

Old World Monkeys The Old World monkeys, or **cercopithecoids,** are related more closely to humans than to New World monkeys. They have the same number of teeth as apes and humans. The Old World monkey species are not as diverse as their New World cousins, but they live in a greater variety of habitats. Some live both in trees and on the ground; others, such as the gelada baboon, are completely **terrestrial,** or ground-living. Macaques are found both in tropical jungles and on snow-covered mountains, and they range from the Rock of Gibraltar to Africa to northern India, Pakistan, and Japan. There are two major subfamilies of Old World monkeys.

Colobine Monkeys The colobine group includes Asian langurs, the African colobus monkeys, and several other species. These monkeys live mostly in trees, and their diet consists principally of leaves and seeds. Their digestive tracts are equipped to obtain maximum nutrition from a high-cellulose diet; they have pouched stomachs, which provide a large surface area for breaking down plant food, and very large intestinal tracts.

Mattias Klum/National Geographic Image Collection

Grooming is an important activity among Old World primates. Here two macaques groom one another.

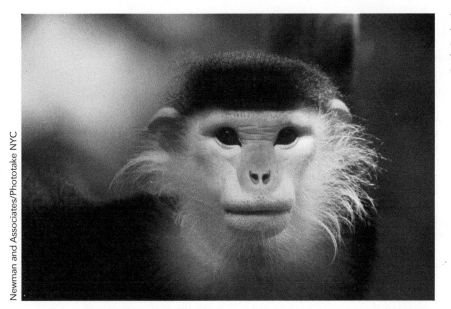

This langur, like all catarrhines, has a relatively narrow nose with nostrils that point downward. Langurs are Asian members of the colobine family and are primarily leaf eaters.

Newman and Associates/Phototake NYC

One of the most noticeable features of colobines is the flamboyant color typical of newborns. For example, in one species, dusky gray mothers give birth to brilliant orange babies.[27] Observational studies suggest that the colobines are also unusual among the primates (except for humans) in that mothers let other group members take care of their infants shortly after birth. But males who are not members of the group are dangerous for infants; males trying to enter and take over a group have been observed to kill infants. Although this description may suggest that a one-male group is the typical group structure, there does not appear to be a typical pattern for a given species. When more than one site of a species has been studied, both one-male and multiple-male groups have been found.[28]

Cercopithecine Monkeys The cercopithecine subfamily of monkeys includes more terrestrial species than any other subfamily of Old World monkeys. Many of these species are characterized by a great deal of **sexual dimorphism** (the sexes look very different); the males are larger, have longer canines, and are more aggressive than the females. Cercopithecines depend more on fruit than do colobines. They are also more capable of surviving in arid and seasonal environments.[29] Pouches inside the cheeks allow cercopithecines to store food for later eating and digestion. An unusual physical feature of these monkeys is the ischial callosities, or callouses, on their bottoms—an adaptation that enables them to sit comfortably in trees or on the ground for long periods of time.[30]

Studies of baboons and macaques suggest that closely related females form the core of a local group, or troop. In large groups, which are common among rhesus monkeys, many social behaviors seem to be determined by degree of biological relatedness. For example, an individual is most likely to sit next to, groom, or help an individual

A troop of baboons in Ethiopia spends most of its time on the ground.

Michael Nichols /National Geographic Image Collection

current research and issues

Researcher at Work: Katharine Milton

Katharine Milton is a professor in the Department of Environmental Science, Policy, and Management at the University of California, Berkeley, and has an avid interest in the scientific study of monkeys. But that is far from how she started out. Born in Alabama, Milton went to Sweet Briar College in Virginia. She was an English major in college and went on to receive her MA in that subject at the University of Iowa. It wasn't until later, while she was living in Argentina, that she discovered her great interest in animal behavior and primates in particular.

After receiving her PhD from New York University, with a dissertation on the "economics" of the howler monkeys of Panama, she was fortunate to be able to study the

woolly spider monkey—a little-known endangered monkey species living in southeastern Brazil. Because so little was known about them, she started out doing a basic review of their diet and behavior. Woolly spider monkeys look like spider monkeys, so they were assumed also to be fruit eaters, as are the spider monkeys. But Milton discovered through systematic observation over a year's time that this "commonsense" view was wrong. As she put it: "Apparently no one ever connected the short life span of captive woolly spider monkeys with the fact that perhaps, just perhaps, they were being fed the wrong food. Zoos, listen up—if you are ever fortunate enough to obtain a woolly spider monkey or two, be sure to give them

leafy matter as their major dietary component, not ripe sugary fruits!"

Much of Milton's research has been devoted to understanding the implications of diet for both nonhuman and human primates. Compared with fruit eaters, leaf-eating primates are generally larger, require relatively less area to feed in, and have relatively smaller brains. Why? Milton suggested that, despite the energy costs of a larger brain, the greater intellectual difficulties of remembering locations of dispersed high-quality food (e.g., fruit, which provides more nutrients by weight than leaves) favored greater mental development in such primates.

Sources: Milton 1988; 2002; 2009

---

who is closely related maternally.[31] Moreover, a closely related subgroup is likely to stay together when a large troop divides.[32]

The Hominoids: Apes and Humans

The **hominoid** group includes three separate families: the lesser apes, or **hylobates** (gibbons and siamangs); the great apes, or **pongids** (orangutans, gorillas, and chimpanzees); and humans, or **hominids.** Several characteristics distinguish the hominoids from the other primates. Their brains are relatively large, especially the areas of the cerebral cortex associated with the ability to integrate data. All hominoids have fairly long arms, short, broad trunks, and no tails. The wrist, elbow, and shoulder joints of hominoids allow a greater range of movement than in other primates. Hominoid hands are longer and stronger than those of other primates. These skeletal features probably evolved along with the hominoids' unique abilities in suspensory locomotion. Unlike other anthropoids, who move quadrupedally along the ground or along tops of tree branches, hominoids often suspend themselves from below the branches and swing or climb hand over hand from branch to branch.[33] This suspensory posture also translates to locomotion on the ground; all hominoids, at least occasionally, move bipedally.

The dentition of hominoids demonstrates some unique features as well (see Figure 5). Hominoid molars are flat and rounded compared to those of other

anthropoids, and have what is called a **"Y-5" pattern** on the lower molars—that is, the lower molars have five cusps with a Y-shaped groove opening toward the cheek running between them. Other anthropoids have what is called a **bilophodont** pattern—their molars have two ridges or "loafs" running perpendicular to the cheeks. All hominoids except for humans also have long canine teeth that project beyond the tops of the other teeth, and a corresponding space on the opposite jaw, called a **diastema,** where the canine sits when the jaws are closed. The contact of the upper canine and the lower third premolar creates a sharp cutting edge, in part due to the premolar being elongated to accommodate the canine.[34] These dental features are related to the hominoids' diets, which often include both fibrous plant materials, which can be efficiently cut with sharp canines against elongated premolars, and soft fruits, which can be efficiently chewed with wide, flat molars.

The skeletal and dental features that the hominoids share point toward their common ancestry. Their proteins and DNA show many similarities, too. This genetic likeness is particularly strong among chimpanzees, gorillas, and humans.[35] For this reason, primatologists think chimpanzees and gorillas are evolutionarily closer to humans than are the lesser apes and orangutans, which probably branched off at some earlier point.

Gibbons and Siamangs   The agile gibbons and their close relatives the siamangs are found in the jungles of

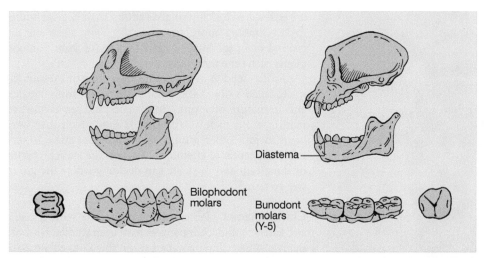

FIGURE 5 Difference in dentition between an Old World monkey (left) and an ape (right).
In Old World monkeys, the cusps of the lower molars form two parallel ridges; in apes, the five cusps form a Y-shaped pattern. Apes also have a space between the lower canine and first premolar, called a diastema.

Source: Adapted from Boaz and Almquist 1999, 164.
Difference in Dentition between an Old World Monkey and an Ape. From Noel Boaz and Alan J. Almquist, *Biological Anthropology.* © 1997. Reprinted by permission of Pearson Education.

Southeast Asia. The gibbons are small, weighing only between 11 pounds and 15 pounds. The siamangs are somewhat larger, but no more than 25 pounds. Both are mostly fruit eaters, although they also eat leaves and insects. They are spectacular **brachiators;** their long arms and fingers let them swing hand over hand through the trees.[36] A gibbon can move more than 30 feet in a single forward swing.

Gibbons and siamangs live in small family groups consisting of an adult pair, who appear to mate for life, and one or two immature offspring. When the young reach adulthood, they are driven from home by the adults. There is little sexual dimorphism—males and females do not differ in size or appearance—nor is there any clear pattern of dominance by either sex. These lesser apes are also highly territorial; an adult pair advertises their territory by singing and defends it by chasing others away.[37]

Orangutans Orangutans survive only on the islands of Borneo and Sumatra. Unlike gibbons and siamangs, they are clearly recognizable as males or females. Males not only weigh almost twice as much as females (up to 200 pounds), but they also have large cheek pads, throat pouches, beards, and long hair.[38] Like gibbons and siamangs, orangutans are primarily fruit eaters and arboreal. They are the heaviest of the arboreal primates, and perhaps they move slowly and laboriously through the trees for this reason. Orangutans are unusual among the higher primates in that, except for mothers and their young, adults spend much of their time alone. Some researchers, however, have found evidence of group behavior. One field study of orangutans on Sumatra found that groups of as many as ten adults fed together in the same tree.[39] And when different researchers pool their information on orangutan behavior, there appear to be regional differences, suggesting the presence of distinct local orangutan cultures.[40] Cultural differences would not likely arise without different groups.

Different ideas have been proposed about the largely solitary habit of the orangutans that live in the mountainous areas of Borneo. One is that any one tree or home range may have insufficient food to support more than a single adult orangutan, a pretty large animal, as animals go. To obtain sufficient food each day without having to travel over a huge area, orangutans thus may live alone

A white-handed gibbon demonstrates its ability as a brachiator.

are well suited for climbing. As adults, their heavier bodies make climbing more precarious.[46] They sleep on the ground or in tub-shaped nests they make from nonfood plants each time they bed down.[47]

Gorillas tend to live in groups consisting of a dominant male, called a silverback, other adult males, adult females, and immature offspring. Both males and females, when mature, seem to leave the groups into which they were born to join other groups. The dominant male is very much the center of attention; he acts as the main protector of the group and the leader in deciding where the group will go next.[48]

Chimpanzees Perhaps because they are more sociable and easier to find, chimpanzees have been studied far more than gorillas. Chimpanzees live in the forested areas of Africa, from Sierra Leone in the west to Tanzania in the east.

There are two distinct species of chimpanzee—the common chimpanzee (*Pan troglodytes*) and the bonobo, or pygmy, chimpanzee (*Pan paniscus*). Although they share many features in common (indeed, they were not recognized as distinct species until 1929), bonobos tend to be more slender than common chimpanzees, with longer limbs and digits, smaller heads, darker faces, and a distinct part in their hair. Unlike common chimpanzees, bonobos show almost no sexual dimorphism in dentition or skeletal structure. More significant seem to be differences in

A young gorilla shows how it knuckle-walks. The back feet are flat on the ground, and only the knuckles of the "hands" touch the ground.

rather than in groups.[41] Another idea is that animals live in groups when they are subject to heavy predation; the large size of orangutans may make them immune to attacks from most animals, so living alone may be a viable option.[42] A third idea, which on the face of it seems opposite to the second, is that living alone may be an adaptation to heavy predation by humans. The orangutan's best defense against humans with guns may be to hide alone in the trees.[43]

Gorillas Gorillas are found in the lowland areas of western equatorial Africa and in the mountain areas of Congo, Uganda, and Rwanda.[44] Unlike the other apes, who are mostly fruit eaters, gorillas mostly eat other parts of plants—stems, shoots (e.g., bamboo), pith, leaves, roots, and flowers. The amount of fruit eaten varies greatly. In many populations, fruit eating is rare; in some, however, fruit is a common part of the diet.[45]

Gorillas are by far the largest of the surviving apes. In their natural habitats, adult males weigh up to 450 pounds and females up to 250 pounds. To support the weight of massive chests, gorillas travel mostly on the ground on all fours in a form of locomotion known as **knuckle walking:** They walk on the thickly padded middle joints of their fingers. Gorillas' arms and legs, especially those of the young,

A bonobo's slender limbs, dark face, and parted hair are some of the traits that distinguish them from common chimpanzees.

Chimpanzees, though they spend much time in the trees, can also move very quickly on the ground.

Anup Shah/Nature Picture Library

social behavior. Bonobos are more gregarious than common chimpanzees, and groups tend to be more stable. Groups also tend to be centered around females rather than males.[49]

Although they are primarily fruit eaters, chimpanzees show many similarities to their close relatives, the gorillas. Both are arboreal and terrestrial. Like gorillas, chimpanzees are good climbers, especially when young, and they spend many hours in the trees. But they move best on the ground, and they come down from the trees and move by knuckle walking when they want to cover long distances. Occasionally, they stand and walk upright, usually when they are traveling through tall grass or are trying to see long distances. Chimpanzees sleep in tree nests that they carefully prepare anew, complete with a bunch of leaves as a pillow, each time they bed down.[50]

Chimpanzees (including bonobos) are less sexually dimorphic than the other great apes. Males weigh a little more than 100 pounds on the average, females somewhat less. But males have longer canines.

For some time it was thought that chimpanzees ate only plant food. Although most of common chimpanzees' diet is vegetarian, a significant amount comes from meat. After three decades of studies at Gombe National Park in Tanzania and elsewhere, researchers have found that common chimpanzees not only eat insects, small lizards, and birds, but they also actively hunt and kill larger animals.[51] They have been observed hunting and eating monkeys, young baboons, and bushbucks in addition to smaller prey. At Gombe, the red colobus monkey is by far the most often hunted animal. So it is not only humans who endanger other primates (see the box "Endangered Primates"); the red colobus monkey population is very small in areas of intense chimpanzee hunting. Hunting appears to be undertaken more often during the dry season when food is scarce.[52] Prey is caught mostly by the males, which hunt either alone or in small groups. It is then shared with—or, perhaps more accurately, begged by—as many as 15 other chimpanzees in friendly social gatherings that may last up to nine hours.[53]

Despite considerable observation, the organization of chimpanzee social groups is still not clear. Groups of common chimpanzees usually are multi-male and multi-female, but the size may range considerably from a few to 100 or so members. In Gombe, males typically remain in their natal group throughout life, and females often move to a neighboring group; but males in Guinea do not tend to stay in their natal groups.[54] It appears that chimpanzees come together and drift apart depending on circumstances such as the availability of food and the risk of predation.[55] Scholars have recently compared information from nine long-term studies of chimpanzee social organization and behavior, and have come to the conclusion that there are behaviors specific to particular groups. These behaviors, which include customary tool use, grooming, and mating displays, do not appear to be determined by the environment, and hence have been interpreted by some scholars as being cultural.[56]

Hominids According to the classification we use here, the hominoids we call hominids include only one living species—modern humans. Humans have many distinctive characteristics that set them apart from other anthropoids and other hominoids, which lead many to place humans in a category separate from the pongids. However, others believe that the differences are not so great as to justify a separate hominid category for humans. For example, humans, chimpanzees, and gorillas are very similar in their proteins and DNA. And it is widely agreed that the lines leading to humans, chimpanzees, and gorillas diverged from a common ancestor perhaps 5 to 6 million years ago.[57] Whether we stress the similarities or differences between humans and apes does not matter that much; what does matter is that we try to understand the reasons for those similarities and differences.

applied anthropology

Endangered Primates

In contrast to many human populations that are too numerous for their resources, many populations of non-human primates face extinction because they are not numerous enough. The two trends—human overpopulation and nonhuman primate extinctions—are related. Were it not for human expansion in many parts of the world, the nonhuman primates living in those habitats would not be endangered. Various lemur and other prosimian species of Madagascar, the mountain gorilla and red colobus monkeys of Africa, and the lion tamarin monkeys of Brazil are among the species most at risk.

Many factors are responsible for the difficulties that nonhuman primates face, but most of them are directly or indirectly the result of human activity. Perhaps the biggest problem is the destruction of tropical rain forest, the habitat of most nonhuman primates, because of encroaching agriculture and cattle ranching and the felling of trees for wood products. The people who live in these areas are partly responsible for the threats to nonhuman primates—population pressure in the human populations increases the likelihood that more forest will be cleared and burned for agriculture, and nonhuman primates are an important source of hunted

food in some areas. But world market forces are probably more important. The increasing need for "American" hamburger in fast-food restaurants has accelerated the search for places to raise beef inexpensively. There is also enormous demand for wood products from tropical forests; Japan imports half of all the timber from rain forests to use for plywood, cardboard, paper, and furniture.

Some would argue that it is important to preserve all species. Primatologists remind us that it is especially important to preserve primate diversity. One reason is the scientific one of needing those populations to study and understand how humans are similar and different and how they came to be that way. Another reason is the usefulness of nonhuman primates in biomedical research on human diseases; we share many of our diseases, and many of our genes, with our primate relatives. (Chimpanzees share 99 percent of their genes with humans.) The film *The Planet of the Apes*, in which the humans are subordinate to the apes, tells us that the primates in zoos could have been us.

So how can nonhuman primates be protected from us? There really are only two major ways: Either human population growth in many

©Tom & Pat Leeson/Photo \hResearchers, Inc.

A golden lion tamarin.

places has to be curtailed, or we have to preserve substantial populations of nonhuman primates in protected parks and zoos. Both are difficult but humanly possible.

Sources: Mittermeier and Sterling 1992, 33–36; Nishida 1992, 303–304.

DISTINCTIVE HOMINID TRAITS

We turn now to some of the features that distinguish us—the hominids—from the other primates. Although we like to think of ourselves as unique, many of the traits we discuss here are at the extreme of a continuum that can be traced from the prosimians through the apes.

Physical Traits

Of all the primates, only hominids consistently walk erect on two feet. Gibbons, chimpanzees (particularly bonobos), and gorillas (and some monkeys too) may stand or walk on two feet some of the time, but only for very short periods. All other primates require thick, heavy musculature to hold their heads erect; this structure is missing in hominids, for our heads are more or less balanced on top

of our spinal columns. A dish-shaped pelvis (peculiar to hominids), a lumbar curve in the spine, straight lower limbs, and arched, nonprehensile feet are all related to **bipedalism.** Because hominids are fully bipedal, we can carry objects without impairing our locomotor efficiency.

Although many primates have an opposable thumb, which enables them to grasp and examine objects, the greater length and flexibility of the hominid thumb allow us to handle objects with greater dexterity. We are capable of both a power grip, to hold large or heavy objects firmly, and a precision grip, to hold small or delicate objects without dropping or breaking them. We also have remarkable hand-eye coordination, as well as a remarkably sophisticated brain.

The hominid brain is large and complex, particularly the **cerebral cortex,** the center of speech and other higher mental activities. The brain of the average adult modern human measures more than 79 cubic inches (1,300 cubic centimeters), compared with 32 cubic inches (525 cubic centimeters) for the gorilla, the primate with the next largest brain. The frontal areas of the hominid brain are also larger than those of other primates, so that hominids have more prominent foreheads than monkeys or gorillas. Hominids have special areas of the brain that are dedicated to speech and language. The large hominid brain requires an enormous amount of blood, and the way blood is carried to and from the brain is also unique.[58]

Hominid teeth reflect our completely omnivorous diet, and they are not very specialized, which may reflect the fact that we use tools and cooking to prepare our food. As discussed earlier, other hominoids have long canines and a diastema, whereas hominid canines do not usually project beyond the tops of the other teeth. This allows hominids to move their jaws both vertically and horizontally when chewing; horizontal movement would be prevented by the long upper canines of the other hominoids. Hominid molars have thicker enamel than the molars of other hominoids, and both horizontal movement and thickened molars may be related to a dietary emphasis on coarse grains and seeds. The hominid jaw is shaped like a parabolic arch, rather than a U-shape, as in the apes, and is composed of relatively thin bones and light muscles. Modern humans have chins; other primates do not.

One other distinctive hominid trait is the sexuality of hominid females, who may engage in intercourse at any time throughout the year; most other primate females engage in sex only periodically, just around the time they can conceive.[59] Hominids are also unusual among the primates in having female-male bonding.[60] Later, in the discussion of the origins of culture, we examine some theories suggesting why male-female bonding, which in modern humans we call "marriage," may have developed. It used to be thought that more or less continuous female sexuality may be related to female-male bonding, but comparative research on mammals and birds contradicts this idea. Those mammals and birds that have more frequent sex are not more likely to have male-female bonding.[61]

Why, then, does hominid female sexuality differ from that of most other primates? One suggestion is that more or less continuous female sexuality became selectively advantageous in hominids after female-male bonding developed in conjunction with local groups consisting of at least several adult males and adult females.[62] More specifically, the combination of group living and male-female bonding—a combination unique to hominids among the primates—may have favored a switch from the common higher-primate pattern of periodic female sexuality to the pattern of more or less continuous female sexuality. Such a switch may have been favored in hominids because periodic rather than continuous female sexuality would undermine female-male bonding in multi-male–multi-female groups.

Field research on nonhuman primates strongly suggests that males usually attempt to mate with any females ready to mate. If the female (or females) a male was bonded to was not interested in sex at certain times, but other females in the group were, it seems likely that the male would try to mate with those other females. Frequent "extramarital affairs" might jeopardize the male-female bond and thereby presumably reduce the reproductive success of both males and females. Hence, natural selection may have favored more or less continuous sexuality in hominid females if hominids already had the combination of group living (and the possibility of "extramarital affairs") and marriage. If bonded adults lived alone, as do gibbons, noncontinuous female sexuality would not threaten bonding, because "extramarital" sex would not be likely to occur. Similarly, seasonal breeding would also pose little threat to male-female bonds, because all females would be sexually active at more or less the same time.[63] So the fact that the combination of group living and male-female bonding occurs only in hominids may explain why continuous female sexuality developed in hominids. The bonobo, or pygmy chimpanzee, female does engage in intercourse throughout the year, but bonobos do not have male-female bonding and the females are not interested in sex quite as often as hominid females.[64]

Behavioral Abilities

In comparison with other primates, a much greater proportion of hominid behavior is learned and culturally patterned. As with many physical traits, we can trace a continuum in the learning abilities of all primates. The great apes, including orangutans, gorillas, and chimpanzees, are probably about equal in learning ability.[65] Old and New World monkeys do much less well in learning tests, and, surprisingly, gibbons perform more poorly than most monkeys.

Toolmaking The same kind of continuum is evident in inventiveness and toolmaking. There is no evidence that any nonhuman primates except great apes use tools, although several species of monkeys use "weapons"— branches, stones, or fruit dropped onto predators below them on the ground. Chimpanzees both fashion and use tools in the wild. As we have noted, they strip leaves from sticks and then use the sticks to "fish" termites from their mound-shaped nests. They use leaves to mop up termites, to sponge up water, or to wipe themselves clean. Indeed, tool use varies enough in chimpanzees that primatologist Christophe Boesch has suggested that local chimpanzee groups have cultural differences in terms of the tools they employ.[66]

One example of chimpanzee tool use suggests planning. In Guinea, West Africa, observers watched a number of chimpanzees crack oil palm nuts with two stones. The "platform" stone had a hollow depression; the other stone was used for pounding. The observers assumed that the stones had been brought by the chimpanzees to the palm trees, because no stones like them were nearby and the chimps were observed to leave the pounding stone on top of or near the platform stone when they were finished.[67] Observers in other areas of West Africa have also reported

Chimps in the wild use tools—in this case, a stone to crack palm nuts. As far as we know, though, they don't use tools to make other tools, as humans do.

C. Bromhall/Animals Animals/ Earth Scenes

that chimpanzees use stones to crack nuts. In one location in Liberia, an innovative female appeared to have started the practice; it seems to have been imitated within a few months by 13 others who previously showed no interest in the practice.[68]

In captivity, chimpanzees have also been observed to be inventive toolmakers. One mother chimpanzee was seen examining and cleaning her son's teeth, using tools she had fashioned from twigs. She even extracted a baby tooth he was about to lose.[69]

Hominids have usually been considered the only toolmaking animal, but observations such as these call for modification of the definition of toolmaking. If we define toolmaking as adapting a natural object for a specific purpose, then at least some of the great apes are toolmakers too. Perhaps it would be more accurate to say hominids are the only habitual toolmaking animal, just as we say hominids are the only habitual bipedal hominoid, even though the other hominoids all can and do walk bipedally sometimes. As far as we know, though, hominids are unique in their ability to use one tool to make another.

Language Only modern humans have spoken, symbolic language. But, as with toolmaking abilities, the line between modern human language and the communications of other primates is not as sharp as we once thought. In the wild, vervet monkeys make different alarm calls to warn of different predators. Observers playing tape recordings of these calls found that monkeys responded to them differently, depending on the call. If the monkeys heard an "eagle" call, they looked up; if they heard a "leopard" call, they ran high into the trees.[70]

Common chimpanzees are also communicative, using gestures and many vocalizations in the wild. Researchers have used this "natural talent" to teach chimpanzees symbolic language in experimental settings. In their pioneering work, Beatrice T. Gardner and R. Allen Gardner raised a female chimpanzee named Washoe and trained her to communicate with startling effectiveness by means of American Sign Language hand gestures.[71] After a year of

training, she was able to associate gestures with specific activities. For example, if thirsty, Washoe would make the signal for "give me" followed by the one for "drink." As she learned, the instructions grew more detailed. If all she wanted was water, she would merely signal for "drink." But if she craved soda pop, as she did more and more, she prefaced the drink signal with the sweet signal—a quick touching of the tongue with her fingers. Later, the Gardners had even more success in training four other common chimpanzees, who were taught by fluent deaf users of American Sign Language.[72]

Bonobos have provided strong evidence that they understand simple grammatical "rules," very much like 2-year-old humans. Pointing to graphic symbols for different particular meanings, a bonobo named Kanzi regularly communicated sequences of types of symbols; for example, he would point to a symbol for a verb ("bite") and then point to a symbol for an object ("ball," "cherry," or "food").[73]

Other Hominid Traits Although many primates are omnivores, eating insects and small reptiles in addition to plants—some even hunt small mammals—only hominids hunt very large animals. Also, hominids are one of the few primates that are completely terrestrial. We do not even sleep in trees, as many other ground-living primates do. Perhaps our ancestors lost their perches when the forests receded, or cultural advances such as weapons or fire may have eliminated the need to seek nightly shelter in the trees. In addition, as we have noted, we have the longest dependency period of any of the primates, requiring extensive parental care and support for up to 20 years or so.

Finally, hominids are unlike almost all other primates in having a division of labor by gender in food-getting and food sharing in adulthood. Among nonhuman primates, both females and males forage for themselves after infancy. Hominids have more gender-role specialization, perhaps because men, unencumbered by infants and small children, were freer to hunt and chase large animals.

PRIMATE ADAPTATIONS

Thus far we have discussed the common features of primates and introduced the different primates that survive in the world today. Now let us examine possible explanations, suggested by research, of some of the ways in which the living primates have adapted to their varying environments.

Body Size

The living primates vary enormously in body size, ranging from the two or so ounces of the average gray mouse lemur to the 350 pounds of the average male gorilla. What accounts for this sizable variation? Three factors seem to predict body size—the time of day the species is active, where it is active (in the trees or on the ground), and the kinds of food eaten.[74] All the nocturnal primates are small; and among the primates active during the day, the arboreal ones tend to be smaller than the terrestrial ones. Finally, species that eat mostly leaves tend to be larger than species that eat mostly fruits and seeds.

Why do these factors predict size? One important consideration is the general relationship in mammals between body weight and energy needs. Generally, larger animals require more absolute energy, but smaller animals require much more energy for their body weight. That being so, smaller animals (and small primates) need more energy-rich food. Insects, fruits, tree gum, and sap are full of calories and tend to be more important in the diet of small primates. Leaves are relatively low in energy, so leaf eaters have to consume a lot of food to get enough energy. They also need large stomachs and intestines to extract the nutrients they need, and a bigger gut in turn requires a bigger skeleton and body.[75] Small primates, which eat insects and other rich foods, probably would compete with birds for food. But most very small primates are nocturnal, whereas most forest-living birds are diurnal. So there is little competition between small primates and birds.

Energy requirements may also explain why arboreal primates are usually smaller. Moving about in trees usually requires both vertical and horizontal motion. The energy required to climb vertically is proportional to weight, so larger animals require more energy to climb. But the energy for traveling horizontally, as on the ground, is not proportionate to weight, so larger animals use energy more efficiently on the ground than in the trees.[76] An additional consideration is the amount of weight that can be supported by small tree branches, where foods such as fruits are mostly located. Small animals can go out to small branches more safely than large animals. Also, ground dwellers might be bigger because large size is a protection against predation.[77]

Relative Brain Size

Larger primates usually have larger brains, but larger animals of all types generally have larger brains (see Figure 6). Thus, primatologists are interested in relative brain size, that is, the ratio of brain size to body size.

Perhaps because hominid primates have the largest brains relatively of any primate, we tend to think a larger brain is "better." However, a large brain does have "costs." From an energy perspective, the development of a large brain requires a great deal of metabolic energy; therefore, it should not be favored by natural selection unless the benefits outweigh the costs.[78]

Fruit-eating primates tend to have relatively larger brains than leaf-eating primates do. This difference may be due to natural selection in favor of more capacity for memory, and therefore relatively larger brains, in fruit eaters. Leaf eaters may not need as much memory, because they depend on food that is more readily available in time and space, and therefore they may not have to remember where food might be found. In contrast, fruit eaters may

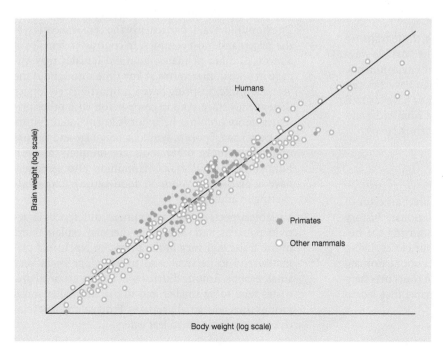

FIGURE 6 As this graph shows, larger animals generally have larger brains. Primates generally have even larger brains than we would expect from their body weight. Note that most of the primates (as indicated by the colored circles) fall above the line showing the relationship between brain weight and body weight. The brains in primates are about twice as heavy as the brains of nonprimate mammals of the same body weight.

Source: From Deacon 1992, 111.
From Terrence Deacon, "Primate Brains and Senses," in Stephen Jones, Robert Martin, and David Pilbeam, eds., *The Cambridge Encyclopedia of Human Evolution* (New York: Cambridge University Press, 1992), p. 111. Reprinted with the permission of Cambridge University Press.

need greater memory and brain capacity because their foods ripen at different times and in separate places that have to be remembered to be found.[79] The brain requires large supplies of oxygen and glucose. Because leaf-eating primates do not have as much glucose in their diets as fruit-eating primates, they may also not have the energy reserves to support relatively large brains.[80]

Group Size

Primate groups vary in size from solitary males and females with young (orangutans) to a few individuals and young (e.g., gibbons) to 100 or more individuals in some Old World monkey troops.[81] What factors might account for such variation?

Nocturnal activity is an important predictor not only of small body size but also of small group size. Nocturnal primates feed either alone or in pairs.[82] John Terborgh has noted that most nocturnal predators hunt by sound, so a nocturnal animal might best avoid attack by being silent.[83] Groups are noisy, and therefore nocturnal animals might be more likely to survive by living alone or in pairs.

On the other hand, a large group might provide advantages in the daytime. The more eyes, ears, and noses a group has, the more quickly a would-be predator might be detected—and perhaps avoided. Also, a larger group would have more teeth and strength to frighten or mob a predator that actually attacked.[84] But this line of reasoning would lead us to expect that all diurnal terrestrial species would have large groups. Yet, not all do. Other factors must be operating. One seems to be the amount and density of food. If food resources occur in small amounts and in separate places, only small groups can get enough to eat; but if food occurs in large patches, there will be enough to support large groups.[85] An additional factor may be competition over resources. One suggestion is that substantial but separated patches of resources are likely to be fought over, and therefore individuals living in larger groups might be more likely to obtain access to them.[86]

Having examined our distinctive traits, those traits we share with other primates, and some of the possible ways primates might have adapted to different environments, we need to ask what selective forces may have favored the emergence of primates, what forces may have favored the line of divergence leading to the first hominids, and what forces led to the emergence of the genus *Homo*.

SUMMARY ● ○ ○

1. Although no living primate can be a direct ancestor of humans, we do share a common evolutionary history with the other surviving primates. Studying the behavioral and anatomical features of our closest living relatives may help us make inferences about primate evolution. Studying distinctive human traits may help us understand why the line of primates that led to humans branched away from the line leading to chimpanzees and gorillas.

2. No one trait is unique to primates. However, primates do share the following features: two bones in the lower part of the leg and in the forearm, a collarbone, flexible prehensile (grasping) hands, stereoscopic vision, a relatively large brain, only one (or sometimes two) offspring at a time, long maturation of the young, and a high degree of dependence on social life and learning.

3. The order Primates is divided into two suborders: the prosimians and the anthropoids. Compared with the anthropoids, prosimians depend more on smell for information. They have mobile ears, whiskers, longer snouts typically, and relatively fixed facial expressions. Anthropoids have rounded braincases; reduced, non-mobile outer ears; and relatively small, flat faces instead of muzzles. They have highly dextrous hands.

4. The Anthropoid order is divided into two main groups: platyrrhines (monkeys of the New World) and catarrhines. The catarrhines are subdivided into cercopithecoids (Old World monkeys) and hominoids (apes and humans). The anthropoid apes consist of the hylobates, or lesser apes (gibbons and siamangs), and the pongids, or great apes (orangutans, gorillas, and chimpanzees).

5. Along with the gorilla, the chimpanzee has proteins and DNA remarkably similar to those of humans, as well as anatomical and behavioral similarities to humans. Wild chimpanzees have been seen to create and use tools, modifying a natural object to fulfill a specific purpose. High conceptual ability is also demonstrated by both the chimpanzee's and the gorilla's facility in learning sign language.

6. The differences between hominids and the other anthropoids show us what makes humans distinctive as a species. Hominids are totally bipedal; they walk on two legs and do not need the arms for locomotion. The hominid brain, particularly the cerebral cortex, is the largest and most complex. In contrast to females of almost all other primates, hominid females may engage in sexual intercourse at any time throughout the year. Hominid offspring have a proportionately longer dependency stage. And in comparison with other primates, more hominid behavior is learned and culturally patterned. Spoken, symbolic language and the use of tools to make other tools are uniquely modern human behavioral traits. Hominids also generally have a division of labor in food-getting and food-sharing in adulthood.

7. Variable aspects of the environment, differences in activity patterns, and variation in diet may explain many of the traits that vary in the primates. Nocturnal primates tend to be small and to live alone or in very small groups. Among diurnal species, the arboreal primates tend to be smaller and to live in smaller social groups than terrestrial primates. Fruit eaters have relatively larger brains than leaf eaters.

GLOSSARY TERMS ○ ● ○

anthropoids	molars
arboreal	nocturnal
bilophodont	omnivorous
bipedalism	opposable thumb
brachiators	platyrrhines
canines	pongids
catarrhines	prehensile
cercopithecoids	premolars
cerebral cortex	primatology
diastema	prosimians
diurnal	quadrupeds
hominids	sexual dimorphism
hominoids	terrestrial
hylobates	vertical clinging and
incisors	leaping
knuckle walking	"Y-5" pattern

CRITICAL QUESTIONS ○ ○ ●

1. How could you infer that a fossil primate lived in the trees?
2. Under what conditions would the ability to communicate be adaptive?
3. Why are humans immature for so long?

PEARSON myanthrolab

Read the chapter by Craig B. Stanford titled "Chimpanzee Hunting Behavior and Human Evolution" on MyAnthroLab. Answer the following questions:

1. How might the study of chimpanzee behavior, and particularly hunting behavior, benefit our understanding of early hominid behavior and of human evolution in general?
2. For many years chimpanzees were thought to be vegetarians. Why did it take so long for chimpanzee hunting to be identified and studied?
3. What do you think is the best answer to the question "Why do chimpanzees hunt"?

NOTES ● ○ ○

1. The classic description of common primate traits is from Napier and Napier 1967. For primate social organization see Smuts et al. 1987.
2. Bearder 1987, 14.
3. Richard 1985, 22ff.
4. R. Martin 1975, 50. The opossum, which is not a primate but lives in trees and has many babies at one time, is a marsupial and has a pouch in which to keep the babies when they are very young.
5. Harlow et al. 1966.
6. Nicolson 1987, 339.
7. Gray 1985 (144–63) provides an overview of research that attempts to explain the variation among primates in the degree of male parental care.
8. Russon 1990, 379.
9. Dohlinow and Bishop 1972, 321–25.
10. Sade 1965; Hausfater et al. 1982.
11. Visaberghi and Fragaszy 1990, 265; Tomasello 1990, 304–05.
12. van Lawick-Goodall 1971, 242.
13. Visaberghi and Fragaszy 1990, 264–65.
14. R. Martin 1992, 17–19; Conroy 1990, 8–15.
15. This simplified chart of primate classification adapts information provided in R. Martin 1992, 21.
16. Doyle and Martin 1979; Tattersall 1982.
17. Richard 1987, 32.
18. Bearder 1987, 13.
19. Charles-Dominique 1977, 258; also R. Martin and Bearder 1979; Bearder 1987, 18–22.
20. MacKinnon and MacKinnon 1980.
21. Cartmill 1992a, 28; Fleagle 1999, 118–22.
22. Napier and Napier 1967, 32–33.
23. Richard 1985, 164–65.
24. Cartmill 1992a, 29; Goldizen 1987, 34; also Eisenberg 1977; Sussman and Kinzey 1984; Fleagle 1999, 168–74.
25. Eisenberg 1977, 15–17.
26. Robinson, Wright, and Kinzey 1987; Crockett and Eisenberg 1987; Robinson and Janson 1987.
27. Hrdy 1977, 18.
28. Hrdy 1977, 18–19.
29. Napier 1970, 80–82.
30. Fedigan 1982, 11.
31. Fedigan 1982, 123–24.
32. P. Lee 1983, 231.
33. Fleagle 1999, 302.
34. LeGros Clark 1964, 184.
35. Pennisi 2007.
36. Preuschoft 1984.
37. Carpenter 1940; Chivers 1974, 1980.
38. Rijksen 1978, 22.
39. Normile 1998.
40. van Schaik et al. 2003.
41. Galdikas 1979, 220–23.
42. Cheney and Wrangham 1987, 236.
43. Rijksen 1978, 321.
44. Fossey 1983, xvi.
45. Tuttle 1986, 99–114.
46. Schaller 1963; 1964.
47. Fossey 1983, 47.
48. Harcourt 1979, 187–92.
49. Susman 1984; White 1996.
50. Goodall 1963; van Lawick-Goodall 1971.
51. Teleki 1973.
52. Stanford 2009.
53. Stanford 2009.
54. Normile 1998.
55. Tuttle 1986, 266–69.
56. Whiten et al. 1999.
57. M. Goodman 1992.
58. Falk 1987.
59. Female bonobos, or pygmy chimpanzees, engage in sexual intercourse nearly as often as human females—see Thompson- Handler et al. 1984.
60. By male-female bonding, we mean that at least one of the sexes is "faithful," that is, typically has intercourse with just one opposite-sex partner throughout at least one estrus or

menstrual cycle or breeding season. Note that the bonding may not be monogamous; an individual may be bonded to more than one individual of the opposite sex. See M. Ember and C. R. Ember 1979.

61. M. Ember and C. R. Ember 1979, 43; also C. R. Ember and M. Ember 1984, 203–04.
62. C. R. Ember and M. Ember 1984, 207.
63. C. R. Ember and M. Ember 1984, 208–09.
64. de Waal and Lanting 1997.
65. Rumbaugh 1970, 52–58.
66. Boesche et al. 1994.
67. Observation by others cited by A. Jolly 1985, 53.
68. Hannah and McGrew 1987.
69. *Newsweek,* "The First Dentist," March 5, 1973, 73.
70. Seyfarth et al. 1980.
71. Gardner and Gardner 1969.
72. Gardner and Gardner 1980.
73. Greenfield and Savage-Rumbaugh 1990.
74. Clutton-Brock and Harvey 1977, 8–9.
75. Aiello 1992; A. Jolly 1985, 53–54.
76. Aiello 1992.
77. A. Jolly 1985, 53–54.
78. Parker 1990, 130.
79. Milton 1981; Clutton-Brock and Harvey 1980.
80. Milton 1988.
81. A. Jolly 1985, 119.
82. Clutton-Brock and Harvey 1977, 9.
83. Terborgh 1983, 224–25.
84. A. Jolly 1985, 120.
85. A. Jolly 1985, 122.
86. Wrangham 1980.

The Origins of Culture and the Emergence of *Homo*

From Chapter 9 of *Anthropology*, 13/e. Carol R. Ember. Melvin Ember. Peter N. Peregrine. Copyright © 2011 by Pearson Education. Published by Prentice Hall. All rights reserved.

The Origins of Culture and the Emergence of *Homo*

n this chapter, we will consider a number of trends in hominid evolution, including the routine use of patterned or nearly standardized stone tools, which is considered one sign of the emergence of culture. It is assumed, but not known for sure, that patterned stone tools were made by the first members of our own genus, **Homo,** for we first see a number of trends in the genus *Homo* that probably started because of habitual stone toolmaking and use—expansion of the brain, modification of the female pelvis to accommodate bigger-brained babies, and reduction in the teeth, face, and jaws.

Even though stone tools are found at various sites in East Africa before the time early *Homo* appeared, most anthropologists surmise that members of early *Homo* species, rather than the australopithecines, made those tools (see Figure 1). After all, early *Homo* had a brain capacity almost one-third larger than that of the australopithecines. But the fact is that none of the earliest stone tools is clearly associated with early *Homo,* so it is impossible as yet to know who made them.[1] We turn now to a discussion of those earliest stone tools and what archaeologists and paleoanthropologists infer about the lifestyles of their makers, the hominids (whoever they were) who lived between about 2.5 million and 1.5 million years ago.   ● ○ ●

EARLY HOMINID TOOLS

The earliest identifiable stone tools found so far come from various sites in East Africa and date from about 2.5 million years ago,[2] and maybe earlier. The oldest tools, some 3,000 in number, were discovered at Gona, Ethiopia. They range from very small flakes (thumb-size) to cobble or core tools that are fist-size.[3] These early tools were apparently made by striking a stone with another stone, a technique called **percussion flaking.** Both the sharp-edged flakes and the sharp-edged cores (the pieces of stone left after flakes are removed) were probably used as tools.

What were those earliest stone tools used for? What do they tell us about early hominid lifestyles? Unfortunately, little can be inferred about lifestyles from the earliest tool sites because little else was found with the tools. In contrast, finds of later tool assemblages at Olduvai Gorge in Tanzania have yielded a rich harvest of cultural information. The Olduvai site was uncovered accidentally in 1911, when a German entomologist followed a butterfly into the gorge and found fossil remains. Louis and Mary Leakey searched the gorge for clues to the evolution of early humans beginning in the 1930s. Of the Olduvai site, Louis Leakey wrote,

> [It] is a fossil hunter's dream, for it shears 300 feet through stratum after stratum of earth's history as through a gigantic layer cake. Here, within reach, lie countless fossils

Artist's reconstruction of a group of *Homo erectus* driving a predator away from an antelope carcass.

and artifacts which but for the faulting and erosion would have remained sealed under thick layers of consolidated rock.[4]

The oldest cultural materials from Olduvai (Bed I) date from Lower Pleistocene times (about 1.6 million years ago). The stone artifacts include core tools and sharp-edged flakes. Flake tools predominate. Among the core tools, so-called choppers are common. Choppers are cores that have been partially flaked and have a side that might have been used for chopping. Other core tools, with flaking along one side and a flat edge, are called scrapers. Whenever a stone has facets removed from only one side of the cutting edge, we call it a **unifacial tool**. If the stone has facets removed from both sides, we call it a **bifacial tool.** Although there are some bifacial tools in the early stone tool assemblages, they are not as plentiful or as elaborated as in later tool traditions. The kind

of tool assemblage found in Bed I and to some extent in later (higher) layers is referred to as **Oldowan** (see Figure 2).[5]

EARLY HOMINID LIFESTYLES

Archaeologists have speculated about the lifestyles of early hominids from Olduvai and other sites. Some of these speculations come from analysis of what can be done with the tools, microscopic analysis of wear on the tools, and examination of the marks the tools make on bones; other speculations are based on what is found with the tools.

Archaeologists have experimented with what can be done with Oldowan tools. The flakes appear to be very versatile; they can be used for slitting the hides of animals, dismembering animals, and whittling wood into sharp-pointed sticks (wooden spears or digging sticks). The larger stone tools (choppers and scrapers) can be used to hack off branches or

77

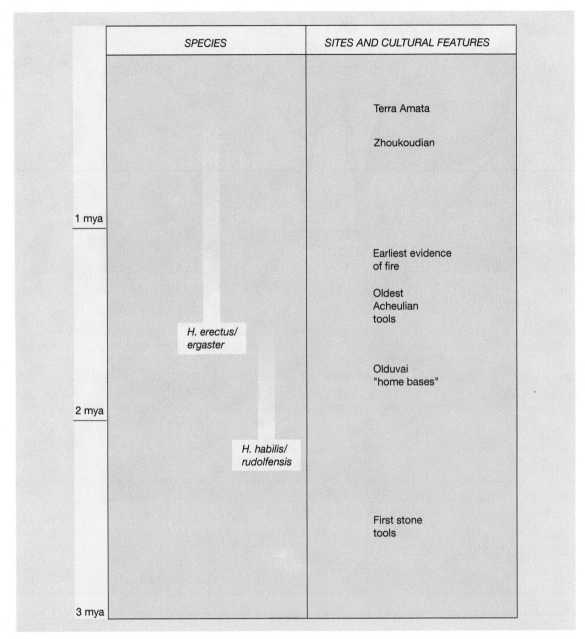

FIGURE 1 Early Evolution of the Genus *Homo*

cut and chop tough animal joints.[6] Those who have made and tried to use stone tools for various purposes are so impressed by the sharpness and versatility of flakes that they wonder whether most of the core tools were really used as tools. The cores could mainly be what remained after wanted flakes were struck off.[7]

Archaeologists surmise that many early tools were also made of wood and bone, but these do not survive in the archaeological record. Present-day populations use sharp-pointed digging sticks for extracting roots and tubers from the ground; stone flakes are very effective for sharpening wood to a very fine point.[8]

None of the early flaked stone tools can plausibly be thought of as weapons. So, if the toolmaking hominids were hunting or defending themselves with weapons, they had to have used wooden spears, clubs, or unmodified stones as missiles. Later, Oldowan tool assemblages also include stones that were flaked and battered into a rounded shape. The unmodified stones and the shaped stones might have been lethal projectiles.[9]

Experiments may indicate what can be done with tools, but they cannot tell us what was *actually* done with them. Other techniques, such as microscopic analysis of the wear on tools, are more informative. Early studies looked at the microscopic scratches formed when a tool was used in different ways. Scratches parallel to the edge of a tool often occur when a tool is used in a sawing motion; perpendicular scratches suggest whittling or scraping.[10] Lawrence Keeley used high-powered microscopes in his experimental investigations of tools and found that different kinds of "polish" develop on tools when they are used on different materials. The polish on tools used for cutting meat is different from the polish on tools used for woodworking. On the basis of microscopic investigation of the

Olduvai Gorge, Tanzania. Bed I, where evidence of early human culture was found, is at the very bottom of the gorge.

© John Reader/Photo Researchers, Inc.

1.5-million-year-old tools from the eastern side of Lake Turkana, Keeley and his colleagues concluded that at least some of the early tools were probably used for cutting meat, others for cutting or whittling wood, and still others for cutting plant stems.[11]

In the 1950s and 1960s, Olduvai Gorge revealed the presence of both Oldowan tools and the remains of broken

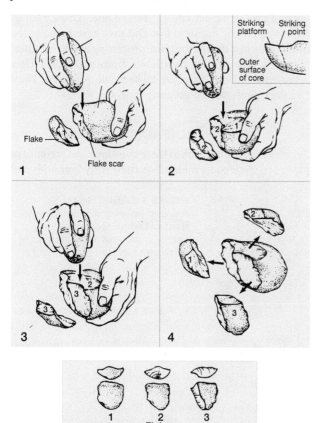

Figure 2 The Production of a Simple Oldowan Chopper Core and the Resultant Flakes

Source: Freyman 1987. Reprinted by permission of the artist, Ed Hanson.
From "The First Technology" by R. Freman in *Scientific American.* Reprinted by permission of the artist, Ed Hanson.

bones and teeth from many different animal species. For many years, it seemed plausible to assume that hominids were the hunters and the animals their prey. But, archaeologists had to reexamine this assumption with the emergence of the field of *taphonomy*, which studies the processes that can alter and distort an assemblage of bones. So, for example, flowing water can bring bones and artifacts together, which may have happened at Olduvai Gorge about 1.8 million years ago. (The area of what is now the gorge bordered the shores of a shallow lake at that time.) Other animals such as hyenas could have also brought carcasses to some of the same places that hominids spent time. Taphonomy requires archaeologists to consider all the possible reasons things may be found together.[12]

But there is little doubt that hominids were cutting up animal carcasses for meat shortly after 2 million years ago. Microscopic analyses show that cut marks on animal bones were unambiguously created by stone flake tools, and microscopic analyses of the polish on stone tools indicate that the polish is consistent with butchering. We still do not know for sure whether the hominids around Olduvai Gorge were just scavenging meat (taking meat from the kills of other animals) or actually hunting the animals.

On the basis of her analysis of cut marks on bone from Bed I in Olduvai Gorge, Pat Shipman suggested that scavenging, not hunting, was the major meat-getting activity of the hominids living there between 2 million and 1.7 million years ago. For example, the cut marks made by the stone tools usually (but not always) overlie teeth marks made by carnivores. This suggests that the hominids were often scavenging the meat of animals killed and partially eaten by nonhominid predators. The fact that the cut marks were sometimes made first, however, suggested to Shipman that the hominids were also sometimes the hunters.[13] On the other hand, prior cut marks may indicate only that the hominids scavenged before carnivores had a chance to consume their prey.

The artifact and animal remains from Bed I and the lower part of Bed II at Olduvai suggest a few other things

© Pictures of Record, Inc.

A replica of an Oldowan stone tool is used to chop into a large bone to extract the nutrient-rich marrow. Few animals have jaws powerful enough to break open the bones of large mammals, but stone tools would have allowed early humans to do so.

about the lifestyles of the hominids there. First, it seems that the hominids moved around during the year; most of the sites in what is now the Olduvai Gorge appear to have been used only in the dry season, as indicated by an analysis of the kinds of animal bones found there.[14] Second, whether the early Olduvai hominids were hunters or scavengers, they apparently exploited a wide range of animals. Although most of the bones are from medium-sized antelopes and wild pigs, even large animals such as elephants and giraffes seem to have been eaten.[15] It is clear, then, that the Olduvai hominids scavenged or hunted for meat, but we cannot tell yet how important meat was in their diet.

There is also no consensus about how to characterize the Olduvai sites that contain concentrations of stone tools and animal bones. In the 1970s, there was a tendency to think of them as home bases to which hominids (presumably male) brought meat to share with others (presumably nursing mothers and young children). Indeed, Mary Leakey identified two locations where she thought early hominids had built simple structures (Figure 3). One

was a stone circle that she suggested formed the base of a small brush windbreak. The other was a circular area of dense debris surrounded by an area virtually without debris. Leakey suggested that the area lacking debris may represent the location of a ring of thorny brush with which early hominids surrounded their campsite in order to keep out predators—much like pastoralists living in the region do today.[16] But archaeologists today are not so sure that these sites were home bases. For one thing, carnivores also frequented the sites. Places with meaty bones lying around may not have been so safe for hominids to use as home bases. Second, the animal remains at the sites had not been completely dismembered and butchered. If the sites had been hominid home bases, we would expect more complete processing of carcasses.[17] Third, natural processes as simple as trees growing through a site can create circular areas of debris such as the ones Leakey identified as structures, and without better evidence that early hominids made them, one cannot be sure that the circles of debris were indeed structures.[18]

If these sites were not home bases, what were they? Some archaeologists are beginning to think that these early sites with many animal bones and tools may just have been places where hominids processed food but did not live. Why would the hominids return repeatedly to a particular site? Richard Potts suggests one possible reason—that hominids left caches of stone tools and stones for toolmaking at various locations to facilitate recurrent food-collecting and processing activities.[19] Future research may tell us more about early hominid life. Did they have home bases, or did they just move from one processing site to another? How did they protect themselves from predators? They apparently did not have fire to keep the predators away. Did they climb trees to get away or to sleep?

Stone Tools and Culture

Regardless of the answers to these questions, the presence of patterned stone tools means that these early hominids had

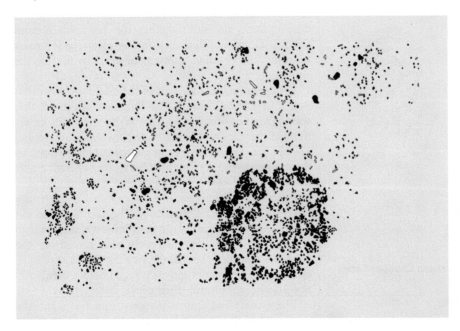

FIGURE 3 Olduvai "Hut"
A ring of stones and bones found in Bed I of Olduvai Gorge that Mary Leakey interpreted as the remains of an ancient hut.

applied anthropology

Stone Tools and Historic Preservation

Historic preservation laws protect archaeological materials in most countries of the world today. What this means is that people cannot remove artifacts, ecofacts, or fossils from the country without permission, nor can they excavate sites or features. Many professional archaeologists and paleoanthropologists work for governments as applied anthropologists protecting and, when necessary, excavating archaeological deposits to prevent them from being destroyed. In our discussion of early hominid sites in Olduvai Gorge and elsewhere, we have touched upon a difficult question in historic preservation—how can one tell a site from a natural disturbance? More specifically, how can paleoanthropologists distinguish early stone tools from ordinary rocks? It is not always easy.

To tell that a core tool is not a naturally flaked rock, paleoanthropologists typically look for three distinct features. First, the tool has to be made of the *right kind of rock*. The rock must be both flakable and durable. You can flake shale, for example, but it is not durable. Many metamorphic rocks are durable, but you cannot flake them because there are too many flaws in the rock. Most stone tools are made from obsidian, quartz, flint, or chert. Second, paleoanthropologists look for *bilateral flaking*. Bilateral flaking occurs when flakes are struck from two sides of a stone to form a cutting edge. Natural processes may knock a couple of flakes from one side of a stone but will rarely knock them off from opposite sides. Third, paleoanthropologists look for *retouching*. Retouching occurs when additional flakes are removed from an existing tool in order to resharpen it. Again, natural processes may knock a series of flakes from one side of a rock but will rarely create something resembling a retouched cutting edge.

Paleoanthropologists may also look for a distinct *striking platform* on flakes. A striking platform is the place where the blow landed that knocked the flake from the core. When a flake is struck from a core, it leaves a clean scar that can be used as a striking platform to knock a flake from the opposite side of the core. On flakes made by humans, the striking platform is often the scar left by a previous flake. Just as bilateral flaking is rare in nature, so too is a flake scar with a clearly prepared striking platform.

With these features, paleoanthropologists can usually distinguish naturally flaked rocks from stone tools. But this is not always the case, and many paleoanthropologists have made mistakes. Indeed, one of the most famous mistakes was made by Louis Leakey, one of the first paleoanthropologists to identify early hominid tools. In the late 1960s, Leakey claimed that a site in California called Calico Hills contained early human tools. This claim was met with disbelief, as no evidence of premodern humans has ever been found in North America, and, as we discuss in the chapter on the Upper Paleolithic world, there is good evidence that modern-looking humans were the continent's first inhabitants. However, because Leakey made the claim, it had to be taken seriously. A group of respected paleoanthropologists met at the site upon Leakey's request to make a determination. Their finding? The alleged stone tools were natural objects, not made by humans.

Calico Hills is an important cautionary tale. How do you know a stone was modified by a hominid, and thus requires protection under historic preservation laws? In addition to the tool's physical features, paleoanthropologists must also consider the context in which it is found. When alleged tools are found in the absence of hominids or with no other clear evidence of stone tool use, as in the case of Calico Hills, and the context does not suggest the possibility of tools, paleoanthropologists should question their presence.

Sources: Andrefsky 1998; Haynes 1973; Patterson 1983.

probably developed *culture*. Archaeologists consider a pattern of behavior, such as a particular way to make a tool that is shared and learned by a group of individuals, to be a sign of cultural behavior. To be sure, toolmaking does not imply that early humans had anything like the complex cultures of humans today. Chimpanzees have patterns of tool use and toolmaking that appear to be shared and learned, but they do not have that much in the way of cultural behavior.

What, exactly, makes human culture so different from other forms of animal behavior? Anthropologists have spent more than a century trying to answer this question, and there is still no widely accepted answer. One thing is clear, however: Culture must be understood as a set of interrelated processes, not as a thing.[20] What are the processes that make up culture? Let's consider some of the more important ones.

First, culture is *learned* as well as *shared*. This is the fundamental difference between culture and most other forms of animal behavior. Culture is not a set of innate behaviors but, rather, a set of learned ones. Culture is something individuals acquire during their lifetimes as they mature and interact with others. Interaction is key here, because not only are cultural behaviors learned, they are learned through interaction with others, through education, and through shared experiences. Culture, then, is a social process, not an individual one. It also includes attitudes, values, and ideals as well as behavior.

Second, culture is generally *adaptive*. What this means is that most of the learned and shared behaviors that make up a culture are thought to have developed and spread through a group of people because they help that group of people survive in a given environment. Thus, cultural behaviors may be favored by natural selection just as genes are. The extent to which human culture is a product of natural selection is hotly debated, but few anthropologists would argue that culture is not a key aspect of human adaptation. What makes culture quite different from the behavioral systems of other animals is that, because culture is learned and shared rather than innate, humans can develop new behaviors quickly and adapt to diverse and changing conditions with relative ease. Adaptation, then, is perhaps the most significant process of culture.

Change is the third major process of culture, for culture is always *changing*. Culture change regularly occurs as new and beneficial means of adaptation are developed and shared. But anthropologists also assume that, when new behaviors or ideas are developed, they tend to become integrated with existing behaviors or ideas. That is, new items that conflict with established ones may lead to one or the other changing. For example, a group of early humans could not have both scavenged meat and, at the same time, prohibited eating meat that they did not themselves kill. Such a situation would create a contradiction, and something would probably have to change. Working out contradictions between new, highly beneficial behaviors and established but less beneficial ones may be one of the reasons that cultures are so dynamic.

It seems clear that the early hominids, like other primates, were social beings. It also seems clear from the archaeological record that early hominids were making and using stone tools on a regular basis. Tools are frequently found in discrete concentrations, and often in association with animal bones and other debris from human activity. And, as we have already noted, a number of paleoanthropologists have argued that such concentrations of debris may represent campsites or even small shelters. Home bases of some sort may have been a part of early hominid culture.

Whether they reflect home bases or not, large numbers of animal bones and tools are found in discrete locations, and these accumulations suggest that groups of individuals used the areas over periods of time. In such a situation, sharing of food is very likely. It seems counterintuitive to think that individuals would have purposely brought food to a common location only to keep it to themselves. Although we must move into the realm of pure speculation, it does seem reasonable to think that closely related individuals, like parents, children, and siblings, would be more likely to associate and share food with one another than more distantly related individuals. This speculation is supported by the fact that, when food sharing takes place among chimpanzees, it is usually among closely related individuals.[21] Thus, the ancient locations of early hominid social activity may be evidence of family groups. How would such a system of social behavior—the creation of a common meeting, resting, and living place for a group of related individuals to share food—have evolved? Let's consider one model.

One Model for the Evolution of Culture

Early *Homo* had a brain almost one-third larger than that of the australopithecines. As we discuss later in the section on trends in hominid evolution, one of the possible consequences of brain expansion was the lessening of maturity at birth. The fact that babies were born more immature may at least partly explain the lengthening of the period of infant and child dependency in hominids. Compared with other animals, we spend not only a longer proportion of our life span, but also the longest absolute period, in a dependent state. Prolonged infant dependency has probably been of great significance in human cultural evolution. According to Theodosius Dobzhansky,

it is this helplessness and prolonged dependence on the ministrations of the parents and other persons that favors . . . the socialization and learning process on which the transmission of culture wholly depends. This may have been an overwhelming advantage of the human growth pattern in the process of evolution.[22]

It used to be thought that the australopithecines had a long period of infant dependency, just as modern humans do, but the way their teeth apparently developed suggests that the early australopithecines followed an apelike pattern of development. Thus, prolonged maturation may be relatively recent, but just how recent is not yet known.[23]

Although some use of tools for digging, defense, or scavenging may have influenced the development of bipedalism, full bipedalism may have made possible more efficient toolmaking and consequently more efficient foraging and scavenging. As we have seen, there are archaeological signs that early hominids may have been scavenging (and perhaps even hunting) animals as far back as the late Pliocene. Indeed, we have fairly good evidence that early hominids were butchering and presumably eating big game some 2 million years ago.

Whenever it was that hominids began to scavenge for game and perhaps hunt regularly, the development of scavenging would have required individuals to travel long distances frequently in search of suitable carcasses. Among groups of early *Homo*, longer infant and child dependency may have fostered the creation of home bases or at least established meeting places. The demands of childbirth and caring for a newborn might have made it difficult for early *Homo* mothers to travel for some time after the birth. Certainly, it would have been awkward for a mother carrying a nursing child to travel long distances to hunt. Although carrying an infant might be possible with a sling, successful hunting might not be so likely with a needy and potentially noisy child along. Because early *Homo* males (and perhaps females without young children) would have been freer to roam farther from home, they probably became the scavengers or hunters. Women with young children may have gathered wild plants within a small area that could be covered without traveling far from the home base or meeting place.

The creation of home bases or meeting places among early *Homo* groups may have increased the likelihood of food sharing. If mothers with young children were limited to gathering plant foods in a relatively small area, the only way to ensure that they and their children could obtain a complete diet would have been to share the other foods obtained elsewhere. With whom would such sharing take place? Most likely with close relatives. Sharing with them would have made it more likely that their offspring would survive to have offspring. Thus, if early *Homo* had home bases and families, those characteristics could have encouraged the development of the learned and shared behaviors we call culture.[24] Obviously this is a "just-so" story—a tale that we may never be able to prove really happened. However, it is a tale that is consistent with the archaeological record.[25]

TRENDS IN HOMINID EVOLUTION

Patterned stone tools do not appear until early *Homo* comes on the scene. With early *Homo*, we see the start of several trends in hominid evolution that appear to reflect the manufacture and use of patterned stone tools—the expansion of the brain, the modification of the female pelvis to accommodate bigger-brained babies, and a general reduction in the size of teeth, face, and jaws.

Expansion of the Brain

The australopithecines had relatively small cranial capacities, about 380–530 cubic centimeters (cc)—not much larger than that of chimpanzees. But around 2.3 million years ago, close to the time that patterned stone tools first appeared, some hominids show evidence of enlarged brain capacity. These hominids, early *Homo*, had cranial capacities averaging about 630–640 cc, which is about 50 percent of the brain capacity of modern humans (which averages slightly more than 1,300 cc). (See Figure 4.) A later member of our genus, *Homo erectus*, which may have first appeared about 1.8 million years ago, had a cranial capacity averaging about 895–1,040 cc, or about 70 percent of the brain capacity of modern humans.[26]

The australopithecines were small, and the earliest *Homo* finds were hardly bigger, so much of the increase in brain size over time might have been a result of later hominids' bigger bodies. When we correct for body size, however, it turns out that brain size increased not only absolutely but also relatively after 2 million years ago. Between about 4 million and 2 million years ago, relative brain size remained just about the same. Only in the last 2 million years has the hominid brain doubled in relative size and tripled in absolute size.[27]

What may have favored the increase in brain size? As we noted earlier, many anthropologists think that the increase is linked to the emergence of stone toolmaking about 2.5 million years ago. The reasoning is that stone toolmaking was important for the survival of our ancestors, and therefore natural selection would have favored bigger-brained individuals because they had motor and conceptual skills that enabled them to be better toolmakers. According to this view, the expansion of the brain and more sophisticated toolmaking would have developed together. Other anthropologists think that the expansion of the brain may have been favored by other factors, such as warfare, hunting, longer life, and language.[28] One intriguing theory is that life in complex social groups requires increased intelligence and memory, and that the creation of home bases and family groups may have fostered the expansion of the hominid brain.[29] Whatever the factors favoring bigger brains, they also provided humans with an expanded capacity for culture. Thus, along with bipedalism, the expansion of the brain marks a watershed in human evolution.

As the hominid brain expanded, natural selection also favored the widening of the female pelvis to allow larger-brained babies to be born.[30] But there was probably a limit to how far the pelvis could widen and still be adapted to bipedalism. Something had to give, and that something was the degree of physical development of the human infant at birth—for instance, the human infant is born with cranial bones so plastic that they can overlap. Because birth takes place before the cranial bones have hardened, the human infant with its relatively large brain can pass through the opening in the mother's pelvis. Human infants are born at a relatively early stage of development, and are wholly dependent on their parents for many years. As we have noted, this lengthy period of infant dependency may have been an important factor in the evolution of culture.

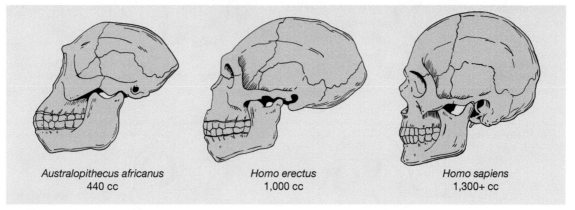

Australopithecus africanus
440 cc

Homo erectus
1,000 cc

Homo sapiens
1,300+ cc

FIGURE 4

Comparison of the estimated cranial capacities of *Australopithecus africanus*, *Homo erectus*, and *Homo sapiens*, demonstrating the expansion of the brain in hominid evolution.

Source: Estimated cranial capacities from Tattersall et al. 2000. Reproduced by permission of Routledge, Inc., part of The Taylor & Francis Group.
Estimated cranial capacities from Tattersall, Delson, and van Couvering, eds., 2000. Reproduced by permission of Routledge, Inc., part of the Taylor and Francis Group.

Reduction of the Face, Teeth, and Jaws

As in the case of the brain, substantial changes in the face, teeth, and jaws do not appear in hominid evolution until after about 2 million years ago. The australopithecines all have cheek teeth that are very large relative to their estimated body weight, perhaps because the diet of the australopithecines was especially high in plant foods,[31] including small, tough objects such as seeds, nuts, and tubers. The australopithecines have thick jawbones, probably also related to their chewing needs. The australopithecines have relatively large faces that project forward below the eyes. But when we get to the *Homo* forms, we see reduction in the size of the face, cheek teeth, and jaws (see Figure 5). It would seem that natural selection in favor of a bigger and stronger chewing apparatus was relaxed. One reason might be that members of the *Homo* genus started to eat foods that were easier to chew. Such foods might have included roots, fruits, and meat. As we discuss later, it may have been the development of habitual tool use and the control of fire that allowed members of the *Homo* genus to change their diet to include foods that are easier to chew, including meat. If food is cooked and easy to chew, individual humans with smaller jaws and teeth would not be disadvantaged, and therefore the face, cheek teeth, and jaw would get smaller on average over time.[32]

The expansion of the brain and reduction of the face occurred at about the same time, and were probably related. A recent discovery in human genetics appears to provide direct evidence of a connection. Researchers studying muscle diseases in modern humans discovered that humans have a unique myosin gene called MYH16 (myosin is a protein in muscle tissue) that is only present in jaw muscles. Comparing MYH16 to related genes in primates, the researchers determined that MYH16 evolved about 2.4 million years ago—around the time the brain began to enlarge and the face and jaw began to shrink. So, the expansion of the brain appears to have been aided by a mutation in myosin that caused jaw muscles to shrink.[33]

Other Evolved Traits

The fossil evidence, which we discuss later in this chapter, suggests when, and in which hominids, changes occurred in brain size and in the face, teeth, and jaws. Other changes in the evolution of hominids cannot yet be confidently dated with regard to time and particular hominid. For example, we know that modern humans are relatively hairless compared with the other surviving primates. But we do not know when hominids became relatively hairless, because fossilized bones do not tell us whether their owners were hairy. On the other hand, we suspect that most of the other characteristically human traits developed after the brain began to increase in size, during the evolution of the genus *Homo*.

What is the evidence that the physical and behavioral changes we have been discussing occurred during the evolution of the *Homo* genus? We shall now consider the earliest *Homo* fossils and how they are associated with brain expansion and the reduction of the face, jaws, and teeth.

EARLY *HOMO*

Hominids with a brain absolutely and relatively larger than that of the australopithecines appear about 2.3 million years ago. These hominids, classified in our own genus,

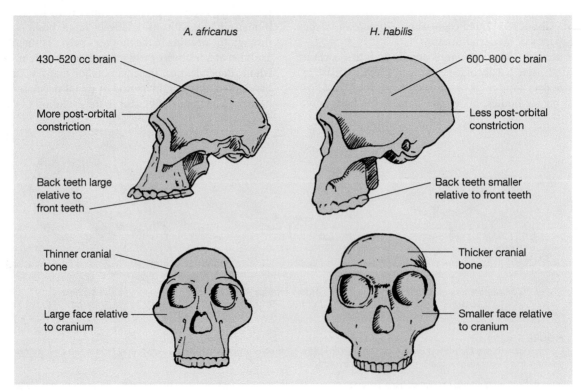

FIGURE 5 Comparison of *A. africanus* and *H. habilis*

Homo, are generally divided into two species: **Homo habilis** and **Homo rudolfensis.** Both are known primarily from the western parts of Kenya and Tanzania, but remains have been found elsewhere in eastern and southern Africa, including the Omo Basin of Ethiopia and Sterkfontein cave in South Africa. Both lived in the same place and time as the robust australopithecine, *Australopithecus boisei,* and may later have lived at the same time as *Homo erectus.*

Homo habilis appears to be the earlier of these two species, appearing around 2.3 million years ago. Compared with the australopithecines, *H. habilis* had a significantly larger brain, averaging 630–640 cc,[34] and reduced molars and premolars.[35] The rest of the skeleton is reminiscent of the australopithecines, including the presence of powerful hands and relatively long arms, suggesting that *H. habilis* was at least partially arboreal. *H. habilis* may also have been sexually dimorphic like the australopithecines, as individuals seem to have greatly differed in size.

Homo rudolfensis is roughly contemporary with *Homo habilis,* and shares many of its features. Indeed, many paleoanthropologists make no distinction between the two species, putting *H. rudolfensis* into *H. habilis.* Those who do see them as distinct species point to the larger and more thickly enameled cheek teeth of *H. rudolfensis,* its flatter and broader face, and its more modernlike limb proportions. Even with its larger teeth and broader face, the dentition of *H. rudolfensis* is considerably reduced over the australopithecines and, as in *H. habilis,* its brain is at least a third larger.

We have little postcranial skeletal material for either early *Homo* species, so it is impossible to tell whether the female pelvis had changed. But, with brains averaging a third larger than that of the australopithecines, it seems likely that some modifications must have developed to allow bigger-brained babies to be born. We do know that changes in the female pelvis to accommodate bigger-brained babies can be seen in *Homo erectus,* and it is this species that we turn to next.

HOMO ERECTUS

Homo erectus evolved very shortly after *Homo habilis,* probably about 1.8 million years ago. **Homo erectus** was the first hominid species to be widely distributed in the Old World. Examples of *H. erectus* were found first in Java, later in China, and still later in Africa (see the box "The First Migrants"). Most paleoanthropologists agree that some human ancestor moved from Africa to Asia at some point. Until recently, it was assumed that it was *H. erectus* who moved, because *H. erectus* lived in East Africa about 1.6 million years ago but not until after about 1 million years ago in Asia.[36] Recent redating, however, suggests that *H. erectus* in Java may be somewhat older, dating to perhaps 1.8 million years ago.[37] And *H. erectus* fossils from Dmanisi, in the southeastern European nation of Georgia, have recently been dated to at least 1.7 million years ago.[38] If this last dating is accurate, early hominids may have moved out of Africa earlier. Indeed, one well-preserved skull found at Dmanisi in 2001 has some features that are reminiscent of *H. habilis*—a brain only about 600 cc, relatively large canines, and a relatively thin browridge.[39] Although the excavators classify the skull as *H. erectus,* it does make one wonder whether *H. habilis* or transitional *habilis-erectus* individuals were the first to leave Africa.

The skull of a Homo habilis/rudolfensis (ER-1470) found by Richard Leakey in 1972. Note its high forehead and large braincase.

The skull of the *Homo erectus/ergaster* boy found at Nariokotome, Kenya. Though an adolescent when he died, he already stood five and a half feet tall.

Original housed in National Museum of Kenya, Nairobi. © 1994 David L. Brill

Brill Atlanta

There is also the question of whether there is only one species *of H. erectus* or whether *H. erectus* contains several distinct species. Some scholars see enough differences between Asian and African populations of *H. erectus* to argue that they should be separated into two distinct species, *Homo erectus* for the Asian populations and **Homo ergaster** for the African ones. Furthermore, *Homo erectus* (or *Homo ergaster*) fossils are also found in Europe. But some paleoanthropologists think that the finds in Europe typically classified as *H. erectus* are actually early examples of *H. sapiens*.[40] Others think that the European fossils and similar ones found in southern Africa and the Near East should be grouped into a distinct species, *Homo heidelbergensis*. There is also *Homo floresiensis*, a diminutive hominid that appears to be a miniature form of *Homo erectus* that evolved only on the isolated island of Flores, Indonesia. It is all a bit confusing. Later we will try to sort it all out.

The Discovery of *Homo erectus*

In 1891, Eugene Dubois, a Dutch anatomist digging in Java, found what he called *Pithecanthropus erectus,* meaning "erect ape man." (We now refer to this hominid as *Homo erectus*.) The discovery was not the first humanlike fossil found; Neandertals were known many years earlier. But no one was certain, not even Dubois himself, whether the fossil he found in Java was an ape or a human.

The actual find consisted of a cranium and a thighbone. For many years, it was thought that the fragments were not even from the same animal. The skull was too large to be that of a modern ape but was smaller than that of an average human, having a cranial capacity between the average ape's 500 cc and the average modern human's 1,300 cc. The thighbone, however, matched that of a modern human. Did the two fragments in fact belong together? The question was resolved many years later by fluorine analysis. If fossils from the same deposit contain the same amount of fluorine, they are the same age. The skull fragment and thighbone found by Dubois were tested for fluorine content and found to be the same age.

A discovery by G. H. R. von Koenigswald in the mid-1930s, also in Java, not only confirmed Dubois's earlier speculations and extended our knowledge of the physical characteristics of *Homo erectus,* but also gave us a better understanding of this early human's place in time. Since then, many more *H. erectus* fossils have been found in Java. These *H. erectus* in Java were thought not to be more than 1 million years old.[41] Now argon–argon dating puts some of the Java specimens back to perhaps 1.8 million years ago.[42]

Between the times of Dubois's and von Koenigswald's discoveries, Davidson Black, a Canadian anatomy professor teaching in Peking (Beijing), China, set out to investigate a large cave at nearby Zhoukoudian where a fossilized tooth had been found. Confident that the tooth came from a hitherto unknown hominid genus, he obtained funds to excavate the area extensively. After two years of excavation, he and his colleagues found a skull in limestone, which they dubbed "Peking Man." Black died in 1934, and his work was carried on by Franz Weidenreich.

It was not until the 1950s that *H. erectus* fossils were uncovered in northern Africa (see Figure 6). Many finds since then have come from East Africa, particularly two sites—Olduvai Gorge in Tanzania and the Lake Turkana region of Kenya. An almost complete skeleton of a boy was found at Nariokotome, on the western side of Lake Turkana, dating from about 1.6 million years ago. The Olduvai finds are from about 1.2 million years ago.[43]

Physical Characteristics of *Homo erectus*

The *Homo erectus* skull generally was long, low, and thickly walled, with a flat frontal area and prominent

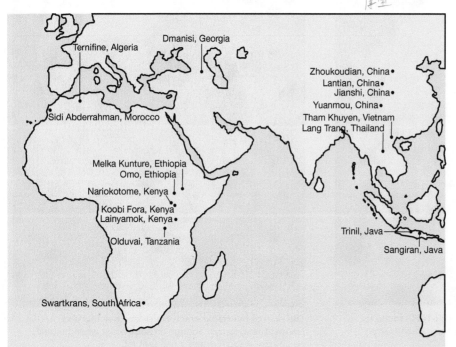

FIGURE 6 *Homo erectus* **Sites**

Source: Ciochon and Fleagle 1993. From Russell L. Ciochon and John G. Fleagle, eds., *The Human Evolution Source Book.* (Upper Saddle River, NJ: Prentice Hall, 1993).

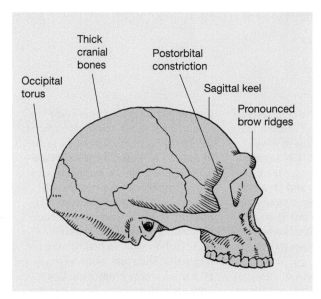

FIGURE 7 *Homo erectus* Features

browridges. It had a unique pentagonal shape when looked at from the back, formed in part by a rounded ridge, called a **sagittal keel,** running along the crest of the skull. There was also a ridge of bone running horizontally along the back of the skull, called an **occipital torus,** which added to the skull's overall long shape (see Figure 7).[44]

Compared with early *Homo, H. erectus* had relatively small teeth. *H. erectus* was the first hominid to have third molars that were smaller than the second or first molars, as in modern humans. The molars also had an enlarged pulp cavity, called **taurodontism,** which may have allowed the teeth to withstand harder use and wear than the teeth of modern humans. But the *H. erectus* jaw was lighter and thinner than in either early *Homo* or the australopithecines, and the face was less **prognathic,** or forward thrusting, in the upper and lower jaw.

The brain, averaging 895–1,040 cc, was larger than that found in any of the australopithecines or early *Homo* species, but smaller than the average brain of a modern human.[45] Endocasts, which provide a picture of the surface of the brain, suggest that it was organized more like the brain of modern humans than like that of australopithecines.

Homo erectus had a prominent, projecting nose, in contrast to the australopithecines' flat, nonprojecting nose.[46] From the neck down, *H. erectus* was practically indistinguishable from *H. sapiens.* In contrast to the smaller australopithecines and early *Homo* species who lived in East Africa around the same time, *H. erectus* was comparable to modern humans in size. The almost complete skeleton of the boy at Nariokotome suggests that he was about five and a half feet tall and about 8 years of age when he died; researchers estimate that he would have been over six feet tall had he lived to maturity. About 1.6 million years ago, the Nariokotome region was probably open grassland, with trees mostly along rivers.[47] *Homo erectus* in East Africa was similar in size to Africans today who live in a similarly open, dry environment.[48] *H. erectus* was also less sexually dimorphic than either the australopithecines or

early *Homo.* The degree of sexual dimorphism in *H. erectus* was comparable to that in modern humans.

Those scholars who group the African populations into a distinct species, *Homo ergaster,* point to several differences between them and other *Homo erectus* populations: The cranial proportions differ in *Homo ergaster;* the browridge is thinner and is arched above each of the eye sockets; the eye sockets are more rounded; and the face is oriented more vertically below the skull, among others. On the other hand, some scholars believe that the differences between *Homo erectus* and modern humans are not large enough to be identified as different species, and argue that *Homo erectus* populations should be lumped into *Homo sapiens.*[49] These arguments will not be settled any time soon, so for now we will stick with the single taxon, *Homo erectus.*

Homo floresiensis

Whether or not there are distinct African and Asian species of *Homo erectus,* most scholars agree that **Homo floresiensis** is a distinct species that is closely related to *Homo erectus. H. floresiensis* has only been found on the Indonesian island of Flores, and only a handful of individuals have been located to date. All are tiny (they stood perhaps three feet tall), and have very small brains, on the order of 380 cc.[50] The structure of the brain, however, seems closely related to that of *H. erectus,* as do the structures of the skull.[51] In other words, *H. floresiensis* appears to be a tiny version of *H. erectus. H. floresiensis* even made tools that look similar to those made by *H. erectus,* and in some cases the tools look even more sophisticated. So, although they were small in stature and had very small brains, *H. floresiensis* seems to have been culturally and intellectually similar to *H. erectus.*[52]

The body of *Homo floresiensis* also seems to resemble *Homo erectus,* or perhaps even *Homo habilis.* The wrist of *H. floresiensis* is not like that of modern humans or

The skull of the dwarf species *Homo floresiensis* next to that of a modern human. Note how small it is in comparison.

National Geographic Image Collection

migrants and immigrants

The First Migrants

Hominids evolved in Africa, yet today hominids are found on every continent. Who were the first hominids to leave Africa, and when did they first leave? For many years, the clear answer was that *Homo erectus* were the first to leave Africa, and they did so perhaps 700,000 to 1 million years ago. In recent years, new findings and sources of evidence have led scholars to question this established answer.

The first new information came from geochemist Carl Swisher, who in the mid-1990s redated the Java sites where *Homo erectus* fossils had been found and determined they dated to perhaps 1.8 million years ago. Because the earliest *H. erectus* fossils in Africa share a similar date, this created a problem—how did *H. erectus* appear in Java at about the same time they appeared in Africa? As this question was being pondered, a remarkable set of new *H. erectus* fossils were being uncovered in Dmanisi, Georgia. Dated at 1.7 million years ago, these fossils made it clear that *H. erectus* left Africa almost as soon

as they had evolved. The discovery of a *Homo habilis*-like fossil at Dmanisi, and of Oldowan-like tools at Riwat, Pakistan and Longgupo, China, suggested that *H. habilis* may have been the first to leave Africa, and *H. erectus* followed a path their predecessors blazed. If they were following an earlier migration, it could explain how *H. erectus* were able to move so quickly across Asia.

A more unusual source of information on when hominids first left Africa comes from the parasites that accompanied them. All hominoids are plagued by lice, but humans host a distinct species, *Pediculus humanus*. Geneticist David Reed and his colleagues found that *P. humanus* diverged from other lice about 5.6 million years ago—about the time the first hominids appeared. More interesting, however, Reed and colleagues discovered that there are two subspecies of *P. humanus* that appear to have diverged about 1.2 million years ago. One subspecies is found worldwide today; the other is restricted to the New World. Reed and

colleagues suggest this is evidence that at least some hominid migrants (probably *H. erectus*) became isolated in Asia by at least 1.2 million years ago, where their lice diverged from that of other hominid populations, only to be picked up much later by modern human migrants who ended up colonizing the New World.

So, who were the first hominid migrants? They may have been *H. habilis*, or they may have been very early *H. erectus*. When did the first hominid migrations out of Africa take place? Probably slightly less than 2 million years ago, but once these hominids left, they moved quickly, and they moved long distances. By 1.6 million years ago, *H. erectus* was in both western and southern Asia, and by 1.2 million years ago, their populations had moved far enough to have become isolated from one another. Whether or not they were the first migrants out of Africa, *H. erectus* migrated fast and far.

Sources: Reed et al. 2004; Tattersall 1997.

Neandertals, but resembles that of the great apes and australopithecines (unfortunately, no wrists of *H. erectus* or *H. habilis* have been found, so no comparison can be made to them).[53] Similarly, the foot of *H. floresiensis* resembles that of *H. erectus* and earlier hominids more than that of modern humans.[54] Once again, *H. floresiensis* appears to be a tiny version of *H. erectus*.

How might a miniature version of *H. erectus* have evolved? The answer is that both dwarfism and gigantism are common phenomena in isolated populations. Dwarfism appears to be an adaptation that occurs when there are few predators—a species in isolation can become smaller, and have a large population, if there are no predators threatening them. This may be what happened on Flores.[55] It is interesting that the island also hosted a number of dwarf species in addition to *H. floresiensis*, including a dwarf elephant that appears to have been one of the favorite foods of *H. floresiensis*. Perhaps even more interesting is the fact that *H. floresiensis* may have survived until as recently as 12,000 years ago—well into the time period when modern humans were living in Indonesia. Could modern humans

and the tiny *H. floresiensis* have met some time in the distant past? It is an intriguing possibility, but there is no evidence to tell us.

The Evolution of *Homo erectus*

The evolution of *Homo erectus* reflects a continuation of the general evolutionary trends we discussed previously. The brain continued to expand, increasing more than a third over early *Homo* (just as early *Homo* had increased more than a third over the australopithecines). The face, teeth, and jaws continued to shrink, taking on an almost modern form. An increasing use and variety of tools may have led to a further development of the brain. *Homo erectus* was eating and probably cooking meat, and this may have led to further reduction in the teeth and jaws.

One additional change in *Homo erectus* is an apparent reduction in the extent of sexual dimorphism to almost modern levels. Recall that the australopithecines and early *Homo* were quite sexually dimorphic. *Homo erectus* does not appear to be as sexually dimorphic as these earlier hominids. What might have caused this change? In other primates, sexual dimorphism appears to be linked to social systems in which males are at the top of dominance hierarchies due to physical size and prowess and such males control sexual access to multiple females in the group. In contrast, lack of sexual dimorphism seems most pronounced in the animals where *pair bonding* exists—that is, where a male and a female form a breeding pair that lasts for a long period of time (there are several distinct variations of male-female bonding in modern human cultures).[56] Could male-female bonding have developed in *Homo erectus*? It seems possible.

Recall that early *Homo* may have established some of the basic elements of human culture, including home bases or meeting places, family groups, and sharing. Another basic element of recent human culture, one that is present in almost all known cultures, is *marriage*. Marriage is a socially recognized sexual and economic bond between two individuals, typically a male and a female, that is intended to continue throughout the lifetimes of the individuals and to produce socially accepted children. It is a specific kind of pair bond with a set of behaviors, expectations, and obligations that extend beyond the pair to those individuals' families. With marriage, then, the competition between males for access to females may have diminished, lessening the importance of sexual dimorphism. But why might marriage have developed in *Homo erectus?*

In animal species where females can feed themselves and their babies after birth, pair bonding is rare. But in species where females cannot feed both themselves and their babies, pair bonding is common. Why? We think it is because a strong male-female bond provides a good solution to the problem of incompatibility between a mother's feeding requirements and tending a newborn baby. A male partner can bring food and/or watch the newborn while the mother gets food.[57] But most primates lack pair bonding. This may be because primate infants are able to cling to their mother's fur soon after birth, so that the mother's hands are free to forage. Human infants demonstrate a residual form of this innate ability to cling during their first few weeks of life. This is called the *Moro reflex*. If a human infant feels it is falling backward, it will automatically stretch out its arms and clench its fists.[58]

This infant chimpanzee has no problem traveling with its mother, as it can cling tightly to her fur. *Homo erectus* mothers probably had no fur to hold on to and had to carry their infants.

We have no way of knowing if *Homo erectus* had fur like other primates, but we think probably not, because we think they may have worn clothing, as we discuss later. The brain in *Homo erectus* may also have already expanded enough that *Homo erectus* infants, like modern human infants, could not adequately support their heads even if they could hold onto their mother's fur. In any case, when early hominids began to depend on scavenging and hunting for food (and for skins to be used in clothing), it would have been difficult and hazardous for a parent with a newborn baby to engage in these activities with a baby along. Marriage would have been an effective solution to this problem because each parent could help protect the baby while the other was away getting food.

Another important aspect of the evolution of *Homo erectus* was the movement of populations out of eastern and southern Africa. As with the lessening of sexual dimorphism, it seems likely that cultural innovations were the key to allowing *Homo erectus* to move into new environments. Why? Because upon entering new environments, *Homo erectus* would have been faced with new (and generally colder) climatic conditions, new and different sources of raw material for tools, and new plants and animals to rely on for food. All animals adapt to such changes through natural selection, but natural selection typically takes a relatively long time and requires physical changes in the adapting organisms. *Homo erectus* was able to adapt to new environments very quickly and without apparent physical changes. This suggests that the primary mechanisms of adaptation for *Homo erectus* were cultural rather than biological.

What cultural adaptations might *Homo erectus* have made? Fire might have been the crucial cultural adaptation to colder climates. As we discuss later, there is tantalizing evidence that *Homo erectus* used fire. But fire can only warm people when they are stationary; it doesn't help when people are out collecting food. To be mobile in colder climates, *Homo erectus* may have begun to wear animal furs for warmth. Some *Homo erectus* tools look like the hide-processing tools used by more recent human groups,[59] and it seems unlikely that *Homo erectus* could have survived in the colder locations where they have been found, in eastern Europe and Asia, without some form of clothing. And if *Homo erectus* was wearing furs for warmth, they must have been hunting. *Homo erectus* could not have depended on scavenging to acquire skins—the skin is the first thing predators destroy when they dismember a carcass. *Homo erectus* needing skins would have had to kill fur-bearing animals themselves if they wanted intact skins and furs for clothing.

As we mentioned earlier, fossil remains themselves cannot provide evidence for whether or not *H. erectus* was hairless. But scientists have found that the genes of modern peoples may offer clues to when our ancestors became hairless. For example, one of the primary genes responsible for hair and skin color, called MC1R, demonstrates uniformity among modern dark-skinned African populations, but diversity among non-Africans. Alan Rogers and colleagues have recently argued that the uniformity in this gene among Africans demonstrates recent, powerful selective pressure in favor of darker skin, and that protection against the tropical sun after the loss of body hair is the likely reason. When did this selective pressure start? Rogers and colleagues estimate it was at least 1.2 million years ago.[60]

It is interesting to consider that, in eastern Africa, *Homo erectus* coexisted with at least one other species of hominid (*A. boisei*), and possibly with as many as three others (*A. boisei, A. africanus,* and *H. habilis/rudolfensis*). Why did *Homo erectus* survive and flourish while these other species went extinct? Again, culture may be the answer. *A. boisei* seems to have been a specialized grasslands species. Their large molars and powerful dental architecture would have allowed them to eat hard grass seeds and other coarse materials that other hominids could not chew. However, they had to compete with the many other grassland animals that also relied on these plants, but reproduced faster and had speed to help them escape from predators. Early *Homo* was apparently a tool user and relied at least in part on scavenging and hunting, but compared to *Homo erectus*, early *Homo* technology was crude and early *Homo* populations may not have been as well organized to scavenge, hunt, and to defend themselves against predators. These differences in culture may have provided advantages to *Homo erectus* that drove early *Homo* to extinction.

This scenario, just like the one we suggested for the evolution of early *Homo*, is a "just-so" story that may or may not be true. But it does fit the facts we now have about *Homo erectus* and the area in which it evolved. Regardless of this story's particular details, there seems no doubt that the development of a more complex culture was vital to the evolution of *Homo erectus*.

LOWER PALEOLITHIC CULTURES

The stone tool traditions of *Homo erectus* are traditionally called **Lower Paleolithic**. These stone tool traditions involve "core" tool techniques, in which a core of stone, rather than a flake, is used as the basic raw material for finished tools (we will talk more about Lower Paleolithic stone tool technology shortly). Because stone tools are the most common cultural material in the archaeological record of these ancient peoples, the entire culture of *Homo erectus* is often termed *Lower Paleolithic,* a practice we follow here.

The archaeological finds of tools and other cultural artifacts dating from 1.5 million years to about 200,000 years ago are assumed to have been produced by *Homo erectus*. But hominid fossils are not usually associated with these materials. Therefore some of the tools during this period were possibly produced by hominids other than *H. erectus*, such as australopithecines earlier and *H. sapiens* later. But the so-called *Acheulian* tool assemblages dating from 1.5 million years ago to more than a million years later are very similar to each other, and *H. erectus* is the only hominid that spans the entire period. Thus, it is conventionally assumed that *H. erectus* was responsible for most if not all of the Acheulian tool assemblages we describe.[61]

The Acheulian Tool Tradition

The stone toolmaking tradition known as the **Acheulian** was named after the site at St. Acheul, France, where the first examples were found. But the oldest Acheulian tools recovered are from East Africa, on the Peninj River, Tanzania, dating back about 1.5 million years.[62] In contrast to Oldowan, Acheulian assemblages have more large tools created according to standardized designs or shapes. Oldowan tools have sharp edges made by a few blows. Acheulian toolmakers shaped the stone by knocking more flakes off most of the edges. Many of these tools were made from very large flakes that had first been struck from very large cores or boulders.

One of the most characteristic and common tools in the Acheulian tool kit is the so-called **hand axe**, which is a teardrop-shaped, bifacially flaked tool with a thinned sharp tip. Other large tools resemble cleavers and picks. There were also many kinds of flake tools, such as scrapers with a wide edge.

Early Acheulian tools appeared to have been made by blows with a hard stone, but later tools are wider and flatter and may have been made with a **soft hammer** of bone or antler.[63] This soft hammer technique of making stone tools was an important innovation. Tools made by a **hard hammer** technique, rock against rock, have limits in terms of their sharpness and form, because only large and thick flakes can be made with a hard hammer technique (unless the flintknapper is very skillful and the stone being used has unique qualities). Flakes created by soft hammer flaking are much thinner and longer than hard hammer flakes, and the flintknapper generally has better control over their size and shape. This means that thinner and sharper tools can be made, as well as tools with complex shapes. Hand axes can be made with either technique, as their shape is simple, but those made using a soft hammer have much thinner and sharper edges.[64]

Were hand axes made for chopping trees, as their name suggests? We cannot be sure what they were used for, but experiments with them suggest that they are not good for cutting trees; they seem more suited for butchering large animals.[65] Lawrence Keeley microscopically examined some Acheulian hand axes, and the wear on them is more consistent with animal butchery. They may also have been used for woodworking, particularly hollowing and shaping wood, and they are also good for digging.[66] William Calvin has even suggested that a hand axe could be used as a projectile thrown like a discus into a herd of animals in the hope of injuring or killing an animal.[67]

Acheulian tools are found widely in Africa, Europe, and western Asia, but bifacial hand axes, cleavers, and picks are not found as commonly in eastern and southeastern Asia.[68] Because *H. erectus* has been found in all areas of the Old World, it is puzzling that the tool traditions seem to differ from west to east. Some archaeologists have suggested that large bifacial tools may be lacking in eastern and southeastern Asia because *H. erectus* in Asia had a better material to make tools out of—bamboo. Bamboo has been used recently in Southeast Asia for many purposes, including incredibly sharp

Homo erectus ate—and probably hunted—large game animals, and they probably also learned to control fire.

arrows and sticks for digging and cutting. Geoffrey Pope has shown that bamboo is found precisely in those areas of Asia where hand axes and other large bifacial tools are largely missing.[69]

Big Game Eating

Some of the Acheulian sites have produced evidence of big game eating. F. Clark Howell, who excavated sites at Torralba and Ambrona, Spain, found a substantial number of elephant remains and unmistakable evidence of human presence in the form of tools. Howell suggests that the humans at those sites used fire to frighten elephants into muddy bogs from which they would be unable to escape.[70] To hunt elephants in this way, the humans would have had to plan and work cooperatively in fairly large groups.

But do these finds of bones of large- and medium-sized animals, in association with tools, tell us that the humans definitely were big game hunters? Some archaeologists who have reanalyzed the evidence from Torralba think that the big game may have been scavenged. Because the Torralba and Ambrona sites are near ancient streams, many of the elephants could have died naturally, their bones accumulating in certain spots because of the flow of water.[71] What seems fairly clear is that the humans did deliberately butcher different kinds of game—different types of tools are found with different types of animals.[72] Thus, whether the humans hunted big game at Torralba and Ambrona is debatable; all we can be sure of, as of now, is that they consumed big game and probably hunted smaller game.

Control of Fire

One way in which *H. erectus* is thought to have hunted is by using *fire drives*—a technique still used by hunting and gathering peoples in recent times. It is highly effective: Animals are driven out of their hiding places and homes by fire and dispatched by hunters positioned downwind of the oncoming flames. Most peoples who use this technique today set fires deliberately, but fires caused by lightning strikes may have also been utilized. Did *H. erectus* set these fires? Because *H. erectus* was the first hominid to be found throughout the Old World and in areas with

freezing winters, most anthropologists presume that *H. erectus* had learned to control fire, at least for warmth. There is archaeological evidence of fire in some early sites, but fires can be natural events. Thus, whether fire was under deliberate control by *H. erectus* is not definitely established.[73]

Suggestive but not conclusive evidence of the deliberate use of fire comes from Kenya in East Africa and is over 1.4 million years old.[74] More persuasive evidence of human control of fire, dating from nearly 800,000 years ago, comes from the site of Gesher Benot Ya'aqov in Israel. Here, researchers found evidence of burned seeds, wood, and stone, as well as concentrations of burned items suggestive of hearths.[75] Evidence of the deliberate use of fire comes from Europe somewhat later. Unfortunately, the evidence of control of fire at Gesher Benot Ya'aqov and European sites is not associated with *H. erectus* fossils, so the link between deliberate use of fire and *H. erectus* cannot definitely be established yet.[76] The lack of clear evidence does not, of course, mean that *H. erectus* did not use fire. After all, *H. erectus* did move into cold areas of the world, and it is hard to imagine how that could have happened without the deliberate use of fire. Such a move is also hard to imagine if *H. erectus* were relatively hairless and did not get warm skins and furs from hunting.

Clothing, therefore, may have been necessary, but fire might have been even more important, and not only for warmth. Cooking would be possible. The control of fire was a major step in increasing the energy under human control. Cooking would have made all kinds of food (not just meat) more safely digestible and therefore more usable.[77] Fires would also have kept predators away, a not inconsiderable advantage given that there were many.

Campsites

Acheulian sites were usually located close to water sources, lush vegetation, and large stocks of herbivorous animals. Some camps have been found in caves, but most were in open areas surrounded by rudimentary fortifications or windbreaks. Several African sites are marked by stony rubble brought there by *H. erectus,* possibly for the dual purpose of securing the windbreaks and providing ammunition in case of a sudden attack.[78]

The presumed base campsites display a wide variety of tools, indicating that the camp was the center of many group functions. More specialized sites away from camp have also been found. These are marked by the predominance of a particular type of tool. For example, a butchering site in Tanzania contained dismembered hippopotamus carcasses and rare heavy-duty smashing and cutting tools. Workshops are another kind of specialized site encountered with some regularity. They are characterized by tool debris and are located close to a source of natural stone suitable for toolmaking.[79]

A camp has been excavated at the Terra Amata site near Nice, on the French Riviera. The camp appears to have been occupied in the late spring or early summer, judging by the pollen found in fossilized human feces. The excavator describes stake holes driven into the sand, paralleled by lines of stones, presumably marking the spots where the people constructed huts of roughly 30 feet by 15 feet (see Figure 8). A basic feature of each hut was a central hearth that seems to have been protected from drafts by a small wall built just outside the northeast corner of the hearth. The evidence suggests that the Terra Amata occupants gathered seafood such as oysters and mussels, did some fishing, and hunted in the surrounding area. The animal remains suggest that they obtained both small and large animals but mostly got the young of larger animals such as stags, elephants, boars, rhinoceroses, and wild oxen. Some of the huts contain recognizable toolmakers' areas, scattered with tool debris; occasionally, the impression of an animal skin shows where the toolmaker actually sat.[80]

Religion and Ritual

Thus far, we have discussed the lifestyles of Lower Paleolithic, but we have not talked about the less material aspects of life, such as religion and ritual. What beliefs did *Homo erectus* hold about the world around them? Did they take part in rituals? Did *H. erectus* have religion? The data we have to answer these questions are limited, but there are some hints that ritual and religion may have been a part of Lower Paleolithic culture.

Remains of *red ochre* (oxidized clay) have been found on a number of Lower Paleolithic sites.[81] This may be significant because, in many later cultures, even modern ones, red ochre has been used in rituals of various types to represent blood or, more generally, life. Ochre seems to be particularly important in burial rituals, and human remains sprinkled with red ochre have been found in many parts of the world and dating as far back as the Middle Paleolithic (about 200,000 years ago). However, there is no evidence that *Homo erectus* buried their dead, nor any evidence that ochre was used in rituals. It may have been used for body decoration, or simply for protection against insects or sunburn.

More significant, and even more controversial, is the suggestion made by the excavators of Zhoukoudian (in northern China) that some of the *H. erectus* remains there showed evidence of ritual cannibalism.[82] The foramen magnum of some specimens had been deliberately enlarged and the facial bones had been deliberately broken away from the cranium on others. A possible reason may have been to remove the brain for ritual consumption. Ritual cannibalism has been widely reported among living peoples, so its presence among ancient peoples is not impossible. But scholars point out that the parts of the skull that seem to have been

Work space

Work space

Hearth

Work space

FIGURE 8 A Reconstruction of the Oval Huts Built at Terra Amata.
These huts were approximately 30 feet by 15 feet.

Source: Copyright © 1969 by Eric Mose.

purposely enlarged (to remove the brain) are those that are also the weakest points on the skull, and may have broken away because of decay or disturbance over the millennia.

At this point, we simply cannot say whether religion and ritual were parts of Lower Paleolithic culture.

SUMMARY ● ○ ○

1. The earliest identifiable stone tools found so far come from various sites in East Africa and date from about 2.5 million years ago. Flake tools predominate, but choppers are also common. Choppers are cores that have been partially flaked and have a side that might have been used for chopping. These early stone tools are referred to as Oldowan.

2. Archaeologists have experimented with what can be done with Oldowan tools. The flakes appear to be very versatile; they can be used for slitting the hides of animals, dismembering animals, and whittling wood. The choppers can be used to hack off branches or cut and chop tough animal joints. Hominids shortly after 2 million years ago were cutting up animal carcasses for meat, mostly obtained through scavenging rather than hunting.

3. There are archaeological sites dating as early as 2 million years ago that contain concentrations of stone tools and animal bones. Some scholars think these might have been early hominid home bases, others do not. If these sites were not home bases, what were they? Some archaeologists are beginning to think that these early sites with many animal bones and tools may just have been places where hominids processed food but did not live.

4. The presence of stone tools and perhaps home bases suggests that early hominids had culture. Culture is a dynamic, adaptive process of learned, shared, and integrated behaviors and ideas.

5. Important physical changes in early hominids that led to the evolution of our genus, *Homo,* include the expansion of the brain, the modification of the female pelvis to allow bigger-brained babies to be born, and the reduction of the face, teeth, and jaws. These physical changes are seen in the species *Homo habilis* and *Homo rudolfensis,* both of which date to around 2.3 million years ago. Early *Homo* appears to have used tools and scavenged or possibly hunted meat, so culture, or the evolution of cultural behavior, seems to have played a role in these physical changes as well.

6. *Homo erectus* emerged about 1.8 million to 1.6 million years ago. It had a larger brain capacity than *Homo habilis* and an essentially modern postcranial skeleton. What differentiates *Homo erectus* most from modern humans is the shape of the skull, which is long, low, and has prominent browridges.

7. *Homo erectus* was the first hominid species to be widely distributed in the Old World. Some of the locations where *Homo erectus* lived in eastern Europe and Asia were quite cold, and *Homo erectus* was able to adapt to these new and often colder environments through culture. Some scholars reserve *Homo erectus* for those populations living outside of Africa, and call the African populations *Homo ergaster.* Outside of Africa, there was at least one additional species of hominid, *Homo floresiensis.*

8. Lower Paleolithic tools and other cultural artifacts from about 1.6 million to about 200,000 years ago were probably produced by *H. erectus.* Acheulian is the name given to the most well-known tool tradition of this period. Acheulian tools include both small flake tools and large tools, but hand axes and other large bifacial tools are characteristic.

9. Although it is presumed that *H. erectus* had learned to use fire to survive in areas with cold winters, there is no definite evidence of the control of fire by *H. erectus.* There is evidence in some sites of big game eating, but whether *H. erectus* hunted those animals is debated. There is little evidence of ritual behavior among *H. erectus.*

GLOSSARY TERMS ○ ● ○

Acheulian	Lower Paleolithic
bifacial tool	occipital torus
hand axe	Oldowan
hard hammer	percussion
Homo	flaking
Homo erectus	prognathic
Homo ergaster	sagittal keel
Homo floresiensis	soft hammer
Homo habilis	taurodontism
Homo rudolfensis	unifacial tool

CRITICAL QUESTIONS ○ ○ ●

1. Why might early hominids have begun to make stone tools? How would stone tools have been more useful than wood or bone tools?

2. How do the physical changes that occur in early hominids correlate with the apparent changes in their behavior?

3. How did *Homo erectus* culture differ from the culture of earlier hominids?

4. When compared to earlier hominids, *Homo erectus* is larger, has a larger brain, and smaller teeth. How might these physical changes correlate with apparent behavioral changes in *Homo erectus*?

5. *Homo erectus* lived in many places in the Old World. What may have enabled them to spread so widely?

PEARSON myanthrolab

Read the chapter by Andrew Kramer titled "The Natural History and Evolutionary Fate of Homo erectus" on MyAnthroLab. Answer the following questions:

1. What is the primary question Kramer attempts to answer in his article? Why is this question important?

2. What methods does Kramer use to determine whether different populations of H. erectus were different species?

3. Describe the difference between "lumpers" and "splitters." How might this difference affect the way each group of scholars views human evolution?

NOTES ● ○ ○

1. Susman 1994.
2. Ibid.
3. Holden 1997.
4. Leakey 1960.
5. Clark 1970, 68; Schick and Toth 1993, 97–99.
6. Schick and Toth 1993, 153–70.
7. Ibid., 129.
8. Ibid., 157–59.
9. Isaac 1984.
10. Whittaker 1994, 283–85.
11. Schick and Toth 1993, 175–76.
12. Speth 2009.
13. Shipman 1986. For the idea that scavenging may have been an important food-getting strategy even for protohominids, see Szalay 1975.
14. Speth and Davis 1976; Blumenschine et al. 2003.
15. Isaac 1971.
16. M. Leakey 1971.
17. Potts 1988, 253–58.
18. Potts 1984.
19. Potts 1988, 278–81.
20. Wolf 1984.
21. Boyd and Silk 2000, 249–50.
22. Dobzhansky 1962, 196.
23. Bromage and Dean 1985; B. H. Smith 1986; Gibbons 2008.
24. Chapais 2008.
25. Gowlett 2008.
26. McHenry 2009; 2009; Tobias 1994.
27. McHenry 1982.
28. McHenry 1982.
29. Dunbar and Shultz 2007; Herrmann et al. 2007; Silk 2007.
30. Simpson et al. 2008.
31. Pilbeam and Gould 1974.
32. Leonard 2002.
33. Stedman et al. 2004.
34. McHenry 2009; Tobias 1994.
35. Simpson 2009.
36. Rightmire 2000.
37. Swisher et al. 1994.
38. Balter and Gibbons 2000; Gabunia et al. 2000.
39. Vekua et al. 2002; Gore 2002.
40. Wolpoff and Nkini 1988. See also Rightmire 2000; Balter 2001.
41. Rightmire 1990, 12–14.
42. Swisher et al. 1994.
43. Rightmire 2000.
44. Fleagle 1999, 534–35; Day 1986, 409–12; Kramer 2009.
45. Rightmire 2000; Tobias 1994.
46. Franciscus and Trinkaus 1988.
47. Feibel and Brown 1993.
48. Ruff and Walker 1993.
49. Wolpoff et al. 1993.
50. Morwood et al. 2004; Brown et al. 2004.
51. Falk et al. 2005
52. Diamond 2004.
53. Tocheri et al. 2007.
54. Jungers et al. 2009.
55. Wong 2005; Weston and Lister 2009.
56. Fleagle 1999, 306.
57. M. Ember and C. R. Ember 1979; cf. Lovejoy 1981.
58. Clayman 1989, 857–58.
59. Bordes 1968, 51–97.
60. Rogers et al. 2004.
61. Phillipson 1993, 57.
62. Schick and Toth 1993, 227, 233.
63. Ibid., 231–33; Whittaker 1994, 27.
64. Bordes 1968, 24–25; Whittaker 1994, 27.
65. Schick and Toth 1993, 258–60; Whittaker 1994, 27.
66. Lawrence Keeley's analysis reported in Schick and Toth 1993, 260; see that page for their analysis of tool use.
67. Calvin 1983.
68. Yamei et al. 2000.
69. Ciochon et al. 1990, 178–83; Pope 1989.
70. Howell 1966.
71. Klein 1987; Binford 1987.
72. L. G. Freeman 1994.
73. A good example of this problem is the ongoing debate about fire use at Zhoukoudian cave, as reported by Weiner et al. 1998.
74. Isaac 1984, 35–36. Other evidence for deliberate use of fire comes from the Swartkrans cave in South Africa and is dated 1 million to 1.5 million years ago; see Brain and Sillen 1988.
75. Goren-Inbar et al. 2004.
76. Binford and Ho 1985.
77. Leonard 2002.
78. Clark 1970, 94–95.
79. Ibid., 96–97.
80. de Lumley 1969.
81. Dickson 1990, 42–44.
82. Dickson 1990, 45; Tattersall and Schwartz 2000, 155.

The Emergence of *Homo sapiens*

From Chapter 10 of *Anthropology*, 13/e. Carol R. Ember. Melvin Ember. Peter N. Peregrine. Copyright © 2011 by Pearson Education. Published by Prentice Hall. All rights reserved.

The Emergence
of *Homo sapiens*

ecent finds in Africa indicate the presence of *Homo sapiens* perhaps 160,000 years ago (see Figure 1). Completely modern-looking humans, ***Homo sapiens sapiens,*** appeared by 50,000 years ago. One paleoanthropologist, Christopher Stringer, characterizes the modern human, *Homo sapiens sapiens,* as having "a domed skull, a chin, small eyebrows, browridges, and a rather puny skeleton."[1] Some of us might not like to be called puny, but except for our larger brain, most modern humans definitely are puny compared with *Homo erectus* and even with earlier forms of our own species, *H. sapiens.* We are relatively puny in several respects, including our thinner and lighter bones, as well as our smaller teeth and jaws.

In this chapter, we discuss the fossil evidence, as well as the controversies, about the transition from *H. erectus* to modern humans, which may have begun 500,000 years ago. We also discuss what we know archaeologically about the Middle Paleolithic cultures between about 300,000 and 40,000 years ago. ● ○ ●

THE TRANSITION FROM *HOMO ERECTUS* TO *HOMO SAPIENS*

Most paleoanthropologists agree that *H. erectus* evolved into *H. sapiens,* but they disagree about how and where the transition occurred. There is also disagreement about how to classify some fossils from about 500,000 years to 200,000 years ago that have a mix of *H. erectus* and *H. sapiens* traits.[2] A particular fossil might be called *H. erectus* by some anthropologists and "archaic" *Homo sapiens* by others. And, as we shall see, still other anthropologists see so much continuity between *H. erectus* and *H. sapiens* that they think it is completely arbitrary to call them different species. According to these anthropologists, *H. erectus* and *H. sapiens* may just be earlier and later varieties of the same species and therefore all should be called *H. sapiens.* (*H. erectus* would then be *H. sapiens erectus.*)

Homo heidelbergensis 海德堡人.

In recent years, some scholars have suggested that the "transitional" fossils share common traits and may actually represent a separate species—***Homo heidelbergensis,*** named after a jaw found in 1907, in the village of Mauer near Heidelberg, Germany.[3] Other specimens that have been suggested as members of this species have been found in many parts of the world: Bodo, Hopefield, Ndutu, Elandsfontein, and Rabat in Africa; Bilzingsleben, Petralona, Arago, Steinheim, and Swanscombe in Europe; and Dali and Solo in Asia. More recently discovered "transitional" specimens from the Atapuerca region of Spain have been classified as a different species, ***Homo antecessor,*** but many scholars believe these specimens should be classified as *H. heidelbergensis.*[4] To simplify things, we will call all these "transitional" specimens *H. heidelbergensis.*

Homo heidelbergensis differs from *Homo erectus* in having smaller teeth and jaws, a much larger brain (on the order of 1,300 cc), a skull that lacks a sagittal keel and occipital torus, a browridge that divides into separate arches above each eye, and a more robust skeleton (see Figure 2). *Homo heidelbergensis* differs from *Homo sapiens* in retaining a large and prognathic face with relatively large teeth and jaws, a browridge, a long, low cranial vault with a sloping forehead, and in its more robust skeleton.[5]

Skull of *Homo neandertalensis*.

Many scholars question whether *Homo heidelbergensis* represents one or several species of Middle Pleistocene hominid, or whether it is indeed a separate species at all. Many would argue that *Homo heidelbergensis* should be considered an archaic *Homo sapiens*. As noted, some scholars also argue that *Homo erectus* should be included in the *Homo sapiens* species.

Neandertals: *Homo sapiens* or *Homo neandertalensis?*

There may be disagreement about how to classify the mixed-trait fossils from 500,000 to 200,000 years ago, but recently an outright battle has emerged about many of the fossils that are less than 200,000 years old. Some anthropologists argue that they were definitely *Homo sapiens* and classify them as *Homo sapiens neandertalensis*. Other anthropologists argue

that they were part of a distinct species, ***Homo neandertalensis,*** more commonly referred to as the **Neandertals.** The Neandertals have been a confusing hominid fossil group since the first specimen was found in 1856. Somehow through the years, the Neandertals have become the victims of their cartoon image, which usually misrepresents them as burly and more ape than human. Actually, they might go unnoticed in a cross-section of the world's population today. Were they part of our species? For a while, the answer seemed to be yes. But recent archaeological and genetic evidence has led most to question the relationship between Neandertals and modern humans, and today the tide seems to have turned against those who would group them together. Let's take a look at some of the history of research on the Neandertals.

In 1856, three years before Darwin's publication of *Origin of Species,* a skullcap and other fossilized bones were

97

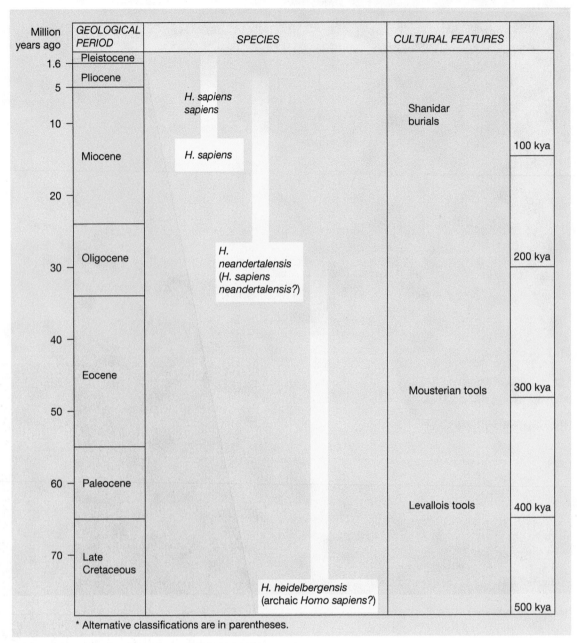

FIGURE 1 Timeline for the Emergence of Modern Humans*

discovered in a cave in the Neander Valley (*tal* is the German word for "valley"), near Düsseldorf, Germany. The fossils in the Neander Valley were the first that scholars could tentatively consider as an early hominid. (The fossils classified as *Homo erectus* were not found until later in the 19th century, and the fossils belonging to the genus *Australopithecus* were not found until the 20th century.) After Darwin's revolutionary work was published, the Neandertal find aroused considerable controversy. A few evolutionist scholars, such as Thomas Huxley, thought that the Neandertal was not that different from modern humans. Others dismissed the Neandertal as irrelevant to human evolution; they saw it as a pathological freak, a peculiar, disease-ridden individual.

However, similar fossils turned up later in Belgium, Yugoslavia, France, and elsewhere in Europe, which meant that the original Neandertal find could not be dismissed as an oddity.[6]

The predominant reaction to the original and subsequent Neandertal-like finds was that the Neandertals were too "brutish" and "primitive" to have been ancestral to modern humans. This view prevailed in the scholarly community until well into the 1950s. A major proponent of this view was Marcellin Boule, who between 1908 and 1913, claimed that the Neandertals would not have been capable of complete bipedalism. Boule, however, misinterpreted the bowed legs and bent spine in the Neandertal skeleton he examined—these were not normal in

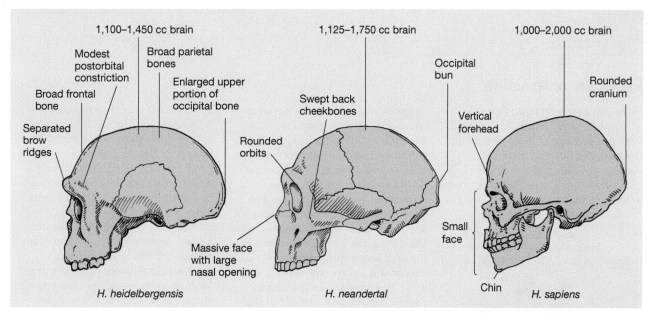

1,100–1,450 cc brain | 1,125–1,750 cc brain | 1,000–2,000 cc brain

Modest postorbital constriction
Broad parietal bones
Enlarged upper portion of occipital bone
Broad frontal bone
Separated brow ridges
Swept back cheekbones
Occipital bun
Rounded cranium
Rounded orbits
Vertical forehead
Massive face with large nasal opening
Small face
Chin

H. heidelbergensis — *H. neandertal* — *H. sapiens*

FIGURE 2 Comparison of the crania of *Homo heidelbergensis*, *Homo neandertalensis*, and *Homo sapiens*, showing important differences.

Neandertals, but were the result of disease in this particular individual. It is now universally agreed that the skeletal traits of the Neandertals are completely consistent with bipedalism.

Perhaps more important, when the much more ancient australopithecine and *H. erectus* fossils were accepted as hominids in the 1940s and 1950s, anthropologists realized that the Neandertals did not look that different from modern humans—despite their sloping foreheads, large browridges, flattened braincases, large jaws, and nearly absent chins (see Figure 2).[7] After all, they did have larger brains (averaging more than 1,450 cc) than modern humans (slightly more than 1,300 cc).[8] Some scholars believe that the large brain capacity of Neandertals suggests that they were capable of the full range of behaviors characteristic of modern humans. Their skeletons did, however, attest to one behavioral trait markedly different from behaviors of most modern humans: Neandertals apparently made very strenuous use of their bodies.[9]

It took almost 100 years for scholars to accept the idea that Neandertals were not that different from modern humans and perhaps should be classified as *Homo sapiens neandertalensis*. But in the last decade, there has been a growing debate over whether the Neandertals in western Europe were ancestral to modern-looking people who lived later in western Europe, after about 40,000 years ago. Neandertals lived in other places besides western Europe. A large number of fossils from central Europe strongly resemble those from western Europe, although some features, such as a projecting midface, are less pronounced.[10] Neandertals have also been found in southwestern Asia (Israel, Iraq) and Central Asia (Uzbekistan). One of the largest collections of Neandertal fossils comes from Shanidar cave in the mountains of northeastern Iraq, where Ralph Solecki unearthed the skeletons of nine individuals (see Figure 3).[11]

A comparison of a Neandertal and a modern human skeleton. Note how similar they are, yet the Neandertal appears more stocky and robust.

What has changed scholars' opinions of the Neandertals so that they are now most commonly seen as not belonging to the *Homo sapiens* group?

In 1997, a group of researchers from the United States and Germany published findings that forced a reconsideration of the Neandertals and their relationship to modern

applied anthropology

Facial Reconstruction

Have you ever wondered how we know what early humans looked like? We have pictures of them throughout this text, but how did the artists determine what to sculpt or draw? The answer lies in the field of forensic anthropology and more particularly in the field of facial reconstruction.

Photo by Ian Tattersall. Courtesy Dept. of Library Services, American Museum of Natural History.

Boule's reconstruction of a Neandertal, as displayed at Chicago's Field Museum in 1929, illustrates how subjective fossil reconstructions can be. It falsely implies that Neandertals could not stand upright or straighten their knees, and that they were more primitive than we know today that they actually were.

Facial reconstruction is based on knowledge of skull musculature and the thickness of soft tissue, determined over many years (the first such analysis was done in 1895) from cadavers and, more recently, magnetic resonance images of living people. From these measurements, forensic anthropologists have established a standard set of 21 to 34 locations on the skull where the average soft tissue thicknesses are known. The first step in facial reconstruction is to mark these locations on a cast of the skull to be reconstructed, using pegs that are the same length as the thickness of muscle and soft tissue at that location. Clay is then used to cover the skull cast to the depth of these pegs (the musculature of the face is first modeled in more sophisticated reconstructions, then clay is used to represent the soft tissues, up to the depth of the pegs).

The size and shape of the nose are reconstructed based on the size and shape of the nasal opening. The size and shape of lips and ears are more difficult to determine, and the skull itself can tell the forensic anthropologist almost nothing about hair or eye color, whether the person had facial hair, or how the person's hair was cut. Those aspects of facial reconstruction require some artistic intuition, and it is helpful to know something about the person, such as sex, age, and ethnicity.

But what about ancient humans? The standard measurements used to reconstruct faces from modern human skulls cannot be assumed to work for ancient skulls. For those, the forensic anthropologists have to go back to the basis of facial reconstruction—muscle and soft tissue. When reconstructing the faces of ancient humans, forensic anthropologists begin with a careful reconstruction of skull musculature, often aided by the comparative anatomy of modern great apes. Once the muscles are in place, glands, fatty tissue, and skin are added, and the face begins to take shape. The size and shape of the nose are determined much like that for modern humans, from the size and shape of the nasal opening. Lips, ears, eyes, and hair are, however, subject to almost pure guesswork—we really have no way of knowing how hairy our ancestors were, whether they had full lips like ours or thin lips like other great apes, or whether their ears were large or small.

Though based on study of the likely muscular anatomy in fossils and the comparative anatomy of modern humans and great apes, it is important to realize that the reconstruction of ancient faces is in part an artistic exercise. We can never know for sure what, for example, *Homo erectus* really looked like. We do not know how hairy they were or how they "styled" their hair. We do not know if their ears were like ours. We do not know the color of their eyes or skin. This is why reconstructions vary in the ways they depict ancient humans. We need to keep in mind when we look at reconstructions that they are educated, perhaps biased, guesses, and not necessarily true depictions of ancient people.

Sources: Prag and Neave 1997; Moser 1998.

humans. These scholars reported that they had been able to extract mitochondrial DNA (mtDNA) from the original Neandertal specimen found in 1856.[12] How similar is Neandertal mtDNA to modern human mtDNA? Not as similar as many scholars would have expected. Among individual modern humans, there are usually five to ten differences in the sequence of mtDNA examined by the U.S.

and German researchers. Between modern humans and the Neandertal specimen, there tend to be about 25 differences—more than three times that among modern humans (see Figure 4). This suggested to the researchers that the ancestors of modern humans and the Neandertal must have diverged about 600,000 years ago.[13] If the last common ancestor of ours and the Neandertal

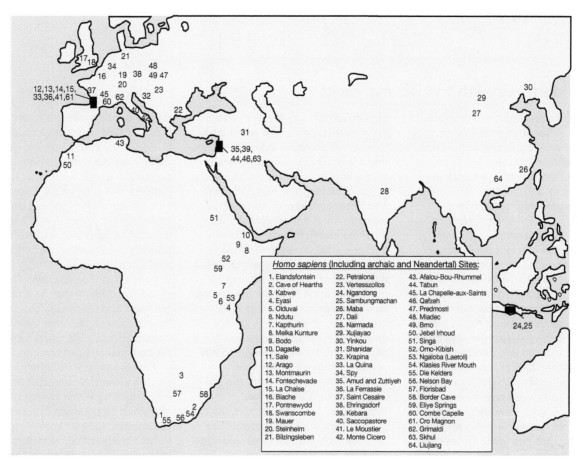

FIGURE 3 *Homo sapiens* **Sites**

Source: Ciochon and Fleagle 1993.
From Russell L. Ciochon and John G. Fleagle, eds., *The Human Evolution Source Book.* (Englewood Cliffs, NJ: Prentice Hall, 1993).

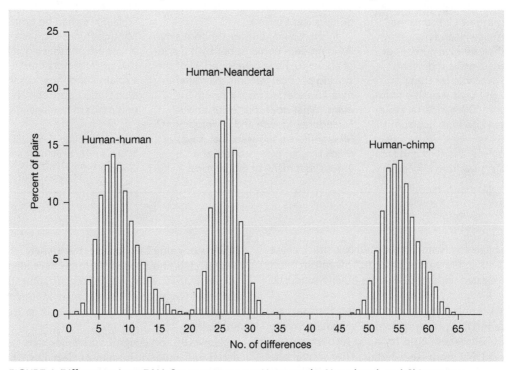

FIGURE 4 Differences in mtDNA Sequences among Humans, the Neandertal, and Chimpanzees
The *x*-axis shows the number of sequence differences; the *y*-axis shows the percent of individuals that share
that number of sequence differences.

Source: Krings 1997, 25.
This was published in Differences in mtDNA Sequences Among Humans, the Neandertal, and Chimpanzees, *Cell,*
90 (1997): 25. Elsevier Science.

current research and issues

Neandertal Growth and Development

One of the reasons many scholars think the Neandertals did not belong to the *Homo sapiens* species is that their material culture was less sophisticated than that of early modern humans who lived at the same time. Because much of contemporary human behavior is dependent on learning that takes place during our long period of infant dependency, could it be that Neandertals matured more rapidly than modern humans and thus had a shorter period of time in which to learn cultural behaviors?

Paleoanthropologist Nancy Minugh-Purvis decided to test this idea by examining growth and development of the skull and face in Neandertals. Minugh-Purvis's study of Neandertal growth and development was feasible largely because Neandertals may have buried their dead. Juvenile and infant skeletons are rare in the archaeological record and often do not preserve well. In juveniles and infants, many of the bones are still growing and thus are relatively delicate. They are also smaller than adult bones, and a wider variety of scavengers can consume them. But because Neandertals may have buried their dead, a number of well-preserved juvenile and infant skeletons are available for study. Indeed, Minugh-Purvis was able to locate more than 100 Neandertal skeletons, ranging in age from newborn to young adult.

To chart the way the skull and face of Neandertals grew from infancy to adulthood, Minugh-Purvis measured the available fossils on a set of standard anthropometric indices—indices that are widely used in physical anthropology to compare the size and shape of bones. She found that newborn Neandertals and modern humans do not differ very much, but that Neandertal infants tend to have thicker cranial bones than modern humans and perhaps heavier musculature. Many of the more striking features of adult Neandertals—a large face with a protruding nose, browridges, and a long skull—are not present in infants. These typical Neandertal characteristics begin to appear in children. For example, a 4-year-old Neandertal from the site of Engis, Belgium, already has browridges. A 7-year-old from the site of La Quinta in France not only has browridges but also a large, protruding nose and face and a long skull. Finally, a 10-year-old from the site of Teshik-Tash in Uzbekistan has all of the typical Neandertal features, and is basically identical to an adult Neandertal except in size.

In short, Neandertals are born similar to modern humans, but by the age of about 10, have developed all of the striking physical features that differentiate Neandertals from modern humans. What does this tell us about Neandertal growth and development? Minugh-Purvis suggests that it was much like our own. Indeed, she argues that many of the physical differences between the Neandertal face and skull and those of modern humans might not be due to genetic differences but rather to behavioral ones. Neandertal teeth show wear patterns that suggest they were used as tools, particularly to hold objects while working on them with the hands. The teeth and jaws were apparently placed under tremendous stress from these uses. Minugh-Purvis suggests that the prognathic face and heavy musculature may be a result of the teeth and jaws being used as tools from a young age, rather than from developmental differences between modern humans and Neandertals.

However, there are other differences between Neandertals and modern humans that cannot be explained by behavior. The overall picture that appears from Minugh-Purvis's study is that Neandertals did indeed mature slightly faster than modern humans. But was their maturation fast enough to account for the lack of cultural elaboration among the Neandertals? Did Neandertals grow so fast they had no time to learn? Minugh-Purvis suggests the differences are not that significant, and that other factors must be sought to explain the differences in cultural elaboration between Neandertals and modern humans.

Sources: Minugh-Purvis 2009; Trinkaus 1987b; Stringer and Gamble 1993.

---

lived that long ago, the Neandertal would be a much more distant relative than previously thought. This research has since been replicated with mtDNA from other Neandertal fossils.[14]

But mtDNA is only part of the story. After their success in sequencing mtDNA, anthropological geneticist Svante Pääbo and his colleagues began trying to recover and sequence nuclear DNA from Neandertals. After several setbacks, Pääbo and collaborators announced in 2009, that they had successfully sequenced the nuclear DNA from two female Neandertals.[15] Analysis of the Neandertal DNA is ongoing but, to date, researchers have found that Neandertals and modern humans have identical versions of the FOXP2 gene, suggesting to some that they may have had language abilities similar to modern humans.[16] Neandertals also had fair skin, and at least some had red hair.[17]

However, some significant differences between Neandertal and modern human nuclear DNA have also been identified. For example, Neandertals apparently lack the modern human version of *microcephalin*, a gene that is associated with brain development.[18] And initial analyses of the nuclear DNA suggest that the ancestral modern human and Neandertal populations split more than a half million years ago, with little or no admixture after that time.[19]

Archaeological findings from Europe and the Near East also seem to indicate that Neandertals and the modern human were different species. It has been known for decades that both modern human and Neandertal fossils are found in the same locations in parts of the Levant, but recent improvements in dating technology and newly discovered fossils have even more clearly demonstrated that the two kinds of hominid coexisted. In fact, several caves in the Mount Carmel region of Israel contain both modern human and Neandertal occupations. The fact that these two groups of hominids coinhabited the Near East for perhaps as much as 30,000 years and did not interbreed or share much in the way of tool technology strongly suggests that the two are different species.[20] And finds in Europe seem to corroborate that assessment. As early modern humans began moving into Europe, they appear to have displaced populations of Neandertals already living there. Sites with tools thought to be associated with Neandertals disappear throughout Europe as sites with tools thought to be associated with modern humans expand their range.[21] Significantly, the area of Europe last colonized by modern humans (Iberia) contains the very latest Neandertal fossils yet found, dating to some 30,000 years ago.[22]

With all this evidence pointing to Neandertals not being part of the modern human species, why is there an ongoing debate? In part, this is because none of the evidence is conclusive, and much of it can be interpreted in alternate ways. There is also evidence suggesting that Neandertals were not all that different physically from modern humans (see the box "Neandertal Growth and Development"). Perhaps more important, however, Neandertal culture, typically referred to as Middle Paleolithic after the predominant tool technology, has some features that make it seem similar to the culture of early modern humans.

MIDDLE PALEOLITHIC CULTURES

The period of cultural history associated with the Neandertals is traditionally called the **Middle Paleolithic** in Europe and the Near East and dates from about 300,000 years to about 40,000 years ago.[23] For Africa, the term *Middle Stone Age* is used instead of Middle Paleolithic. The tool assemblages from this period are generally referred to as Mousterian in Europe and the Near East and as *post-Acheulian* in Africa.

Tool Assemblages

The Mousterian   The Mousterian type of tool complex is named after the tool assemblage found in a rock shelter at Le Moustier in the Dordogne region of southwestern France. Compared with an Acheulian assemblage, a **Mousterian tool assemblage** has a smaller proportion of large core tools such as hand axes and cleavers and a bigger proportion of small flake tools such as scrapers.[24] Although many flakes struck off from a core were used "as is," the Mousterian is also characterized by flakes that were often altered or "retouched" by striking small flakes or chips from one or more edges (see Figure 5).[25] Studies of the wear on scrapers suggest that many were used for scraping hides or working wood. The fact that some of the tools, particularly points, were thinned or shaped on one side suggests that they were hafted or attached to a shaft or handle.[26]

Toward the end of the Acheulian period, a technique developed that enabled toolmakers to produce flake tools of a predetermined size instead of simply chipping flakes away from the core at random. In this **Levalloisian method,** toolmakers first shaped the core and prepared a "striking platform" at one end. Flakes of predetermined and standard sizes could then be knocked off. Although some Levallois flakes date as far back as 400,000 years ago, they are found more frequently in Mousterian tool kits.[27]

The tool assemblages in particular sites may be characterized as Mousterian, but one site may have more or fewer scrapers, points, and so forth, than another site. A number of archaeologists have suggested possible reasons for this variation. For example, Sally Binford and Lewis Binford suggested that different activities may have occurred in different sites. Some sites may have been used for butchering and other sites may have been base camps; hence, the kinds of tools found in different sites should vary.[28] And Paul Fish has suggested that some sites may have more tools produced by the Levalloisian technique because larger pieces of flint were available.[29]

The Post-Acheulian in Africa   Like Mousterian tools, many of the post-Acheulian tools in Africa during the Middle Stone Age were struck off prepared cores in the Levalloisian way. The assemblages consist mostly of various types of flake tools. A well-described sequence of such tools comes from the area around the mouth of the Klasies River on the southern coast of South Africa. This area contains rock shelters and small caves in which early and later *Homo sapiens* lived. The oldest cultural remains in one of the caves may date back 120,000 years.[30] These earliest tools include parallel-sided flake blades (probably used as knives), pointed flakes (possibly spearpoints), burins or gravers (chisel-like tools), and scrapers. Similar tools discovered at Border cave, South Africa, may have been used almost 200,000 years ago.[31]

Homesites

Most of the excavated Middle Paleolithic homesites in Europe and the Near East are located in caves and rock shelters. The same is true for the excavated Middle Stone Age homesites in sub-Saharan Africa. We might conclude, therefore, that Neandertals (as well as many early modern humans) lived mostly in caves or rock shelters. But that

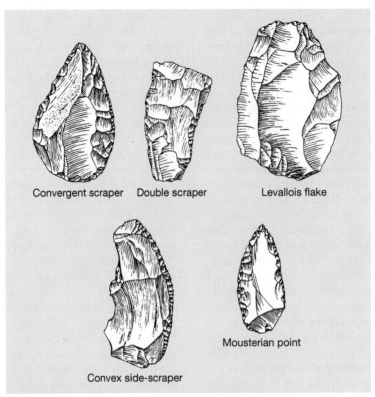

Convergent scraper   Double scraper   Levallois flake

Convex side-scraper

Mousterian point

FIGURE 5 Stone Tools of the Typical Mousterian Industry
Flakes were carefully retouched, usually on two sides. Mousterian tools, associated Neandertals, are part of what archaeologists call the Middle Paleolithic, about 200,000 to 35,000 years before the present.

conclusion could be incorrect. Caves and rock shelters may be overrepresented in the archaeological record because they are more likely to be found than are sites that originally were in the open but now are hidden by thousands of years, and many feet, of sediment. Sediment is the dust, debris, and decay that accumulate over time; when we dust the furniture and vacuum the floor, we are removing sediment.

Still, we know that many Neandertals lived at least part of the year in caves. This was true, for example, along the Dordogne River in France. The river gouged deep valleys in the limestone of that area. Below the cliffs are rock shelters with overhanging roofs and deep caves, many of which were occupied during the Middle Paleolithic. Even if the inhabitants did not stay all year, the sites do seem to have been occupied year after year.[32] Although there is evidence of some use of fire in earlier cultures, Middle Paleolithic humans seem to have relied more on fire. There are thick layers of ash in many rock shelters and caves and evidence that hearths were used to increase the efficiency of the fires.[33]

Quite a few Neandertal homesites were in the open. In Africa, open-air sites were located on floodplains, at the edges of lakes, and near springs.[34] Many open-air sites have been found in Europe, particularly eastern Europe. The occupants of the well-known site at Moldova in western Russia lived in river-valley houses framed with wood and covered with animal skins. Bones of mammoths, huge elephants now extinct, surround the remains of hearths and were apparently used to help hold the animal skins in place. Even though the winter climate near the edge of the glacier nearby was cold at that time, there still would have been animals to hunt because the plant food for the game was not buried under deep snow.

The hunters probably moved away in the summer to higher land between the river valleys. In all likelihood, the higher ground was grazing land for the large herds of animals the Moldova hunters depended on for meat. In the winter river valley sites, archaeologists have found skeletons of wolf, arctic fox, and hare with their paws missing. These animals probably were skinned for pelts that were made into clothing.[35]

Getting Food

How Neandertals and early modern humans got their food probably varied with their environment. In Africa, they lived in savanna and semiarid desert. In western and eastern Europe, they had to adapt to cold; during periods of increased glaciation, much of the environment was steppe grassland and tundra.

The European environment during this time was much richer in animal resources than the tundra of northern countries is today. Indeed, the European environment

Neandertals appear to have hunted a wide variety of game. In this reconstruction, two Neandertals are shown attacking a mastodon they have trapped in a pit.

Dallas and John Heaton/Stock Connection

inhabited by Neandertals abounded in game, both big and small. The tundra and alpine animals included reindeer, bison, wild oxen, horses, mammoths, rhinoceroses, and deer, as well as bears, wolves, and foxes.[36] Some European sites have also yielded bird and fish remains. For example, people in a summer camp in northern Germany apparently hunted swans and ducks and fished for perch and pike.[37] Little, however, is known about the particular plant foods the European Neandertals may have consumed; the remains of plants are unlikely to survive thousands of years in a nonarid environment.

In Africa, too, early *Homo sapiens* varied in how they got food. For example, we know that the people living at the mouth of the Klasies River in South Africa ate shellfish as well as meat from small grazers such as antelopes and large grazers such as eland and buffalo.[38] But archaeologists disagree about how the Klasies River people got their meat when they began to occupy the caves in the area.

Richard Klein thinks they hunted both large and small game. Klein speculates that, because the remains of eland of all ages have been found in Cave 1 at the Klasies River site, the people there probably hunted the eland by driving them into corrals or other traps, where animals of all ages could be killed. Klein thinks that buffalo were hunted differently. Buffalo tend to charge attackers, which would make it difficult to drive them into traps. Klein believes that, because bones from mostly very young and very old buffalo are found in the cave, the hunters were able to stalk and kill only the most vulnerable animals.[39]

Lewis Binford thinks the Klasies River people hunted only small grazers and scavenged the eland and buffalo meat from the kills of large carnivores. He argues that sites should contain all or almost all of the bones from animals that were hunted. According to Binford, because more or less complete skeletons are found only from small animals, the Klasies River people were not, at first, hunting all the animals they used for food.[40]

But evidence suggests that people were hunting big game as much as 400,000 years ago. Wooden spears that old were found in Germany in association with stone tools and the butchered remains of more than ten wild horses. The heavy spears resemble modern aerodynamic javelins, which suggests they would have been thrown at large animals such as horses, not at small animals. This new evidence strongly suggests that hunting, not just scavenging, may be older than archaeologists once thought.[41]

Funeral and Other Rituals?

Some Neandertals appear to have been deliberately buried. At Le Moustier, the skeleton of a boy 15 or 16 years old was found with a beautifully fashioned stone axe near his hand. At La Ferrassie, five children and two adults were apparently interred together in a family plot. These finds, along with several at Shanidar cave in Iraq, have aroused speculation about the possibility of funeral rituals.

The most important evidence at Shanidar consists of pollen around and on top of a man's body. Pollen analysis suggests that the flowers included ancestral forms of modern grape hyacinths, bachelor's buttons, hollyhocks, and yellow flowering groundsels. John Pfeiffer speculated about this find:

> A man with a badly crushed skull was buried deep in the cave with special ceremony. One spring day about 60,000 years ago members of his family went out into the hills, picked masses of wild flowers, and made a bed of them on the ground, a resting place for the deceased. Other flowers were probably laid on top of his grave; still others seem to have been woven together with the branches of a pinelike shrub to form a wreath.[42]

Can we be sure? Not really. All we really know is that there was pollen near and on top of the body. It could have gotten there because humans put flowers in the grave, or it could have gotten there for other, even accidental, reasons. Some scholars have argued that other Shanidar burials are actually the remains of people who were trapped under rockfalls within the cave and killed—they were not deliberately buried at all, but rather buried accidentally.[43]

An artist's reconstruction of the Neandertal burial at Shanidar cave.

Luigi Galante © Dorling Kindersley

Neandertals may have taken part in other rituals as well, but, like funeral rituals, the evidence is ambiguous. At Drachenloch cave in the Swiss Alps, for example, a stone-lined pit holding the stacked skulls of seven cave bears was found in association with a Neandertal habitation. Why preserve these skulls? One reason might be for rituals intended to placate or control bears. Cave bears were enormous—some nearly nine feet tall—and competed with Neandertals for prime cave living sites. Perhaps the Neandertals preserved the skulls of bears they killed in the cave as a way of honoring or appeasing either the bears or their spirits. But, as with funeral rituals, the evidence is not completely persuasive. In our own society, some may hang a deer or moose head on the wall without any associated ritual. At this point, we cannot say for certain whether or not Neandertals engaged in ritual behavior.[44]

THE EMERGENCE OF MODERN HUMANS

Cro-Magnon humans, who appear in western Europe about 35,000 years ago, were once thought to be the earliest specimens of modern humans, or *Homo sapiens sapiens.* (The Cro-Magnons are named after the rock shelter in France where they were first found, in 1868.[45]) But we now know that modern-looking humans appeared earlier outside of Europe. As of now, the oldest unambiguous

fossils classified as *H. sapiens* come from Ethiopia and date to perhaps 160,000 years ago.[46] Additional fossils, discovered in one of the Klasies River mouth caves in South Africa, are possibly as old as 100,000 years.[47] Other *Homo sapiens* fossils of about the same age have been found in Border cave in South Africa.[48] Remains of anatomically modern humans (*Homo sapiens sapiens*) found at two sites in Israel, at Skhul and Qafzeh, which used to be thought to date back 40,000 years to 50,000 years, may be 90,000 years old.[49] There are also anatomically modern human finds in Borneo, at Niah, from about 40,000 years ago and in Australia, at Lake Mungo, from about 30,000 years ago.[50]

These modern-looking humans differed from the Neandertals and other early *H. sapiens* in that they had higher, more bulging foreheads, thinner and lighter bones, smaller faces and jaws, chins (the bony protuberances that remain after projecting faces recede), and only slight browridges (or no ridges at all; see Figure 2).

Theories about the Origins of Modern Humans

Two theories about the origins of modern humans continue to be debated among anthropologists. One, which can be called the *single-origin theory,* suggests that modern humans emerged in just one part of the Old World and then spread to other parts, replacing Neandertals. (Africa

This *Homo sapiens* skull from Ethiopia is the oldest member of our species yet found, dating to 160,000 years ago.

© 2001 David L. Brill/Atlanta.

is generally thought to be the place of modern humans' origin.) The second theory, which has been called the multiregional theory, suggests that modern humans evolved in various parts of the Old World after *Homo erectus* spread out of Africa.[51]

Single-Origin Theory According to the single-origin theory, the Neandertals did not evolve into modern humans. Rather, Neandertals became extinct after 30,000 years ago because they were replaced by modern humans. The presumed place of origin of the first modern humans has varied over the years as new fossils have been discovered. In the 1950s, the source population was presumed to be Neandertals in the Near East, who were referred to as "generalized" or "progressive" Neandertals. Later, when earlier *Homo sapiens* were found in Africa, paleoanthropologists postulated that modern humans emerged first in Africa and then moved to the Near East and from there to Europe and Asia. Single-origin theorists think that the originally small population of *H. sapiens sapiens* had some biological or cultural advantage, or both, that allowed them to spread and replace Neandertals.

The main evidence for the single-origin theory comes from the genes of living peoples. In 1987, Rebecca Cann and her colleagues presented evidence that the mtDNA from people in the United States, New Guinea, Africa, and East Asia showed differences, suggesting that their common ancestor lived only 200,000 years ago. Cann and colleagues further claimed that, because the amount of variation among individuals was greatest in African populations, the common ancestor of all lived in Africa.[52] (It is generally the case that people living in a homeland exhibit more variation than any emigrant descendant population.) Thus was born what the media called the "mitochondrial Eve" and the "Eve hypothesis" for the origins of modern humans. Of course, there wasn't just one "Eve"; there must have

been more than one of her generation with similar mtDNA.

There were many problems with early mtDNA studies, but those problems have been addressed over the years and new and better mtDNA analyses have been performed. Most scholars now agree that the mtDNA of modern humans shows a remarkably small degree of variation (in fact, less than half the variation found in most chimpanzee populations), which strongly suggests that we all share a very recent, common ancestry.[53] More detailed analyses of mtDNA diversity in modern humans have allowed scholars to identify the ancestral roots of contemporary populations around the world, and these analyses also point to modern human origins in East Africa and a subsequent spread out of that region (see Figure 6).[54]

Evidence for an East African origin of modern humans and the subsequent expansion also comes from research on variation in the Y chromosome. The Y chromosome is the chromosome that determines whether a person is male. A female inherits an X chromosome from both her mother and father, whereas a male inherits an X chromosome from his mother and a Y chromosome from his father. Only men have a Y chromosome, and because there is only one copy in any given man, the Y chromosome is the only nuclear chromosome that, like mtDNA, does not undergo recombination. Although the Y chromosome can be affected by selection, it is thought that most variation in the Y chromosome, like variation in mtDNA, is caused by random mutations. Variation in the Y chromosome can therefore be analyzed in much the same way as variation in mtDNA.[55]

The results of research on variation in the Y chromosome mirror those on variation in mtDNA to a remarkable extent. Analysis of Y chromosome variation points to Africa as the source of modern humans, andsuggests an exodus from Africa of modern humans. One of the major

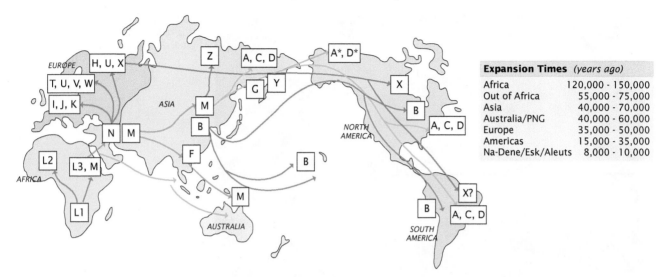

Expansion Times *(years ago)*

Africa	120,000 - 150,000
Out of Africa	55,000 - 75,000
Asia	40,000 - 70,000
Australia/PNG	40,000 - 60,000
Europe	35,000 - 50,000
Americas	15,000 - 35,000
Na-Dene/Esk/Aleuts	8,000 - 10,000

FIGURE 6 Mitochondrial Evidence for a Single Origin of Modern Humans
This map shows the current location and suspected origin of mitochondrial DNA haplogroups in modern human populations. A haplogroup reflects a population that shares a unique mutation in their mtDNA. Such mutations, their age as determined by the molecular clock, and their relationship to other haplogroups that suggest a shared ancestral homeland, provide strong evidence for an African origin of modern humans.

Source: http://www.familytreedna.com/images/migration_map_tut.gif
From FamilyTreeDNA.com.

differences between mtDNA studies and those employing the Y chromosome is in the dating of the most recent common ancestor. As noted previously, studies of mtDNA suggest the most recent common ancestor lived about 200,000 years ago, whereas studies of the Y chromosome suggest the most recent ancestor lived only about 100,000 years ago.[56] Additional research, including new research on variation in nuclear DNA, may help to resolve these differences. For now, however, it seems clear that the modern human gene pool has a single, and fairly recent, origin in Africa.[57] The color map titled "The Spread of Modern Humans" provides a summary of how most scholars believe humans spread around the world.

The mtDNA analyses of Neandertals, and the archaeological evidence suggesting that Neandertals and modern humans lived without apparent interaction in Europe and the Near East, also tend to support the single-origin theory. The *Homo sapiens* skeletal material from Ethiopia, Africa, in the 150,000–200,000-year-ago time range, further supports the single-origin theory.[58] However, such evidence does not necessarily contradict the validity of the multiregional theory of human origins.

Multiregional Theory According to the multiregional theory, *Homo erectus* populations in various parts of the Old World gradually evolved into anatomically modern-looking humans. The few scholars who continue to support this view believe that the "transitional" or "archaic" *H. sapiens* and the Neandertals represent phases in the gradual development of more "modern" anatomical features. Indeed, as we have noted, some of these scholars see so much continuity between *Homo erectus* and modern humans that they classify *Homo erectus* as *Homo sapiens erectus*.

Continuity is the main evidence multiregional theorists use to support their position. In several parts of the world, there seem to be clear continuities in distinct skeletal features between *Homo erectus* and *Homo sapiens*. For example, *Homo erectus* fossils from China tend to have broader faces with more horizontal cheekbones than specimens from elsewhere in the world, traits that also appear in modern Chinese populations.[59] Southeast Asia provides more compelling evidence, according to multiregional theorists. There, a number of traits—relatively thick cranial bones, a receding forehead, an unbroken browridge, facial prognathism, relatively large cheekbones, and relatively large molars—appear to persist from *Homo erectus* through modern populations (see Figure 7).[60] But others suggest that these traits cannot be used to establish a unique continuation from *Homo erectus* in Southeast Asia because these traits are found in modern humans all over the world. And still others argue that the traits are not as similar as the multiregional theorists claim.[61]

In support of their position, multiregional theorists argue that the mtDNA and Y chromosome evidence supports multiregional evolution rather than a single-origin theory of modern humans, that genetic variation in modern humans may reflect the emigration of *Homo erectus* out of Africa rather than the emigration of *Homo sapiens sapiens*. This interpretation would mean that the accepted rates of mutation in both mtDNA and the Y chromosome are wrong, that both actually mutate much more slowly than currently thought.[62] However, this interpretation is contradicted by established correlations between differences in mtDNA among human groups known to have colonized New Guinea and Australia at particular points in time, which seem to fit the accepted rate of mutation, and with the divergence between humans and apes, the date of

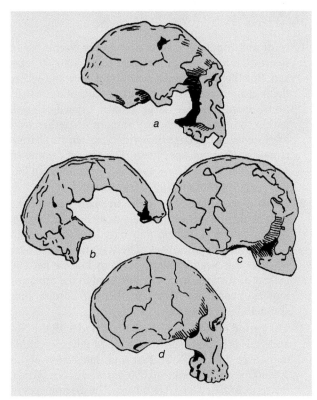

FIGURE 7 Fossil Evidence for Regional Continuity
Continuity in Southeast Asian and Australian populations:
Skulls of (a) *Homo erectus*, (b) early *Homo sapiens*, and
(d) modern *Homo sapiens*, all from Southeast Asia and
Australia, have similar foreheads, browridges, and occipital
and facial shapes, whereas skulls from Africa, represented here
by (c), an early *Homo sapiens*, have different forms. The similarity in Southeast Asian and Australian populations over more
than 500,000 years argues for regional continuity rather than
replacement.

been some replacement of one population by another,
some local continuous evolution, and some interbreeding between early modern humans who spread out of
Africa, and populations encountered in North Africa,
Europe, and Asia.[64] As biologist Alan Templeton has
noted, the debates over a single-origin versus multiregional evolution

> are based on the myth that replacement of one phys-
> ical feature in a fossil series with another feature can
> only be created by one population replacing another
> (by exterminating them, for example), but such fossil
> patterns could be a reflection of one genotype re-
> placing another through gene flow and natural selec-
> tion. Morphological replacement should not be
> equated with population replacement when one is
> dealing with populations that can interbreed.[65]

Interestingly, data on the genetic diversity of human
body lice seems to support an intermediate theory of
human origins. Humans are plagued by a single species of
hair lice, *Pediculus humanus*, which happens to have two
distinct genetic lineages. One is found worldwide, the
other only in the Americas. These two genetic lineages of
lice appear to have diverged over one million years ago. If
modern humans evolved less than 200,000 years ago (and
the worldwide louse lineage suggests it experienced some
dramatic changes about 100,000 years ago, which may relate to modern humans leaving Africa), then how did the
other lineage continue? One answer is that they were
transferred to modern humans from a previously isolated
population of *Homo erectus* in Asia.[66] But if that were the
case, then very close contact—either body to body or
sharing clothing—would had to have taken place between
modern and archaic humans.

which also seems to accord with the accepted faster rate of
mtDNA mutation.

To explain why human evolution would proceed gradually and in the same direction in various parts of the Old
World, multiregional theorists point to cultural improvements in cutting-tool and cooking technology that occurred all over the Old World. These cultural improvements
may have relaxed the prior natural selection for heavy bones
and musculature in the skull. The argument is that, unless
many plant and animal foods were cut into small pieces and
thoroughly cooked in hearths or pits that were efficient
thermally, they would be hard to chew and digest. Thus,
people would have needed robust jaws and thick skull
bones to support the large muscles that enabled them to cut
and chew their food. But robust bone and muscle would no
longer be needed after people began to cut and cook more
effectively.[63]

Intermediate Theories The single-origin and
multiregional theories are not the only possible interpretations of the available fossil record. There is also
the intermediate interpretation that there may have

WHAT HAPPENED TO THE NEANDERTALS?

Regardless of which theory (single-origin, multiregional,
or intermediate) is correct, it seems clear that Neandertals
and modern humans (*H. sapiens sapiens*) coexisted in
Europe and the Near East for at least 20,000 years, and
maybe as long as 60,000 years. What happened to the
Neandertals? Three answers have generally been considered. First, they interbred with modern humans and the
unique Neandertal characteristics slowly disappeared from
the interbreeding population. Second, they were killed off
by modern humans. Third, they were driven to extinction
due to competition with modern humans. Let's take a look
at each of these scenarios.

Interbreeding The interbreeding scenario seems the
most probable, yet evidence supporting it is weak. If modern humans and Neandertals interbred, we should be able
to find "hybrid" individuals in the fossil record. In fact, a

group of scholars has argued that an Upper Paleolithic skeleton from Portugal demonstrates a combination of modern human and Neandertal features.[67] The finding remains controversial, however, because it is a child's skeleton (approximately 4 years old) and its Neandertal-like features have not been corroborated by other scholars. More significantly, if the interbreeding hypothesis is correct, then the mtDNA analysis we have discussed several times in this chapter must be wrong. On the other hand, recent research on Neandertal tools suggests that some Neandertal groups adopted new techniques of tool manufacture that are thought to be uniquely associated with modern humans.[68] If Neandertals were learning from modern humans, then the idea that they could have interbred and perhaps been absorbed within the modern human population gains credibility.

Genocide The genocide scenario, that modern humans killed off Neandertals, has appeal as a sensational story, but little evidence. Not a single "murdered" Neandertal has ever been found, and one might wonder, in a fight between the powerful Neandertals and the more gracile modern humans, who might get the better of whom.

Extinction Finally, the extinction scenario, that Neandertals simply could not compete with modern humans, seems to have the best archaeological support. As we discussed earlier, there appear to be "refugee" populations of Neandertals in Iberia as recently as perhaps 30,000 years ago. The "retreat" of Neandertals from the Near East, eastern Europe, and finally western Europe following the movement of modern humans into the region seems to support the "refugee" interpretation.[69] More importantly, physical anthropologist Erik Trinkaus has argued, based on both physical characteristics of the Neandertal skeleton and their apparent patterns of behavior, that Neandertals were less efficient hunters and gatherers than modern humans.[70] And not only may Neandertals have been less efficient than modern humans in getting food, they may have needed more of it. Steve Churchill has suggested that Neandertals' stocky bodies and great muscle mass might have required 25 percent more calories than modern humans.[71] If this is true, a modern human group would have been able to live and reproduce more easily than a Neandertal group in the same territory, and this would likely drive the Neandertals away. When there were no new territories to run to, the Neandertals would go extinct—precisely what the archaeological record seems to suggest.[72]

But were modern humans and their cultures really that much more efficient than Middle Paleolithic cultures? The Upper Paleolithic does seem to mark a watershed in the evolution of human culture, allowing humans to expand their physical horizons throughout the world and their intellectual horizons into the realms of art and ritual.

SUMMARY ● ○ ○

1. Most anthropologists agree that *Homo erectus* began to evolve into *Homo sapiens* after about 500,000 years ago. But there is disagreement about how and where the transition occurred. The mixed traits of the transitional fossils include large cranial capacities (well within the range of modern humans), together with low foreheads and large browridges, which are characteristic of *H. erectus* specimens. The earliest definite *H. sapiens*, who did not look completely like modern humans, appeared about 160,000 years ago.

2. *Homo sapiens* have been found in many parts of the Old World—in Africa and Asia as well as in Europe. Some of these *H. sapiens* may have lived earlier than the Neandertals of Europe. There is still debate over whether the Neandertals in western Europe became extinct or survived and were ancestral to the modern-looking people who lived in western Europe after about 40,000 years ago.

3. The period of cultural history associated with the Neandertals is traditionally called the Middle Paleolithic in Europe and the Near East and dates from about 300,000 years to about 40,000 years ago. For Africa, the term *Middle Stone Age* is used. The assemblages of flake tools from this period are generally referred to as Mousterian in Europe and the Near East and as post-Acheulian in Africa. Compared with an Acheulian assemblage, a Mousterian tool assemblage has a smaller proportion of large hand axes and cleavers and a larger proportion of small flake tools such as scrapers. Some Mousterian sites show signs of intentional burial.

4. Fossil remains of fully modern-looking humans, *Homo sapiens sapiens*, have been found in Africa, the Near East, Asia, and Australia, as well as in Europe. The oldest of these fossils have been found in East Africa and may be 160,000 years old.

5. Two theories about the origins of modern humans continue to be debated among anthropologists. One, the *single-origin theory*, suggests that modern humans emerged in just one part of the Old World—the Near East and, more recently, Africa have been the postulated places of origin—and spread to other parts of the Old World, superseding Neandertals. The second theory, the *multiregional theory*, suggests that modern humans emerged in various parts of the Old World, becoming the varieties of humans we see today.

GLOSSARY TERMS ○ ● ○

Cro-Magnon	Levalloisian method
Homo antecessor	Middle Paleolithic
Homo heidelbergensis	Mousterian tool
Homo neandertalensis	assemblage
Homo sapiens sapiens	Neandertal

CRITICAL QUESTIONS ○ ○ ●

1. If the single-origin or "out-of-Africa" theory were correct, by what mechanisms could *Homo sapiens* have been able to replace *Homo erectus* and *Homo neandertalensis* populations?

2. If modern human traits emerged in *Homo erectus* populations in different areas more or less at the same time, what mechanisms would account for similar traits emerging in different regions?

3. How do Middle Paleolithic cultures differ from Lower Paleolithic cultures?

PEARSON
myanthrolab

Read the chapter by David Frayer titled "Testing Theories and Hypotheses about Modern Human Origins" on MyAnthroLab. Answer the following questions:

1. What does Frayer identify as the key elements of debate between the "Out of Africa" (or, as he calls it, "Noah's Ark") and "Multiregional" models of modern human origins?

2. What problems does Frayer identify with mitochondrial DNA evidence of modern human origins?

3. Frayer is in the minority among physical anthropologists today in supporting the multiregional model of human evolution. What reasons does he give for rejecting the more broadly accepted "Out of Africa" model?

NOTES ● ○ ○

1. Stringer 1985.
2. Ibid.
3. Rightmire 1997.
4. Carbonell et al. 2008.
5. Rightmire 1997; Fleagle 1999, 535–37.
6. Spencer 1984.
7. Trinkaus 1985.
8. Stringer 2000.
9. Trinkaus and Shipman 1993a; 1993b.
10. F. Smith 1984, 187.
11. Trinkaus 1984, 251–53.
12. Krings et al. 1997.
13. Ibid.
14. Ovchinnikov et al. 2000; Green et al. 2008.
15. Pennisi 2009.
16. Krause et al. 2007.
17. Lalueza-Fox et al. 2007.
18. Pennisi 2009.
19. Serre et al. 2004; Hodgson and Driscoll 2008.
20. Tattersall 1999, 115–16; Gibbons 2001.
21. Mellars 1996: 405–19.
22. Mellars 1998.
23. Strauss 1989.
24. Schick and Toth 1993, 288–92.
25. Klein 1989, 291–96.
26. Schick and Toth 1993, 288–92; Whittaker 1994, 30–31.
27. Klein 1989, 421–22.
28. Binford and Binford 1969.
29. Fish 1981, 377.
30. Butzer 1982, 42.
31. Phillipson 1993, 63.
32. For the controversy about whether the inhabitants of the Dordogne Valley lived in their homesites year-round, see Binford 1973.
33. Schick and Toth 1993, 292.
34. Klein 1977.
35. Klein 1974.
36. Bordes 1961.
37. T. Patterson 1981.
38. Phillipson 1993, 64.
39. Klein 1983, 38–39.
40. Binford 1984, 195–97. To explain the lack of complete skeletons of large animals, Klein (1983) suggests that the hunters may have butchered the large animals elsewhere because they could carry home only small cuts.
41. Wilford 1997.
42. Pfeiffer 1978, 155.
43. Trinkaus 1984.
44. Chase and Dibble 1987.
45. Stringer et al. 1984, 107.
46. Singer and Wymer 1982, 149.
47. Gibbons 2003.
48. Bräuer 1984, 387–89, 394; Rightmire 1984, 320.
49. Valladas et al. 1988.
50. Stringer et al. 1984, 121.
51. For arguments supporting the single-origin theory, see the chapters by Günter Bräuer, F. Clark Howell, and C. B. Stringer et al., in F. Smith and Spencer 1984. For arguments supporting the multiregional theory, see the chapters by C. L. Brace et al., David W. Frayer, Fred H. Smith, and Milford H. Wolpoff et al. in the same volume.
52. Cann et al. 1987.
53. Vigilant et al. 1991.
54. Stoneking 1997.
55. Hammer and Zegura 1996.
56. Hammer and Zegura 2002.
57. Cavalli-Sforza and Feldman 2003.
58. Stringer 2003.
59. Wolpoff 1999, 501–504, 727–31; Frayer et al. 1993.
60. Wolpoff 1999, 735–43; Frayer et al. 1993.
61. D. Lieberman 1995.
62. Templeton 1993.
63. Trinkaus 1986.
64. Eswaran 2002.
65. Templeton 1996. See also Ayala 1995; 1996.
66. Reed et al. 2004.
67. Duarte et al. 1999.
68. Bahn 1998.
69. Tattersall 1999, 198–203.
70. Trinkaus 1986; see also Trinkaus and Howells 1979.
71. Culotta 2005.
72. Klein 2003.

Origins of Food Production and Settled Life

From Chapter 12 of *Anthropology*, 13/e. Carol R. Ember. Melvin Ember. Peter N. Peregrine. Copyright © 2011 by Pearson Education.
Published by Prentice Hall. All rights reserved.

Origins of Food Production and Settled Life

oward the end of the period known as the Upper Paleolithic, people seem to have obtained most of their food from hunting migratory herds of large animals, such as wild cattle, antelope, bison, and mammoths. These hunter-gatherers were probably highly mobile to follow the migrations of the animals. Beginning about 14,000 years ago, people in some regions began to depend less on big game hunting and more on relatively stationary food resources, such as fish, shellfish, small game, and wild plants (see Figure 1). In some areas, particularly Europe and the Near East, the exploitation of local, relatively permanent resources may account for an increasingly settled way of life. The cultural period in which these developments took place is usually now called the **Epipaleolithic** in the Near East and the **Mesolithic** in Europe. Other areas of the world show a similar switch to what is called *broad-spectrum* food-collecting, but they do not always show an increasingly settled lifestyle, as, for example, in Mesoamerica where this period is called the **Archaic**.

We see the first clear evidence of a changeover to **food production**—the cultivation and domestication of plants and animals—in the Near East, about 8000 B.C.[1] This shift, called the *Neolithic revolution* by archaeologist V. Gordon Childe, occurred, probably independently, in other areas of the Old and New Worlds within the next few thousand years. In the Old World, there were independent centers of domestication in China, Southeast Asia (what is now Malaysia, Thailand, Cambodia, Vietnam, and New Guinea), and Africa around 6000 B.C.[2] In the New World, there were centers of cultivation and domestication in the highlands of Mesoamerica (about 7000 B.C.), the central Andes around Peru (about 7000 B.C.), and the Eastern Woodlands of North America (about 2000 B.C., but perhaps earlier).[3] Most of the world's major food plants and animals were domesticated well before 2000 B.C. Also developed by that time were techniques of plowing, fertilizing, fallowing, and irrigation.[4] Figure 2 shows the regions of the world that domesticated today's main food crops, and the color map on "The Spread of Agriculture" gives more detail on how plants and animals spread from their regions of domestication.

In this chapter, we discuss what is believed about the origins of food production and settled life, called **sedentarism**—how and why people in different places may have come to cultivate and domesticate plants and animals and to live in permanent villages. **Agriculture** (which we use here to refer to all types of domestic plant cultivation) and a sedentary life did not necessarily develop together. In some regions of the world, people began to live in permanent villages before they cultivated and domesticated plants and animals, whereas people in other places planted crops

without settling down permanently. Much of our discussion focuses on the Near East and Mesoamerica, the areas we know best archaeologically for the developments leading to food production and settled life. As much as we can, however, we try to indicate how data from other areas appear to suggest patterns different from, or similar to, those in the Near East and Mesoamerica.

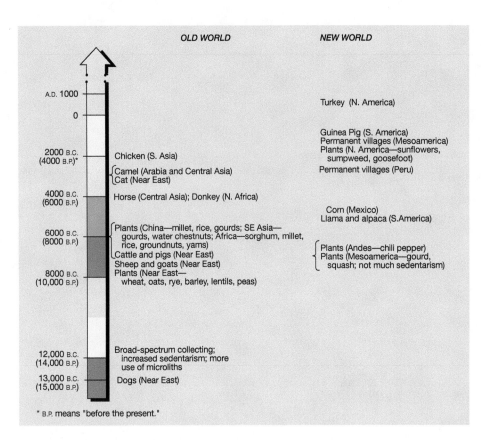

FIGURE 1 The Evolution of Domestication

Source: Dates for animal domestication are from Clutton-Brock 1992. Dates for animal domestication are from Juliet Clutton-Brock, "Domestication of Animals," in Stephen Jones, Robert Martin, and David Pilbeam, eds., The Cambridge Encyclopedia of Human Evolution (New York: Cambridge University Press, 1992), p. 384. Reprinted with the permission of Cambridge University Press.

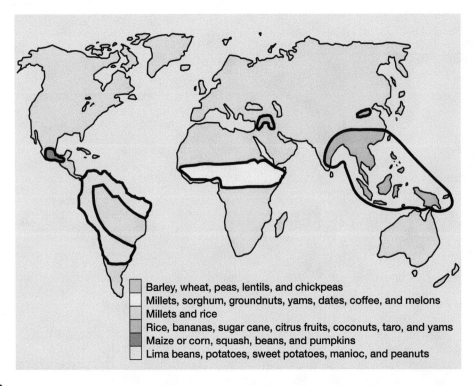

FIGURE 2 Original Locations of the World's Main Food Crops
The world's main food crops were originally domesticated in different regions.

Source: Hole 1992.
From Frank Hole, "Origins of Agriculture," in Stephen Jones, Robert Martin, and David Pilbeam, eds., The Cambridge Encyclopedia of Human Evolution (New York: Cambridge University Press, 1992), p. 376. Reprinted with the permission of Cambridge University Press.

PREAGRICULTURAL DEVELOPMENTS

Much of our discussion here focuses on the Near East and Mesoamerica, the areas we know best archaeologically for the developments leading to food production and settled life. As much as we can, however, we try to indicate how data from other areas appear to suggest patterns different from, or similar to, those in the Near East and Mesoamerica.

The Near East

In the Near East, there seems to have been a shift from mobile big game hunting to the utilization of a broad spectrum of natural resources at the end of the Upper Paleolithic, similar to those changes that happened in Europe.[5] There is evidence that people subsisted on a variety of resources, including fish, mollusks, and other water life; wild deer, sheep, and goats; and wild grains, nuts, and legumes.[6] The increased utilization of stationary food sources such as wild grain may partly explain why some people in the Near East began to lead more sedentary lives during the Epipaleolithic.

Even today, a traveler passing through the Anatolian highlands of Turkey and other mountainous regions in the Near East may see thick stands of wild wheat and barley growing as densely as if they had been cultivated.[7] Wielding flint sickles, Epipaleolithic people could easily have harvested a bountiful crop from such wild stands. Just how productive these resources can be was demonstrated in a field experiment duplicating prehistoric conditions. Using the kind of flint-blade sickle an Epipaleolithic worker would have used, researchers were able to harvest a little over two pounds of wild grain in an hour. A family of four, working only during the few weeks of the harvest season, probably could have reaped more wheat and barley than they needed for the entire year.[8]

The amount of wild wheat harvested in the experiment prompted Kent Flannery to conclude, "Such a harvest would almost necessitate some degree of sedentism—after all, where could they go with an estimated metric ton of clean wheat?"[9] Moreover, the stone equipment used for grinding would have been a clumsy burden to carry. Part of the harvest would probably have been set aside for immediate consumption, ground, and then cooked either by roasting or boiling. The rest of the harvest would have been stored to supply food for the remainder of the year. A grain diet, then, could have been the impetus for the construction of roasters, grinders, and storage pits by some preagricultural people, as well as for the construction of solid, fairly permanent housing. Once a village was built, people may have been reluctant to abandon it. We can visualize the earliest preagricultural settlements clustered around such naturally rich regions, as archaeological evidence indeed suggests they were.

The Natufians of the Near East Eleven thousand years ago, the Natufians, a people living in the area that is now Israel and Jordan, inhabited caves and rock shelters and built villages on the slopes of Mount Carmel in Israel. At the front of their rock shelters, they hollowed out basin-shaped depressions in the rock, possibly for storage pits. Examples of Natufian villages are also found at the Eynan site in Israel.

Eynan is a stratified site containing the remains of three villages in sequence, one atop another. Each village consisted of about 50 circular *pit houses*. The floor of each house was sunk a few feet into the ground, so that the walls of the house consisted partly of earth, below ground level, and partly of stone, above ground level. Pit houses had the advantage of retaining heat longer than houses built above the ground. The villages appear to have had stone-paved walks; circular stone pavements ringed with what seem to be permanent hearths; and the dead were interred in village cemeteries.

The tools suggest that the Natufians harvested wild grain intensively. Sickles recovered from their villages have a specific sheen, which experiments have shown to be the effect of flint striking grass stems, as the sickles would have been used in the cutting of grain. The Natufians are the earliest Epipaleolithic people known to have stored surplus crops. Beneath the floors of their stone-walled

Hayonim, one of the many caves in which the Natufians built relatively permanent settlements. Archaeologists are at work at the site.

houses, they constructed plastered storage pits. In addition to wild grains, the Natufians exploited a wide range of other resources.[10] The remains of many wild animals are found in Natufian sites; Natufians appear to have concentrated on hunting gazelle, which they would take by surrounding whole herds.[11]

The Natufians, as well as foragers in other areas at the time, show many differences as compared with foragers in earlier periods.[12] Not only was Natufian foraging based on a more intensive use of stationary resources such as wild grain, but the archaeological evidence suggests increasing social complexity. Natufian sites on the average were five times larger than those of their predecessors. Communities were occupied for most of the year, if not year-round. Burial patterns suggest more social differences between people. Although the available wild cereal resources appear to have enabled the Natufians to live in relatively permanent villages, their diet seems to have suffered. Their tooth enamel shows signs of nutritional deficiency, and their stature declined over time.[13]

Mesoamerica

A similar shift toward more broad-spectrum hunting and gathering occurred in the New World at the end of the Paleo-Indian period, about 10,000 years ago. Climate change seems to have been vital here too, as it was in the Old World. The retreat of glacial ice from North America and overall warmer and wetter climate brought dramatic changes to plant and animal communities throughout North America and Mesoamerica. Pleistocene megafauna, such as mammoths, mastodon, rhinoceros, giant ground sloth, and others, as well as a variety of smaller game animals, such as the horse, all went extinct in a relatively short period of time.[14] Hunting strategies shifted toward a broader range of game species, particularly deer, antelope, bison, and small mammals. At the same time, deciduous woodlands and grasslands expanded, providing a range of new plants to exploit. Ground stone woodworking tools such as axes and adzes first appeared, as did nut-processing tools such as mortars and pestles. Shellfish began to be exploited in some areas. Throughout North America and Mesoamerica, people began to expand the range of plants and animals they relied upon.[15]

The Archaic Peoples of Highland Mesoamerica In Highland Mesoamerica, the mountainous regions of central and southern Mexico, we also see a shift from big game hunting to a broader use of resources, in part due to a change in climate more like today's. Altitude became an important factor in the hunting and collecting regime, as different altitudes have different plant and animal resources. Valleys tend to have scrubby, grassland vegetation, whereas foothills and mountains have "thorn forests" of cactuses and succulents, giving way to oak and pine forests at higher altitudes, where there is more moisture. This vertical zonation means that a wide range of plants and animals were available in relatively close proximity—different environments were close by—and the Archaic peoples took advantage of these varied conditions to hunt and collect a broad range of resources.[16]

About 8,000 years ago, the Archaic peoples in Mesoamerica appear to have moved seasonally between communities of two different sizes: camps with 15 to 30 residents (*macrobands*) and camps with only 2 to 5 residents (*microbands*). Macroband camps were located near seasonally abundant resources, such as acorns or mesquite pods. Several families would have come together when these resources were in season, both to take advantage of them and to work together to harvest them while they were plentiful, perhaps to perform rituals, and simply to socialize. Microband camps were also inhabited seasonally, probably by a single family, when groups were not assembled into macroband camps. Remains of these microband camps are often found in caves or rock shelters from which a variety of environments could be exploited by moving either upslope or downslope from the campsite.[17]

Unlike the Natufians of the Near East, there is no evidence of social differences among the Archaic peoples of Highland Mesoamerica. The largest social unit, the macroband camp, was probably composed of related family groups, and leadership in these groups was probably informal. There is little evidence of ritual behavior beyond the presence of what may have been a ceremonial dance floor at Gheo-Shih, a macroband campsite in the Valley of Oaxaca. In short, lifestyles remained much like the simple and egalitarian ones of the Paleo-Indians, despite the transition to a much broader strategy of foraging.

Other Areas

People in other areas of the world also shifted from hunting big game to collecting many types of food before they began to practice agriculture. The still-sparse archaeological record suggests that such a change occurred in Southeast Asia, which may have been one of the important centers of original plant and animal domestication.[18] The faunal remains in inland sites there indicate that many different sources of food were being exploited from the same base camps. For example, at these base camps, we find the remains of animals from high mountain ridges as well as lowland river valleys, birds and primates from nearby forests, bats from caves, and fish from streams. The few coastal sites indicate that many kinds of fish and shellfish were collected and that animals such as deer, wild cattle, and rhinoceros were hunted.[19] The preagricultural developments in Southeast Asia probably were responses to changes in the climate and environment, including a warming trend, more moisture, and a higher sea level.[20]

In Africa, too, the preagricultural period was marked by a warmer, wetter environment. The now-numerous lakes, rivers, and other bodies of water provided fish, shellfish, and other resources that apparently allowed people to settle more permanently than they had before. For example, there were lakes in what is now the southern and central Sahara Desert, where people fished and hunted hippopotamuses and crocodiles. This pattern of broad-spectrum food-collecting seems also to have been characteristic of the areas both south and north of the Sahara.[21] One area showing increased sedentarism is the Dakhleh Oasis in the Western Desert of Egypt. Between 9,000 years and 8,500 years ago, the inhabitants lived in circular stone

These young Fulbe-Waila girls in Chad are collecting seeds much like preagricultural peoples did.

Frank Kroenke/Das Fotoarchiv/Peter Arnold, Inc.

huts on the shores of rivers and lakes. Bone harpoons and pottery are found there and in other areas from the Nile Valley through the central and southern Sahara westward to what is now Mali. Fishing seems to have allowed people to remain along the rivers and lakes for much of the year.[22]

Why Did Broad-Spectrum Collecting Develop?

It is apparent that the preagricultural switch to broad-spectrum collecting was fairly common throughout the world. Climate change was probably at least partly responsible for the exploitation of new sources of food. For example, the worldwide rise in sea level because of glacial melting may have increased the availability of fish and shellfish. Changes in climate may have also been partly responsible for the decline in the availability of big game, particularly the large herd animals. In addition, it has been suggested that another possible cause of that decline was human activity, specifically overkilling of some of these animals.[23] The evidence suggesting overkill is that the extinction in the New World of many of the large Pleistocene animals, such as the mammoth, coincided with the movement of humans from the Bering Strait region into the Americas.[24]

The overkill hypothesis has been questioned on the basis of bird as well as mammal extinctions in the New World. An enormous number of bird species also became extinct during the last few thousand years of the North American Pleistocene, and it is difficult to argue that human hunters caused all of those extinctions. Because the bird and mammal extinctions occurred simultaneously, it is likely that most or nearly all the extinctions were due to climatic and other environmental changes.[25] Then again, the example of the New Zealand moas, which went extinct soon after humans colonized the islands, may be instructive. Moas had low reproductive rates; computer simulations suggest their population would have been very sensitive to increases in adult mortality. Because many large animals have low reproductive rates like moas,

human overhunting may have been responsible for their extinction.[26]

The decreasing availability of big game may have stimulated people to exploit new food resources. But they may have turned to a broader spectrum of resources for another reason—population growth (see Figure 3). As Mark Cohen has noted, hunter-gatherers were "filling up" the world, and they may have had to seek new, possibly less desirable sources of food.[27] (We might think of shellfish as more desirable than mammoths, but only because we don't have to do the work to get such food. A lot of shellfish have to be collected, shelled, and cooked to produce the amount of animal protein obtainable from one large animal.)

Broad-spectrum collecting may have involved exploitation of new sources of food, but that does not necessarily mean that people were eating better. A decline in stature often indicates a poorer diet. During the preagricultural period, height apparently declined by as much as two inches in many parts of the Old World (Greece, Israel, India, and northern and western Europe).[28] This decline may have been a result of decreasing nutrition, but it could also be that natural selection for greater height was relaxed because leverage for throwing projectiles such as spears was not so favored after the decline of big game hunting. (Greater limb-bone length, and therefore greater height, would enable a hunter to throw a spear with more force and farther.[29]) In other areas of the world, such as Australia and what is now the midwestern United States, skeletal evidence also suggests a decline in the general level of health with the rise of broad-spectrum collecting.[30]

Broad-Spectrum Collecting and Sedentarism

Does the switch to broad-spectrum collecting explain the increasingly sedentary way of life we see in various parts of the world in preagricultural times? The answer seems to be both yes and no. In some areas of the world—some sites in Europe, the Near East, Africa, and Peru—settlements

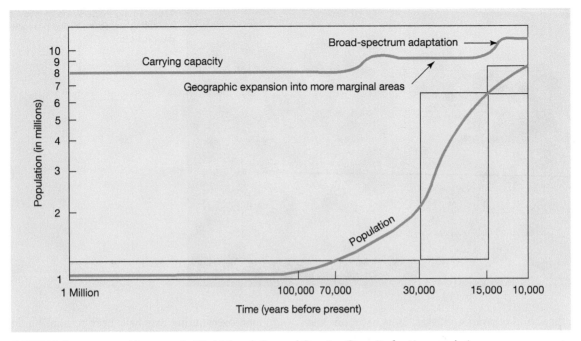

FIGURE 3 Reconstructed Increases in World Population and Carrying Capacity for Humans during the Pleistocene
Estimates of human population suggest that substantial increases preceded the movement of humans into more marginal areas. Further population increase preceded the emergence of broad-spectrum collecting.

Source: Hassan 1981.
Figure adapted from *Demographic Archaeology* by F. A. Hassan. (New York: Academic Press, 1981).

became more permanent. In other areas, such as the semi-arid highlands of Mesoamerica, the switch to broad-spectrum collecting was not associated with increasing sedentarism. Even after the Highland Mesoamericans began to cultivate plants, they still did not live in permanent villages.[31] Why?

It would seem that it is not simply the switch to broad-spectrum collecting that accounts for increasing sedentarism in many areas. Rather, a comparison of settlements on the Peruvian coast suggests that the more permanent settlements were located nearer, within three and a half miles, to most, if not all, of the diverse food resources exploited during the year. The community that did not have a year-round settlement seems to have depended on more widely distributed resources. What accounts for sedentarism may thus be the nearness[32] or the high reliability and yield[33] of the broad-spectrum resources, rather than the broad spectrum itself.

Sedentarism and Population Growth

Although some population growth undoubtedly occurred throughout the hunting and gathering phase of world history, some anthropologists have suggested that populations would have increased dramatically when people began to settle down. The evidence for this suggestion comes largely from a comparison of recent nomadic and sedentary !Kung populations.

The settling down of a nomadic group may reduce the typical spacing between births.[34] Nomadic !Kung have children spaced four years apart on the average; in contrast,

recently sedentarized !Kung have children about three years apart. Why might birth spacing change with settling down? There are several possibilities.

The spacing of children far apart can occur in a number of ways. One way, if effective contraceptives are not available, is prolonged sexual abstinence after the birth of a child—the postpartum sex taboo—which is common in recent human societies. Another way is abortion or infanticide.[35] Nomadic groups may be motivated to have children farther apart because of the problem of carrying small children. Carrying one small child is difficult enough; carrying two might be too burdensome. Thus, sedentary populations could have their children spaced more closely because carrying children would not always be necessary.

Although some nomadic groups may have deliberately spaced births by abstinence or infanticide, there is no evidence that such practices explain why four years separate births among nomadic !Kung. There may be another explanation, involving an unintended effect of how babies are fed. Nancy Howell and Richard Lee have suggested that the presence of baby foods other than mother's milk may be responsible for the decreased birth spacing in sedentary agricultural !Kung groups.[36] It is now well established that the longer a mother nurses her baby without supplementary foods, the longer it is likely to be before she starts ovulating again. Nomadic !Kung women have little to give their babies in the way of soft, digestible food, and the babies depend largely on mother's milk for two to three years. But sedentary !Kung mothers can give their babies soft foods such as cereal (made from cultivated grain) and milk from domesticated animals. Such changes in feeding

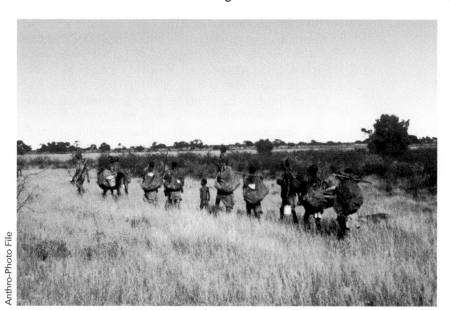

A !Kung group moving camp. When hunters and gatherers move, they have to carry their children and all their possessions with them. Spacing births an average of four years apart helps to ensure that a woman will not have to carry more than two children at a time.

Anthro-Photo File

practices may shorten birth spacing by shortening the interval between birth and the resumption of ovulation. In preagricultural sedentary communities, it is possible that baby foods made from wild grains might have had the same effect. For this reason alone, therefore, populations may have grown even before people started to farm or herd.

Another reason sedentary !Kung women may have more babies than nomadic !Kung women has to do with the ratio of body fat to body weight. Some investigators suspect that a critical minimum of fat in the body may be necessary for ovulation. A sedentary !Kung woman may have more fatty tissue than a nomadic !Kung woman, who walks many miles daily to gather wild plant foods, often carrying a child with her. Thus, sedentary !Kung women might resume ovulating sooner after the birth of a baby, and so for that reason alone may be likely to have more closely spaced children. If some critical amount of fat is necessary for ovulation, that would explain why many women who have little body fat in our own society—long-distance runners, gymnasts, and ballet dancers are examples—do not ovulate regularly.[37]

Microlithic Technology

Technologically, these preagricultural cultures did not differ radically from Upper Paleolithic cultures.[38] The trend toward smaller and lighter tools continued. Microliths, small blades half an inch to two inches long, which were made in late Upper Paleolithic times, were now used in quantity. In place of the one-piece flint implement, the preagricultural peoples in Europe, Asia, and Africa equipped themselves with *composite* tools—that is, tools made of more than one material.

Microliths, too small to be used one at a time, could be fitted into grooves in bone or wood to form arrows, harpoons, daggers, and sickles. A sickle, for example, was made by inserting several microliths into a groove in a wooden or bone handle. Resin held the blades in place. A broken mi-

Steve Gorton © Dorling Kindersley

A sickle made with microliths.

crolith could be replaced like a blade in a modern razor. Besides being adaptable for many uses, microliths could be made from many varieties of available stone. Because they did not need the large nodules to make large core and flake tools, people using microliths could work with smaller nodules to make the small blades.[39]

THE DOMESTICATION OF PLANTS AND ANIMALS

Neolithic means "of the new stone age"; the term originally signified the cultural stage in which humans invented pottery and ground-stone tools. We now know, however, that both were present in earlier times, so we cannot define a Neolithic state of culture purely on the basis of the presence of pottery and ground-stone tools. At present,

FIGURE 4 Seed Heads of Wild and Domesticated Wheat
Note the larger and more numerous seeds on domesticated wheat.

Source: Feder 2000.
From *Past in Perspective*, 2nd ed., by K. Feder. (Mountain View, CA: Mayfield, 2000).

archaeologists generally define the **Neolithic** in terms of the presence of domesticated plants and animals. In this type of culture, people began to produce food rather than merely collect it.

The line between food-collecting and food-producing occurs when people begin to plant crops and to keep and breed animals. How do we know when this transition occurred? In fact, archaeologically we do not see the beginning of food production; we can see signs of it only after plants and animals show differences from their wild varieties. When people plant crops, we refer to the process as cultivation. It is only when the crops cultivated and the animals raised are *modified*—different from wild varieties—that we speak of plant and animal **domestication.**

We know, in a particular site, that domestication occurred if plant remains have characteristics different from those of wild plants of the same types (see Figure 4). For example, wild grains of barley and wheat have a fragile **rachis**—the seed-bearing part of the stem—which shatters easily, releasing the seeds. Domesticated grains have a tough rachis, which does not shatter easily. In addition, the grain of wild barley and wheat has a tough shell protecting the seed from premature exposure, whereas domesticated grain has a brittle shell that can be easily separated, which facilitates preparing the seed for grinding into flour.

How did the domesticated plants get to be different from the wild varieties? Artificial or human selection, deliberate or accidental, obviously was required. Consider how the rachis of wheat and barley may have changed. As we said, when wild grain ripens in the field, the rachis shatters easily, scattering the seed. This trait is selectively advantageous under wild conditions; it is nature's method of propagating the species. Plants with a tough rachis, therefore, have only a slight chance of reproducing themselves under natural conditions, but they are more desirable for planting. When humans arrived with sickles and flails to collect the wild stands

of grain, the seeds harvested probably contained a high proportion of tough-rachis mutants, because these could best withstand the rough treatment of harvest processing. If planted, the harvested seeds would be likely to produce tough-rachis plants. If, in each successive harvest, seeds from tough-rachis plants were the least likely to be lost, tough-rachis plants would come to predominate.[40]

Domesticated species of animals also differ from the wild varieties. For example, the horns of wild goats in the Near East are shaped differently from those of domesticated goats.[41] But differences in physical characteristics may not be the only indicators of domestication. Some archaeologists believe that imbalances in the sex and age ratios of animal remains at particular sites also suggest that domestication had occurred. For example, at Zawi Chemi Shanidar in Iraq, the proportion of young to mature sheep remains was much higher than the ratio of young to mature sheep in wild herds. One possible inference to be drawn is that the animals were domesticated, the adult sheep being saved for breeding purposes whereas the young were eaten. (If mostly young animals were eaten, and only a few animals were allowed to grow old, most of the bones found in a site would be from the young animals that were killed regularly for food.[42])

Domestication in the Near East

For some time, most archaeologists have thought that the Fertile Crescent (see Figure 5), the arc of land stretching up from Israel and the Jordan Valley through southern Turkey and then downward to the western slopes of the Zagros Mountains in Iran, was one of the earliest centers of plant and animal domestication. We know that several varieties of domesticated wheat were being grown there after about 8000 B.C., as were oats, rye, barley, lentils, peas, and various fruits and nuts (apricots, pears, pomegranates, dates, figs, olives, almonds, and pistachios).[43] It appears that animals were first domesticated in the Near East. Dogs were first domesticated before the rise of agriculture, around 13,000 B.C. (see the box "Did Dogs (and Cats) Domesticate Themselves?"), goats and sheep around 7000 B.C., and cattle and pigs around 6000 B.C.[44]

Let us look at two early Neolithic sites in the Near East to see what life there may have been like after people began to depend on domesticated plants and animals for food.

Ali Kosh   At the stratified site of Ali Kosh in what is now southwestern Iran (see Figure 5), we see the remains of a community that started out about 7500 B.C., living mostly on wild plants and animals. Over the next 2,000 years, until about 5500 B.C., agriculture and herding became increasingly important. After 5500 B.C., we see the appearance of two innovations—irrigation and the use of domesticated cattle—that seem to have stimulated a minor population explosion during the following millennium.

From 7500 to 6750 B.C., the people at Ali Kosh cut little slabs of raw clay out of the ground to build small, multi-room structures. The rooms excavated by archaeologists are seldom more than 7 feet by 10 feet, and there is no evidence that the structures were definitely houses where

current research and issues

Did Dogs (and Cats) Domesticate Themselves?

Early evidence of a close relationship between dogs and people comes from an archaeological site in northern Israel dating to nearly 12,000 years ago. At that site, archaeologists found the grave of an elderly woman, lying on her right side with her legs folded up, with a dog under her left hand.

The Embers' dog was always happy to greet them when they came home. She also was a retriever, an alarm system, could follow a scent, and ate everything that dropped on the floor. Do any of these attributes explain why humans all over the world have had domesticated descendants of wolves around the house for the last 10,000 to 15,000 years?

Dogs were probably the first animals domesticated by humans, probably about 15,000 years ago, and several thousand years before plants, sheep, and goats were domesticated in the Near East. Humans were starting to settle down in semipermanent camps and villages, as they began to depend less on big game (which they would have had to follow over long distances) and more on relatively stationary food resources, such as fish, shellfish, small game, and wild plants rich in carbohydrates, proteins, and oils.

Why would humans have been interested in taming wolves at that time? One theory is that humans were shifting their prey from large animals to small, and they needed dogs for tracking wounded game or for retrieving killed game from bodies of water or underbrush. Dogs might also have been useful as alarm-givers in case predators came close. Finally, dogs might have helped to keep a camp clean by scavenging garbage.

The Embers think that this last use of dogs suggests an alternative theory of dog domestication. Perhaps it wasn't so much that humans domesticated dogs, but that some wolves domesticated themselves by hanging around human camps. Why would wolves be interested in those humans

who were first settling down? It couldn't have been the possibility of a human dinner, because that would have been a possibility for millions of years before. So perhaps something else lured wolves to those early settled camps and villages. What was different about those early settlements? For the first time in human history, people were staying put for considerable periods of time—months at a time, year after year—because they could count on being able to "harvest" and live on the wild resources of the area. If they lived in a place for years, even if only seasonally, they would eventually have a problem with garbage.

The residues of meals, in particular, would have been a problem. They might not only come to stink; they might also attract rodents and bigger threats to health and children. What could the people do about this problem? Well, as any camper nowadays realizes, they could have buried the garbage so that its scent would not attract unwelcome visitors. But eventually they would have run out of room for garbage pits in or close to the settlement. Of course, they could have moved the settlement. But maybe they didn't want to. After all, they had spent a lot of time and effort building a permanent house that was warm in the winter and dry in the rains. And they had a lot of things stored there. So what could they do?

Maybe people didn't have to do anything. Maybe those wolves hanging around the neighborhood solved the problem for our ancestors. How? By scavenging, which is something most dogs (particularly larger ones, like the first domesticated dogs) do quite naturally and efficiently. The Embers' dog ate anything (except maybe undressed lettuce). So even a few tame wolves or domesticated dogs could have kept a garbage pit or pile from stinking and growing. And the people "feeding" that pit or pile could stay put in one place for a

long time, safe from smells, vermin, and disease. Dogs may have mostly domesticated themselves because it was good for some of them as well as for those preagricultural humans.

A similar theory may explain the domestication of cats. Cats are especially good at catching and killing mice. Masses of mice skeletons (of the house mouse) begin to appear in basements of Near East dwellings after the emergence of agriculture. It is possible that humans purposely tried to domesticate cats to catch mice, but it is more likely that cats would have domesticated themselves by adapting to life near or in a granary or storage cellar. Of course, humans might have helped the process of domestication a little, by killing the more ferocious wild cats that were attracted to the settlement. The same was probably true for the wolves attracted to garbage. Even if you didn't at first want to "pet" the canids or felids that were hanging around, you wouldn't want them to attack humans. Wolves in the wild have a dominance-submission hierarchy, so they would be preadapted to heeding a "dominant" human; those that were not sufficiently submissive could be killed.

How could these theories of dog and cat domestication be tested? If dogs domesticated themselves as scavengers, archaeologists should find evidence of dog domestication (e.g., changes in anatomy) only in sites that were occupied for a good part of the year over a period of years. Only under those circumstances would garbage be a problem and dogs a solution. Similarly, evidence of cat domestication should be found only in sites that show signs of year-to-year grain storage. Only then would rodents be a problem and cats a solution. We hope archaeologists will make these tests in the future.

Sources: Budiansky 1992; Driscoll et al. 2007; 2009; Clutton-Brock 1984; Robinson 1984.

FIGURE 5 Early Agricultural Settlements in the Near East
Modern cities are represented by a dot, early settlements by a square. The yellow color indicates the area known as the Fertile Crescent.

people actually spent time or slept. Instead, they may have been storage rooms. On the other hand, house rooms of even smaller size are known in other areas of the world, so it is possible that the people at Ali Kosh in its earliest phase were actually living in those tiny, unbaked, "brick" houses. There is a bit of evidence that the people at Ali Kosh may have moved for the summer (with their goats) to the grassier mountain valleys nearby, which were just a few days' walk away.

We have a lot of evidence about what the people at Ali Kosh ate. They got some of their food from cultivated emmer wheat and a kind of barley and a considerable amount from domesticated goats. We know the goats were domesticated because wild goats do not seem to have lived in the area. Also, the fact that virtually no bones from elderly goats were found in the site suggests that the goats were domesticated and herded rather than hunted. Moreover, it would seem from the horn cores found in the site that mostly young male goats were eaten, so the females probably were kept for breeding and milking. But with all these signs of deliberate food production, there is an enormous amount of evidence—literally tens of thousands of seeds and bone fragments—that the people at the beginning of Ali Kosh depended mostly on wild plants (legumes and grasses) and wild animals (including gazelles, wild

oxen, and wild pigs). They also collected fish, such as carp and catfish, and shellfish, such as mussels, as well as waterfowl that visited the area during part of the year.

The flint tools used during this earliest phase at Ali Kosh were varied and abundant. Finds from this period include tens of thousands of tiny flint blades, some only a few millimeters wide. About 1 percent of the chipped stone that archaeologists found was **obsidian,** or volcanic glass, which came from what is now eastern Turkey, several hundred miles away. Thus, the people at Ali Kosh during its earliest phase definitely had some kind of contact with people elsewhere. This contact is also suggested by the fact that the emmer wheat they cultivated did not have a wild relative in the area.

From 6750 to 6000 B.C., the people increased their consumption of cultivated food plants; 40 percent of the seed remains in the hearths and refuse areas were now from emmer wheat and barley. The proportion of the diet coming from wild plants was much reduced, probably because the cultivated plants have the same growing season and grow in the same kind of soil as the wild plants. Grazing by the goats and sheep that were kept may also have contributed to the reduction of wild plant foods in the area and in the diet. The village may or may not have grown larger, but the multiroom houses definitely had. The rooms were now larger than 10 feet by 10 feet; the walls were much thicker; and a mud mortar now held the clay-slab bricks together. Also, the walls now often had a coat of smooth mud plaster on both sides. The stamped-mud house floors were apparently covered with rush or reed mats (you can see the imprints of them). There were courtyards with domed brick ovens and brick-lined roasting pits. Understandably, considering the summer heat in the area, none of the ovens found was inside a house.

Even though the village probably contained no more than 100 individuals, it participated in an extensive trading network. Seashells were probably obtained from the Persian Gulf, which is some distance to the south; copper may have come from what is now central Iran; obsidian was still coming from eastern Turkey; and turquoise somehow made its way from what is now the border between Iran and Afghanistan. Some of these materials were used as ornaments worn by both sexes—or so it seems from the remains of bodies found buried under the floors of houses.

After about 5500 B.C., the area around Ali Kosh began to show signs of a much larger population, apparently made possible by a more complex agriculture employing irrigation and plows drawn by domesticated cattle. In the next thousand years, by 4500 B.C., the population of the area probably tripled. This population growth was apparently part of the cultural developments that culminated in the rise of urban civilizations in the Near East.[45]

Population growth may have occurred in and around Ali Kosh but did not continue in all areas of the Near East after domestication. For example, one of the largest early villages in the Near East, 'Ain Ghazal (on the outskirts of what is now Amman, Jordan), suffered a decline in population and standard of living over time, perhaps because the environment around 'Ain Ghazal could not permanently support a large village.[46]

Catal Hüyük On a windswept plateau in the rugged, mountainous region of southern Turkey stand the remains of a mud-brick town known as Catal Hüyük. *Hüyük* is the Turkish word for a mound formed by a succession of settlements, one built on top of another.

About 5600 B.C., Catal Hüyük was an adobe town. Some 200 houses have been excavated, and they are interconnected in *pueblo fashion* (each flat-roofed structure housed a number of families). The inhabitants decorated the walls of the houses with imaginative murals, and their shrines with symbolic statuary. The murals depict what seem to be religious scenes and everyday events. Archaeologists peeling away frescoes found layer upon layer of murals, indicating that old murals were plastered over to make way for fresh paintings. Several rooms are believed to have been shrine rooms. They contain many large bull murals and clay bull figurines and have full-sized clay heads of cattle on the walls. Other "shrine room" murals depict scenes of life and death, painted in red and black, respectively. Clay statuettes of a pregnant woman and of a bearded man seated on a bull have also been found in these rooms.

Farming was well advanced at Catal Hüyük. Lentils, wheat, barley, and peas were grown in quantities that produced a surplus. Archaeologists were astonished at the richly varied handicrafts, including beautifully carved wooden bowls and boxes that the people of the town produced. These people also had obsidian and flint daggers, spearheads, lance heads, scrapers, awls, and sickle blades. Bowls, spatulas, knives, ladles, and spoons were made from bone. The houses contained belt hooks, toggles, and pins carved from bone. Evidence also suggests that men and women wore jewelry fashioned from bone, shell, and copper, and that they used obsidian mirrors.[47]

Because Catal Hüyük is located in a region with few raw materials, the town evidently depended on exchange with other areas to secure the rich variety of materials it used. Shells were procured from the Mediterranean, timber from the hills, obsidian from 50 miles away, and marble from western Turkey.

Excavation in the pueblo-like structures of Neolithic Catal Hüyük.

© Yann Arthus-Bertrand/CORBIS

Domestication in Mesoamerica

A very different pattern of domestication is seen in Mesoamerica. Here the seminomadic Archaic hunting and gathering lifestyle persisted long after people first domesticated plants.[48] How can this be? Don't people have to settle near their crops to take care of them? Once they have domesticated plants, don't they stop collecting wild plants? The answer is no. In Mesoamerica, people sowed a variety of plants, but after doing so, they went on with their seasonal rounds of hunting and gathering, and came back later to harvest what they had sown. Many of the early domesticates in Mesoamerica were not basic to subsistence, even if they were highly desirable. Domestication may have been a way for Archaic peoples to make desirable plants more common in their environment. For example, one of the first domesticates was the bottle gourd. These were not eaten but were used to carry water. Joyce Marcus and Kent Flannery hypothesize that people deliberately domesticated the bottle gourd by planting them in areas where they did not grow naturally, so that as groups moved through those areas, they always had access to gourds for carrying water.[49]

Bottle gourds are only one of many early domesticates from Highland Mesoamerica. Others include tomatoes, cotton, a variety of beans and squashes, and, perhaps most importantly, maize. The earliest domesticated form of maize (corn), dating from about 5000 B.C., has been found in Tehuacán, Mexico. Genetic studies of maize show that it was domesticated from teosinte, a tall wild grass that still grows widely in Mexico (see Figure 6).[50] Indeed, these genetic studies suggest that changes occured in only two genes, one related to the kernel glumes (outer casing), and one related to the stalk shape.[51] The genes of modern corn were already established 4,000 years to 6,000 years ago.

Teosinte is quite different from maize in several important ways, but small genetic changes led to major phenotypic changes. The genetic malleability of maize may be one reason it has become one of the most important domesticated crops on earth. Teosinte stalks do look a lot like maize, but teosinte has a "spike" to which 7 to 12 individual seeds are attached in a single row, unlike the maize cob, which has many seeds in many rows. Each teosinte seed has its own brittle shell, whereas the entire maize cob is covered with a tough husk. However, early maize was also considerably different from modern maize. The oldest maize cobs—dating to about 7,000 years ago—are tiny, only about an inch long. They have only a half-dozen rows of seeds, and each seed is tiny. One interesting fact about both ancient and modern maize is that it is almost completely dependent on humans to reproduce—the shift from seeds with brittle coats to cobs with a tough husk meant that someone had to open the husk without damaging the seeds for them to be dispersed and reproduce.[52]

Like maize and the bottle gourd, beans and squash were probably domesticated by simple manipulation of wild varieties. Runner beans, for example, grow naturally in the soils on the slopes outside of rock shelters and caves. It is not a stretch of the imagination to envision Archaic

Teosinte

Maize

FIGURE 6 Teosinte Plant, Spike, and Seeds and Maize Plant, Cob, and Kernels
Note how much larger the domesticated maize cob and kernels are compared to the teosinte spike and seeds.

Source: Feder 2000.
From *Past in Perspective*, 2nd ed., by K. Feder. (Mountain View, CA: Mayfield, 2000).

peoples harvesting these beans (for their roots to begin with—nondomestic runner bean seeds are tiny and probably were not eaten) and selectively planting those with desired qualities, like large seeds. Similarly, the Archaic peoples likely only ate the seeds of wild squashes, as the flesh of wild squashes often has an unattractive smell and taste. But they may have selectively planted mutants with good-tasting flesh and larger seeds, eventually producing the domestic varieties over time.[53]

People who lived in Mesoamerica, Mexico, and Central America are often credited with the invention of planting maize, beans, and squash together in the same field. This planting strategy provides some important advantages. Maize takes nitrogen from the soil; beans, like all legumes, put nitrogen back into the soil. The maize stalk provides a natural pole for the bean plant to twine around, and the low-growing squash can grow around the base of the tall maize plant. Beans supply people with the amino acid lysine, which is missing in maize. Thus, maize and beans together provide all the essential amino acids that humans need to obtain from their food. Teosinte may have provided the model for this unique combination, as wild runner beans and wild squash occur naturally where teosinte grows.[54]

Guila Naquitz The Guila Naquitz cave, excavated in the 1960s by Kent Flannery, provides a good picture of early domestication in Highland Mesoamerica. Here, small groups of people, probably only a single family at a time, lived intermittently (and probably seasonally) over a period of 2,000 years (circa 8900 B.C.–6700 B.C.), the period during which plants were domesticated. The cave itself is located in the thorn forest of the upper piedmont above the floor of the Valley of Oaxaca. The residents of Guila Naquitz hunted deer and peccary (a wild piglike animal) with spears and spear throwers, and trapped small animals such as rabbits. They also collected plant foods from the surrounding area, particularly prickly pear fruits, cherries, acorns, and piñion nuts from the forests above the cave, along with agave hearts, onions, and various other nuts and fruits from a variety of thorn forest plants.[55]

Also found in the Guila Naquitz cave are the remains of domesticated plants, including bottle gourd and several varieties of squashes. How did these come to be in the cave? Were the inhabitants planting fields of squashes? Probably not in the way one thinks of planting a field today. Squashes are common wild plants in Highland Mesoamerica, and thrive in disturbed soils such as those outside of caves. It may be that the inhabitants of the Guila Naquitz cave knew squashes would grow easily near their cave, and so actively planted some with better-tasting flesh or larger seeds than those that might naturally grow there.[56] Domestication and the use of domesticated plants would be rather informal—a supplement to a diet already rich in animal and plant species. This picture seems much different from that at Near Eastern sites such as Ali Kosh and Catal Hüyük. Domestication in Guila Naquitz appears to have been accomplished by hunters and gatherers who supplemented their basic diet with some desired

plants (squashes with tasty flesh, for example); there was no "revolution" that enabled the people to rely on domesticated plants.

Domestication Elsewhere in the World

South America and the Eastern United States Outside of Mesoamerica, evidence of independent domestication of plants comes from at least two areas in the New World: South America and the eastern United States. The first plants to be domesticated in the New World were members of the cucurbit family, including the bottle gourd and a variety of squashes, all probably domesticated some time after 7500 B.C. In addition to these and other plants domesticated in Mesoamerica, we can trace more than 200 domesticated plants to the Andes in South America, including potatoes, lima beans, peanuts, amaranth, and quinoa. The first clear domesticates were squashes and gourds, which may date back to 8000 B.C., which makes domestication in the Andes as old as in Mesoamerica, and perhaps even older.[57] The origins of the root crops manioc and sweet potato are less certain, but those crops probably originated in lowland tropical forest regions of South America.[58]

Many of the plants grown in North America, such as corn, beans, and squash, were apparently introduced from Mesoamerica. However, at least three seed plants were probably domesticated independently in North America at an earlier time—sunflowers, sumpweed, and goosefoot. Sunflowers and sumpweed contain seeds that are highly nutritious in terms of protein and fat; goosefoot is high in starch and similar to corn in food value.[59] Sumpweed is an unusually good source of calcium, rivaled only by greens, mussels, and bones. It is also a very good source of iron (better than beef liver) and thiamine.[60] These plants may have been cultivated in the area of Kentucky, Tennessee, and southern Illinois beginning around 2000 B.C. (Corn was introduced about A.D. 200.)

All of the domesticates before corn are nutritionally superior to corn, so why did North American agriculturalists switch to a reliance on corn in the last 1,000 years?[61] In archaeologist Bruce Smith's words, "With the exception of the sunflower, North American seed crops are not exactly household words."[62] Crop yields of corn would have had to be quite high to surpass the yields of those other crops, so perhaps the crucial factors were the time of harvest and the amount of effort required. Goosefoot, for example, was comparable to corn nutritionally. But harvesting and preparing it for storage took a lot of work and also had to be done during the fall, the time of year when deer could be hunted intensively. So perhaps the incompatibility of goosefoot production and deer hunting, and the ease of harvesting corn and preparing it for storage, explain the switch to corn.[63]

On the whole, domestic animals were less important economically in the New World than they were in many parts of the Old World. In North America, dogs and turkeys were the main domesticated animals before the arrival of the Spanish. Dogs in North and South America

applied anthropology

Raised Field Agriculture

Most agricultural systems in the Americas today rely upon either animal power or large machines to cultivate the soil and harvest food. But in the past, people had no traction animals or machines to help with agricultural production. How did the ancient farmers in the Americas till the soil and harvest crops? The answer is that they used human labor. In most cases, animal or mechanical power is much more efficient than human power, and allows more food to be grown on the same piece of land. Archaeologists, however, have found that some ancient, human-powered agricultural systems are actually better suited to specific local environments, and produce more food than modern, mechanized systems. These archaeologists have started to use their knowledge of ancient food production to help modern communities improve their lives.

Archaeologist Clark Erickson calls this work "applied archaeology," and he has been conducting applied archaeological work in South America since the early 1980s. One of his most significant projects involved the reconstruction of raised fields in the community of Huatta near Lake Titicaca in highland Peru. The environment there is relatively harsh. Agricultural development projects in the 1960s tried and failed to make the land surrounding Huatta productive. But Erickson recognized that most of the area surrounding the community had once been highly productive raised fields, and he wondered if rebuilding these ancient agricultural structures might help the community.

Raised field agriculture in the Lake Titicaca basin.

Courtesy Clark Erikson

Raised fields are created by piling soil into a long mound, which becomes surrounded by a ditch as soil is taken from it and piled on the mound. Over time, the ditch fills with water and aquatic plants. The aquatic plants are harvested annually and placed on top of the mound as fertilizer. The water in the ditch both keeps the mound soil moist and helps control the soil temperature. As a system, raised fields form a self-sustaining agricultural microenvironment. The major drawback is that mechanized equipment cannot be used easily on these mounds and ditches, so significant amounts of human labor are often required.

In 1981, Erickson began working with members of the Huatta community to rebuild several of the ancient raised fields. By 1986, it was clear that raised field agriculture was well suited to the area. Raised fields were not as labor-intensive as initially thought, and were as productive as nearby agricultural fields built upon better soils. More significantly, the "manure" from aquatic plants maintained the soils in the raised fields and actually improved them over time. So, although more labor-intensive, raised fields were able to bring otherwise marginal land into full agricultural production. Today, large areas of the Lake Titicaca basin have been returned to raised field agriculture.

Sources: Erickson 1988; 1989; 1998.

---

probably accompanied the first colonizers of the Americas, as all domestic dogs appear to be descended from a common Asian ancestor.[64] Domesticated turkeys from about A.D. 500 have been found in pueblos in the American Southwest.[65] Their feathers were used for arrows, ornaments, and weaving, and their bones for tools; but they do not seem to have been used frequently for food. However, turkeys were an important food in Mexico, where they may have been independently domesticated, and in

Central America. When Cortes came to Mexico in 1519, he found domesticated turkeys in great quantities.[66]

The central Andes was the only part of the New World where animals were a significant part of the economy. Used for meat, transportation, and wool, llamas and alpacas (members of the camel family) were domesticated as early as 5000 B.C. in the Andes.[67] Guinea pigs, misnamed because they are neither pigs nor from Guinea, are rodents that were domesticated in the Andes sometime later. They were an important source of food even before domestication.[68] Since they were domesticated, they have been raised in people's dwellings.

Animal domestication in the New World differed from that in the Old World because different wild species were found in the two hemispheres. The Old World plains and forests were the homes for the wild ancestors of the cattle, sheep, goats, pigs, and horses we know today. In the New World, the Pleistocene herds of horses, mastodons, mammoths, and other large animals were long extinct, allowing few opportunities for domestication of large animals.[69]

East Asia The archaeological record for the domestication of seed crops is better known than for soft-flesh crops because the latter do not preserve well. The earliest clear evidence of cereal cultivation outside the Near East is from China. Late in the 6th millennium B.C. in North China, there were sites where foxtail millet was cultivated. Storage pits, storage pots, and large numbers of grinding stones suggest that millet was an enormously important item in the diet. The wild animal bones and the hunting and fishing tools that have been found suggest that people still depended on hunting and fishing somewhat, even though domesticated pigs (as well as dogs) were present. In South China, from about the same time, archaeologists have found a village by the edge of a small lake where people cultivated rice, bottle gourds, water chestnuts, and the datelike fruit called jujube. The people in South China also raised water buffalo, pigs, and dogs. And, as in the North China sites, some of their food came from hunting and fishing.[70]

Mainland Southeast Asia may have been a place of domestication as early as the Near East was. The dating of domestication in Southeast Asia is not yet clear; the dates of the oldest site with probable domesticates—Spirit cave in northwest Thailand—range from about 9500 B.C. to 5500 B.C. Some of the plants found at Spirit cave are not clearly distinguishable from wild varieties, but others, such as gourds, betel nut, betel leaf, and water chestnut, were probably domesticates.[71]

Most of the early cultivation in mainland Southeast Asia seems to have occurred in the plains and low terraces around rivers, although the main subsistence foods of early cultivators were probably the fish and shellfish in nearby waters. The first plants to be domesticated probably were not cereal grains, as they were in the Near East. Indeed, some early cultivated crops may not have been used for food at all. In particular, bamboo may have been used to make cutting tools and for a variety of building purposes, and gourds were probably used as containers or bowls. We do not know yet exactly when rice was first domesticated, but there is definite evidence of cultivated rice in Thailand after 4000 B.C.

Bananas and taro may have been first domesticated in New Guinea. Recent analyses of soils from archaeological deposits at Kuk Swamp have identified phytoliths (small silica crystals formed between plant cells that are unique to particular species of plants) from bananas and taro dating from almost 7,000 years ago.[72] Archaeologists have known that agricultural fields with soil mounds and irrigation features have a long history in New Guinea, dating

Bananas and taro were domesticated in New Guinea nearly 7,000 years ago. Bananas are now grown in many tropical regions, including Ghana pictured here.

back as far as 10,000 years. The new findings of very early taro and banana cultivation suggest that New Guinea may have been the location where these plants were first domesticated. Other major food plants domesticated in Southeast Asia include yams, breadfruit, and coconuts.[73]

Africa Some plants and animals were domesticated first in Africa. Most of the early domestications probably occurred in the wide, broad belt of woodland-savanna country south of the Sahara and north of the equator. Among the cereal grains, sorghum was probably first domesticated in the central or eastern part of this belt, bulrush millet and a kind of rice (different from Asian rice) in the western part, and finger millet in the east. Groundnuts (peanuts) and yams were first domesticated in West Africa.[74] We do know that farming became widespread in the northern half of Africa after 6000 B.C.; investigators continue to debate whether the earliest crops grown there were indigenous or borrowed from the Near East. There is little doubt, however, that some of the plant foods were first domesticated in sub-Saharan Africa because the wild varieties occur there.[75] Many of the important domestic animals in Africa today, especially sheep and goats, were first domesticated elsewhere in the Old World, but one form of cattle, as well as donkey and guinea fowl, were probably first domesticated in Africa.[76]

A farmer inspecting his sorghum crop in Sudan. Sorghum is one of several plant species domesticated in Africa.

WHY DID FOOD PRODUCTION DEVELOP?

We know that an economic transformation occurred in widely separate areas of the world beginning after about 10,000 years ago, as people began to domesticate plants and animals. But why did domestication occur? And why did it occur independently in many different places within a period of a few thousand years? Considering that people depended only on wild plants and animals for millions of years, the differences in exactly when domestication first occurred in different parts of the world seem small. The spread of domesticated plants seems to have been more rapid in the Old World than in the New World, perhaps because the Old World spread was more along an east-west axis (except for the spread to sub-Saharan Africa), whereas the New World spread was more north-south. Spreading north and south may have required more time to adapt to variation in day lengths, climates, and diseases.[77]

There are many theories of why food production developed; most have tried to explain the origin of domestication in the area of the Fertile Crescent. Gordon Childe's theory, popular in the 1950s, was that a drastic change in climate caused domestication in the Near East.[78] According to Childe, the postglacial period was marked by a decline in summer rainfall in the Near East and northern Africa. As the rains decreased, people were forced to retreat into shrinking pockets, or oases, of food resources surrounded by desert. The lessened availability of wild resources provided an incentive for people to cultivate grains and to domesticate animals, according to Childe.

Robert Braidwood criticized Childe's theory for two reasons. First, Braidwood believed that the climate changes may not have been as dramatic as Childe had assumed, and therefore the "oasis incentive" may not have existed. Second, the climatic changes that occurred in the Near East after the retreat of the last glaciers had probably occurred at earlier interglacial periods too, but there had never been a similar food-producing revolution before. Hence, according to Braidwood, there must be more to the explanation of why people began to produce food than simply changes in climate.[79]

Braidwood and Gordon Willey claimed that people did not undertake domestication until they had learned a great deal about their environment and until their culture had evolved enough for them to handle such an undertaking: "Why did incipient food production not come earlier? Our only answer at the moment is that culture was not ready to achieve it."[80]

But most archaeologists now think we should try to explain why people were not "ready" earlier to achieve domestication. Both Lewis Binford and Kent Flannery suggest that some change in external circumstances must have induced or favored the changeover to food production.[81] As Flannery pointed out, there is no evidence of a great economic incentive for hunter-gatherers to become food producers. In fact, some contemporary hunter-gatherers obtain adequate nutrition with far *less* work than many agriculturalists. So what might push food collectors to become food producers?

Binford and Flannery thought that the incentive to domesticate animals and plants may have been a desire to reproduce what was wildly abundant in the most bountiful or optimum hunting and gathering areas. Because of population growth in the optimum areas, people might have moved to surrounding areas containing fewer wild resources. In those marginal areas, people might have first turned to food production to reproduce what they used to have.

The Binford-Flannery model seems to fit the archaeological record in the Levant, the southwestern part of the Fertile Crescent, where population increase did precede the first signs of domestication.[82] But, as Flannery admitted, in some regions, such as southwestern Iran, the optimum hunting and gathering areas do not show population increase before the emergence of domestication.[83]

The Binford-Flannery model focuses on population pressure in a small area as the incentive to turn to food production. Mark Cohen theorizes that population pressure on a global scale explains why so many of the world's peoples adopted agriculture within the span of a few thousand years.[84] He argues that hunter-gatherers all over the world gradually increased in population so that the world was more or less filled with foragers by about 10,000 years ago. Thus, people could no longer relieve population pressure by moving to uninhabited areas. To support their increasing populations, they would have had to exploit a broader range of less desirable wild foods; that is, they would have had to switch to broad-spectrum collecting, or they would have had to increase the yields of the most desirable wild plants by weeding, protecting them from animal pests, and perhaps deliberately planting the most productive among them. Cohen thinks that people might have tried a variety of these strategies but would generally have ended up depending on cultivation because that would have been the most efficient way to allow more people to live in one place.

Recently, some archaeologists have returned to the idea that climatic change (not the extreme variety that Childe envisaged) might have played a role in the emergence of agriculture. It seems clear from the evidence now available that the climate of the Near East about 13,000 years to 12,000 years ago became more seasonal: The summers got hotter and drier than before and the winters became colder. These climatic changes may have favored the emergence of annual species of wild grain, which archaeologically we see proliferating in many areas of the Near East.[85] People such as the Natufians intensively exploited the seasonal grains, developing an elaborate technology for storing and processing the grains and giving up their previous nomadic existence to do so. The transition to agriculture may have occurred when sedentary foraging no longer provided sufficient resources for the population. This could have happened because sedentarization led to population increase and therefore resource scarcity,[86] or because local wild resources became depleted after people settled down in permanent villages.[87] In the area of Israel and Jordan where the Natufians lived, some of the people apparently turned to agriculture, probably to increase the supply of grain, whereas other people returned to nomadic foraging because of the decreasing availability of wild grain.[88]

Change to a more seasonal climate might also have led to a shortage of certain nutrients for foragers. In the dry seasons, certain nutrients would have been less available. For example, grazing animals get lean when grasses are not plentiful, so meat from hunting would have been in short supply in the dry seasons. Although it may seem surprising, some recent hunter-gatherers have starved when they had to rely on lean meat. If they could have increased their carbohydrate or fat intake somehow, they might have been more likely to get through the periods of lean game.[89] So it is possible that some foragers in the past thought of planting crops to get them through the dry seasons when hunting, fishing, and gathering did not provide enough carbohydrates and fat for them to avoid starvation.

Mesoamerica presents a very different picture, because the early domesticates were not important to subsistence. Theories about population pressure and nutrient shortage don't seem to fit Mesoamerica well. However, there were apparently shortages of desired plants, such as bottle gourds, and domestication may well have occurred as humans actively sowed these desired plants. The difference between this model and the ones described previously is that humans in Mesoamerica were apparently not forced into domestication by climate change or population pressure, but actively turned to domestication to obtain more of the most desired or useful plant species. The most interesting case is maize, which only became a staple food some 2,500 or more years after it was first domesticated. Why did it become a staple? Probably both because it was a suitable staple crop (especially when intercropped with beans and squash, as discussed earlier) and because people liked it, so they grew it in large quantities. Over time, and perhaps because of conflict, population pressure, and other forces similar to those that apparently led to domestication in the Near East, people in Mesoamerica and later North and South America came to rely on maize as their dietary mainstay.

CONSEQUENCES OF THE RISE OF FOOD PRODUCTION

We know that intensive agriculture (permanent rather than shifting cultivation) probably developed in response to population pressure, but we do not know for sure that population pressure was even partly responsible for plant and animal domestication in the first place. Still, population growth certainly accelerated after the rise of food production (see Figure 7). There were other consequences too. Paradoxically, perhaps, health seems to have declined. Material possessions, though, became more elaborate.

Accelerated Population Growth

As we have seen, settling down (even before the rise of food production) may have increased the rate of human population growth. But population growth definitely accelerated after the emergence of farming and herding, possibly because the spacing between births was reduced further and therefore fertility (the number of births per mother) increased. Increased fertility may have been advantageous because of the greater value of children in farming and herding economies; there is evidence from recent population studies that fertility rates are higher where children contribute more to the economy.[90]

Not only may parents desire more children to help with chores; the increased workload of mothers may also (but inadvertently) decrease birth spacing. The busier a mother is, the less frequently she may nurse and the more likely her baby will be given supplementary food by other caretakers such as older siblings.[91] Less frequent nursing[92] and greater reliance on food other than mother's milk may result in an earlier resumption of ovulation after the birth of a baby. (Farmers and herders are likely to have animal milk to feed to babies, and also cereals that have been transformed by cooking into soft, mushy porridges.) Therefore, the spacing between births may have decreased (and the number of births per mother, in turn, increased) when mothers got busier after the rise of food production.

FIGURE 7 Population Growth since 10,000 Years Ago
The rate of population growth accelerated after the emergence of farming and herding 10,000 years ago. The rate of growth accelerated even more dramatically in recent times.

Source: Coale 1974.
Adapted from Ansley J. Coale, *The History of the Human Population.* Copyright © 1974 by Scientific American Inc.

131

current research and issues

You Are What You Eat: Chemical Analyses of Bones and Teeth

Archaeologists study ancient diets in several ways, most of them indirect. They can indirectly infer some of what ancient people ate from recovered food wastes. For example, if you find a lot of corncobs, chances are that the people ate a lot of corn. Plant and animal foods can be identified in the charred remains of cooking fires and (when preserved) in the ancient people's feces, or coprolites. Such inferences are usually biased in favor of hard food sources such as seeds, nuts, and grains (which are likely to be preserved); rarely are the remains of soft plants such as bananas or tubers found. Archaeologists can also indirectly infer diet from the artifacts they find, particularly, of course, ones we can be pretty sure were used in obtaining or processing food. So, for example, if you find a stone with a flat or concave surface that looks like what people use in some places to grind corn, it is very likely that the ancient people also ground grain (or other hard things such as seeds) for food. But plant remains or implements do not tell us how much people relied on particular sources of food.

There is a more direct way to study ancient diets. Anthropologists have discovered that, in many ways, "you are what you eat." In particular, chemical analyses of bones and teeth, the most common remains found in excavations, can reveal distinctive traces of the foods that metabolically went into the bones and teeth.

One kind of informative chemical analysis involves the ratio of strontium to calcium in bone. This analysis can indicate the relative amounts of plant and animal food in the diet. So, for example, we know from strontium analysis of bones that, just before the beginnings of cereal agriculture in the Near East, people were eating a lot of plant food, probably wild cereals that were intensively collected. Then there was a temporary decline in such collecting, suggesting overexploitation of the wild resources or at least their decreasing availability. This problem was presumably solved by the cultivation and domestication (modification) of cereals.

Carbon isotope ratios also can tell us what types of plants people were eating. Trees, shrubs, and temperate-zone grasses (such as rice) have carbon isotope ratios that are different from those of tropical and subtropical grasses (such as millet and corn). People in China were relying heavily on cereals about 7,000 years to 8,000 years ago, but the cereals were not the same in the north and south. Contrary to what we might expect, the carbon isotope ratios tell us that an originally temperate-zone cereal (rice) was the staple in subtropical southern China; in the more temperate north, an originally tropical or subtropical grass (millet) was most important. The dependence on millet in the north was enormous. It is estimated that 50 percent to 80 percent of the diet between 5000 B.C. and 500 B.C. came from millet.

In the New World, seed crops such as sunflower, sumpweed, and goosefoot were domesticated in eastern North America long before corn, introduced from Mexico, became the staple. We know this partly from the archaeology; the remains of the early seed crops are older than the remains of corn. Corn, an originally subtropical plant, has a carbon isotope ratio that is different from the ratio for the earlier, temperate-zone seed crops. Thus, the shift in carbon isotope ratios after A.D. 800 to A.D. 900 tells us that corn had become the staple.

Physical anthropologists and archaeologists traditionally use nonchemical analyses of human bones and teeth to study similarities and differences between peoples in different geographic regions, between living humans and possible fossil ancestors, and between living humans and other surviving primates. Much of the research involved surface measurements, particularly of the skull (outside and inside). In recent years, physical anthropologists and archaeologists have begun to study the "insides" of bones and teeth. The new kinds of chemical analysis mentioned here are part of that trend. In N. J. van der Merwe's pithy words: "The emphasis in studies of human evolution has … shifted from a preoccupation with the brain to an equal interest in the stomach."

Sources: van der Merwe 1992; Larsen 2002, 2009.

Declining Health

Although the rise of food production may have led to increased fertility, this does not mean that health generally improved. In fact, it appears that health declined at least sometimes with the transition to food production. The two trends may seem paradoxical, but rapid population growth can occur if each mother gives birth to a large number of babies, even if many of them die early because of disease or poor nutrition.

The evidence that health may have declined sometimes after the rise of food production comes from studies of the bones and teeth of some prehistoric populations, before and after the emergence of food production (see the box titled "You Are What You Eat"). Nutritional and disease problems are indicated by such features as incomplete formation of tooth enamel, nonaccidental bone lesions (incompletely filled-in bone), reduction in stature, and decreased life expectancy. Many of the studied prehistoric populations that relied heavily on agriculture seem to show less adequate nutrition and higher infection rates than populations living in the same areas before agriculture.[93] Some of the agricultural populations are shorter and had lower life expectancies.

The reasons for a decline in health in those populations are not yet clear. Greater malnutrition can result from an overdependence on a few dietary staples that lack some

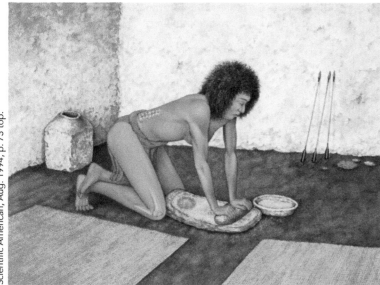

As this reconstruction shows, transforming grain into flour was a "daily grind," putting a great deal of stress on the lower back and knees. Studies of Neolithic skeletons of women show marks of stress on bone and arthritis, probably reflecting their long hours of work at the grinding stone.

Source: "The Eloquent Bones of Abu Hureyras", Roberto Osti. Courtesy of Scientific American, Aug. 1994, p. 73 top.

necessary nutrients. Overdependence on a few sources of food may also increase the risk of famine because the fewer the staple crops, the greater the danger to the food supply posed by a weather-caused crop failure. But some or most nutritional problems may be the result of social and political factors, particularly the rise of different socioeconomic classes of people and unequal access, between and within communities, to food and other resources.[94]

Social stratification or considerable socioeconomic inequality seems likely to develop after the rise of food production. The effects of stratification and political dominance from afar on the general level of health may be reflected in the skeletal remains of prehistoric Native Americans who died in what is now Illinois between A.D. 950 and A.D. 1300, the period spanning the changeover in that region from hunting and gathering to agriculture. The agricultural people living in the area of Dickson Mounds—burial sites named after the doctor who first excavated them—were apparently in much worse health than their hunter-gatherer ancestors. But curiously, archaeological evidence suggests that they were still also hunting and fishing. A balanced diet was apparently available, but who was getting it? Possibly it was the elites at Cahokia, 110 miles away, where perhaps 15,000 to 30,000 people lived, who were getting most of the meat and fish. The individuals near Dickson Mounds who collected the meat and fish may have gotten luxury items such as shell necklaces from the Cahokia elites, but many of the people buried at Dickson Mounds were clearly not benefiting nutritionally from the relationship with Cahokia.[95]

The Elaboration of Material Possessions

In the more permanent villages that were established after the rise of food production about 10,000 years ago, houses became more elaborate and comfortable, and construction methods improved. The materials used in construction depended on whether timber or stone was locally available or whether a strong sun could dry mud bricks. Modern architects might find to their surprise that bubble-shaped houses were known long ago in Neolithic Cyprus. Families in the island's town of Khirokitia made their homes in large, domed, circular dwellings shaped like beehives and featuring stone foundations and mud-brick walls. Often, more space was created by dividing the interior horizontally and firmly propping a second floor on limestone pillars.

Sizable villages of solidly constructed, gabled wooden houses were built in Europe on the banks of the Danube and along the rims of Alpine lakes.[96] Many of the gabled wooden houses in the Danube region were long, rectangular structures that apparently sheltered several family units. In Neolithic times, these longhouses had doors, beds, tables, and other furniture that closely resembled those in modern-day societies. We know the people had furniture because miniature clay models have been found at their sites. Several of the chairs and couches seem to be models of padded and upholstered furniture with wooden frames, indicating that Neolithic European artisans were creating fairly sophisticated furnishings.[97] Such furnishings were the result of an advanced tool technology put to use by a people who, because they were staying in one area, could take time to make and use furniture.

For the first time, apparel made of woven textiles appeared. This development was not simply the result of the domestication of flax (for linen), cotton, and wool-growing sheep. These sources of fiber alone could not produce cloth. It was the development by Neolithic society of the spindle and loom for spinning and weaving that made textiles possible. True, textiles can be woven by hand without a loom, but to do so is a slow, laborious process, impractical for producing garments.

The pottery of the early Neolithic was similar to the plain earthenware made by some preagricultural groups and included large urns for grain storage, mugs, cooking pots, and dishes. To improve the retention of liquid, potters in the Near East may have been the first to glaze the earthenware's porous surface. Later, Neolithic ceramics

Sophisticated ceramics like this 5,000-year-old Chinese funeral urn first appeared in the Neolithic era as part of the elaboration of material possessions.

Source: Dagli Orti/Picture Desk, Inc./Kobal Collection

became more artistic. Designers shaped the clay into graceful forms and painted colorful patterns on the vessels.

It is probable that virtually none of these architectural and technological innovations could have occurred until humans became fully sedentary. Nomadic hunting and gathering peoples would have found it difficult to carry many material goods, especially fragile items such as pottery. Only when humans settled in one place would these goods have provided advantages, enabling villagers to cook and store food more effectively and to house themselves more comfortably.

There is also evidence of long-distance trade in the Neolithic, as we have noted. Obsidian from southern Turkey was being exported to sites in the Zagros Mountains of Iran and to what are now Israel, Jordan, and Syria in the Levant. Great amounts of obsidian were exported to sites about 190 miles from the source of supply; more than 80 percent of the tools that residents of those areas used were made of this material.[98] Marble was being sent from western to eastern Turkey, and seashells from the coast were traded to distant inland regions. Such trade suggests a considerable amount of contact among various Neolithic communities.

About 3500 B.C., cities first appeared in the Near East. These cities had political assemblies, kings, scribes, and specialized workshops. The specialized production of goods and services was supported by surrounding farming villages, which sent their produce to the urban centers. A dazzling transformation had taken place in a relatively short time. People had not only settled down, but they had also become "civilized," or urbanized. (The word *civilized* literally means to make "citified.") Urban societies seem to have developed first in the Near East and somewhat later

around the eastern Mediterranean, in the Indus Valley of northwestern India, in northern China, and in Mexico and Peru.

SUMMARY ● ○ ○

1. In the period immediately before plants and animals were domesticated, there seems to have been a shift in many areas of the world to less dependence on big game hunting and greater dependence on what is called broad-spectrum collecting. The broad spectrum of available resources frequently included aquatic resources such as fish and shellfish and a variety of wild plants, deer, and other game. Climatic changes may have been partly responsible for the change to broad-spectrum collecting.

2. In some sites in Europe, the Near East, Africa, and Peru, the switch to broad-spectrum collecting seems to be associated with the development of more permanent communities. In other areas, such as the semiarid highlands of Mesoamerica, permanent settlements may have emerged only after the domestication of plants and animals.

3. The shift to the cultivation and domestication of plants and animals has been referred to as the Neolithic revolution, and it occurred, probably independently, in a number of areas. To date, the earliest evidence of domestication comes from the Near East at about 8000 B.C. Dating for the earliest domestication in other areas of the Old World is not so clear, but the presence of different domesticated crops in different regions suggests that there were independent centers of domestication in China, Southeast Asia (what is now Malaysia, Thailand, Cambodia, and Vietnam), New Guinea, and Africa some time around or after 6000 B.C. In the New World, there appear to have been several early areas of cultivation and domestication: the highlands of Mesoamerica (about 7000 B.C.), the central Andes around Peru (about the same time, but perhaps even earlier), and the Eastern Woodlands of North America (about 2000 B.C.).

4. Theories about why food production originated remain controversial, but most archaeologists think that certain conditions must have pushed people to switch from collecting to producing food. Some possible causal factors include (1) population growth in regions of bountiful wild resources (which may have pushed people to move to marginal areas where they tried to reproduce their former abundance); (2) global population growth (which filled most of the world's habitable regions and may have forced people to utilize a broader spectrum of wild resources and to domesticate plants and animals); and (3) the emergence of hotter and drier summers and colder winters (which may have favored sedentarism near seasonal stands of wild grain; population growth in such areas

may have forced people to plant crops and raise animals to support themselves).

5. Regardless of why food production originated, it seems to have had important consequences for human life. Populations generally increased substantially after plant and animal domestication. Even though not all early cultivators were sedentary, sedentarism did increase with greater reliance on agriculture. Somewhat surprisingly, some prehistoric populations that relied heavily on agriculture seem to have been less healthy than earlier populations that relied on foraging. In the more permanent villages that were established after the rise of food production, houses and furnishings became more elaborate, and people began to make textiles and to paint pottery. These villages have also yielded evidence of increased long-distance trade.

GLOSSARY TERMS ○ ● ○

agriculture	Mesolithic
Archaic	Neolithic
domestication	obsidian
Epipaleolithic	rachis
food production	sedentarism

CRITICAL QUESTIONS ○ ○ ●

1. What factors might cause people to work harder to get food? Explain your answer.

2. How might people have domesticated sheep, goats, and cattle?

3. Do the various theories of the rise of food production explain why domestication occurred in many areas of the world within a few thousand years?

PEARSON
myanthrolab

Read the chapter by Mark Nathan Cohen titled "Were Early Agriculturalists Less Healthy than Food Collectors?" on MyAnthroLab. Answer the following questions:

1. Describe the basic arguments behind Cohen's question. What benefits did agriculture provide to human groups? What problems may have resulted from agriculture?

2. What does Cohen suggest his comparative data from modern foragers and modern agriculturalists demonstrate about the relative health of the two groups? Do data from ancient skeletons demonstrate a similar or a different pattern?

NOTES ● ○ ○

1. N. Miller 1992.
2. Crawford 1992; Phillipson 1993, 118; MacNeish 1991, 256; 268.
3. Flannery 1986, 6–8; Pearsall 1992; B. Smith 1992a.
4. Hole 1992.
5. Binford 1971.
6. Flannery 1973a.
7. Simcha et al. 2000.
8. Harlan 1967.
9. Flannery 1971.
10. Mellaart 1961.
11. Henry 1989, 214–15.
12. Brown and Price 1985.
13. Henry 1989, 38–39, 209–10; 1991. See Olszewski 1991 for some questions about the degree of social complexity in Natufian sites.
14. Martin and Wright 1967.
15. A recent analysis of these changes can be found in Kuehn 1998; see also J. Brown 1985.
16. Marcus and Flannery 1996, 49–50.
17. Ibid., 50–53.
18. Balter 2007; Jones and Liu 2009.
19. Gorman 1970.
20. Chang 1970; Gorman 1970.
21. J. Clark 1970, 171–72.
22. Phillipson 1993, 111–12.
23. Alroy 2001.
24. Martin 1973.
25. Grayson 1977; 1984. See also L. G. Marshall 1984; Guthrie 1984; Barnosky et al. 2004.
26. Holdaway and Jacomb 2000.
27. Cohen 1977b, 12; 85.
28. Cohen 1989, 112–13.
29. Frayer 1981.
30. Cohen 1989, 113–15.
31. Flannery 1973b.
32. Patterson 1971.
33. G. Johnson 1977; D. Harris 1977.
34. Sussman 1972; Lee 1972.
35. For some examples of societies that have practiced infanticide, D. Harris 1977.
36. Howell 1979; Lee 1979.
37. Frisch 1980; Howell 1979.
38. Phillipson 1993, 60–61.
39. Semenov 1970, 63; 203–204; Whittaker 1994, 36–37.
40. Zohary 1969.
41. Flannery 1965.
42. Ibid. For the view that a high proportion of immature animals does not necessarily indicate domestication, see Collier and White 1976.
43. Hole 1992; MacNeish 1991, 127–28.
44. Clutton-Brock 1992; Chessa et al. 2009.
45. Hole et al. 1969.
46. Simmons et al. 1988.
47. Mellaart 1964.
48. Flannery 1986, 3–5; Pringle 1998.
49. Marcus and Flannery 1996, 64–66.
50. Flannery 1986, 6–8.
51. Fedoroff 2003.
52. Flannery 1986, 8–9; Marcus and Flannery 1996, 66–67.
53. Marcus and Flannery 1996, 65–66.
54. Ibid., 66–68.
55. Flannery 1986, 31–42.
56. Ibid., 502.
57. Piperno and Stothert 2003.
58. MacNeish 1991, 37, 47; Hole 1992.
59. B. Smith 1992b, 163, 287.
60. Asch and Asch 1978.
61. B. Smith 1992a; 1992b, 39, 274–75, 292.
62. B. Smith 1992b, 6.

63. Ibid., 180.
64. Savolainen et al. 2002.
65. Clutton-Brock 1992.
66. Crawford 1984.
67. Clutton-Brock 1992.
68. Müller-Haye 1984.
69. Wenke 1984, 350, 397–98.
70. Chang 1981; MacNeish 1991, 159–63.
71. MacNeish 1991, 267–68.
72. Neumann 2003; Denham et al. 2003.
73. Hole 1992.
74. Phillipson 1993, 118.
75. MacNeish 1991, 314.
76. Hanotte et al. 2002; Clutton-Brock 1992.
77. Diamond 1997a; 1997b.
78. Cited in MacNeish 1991, 6.
79. Braidwood 1960.
80. Braidwood and Willey 1962.
81. Binford 1971; Flannery 1973a.
82. Wright 1971.
83. Flannery 1986, 10–11.
84. Cohen 1977a; 1977b, 279.
85. Byrne 1987, referred to in Blumler and Byrne 1991; see also Henry 1989, 30–38; McCorriston and Hole 1991.
86. Henry 1989, 41.
87. McCorriston and Hole 1991.
88. Henry 1989, 54.
89. Speth and Spielmann 1983.
90. B. White 1973; see also Kasarda 1971.
91. C. R. Ember 1983.
92. Konner and Worthman 1980.
93. Roosevelt 1984; see also M. N. Cohen and Armelagos 1984b, 585–602; Cohen 1987; 2009. For evidence suggesting that the transition to food production was not generally associated with declining health, see Wood et al. 1992; Starling and Stock 2007.
94. Roosevelt 1984
95. Goodman and Armelagos 1985; see also A. H. Goodman et al. 1984; Cohen 2009.
96. Clark and Piggott 1965, 240–42.
97. Ibid., 235.
98. Renfrew 1969.

Origins of Cities and States

From Chapter 13 of *Anthropology*, 13/e. Carol R. Ember. Melvin Ember. Peter N. Peregrine. Copyright © 2011 by Pearson Education. Published by Prentice Hall. All rights reserved.

Origins of Cities and States

From the time agriculture first developed until about 6000 B.C., people in the Near East lived in fairly small villages. There were few differences in wealth and status from household to household, and apparently there was no governmental authority beyond the village. There is also no evidence that these villages had any public buildings or craft specialists or that one community was very different in size from its neighbors. In short, these settlements had none of the characteristics we commonly associate with "civilization."

But sometime around 6000 B.C., in parts of the Near East—and at later times in other places—a great transformation in the quality and scale of human life seems to have begun. For the first time, we can see evidence of differences in status among households. For example, some are much bigger than others. Communities begin to differ in size and to specialize in certain crafts. And there are signs that some political officials had acquired authority over several communities, that what anthropologists call "chiefdoms" had emerged.

Somewhat later, by about 3500 B.C., we can see many, if not all, of the conventional characteristics of **civilization:** the first inscriptions, or writing; cities; many kinds of full-time craft specialists; monumental architecture; great differences in wealth and status; and the kind of strong, hierarchical, centralized political system we call the **state** (see Figure 1).

This type of transformation has occurred many times and in many places in human history. The color map titled "The First Civilizations" shows the locations where early civilizations arose. The most ancient civilizations arose in the Near East around 3500 B.C., in northwestern India and in Peru about 2500 B.C., in northern China around 1750 B.C., in Mexico a few hundred years before the time of Christ, and in tropical Africa somewhat later.[1] At least some of these civilizations evolved independently of the others—for example, those in the New World and those in the Old World. Why did they do so? What conditions favored the emergence of centralized, statelike political systems? What conditions favored the establishment of cities? We ask this last question separately, because archaeologists are not yet certain that all the ancient state societies had cities when they first developed centralized government. In this chapter, we discuss some of the things archaeologists have learned or suspect about the growth of ancient civilizations. Our discussion focuses primarily on the Near East and Mexico because archaeologists know the most about the sequences of cultural development in those two areas.

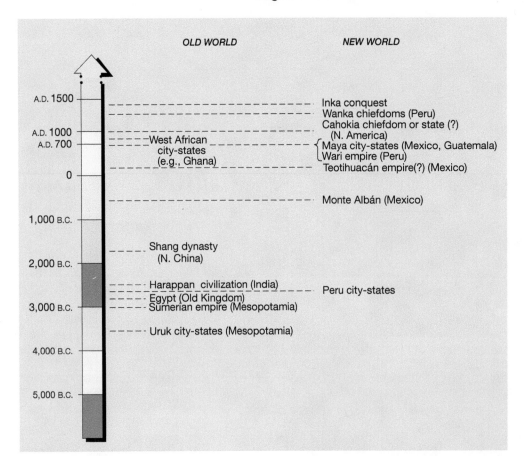

FIGURE 1 The Emergence of Civilization

OLD WORLD   NEW WORLD

A.D. 1500 — Inka conquest
— Wanka chiefdoms (Peru)
A.D. 1000 — Cahokia chiefdom or state (?)
A.D. 700 (N. America)
— West African — Maya city-states (Mexico, Guatemala)
city-states — Wari empire (Peru)
(e.g., Ghana)
0 — Teotihuacán empire(?) (Mexico)

— Monte Albán (Mexico)

1,000 B.C.

2,000 B.C. — Shang dynasty
(N. China)

— Harappan civilization (India) — Peru city-states
3,000 B.C. — Egypt (Old Kingdom)
— Sumerian empire (Mesopotamia)

— Uruk city-states (Mesopotamia)

4,000 B.C.

5,000 B.C.

ARCHAEOLOGICAL INFERENCES ABOUT CIVILIZATION

Archaeologists rather than historians have studied the most ancient civilizations because those civilizations evolved before the advent of writing. How do archaeologists infer that a particular people in the preliterate past had social classes, cities, or a centralized government?

As we have noted, it appears that the earliest Neolithic societies were *egalitarian;* that is, people did not differ much in wealth, prestige, or power. Some later societies show signs of social inequality, indicated by burial finds. Archaeologists generally assume that inequality in death reflects inequality in life, at least in status and perhaps also in wealth and power. Thus, we can be fairly sure that a society had differences in status if only some people were buried with special objects, such as jewelry or pots filled with food. And we can be fairly sure that high status was assigned at birth rather than achieved in later life if we find noticeable differences in children's tombs. For example, some (but not all) child burials from as early as 5500 B.C. to 5000 B.C. at Tell es-Sawwan in Iraq, and from about 800 B.C. at La Venta in Mexico, are filled with statues and ornaments, suggesting that some children had high status from birth.[2] But burials indicating differences in status do not necessarily mean a society had significant differences in wealth. Only when archaeologists find other substantial differences, as in house size and furnishings, can we be sure the society had different socioeconomic classes of people.

Reconstruction of the burial of a prehistoric Peruvian king, known as the "Lord of Sipan." Note the carefully laid-out wood tomb and the ornate cloth and gold items buried with the individual. Archaeologists assume that such special treatment indicates elite status.

Nigel Hicks © Dorling Kindersley, Courtesy of Museo Tumbas Reales de Sipan

new perspectives on gender

Effects of Imperialism on Women's Status

Archaeologists, and particularly women archaeologists, have begun to pay attention to the gender implications of archaeological materials. Do the findings from excavated houses imply anything about what women and men did where they lived? What do the findings in houses and other places suggest about the division of labor by gender? Can archaeology tell us about women's status in the culture and how it may have changed over time? Recent research suggests that if you look for gender-related results, you can often find some. As the title of a recent book indicated, new kinds of archaeology can be "engendered." For example, archaeologist Cathy Costin has studied the effects of Inka (Inca) imperialism on women's status in a conquered area.

Costin participated in a research project that studied culture change in the Yanamarca Valley of highland Peru. The project focused on the development of chiefdoms among the indigenous Wanka ethnic group between A.D. 1300 and A.D. 1470 and on the effects of the Inka conquest at the end of that period. According to the archaeology, most people before the Inka conquest were farmers, but some households specialized part-time in the production of pottery, stone tools, and perhaps textiles. Documents written after the arrival of the Spanish suggest that the Wanka had developed chiefdoms about A.D. 1300, possibly as a result of intensified warfare among the various communities. A high level of conflict is inferred from the locations and configurations of the settlements: Most people lived in fortified (walled) communities located on hills above the valley floor. According to the documentary sources, the Wanka chiefs had achieved their positions because of success as war leaders.

We know from documents that the Inka conquered the Wanka during the reign of the emperor Pachakuti (about

A.D. 1470). The Wanka region became a province within the Inka Empire, and bureaucrats from the capital at Cuzco came to govern the Wanka. The Inka conquerors, including military personnel, formed the highest class in the valley. The Wanka chiefs became vassals of the Inka state and imitators of Inka ways, using Inka-like pottery and building Inka-style additions to their homes. The economy of the valley became more specialized, apparently to meet the needs of the Inka. People in some villages still mostly farmed, but most households in other villages specialized in the production of pottery, stone tools, and other crafts. Skeletal remains indicate that the commoners became healthier and lived longer after the Inka conquest.

How did the Inka conquest affect the status of women? One key to an answer was suggested by the presence in the excavations of several thousand perforated, round ceramic objects. They were spindle whorls, weights used in spinning to keep the thread tight and even. The thread (from llama and alpaca wool) was made into cloth, which became the major form of tax payment after the Inka took over. Each village had to produce a certain amount of cloth for the state tax collectors. The cloth collected was used to clothe men serving in the army and to "pay" other government personnel. The burden of producing the cloth fell on the traditional spinners and weavers, who we know from the post-Spanish documents were females of all ages.

Just before the Inka conquest, all households excavated had spindle whorls, indicating that the female occupants in all households spun and made cloth. More whorls were found the farther up the mountain the house was located, indicating that women who lived closer to the high grasslands, where the flocks of llamas and alpacas were kept, spun more thread

than did women who lived farther down from the pastures. We might expect that elite women would do less work. But, to the contrary, the women in elite households seem to have produced more cloth than the women in commoner households, judging by the number of whorls in the households.

After the Inka conquest, households appear to have produced twice the amount of thread they did before, because there are twice the number of recovered spindle whorls. There is no indication, archaeological or documentary, that the women were freed from other tasks to make more time for spinning, so it would appear that women had to work harder under Inka domination to produce thread and cloth. But the producers do not appear to have benefited from the increased cloth production. Much if not most of the cloth produced was removed from the villages and taken to Inka storage facilities in the capital and redistributed from there.

In addition to working harder for the Inka, women seem to have fared worse than the men when it came to nutrition. Christine Hastorf's chemical analysis of bones from graves of the Inka period suggests that women ate less maize (corn) than did men. It seems that the men were "eating out" more than women. Maize was often consumed as chicha beer, a key component of state-sponsored feasts, which more men than women probably attended. Men also worked more in state-organized agricultural and production projects, where they probably were rewarded with meat, maize, and chicha for their service to the state.

So, under Inka domination, Wanka women had to produce more and received less. Is this a general effect of imperialism? And, if so, why?

Sources: Brumfiel 1992; Costin 2009; Gero and Conkey 1991.

Some archaeologists think that states first evolved around 3500 B.C. in greater Mesopotamia, the area now shared by southern Iraq and southwestern Iran. Archaeologists do not always agree on how a state should be defined, but most think that hierarchical and centralized decision making affecting a substantial population is the key criterion. Other characteristics are usually, but not always, found in these first states. They usually have cities with a substantial part of the population not involved directly in the collection or production of food (which means that people in cities are heavily dependent on people elsewhere); full-time religious and craft specialists; public buildings; and often an official art style. There is a hierarchical social structure topped by an elite class from which the leaders are drawn. The government tries to claim a monopoly on the use of force. (Our own state society says that citizens do not have the right "to take the law into their own hands.") The state uses its force or threat of force to tax its population and to draft people for work or war.[3]

How can archaeologists tell, from the information provided by material remains, whether a society was a state or not? This depends in part on what is used as the criterion for a state. For example, Henry Wright and Gregory Johnson defined a state as a centralized political hierarchy with at least three levels of administration.[4] But how might archaeologists infer that such a hierarchy existed in some area? Wright and Johnson suggested that the way settlement sites differ in size is one indication of how many levels of administration there were in an area.

During the early Uruk period (just before 3500 B.C.), in what is now southwestern Iran, there were some 50 settlements that seem to fall into three groups in terms of size.[5] There were about 45 small villages, three or four "towns," and one large center, Susa. These three types of settlements seem to have been part of a three-level administration hierarchy, because many small villages could not

trade with Susa without passing through a settlement intermediate in size. Because a three-level hierarchy is Wright and Johnson's criterion of a state, they think a state had emerged in the area by early Uruk times.

Evidence from the next period, middle Uruk, suggests more definitely that a state had emerged. This evidence takes the form of clay seals that were apparently used in trading.[6] *Commodity sealings* were used to keep a shipment of goods tightly closed until it reached its destination, and *message sealings* were used to keep track of goods sent and received. The clay seals found in Susa include many message seals and *bullae,* clay containers that served as bills of lading for goods received. The villages, in contrast, had few message seals and bullae. Again, this finding suggests that Susa administered the regional movement of goods and that Susa was the "capital" of the state.

Let us turn now to the major features of the cultural sequences leading to the first states in southern Iraq.

CITIES AND STATES IN SOUTHERN IRAQ

Farming communities older than the first states have not been found in the arid lowland plains of southern Iraq—the area known as Sumer, where some of the earliest cities and states developed (see Figure 2). Perhaps silt from the Tigris and Euphrates rivers has covered them. Or, as has been suggested, Sumer may not have been settled by agriculturalists until people learned how to drain and irrigate river-valley soils otherwise too wet or too dry for cultivation. At any rate, small communities depending partly on agriculture had emerged in the hilly areas north and east of Sumer early in the Neolithic. Later, by about 6000 B.C., a mixed herding and farming economy developed in those areas.

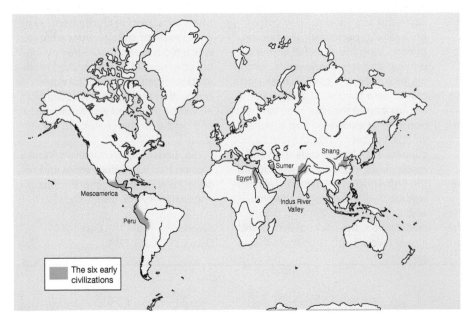

FIGURE 2 Six Early Civilizations

Source: Service 1975.
"Map of the Six Early Civilizations", from The Origins of the State Ad Civilization: The Process of Cultural Evolution by Elman R. Service. Copyright © 1975 by W. W. Norton & Company, Inc. Used by permission of W. W. Norton & Company, Inc.

The Formative Era

Elman Service called the period from about 5000 B.C. to 3500 B.C. the *formative era,* for it saw the coming together of many changes that seem to have played a part in the development of cities and states. Service suggested that, with the development of small-scale irrigation, lowland river areas began to attract settlers. The rivers provided not only water for irrigation but also mollusks, fish, and waterbirds for food. And they provided routes by which to import needed raw materials, such as hardwood and stone, that were lacking in Sumer.

Changes during this period suggest an increasingly complex social and political life. Differences in status are reflected in the burial of statues and ornaments with children. Different villages specialized in the production of different goods—pottery in some, copper and stone tools in others.[7] Temples were built in certain places that may have been centers of political as well as religious authority for several communities.[8] Furthermore, some anthropologists think that chiefdoms, each having authority over several villages, had developed by this time.[9]

Sumerian Civilization

By about 3500 B.C., there were quite a few cities in the area of Sumer. Most were enclosed in a fortress wall and surrounded by an agricultural area. About 3000 B.C., all of Sumer was unified under a single government. After that time, Sumer became an empire. It had great urban centers. Imposing temples, commonly set on artificial mounds, dominated the cities. In the city of Warka, the temple mound was about 150 feet high. The empire was very complex and included an elaborate system for the administration of justice, codified laws, specialized government officials, a professional standing army, and even sewer systems in the cities. Among the many specialized crafts were brickmaking, pottery, carpentry, jewelry making, leatherworking, metallurgy, basketmaking, stonecutting, and sculpture. Sumerians learned to construct and use wheeled wagons, sailboats, horse-drawn chariots, and spears, swords, and armor of bronze.[10]

As economic specialization developed, social stratification became more elaborate. Sumerian documents describe a system of social classes: nobles, priests, merchants, craftworkers, metallurgists, bureaucrats, soldiers, farmers, free citizens, and slaves. Slaves were common in Sumer; they often were captives, brought back as the spoils of war.

We see the first evidence of writing around 3000 B.C. The earliest Sumerian writings were in the form of ledgers containing inventories of items stored in the temples and records of livestock or other items owned or managed by the temples. Sumerian writing was wedge-shaped, or **cuneiform,** formed by pressing a stylus against a damp clay tablet. For contracts and other important documents, the tablet was fired to create a virtually permanent record. Egyptian writing, or hieroglyphics, appeared about the same time. **Hieroglyphics** were written on rolls woven from papyrus reeds, from which our word *paper* derives. The color map on "The Spread of Writing" provides more information about early writing and its spread to other areas.

CITIES AND STATES IN MESOAMERICA

Cities and states emerged in Mesoamerica—Mexico and Central America—later than they did in the Near East. The later appearance of civilization in Mesoamerica may be linked to the later emergence of agriculture in the New World and possibly to the near-absence of large animals such as cattle and horses that could be domesticated.[11] We focus primarily on the developments that led to the rise of the city-state of Teotihuacán, which reached its height shortly after the time of Christ. Teotihuacán is located in a

Examples of two of the earliest writing systems on earth. On the left is a cuneiform tablet and on the right is a section of a hieroglyphic panel.

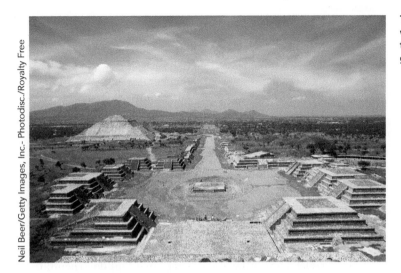

The city of Teotihuacán, which had its peak in A.D. 500, was a planned city built on a grid pattern. At the center was the Pyramid of the Sun, seen in the background on the left here.

valley of the same name, which is the northeastern part of the larger Valley of Mexico.

The Formative Period

The formative period in the area around Teotihuacán (1000 B.C. to 300 B.C.) was characterized initially by small, scattered farming villages on the hilly slopes just south of the Teotihuacán Valley. There were probably a few hundred people in each hamlet, and each of these scattered groups was probably politically autonomous. After about 500 B.C., there seems to have been a population shift to settlements on the valley floor, probably in association with the use of irrigation. Between about 300 B.C. and 200 B.C., small "elite" centers emerged in the valley; each had an earthen or stone raised platform. Residences or small temples of poles and thatch originally stood on these platforms. That some individuals, particularly those in the elite centers, were buried in special tombs supplied with ornaments, headdresses, carved bowls, and a good deal of food indicates some social inequality.[12] The various elite centers may indicate the presence of chiefdoms.

The City and State of Teotihuacán

About 150 years before the time of Christ, no more than a few thousand people lived in scattered villages in the Teotihuacán Valley. In A.D. 100, there was a city of 80,000. By A.D. 500, well over 100,000 people, or approximately 90 percent of the entire valley population, seem to have been drawn or coerced into Teotihuacán.[13]

The layout of the city of Teotihuacán, which shows a tremendous amount of planning, suggests that the valley was politically unified under a centralized state from its beginning. Mapping has revealed that the streets and most of the buildings are laid out in a grid pattern following a basic modular unit of over 613 square feet (57 square meters). Residential structures are often squares of this size, and many streets are spaced according to multiples of the basic unit. Even the river that ran through the center of the city was channeled to conform to the grid pattern. Perhaps the most outstanding feature of the city is the colossal scale of its architecture. Two pyramids dominate the

metropolis, the so-called Pyramid of the Moon and the Pyramid of the Sun. At its base, the latter is as big as the great Pyramid of Cheops in Egypt.

The thousands of residential structures built after A.D. 300 follow a standard pattern. Narrow streets separate the one-story buildings, each of which has high, windowless walls. Patios and shafts provide interior light. The layout of rooms suggests that each building consisted of several apartments; more than 100 people may have lived in one of these apartment compounds. There is variation from compound to compound in the size of rooms and the elaborateness of interior decoration, suggesting considerable variation in wealth.[14]

At the height of its power (A.D. 200 to A.D. 500), the metropolis of Teotihuacán encompassed an area larger than imperial Rome.[15] Much of Mesoamerica seems to have been influenced by Teotihuacán. Archaeologically, its influence is suggested by the extensive spread of Teotihuacán-style pottery and architectural elements. Undoubtedly, large numbers of people in Teotihuacán were engaged in production for, and the conduct of, long-distance trade. Perhaps 25 percent of the city's population worked at various specialized crafts, including the manufacture of projectile points and cutting and scraping tools from volcanic obsidian. Teotihuacán was close to major deposits of obsidian, which was apparently in some demand over much of Mesoamerica. Materials found in graves indicate that there was an enormous flow of foreign goods into the city, including precious stones, feathers from colorful birds in the tropical lowlands, and cotton.[16]

The City of Monte Albán

Teotihuacán probably was not the earliest city-state in Mesoamerica. There is evidence of political unification somewhat earlier, about 500 B.C., in the Valley of Oaxaca, in southern Mexico, with the city of Monte Albán at its center. Monte Albán presents an interesting contrast to Teotihuacán. Whereas Teotihuacán seems to have completely dominated its valley, containing almost all its inhabitants and craftspeople, Monte Albán did not. The various villages in the Valley of Oaxaca seem to have specialized in different crafts, and Monte Albán did not monopolize craft production. After the political unification of the valley, cities and towns other than Monte Albán remained important; the population of Monte Albán grew only to 30,000 or so. Unlike Teotihuacán, Monte Albán was not an important commercial or market center, it was not laid out in a grid pattern, and its architecture was not much different from that of other settlements in the valley.[17]

Monte Albán did not have the kinds of resources that Teotihuacán had. It was located on top of a mountain in the center of the valley, far from either good soil or permanent water supplies that could have been used for irrigation. Even finding drinking water must have been difficult. No natural resources for trade were nearby, nor is there much evidence that Monte Albán was used as a ceremonial center. Because the city was at the top of a steep mountain, it is unlikely that it could have been a central marketplace for valleywide trade.

Why, then, did Monte Albán rise to become one of the early centers of Mesoamerican civilization? Richard Blanton suggested it may have originally been founded in the late formative period (500 B.C. to 400 B.C.) as a neutral place where representatives of the different political units in the valley could reside to coordinate activities affecting the whole valley. Thus, Monte Albán may have been like the cities of Brasília, Washington, DC, and Athens, all of which were originally founded in "neutral," nonproductive areas. Such a center, lacking obvious resources, would not, at least initially, threaten the various political units around it. Later it might become a metropolis dominating a more politically unified region, as Monte Albán came to do in the Valley of Oaxaca.[18]

Other Centers of Mesoamerican Civilization

In addition to Teotihuacán and Oaxaca, there were other Mesoamerican state societies that developed somewhat later. For example, there are a number of centers with monumental architecture, presumably built by speakers of Mayan languages, in the highlands and lowlands of modern-day Guatemala and the Yucatán Peninsula of modern-day Mexico. On the basis of surface appearances, the Mayan centers do not appear to have been as densely populated as Teotihuacán or Monte Albán. But it is now evident that the Mayan centers were more densely populated and more dependent on intensive agriculture than was once thought,[19] and recent translations of Mayan picture writing indicate a much more developed form of writing than previously thought.[20] It is apparent now that Mayan urbanization and cultural complexity were underestimated because of the dense tropical forest that now covers much of the area of Mayan civilization.

THE FIRST CITIES AND STATES IN OTHER AREAS

So far, we have discussed the emergence of cities and states in southern Iraq and Mesoamerica whose development is best, if only imperfectly, known archaeologically. But other state societies probably arose more or less independently in

many other areas of the world as well (see Figure 2). We say "independently" because such states seem to have emerged without colonization or conquest by other states.

Almost at the same time as the Sumerian empire, the great dynastic age was beginning in the Nile Valley in Egypt. The Old Kingdom, or early dynastic period, began about 3100 B.C., with a capital at Memphis. The archaeological evidence from the early centuries is limited, but most of the population appears to have lived in largely self-sufficient villages. Many of the great pyramids and palaces were built around 2500 B.C.[21]

Elsewhere in Africa, states also arose. In what is present-day Ethiopia, the Axum (or Aksum) state evolved beginning sometime early in the 1st millennium A.D., and ultimately became a center of trade and commerce between Africa and the Arabian Peninsula. Among the unique accomplishments of the Axum state were multistory stone residences built in a singular architectural style. Axum is also notable as being perhaps the first officially Christian state in the world.[22]

In sub-Saharan Africa, by A.D. 800, the savanna and forest zones of western Africa had a succession of city-states. One of them was called Ghana, and it became a major source of gold for the Mediterranean world (as did other states in what came to be known as the "Gold Coast").[23] In the Congo River basin, a powerful kingdom had evolved

Archaeologists examining hieroglyphs in the ruins of Abusir at the ancient capital of Egypt, Memphis.

Kenneth Garrett/NGS Image Collection

Artist's reconstruction of the ancient city of Harappa. Despite large public works like this water control system, there was little display of grandeur at Harappa. Unlike many other ancient civilizations, all Harappan cities were laid out according to the same basic plan.

by A.D. 1200, with cities described as having tens of thousands of residences and a king that was recognized as an equal by the Portuguese king in the early 1500s.[24] Farther south, states apparently arose in several areas early in the 2nd millennium A.D. One of these was responsible for the large, circular stone structures known today as the Great Zimbabwe.[25]

In the Indus Valley of northwestern India, a large state society had developed by 2300 B.C. This Harappan civilization did not have much in the way of monumental architecture, such as pyramids and palaces, and it was also unusual in other respects. The state apparently controlled an enormous territory—over a million square kilometers. There was not just one major city but many, each built according to a similar pattern and with a municipal water and sewage system.[26]

The Shang dynasty in northern China (1750 B.C.) has long been cited as the earliest state society in the Far East.

But recent research suggests that an even earlier one, the Xia dynasty, may have emerged in the same general area by 2200 B.C.[27] In any case, the Shang dynasty had all the earmarks of statehood: a stratified, specialized society; religious, economic, and administrative unification; and a distinctive art style.[28]

In South America, a group of distinct state societies may have emerged as early as 2500 B.C. in the Supe and Pativilca valleys north of Lima, Peru. The valley contains a group of large cities that seem to have been interdependent—cities on the coast supplied inland cities with fish, whereas inland cities served as political and economic centers. The cities contain plaza areas and large pyramids, which are thought to be temple structures.[29] After 200 B.C. the major river valleys leading from the Andes to the sea witnessed the development of a complex agricultural system dependent on irrigation. The separate, but similar, states participated in a widespread system of religious symbols and beliefs called Chavín. The various states included the well-known Moche state, creators of some of the most remarkable effigy ceramics ever known, and the Nazca state, the people of which constructed a huge landscape of intaglios (inscribed images and lines) on the hard ground of highland deserts. By A.D. 700, these regional states were integrated into a large, militaristic empire called Wari (or Huari).[30]

And in North America, a huge settlement, with over 100 earthen mounds (one of them, Monk's Mound, is the largest pre-Columbian structure north of Mexico), and covering an area of more than 5 square miles (13 square kilometers), developed near present-day St. Louis late in the 1st millennium A.D. The site is called Cahokia, and it was certainly the center of a large and powerful chiefdom. Whether it had achieved a state level of organization is controversial. There is evidence for religious and craft specialists and there is clear social stratification, but whether or not the leaders of Cahokian society were able to govern by force is still unclear.[31]

Artist's reconstruction of what Cahokia may have looked like during its fluorescence.

THEORIES ABOUT THE ORIGIN OF THE STATE

We have seen that states developed in many parts of the world. Why did they evolve when and where they did? A number of theories have been proposed. We consider those that archaeologists have discussed frequently.[32]

Irrigation

Irrigation seems to have been important in many of the areas in which early state societies developed. Irrigation made the land habitable or productive in parts of Mesoamerica, southern Iraq, the Nile Valley, China, and South America. It has been suggested that the labor and management needed for the upkeep of an irrigation system led to the formation of a political elite, the overseers of the system, who eventually became the governors of the society.[33] Proponents of this view believe that both the city and civilization were outgrowths of the administrative requirements of an irrigation system.

Critics note that this theory does not seem to apply to all areas where cities and states may have emerged independently. For example, in southern Iraq, the irrigation systems serving the early cities were generally small and probably did not require extensive labor and management. Large-scale irrigation works were not constructed until after cities had been fully established.[34] Thus, irrigation could not have been the main stimulus for the development of cities and states in Sumer. Even in China, for which the irrigation theory was first formulated, there is no evidence of large-scale irrigation as early as Shang times.[35]

Although large-scale irrigation may not always have preceded the emergence of the first cities and states, even small-scale irrigation systems could have resulted in unequal access to productive land and so may have contributed to the development of a stratified society.[36] In addition, irrigation systems may have given rise to border and other disputes between adjacent groups, thereby prompting people to concentrate in cities for defense and stimulating the development of military and political controls.[37] Finally, as Robert Adams and Elman Service both suggested, the main significance of irrigation, either large or small scale, may have been its intensification of production, a development that in turn may have indirectly stimulated craft specialization, trade, and administrative bureaucracy.[38]

Population Growth, Circumscription, and War

Robert Carneiro has suggested that states may emerge because of population growth in an area that is physically or socially limited. Competition and warfare in such a situation may lead to the subordination of defeated groups, who are obliged to pay tribute and to submit to the control of a more powerful group.[39] Carneiro illustrated his theory by describing how states may have emerged on the northern coast of Peru.

After the people of that area first settled into an agricultural village life, population grew at a slow, steady rate. Initially, new villages were formed as population grew. But in the narrow coastal valleys—blocked by high mountains, fronted by the sea, and surrounded by desert—this splintering-off process could not continue indefinitely. The result, according to Carneiro, was increasing land shortage and warfare between villages as they competed for land. Because the high mountains, the sea, and the desert blocked any escape for losers, the defeated villagers had no choice but to submit to political domination. In this way, chiefdoms may have become kingdoms as the most powerful villages grew to control entire valleys. As chiefs' power expanded over several valleys, states and empires may have been born.

Carneiro noted that physical or environmental circumscription may not be the only kind of barrier that gives rise to a state. Social circumscription may be just as important. People living at the center of a high-density area may find that their migration is blocked by surrounding settlements just as effectively as it could be by mountains, sea, and desert.

Marvin Harris suggested a somewhat different form of circumscription. He argued that the first states with their coercive authority could emerge only in areas that supported intensive grain agriculture (and the possibility of high food production) and were surrounded by areas that could not support intensive grain agriculture. So people in such areas might put up with the coercive authority of a state because they would suffer a sharp drop in living standards if they moved away.[40]

Carneiro suggested that his theory applies to many areas besides the northern coast of Peru, including southern Iraq and the Indus and Nile valleys. Although there were no geographic barriers in areas such as northern China or the Mayan lowlands on the Yucatán Peninsula, the development of states in those areas may have been the result of social circumscription. Carneiro's theory seems to be supported for southern Iraq, where there is archaeological evidence of population growth, circumscription, and warfare.[41] And there is evidence of population growth before the emergence of the state in the Teotihuacán Valley.[42]

But population growth does not necessarily mean population pressure. For example, the populations in the Teotihuacán and Oaxaca valleys apparently did increase prior to state development, but there is no evidence that they had even begun to approach the limits of their resources. More people could have lived in both places.[43] Nor is population growth definitely associated with state formation in all areas where early states arose. For example, according to Wright and Johnson, there was population growth long before states emerged in southwestern Iran, but the population apparently declined just before the states emerged.[44]

In addition, Carneiro's circumscription theory leaves an important logical question unanswered: Why would the victors in war let the defeated populations remain and pay tribute? If the victors wanted the land so much in the first place, why wouldn't they try to exterminate the defeated and occupy the land themselves, which has happened many times in history?

Local and Long-Distance Trade

It has been suggested that trade was a factor in the emergence of the earliest states.[45] Wright and Johnson theorized that the organizational requirements of producing items for export, redistributing the items imported, and defending trading parties would foster state formation.[46] Does the archaeological evidence support such a theory?

In southern Iraq and the Mayan lowlands, long-distance trade routes may indeed have stimulated bureaucratic growth. In the lowlands of southern Iraq, as we have seen, people needed wood and stone for building, and they traded with highland people for those items. In the Mayan lowlands, the development of civilization seems to have been preceded by long-distance trade. Farmers in the lowland regions traded with faraway places to obtain salt, obsidian for cutting blades, and hard stone for grinding tools.[47] In southwestern Iran, long-distance trade did not become very important until after Susa became the center of a state society, but short-distance trade may have played the same kind of role in the formation of states.

Kwang-chih Chang put forward a similar theory for the origin of states in China. He suggested that Neolithic societies in the Yellow River valley developed a long-distance trade network, which he called an *interaction sphere*, by about 4000 B.C. Trade spread cultural elements among the societies in the interaction sphere, so that they came to share some common elements (see Figure 3). Over time, these societies came to depend on each other both as trade partners and as cultural partners, and around 2000 B.C., they unified into a single political unit under the Shang dynasty.[48] Thus, Chang sees political unification in China as an outgrowth of a preexisting system of trade and cultural interaction.

The Various Theories: An Evaluation

Why do states form? As of now, no one theory seems to fit all the known situations. The reason may be that different conditions in different places may have favored the emergence of centralized government. After all, the state, by definition, implies an ability to organize large populations for a collective purpose. In some areas, this purpose may have been the need to organize trade with local or far-off regions. In other cases, the state may have emerged as a way to control defeated populations in circumscribed areas. In still other instances, a combination of factors may have fostered the development of the state type of political system.[49]

THE CONSEQUENCES OF STATE FORMATION

We have considered several areas where states arose, as well as a number of theories to explain the origin of states. But what were the consequences for the people living in those societies? The consequences seem to have been dramatic.

One of the ways states change the lifestyles of people is by allowing for larger and denser populations.[50] As we have already seen, agriculture itself gives populations the potential to grow, and the development of a state only furthers that potential. Why? Because a state is able to build infrastructure—irrigation systems, roadways, markets—that allows both the production and distribution of agricultural products to become more efficient. States are able to coordinate information as well, and can use that information to manage agricultural production cycles and to anticipate or manage droughts, blights, or other natural disasters. States are also able to control access to land (through laws and a military) and thus can both maintain farmers on the land and prevent others (from either within or outside of the state) from removing the farmers or interfering with their ability to produce food.

With increased efficiency of agricultural production and distribution, states also allow many (if not most) people in the society to be relieved of food production. These people are freed to become craftspeople, merchants, and artists, as well as bureaucrats, soldiers, and political leaders. People may also live apart from agricultural fields, and thus cities with dense populations can arise. Cities can also arise in locations that are not suited to agriculture but that perhaps are suited to trade (such as the cities on rivers in southern Mesopotamia) or defense (such as on top of a mountain, as in the case of Monte Albán). Art, music, and literature often flourish in such contexts, and these too are often consequences of the rise of states. Organized religion also often develops after states appear. Thus, all the hallmarks we associate with civilization can be seen as resulting from the evolution of states.[51]

The development of states can have many negative impacts as well. When states develop, people become

FIGURE 3 Expansion of Regional Neolithic Cultures in China, 4000 B.C. to 3000 B.C.

Source: Chang 1986.
From *Archaeology of Ancient China*, 4th ed., by K.-C. Chang (New Haven: Yale, 1986).

migrants and immigrants

Imperialism, Colonialism, and the State

The first city-states seem to have emerged during the Uruk period, roughly the 4th millennium B.C., in the river valleys of southern Mesopotamia, now southern Iraq. From their very beginnings, these first city-states had "foreign trade." This trade may have been indispensable; the riverine environment, though fertile when drained and irrigated, lacked necessary raw materials such as hardwood and stone. The trade with other areas could have been peaceful and balanced, as between equals. After all, it is possible that when one area has something that another wants, and vice versa, the people on both sides could voluntarily arrange to satisfy each other's needs by bargaining and negotiating. But the archaeological evidence from the preliterate Uruk period, as well as the documentary evidence for shortly afterward, suggests that the first city-states in Mesopotamia were engaged in imperialism and colonialism from their very beginnings.

Just like the British and French, who first came to North America to explore and trade and often used force to protect their settlements and access to trade items, the Uruk city-states seem also to have dominated their peripheral, less developed trading "partners." For example, before 3000 B.C. there were fortified towns with Uruk-style pottery and administrative artifacts at river junctions in the north of Mesopotamia. Why did the Uruk people go there? One possibility is that they deliberately built outposts to secure their access to needed trade goods, including hides and dried meat.

There was no single state involved in this imperialism and colonialism. Southern Mesopotamia (Sumer) was not politically unified until after 3000 B.C. Rather, the various Uruk period polities of the Tigris and Euphrates river valleys seem to have been intensely competitive. The walls around the cities indicate that they were probably subject to attack by their rivals at any time. The picture is

reminiscent of the Greek city-states described by Thucydides. It is also like the picture we get from the hieroglyphic writings of the Maya city-states in and around southern Mexico (A.D. 300 to A.D. 800), which, in a mixture of history and propaganda, extol the triumphs of the various rivalrous rulers. And, of course, we are all familiar with how Britain and Spain and Holland and France were rivalrous before and after the New World was discovered.

We know that the Greek city-states were imperialistic colonizers because we have historical evidence of the fact. Greek speakers, from Athens and other polities, established colonies all over the Mediterranean—Syracuse in Sicily and Marseilles in France, for example. But what about the Uruk city-states? Why should we think they too were imperialistic colonizers? Archaeologist Guillermo Algaze recently reviewed the evidence. First, there was the colonization of the plains of southwestern Iran, which people could get to from southern Mesopotamia in seven to ten days by foot or donkey caravan. Then, and maybe overlapping with the expansion into southwestern Iran, the Uruk polities established outposts or took over already existing settlements to the north and northwest, on the plains of what are now northern Iraq and Syria; these latter settlements were apparently all located at intersections of the important waterways and overland routes.

According to Algaze, the Uruk enclaves and outposts outside southern Mesopotamia fit what comparative historian Philip Curtin calls trade diaspora. Curtin thinks that such movements develop after the emergence of cities, with their vulnerable populations. (An urban population is vulnerable because a city, by definition, is inhabited mostly by people who are dependent for their food on people who live outside the city.) Diaspora have taken various forms, but they all represent ways to organize exchange between areas with different but

complementary resources. At one end of the range of possibilities—involving little or no political organization—commercial specialists remove themselves from their own society and settle as aliens somewhere else. At the other end of the range of variation—the most politically organized—the expanding polity is involved from the beginning in the founding of outposts that secure the required trade.

Algaze thinks that the Uruk expansion was motivated by a lack of resources in southern Mesopotamia. But is that a complete explanation? Other areas of the world, at the time and since, have lacked resources, but they did not all become imperialistic colonizers. So what else, in addition to the need for external resources, might explain the Uruk expansion? And how can we explain why it eventually stopped? Algaze notes that, when the Uruk settlers moved into southwestern Iran, they were entering an area that was not so densely settled, so they may have encountered only minimal resistance. Indeed, the various Uruk period enclaves and outposts outside southern Mesopotamia were apparently larger and more complex than any previous communities in the peripheral areas. Perhaps, then, imperialism and colonialism are possible only in a world of unequals.

Years ago, anthropologist Stanley Diamond argued that "imperialism and colonialism are as old as the State." Does this mean that states are likely to practice imperialism and colonialism if they can get away with it? Or are only some conditions likely to predispose states to imperialism and colonialism? How strongly are imperialism and colonialism linked to state organization anyway? What makes a humane state possible? Perhaps future research, particularly cross-cultural and cross-historical research, will tell us.

Sources: Algaze 1993; Curtin 1984; Diamond 1974; Marcus 2009; Zeder 1994, 97–126.

Shown is a street in the old city of Jaipur, India. The rise of states allows cities with dense populations to develop and, along with them, the many potentials and problems that cities and their populations create.

© Paul Harris/Stone/Getty Images, Inc.

governed by force and are no longer able to say "no" to their leaders. Police and military forces can become instruments of oppression and terror.[52] On a less obvious level, the class stratification of states creates differences in access to resources and an underclass of poor, uneducated, and frequently unhealthy people. Health issues are exacerbated by the concentration of people in cities, an environment in which epidemic diseases can flourish.[53] Without direct access to food supplies, people in cities also face the threat of malnutrition or outright starvation if food production and distribution systems fail.[54]

All states appear to be expansionistic, and the emergence of state warfare and conquest seems one of the most striking negative impacts of the evolution of states. In fact, more human suffering can probably be linked to state expansion than to any other single factor. Why do states expand? One basic reason may be that they are able to (see the box "Imperialism, Colonialism, and the State"). States have standing armies ready to fight or be sent to conquer enemies. Another reason for state expansion might be related to the threat of famine and disease, which is more likely with intensive agriculture.[55] The Embers have found that, in recent societies, resource unpredictability is strongly associated with a higher frequency of warfare, and states fearful of shortfalls in resources may resort to war ahead of time as a means of gaining access to more resources (or of limiting the unpredictability of resources).[56] A third answer to the question of why states tend to expand might be that belligerence is simply part of the nature of states. States often arise through military

means, and it may be vital to the continuation of some states that military power be continually demonstrated.[57] Regardless of the causes, war and conquest are the consequences of state formation. Often, too, defeat in war is the fate of states.

THE DECLINE AND COLLAPSE OF STATES

When you look over the list of ancient states we have discussed in this chapter—Monte Albán, Teotihuacán, Sumer, pharonic Egypt—you will notice one element common to them all: Each eventually collapsed; none maintained its power and influence into historic times. Why? It is an important question because, if collapse is the ultimate fate of many if not all states, then we can anticipate that our own state is likely to collapse eventually. Perhaps knowing something about how and why other states have fallen can prevent (or at least hold off) the fall of our own.

One suggested explanation for the decline and collapse of states is environmental degradation. If states originally arose where the environment was conducive to intensive agriculture and harvests big enough to support social stratification, political officials, and a state type of political system, then perhaps environmental degradation—declining soil productivity, persistent drought, and the like—contributed to the collapse of ancient states. Archaeologist Harvey Weiss has suggested that persistent drought helped to bring about the fall of the ancient Akkadian empire, in the Near East. By 2300 B.C., the Akkadians had established an empire stretching over 800 miles (1,300 kilometers) from the Persian Gulf in what is now Iraq to the headwaters of the Euphrates River in what is now Turkey. But a century later, the empire collapsed. Weiss thinks that a long-term drought brought the empire down, as well as other civilizations around at that time too. Many archaeologists doubted there was such a widespread drought, but new evidence indicates that the worst dry spell of the past 10,000 years began just as the Akkadians' northern stronghold was being abandoned.[58] The evidence of the drought, windblown dust in sediment retrieved from the bottom of the Persian Gulf, indicates that the dry spell lasted 300 years. Other geophysical evidence suggests that the drought was worldwide.[59]

Environmental degradation may also have contributed to the collapse of Mayan civilization.[60] The Mayans built large temple complexes in the lowland regions of Mexico and the Yucatán Peninsula beginning about A.D. 250, but after about A.D. 750, construction ceased, and by about A.D. 900, the temple complexes appear to have been all but abandoned. Lake sediments show that the region the Maya inhabited experienced an extended period of drought lasting between roughly A.D. 800 and A.D. 1000. The Maya, who depended on rainfall agriculture for subsistence, may not have been able to produce enough food in areas around temple complexes during this long period of drought to feed the resident populations. People would have been forced to move into less populated areas to survive, and the temple complexes would have slowly been abandoned.[61]

applied anthropology

The Archaeology of Environmental Collapse

In *The Life of Reason*, philosopher George Santayana (1905) wrote "Those who cannot remember the past are condemned to repeat it." Archaeologists have long sought to provide a way for government agencies to remember the past so that mistakes will not be repeated. Today, the world's governments are struggling with problems of environmental degradation and global warming, but this is nothing new to archaeologists. States have routinely damaged or even destroyed their environments and either developed solutions or have collapsed.

In the 1990s, the European Union (EU) decided that an archaeological perspective might help them to better understand the problem of land degradation within Europe. A team of archaeologists, geographers, environmental scientists, and others developed the ARCHAEOMEDES project for the EU, with the expressed purpose of developing a long-term perspective on the problem of land degradation. To date, the ARCHAEOMEDES team has completed case studies on four situations of land degradation spanning the range of human history in Europe from the Bronze Age to the present, and more are planned.

One example is the Rhône Valley of southeastern France. During the first few centuries A.D., the Rhône experienced a major period of Roman colonization. Hundreds of new towns emerged, transportation and water management systems were put in place, and thousands of acres were brought into agricultural production. Much of the agricultural production was market-oriented, particularly olive oil and wine. But, by the fifth century A.D., much of the region had been deserted, and agricultural land had been degraded (mainly by erosion) to the point that some has not yet recovered. What happened?

The ARCHAEOMEDES team found that the answer was complex. Minor climatic fluctuations increased the amount of rainfall and runoff from the Alps, causing periodic floods that forced farmers to abandon large parts of the Rhône floodplain. But water control systems the Romans put in place exacerbated the problem, extending flooding to other areas and fostering high levels of erosion.

The ARCHAEOMEDES team concluded that the environmental crisis of the first centuries A.D. in the Rhône Valley were largely political and economic in their origins. The changes Roman colonists imposed on the Rhône Valley triggered land degradation because the infrastructure could only be sustained during good times. When too much rain fell, flooding could not be controlled, and the system collapsed. The lesson seems clear. The environment itself did not collapse; human alterations to the environment could not adapt to "normal" fluctuations in the climate, and sparked an environmental crisis. It is a lesson the ARCHAEOMEDES team hopes European governments will take to heart.

Sources: Redman 1999; van der Leeuw 1998; van der Leeuw et al. 2002.

Environmental degradation may occur for reasons other than natural events. The behavior of humans may sometimes be responsible. Consider the collapse of Cahokia, a city of at least 15,000 people that thrived for a while in the area where the Missouri and Mississippi rivers converge. In the 12th century A.D., Cahokia had large public plazas, a city wall constructed from some 20,000 logs, and massive mounds. But within 300 years, only the mounds were left. Silt from flooding covered former croplands and settled areas. Geographer Bill Woods thinks that overuse of woodlands for fuel, construction, and defense led to deforestation, flooding, and persistent crop failure. The result was the abandonment of Cahokia. Timber depletion is also indicated by studies of charcoal from excavations in the area. Apparently the quality of wood used in construction declined over time, suggesting that choice trees got scarcer.[62]

Cahokia is just one example of degradation that may have been caused by human behavior. Another example is the increasing saltiness of soils caused by evaporation of water from fields that have been irrigated over long periods of time, as in what is now southern Iraq.

Civilizations may sometimes decline because human behavior has increased the incidence of disease. As we noted, many lowland Mayan cities were abandoned between A.D. 800 and A.D. 1000, possibly because of drought. But another factor may have been the increasing incidence of yellow fever. The clearing of forests and the consequent increase of breeding sites for mosquitoes may have favored the spread of the disease from areas farther south in Central America. Or the planting of particular trees by the Mayans in their urban areas may have increased the populations of coresident monkeys who carried the disease (which mosquitoes transmitted to people).[63]

Another reason that some states have collapsed appears to be overextension. This is often one of the reasons given for the decline of the Roman Empire. By the time of its fall, beginning in the 2nd century A.D., the empire had expanded throughout the Mediterranean region and into northwestern Europe. That huge area may simply have been too large to administer. "Barbarian" incursions on the peripheries of the empire went unchecked because it was too difficult, and too costly, to reinforce these far-flung frontiers. Sometimes these incursions became

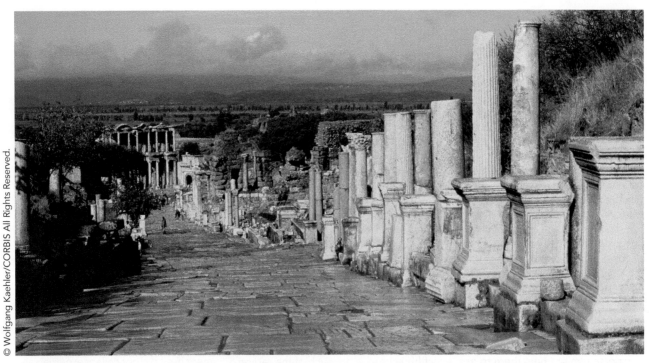

The history of Ephesus, a former city lying in ruins in what is now western Turkey, illustrates the waxing and waning of states and empires. From about 1000 B.C. to 100 B.C., it was controlled by the Greeks, Lydians, Persians, Macedonians, and Romans, among others.

wholesale invasions that were exacerbated by famines, plagues, and poor leadership. By the time the last Roman emperor of the West was deposed in A.D. 476, the empire had withered to virtually nothing.[64]

Finally, internal conflict because of leaders' mismanagement or exploitation has been put forward to explain the collapse of states. For example, Peter Charanis has argued that the Byzantine Empire (the eastern half of the Roman Empire) collapsed because large, powerful landholders had been allowed to take over the land of too many small holders, creating a group of overtaxed, exploited peasants with no interest in maintaining the empire. When the landholders began vying with the emperor for power, civil wars erupted, leading to disunity that left the empire vulnerable to conquest.[65]

Many other ideas have been put forward to explain collapse, ranging from catastrophes to almost mystical factors such as "social decadence," but, as with theories for the origin of states, no single explanation seems to fit all or even most of the situations. Although it is still not clear what specific conditions led to the emergence, or collapse, of the state in each of the early centers of civilization, the question of why states form and decline is a lively focus of research today. More satisfactory answers may come out of ongoing and future investigations.

SUMMARY ● ○ ○

1. Archaeologists do not always agree on how a state should be defined, but most seem to agree that hierarchical and centralized decision making affecting a substantial population is the key criterion. Most states have cities with public buildings, full-time craft and religious specialists, an official art style, and a hierarchical social structure topped by an elite class from which the leaders are drawn. Most states maintain power with a monopoly on the use of force. The state uses force or the threat of force to tax its population and to draft people for work or war.

2. Early state societies arose within the Near East in what is now southern Iraq and southwestern Iran. Southern Iraq, or Sumer, was unified under a single government just after 3000 B.C. It had writing, large urban centers, imposing temples, codified laws, a standing army, wide trade networks, a complex irrigation system, and a high degree of craft specialization.

3. Probably the earliest city-state in Mesoamerica developed around 500 B.C. in the Valley of Oaxaca, with a capital at Monte Albán. Somewhat later, in the northeastern section of the Valley of Mexico, Teotihuacán developed. At the height of its power, A.D. 200 to A.D. 500, the city-state of Teotihuacán appears to have influenced much of Mesoamerica.

4. City-states arose early in other parts of the New World: in Guatemala, the Yucatán Peninsula of Mexico, Peru, and possibly near St. Louis, Missouri. In the Old World, early states developed in Africa, the Indus Valley of India, and northern China.

5. There are several theories of why states arose. The irrigation theory suggests that the administrative needs of maintaining extensive irrigation systems may have been the impetus for state formation. The circumscription theory suggests that states emerge when competition and warfare in circumscribed areas lead to the subordination of defeated groups, which are obliged to submit to the control of the most powerful

group. Theories involving trade suggest that the organizational requirements of producing exportable items, redistributing imported items, and defending trading parties would foster state formation. Which is correct? At this point, no one theory is able to explain the formation of every state. Perhaps different organizational requirements in different areas all favored centralized government.

6. When states arise, they have a dramatic impact. Populations grow and become concentrated in cities. Agriculture becomes more efficient, allowing many people to be removed from food production. States provide a context in which what we commonly call civilization—art, music, literature, and organized religion—can develop and flourish. But states also provide a context in which warfare and political terror can flourish. The social differentiation found in states produces an underclass of poor and often unhealthy people. States are prone to epidemic disease and periodic famine.

7. All ancient states collapsed eventually. Although we have no good answers to the question of why states collapse, research into this question may have implications for prolonging the lives of our modern state systems.

GLOSSARY TERMS ○ ● ○

civilization	hieroglyphics
cuneiform	state

CRITICAL QUESTIONS ○ ○ ●

1. Cities and states did not appear until after the emergence of food production. Why might food production be necessary, but not sufficient, for cities and states to develop?

2. Like the emergence of food production, the earliest cities and states developed within a few thousand years of each other. What might be the reasons?

3. Can you imagine a future world without states? What conditions might lead to that "state" of the world?

PEARSON
myanthrolab

Read the chapter by Joyce Marcus titled "Maya Hieroglyphs: History or Propaganda?" on MyAnthroLab. Answer the following questions:

1. Marcus describes a series of "pendulum swings" in the study of Mayan writing. What does she mean by a "pendulum swing"? Give an example.

2. How has the decipherment of Mayan writing led scholars to question the histories it apparently was used to convey?

3. What does Marcus mean by Maya "propaganda"? How might Mayan kings have used "propaganda"?

NOTES ● ○ ○

1. Wenke 1990; Connah 1987; Service 1975.
2. Flannery 1972.
3. Flannery 1972; Redman 1978, 215–16.
4. Wright and Johnson 1975.
5. The discussion in the remainder of this section draws from Wright and Johnson 1975; see also G. Johnson 1987.
6. Wright and Johnson 1975.
7. Flannery 1972.
8. Service 1975, 207.
9. Service 1975; Flannery 1972.
10. This description of Sumerian civilization is based on Kramer 1963.
11. Diamond 1989.
12. Helms 1975, 34–36, 54–55; Sanders et al. 1979.
13. Millon 1967.
14. Millon 1976.
15. Millon 1967.
16. Helms 1975, 61–63; Weaver 1993.
17. Blanton 1981; J. Marcus 1983.
18. Blanton 1976; 1978.
19. B. Turner 1970; Harrison and Turner 1978.
20. Houston 1988.
21. Wenke 1984, 289.
22. Connah 1987, 67.
23. Fagan 1989, 428–30.
24. Connah 1987, 216–17.
25. Vogel 2009.
26. Wenke 1984, 305–20.
27. Chang 1981.
28. Chang 1968, 235–55.
29. Solis et al. 2001; Haas et al. 2004.
30. For an overview, see Lumbreras 1974.
31. M. Fowler 1975.
32. For a more complete review of the available theories, see various chapters in Cohen and Service 1978; see also Chapter 1 in Zeder 1991.
33. Wittfogel 1957.
34. Adams 1960; H. T. Wright 1986.
35. Wheatley 1971, 291.
36. Adams 1960.
37. Adams 1981: 244.
38. Adams 1981, 243; Service 1975, 274–75.
39. Carneiro 1970; Sanders and Price 1968, 230–32.
40. M. Harris 1979, 101–02.
41. T. C. Young 1972.
42. Sanders and Price 1968, 141.
43. Blanton et al. 1981, 224. For the apparent absence of population pressure in the Teotihuacàn Valley, see Brumfiel 1976. For the Oaxaca Valley, see Feinman et al. 1985.
44. Wright and Johnson 1975. Carneiro 1988, however, argued the opposite, that the population grew just before the states emerged in southwestern Iran. Whether or not population declined, Frank Hole (1994) has suggested that climate change around that time may have forced local populations to relocate, some to centers that became cities.
45. Polanyi et al. 1957, 257–62; Sanders 1968.
46. Wright and Johnson 1975.
47. Rathje 1971.
48. Chang 1986, 234–94.
49. For a discussion of how political dynamics may play an important role in state formation, see Brumfiel 1983.
50. Johnson and Earle 1987, 324–26.
51. Childe 1950.
52. Service 1975, 12–15, 89–90.

53. J. Diamond 1997a, 205–07.
54. Dirks 1993.
55. Johnson and Earle 1987, 243–48, 304–06.
56. C. R. Ember and M. Ember 1992.
57. Ferguson and Whitehead 1992.
58. Weiss et al. 1993.
59. Kerr 1998; Grossman 2002.
60. Haug et al. 2003.
61. DeMenocal 2001; Haug et al. 2003; Hodell et al. 2001.
62. Holden 1996.
63. Wilkinson 1995.
64. Tainter 1988, 128–52.
65. Charanis 1953.

Culture and Culture Change

From Chapter 14 of *Anthropology*, 13/e. Carol R. Ember. Melvin Ember. Peter N. Peregrine. Copyright © 2011 by Pearson Education. Published by Prentice Hall. All rights reserved.

Culture and Culture Change

W e all consider ourselves to be unique individuals with our own set of personal opinions, preferences, habits, and quirks. Indeed, all of us are unique; and yet most of us also share many feelings, beliefs, and habits with most of the people who live in our society. If we live in North America, we are likely to have the feeling that eating dogs is wrong, have the belief that bacteria or viruses cause illness, and have the habit of sleeping on a bed. Most people hardly ever think about the ideas and customs they share with other people in their society, assuming them to be "natural." These ideas and behaviors are part of what we mean by *culture*. We only begin to become aware that our culture is different when we become aware that other peoples have different feelings, different beliefs, and different habits from ours. So most North Americans would never even think of the possibility of eating dog meat if they did not know that people in some other societies commonly do so. They would not realize that their belief in germs was cultural if they were not aware that people in some societies think that witchcraft or evil spirits causes illness. They might not become aware that it is their custom to sleep on beds if they were not aware that people in many societies sleep on the floor or on the ground. Only when we compare ourselves with people in other societies may we become aware of cultural differences and similarities. This is, in fact, the way that anthropology as a profession began. When Europeans began to explore and move to faraway places, they were forced to confront the sometimes striking facts of cultural variation.

Most of us are aware that "times have changed," especially when we compare our lives with those of our parents. Some of the most dramatic changes have occurred in attitudes about sex and marriage, changes in women's roles, and changes in technology. But such culture change is not unusual. Throughout history, humans have replaced or altered customary behaviors and attitudes as their needs have changed. Just as no individual is immortal, no particular cultural pattern is impervious to change. Anthropologists want to understand how and why such change occurs. Culture change may be gradual or rapid. Although there has always been contact between different societies, contact between faraway cultures through exploration, colonization, trade, and more recently multinational business has accelerated the pace of change within the last 600 years or so. Globalization has made the world more and more interconnected. We conclude this chapter with a discussion of the future of cultural diversity.

● ○ ●

DEFINING CULTURE

In everyday usage, the word *culture* refers to a desirable quality we can acquire by attending a sufficient number of plays and concerts and visiting art museums and galleries. Anthropologists, however, have a different definition, as Ralph Linton explained:

Culture refers to the total way of life of any society, not simply to those parts of this way which the society regards as higher or more desirable. Thus culture, when applied to our own way of life, has nothing to do with playing the piano or reading Browning. For the social scientist such activities are simply elements within the totality of our culture. This totality also includes such mundane activities as washing dishes or driving an automobile, and for the purposes of cultural studies these stand quite on a par with "the finer things of life." It follows that for the social scientist there are no uncultured societies or even individuals. Every society has a culture, no matter how simple this culture may be, and every human being is cultured, in the sense of participating in some culture or other.[1]

Culture, then, refers to innumerable aspects of life, including many things we consider ordinary. Linton emphasized common habits and behaviors in what he considered culture, but the totality of life also includes not just what people do, but also how they commonly think and feel. As we define it here, **culture** is the set of learned behaviors and ideas (including beliefs, attitudes, values, and ideals) that are characteristic of a particular society or other social group. Behaviors can also produce products or *material culture*—things like houses, musical instruments, and tools that are the products of customary behavior.

Different kinds of groups can have cultures. People come to share behaviors and ideas because they communicate with and observe each other. Although groups from families to societies share cultural traits, anthropologists have traditionally been concerned with the cultural characteristics of *societies*. Many anthropologists define **society** as a group of people who occupy a particular territory and speak a common language not generally understood by neighboring peoples. By this definition, societies may or may not correspond to countries. There are many countries, particularly newer ones, that have within their boundaries different peoples speaking mutually unintelligible languages. By our definition of society, such countries are composed of many different societies and therefore many cultures. Also, by our definition of society, some societies may even include more than one country. For example, we would have to say that Canada and the United States form a single society because the two groups generally speak English, live next to each other, and share many common ideas and behaviors. That is why we refer to "North American culture" in this chapter. The terms *society* and *culture* are not synonymous. Society refers to a group of people; culture refers to the learned and shared behaviors, ideas, and characteristic of those people. As we will discuss shortly, we also have to be careful to describe culture as of particular time period; what is characteristic of one time may not be characteristic of another.

Culture Is Commonly Shared

If only one person thinks or does a certain thing, that thought or action represents a personal habit, not a pattern of culture. For a thought or action to be considered cultural, some social group must commonly share it. We usually share many behaviors and ideas with our families and friends. We commonly share cultural characteristics with those whose ethnic or regional origins, religious affiliations, and occupations are the same as or similar to our own. We share certain practices and ideas with most people in our society. We also share some cultural traits with people beyond our society who have similar interests (such as rules for international sporting events) or similar roots (as do the various English-speaking nations).

When we talk about the commonly shared customs of *a* society, which constitute the traditional and central concern of cultural anthropology, we are referring to *a* culture. When we talk about the commonly shared customs of a group within a society, which are a central concern of sociologists and increasingly of concern to anthropologists, we are referring to a **subculture.** (A subculture is not necessarily the same as an ethnic group. When we study the commonly shared customs of some group that includes different societies, we are talking about a phenomenon for which we do not have a single word—for example, as when we refer to *Western culture* (the cultural characteristics of societies in or derived from Europe) or the *culture of poverty* (the presumed cultural characteristics of poor people the world over).

We must remember that, even when anthropologists refer to something as cultural, there is always individual variation, which means that not everyone in a society shares a particular cultural characteristic of that society. For example, it is cultural in North American society for adults to live apart from their parents. But not all adults in our society do so, nor do all adults wish to do so. The custom of living apart from parents is considered cultural because

A daughter braids her doll's hair, imitating what her mother is doing.

most adults practice that custom. In every society studied by anthropologists—in the simplest as well as the most complex—individuals do not all think and act the same.[2] Indeed, individual variation is a major source of new culture.[3]

Culture Is Learned

Not all things shared generally by a group are cultural. Typical hair color is not cultural, nor is eating. For something to be considered cultural, it must be learned as well as shared. A typical hair color (unless dyed) is not cultural because it is genetically determined. Humans eat because they must; but what and when and how they eat are learned and vary from culture to culture. Most North Americans do not consider dog meat edible, and indeed the idea of eating dogs horrifies them. But in China, as in some other societies, dog meat is considered delicious. In North American culture, many people consider a baked ham to be a holiday dish. In several societies of the Middle East, however, including those of Egypt and Israel, eating the meat of a pig is forbidden by sacred writings.

To some extent, all animals exhibit learned behaviors, some of which most individuals in a population may share and may therefore consider cultural. But different animal species vary in the degree to which their shared behaviors are learned or are instinctive. The sociable ants, for instance, despite all their patterned social behavior, do not appear to have much, if any, culture. They divide their labor, construct their nests, form their raiding columns, and carry off their dead—all without having been taught to do so and without imitating the behavior of other ants. Our closest biological relatives, the monkeys and the apes, not only learn a wide variety of behaviors on their own, they also learn from each other. Some of their learned responses are as basic as those involved in maternal care; others are as frivolous as the taste for candy. Frans de Waal reviewed seven long-term studies of chimpanzees and identified at least 39 behaviors that were clearly learned from others.[4] If shared and socially learned, these behaviors could be described as cultural.

The proportion of an animal's life span occupied by childhood roughly reflects the degree to which the animal depends on learned behavior for survival. Monkeys and apes have relatively long childhoods compared to other animals. Humans have by far the longest childhood of any animal, reflecting our great dependence on learned behavior. Although humans may acquire much learned behavior by trial and error and imitation, as do monkeys and apes, most human ideas and behaviors are learned from others. Much of it is probably acquired with the aid of spoken, symbolic language. Using language, a human parent can describe a snake and tell a child that a snake is dangerous and should be avoided. If symbolic language did not exist, the parent would have to wait until the child actually saw a snake and then, through example, show the child that such a creature is to be avoided. Without language, we probably could not transmit or receive information so efficiently and rapidly, and thus would not be heir to so rich and varied a culture.

To sum up, we may say that something is cultural if it is a learned behavior or idea (belief, attitude, value, ideal) that the members of a society or other social group generally share.

Controversies About the Concept of Culture

Although we have explained what we mean by culture and we have tried to give the definition most anthropologists use, some would disagree with the definition. One of the disagreements is whether the concept of culture should refer just to the rules or ideas behind behavior,[5] or should also include the behaviors or the products of behavior, as is our choice here.

Cognitive anthropologists are most likely to say that culture refers to rules and ideas behind behavior, and therefore that culture resides in people's heads.[6]

Every individual will have slightly different constructs that are based in part on their own unique experiences. Because many people in a society share many of the same experiences, they will share many ideas—those shared ideas anthropologists describe as culture. This view allows for individual differences within a society, and also suggests that individual variation is the source of new culture.

Observers of human life often point to the seeming force of "culture," the profound effect on individuals of living in social groups. As we will see shortly in the section on cultural constraints, these social constraints suggest that culture exists outside of individuals. In the strongest view, one that was more acceptable in the past, culture is thought of as having a "life" of its own that could be studied without much regard for individuals at all.[7] According to this view, people are born blank slates, which culture can put its stamp on in each generation. Individuals may acquire their culture in the course of growing up, but understanding culture does not require understanding psychological processes.

There are a number of problems if we view culture as having a "life" of its own. First, where does it reside exactly? Second, if individuals do not matter, what are the mechanisms of culture change? And lastly, if psychological processes are irrelevant, how is it that there is considerable similarity across cultures?

As we will see in the next section, people do behave differently in social groups in ways that they might not even imagine ahead of time. Mob behavior is an extreme, but telling example. Therefore, we think we should look at behavior as well as rules or ideas in people's heads in describing a culture. It is not necessary to postulate that culture has a "life" of its own to explain why people sometimes behave differently in social groups. Humans are social beings and respond to others. So, in contrast to many cognitive anthropologists, we include behavior and the products of behavior in describing culture. But like cognitive anthropologists, we believe that one must consider individual variation in describing culture to sort out what is individual and what is shared. Those commonly shared and learned behaviors as well as ideas are the stuff of culture.

CULTURAL CONSTRAINTS

The noted French sociologist Émile Durkheim stressed that culture is something *outside* us, exerting a strong coercive power on us. We do not always feel the constraints of our culture because we generally conform to the types of conduct and thought it requires. Social scientists refer to standards or rules about what is acceptable behavior as **norms.** The importance of a norm usually can be judged by how members of a society respond when the norm is violated.

Cultural constraints are of two basic types, *direct* and *indirect.* Naturally, the direct constraints are the more obvious. For example, if you choose to wear a casual shorts outfit to a wedding, you will probably be subject to some ridicule and a certain amount of social isolation. But if you choose to wear nothing, you may be exposed to a stronger, more direct cultural constraint—arrest for indecent exposure.

Although indirect forms of cultural constraint are less obvious than direct ones, they are no less effective. Durkheim illustrated this point when he wrote, "I am not obliged to speak French with my fellow-countrymen, nor to use the legal currency, but I cannot possibly do otherwise. If I tried to escape this necessity, my attempt would fail miserably."[8] In other words, if Durkheim had decided he would rather speak Icelandic than French, nobody would have tried to stop him. But hardly anyone would have understood him either. And although he would not have been put into prison for trying to buy groceries with Icelandic money, he would have had difficulty convincing the local merchants to sell him food.

In a series of classic experiments on conformity, Solomon Asch revealed how strong social pressure can be. Asch coached the majority of a group of college students to give deliberately incorrect answers to questions involving visual stimuli. A "critical subject," the one student in the room who was not so coached, had no idea that the other participants would purposely misinterpret the evidence presented to them. Asch found that, in one-third of the experiments, the critical subjects consistently gave incorrect answers, seemingly allowing their own correct perceptions to be distorted by the obviously incorrect statements of the others. And in another 40 percent of the experiments, the critical subject yielded to the opinion of the group some of the time.[9] These studies have been replicated in the United States and elsewhere. Although the degree of conformity appears to vary in different societies, most studies still show conformity effects.[10] Many individuals still do not give in to the wishes of the majority, but a recent study using MRIs has shown that perceptions can actually be altered if participants consciously alter their answers to conform to others.[11]

ATTITUDES THAT HINDER THE STUDY OF CULTURES

Many of the Europeans who first traveled to faraway places were revolted or shocked by customs they observed. Such reactions are not surprising. People commonly feel that their own behaviors and attitudes are the correct ones and that people who do not share those patterns are immoral or inferior.[12] People who judge other cultures solely in terms of their own culture are **ethnocentric**—that is, they hold an attitude called **ethnocentrism.** Most North Americans would think that eating dogs or insects is disgusting, but most do not feel the same way about eating beef. Similarly, they would react negatively to child betrothal or digging up the bones of the dead.

Our own customs and ideas may appear bizarre or barbaric to an observer from another society. Hindus in

Because we are ethnocentric about many things, it is often difficult to criticize our own customs, some of which might seem shocking to a member of another society. The elderly in America often spend their days alone. In contrast, the elderly in Japan often live in a three-generational family.

N. Martin Haudrich/Photo \hResearchers, Inc.

James L. Stanfield/National Geographic Image Collection

India, for example, would consider our custom of eating beef disgusting. In their culture, the cow is a sacred animal and may not be slaughtered for food. In many societies, a baby is almost constantly carried by someone, in someone's lap, or asleep next to others.[13] People in such societies may think it is cruel of us to leave babies alone for long periods of time, often in devices that resemble cages (cribs and playpens). Even our most ordinary customs—the daily rituals we take for granted—might seem thoroughly absurd when viewed from an outside perspective. An observer of our society might justifiably take notes on certain strange behaviors that seem quite ordinary to us, as the following description shows:

> The daily body ritual performed by everyone includes a mouth-rite. Despite the fact that these people are so punctilious about the care of the mouth, this rite involves a practice which strikes the uninitiated stranger as revolting. It was reported to me that the ritual consists of inserting a small bundle of hog hairs into the mouth, along with certain magical powders, and then moving the bundle in a highly formalized series of gestures. In addition to the private mouth-rite, the people seek out a holy-mouth man once or twice a year. These practitioners have an impressive set of paraphernalia, consisting of a variety of augers, awls, probes, and prods. The use of these objects in the exorcism of the evils of the mouth involves almost unbelievable ritual torture of the client. The holy-mouth man opens the client's mouth and, using the above-mentioned tools, enlarges any holes which decay may have created in teeth. Magical materials are put into these holes. If there are no naturally occurring holes in the teeth, large sections of one or more teeth are gouged out so that the supernatural substance can be applied. In the client's view, the purpose of these ministrations is to arrest decay and to draw friends. The extremely sacred and traditional character of the rite is evident in the fact that the natives return to the holy-mouth man year after year, despite the fact that their teeth continue to decay.[14]

We are likely to protest that to understand the behaviors of a particular society—in this case, our own—the observer must try to find out what the people in that society say about why they do things. For example, the observer might find out that periodic visits to the "holy-mouth man" are for medical, not magical, purposes. Indeed, the observer, after some questioning, might discover that the "mouth-rite" has no sacred or religious connotations whatsoever. Actually, Horace Miner, the author of the passage on the "daily rite ritual," was not a foreigner. An American, he described the "ritual" the way he did to show how the behaviors involved might be interpreted by an outside observer.

Ethnocentrism hinders our understanding of the customs of other people and, at the same time, keeps us from understanding our own customs. If we think that everything we do is best, we are not likely to ask why we do what we do or why "they" do what "they" do.

We may not always glorify our own culture. Other ways of life may sometimes seem more appealing. Whenever we are weary of the complexities of civilization, we may long for a way of life that is "closer to nature" or "simpler" than our own. For instance, a young North American whose parent is holding two or three jobs just to provide the family with bare necessities might briefly be attracted to the lifestyle of the !Kung of the Kalahari Desert in the 1950s. The !Kung shared their food and therefore were often free to engage in leisure activities during the greater part of the day. They obtained all their food by men hunting animals and women gathering wild plants. They had no facilities for refrigeration, so sharing a large freshly killed animal was clearly more sensible than hoarding meat that would soon rot. Moreover, the sharing provided a kind of social security system for the !Kung. If a hunter was unable to catch an animal on a certain day, he could obtain food for himself and his family from someone else in his band. Then, at some later date, the game he caught would provide food for the family of another, unsuccessful hunter. This system of sharing also ensured that people too young or too old to help with collecting food would still be fed.

Could we learn from the !Kung? Perhaps we could in some respects, but we must not glorify their way of life either or think that their way of life might be easily imported into our own society. Other aspects of !Kung life would not appeal to many North Americans. For example, when the nomadic !Kung decided to move their camps, they had to carry all the family possessions, substantial amounts of food and water, and all young children below age 4 or 5. This is a sizable burden to carry for any distance. The nomadic !Kung traveled about 1,500 miles in a single year and families had few possessions.[15] It is unlikely that most North Americans would find the !Kung way of life enviable in all respects.

Both ethnocentrism and its opposite, the glorification of other cultures, hinder effective anthropological study.

CULTURAL RELATIVISM

The early evolutionists tended to think of Western cultures as being at the highest or most progressive stage of evolution. Not only were these early ideas based on very poor evidence of the details of world ethnography, they could also be ethnocentric glorifications of Western culture.

But Franz Boas and many of his students—like Ruth Benedict, Melville Herskovits, and Margaret Mead—felt otherwise.[16] They stressed that the early evolutionists did not sufficiently understand the details of the cultures they theorized about, nor did they understand the context in which these customs appeared. Challenging the attitude that Western cultures were obviously superior, the Boasians insisted that a society's customs and ideas should be described objectively and understood in the context of that society's problems and opportunities. This attitude is known as **cultural relativism.** Does cultural relativism mean that the actions of another society, or of our own, should not be judged? Does our insistence on objectivity mean that anthropologists should not make moral judgments about the cultural phenomena they observe and try to explain? Does it mean that anthropologists should not try to bring about change? Not necessarily. Although the concept of cultural relativism remains an important anthropological tenet, anthropologists differ in their interpretation of the principle of cultural relativism.

Many anthropologists are uncomfortable with the strong form of cultural relativism that suggests that all patterns of culture are equally valid. What if the people practice slavery, violence against women, torture, or genocide? If the strong doctrine of relativism is adhered to, then these cultural practices are not to be judged, and we should not try to eliminate them. A weaker form of cultural relativism asserts that anthropologists should strive for objectivity in describing a people and should be wary of superficial or quick judgment in their attempts to understand the reasons for cultural behavior. Tolerance should be the basic mode unless there is strong reason to behave otherwise.[17] The weak version of cultural relativity does not preclude anthropologists from making judgments or from trying to change behavior they think is harmful. But judgments need not, and should not, preclude accurate description and explanation.

Human Rights and Relativism

The news increasingly reports behaviors that Western countries consider to be violations of human rights. Examples range from jailing people for expressing certain political ideas to ethnic massacre. But faced with criticism from the West, people in other parts of the world are saying that the West should not dictate its ideas about human rights to other countries. Indeed, many countries say they have different codes of ethics. Are the Western countries being ethnocentric by taking their own cultural ideas and applying them to the rest of the world? Should we instead rely on the strong version of the concept of cultural relativism, considering each culture on its own terms? If we do that, it may not be possible to create a universal standard of human rights.

What we do know is that all cultures have ethical standards, but they do not emphasize the same things. For example, some cultures emphasize individual political rights; others emphasize political order. Some cultures emphasize protection of individual property; others emphasize the sharing or equitable distribution of resources. People in the United States may have freedom to dissent, but they can be deprived of health insurance or of food if they lack the money to buy them. Cultures also vary markedly in the degree to which they have equal rights for minorities and women. In some societies, women are killed when a husband dies or when they disobey a father or brother.

Some anthropologists argue strongly against cultural relativism. For example, Elizabeth Zechenter says that cultural relativists claim there are no universal principles of morality, but insist on tolerance for all cultures. If tolerance is one universal principle, why shouldn't there be others? In addition, she points out that the concept of cultural relativism is often used to justify traditions desired by the dominant and powerful in a society. She points to a case in 1996, in Algeria, where two teenage girls were raped and murdered because they violated the fundamentalist edict against attending school. Are those girls any less a part of the culture than the fundamentalists? Would it make any difference if most Algerian women supported the murders? Would that make it right? Zechenter does not believe that international treaties such as the Universal Declaration of Human Rights impose uniformity among diverse cultures. Rather, they seek to create a floor below which no society is supposed to fall.[18]

Can the concept of cultural relativism be reconciled with the concept of an international code of human rights? Probably not completely. Paul Rosenblatt recognizes the dilemma but nonetheless thinks that something has to be done to stop torture and "ethnic cleansing," among other practices. He makes the case that "to the extent that it is easier to persuade people whose viewpoints and values one understands, relativism can be a tool for change . . . a relativist's awareness of the values and understanding of the elite makes it easier to know what arguments would be persuasive. For example, in a society in which the group rather than the individual has great primacy, it might be persuasive to show how respect for individual rights benefits the group."[19]

DESCRIBING A CULTURE

Earlier we discussed *participant-observation* and some other methods of research that cultural anthropologists use in doing fieldwork. But here we focus on another question: If all individuals are unique and all cultures have some internal variation, how do anthropologists discover what may be cultural? Understanding what is cultural involves two parts—separating what is shared from what is very individually variable, and understanding whether common behaviors and ideas are learned.

To understand better how an anthropologist might make sense of diverse behaviors, let us examine the diversity at a professional football game in the United States. When people attend a football game, various members of the crowd behave differently while "The Star-Spangled Banner" is being played. As they stand and listen, some people remove their hats; a child munches popcorn; a veteran of the armed forces stands at attention; a teenager searches the crowd for a friend; and the coaches take a final opportunity to intone secret chants and spells designed to sap the strength of the opposing team. Yet, despite these individual variations, most of the people at the game respond in a basically similar manner: Nearly everyone stands silently, facing the flag. Moreover, if you go to several football games, you will observe that many aspects of the event are notably similar. Although the plays will vary from game to game, the rules of the game are never different, and although the colors of the uniforms of the

In deciding what is cultural behavior, anthropologists look for commonalities, understanding that there is always considerable variation. In North American culture, unmarried couples are allowed and even encouraged to spend time with each other, but how they spend their time varies.

teams are different, the players never appear on the field dressed in swimsuits.

Although the variations in individual reactions to a given stimulus are theoretically limitless, in fact they tend to fall within easily recognizable limits. A child listening to the anthem may continue to eat popcorn but will probably not do a rain dance. Similarly, the coaches will unlikely react to that same stimulus by running onto the field and embracing the singer. Variations in behavior, then, are confined within socially acceptable limits, and part of the anthropologists' goals is to find out what those limits are. They may note, for example, that some limitations on behavior have a practical purpose: A spectator who disrupts the game by wandering onto the field would be required to leave. Other limitations are purely traditional. In our society, it is considered proper for a man to remove his overcoat if he becomes overheated, but others would undoubtedly frown upon his removing his trousers even if the weather were quite warm. Using observation and interviewing, anthropologists discover the customs and the ranges of acceptable behavior that characterize the society under study.

Similarly, anthropologists interested in describing courtship and marriage in our society would encounter a variety of behaviors. Dating couples vary in where they go (coffee shops, movies, restaurants, bowling alleys), what behaviors they engage in on dates, how long they date before they split up or move on to more serious relationships. If they decide to marry, ceremonies may be simple or elaborate and involve either religious or secular rituals. Despite this variability, the anthropologists would begin to detect certain regularities in courting practices. Although couples may do many different things on their first and subsequent dates, they nearly always arrange the dates by themselves; they try to avoid their parents when on dates; they often manage to find themselves alone at the end of a date; they put their lips together frequently; and so forth. After a series of more and more closely spaced encounters, a man and woman may decide to declare themselves publicly as a couple, either by announcing that they are engaged or by revealing that they are living together or intend to do so. Finally, if the two of them decide to marry, they must in some way have their union recorded by the civil authorities.

In our society, a person who wishes to marry cannot completely disregard the customary patterns of courtship. If a man saw a woman on the street and decided he wanted to marry her, he could conceivably choose a quicker and more direct form of action than the usual dating procedure. He could get on a horse, ride to the woman's home, snatch her up in his arms, and gallop away with her. In Sicily, until the last few decades, such a couple would have been considered legally married, even if the woman had never met the man before or had no intention of marrying. But in North American society, any man who acted in such a fashion would be arrested and jailed for kidnapping and would probably have his sanity challenged. Although individual behaviors may vary, most social behavior falls within culturally acceptable limits.

In the course of observing and interviewing, anthropologists also try to distinguish actual behavior from the ideas about how people in particular situations ought to feel and behave. In everyday terms, we speak of these ideas as *ideals;* in anthropology, we refer to them as *ideal cultural traits*. Ideal cultural traits may differ from actual behavior because the ideal is based on the way society used to be. (Consider the ideal of "free enterprise," that industry should be totally free of governmental regulation.) Other ideals may never have been actual patterns and may represent merely what people would like to see as correct behavior. Consider the idealized belief, long cherished in North America, that everybody is "equal before the law," that everybody should be treated in the same way by the police and courts. Of course, we know that this is not always true. The rich, for example, may receive less jail time and be sent to nicer prisons. Nevertheless, the ideal is still part of our culture; most of us continue to believe that the law should be applied equally to all.

When dealing with customs that are overt or highly visible within a society—for example, the custom of sending children to school—an investigator can determine the existence of such practices by direct observation and by interviewing a few knowledgeable people. But when

Distance between people conversing varies cross-culturally. The faces of the Rajput Indian men on the left are much closer than the faces of the American women on the right.

dealing with a domain of behavior that may include many individual variations, or when the people studied are unaware of their pattern of behavior and cannot answer questions about it, the anthropologist may need to collect information from a larger sample of individuals to establish what the cultural trait is.

One example of a cultural trait that most people in a society are not aware of is how far apart people stand when they are having a conversation. Yet there is considerable reason to believe that unconscious cultural rules govern such behavior. These rules become obvious when we interact with people who have different rules. We may experience considerable discomfort when another person stands too close (indicating too much intimacy) or too far (indicating unfriendliness). Edward Hall reported that Arabs customarily stand quite close to others, close enough, as we have noted, to be able to smell the other person. In interactions between Arabs and North Americans, then, the Arabs will move closer at the same time that the North Americans back away.[20]

If we wanted to arrive at the cultural rule for conversational distance between casual acquaintances, we could study a sample of individuals from a society and determine the *modal response,* or *mode.* The mode is a statistical term that refers to the most frequently encountered response in a given series of responses. So, for the North American pattern of casual conversational distance, we would plot the actual distance for many observed pairs of people. Some pairs may be 2 feet apart, some 2.5, and some 4 feet apart. If we count the number of times every particular distance is observed, these counts provide what we call a *frequency distribution.* The distance with the highest frequency is the *modal pattern.* Very often

the frequency distribution takes the form of a *bell-shaped curve,* as shown in Figure 1.

There, the characteristic being measured is plotted on the horizontal axis (in this case, the distance between conversational pairs), and the number of times each distance is observed (its frequency) is plotted on the vertical axis. If we were to plot how a sample of North American casual conversational pairs is distributed, we would probably get a bell-shaped curve that peaks at around 3 feet.[21] Is it any wonder, then, that we sometimes speak of keeping others "at arm's length"?

Although we may be able to discover by interviews and observation that a behavior, thought, or feeling is widely shared within a society, how do we establish that something commonly shared is learned, so that we can call it cultural? Establishing that something is or is not learned may be difficult. Because children are not reared apart from adult caretakers, the behaviors they exhibit as part of their genetic inheritance are not clearly separated from those they learn from others around them. We suspect that particular behaviors and ideas are largely learned if they vary from society to society. We also suspect genetic influences when particular behaviors or ideas are found in all societies. For example, children the world over seem to acquire language at about the same age, and the structure of their early utterances seems to be similar. These facts suggest that human children are born with an innate grammar. However, although early childhood language seems similar the world over, the particular languages spoken by adults in different societies show considerable variability. This variability suggests that

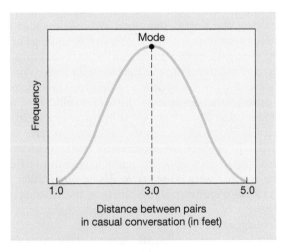

FIGURE 1 Frequency Distribution Curve

particular languages have to be learned. Similarly, if the courtship patterns of one society differ markedly from those of another, we can be fairly certain that those courtship patterns are learned and therefore cultural.

CULTURE IS PATTERNED

Anthropologists have always known that culture is not a hodgepodge of unrelated behaviors and ideas—that a culture is mostly integrated. In saying that a culture is mostly *integrated,* we mean that the elements or traits that make up that culture are not just a random assortment of customs but are mostly adjusted to or consistent with one another.

A culture may also tend to be integrated for psychological reasons. The ideas of a culture are stored in the brains of individuals. Research in social psychology has suggested that people tend to modify beliefs or behaviors that are not cognitively or conceptually consistent with other information.[22] We do not expect cultures to be completely integrated, just as we do not expect individuals to be completely consistent. But if a tendency toward cognitive consistency is found in humans, we might expect that at least some aspects of a culture would tend to be integrated for that reason alone. How this pressure for consistency works is not hard to imagine. Children, for example, seem to be very good at remembering *all* the things their parents say. If they ask for something and the parents say no, they may say, "But you said I could yesterday." This pressure for consistency may even make parents change their minds! Of course, not everything one wants to do is consistent with the rest of one's desires, but there surely is pressure from within and without to make it so.

Humans are also capable of rational decision making; they can usually figure out that certain things are not easy to do because of other things they do. For example, if a society has a long postpartum sex (a custom in which couples abstain from sex for a year or more after the birth of a baby), we might expect that most people in the society could figure out that it would be easier to observe the taboo if husband and wife did not sleep in the same bed. Or if people drive on the left side of the road, as in England, it is easier and less dangerous to drive a car with a steering wheel on the right because that placement allows you to judge more accurately how close you are to cars coming at you from the opposite direction.

Consistency or integration of culture traits may also be produced by less conscious psychological processes. Religion and magic, and the arts, people may generalize (transfer) their experiences from one area of life to another. For example, where children are taught that it is wrong to express anger toward family and friends, it turns out that folktales parallel the childrearing; anger and aggression in the folktales tend to be directed only toward strangers, not toward family and friends. It seems as if the expression of anger is too frightening to be expressed close to home, even in folktales.

Adaptation to the environment is another major reason for traits to be patterned. Customs that diminish the survival chances of a society are not likely to persist. Either the people clinging to those customs will become extinct, taking the customs with them, or the customs will be replaced, thereby possibly helping the people to survive. By either process, **maladaptive customs**—those that diminish the chances of survival and reproduction—are likely to disappear. The customs of a society that enhance survival and reproductive success are **adaptive customs** and are likely to persist. Hence, we assume that if a society has survived long enough to be described in the annals of anthropology (the "ethnographic record"), much, if not most, of its cultural repertoire is adaptive, or was at one time.

When we say that a custom is adaptive, however, we mean it is adaptive only with respect to a specific physical and social environment. What may be adaptive in one environment may not be adaptive in another. Therefore, when we ask why a society may have a particular custom, we really are asking if that custom makes sense as an adaptation to that society's particular environmental conditions. If certain customs are more adaptive in particular settings, then those "bundles" of traits will generally be found together under similar conditions. For example, the !Kung, as we have mentioned, subsisted by hunting wild animals and gathering wild plants. Because wild game is mobile and different plants mature at different times, a nomadic way of life may be an adaptive strategy. That food-getting strategy cannot support that many people in one area, so small social groups make more sense than large communities. Because people move frequently, it is probably more adaptive to have few material possessions. As we will see, these cultural traits usually occur together when people depend on hunting and gathering for their food.

We must remember that not all aspects of culture are consistent, nor is a society forced to adapt its culture to changing environmental circumstances. Even in the face of changed circumstances, people may choose not to change their customs. For example, the Tapirapé of central Brazil did not alter their custom of limiting the number of births, even though they suffered severe population losses after contact with Europeans and their diseases. The Tapirapé population fell to fewer than 100 people from over 1,000. Clearly, they were on the way to extinction, yet they continued to value small families. Not only did they believe that a woman should have no more than three children, but they took specific steps to achieve this limitation. They practiced infanticide if twins were born, if the third child was of the same sex as the first two children, and if the possible fathers broke certain taboos during pregnancy or in the child's infancy.[23]

Of course, it is also possible that a people will behave maladaptively, even if they try to alter their behavior. After all, although people may alter their behavior according to what they perceive will be helpful to them, what they perceive to be helpful may not prove to be adaptive. The tendency for a culture to be integrated or patterned, then, may be cognitively and emotionally, as well as adaptively, induced.

HOW AND WHY CULTURES CHANGE

When you examine the history of a society, it is obvious that its culture has changed over time. Some of the shared behaviors and ideas that were common at one time are modified or replaced at another time. That is why, in describing a culture, it is important to understand that a description pertains to a particular time period. (Moreover, in many large societies, the description may only be appropriate for a particular subgroup.) For example, the !Kung of the 1950s were mostly dependent on the collection of wild plants and animals and moved their campsites frequently, but later they became more sedentary to engage in wage labor. Whether we focus on some aspect of past behavior or on contemporary behavior depends on what question we want to answer. If we want to maximize our understanding of cultural variation, such as variation in religious belief and practice, it may be important to focus on the earliest descriptions of a group before they were converted to a major world religion. On the other hand, if we want to understand why a people adopted a new religion or how they altered their religion or resisted change in the face of pressure, we need to examine the changes that occurred over time.

In the remainder of this chapter, we will discuss how and why cultures change and briefly review some of the widespread changes that have occurred in recent times. In general, the impetus for change may come from within the society or from without. From within, the unconscious or conscious pressure for consistency will produce culture change if enough people adjust old behavior and thinking to new. And change can also occur if people try to invent better ways of doing things. Michael Chibnik suggests that people who confront a new problem conduct mental or small "experiments" to decide how to behave. These experiments may give rise to new cultural traits.[24] A good deal of culture change may be stimulated by changes in the external environment. For example, if people move into an arid area, they will either have to give up farming or develop a system of irrigation. In the modern world, changes in the social environment are probably more frequent stimuli for culture change than changes in the physical environment. Many North Americans, for example, started to think seriously about conserving energy and about using sources of energy other than oil only after oil supplies from the Middle East were curtailed in 1973 and 1974. As we noted earlier, a significant amount of the radical and rapid culture change that has occurred in the last few hundred years has been due to the imperial expansion of Western societies into other areas of the world. Native Americans, for instance, were forced to alter their lifestyles drastically when they were driven off their lands and confined to reservations.

Discovery and Invention

Discoveries and inventions, which may originate inside or outside a society, are ultimately the sources of all culture change. But they do not necessarily lead to change. If an invention or discovery is ignored, no change in culture results. Only when society accepts an invention or discovery and uses it regularly can we begin to speak of culture change.

The new thing discovered or invented, the innovation, may be an object—the wheel, the plow, the computer—or it may involve behavior and ideas—buying and selling, democracy, monogamy. According to Ralph Linton, a discovery is any addition to knowledge, and an invention is a new application of knowledge.[25] Thus, a person might discover that children can be persuaded to eat nourishing food if the food is associated with an imaginary character that appeals to them. And then someone might exploit that discovery by inventing a character named Popeye who appears in a series of animated cartoons, acquiring miraculous strength by devouring cans of spinach.

Unconscious Invention In discussing the process of invention, we should differentiate between various types of inventions. One type is the consequence of a society's setting itself a specific goal, such as eliminating tuberculosis or placing a person on the moon. Another type emerges less intentionally. This second process of invention is often referred to as *accidental juxtaposition* or *unconscious invention*. Linton suggested that some inventions, especially those of prehistoric days, were probably the consequences of literally dozens of tiny initiatives by "unconscious" inventors. These inventors made their small contributions, perhaps over many hundreds of years, without being aware of the part they were playing in bringing one invention, such as the wheel or a better form of hand ax, to completion.[26] Consider the example of children playing on a fallen log, which rolls as they walk and balance on it, coupled with the need at a given moment to move a slab of granite from a cave face. The children's play may have suggested the use of logs as rollers and thereby set in motion a series of developments that culminated in the wheel.

In reconstructing the process of invention in prehistoric times, however, we should be careful not to look back on our ancestors with a smugness generated by our more highly developed technology. We have become accustomed to turning to the science sections of our magazines and newspapers and finding, almost daily, reports of miraculous new discoveries and inventions. From our point of view, it is difficult to imagine such a simple invention as the wheel taking so many centuries to come into being. We are tempted to surmise that early humans were less intelligent than we are. But the capacity of the human brain has been the same for perhaps 100,000 years; there is no evidence that the inventors of the wheel were any less intelligent than we are.

Intentional Innovation Some discoveries and inventions arise out of deliberate attempts to produce a new idea or object. It may seem that such innovations are obvious responses to perceived needs. For example, during the Industrial Revolution, there was a great demand for inventions that would increase productivity. James Hargreaves, in 18th-century England, is an example of an inventor

current research and issues

Culture Change and Persistence in China

In the years since the 1949 Communist takeover in China, the central government has initiated a variety of changes in family life. Many of these changes were literally forced; people who resisted them were often resettled or jailed. Ancestor worship and lineage organization were attacked or declared illegal. Most private property was abolished, undermining family loyalties. Why participate in family activities if there could be no economic reward? Still, the actions of the central government did not completely change family life. Even coercion has its limits.

The government may have wanted to restrict the family and kinship, but its investments in public health and famine relief reduced mortality, thereby strengthening family ties. Fewer infants died, more children lived long enough to marry, old age became more common—all of these developments allowed people in all social classes to have larger and more complex networks of kin than were possible before 1949. To be sure, government policies undercut the power and authority of extended family patriarchs. But the new healthier conditions were conducive to large, multigenerational households with economic as well as social ties to other kin.

As China became more accessible to anthropologists and other researchers from abroad, many investigators came to study the variability and similarity in Chinese family life. Most of these studies focused on the dominant Han Chinese (the Han constitute about 95 percent of the total population of China); investigators have also studied many of the 55 "recognized" minority cultures in China. Burton Pasternak, a U.S. anthropologist, Janet Salaff, a Canadian sociologist, and Chinese sociologists studied four communities of Han who had moved outside the Great Wall to colonize the Inner Mongolian frontier (Inner Mongolia is part of China). The results of their study suggest that, despite strong pressures from the government, what changes or persists in a culture mainly reflects what is possible ecologically and economically. A tradition of intensive agriculture cannot persist in the absence of sufficient watering. The government's insistence on one child per family cannot withstand a family's need for more children.

Han farmers who crossed the Great Wall were searching for a better life. They found difficulties in climate and soil that forced many to return home. But many adjusted to the grasslands and remained. Some continued to depend on farming on the fringes of the grasslands. Others farther out on the grasslands became herders. The Han who switched to herding are now in many respects more like the native Mongol herders than like Han or Mongol farmers. The gender division of labor among the Han pastoralists became much sharper than among the Han farmers because men are often far away with the herds. Pastoralist children, not that useful in herding because mistakes can be very costly, are more likely than farm children to stay in school for a long time. Perhaps because of the greater usefulness of children on the farm, Han farm families have more children than Han pastoralists. But both groups have more than one child per family. Herdsmen are less likely than farmers to need cooperative labor, so Han pastoralists are more likely to live as an independent family living apart from kin than as an extended family (which was traditional). In short, the adjustment of the Han to the grasslands seems to be explained more by ecological requirements than by ethnic traditions.

Although an increasing number of Han have become more like Mongols in their pastoral adaptations, many Mongols have adopted an urban way of life and moved away from their pastoral life. The Chinese government was initially responsible for encouraging non-Mongols to move into Inner Mongolia, particularly into its new capital, Hohhot. At the same time, many Mongols moved from the grasslands and into the capital city. Chinese government policy was intended to make each non-Han ethnic group a minority in its traditional land, but the government paradoxically also tried to encourage minority ethnic pride in their traditional culture. So the city of Hohhot is filled with images of the traditional herding culture in its buildings and monuments.

As described by anthropologist William Jankowiak, who studied the Mongols in the capital city of Hohhot, the results were not what the Chinese government intended. In many ways, to be sure, the urban Mongols had abandoned their traditional culture and assimilated to the dominant Han culture. But we see the force of ecology more than the hand of tradition in the outcome. Many Mongols in the city no longer speak the Mongol language. Parents find it difficult to get children to speak Mongol when they live among Han. The scarcity of housing makes it difficult for the Mongols to form an ethnic enclave, or even live near kin as they did in the past. In contrast to life in the rural areas, which revolves around kinship, city life requires interacting with strangers as well as relatives. Indeed, nonkin are often more important to you than kin. As one person said to Jankowiak, "We hide from our cousins but not our friends."

Sources: Davis and Harrell 1993; Pasternak 2009; Jankowiak 2004.

who responded to an existing demand. Textile manufacturers were clamoring for such large quantities of spun yarn that cottage laborers, working with foot-operated spinning wheels, could not meet the demand. Hargreaves, realizing that prestige and financial rewards would come to the person who invented a method of spinning large quantities of yarn in a short time, set about the task and developed the spinning jenny.

But perceived needs and the economic rewards that may be given to the innovator do not explain why only some people innovate. We know relatively little about why some people are more innovative than others. The ability to innovate may depend in part on individual characteristics such as high intelligence and creativity. And creativity may be influenced by social conditions.

A study of innovation among Ashanti artist carvers in Ghana suggests that creativity is more likely in some socioeconomic groups than in others.[27] Some carvers produced only traditional designs; others departed from tradition and produced "new" styles of carving. Two groups were found to innovate the most—the wealthiest and the poorest carvers. These two groups of carvers may tolerate risk more than the middle socioeconomic group. Innovative carving entails some risk because it may take more time and it may not sell. Wealthy carvers can afford the risk, and they may gain some prestige as well as income if their innovation is appreciated. The poor are not doing well anyway, and they have little to lose by trying something new.

Some societies encourage innovativeness more than others, and this can vary substantially over time. Patricia Greenfield and her colleagues describe the changes in weaving in a Mayan community in the Zinacantán region of Chiapas, Mexico.[28] In 1969 and 1970, innovation was not valued. Rather, tradition was; there was the old "true way" to do everything, including how one dressed. There were only four simple weaving patterns, and virtually all males wore ponchos with the same pattern. By 1991, virtually no poncho was the same and the villagers had developed elaborate brocaded and embroidered designs. In a period of 20 years, innovation had increased dramatically.

Two other things had also changed. The economy was more commercialized; textiles as well as other items were now bought and sold. The other change was a shift to a much less directed teaching style. Earlier, mothers would give highly structured instruction to their daughters, often with "four hands" on the loom. Later, girls were allowed to learn more by themselves, by trial and error, and they produced more abstract and varied designs.

Who Adopts Innovations? Once someone discovers or invents something, there is still the question of whether others will adopt the innovation. Many researchers have studied the characteristics of "early adopters." Such individuals tend to be educated, high in social status, upwardly mobile, and, if they are property owners, have large farms and businesses. The individuals who most need technological improvements—those who are less well off—are generally the last to adopt innovations. The theory is that only the wealthy can afford to take the substantial risks associated with new ways of doing things. In periods of rapid technological change, therefore, the gap between rich and poor is likely to widen because the rich adopt innovations sooner, and benefit more from them, than the poor.[29]

Does this imply that the likelihood of adopting innovations is a simple function of how much wealth a possible adopter possesses? Not necessarily. Frank Cancian reviewed several studies and found that upper-middle-class individuals show more conservatism than lower-middle-class individuals. Cancian suggested that, when the risks are unknown, the lower-middle-class individuals are more receptive to innovation because they have less to lose. Later on, when the risks are better known—that is, as more people adopt the innovation—the upper-middle class catches up to the lower-middle class.[30] So the readiness to accept innovation, like the likelihood of creativity among Ashanti carvers, may not be related to socioeconomic position in a linear way.

The speed of accepting an innovation may depend partly on how new behaviors and ideas are typically

Mayan woman from San Martin Jilotepeque working on a hip-strap loom. Designs became more individual and complex by the 1990s.

Dorling Kindersley © Jamie Marshall

transmitted in a society. In particular, is a person exposed to many versus few "teachers"? If children learn most of what they know from their parents or from a relatively small number of elders, then innovation will be slow to spread throughout the society, and culture change is likely to be slow. Innovations may catch on more rapidly if individuals are exposed to various teachers and other "leaders" who can influence many in a relatively short time. And the more peers we have, the more we might learn from them.[31] Perhaps this is why the pace of change appears to be so quick today. In societies like our own, and increasingly in the industrializing world, it is likely that people learn in schools from teachers, from leaders in their specialties, and from peers.

Costs and Benefits An innovation that is technologically superior is not necessarily going to be adopted. There are costs as well as benefits for both individuals and large-scale industries. Take the computer keyboard. The keyboard used most often on computers today is called the QWERTY keyboard (named after the letters on the left side of the line of keys below the row of number keys). This keyboard was actually invented to slow typing speed down! Early typewriters had mechanical keys that jammed if the typist went too fast.[32] Computer keyboards don't have that problem, so an arrangement of keys that allowed faster typing would probably be better. Different keyboard configurations have been invented, but they haven't caught on. Most people probably would find it too hard or too time-consuming to learn a new style of typing, so the original style of keyboard persists.

In large-scale industries, technological innovations may be very costly to implement. A new product or process may require revamping a manufacturing or service facility and retraining workers. Before a decision is made to change, the costs of doing so are weighed against the potential benefits. If the market is expected to be large for a new product, the product is more likely to be produced. If the market is judged small, the benefits may not be sufficient inducement to change. Companies may also judge the value of an innovation by whether competitors could copy it. If the new innovation can be easily copied, the inventing company may not find the investment worthwhile. Although the market may be large, the inventing company may not be able to hold onto market share if other companies could produce the product quickly without having to invest in research and development.[33]

Diffusion

The source of new cultural elements in a society may also be another society. The process by which cultural elements are borrowed from another society and incorporated into the culture of the recipient group is called **diffusion.** Borrowing sometimes enables a group to bypass stages or mistakes in the development of a process or institution. For example, Germany was able to accelerate its program of industrialization in the 19th century because it was able to avoid some of the errors its English and Belgian competitors made by taking advantage of technological borrowing. Japan did the same somewhat later. Indeed, in recent years, some of the earliest industrialized countries have fallen behind their imitators in certain areas of production, such as automobiles, televisions, cameras, and computers.

In a well-known passage, Linton conveyed the far-reaching effects of diffusion by considering the first few hours in the day of an American man in the 1930s. This man

> . . . awakens in a bed built on a pattern which originated in the Near East but which was modified in northern Europe before it was transmitted to America. He throws back covers made from cotton, domesticated in India, or linen, domesticated in the Near East, or silk, the use of which was discovered in China. All of these materials have been spun and woven by processes invented in the Near East. . . . He takes off his pajamas, a garment invented in India, and washes with soap invented by the ancient

A Masai man in Kenya can call home or around the world from the plains of Kenya.

169

Gauls. He then shaves, a masochistic rite which seems to have derived from either Sumer or ancient Egypt.

Before going out for breakfast he glances through the window, made of glass invented in Egypt, and if it is raining puts on overshoes made of rubber discovered by the Central American Indians and takes an umbrella, invented in southeastern Asia. . . .

On his way to breakfast he stops to buy a paper paying for it with coins, an ancient Lydian invention. . . . His plate is made of a form of pottery invented in China. His knife is of steel, an alloy first made in southern India, his fork a medieval Italian invention, and his spoon a derivative of a Roman original. . . . After his fruit (African watermelon) and first coffee (an Abyssinian plant), . . . he may have the egg of a species of bird domesticated in Indo-China, or thin strips of the flesh of an animal domesticated in eastern Asia which have been salted and smoked by a process developed in northern Europe. . . .

While smoking (an American Indian habit), he reads the news of the day, imprinted in characters invented by the ancient Semites upon a material invented in China by a process invented in Germany. As he absorbs the accounts of foreign troubles he will, if he is a good conservative citizen, thank a Hebrew deity in an Indo-European language that he is 100 percent American.[34]

Patterns of Diffusion The following are the three basic patterns of diffusion: direct contact, intermediate contact, and stimulus diffusion.

1. **Direct contact.** Elements of a society's culture may first be taken up by neighboring societies and then gradually spread farther and farther afield. The spread of the use of paper (a sheet of interlaced fibers) is a good example of extensive diffusion by direct contact. The invention of paper is attributed to the Chinese Ts'ai Lun in A.D. 105. Within 50 years, paper was being made in many places in central China. Although the art of papermaking was kept secret for about 500 years, paper was distributed as a commodity to much of the Arab world through the markets at Samarkand. But when Samarkand was attacked by the Chinese in A.D. 751, a Chinese prisoner was forced to set up a paper mill. Paper manufacture then spread to the rest of the Arab world; it was first manufactured in Baghdad in A.D. 793, Egypt about A.D. 900, and Morocco about A.D. 1100. Papermaking was introduced as a commodity in Europe by Arab trade through Italian ports in the 12th century. The Moors built the first European paper mill in Spain about 1150. The technical knowledge then spread throughout Europe, with paper mills built in Italy in 1276, France in 1348, Germany in 1390, and England in 1494.[35] In general, the pattern of accepting the borrowed invention was the same in all cases: Paper was first imported as a luxury, then in ever-expanding quantities as a staple product. Finally, and usually within one to three centuries, local manufacture began.

2. **Intermediate contact.** Diffusion by intermediate contact occurs through the agency of third parties. Frequently, traders carry a cultural trait from the society that originated it to another group. As an example of diffusion through intermediaries, Phoenician traders spread the alphabet—which may have been invented by another Semitic group—to Greece. At times, soldiers serve as intermediaries in spreading a culture trait. European crusaders, such as the Knights Templar and the Knights of St. John, acted as intermediaries in two ways: They carried Christian culture to Muslim societies of North Africa and brought Arab culture back to Europe. In the 19th century, Western missionaries in all parts of the world encouraged natives to wear Western clothing. Hence, in Africa, the Pacific Islands, and elsewhere, native peoples can be found wearing shorts, suit jackets, shirts, ties, and other typically Western articles of clothing.

3. **Stimulus diffusion.** In stimulus diffusion, knowledge of a trait belonging to another culture stimulates the invention or development of a local equivalent. A classic example of stimulus diffusion is the Cherokee syllabic writing system created by a Native American named Sequoya so that his people could write down their language. Sequoya got the idea from his contact with Europeans. Yet, he did not adopt the English writing system; indeed, he did not even learn to write English. What he did was utilize some English alphabetic symbols, alter others, and invent new ones. All the symbols he used represented Cherokee syllables and in no way echoed English alphabetic usage. In other words, Sequoya took English alphabetic ideas and gave them a new, Cherokee form. The stimulus originated with Europeans; the result was peculiarly Cherokee.

The Selective Nature of Diffusion Although there is a temptation to view the dynamics of diffusion as similar to a stone sending concentric ripples over still water, this would be an oversimplification of the way diffusion actually occurs. Not all cultural traits are borrowed as readily as the ones we have mentioned, nor do they usually expand in neat, ever-widening circles. Rather, diffusion is a selective process. The Japanese, for instance, accepted much from Chinese culture, but they also rejected many traits. Rhymed tonal poetry, civil service examinations, and foot binding, which the Chinese favored, were never adopted in Japan. The poetry form was unsuited to the structure of the Japanese language; the examinations were unnecessary in view of the entrenched power of the Japanese aristocracy; and foot binding was repugnant to a people who abhorred body mutilation of any sort.

Not only would we expect societies to reject items from other societies that are repugnant, we would also expect them to reject ideas and technology that do not satisfy some psychological, social, or cultural need. After all, people are not sponges; they don't automatically soak up the things around them. If they did, the amount of cultural variation in the world would be extremely small, which is clearly not the case. Diffusion is also selective because cultural traits differ in the extent to which they can be communicated. Elements of material culture, such as mechanical processes and techniques, and other traits, such as physical sports and the like, are not especially difficult to demonstrate. Consequently, they are accepted or rejected on their merits. But the moment we move out of the material context, we encounter real difficulties. Linton identified the problem in these words:

> Although it is quite possible to describe such an element of culture as the ideal pattern for marriage . . . it is much less complete than a description of basketmaking. . . . The most thorough verbalization has difficulty in conveying the series of associations and conditioned emotional responses which are attached to this pattern [marriage] and which gave it meaning and vitality within our own society. . . . This is even more true of those concepts which . . . find no direct expression in behavior aside from verbalization. There is a story of an educated Japanese who after a long discussion on the nature of the Trinity with a European friend . . . burst out with: "Oh, I see now, it is a committee."[36]

Finally, diffusion is selective because the overt form of a particular trait, rather than its function or meaning, frequently seems to determine how the trait will be received. For example, the enthusiasm in women for bobbed hair (short haircuts) that swept through much of North America in the 1920s never caught on among the Native Americans of northwestern California. To many women of European ancestry, short hair was a symbolic statement of their freedom. To Native American women, who traditionally cut their hair short when in mourning, it was a reminder of death.[37]

In the process of diffusion, then, we can identify a number of different patterns. We know that cultural borrowing is selective rather than automatic, and we can describe how a particular borrowed trait has been modified by the recipient culture. But our current knowledge does not allow us to specify when one or another of these outcomes will occur, under what conditions diffusion will occur, and why it occurs the way it does.

Acculturation

On the surface, the process of change called **acculturation** seems to include much of what we have discussed under the label of diffusion, because acculturation refers to the changes that occur when different cultural groups come into intensive contact. As in diffusion, the source of new cultural items is the other society. But more often than not, anthropologists use the term *acculturation* to describe a situation in which one of the societies in contact is much more powerful than the other. Thus, acculturation can be seen as a process of extensive cultural borrowing in the context of superordinate-subordinate relations between societies.[38] There is probably always some borrowing both ways, but generally the subordinate or less powerful society borrows the most.

External pressure for culture change can take various forms. In its most direct form—conquest or colonialization—the dominant group uses force or the threat of force to try to bring about culture change in the other group. For example, in the Spanish conquest of Mexico, the conquerors forced many of the native groups to accept Catholicism. Although such direct force is not always exerted in conquest situations, dominated peoples often have little choice but to change. Examples of such indirectly forced change abound in the history of Native Americans in the United States. Although the federal government made few direct attempts to force people to adopt American culture, it did drive many native groups from their lands, thereby obliging them to give up many aspects of their traditional ways of life. To survive, they had no choice but to adopt many of the dominant society's traits. When Native American children were required to go to schools, which taught the dominant society's values, the process was accelerated.

A subordinate society may acculturate to a dominant society even in the absence of direct or indirect force. Perceiving that members of the dominant society enjoy more secure living conditions, the dominated people may identify with the dominant culture in the hope that they will be able to share some of its benefits by doing so. Or, they may elect to adopt cultural elements from the dominant society because they perceive that the new element has advantages. For example, in Arctic areas, many Inuit and Lapp groups seemed eager to replace dog sleds with snowmobiles without any coercion.[39] There is evidence that the Inuit weighed the advantages and disadvantages of the snowmobile versus the dog sled and that its adoption was gradual. Similarly, rifles were seen as a major technological improvement, increasing the success rate in hunting, but the Inuit did not completely abandon their former ways of hunting. More recently the Inuit are trying out GPS devices for navigating.[40]

Acculturation processes vary considerably depending upon the wishes of the more powerful society, the attitudes of the less powerful, and whether there is any choice. More powerful societies do not always want individuals from another culture to assimilate or "melt into" the dominant culture completely; instead, they may prefer and even actively promote a *multicultural* society. Multiculturalism can be voluntary or it may arise out of deliberate segregation. Then too, even though the less powerful group may be pressured by the dominant group to acquire some of their culture traits, they may resist or even reject those cultural elements, at least for a considerable length of time.

Many millions of people, however, never had a chance to acculturate after contact with Europeans. They simply died, sometimes directly at the hands of the conquerors, but probably more often as a result of the new diseases the Europeans inadvertently brought with them. Depopulation because of measles, smallpox, and tuberculosis was particularly common in North and South America and on the islands of the Pacific. Those areas had previously been isolated from contact with Europeans and from the diseases of that continuous landmass we call the Old World—Europe, Asia, and Africa.[41]

171

applied anthropology

Why the Bedouin Do Not Readily Settle Down

Most countries of the world today want to "develop." They want to increase their crop yields and their exports, build major roads and irrigation projects, and industrialize. Anthropologists interested in development have pointed out that many development schemes have failed in part because they do not adequately consider the culture of the people whose lives they affect. Thus, the international agencies that lend money have increasingly turned for advice to anthropologists to help plan and evaluate development projects.

Governments often view traditional ways of life negatively and fail to recognize that the old ways of life may be adaptive. Because culture is integrated, people cannot be expected to change an aspect of culture that is central to their lives. It is not that people do not want to change, but change is unlikely if it doesn't integrate well with other aspects of their lifestyle.

In many countries of the Middle East, governments want the Bedouin—people who herd animals over vast stretches of semiarid grassland—to settle down. Governments have tried to settle them by force or by enticements, but settlement schemes have failed time after time. In retrospect, such failures are not surprising. The Bedouin continue to try to herd animals near newly constructed settlements, but such grazing often results in human-made deserts near the settlements, so the settlements are abandoned. The traditional Bedouin pattern of herding animals depends on mobility. When the animals eat the tops of the grasses in a particular place, the people need to move on. When water starts drying up in one location, the herds need to be moved. Overgrazing near a settlement and plowing land in a semiarid environment can lead to quick erosion of the soil and the loss of plant cover. After the failure of many settlement schemes, governments may try to encourage a return to more traditional methods of grazing.

It is not that the Bedouin are reluctant to change in all respects. Many Bedouin readily gave up relying on camels for transport in favor of trucks. Trucks are a modern adaptation, yet they still allow mobility. Now the Bedouin are able to get water from wells and transport water to their animals by truck. The adoption of trucks led to other changes in Bedouin life. Small animals can be more readily transported to new pastures by truck, so many Bedouin have given up their dependence on camels and shifted to sheep and goat herding. Money is required to buy trucks and pay for gasoline and repairs, so more time is spent working for wages in temporary jobs.

In the 1980s, Dawn Chatty was asked by the government of the Middle Eastern country of Oman to help design a project to extend basic social services to the Bedouin without coercing them to alter their way of life. It isn't often that governments fund in-depth studies to understand the needs of the people being affected, but Chatty was able to persuade the Oman government that such a study was necessary as a first step. With United Nations funding, she began a study of the Harasiis pastoralists of southern Oman to evaluate their needs. The government wanted some action right away, so the project soon incorporated a mobile health unit that could begin a program of primary care as well as immunization against measles, whooping cough, and polio. After a period of evaluation, the project team also recommended an annual distribution of tents, the establishment of dormitories so children could live at schools, a new system of water delivery, and veterinary and marketing assistance.

Unfortunately, a development project often ends without any guarantee that health and other services will continue to be provided. As Chatty found out, long-term change is not as easy to achieve as short-term change. Along with other applied anthropologists, she continues to push for what Michael Cernea called "putting people first."

Sources: Chatty 1996; Cernea 1991, 7.

The story of Ishi, the last surviving member of a group of Native Americans in California called the Yahi, is a moving testimonial to the frequently tragic effect of contact with Europeans. In the space of 22 years, the Yahi population was reduced from several hundred to near zero. The historical record on this episode of depopulation suggests that European Americans murdered 30 to 50 Yahi for every European American murdered, but perhaps 60 percent of the Yahi died in the 10 years following their initial exposure to European diseases.[42]

Nowadays, many powerful nations—and not just Western ones—may seem to be acting in more humanitarian ways to improve the life of previously subjugated as well as other "developing" peoples. For better or worse, these programs, however, are still forms of external pressure. The tactic used may be persuasion rather than force, but most of the programs are nonetheless designed to bring about acculturation in the direction of the dominant societies' cultures. For example, the introduction of formal schooling cannot help but instill new values that may contradict traditional cultural patterns. Even health care programs may alter traditional ways of life by undermining the authority of shamans and other leaders and by increasing population beyond the number that can be supported in traditional ways. Confinement to "reservations" or other kinds of direct force are not the only ways a dominant society can bring about acculturation.

The process of acculturation also applies to immigrants, most of whom, at least nowadays, choose to leave one country for another. Immigrants are almost always a minority in the new country and therefore are in a subordinate position. If the immigrant's culture changes, it is almost always in the direction of the dominant culture. Immigrant groups vary considerably in the degree and speed with which they adopt the new culture and the social roles of the new society in which they live. An important area of research is explaining the variation in acculturation and assimilation. (*Assimilation* is a concept very similar to acculturation, but *assimilation* is a term more often used by sociologists to describe the process by which individuals acquire the social roles and culture of the dominant group.) Why do some immigrant groups acculturate or assimilate faster than others? A comparative study by Robert Schrauf assessed the degree to which immigrant groups coming to North America retained their native language over time. He looked at whether they lived in tightly knit communities, retained religious rituals, had separate schools and special festivals, visited their homeland, did not intermarry, or worked with others of their ethnic group. All of these factors might be expected to lead to retention of the native language (and presumably other cultural patterns), but only living in tightly knit communities and retaining religious rituals strongly predicted retaining the native language over a long period of time.[43]

CULTURE CHANGE AND ADAPTATION

Earlier in this chapter when we discussed the fact that culture is patterned, we indicated that adaptation to the environment is one reason why certain culture traits will cluster, because more than one trait is likely to be *adaptive* in a particular environment. We make the assumption that most of the customary behaviors of a culture are probably *adaptive*, or at least not maladaptive, in that environment. Even though customs are learned and not genetically inherited, cultural adaptation may resemble biological adaptation in one major respect. The frequency of certain genetic alternatives is likely to increase over time if those genetic traits increase their carriers' chances of survival and reproduction. Similarly, the frequency of a new learned behavior will increase over time and become customary in a population if the people with that behavior are most likely to survive and reproduce.

One of the most important differences between cultural evolution and genetic evolution is that individuals often can decide whether or not to accept and follow the way their parents behave or think, whereas they cannot decide whether or not to inherit certain genes. When enough individuals change their behavior and beliefs, we say that the culture has changed. Therefore, it is possible for culture change to occur much more rapidly than genetic change.

A dramatic example of intentional cultural change was the adoption and later elimination of the custom of *sepaade* among the Rendille, a pastoral population that herds camels, goats, and sheep in the desert in northern Kenya. According to the *sepaade* tradition, some women had to wait to marry until all their brothers were married. These women could well have been over 40 by the time they married. The Rendille say that this tradition was a result of intense warfare between the Rendille and the Borana during the mid-19th century. Attacked by Borana on horseback, the male warriors had to leave their camels unattended and the frightened camels fled. The daughters of one male age-set were appointed to look after the camels, and the *sepaade* tradition developed. In 1998, long after warfare with the Borana ceased, the elders decided to free the *sepaade* from their obligation to postpone their own marriages. Interviews with the Rendille in the 1990s revealed that many individuals were fully aware of the reason for the tradition in the first place. Now, they said, there was peace, so there was no longer any reason for the *sepaade* tradition to continue.[44]

The adoption of the *sepaade* is an example of culture change in a changing environment. But what if the environment is stable? Is culture change more or less likely? Robert Boyd and Peter Richerson have shown mathematically that, when the environment is relatively stable and individual mistakes are costly, staying with customary modes of behavior (usually transmitted by parents) is probably more adaptive than changing.[45] But what happens when the environment, particularly the social environment, is changing? There are plenty of examples in the modern world: People have to migrate to new places for work; medical care leads to increased population so that land is scarcer; people have had land taken away from them and are forced to make do with less land; and so on.

It is particularly when circumstances change that individuals are likely to try ideas or behaviors that are different from those of their parents. Most people would want to adopt behaviors that are more suited to their present circumstances, but how do they know which behaviors are better? There are various ways to find out. One way is by experimenting, trying out various new behaviors. Another way is to evaluate the experiments of others. If a person who tries a new technique seems successful, we would expect that person to be imitated, just as we would expect people to stick with new behaviors they have personally tried and found successful. Finally, one might choose to do what most people in the new situation decide to do.[46]

Why one choice rather than another? In part, the choice may be a function of the cost or risk of the innovation. It is relatively easy, for example, to find out how long it takes to cut down a tree with an introduced steel ax, as compared with a stone ax. Not surprisingly, innovations such as a steel ax catch on relatively quickly because comparison is easy and the results clear-cut. But what if the risk is very great? Suppose the innovation involves adopting a whole new way of farming that you have never practiced before. You can try it, but you might not have any food if you fail. As we discussed earlier, risky innovations are likely to be tried only by those individuals who can afford the risk. Other people may then evaluate their success and adopt the new strategy if it looks promising. Similarly, if you migrate to a new area, say, from a high-rainfall area to a drier one, it may pay to look around to see what most people in the new

Currier & Ives, "Give Me Liberty or Give Me Death!", 1775. Lithograph, 1876. c. The Granger Collection, New York

Revolutionary leaders are often from high-status backgrounds. Here we see a depiction of Patrick Henry giving his famous speech to the aristocratic landowners in the Virginia General Assembly on March 23, 1775. Urging the Virginians to fight the British, Henry said that the choice was "liberty or death."

Source: Currier & Ives, "Give Me Liberty or Give Me Death!", 1775. Lithograph, 1876. c. The Granger Collection, New York.

place do; after all, the people in the drier area probably have customs that are adaptive for that environment.

We can expect, then, that the choices individuals make may often be adaptive ones. But it is important to note that adopting an innovation from someone in one's own society or borrowing an innovation from another society is not always or necessarily beneficial, either in the short or the long run. First, people may make mistakes in judgment, especially when some new behavior seems to satisfy a physical need. Why, for example, have smoking and drug use diffused so widely even though they are likely to reduce a person's chances of survival? Second, even if people are correct in their short-term judgment of benefit, they may be wrong in their judgment about long-run benefit. A new crop may yield more than the old crop for five consecutive years, but the new crop may fail miserably in the sixth year because of lower-than-normal rainfall or because the new crop depleted soil nutrients. Third, people may be forced by the more powerful to change, with few if any benefits for themselves.

Whatever the motives for humans to change their behavior, the theory of natural selection suggests that new behavior is not likely to become cultural or remain cultural over generations if it has harmful reproductive consequences, just as a genetic mutation with harmful consequences is not likely to become frequent in a population.[47] Still, we know of many examples of culture change that seem maladaptive—the switch to bottle-feeding rather than nursing infants, which may spread infection because contaminated water is used, or the adoption of alcoholic beverages, which may lead to alcoholism and early death.

Revolution

Certainly the most drastic and rapid way a culture can change is as a result of **revolution**—replacement, usually violent, of a country's rulers. Historical records, as well as our daily newspapers, indicate that people frequently rebel against established authority. Rebellions, if they occur, almost always occur in state societies, where there is a dis-

tinct ruling elite. They take the form of struggles between rulers and ruled, between conquerors and conquered, or between representatives of an external colonial power and segments of the native society. Rebels do not always succeed in overthrowing their rulers, so rebellions do not always result in revolutions. And even successful rebellions do not always result in culture change; the individual rulers may change, but customs or institutions may not. The sources of revolution may be mostly internal, as in the French Revolution, or partly external, as in the Russian-supported 1948 revolution in Czechoslovakia and the United States-supported 1973 revolution against President Allende in Chile.

The American War of Independence toward the end of the 18th century is a good example of a colonial rebellion, the success of which was at least partly a result of foreign intervention. The American rebellion was a war of neighboring colonies against the greatest imperial power of the time, Great Britain. In the 19th century and continuing into the middle and later years of the 20th century, there would be many other wars of independence, in Latin America, Europe, Asia, and Africa. We don't always remember that the American rebellion was the first of these anti-imperialist wars in modern times, and the model for many that followed. And just like many of the most recent liberation movements, the American rebellion was also part of a larger worldwide war, involving people from many rival nations. Thirty thousand German-speaking soldiers fought, for pay, on the British side; an army and navy from France fought on the American side. There were volunteers from other European countries, including Denmark, Holland, Poland, and Russia.

One of these volunteers was a man named Kosciusko from Poland, which at the time was being divided between Prussia and Russia. Kosciusko helped win a major victory for the Americans, and subsequently directed the fortification of what later became the American training school for army officers, West Point. After the war, he returned to Poland and led a rebellion against the Russians, which was only briefly successful. In 1808, he published the *Manual on the Maneuvers of Horse Artillery,* which was used for many years by the American army. When he died, he left money to buy freedom and education for American slaves. The executor of Kosciusko's will was Thomas Jefferson.

As in many revolutions, those who were urging revolution were considered "radicals." At a now-famous debate in Virginia in 1775, delegates from each colony met at a Continental Congress. Patrick Henry put forward a resolution to prepare for defense against the British armed forces. The motion barely passed, by a vote of 65 to 60. Henry's speech is now a part of American folklore. He rose to declare that it was insane not to oppose the British and that he was not afraid to test the strength of the colonies against Great Britain. Others might hesitate, he said, but he would have "liberty or death." The "radicals" who supported Henry's resolution included many aristocratic landowners, two of whom, George Washington and Thomas Jefferson, became the first and third occupants of the highest political office in what became the United States of America.[48]

Not all peoples who are suppressed, conquered, or colonialized eventually rebel against established authority. Why this is so, and why rebellions and revolts are not always successful in bringing about culture change, are still open questions. But some possible answers have been investigated. One historian who examined the classic revolutions of the past, including the American, French, and Russian revolutions, suggested some conditions that may give rise to rebellion and revolution:

1. **Loss of prestige of established authority,** often as a result of the failure of foreign policy, financial difficulties, dismissals of popular ministers, or alteration of popular policies. France in the 18th century lost three major international conflicts, with disastrous results for its diplomatic standing and internal finances. Russian society was close to military and economic collapse in 1917, after three years of World War I.

2. **Threat to recent economic improvement.** In France, as in Russia, those sections of the population (professional classes and urban workers) whose economic fortunes had only shortly before taken an upward swing were "radicalized" by unexpected setbacks, such as steeply rising food prices and unemployment. The same may be said for the American colonies on the brink of their rebellion against Great Britain.

3. **Indecisiveness of government,** as exemplified by lack of consistent policy, which gives the impression of being controlled by, rather than in control of, events. The frivolous arrogance of Louis XVI's regime and the bungling of George III's prime minister, Lord North, with respect to the problems of the American colonies are examples.

4. **Loss of support of the intellectual class.** Such a loss deprived the prerevolutionary governments of France and Russia of any avowed philosophical support and led to their unpopularity with the literate public.[49]

The classic revolutions of the past occurred in countries that were industrialized only incipiently at best. For the most part, the same is true of the rebellions and revolutions in recent years; they have occurred mostly in countries we call "developing." The evidence from a worldwide survey of developing countries suggests that rebellions have tended to occur where the ruling classes depended mostly on the produce or income from land, and therefore were resistant to demands for reform from the rural classes that worked the land. In such agricultural economies, the rulers are not likely to yield political power or give greater economic returns to the workers, because to do so would eliminate the basis (landownership) of the rulers' wealth and power.[50]

Finally, a particularly interesting question is why revolutions sometimes, perhaps even usually, fail to measure up to the high hopes of those who initiate them. When rebellions succeed in replacing the ruling elite, the result is often the institution of a military dictatorship even more restrictive and repressive than the government that existed before. The new ruling establishment may merely substitute one set of repressions for another, rather than bring any real change to the nation. On the other hand, some revolutions have resulted in fairly drastic overhauls of societies.

The idea of revolution has been one of the central myths and inspirations of many groups both in the past and in the present. The colonial empire building of countries such as England and France created a worldwide situation in which rebellion became nearly inevitable. In numerous technologically underdeveloped lands, which have been exploited by more powerful countries for their natural resources and cheap labor, a deep resentment has often developed against the foreign ruling classes or their local clients. Where the ruling classes, native or foreign, refuse to be responsive to those feelings, rebellion becomes the only alternative. In many areas, it has become a way of life.

GLOBALIZATION: PROBLEMS AND OPPORTUNITIES

Investment capital, people, and ideas are moving around the world at an ever faster rate.[51] Transportation now allows people and goods to circle the globe in days; telecommunications and the Internet make it possible to send a message around the world in seconds and minutes. Economic exchange is enormously more global and transnational. The word **globalization** is often used nowadays to refer to "the massive flow of goods, people, information, and capital across huge areas of the earth's surface."[52] The process of globalization has resulted in the worldwide spread of cultural features, particularly in the domain of economics and international trade. We buy from the same companies (that have factories all over the world), we sell our products and services for prices that are set by world market forces. We can eat pizza, hamburgers, curry, or sushi in most urban centers. In some ways, cultures are changing in similar directions. They have become more commercial, more urban, and more international. The job has become more important, and kinship less important,

175

Television has dramatically enhanced world communication. We can see what's happening on the other side of the world almost in real time. People in Niger watch television powered by another important invention, solar panels.

John Chiasson

as people travel to and work in other countries, and return just periodically to their original homes. Ideas about democracy, the rights of the individual, and alternative medical practices and religions have become more widespread; people in many countries of the world watch the same TV shows, wear similar fashions, and listen to the same or similar music. In short, people are increasingly sharing behaviors and beliefs with people in other cultures, and the cultures of the world are less and less things "with edges," as Paul Durrenberger says.[53]

Globalization began in earnest about A.D. 1500, with exploration by and expansion of Western societies.[54] In the last few decades, globalization has greatly intensified such that there are very few places in the world that have not been affected.[55] Thus, much of the culture change in the modern world has been externally induced, if not forced. This is not to say that cultures are changing now only because of external pressures; but externally induced changes have been the changes that anthropologists and other social scientists most frequently study. Most of the external pressures have come from Western societies, but not all. Far Eastern societies, such as Japan and China, have also stimulated culture change. And the expansion of Islamic societies after the 8th century A.D. made for an enormous amount of culture change in the Near East, Africa, Europe, and Asia.

But diffusion of a culture trait does not mean that it is incorporated in exactly the same way, and the spread of certain products and activities through globalization does not mean that change happens in the same way everywhere. For example, the spread of multinational fast-food restaurants like McDonald's or Kentucky Fried Chicken has come to symbolize globalization. But the behavior of the Japanese in such restaurants is quite different from behavior in the United States. Perhaps the most surprising difference is that the Japanese in McDonald's actually have more familial intimacy and sharing than in more traditional restaurants. We imagine that establishments like McDonald's promote fast eating. But Japan has long had fast food—noodle shops at train stations, street vendors,

and boxed lunches. Sushi, which is usually ordered in the United States at a sit-down restaurant, is usually served in Japan at a bar with a conveyor belt—individuals only need to pluck off the wanted dish as it goes by. Observations at McDonald's in Japan suggest that mothers typically order food for the family while the father spends time with the children at a table, a rare event since fathers often work long hours and cannot get home for dinner often. Food, such as French fries, is typically shared by the family. Even burgers and drinks are passed around, with many people taking a bite or a sip. Such patterns typify long-standing family practices. Japan has historically borrowed food, such as the Chinese noodle soup, now called ramen. Indeed, in a survey, ramen was listed as the most representative Japanese food. The burger was the second most-often listed. McDonald's has become Japanese—the younger generation does not even know that McDonald's is a foreign company—they think it is Japanese.[56]

Globalization is not new. The world has been global and interdependent since the 16th century.[57] What we currently call "globalization" is a more widespread version of what we used to call by various other names—diffusion, acculturation, colonialism, imperialism, or commercialization. But globalization is now on a much grander scale; enormous amounts of international investment fuel world trade. Shifts in the world marketplace may drastically affect a country's well-being more than ever before. For example, 60 percent of Pakistan's industrial employment is in textile and apparel manufacturing, but serious unemployment resulted when that manufacturing was crippled by restrictive American import policies and fears about war between India and Afghanistan.[58]

As we have seen in this chapter, there are many negative effects of colonialism, imperialism, and globalization. Many native peoples in many places lost their land and have been forced to work for inadequate wages in mines and plantations and factories that foreign capitalists own. Frequently, there is undernutrition if not starvation. Global travel has resulted in the quick spread of diseases such as HIV and severe acute respiratory syndrome (SARS), and increasing deforestation has led to a spread of malaria.[59] But are there any positive consequences? The "human development indicators" collected by the United Nations suggest an improvement in many respects, including increases in life expectancy and literacy in most countries. Much of the improvement in life expectancy is undoubtedly due to the spread of medicines developed in the advanced economies of the West. There is generally less warfare as colonial powers enforced pacification within the colonies that later became independent states. Most important, perhaps, has been the growth of middle classes all over the world, whose livelihoods depend on globalizing commerce. The middle classes in many countries have become strong and numerous enough to pressure governments for democratic reforms and the reduction of injustice.

World trade is the primary engine of economic development. Per capita income is increasing. Forty years ago, the countries of Asia were among the poorest countries in the world in terms of per capita income. Since then, because of their involvement in world trade, their incomes have risen enormously. In 1960, South Korea was as poor as India. Now its per capita income is 20 times higher than India's. Singapore is an even more dramatic example. In the late 1960s, its economy was a disaster. Today, its per capita income is higher than Britain's.[60] Mexico used to be a place where North Americans built factories to produce garments for the North American market. Now its labor is no longer so cheap. But because it has easy access to the North American market and because its plentiful labor is acquiring the necessary skills, Mexico is now seeing the development of high-tech manufacturing with decent salaries.[61]

There is world trade also in people. Many countries of the world now export people to other countries. Mexico has done so for a long time. Virtually every family in a Bangladesh village depends on someone who works overseas and sends money home. Without those remittances, many would face starvation. The government encourages people to go abroad to work. Millions of people from Bangladesh are now overseas on government-sponsored work contracts.[62]

But does a higher per capita income mean that life has improved generally in a country? Not necessarily. Inequality within countries can increase with technological improvements because the rich often benefit the most. In addition, economic wealth is increasingly concentrated in a relatively small number of countries. Obviously, then, not everyone is better off even if most countries are doing better on average. Poverty has become more common as countries have become more unequal.

Although many of the changes associated with globalization seem to be driven by the economic and political power of the richer countries, the movement of ideas, art, music, and food is more of a two-way process. A large part of that process involves the migration of people who bring their culture with them. As we will see in the box titled "Migrants and Immigrants," movements of people have played a large role in the entry of food such as tortilla chips and salsa, sushi, and curries into the United States,

music like reggae and many types of dance music from Latin America, and African carvings and jewelry such as beaded necklaces. Recently there has even been increased interest in acquiring indigenous knowledge of plants, the knowledge of indigenous healers, and learning about shamanistic trances. As indigenous knowledge comes to be viewed as potentially valuable, shamans have been able to speak out on national and international issues. In Brazil, shamans have organized to speak out against "biopiracy"—what is perceived as the unethical appropriation of biological knowledge for commercial purposes. In a more globalized world, shamans and other indigenous activists can be heard by more people than ever before. Despite the fact that indigenous people constitute less than one percent of the Brazilian population, some activist groups have been able to keep in touch with international environmentalists, using tape recorders and video cameras to convey information about their local situation.[63]

It is probably not possible to go back to a time when societies were not so dependent on each other, not so interconnected through world trade, not so dependent on commercial exchange. Even those who are most upset with globalization find it difficult to imagine that it is possible to return to a less connected world. For better or worse, the world is interconnected and will remain so. The question now is whether the average economic improvements in countries will eventually translate into economic improvements for most individuals.

ETHNOGENESIS: THE EMERGENCE OF NEW CULTURES

Many of the processes that we have discussed—the expansion and domination by the West and other powerful nations, the deprivation of the ability of peoples to earn their livelihoods by traditional means, the imposition of schools or other methods to force acculturation, the attempts to convert people to other religions, and globalization—have led to profound changes in culture. But if culture change in the modern world has made cultures more alike in some ways, it has not eliminated cultural differences. Indeed, people are still very variable culturally from one place to the next. New differences have also emerged. Often, in the aftermath of violent events such as depopulation, relocation, enslavement, and genocide by dominant powers, deprived peoples have created new cultures in a process called **ethnogenesis**.[64]

Some of the most dramatic examples of ethnogenesis come from areas where escaped slaves (called Maroons) created new cultures. Maroon societies emerged in the past few hundred years in a variety of New World locations, from the United States to the West Indies and northern parts of South America. One of the new cultures, now known as Aluku, emerged when slaves fled from coastal plantations in Suriname to the swampy interior country along the Cottica River. After a war with the Dutch colonists, this particular group moved to French Guiana.

migrants and immigrants

Increasing Cultural Diversity within the Countries of the World

The modern world is culturally diverse in two ways. There are native cultures in every part of the world, and today most countries have people from different cultures who have arrived relatively recently. Recent arrivals may be migrants coming for temporary work, or they may be refugees, forced by persecution or genocide to migrate, or they may be immigrants who voluntarily come into a new country. Parts of populations have moved away from their native places since the dawn of humanity. The first modern-looking humans moved out of Africa only in the last 100,000 years. People have been moving ever since. The people we call Native Americans were actually the first to come to the New World; most anthropologists think they came from northeast Asia. In the last 200 years, the United States and Canada have experienced extensive influxes of people. As is commonly said, they have become nations of migrants and immigrants, and Native Americans are now vastly outnumbered by the people and their descendants who came from Europe, Africa, Asia, Latin America, and elsewhere. North America not only has native and regional subcultures, but also ethnic, religious, and occupational subcultures, each with its own distinctive set of culture traits. Thus, North American culture is partly a

"melting pot" and partly a mosaic of cultural diversity. Many of us, not just anthropologists, like this diversity. We like to go to ethnic restaurants regularly. We like salsa, sushi, and spaghetti. We compare and enjoy the different geographic varieties of coffee. We like music and artists from other countries. We often choose to wear clothing that may have been manufactured halfway around the world. We like all of these things not only because they may be affordable. We like them mostly, perhaps, because they are different.

Many of the population movements in the world today, as in the past, are responses to persecution and war. The word *diaspora* is often used nowadays to refer to these major dispersions. Most were and are involuntary; people are fleeing danger and death. But not always. Scholars distinguish different types of diaspora, including "victim," "labor," "trade," and "imperial" diasporas. The Africans who were sold into slavery, the Armenians who fled genocide in the early 20th century, the Jews who fled persecution and genocide in various places over the centuries, the Palestinians who fled to the West Bank, Gaza, Jordan, and Lebanon in the mid-20th century, and the Rwandans who fled genocide toward the end of the 20th century may have

mostly been victims. The Chinese, Italians, and the Poles may have mostly moved to take advantage of job opportunities, the Lebanese to trade, and the British to extend and service their empire. Often these categories overlap; population movements can and have occurred for more than one reason. Some of the recent diasporas are less one-way than in the past. People are more "transnational," just as economics and politics are more "globalized." The new global communications have facilitated the retention of homeland connections—socially, economically, and politically. Some diasporic communities play an active role in the politics of their homelands, and some nation-states have begun to recognize their far-flung emigrants as important constituencies.

As cultural anthropologists increasingly study migrant, refugee, and immigrant groups, they focus on how the groups have adapted their cultures to new surroundings, what they have retained, how they relate to the homeland, how they have developed an ethnic consciousness, and how they relate to other minority groups and the majority culture.

Sources: M. Ember et al. 2005; Levinson and M. Ember 1997.

The escaped slaves, originating from widely varying cultures in Africa or born on Suriname plantations, organized themselves into autonomous communities with military headmen.[65] They practiced slash-and-burn cultivation, with women doing most of the work. Although settlements shifted location as a way of evading enemies, coresidence in a community and collective ownership of land became important parts of the emerging identities. Communities took on the names of the specific plantations from which their leaders had escaped. Principles of inheritance through the female line began to develop, and full-fledged matriclans became the core of each village. Each village had its own shrine, the *faaka tiki*, where residents invoked the clan ancestors, as well as a special house where the deceased were brought to be honored and feted before being taken to the forest for burial. Clans also in-

herited avenging spirits with whom they could communicate through mediums.

The Aluku case is a clear example of ethnogenesis because the culture did not exist 350 years ago. It emerged and was created by people trying to adapt to circumstances not of their own making. In common with other cases of emerging ethnic identity, the Aluku came not only to share new patterns of behavior but also to see themselves as having a common origin (a common ancestor), a shared history, and a common religion.[66]

The emergence of the Seminole in Florida is another case of ethnogenesis. The early settlers who moved to what is now Florida and later became known as Seminole largely derived from the Lower Creek Kawita chiefdom. The Kawita chiefdom, like other southeastern Muskogean chiefdoms, was a large, complex, multiethnic paramount

Osceola, a Seminole chief, born of a British father and a Creek mother. He led his people against the settlers in the Seminole Wars but was captured and died in confinement at Fort Moultrie, South Carolina.

chiefdom. Its ruler, Kawita, relied on allegiance and tribute from outlying districts; ritual and linguistic hegemony was imposed by the ruler.[67]

A combination of internal divisions among the Lower Creek, vacant land in northern Florida, and weak Spanish control over northern Florida apparently prompted dissidents to move away and settle in three different areas in Florida. Three new chiefdoms were established, essentially similar to those the settlers left and still under the supposed control of Kawita.[68] But the three chiefdoms began to act together under the leadership of Tonapi, the Talahassi chief. After 1780, over a period of 40 or so years, the three Seminole chiefdoms formally broke with Kawita. Not only was geographic separation a factor, but the political and economic interests of the Creek Confederacy and of the Seminole had diverged. For example, the Creek supported neutrality in the American Revolution, but the Seminole took the side of the British. During this time, the British encouraged slaves to escape by promising freedom in Florida. These Maroon communities allied themselves with the emerging Seminole. The composition of the Seminole population again changed dramatically after the War of 1812 and the Creek War of 1814.[69] First, a large number of Creek refugees, mostly Upper Creek Talapusa (who spoke a different Muskogean language), became Seminole. Second, the Seminole ranks were also expanded by a large number of escaped slaves and Maroons who fled when the Americans destroyed a British fort in 1816. Larger-scale political events continued to influence Seminole history. When the Americans conquered Florida, they insisted on dealing with one unified Seminole council, they removed the Seminole to a reserve in Florida, and later, after the second Seminole war, removed most of them to Oklahoma.[70]

It would seem from this and other cases that cultural identities can be shaped and reshaped by political and economic processes.

CULTURAL DIVERSITY IN THE FUTURE

Measured in terms of travel time, the world today is much smaller than it has ever been. It is possible now to fly halfway around the globe in the time it took people less than a century ago to travel to the next state. In the realm of communication, the world is even smaller. We can talk to someone on the other side of the globe in a matter of minutes, we can send that person a message (by fax or Internet) in seconds, and through television we can see live coverage of events in that person's country. More and more people are drawn into the world market economy, buying and selling similar things and, as a consequence, altering the patterns of their lives in sometimes similar ways. Still, although modern transportation and communication facilitate the rapid spread of some cultural characteristics to all parts of the globe, it is highly unlikely that all parts of the world will end up the same culturally. Cultures are bound to retain some of their original characteristics or develop distinctive new adaptations. Even though television has diffused around the world, local people continue to prefer local programs when they are available. And even when people all over the world watch the same program, they may interpret it in very different ways. People are not just absorbing the messages they get; they often resist or revise them.[71]

Until recently, researchers studying culture change generally assumed that the differences between people of different cultures would become minimal. But in the last 30 years or so, it has become increasingly apparent that, although many differences disappear, many people are affirming ethnic identities in a process that often involves deliberately introducing cultural difference.[72] Eugeen Roosens describes the situation of the Huron of Quebec, who in the late 1960s seemed to have disappeared as a distinct culture. The Huron language had disappeared and the lives of the Huron were not obviously distinguishable from those of the French Canadians around them. The Huron then developed a new identity as they actively worked to promote the rights of indigenous peoples like themselves. That their new defining cultural symbols bore no resemblance to the past Huron culture is beside the point.

One fascinating possibility is that ethnic diversity and ethnogenesis may be a result of broader processes. Elizabeth Cashdan found that ethnic diversity appears to be related to environmental unpredictability, which is associated with greater distance from the equator.[73] There appear to be many more cultural groups nearer to the equator than in very northern and southern latitudes. Perhaps, Cashdan suggests, environmental unpredictability in the north and south necessitates wider ties between social groups to allow cooperation in case local resources fail. This may minimize the likelihood of cultural divergence, that is, ethnogenesis. Hence, there will be fewer cultures further from the equator.

Future research on culture change should increase our understanding of how and why various types of change are occurring. If we can increase our understanding of culture change in the present, we should be better able to understand similar processes in the past. We may be guided in our efforts to understand culture change by the large number of cross-cultural correlations that have been discovered between a particular cultural variation and its presumed causes.[74] All cultures have changed over time; variation is the product of differential change. Thus, the variations we see are the products of change processes, and the discovered predictors of those variations may suggest how and why the changes occurred. The task of discovering which particular circumstances favor which particular patterns is a large and difficult one.

SUMMARY ● ○ ○

1. Despite individual differences, the members of a particular society share many behaviors and ideas that constitute their culture.

2. Culture may be defined as the set of learned behaviors and ideas (including beliefs, attitudes, values, and ideals) that are characteristic of a particular society or other social group.

3. The type of group within which cultural traits are shared can vary from a particular society or a segment of that society to a group that transcends national boundaries. When anthropologists refer to *a* culture, they usually are referring to the cultural patterns of a particular society—that is, a particular territorial population speaking a language not generally understood by neighboring territorial populations. Although other animals exhibit some cultural behavior, humans are unusual in the number and complexity of the learned patterns that they transmit to their young. And they have a unique way of transmitting their culture: through spoken, symbolic language.

4. Ethnocentrism, judging other cultures in terms of your own, and its opposite—the glorification of other cultures—impede anthropological inquiry. An important tenet in anthropology is the principle of cultural relativism: the attitude that a society's customs and ideas should be studied objectively and understood in the context of that society's culture. But when it comes to some cultural practices such as violence against women, torture, slavery, or genocide, most anthropologists can no longer adhere to the strong form of cultural relativism that asserts that all cultural practices are equally valid.

5. Anthropologists seek to discover the customs and ranges of acceptable behavior that constitute the culture of a society under study. In doing so, they focus on general or shared patterns of behavior rather than on individual variations. When dealing with practices that are highly visible, or with beliefs that are almost unanimous, the investigator can rely on observation on or interviewing off a few knowledgeable people. With less obvious behaviors or attitudes, anthropologists must collect information from a sample of individuals. The mode of a frequency distribution can then be used to express the cultural pattern.

6. Cultures have patterns or clusters of traits. They tend to be integrated for psychological and adaptive reasons.

7. Culture is always changing. Because culture consists of learned patterns of behavior and belief, cultural traits can be unlearned and learned anew as human needs change. The sources of change may be external and/or internal.

8. Discoveries and inventions, though ultimately the sources of all culture change, do not necessarily lead to change. Only when society accepts an invention or discovery and uses it regularly can culture change be said to have occurred. Some inventions are probably the result of dozens of tiny, perhaps accidental, initiatives over a period of many years. Other inventions are consciously intended. Why some people are more innovative than others is still only incompletely understood. There is some evidence that creativity and a readiness to adopt innovations may be related to socioeconomic position.

9. The process by which cultural elements are borrowed from another society and incorporated into the culture of the recipient group is called diffusion. Cultural traits do not necessarily diffuse; that is, diffusion is a selective, not automatic, process. A society accepting a foreign cultural trait is likely to adapt it in a way that effectively harmonizes it with the society's own traditions.

10. When a group or society is in contact with a more powerful society, the weaker group is often obliged to acquire cultural elements from the dominant group. This process of extensive borrowing in the context of superordinate-subordinate relations between societies is called acculturation. Acculturation processes vary considerably depending upon the wishes of the more powerful society, the attitudes of the less powerful, and whether there is any choice.

11. Even though customs are not genetically inherited, cultural adaptation may be similar to biological adaptation in one major respect. Traits (cultural or genetic) that are more likely to be reproduced (learned or inherited) are likely to become more frequent in a population over time. Particularly when the environment changes, individuals may try out ideas and behaviors that are different than their parents.

12. Perhaps the most drastic and rapid way a culture can change is by revolution—a usually violent replacement

of the society's rulers. Rebellions occur primarily in state societies, where there is a distinct ruling elite. However, not all peoples who are suppressed, conquered, or colonized eventually rebel or successfully revolt against established authority.

13. Globalization—the widespread flow of people, information, technology, and capital over the earth's surface—has minimized cultural diversity in some respects, but it has not eliminated it.

14. Ethnogenesis is the process by which new cultures are created.

GLOSSARY TERMS ○ ● ○

acculturation	ethnogenesis
adaptive customs	globalization
cultural relativism	maladaptive customs
culture	norms
diffusion	revolution
ethnocentric	society
ethnocentrism	subculture

CRITICAL QUESTIONS ○ ○ ●

1. Would it be adaptive for a society to have everyone adhere to the cultural norms? Explain your answer.

2. Some anthropologists think of culture as being "outside" individuals; others think of culture as being "inside" individuals in the form of individual cognitive maps as to how people should behave. How would these different views affect research methods and the resultant cultural descriptions? How would these views affect the understanding of culture change?

3. Not all people faced with external pressure to change do so or do so at the same rate. What factors might explain why some societies rapidly change their culture?

4. Does the concept of cultural relativism promote international understanding, or does it hinder attempts to have international agreement on acceptable behavior, such as human rights?

PEARSON
myanthrolab

Read the chapter by Regina Smith Oboler, "Nandi: From Cattle-Keepers to Cash-Crop Farmers," on MyAnthroLab, and answer the following questions:

1. Who are the Nandi? Give a brief description of them, and include the time period and community being described by Oboler.

2. As you read about the Nandi, you may be surprised by some of their customs. Indicate which specific customs surprise you. Describe whether you think you are reacting simply because their customs are different from your customs, whether you are being ethnocentric, or if you prefer their customs.

3. Anthropologists have to learn not to judge behavior in another culture in terms of their own culture. Give an example from Regina Smith Oboler's fieldwork among the Nandi.

NOTES ● ○ ○

1. Linton 1945, 30.
2. Sapir 1938, cited by Pelto and Pelto 1975, 1.
3. Pelto and Pelto 1975, 14–15.
4. de Waal 2001, 269.
5. de Munck 2000, 22.
6. Ibid. 2000, 22.
7. Ibid. 2000, 8.
8. Durkheim 1938/1895, 3.
9. Asch 1956.
10. Bond and Smith 1996.
11. Berns et al. 2005.
12. M. F. Brown 2008, 372.
13. Hewlett 2004.
14. Miner 1956, 504–05, reproduced by permission of the American Anthropological Association. Although Miner is not a foreign visitor, he wrote this description in a way that shows how these behaviors might be seen from an outside perspective.
15. Lee 1972.
16. M. F. Brown 2008, 364.
17. Hatch 1997.
18. Zechenter 1997.
19. Rosenblatt 2009.
20. Hall 1966, 159–60.
21. Ibid., 120.
22. R. Brown 1965, 549–609.
23. Wagley 1974.
24. Chibnik 1981, 256–68.
25. Linton 1936, 306.
26. Ibid., 310–11.
27. Silver 1981.
28. Greenfield et al. 2000.
29. Rogers 1983, 263–69.
30. Cancian 1980.
31. Hewlett and Cavalli-Sforza 1986; Cavalli-Sforza and Feldman 1981.
32. Valente 1995, 21.
33. W. Cohen 1995.
34. Linton 1936, 326–27.
35. *Britannica Online* 1998; *Academic American Encyclopedia* 1980.
36. Linton 1936, 338–39.
37. G. M. Foster 1962, 26.
38. Bodley 2008.
39. Pelto and Müller-Wille 1987, 207–43.
40. Aporta and Higgs 2005.
41. Bodley 2008.
42. T. Kroeber 1967, 45–47.
43. Schrauf 1999.
44. Roth 2001.
45. Boyd and Richerson 1996/1985, 106.
46. Ibid., p. 135.
47. D. T. Campbell 1965. See also Boyd and Richerson 1996/1985 and Durham 1991.

48. The historical information we refer to comes from a book by Nevins 1927. For how radical the American Revolution was, see G. Wood 1992.
49. Brinton 1938.
50. Paige 1975.
51. Bestor 2001, 76.
52. Trouillot 2001, 128.
53. Durrenberger 2001a; see also Hannerz 1996.
54. McNeill 1967, 283–87; Guest and Jones 2005, 4.
55. Guest and Jones 2005, 4
56. Traphagan and Brown 2002.
57. Trouillot 2001, 128.
58. Bradsher 2002, 3.
59. Guest and Jones 2005.
60. Yergin 2002, A29.
61. G. Thompson 2002, A3.
62. Sengupta 2002, A3.
63. Conklin 2002.
64. J. D. Hill 1996, 1.
65. Bilby 1996, 127–28, referring to Hoogbergen 1990, 23–51.
66. Bilby 1996, 128–37.
67. Sattler 1996, 42.
68. Ibid., 50–51.
69. Ibid., 54.
70. Ibid., 58–59.
71. Kottak 1996, 136; 153.
72. Roosens 1989, 9.
73. Cashdan 2001.
74. C. R. Ember and Levinson 1991.

Communication and Language

From Chapter 15 of *Anthropology*, 13/e. Carol R. Ember. Melvin Ember. Peter N. Peregrine. Copyright © 2011 by Pearson Education. Published by Prentice Hall. All rights reserved.

Communication and Language

F ew of us can remember when we first became aware that words signified something. Yet that moment was a milestone for us, not just in the acquisition of language but in becoming acquainted with all the complex, elaborate behavior that constitutes our culture. Without language, the transmission of complex traditions would be virtually impossible, and each person would be trapped within his or her own world of private sensations.

Helen Keller, left deaf and blind by illness at the age of 19 months, gives a moving account of the afternoon she first established contact with another human being through words:

> [My teacher] brought me my hat, and I knew I was going out into the warm sunshine. This thought, if a wordless sensation may be called a thought, made me hop and skip with pleasure.
>
> We walked down the path to the well house, attracted by the fragrance of the honeysuckle with which it was covered. Someone was drawing water and my teacher placed my hand under the spout. As the cool stream gushed over one hand she spelled into the other the word water, first slowly, then rapidly. Suddenly I felt a misty consciousness as of something forgotten—a thrill of returning thought; and somehow the mystery of language was revealed to me. I knew then that w-a-t-e-r meant the wonderful cool something that was flowing over my hand. That living word awakened my soul, gave it light, hope, joy, set it free! There were barriers still, it is true, barriers that could in time be swept away.
>
> I left the well house eager to learn. Everything had a name, and each name gave birth to a new thought. As we returned to the house every object which I touched seemed to quiver with life. That was because I saw everything with the strange, new sight that had come to me.[1]

● ○ ●

COMMUNICATION

Against all odds, Helen Keller had come to understand the essential function that language plays in all societies—namely, that of communication. The word *communicate* comes from the Latin verb *communicare*, "to impart," "to share," "to make *common*." We communicate by agreeing, consciously or unconsciously, to call an object, a movement, or an abstract concept by a common name. For example, speakers of English have agreed to call the color of grass *green*, even though we have no way of comparing precisely how two people actually experience this color. What we share is the agreement to call similar sensations *green*. Any system of language consists of publicly accepted symbols by which individuals try to share private experiences. Spoken or vocal language is probably the major transmitter of culture, allowing us to share and pass on our complex configuration of attitudes, beliefs, and patterns of behavior.

185

Nonverbal Human Communication

As we all know from experience, the spoken word does not communicate all that we know about a social situation. We can usually tell when someone says, "It was good to meet you," whether he or she really means it. We can tell if people are sad from their demeanor, even if they just say, "I'm fine," in response to the question "How are you?"

Obviously, our communication is not limited to spoken language. We communicate directly through facial expression, body stance, gesture, and tone of voice and indirectly through systems of signs and symbols, such as writing, algebraic equations, musical scores, dancing, painting, code flags, and road signs. As Anthony Wilden put it, "every act, every pause, every movement in living and social systems is also a message; silence is communication; short of death it is impossible for an organism or person not to communicate."[2] How can silence be a communication? Silence may reflect companionship, as when two people work side by side on a project, but silence can also communicate unfriendliness. An anthropologist can learn a great deal from what people in a society do not talk about. For example, in India, sex is not supposed to be talked about. HIV infection is spreading very fast in India, so the unwillingness of people to talk about sex makes it extraordinarily difficult for medical anthropologists and health professionals to do much to reduce the rate of spread.[3]

Some nonverbal communication appears to be universal in humans. For example, humans the world over appear to understand facial expression in the same way; that is, they are able to recognize a happy, sad, surprised, angry, disgusted, or afraid face. How the face is represented in art appears to evoke similar feelings in many different cultures. Masks intended to be frightening have sharp, angular features and inward- and downward-facing eyes and eyebrows.

Nonverbal communication is also culturally variable. The distance between people standing together is culturally variable. In the realm of facial expression, different cultures have different rules about the emotions that are acceptable to express. One study compared how Japanese and Americans express emotion. Individuals from both groups were videotaped while they were shown films intended to evoke feelings of fear and disgust. When the subjects saw the films by themselves, without other people present, they showed the same kinds of facial expressions of fear and disgust. But there was a cultural effect too. When an authority figure was present during the videotaping, the Japanese subjects tried to mask their negative feelings with a half-smile more often than did the Americans.[4] Many gestures are culturally variable. In some cultures, an up and down nod of the head means "yes," in others it means "no."

Kinesics is the study of communication by nonverbal or nonvocal means, including posture, mannerisms, body movement, facial expressions, and signs and gestures. Informally, we may refer to nonverbal communication as "body language." As noted previously, some aspects of body language, such as facial expressions of emotion, may be human universals. Specific signs and gestures are often culturally

variable and the cause of cultural misunderstandings. Nonverbal communication can even involve the voice. Consider how we might know that a person is not fine even though she just said "I'm fine." We can tell a lot by tone of voice. A depressed person might speak very quietly and use a flat tone of voice. If a person thought about explaining what was really wrong but thought better of it, a significant pause or silence might come before the words, "I'm fine." Even a person's **accent** (differences in pronunciation) can tell a lot about the person's background, such as place of origin and education. There are also nonverbal (nonword) sounds that people make—grunts, laughs, giggles, moans, and sighs. **Paralanguage** refers to all the optional vocal features or silences that communicate meaning apart from the language itself. Although body language and some forms of paralanguage enable humans to communicate without spoken language, language spoken by humans probably never occurs without kinetic communication and paralanguage.[5]

Nonhuman Communication

Systems of communication are not unique to human beings, nor is communication by sound. Other animal species communicate in a variety of ways. One way is by sound. A bird may communicate by a call that "this is my territory"; a squirrel may utter a cry that leads other squirrels to flee from danger. Another means of animal

Apes lack the human capacity for speech, so researchers have explored the capacity of chimpanzees and other apes to communicate with hand gestures. Researcher Joyce Butler teaches Nim, a chimpanzee, a sign for "drink." A family employs sign language to communicate with a deaf child.

Susan Kuklin/Science Source/Photo Researchers, Inc.

Ellen Senisi/The Image Works

communication is odor. An ant releases a chemical when it dies, and its fellows then carry it away to the compost heap. Apparently the communication is highly effective; a healthy ant painted with the death chemical will be dragged to the funeral heap again and again. Bees use another means of communication, body movement, to convey the location of food sources. Karl von Frisch discovered that the black Austrian honeybee—by choosing a round dance, a wagging dance, or a short, straight run—can communicate not only the precise direction of the source of food but also its distance from the hive.[6]

One of the biggest scholarly debates is the degree to which nonhuman animals, particularly nonhuman primates, differ from humans in their capacity for language. Some scholars see so much discontinuity that they postulate that humans must have acquired (presumably through mutation) a specific genetic capability for language. Others see much more continuity between humans and nonhuman primates and point to research that shows much more cognitive capacity in nonhuman primates than previously thought possible. They point out that the discontinuity theorists are constantly raising the standards for the capacities thought necessary for language.[7] For example, in the past, only human communication was thought to be symbolic. But recent research suggests that some monkey and ape calls in the wild are also symbolic.

When we say that a call, word, or sentence is **symbolic communication,** we mean at least two things. First, the communication has meaning even when its *referent* (whatever is referred to) is not present. Second, the meaning is arbitrary; the receiver of the message could not guess its meaning just from the sound(s) and does not know the meaning instinctively. In other words, symbols have to be learned. There is no compelling or "natural" reason that the word *dog* in English should refer to a smallish four-legged omnivore.

Vervet monkeys in Africa are not as closely related to humans as are African apes. Nevertheless, scientists who have observed vervet monkeys in their natural environment consider at least three of their alarm calls to be symbolic because each of them *means* (refers to) a different kind of predator—eagles, pythons, or leopards—and monkeys react differently to each call. For example, they look up when they hear the "eagle" call. Experimentally, in the absence of the referent, investigators have been able to evoke the normal reaction to a call by playing it back electronically. Another indication that the vervet alarm calls are symbolic is that infant vervets appear to need some time to learn the referent for each. When they are very young, infants apply a particular call to more animals than adult vervets apply the call to. So, for example, infant vervets will often make the eagle warning call when they see any flying bird. The infants learn the appropriate referent apparently through adult vervets' repetition of infants' "correct" calls; in any case, the infants gradually learn to restrict the call to eagles. This process is probably not too different from the way a North American infant in an English-speaking family first applies the "word" *dada* to all adult males and gradually learns to restrict it to one person.[8] Or to how the Embers' daughter Kathy said "dog"

to all pictures of four-footed animals, including elephants, when she was 18 months old.

All of the nonhuman vocalizations we have described so far enable individual animals to convey messages. The sender gives a signal that is received and "decoded" by the receiver, who usually responds with a specific action or reply. How is human vocalization different? Because monkeys and apes appear to use symbols at least some of the time, it is not appropriate to emphasize symbolism as the distinctive feature of human language. However, there is a significant quantitative difference between human language and other primates' systems of vocal communication. All human languages employ a much larger set of symbols.

Another often-cited difference between human and nonhuman vocalizations is that the other primates' vocal systems are *closed*—that is, different calls are not combined to produce new, meaningful utterances. In contrast, human languages are *open* systems, governed by complex rules about how sounds and sequences of sounds can be combined to produce an infinite variety of meanings.[9] For example, an English speaker can combine *care* and *full* (*careful*) to mean one thing, then use each of the two elements in other combinations to mean different things. *Care* can be used to make *carefree, careless,* or *caretaker; full* can be used to make *powerful* or *wonderful*. And because language is a system of shared symbols, it can be re-formed into an infinite variety of expressions and be understood by all who share these symbols. In this way, for example, T. S. Eliot could form a sentence never before formed—"In the room the women come and go/talking of Michelangelo"[10]—and all speakers of English could understand the sense of his sentence, though not necessarily his private meaning.

Although no primatologist disputes the complexity and infinite variety with which human languages can combine sounds, other primates (cotton-top tamarins, pygmy marmosets, capuchin monkeys, and rhesus macaques) also combine calls in orderly sequences,[11] but not nearly as much as humans do.

Another trait thought to be unique to humans is the ability to communicate about past or future events. But Sue Savage-Rumbaugh has observed wild bonobos leaving what appear to be messages to other bonobos to follow a trail. They break off vegetation where trails fork and point the broken plants in the direction to follow.

Perhaps most persuasive are the successful attempts to teach apes to communicate with humans and with each other using human-created signs. These successes have led many scholars to question the traditional assumption that the gap between human and other animal communication is enormous. Even a parrot, which has a small brain, has been taught to communicate with a human trainer in ways once thought impossible. Alex (the parrot) could correctly answer questions in English about what objects were made of, how many objects of a particular type there were, and even what made two objects the same or different.[12] When he was not willing to continue a training session, Alex would say, "I'm sorry . . . Wanna go back."[13]

Chimpanzees Washoe and Nim and the gorilla Koko were taught hand signs based on American Sign Language (ASL; used by the hearing impaired in the United States).

The chimpanzee Sarah was trained with plastic symbols. Subsequently, many chimpanzees were trained on symbol keyboards connected to computers. Some of the best examples of linguistic ability come from a chimpanzee named Kanzi. In contrast to other apes, Kanzi initially learned symbols just by watching his mother being taught, and he spontaneously began using the computer symbols to communicate with humans, even indicating his intended actions. Kanzi did not need rewards or to have his hands put in the right position. And he understood a great deal of what was spoken to him in English. For example, when he was 5 years old, Kanzi heard someone talk about throwing a ball in the river, and he turned around and did so. Kanzi has come close to having a primitive English grammar when he strings symbols together.[14] If chimpanzees and other primates have the capacity to use nonspoken language and even to understand spoken language, then the difference between humans and nonhumans may not be as great as people used to think.

Are these apes really using language in some minimal way? Many investigators do agree about one thing—nonhuman primates have the ability to "symbol," to refer to something (or a class of things) with an arbitrary "label" (gesture or sequence of sounds).[15] For example, Washoe originally learned the sign *dirty* to refer to feces and other soil and then began to use it insultingly, as in "dirty Roger," when her trainer Roger Fouts refused to give her things she wanted.

When we discuss the structure of sounds (phonology) later in this chapter, we will see that every human language has certain ways of combining sounds and ways of not combining those sounds. Apes do not have anything comparable to linguistic rules for allowed and disallowed combinations of sounds. In addition, humans have many kinds of discourse. We make lists and speeches, tell stories, argue, and recite poetry. Apes do none of these things.[16] But apes do have at least some of the capacities for language. Therefore, understanding their capacities may help us better understand the evolution of human language.

THE ORIGINS OF LANGUAGE

How long humans have had spoken language is not known. Some think that the earliest *Homo sapiens,* perhaps 100,000 years ago, may have had the beginnings of language. Others believe that language developed only after 100,000 years ago, with the emergence of modern humans. Because the only unambiguous remains of language are found on written tablets, and the earliest stone tablets date back only about 5,000 years,[17] pinpointing the emergence of earliest languages remains speculative. Theories about when language developed are based on nonlinguistic information such as when cranial capacity expanded dramatically, when complex technology and symbolic artifacts (such as art) started to be made, and when the anatomy of the throat, as inferred from fossil remains, began to resemble what we see in modern humans.

Noam Chomsky and other theoreticians of grammar suggest that there is an innate *language-acquisition device* in the human brain, as innate to humans as call systems

are to other animals.[18] If humans are unique in having an innate capacity for language, then some mutation or series of mutations had to be favored in human evolution, not before the human line separated from apes. Whether such a mechanism in fact exists is not clear. But we do know that the actual development of individual language is not completely biologically determined; if it were, all human beings would speak the same brain-generated language. Instead, about 4,000 to 5,000 mutually unintelligible languages have been identified. More than 2,000 of them were still spoken as of recently, most by peoples who did not traditionally have a system of writing.

Can we learn anything about the origins of language by studying the languages of nonliterate (without writing) and technologically simpler societies? The answer is no, because such languages are not simpler or less developed than ours. The sound systems, vocabularies, and grammars of technologically simpler peoples are in no way inferior to those of peoples with more complex technology.[19] Of course, people in other societies, and even some people in our own society, will not be able to name the sophisticated machines used in our society. All languages, however, have the potential for doing so. As we will see later in this chapter, all languages possess the amount of vocabulary their speakers need, and all languages expand in response to cultural changes. A language that lacks terminology for some of our conveniences may have a rich vocabulary for events or natural phenomena that are of particular importance to the people in that society.

If there are no primitive languages, and if the earliest languages have left no traces that would allow us to reconstruct them, does that mean we cannot investigate the origins of language? Some linguists think that understanding the way children acquire language, which we discuss shortly, can help us understand the origins of language. Other linguists have suggested that an understanding of how Creole languages develop will also tell us something about the origins of language.

Pidgin and Creole Languages

In many contact situations where one group is much more powerful than the other, people shift to the dominant language, and their native language gradually becomes lost (see the boxes "Can Languages Be Kept from Extinction?" and "Why Are 'Mother Tongues' Retained, and for How Long?"). However, some contact situations led to a different result—the development of a new language, different from the dominant language or the previous native languages.

Some languages developed where European colonial powers established commercial enterprises that relied on imported labor, generally slaves. The laborers in one place often came from many different societies and, in the beginning, would speak with their masters and with each other in some kind of simplified way, using linguistic features of one or more of the languages. Often, most of the vocabulary is drawn from the masters' language.[20] These *pidgin languages* become a new way of communicating. Pidgins are simplified languages and lack many of the building blocks found in the languages of whole societies,

applied anthropology

Can Languages Be Kept from Extinction?

Not only animal and plant species are endangered; many peoples and their languages are too. In the last few hundred years, and continuing in some places today, Western expansion and colonization have led to the depopulation and extinction of many native societies, mainly as a result of introduced disease and campaigns of extermination. Thus, many languages disappeared with the peoples that spoke them. More than 50 of approximately 200 aboriginal languages in Australia disappeared relatively quickly as a result of massacre and disease.

Today, native languages are endangered more by the fact that they are not being passed on to children. Political and economic dominance by speakers of Western languages undoubtedly play an enormous role in this process. First, schooling is usually conducted in the dominant language. Second, when another culture is dominant, the children may prefer (often with the encouragement of their parents) to speak in the language perceived to have higher prestige.

Almost all the languages of aboriginal Australia are now gone. This is a worldwide trend. Michael Krauss, a linguist who tracks disappearing languages, estimates that 90 percent of the world's languages are endangered in the current century. A common estimate of the number of existing languages is 6,000. If the 90 percent endangered estimate is correct, only 600 human languages will be left at the end of this century.

What can be done? For a long time, linguists have worked on describing languages that are endangered, often working closely with the few remaining speakers. Although description is essential to language preservation, linguists are increasingly engaging actively in efforts to revitalize endangered languages by participating in community programs and by playing active roles in organizations that are preserving, often in digitized archives, endangered languages and recordings of speech. After all, without speakers or any written records, languages are truly lost. The following are a few examples of "dead" languages being brought back to life. Kaurna, a language of Australia, abandoned for over a century, is now used in songs, ritual events, public speeches, and everyday greetings. It has moved from no use to some use. Hebrew is an often-cited example of a "dead" language that was brought back to life because more than 5 million people now speak it. However, Hebrew, like Latin, was never really "dead" in the same sense as Kaurna. Hebrew has been used in religious contexts for over 16 centuries and had extensive written literature. But the Hebrew case indicates something fundamental—for successful revitalization to occur, a community of people must be strongly motivated to revive it. Anthropological linguists may help design and implement revitalization programs, but they are unlikely to be successful without the interest of the community.

Total immersion programs are probably the most likely to work, but they are the most costly and difficult to implement. School programs employing total immersion during the school day beginning with preschool have had considerable success among the Maori of New Zealand, as well as among Hawaiians of the United States and the Mohawk of Canada. Bilingual programs are perhaps the most popular programs, but they use only partial immersion. Krauss, who is particularly interested in preserving native Alaskan languages, developed materials on native languages with help from the state government of Alaska to assist teachers in bilingual programs. UNESCO favors a very different approach, to teach adults first, who can then teach their children naturally.

Computer technology provides new avenues for revitalizing languages. H. Russell Bernard believes that "to keep a language truly alive we must produce authors." With the help of computer technology, which allows reconfiguring a keyboard to produce special characters for sounds, Bernard has taught native speakers to write their native languages directly on computers. These texts then become the basis for dictionaries. So far, more than 80 people, speaking 12 endangered languages, have become authors in Mexico and South America. Although these authors may not be using the standardized characters linguists use to represent sounds, they are producing "written" materials that might otherwise be lost forever. These texts provide more than just information about language. In their works, the authors convey ideas about curing illness, acquiring food, raising children, and settling disputes. On a broader scale, the Web provides a way for far-flung people to access language materials, pick up advice for teaching languages, and even feel more part of a "community" with those whose language is shared.

We are not sure when humans first developed spoken language. But the enormous linguistic diversity on this planet took a long time to develop. As Krauss points out, "Each language is a unique repository of facts and knowledge about the world that we can ill afford to lose" (quoted in Kolbert 2005). Unfortunately, it may take only a short time for that diversity to become a thing of the past.

Sources: Crystal 2000, 4, 142, 154; Holmes 2001, 65–71; Grenoble and Whaley 2006; Kolbert 2005; Shulman 1993.

building blocks such as prepositions (*to, on,* and so forth) and auxiliary verbs (designating future and other tenses). If a pidgin language is used merely as system of communicating in a limited setting, it may not develop into a fully developed language. However, children may begin to use pidgin as their first language. The pidgin language may expand and become more complex grammatically.[21] Many pidgin languages developed into and were replaced by so-called *creole languages,* which incorporate much of the vocabulary of another language (often the masters' language) but also have a grammar that differs from it and from the grammars of the laborers' native languages.[22]

Derek Bickerton argues that there are striking grammatical similarities in creole languages throughout the world. This similarity, he thinks, is consistent with the idea that some grammar is inherited by all humans. Creole languages, therefore, may resemble early human languages. All creoles use intonation instead of a change in word order to ask a question. The creole equivalent of the question "Can you fix this?" would be "You can fix this?" The creole version puts a rising inflection at the end; in contrast, the English version reverses the subject and verb without much inflection at the end. All creoles express the future and the past in the same grammatical way, by the use of particles (such as the English *shall*) between subject and verb, and they all employ double negatives, as in the Guyana English Creole "Nobody no like me."[23]

It is possible that many other things about language are universal, that all languages are similar in many respects, because of the way humans are "wired" or because people in all societies have similar experiences. For example, names for frogs may usually contain *r* sounds because frogs make them.[24]

Children's Acquisition of Language

Apparently a child is equipped from birth with the capacity to reproduce all the sounds used by the world's languages and to learn any system of grammar. Research on 6-month-old infants finds that they can distinguish sounds of approximately 600 consonants and 200 vowels—all the sounds of all the languages of the world. But, by about the time of their first birthdays, babies become better at recognizing the salient sounds and sound clusters of their parents or caretakers and become less adept at distinguishing those of other languages.[25]

Children's acquisition of the structure and meaning of language has been called the most difficult intellectual achievement in life. If that is so, it is pleasing to note that they accomplish it with relative ease and vast enjoyment. As we have noted, many believe that this "difficult intellectual achievement" may in reality be a natural response to the capacity for language that is one of humans' genetic characteristics. All over the world, children begin to learn language at about the same age, and in no culture do children wait until they are 7 or 10 years old. By 12 or 13 months of age, children are able to name a few objects and actions, and by 18 to 20 months, they can make one key word stand for a whole sentence: "Out!" for "Take me out for a walk right now"; "Juice!" for "I want some juice

now." Evidence suggests that children acquire the concept of a word as a whole, learning sequences of sounds that are stressed or at the ends of words (e.g., "raffe" for giraffe). Even children with hearing impairments who are learning signs in ASL tend to acquire and use signs in a similar fashion.[26]

Children the world over tend to progress to two-word sentences at about 18 to 24 months of age. In their sentences, they express themselves in "telegraph" form—using nounlike words and verblike words but leaving out the seemingly less important words. So a two-word sentence such as "Shoes off" may stand for "Take my shoes off," or "More milk" may stand for "Give me more milk, please."[27] They do not utter their two words in random order, sometimes saying "off" first, other times saying "shoes" first. If children say, "Shoes off," then they will also say, "Clothes off" and "Hat off." They seem to select an order that fits the conventions of adult language, so they are likely to say, "Daddy eat," not "Eat Daddy." In other words, they tend to put the subject first, as adults do. And they tend to say "Mommy coat" rather than "Coat Mommy" to indicate "Mommy's coat."[28] Adults do not utter sentences such as "Daddy eat," so children seem to know a lot about how to put words together with little or no direct teaching from their caretakers. Consider the 5-year-old who, confronted with the unfamiliar "Gloria in Excelsis," sings quite happily, "Gloria eats eggshells." To make the words fit the structure of English grammar is more important than to make the words fit the meaning of the Christmas pageant.

If there is a basic grammar imprinted in the human mind, we should not be surprised that children's early and later speech patterns seem to be similar in different languages. We might also expect children's later speech to be similar to the structure of creole languages. And it is, according to Derek Bickerton.[29] The "errors" children make in speaking are consistent with the grammar of creoles. For example, English-speaking children 3 to 4 years old tend to ask questions by intonation alone, and they tend to use double negatives, such as "I don't see no dog," even though the adults around them do not speak that way and consider the children's speech "wrong."

But some linguists argue that the evidence for an innate grammar is weak because children the world over do not develop the same grammatical features at similar ages. For example, word order is a more important determinant of meaning in English than in Turkish; the endings of words are more important in Turkish. The word at the beginning of the sentence in English is likely to be the subject. The word with a certain ending in Turkish is the likely subject. Consistent with this difference, English-speaking children learn word order earlier than Turkish children do.[30]

Future research on children's acquisition of language and on the structure of creole languages may bring us closer to an understanding of the origins of human language. But, even if much of grammar is universal, we still need to understand how and why the thousands of languages in the world vary, which brings us to the conceptual tools linguists have had to invent to study languages.

migrants and immigrants

Why Are "Mother Tongues" Retained, and for How Long?

The longer an immigrant group lives in another country, the more they incorporate the culture of their new home. At some point, the original language is no longer even partially understood. Consider people who originally came from Wales, the region west of England in Great Britain. In that region, until about 100 years ago, most people spoke the Welsh language, which belongs to the Celtic subfamily of Indo-European along with Irish and Scottish Gaelic and Breton. (Celtic is a different subfamily from the one English belongs to, which is Germanic.) In 1729, the Welsh in Philadelphia established the Welsh Society, the oldest ethnic organization in the United States. Many of the members, if not all, spoke Welsh in addition to English at that time. But, by the 20th century, hardly any of their descendants did.

If immigrant groups eventually lose their "mother tongues" in many if not most countries, this doesn't mean that the process occurs at the same speed in every group. Why is that? Why do some immigrant groups lose their language faster than others? Is it because they do not live in tightly knit ethnic enclaves? Or because they marry outside their ethnic group? Or because they do not have traditional festivals or celebrations marking their separate identity? A comparative study by Robert Schrauf discovered the most likely reasons. First, Schrauf assessed the degree to which immigrant groups coming to North America retained their native language over time. The greatest retention was defined as when the third generation (the grandchildren of immigrants) continued to use the native language. Examples were Chicanos, Puerto Ricans, Cubans, and Haitians. On the other hand, the third generation in some groups had no comprehension of the native language except for isolated words. Even the second generation (the children of immigrants) mostly spoke and understood only English. Examples were Italians, Armenians, and Basques. Chinese and Koreans were in the middle, with some evidence that the third generation understands a little of the native language. Schrauf then measured seven social factors that might explain longer versus shorter retention of the mother tongue. He looked at whether the group lived in tightly knit communities, retained religious rituals from the old country, had separate schools and special festivals, visited their homeland, did not intermarry, or worked with others of their ethnic group.

Schrauf used data on 11 North American ethnic groups drawn from the HRAF Collection of Ethnography. The major advantage of the HRAF materials is that ethnographies written for more general purposes, or for purposes other than linguistic ones, contain a wealth of information concerning sociocultural features of ethnic groups that may be tested for their possible effects on language retention and loss.

We might suspect that all of the factors Schrauf measured would lead people to retain their native language (and presumably other native cultural patterns). But not all do, apparently. Only living in tightly knit communities and retaining religious rituals strongly predict retention of the mother tongue in the home into the third generation. Why? Possibly because living in an ethnic community and religious rituals are experienced early in life: Conditions associated with early socialization might have more lasting effects than conditions experienced later in life, such as schooling, visits to the homeland, marriage, and work. Participation in celebrations and festi-

Living in an ethnic neighborhood as in San Francisco's Chinatown encourages retention of the mother tongue.

vals is probably important too, but it does not have quite as strong an effect, perhaps because celebrations and festivals are not everyday experiences.

As always, in the case of research, this study raises questions for future research. Would the same effects be found outside of North America? Would the results be the same if we looked also at other immigrant groups in North America? Does frequent travel back to the homeland help language retention? Do some immigrant groups live in close-knit communities because of discrimination or choice? If choice, are some groups more interested in assimilating than others? And if so, why?

Sources: Caulkins 1997; Schrauf 1999.

Ellen Isaacs/age fotostock/Art Life Images

A lot of language instruction occurs by pointing to something and saying what it is called.

DESCRIPTIVE LINGUISTICS

In every society, children do not need to be taught "grammar" to learn how to speak. They begin to grasp the essential structure of their language at a very early age, without direct instruction. If you show English-speaking children a picture of one "gork" and then a picture of two of these creatures, they will say there are two "gorks." Somehow they know that adding an *s* to a noun means more than one. But they do not know this consciously, and adults may not either. One of the most surprising features of human language is that meaningful sounds and sound sequences are combined according to rules that the speakers often do not consciously know.

These rules should not be equated with the "rules of grammar" you were taught in school so that you would speak "correctly." Rather, when linguists talk about rules, they are referring to the patterns of speaking that are discoverable in actual speech. Needless to say, there is some overlap between the actual rules of speaking and the rules taught in school. But there are rules that children never hear about in school, because their teachers are not linguists and are not aware of them. When linguists use the term *grammar*, they are *not* referring to the prescriptive rules that people are supposed to follow in speaking. Rather, *grammar* to the linguist consists of the actual, often unconscious principles that predict how most people talk. As we have noted, young children may speak two-word sentences that conform to a linguistic rule, but their speech is hardly considered "correct."

Discovering the mostly unconscious rules operating in a language is a very difficult task. Linguists have had to invent special concepts and methods of transcription (writing) to permit them to describe: (1) the rules or principles that predict how sounds are made and how they are used (slightly varying sounds are often used interchangeably in words without creating a difference in meaning—this aspect of language is called **phonology**); (2) how sound sequences (and sometimes even individual sounds) convey meaning and how meaningful sound sequences are strung together to form words (this aspect is called **morphology**);

and (3) how words are strung together to form phrases and sentences (this aspect is called **syntax**).

Understanding the language of another people is an essential part of understanding the culture of that people. Although sometimes what people say is contradicted by their observed behavior, there is little doubt that it is hard to understand the beliefs, attitudes, values, and worldview of a people without understanding their language and the nuances of how that language is used. Even behavior, which theoretically one can observe without understanding language, usually cannot be readily understood without interpretation. Imagine that you see people go by a certain rock and seemingly walk out of their way to avoid it. Suppose they believe that an evil spirit resides there. How could you possibly know that without being able to ask and to understand their answer?

Phonology

Most of us have had the experience of trying to learn another language and finding that some sounds are exceedingly difficult to make. Although the human vocal tract theoretically can make a very large number of different sounds—**phones,** to linguists—each language uses only some of them. It is not that we cannot make the sounds that are strange to us; we just have not acquired the habit of making those sounds. And until the sounds become habitual for us, they continue to be difficult to make.

Finding it difficult to make certain sounds is only one of the reasons we have trouble learning a "foreign" language. Another problem is that we may not be used to combining certain sounds or making a certain sound in a particular position in a word. Thus, English speakers find it difficult to combine *z* and *d*, as Russian speakers often do (because we never do so in English), or to pronounce words in Samoan, a South Pacific language, that begin with the sound English speakers write as *ng*, even though we have no trouble putting that sound at the end of words, as in the English *sing* and *hitting*.

To study the patterning of sounds, linguists who are interested in *phonology* have to write down speech utterances as sequences of sound. This task would be almost impossible if linguists were restricted to using their own alphabet (say, the one we use to write English), because other languages use sounds that are difficult to represent with the English alphabet or because the alphabet we use in English can represent a particular sound in different ways. (English writing represents the sound *f* by *f* as in *food*, but also as *gh* in *tough* and *ph* in *phone*.) In addition, in English, different sounds may be represented by the same letter. English has 26 letters but more than 40 significant sounds (sounds that can change the meaning of a word).[31] To overcome these difficulties in writing sounds with the letters of existing writing systems, linguists have developed systems of transcription with special alphabets in which each symbol represents only one particular sound.

Once linguists have identified the sounds or phones used in a language, they try to identify which sounds affect meaning and which sounds do not. One way is to start with a simple word like *lake* and change the first sound to *r* to make the word *rake*. A linguist will ask if this new combination of sounds means the same thing. An English speaker would say *lake* means something completely different from *rake*. These minimal contrasts enable linguists to identify a **phoneme** in a language—a sound or set of sounds that makes a difference in meaning in that language.[32] So the sound *l* in *lake* is different phonemically from the sound *r* in *rake*. The ways in which sounds are grouped together into phonemes vary from language to language. We are so used to phonemes in our own language that it may be hard to believe that the contrast between *r* and *l* may not make a difference in meaning in some languages. For example, in Samoan, *l* and *r* can be used interchangeably in a word without changing the meaning (therefore, these two sounds belong to the same phoneme in Samoan). So Samoan speakers may say "Leupena" sometimes and "Reupena" at other times when they are referring to someone who in English would be called "Reuben."

English speakers may joke about languages that "confuse" *l* and *r*, but they are not usually aware that we do the same thing with other sets of sounds. For example, in English, the word we spell *and* may be pronounced quite differently by two different English speakers without changing the meaning, and no one would think that a different word was spoken. We can pronounce the *a* in *and* as in the beginning of the word *air*, or we can pronounce it as the *a* in *bat*. If you say those varying *a* sounds and try to think about how you are forming them in your mouth, you will realize that they are two different sounds. English speakers might recognize a slight difference in pronunciation but pay little or no attention to it because the two ways to pronounce the *a* in *and* do not change the meaning. Now think about *l* and *r*. If you form them in your mouth, you will notice that they are only slightly different with respect to how far the tongue is from the ridge behind the upper front teeth. Languages do tend to consider sounds that are close as belonging to the same phoneme, but why they choose some sounds and not others to group together is not yet fully understood.

Some recent research suggests that infants may learn early to ignore meaningless variations of sound (those that are part of the same phoneme) in the language they hear at home. It turns out that, as early as 6 months of age, infants "ignore" sound shifts within the same phoneme of their own language, but they "hear" a sound shift within the phoneme of another language. Researchers are not sure how babies learn to make the distinction, but they seem to acquire much of the phonology of their language very early indeed.[33]

After discovering which sounds are grouped into phonemes, linguists can begin to discover the sound sequences that are allowed in a language and the usually unconscious rules that predict those sequences. For example, words in English rarely start with three nonvowel sounds. But when they do, the first sound or phone is always an *s*, as in *strike* and *scratch*.[34] (Some other words in English may start with three consonants but only two sounds are involved, as in *chrome*, where the *ch* stands for the sound in *k*.) Linguists' descriptions of the patterning of sounds (phonology) in different languages may allow them to investigate why languages vary in their sound rules.

Why, for example, are two or more consonants strung together in some languages, whereas in other languages, vowels are *almost* always put between consonants? The Samoan language now has a word for "Christmas" borrowed from English, but the borrowed word has been changed to fit the rules of Samoan. In the English word, two consonants come first, *k* and *r*, which we spell as *ch* and *r*. The Samoan word is *Kerisimasi* (pronounced as if it were spelled Keh-ree-see-mah-see). It has a vowel after each consonant, or five consonant-vowel syllables.

Why do some languages like Samoan alternate consonants and vowels more or less regularly? Recent cross-cultural research suggests three predictors of this variation. One predictor is a warmer climate. Where people live in warmer climates, the typical syllable is more likely to be a consonant-vowel syllable. Linguists have found that consonant-vowel syllables provide the most contrast in speech. Perhaps when people converse outdoors at a distance, which they are likely to do in a warmer climate, they need more contrast between sounds to be understood. A second predictor of consonant-vowel alternation is literacy. Languages that are written have fewer consonant-vowel syllables. If communication is often in written form, meaning does not have to depend so much on contrast between adjacent sounds. A third (indeed the strongest) predictor of consonant-vowel alternation is the degree to which babies are held by others. Societies with a great deal of baby-holding have a lot of consonant-vowel syllables. One theory is that, when babies are held on a person much of the day, they begin to associate regular rhythm with pleasurable experiences. The baby senses the regular rhythm of the caretaker's heartbeats or the caretaker's rhythmic work, and the reward value of that experience generalizes to a preference for all regular rhythms in adult life, including apparently a regular consonant-vowel alternation in adult speech. Compare the rhythm of the Samoan word *Kerisimasi* with the English word *Christmas*.[35]

Morphology

A phoneme in a language usually does not mean something by itself. Usually phonemes are combined with other phonemes to form a meaningful sequence of sounds. *Morphology* is the study of sequences of sounds that have meaning. Often these meaningful sequences of sounds make up what we call *words*, but a word may be composed of a number of smaller meaningful units. We take our words so much for granted that we do not realize how complicated it is to say what words are. People do not usually pause very much between words when they speak; if we did not know our language, a sentence would seem like a continuous stream of sounds. This is how we first hear a foreign language. Only when we understand the language and write down what we say do we separate (by spaces) what we call words. But a word is really only an arbitrary sequence of sounds that has a meaning; we would not "hear" words as separate units if we did not understand the language spoken.

Because anthropological linguists traditionally investigated unwritten languages, sometimes without the aid of interpreters, they had to figure out which sequences of sounds conveyed meaning. And because words in many languages can often be broken down into smaller meaningful units, linguists had to invent special words to refer to those units. Linguists call the smallest unit of language that has a meaning a **morph.** Just as a phoneme may have one or more phones, one or more morphs with the same meaning may make up a **morpheme.** For example, the prefix *in-*, as in *indefinite*, and the prefix *un-*, as in *unclear*, are morphs that belong to the morpheme meaning *not*. Although some words are single morphs or morphemes (e.g., *for* and *giraffe* in English), many words are a combination of morphs, generally prefixes, roots, and suffixes. Thus *cow* is one word, but the word *cows* contains two meaningful units—a root (*cow*) and a suffix (pronounced like *z*) meaning more than one. The **lexicon** of a language, which a dictionary approximates, consists of words and morphs and their meanings.

It seems likely that the intuitive grasp children have of the structure of their language includes a recognition of morphology. Once they learn that the morph /-z/ added to a noun-type word indicates more than one, they plow ahead with *mans, childs;* once they grasp that the morpheme class pronounced /-t/ or /-d/ or /-ed/ added to the end of a verb indicates that the action took place in the past, they apply that concept generally and invent *runned, drinked, costed*. They see a ball roll near*er* and near*er*, and they transfer that concept to a kite, which goes upp*er* and upp*er*. From their mistakes as well as their successes, we can see that children understand the regular uses of morphemes. By the age of 7, they have mastered many of the irregular forms as well—that is, they learn which morphs of a morpheme are used when.

The child's intuitive grasp of the dependence of some morphemes on others corresponds to the linguist's recognition of free morphemes and bound morphemes. A *free* morpheme has meaning standing alone—that is, it can be a separate word. A *bound* morpheme displays its meaning only when attached to another morpheme. The morph pronounced /-t/ of the bound morpheme meaning *past tense* is attached to the root *walk* to produce *walked;* but the /-t/ cannot stand alone or have meaning by itself.

In English, the meaning of an utterance (containing a subject, verb, object, and so forth) usually depends on the order of the words. "The dog bit the child" is different in meaning from "The child bit the dog." But in many other languages, the grammatical meaning of an utterance does not depend much, if at all, on the order of the words. Rather, meaning may be determined by how the morphs in a word are ordered. For example, in Luo, a language of East Africa, the same bound morpheme may mean the subject or object of an action. If the morpheme is the prefix to a verb, it means the subject; if it is the suffix to a verb, it means the object. Another way that grammatical meaning may be conveyed is by altering or adding a bound morpheme to a word to indicate what part of speech it is. For example, in Russian, when the subject of a sentence, the word for *mail* is pronounced something like *pawchtah*. When *mail* is used as the object of a verb, as in "I gave her the mail," the ending of the word changes to *pawchtoo*. And if I say, "What was in the mail?" the word becomes *pawchtyeh*.

Some languages have so many bound morphemes that they might express as a complex but single word what is considered a sentence in English. For example, the English sentence, "He will give it to you" can be expressed in Wishram, a Chinookan dialect that was spoken along the Columbia River in the Pacific Northwest, as *acimluda* (a-c-i-m-l-ud-a, literally "will-he-him-thee-to-give-will"). Note that the pronoun *it* in English is gender-neutral; Wishram requires that *it* be given a gender, in this case, "him."[36]

Syntax

Because language is an open system, we can make up meaningful utterances that we have never heard before. We are constantly creating new phrases and sentences. Just as they do for morphology, speakers of a language seem to have an intuitive grasp of *syntax*—the rules that predict how phrases and sentences are generally formed. These "rules" may be partly learned in school, but children know many of them even before they get to school. In adulthood, our understanding of morphology and syntax is so intuitive that we can even understand a nonsense sentence, such as this famous one from Lewis Carroll's *Through the Looking-Glass:*

> *'Twas brillig, and the slithy toves*
> *Did gyre and gimble in the wabe*

Simply from the ordering of the words in the sentence, we can surmise which part of speech a word is, as well as its function in the sentence. *Brillig* is an adjective; *slithy*, an adjective; *toves*, a noun and the subject of the sentence; *gyre* and *gimble*, verbs; and *wabe*, a noun and the object of a prepositional phrase. Of course, an understanding of morphology helps too. The *-y* ending in *slithy* is an indication that the latter is an adjective, and the *-s* ending in *toves* tells us that we most probably have more than one of these creatures. In addition to producing and understanding an infinite variety of sentences, speakers of a language can tell when a sentence is not "correct" without consulting grammar books. For example, an English speaker can tell that "Child the dog the hit" is not an acceptable sentence but "The child hit the dog" is fine. There must, then, be a set of rules underlying how phrases and sentences are constructed in a language.[37] Speakers of a language know these implicit rules of syntax but are not usually consciously aware of them. The linguist's description of the syntax of a language tries to make these rules explicit.

HISTORICAL LINGUISTICS

The field of **historical linguistics** focuses on how languages change over time. Written works provide the best data for establishing such changes. For example, the following brief passage from Chaucer's *Canterbury Tales,* written in the English of the 14th century, has recognizable elements but is different enough from modern English to require a translation.

> A Frere ther was, a wantowne and a merye,
> A lymytour, a ful solempne man.
> In alle the ordres foure is noon that kan
> So muche of daliaunce and fair language.
> He hadde maad ful many a mariage
> Of yonge wommen at his owene cost.

> A Friar there was, wanton and merry,
> A limiter [a friar limited to certain districts], a
>   very important man.
> In all the orders four there is none that knows
> So much of dalliance [flirting] and fair
>   [engaging] language.
> He had made [arranged] many a marriage
> Of young women at his own cost.[38]

In this passage, we can recognize several changes. Many words are spelled differently today, and in some cases, meaning has changed: *Full,* for example, would be translated today as *very.* What is less evident is that changes in pronunciation have occurred. For example, the *g* in

An illustration accompanies the ornate script text on a page from Chaucer's famed *The Canterbury Tales.*

mariage (marriage) was pronounced *zh,* as in the French from which it was borrowed, whereas now it is usually pronounced like either *g* in *George.*

Because languages spoken in the past leave no traces unless they were written, and most of the languages known to anthropology were not written by their speakers, you might think that historical linguists can study linguistic change only by studying written languages such as English. But that is not the case. Linguists can reconstruct changes that have occurred by comparing contemporary languages that are similar. Such languages show phonological, morphological, and syntactical similarities because they usually derive from a common ancestral language. For example, Romanian, Italian, French, Spanish, and Portuguese have many similarities. On the basis of these similarities, linguists can reconstruct what the ancestral language was like and how it changed into what we call the Romance languages. Of course, these reconstructions can easily be tested and confirmed because we know from many surviving writings what the ancestral language, Latin, was like; we also know from documents how Latin diversified as the Roman Empire expanded. Thus, common ancestry is frequently the reason why neighboring, and sometimes even separated, languages show patterns of similarity.

But languages can be similar for other reasons too. Contact between speech communities, often with one group dominant over another, may lead one language to borrow from the other. For example, English borrowed a lot of vocabulary from French after England was conquered by the French-speaking Normans in A.D. 1066. Languages may also show similarities even though they do not derive from a common ancestral language and even though there has been no contact or borrowing between them. Such similarities may reflect common or universal features of human cultures or human brains or both. (As we noted earlier in the chapter, the grammatical similarities exhibited by creole languages may reflect how the human brain is "wired.") Finally, even unrelated and separated languages may show some similarities because of the phenomenon of convergence; similarities can develop because some processes of linguistic change may have only a few possible outcomes.

Language Families and Culture History

Latin is the ancestral language of the Romance languages. We know this from documentary (written) records. But if the ancestral language of a set of similar languages is not known from written records, linguists still can reconstruct many features of that language by comparing the derived languages. (Such a reconstructed language is called a **protolanguage.**) That is, by comparing presumably related languages, linguists can become aware of the features that many of them have in common, features that were probably found in the common ancestral language. The languages that derive from the same protolanguage are called a *language family.* Most languages spoken today can be grouped into fewer than 30 families. The language family that English belongs to is called *Indo-European,* because it includes most of the languages of Europe and some of the languages of India. (Persian, spoken in Iran, and Kurdish also belong to this family.) About 50 percent of the world's population (now more than 6 billion people) speak Indo-European languages.[39] Another very large language family, now spoken by more than a billion people, is Sino-Tibetan, which includes the languages of northern and southern China as well as those of Tibet and Burma.[40]

The field of historical linguistics got its start in 1786, when a British scholar living in India, Sir William Jones, noticed similarities between Sanskrit, a language spoken and written in ancient India, and classical Greek, Latin, and more recent European languages.[41] In 1822, Jakob Grimm, one of the brothers Grimm of fairy tale fame, formulated rules to describe the sound shifts that had occurred when the various Indo-European languages diverged from each other. So, for example, in English and the other languages in the Germanic branch of the Indo-European family, *d* regularly shifted to *t* (compare the English *two* and *ten* with the Latin *duo* and *decem*), and *p* regularly shifted to *f* (compare the English *father* and *foot,* to Latin's *pater* and *pes*). Scholars generally agree that the Indo-European languages derive from a language spoken 5,000 years to 6,000 years ago.[42] The ancestral Indo-European language, many of whose features have now been reconstructed, is called *proto-Indo-European,* or *PIE* for short.

Where did PIE originate? Some linguists believe that the approximate location of a protolanguage is suggested by the words for plants and animals in the derived languages. More specifically, among these different languages, the words that are **cognates**—that is, words that are similar in sound and meaning—presumably refer to plants and animals that were present in the original homeland. So, if we know where those animals and plants were located 5,000 years to 6,000 years ago, we can guess where PIE people lived. Among all the cognates for trees in the Indo-European languages, Paul Friedrich has identified 18 that he believes were present in the eastern Ukraine in 3000 B.C. On this basis, he suggests that the eastern Ukraine was the PIE homeland.[43] Also consistent with this hypothesis is the fact that the Balto-Slavic subfamily of Indo-European, which includes most of the languages in and around the former Soviet Union, has the most tree names (compared with other subfamilies) that are similar to the reconstructed form in proto-Indo-European.[44]

Marija Gimbutas thinks we can even identify the proto-Indo-Europeans archaeologically. She believes that the PIE people were probably the people associated with what is known as the Kurgan culture (5000 B.C. to 2000 B.C.), which spread out from the Ukraine around 3000 B.C. The Kurgan people were herders, raising horses, cattle, sheep, and pigs. They also relied on hunting and grain cultivation. Burials suggest differences in wealth and special status for men.[45] Why the Kurgan and linguistically similar people were able to expand to many places in Europe and the Near East is not yet clear. Some have suggested that horses and horse-drawn wagons and perhaps horseback riding provided important military advantages.[46] In any case, it is clear that many Kurgan cultural elements were distributed after 3000 B.C. over a wide area of the Old World.

Colin Renfrew disagrees with the notion that the Ukraine was the homeland of PIE. He thinks that PIE is 2,000 years to 3,000 years older than Kurgan culture and that the PIE people lived in a different place. Renfrew locates the PIE homeland in eastern Anatolia (Turkey) in 7000 B.C. to 6000 B.C., and he suggests, on the basis of archaeological evidence, that the spread of Indo-European to Europe and what is now Iran, Afghanistan, and India accompanied the spread of farming to those areas.[47]

Just as some historical linguists and archaeologists have suggested when and where the PIE people may have lived originally and how they may have spread, other linguists and archaeologists have suggested culture histories for other language families. For example, the Bantu languages in Africa (spoken by perhaps 100 million people) form a subfamily of the larger Niger-Congo family of languages. Bantu speakers currently live in a wide band across the center of Africa and down the eastern and western sides of southern Africa. All of the Bantu languages presumably derive from people who spoke proto-Bantu. But where was their homeland?

As in the case of proto-Indo-European, different theories have been proposed. But most historical linguists now agree with Joseph Greenberg's suggestion that the origin of Bantu was in what is now the Middle Benue area of eastern Nigeria.[48] The point of origin is presumably where there is the greatest diversity of related languages and *dialects* (varying forms of a language); it is assumed that the place of origin has had the most time for linguistic diversity to develop, compared with an area only recently occupied by a related language. For example, England has more dialect diversity than New Zealand or Australia.

Why were the Bantu able to spread so widely over the last few thousand years? Anthropologists have only begun to guess.[49] Initially, the Bantu probably kept goats and practiced some form of agriculture and thereby were able to spread, displacing hunter-gatherers in the area. As the Bantu speakers expanded, they began to cultivate certain cereal crops and herd sheep and cattle. Around this time, after 1000 B.C., they also began to use and make iron tools, which may have given them significant advantages. In any case, by 1,500 years to 2,000 years ago, Bantu speakers had spread throughout central Africa and into the northern reaches of southern Africa. But speakers of non-Bantu languages still live in eastern, southern, and southwestern Africa.

THE PROCESSES OF LINGUISTIC DIVERGENCE

Historical or comparative linguists hope to do more than record and date linguistic divergence. Just as physical anthropologists may attempt to develop explanations for human variation, so linguists investigate the possible causes of linguistic variation. Some of the divergence undoubtedly comes about gradually. When groups of people speaking the same language lose communication with one another because they become separated, either physically or socially, they begin to accumulate small changes in phonology, morphology, and syntax (which occur continuously in any language). These variant forms of language are considered **dialects** when the differences in phonology, morphology, and syntax are not great enough to produce unintelligibility. (Dialects should not be confused with accents, which are merely differences in pronunciation.) Eventually, if the separation continues, the former dialects of the same language will become separate languages; that is, they will become mutually unintelligible, as German and English now are. Just as culture change originates from individual changes, language change originates from individual speakers, either from spontaneous innovation or from borrowing. Only when innovative speech patterns are picked up by others does linguistic change occur.[50]

Geographic barriers, such as large bodies of water, deserts, and mountains, may separate speakers of what was once the same language, but distance by itself can also produce divergence. For example, if we compare dialects of English in the British Isles, it is clear that the regions farthest away from each other are the most different linguistically (compare the northeast of Scotland and London).[51] In northern India, hundreds of semi-isolated villages and regions developed hundreds of local dialects. Today, the inhabitants of each village understand the dialects of the surrounding villages and, with a little more difficulty, the dialects of the next circle of villages. But slight dialect shifts accumulate village by village, and it seems as if different languages are being spoken at the opposite ends of the region, which are separated by more than a thousand miles.[52]

Even where there is little geographic separation, there may still be a great deal of dialect differentiation because of social distance. So, for example, the spread of a linguistic feature may be halted by religious, class, or other social differences that inhibit communication.[53] In the village of Khalapur in northern India, John Gumperz found substantial differences in speech between the Untouchables and other groups. Members of the Untouchables have work contacts with members of other groups but no friendships.[54]

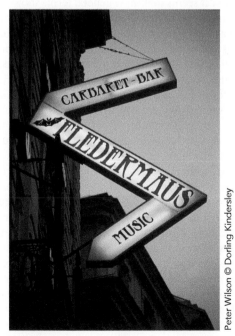

The Fledermaus cabaret bar in Vienna uses some English words in its sign out front.

Peter Wilson © Dorling Kindersley

Without friendships and the easy communication between friends, dialect differentiation can readily develop.

Whereas isolation brings gradual divergence between speech communities, contact results in greater resemblance. This effect is particularly evident when contact between mutually unintelligible languages introduces borrowed words, which usually name some new item borrowed from the other culture—*tomato, canoe, sushi,* and so on. Bilingual groups within a culture may also introduce foreign words, especially when the mainstream language has no real equivalent. Thus, *salsa* has come into English, and *le weekend* into French.

Conquest and colonization often result in extensive and rapid borrowing, if not linguistic replacement. The Norman conquest of England introduced French as the language of the new aristocracy. It was 300 years before the educated classes began to write in English. During this time, the English borrowed words from French and Latin, and the two languages—English and French—became more alike than they would otherwise have been. About 50 percent of the English general vocabulary originated in French. As this example suggests, different social classes may react to language contact differently. For example, English aristocrats eventually called their meat "pork" and "beef" (derived from the French words), but the people who raised the animals and prepared them for eating continued (at least for a while) to refer to the meat as "pig" and "bull," the original Anglo-Saxon words.

In those 300 years of extensive contact, the grammar of English remained relatively stable. English lost most of its inflections or case endings, but it adopted little of the French grammar. In general, the borrowing of words, particularly free morphemes,[55] is much more common than the borrowing of grammar.[56] As we might expect, borrowing by one language from another can make the borrowing language more different from its *sibling languages* (those derived from a common ancestral language) than it would otherwise be. Partly as a result of the French influence, the English vocabulary looks quite different from the languages to which it is actually most similar in terms of phonology and grammar—German, Dutch, and the Scandinavian languages.

RELATIONSHIPS BETWEEN LANGUAGE AND CULTURE

Some attempts to explain the diversity of languages have focused on the possible interactions between language and other aspects of culture. On the one hand, if it can be shown that a culture can affect the structure and content of its language, then it would follow that linguistic diversity derives at least in part from cultural diversity. On the other hand, the direction of influence between culture and language might work in reverse: Linguistic features and structures might affect other aspects of the culture.

Cultural Influences on Language

One way a society's language may reflect its corresponding culture is in **lexical content,** or vocabulary. Which experiences, events, or objects are singled out and given words may be a result of cultural characteristics.

Basic Words for Colors, Plants, and Animals

Early in the 20th century, many linguists pointed to the lexical domain (vocabulary) of color words to illustrate the supposed truth that languages vary arbitrarily or without apparent reason. Different languages not only had different numbers of basic color words (from 2 to 12 or so; for example, the words *red*, *green*, and *blue* in English), but they also, it was thought, had no consistency in the way they classified or divided the colors of the spectrum. But findings from a comparative (cross-linguistic) study contradicted these traditional presumptions about variation in the number and meaning of basic color words. On the basis of their study of at first 20 and later over 100 languages, Brent Berlin and Paul Kay found that languages did not encode color in completely arbitrary ways.[57]

Although different languages do have different numbers of basic color words, most speakers of any language are very likely to point to the same color chips as the best representatives of particular colors. For example, people the world over mean more or less the same color when they are asked to select the best "red." Moreover, there appears to be a nearly universal sequence by which basic color words are added to a language.[58] If a language has just two basic color words, its speakers will always refer to "black" (or dark) hues and "white" (or light) hues. If a language has three basic color words, the third word will nearly always be "red." The next category to appear is either "yellow" or "grue" (green/blue), then different words for green and blue, and so on. To be sure, we usually do not see the process by which basic color words are added to a language. But we can infer the usual sequence because, for example, if a language has a word for "yellow," it will almost always have a word for "red," whereas having a word for "red" does not mean that the language will have a word for "yellow."

What exactly is a *basic* color word? All languages, even the ones with only two basic color terms, have many different ways of expressing how color varies. For example, in English, we have words such as turquoise, blue-green, scarlet, crimson, and sky blue. Linguists do not consider these to be basic color words. In English, the basic color words are *white, black, red, green, yellow, blue, brown, pink, purple, orange,* and *gray.* One feature of a basic color word is that it consists of a single morph; it cannot include two or more units of meaning. This feature eliminates combinations such as *blue-green* and *sky blue.* A second feature of a basic color word is that the color it represents is not generally included in a higher-order color term. For example, scarlet and crimson are usually considered variants of red, turquoise a variant of blue. A third feature is that basic terms tend to be the first-named words when people are asked for color words. Finally, for a word to be considered a basic color word, many individual speakers of the language have to agree on the central meaning (in the color spectrum) of the word.[59]

Why do different societies (languages) vary in number of basic color terms? Berlin and Kay suggest that the number of basic color terms in a language increases with technological specialization as color is used to decorate and distinguish objects.[60] Cross-linguistic variation in the number of basic color terms does not mean that some languages make more color distinctions than others. Every language could make a particular distinction by combining words (e.g., "fresh leaf" for green); a language need not have a separate basic term for that color.

There may also be many basic color terms because of a biological factor.[61] Peoples with darker (more pigmented) eyes seem to have more trouble distinguishing colors at the dark (blue-green) end of the spectrum than do peoples with lighter eyes. It might be expected, then, that peoples who live nearer the equator (who tend to have darker eyes, presumably for protection against damaging ultraviolet radiation) would tend to have fewer basic color terms. And they do.[62] Moreover, it seems that both cultural and biological factors are required to account for cross-linguistic variation in the number of basic color terms. Societies tend to have six or more such terms (with separate terms for blue and green) only when they are relatively far from the equator and only when their cultures are more technologically specialized.[63] Technological specialization tends to go with larger communities, more centralized governments, occupational specialization, and more social inequality. Societies with such traits are often referred to in a shorthand way as more "complex," which should not be taken to mean "better."

Echoing Berlin and Kay's finding that basic color terms seem to be added in a more or less universal sequence, Cecil Brown has found what seem to be developmental sequences in other lexical domains. Two such domains are general, or *life-form,* terms for plants and for animals. Life-form terms are higher-order classifications. All languages have lower-order terms for specific plants and animals. For example, English has words such as *oak, pine, sparrow,* and *salmon.* English speakers make finer distinctions too—*pin oak, white pine, white-throated sparrow,* and *red salmon.* But why, in some languages, do people have a larger number of general terms such as *tree, bird,* and *fish?* It seems that these general terms show a universal developmental sequence too. That is, general terms seem to be added in a somewhat consistent order. After "plant" comes a term for "tree"; then one for "grerb" (small, green, leafy, nonwoody plant); then "bush" (for plants between tree and grerb in size); then "grass"; then "vine."[64] The life-form terms for animals also seem to be added in sequence; after "animal" comes a term for "fish," then "bird," then "snake," then "wug" (for small creatures other than fish, birds, and snakes—for example, worms and bugs), then "mammal."[65]

More complex societies tend to have a larger number of general, or life-form, terms for plants and animals than do simpler societies, just as they tend to have a larger number of basic color terms. Why? And do all realms or domains of vocabulary increase in size as social complexity increases? If we look at the total vocabulary of a language (as can be counted in a dictionary), more complex societies do have larger vocabularies.[66] But we have to remember that complex societies have many kinds of specialists, and dictionaries will include the terms such specialists use. If we look instead at the nonspecialist, **core vocabulary** of languages, it seems that all languages have a core vocabulary of about the same size.[67] Indeed, although some domains increase in size with social complexity, some remain the same and still others decrease. An example of a smaller vocabulary domain in complex societies is that of specific names for plants. Urban North Americans may know general terms for plants, but they know relatively few names for specific plants. The typical individual in a small-scale society can commonly name 400 to 800 plant species; a typical person in our own and similar societies may be able to name only 40 to 80.[68] The number of life-form terms is larger in societies in which ordinary people know less about particular plants and animals.[69]

The evidence now available strongly supports the idea that the vocabulary of a language reflects the everyday distinctions that are important in the society. Those aspects of environment or culture that are of special importance will receive greater attention in the language.

Grammar Most of the examples we could accumulate would show that a culture influences the names of things visible in its environment. Evidence for cultural influence on the grammatical structure of a language is less extensive. Harry Hoijer draws attention to the verb categories in the language of the Navajo, a traditionally nomadic people. These categories center mainly in the reporting of events, or "eventings," as he calls them. Hoijer notes that, in "the reporting of actions and events, and the framing of substantive concepts, Navajo emphasizes movement and specifies the nature, direction, and status of such movement in considerable detail."[70] For example, Navajo has one category for eventings that are in motion and another for eventings that have ceased moving. Hoijer concludes that the emphasis on events in the process of occurring reflects the Navajo's nomadic experience over the centuries, an experience also reflected in their myths and folklore.

A linguistic emphasis on events may or may not be generally characteristic of nomadic peoples; as yet, no one has investigated the matter cross-culturally or comparatively. But there are indications that systematic comparative research would turn up other grammatical features that are related to cultural characteristics. For example, many languages lack the possessive transitive verb we write as "have," as in "I have." Instead, the language may say something such as "it is to me." A cross-cultural study has suggested that a language may develop the verb "have" after the speakers of that language have developed a system of private property or personal ownership of resources.[71] The concept of private property is far from universal and tends to occur only in complex societies with social inequality. In contrast, many societies have some kind of communal ownership, by kin groups or communities. How people talk about owning seems to reflect how they own; societies that lack a concept of private property also lack the verb "have."

Linguistic Influences on Culture: The Sapir-Whorf Hypothesis

There is general agreement that culture influences language. But there is less agreement about the opposite possibility— that language influences other aspects of culture. Edward

Sapir and Benjamin Lee Whorf suggested that language is a force in its own right, that it affects how individuals in a society perceive and conceive reality. This suggestion is known as the *Sapir-Whorf hypothesis*.[72] In comparing the English language with Hopi, Whorf pointed out that English-language categories convey discreteness with regard to time and space, but Hopi does not. English has a discrete past, present, and future, and things occur at a definite time. Hopi expresses things with more of an idea of ongoing processes without time being apportioned into fixed segments. According to Ronald Wardhaugh, Whorf believed that these language differences lead Hopi and English speakers to see the world differently.[73]

As intriguing as that idea is, the relevant evidence is mixed. Linguists today do not generally accept the view that language coerces thought, but some suspect that particular features of language may facilitate certain patterns of thought.[74] The influences may be clearest in poetry and metaphors, where words and phrases are applied to other than their ordinary subjects, as in "all the world's a stage."[75] One of the serious problems in testing the Sapir-Whorf hypothesis is that researchers need to figure out how to separate the effects of other aspects of culture from the effects of language.

One approach that may reveal the direction of influence between language and culture is to study how children in different cultures (speaking different languages) develop concepts as they grow up. If language influences the formation of a particular concept, we might expect that children will acquire that concept earlier in societies where the languages emphasize that concept. For example, some languages make more of gender differences than others. Do children develop gender identity earlier when their language emphasizes gender? (Very young girls and boys seem to believe they can switch genders by dressing in opposite-sex clothes, suggesting that they have not yet developed a stable sense that they are unchangeably girls or boys.) Alexander Guiora and his colleagues have studied children growing up in Hebrew-speaking homes (Israel), English-speaking homes (the United States), and Finnish-speaking homes (Finland). Hebrew has the most gender emphasis of the three languages; all nouns are either masculine or feminine, and even second-person and plural pronouns are differentiated by gender. English emphasizes gender less, differentiating by gender only in the third-person singular (*she* or *her* or *hers; he* or *him* or *his*). Finnish emphasizes gender the least; although some words, such as *man* and *woman,* convey gender, differentiation by gender is otherwise lacking in the language. Consistent with the idea that language may influence thought, Hebrew-speaking children acquire the concept of stable gender identity the earliest on the average, Finnish-speaking children the latest.[76]

Another approach is to predict from language differences how people may be expected to perform in experiments. Comparing the Yucatec Mayan language and English, John Lucy predicted that English speakers might recall the *number* of things presented more than Yucatec Mayan speakers. For most classes of nouns, English requires a linguistic way of indicating whether something is singular or plural. You cannot say "I have dog" (no indication of number), but must say "I have a dog," "I have dogs," or "I have one (two, three, several, many) dogs." Yucatec Maya, like English, can indicate a plural, but allows the noun to be neutral with regard to number. For example, the translated phrase there-is-dog-over-there (*yàan pèek té'elo'*) can be left ambiguous about whether there is one or more than one dog. In English, the same ambiguity would occur in the sentence "I saw deer over there," but English does not often allow ambiguity for animate or inanimate nouns.[77] In a number of experiments, Yucatec Mayan and American English speakers were equally likely to recall the objects in a picture, but they differed in how often they described the number of a particular object in the picture. Yucatec Mayan speakers did so less often, consistent with their language's lack of insistence on indicating number.[78] So the salience of number in the experiments was probably a consequence of how the languages differ. Of course, it is possible that salience of number is created by some other cultural feature, such as dependence on money in the economy.

THE ETHNOGRAPHY OF SPEAKING

Traditionally, linguists concentrated on trying to understand the structure of a language, the usually unconscious rules that predict how the people of a given society typically speak. In recent years, many linguists have begun to study how people in a society vary in how they speak. This type of linguistic study, *sociolinguistics,* is concerned with the *ethnography of speaking*—that is, with cultural and subcultural patterns of speech variation in different social contexts.[79] The sociolinguist might ask, for example, what kinds of things one talks about in casual conversation with a stranger. A foreigner may know English vocabulary and grammar well but may not know that one typically chats with a stranger about the weather or where one comes from, and not about what one ate that day or how much money one earns. A foreigner may be familiar with much of the culture of a North American city, but if that person divulges the real state of his or her health and feelings to the first person who says, "How are you?" he or she has much to learn about "small talk" in North American English.

Similarly, North Americans tend to get confused in societies where greetings are quite different from ours. People in some other societies may ask as a greeting, "Where are you going?" or "What are you cooking?" Some Americans may think such questions are rude; others may try to answer in excruciating detail, not realizing that only vague answers are expected, just as we don't really expect a detailed answer when we ask people how they are.

Social Status and Speech

That a foreign speaker of a language may know little about the small talk of that language is but one example of the sociolinguistic principle that what we say and how we say it are not wholly predictable by the rules of our language.

Rhoda Sidney

Renate Hiller

Strangers shake hands when they meet; friends may touch each other more warmly. How we speak to others also differs according to the degree of friendship.

Who we are socially and whom we are talking to may greatly affect what we say and how we say it.

In a study interviewing children in a New England town, John Fischer noted that, in formal interviews, children were likely to pronounce the ending in words such as *singing* and *fishing,* but in informal conversations, they said "*singin'*" and "*fishin'*." Moreover, he noted that the phenomenon also appeared to be related to social class; children from higher-status families were less likely to drop the ending than were children from lower-status families. Subsequent studies in English-speaking areas tend to support Fischer's observations with regard to this speech pattern. Other patterns are observed as well. For example, in Norwich, England, lower classes tend to drop the *h* in words such as *hammer,* but in all classes, the pattern of dropping the *h* increases in casual situations.[80] With respect to grammatical differences, in inner-city Detroit, lower class African Americans are more likely to use double negatives as in "It ain't nobody's business," in contrast to middle-class African Americans who usually say "It isn't anybody's business."[81]

Research has shown that English people from higher-class backgrounds tend to have more *homogeneous* speech, conforming more to what is considered standard English (the type of speech heard on television or radio), whereas people from lower-class backgrounds have very *heterogeneous* speech, varying in their speaking according to the local or dialect area they come from.[82] In some societies, social status differences may be associated with more marked differentiation of words. Clifford Geertz, in his study of Javanese, showed that the vocabularies of the three rather sharply divided groups in Javanese society—peasants, townspeople, and aristocrats—reflect their separate positions. For example, the concept *now* is expressed differently in these three groups. A peasant will use *saiki* (considered the lowest and roughest form of the word); a townsman will use *saniki* (considered somewhat more elegant); and an aristocrat will use *samenika* (the most elegant form).[83]

Status relationships between people can also influence the way they speak to each other. Terms of address are a good example. In English, forms of address are relatively simple. One is called either by a first name or by a title (such as *Doctor, Professor, Ms.,* or *Mister*) followed by a last name. A study by Roger Brown and Marguerite Ford indicates that terms of address in English vary with the nature of the relationship between the speakers.[84] The reciprocal use of first names generally signifies an informal or intimate relationship between two people. A title and last name used reciprocally usually indicates a more formal or businesslike relationship between individuals who are roughly equal in status. Nonreciprocal use of first names and titles in English is reserved for speakers who recognize a marked difference in status between them. This status difference can be a function of age, as when a child refers to her mother's friend as Mrs. Miller and is in turn addressed as Sally, or can be due to occupational hierarchy, as when a person refers to his boss as Ms. Ramirez and is in turn addressed as Joe. In some cases, generally between boys and between men, the use of the last name alone represents a middle ground between the intimate and the formal usages.

Gender Differences in Speech

In many societies, the speech of men differs from the speech of women. The variation can be slight, as in our own society, or more extreme, as with the Carib Indians in the Lesser Antilles of the West Indies, among whom women and men use different words for the same concepts.[85] In Japan, males and females use entirely different words for numerous concepts (e.g., the male word for water is *mizu;* the female version is *ohiya*), and females often add the polite prefix *o-* (females will tend to say *ohasi* for chopsticks; males will tend to say *hasi*).[86] In the United States and other Western societies, there are differences in the speech of females and males, but they are not as dramatic as in the Carib and Japanese cases. For example, earlier we noted the tendency for the *g* to be dropped in words such as *singing* when the situation is informal and when the social class background is lower. But there is also a gender difference. Women are more likely than men to keep the *g* sound and less likely than men to drop the *h* in words such as *happy.* In Montreal,

women are less likely than men to drop the *l* in phrases such as *il fait* ("he does") or in the idiom *il y a* ("there is/are").[87] And in Detroit, in each social class, African American women are less likely than men to use double negatives.[88]

Gender differences occur in intonation and in phrasing of sentences as well. Robin Lakoff found that, in English, women tend to answer questions with sentences that have rising inflections at the end instead of a falling intonation associated with a firm answer. Women also tend to add questions to statements, such as "They caught the robber last week, didn't they?"[89]

One explanation for the gender differences, particularly with regard to pronunciation, is that women in many societies may be more concerned than men with being "correct."[90] (This is not in the linguist's sense; it is important to remember that linguists do not consider one form of speech more correct than another, just as they do not consider one dialect superior to another. All are equally capable of expressing a complex variety of thoughts and ideas.) In societies with social classes, what is considered more correct by the average person may be what is associated with the upper class. In other societies, what is older may be considered more correct. For example, in the Native American language of Koasati, which used to be spoken in Louisiana, males and females used different endings in certain verbs. The differences seemed to be disappearing in the 1930s, when the research on Koasati was done. Young girls had begun to use the male forms and only older women still used the female forms. Koasati men said that the women's speech was a "better" form of speech.[91] Gender differences in speech may parallel some of the gender differences noted in other social behavior: Girls are more likely than boys to behave in ways that are acceptable to adults.

There are not enough studies to know just how common it is for women to exhibit more linguistic "correctness." We do know of some instances where it is not the case. For example, in a community in Madagascar where people speak Merina, a dialect of Malagasy, it is considered socially correct to avoid explicit directives. So, instead of directly ordering an action, a Merina speaker will try to say it indirectly. Also, it is polite to avoid negative remarks, such as expressing anger toward someone. In this community, however, women, not men, often break the rules; women speak more directly and express anger more often.[92] This difference may be related to the fact that women are more involved in buying and selling in the marketplace.

Some researchers have questioned whether it is correctness that is at issue. Rather, we may be dealing in these examples with unequal prestige and power. Women may try to raise their status by conforming more to standard speech. When they answer a question with a rising inflection, they may be expressing uncertainty and a lack of power. Alternatively, perhaps women want to be more cooperative conversationalists. Speaking in a more "standard" fashion is consistent with being more likely to be understood by others. Answering a question with another question leads to continued conversation.[93]

new perspectives on gender

Does the English Language Promote Sexist Thinking?

Does English promote sexist thinking, or does the language merely reflect gender inequalities that already exist? For those who wish to promote gender equality, the answers to these questions are important because, if language influences thought (along the lines put forward by Edward Sapir and Benjamin Whorf), then linguistic change will be necessary to bring about change in the culture of gender. If it is the other way around, that is, if language reflects inequality, then social, economic, and political changes have to come before we can expect substantial linguistic change to occur.

Leaving aside for the moment which changes first, how does English represent gender inequity? Consider the following written by Benjamin Lee Whorf: "Speech is the best show man puts on. . . . Language helps man in his thinking." Although *man* in English technically refers to all humans and *his* technically refers to the thinking of a single person of either gender, the frequent use of such words could convey the idea that males are more important. Similarly, do the words *chairman, policeman, businessman,* and *salesman* convey that males are supposed to have those jobs? What is conveyed when there are two words for the two genders, as in *actor* and *actress* and *hero* and *heroine*? Usually the base word is male and the suffix is added for the female form. Does the suffix convey that the female form is an afterthought or less important?

It is not just the structure of the language that may convey gender inequality. How come in the pairs *sir/madam, master/mistress, wizard/witch,* the female version has acquired negative connotations? Men might be called animal names, such as wolves, rats, or pigs. But more animal images seem to be applied to women. They can be *chicks, henpeckers, cows, dogs, bitches, kittens,* or *birds*. Coming back to the original questions, how would we know whether language promotes sexism or sexism influences language? One way to find out is to do experimental studies, such as the one conducted by Fatemeh Khosroshashi. Some individuals were asked to read texts written with *man, he,* and *his* referring to people; others were asked to read texts with more gender-neutral phrasing. Individuals were subsequently asked to draw pictures to go with the texts. The ones who read the texts with more male terminology drew more accompanying pictures of men, strongly suggesting that the use of the terms *man, he,* and *his* conveyed the thought that the people in the text were men, not women, *because* of the vocabulary used. We need more such studies to help address the intellectual question of which comes first, linguistic or nonlinguistic culture.

It would be important to know whether societies with more "male-oriented" language are more male-dominated than are societies without such distinctions. We don't have that kind of comparative research yet. But one study by Robert and Ruth Munroe looked at the *proportion* of female and male nouns in ten languages (six Indo-European, four other than Indo-European) in which nouns have gender. Although none of those societies could be described as having a female bias, the Munroes were able to ask whether those societies with less male bias in social customs (e.g., all children are equally likely to inherit property) have a higher proportion of female nouns than male nouns (more female than male nouns). The answer appears to be yes. Although this study does not reveal what came first, studies like it are important if we want to discover how language differences may be related to other aspects of culture. If male-oriented languages are not related to male dominance, then it is not likely that sexist thinking is a consequence of language.

On the assumption that language may influence thought, many are pushing for changes in the way English is used, if not structured. It is hard to get English speakers to adopt a gender-neutral singular pronoun to replace *he*. Attempts to do so go back to the 18th century and include suggestions of *tey, thon, per,* and *s/he*. Although these efforts have not succeeded, the way English is written and spoken has begun to change. Words or phrases such as *chair* (or *chairperson*), *police officer,* and *sales assistant* (*salesperson*) have begun to replace their former *man* versions. If Whorf were writing his sentence now, it probably would be written: "Speech is the best show humans put on. . . . Language helps people think."

Sources: Holmes 2001, 305–16; Khosroshashi 1989; Lakoff 1973; Munroe and Munroe 1969; Romaine 1994, 105–16; Wardhaugh 2002, 317.

Men and women typically differ in what they talk about, or do not talk about. Deborah Tannen offers some examples. When women hear about someone else's troubles, they are likely to express understanding of the other's feelings; in contrast, men are likely to offer solutions. Men tend not to ask for directions; women do. Women tend to talk a lot in private settings; men talk more in public settings. These and other differences can cause friction and misunderstanding between the genders. When women express their troubles and men offer solutions, women feel that their feelings are not understood; men are frustrated that the women do not take their solutions seriously. Men may prefer to sit at home quietly and feel put upon to have to engage in conversation; women feel slighted when men avoid extended conversations with them. Why these differences? Tannen suggests that misunderstanding between men and women arises because boys and girls grow up in somewhat different cultures. Girls typically play in small groups, talk frequently, and are intimate with others. Boys more often play in large groups in which jockeying for status and attention are more of a concern. Higher-status individuals give directions and solutions; they do not seek directions or solutions. So asking for directions is like acknowledging lower status. But large play groups resemble public settings, and so later in life, men feel more comfortable speaking in public. Women, in contrast, are more comfortable speaking in small, intimate groups.[94]

Multilingualism and Code-Switching

For many people, the ability to speak more than one language is a normal part of life. One language may be spoken at home and another in school, the marketplace, or government. Or more than one language may be spoken at home if family members come from different cultures and still other languages are spoken outside. Some countries explicitly promote multilingualism. For example, Singapore has four official languages—English, Mandarin (one of the Chinese languages), Tamil, and Malay. English is stressed for trade, Mandarin as the language of communication with most of China, Malay as the language of the general region, and Tamil as the language of an important ethnic group. Moreover, most of the population speaks Hokkien, another Chinese language. Education is likely to be in English and Mandarin.[95]

What happens when people who know two or more languages communicate with each other? Very often you find them **code-switching,** using more than one language in the course of conversing.[96] Switching can occur in the middle of a Spanish-English bilingual sentence, as in "No van a bring it up in the meeting" ("They are not going to bring it up in the meeting").[97] Or switching can occur when the topic or situation changes, such as from social talk to schoolwork. Why do speakers of more than one language sometimes switch? Although speakers switch for a lot of different reasons, what is clear is that the switching is not a haphazard mix that comes from laziness or ignorance. Code-switching involves a great deal of knowledge of two or more languages and an awareness of what is considered appropriate or inappropriate in the community. For example, in the Puerto Rican community in New York City, code-switching within the same sentence seems to be common in speech among friends, but if a stranger who looks like a Spanish speaker approaches, the language will shift entirely to Spanish.[98]

Although each community may have its own rules for code-switching, variations in practice may need to be understood in terms of the broader political and historical context. For example, German speakers in Transylvania, where Romanian is the national language, hardly ever code-switch to Romanian. Perhaps the reason is that, before the end of World War II, German speakers were a privileged economic group who looked down upon landless Romanians and their language. Under socialism, the German speakers lost their economic privilege, but they continued to speak German among

themselves. In the rare cases that Romanian is used among German speakers, it tends to be associated with low-status speech, such as singing bawdy songs. The opposite situation occurred in a Hungarian region of German-speaking Austria. The people of this agricultural region, annexed to Austria in 1921, were fairly poor peasant farmers. After World War II, business expansion began to attract labor from rural areas, so many Hungarians eagerly moved into jobs in industry. Younger generations saw German as a symbol of higher status and upward mobility; not surprisingly, code-switching between Hungarian and German became part of their conversations. Indeed, in the third generation, German has become the language of choice, except when speaking to the oldest Hungarians. The Hungarian-Austrian situation is fairly common in many parts of the world, where the language of the politically dominant group ends up being "linguistically dominant."[99]

WRITING AND LITERACY

Most of us have come to depend on writing for so many things that it is hard to imagine a world without it. Yet humans spent most of their history on earth without written language and many, if not most, important human achievements predate written language. Parents and other teachers passed on their knowledge by oral instruction and

Children do not need help learning the language spoken in their homes. However, reading and writing cannot usually be learned without instruction. Nowadays, children in most cultures are expected to learn to read and write in school. These Trobriand children from Papua New Guinea are allowed to wear their traditional clothes to school once a week.

demonstration. Stories, legends, and myths abounded—the stuff we call oral literature—even in the absence of writing. This is not to say that writing is not important. Far more information and far more literature can be preserved for a longer period of time with a writing system. The earliest writing systems are only about 6,000 years old and are associated with early cities and states. Early writing is associated with systematic record-keeping—keeping of ledgers for inventorying goods and transactions. In early times, probably only the elite could read and write—indeed only recently has universal literacy (the ability to read and write) become the goal of most countries. But in most countries, the goal of universal literacy is far from achieved. Even in countries with universal education, the quality of education and the length of education varies considerably between subcultures and genders. Just as some ways of speaking are considered superior to others, a high degree of literacy is usually considered superior to illiteracy.[100] But literacy in what language or languages? As we discussed in the box on endangered languages, recent efforts to preserve languages have encouraged writing of texts in languages that were only spoken previously. Obviously, there will be few texts in those languages; other languages have vast numbers of written texts. As more accumulated knowledge is written and stored in books, journals, and databases, attainment of literacy in those written languages will be increasingly critical to success. And texts do not only convey practical knowledge—they may also convey attitudes, beliefs, and values that are characteristic of the culture associated with the language in which the texts are written.

SUMMARY ● ○ ○

1. The essential function language plays in all societies is that of communication. Although human communication is not limited to spoken language, such language is of overriding importance because it is the primary vehicle through which culture is shared and transmitted.

2. Systems of communication are not unique to humans. Other animal species communicate in a variety of ways—by sound, odor, body movement, and so forth. The ability of chimpanzees and gorillas to learn and use sign language suggests that symbolic communication is not unique to humans. Still, human language is distinctive as a communication system in that its spoken and symbolic nature permits an infinite number of combinations and recombinations of meaning.

3. Nonverbal human communication includes posture, mannerisms, body movement, facial expressions, and signs and gestures. Nonverbal human communication also includes tone of voice, accent, nonword sounds, and all the optional vocal features that communicate meaning apart from the language itself.

4. Descriptive (or structural) linguists try to discover the rules of phonology (the patterning of sounds), morphology (the patterning of sound sequences and words), and syntax (the patterning of phrases and sentences) that predict how most speakers of a language talk.

5. By comparative analysis of cognates and grammar, historical linguists test the notion that certain languages derive from a common ancestral language, or protolanguage. The goals are to reconstruct the features of the protolanguage, to hypothesize how the offspring languages separated from the protolanguage or from each other, and to establish the approximate dates of such separations.

6. When two groups of people speaking the same language lose communication with each other because they become separated either physically or socially, they begin to accumulate small changes in phonology, morphology, and syntax. If the separation continues, the two former dialects of the same language will eventually become separate languages—that is, they will become mutually unintelligible.

7. Whereas isolation brings about divergence between speech communities, contact results in greater resemblance. This effect is particularly evident when contact between people who speak mutually unintelligible languages introduces borrowed words, most of which name some new item borrowed from the other culture.

8. Some attempts to explain the diversity of languages have focused on the possible interaction between language and other aspects of culture. On the one hand, if it can be shown that a culture can affect the structure and content of its language, then it would follow that linguistic diversity derives at least in part from cultural diversity. On the other hand, the direction of influence between culture and language might work in reverse; the linguistic structures might affect other aspects of the culture.

9. In recent years, some linguists have begun to study variations in how people actually use language when speaking. This type of linguistic study, called sociolinguistics, is concerned with the ethnography of speaking—that is, with cultural and subcultural patterns of speaking in different social contexts.

10. In bilingual or multilingual populations, code-switching (using more than one language in the course of conversing) has become increasingly common.

11. Written language dates back only about 6,000 years, but writing and written records have become increasingly important; literacy is now a major goal of most countries.

GLOSSARY TERMS ○ ● ○

accent	morpheme
code-switching	morphology
cognates	paralanguage
core vocabulary	phoneme
dialects	phones
historical linguistics	phonology
kinesics	protolanguage
lexical content	syntax
lexicon	symbolic
morph	communication

CRITICAL QUESTIONS ○ ○ ●

1. Why might natural selection have favored the development of true language in humans but not in apes?

2. Would the world be better off with many different languages spoken or with just one universal language? Why do you think so?

3. Discuss some new behavior or way of thinking that led people to adopt or invent new vocabulary or some new pattern of speech.

4. How does some aspect of your speech differ from your parents or others of the previous generation? Why do you think it has changed?

PEARSON
myanthrolab

Read the chapter by Jane H. Hill, "Do Apes Have Language?" on MyAnthroLab and answer the following questions.

1. Jane Hill raises the question of whether apes have language. Briefly, what is her answer to the question?

2. Chimpanzees have learned signs from American Sign Language but they have not been able to learn to speak words. Why not?

NOTES ● ○ ○

1. Keller 1974/1902, 34.
2. Wilden 1987, 124, referred to in Christensen et al. 2001.
3. Lambert 2001.
4. Ekman and Keltner 1997, 32.
5. Poyatos 2002, 103–5, 114–18.
6. von Frisch 1962.
7. King 1999a; Gibson and Jessee 1999, 189–90.
8. Seyfarth and Cheney 1982, 242, 246.
9. Hockett and Ascher 1964.
10. T. S. Eliot 1963.
11. Snowdon 1999, 81.
12. Pepperberg 1999.
13. Mukerjee 1996, 28.
14. Savage-Rumbaugh 1992, 138–41.
15. J. H. Hill 1978, 94; J. H. Hill 2009.
16. Ibid.
17. Senner 1989.
18. Chomsky 1975.
19. Southworth and Daswani 1974, 312. See also Boas 1911/1964, 121–23.
20. Akmajian et al. 2001, 296.
21. Ibid., 298.
22. Bickerton 1983.
23. Ibid., 122.
24. B. Berlin 1992; Hays 1994.
25. G. Miller 2004.
26. Gleitman and Wanner 1982; Blount 1981.
27. R. Brown 1980, 93–4.
28. de Villiers and de Villiers 1979, 48; see also Wanner and Gleitman 1982.
29. Bickerton 1983, 122.
30. E. Bates and Marchman 1988 as referred to by Snowdon 1999, 88–91.
31. Crystal 1971, 168.
32. Ibid., 100–1.
33. Barinaga 1992, 535.
34. Akmajian et al. 1984, 136.
35. R. L. Munroe et al. 1996; M. Ember and C. R. Ember 1999. The theory about the effect of baby-holding on consonant-vowel alternation is an extension of the theory that regular baby-holding encourages a preference for regular rhythm in music; see Ayres 1973.
36. Sapir and Swadesh 1964, 103.
37. Akmajian et al. 2001, 149–54.
38. Chaucer 1926, 8. Our modern English translation is based on the glossary in this book.
39. Katzner 2002, 10.
40. Akmajian et al. 2001, 334.
41. Baldi 1983, 3.
42. Ibid., 12.
43. Friedrich 1970, 168.
44. Ibid., 166.
45. Gimbutas 1974, 293–95. See Skomal and Polomé 1987.
46. Anthony et al. 1991.
47. Renfrew 1987.
48. Greenberg 1972; see also Phillipson 1976, 71.
49. Phillipson 1976, 79.
50. Holmes 2001, 194–95.
51. Trudgill 1983, 34.
52. Gumperz 1961, 976–88.
53. Trudgill 1983, 35.
54. Gumperz 1971, 45.
55. Weinreich 1968: 31.
56. But see Thomason and Kaufman 1988 for a discussion of how grammatical changes due to contact may be more important than was previously assumed.
57. Berlin and Kay 1969.
58. Ibid.
59. Ibid., 5–6.
60. Ibid., 104; Witkowski and Brown 1978.
61. Bornstein 1973, 41–101.
62. M. Ember 1978, 364–67.
63. Ibid.
64. C. H. Brown 1977.
65. C. H. Brown 1979.
66. Witkowski and Burris 1981.
67. Ibid.
68. C. H. Brown and Witkowski 1980, 379.
69. C. H. Brown 1984, 106.
70. Hoijer 1964, 146.
71. Webb 1977, 42–9; see also Rudmin 1988.
72. Sapir 1931, 578; see also J. B. Carroll 1956.
73. Wardhaugh 2002, 222.
74. Denny 1979, 97.
75. Friedrich 1986.
76. Guiora et al. 1982.
77. Lucy 1992, 46.
78. Ibid., 85–148.
79. Hymes 1974, 83–117.
80. Fischer 1958; Wardhaugh 2002, 160–88.
81. Chambers 2002, 352; citing research by Shuy.
82. Trudgill 1983, 41–2.
83. Geertz 1960, 248–60; see also Errington 1985.
84. R. Brown and Ford 1961.
85. Wardhaugh 2002, 315.
86. Shibamoto 1987, 28.

87. Holmes 2001, 153.
88. Chambers 2002, 352, citing research by Shuy.
89. Lakoff 1973; Lakoff 1990.
90. Wardhaugh 2002, 328; Holmes 2001, 158–59; Trudgill 1983, 87–88.
91. M. R. Haas 1944, 142–49.
92. Keenan 1989.
93. Holmes 2001, 289.
94. Tannen 1990, 49–83.
95. Wardhaugh 2002, 100.
96. Heller 1988, 1.
97. Pfaff 1979.
98. Wardhaugh 2002, 108.
99. Gal 1988, 249–55.
100. Collins and Blot 2003, 1–3.

Getting Food

Getting Food

or most people in our society, getting food consists of a trip to the supermarket. Within an hour, we can gather enough food from the shelves to last us a week. Seasons don't daunt us. Week after week, we know food will be there. But we do not think of what would happen if the food were not delivered to the supermarket. We wouldn't be able to eat, and without eating for a while, we would die. Despite the old adage "Man [or woman] does not live by bread alone," we could not live at all without bread or the equivalent. Food-getting activities, then, take precedence over other activities important to survival. Reproduction, social control (the maintenance of peace and order within a group), defense against external threat, and the transmission of knowledge and skills to future generations—none could take place without energy derived from food. But it is not merely energy that is required for survival and long-term reproduction. Food-getting strategies need to provide the appropriate combination of nutrients throughout varying seasons and changing environmental conditions. Food-getting activities are also important because the way a society gets its food strongly predicts other aspects of a culture, from community size and permanence of settlement to type of economy and degree of inequality and type of political system, and even art styles and religious beliefs and practices.

In contrast with our own and similar societies, most societies have not had food-getting specialists. Rather, almost all able-bodied adults were largely engaged in getting food for themselves and their families. Such economies are described as **subsistence economies**. For millions of years, humans obtained their food by gathering wild plants, hunting or scavenging wild animals, and fishing. Agriculture is a relatively recent phenomenon, dating back only about 10,000 years. And industrial or mechanized agriculture is hardly more than a century old. Harvesting machines have been used a little bit longer, but self-propelled machines had to wait for the internal combustion engine and the rise of the oil industry.

In this chapter, we look at the ways different societies get food and discuss some of the features associated with the different patterns. We ask why societies vary in their food-getting strategies. We shall see that the physical environment by itself has only a limited or restraining effect on how a society gets most of its food. To explain the variation more fully, we discuss at the end of the chapter why societies in the prehistoric past switched from collecting wild food resources to cultivating plants and raising animals. ● ○ ●

FORAGING

Foraging or *food collection* may be generally defined as a food-getting strategy that obtains wild plant and animal resources through gathering, hunting, scavenging, or fishing. Although this was the way humans got their food for most of human history, foragers in

the world today, also commonly referred to as **hunter-gatherers,** are not very numerous, and most of them live in what have been called the *marginal areas* of the earth—deserts, the Arctic, and dense tropical forests—habitats that do not allow easy exploitation by modern agricultural technologies. In the last few hundred years, only about 5 million people are or were foragers.[1]

Anthropologists are interested in studying the relatively few foraging societies still available for observation because these groups may help us understand some aspects of human life in the past, when all people were foragers. But we must be cautious in drawing inferences about the past from our observations of recent and contemporary foragers, for three reasons. First, early foragers lived in almost all types of environments, including some very bountiful ones. Therefore, what we observe among recent and contemporary foragers, who generally live in deserts, the Arctic, and tropical forests, may not be comparable to what would have been observable in more favorable environments in the past.[2] Second, contemporary foragers are not relics of the past. Like all contemporary societies, they have evolved and are still evolving. Indeed, recent research reveals considerable variation in economic behavior as well as in social structure in foraging groups that share common ancestry; this implies that recent foragers have responded to differences in local environmental conditions.[3] Third, recent and contemporary foragers have been interacting with kinds of societies that did not exist until after 10,000 years ago—agriculturalists, pastoralists, and intrusive, powerful state societies.[4] For example, evidence from South Asia and Southeast Asia suggests that trade with agriculturalists was probably an important component of foragers' economic strategies for millennia.[5] And, in the recent past, foraging people have increasingly depended on agriculture and commercial activities as well as trade. In short, what we see recently may be very different from the distant past when foraging was the only means of subsistence.

Let us examine two areas of the world with very different environments where recent foragers lived: Australia and the North American Arctic.

Australian Aborigines

Before Europeans came to the Australian continent, all the aboriginal people who lived there depended on foraging. Although the way of life of Australian aborigines is now considerably altered, we consider the life of the Ngatatjara, as described by Richard Gould in the 1960s, when they still lived by gathering wild plants and hunting wild animals in the Gibson Desert of western Australia.[6] (We mostly use the present tense in our discussion because that is the custom in ethnographic writing, but readers should remember that we are referring to aboriginal life in the 1960s.)

The desert environment of the Ngatatjara averages less than 8 inches of rain per year, and the temperature in summer may rise to 118°F. The few permanent water holes are separated by hundreds of square miles of sand, scrub, and rock. Even before Europeans arrived in Australia, the area was sparsely populated—fewer than one person per 35 to 40 square miles. Now there are even fewer people, because the aboriginal population was decimated by introduced diseases and mistreatment after the Europeans arrived.

On a typical day, the camp begins to stir just before sunrise, while it is still dark. Children are sent to fetch water, and the people breakfast on water and food left over from the night before. In the cool of the early morning, the adults talk and make plans for the day. The talking goes on for a while. Where should they go for food—to places they have been to recently or to new places? Sometimes there are other considerations. For example, one woman may want to search for plants whose bark she needs to make new sandals. When the women decide which plants they want to gather and where they think those plants are most likely to be found, they take up their digging sticks and set out with large wooden bowls of drinking water on their heads. Their children ride on their hips or walk alongside. Meanwhile, the men may have decided to hunt emus, 6-foot-tall ostrichlike birds that do not fly. The men go to a creek bed where they will wait to ambush any game that may come along. They lie patiently behind a screen of brush they have set up, hoping for a chance to throw a spear at an emu or even a kangaroo. They can throw only once, because the game will run away if they miss.

By noon, the men and women are usually back at camp, the women with their wooden bowls each filled with up to 15 pounds of fruit or other plant foods, the men more often than not with only some small game, such as lizards and rabbits. The men's food-getting is less certain of success than the women's, so most of the Ngatatjara aborigines' diet is plant food. The daily cooked meal is eaten toward evening, after an afternoon spent resting, gossiping, and making or repairing tools.

The aborigines traditionally were nomadic, moving their campsites fairly frequently. The campsites were isolated and inhabited by only a small number of people, or they were clusters of groups including as many as 80 people. The aborigines never established a campsite right next to a place with water. If they were too close, their presence would frighten away game and might cause tension with neighboring bands, who would also wait for game to come to the scarce watering spots.

Today, many aborigines live in small settled villages. For example, in the 1980s, Victoria Burbank worked in a village she calls "Mangrove" in the Northern Territory of Australia. The once-nomadic aborigines now live in a village of about 600, which was founded in the 1950s around a Protestant mission. Their houses have stoves, refrigerators, toilets, washing machines, and even television sets. Their children attend school full-time, and there is a health clinic for their medical needs. They still do some foraging, but most of their food comes from the store. Some earn wages, but many subsist on government welfare checks.[7]

The Inuit (Eskimo)

The diet of the Australian aborigines was mainly wild plant foods. But for the Inuit (Eskimo) peoples, who live year-round in the North American Arctic, plants are too scarce to be the most important part of the diet. From Greenland and Labrador in the east to Alaska in the west, the Inuit used to depend almost entirely on sea and land

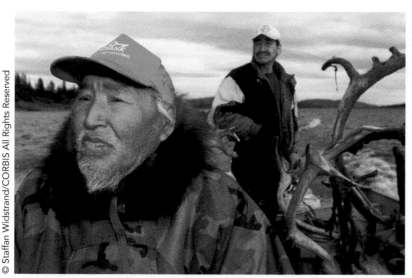

mammals and fish. (The term *Eskimo* is used widely in the West, but it is not a word in any of the native languages in that area. Many of the native Arctic groups, particularly those now living in Canada, prefer to be called Inuit.) We focus here on the traditional life of the north Alaskan Inupiaq in the beginning of the 19th century, as reconstructed by Ernest Burch (the "ethnographic present" in the following discussion).[8] Northern Alaska is relatively "warm" for its latitude but not for most of us farther south; little sun and below-zero temperatures for a month or so in the winter are hardly warm. Rivers and lakes freeze in October and do not thaw until May. Even the ocean freezes for part of the winter.

What the Inupiaq get for food depends mostly on the season, but the critical resources are sea mammals (ranging in size from whales to seals), fish, and caribou or wild reindeer. The usual technique for hunting sea mammals is to hurl a toggle harpoon into the animal from a kayak. It is very difficult to kill a moving sea mammal, so hunters attach a line to the animal with the harpoon; on the other end of the line is a sealskin float that indicates where the harpooned sea mammal can be located. The sea mammal gets more and more tired pulling the float until the hunter is able to kill it with a lance. One man alone can manage to hunt smaller sea mammals, but groups of men are needed to hunt whales. In the winter, when the sea ice is frozen, hunters use a different hunting technique. Hunters must locate a breathing hole and then wait, immobile and attentive, for hours or sometimes days until a seal comes up for air. The instant a seal surfaces, the hunters must aim perfectly with the harpoon.

The women butcher the animal, prepare it for eating or storage, and process the skin. Women sew all of the skin clothing. They also hunt small animals, such as hares, and do much of the fishing. Various techniques are used for fishing—hook and line, spearing, and ambushing with nets and dams. Women make the fishing nets, and it takes the better part of a year to make one. Although there are not many plants to gather, the women do that too.

Related families usually live together and move camp by boat or sled to be in the best place to intercept the migratory animals and fish. For instance, caribou migrate, so the Inupiaq try to catch them by building a corral in a place through which they are expected to pass. A network of interrelated families lives and moves in a territory of thousands of square miles, moving outside it only when they have made arrangements with other groups to do so.

Much has changed since the time just described. Now the Inupiaq live in villages or towns with many modern conveniences. In the village of Kivalina, there are permanent houses with electricity, telephones, and television sets. Dog teams have been replaced by all-terrain vehicles and snowmobiles. There are powerful outboard motors rather than skin boats. Many men and women have full-time wage-paying jobs. But even though the people may buy most of their food, there is still a preference for traditional foods, so the Inupiaq still hunt and fish on the weekends.

General Features of Foragers

Despite the differences in terrain and climate under which they live and the different food-collecting technologies they use, Australian aborigines, Inuit, and most other recent foragers have certain characteristic cultural patterns. Most live in small communities in sparsely populated territories and follow a nomadic lifestyle, forming no permanent settlements. As a rule, they do not recognize individuals' land rights. Their communities generally do not have different classes of people and tend to have no specialized or full-time political officials.[9] Division of labor in foraging societies is based largely on age and gender: Men exclusively hunt large marine and land animals and usually do most of the fishing, and women usually gather wild plant foods.[10] Foragers must decide what plants or animals to target. Optimal foraging theory helps explain some of the decisions foragers make.

Is there a typical pattern of food-getting among foragers? Many anthropologists have assumed that foragers typically get their food more from gathering than from hunting, and that women contribute more than men to

TABLE 1	Variation in Food-Getting and Associated Features			
	Food Collectors		Food Producers	
	Foragers	Horticulturalists	Pastoralists	Intensive Agriculturalists
Population density	Lowest	Low to moderate	Low	Highest
Maximum community size	Small	Small to moderate	Small	Large (towns and cities)
Nomadism/ permanence of settlements	Generally nomadic or seminomadic	More sedentary: communities may move after several years	Generally nomadic or seminomadic	Permanent communities
Food shortages	Infrequent	Infrequent	Frequent	Frequent
Trade	Minimal	Minimal	Very important	Very important
Full-time craft specialists	None	None or few	Some	Many (high degree of craft specialization)
Individual differences in wealth	Generally none	Generally minimal	Moderate	Considerable
Political leadership	Informal	Some part-time political officials	Part- and full-time political officials	Many full-time political officials

subsistence, because women generally do the gathering.[11] Although gathering is the most important food-getting activity for some foragers (e.g., the Ngatatjara aborigines and the !Kung of southern Africa), this is not true for most food-collecting societies known to us. A survey of 180 such societies indicates that there is a lot of variation with regard to which food-getting activity is most important to the society. Gathering is the most important activity for 30 percent of the surveyed societies, hunting for 25 percent, and fishing for 38 percent. (That is why we prefer the term *foragers* rather than the often-used *hunter-gatherers*; the term "foragers" allows us to recognize the importance of fishing.) In any case, because men generally do the fishing as well as the hunting, the men usually contribute more to food-getting than do the women among recent foragers.[12]

Because foragers move their camps often and walk great distances, it may seem that the food-collecting way of life is difficult. Although we do not have enough quantitative studies to tell us what is typical of most foragers, studies of two Australian aborigine groups[13] and of one !Kung group[14] indicate that those foragers do not spend many hours getting food. For example, !Kung adults spend an average of about 17 hours per week collecting food. Even when you add the time spent making tools (about 6 hours a week) and doing housework (about 19 hours a week), the !Kung seem to have more leisure time than many agriculturalists, as we discuss later.

Complex Foragers

When we say that foragers tend to have certain traits, this does not mean that all of them have those traits. There is considerable variability among societies that depend on

foraging. Foraging societies that depend heavily on fishing (such as on the Pacific Coast of the northwestern United States and Canada or on the south coast of New Guinea) are more likely to have bigger and more permanent communities and more social inequality than foraging societies elsewhere who mostly depend on game and plants.[15] The Pacific Coast and New Guinea coastal people also tend to have higher population densities, food storage, occupational specialization, resource ownership, slavery, and competitiveness.[16] Two foraging groups that depended heavily on annual salmon runs were the Tlingit of southeastern Alaska and the Nimpkish of British Columbia. Both groups had a three-tiered class system with a high class, commoners, and slaves. The high-status individuals were obliged to stage competitive elaborate feasts and distributions of valuables.[17] This type of inequality and competitiveness was very different from what we find in typical foragers, who generally show little social differentiation. In a worldwide study of foragers, those societies that were more dependent on fishing also tended to have more fighting between communities, compared with other foragers. Perhaps this is because some fishing sites were more predictable than others and people were willing to fight to defend them.[18]

In New Guinea, about 40 societies depend almost exclusively on foraging. Wild sago provides most of the carbohydrates for these foragers, but they vary considerably on how they obtain animal protein. Paul Roscoe has found that the amount of dependence upon fishing is strongly associated with density of population and settlement size.[19] For example, societies with more than 75 percent dependence upon fishing have average community sizes of about 350 people, as compared with community size of about 50 for those with less than 25 percent dependence upon fishing. Some villages were much larger. One Asmat village had over 1,400 people and a Waropen village over 1,700.

FOOD PRODUCTION

Beginning about 10,000 years ago, people in widely separated geographic locations made the revolutionary changeover to food production. That is, they began to cultivate and then domesticate plants and animals. (Domesticated plants and animals are different from the ancestral wild forms.) With domestication of these food sources, people acquired control over certain natural processes, such as animal breeding and plant seeding. Today, most peoples in the world depend for their food on some combination of domesticated plants and animals.

Anthropologists generally distinguish three major types of food production systems—*horticulture, intensive agriculture,* and *pastoralism.*

Horticulture

The word **horticulture** may conjure up visions of people with "green thumbs" growing orchids and other flowers in greenhouses. But to anthropologists, the word means the growing of crops of all kinds with relatively simple tools and methods, in the absence of permanently cultivated fields. The tools are usually hand tools, such as the digging stick or hoe, not plows or other equipment pulled by animals or tractors. And the methods used do not include fertilization, irrigation, or other ways to restore soil fertility after a growing season.

There are two kinds of horticulture. The more common one involves a dependence on **extensive or shifting cultivation.** The land is worked for short periods and then left idle for some years. During the years when the land is not cultivated, wild plants and brush grow; when the fields are later cleared by *slash-and-burn techniques,* nutrients are returned to the soil. The other kind of horticulture involves a dependence on long-growing tree crops. The two kinds of horticulture may be practiced in the same society, but in neither case is there permanent cultivation of field crops.

Most horticultural societies do not rely on crops alone for food. Many also hunt or fish; a few are nomadic for part of the year. For example, the Kayapo of the Brazilian Amazon leave their villages for as long as three months at a time to trek through the forest in search of game. The entire village participates in a trek, carrying large quantities of garden produce and moving their camp every day.[20] Other horticulturalists raise domestic animals, but these are usually not large animals, such as cattle and camels.[21] More often than not, horticulturalists raise smaller animals, such as pigs, chickens, goats, and sheep.

Let us look now at two horticultural societies, the Yanomamö of the Brazilian-Venezuelan Amazon and the Samoans of the South Pacific.

The Yanomamö Dense tropical forest covers most of Yanomamö territory. From the air, the typical village is located in a forest clearing and looks like a single, large, circular lean-to with its inner side open to the central plaza. Each individual family has its own portion of the

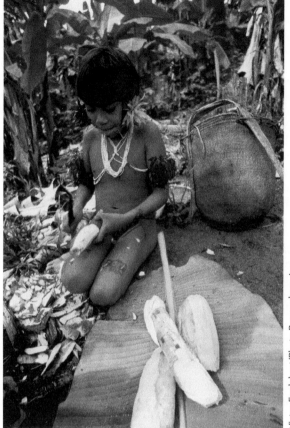

A Yanomamö boy peels cassava.

lean-to under the common roof. Each family's portion of the lean-to has a back wall (part of the closed back wall around the circular village structure), but the portions are open on the sides to each other as well as onto the central plaza of the village. The Yanomamö get most of their calories from garden produce, but according to Raymond Hames, the Yanomamö actually spend most of their time foraging.[22]

Before the people can plant, the forest must be cleared of trees and brush. Like most shifting cultivators, the Yanomamö use a combination of techniques: slashing the undergrowth, felling trees, and using controlled burning to clear a garden spot—in other words, **slash-and-burn** horticulture. Before the 1950s, the Yanomamö had only stone axes, so felling trees was quite difficult. Now they have steel machetes and axes given or traded to them by missionaries.

Because of the work involved in clearing a garden, the Yanomamö prefer to make use of forest patches that have little thorny brush and not too many large trees.[23] After the ground is cleared, the Yanomamö plant plantains, manioc, sweet potatoes, taro, and a variety of plants for medicine, condiments, and craft materials. Men do the heavy clearing work to prepare a garden, and they as well as women plant the crops. Women usually go to the gardens daily to weed and harvest. After two or three years, the yields diminish and the forest starts growing back, making continued cultivation less desirable and more difficult, so they abandon the garden and clear a new one. If they can, they clear adjacent forest, but if gardens are far from the village, they will move the village to a new location. Villages are moved about every five years because of gardening needs and warfare. There is a great deal of inter-village raiding, so villages are often forced to flee to another location.

Extensive cultivation requires a lot of territory because new gardens are not cleared until the forest grows back. What is often misunderstood is why it is so important to shift gardens. Not only is a burned field easier to plant, but the organic matter that is burned provides necessary nutrients for a good yield. If horticulturalists come back too quickly to a spot with little plant cover, a garden made there will not produce a satisfactory yield.

The Yanomamö crops do not provide much protein, so hunting and fishing are important to their diet. Men hunt birds, peccaries, monkeys, and tapir with bows and arrows. Women, men, and children enjoy fishing. They catch fish by hand, with small bows and arrows, and by stream poisoning. Everybody gathers honey, hearts of palm, Brazil nuts, and cashews, although the men usually climb trees to shake down the nuts. Much of the foraging is done from the village base, but the Yanomamö, like the Kayapo, may go on treks to forage from time to time.

The Samoans The Samoans numbered about 56,000 people in 1839, soon after European missionaries arrived.[24] The islands of Samoa, which are about 2,300 miles south of the Hawaiian Islands, are volcanic in origin, with central ridges and peaks as high as 6,000 feet. Though the land is generally steep, the islands have a lush plant cover watered by up to 200 inches of rain a year (about five times the amount of rain that falls on New York City in a year). All that rain does not interfere much with outdoor activity, because the torrential showers do not last long and the water disappears quickly into the porous volcanic soil. The temperature is relatively constant, rarely falling below 70°F or rising above 88°F. Strong cooling trade winds blow most of the year, generally from the east or southeast, and on the coasts one hears a continuous low rumble from the huge Pacific swells that break upon the fringing coral reefs offshore.

Samoan horticulture involves mostly three tree crops requiring little work except in harvesting. Once planted, and with hardly more than a few years of waiting, the breadfruit tree continues to produce about two crops a year for up to a half century. Coconut trees may continue to produce for a hundred years. And banana trees make new stalks of fruit, each weighing more than 50 pounds, for many years; merely cutting down one stalk induces the plant to grow another. Young men do most of the harvesting of tree crops. Women do the occasional weeding.

The Samoans also practice some shifting cultivation; men periodically clear small patches of land for taro, a root crop that is a staple food. The taro patches can produce a few crops before they must be allowed to revert to bush so that soil fertility can be restored. But even taro cultivation does not require much work; planting requires nothing more than slightly burying the top sliced off a root just harvested. Young men do most of the planting and harvesting. The taro patches are weeded infrequently, mostly by women. This kind of casual farming behavior prompted Captain Bligh, of *Mutiny on the Bounty* fame, to describe the Tahitians as lazy.[25] Captain Bligh's attitude was ethnocentric. South Pacific islanders such as the Samoans and Tahitians cannot weed as often as European farmers without risking the erosion of their soil, because, in contrast with European farmlands, which are generally flat or only slightly sloping, the land of Samoa and Tahiti is mostly steep. The Samoan and Tahitian practice of not weeding crops and growing them in glorious and messy confusion minimizes soil erosion; the deep and shallow root structures of the various plants growing together prevent the loose volcanic soil from being washed away by the torrential showers.

The Samoans keep chickens and pigs, which they eat only occasionally. The major source of animal protein in the Samoan diet is fish, caught inside and outside the reef. Younger men may swim in the deep sea outside the reef and use a sling to spear fish; older men are more likely to stand

The islands of American Samoa have very little flat land for cultivation. To prevent soil erosion, crops are interspersed among the naturally occurring brush. If land were completely cleared and single-cropped, the frequent torrential rains would quickly wash away the loose volcanic topsoil.

© Melvin Ember

on the reef and throw a four-pointed spear at fish swimming inside the reef. For many years, people in the villages of Samoa have sold copra, the sun-dried meat of the ripe coconut, to the world market for coconut oil. Men generally cut the copra from the shells after the ripe coconuts fall by themselves to the ground. With the cash earned from the sale of copra, people buy imported items such as machetes, kerosene, and flour. People in most villages still produce most of the foods they eat, but many have migrated to towns on the bigger islands and to cities in Hawaii and on the U.S. mainland to find wage-paying jobs.

General Features of Horticulturalists   In most horticultural societies, simple farming techniques have tended to yield more food from a given area than is generally available to foragers. Consequently, horticulture is able to support larger, more densely populated communities. The way of life of horticulturalists is more sedentary than that of foragers, although communities may move after some years to farm a new series of plots. (Some horticulturalists have permanent villages because they depend mostly on food from trees that keep producing for a long time.) In contrast with most recent food-collecting groups, horticultural societies exhibit the beginnings of social differentiation. For example, some individuals may be part-time craftworkers or part-time political officials, and certain members of a kin group may have more status than other individuals in the society.

Intensive Agriculture

People engaged in **intensive agriculture** use techniques that enable them to cultivate fields permanently. Essential nutrients may be put back in the soil through the use of fertilizers, which may be organic material (most commonly dung from humans or other animals) or inorganic (chemical) fertilizers. But there are other ways to restore nutrients. The Luo of western Kenya plant beans around corn plants. Bacteria growing around the roots of the bean plant replace lost nitrogen, and the corn plant conveniently provides a pole for the bean plant to wind around as it grows. Some intensive agriculturalists use irrigation from streams and rivers to ensure an adequate supply of waterborne nutrients. Crop rotation and plant stubble that has been plowed under also restore nutrients to the soil.

In general, the technology of intensive agriculturalists is more complex than that of horticulturalists. Plows rather than digging sticks are generally employed. But there is enormous variation in the degree to which intensive agriculturalists rely on mechanization rather than hand labor. In some societies, the most complex machine is an animal-drawn plow; in the corn and wheat belts of the United States, huge tractors till, seed, and fertilize 12 rows at a time.[26]

Let's look at two groups of intensive agriculturalists, those of rural Greece and those of the Mekong Delta in Vietnam.

Rural Greece   The village of Vasilika is situated at the foot of Mount Parnassus on the Boeotian plain. As described by Ernestine Friedl in the 1950s, its population was about 220 inhabitants.[27] Grapevines and wheat are cultivated for domestic use. The agricultural year begins in March, with pruning of the vines and hoeing of the fields, tasks regarded as men's work. Winemaking begins in September, after the grain harvest, and involves the whole family. Men, women, and children talk and joke as they pick the grapes and put them into large baskets. After they remove the leaves and stems, men trample the fruit, and the newly pressed grape juice, or *must*, is transferred to barrels. After adding whatever sugar and alcohol are needed, farmers also add resin to give the wine its characteristic flavor.

The villagers use horses to plow their wheat fields in October, and in November, they sow the seed by hand. The wheat crop is harvested the following summer, usually by machine. Wheat constitutes the staple village food and is eaten as bread, as a cereal (called *trakhana*), or as noodles. It is also commonly bartered for other food items, such as fish, olive oil, and coffee.

Cotton and tobacco are the main **cash crops**—that is, crops raised for sale. In this dry plains country, the success of the cotton crop depends on irrigation, and the villagers use efficient diesel pumps to distribute water. The real work in the cotton fields begins after the spring plowing and seeding have been completed. Then the young plants must be hoed and mulched, a task done mostly by women. The season of cotton cultivation is especially hard on women, who must do all the cooking and household chores in addition to working in the cotton fields. Irrigation, which begins in July, is men's work. It is usually done three times a season and involves the clearing of shallow ditches, the mounting of pumps, and the channeling of water. Cotton picking, which starts in October, is considered women's work. For picking, as well as hoeing and harvesting, a farmer owning more than five acres usually hires women from the same village or neighboring villages and sometimes even from distant towns. The cotton ginning is carried out by centrally located contractors, who are paid on the spot with 6 percent of each farmer's crop. Most of the seed reclaimed in the ginning is used for the next year's planting. The remainder is pressed into cakes to serve as supplementary food for ewes at lambing time. Tobacco yields a larger cash income than cotton, and the tobacco crop fits well into what would otherwise be slack periods in cultivation.

Raising animals plays a relatively minor role in the villagers' economic life. Each farmer has a horse or two for heavy draft work, a mule or donkey, about two dozen sheep, and some fowl.

Farmers at Vasilika are responsive to modern developments; they are prepared to experiment to a certain extent, especially with mechanization. Where the amount of acreage under cultivation warrants the expense, tractors are hired for plowing. Specialists are regularly called in to handle harvesting, cotton ginning, and similar tasks. Indeed, the Greek farmer is content to be a farmer and to rely on the skills of others to repair his roof, maintain his

Vietnamese farmers in the Mekong Delta working in a flooded rice paddy. Much of the delta was originally tropical forest.

© KEREN SU/DanitaDelimont.com

water pump, and provide the mechanical know-how for crop production.

Rural Vietnam: The Mekong Delta

The village of Khanh Hau, situated along the flat Mekong Delta, comprised about 600 families when Gerald Hickey described it in the late 1950s, before the Vietnam War.[28] The delta area has a tropical climate, with a rainy season that lasts from May to November. As a whole, the area has been made habitable only through extensive drainage.

Wet rice cultivation is the principal agricultural activity of Khanh Hau. It is part of a complex, specialized arrangement that involves three interacting components: (1) a complex system of irrigation and water control; (2) a variety of specialized equipment, including plows, waterwheels, threshing sledges, and winnowing machines; and (3) a clearly defined set of socioeconomic roles—from those of landlord, tenant, and laborer to those of rice miller and rice merchant.

In the dry season, the farmer decides what sort of rice crop to plant, whether of long (120 days) or short (90 days) maturation. The choice depends on the capital at his disposal, the current cost of fertilizer, and the anticipated demand for rice. The seedbeds are prepared as soon as the rains have softened the ground in May. The soil is turned over (plowed) and broken up (harrowed) as many as six separate times, with two-day intervals for "airing" between operations. During this time, the rice seeds are soaked in water for at least two days to stimulate sprouting. Before the seedlings are planted, the paddy is plowed once more and harrowed twice in two directions at right angles.

Planting is a delicate, specialized operation that must be done quickly and is performed most often by hired male laborers. But efficient planting is not enough to guarantee a good crop. Proper fertilization and irrigation are equally important. In the irrigating, steps must be taken to ensure that the water level remains at exactly the proper depth over the entire paddy. Water is distributed by means of scoops, wheels, and mechanical pumps. Successive crops of rice ripen from late September to May; all members of the family may be called upon to help with the harvest. After each crop is harvested, it is threshed, winnowed, and dried. Normally, the rice is sorted into three portions: one is set aside for use by the household in the following year; one is for payment of hired labor and other services (such as loans from agricultural banks); and one is for cash sale on the market. Aside from the harvesting, women do little work in the fields, spending most of their time on household chores. In families with little land, however, young daughters help in the fields and older daughters may hire themselves out to other farmers.

The villagers also cultivate vegetables, raise pigs, chickens, and the like, and frequently engage in fishing. The village economy usually supports three or four implement makers and a much larger number of carpenters.

General Features of Intensive Agricultural Societies

Societies with intensive agriculture are more likely than horticulturalists to have towns and cities, a high degree of craft specialization, complex political organization, and large differences in wealth and power. Studies suggest that intensive agriculturalists work longer hours than horticulturalists.[29] For example, men engaged in intensive agriculture average nine hours of work a day, seven days a week; women average almost 11 hours of work per day. Most of the work for women in intensive agricultural societies involves food processing and work in and around the home, but they also spend a lot of time working in the fields.

Intensive agricultural societies are more likely than horticultural societies to face famines and food shortages, even though intensive agriculture is generally more productive than horticulture.[30] Why, if more food can be produced per acre, is there more risk of shortage among intensive agriculturalists? Intensive agriculturalists may be more likely to face food shortages because they are often producing crops for a market. Producing for a market pushes farmers to cultivate plants that give them the highest yield rather than cultivating plants that are drought-resistant or that require fewer nutrients. Farmers producing for a market also tend to concentrate on one crop. Crop diversity is often a protection against total crop failure because fluctuations in weather, plant diseases, or insect pests are not likely to affect all the crops. There are also fluctuations in market demand. If the market demand drops and the price falls for a particular crop, farmers may not have enough cash to buy the other food they need.

The Commercialization and Mechanization of Agriculture

Some intensive agriculturalists produce very little for sale; most of what they produce is for their own use. But there is a worldwide trend for intensive agriculturalists to produce more and more for a market. This trend is called **commercialization,** which may occur in any area of life and which involves increasing dependence on buying and selling, usually with money as the medium of exchange. Some of the push toward commercialization comes from external pressures, from governments that impose taxes that must be paid by money. But some of the shift occurs when subsistence farmers choose to plant a cash crop to earn money for various reasons. For example, the Malaiyali farmers of India grow a cash crop, tapioca (cassava), as a way of responding to unpredictable rainfall. Tapioca is fairly drought-tolerant, grows in poor soils, and can be planted later in the year when the rainfall has become more predictable.[31]

The increasing commercialization of agriculture is associated with several other trends. One is that farmwork is becoming more mechanized as hand labor becomes scarce, because of migration to industrial and service jobs in towns and cities, or because hired hand labor has become too expensive. A second trend is the emergence and spread of *agribusiness,* large corporation-owned farms that may be operated by multinational companies and worked entirely by hired, as opposed to family, labor. For example, consider how cotton farming has changed in the southeastern United States. In the 1930s, tractors replaced mules and horses used in plowing. This change allowed some landowners to evict their sharecroppers and expand their holdings. After World War II, mechanical cotton pickers replaced most of the harvest laborers. But a farmer had to have a good deal of money to acquire those machines, each of which cost many tens of thousands of dollars.[32] So the mechanization of cotton farming sent many rural farm laborers off to the cities of the North in search of employment, and the agricultural sector increasingly became big business. A third trend associated with the commercialization of agriculture, including animal raising, is a reduction in the proportion of the population engaged in food production. In the United States today, for example, less than 1 percent of the total population work on farms.[33] A fourth trend is that much of what people produce for sale nowadays is shipped to or received from markets in other countries. For example, in the summer months, fruits and vegetables are often shipped to markets where consumers have little local fresh produce. The spread of different kinds of food is not new (see the box "Food on the Move") but is accelerating in today's world.

"Market Foraging" in Industrial Societies

Food in countries such as the in United States and Canada comes largely from intensive agriculture and animal husbandry practiced by a small proportion of the population. Those food specialists make their living by selling animal and plant products to marketers, distributors, and food processors. Indeed, most people know very little about how to grow crops or raise animals. Food appears in markets or supermarkets already processed by other specialists. It comes in paper or plastic packages, looking far different from how it originally looked in the field or on the feedlot. Thus, most of us are "market foragers," collecting our food from stores. In some ways, as we shall see in the chapter on culture and the individual, we behave very much like foragers of wild plants and animals. But there are also enormous differences between our kind of foraging and the original kind. If our society did not have very productive intensive agriculture and animal husbandry, we would not have towns and cities, thousands of different full-time occupations (hardly any of which are involved in food-getting), a centralized government, or many of our other characteristics.

Pastoralism

Most agriculturalists keep and breed some animals (practice animal husbandry), but a small number of societies depend mostly for their living on domesticated herds of animals that feed on natural pasture.[34] We call such a system **pastoralism.** We might assume that pastoralists breed animals to eat their meat, but most do not. Pastoralists more often get their animal protein from live animals in the form of milk, and some pastoralists regularly take blood, which is rich in protein, from their animals to mix with other foods. The herds often indirectly provide food because many pastoralists trade animal products for plant foods and other necessities. In fact, a large proportion of their food may actually come from trade with agricultural groups.[35] For example, some pastoral groups in the Middle East derive much of their livelihood from the sale of what we call oriental rugs, which are made from the wool of their sheep on hand looms. Two pastoral societies we shall examine are the Basseri of southern Iran and the Lapps of Scandinavia.

The Basseri

The Basseri, described by Fredrik Barth as of the 1960s, are a tribe of about 16,000 tent-dwelling nomads.[36] Their herds consist principally of sheep and goats, though donkeys and camels are raised for pulling or carrying, and the wealthier men have horses for riding. Theirs is a dry, arid habitat, with rainfall averaging no more than 10 inches a year. The Basseri's pastoral way of life is based on a regular, migratory exploitation of the grazing lands within their territory, which measures about 15,000 square miles in all. In winter, when the mountains to the north are covered with snow, the plains and foothills to the south offer extensive pasturage. During the spring, grazing is

migrants and immigrants

Food on the Move

People in North America get most of their food from stores. Most people do not know where the food comes from originally—where it was first grown or raised. This is partly because relatively few are directly involved in food-getting (less than 1 percent of the workers in the United States). Even when you count all the activities related to food-getting, such as marketing and transportation, only 14 percent of U.S. workers have anything to do with the production and distribution of food. But nowadays, many of the foods we buy in markets—tacos, salsa, bagels, pasta, pizza, sausage, soy sauce, and teriyaki—have become mainstream "North American" food. Where did these foods come from? Originally, they were eaten only by ethnic and immigrant minorities who came to the United States and Canada. Some, but not all, of their foods caught on and became widely consumed. They became, in short, as "American" as apple pie.

The ingredients in many of these food items resulted from previous movements of people even further back in time. Consider the ingredients in pizza, a favorite food now for many of us. The dough is made from wheat flour, which was first grown in the Middle East, perhaps as much as 10,000 years ago. How do anthropologists know that? Archaeologists have discovered wheat kernels that old in Middle Eastern sites, and they have found flat stones and stone rolling pins from that time that we know were used to grind kernels into flour (we can tell from microscopic analysis of the residue on the stone). What about other ingredients that may be found in pizza? Cheese was first made in the Middle East too, at least 5,000 years ago (we have writings from that time that mention cheese). Tomatoes were first grown in South America, probably several thousand years ago. They got to Italy, the birthplace of the tomato pie (which became transformed into pizza), less than 200 years ago. Just 100 years ago, tomatoes (the key ingredient in pizza for some) were so new in eastern Europe that people were afraid to eat them because their leaves are poisonous to humans and some other animals. Another food we associate with Italian cuisine, spaghetti-type noodles, came to Italy (from China) less than 500 years ago. So the major ingredients of pizza, just like round-noodle pasta, are all not native to Italy.

The amazing thing about foods is that they so often travel far and wide, generally carried by the people who like to eat them. And some of our foods, when alive, also travel widely. For example, the bluefin tuna (which can weigh more than a thousand pounds) swims thousands of miles from feeding to breeding grounds in the North Atlantic, Mediterranean, and Caribbean. This largest of all existing fishes is being hunted into extinction because its meat is so prized for what the Japanese call *sushi*, a kind of food that has spread from Japan throughout the world.

Sources: Diament 2005, pp. A32–34; Revkin 2005, F1, F4.

---

excellent on a plateau near the center of the territory. By summer, when most of the lower-lying pastures have dried up, sufficient food for the herds can be found in the mountains at an altitude of nearly 6,000 feet.

Annual migrations are so important to the economies of the Basseri and other pastoralist societies of that region that they have developed the concept of *il-rah*, or "tribal road." A major pastoral tribe such as the Basseri has a traditional route and schedule. The route, consisting of the localities in the order in which each is visited, follows existing passes and lines of communication. The schedule, which regulates the length of time each location will be occupied, depends on the maturation of different pastures and the movements of other tribes. The *il-rah* is regarded, in effect, as the property of the tribe. Local populations and authorities recognize the tribe's right to pass along roads and cultivated lands, to draw water from the public wells, and to pasture flocks on public land.

The Basseri herd sheep and goats together, with one shepherd (a boy or unmarried man) responsible for a flock of 300 to 400 animals. Children of both sexes are usually responsible for herding the baby animals (lambs and kids).

Milk and its by-products are the most important commodities, but wool, hides, and meat are also important to the economy of the Basseri. Both wool and hides are traded, but they are even more useful within the tribe. The Basseri, especially the women, are skilled spinners and weavers, and much of their time is spent at these activities. Saddlebags and pack bags are woven on horizontal looms from homespun wool and hair, as are carpets, sleeping rugs, and the characteristic black tents made of panels of woven goat hair. Woven goat hair provides an exceptionally versatile cloth. For winter use, it retains heat and repels water; in the summer, it insulates against heat and permits free circulation of air. Lambskin hides also serve many purposes. When plucked and turned inside out, they are made into storage bags to hold water, buttermilk, sour milk, and other liquids.

Most of the Basseri must trade for the necessities and luxury items they do not produce within the community. The staple items they sell are butter, wool, lambskins, rope, and occasionally livestock.

The Lapps The Lapps or Saami practice reindeer herding in northwestern Scandinavia where Finland, Sweden,

A Saami reindeer herder feeds two of her animals in the snow.

and Norway share common frontiers. It is a typical Arctic habitat: cold, windswept, with long, dark days for half the year. Considerable change has occurred recently, so we first discuss the food-getting strategy in the 1950s, as described by Ian Whitaker and T. I. Itkonen.[37]

The Lapps herd their reindeer either intensively or, more often, extensively. In the *intensive system,* the herd is constantly under observation within a fenced area for the whole year. Intensively herded reindeer and other animals are accustomed to human contact. Hence, the summer corralling of the females for milking and the breaking in of the ox-reindeer for use as work animals are not difficult tasks. The *extensive system* involves allowing the animals to migrate over a large area. It requires little surveillance and encompasses large herds. Under this system, the reindeer are allowed to move through their seasonal feeding cycles watched by only one or two scouts. The other Lapps stay with the herd only when it has settled in its summer or winter habitat. But milking, breaking in, and corralling are harder in the extensive than in the intensive system because the animals are less accustomed to humans.

Even under the extensive system, which theoretically permits Lapps to engage in subsidiary economic activities such as hunting and fishing, the reindeer herd is the essential, if not the only, source of income. A family might possess as many as 1,000 reindeer, but usually the figure is half that number. Studies show 200 to be the minimum number of reindeer needed to provide for a family of four or five adults. Women may have shared the herding chores in the past under the intensive system, but now, under the extensive system, men do the herding. Women still do the milking. The Lapps eat the meat of the bull reindeer; the female reindeer are kept for breeding purposes. Bulls are slaughtered in the fall, after the mating season. Meat and hides are frequently sold or bartered for other food and necessities.

Reindeer are still herded nowadays, but snowmobiles, all-terrain vehicles, and even helicopters have replaced sleds for herding. Ferries move reindeer to and from different pastures, and the herders communicate by field telephones. With faster transportation, many Lapps now live in permanent homes and can still get to their herds in hours. Lapp children spend much of their time in school

and, consequently, do not learn much of the herding ways. The Norwegian government now regulates pastoralism, licensing pastoralists and trying to limit the number of reindeer they can herd.[38] And many Lapps (they prefer to call themselves Saami) no longer have reindeer.

General Features of Pastoralism In recent times, pastoralism has been practiced mainly in grassland and other semiarid habitats that are not especially suitable for cultivation without some significant technological input such as irrigation. Most pastoralists are nomadic, moving camp fairly frequently to find water and new pasture for their herds. But other pastoralists have somewhat more sedentary lives. They may move from one settlement to another in different seasons, or they may send some people out to travel with the herds in different seasons. Pastoral communities are usually small, consisting of a group of related families.[39] Individuals or families may own their own animals, but the community makes decisions about when and where to move the herds.

As we have noted, there is a great deal of interdependence between pastoral and agricultural groups. That is, trade is usually necessary for pastoral groups to survive. Like agriculturalists, pastoralists are more vulnerable than foragers and horticulturalists to famine and food shortages. Pastoralists usually inhabit drought-prone regions, but recent pastoralists have had their access to grazing lands reduced, and political pressures have pushed them to decrease their movement over large areas. Mobility kept the risk of overgrazing to a minimum, but overgrazing in small territories has increased the risk of desertification.[40]

ENVIRONMENTAL RESTRAINTS ON FOOD-GETTING

Of great interest to anthropologists is why different societies have different methods of getting food. Archaeological evidence suggests that major changes in food-getting, such as the domestication of plants and animals, have been independently invented in at least several areas of the world. Yet, despite these comparable inventions and their subsequent spread by diffusion and migration, there is still wide diversity in the means by which people obtain food.

How much does the physical environment affect food-getting? Anthropologists have concluded that the physical environment by itself has a restraining, rather than a determining, effect on the major types of subsistence. Because they have very short growing seasons, cold regions of the earth are not particularly conducive to growing plants. No society we know of has practiced agriculture in the Arctic; instead, people who live there rely primarily on animals for food. But both foraging (as among the Inuit) and food production (as among the Lapps) can be practiced in cold areas. Indeed, cross-cultural evidence indicates that neither foraging nor food production is significantly associated with any particular type of habitat.[41]

We know that foraging has been practiced at one time or another in almost all areas of the earth. The physical

applied anthropology

The Effect of Food-Getting on the Environment

Many people are now aware of industrial pollution—the dumping of industrial wastes in the ground or into rivers, the spewing of chemicals into the air through smokestacks—but we don't often realize how much humans have altered the environment by the ways they collect and produce food. Consider irrigation. Irrigation has made agriculture productive in arid or unpredictable rainfall environments. There are various ways to capture water for irrigation. Water can be channeled from rivers; rainwater can be caught in terraces carved out of hillsides; ancient water can be pumped up from vast underground reservoirs called aquifers. But much of the water use is wasteful, seeping into the channels or evaporating into the air before reaching the plants. Plants absorb water and leave behind the salts. But the extensive evaporation of water during irrigation mostly leads to higher concentration of minerals and salts. If drainage is poor and if the water table rises, the salt concentrations are not washed away. Often, the more a piece of land has been irrigated, the saltier the ground becomes. Eventually, the soil becomes too salty to grow crops effectively and crops have to be grown elsewhere.

Some archaeologists have suggested that the accumulation of toxic salts in the soil at least partly explains the doom or decline of various groups in the past. For example, salinization probably contributed to the decline of Sumer, an early empire in Mesopotamia, and other early states in what is now southern Iraq and southwestern Iran. Over time, the concentration of people shifted from the lower portion of the Tigris-Euphrates river system to the upper portion as irrigated land lower down became unusable for farming. Today, much of the soil is still too salty for cultivation. Recent irrigation schemes during Saddam Hussein's regime have seriously degraded the downstream Iraqi marshes. Less than 10 percent of the marsh wetlands remain, putting over 60 bird species at risk. In addition, the loss of the marshlands has reduced the ability of the marshland to filter the water before it reaches the Persian Gulf, which has led to declines in productivity of the coastal fisheries. The severity of the degradation in the region has been compared with the deforestation of the Amazon.

The lessons of history have not been learned yet. The San Joaquin Valley of California, perhaps the most productive agricultural area in the world, now has a serious salinization problem. One solution in many of the areas of the Great American Desert is to pump water up from underground. Indeed, in many places, there is a great deal of water underground. For example, the Ogallala aquifer, which underlies parts of Nebraska, Kansas, Texas, Oklahoma, Colorado, and New Mexico, contains water left from the ice ages. But the pumping solution, if it is a solution, is only a short-term fix, for the huge Ogallala aquifer is also the fastest-disappearing aquifer. The only question is how long it will take to disappear totally.

Too many people raising too many animals can also have serious effects on the environment. We can easily imagine how the possibility of profit might inspire people to try to raise more animals than the land will support. For example, 300 years ago, the Great American Desert was a vast grassland. It supported large herds of buffalo, which were all but exterminated by overhunting in the next 200 years. The European-American settlers soon discovered they could raise cattle and sheep on this grassland, but many parts of it were overgrazed. It took the swirling dust storms of the 1930s to make people realize that overgrazing as well as poor farming practices could be disastrous. The problems are not just recent ones. The Norse colonized Greenland and Iceland around A.D. 800, but overgrazing of pasture undoubtedly contributed to soil erosion and the disappearance or decline of the colonies by A.D. 1500.

Are environmental problems associated only with food production? Although food producers may be the worst offenders, there is reason to think that foragers may also have sometimes overfished, overgathered, or overhunted. For example, some scholars suspect that the movement of humans into the New World was mainly responsible for the disappearance of the mammoth. Unfortunately, there is little evidence that humans have been good conservers in the past. That does not mean that humans cannot do better in the future—but they have to want to.

Source: Los Angeles Times 1994; Reisner 1993; Hillel 2000; Curtis et al. 2005; Dirks 2009.

environment does seem to have some effect on what kind of foraging is practiced, that is, on the extent to which foragers will depend on plants, animals, or fish. Farther away from the equator, foragers depend much less on plants for food and much more on animals and fish.[42] Lewis Binford argues that fishing becomes increasingly important in cold climates because foragers need nonportable housing in severe winters to protect themselves from the cold. Therefore, they cannot rely on large animals, which usually have to feed themselves by moving over considerable distances in the winter. Fishing is more localized than hunting, and therefore foragers who rely on fishing can stay in their nonportable houses in winter.[43]

There is one habitat that may have precluded foraging until recent times. If it were not for the nearness of food producers, particularly agriculturalists, recent foragers such as the Mbuti of central Africa could probably not have supported themselves in the tropical forest habitats where they now live.[44] Tropical forests are lush in plants, but they do not provide much in the way of reachable fruits, seeds,

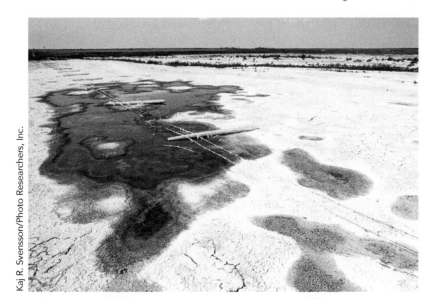

Areas that have practiced irrigation for long time periods begin to suffer from salinization and become unsuitable for agriculture as in parts of Alberta, Canada.

Kaj R. Svensson/Photo Researchers, Inc.

and flowers that humans can eat. Animals are available in tropical forests, but typically they are lean and do not provide humans with sufficient carbohydrates or fat. Like the Mbuti groups who hunt and gather in the forest, many tropical foragers trade for agricultural products; other collectors cultivate some crops in addition to hunting and gathering. It would seem, then, that foragers could not survive in tropical forests were it not for the carbohydrates they obtain from agriculturalists.

When we contrast horticulture and intensive agriculture, the physical environment appears to explain some of the variation. Approximately 80 percent of all societies that practice horticulture or simple agriculture are in the tropics, whereas 75 percent of all societies that practice intensive agriculture are not in tropical forest environments.[45] Tropical forests have abundant rainfall. But despite the attractiveness of lush vegetation and brilliant coloring, tropical forestlands do not usually offer favorable environments for intensive agriculture. Perhaps the heavy rainfall quickly washes away certain minerals from cleared land. Also, the difficulty of controlling insect pests and weeds, which abound in tropical forests,[46] may make intensive agriculture less productive.

But difficulty is not impossibility. Today, there are some areas, for instance, the Mekong Delta in Vietnam, whose tropical forests have been cleared and prevented from growing again by the intensive cultivation of rice in paddies. And, although cultivation is not normally possible in dry lands, because of insufficient natural rainfall to sustain crops, agriculture can be practiced where there are oases—small, naturally watered areas where crops can be grown with a simple technology—or rivers that can be tapped by irrigation, one of the techniques used with intensive agriculture.

The animals that pastoralists raise depend primarily on grass for food, so it is not surprising that pastoralism is typically practiced in grassland regions of the earth. These regions may be **steppes** (dry, low grass cover), **prairies** (taller, better-watered grass), or savannas (tropical grasslands). The grassland habitat favors large game and hence supports both hunting and pastoral technologies, except

where machine technology makes intensive agriculture possible, as in parts of the United States, Canada, and Ukraine.

Very different strategies of food-getting have been practiced in the same environment over time. A dramatic illustration is the history of the Imperial Valley in California. The complex systems of irrigation now used in that dry-land area have made it a very productive region. Yet, about 400 years ago, this same valley supported only hunting and gathering groups who subsisted on wild plants and animals.

It is evident from the Imperial Valley example and many others like it that the physical environment does not by itself account for the system of food-getting in an area. Even a polar environment could have agriculture with heated greenhouses, though it would be too expensive. Technological advances as well as enormous capital investment in irrigation, labor, and equipment have made intensive agriculture possible in the Imperial Valley. But the agriculture there is precarious, depending on sources of water and power from elsewhere. In a prolonged drought, it may be difficult or too expensive to obtain the needed water. And should the prices for vegetables fall, the farming businesses in the Imperial Valley could find themselves

This area of Montana is cultivated now. In the past, only foraging was practiced.

ALEX S. MACLEAN/Peter Arnold, Inc.

unable to finance the investment and borrowing of capital that they need to continue. So technological, social, and political factors rather than environmental factors mostly determine what kind of food-getting can be practiced in a given environment.

THE ORIGIN, SPREAD, AND INTENSIFICATION OF FOOD PRODUCTION

To understand why most people today are food producers rather than food collectors, we need to consider why plant and animal domestication may have emerged in the first place. There are several theories of why people started to produce food. Most of the theories currently considered that people made the changeover because they were pushed into it. The possible reasons include:

1. Population growth in regions of bountiful wild resources pushed people to move to marginal areas, where they tried to reproduce their former abundance.

2. Global population growth filled up most of the world's habitable regions and forced people to utilize a broader spectrum of wild resources and to domesticate plants and animals.

3. Climatic change—hotter, drier summers and colder winters—favored settling near seasonal stands of wild grain; population growth in such areas would force people to plant crops and raise animals.

Whatever the reasons for the switch to food production, we still need to explain why food production has supplanted foraging as the primary mode of subsistence. We cannot assume that collectors would automatically adopt production as a superior way of life once they understood the process of domestication. After all, as we have noted, domestication may entail more work and provide less security than the food-collecting way of life.

The spread of agriculture may be linked to the need for territorial expansion. As a sedentary, food-producing population grew, it may have been forced to expand into new territory. Some of this territory may have been vacant, but much of it was probably already occupied by foragers. Although food production is not necessarily easier than collection, it is generally more productive per unit of land. Greater productivity enables more people to be supported in a given territory. In the competition for land between the faster-expanding food producers and the foragers, the food producers may have had a significant advantage: They had more people in a given area. Thus, the foraging groups may have been more likely to lose out in the competition for land. Some groups may have adopted cultivation, abandoning the foraging way of life to survive. Other groups, continuing as foragers, may have been forced to retreat into areas the cultivators did not desire. Today, as we have seen, the small number of remaining foragers inhabit areas not particularly suitable for cultivation—dry lands, dense tropical forests, and polar regions.

Just as prior population growth might account for the origins of domestication, further population growth and ensuing pressure on resources at later periods might also at least partly explain the transformation of horticultural systems into intensive agricultural systems. Ester Boserup suggested that intensification of agriculture, with a consequent increase in yield per acre, is not likely to develop naturally out of horticulture, because intensification requires much more work.[47] She argued that people will be willing to intensify their labor only if they have to. Where emigration is not feasible, the prime mover behind intensification may be prior population growth. The need to pay taxes or tribute to a political authority may also stimulate intensification.

Boserup's argument about intensification is widely accepted. However, her assumption that more work is required with intensive agriculture has recently been questioned. Comparing horticultural (swidden or shifting) rice production with rice produced on permanent fields using irrigation, Robert Hunt found that *less*, not more, labor is required with irrigation.[48] Still, population increase may generally provide the impetus to intensify production to increase yields to support the additional people.

Intensive agriculture has not yet spread to every part of the world. Horticulture continues to be practiced in certain tropical regions, and there are still some pastoralists and foragers. Some environments may make it somewhat more difficult to adopt certain subsistence practices. For example, intensive agriculture cannot supplant horticulture in some tropical environments without tremendous investments in chemical fertilizers and pesticides, not to mention the additional labor required.[49] And enormous amounts of water may be required to make agriculturalists out of foragers and pastoralists who now exploit semiarid environments. However, difficulty is not impossibility. Anna Roosevelt points out that, although horticulture was a common food-getting strategy in Amazonia in recent times, archaeological evidence indicates that there were complex societies practicing intensive agriculture on raised, drained fields in the past.[50] The physical environment does not completely control what can be done with it.

SUMMARY ● ○ ○

1. Foraging—hunting, gathering, and fishing—depends on wild plants and animals and is the oldest human food-getting technology. There is a lot of variation with regard to which food-getting activity is most important to a society. Recent foragers depended most on fishing, followed by gathering and hunting. Today, only a small number of societies depend largely on foraging, and they tend to inhabit marginal environments.

2. Foragers can be found in various physical habitats. Most foragers are nomadic, and population density is low. Usually, the small bands consist of related families, with the division of labor along age and

gender lines only. Personal possessions are limited, individuals' land rights are seldom recognized, and people are not differentiated by class.

3. Beginning about 10,000 years ago, certain peoples in widely separated geographic locations began to make the revolutionary changeover to food production—the cultivation and raising of plants and animals. Over the centuries, food production began to supplant food collection as the predominant mode of subsistence.

4. Horticulturalists farm with relatively simple tools and methods and do not cultivate fields permanently. Their food supply is sufficient to support larger, more densely populated communities than can be fed by foraging. Their way of life is sedentary, although communities may move after some years to farm a new series of plots.

5. Intensive agriculture is characterized by techniques such as fertilization and irrigation that allow fields to be cultivated permanently. In contrast with horticultural societies, intensive agriculturalists are more likely to have towns and cities, a high degree of craft specialization, large differences in wealth and power, and more complex political organization. They are also more likely to face food shortages. In the modern world, intensive agriculture is increasingly mechanized and geared to production for a market.

6. Pastoralism is a subsistence technology involving principally the raising of large herds of animals. It is generally found in low-rainfall areas. Pastoralists tend to be nomadic, to have small communities consisting of related families, and to depend significantly on trade because they do not produce items (including certain types of food) they need.

7. Anthropologists generally agree that the physical environment normally exercises a restraining rather than a determining influence on how people in an area get their food; technology as well as social and political factors may be more important.

8. We see the first evidence of a changeover to food production in the Near East about 10,000 years ago (8000 B.C.). Theories about why food production originated remain controversial, but most archaeologists think that certain conditions must have pushed people to switch from collecting to producing food. Some possible causal factors include (1) population growth in regions of bountiful wild resources, which may have pushed people to move to marginal areas where they tried to reproduce their former abundance; (2) global population growth, which filled most of the world's habitable regions and may have forced people

to utilize a broader spectrum of wild resources and to domesticate plants and animals; and (3) the emergence of hotter and drier summers and colder winters, which may have favored sedentarization near seasonal stands of wild grain; population growth in such areas may have forced people to plant crops and raise animals to support themselves.

9. Because food producers can support more people in a given territory than foragers can, they may have had a competitive advantage in confrontations with foragers.

GLOSSARY TERMS ○ ● ○

cash crops	intensive agriculture
commercialization	pastoralism
extensive or shifting cultivation	prairie
	slash-and-burn
foraging	steppe
horticulture	subsistence economies
hunter-gatherers	

CRITICAL QUESTIONS ○ ○ ●

1. Why might meat be valued more than plant foods in many societies?

2. Why might foragers be less likely than intensive agriculturalists to suffer from food shortages?

3. Why do certain foods in a society come to be preferred?

PEARSON
myanthrolab

Read the chapter by Burton Pasternak, "Han: Pastoralists and Farmers on a Chinese Frontier," on MyAnthroLab and answer the following questions.

1. The Han Chinese traditionally depended on intensive agriculture. The Mongols traditionally depended on pastoralism. What happened to the Han when they moved beyond the Great Wall to a grassland environment?

2. How has the change to more pastoralism affected marriage and family among the Han?

3. How have the Mongols changed?

NOTES ● ○ ○

1. Hitchcock and Beisele 2000, 5.
2. C. R. Ember 1978b.
3. Kent 1996.
4. Schrire 1984a; Myers 1988.
5. Morrison and Junker 2002.
6. The discussion of the Australian aborigines is based on R. A. Gould 1969.
7. Burbank 1994, 23; Burbank 2009b.
8. Burch 2009; 1988.
9. Data from Textor 1967 and Service 1979.
10. Murdock and Provost 1973, 207.
11. R. B. Lee 1968; DeVore and Konner 1974.
12. C. R. Ember 1978b.
13. McCarthy and McArthur 1960.
14. R B. Lee 1979, 256–58, 278–80.
15. Palsson 1988; Roscoe 2002.
16. Keeley 1991; R. L. Kelly 1995, 293–315.
17. Mitchell 2009; Tollefson 2009.
18. C. Ember 1975.
19. Roscoe 2002.
20. D. Werner 1978.
21. Textor 1967.
22. This section is largely based on Hames 2009.
23. Chagnon 1983, 60.
24. This section is based mostly on Melvin Ember's fieldwork on the islands of American Samoa in 1955 to 1956.
25. Oliver 1974, 252–53.
26. S. S. King 1979.
27. Friedl 1962.
28. Hickey 1964, 135–65.
29. C. R. Ember 1983, 289.
30. Textor 1967; Dirks 2009; Messer 1996, 244.
31. Finnis 2006.
32. Barlett 1989, 253–91.
33. U.S. Environmental Protection Agency 2009.
34. Salzman 1996.
35. Lees and Bates 1974; A. L. Johnson 2002.
36. Barth 1965.
37. Whitaker 1955; Itkonen 1951.
38. Paine 1994.
39. Textor 1967.
40. Dirks 2009.
41. Data from Textor 1967.
42. L. R. Binford 1990; see also Low 1990a, 242–43.
43. The few foragers in cold areas relying primarily on hunting have animals (dogs, horses, reindeer) that can carry transportable housing; see L. R. Binford 1990.
44. Bailey et al. 1989.
45. Data from Textor 1967.
46. Janzen 1973. For an argument supporting the "weeding" explanation, see Carneiro 1968.
47. Boserup 1993 [1965].
48. R. C. Hunt 2000.
49. Janzen 1973.
50. Roosevelt 1992.

Social Stratification: Class, Ethnicity, and Racism

From Chapter 18 of *Anthropology*, 13/e. Carol R. Ember. Melvin Ember. Peter N. Peregrine. Copyright © 2011 by Pearson Education. Published by Prentice Hall. All rights reserved.

Social Stratification: Class, Ethnicity, and Racism

A long-enduring value in the United States is the belief that "all men are created equal." These famous words from the American Declaration of Independence do not mean that all people are equal in wealth or status but rather that all (including women nowadays) are supposed to be equal before the law. Equality before the law is the ideal. But the ideal is not always the actuality. Some people have advantages in legal treatment, and they generally also tend to have advantages of other kinds, including economic advantages. Without exception, recent and modern industrial and postindustrial societies such as our own are *socially stratified*—that is, they contain social groups such as families, classes, or ethnic groups that have unequal access to important advantages such as economic resources, power, and prestige.

Hasn't such inequality always existed? Anthropologists, based on first-hand observations of recent societies, would say not. To be sure, even the simplest societies (in the technological sense) have some differences in advantages based on age, ability, or gender—adults have higher status than children, the skilled more than the unskilled, men more than women. But anthropologists would argue that *egalitarian* societies exist where *social groups* (e.g., families) have more or less the same access to rights or advantages. The economic systems of many food collectors and horticulturalists promote equal access to economic resources for all families in the community. Moreover, such societies also tend to emphasize the sharing of food and other goods, which tends to equalize any small inequalities in resources between families. Until about 10,000 years ago, all human societies depended on food they hunted, gathered, and/or fished. And so we might expect that egalitarianism characterized most of human history. That is indeed what archaeologists suggest. Substantial inequality generally appears only with permanent communities, centralized political systems, and intensive agriculture, which are cultural features that began to appear in the world only in the last 10,000 years. Before that time, then, most societies were probably egalitarian. In the world today, egalitarian societies have all but disappeared because of two processes—the global spread of commercial or market exchange and the voluntary or involuntary incorporation of many diverse people into large, centralized political systems. In modern societies, some groups have more advantages than others. These groups may include *ethnic* groups. That is, ethnic diversity is almost always associated with differential access to advantages. When ethnic diversity is also associated with differences in physical features such as skin color, the social stratification may involve *racism*, the belief that some "racial" groups are inferior.

Systems of social stratification are strongly linked to the customary ways in which economic resources are allocated, distributed, and converted through labor into goods and services. So we would not expect much inequality if all people had relatively equal access to economic resources. But stratification cannot be understood solely in terms of economic resources; there are other benefits such as prestige and power that may be unequally distributed. We first examine how societies vary in their systems of stratification. Then we turn to possible explanations of why they vary.

● ○ ●

VARIATION IN DEGREE OF SOCIAL INEQUALITY

Societies vary in the extent to which social groups, as well as individuals, have unequal access to advantages. In this chapter, we are concerned with differential or unequal access to three types of advantages: (1) wealth or economic resources, (2) power, and (3) prestige. **Economic resources** are things that have value in a culture; they include land, tools and other technology, goods, and money. **Power,** a second but related advantage, is the ability to make others do what they do not want to do; power is influence based on the threat of force. When groups in a society have rules or customs that give them unequal access to wealth or resources, they generally also have unequal access to power. So, for example, when we speak of a "company town" in the United States, we are referring to the fact that the company that employs most of the residents of the town usually has considerable control over them. Finally, there is the advantage of **prestige.** When we speak of prestige, we mean that someone or some group is accorded particular respect or honor. Even if it is true that there is always unequal access by individuals to prestige (because of differences in age, gender, or ability), some societies in the ethnographic record have no social groups with unequal access to prestige.

Thus, anthropologists conventionally distinguish three types of society in terms of the degree to which different social groups have unequal access to advantages: *egalitarian, rank,* and *class societies* (see Table 1). Some societies in the ethnographic record do not fit easily into any of these three types; as with any classification scheme, some cases seem to straddle the line between types.[1] **Egalitarian societies** contain no social groups with greater or lesser access to economic resources, power, or prestige. **Rank societies** do not have very unequal access to economic resources or to power, but they do contain social groups with unequal access to prestige. Rank societies, then, are partly stratified. **Class societies** have unequal access to all three advantages—economic resources, power, and prestige.

EGALITARIAN SOCIETIES

Egalitarian societies can be found not only among foragers such as the !Kung, Mbuti, Australian aborigines, Inuit, and Aché, but also among horticulturalists such as the Yanomamö and pastoralists such as the Lapps. An important point to keep in mind is that egalitarian does not mean that all people within such societies are the same. There will always be differences among individuals in age and gender and in such abilities or traits as hunting skill, perception, health, creativity, physical prowess, attractiveness, and intelligence. According to Morton Fried, egalitarian means that, within a given society, "there are as many positions of prestige in any given age/sex grade as there are persons capable of filling them."[2] For instance, if a person can achieve high status by fashioning fine spears, and if many people in the society fashion such spears, then many acquire high status as spear makers. If high status is also acquired by carving bones into artifacts, and if only three people are considered expert carvers of bones, then only those three achieve high status as carvers. But the next generation might produce eight spear makers and 20 carvers. In an egalitarian society, the number of prestigious positions is adjusted to fit the number of qualified candidates. We would say, therefore, that such a society is not socially stratified.

There are, of course, differences in position and prestige arising out of differences in ability. Even in an egalitarian society, differential prestige exists. But, although some people may be better hunters or more skilled artists than others, there is still *equal access* to status positions for people of the same ability. Any prestige gained by achieving high status as a great hunter, for instance, is neither transferable nor inheritable. Because a man is a great hunter, it is not assumed that his sons are also great hunters. There also may be individuals with more influence, but it cannot be inherited, and there are no groups with appreciably more influence over time. An egalitarian society keeps inequality at a minimal level.

TABLE 1	Stratification in Three Types of Societies			
	SOME SOCIAL GROUPS HAVE GREATER ACCESS TO:			
Type of Society	Economic Resources	Power	Prestige	Examples
Egalitarian	No	No	No	!Kung, Mbuti, Australian aborigines, Inuit, Aché, Yanomamö
Rank	No	No	Yes	Samoans, Tahiti, Trobriand Islands, Ifaluk
Class/caste	Yes	Yes	Yes	United States, Canada, Greece, India, Inca

Any differences in prestige that do exist are not related to economic differences. Egalitarian groups depend heavily on *sharing*, which ensures equal access to economic resources despite differences in acquired prestige. For instance, in some egalitarian communities, some members achieve higher status through hunting. But even before the hunt begins, how the animal will be divided and distributed among the members of the band has already been decided according to custom. The culture works to separate the status that members achieve—recognition as great hunters—from actual possession of the wealth, which in this case would be the slain animal.

Just as egalitarian societies do not have social groups with unequal access to economic resources, they also do not have social groups with unequal access to power. Unequal access to power by social groups seems to occur only in state societies, which have full-time political officials and marked differences in wealth. Egalitarian societies use a number of customs to keep leaders from dominating others. Criticism and ridicule can be very effective. The Mbuti of central Africa shout down an overassertive leader. When a Hadza man (in Tanzania) tried to get people to work for him, other Hadza made fun of him. Disobedience is another strategy. If a leader tries to command, people just ignore the command. In extreme cases, a particularly domineering leader may be killed by community agreement; this behavior was reported among the !Kung and the Hadza. Finally, particularly among more nomadic groups, people may just move away from a leader they don't like. The active attempts to put down upstarts in many egalitarian societies prompts Christopher Boehm to suggest that dominance comes naturally to humans. Egalitarian societies work hard to reverse that tendency.[3] The Mbuti provide an example of a society almost totally equal: "Neither in ritual, hunting, kinship nor band relations do they exhibit any discernible inequalities of rank or advantage."[4] Their hunting bands have no leaders, and recognition of the achievement of one person is not accompanied by privilege of any sort. Economic resources such as food are communally shared, and even tools and weapons are frequently passed from person to person. Only within the family are rights and privileges differentiated.

Foraging societies with extensive sharing of resources are more readily labeled egalitarian as compared with some pastoral societies where households may vary considerably in the number of animals they own. Should we consider a pastoral society with unequal distribution of animals egalitarian? Here there is controversy. One important issue is whether unequal ownership persists through time—that is, inherited. If vagaries of weather, theft, and gifts of livestock to relatives make livestock ownership fluctuate over time, wealth differences may mostly be temporary. A second important issue is whether the inequalities in livestock ownership make any difference in the ease of acquiring other "goods," such as prestige and political power. If wealth in livestock is ephemeral and is not associated with differential access to prestige and power, then some anthropologists would characterize such pastoral societies as egalitarian.[5] It is easy to imagine how an egalitarian society with some wealth differences, as opposed to one with no wealth differences, could become a rank or a class society. All you would need is a mechanism for retaining more wealth in some families over time.

RANK SOCIETIES

Most societies with social *ranking* practice agriculture or herding, but not all agricultural or pastoral societies are ranked. Ranking is characterized by social groups with unequal access to prestige or status but *not* significantly unequal access to economic resources or power. Unequal

In egalitarian societies, such as among the Mbuti hunter-gatherers, houses tend to look the same.

Wendy Stone/CORBIS- NY

access to prestige is often reflected in the position of chief, a rank which only some members of a specified group in the society can achieve.

Unusual among rank societies were the 19-century Native Americans who lived along the northwestern coast of the United States and the southwestern coast of Canada. An example were the Nimpkish, a Kwakiutl group.[6] These societies were unusual because their economy was based on food collecting. But huge catches of salmon—which were preserved for year-round consumption—enabled them to support fairly large and permanent villages. These societies were similar to food-producing societies in many ways, not just in their development of social ranking. Still, the principal means of proving one's high status was to give away wealth. The tribal chiefs celebrated solemn rites by grand feasts called *potlatches,* at which they gave gifts to every guest.[7]

In rank societies, the position of chief is at least partly hereditary. The criterion of superior rank in some Polynesian societies, for example, was genealogical. Usually the eldest son succeeded to the position of chief, and different kinship groups were differentially ranked according to their genealogical distance from the chiefly line. In rank societies, chiefs are often treated with deference by people of lower rank. For example, among the Trobriand Islanders of Melanesia, people of lower rank must keep their heads lower than a person of higher rank. So, when a chief is standing, commoners must bend low. When commoners have to walk past a chief who happens to be sitting, he may rise and they will bend. If the chief chooses to remain seated, they must crawl.[8]

Although there is no question that chiefs in a rank society enjoy special prestige, there is some controversy over whether they really do not also have material advantages. Chiefs may sometimes look as if they are substantially richer than commoners, for they may receive many gifts and have larger storehouses. In some instances, the chief may even be called the "owner" of the land. However, Marshall Sahlins maintains that the chief's storehouses only house temporary accumulations for feasts or other redistributions. And although the chief may be designated the "owner" of the land, others have the right to use the land. Furthermore, Sahlins suggests that the chief in a rank society lacks power because he usually cannot make people give him gifts or force them to work on communal projects. Often the chief can encourage production only by working furiously on his own cultivation.[9]

This picture of economic equality in rank societies is beginning to be questioned. Laura Betzig studied patterns of food sharing and labor on Ifaluk, a small atoll in the Western Carolines.[10] Chiefly status is inherited genealogically in the female line, although most chiefs are male.

Wendy Stone/Odyssey/Chicago/Odyssey Productions, Inc.

In societies with rank and class, deference is usually shown to political leaders, as in the case of this Fon chief in the lowlands of Cameroon, Africa.

As in other chiefly societies, Ifaluk chiefs are accorded deference. For example, during collective meals prepared by all the island women, chiefs were served first and were bowed to. The Ifaluk chiefs are said to control the fishing areas. Were the catches equitably distributed? Betzig measured the amount of fish each household got. All the commoners received an equal share, but the chiefs got extra fish; their households got twice as much per person as other households. Did the chiefs give away more later?

Theoretically, generosity is supposed to even things out, but Betzig found that the gifts from chiefs to other households did not equal the amount the chiefs received from others. Furthermore, although everyone gave to the chiefs, the chiefs gave mostly to their close relatives. On Ifaluk, the chiefs did not work harder than others; in fact, they worked less. Is this true in other societies conventionally considered to be rank societies? We do not know. However, we need to keep in mind that the chiefs in Ifaluk were not noticeably better off either. If they lived in palaces with servants, had elaborate meals, or were dressed in fine clothes and jewelry, we would not need measures of food received or a special study to see if the chiefs had greater access to economic resources, because their wealth would be obvious. But rank societies may not have had as much economic equality as we used to think.

CLASS SOCIETIES

In class societies, as in rank societies, there is unequal access to prestige. But, unlike rank societies, class societies are characterized by groups of people that have substantially greater or lesser access to economic resources and power. That is, not every social group has the same opportunity to obtain land, animals, money, or other economic benefits or the same opportunity to exercise power that other groups have. Fully stratified or class societies range from somewhat open to virtually closed class, or *caste*, systems.

Open Class Systems

A **class** is a category of people who all have about the same opportunity to obtain economic resources, power, and prestige. Different classes have differing opportunities. We call class systems *open* if there is some possibility of moving from one class to another. Since the 1920s, there have been many studies of classes in towns and cities in the United States. Researchers have produced profiles of these different communities—known variously as Yankee City, Middletown, Jonesville, and Old City—all of which support the premise that the United States has distinguishable, though somewhat open, social classes. Both W. Lloyd Warner and Paul Lunt's Yankee City study[11] and Robert and Helen Lynd's Middletown study[12] concluded that the social status or prestige of a family is generally correlated with the occupation and wealth of the head of the family. Class systems are by no means confined to the United States. They are found in all nations of the modern world.

Although class status is not fully determined at birth in open class societies, there is a high probability that most people will stay close to the class into which they were born and will marry within that class. Classes tend to perpetuate themselves through the inheritance of wealth. John Brittain suggested that, in the United States, the transfer of money through bequests accounts for much of the wealth of the next generation. As we might expect, the importance of inheritance seems to increase at higher levels of wealth. That is, the wealth of richer people comes more from inheritance than does the wealth of not-so-rich people.[13]

Other mechanisms of class perpetuation may be more subtle, but they are still powerful. In the United States, many institutions make it possible for an upper-class person to have little contact with other classes. Private day and boarding schools put upper-class children in close contact mostly with others of their class. Attending these schools makes it more likely they will get into universities with higher prestige. Debutante balls and exclusive private parties ensure that young people meet the "right people." Country clubs, exclusive city clubs, and service in particular charities continue the process of limited association. People of the same class also tend to live in the same neighborhoods. Before 1948, explicit restrictions kept certain groups out of particular neighborhoods, but after the U.S. Supreme Court ruled such discrimination unconstitutional, more subtle methods were developed. For instance, zoning restrictions may prohibit multiple-family dwellings in a town or neighborhood and lots below a certain acreage.[14]

Identification with a social class begins early in life. In addition to differences in occupation, wealth, and prestige, social classes vary in many other ways, including religious

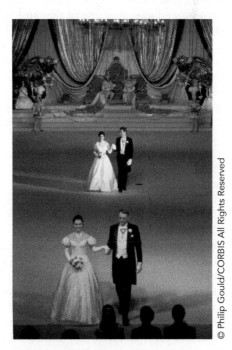

People of the same social class tend to socialize together, where they live, where they vacation, or through shared activities. Debutantes and their escorts are presented at the Krewe of Rex ball during Mardi Gras in New Orleans.

affiliation, closeness to kin, ideas about childrearing, job satisfaction, leisure-time activities, style of clothes and furniture, and (as noted in the chapter on communication and language) even in styles of speech.[15] People from each class tend to be more comfortable with those from the same class; they talk similarly and are more likely to have similar interests and tastes.

Class boundaries, though vague, have been established by custom and tradition; sometimes they have been reinforced by the enactment of laws. Many of our laws serve to protect property and thus tend to favor the upper and upper-middle classes. The poor, in contrast, seem to be disadvantaged in our legal system. The crimes the poor are most likely to commit are dealt with harshly by the courts, and poor people rarely have the money to secure effective legal counsel.

In open class systems, it is not always clear how many classes there are. In Stanley Barrett's study of "Paradise," Ontario, some people thought that there were only two classes in the past. One person said, "There was the hierarchy, and the rest of us." Another said that there were three classes: "The people with money, the in-between, and the ones who didn't have anything." Many said there were four: "The wealthy businessmen, the middle class, blue collar workers, and the guys that were just existing."[16] A few insisted that there were five classes. With the breakdown of the old rigid class structure, there are more people in the middle.[17]

Degree of Openness

Some class systems are more open than others; that is, it is easier in some societies to move from one class position to another. Social scientists typically compare the class of people with the class of their parent or parents to measure the degree of mobility. Although most people aspire to move up, mobility also includes moving down. Obtaining more education, particularly a university education, is one of the most effective ways to move upward in contemporary societies. For example, in the United States, individuals with a college bachelor's degree average 75 percent more income than those with only a high school diploma. And individuals with professional degrees earn on average 119 percent more than those with a bachelor's degree.[18] In many countries, educational attainment predicts one's social class better than parents' occupation does.[19]

How do the United States and Canada compare with other countries in degree of class mobility? Canada, Finland, and Sweden have more mobility than the United States and Britain. Mexico and Peru have less mobility than the United States and Brazil, and Colombia considerably less.[20]

Class openness also varies over time. In "Paradise," Ontario, Barrett found that the rigid stratification system of the 1950s opened up considerably as new people moved into the community. No one disputed who belonged to the elite in the past. They were of British background, lived in the largest houses, had new cars, and vacationed in Florida. Moreover, they controlled all the leadership positions in the town. By the 1980s, though, the leaders came mostly from the middle and working classes.[21]

Degree of Inequality

Degree of class mobility, however, is not the same as degree of economic inequality. For example, Japan, Italy, and Germany have less mobility than the United States, but less inequality (see later). Degree of inequality can vary considerably over time. In the United States, inequality has fluctuated considerably from the 1900s to the present. The greatest inequality was just before the 1929 stock market crash, when the top 1 percent had 42.6 percent of all the wealth. The least inequality was in the mid-1970s, after the stock market declined by 42 percent. Then the top 1 percent controlled 17.6 percent of the wealth.

Change over time in the degree of inequality sometimes appears to have economic causes; for example, the 1929 crash made the wealthy less wealthy. But some of the change over time is due to shifts in public policy. During the New Deal of the 1930s, tax changes and work programs shifted more income to ordinary people; in the 1980s, tax cuts for the wealthy helped the rich get richer. In the 1990s, the rich continued to get richer and the poor got poorer.[22] By 2006, inequality was more concentrated at the top than since the 1929 crash. Only since the severe recession between 2007 and 2009 have the rich gotten somewhat poorer.[23] One way of calculating the disparity between rich and poor is to use the ratio of income held by the top fifth of the households divided by the income held by the bottom fifth. Comparatively speaking, the United States presently has more inequality than any of the countries in western Europe, with a ratio of 8.5 to 1 (see Figure 1). That is, the top 20 percent of U.S. households controls 8.5 times the wealth controlled by the bottom 20 percent. Norway, on the other hand, has a ratio of about 4 to 1. And Germany has a ratio of about 4.3 to 1. The degree of inequality in the United States exceeds that of India, with a ratio of about 4.7 to 1. Brazil is one of the most unequal countries, with ratios of 32 to 1.

Recognition of Class

Societies that have open class systems vary in the degree to which members of the society recognize that there are classes, albeit somewhat open classes. The United States is unusual in that, despite objective evidence of multiple social classes, many people deny their existence. The ideology that hard work and strong character can transform anyone into a success appears to be so powerful that it masks the realities of social inequality.[24] A recent poll found that more people in the United States now believe that the chance of moving up has improved in the last few decades, when in reality mobility has declined.[25] When we were growing up, we were told that "Anyone can be President of the United States." As "proof," people pointed to a few individuals who rose from humble beginnings. But consider the odds. How many presidents have come from poor families? How many were not European in background? How many were not Protestant? So far, almost all of the presidents of the United States have been mainly

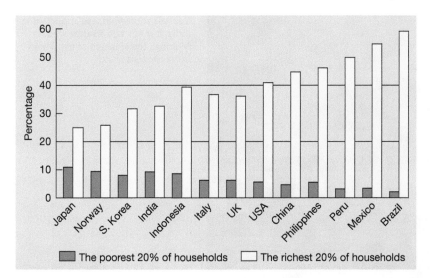

FIGURE 1 Proportion of National Income Earned by the Richest 20 Percent of Households Compared with the Poorest 20 Percent: Selected Country Comparisons. The countries are ordered by their Gini coefficients, a widely used measure of degree of income inequality.

Source: These data are abstracted from World Bank 2004, 60–62.

These data are abstracted from Proportion of National Income Earned by the Richest 20 Percent of Households. From World Bank. 2004. World Development Indicators 2004. Washington, DC: World Bank Publications. ISBN/ISSN: 01635085.

European in ancestry, all but one have been Protestant, and all have been male. And only a handful came from humble beginnings. The paradox of an open class system is that, to move up in the social ladder, people seem to have to believe that it is possible to do so. However, it is one thing to believe in mobility; it is another thing to deny the existence of classes. Why might people need to deny that classes exist?

Caste Systems

Some societies have classes (called castes) that are virtually closed. A **caste** is a ranked group in which membership is determined at birth, and marriage is restricted to members of one's own caste. The only way you can belong is by being born into the group; and because you cannot marry outside the group, your children cannot acquire another caste status either. In India, for example, there are several thousand hereditary castes. Although the precise ranking of these thousands of groups is not clear, there appear to be four main levels of hierarchy. The castes in India are often thought to be associated with different occupations, but that is not quite true. Most Indians live in rural areas and have agricultural occupations, but their castes vary widely.[26]

Castes may exist in conjunction with a more open class system. Indeed, in India today, members of a low caste who can get wage-paying jobs, chiefly those in urban areas, may improve their social standing in the same ways available to people in other class societies. In general, however, they still cannot marry someone in a higher caste, so the caste system is perpetuated.

Questions basic to all stratified societies, and particularly to a caste society, were posed by John Ruskin, a 19th-century British essayist: "Which of us . . . is to do the hard and dirty work for the rest—and for what pay? Who is to do the pleasant and clean work, and for what pay?"[27] In India, those questions have been answered by the caste system, which mainly dictates how goods and services are exchanged, particularly in rural areas.[28] Who is to do the hard and dirty work for the rest of society is clearly established: A large group of Untouchables forms the bottom of the hierarchy. Among the Untouchables are subcastes such as the Camars, or leatherworkers, and the Bhangis, who traditionally are sweepers. At the top of the hierarchy, performing the pleasant and clean work of priests, are the Brahmans. Between the two extremes are thousands of castes and subcastes.[29] In a typical village, a potter makes clay drinking cups and large water vessels for the entire village population. In return, the principal landowner gives him a house site and supplies him twice yearly with grain. Some other castes owe the potter their services: The barber cuts his hair; the sweeper carries away his rubbish; the washer washes his clothes; the Brahman performs his children's weddings. The barber serves every caste in the village except the Untouchables; he, in turn, is served by half of the others. He has inherited the families he works for, along with his father's occupation. All castes help at harvest and at weddings for additional payment, which sometimes includes a money payment.

This description is, in fact, an idealized picture of the caste system of India. In reality, the system operates to the advantage of the principal landowning caste—sometimes the Brahmans and sometimes other castes. Also, it is not carried on without some resentment; signs of hostility are shown toward the ruling caste by the Untouchables and other lower castes. The resentment does not appear to be against the caste system as such. Instead, the lower castes exhibit bitterness at their own low status and strive for greater equality. For instance, one of the Camars' traditional services is to remove dead cattle; in return, they can have the meat to eat and the hide to tan for their leatherworking. Because handling dead animals and eating beef are regarded as unclean acts, the Camars of one village refused to continue this service. Thus, they lost a source of free hides and food in a vain attempt to escape unclean status.

Since World War II, the economic basis of the caste system in India has been undermined somewhat by the growing practice of giving cash payment for services. For instance, the son of a barber may be a teacher during the week, earning a cash salary, and confine his haircutting to weekends. But he still remains in the barber caste (Nai) and must marry within that caste.

233

Caste is somewhat less important in India, but has not disappeared. In Mumbai, the washers of the Dhobi caste process laundry.

© sinopictures/Peter Arnold, Inc.

Perpetuation of the caste system is ensured by the power of those in the upper castes, who derive three main advantages from their position: economic, prestige, and sexual gains. The economic gain is the most immediately apparent. An ample supply of cheap labor and free services is maintained by the threat of sanctions. Lower-caste members may have their use of a house site withdrawn; they may be refused access to the village well or to common grazing land for animals; or they may be expelled from the village. Prestige is also maintained by the threat of sanctions; people in the higher castes expect deference and servility from those in the lower castes. The sexual gain is less apparent but equally real. The high-caste male has access to two groups of females, those of his own caste and those of lower castes. High-caste females are kept free of the "contaminating" touch of low-caste males because low-caste males are allowed access only to low-caste women. Moreover, the constant reminders of ritual uncleanness serve to keep those of the lower castes "in their place." People in higher castes do not accept water from Untouchables, sit next to them, or eat at the same table with them.

Japan also had a caste group within a class society. Now called *burakumin* (instead of the pejorative *eta*), this group traditionally had occupations that were considered unclean.[30] Comparable to India's Untouchables, they were a hereditary, endogamous (in-marrying) group. Their occupations were traditionally those of farm laborer, leatherworker, and basket weaver; their standard of living was very low. The burakumin are physically indistinguishable from other Japanese.[31] Despite that, the burakumin were considered a separate "race" by some for centuries.[32] The Japanese government officially abolished discrimination against the burakumin in 1871, but the burakumin did not begin organizing to bring about change until the 20th century. As of 1995, 73 percent of burakumin marriages were with non-burakumin. In public opinion polls, two-thirds of burakumin now said

that they had not encountered discrimination. However, most burakumin still live in segregated neighborhoods where unemployment, crime, and alcoholism rates are high.[33]

In a considerable number of sub-Saharan African societies, some occupational specialties are only performed by certain castes. The specialties usually involve metalworking, pottery, woodworking, leatherworking, playing musical instruments, and praise-singing. There may be different castes for different specialties or one caste for many specialties. In some cases, the caste consists of people who traditionally hunted and gathered. In almost all cases, the specialists had to marry within their own group and their social position was inherited. These castes usually constituted only a small minority of the society's population and were not the lowest ranking groups in society. Only slaves had a lower rank. Some of the castes took on additional tasks, such as go-betweens for arranging marriages, messengers, and circumcisers. The caste vocational distinctions have weakened in recent times as people have become more educated.[34]

In Rwanda, long before the ethnic division arose between the Hutu and Tutsi (see discussion later in the ethnicity section), the Twa, who comprised less than 1 percent of the population, were subject to serious discrimination. Their bodies were viewed as dangerous and polluting and they were avoided whenever possible. For example, if a Twa were present while others were eating or drinking, separate utensils were reserved only for Twa. The Twa traditional occupations were foraging, making pottery, entertaining, and serving as torturers or executioners for the Rwandan king. Mutton was considered a Twa food and other Rwandans would not eat mutton.[35]

In the United States, African Americans used to have more of a castelike status determined partly by the inherited characteristic of skin color. Until recently, some states had laws prohibiting an African American from marrying a European American. When interethnic marriage did

current research and issues

The Gap Between Poor and Rich Countries

When people support themselves by what they collect and produce themselves, as most people did until a few thousand years ago, it is difficult to compare the standards of living of different societies because we cannot translate what people have into market or monetary value. Only where people are at least partly involved in the world market economy can we measure the standard of living in monetary terms. Today, this comparison is possible for most of the world. Many people in most societies depend on buying and selling for a living; and the more people who depend on international exchange, the more possible it is to compare them in terms of standard economic indicators. We do not have such indicators for all the different societies, but we do have them for many countries. Those indicators suggest that the gap between the rich and poor countries in the world is not only very substantial but has generally increased in the last couple of decades.

To convey just how economically unequal the world has become, let us compare economic data for the years 1960, 1978, and 2000. In 1960, about a third of 126 countries (41) were classified as rich, and 17 percent were in the next lower rank—contenders to be rich. By 1978, about one-quarter (or 11) of the rich countries slipped down into the ranks of the contenders and about 7 percent (three) moved into the Third World category. By 2000, an additional five rich countries

slipped down. During the same time frame, only four countries moved up to join the rich—Singapore, Hong Kong, Taiwan, and South Korea. During the same time periods, almost all of the poorest countries stayed at the bottom, and if there was movement among the non-rich countries, it was mostly downward. Western countries increased their hold on the world's wealth during this period. Of the 41 originally rich countries in 1960, almost half (19) were non-Western. In 2000, there were fewer rich countries—only 31—but only 30 percent (nine) were non-Western.

If the world as a whole is seeing improvements in technology and economic development, why is the gap between the rich and poor countries increasing? Often the rich within a society benefit most from new technology, at least initially. They are not only the most likely to be able to afford it, they also are the only ones who can afford to take the risks that it involves. The same may be true for nations. Those that already have capital are more likely than the poorer nations to take advantage of improvements in technology. In addition, the poorer countries generally have the highest rates of population growth, so income per capita can fall if population increases faster than the rate of economic development. Economists tell us that a developing country may, at least initially, experience an increase in inequality, but the inequality often decreases over time.

Will the inequalities among countries also decrease as the world economy develops further?

If it is true that the disparity between rich and poor countries has increased in recent years, it is also true that the world has seen improvement in some respects. The United Nations has computed a "human development index" for 177 countries, combining measures of life expectancy, literacy, and a measure of per capita purchasing power. According to this index, most countries, including developing countries, have improved substantially between 1990 and 2005. For example, Bangladesh, China, and Uganda have increased their ranking by about 20 percent between 1990 and 2005. Some countries are doing worse—most of these are in sub-Saharan Africa or had been parts of the former Soviet Union. World leaders at the United Nations Millennium Declaration have committed themselves to a number of goals by the year 2015, including halving the proportion of people living in extreme poverty and halving the proportion of people suffering from hunger. Even if those goals are achieved, much more will remain to be done if we are to achieve a more equal world.

Sources: United Nations Development Programme 2007; UN News Centre 2005; Milanovic 2005.

occur, children of the union were often regarded as having lower status than European American children, even though they may have had blond hair and light skin. In the South, where treatment of African Americans as a caste was most apparent, European Americans refused to eat with African Americans or sit next to them at lunch counters, on buses, and in schools. Separate drinking fountains and toilets reinforced the idea of ritual uncleanness. The economic advantages and gains in prestige that European Americans enjoyed are well documented.[36]

In the following sections on slavery, racism, and inequality, we discuss the social status of African Americans in more detail.

Slavery

Slaves are people who do not own their own labor, and as such they represent a class. We may associate slavery with a few well-known examples, such as ancient Egypt, Greece, and Rome or the southern United States, but slavery has existed in some form in almost every part of the world at one time or another, in simpler as well as in more complex societies. Slaves are often obtained from other cultures directly: kidnapped, captured in war, or given as tribute. Or they may be obtained indirectly as payment in barter or trade. Slaves sometimes come from the same culture; one became a slave as payment of a debt, as a punishment for a crime, or even as a chosen alternative to poverty. Slave societies vary in the degree to which it is possible to become freed from slavery.[37] Sometimes the slavery system has been a closed class, or caste, system, sometimes a relatively open class system. In different slave-owning societies, slaves have had different, but always some, legal rights.[38]

In ancient Greece, slaves often were conquered enemies. Because city-states were constantly conquering one another or rebelling against former conquerors, slavery was a threat to everyone. After the Trojan War, the transition of Hecuba from queen to slave was marked by her cry, "Count no one happy, however fortunate, before he dies."[39] Nevertheless, Greek slaves were considered human beings, and they could even acquire some higher-class status along with freedom. Andromache, Hecuba's daughter-in-law, was taken as a slave and concubine by one of the Greek heroes. When his legal wife produced no children, Andromache's slave son became heir to his father's throne. Although slaves had no rights under law, once they were freed, either by the will of their master or by purchase, they and their descendants could become assimilated into the dominant group. In other words, slavery in Greece was not seen as the justified position of inferior people. It was regarded, rather, as an act of fate—"the luck of the draw"—that relegated one to the lowest class in society.

Among the Nupe, a society in central Nigeria, slavery was of quite another type.[40] The methods of obtaining slaves—as part of the booty of warfare and, later, by purchase—were similar to those of Europeans, but the position of the slaves was very different. Mistreatment was rare. Male slaves were given the same opportunities to earn money as other dependent males in the household—younger brothers, sons, or other relatives. A slave might be given a garden plot of his own to cultivate, or he might be given a commission if his master was a craftsman or a tradesman. Slaves could acquire property, wealth, and even slaves of their own. But all of a slave's belongings went to the master at the slave's death.

Manumission—the granting of freedom to slaves—was built into the Nupe system. If a male slave could afford the marriage payment for a free woman, the children of the resulting marriage were free; the man himself, however, remained a slave. Marriage and concubinage were the easiest ways out of bondage for a slave woman. Once she had produced a child by her master, both she and the child had free status. The woman, however, was only figuratively free; if a concubine, she had to remain in that role. As might be expected, the family trees of the nobility and the wealthy were liberally grafted with branches descended from slave concubines.

The most fortunate slaves among the Nupe were the house slaves. They could rise to positions of power in the household as overseers and bailiffs, charged with law enforcement and judicial duties. (Recall the Old Testament story of Joseph, who was sold into slavery by his brothers. Joseph became a household slave of the pharaoh and rose to the position of second in the kingdom because he devised an ingenious system of taxation.) There was even a titled group of Nupe slaves, the Order of Court Slaves, who were trusted officers of the king and members of an elite. Slave status in general, though, placed one at the bottom of the social ladder. In the Nupe system, few slaves, mainly princes from their own societies, ever achieved membership in the titled group. Nupe slavery was abolished at the beginning of the 20th century.

In the United States, slavery originated as a means of obtaining cheap labor, but the slaves soon came to be regarded as deserving of their low status because of their alleged inherent inferiority. Because the slaves were from Africa and were dark-skinned, some European Americans justified slavery and the belief in "black" people's inferiority by quoting scripture out of context ("They shall be hewers of wood and drawers of water"). Slaves could not marry or make any other contracts, nor could they own property. In addition, their children were also slaves, and the master had sexual rights over the female slaves. Because the status of slavery was determined by birth in the United States, slaves constituted a caste. During the days of slavery, therefore, the United States had both a caste and a class system. It is widely assumed that slavery occurred only in the southern United States, but although not on as large a scale, slavery existed in the northern states as well. New Jersey was the last northern state to legally give up slavery around the time of the U.S. Civil War.[41]

Even after the abolition of slavery, as we have noted, some castelike elements remained. It is important to note that these castelike elements were not limited to the American South where slavery had been practiced. For example, although Indiana was established as a "free" state in 1816, in its first constitution, "negros" did not have the right to vote nor could they intermarry with "whites." In the constitution of 1851, Indiana did not allow "negros" to come into the state, nor did it allow the existing African American residents to attend public schools even though they had to pay school taxes.[42] In Muncie, Indiana, in the first half of the 20th century, there was customary segregation in shows, restaurants, and parks. Not until the 1950s was the public swimming pool desegregated.[43]

As for why slavery may have developed in the first place, cross-cultural research is as yet inconclusive. We do know, however, that slavery is not an inevitable stage in economic development, contrary to what some have assumed. In other words, slavery is not found mainly in certain economies, such as those dependent on intensive agriculture. Unlike the United States until the Civil War, many societies with intensive agriculture did not develop any variety of slavery. Also, the hypothesis that slavery develops where available resources are plentiful but labor is scarce is not supported by the cross-cultural evidence. All we can say definitely is that slavery does not occur in developed or industrial economies; either it disappears or it was never present in them.[44]

RACISM AND INEQUALITY

Racism is the belief that some "races" are inferior to others. In a society composed of people with noticeably different physical features, such as differences in skin color, racism is almost invariably associated with social stratification. Those "races" considered inferior make up a larger proportion of the lower social classes or castes. Even in more open class systems, where individuals from all backgrounds can achieve higher status positions, individuals from groups deemed inferior may be subject to discrimination in housing or may be more likely to be searched or stopped by the police.

In some societies, such as the United States, the idea that humans are divided into "races" is taken so much for granted that people are asked for their "race" on the census. Most Americans probably assume that the classification of people into categories such as "white" or "black" reflects important biological categories. But that is not so. We now know from genetic research that there is enormous genetic diversity within the African continent, in fact, more than between Africa and any other continent.[45] There is no clear boundary where one trait is present or absent. For example, in the area around Egypt, there is a gradient of skin color as you move from north to south in the Nile Valley. Nose shape varies with humidity, but its gradient is not the same as the gradient for skin color, so the two distributions are quite different. Both of these characteristics make it impossible to draw discrete boundaries between groups on the basis of external traits such as skin color and nose shape. The genetic diversity within Africa is consistent with the fossil evidence that the African continent is where both early humans and modern humans emerged. This is as you may remember, parallel to linguistic diversity—English developed in England, and

there we find the most dialect diversity. Modern humans emerged first in Africa, so it is accurate to say that we are all African, and members of the "human race."

You may have noticed that we put "race" in quotes to reflect the fact that most anthropologists are now persuaded that the biological concept of "race" is not scientifically useful when applied to humans. However, "race" is a social concept that is important as a classifier in some societies.

Race as a Social Category

Racial classifications are social categories to which individuals are assigned, by themselves and others, to separate "our" group from others. We have seen that people tend to be *ethnocentric*, to view their culture as better than other cultures. Racial classifications may reflect the same tendency to divide "us" from "them," except that the divisions are supposedly based on biological differences.[46] The "them" are almost always viewed as inferior to "us."

We know that racial classifications have often been, and still are, used by certain groups to justify discrimination, exploitation, or genocide. The "Aryan race" was supposed to be the group of blond-haired, blue-eyed, white-skinned people whom Adolf Hitler wanted to dominate the world, to which end he and others attempted to destroy as many members of the Jewish "race" as they could. (An estimated 6 million Jews and others were murdered in what is now called the Holocaust.[47]) But who were the Aryans? Technically, Aryans are any people, including the German-speaking Jews in Hitler's Germany, who speak one of the Indo-European languages. The Indo-European languages include such disparate modern tongues as Greek, Spanish, Hindi, Polish, French, Icelandic, German, Gaelic, and English. And many Aryans speaking these languages have neither blond hair nor blue eyes. Similarly, all kinds of people may be Jews, whether or not they descend from the

Some of our physical differences give the impression that it is possible to divide us into races. But when these physical characteristics are subjected to detailed study, that cannot be concluded at all. Instead it becomes obvious that our physical diversity reflects continuous changes from one extreme to the other. To place any boundaries within this continuous diversity would be, therefore, completely arbitrary. Human diversity is in fact infinitely more complicated than the idea we have constructed of it. This is why attempts to make racial classifications that are typically made don't yield any coherent results; there is nothing scientific about "race".

It is an illusion that there are races. The diversity of human beings is so great and so complicated that it is impossible to classify the 5.8 billions of individuals into discrete "races."

applied anthropology

Unequal in Death: African Americans Compared with European Americans

Everyone dies of something. Yet, if you consider cardiovascular disease, the leading cause of death in the United States, it turns out that after controlling for the effects of age and gender, African Americans die more often from that disease than European Americans. The same kind of disparity occurs also with almost every other major cause of death—cancer, cirrhosis of the liver, kidney disease, diabetes, injuries, infant mortality, and homicide. Medical anthropologists and health policy researchers want to know why. Without such understanding, it is hard to know how to reduce the disparity.

One reason may be subtle discrimination by the medical profession itself. For example, a European American with chest pain in the United States is more likely than an African American to be given an angiogram, a medical procedure that injects radioactive dye into the heart to look for deficits in blood flow through the coronary arteries that supply blood to the heart. And even if coronary heart disease is detected by an angiogram, an African American is less likely to receive bypass surgery. Thus, the death rate from cardiovascular disease may be higher for African Americans than for European Americans because of unequal medical care. Seeing a patient physically appears to make a difference. When heart specialists reviewed cases to make decisions about subsequent treatment after catheterization, recommendations did not differ by "race" when the doctors did not know the "race" of the patient.

Yet, although some difference in mortality may be due to disparity in medical treatment, this could only be part of the picture. African Americans may be more prone to cardiovascular disease because they are about twice as likely as European Americans to have high rates of hypertension (high blood pressure). But, why the disparity in hypertension? Three possible explanations, not mutually exclusive, are discussed in the research literature. The first is a possible difference in genetics. The second is a difference in lifestyle. The third is class difference.

Most of the Africans that came to the Americas were forcibly taken as slaves between the 16th and 19th centuries, largely from West Africa. In one comparative study of hypertension, African Americans had much higher blood pressure than Africans in Nigeria and Cameroon, even in urban areas. People with African ancestry in the Caribbean were in the middle of the range. Lifestyle differences were also vast—the West Africans had plenty of exercise, were lean, and ate low-fat and low-salt diets. Any possible difference in genes would seem to be insignificant. Jared Diamond has suggested that individuals who could retain salt would have been most likely to survive the terrible conditions of the sailing ships that brought slaves to the New World. Many died from diarrhea and dehydration (salt-depleting conditions) on those voyages. Retention of salt would have been a genetic advantage then, but disadvantageous in places such as the United States with high-salt, high-fat diets. Critics of this theory suggest that salt-depleting diseases were not the leading causes of death in the slave voyages; tuberculosis and violence were more frequent causes of death. Furthermore, critics say that the slave ship theory would predict little genetic diversity in African American populations with respect to hypertension, but in fact there is great diversity.

Hypertension could be related also to differences in lifestyle and wealth. As we noted in the section on racism and inequality, African Americans in the United States are disproportionately poorer. Study after study has noted that healthier lifestyle habits are generally correlated with higher positions on the socioeconomic ladder. Moreover, individuals from higher social positions are more likely to have health insurance and access to care in superior hospitals. But even after correcting for factors such as obesity, physical activity, and social class, the health differential persists—African Americans still have a much higher incidence of hypertension than European Americans.

William Dressler suggests that stress is another possible cause of higher rates of hypertension. Despite increased economic mobility in recent years, African Americans are still subject to prejudice and may consequently have more stress even if they have higher income. Stress is related to higher blood pressure. In a color-conscious society, a very dark-skinned individual walking in a wealthy neighborhood at night may be thought not to live there and may be stopped by the police. If Dressler is correct, darker-skinned African Americans who have objective indicators of higher status should have much higher blood pressure than would be expected from their relative education, age, body mass, or social class alone. And that seems to be true. Racism may affect health.

Sources: Smedley et al. 2003, 3; Geiger 2003; Dressler 1993; Cooper et al. 1999, 56–63; Diamond 1991.

ancient Near Eastern population that spoke the Hebrew language. There are light-skinned Danish Jews and darker Jewish Arabs. One of the most orthodox Jewish groups in the United States is based in New York City and is composed entirely of African Americans.

The arbitrary and social basis of most racial classifications becomes apparent when you compare how they differ from one place to another. Consider, for example, what used to be thought about the "races" in South Africa. Under apartheid, which was a system of racial segregation and discrimination, someone with mixed "white" and "black" ancestry was considered "colored." However, when important people of African ancestry (from other countries) would visit South Africa, they were often considered "white." Chinese were considered "Asian"; but the Japanese, who were important economically to South Africa, were considered "white."[48] In some parts of the United States, laws against interracial marriage continued in force through the 1960s. You would be considered a "negro" if you had an eighth or more "negro" ancestry (if one or more of your eight grandparents were "negro").[49] In some states, an even smaller proportion made you "negro." Some refer to this concept as the "one-drop" rule—just a tiny bit of "negro" (now called "black") ancestry was sufficient to determine your "racial" classification.[50] So only a small amount of "negro" ancestry made a person "negro." But a small amount of "white" ancestry did not make a person "white." Biologically speaking, this makes no sense, but socially it was another story.[51]

In much of Latin America and the Caribbean, the reverse rule is the case. A small amount of European blood can make you "white." When people from Dominica, Haiti, or Cuba come to the United States, they often find that their "race" has changed. They might have been considered "white" at home, but they are considered "black" in the United States. In contrast to the United States with a two-part division of "white" and "black," concepts of race in Latin America are on more of a continuum from light to dark, with important middle positions (such as "mestizo"). Wealth makes a difference too—if you are dark-skinned, but wealthy, you will tend to be considered "whiter."[52]

If people of different "races" are viewed as inferior, they are more likely going to end up on the lower rungs of the social ladder in a socially stratified society. Discrimination will keep them out of the better-paying or higher-status jobs and in neighborhoods that are poorer. As the box "Unequal in Death" shows, people of different "races" also suffer from differential access to health care and have more health problems.

ETHNICITY AND INEQUALITY

If "race" is not a scientifically useful category because people cannot be clearly divided into different "racial" categories based on sets of physical traits, then racial classifications such as "black" and "white" in the United States might better be described as *ethnic* classifications. How else can we account for the following facts? Groups that are thought of as "white" now in the United States were earlier thought of as belonging to inferior "races." For example, in the latter half of the 19th century, newspapers would often talk about the new immigrants from Ireland as belonging to the Irish "race." Similarly, before World War II, Jews were thought of as a separate "racial" group, and only became "white" afterward.[53] It is hard to escape the idea that changes in "racial" classification occurred as the Irish, Jews, and other immigrant groups became more accepted by the majority in the United States.[54]

It is apparent that *ethnic groups* and *ethnic identities* emerge as part of a social and political process. The process of defining **ethnicity** usually involves a group of people emphasizing common origins and language,

Members of minority ethnic groups are more often at the bottom of the socioeconomic "ladder," but not always, as these pictures from the United States illustrate.

239

shared history, and selected cultural differences such as a difference in religion. Those doing the defining can be outside or inside the ethnic group. Outsiders and insiders often perceive ethnic groups differently. In a country with one large core majority group, often the majority group doesn't think of itself as an ethnic group. Rather, they consider only the minority groups to have ethnic identities. For example, in the United States, it is not common for the majority to call themselves European Americans, but other groups may be called African Americans, Asian Americans, or Native Americans. The minority groups, on the other hand, may also have different named identities.[55] Asian Americans may identify themselves more specifically as Japanese Americans, Korean Americans, Chinese Americans, or Hmong. The majority population often uses derogatory names to identify people who are different. The majority may also tend to lump people of diverse ethnicities together. Naming a group establishes a boundary between it and other ethnic groups.[56]

Ethnic differences can sometimes arise from class differences. Rwanda is a good case in point. By the end of the 19th century, Rwandans were part of a kingdom with significant class distinctions, but the distinctions between Hutu and Tutsi, so important in recent times, were not very important or clear.[57] Cattle were an important form of wealth and, although many people known as Tutsi were cattle herders and many known as Hutu were agriculturalists, many Tutsi and Hutu were both. If Hutu acquired wealth and intermarried with Tutsi, they could move up in rank. A Tutsi could lose cattle and turn to cultivation.[58] Colonialism did not create differentiation between Tutsi and Hutu, but it did accentuate it. For example, the Belgian administration tried to reinforce the power of the "natural rulers" (the Tutsi), and they issued identity cards in the 1930s to distinguish Tutsi, Hutu, and Twa (the Twa were discussed earlier in the caste section). During the colonial period, the idea developed that the three groups were biologically different from each other. It was commonly thought that the taller Tutsi were different people who originally conquered the others.[59]

When the Hutu united to demand more of the rewards of their labor in 1959, the king and many of the Tutsi ruling elite were driven out of the country. The Hutu then established a republican form of government and declared independence from Belgium in 1962. In 1990, Tutsi rebels invaded from Uganda, and attempts were made to negotiate a multiparty government. However, civil war continued, and in 1994 alone, over a million people, mostly Tutsi, were killed. Almost 2 million refugees, mostly Hutu, fled to Zaire as the Tutsi-led rebels established a new government.[60] In the intervening years, the Rwandan government has made progress in bringing home the refugees, bringing those who committed genocide to trial, and integrating different groups into the government.[61]

Ethnic identity may be manipulated, by insiders and by outsiders, in different situations. A particularly repressive regime that emphasizes nationalism and loyalty to the state may not only suppress the assertiveness of ethnic claims; it may also act to minimize communication among people who might otherwise embrace the same ethnic identity.[62] More democratic regimes may allow more expression of difference and celebrate ethnic difference. However, manipulation of ethnicity does not come just from the top. It may be to the advantage of minority groups to lobby for more equal treatment as a larger entity, such as Asian American, rather than as Japanese, Chinese, Hmong, Filipino, or Korean American. Similarly, even though there are hundreds of Native American groups, originally speaking different languages, there may be political advantages for all if they are treated as Native Americans.

In many multiethnic societies, ethnicity and diversity are things to be proud of and celebrated. Shared ethnic identity often makes people feel comfortable with similar people and gives them a strong sense of belonging. Still, ethnic differences in multiethnic societies are usually associated with inequities in wealth, power, and prestige. In other words, ethnicity is part of the system of *stratification*.

Although some people believe that inequities are deserved, the origins of ethnic stereotypes, prejudice, and discrimination usually follow from historical and political events that give some groups dominance over others. For example, even though there were many early stories of help given by native peoples to the English settlers in the 17th century in the land now known as North America, the English were the invaders, and negative stereotypes about native peoples developed to justify taking their land and their lives. Referring to the negative stereotypes of Native Americans that developed, J. Milton Yinger said, "One would almost think that it had been the Indian who had invaded Europe, driven back the inhabitants, cut their population to one-third of its original size, unilaterally changed treaties, and brought the dubious glories of firewater and firearms."[63]

Similarly, as we noted in the section on slavery, African slaves were initially acquired as cheap labor, but inhumane treatment of slaves was justified by beliefs about their inferiority. Unfortunately, stereotypes can become self-fulfilling prophesies, especially if those discriminated against come to believe the stereotypes. It is easy to see how this can happen. If there is a widespread belief that a group is inferior, and that group is given inferior schools and little chance for improvement or little chance for a good job, the members of that group may acquire few skills and not try hard. The result is often a vicious cycle.[64]

And yet, the picture is not all bleak. Change has occurred. The ethnic identity a minority group forges can help promote political activism, such as the nonviolent civil rights movement in the United States in the 1960s. That activism, helped by some people in the more advantaged groups, helped break down many of the legal barriers and segregationist practices that reinforced inequality.

The traditional barriers in the United States have mostly been lifted in recent years, but the "color line" has not disappeared. African Americans are found in all social classes, but they remain underrepresented in the wealthiest group and overrepresented at the bottom. Discrimination may be lessened, but it is still not gone. In research done with matched pairs of "whites" and "blacks" applying for jobs or for housing, discrimination is still evident.[65] Thus, African Americans may have to be better than others to get promoted, or it may be assumed that they got ahead just because they were African American and were hired because of affirmative action programs. European Americans often expect African Americans to be "ambassadors," to be called on mainly for knowledge about how to handle situations involving other African Americans. African Americans may work with others, but they usually go home to African American neighborhoods. Or they may live in mixed neighborhoods and experience considerable isolation. Few African Americans can completely avoid the anguish of racism.[66]

THE EMERGENCE OF STRATIFICATION

Anthropologists are not certain why social stratification developed. Nevertheless, they are reasonably sure that higher levels of stratification emerged relatively recently in human history. Archaeological sites dating before about 8,000 years ago do not show extensive evidence of inequality. Houses do not appear to vary much in size or content, and different communities of the same culture are similar in size and otherwise. Signs of inequality appear first in the Near East, about 2,000 years after agriculture emerged in that region. Inequality in burial suggests inequality in life. Particularly telling are unequal child burials. It is unlikely that children could achieve high status by their own achievements. So, when archaeologists find statues and ornaments only in some children's tombs, as at the 7,500-year-old site of Tell es-Sawwan in Iraq,[67] the grave goods suggest that those children belonged to a higher-ranking family or a higher class.

Another indication that stratification is a relatively recent development in human history is the fact that certain cultural features associated with stratification also developed relatively recently. For example, most societies that depend primarily on agriculture or herding have social classes.[68] Agriculture and herding developed within the past 10,000 years, so we may assume that most food collectors in the distant past lacked social classes. Other recently developed cultural features associated with class stratification include fixed settlements, political integration beyond the community level, the use of money as a medium of exchange, and the presence of at least some full-time specialization.[69]

In 1966, the comparative sociologist Gerhard Lenski suggested that the trend toward increasing inequality since 8,000 years ago was reversing. He argued that inequalities of power and privilege in industrial societies—measured in terms of the concentration of political power and the distribution of income—are less pronounced than inequalities in complex preindustrial societies. Technology in industrialized societies is so complex, he suggested, that those in power are compelled to delegate some authority to subordinates if the system is to work. In addition, a decline in the birth rate in industrialized societies, coupled with the need for skilled labor, has pushed the average wage of workers far above the subsistence level, resulting in greater equality in the distribution of income. Finally, Lenski also suggested that the spread of the democratic ideology, and particularly its acceptance by elites, has significantly broadened the political power of the lower classes.[70] A few studies have tested and supported Lenski's hypothesis that inequality has decreased with industrialization. In general, nations that are highly industrialized exhibit a lower level of inequality than nations that are only somewhat industrialized.[71] But, as we have seen, even the most industrialized societies may still have an enormous degree of inequality.

Why did social stratification develop in the first place? On the basis of his study of Polynesian societies, Marshall Sahlins suggested that an increase in agricultural productivity results in social stratification.[72] According to Sahlins, the degree of stratification is directly related to the production of a surplus, which is made possible by greater technological efficiency. The higher the level of productivity and the larger the agricultural surplus, the greater the scope and complexity of the distribution system. The status of the chief, who serves as redistributing agent, is enhanced. Sahlins argued that the differentiation between distributor and producer inevitably gives rise to differentiation in other aspects of life:

First, there would be a tendency for the regulator of distribution to exert some authority over production itself—especially over productive activities which necessitate subsidization, such as communal labor or specialist labor. A degree of control of production implies a degree of control over the utilization of resources, or, in other words, some preeminent property rights. In turn, regulation of these economic processes necessitates the exercise of authority in interpersonal affairs; differences in social power emerge.[73]

Sahlins later rejected the idea that a surplus leads to chiefships, postulating instead that the relationship may be the other way around—that is, leaders encourage the development of a surplus so as to enhance their prestige through feasts, potlatches, and other redistributive events.[74] Of course, both trajectories are possible—surpluses may generate stratification, and stratification may generate surpluses; they are not mutually exclusive.

Lenski's theory of the causes of stratification is similar to Sahlins's original idea. Lenski, too, argued that production of a surplus is the stimulus in the development of stratification, but he focused primarily on the conflict that arises over control of that surplus. Lenski concluded that the distribution of the surplus will be determined on the basis of power. Thus, inequalities in power promote unequal access to economic resources and simultaneously give rise to inequalities in privilege and prestige.[75]

The "surplus" theories of Sahlins and Lenski do not really address the question of why the redistributors or leaders will want, or be able, to acquire greater control over resources. After all, the redistributors or leaders in many rank societies do not have greater wealth than others, and custom seems to keep things that way. One suggestion is that, as long as followers have mobility, they can vote with their feet by moving away from leaders they do not like. But when people start to make more permanent "investments" in land or technology (e.g., irrigation systems or weirs for fishing), they are more likely to put up with a leader's aggrandizement in exchange for protection.[76] Another suggestion is that access to economic resources becomes unequal only when there is population pressure on resources in rank or chiefdom societies.[77] Such pressure may be what induces redistributors to try to keep more land and other resources for themselves and their families.

C. K. Meek offered an example of how population pressure in northern Nigeria may have led to economic stratification. At one time, a tribal member could obtain the right to use land by asking permission of the chief and presenting him with a token gift in recognition of his higher status. But, by 1921, the reduction in the amount of available land had led to a system under which applicants offered the chief large payments for scarce land. As a result of these payments, farms came to be regarded as private property, and differential access to such property became institutionalized.[78]

Future research by archaeologists, sociologists, historians, and anthropologists should provide more understanding of the emergence of social stratification in human societies and how and why it may vary in degree.

SUMMARY ● ○ ○

1. Without exception, recent and modern industrial and postindustrial societies such as our own are socially stratified—that is, they contain social groups such as families, classes, or ethnic groups that have unequal access to important advantages, such as economic resources, power, and prestige. Anthropologists, based on firsthand observations, would say that such inequality has not always existed among the societies they have studied. Although even the simplest societies (in the technological sense) have some differences in advantages based on age, ability, or gender—adults have higher status than children, the skilled more than the unskilled, men more than women—anthropologists would argue that egalitarian societies exist where social groups (e.g., families) have more or less the same access to rights or advantages.

2. The presence or absence of customs or rules that give certain groups unequal access to economic resources, power, and prestige can be used to distinguish three types of societies. In egalitarian societies, social groups do not have unequal access to economic resources, power, or prestige; they are unstratified. In rank societies, social groups do not have very unequal access to economic resources or power, but they do have unequal access to prestige. Rank societies, then, are partially stratified. In class societies, social groups have unequal access to economic resources, power, and prestige. They are more completely stratified than are rank societies.

3. Stratified societies range from somewhat open class systems to caste systems, which are extremely rigid, because caste membership is fixed permanently at birth.

4. Slaves are people who do not own their own labor; as such, they represent a class and sometimes even a caste. Slavery has existed in various forms in many times and places, regardless of "race" and culture. Sometimes slavery is a rigid and closed, or caste, system; sometimes it is a relatively open class system.

5. Within a society composed of people from widely divergent backgrounds and different physical features, such as skin color, racism is almost invariably associated with social stratification. Those "races" considered inferior make up a larger proportion of the lower social classes or castes. In the opinion of many biological anthropologists, "race" is not a scientifically useful device for classifying humans. "Racial" classifications should be recognized for what they mostly are—social categories to which individuals are assigned, by themselves and others, on the basis of supposedly shared biological traits.

6. In multiethnic societies, ethnic differences are usually associated with inequities in wealth, power, and prestige. In other words, ethnicity is part of the system of stratification.

7. Social stratification appears to have emerged relatively recently in human history, about 8,000 years ago. This conclusion is based on archaeological evidence and on the fact that certain cultural features associated with stratification developed relatively recently.

8. One theory suggests that social stratification developed as productivity increased and surpluses were produced. Another suggestion is that stratification can develop only when people have "investments" in land or technology and therefore cannot move away from leaders they do not like. A third theory suggests that stratification emerges only when there is population pressure on resources in rank societies.

GLOSSARY TERMS ○ ● ○

caste	manumission
class	power
class societies	prestige
economic resources	rank societies
egalitarian societies	slaves
ethnicity	

CRITICAL QUESTIONS ○ ○ ●

1. What might be some of the social consequences of large differences in wealth? Explain your reasoning.

2. Is an industrial or a developed economy incompatible with a more egalitarian distribution of resources? Why or why not?

3. In a multiethnic society, does ethnic identity help or hinder social equality? Explain your answer.

4. Why do you suppose the degree of inequality has decreased in some countries in recent years?

PEARSON
myanthrolab

Read "Haitians: From Political Repression to Chaos" by Robert Lawless on MyAnthroLab. Answer the questions below.

1. In what ways does Lawless suggest that the elite in Haiti maintain their power?

2. Why does Lawless say that "Voodoo" is an egalitarian religion?

3. Explain what role slavery played in Haitian history.

NOTES ● ○ ○

1. In an analysis of many native societies in the New World, Gary Feinman and Jill Neitzel argue that egalitarian and rank societies ("tribes" and "chiefdoms," respectively) are not systematically distinguishable. See Feinman and Neitzel (1984, 57).
2. Fried 1967, 33.
3. Boehm 1993, 230–31; Boehm 1999.
4. M. G. Smith 1966, 152.
5. Salzman 1999.
6. D. Mitchell 2009.
7. Drucker 1965, 56–64.
8. Service 1978, 249.
9. Sahlins 1958, 80–81.
10. Betzig 1988.
11. W. L. Warner and Lunt 1941.
12. Lynd and Lynd 1929; and Lynd and Lynd 1937.
13. Brittain 1978.
14. Higley 1995, 1–47.
15. Argyle 1994.
16. S. R. Barrett 1994, 17–19, 34–35.
17. Ibid., 155.
18. U.S. Census Bureau 2002.
19. Treiman and Ganzeboom 1990, 117; Featherman and Hauser 1978, 4, 481.
20. Solon 2002; Behrman et al. 2001.
21. S. R. Barrett 1994, 17, 41.
22. K. Phillips 1990; U.S. Census Bureau 1993; *New York Times* 1997, A26; Johnston 1999, 16.
23. Leonhardt and Fabrikant 2009.
24. Durrenberger 2001b, who refers to Goldschmidt 1999 and Newman 1988; 1993.
25. Scott and Leonhardt 2005.
26. Klass 2009.
27. Ruskin 1963, 296–314.
28. O. Lewis 1958.
29. Ibid.
30. Kristof 1995, A18.
31. For more information about caste in Japan, see Berreman 1973 and 1972, 403–14.
32. Takezawa 2006.
33. Kristof 1995; Kristof 1997.
34. Tamari 1991; 2005.
35. Taylor 2005.
36. Berreman 1960, 120–27.
37. O. Patterson 1982, vii–xiii, 105.
38. Pryor 1977, 219.
39. Euripides 1937, 52.
40. Nadel 1942.
41. Harper 2003.
42. Lassiter et al. 2004, 49–50.
43. Ibid., 59–67.
44. Pryor 1977, 217–47.
45. Brooks et al. 1993; Tishkoff et al. 2009.
46. M. D. Williams 2004.
47. S. S. Friedman 1980, 206.
48. M. H. Ross 2009a.
49. Marks 1994, 32.
50. Fluehr-Lobban 2006, 12.
51. Marks 1994, 32.
52. Fluehr-Lobban 2006, 12.
53. Armelagos and Goodman 1998, 365.
54. O. Patterson 2000.
55. M. Nash 1989, 2.
56. Ibid., 10.
57. Newbury 1998.
58. C. Taylor 2005.
59. Newbury 1998.
60. *Britannica Online* 1995.
61. See Rwanda in later Books of the Year from Britannica Online http://search.eb.com/search?query=rwanda&x=0&y= 0&ct=.
62. Barth 1994, 27.
63. Yinger 1994, 169.
64. Ibid., 169–71.
65. Ibid., 216–17.
66. Benjamin 1991; see also M. D. Williams 2004.
67. Flannery 1972.
68. Data from Textor 1967.
69. Ibid.
70. Lenski 1984/1966, 308–18.
71. Treiman and Ganzeboom 1990, 117; Cutright 1967, 564.
72. Sahlins 1958.
73. Ibid., 4.
74. Sahlins 1972.
75. Lenski 1984/1966.
76. Gilman 1990.
77. Fried 1967, 201ff; and Harner 1975.
78. Meek 1940, 149–50.

Culture and the Individual

From Chapter 19 of *Anthropology*, 13/e. Carol R. Ember. Melvin Ember. Peter N. Peregrine. Copyright © 2011 by Pearson Education. Published by Prentice Hall. All rights reserved.

Culture
and the Individual

nthropology, with its focus on culture, may seem to ignore the individual. To be sure, individuals provide information about culture, but their psychological characteristics, a central concern of psychology, are often considered irrelevant. However, there are anthropologists who think that understanding individuals and psychological processes is vital to anthropological understanding. Take culture change as an example. *Individuals* are ultimately the source of culture change. They discover and invent, they adopt new behaviors or ideas from others, or they resist or accommodate to changes other societies try to impose. Culture changes only when enough individuals alter their ideas or their patterns of behavior. Individuals are the *agents* of change.

Anthropologists who are interested in the relationships between culture and the individual and the importance of understanding psychological processes call themselves *psychological anthropologists*. Psychologists who study people in two or more societies call themselves *cross-cultural psychologists*. Four main questions seem to characterize psychological anthropology: (1) To what extent do all human beings develop psychologically in the same ways? (2) If there are differences, what are they and what may account for them? (3) How do people in different societies conceive of individuals and their psychological development? and (4) How can understanding individuals or psychological processes help us understand culture and culture change? This chapter discusses some of the attempts of researchers to answer some of these questions.

● ○ ●

THE UNIVERSALITY OF PSYCHOLOGICAL DEVELOPMENT

Anthropologists became interested in psychology in the early years of the 20th century partly because they did not believe that human nature was completely revealed in Western societies, as psychologists then generally assumed. Only recently have many psychologists joined anthropologists in questioning the assumption that humans are exactly the same psychologically in all societies. Psychologist Otto Klineberg, for example, scolded his psychologist colleagues in 1974: "My contact with anthropology affected me somewhat like a religious conversion. How could psychologists speak of *human* attributes and *human* behavior when they knew only one kind of human being?"[1]

How can we know what is universal about human behavior and what is variable until we study all kinds of humans? Because humans the world over are the same species and share a very large proportion of their genes, we might assume that there is a good deal of similarity across societies in the way people develop psychologically from birth to maturity or in the ways they think, feel, and behave. Here we discuss some universals that are related that to psychology. Donald Brown compiled a list of probable human universals in the psychological

realm.[2] They include the ability to create taxonomies, make binary contrasts, order phenomena, use logical operators (e.g., *and, not, equals*), plan for the future, and have an understanding of the world and what it is about.

With regard to ideas about people, it seems universal to have a concept of the self or person, to recognize individual faces, to try to discern other peoples' intentions from observable clues in their faces, utterances, and actions, and to imagine what others are thinking. With regard to emotions, people seem universally to be able to empathize with the feelings of others; facially communicate and recognize, as well as hide or mimic, the emotions of happiness, sadness, anger, fear, surprise, disgust, and contempt; smile when friendly; cry when in pain or unhappy; play for fun; show and feel affection for others; feel sexual attraction, envy, and jealousy; and have similar childhood fears (e.g., fear of strangers). Indeed, it seems that people in different cultures even conceive of love in much the same ways, despite love's reputation as something mysterious and culturally variable.[3]

What about psychological development? Certain aspects of language acquisition appear to be universal across cultures. In what respects is psychological development the same the world over? In what respects is it different?

Early Research on Emotional Development

When Margaret Mead went to American Samoa in the mid-1920s, psychologists believed that adolescence was universally a period of "storm and stress" because of the physiological changes that occur at puberty. Mead's observations of, and interviews with, Samoan adolescent girls led her to doubt the idea that adolescence was necessarily a time of turmoil. Samoan girls apparently showed little evidence of emotional upheaval and rebelliousness, and therefore it was questionable whether psychological development in adolescence was the same in all societies.[4]

Bronislaw Malinowski, another early anthropologist, questioned the universality of an assumption about emotional development, in this case Freud's assumption that young boys universally see themselves, unconsciously, as sexual rivals of their fathers for possession of their mothers. Freud called these feelings the *Oedipus complex,* after the character in Greek mythology who killed his father and married his mother without knowing that they were his parents. Freud thought that all boys before the age of 7 or so would show hostility toward their fathers, but Malinowski disagreed on the basis of his fieldwork in the Trobriand Islands.[5]

Malinowski suggested that young boys in male-oriented societies may feel hostility toward the father not as a sexual rival but as the disciplinarian. Malinowski proposed this theory because he thought that the Oedipus complex works differently in societies organized around the female line, such as the matrilineal Trobriands. In matrilineal

societies, the mother's brother is the main authority figure in the matrilineal kin group—than toward their father.

Derek Freeman criticized Mead's conclusions about Samoa,[6] and Melford Spiro challenged Malinowski's conclusions about the Trobriand Islanders.[7] Mead and Malinowski may or may not have been correct about the societies they studied, but the issues they raised remain crucial to the question of whether psychological development is similar across societies. To find out, we need research in many societies, not just a few. Only on the basis of extensive cross-cultural research will we be able to decide whether stages of emotional development can be affected by cultural differences.

For example, only recently has adolescence been systematically studied cross-culturally. Alice Schlegel and Herbert Barry reported that adolescence is generally not a period of overt rebelliousness. The reason, they suggested, is related to the fact that most people in most societies live with or near (and depend on) close kin before and after they grow up. Only in societies like our own, where children leave home when they grow up, might adolescents be rebellious, possibly to prepare emotionally for going out on their own.[8]

Adolescence in many societies is a time for developing work skills. An Asmat boy in Indonesian New Guinea is learning to carve, and an adult is supervising.

Research on Cognitive Development

One day the Embers went out for pizza. The pizza maker was laughing hilariously, and we asked what was so funny. He told us: "I just asked the guy ahead of you, 'How many slices do you want me to cut the pizza into, six or eight?' 'Six,' he said, 'I'm not very hungry.'" According to a theory of cognitive (intellectual) development suggested by Jean Piaget, the renowned Swiss psychologist, the "not very hungry" guy may not have acquired the concept of *conservation,* which characterizes a stage of thinking normally acquired by children between the ages of 7 and 11 in Western societies.[9] The pizza customer ahead of us, like many very young children, seemed not to understand that certain properties of an object, such as quantity, weight, and volume, remain constant even if the object is divided into small pieces or removed to a container of a different shape. They have not acquired the mental image of *reversibility,* the ability to imagine that if you put the pizza back together again it would be the same size whether you had cut it into eight or six slices. To the child or adult who has not acquired the ability to reverse actions mentally, eight slices may seem like more pizza than six slices, because eight is more than six.

Piaget's theory says that the development of thinking in humans involves a series of stages, each of which is characterized by different mental skills. To get to a higher stage of thinking, one has to pass through a lower stage. So Piaget's theory would predict that the pizza customer would not be able to think systematically about the possible outcomes of hypothetical situations, a defining feature of Piaget's *formal-operational* stage, because he had not acquired the notion of conservation and the other mental skills that characterize the previous, *concrete-operational* stage of cognitive development.

What does the evidence suggest about the universality of Piaget's supposed stages? And do people the world over get to each stage at the same age? The first stage of development, *sensorimotor,* has not been investigated in many societies, but the results of studies conducted so far are remarkably consistent. They support Piaget's notion that there is a predictable order in the sequence of stages.[10] And, on the basis of their reactions to the same conditions, babies in different places seem to think similarly. For example, a comparison of French babies and Baoulé babies in the Ivory Coast showed that the Baoulé babies, who had never seen objects such as red plastic tubes and paper clips, nevertheless tried to pass the clips through the tubes in the same way the French babies did. The two sets of babies even made the same kinds of errors.[11] And even though they had few toys, the Baoulé babies showed advances over French babies on such tasks as using instruments to increase the reach of the arm. But Baoulé babies are allowed to touch all kinds of objects, even things that Europeans consider dangerous.[12]

Most of the cross-cultural studies of Piaget's stages have focused on the transition between the second, *preoperational,* and third, *concrete-operational,* stages, particularly the attainment of the concept of conservation. The results of many of these studies are somewhat puzzling. Although older children are generally more likely to show conservation than younger children, it is not clear what to make of the apparent finding that the attainment of conservation is much delayed in many non-Western populations. Indeed, in some places, most of the adults tested do not appear to understand one or more of the conservation properties.

Can this be true? Do people in different cultures differ that much in intellectual functioning, or is there some problem with the way conservation is measured? Is it possible that an adult who just brought water from the river in a large jug and poured it into five smaller containers does not know that the quantity of water is still the same? We may also be skeptical about the findings on the formal-operational stage. Most of the studies of formal-operational thinking have found little evidence of such thinking in non-Western populations. But people in nonliterate societies surely have formal-operational thinking if they can navigate using the stars, remember how to return to camp after a 15-mile trek, or identify how people are related to each other three and more generations back.

One reason to be skeptical about the apparent findings regarding delay of conservation and formal-operational thinking is that most of the cross-cultural psychologists have taken tests developed in our own and other Western countries to measure cognitive development elsewhere.[13] This procedure puts non-Westerners at a considerable disadvantage, because they are not as familiar as Westerners with the test materials and the whole testing situation. In tests of conservation, for example, researchers have often used strange-looking glass cylinders and beakers. Some researchers who have used natively familiar materials, however, have gotten different results. Douglass Price-Williams found no difference between Tiv, in West Africa, and European children in understanding the conservation of earth, nuts, and number.[14] Also, some researchers have retested children after brief training sessions and found that they improved substantially. It would seem, then, that children anywhere can acquire the concept of conservation if they have had preparatory life experiences or appropriate training.[15]

The results of tests elsewhere on formal-operational thinking may also be questionable. Such tests ask questions dealing with content that is taught in science and mathematics classes. It should not be surprising, then, that schooled individuals usually do better than the unschooled on tests of formal-operational thinking. Where compulsory schooling is lacking, we should not expect people to do well on tests of such thinking.[16]

In trying to find out what may be universal in emotional and cognitive development, researchers have discovered some apparent differences between societies. These differences, to which we now turn, need to be explored and explained.

THE ANTHROPOLOGY OF CHILDHOOD

One thing is common in all human societies—a long period in which the young are dependent on parents and other caretakers. This is one of the most notable human characteristics that differentiates us from our closest biological relatives. Also unusual is the parental role fathers play and the long stage of life following reproduction.[17] In many animals, life ends shortly after reproduction ends. Human females typically stop being able to reproduce much earlier than males, but this gives them a long period of time to be grandmothers and help their children with their reproduction. Exactly why the long period of dependency evolved is a matter of some debate,[18] but this period of time, which we are loosely calling childhood (including here infancy and adolescence), is critical for understanding what kind of people we become. It provides a long period of time to acquire much of the complexity of human social and cultural life. Childhood is also a time when learning from nonparental figures can lead to rapid changes in ideas and behavior. Consider the changes in technology in the world today. Children are much more comfortable, as well as much more adept, with technological innovations than their parents. Children often become the teachers of their parents, showing the parents how to use the new technology.

Anthropologists interested in childhood are increasingly looking at children as agents and actors, not just as recipients of socialization. Children not only have their own culture they can tell us about, but they also have opinions, anxieties, and fears that only they can express. But their voices are often ignored, just as women's voices were often ignored in the past.[19]

It is generally agreed that our personalities are the result of an interaction between genetic inheritance and life experiences. But a considerable portion of one's life experiences, as well as one's genes, is shared with others. Parents undoubtedly exert a major influence on the way we grow up. Because family members share similar life experiences and genes, they may be somewhat similar in personality. But we have to consider why a particular family raises children the way it does. Much of the way parents rear children is influenced by their culture—by typical patterns of family life and by shared conceptions of the way to bring up children.

Socialization is a term both anthropologists and psychologists use to describe the development, through the influence of parents and other people, of patterns of behavior, and attitudes and values, in children that conform to cultural expectations. (The term **enculturation** has a similar meaning.) But, although these terms imply a mechanism to replicate culture (the "cookie-cutter" view of culture), we know that parents don't always follow societal dictates. Moreover, most parents consciously or unconsciously change with changing times, particularly as their family circumstances change. If a family no longer relies on agriculture because they now rely on wage labor, their expectations and their treatment of children will probably change.

It is not easy to determine the extent to which members of a society share conceptions about childrearing. As we look at families in our own society, we see differences in upbringing that reflect different ideas about the "right" way to raise children. Some parents seem to go along with "conventional" ideas about childrearing; others seem determined to bring up their children in ways that buck the conventional. Still, in a study of California families headed by single mothers, unmarried couples, or living in communes, researchers found that these so-called "unconventional parents" actually did not differ that much from "conventional" parents (married, living in nuclear families) compared with parents in other societies.[20] For example, even though unconventional California mothers breast-fed their children for a significantly longer period than conventional mothers did, both groups usually stopped breast-feeding after about a year, which is far below the worldwide average. In 70 percent of the world's societies, mothers typically breast-feed children for at least two years; last-born children may be weaned even later. In a few societies, such as the Chenchu of India, children typically were not weaned until they were 5 or 6 years old.[21] In the California study, no parent, conventional or unconventional, was observed to carry a baby more than 25 percent of the time, but it is common in many preindustrial societies for babies to be held more than half the day.[22] The point here is that, although some parents tried to be different, and indeed were different, they were in many respects not that different from each other when compared on a worldwide scale. But did the unconventional parents bring about culture change? The parental style of holding babies may not be that common in American culture, but it is much more common than it used to be. So although the new behaviors are not yet customary, cultural patterns have shifted.

Explaining Variation in Childhood and Beyond

When we discuss variation in how children are brought up in the following sections, there are two common types of explanation. The first has to do with general belief systems about children. Societies do not just have ideas about individual aspects of childrearing, such as how often to nurse

Children are adept at using new technology, as this young monk in Burma (Myanmar) demonstrates as he plays a video game.

and for how long, and where to put children to sleep, but societies also have their own theories about childhood. These theories suggest why societies do what they do. In heterogenous societies, different ethnic groups and different classes of people often have different theories. But what might explain these different belief systems? Some belief systems and consequently some childrearing systems may have consequences for survival. Adaptational explanations may suggest why different childrearing customs are adapted to different environments. Finally, there is the possibility that some aspects of personality have genetic or physiological explanations.

Parents' Belief Systems   In most of the world, parents do not read books about how to bring up children. Indeed, they may not consciously think at all about their behavior toward children. But parents in all cultures do have ideas about what kinds of children they want to raise and how children should be treated. Many of these ideas are culturally patterned; they have been called "ethnotheories."[23] For example, Sara Harkness and Charles Super, who studied Dutch parents and infants, found that Dutch parents believe in what they term the "three Rs"—*rust* (rest), *regelmaat* (regularity), and *reinheid* (cleanliness). Parents follow a calm and regular routine for babies, try not to overstimulate their children by giving them too many things to look at, and surprisingly, for Americans, have babies who sleep a great deal more. (At six months of age, Dutch babies slept an average of 15 hours a day compared with 13 hours for American babies.) When an American mother will think a baby is bored and give her another toy, a Dutch mother will think the baby is tired and put her to sleep.[24]

Although it is important to understand parental ethnotheories, it is also important to evaluate whether parents behave in accordance with their theories, and whether parental behaviors produce the effects that parents want. Researchers need to observe parent-child behavior, not just understand what parents say they want to do, and they need to observe outcomes in children. Some behaviors by parents and other caretakers do not have the intended effects. American parents, particularly middle-class parents, stress independence and self-reliance, but behavior observations suggest that children frequently seek attention from parents and parents reward this kind of dependency. Even countercultural parents who reject many middle-class values behave in the same ways with their children.[25]

Adaptational Explanations   Cultural anthropologists seek not only to establish connections between childrearing customs and personality traits but also to learn why those customs differ in the first place. Some anthropologists believe that childrearing practices are largely adaptive—that a society produces the kinds of personalities best suited to performance of the activities necessary for the survival of the society. As John Whiting and Irvin Child expressed it, "The economic, political and social organs of a society—the basic customs surrounding the nourishment, sheltering, and protection of its members . . . seem a likely source of influence on child training practices."[26]

The belief that childrearing practices are adaptive does not mean that societies always produce the kinds of people they need. Just as in the biological realm, where we see poor adaptations and extinctions of species and subspecies, so we may expect that societies sometimes produce personality traits that are maladapted to the requirements of living in that society. So we cannot assume that a trait must be adaptive just because it is present. We cannot come to that conclusion unless we carefully investigate whether the trait is beneficial or harmful.[27] But we do expect that most societies that have survived to be recorded have produced personality traits that are mostly adaptive.

The anthropology of childrearing involves comparison. Our own cultural conceptions begin to become apparent only when we examine other societies and their patterns of childrearing.

Possible Genetic and Physiological Influences
Some researchers have suggested that genetic or physiological differences between populations predispose them to have different personality characteristics. Daniel Freedman found differences in "temperament" in newborn babies of different ethnic groups; because he observed newborns, the differences between them were presumed to be genetic. Comparing Chinese and European American newborns with the families matched on income, number of previous children, and so on, Freedman found that European American babies cried more easily, were harder to console, and fought experimental procedures more. Chinese babies, on the other hand, seemed calmer and more adaptable. Navajo babies were similar to the Chinese, showing even more calmness.[28] Freedman also suggested that an infant's behavior can influence how the parents respond. A calm baby may encourage a calm parental response; a more active baby may encourage a more active response.[29] So, in Freedman's view, babies' genetically determined behavior can lead to ethnic differences in adult personality and caretaking styles. But we cannot rule out nongenetic explanations of babies' behavior. For example, the mother's diet or her blood pressure could affect the baby's behavior. And it may be that the baby can learn even in the womb. After all, babies in the womb apparently can hear and respond to sounds and other stimuli. Therefore, it is possible that in societies in which pregnant women are calm, their babies may have learned calmness even before they were born. Last, we still do not know if the initial differences observed in newborn babies persist to become personality differences in adulthood.

Just as the diet of the mother, including the intake of alcohol and drugs, may affect the developing fetus, the diet of infants and children may also affect their intellectual development and their behavior. Studies have shown that malnutrition is associated with lower levels of activity, less attentiveness, lack of initiative, and low tolerance of frustration. Behavior of children can change with short-term nutrition supplements. For example, Guatemalan children who were given nutritional supplements were observed to have less anxiety, more exploratoriness, and greater involvement in games than children who were not given supplements.[30] The problem of malnutrition is not just a matter

One major difference in childrearing between the West and other places is the degree to which caretakers hold infants during the day. In the United States and other Western countries, infants spend much of the day in a crib, playpen, or stroller. The Dao babies from Yunnan Province in China (on the right) spend a good deal of time in physical contact with their mother or other caretaker.

of nutrition. Other kinds of care may also be reduced. For example, caretakers of malnourished children may interact with them less than do caretakers of healthy children. As a malnourished child shows reduced activity, caretakers tend to respond to the child with lower frequency and less enthusiasm. Then the child withdraws from interaction, creating a potentially serious vicious cycle.[31] Another possible influence, which we discuss later, is how hypoglycemia may affect adult expressions of aggression.

CROSS-CULTURAL VARIATION IN CHILDREARING

In what follows, we examine some aspects of childhood that appear to vary cross-culturally.[32] When we can, we discuss possible explanations for these patterns.

Parental Responsiveness to Infants and Baby-Holding

Consider how societies vary in how quickly parents respond to an infant's needs, in other words, the degree of "indulgence." In many aspects of indulgence—amount of time holding, feeding on demand, responding to crying—industrialized societies such as the United States tend to indulge babies less than do preindustrialized societies. In contrast to those preindustrial societies in which babies are held more than half the day, sometimes almost all day, consider the United States, England, and the Netherlands, where babies may spend most of the day in devices such as playpens, rockers, swings, or cribs. It is estimated that babies are held or touched only 12 percent to 20 percent of their daytime hours in these countries and in Japan. The same pattern continues at nighttime. In most preindustrial societies, babies are much more apt to be close to another person, usually sleeping with the mother in the same bed or, if not in the same bed, in the same room. During the

day, babies are breast-fed in all preindustrial societies, usually on demand. In industrialized societies, bottle-feeding is common, and feeding is usually spaced out every few hours; in some preindustrial societies, babies are breast-fed 20 to 40 times a day. And in many preindustrial societies, people respond very quickly to an infant's crying. For example, among the Efe of the Ituri Forest in central Africa, a 3-month-old infant who cries gets a response within 10 seconds 75 percent of the time. In the United States, a caregiver deliberately *does not* respond at all about 45 percent of the time.[33]

The cross-cultural variation just described seems to reflect cultural attitudes toward childrearing. Parents in the United States say that they do not want their babies to be dependent and clingy; they want to produce independent and self-reliant children. Whether children become self-reliant because of our kind of childrearing is debatable,[34] but our attitudes about childrearing are certainly consistent with our practices.

We think of a quick response of parents to infants as "indulgence," but although many mothers respond quickly to the baby's physical needs, this does not mean that mothers interact with them when they respond, by looking at the baby in the eye, responding to babbling, or kissing and hugging them. Often the mother is doing something else while she nurses the baby.[35]

Ruth and Robert Munroe studied the effects of more versus less holding by the mother in infancy on Logoli children.[36] The Munroes had observational information on how often infants were held, and they were able to interview many of these individuals as children five years later. They were interested in seeing whether children who had been held more often by their mothers were more secure, trusting, and optimistic. So they designed a series of personality measures appropriate for young children. As a measure of optimism, they showed children smiling faces and nonsmiling faces and asked which they preferred. As measures of trust, they looked to see how long a child was willing to stay in a room with a stranger or play with new toys.

The results of the study suggest that children who were often held or carried by their mothers as infants are significantly more trusting and optimistic at age 5 than are other children. Somewhat to their surprise, the Munroes found that, although time held by other caregivers did not predict more trust and optimism, the sheer number of different people who had held the infant did predict more trust and optimism. Holding by the mother was important, but trust was even greater if a large number of other people had held the baby. One possible explanation is that a highly trusting mother is likely to allow many others to hold the baby; by doing so, she conveys trust to the baby.

Robert LeVine suggested an adaptational explanation for the frequent holding and feeding of infants and quick response of caretakers in preindustrial societies.[37] Only 1 percent of infants die in industrial societies in the first year of life, but typically more than 20 percent die in preindustrial societies. What can parents do? Parents often do not have access to modern medical care, but they can respond to a baby's fussing immediately if the baby is with them. Also, babies may be safer off the ground if there are cooking fires, dangerous insects, and snakes in the vicinity. When survival is not so much at issue, LeVine suggests, parents can safely leave babies more on their own.

High mortality of infants may also explain why mothers in many of these same societies rarely interact with their infants in more emotional ways—it may help protect them emotionally in case of the infant's early death.

We really don't know much about the long-range effects of short or long response times on the infant. As long as a baby is fed fairly regularly and held some of the time, it might make little difference to the ultimate outcome. We can be more sure that, if a baby's needs are seriously ignored, there will be negative physical and social consequences.

Parent-Child Play

In Western societies, it is commonly thought that "good" parents should provide their children with toys and play

with them frequently, starting from birth and continuing through adolescence. Parents who do not do this are viewed as deficient. Yet, cross-culturally, parent-child play is exceedingly rare except perhaps in foraging groups. It is not that play is rare. Children the world over play by themselves or with peers. Often, they make their own toys or pretend objects. Adults play too, usually games, but they don't play as often as children. And when children and adults play, they generally do so separately.[38]

Inuit mothers and babies are together for long periods in their houses when the weather is harsh. Under traditional conditions, there are often no playmates or other caretakers nearby, so perhaps it is not surprising that mothers play with their infants and young children, and make toys for them. Play with infants also occurs in many small foraging bands, but it is typically play with others beside their mothers.[39]

Lack of play with parents may be related to the same factor that probably explains high responsiveness to infant physical needs—high mortality of infants and the psychological need of parents to create emotional distance. But some societal ethnotheories suggest to parents that not playing may be better than play. The Yucatec Maya believe that "a quiet baby is a healthy baby" and, rather than stimulate babies, they are lulled to sleep whenever possible.[40] Babies are commonly thought to be "brainless" and so there is no point to interaction. On Ifaluk, in the Caroline Islands, parents say that "Infants younger than two years of age do not have any thoughts/feelings—*nunuwan*. Without nunuwan, . . . it's useless . . . talking to babies younger than two."[41]

We turn now to the period of time after infancy.

Parental Acceptance and Rejection of Children

What about the overall quality of parenting? Are there positive effects on personality when parents show love, warmth, and affection to their children and negative effects when parents are indifferent or hostile to their children?

Children the world over play, sometimes with toys they make themselves.

These questions are difficult to investigate cross-culturally because cultures vary in the ways feeling is expressed. If love and affection are not expressed in the same ways, outsiders may misinterpret parental behavior. Nevertheless, Ronald Rohner and his colleagues did extensive work on the effects of parental acceptance and rejection on children after infancy. In a cross-cultural comparison of 101 societies, using measures based on ethnographic materials, Rohner found that children tend to be hostile and aggressive when they are neglected and not treated affectionately by their parents. In societies in which children tend to be rejected, adults seem to view life and the world as unfriendly, uncertain, and hostile.[42] A large number of other studies have compared individuals in different cultures to see if the cross-cultural findings were supported. In general, they were. In addition to finding the world more unfriendly and hostile, individuals who think they were rejected are likely to be hostile and aggressive, emotionally unresponsive or unstable, and have negative evaluations of themselves.[43]

Under what conditions is parental rejection likely in childhood? The Rohner study suggests that rejection is likely where mothers get no relief from child care; when fathers and grandparents play a role in child care, rejection is less likely. Foraging societies (those dependent on wild food resources) tend to show warmth and affection to their children. More complex societies are less likely to be affectionate to their children.[44] It is not clear why this should be, but perhaps parental rejection is more likely where parents have less leisure time. Less leisure time may make parents more tired and irritable and therefore have less patience with their children. As we noted in the chapter on economic systems, leisure time probably decreases as cultural complexity increases. More complex societies, which rely on intensive agriculture, also tend to have more economic uncertainty. Not only do they tend to have more risk of famines and food shortages, but they also tend to have social inequality. In societies with social classes, many families may not have enough food and money to satisfy their needs, and this factor can also produce frustration in the parents. Whatever the reasons for parental rejection, it seems to perpetuate itself: Children who were rejected tend to reject their own children.

Compliance or Assertiveness

Herbert Barry, Irvin Child, and Margaret Bacon cross-culturally investigated the possibility that child-training practices are adapted to the economic requirements of a society. Such requirements, they theorized, might explain why some societies strive to develop "compliant" (responsible, obedient, nurturant) children, whereas others aim more for "assertiveness" (independence, self-reliance, and achievement).[45] The cross-cultural results indicated that agricultural and herding societies are likely to stress responsibility and obedience, whereas hunting and gathering societies tend to stress self-reliance and individual assertiveness. The investigators suggested that agricultural and herding societies cannot afford departures from established routine, because departures might jeopardize the food supply for long periods. Such societies, therefore, are

Children in many societies learn a lot by imitation as well as by instruction.

likely to emphasize compliance with tradition. Departures from routine in a hunter-gatherer society cannot cause much damage to a food supply that has to be collected anew almost every day. So hunter-gatherers can afford to emphasize individual initiative.

Although our own society relies on food production and has large stores of accumulated food, we seem more like hunter-gatherers in emphasizing individual initiative. Are we, then, exceptions to the Barry et al. findings? Not really. Hardly any of us are farmers (in the United States, less than 2 percent of the total population is still on the farm), and most of us expect that we can "forage" in the supermarket or "store" just about anytime. Perhaps more important is the fact that our highly commercial economy, with most people dwelling in or near cities, requires us to compete to get jobs to make a living. In our kind of economy, then, individual initiative is important too. Consider the results of a cross-national comparison of eight countries in which the researchers asked parents what quality they most wanted their school-age children to have. Parents in the more rural countries (Indonesia, Philippines, and Thailand) seldom mentioned independence and self-reliance but those in the more urban countries (Korea, Singapore, and the United States) did.[46]

Attitudes Towards Aggression

Societies also differ considerably in their attitudes toward aggression in children. Some societies actively encourage children to be aggressive, not only to each other but even to the parents. Among the Xhosa of southern Africa, 2- or 3-year-old boys will be prodded to hit each other in the face and women look on laughing. Similar behavior is described for the Gapun of Papua New Guinea; even raising a knife to an older sibling is rewarded.[47] Yanomamö boys of the Venezuelan-Brazilian Amazon are encouraged to be aggressive and are rarely punished for hitting either their parents or the girls in the village. One father, for example, lets his son Ariwari

> beat him on the face and head to express his anger and temper, laughing and commenting on his ferocity. Although Ariwari is only about 4 years old, he has already learned that the appropriate response to a flash of anger is to strike someone with his hand or with an object, and it is not uncommon for him to give his father a healthy smack in the face whenever something displeases him. He is frequently goaded into hitting his father by teasing, being rewarded by gleeful cheers of assent from his mother and from the other adults in the household.[48]

In contrast, the Semai of central Malaya are famous for their timidity. Robert Dentan reports that they say that they do not get angry.[49] Whereas other societies clearly and actively encourage aggression, the Semai communicate nonviolence in more subtle ways. They say, in fact, that they do not teach children. The Semai expect children to be nonviolent and are shocked when they are not. When a child loses his or her temper, an adult will simply cart the child off. The Semai do not physically punish a child's

aggression, and this approach may be one of the most important teaching devices of all. With such teaching—by example—a child rarely sees an aggressive model and thus has no aggression to imitate.[50] In comparison, hardly any North American parents would encourage children to hit them in the face or encourage them to hit other children. Yet many probably use physical punishment sometimes, and many feel that boys especially should "stand up for themselves" if another child provokes a fight.

With regard to aggression, research has shown that children who are physically punished when they are aggressive (the parents trying to minimize aggression) actually exhibit more aggression than children who are not physically punished. Children who are hit may learn not to hit their parents and other caretakers, but the aggression caretakers exhibit seems to be a model for children's aggressive behavior. If children see a parent or other caretaker acting aggressively, they may conclude that it is okay for them to act aggressively.[51]

A society's involvement in war cross-culturally predicts parental encouragement of aggression, particularly in boys. Socialization for aggression appears to decrease after a society is pacified or forced to stop fighting.[52]

Task Assignment

In our society, young children are not expected to help much with chores. If they do have chores, such as tidying up their rooms, they are not likely to affect the welfare of the family or its ability to survive. In contrast, in some societies known to anthropology, young children, even 3- and 4-year-olds, are expected to help prepare food, care for animals, and carry water and firewood, as well as clean. A child between 5 years and 8 years of age may even be given the responsibility of caring for an infant or toddler for much of the day while the mother works in the fields.[53] What are the effects of such task assignment on personality development?

We now have evidence from more than 10 cultures that children who regularly babysit are more nurturant—that is, offer more help and support to others—than are other children, even when the children who babysit are not babysitting. Some of this evidence comes from a project known as the Six Cultures study, in which different research teams observed children's behavior in Kenya (Nyansongo), Mexico, India, the Philippines, Okinawa, and the United States (New England).[54] Ruth and Robert Munroe collected data on children's behavior in four other cultures that show the same relationship between babysitting and nurturant behavior; the Munroes' data come from Kenya (Logoli), Nepal, Belize, and American Samoa.[55] Clearly, children who babysit infrequently are less attuned to others' needs than are children who babysit often.

Why might task assignment affect the behaviors of children? One possibility is that children learn certain behaviors during performance of the task, and these behaviors become habitual. For example, a responsible babysitter is supposed to offer help. Mothers might directly instruct the babysitter to make sure that happens. But there is probably also an intrinsic satisfaction in doing a job well. For example, it is pleasurable to see an infant smile and laugh, but it is unpleasant to hear a baby cry. We might therefore expect that a child who is assigned babysitting would learn that comforting a baby brings its own rewards.[56]

Children's Settings

Children who are assigned many tasks may spend their day in different kinds of settings, and these settings may indirectly influence behavior. For example, children who are asked to do many household chores are apt to be around both adults and younger children. Children who are assigned few or no tasks are freer to play with their age-mates. Beatrice Whiting suggests that one of the most powerful socializing influences on children is the type of setting they are placed in and the "cast of characters" there.[57] How does the setting influence a child's behavior? We have already noted that being around younger children may make older children more nurturant. Aggressive behaviors also appear to be influenced by who is in the child's setting. Results from the Six Cultures project suggest that children tend to be more aggressive the more they are in the company of other children of roughly the same age. In contrast, children tend to inhibit aggression when adults are on the scene.[58] Boys usually exhibit more aggression than girls. Part of that difference may be due to the fact that girls are generally assigned more work in and around the home (where adults are), whereas boys are

more often free to play with their peers. Parents may not be deliberately trying to inculcate certain behaviors, but they may produce certain behaviors by arranging the settings in which children spend their time.

Schooling One of the most important settings for children in some societies is school. Most researchers focus on the parents when they investigate how children are brought up. But in our own and other societies, children may spend a substantial part of their time in school from the age of 3 or so. What influence does school have on children's social behavior and on how they think as measured by tests? To investigate the effect of schooling, researchers have compared children or adults who have not gone to school with those who have. All of this research has been done in societies that do not have compulsory schooling; otherwise, we could not compare the schooled with the unschooled. We know relatively little about the influence of school on social behavior. In contrast, we know more about how schooling influences performance on cognitive tests.

Schooling clearly predicts "superior" performance on many cognitive tests, and within the same society, schooled individuals will generally do better than the unschooled on those tests. So, for example, unschooled individuals in non-Western societies are not as likely as schooled individuals to perceive depth in two-dimensional pictures, do not perform as well on tests of memory, are not as likely to classify items in certain ways, and do not display evidence of formal-operational thinking.[59] But schooling does not

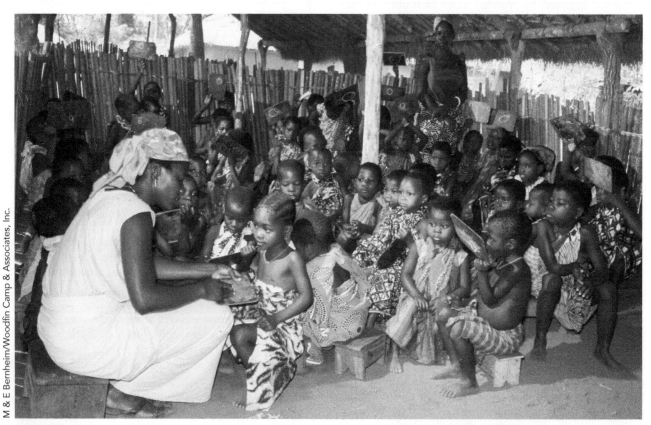

Attending school has become customary in many parts of the world, as among the Baoulé of the Ivory Coast. Schooling seems to affect cognitive development, but we do not know exactly why or how.

M & E Bernheim/Woodfin Camp & Associates, Inc.

In many societies, children work. Kurdish boys in Iraq herd the family's sheep.

AP Wide World Photos

always produce superior performance on tests of inferential reasoning.[60]

Why does schooling have these effects? Although it is possible that something about schooling creates higher levels of cognitive thinking in some respects, there are other possible explanations. The observed differences may be due to the advantages that schoolchildren have because of their experiences in school, advantages that have nothing to do with general cognitive ability. For example, consider research that asks people to classify or group drawings of geometric shapes that belong together. Suppose a person is shown three cards—a red circle, a red triangle, and a white circle—and is asked which two are most alike. A person could choose to classify in terms of color or in terms of shape. In the United States, young children usually classify by color, and they classify more often by shape as they get older. Many psychologists assume that classification by color is more "concrete" and classification by shape or function is more "abstract." Unschooled adults in many parts of Africa sort by color, not by shape. Does this mean that they are classifying less abstractly? Not necessarily. It may just be that unschooled Africans classify differently because they are likely to be unfamiliar with the test materials (drawings on paper, geometric shapes).

How can people classify "abstractly" (e.g., by shape) if they have never had the experience of handling or seeing shapes that are drawn in two dimensions? Is it likely that they would classify things as triangles if they had never seen a three-pointed figure with straight sides? In contrast, consider how much time teachers in the United States spend drilling children on various geometric shapes. People who are familiar with certain materials may for that reason alone do better on cognitive tests that use those materials.[61]

A comparative study of Liberian rice farmers in West Africa and U.S. undergraduates also illustrates the point that choice of materials may influence research results. The comparison involved a set of materials familiar to the rice farmers—bowls of rice—and a set of materials familiar to the undergraduates—geometric cards. Rice farmers appeared to classify more "abstractly" than undergraduates when they were asked to classify rice, and undergraduates seemed to classify more "abstractly" than rice farmers when they classified geometric cards.[62]

Schooled individuals may also enjoy an advantage on many cognitive tests just because they are familiar with tests and the way tests ask them to think of new situations. For example, consider the reaction of an unschooled person in central Asia who was asked the following question by a Russian psychologist interested in measuring logical thinking: "In the Far North where there is snow, all bears are white. Novaya Zemlya is in the Far North and there is always snow there. What color are the bears there?" The reply was, "We don't talk about what we haven't seen." Such a reply was typical of unschooled individuals; they did not even try to answer the question because it was not part of their experience.[63] Clearly, we cannot judge whether people think logically if they do not want to play a cognitive game.

Much research needs to be done on exactly how and why schooling affects cognition. Is it important which specific things are taught? Is it important to be asked to attend to questions that are out of context? Is being literate a factor? This last question was the subject of research among the Vai of Liberia, who had a somewhat unusual situation in that schooling and literacy were not completely confounded. The Vai had an indigenous script learned outside of school. Thus, researchers Sylvia Scribner and Michael Cole were able to see how Vai individuals who were literate but not formally schooled compared with others who were formally schooled (and literate) and those who were unschooled (and illiterate). They found some, but relatively minor, effects of literacy itself; the number of years of schooling affected cognitive test performance much more. Similar results come from a study of the Cree of northern Ontario who have their own syllabic script learned outside of school.[64] These comparisons suggest that some other aspects of schooling are more important than literacy as determinants of cognitive performance.

By studying other societies where schooling is not universal, we may be better able to understand just what role schooling plays in cognitive and other development. That schooling makes for so much difference in cognitive

applied anthropology

Schools: Values and Expectations

Most people think of schools as teaching skills such as reading and writing and subjects such as history, math, biology, or social science. But schools also convey much more about the society and individuals' places in it. They do not just teach content. We focus here on cultural values and expectations.

Joseph Tobin, David Wu, and Dana Davidson videotaped preschool classroom scenes in Japan, China, and the United States. In each country, they asked children, teachers, parents, and school administrators to comment on the scenes in all three countries. We can get a feel for how different values are implicitly taught in each country by reviewing the comments.

When individuals in the United States viewed the Japanese tape, two things generally bothered them. One was the fact that children in Japan often did the same things simultaneously as a group. For example, the teacher showed what to fold first and subsequently to make an origami bird figure, and the children followed along. Parents and teachers in the United States said that children should have more choice in what to do and how to do it. The second

thing that bothered people in the United States, as well as in China, was that the teacher in Japan appeared to ignore what we might consider "unruly" behavior by the children. For example, when children got restless during a group workbook activity, they would leave their seats, joke with friends, or go to the bathroom. In the tape, a particularly troublesome boy talked loudly, sometimes purposely hurt other children, and threw things around, but the teacher seemed to ignore these behaviors. People in the United States and China thought that the teacher should try to do something in such situations. In Japan, however, most of the teachers preferred not to call attention to, or single out, a troublesome child. Japanese teachers expect such a child eventually to behave more appropriately, and they encourage the other children to exert social pressure in that direction. In Lois Peak's words: "Learning to go to school in Japan is primarily defined as training in group life."

Most of the activities in the Chinese preschool were highly structured. For example, the first task of the day was building with blocks, but in contrast to the style at the

Japanese preschool, the children in China were expected to complete the task on their own and to do so in silence. If they spoke, the teacher reprimanded them. They used a picture as a guide for what to do. When they were done, the teachers checked their work. If they got it right, they took it apart and rebuilt it; if they got it wrong, they were asked to correct it. An arithmetic lesson followed. Children then ate the lunch that was brought for them into the classroom. Teachers monitored the lunch to make sure that the children ate all their food and ate in silence. After an afternoon nap, the children listened to a patriotic story and then had relay races, which were followed by 15 minutes of free play. Supper was served at 5:00 P.M. and parents came at 6:00. In seeing the videotapes, Americans and Japanese were bothered by the rigidity and "overcontrol" of the children and by the lack of privacy in their communal bathroom.

In the U.S. preschool, in Honolulu, as in Japan, parents brought their children at different times, but some parents stayed with the child for as long as a half hour. Compared with the other preschools, the U.S.

performance raises the serious issue of how much of what we observe about child development in our society and in other Western societies is simply a function of what children are taught in school. After all, children who grow up in this society not only get older each year, they also go one year further in school. Schools are not just places to learn a particular curriculum. Children learn to interact with one another and with adults who are not parents and family. Therefore, we might expect that schools not only shape cognition but also convey important cultural attitudes, values, and appropriate ways of behaving toward others (see the box "Schools: Values and Expectations").

Schooling does seem to predict having a personality trait we call "patience." The more schooling you have, the more patience you have. In a study conducted among the Tsimane, a horticultural people living in the Bolivian Amazon, patience or a tolerance for delayed gratification is associated with a wide range of advantages, including higher income, more wealth, and better health. These positive

outcomes may be partly the result of respect for authority, obedience, and conformity, which schooling may instill.[65]

PSYCHOLOGICAL VARIATION IN ADULTHOOD

So far, we have focused on the anthropology of childhood. But there are characteristics of adults (as well as children) that appear to vary as well. Some of these concepts, such as ideas about the self, may shape childrearing as well.

Concepts of the Self Anthropologists have begun to study different cultural ideas of personhood or concept of the "self." Many have concluded that the concept of self in many non-Western societies is quite different from the Western conception. Clifford Geertz described the Western conception of the person as "bounded, unique, . . . a dynamic center of awareness, emotion, judgment, and action organized into a distinctive whole."[66] He claimed, preschool emphasized individual participation and individualized activity. For example, "show and tell" was voluntary; sometimes only three kids decided to get up and talk. In an activity involving a felt board, each child was asked to add something to the board. Much of the rest of the day was spent in "learning centers"; the teachers helped the children decide which center they would like to go to. Children started at one activity but could change if they wished. Even lunch was more individual. All children took their lunch boxes to a big table where they all ate and talked animatedly. The U.S. teacher, in contrast to the Japanese teacher, intervened when a child misbehaved, such as when one boy grabbed a block from another. Without raising her voice, the teacher asked the two children to talk to each other about the disagreement. She resorted to a "time-out" (a period of isolation) when the dispute was not settled by talking.

Even though they do not teach values explicitly, these preschools clearly convey values. The value of the individual appears to be stressed most in the U.S. preschool, where most of the daily activities allowed individual choice of some kind. In both Japan and China, group activities predominated, although the Japanese preschool allowed flexible arrival times, more free play, and more freedom to talk or move about than the Chinese preschool. Second

is the source of control. The Japanese teachers relied informally on the group to control the children's behavior. For example, after nine months, the unruly boy sat by himself at lunch; the other children did not want to sit with him. In contrast, the Chinese teachers saw to it that the children behaved like others in the group by exerting strong control over the children's behavior. The U.S. teachers also intervened in response to unruly behavior.

Cultural values are not unchanging. For example, although many Japanese educational administrators thought that the Japanese preschool was quite "Japanese" in style, and therefore satisfactory, a considerable number of Japanese parents and teachers were critical of the school and said there were "better" schools in Japan that were more like the U.S. preschool. And some Japanese thought that more attention should be paid to the individual needs of troubled children. When some Chinese saw the tapes of the Chinese school, they complained that it was too "old-fashioned."

Recent research also shows how much cultural expectations shape school performance. Most of this research has focused on minority students. Most of them are not often expected to do well by their teachers and others because of cultural stereotypes. Indeed, in most tests in school, these students do less well. The important

question is whether stereotyped expectations hamper performance, or whether performance has to do with factors having nothing to do with school. Many experiments have confirmed that, even after controlling for factors like family wealth, even subtle reminders of cultural stereotypes cause performance to suffer. The cues can be as simple as saying that the test measures intelligence (in contrast to the control group told that they will not be evaluated on their performance) or asking the person for their "race" (in contrast to not asking) as one of a number of background questions.

What can be done to improve performance? Some suggestions are to tell students that human abilities and skills are changeable, not fixed; another is to give them challenging work that conveys that they are capable. One of the most fascinating studies was a comparison of African American and European American students before and after Barack Obama was elected President of the United States. Before the election, the African Americans, even though matched on ability, did worse than the European Americans. After the election, the differences practically disappeared. This study strongly suggests that conditions in the larger society affect performance.

Sources: Tobin et al. 1989; Peak 1991; Lock 2009; Aronson 2002; Nisbett 2009.

---

on the basis of his fieldwork in Java, Bali, and Morocco, that those societies have very different conceptions of a person, not only different from each other but quite different from the Western conception. For example, Geertz said that the Balinese describe a person as having many different roles, like an actor who plays different characters. The unique characteristics of a person are not emphasized; what is emphasized are the "masks" people wear and the "parts" they play.

Geertz focused on the variation and uniquenesses in different cultures' conceptions of the self. But other scholars think that there are recognizable and predictable patterns in this variation. One of the most talked-about patterns is the Western emphasis on the self as an autonomous individual and the non-Western emphasis on the relations a person has with others.[67] Labels used to describe such Western and non-Western cultural differences are "individualism" versus "holism" or "collectivism," "egocentric" versus "sociocentric," and the like.[68] For example,

the Japanese concept of self is often described as "relational" or "situational"; people exist in networks of relationships and the ideal person has the ability to shift easily from one social situation to another.[69]

There are two major objections to the idea that the Western sense of self should be contrasted with the non-Western. The first is that studies of other cultures have suggested other dimensions of variation besides "individualism" versus "collectivism." For example, the traditional Inuit concept *inummarik*, "a genuine person," seems to include a lifelong process of ecological involvement—interacting with animals and the environment as well as people.[70] A culture's concept of self, then, may include other dimensions besides individual versus collective. A second objection to the Western/non-Western contrast is that it may not be based on adequate evidence. As Melford Spiro pointed out, it is necessary to find out how a sample of individuals in a society actually view themselves. The ideal in the culture might be different from the actual.[71]

For example, individuals even in the United States do not just describe themselves as autonomous. When Jane Wellenkamp and Douglas Hollan interviewed Americans about their feelings about the death of someone close, they got statements about autonomy (such as "I can stand on my own" and "At least you have yourself"), but they also got statements reflecting interdependence ("You realize that they're gone and that a part of you has gone with them").[72] This is not to say that the autonomy of the individual isn't important in the United States. It is. But individuals also realize that they are interdependent. How we actually think of ourselves may not be so different from how people in other societies think of themselves.

If a cultural theme such as individualism is important, societies may express or convey this theme in many ways. It may start right after birth, as when a baby is put in a crib or bassinet to sleep alone rather than with someone in the family. Young children may be given their "own" toys. They may go to preschool or day care, where they are encouraged to make their own choices (see the Box "Schools: Values and Expectations"). And schools for older children may require individual, not group, achievement. Does the theme of individualism have to be taught explicitly? Probably not, because it can be conveyed in so many different ways.

Perceptual Style: Field Independence or Dependence

Might the environment influence the way people in different societies think and perceive (interpret sensory information)? John Berry suggested that different perceptual and cognitive processes may be selected and trained for in societies that differ in their adaptational requirements.[73] Berry's particular focus was on what psychologists call *field independence* and *field dependence*.[74] Field independence means being able to isolate a part of a situation from the whole. The opposite perceptual style, field dependence, means that parts are not perceived separately; rather, the whole situation is focused on.

The contrast between field independence and field dependence may become clear if we look at some of the ways they are measured. In the rod-and-frame test, a person seated in a darkened room is asked to adjust a tilted luminous rod so that it is upright within a luminous frame. Individuals are considered field dependent if they adjust the rod to line up with the frame when the frame is tilted. Individuals are considered field independent if they adjust the rod to a truly upright position even though the frame is tilted. Field independence is also measured by the ability to see a simply drawn figure when it is included but somewhat hidden in a more complex picture.

Why should some societies produce people who are more field independent or dependent? Berry suggested that people who rely a lot on hunting must be field independent to be successful, because hunting requires the visual isolation of animals from their backgrounds. Hunters must also learn to visualize themselves in precise relationship to their surroundings so that they can find

animals and get back home. In a comparative study of communities in four societies, Berry found that degree of reliance on hunting predicted field independence. The more a community relied on hunting, the more the individuals showed field independence on tests. Those communities more reliant on agriculture tested out to be more field dependent. How might hunters develop field independence as a cognitive style? Different child training might be involved. In the United States and a few other societies, it has been found that children whose parents are very strict are less likely to develop field independence than are children whose parents are lenient.[75] It seems that emotional independence from parents is necessary for the perceptual style of field independence to develop. No matter what the precise mechanism is, we know from the Barry et al. (1959) study that hunter-gatherers are more likely to train children to be individualistic and assertive, and that agriculturalists and herders are more likely to train their children to be compliant. So hunter-gatherers may cause their children to develop field independence by stressing emotional independence in childhood.

Investigations have shown that there are gender differences in the United States and other (but not all) cultures in degree of field dependence versus independence.[76] Perhaps these differences reflect the fact that girls are encouraged to be obedient and responsible and boys to be independent and self-reliant. And perhaps, too, gender differences in field dependence versus independence may be related to the fact that girls work more in and around the home, close to others. If so, we might expect that girls more field dependent are also likely to have a morality that stresses interpersonal concerns (see the box "Do Women Have a Different Morality?").

Expression of Aggression

Leaving aside behavior during warfare, which we discuss further in the chapter on political life, societies vary markedly in the degree to which adults express anger and act aggressively toward others. Not surprisingly, many of the societies that encourage children to be more aggressive also appear to have more aggressive adults. The Semai and the Yanomamö are good examples. The Semai are famous for their timidity and have never been described as hostile.[77] The Yanomamö, on the other hand, frequently show aggression within a village. Shouting and threatening to obtain demands are frequent, as are wife-beatings and bloody fights with clubs.[78] Cross-culturally, all kinds of aggression tend to co-occur, so much so that many researchers discuss a "culture of violence."[79] What drives this pattern is debatable, but as we discussed earlier, there is some evidence that when war ceases, socialization for aggression ceases. So, adults who grow up in more peaceful times may exhibit less aggression of all types.

Whether adults express aggression freely may also be related to a group's economy. In a comparative study of personality differences between pastoralists and farmers in four societies in East Africa, Robert Edgerton found

new perspectives on gender

Do Women Have a Different Morality?

There is widespread agreement that as children mature they develop a sense of self that distinguishes themselves from others. But what kind of sense of self do they develop? Some researchers suggest that different cultures have different conceptions of the self. In particular, the West seems to emphasize the separateness of each person; other cultures emphasize the connection of the self to others.

Several psychologists, including Carol Gilligan, proposed that women, in contrast to men, are more likely to develop a sense of themselves that involves social interaction and connectedness. Gilligan proposed that women also tend to have a different sense of morality, one that is more apt to consider the feelings of others and the preservation of relationships. Men, she suggested, are more likely to emphasize rules or principles that are applied equally and impartially to individuals. Is there any substantial evidence for her claims about gender differences in morality?

Some studies have interviewed females and males and explicitly compared their statements about themselves and about solutions to moral dilemmas. The responses are coded for the degree to which the self is described as "autonomous" or

as "connected" and the degree to which responses to moral dilemmas are couched in "justice" or "care" terms. "Well, you have to think about whether it is right . . . or whether it is wrong" is an example of a statement couched in "justice" terms. "I wanted them to get along. . . . I didn't want anybody getting in fights or anything" is an example of a statement couched in "care" terms.

So far the research, conducted mostly in the United States among well-educated populations, suggests that, although women more often than men do tend to describe themselves as "connected" and more often display a "caring" morality, there is no absolute separation between the genders. Most people, regardless of gender, give "connected" and "autonomous" statements about themselves, and most people express "justice" and "care" concerns with regard to moral dilemmas. If there is a difference between the genders in a culture, it is only in tendency, not in a completely different approach to morality.

Although moral development in childhood has been studied in several cultures, there is relatively little research that directly addresses the issues raised by Gilligan. To be sure, research by David Stimpson and his

colleagues compared educated university students in Korea, China, Thailand, and the United States and found support for the idea that women were more concerned with affection, compassion, and sensitivity to the needs of others, as compared with men. But that study did not specifically ask for responses to moral dilemmas. Some other researchers suggest that the picture may be more complicated, because concepts of morality may vary quite a bit from the two types described by Gilligan. For example, Joan Miller found that middle-class Hindu Indians generally had a very strong sense of interpersonal morality compared with people in the United States. But the Hindu Indian morality was not based on individual concern for others; rather, their responses to moral dilemmas were strongly influenced by considerations of social duty. And Miller found no gender differences in responses.

All we can conclude so far is that the genders may have somewhat different moralities in some cultures. We need more research on how morality may vary by gender as well as by culture.

Sources: Gilligan 1982; Lyons 1988; Gilligan and Attanucci 1988; Stimpson et al. 1992; J. G. Miller 1994.

that pastoralists were more willing than farmers to express aggression openly. As a matter of fact, pastoralists seemed freer to express all kinds of emotion, including sadness and depression. Although farmers displayed reluctance to express overt aggression themselves, they were quite willing to talk about witchcraft and sorcery practiced by others. How can we explain these personality differences? Edgerton proposed that the lifestyle of farmers, who must spend their lives cooperating with a fixed set of neighbors, requires them to contain their feelings, particularly hostile feelings. (But these feelings may not go away, and so the farmers might "see them" in others.) Pastoralists, on the other hand, can more readily move away in conflict situations because they are not as dependent on a fixed set of individuals. Not only might they be able to express aggression more openly, but such aggression may even be adaptive. The pastoralists studied

by Edgerton engaged frequently in raids and counter-raids involving cattle stealing, and the most aggressive individuals may have had the best chance of surviving the skirmishes.[80]

Physiological (not necessarily genetic) differences between populations may also be responsible for some personality differences in adulthood. Such differences could also have an effect in childhood. Research by Ralph Bolton suggests that a physiological condition known as hypoglycemia may be responsible for the high levels of aggression recorded among the Qolla of Peru.[81] (People with hypoglycemia experience a big drop in their blood sugar level after they ingest food.) Bolton found that about 55 percent of the males he tested in a Qolla village had hypoglycemia. Moreover, those men with the most aggressive life histories tended to be hypoglycemic. Whether hypoglycemia is induced by genetic or environmental factors or both, the condition can be alleviated by a change in diet.

PSYCHOLOGICAL EXPLANATIONS OF CULTURAL VARIATION

Psychological anthropologists, as well as other social scientists, have also investigated the possible *consequences* of psychological variation, particularly how psychological characteristics may help us understand certain aspects of cultural variation. For example, David McClelland's research suggests that societies that develop high levels of achievement motivation (a personality trait) in individuals will be likely to experience high rates of economic growth. Economic decline, McClelland suggested, will follow a decline in achievement motivation.[82] Differences in achievement motivation may even have political consequences. For example, Robert LeVine, who studied achievement motivation in three Nigerian ethnic groups, noted that the traditionally more influential groups may have resented the entry of one of them, the Ibo, into higher education and into many emerging professions.[83] Soon after LeVine's book was published, the friction between the rival groups escalated into rebellion by the Ibo and the defeat of a separatist Ibo state named Biafra.

Psychological factors may also help us explain why some aspects of culture are statistically associated with others. Abram Kardiner originally suggested that cultural patterns influence personality development through child training and that the resulting personality characteristics in turn influence the culture. He believed that **primary institutions**, such as family organization and subsistence techniques, give rise to certain personality characteristics. Once the personality is formed, though, it can have its own impact on culture. In Kardiner's view, the **secondary institutions** of society, such as religion and art, are shaped by common—he called them *basic*—personality characteristics. Presumably, these secondary institutions have little relation to the adaptive requirements of the society. But they may reflect and express the motives, conflicts, and anxieties of typical members of the society.[84] Thus, if we can understand why certain typical personality characteristics develop, we might, for example, be able to understand why certain kinds of art are associated with certain kinds of social systems.

Whiting and Child used the phrase **personality integration of culture** to refer to the possibility that an understanding of personality might help us explain connections between primary and secondary institutions.[85] As examples of how personality may integrate culture, we turn to some suggested explanations for cultural preferences in games and for the custom of male initiation ceremonies.

In a cross-cultural study conducted by John Roberts and Brian Sutton-Smith, cultural preferences for particular types of games were found to be related to certain aspects of childrearing. The researchers suggested that these associations are a consequence of conflict generated in many people in a society by particular types of childrearing pressures. Games of strategy, for example, are associated with child training that emphasizes obedience. Roberts and Sutton-Smith proposed that severe obedience training can create a conflict between the need to obey and the desire not to obey, a conflict that arouses anxiety. Such anxiety may or may not manifest itself against the person who instigates the anxiety. But the conflict and the aggression itself can be played out on the miniature battlefields of games of strategy such as chess or the Japanese game of *go*.[86] Politically complex and socially stratified societies are particularly likely to emphasize obedience, so it is not surprising that such societies are most likely to have games of strategy.[87] Similarly, games of chance may represent defiance of societal expectations of docility and responsibility. The general interpretation suggested by Roberts and Sutton-Smith is that

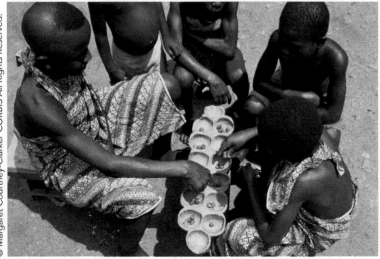

Children in Ghana playing *mancala*, a game of strategy that is now also played in North America.

players—and societies—initially become curious about games, learn them, and ultimately develop high involvement in them because of the particular kinds of psychological conflicts that are handled or expressed, but not necessarily resolved, by the games.

The possible role of psychological processes in connecting different aspects of culture is also illustrated in cross-cultural work on initiation ceremonies for boys at adolescence. In the ceremonies, boys are subjected to painful tests of manhood, usually including genital operations, which indicate the boys' transition to adulthood. Roger Burton and John Whiting found that initiation ceremonies tend to occur in male-oriented societies in which infant boys initially sleep exclusively with their mothers. They suggest that initiation rites in such societies are intended to break a conflict in sex identity. The conflict is believed to exist because boys in these societies would initially identify with their mothers, who exercise almost complete control over them in infancy. Later, when the boys discover that men dominate the society, they will identify secondarily with their fathers. This sex-role conflict is assumed to be resolved by the initiation ceremony, which demonstrates a boy's manhood, thus strengthening the secondary identification.[88]

Some researchers feel that psychological explanations for variation in culture may help us understand why gods in some societies are viewed as mean, why artists in some societies prefer repetitive designs, and why strangers in some societies tend to be the "bad ones" in folktales. Psychological anthropologists often assume that conceptions of gods and artistic creations are not constrained by any objective realities, so people are free to create them as they wish. In other words, people may tend to project their personalities—their feelings, their conflicts, their concerns—into these areas. This idea of projection underlies what psychologists call **projective tests**. In such tests, which presumably reveal personality characteristics, subjects are given stimuli that are purposely ambiguous. So, for example, in the Thematic Apperception Test (TAT), subjects are shown vague drawings and are asked what they think is going on in them, what happened before, and how they think things will turn out. Because the test materials give few instructions about what to say, it is assumed that subjects will interpret the materials by projecting their own personalities. Some aspects of religion and the arts may be similar to TAT stories and may express or reflect the common personality characteristics of a society.

INDIVIDUALS AS AGENTS OF CULTURAL CHANGE

Many of the processes we have been talking about involve culture change. For instance, in the section on expression of aggression, we referred to research by Edgerton, suggesting that pastoralists may be freer than farmers to express their aggressiveness as well as other emotions because they can move away in conflict situations. Farmers have to live their whole lives in close proximity to neighbors. The research suggests that, if pastoralists settle down and start farming, they may learn that it is important for them to repress some of their emotions. But even if individuals don't change when they settle down, change may occur in the next generation because the less aggressive may be imitated if they are perceived to be more successful. Either of these possibilities points to the importance of the individual in bringing about change. Ethnographers are focusing more explicitly now on how individual *agency* may bring about change.

Let us look at a few examples of how women are helping to bring about change in strongly patriarchal societies.

Large-scale changes in China have been pushed by the government since 1949, including the introduction of new marriage laws, the attack on patrilineal ideology, and the introduction of public ownership. But Yunxiang Yan, who studied women in rural north China, points out that the efforts of young women themselves, particularly those transitioning from teenager to young daughter-in-law, have contributed substantially to change. Young women traditionally had little to say about whom they married, the negotiations that took place before marriage, or when their husband would split from his extended family and form a new household. Because they were going to move into their husband's household after marriage, young women traditionally had little status in the household in which they grew up. In their husband's household, they became the in-marrying stranger. Yan observes that she began to notice from the complaints of women about their daughters and daughters-in-laws, and men's complaints about women, that young women were bringing about change. The ability of a woman to veto a marriage proposal was recognized in law in the early 1950s, but it was young women that used their veto power, sometimes repeatedly, that brought about change. Now women may select a husband. Young women have become more expressive emotionally and expect a more passionate and intimate relationship with their potential spouses and later with their husbands. Premarital sex has now become common. Young women have also pushed transformation of the custom of bridewealth (the gift of goods from the groom's family to the bride's family). They began to go with the groom to pick out items, they demanded that gifts be converted into cash to be given to the bride, and they started to engage in the negotiations between the families. Finally, young women have pushed for an early division of the extended family, so that less and less time is spent in the husband's family's household.[89] But why some women push more for change than other women is a question still to be investigated.

The world over, higher education is almost always associated with lower fertility. Jennifer Johnson-Hanks wanted to understand at the individual level why this may come about. Her research took place among the Beti in southern Cameroon. As in China, social organization was oriented around males. The Beti value the development of each individual child's potential, and in recent times with the introduction of schools, they value education for their children. School is not free, so parents have to sacrifice to send their children to school. Schoolgirls stress that schooling gives them more options, not only to get better paying jobs in the future, but also to have more freedom and less dependency on a husband. Schoolgirls emphasize that schooling allows them to be honorable. Honor brings privilege and prestige, but the concept also involves becoming more rational and controlling choices, including being more choosy about men with whom to be involved, and controlling the conditions under which they become mothers. It is not that young women believe in abstaining from sex—sex is viewed as natural and important, but young women employ strategies to delay motherhood. These include periodic abstinence, aborting pregnancies, and giving up children to fosterage if they are not ready to be mothers. Rationality also entails knowing that you cannot have a lot of children if there are not enough resources.[90]

In Senegal, after independence, development programs favored men by promoting plow agriculture and distributing seed to heads of households. But judging by the Wolof peanut farmers that Donna Perry studied, men's advantages were short-lived. In the mid-1980s, agricultural cooperatives were dissolved and economic supports were eliminated. Cash-cropping by small farm households has diminished, and men appear to be suffering a crisis of masculinity as their wives trade more in the weekly markets (*loumas*). Men express their frustration: "You wake up in the morning now and don't even know who the head of the household is!"[91] It is hard to know in advance where this anxiety will lead. It could be that, as males' authority diminishes, they will become more conservative in an attempt to recapture the old ways. Or, males and females could move toward more shared authority. Conflict may play out at the individual level, which may lead to culture change.

SUMMARY ● ○ ○

1. Anthropologists who are interested in the relationships between culture and the individual and the importance of understanding psychological processes call themselves psychological anthropologists. Four main questions characterize psychological anthropology: (1) To what extent do all human beings develop psychologically in the same ways? (2) If there are differences, what are they and what may account for them? (3) How do people in different societies conceive of individuals and their psychological development? and (4) How can understanding individuals or psychological processes help us understand culture and culture change?

2. Early research in psychological anthropology was concerned mainly with how cultural differences seem to affect supposedly universal stages of emotional development. Some doubt has been cast on the idea that adolescence is necessarily a time of "storm and stress" and that the Oedipus complex, at least in the form stated by Freud, is universal. But there appear to be some universals in the psychological realm, including creating taxonomies, plans for the future, a concept of the self or person, trying to discern the intention of others, the ability to recognize emotions and to play, and to feel affection, sexual attraction, envy, and jealousy.

3. Recent research on universals in psychological development has been concerned more with cognitive, or intellectual, development. In looking for universals, many researchers have discovered some apparent differences. Most of the tests used in research may favor people in Western cultures and those who attend formal schools.

4. To understand cross-cultural variation in psychological characteristics, many researchers have tried to discover if variation in childrearing customs can account for the observed psychological differences.

5. Humans have a long period in which the young are dependent on caretakers. *Socialization* is a term anthropologists and psychologists use to describe the development, through the influence of parents and others, of patterns of behavior in children that conform to cultural expectations. But children are also agents and actors, not just recipients of socialization. They can learn from others, such as peers, in ways that may lead to rapid changes in behavior.

6. Many of the ideas parents have about childrearing come from societal belief systems or "ethnotheories" about children and how they should be treated. Some anthropologists believe societies produce the kinds of personality best suited to performance of the activities necessary for the survival of the society.

7. Societies vary considerably in how quickly they respond to an infant's needs, how much infants are held, how much parents play with infants and young children, how much warmth and affection they show children, how much they expect children to comply with adults or assert themselves, and how aggressive they want children to be. There is also considerable variation in how much children are assigned chores and responsibilities and go to school.

8. One of the most profound effects on cognitive thinking appears to be how much schooling a person has.

9. Some adult differences in psychological traits have been documented in different societies. These include a difference in perceptual style known as field independence versus field dependence (that may be related to economic differences) and difference in display of aggression (that may be also related to economic differences as well as to involvement in war).

10. Psychological anthropologists are interested not only in the possible causes of psychological differences between societies but also in the possible consequences of psychological variation, particularly how psychological

characteristics may help us understand statistical associations between various aspects of culture.

11. Recently, anthropologists have explored how individuals can be agents of culture change.

GLOSSARY TERMS ○ ● ○

enculturation
personality integration
  of culture
primary institutions

projective tests
secondary
  institutions
socialization

CRITICAL QUESTIONS ○ ○ ●

1. Do you think indulging children makes them more or less self-reliant as adults? Why do you think so?

2. What may explain adolescent rebelliousness?

3. Agriculturalists and foragers seem to have somewhat different personalities, so the method of food-getting may be related to personality. Do you think there is a similar relationship between occupation and personality? If so, why?

PEARSON
myanthrolab

Read the chapter by Susan Schaefer Davis titled "Morocco: Adolescents in a Small Town" on MyAnthroLab, and answer the following questions:

1. Why do many (but not all) cultures have a stage of life called "adolescence"?

2. Do you think that rebelliousness is inevitable in adolescence?

3. Describe some of the aspects of adolescence that are different in Morocco from your own culture.

NOTES ● ○ ○

1. Quoted in Klineberg, "Foreword," in Segall 1979, v.
2. D. E. Brown 1991.
3. C. C. Moore 1997, 8–9; see also C. C. Moore et al. 1999.
4. M. Mead 1961.
5. Malinowski 1927.
6. D. Freeman 1983. For reasons to be skeptical about Freeman's criticism, see M. Ember 1985, 906–909.
7. Spiro 1982.
8. Schlegel and Barry 1991, 44.
9. Piaget 1970, 703–32.
10. Berry et al. 1992, 40.
11. Ibid., 40–41.
12. Dasen and Heron 1981, 305–06.
13. C. R. Ember 1977; and Rogoff 1981.
14. Price-Williams 1961.
15. Segall et al. 1990, 149.
16. Rogoff 1981, 264–67.
17. Kaplan et al. 2000, 156.
18. Lancy 2008, 4–7.
19. A. James 2007.
20. Weisner et al. 1983.
21. J. W. M. Whiting and Child 1953, 69–71.
22. Weisner et al. 1983, 291; Hewlett 2004.
23. For a review of the concept of ethnotheories about parenting, see Super and Harkness 1997.
24. Harkness and Super 1997, in Small 1997, 45.
25. Weisner 2004.
26. J. W. M. Whiting and Child 1953, 310.
27. Edgerton 1992, 206.
28. D. G. Freedman 1979.
29. Ibid., 40–41. For a discussion of possible genetic influences on the social environment, see Scarr and McCartney 1983.
30. See Dasen et al. 1988 for references to research, particularly by Barrett 1984.
31. Dasen et al. 1988, 117–18, 126–28.
32. See R. A. LeVine 2007, for an overview of ethnographic studies of childhood.
33. See the research cited in Hewlett 2004; see also Small 1997.
34. Ibid.
35. Lancy 2008, 113–14.
36. R. H. Munroe and Munroe 1980.
37. R. A. LeVine 1988, 4–6; see also discussion in Hewlett 2004.
38. Lancy 2007.
39. Ibid., 274.
40. Ibid., 275 referring to Howrigan 1988, 41.
41. Lancy 2007, 275, quoting Le 2000, 216, 218.
42. Rohner 1975, 97–105.
43. See research reported in Rohner and Britner 2002, 16–47.
44. Rohner 1975, 112–16.
45. Barry et al. 1959. For a somewhat different analysis of the Barry et al. data, see Hendrix 1985.
46. Hoffman 1988, 101–03.
47. Lancy 2008, 180–81, reporting on Mayer and Mayer 1970, 165, and Kulick 1992, 119.
48. Chagnon 1983, 115.
49. Dentan 1968, 55-56.
50. Ibid., 61.
51. Straus 2001.
52. C. R. Ember and Ember 1994.
53. B. B. Whiting and Whiting 1975, 94; see also R. H. Munroe et al. 1984.
54. B. B. Whiting and Edwards 1988, 265.
55. R. H. Munroe et al. 1984, 374–76; see also C. R. Ember 1973.
56. B. B. Whiting and Whiting 1975, 179.
57. B. B. Whiting and Edwards 1988, 35.
58. Ibid., 152–63; and C. R. Ember 1981, 560.
59. C. R. Ember 1977; Rogoff 1981.
60. Rogoff 1981, 285.
61. For how school experiences may improve particular cognitive skills, rather than higher levels of cognitive development in general, see Rogoff 1990, 46–49.
62. Irwin et al. 1974.
63. Luria 1976, 108; quoted in Rogoff 1981, 254.
64. Scribner and Cole 1981; Berry and Bennett 1989, 429–50, as reported in Berry et al. 1992, 123–24.
65. Godoy et al. 2004; Bowles et al. 2001.
66. Geertz 1984, 123–36.
67. Although Melford Spiro (1993) does not believe that this Western/non-Western pattern exists, readers are referred to his article for the many references to the works of those who do.

68. For a review of the literature on "individualism" versus "collectivism," which is mostly based on studies of educated individuals from industrialized cultures, see Triandis 1995. Using data collected by anthropologists on mostly preindustrial cultures, Carpenter (2000, 38–56), finds support for the idea that the concept of self differs in individualist as compared with collectivist cultures.
69. Bachnik 1992.
70. Stairs 1992.
71. Spiro 1993.
72. Research reported in Hollan 1992, 289–90.
73. Berry 1976.
74. Witkin 1967, 233–50.
75. Dawson 1967, 115–28, 171–85; and Berry 1971, 324–36.
76. C. R. Ember 2009; Halpern 2000, 110–12.
77. Dentan 1968, 55–56.
78. Chagnon 1983.
79. C. R. Ember and M. Ember 1994.
80. Edgerton 1971.
81. Bolton 1973.
82. McClelland 1961.
83. LeVine 1966, 2.
84. Kardiner 1946/1939, 471.
85. J. W. M. Whiting and Child 1953, 32–38.
86. J. M. Roberts and Sutton-Smith 1962, 178.
87. J. M. Roberts et al. (1959, 597–605) first established the relationship between games of strategy and social stratification and political complexity. Chick (1998) has replicated those findings.
88. R. V. Burton and Whiting 1961. See also R. L. Munroe, Munroe, and Whiting 1981. For a review of cross-cultural research on initiation, see Burbank 2009a.
89. Yan 2006.
90. Johnson-Hanks 2006.
91. Perry 2005, 217.

Sex, Gender, and Culture

Sex, Gender, and Culture

umans come in two major varieties or sexes—female and male. Each has different reproductive organs. The contrast between them is one of the facts of life shared with most animal species. But having different organs of reproduction does not explain why males and females may also differ in other physical ways. There are some animal species—such as pigeons, gulls, and laboratory rats—in which the two sexes differ little in appearance.[1] The fact that we are a species with two sexes does not explain why human females and males typically look different, nor why human males and females should differ in behavior or be treated differently by society. Yet, no society we know of treats females and males in exactly the same way; indeed, females usually have fewer advantages than males. Egalitarian societies have no *social groups* with unequal access to resources, power, and prestige. But within social groups (e.g., families), even egalitarian societies usually allow males greater access to economic resources, power, and prestige.

Because many of the differences between females and males may reflect cultural expectations and experiences, many researchers now prefer to speak of those as **gender differences**, reserving the term **sex differences** for purely biological differences.[2] Unfortunately, biological and cultural influences are not always clearly separable, so it is sometimes hard to know which term to use. As long as societies treat males and females differently, we may not be able to separate the effects of biology from the effects of culture, and both may be present. As we discuss differences and similarities between females and males, keep in mind that not all cultures conceive of gender as including just two categories. Sometimes "maleness" and "femaleness" are thought of as opposite ends of a continuum, or there might be three or more categories of gender, such as "female," "male," and "other."[3]

In this chapter, we discuss what we know cross-culturally about how and why females and males may differ physically, in gender roles, and in personality. We also discuss how and why sexual behavior and attitudes about sex vary from culture to culture. First, we focus on how concepts about gender vary cross-culturally.

● ○ ●

GENDER CONCEPTS

In the United States and many Western societies, there are only two genders—female or male. Your gender is assigned at birth based on external biological attributes. However, not all individuals feel comfortable with their gender assignment. The term *transgender* is now used to describe people who don't feel that their assigned gender fits them well.

The division into just two genders—male/female—is very common cross-culturally. But a strict dichotomy is far from universal. Some societies, like the Cheyenne Native Americans of the Great Plains, recognized male, female, and a third gender, referred to by the Cheyennes as "two-spirits." "Two-spirit" people were usually biological males. The gender status of "two-spirit" was often recognized after a boy finished his vision quest, usually in his preadolescent years. A two-spirit person would wear women's dress and take on many of the activities of women. A two-spirit might even be taken as a second wife by a man, but whether the man and the two-spirit person engaged in sex is unknown. The role of a "two-spirit" person was not equivalent to becoming a woman, because two-spirits played special roles at weddings and childbirth. Europeans referred to a two-spirit individual as a *berdache*.[4] Accounts of "two-spirit" biological females who take on the role of men are relatively rare, but they do occur in a number of native North American societies, such as the Kaska of Yukon Territory, the Klamath of southern Oregon, and the Mohave of the Colorado River area in the southwestern United States. These biological female "two-spirits" could marry women, and such relationships were known to be lesbian relationships [5]

In Oman, there is a third gender role called *xanith*. Anatomically male, *xaniths* speak of themselves as "women." However, *xaniths* have their own distinctive dress—they wear clothes that are neither male nor female. In fact, their clothes and dress seem in-between. Men wear white clothes, women bright patterns, and *xaniths* wear unpatterned pastels. Men have short hair, women long, and *xaniths* are medium-length. Women are generally secluded in their houses and can only go out with permission from their husbands, but the *xanith* is free to come and go and works as a servant and/or a homosexual prostitute. But the *xanith* gender role is not necessarily forever. A *xanith* may decide to marry, and if he is able to have intercourse with his bride, he becomes a "man." An older *xanith* who is no longer attractive may decide to become an "old man."[6]

PHYSIQUE AND PHYSIOLOGY

As we noted earlier, males and females cannot readily be distinguished in some animal species. Although they differ in chromosome makeup and in their external and internal organs of reproduction, they do not differ otherwise. In contrast, humans are *sexually dimorphic*—that is, the two sexes of our species are generally different in size and appearance. Females have proportionately wider pelvises. Males typically are taller and have heavier skeletons. Females have a larger proportion of their body weight in fat; males have a larger proportion of body weight in muscle. Males typically have greater grip strength, proportionately larger hearts and lungs, and greater aerobic capacity (greater intake of oxygen during strenuous activity).

North American culture tends to view "taller" and "more muscled" as better, which may reflect a bias toward males. But how did these differences come about? Natural selection may have favored these traits in males but selected against them in females. Because females bear children, selection may have favored earlier cessation of growth, and therefore less ultimate height so that the nutritional needs of a fetus would not compete with a growing mother's needs.[7] (Females achieve their ultimate height shortly after puberty, but boys continue to grow for years after puberty.) Similarly, there is some evidence that females are less affected than males by nutritional shortages, presumably because they tend to be shorter and have proportionately more fat.[8] Natural selection may have favored more proportionate "fatness" in females because that resulted in greater reproductive success.

Athletes can build up their muscle strength and increase their aerobic work capacity through training. Given that fact, cultural factors, such as how much a society expects and allows males and females to engage in muscular activity, could influence the degree to which females and males differ muscularly and in aerobic capacity. Similar training may account for the recent trend toward decreasing differences between females and males in certain athletic events, such as marathons and swim meets. Even

Hmong women carry large loads of firewood to market.

JORGEN SCHYTTE/Peter Arnold, Inc.

when it comes to female and male physique and physiology, then, what we see may be the result of both culture and genes.[9]

GENDER ROLES

Productive and Domestic Activities

All societies assign or divide labor somewhat differently between females and males. Because role assignments have a clear cultural component, we speak of them as **gender roles**. What is of particular interest here about the gender division of labor is not so much that every society has different work for males and females but rather that so many societies divide up work in similar ways. The question, then, is: Why are there universal or near-universal patterns in such assignments?

Table 1 summarizes the worldwide patterns indicating which activities are performed by which gender in all or almost all societies, which activities are usually performed by one gender, and which activities are commonly assigned to either gender or both. If every culture assigned work arbitrarily to the genders, there wouldn't be any patterns in the table. Although many tasks are assigned to both genders (the middle column), clearly some patterns are worldwide. One of the most striking is in primary subsistence activities; males almost always hunt and trap animals and females usually gather wild plants. Does this and the other distributions of activities in the table suggest

why females and males generally do different things? Scholars have suggested four explanations or theories that we label: *strength theory*, *compatibility-with-child-care theory*, *economy-of-effort theory*, and *expendability theory*.

The *strength theory* focuses on the generally greater strength of males and their superior capacity to mobilize their strength in quick bursts of energy (because of greater aerobic work capacity). Certainly, males may generally best perform activities that require lifting heavy objects (hunting large animals, butchering, clearing land, or working with stone, metal, or lumber), throwing weapons, and running with great speed (as in hunting). And none of the activities females usually perform, with the possible exception of collecting firewood, seem to require the same degree of physical strength or quick bursts of energy. But the strength theory is not completely convincing, if only because it cannot readily explain all the observed patterns. For example, it is not clear that the male activities of trapping small animals, collecting wild honey, or making musical instruments require much physical strength. Moreover, as we will see shortly, women do hunt in some societies, suggesting that differences in strength cannot play a very important role.

The *compatibility-with-child-care theory* emphasizes that women's tasks need to be compatible with child care. Although males can take care of infants, most traditional societies rely on breast-feeding of infants, which men cannot do. (In most societies, women breast-feed their children for two years on the average.) Women's tasks may be those that do not take them far from home for long

TABLE 1	Worldwide Patterns in the Division of Labor by Gender				
Type of Activity	Males Almost Always	Males Usually	Either Gender or Both	Females Usually	Females Almost Always
Primary subsistence activities	Hunt and trap animals, large and small	Fish Herd large animals Collect wild honey Clear land and prepare soil for planting	Collect shellfish Care for small animals Plant crops Tend crops Harvest crops Milk animals	Gather wild plants	
Secondary subsistence and household activities		Butcher animals	Preserve meat and fish	Care for children Cook Prepare vegetable foods, drinks, and dairy products Launder Fetch water Collect fuel	Care for infants
Other	Lumber Mine and quarry Make boats, musical instruments, and bone, horn, and shell objects Engage in combat	Build houses Make nets and rope Exercise political leadership	Prepare skins Make leather products, baskets, mats, clothing, and pottery	Spin yarn	

Source: Mostly adapted from Murdock and Provost 1973, 203–25. The information on political leadership and warfare comes from Whyte 1978a, 217. The information on child care comes from Weisner and Gallimore 1977, 169–80.

periods, do not place children in potential danger if they are taken along, and that can be stopped and resumed if an infant needs care.[10]

The compatibility theory may explain why *no* activities other than infant care are listed in the right-hand column of Table 1. That is, it may be that there are practically no universal or near-universal women-only activities because until recently most women have had to devote much of their time to nursing and caring for infants, as well as caring for other children. This theory may also explain why men usually perform tasks such as hunting, trapping, fishing, collecting honey, lumbering, and mining. Those tasks are dangerous for infants to be around, and in any case, would be difficult to coordinate with infant care.[11]

Finally, the compatibility theory may also explain why men seem to take over certain crafts in societies with full-time specialization. Although the distinction is not shown in Table 1, crafts such as making baskets, mats, and pottery are women's activities in noncommercial societies but tend to be men's activities in societies with full-time craft specialists.[12] Similarly, weaving tends to be a female activity unless it is produced for trade.[13] Full-time specialization and production for trade may increase incompatibility with child care. Cooking is a good example in our own society. Many women are excellent cooks and traditionally did most of the cooking at home, but chefs and bakers tend to be men. Women might be more likely to work as chefs if they could leave their babies and young children in safe places to be cared for by other people or if the hours chefs and bakers work were not so long.

But the compatibility theory does not explain why men usually prepare soil for planting, make objects out of wood, or work bone, horn, and shell. All of those tasks could probably be stopped to tend to a child, and none of them is any more dangerous to children nearby than is cooking. Why, then, do males tend to do them? The *economy-of-effort theory* may help explain patterns that cannot readily be explained by the strength and compatibility theories. For example, it may be advantageous for men to make wooden musical instruments because men generally lumber.[14] Lumbering may give men more knowledge about the physical properties of various woods and make it more likely that they know how to work with different woods. The economy-of-effort interpretation also suggests that it would be advantageous for one gender to perform tasks that are physically located near each other. If women have to be near home to take care of nursing and young children, it would be economical for them to perform other chores in or near the home.

Expendability theory suggests that men, rather than women, will tend to do the dangerous work in a society because the loss of men is less disadvantageous reproductively than the loss of women. If some men lose their lives in hunting, deep-water fishing, mining, quarrying, lumbering, and the like, reproduction need not suffer as long as most fertile women have sexual access to men—for example, if the society permits two or more women to be married to the same man.[15] If something is dangerous, why would anybody, male or female, be willing to do it?

In many farming societies, women can do some agriculture and take care of their young children at the same time, as this mother in Zambia demonstrates.

Perhaps only when society glorifies those roles and endows them with high prestige and other rewards.

Although the various theories, singly or in combination, seem to explain much of the division of labor by gender, there are some unresolved problems. Critics of the strength theory have pointed out that women in some societies do engage in very heavy labor.[16] If women in some societies can develop the strength to do such work, perhaps strength is more a function of training than traditionally has been believed.

The compatibility theory also has some problems. It suggests that labor is divided to conform to the requirements of child care. But sometimes it seems the other way around. For example, women who spend a good deal of time in agricultural work outside the home often ask others to watch and feed their infants while they are unavailable to nurse.[17] Consider, too, the mountain areas of Nepal, where agricultural work is incompatible with child care; heavy loads must be carried up and down steep slopes, fields are far apart, and labor takes up most of the day. Yet women do this work anyway and leave their infants with others for long stretches of time.[18]

Furthermore, in some societies, women hunt—one of the activities most incompatible with child care and generally not done by women. Many Agta women of the Philippines regularly hunt wild pig and deer; women alone or in groups kill almost 30 percent of the large game.[19] The women's hunting does not seem to be incompatible with child care. Women take nursing babies on hunting trips, and the women who hunt do not have lower reproductive rates than the women who choose not to hunt. Agta women may find it possible to hunt because the hunting grounds are only about a half hour from camp, the dogs that accompany the women assist in the hunting and protect the women and babies, and the women generally hunt in groups, so others can help carry babies as well as carcasses. Hunting by women is also fairly common among the Aka, forest foragers in the Central African Republic. Aka women participate in and sometimes lead in organizing cooperative net-hunting, in which an area is circled and animals are flushed out and caught in nets. Women spend approximately 18 percent of their time net-hunting, which is more than men do.[20] In the Canadian subarctic, teams of Chipewyan women would hunt small animals such as muskrats or rabbits, and would commonly join their husbands to hunt large animals such as moose. However, women noted that they would avoid hunting moose after their fourth or fifth month of pregnancy, so they mainly were part of the team when they were newly married and later when they were older. Women did not participate in long-distance hunts,[21] which also suggests that compatibility with child care was a consideration.

As the cases just described suggest, we need to know a lot more about labor requirements. More precisely, we need to know exactly how much strength is required in particular tasks, how dangerous those tasks are, and whether a person could stop working at a task to care for a child. So far, we have mostly guesses. When there is more systematically collected evidence on aspects of particular tasks, we will be in a better position to evaluate the various theories. In any case, none of the available theories implies that the worldwide patterns of division of labor shown in Table 1 will persist. As we know from our own and other industrial societies, a strict gender division of labor begins to disappear when machines replace human strength, when women have fewer children, and when women can assign child care to others.

RELATIVE CONTRIBUTIONS TO WORK

In the United States, there is a tendency to equate "work" with a job earning income. Until relatively recently, being a "homemaker" was not counted as an occupation. Anthropologists also tended to ignore household work; indeed, most of the research on division of labor by gender focuses on **primary subsistence activities**—gathering, hunting, fishing, herding, and farming—and relatively less attention is paid to gender contributions to **secondary subsistence activities,** those that involve the processing and preparation of food for eating or storing. With a few exceptions, food almost never can be consumed without preparation of some kind. For example, hunting cannot contribute much to the diet unless the meat is brought back home (cut up or carried whole) and butchered. If the animal is large, the meat often has to be prepared for distribution and/or storage. And as skins and other parts are often used for clothing or tools, someone has to prepare those. As Hetty Jo Brumbach and Robert Jarvenpa point out, the Western model of hunting focuses on the "kill" (perhaps derived from the notion of sport-hunting) and ignores the complexity of processes associated with it. This view may hide women's role in "hunting" and emphasizes the male role as the "hunter."[22]

Overall Work

We can also ask whether males or females generally do more work. We do not yet have that many studies of how females and males spend their time, but studies of horticultural and intensive agricultural societies so far suggest that, if we count all the kinds of economic activities shown in Table 1, women typically work more total hours per day than men.[23] We do not know if this is a truly cross-cultural universal. However, we do know that, in many societies where women earn wages, they are still responsible for the bulk of the household work as well as the child care at home.

Subsistence Work

If we focus on contribution to primary subsistence activities, which are generally located further from the home, female and male contributions are more variable cross-culturally. Estimates of time actually working are not generally available, so most comparisons estimate how much each gender contributes to the diet in terms of caloric intake from primary subsistence activities.

In some societies, women have traditionally contributed more to the economy than men by any measure. For example, among the Tchambuli of New Guinea in the 1930s, the women did all the fishing—going out early in the morning by canoe to their fish traps and returning when the sun was hot. Some of the catch was traded for sago (a starch) and sugarcane, and it was the women who went on the long canoe trips to do the trading.[24]

In contrast, men did almost all of the primary subsistence work among the Toda of India. As they were described early in the 20th century, they depended for subsistence almost entirely on the dairy products of their water buffalo, either by using the products directly or by selling them for grain. Women were not allowed to have anything to do with dairy work; only men tended the buffalo and prepared the dairy products. Women's work was largely household work. Women prepared the purchased grain for cooking, cleaned house, and decorated clothing.[25]

A survey of a wide variety of societies has revealed that these extremes are not common. Usually both women and men contribute a good deal to primary food-getting activities, but men usually contribute more in most societies.[26] Because women are almost always occupied with infant and child care responsibilities, it is not surprising that men usually do most of the primary subsistence work, which generally has to be done away from the home.

Why do women in some societies do as much or more than men in primary subsistence work? Some of the variation is explained by the type of food-getting activities in the society. In societies that depend on hunting, fishing, and herding for most of their calories—generally male activities—men usually contribute more than women.[27] For example, among the Inuit who traditionally depended mostly on hunting and fishing, as well as among the Toda who depended mostly on herding, men did most of the primary subsistence work. In societies that depend on gathering, primarily women's work, women tend to do most of the food-getting.[28] The !Kung are an example. But the predominant type of food-getting is not always predictive. For example, among the Tchambuli who depended mostly on fishing, women did most of the work. Most societies depend upon some form of food production, rather than foraging. With the exception of clearing land, preparing the soil, and herding large animals, which are usually men's tasks, men, women, or both do the work of planting, crop tending (weeding, irrigating), and harvesting (see Table 1). So we need some explanation of why women do most of the farming work in some societies but men do it in others. Different patterns predominate in different areas of the world. In Africa, south of the Sahara, women generally do most of the farming. In much of Asia and Europe and the areas around the Mediterranean, men do more.[29]

The type of agriculture may help explain some of the variation. Many have pointed out that men's contribution to primary subsistence tends to be much higher than women's in intensive agricultural societies, particularly with plow agriculture. In contrast, women's contribution is relatively high compared with men's and sometimes higher in horticultural societies. According to Ester Boserup, when population increases and there is pressure to make more intensive use of the land, cultivators begin to use the plow and irrigation, and males start to do more.[30] But it is not clear why.

Why should women not contribute a lot to farming just because plows are used? In trying to answer this question, most researchers shift to considering how much time males and females spend in various farming tasks, rather than estimating the total caloric contribution of females versus males. The reason for this shift is that gender contribution to farming varies substantially over the various phases of the production sequence, as well as from one crop to another. Thus, the total amount of time females versus males work at farming tasks is easier to estimate than how much each gender contributes to the diet in terms of calories. How would caloric contribution be judged, for example, if men do the clearing and plowing, women do the planting and weeding, and both do the harvesting?

Perhaps plow agriculture increases male contribution to subsistence because plowing takes longer and minimizes weeding time. Cross-culturally, men usually clear land. (This doesn't mean that women are not able to plow because there are examples of women plowing when necessary.[31]) It has been estimated that, in one district in Nigeria, 100 days of work are required to clear one acre of virgin land for plowing by tractor; only 20 days are required to prepare the land for shifting cultivation. Weeding is a task that probably can be combined with child

Grinding corn is very time-consuming hard work. A woman in the highlands of Guatemala is grinding corn for tortillas.

care, and perhaps women may have mostly performed it previously for that reason.[32] But the fact that men do the plowing, which may take a lot of time, does not explain why women do relatively fewer farming tasks, including weeding, in societies that have the plow.[33]

Another explanation is that household chores increase substantially with intensive agriculture and limit the time women can spend in the fields. Intensive agriculturalists rely heavily on grain crops (such as corn, wheat, oats) that are usually dried before storing. To make these dried foods edible, they either have to be cooked in water for a long time or they have to be processed first to make cooking faster. Cooking usually requires collecting water and firewood, neither usually close by, and both tasks are usually done by women. The longer the cooking time, the more time is needed and the more water and firewood is needed. In addition, there is more cleaning of pots and utensils. Soaking, grinding, or pounding can reduce cooking time for hard grains, but the process that speeds up cooking the most—grinding—is itself very time-consuming unless done by machine.[34] Then there is also child care and the additional housework that children entail. Household work may increase substantially with intensive agriculture because women in such societies have *more* children than women in horticultural societies.[35] If household work increases in these ways, it is easy to understand why women cannot contribute more time than men, or as much time as men, to intensive agriculture. But women's contribution, although less than men's, is nonetheless substantial; they seem to work outside the home four and a half hours a day, seven days a week, on the average.[36]

We still have not explained why women contribute so much to horticulture in the first place. They may not have as much household work as intensive agricultural women, but neither do the men. Why, then, don't men do relatively more in horticulture also? Men in horticultural societies are often drawn away from cultivation into other types of activities. One of the most common is warfare, in which all able-bodied men are expected to participate. There is evidence that, if males are engaged in warfare when primary subsistence work has to be done, the women must do that subsistence work.[37] Men may also be withdrawn from primary subsistence work if they have to work in distant towns and cities for wages or if they periodically go on long-distance trading trips.[38]

When women contribute a lot to primary food-getting activities, we might expect effects on their childrearing. Several cross-cultural studies suggest that this expectation is correct. In societies with a high female contribution to primary subsistence (in terms of contributing calories), infants are fed solid foods earlier (so that other people besides mothers can feed them) than in societies with a low female contribution.[39] Girls are likely to be trained to be industrious (probably to help their mothers), and girl babies are more valued.[40]

POLITICAL LEADERSHIP AND WARFARE

In almost every known society, men rather than women are generally the leaders in the political arena. One cross-cultural survey found that, in about 88 percent of the surveyed societies, only men were leaders. In 10 percent of societies in which some women occupied leadership positions, the women were either outnumbered by or less powerful than the male leaders.[41] In the remaining 2 percent, leadership was fairly evenly distributed between men and women. If we look at countries, not cultures, women on the average make up only around 10 percent of the representatives in national parliaments or legislative bodies.[42] Whether or not we consider warfare to be part of the political sphere of life, we find an almost universal dominance of males in that arena. In 87 percent of the world's societies, women never participate actively in war.[43] (See the box "Why Do Some Societies Allow Women to Participate in Combat?" for a discussion of women in combat in the remaining 13 percent of societies.)

Even in *matrilineal* societies, which seem to be oriented around women, men usually occupy formal political positions. Among the Iroquois of what is now New York State, women had control over resources, but men, not women, held political office. The highest political body among the League of the Iroquois, which comprised five tribal groups, was a council of 50 male chiefs. Nonetheless, women had considerable informal influence on political affairs. Women could nominate, elect, and impeach their male representatives. Women also could decide between life and death for prisoners of war, forbid the men of their households to go to war, and intervene to bring about peace.[44]

Why have men (at least so far) almost always dominated the political sphere of life? Some scholars have suggested that men's role in warfare gives them the edge in all kinds of political leadership, particularly because they control weapons, an important resource.[45] But evidence suggests that force is rarely used to obtain leadership positions;[46] superior strength is not the deciding factor. Still, warfare may be related to political leadership for another reason. Warfare clearly affects survival, and it occurs regularly in most societies. Therefore, decision making about war may be among the most important kinds of politics in most societies. If so, then the people who know the most about warfare should be making the decisions about it.

To explain why males and not females usually engage in fighting, let us refer to three of the possible explanations of the worldwide patterns in the gender division of labor. Warfare, like hunting, probably requires strength (for throwing weapons) and quick bursts of energy (for running). And certainly combat is one of the most dangerous and uninterruptible activities imaginable, hardly compatible with child care. Also, even if they do not at the time have children, women may generally be kept out of combat because their potential fertility is more important to a population's reproduction and survival than their potential usefulness as warriors.[47] So the strength theory, the compatibility theory, and the expendability theory might all explain the predominance of men in warfare.

Two other factors may be involved in male predominance in politics. One is the generally greater height of men. Why height should be a factor in leadership is unclear, but studies suggest that taller people are more likely to be leaders.[48] Finally, there is the possibility that men

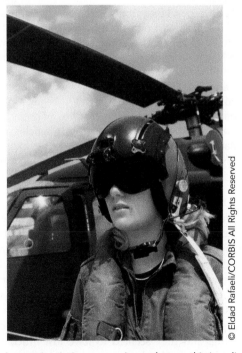

Women in some societies engage in combat, as this Israeli helicopter gunner does.

new perspectives on gender

Why Do Some Societies Allow Women to Participate in Combat?

U.S. women can serve in the military but are not in units directly engaged in combat. Some women feel that such exclusion is unfair and decreases their chances of promotion in the military. Other people, including some women, insist that female participation in combat would be detrimental to military performance or is inappropriate for women. Women in the U.S. military have been attacked in the course of their duties in Iraq and some have died. Some countries currently allow women to engage in combat. And in the 18th and 19th centuries, women made up one wing of the standing army in the West African Kingdom of Dahomey and at one point constituted one-third of the armed forces. Most societies, however, have excluded women from combat, and some have excluded women from any involvement in military activities or planning.

Why, then, do some societies allow women to be warriors? Psychologist David Adams compared about 70 societies studied by anthropologists to try to answer that question. Although most societies exclude women from war, Adams found that women are active warriors, at least occasionally, in 13 percent of the sample societies. In native North America, such societies included the Comanche, Crow, Delaware, Fox, Gros Ventre, and Navajo. In the Pacific, there were active warrior women among the Maori of New Zealand, on Majuro Atoll in the Marshall Islands, and among the Orokaiva of New Guinea. In none of

these societies were the warriors usually women, but women were allowed to engage in combat if they wanted to.

How are the societies with women warriors different from those that exclude women from combat? They differ in one of two ways. Either they conduct war only against people in other societies (this is called "purely external" war) or they marry within their own community. Adams argues that these two conditions, which are not particularly common, preclude the possibility of conflicts of interest between wives and husbands, and therefore women can be permitted to engage in combat because their interests are the same as those of their husbands. Because marriages in most cases involve individuals from the same society, husbands and wives will have the same loyalties if the society has purely external war. And even if war occurs between communities and larger groups in the same society (what we call "internal" war), there will be no conflict of interest between husband and wife if they both grew up in the same community. In contrast, there is internal war at least occasionally in most societies, and wives usually marry in from other communities. In this situation, there may often be a conflict of interest between husband and wife; if women were to engage in combat, they might have to fight against their fathers, paternal uncles, and brothers. And wouldn't we expect the wives to try to warn kin in their home communities if the

husbands planned to attack them? Indeed, the men's likely fear of their wives' disloyalty would explain why women in these societies are forbidden to make or handle weapons or go near meetings in which war plans are discussed.

Many countries today engage in purely external war, so other things being equal, we would not expect conflicts of interest to impede women's participation in combat. Therefore, extrapolating from Adams's findings, we might expect that the barriers against female participation in combat will disappear completely. But other conditions may have to be present before women and men participate equally in combat. In Adams's study, not all societies with purely external war or intracommunity marriage had women warriors. So we may also have to consider the degree to which the society seeks to maximize reproduction (and therefore protect women from danger) and the degree to which the society depends on women for subsistence during wartime.

There are other related questions to explore: Does military participation by women increase women's participation in politics? Does the presence of war in a society decrease or increase women's political participation? Does women's participation in politics or in the military change the nature of war?

Source: From D. B. Adams 1983; J. S. Goldstein 2001; 2004.

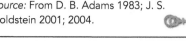

dominate politics because they get around more in the outside world than do women. Men's activities typically take them farther from home; women tend to work more around the home. If societies choose leaders at least in part because of what they know about the larger world, then men will generally have some advantage. In support of this reasoning, Patricia Draper found that, in settled !Kung groups, women no longer engaged in long-distance gathering, and they seemed to have lost much of their former influence in decision making.[49] Involvement in child care may also detract from influence in decision making. In a study of village leadership among the Kayapo

of Brazil, Dennis Werner found that women with heavy child care burdens were less influential than women not as involved in child care; he suggests that they had fewer friends and missed many details of what was going on in the village.[50]

These various explanations suggest why men generally dominate politics, but we still need to explain why women participate in politics more in some societies than in others. Marc Ross investigated this question in a cross-cultural survey of 90 societies.[51] In that sample, the degree of female participation in politics varied considerably. For example, among the Mende of Sierra Leone, women regularly held high office, but among the Azande of Zaire, women took no part in public life. One factor that predicts the exclusion of women from politics is the organization of communities around male kin. As we will see later, when they marry, women usually have to leave their communities and move to their husband's place. If women are "strangers" in a community with many related males, then the males will have political advantages because of their knowledge of community members and past events.

THE RELATIVE STATUS OF WOMEN

There are probably as many definitions of status as there are researchers interested in the topic. To some, the relative status of the sexes means how much importance society confers on females versus males. To others, it means how much power and authority men and women have relative to each other. And to still others, it means what kinds of rights women and men possess to do what they want to do. In any case, many social scientists ask why the status of women appears to vary from one society to another. Why do women have few rights and little influence in some societies and more of each in other societies? In other words, why is there variation in degree of **gender stratification**?

In the small Iraqi town of Daghara, women and men live very separate lives.[52] In many respects, women appear to have very little status. Like women in some other parts of the Islamic world, women in Daghara live their lives mostly in seclusion, staying in their houses and interior courtyards. If women must go out, which they can do only with male approval, they must shroud their faces and bodies in long black cloaks. These cloaks must be worn in mixed company, even at home. Women are essentially excluded from political activities. Legally, they are considered to be under the authority of their fathers and husbands. Even the sexuality of women is controlled. There is strict emphasis on virginity before marriage. Because women are not permitted even casual conversations with strange men, the possibilities for extramarital or even premarital relationships are very slight. In contrast, hardly any sexual restrictions are imposed on men.

But some societies such as the Mbuti seem to approach equal status for males and females. Like most food collectors, the Mbuti have no formal political organization to make decisions or to settle disputes. Public disputes occur, and both women and men take part in the uproar that is part of such disputes. Not only do women make their positions known, but their opinions are often heeded. Even in domestic quarrels involving physical violence between husband and wife, others usually intervene to stop them, regardless of who hit whom first.[53] Women control the use of dwellings; they usually have equal say over the disposal of resources they or the men collect, over the upbringing of their children, and about whom their children should marry. One of the few signs of inequality is that women are somewhat more restricted than men with respect to extramarital sex.[54]

There are many theories about why women have relatively high or low status. One of the most common is that women's status will be high when they contribute substantially to primary subsistence activities. This theory would predict that women should have very little status when food-getting depends largely on hunting, herding, or intensive agriculture. A second theory suggests that men will be more valued and esteemed than women where warfare is particularly important. A third theory suggests that men will have higher status where there are centralized political hierarchies. The reasoning in this theory is essentially the same as the reasoning in the warfare theory: Men usually play the dominant role in political behavior, so men's status should be higher wherever political behavior is more important or frequent. Finally, there is the theory that women will have higher status where kin groups and couples' places of residence after marriage are organized around women.

One of the problems in evaluating these theories is that decisions have to be made about the meaning of *status*. Does it mean value? Rights? Influence? And do all these aspects of status vary together? Cross-cultural research by Martin Whyte suggests that they do not. For each sample society in his study, Whyte rated 52 items that might be used to define the relative status of the sexes. These items included such things as which sex can inherit property, who has final authority over disciplining unmarried children, and whether the gods in the society are male, female, or both. The results of the study indicate that very few of these items are related. Therefore, Whyte concluded, we cannot talk about status as a single concept. Rather, it seems more appropriate to talk about the relative status of women in different spheres of life.[55]

Even though Whyte found no necessary connection between one aspect of status and another, he decided to ask whether some of the theories correctly predict why some societies have many, as opposed to few, areas in which the status of women is high. Let us turn first to the ideas *not* supported by the available cross-cultural evidence. Contrary to popular belief, the idea that generally high status stems from a greater caloric contribution to primary subsistence activities is not supported.[56] For example, women seem to have higher status the more a society depends upon hunting, but women do little of the primary subsistence work in hunting societies. And it is commonly thought that warfare should bolster male status, but there is no consistent evidence that a high frequency of warfare generally lowers women's status in different spheres of life.[57]

What does predict higher status for women in many areas of life? Although the results are not strong, there is some support in Whyte's study for the theory that women have somewhat higher status where kin groups and marital residence are organized around women. The Iroquois are a good example. Even though Iroquois women could not hold formal political office, they had considerable authority within and beyond the household. Related women lived together in longhouses with husbands who belonged to other kin groups. In the

new perspectives on gender

Women's Electoral Success on the Northwest Coast

Political life has changed dramatically since first contact with Europeans for most Native American groups, including the Coast Salish of western Washington State and British Columbia. With impetus from the U.S. and Canadian governments, each of the recognized Coast Salish communities now has an elected council. But who is getting elected? Even though women did not have much of a role in traditional politics, now the Coast Salish groups are electing a lot of women. From the 1960s to the 1980s, women held over 40 percent of the council seats in the 12 Washington State groups, and in the 1990s, women held 28 percent of the seats in the 50 British Columbian groups. The proportion of women on the councils varies from 6 percent among the Tulalip to 62 percent among the Stillaguamish. What accounts for the women's electoral success? And why does that success vary from one group to another, even though the groups are closely related culturally?

According to Bruce Miller, who did a comparative study of women's electoral success in Coast Salish communities, women generally have more of a political role now perhaps because new economic opportunities in the service and technical sectors allow women to contribute more to the household economy. But why do women win proportionately more council seats in some communities than in others? Miller found that women win proportionately more seats in communities with less income, the least income derived from fishing, and the smallest populations. Why should lower household income predict more electoral success for women? Miller suggests that it is not so much the amount of income but rather the degree to which women (compared with men) contribute to household income. In groups with economic difficulties, the jobs women are able to get play a vital role in the household. Federally funded programs such as the War on Poverty helped women to acquire technical skills and jobs. Simultaneously many men in some communities lost their jobs in logging and agriculture.

But a high dependence on fishing income seems to favor men politically. Families that operate vessels with a large drawstring net to catch fish at sea can make hundreds of thousands of dollars a year. Men predominantly do such fishing, and where there is such lucrative fishing, the successful men dominate the councils. Even though women may have jobs too, their income is not as great as the successful fisherman's.

Why should women be more successful politically in smaller communities? Miller suggests that women have a better chance to be known personally when the community is small, even though working outside the home in technical or service jobs cuts down on the time women can devote to tribal ceremonials and other public events.

Does female income relative to male and community size help explain the relative political success of women elsewhere? We do not know yet, but subsequent research may help us find out.

Source: B. G. Miller 1992.
B. G. Miller 1992. "Women and Politics: Comparative Evidence from the Northwest Coast," Ethnology 32(4): 367–82. © 1992 by University of Pittsburgh.

Ann Mohs/Bruce Miller

Women as well as men serve on political councils in many Coast Salish communities. Here, we see a swearing-in ceremony for the Special Chiefs' Council in Sardis, British Columbia.

applied anthropology

Economic Development and Women's Status

Based on the writings of Ester Boserup and subsequent scholarship on women in development, the prevailing opinion was that development usually made things worse for women. Development agents commonly targeted men for learning new technology and how to produce crops for sale. Today, women in developing countries are still largely left out and women still face difficulties, but recent research has documented how women often find creative solutions to participating in commercial enterprises. In many cases, involvement in commercial activity leads to improvement in women's lives, at least as judged from material and status benefits they receive. Producing for a market might range in scale from raising a few extra pigs for sale in southwestern China, to more complex involvement such as contract farming for crop exports in Kenya, or market trading in Ghana.

Some of the creative strategies women use in Kenya to get around their structural disadvantages include buying or renting land with their proceeds, "pooling" small pieces of land to meet minimum requirements for commercial growers, joining women's rotating credit associations, and looking to the private sector for training and materials for contract agriculture.

Almost everywhere, women in developing countries use money from their commercial enterprise to purchase things for their households. At first the money might go to food purchases, household goods, and education for their children. If their incomes or savings grow, women may pay for large appliances, furniture, and farm machinery and vehicles. Women, in contrast to men, tend to plow all their earnings into household expenditures.

Most of these recent studies suggest that bringing money into the household generally translates into lasting changes, including increased educational opportunities, greater say in household decisions, and higher social status in the community.

Some opportunities for women open up when men move into other domains. For example, among the Asante of Ghana, many men moved out of market trading to take advantage of more lucrative cocoa production. Women had long been traders along with men, but with the departure of men, women took over many of men's former market niches and began to engage in longer-distance trade. And, in Kenya, male migration has increased the number of women who manage the farm and head households.

The places we have discussed so far are largely agricultural. Women's work is primarily in or near the household. Commercial involvement gets women more into the public sector. But what about industrial societies, where only a small proportion of people engage in farming? According to a survey of 61 countries, gender equality is more favored in industrializing countries than in agricultural societies. With industrialization, infant and child mortality decline, lessening the pressure on women to reproduce. Perhaps this frees them to pursue education and work outside the home. Postindustrial countries, with even lower fertility rates, are even more accepting of gender equality. As women learn more and get out in the world more, gender inequality appears to decline.

Sources: Anita Spring 2000a; 2000b; 2000c; Bossen 2000; G. Clark 2000; Doyle 2005.

---

longhouse, the women's authority was clear, and they could ask objectionable men to leave. The women controlled the allocation of the food they produced. Allocation could influence the timing of war parties, because men could not undertake a raid without provisions. Women were involved in the selection of religious leaders, half of whom were women. Even in politics, although women could not speak or serve on the council, they largely controlled the selection of councilmen and could institute impeachment proceedings against those to whom they objected.[58]

In preindustrial societies, women have generally lower status in societies with more political hierarchy.[59] Lower status for women is also associated with other indicators of cultural complexity—social stratification, plow and irrigation agriculture, large settlements, private property, and craft specialization. Only one type of influence for women increases with cultural complexity—informal influence. But, informal influence may simply reflect a lack of *real* influence.[60] Why cultural complexity in preindustrial societies is associated with women having less authority in the home, less control over property, and

more restricted sexual lives is not yet understood. However, the relationship between cultural complexity and gender equality appears to be reversed in industrial and postindustrial societies. Judging by a comparative study of gender attitudes in 61 countries, it seems that countries relying on agriculture such as Nigeria and Peru have the least favorable attitudes toward gender equality, industrial societies such as Russia and Taiwan have moderately favorable attitudes, and postindustrial societies such as Sweden and the United States have the most favorable attitudes toward gender equality.[61] One of the critical differences explaining this reversal may be the role that formal education plays in industrial and postindustrial societies. Education almost always increases status, and the more girls and young women are educated, the greater the likelihood that their status will increase. Furthermore, although the mechanisms are not well understood, education usually results in lowered fertility, which perhaps frees women to pursue other interests. As we discussed earlier, one study among the Kayapo found that women with more children are considered less influential.[62]

Western colonialism appears to have been generally detrimental to women's status. Although the relative status of men and women may not have been equal before the Europeans arrived, colonial influences seem generally to have undermined the position of women. There are plenty of examples of Europeans restructuring landownership around men and teaching men modern farming techniques, even in places where women were usually the farmers. In addition, men more often than women could earn cash through wage labor or through sales of goods (such as furs) to Europeans.[63] We are beginning to understand some of the conditions that may enhance or decrease certain aspects of women's status. If we can understand which of these conditions are most important, society may be able to reduce gender inequality if it wants to.[64]

PERSONALITY DIFFERENCES

Much of the research on gender differences in personality has taken place in the United States and other Western countries where psychology is a major field of study. Although such studies are informative, they do not tell us whether the observed differences hold true in cultures very different from our own. Fortunately, we now have systematic observational studies for various non-Western societies. These studies recorded the minute details of behavior of substantial numbers of males and females. Any conclusions about female-male differences in aggressiveness, for example, are based on actual counts of the number of times a particular individual tried to hurt or injure another person during a given amount of observation time. Almost all of these differences are subtle and a matter of degree, not a matter of a behavior being present or absent in females or males.

Which differences in personality are suggested by these systematic studies? Most of them have observed children in different cultural settings. The most consistent difference is in the area of aggression; boys try to hurt others more frequently than girls do. In an extensive comparative study of children's behavior, the Six Cultures project, this difference showed up as early as 3 years to 6 years of age.[65] In the Six Cultures project, six different research teams observed children's behavior in Kenya (among the Gusii),

Mexico, India, the Philippines, Okinawa, and the United States. A more recent cross-cultural comparison of four other cultures (the Logoli of Kenya, Nepal, Belize, and American Samoa) supports the sex difference in aggression.[66] Studies in the United States are consistent with the cross-cultural findings: In a large number of observation and experimental studies, boys exhibited more aggression than girls.[67]

Other female-male differences have turned up with considerable consistency, but we have to be cautious in accepting them, either because they have not been documented as well or because there are more exceptions. There seems to be a tendency for girls to exhibit more responsible behavior, including nurturance (trying to help others). Girls seem more likely to conform to adult wishes and commands. Boys try more often to exert dominance over others to get their own way. In play, boys and girls show a preference for their own gender. Boys seem to play in large groups, girls in small ones. And boys seem to maintain more distance between each other than girls do.[68]

If we assume that these differences are consistent across cultures, how can we explain them? Many writers and researchers believe that because certain female-male differences are so consistent, they are probably rooted in the biological differences between the two sexes. Aggression is one of the traits talked about most often in this connection, particularly because this male-female difference appears so early in life.[69] But an alternative argument is that societies bring up boys and girls differently because they almost universally require adult males and females to perform different types of roles. If most societies expect adult males to be warriors or to be prepared to be warriors, shouldn't we expect most societies to encourage or idealize aggression in males? And if females are almost always the caretakers of infants, shouldn't we also expect societies generally to encourage nurturant behaviors in females?

Researchers tend to adopt either the biological or the socialization view, but it is possible that both kinds of causes are important in the development of gender differences. For example, parents might turn a slight genetic difference into a large gender difference by maximizing that difference in the way they socialize boys versus girls.

Cross-culturally, girls more often play in small, intimate groups, boys in larger groups.

It is difficult for researchers to distinguish the influence of genes and other biological conditions from the influence of socialization. We have research indicating that parents treat boy and girl infants differently as early as birth.[70] In spite of the fact that objective observers can see no major "personality" differences between girl and boy infants, parents often claim to.[71] But parents may unconsciously want to see differences and may therefore produce them in socialization. So even early differences could be learned rather than genetic. Remember, too, that researchers cannot do experiments with people; for example, parents' behavior cannot be manipulated to find out what would happen if boys and girls were treated in exactly the same ways.

However, there is considerable experimental research on aggression in nonhuman animals. These experiments suggest that the hormone androgen is partly responsible for higher levels of aggression. For example, in some experiments, females injected with androgen at about the time the sexual organs develop (before or shortly after birth) behave more aggressively when they are older than do females without the hormone. These results may or may not apply to humans of course, but some researchers have investigated human females who were "androgenized" in the womb because of drugs given to their mothers to prevent miscarriage. By and large, the results of these studies are similar to the experimental studies—androgenized human females show similar patterns of higher aggression.[72] Some scholars take these results to indicate that biological differences between males and females are responsible for the male-female difference in aggression;[73] others suggest that even these results are not conclusive, because females who get more androgen show generally disturbed metabolic systems, and general metabolic disturbance may itself increase aggressiveness. Furthermore, androgen-injected females may look more like males because they develop male-like genitals; therefore, they may be treated like males.[74]

Is there any evidence that socialization differences may account for differences in aggression? Although a cross-cultural survey of ethnographers' reports on 101 societies does show that more societies encourage aggression in boys than in girls, most societies show no difference in aggression training.[75] The few societies that do show differences in aggression training can hardly account for the widespread sex differences in actual aggressiveness. But the survey does not necessarily mean that there are no consistent differences in aggression training for boys and girls. All it shows is that there are no *obvious* differences. For all we know, the learning of aggression and other "masculine" traits by boys could be produced by subtle types of socialization.

One possible type of subtle socialization that could create gender differences in behavior is the chores children are assigned. It is possible that little boys and girls learn to behave differently because their parents ask them to do different kinds of work. Beatrice and John Whiting reported from the Six Cultures project that, in societies where children were asked to do a great deal of work, they generally showed more responsible and nurturant behavior. Because girls are almost always asked to do more work than boys, they may be more responsible and nurturant for this reason alone.[76] If this reasoning is correct, we should find that, if boys are asked to do girls' work, they will learn to behave more like girls.

A study of Luo children in Kenya by Carol Ember supports this view.[77] Girls were usually asked to babysit, cook, clean house, and fetch water and firewood. Boys were usually asked to do very little because boys' traditional work was herding cattle, and most families in the community studied had few cattle. But for some reason, more boys than girls had been born, and many mothers without girls at home asked their sons to do girls' chores. Systematic behavior observations showed that much of the behavior of the boys who did girls' work was intermediary between the behavior of other boys and the behavior of girls. The boys who did girls' work were more like girls in that they were less aggressive, less domineering, and more responsible than other boys, even when they weren't working. So it is possible that task assignment has an important influence on how boys and girls learn to behave. These and other subtle forms of socialization need to be investigated more thoroughly.

Misconceptions About Differences in Behavior

Before we leave the subject of behavior differences, we should note some widespread beliefs about them that research does not support. Some of these mistaken beliefs are that girls are more dependent than boys, that girls are more sociable, and that girls are more passive. The results obtained by the Six Cultures project cast doubt on all these notions.[78] First, if we think of dependency as seeking help and emotional support from others, girls are generally no more likely to behave this way than boys. To be sure, the results do indicate that boys and girls have somewhat different styles of dependency. Girls more often seek help and contact; boys more often seek attention and approval. As for sociability, which means seeking and offering friendship, the Six Cultures results showed no reliable differences between the sexes. Of course, boys and girls may be sociable in different ways because boys generally play in larger groups than girls. As for the supposed passivity of girls, the evidence is also not particularly convincing. Girls in the Six Cultures project did not consistently withdraw from aggressive attacks or comply with unreasonable demands. The only thing that emerged as a female-male difference was that older girls were less likely than boys to respond to aggression with aggression. But this finding may not reflect passivity as much as the fact that girls are less aggressive than boys, which we already knew.

So some of our common ideas about female-male differences are unfounded. Others, such as those dealing with aggression and responsibility, cannot be readily dismissed and should be investigated further.

As we noted, an observed difference in aggression does not mean that males are aggressive and females are not. Perhaps because males are generally more aggressive, aggression in females has been studied less often. For that reason, Victoria Burbank focused on female aggression in an Australian aborigine community she calls Mangrove. During the 18 months that she was there, Burbank observed some act of aggression almost every other day. Consistent with the cross-cultural evidence, men initiated aggression more often than women, but women were initiators about 43 percent of the time. The women of Mangrove engaged in almost all the same kinds of aggression as men did, including fighting, except that it tended not to be as lethal as male violence. Men most often used lethal weapons; when women fought with weapons, they mostly used sticks, not spears, guns, or knives. Burbank points out that, in contrast to Western cultures, female aggression is not viewed as unnatural or deviant but rather as a natural expression of anger.[79]

SEXUALITY

In view of the way the human species reproduces, it is not surprising that sexuality is part of our nature. But no society we know of leaves sexuality to nature; all have at least some rules governing "proper" conduct. There is much variation from one society to another in the degree of sexual activity permitted or encouraged before marriage, outside marriage, and even within marriage. And societies vary markedly in their tolerance of nonheterosexual sexuality.

Cultural Regulations of Sexuality: Permissiveness Versus Restrictiveness

All societies seek to regulate sexual activity to some degree, and there is a lot of variation cross-culturally. Some societies allow premarital sex; others forbid it. The same is true for extramarital sex. In addition, a society's degree of restrictiveness is not always consistent throughout the life span or for all aspects of sex. For example, a number of societies ease sexual restrictions somewhat for adolescents, and many become more restrictive for adults.[80] Then, too, societies change over time. The United States has traditionally been restrictive, but until recently—before the emergence of the AIDS epidemic—more permissive attitudes were gaining acceptance.

Premarital Sex The degree to which sex before marriage is approved or disapproved of varies greatly from society to society. The Trobriand Islanders, for example, approved of and encouraged premarital sex, seeing it as an important preparation for later marriage roles. Both girls and boys were given complete instruction in all forms of sexual expression at the onset of puberty and were allowed plenty of opportunity for intimacy. Some societies not only allow premarital sex on a casual basis but specifically encourage trial marriages between adolescents. Among the Ila-speaking peoples of central Africa, at harvest time, girls were given houses of their own where they could play at being wife with the boys of their choice.[81]

On the other hand, premarital sex was discouraged in many societies. For example, among the Tepoztlan Indians of Mexico, a girl's life became "crabbed, cribbed, confined"

from the time of her first menstruation. She was not to speak to or encourage boys in the least way. To do so would be to court disgrace, to show herself to be crazy. The responsibility of guarding the chastity and reputation of one or more daughters of marriageable age was often a burden for the mother. One mother said she wished her 15-year-old daughter would marry soon because it was inconvenient to "spy" on her all the time.[82] In many Muslim societies, a girl's premarital chastity was tested after her marriage. After the wedding night, blood-stained sheets were displayed as proof of the bride's virginity.

Cultures do not remain the same; attitudes and practices can change markedly over time, as in the United States. In the past, sex was generally delayed until after marriage; in the 1990s, most Americans accepted or approved of premarital sex.[83]

Sex in Marriage Not surprisingly, there are many common features in the sexual relations in married couples, but there is considerable cross-cultural variation in many respects. In most societies, some form of face-to-face sexual intercourse or coitus is the usual pattern, most preferring the woman on her back and the man on top. Couples in most cultures prefer privacy. This is easier in societies with single-family dwellings or separate rooms, but privacy is difficult to attain in the house in societies with unpartitioned dwellings and multiple families living there. For example, the Siriono of Bolivia had as many as 50 hammocks 10 feet apart in their houses. Not surprisingly, couples in such societies prefer to have sex outdoors in a secluded location.[84]

Night is often preferred for sex, but some cultures specifically opted for day. For example, the Chenchu of India believed that a child conceived at night might be born blind. In some societies, couples engage in sex quickly with little or no foreplay; in others, foreplay may take hours.[85] Attitudes toward marital sex and the frequency of it vary widely from culture to culture. In one cross-cultural survey, frequent marital sex is generally viewed as a good thing, but frequent sex is viewed as undesirable, causing weakness, illness, and sometimes death in 9 percent of the societies.[86] People in most societies abstain from intercourse during menstruation, during at least part of pregnancy, and for a period after childbirth. Some societies prohibit sexual relations before various activities, such as hunting, fighting, planting, brewing, and iron smelting. Our own society is among the most lenient regarding restrictions on intercourse within marriage, imposing only rather loose restraints during mourning, menstruation, and pregnancy.[87]

Extramarital Sex Extramarital sex is not uncommon in many societies. In about 69 percent of the world's societies, men have extramarital sex more than occasionally, and in about 57 percent of the societies women do so. The frequency of such sexual activity is higher than we might expect, given that only a slight majority of societies say they allow extramarital sex for men, and only a small number (11 percent) say they allow it for women.[88]

In quite a few societies, then, there is quite a difference between the restrictive code and actual practice. The

Some cultures are more relaxed about sexuality than others. Does public sculpture reflect that? A park in Oslo, Norway, is dedicated to sculptures by Gustav Vigeland.

Navajo of the 1940s were said to forbid adultery, but young married men under the age of 30 had about a quarter of their heterosexual contacts with women other than their wives.[89] And although people in the United States in the 1970s almost overwhelmingly rejected extramarital sex, 41 percent of married men and about 18 percent of married women had had extramarital sex. In the 1990s, proportionately more men and women reported that they had been faithful to their spouses.[90] Cross-culturally, most societies have a double standard with regard to men and women, with restrictions considerably greater for women.[91] A substantial number of societies openly accept extramarital relationships. The Chukchee of Siberia, who often traveled long distances, allowed a married man to engage in sex with his host's wife, with the understanding that he would offer the same hospitality when the host visited him.[92]

Although a society may allow extramarital sex, a recent cross-cultural study of individual reactions to extramarital sex finds that men and women try a variety of strategies to curtail such sex. Men are much more likely than women to resort to physical violence against their wives; women are more likely to distance themselves from their husbands. Gossip may be employed to shame the relationship and a higher authority may be asked to intervene in more complex societies. The researchers conclude that married women and men universally consider extramarital sex inappropriate, even in societies that permit it sometimes.[93]

Homosexuality When most anthropologists discuss homosexuality, they usually refer to sex between males or sex between females. But although the biological male-female dichotomy corresponds to the gender male-female dichotomy in the West, other societies do not have the same gender concepts, so that the meaning of homosexuality may be different in different societies. For example, the Navajo of the American Southwest traditionally recognized four genders. Only relationships between people of the same gender would be considered homosexual, and they considered such relationships inappropriate.[94] Biologically speaking, some of the cross-gender relationships

would be considered homosexual in the Western view. Most of the research to date has adopted the biological view that homosexuality is between people of the same biological sex.

The range in permissiveness or restrictiveness toward homosexual relations is as great as that for any other kind of sexual activity. Among the Lepcha of the Himalayas, a man was believed to become homosexual if he ate the flesh of an uncastrated pig. But the Lepcha said that homosexual behavior was practically unheard of, and they viewed it with disgust.[95] Perhaps because many societies deny that homosexuality exists, little is known about homosexual practices in the restrictive societies. Among the permissive ones, there is variation in the type and pervasiveness of homosexuality. In some societies, homosexuality is accepted but limited to certain times and certain individuals. For example, among the Papago of the southwestern United States, there were "nights of saturnalia" in which homosexual tendencies could be expressed. The Papago also had many male transvestites who wore women's clothing, did women's chores, and, if not married, could be visited by men.[96] A woman did not have the same freedom of expression. She could participate in the saturnalia feasts but only with her husband's permission, and female transvestites were nonexistent.

Homosexuality occurs even more widely in other societies. The Berber-speaking Siwans of North Africa expected all males to engage in homosexual relations. In fact, fathers made arrangements for their unmarried sons to be given to an older man in a homosexual arrangement. Siwan custom limited a man to one boy. Fear of the Egyptian government made this a secret matter, but before 1909, such arrangements were made openly. Almost all men were reported to have engaged in a homosexual relationship as boys; later, when they were between 16 and 20, they married girls.[97] Such prescribed homosexual relationships between people of different ages are a common form of homosexuality.[98] Among the most extremely pro-homosexual societies, the Etoro of New Guinea preferred homosexuality to heterosexuality. Heterosexuality was prohibited as many as 260 days a year and was forbidden in or near the house and gardens. Male homosexuality, on the other hand, was not prohibited at any time and was believed to make crops flourish and boys become strong.[99] Even among the Etoro, however, men were expected to marry women after a certain age.[100]

Only recently have researchers paid much attention to erotic relationships between females. Although early studies found relatively few societies with female-female sexual relationships, Evelyn Blackwood located reports of 95 societies with such practices, suggesting that it is more common than previously thought.[101] As with male homosexuality, some societies institutionalize same-sex sexual relationships—the Kaguru of Tanzania have female homosexual relationships between older and younger women as part of their initiation ceremonies, reminiscent of the male-male "mentor" relationships in ancient Greece.

Cross-culturally, it is extremely unusual to find "gays" or exclusive male or female homosexuals. In most societies, males and females are expected to marry, and homosexuality, if tolerated or approved, either occurs as a phase in one's life or occurs along with heterosexuality.[102]

Reasons for Restrictiveness

Before we deal with the question of why some societies are more restrictive than others, we must first ask whether all forms of restrictiveness go together. The research to date suggests that societies that are restrictive with regard to one aspect of heterosexual sex tend to be restrictive with regard to other aspects. Thus, societies that frown on sexual expression by young children also punish premarital and extramarital sex.[103] Furthermore, such societies tend to insist on modesty in clothing and are constrained in their talk about sex.[104] But societies that are generally restrictive about heterosexuality are not necessarily restrictive about homosexuality. Societies restrictive about premarital sex are neither more nor less likely to restrict homosexuality. In the case of extramarital sex, the situation is somewhat different. Societies that have a considerable amount of male homosexuality tend to disapprove of males having extramarital heterosexual relationships.[105] If we are going to explain restrictiveness, then, it appears we have to consider heterosexual and homosexual restrictiveness separately.

Let us consider homosexual restrictiveness first. Why do homosexual relationships occur more frequently in some societies, and why are some societies intolerant of such relationships? There are many psychological interpretations of why some people become interested in homosexual relationships, and many of these interpretations relate the phenomenon to early parent-child relationships. So far, the research has not yielded any clear-cut predictions, although several cross-cultural predictors about male homosexuality are intriguing.

One such finding is that societies that forbid abortion and infanticide for married women (most societies permit these practices for illegitimate births) are likely to be intolerant of male homosexuality.[106] This and other findings are consistent with the point of view that homosexuality is less tolerated in societies that would like to increase population. Such societies may be intolerant of all kinds of behaviors that minimize population growth. Homosexuality would have this effect, if we assume that a higher frequency of homosexual relations is associated with a lower frequency of heterosexual relations. The less frequently heterosexual relations occur, the lower the number of conceptions there might be. Another indication that intolerance may be related to a desire for population growth is that societies with famines and severe food shortages are more likely to allow homosexuality. Famines and food shortages suggest population pressure on resources; under these conditions, homosexuality and other practices that minimize population growth may be tolerated or even encouraged.[107]

The history of the Soviet Union may provide some other relevant evidence. In 1917, in the turmoil of revolution, laws prohibiting abortion and homosexuality were revoked and reproduction was discouraged. But, in the period between 1934 and 1936, the policy was reversed. Abortion and homosexuality were again declared illegal, and homosexuals were arrested. At the same time, awards were given to mothers who had more children.[108] Population pressure may also explain why our own society has become somewhat more tolerant of homosexuality recently. Of course, population pressure does not explain why certain individuals become homosexual or why most individuals in some societies engage in such behavior, but it might explain why some societies view such behavior more or less permissively.

Let us now turn to heterosexual behavior. What kinds of societies are more permissive than others? Although we do not yet understand the reasons, we do know that greater restrictiveness toward premarital sex tends to occur in more complex societies—societies that have hierarchies of political officials, part-time or full-time craft specialists, cities and towns, and class stratification.[109] It may be that, as social inequality increases and various groups come to have differential wealth, parents become more concerned with preventing their children from marrying "beneath them." Permissiveness toward premarital sexual relationships might lead a person to become attached to someone not considered a desirable marriage partner. Even worse, from the family's point of view, such "unsuitable" sexual liaisons might result in a pregnancy that could make it impossible for a girl to marry "well." Controlling mating, then, may be a way of trying to control property. Consistent with this view is the finding that virginity is emphasized in rank and stratified societies, in which families are likely to exchange goods and money in the course of arranging marriages.[110]

The biological fact that humans depend on sexual reproduction does not by itself help explain why females and males differ in so many ways across cultures, or why societies vary in the way they handle male and female roles. We are only beginning to investigate these questions. When we eventually understand more about how and why females and males are different or the same in roles, personality, and sexuality, we may be better able to decide how much we want the biology of sex to shape our lives.

SUMMARY ● ○ ○

1. That humans reproduce sexually does not explain why males and females tend to differ in appearance and behavior, and to be treated differently, in all societies.

2. All or nearly all societies assign certain activities to females and other activities to males. These worldwide gender patterns of division of labor may be explained by male-female differences in strength, by differences in compatibility of tasks with child care, or by economy-of-effort considerations and/or the expendability of men.

3. Perhaps because women almost always have infant and child care responsibilities, men in most societies contribute more to primary subsistence activities, in terms of calories. But women contribute substantially to primary subsistence activities in societies that depend heavily on gathering and horticulture and in which warfare occurs while primary subsistence work has to be done. When primary and secondary subsistence work is counted, women typically work more hours than men. In most societies, men are the leaders in the political arena, and warfare is almost exclusively a male activity.

4. The relative status of women compared with that of men seems to vary from one area of life to another. Whether women have relatively high status in one area does not necessarily indicate that they will have high status in another. Less complex societies, however, seem to approach more equal status for males and females in a variety of areas of life.

5. Recent field studies have suggested some consistent female-male differences in personality: Boys tend to be more aggressive than girls, and girls seem to be more responsible and helpful than boys.

6. Although all societies regulate sexual activity to some extent, societies vary considerably in the degree to which various kinds of sexuality are permitted. Some societies allow both masturbation and sex play among children, whereas others forbid such acts. Some societies allow premarital sex; others do not. Some allow extramarital sex in certain situations; others forbid it generally.

7. Societies that are restrictive toward one aspect of heterosexual sex tend to be restrictive with regard to other aspects. And more complex societies tend to be more restrictive toward premarital heterosexual sex than less complex societies.

8. Societal attitudes toward homosexuality are not completely consistent with attitudes toward sexual relationships between the sexes. Societal tolerance of homosexuality is associated with tolerance of abortion and infanticide and with famines and food shortages.

GLOSSARY TERMS ○ ● ○

gender differences
gender roles
gender stratification
primary subsistence
 activities
secondary subsistence
 activities
sex differences

CRITICAL QUESTIONS ○ ○ ●

1. Would you expect female-male differences in personality to disappear in a society with complete gender equality in the workplace?

2. Under what circumstances would you expect male-female differences in athletic performance to disappear?

3. What conditions may make the election of a female head of state most likely?

PEARSON
myanthrolab

Read "Andean Mestizos: Growing Up Female and Male" by Lauris McKee in MyAnthroLibrary and answer the following questions:

1. Which of the Andean Mestizos' ideas about conception, pregnancy, and birth are different from those of your own culture? (Identify your own culture in your answer).

2. According to McKee, what do the Mestizos say is the reason for the shorter breastfeeding of girls?

3. What are the consequences of the gender difference in breast-feeding? Are the parents aware of these consequences?

NOTES ● ○ ○

1. Leibowitz 1978, 43–44.
2. Schlegel 1989, 266; Epstein 1988, 5–6; Chafetz 1990, 28.
3. Jacobs and Roberts 1989.
4. Segal 2004; Segal also cites the work of W. Williams 1992.
5. Lang 1999, 93–94; Blackwood 1984b.
6. Wikan 1982, 168–86.
7. Stini 1971.
8. Frayer and Wolpoff 1985, 431–32.
9. For reviews of theories and research on sexual dimorphism and possible genetic and cultural determinants of variation in degree of dimorphism over time and place, see Frayer and Wolpoff 1985 and Gray 1985, 201–09, 217–25.
10. J. K. Brown 1970b, 1074.
11. Among the Aché hunter-gatherers of Paraguay, women collect the type of honey produced by stingless bees (men collect other honey); this division of labor is consistent with the compatibility theory. See Hurtado et al. 1985, 23.
12. Murdock and Provost 1973, 213; Byrne 1994.
13. R. O'Brian 1999.
14. D. R. White et al. 1977, 1–24.
15. Mukhopadhyay and Higgins 1988, 473.
16. J. K. Brown 1970b, 1073–78; and D. R. White et al. 1977.
17. Nerlove 1974.
18. N. E. Levine 1988.
19. M. J. Goodman et al. 1985.
20. Noss and Hewlett 2001.
21. Brumbach and Jarvenpa 2006a; Jarvenpa and Brumbach 2006.
22. Brumbach and Jarvenpa 2006b.
23. C. R. Ember 1983, 288–89.
24. Mead 1950 [originally published 1935], 180–84.
25. Rivers 1967 [originally published 1906], 567.
26. M. Ember and Ember 1971, 573, Table 1.

27. Schlegel and Barry 1986.
28. Wood and Eagly 2002, 706, drawing on data from H. Kaplan et al. 2000.
29. Boserup 1970, 22–25; see also Schlegel and Barry 1986, 144–45.
30. Boserup 1970, 22–25.
31. Bossen 2000.
32. Ibid., 31–34.
33. C. R. Ember 1983, 286–87; data from Murdock and Provost 1973, 212; Bradley 1995.
34. C. R. Ember 1983.
35. Ibid.
36. Ibid., 287–93.
37. M. Ember and Ember 1971, 579–80.
38. Ibid., 581; see also Sanday 1973, 1684.
39. Nerlove 1974.
40. Schlegel and Barry 1986.
41. Whyte 1978a, 217.
42. Nussbaum 1995, 2, based on data from Human Development Report 1993.
43. Whyte 1978a; D. B. Adams 1983.
44. J. K. Brown 1970a.
45. Sanday 1974; and Divale and Harris 1976.
46. Quinn 1977, 189–90.
47. Graham 1979.
48. D. Werner 1982; and Stogdill 1974, cited in ibid.; see also Handwerker and Crosbie 1982.
49. Draper 1975, 103.
50. D. Werner 1984.
51. M. H. Ross 1986.
52. This description is based on the fieldwork of Elizabeth and Robert Fearnea (1956–1958), as reported in M. K. Martin and Voorhies 1975, 304–31.
53. Begler 1978.
54. Ibid. See also Whyte 1978a, 229–32.
55. Whyte 1978b, 95–120; see also Quinn 1977.
56. Whyte 1978b, 124–29, 145; see also Sanday 1973.
57. Whyte 1978b, 129–30.
58. J. K. Brown 1970a.
59. Whyte 1978b, 135–36.
60. Ibid., 135.
61. Doyle 2005.
62. D. Werner 1984.
63. Quinn 1977, 85; see also Etienne and Leacock 1980, 19–20.
64. Chafetz 1990, 11–19.
65. B. B. Whiting and Edwards 1973.
66. R. L. Munroe et al. 2000, 8–9.
67. Maccoby and Jacklin 1974.
68. For a more extensive discussion of behavior differences and possible explanations of them, see C. R. Ember 1981.
69. B. B. Whiting and Edwards 1973.
70. For references to this research, see C. R. Ember 1981, 559.
71. Rubin et al. 1974.
72. For a discussion of this evidence, see Ellis 1986, 525–27; C. R. Ember 1981.
73. For example, Ellis (1986) considers the evidence for the biological view of aggression "beyond reasonable dispute."
74. For a discussion of other possibilities, see C. R. Ember 1981.
75. Rohner 1976.
76. B. B. Whiting and Whiting 1975; see also B. B. Whiting and Edwards 1988, 273.
77. C. R. Ember 1973, 424–39.
78. B. B. Whiting and Edwards 1973, 175–79; see also Maccoby and Jacklin 1974.
79. Burbank 1994.
80. Heise 1967.
81. C. S. Ford and Beach 1951, 191.
82. O. Lewis 1951, 397.
83. Farley 1996, 60.
84. C. S. Ford and Beach 1951, 23–25, 68–71.
85. Ibid., 40–41, 73.
86. Broude 2009.
87. C. S. Ford and Beach 1951, 82–83.
88. Broude and Greene 1976.
89. Kluckhohn 1948, 101.
90. M. Hunt 1974, 254–57; Lewin 1994.
91. Broude 1980, 184.
92. C. S. Ford and Beach 1951, 114.
93. Jankowiak et al. 2002.
94. Lang 1999, 97, citing Thomas 1993.
95. J. Morris 1938, 191.
96. Underhill 1938, 117, 186.
97. 'Abd Allah 1917, 7, 20.
98. Cardoso and Werner 2004.
99. R. C. Kelly 1974.
100. Cardoso and Werner 2004.
101. Blackwood and Wieringa 1999, 49; Blackwood 1984a.
102. Cardoso and Werner 2004, 207.
103. Data from Textor 1967.
104. W. N. Stephens 1972, 1–28.
105. Broude 1976, 243.
106. D. Werner 1979; D. Werner 1975.
107. D. Werner 1979, 345–62; see also D. Werner 1975, 36.
108. D. Werner 1979, 358.
109. Data from Textor 1967.
110. Schlegel 1991.

Marriage and the Family

From Chapter 21 of *Anthropology*, 13/e. Carol R. Ember. Melvin Ember. Peter N. Peregrine. Copyright © 2011 by Pearson Education.
Published by Prentice Hall. All rights reserved.

Marriage and the Family

Nearly all societies known to anthropology have had the custom of marriage. Why marriage is customary in nearly every society we know of is a classic and perplexing question, and one we attempt to deal with in this chapter.

The near universality of marriage customs does not mean that everyone in a society gets married. In addition, when we say that marriage is nearly universal, we do not mean that marriage and family customs are the same in all societies. On the contrary, there is much variation from society to society in how one marries, whom one marries, and even how many people a person can be married to simultaneously. Indeed, although each marriage usually involves one pair at time, most societies in recent times have allowed a man to be married to more than one woman at a time.

Families are universal; all societies have parent-child groups, but the form and size of the family can vary from society to society. Some societies have large extended families with two or more related parent-child groups; others have smaller independent families. Today, marriage is not always the basis for family life. One-parent families are becoming increasingly common in our own and other societies. Marriage has not disappeared in these places—it is still customary to marry—but more individuals are choosing now to have children without being married.

MARRIAGE

When anthropologists speak of marriage, they do not mean to imply that couples everywhere must get marriage certificates or have wedding ceremonies, as in our own society. **Marriage** merely means a socially approved sexual and economic union, usually between a woman and a man. It is presumed, by both the couple and others, to be more or less permanent, and it subsumes reciprocal rights and obligations between the two spouses and between spouses and their future children.[1] Marriage to more than one spouse at a time is quite common, as we shall see.

It is a socially approved sexual union in that a married couple does not have to hide the sexual nature of their relationship. A woman might say, "I want you to meet my husband," but she could not say, "I want you to meet my lover" without causing some embarrassment in most societies. Although the union may ultimately be dissolved by divorce, couples in all societies begin marriage with some idea of permanence in mind. Implicit too in marriage are reciprocal rights and obligations. These may be more or less specific and formalized regarding matters of property, finances, and childrearing.

Marriage entails both a sexual and an economic relationship, as George Peter Murdock noted: "Sexual relations can occur without economic cooperation, and there can be a division of labor between men and women without sex. But marriage unites the economic and the sexual."[2]

As we will see, the event that marks the commencement of marriage varies in different societies. A Winnebago bride, for example, knew no formal ritual such as a wedding ceremony. She went with her groom to his parents' house, took off her "wedding" clothes and finery, gave them to her mother-in-law, received plain clothes in exchange, and that was that.[3]

Bride, groom, and other guests at a wedding in the village at Yorilgan in Uzbekistan, Central Asia.

The Na Exception

The Na of Yunnan in southwest China, with a population of about 30,000, did not customarily marry or live with their sexual partners. People lived their whole lives in a residential group made up of maternal kin (grandmother, great-uncles, brothers, sisters, and their children). This group was the family, cooperating economically and raising the children together. Furtive sex was the norm.[4] Men would visit women, usually after midnight, and leave before anyone would notice them. There was no other tie between the lovers, nor any encouragement for the relationship to be long-standing. Only a few couples stayed together (the Na do not have words for marriage); but this usually occurred among aristocrats. On and off since 1959, the Chinese government has tried to impose monogamy and fines for illegitimate births, without much success. However, young people's attitudes are changing, largely because of education. At school, children are asked for their father's name, which embarrasses them because they usually don't know it. And the books often refer to married couples.

In the 19th century, the Nayar, a subcaste in India, also lacked the custom of marriage.[5] The Na and the Nayar may both have had frequently absent men. In the Nayar case, the men hired themselves out to fight for princes in various parts of India. In the Na case, between the 1920s and the 1950s, the Na raised horses and mules for caravans they organized to transport merchandise throughout the western part of Yunnan. Of course, the relative absence of men cannot be the only reason for the absence of marriage in these groups; long-distance travel by men occurs in some other ethnic groups along with marriage.

Rare Types of Marriage

In addition to the usual male-female marriages, some societies recognize marriages between people of the same biological sex. Such marriages are not typical in any known society. These same-sex marriages may be socially approved unions, modeled after regular marriages, and they often entail a considerable number of reciprocal rights and obligations. Sometimes the marriages involve an individual who is considered a

The bride's relatives arrive at the groom's home bearing gifts and Piki bread from the bride's family at a traditional Hopi engagement ceremony in Arizona.

David McLain/Aurora Photos, Inc.

"woman" or "man," even though "she" or "he" is not that sex biologically. The Cheyenne Indians allowed a married man to take as a second wife a biological man belonging to the third gender, "two-spirits."

Although it is not clear that the Cheyenne male-male marriages involved homosexual relationships, it is clear that temporary homosexual marriages did occur among the Azande of Africa. Before the British took control over what is now Sudan, Azande warriors who could not afford wives often married "boy-wives" to satisfy their sexual needs. As in normal marriages, gifts (although not as substantial) were given by the "husband" to the parents of his boy-wife. The husband performed services for the boy's parents and could sue any other lover of the boy in court for adultery. The boy-wives not only had sexual relations with their husbands but also performed many of the chores female wives traditionally performed for their husbands.[7]

Female-female marriages are reported to have occurred in many African societies, but there is no evidence of any sexual relationship between the partners. It seems, rather, that female-female marriages were a socially approved way for a woman to take on the legal and social roles of a father and husband.[8] For example, among the Nandi, a pastoral and agricultural society of Kenya, about 3 percent of the marriages are female-female marriages. Such marriages appear to be a Nandi solution to the problem of a regular marriage's failure to produce a male heir to property. The Nandi solution is to have the woman, even if her husband is still alive, become a "husband" to a younger female and "father" the younger woman's children. The female husband provides the marriage payments required for obtaining a wife, renounces female work, and takes on the obligations of the husband to that woman. Although no sexual relations are permitted between the female husband and the new wife (or between the female husband and her own husband), the female husband arranges a male consort so that the new wife can have children. Those children, however, consider the female husband to be their father because she (or more aptly the gender role "he") is the socially designated father. If asked who their father is, a child of such a marriage will name the female who is the husband.[9]

WHY IS MARRIAGE NEARLY UNIVERSAL?

Because virtually all societies practice female-male marriage as we have defined it, we can assume that the custom is adaptive. But saying that does not specify exactly how it may be adaptive. Several interpretations have traditionally been offered to explain why all human societies have the custom of marriage. Each suggests that marriage solves problems found in all societies—how to share the products of a gender division of labor; how to care for infants, who are dependent for a long time; and how to minimize sexual competition. To evaluate the plausibility of these interpretations, we must ask whether marriage provides the best or the only reasonable solution to each problem. After all, we are trying to explain a custom that is virtually universal. The comparative study of other animals, some of which have something like marriage, may help us to evaluate these explanations.

Gender Division of Labor

Every society known to anthropology has had a gender division of labor. Males and females in every society perform different economic activities. This gender division of labor has often been cited as a reason for marriage.[10] As long as there is a division of labor by gender, society has to have some mechanism by which women and men share the products of their labor. Marriage would be one way to solve that problem. But it seems unlikely that marriage is the only possible solution. The hunter-gatherer rule of sharing could be extended to include all the products brought in by both women and men. Or a small group of men and women, such as brothers and sisters, might be pledged to cooperate economically. Thus, although marriage may solve the problem of sharing the fruits of a division of labor, it clearly is not the only possible solution.

Prolonged Infant Dependency

Humans exhibit the longest period of infant dependency of any primate. The child's prolonged dependence places the greatest burden on the mother, who is the main child caregiver in most societies. The burden of prolonged child care by human females may limit the kinds of work they can do. They may need the help of a man to do certain types of work, such as hunting, that are incompatible with child care. Because of this prolonged dependency, it has been suggested, marriage is necessary.[11] But here the argument becomes essentially the same as the division-of-labor argument, and it has the same logical weakness. It is not clear why a group of women and men, such as a hunter-gatherer band, could not cooperate in providing for dependent children without marriage.

Sexual Competition

Unlike most other female primates, the human female may engage in intercourse at any time throughout the year. Some scholars have suggested that more or less continuous female sexuality may have created a serious problem—considerable sexual competition between males for females. It is argued that society had to prevent such competition to survive, that it had to develop some way of minimizing the rivalry among males for females to reduce the chance of lethal and destructive conflict.[12]

There are several problems with this argument. First, why should continuous female sexuality make for more sexual competition in the first place? One might argue the other way around. There might be more competition over the scarcer resources that would be available if females were less frequently interested in sex. Second, males of many animal species, even some that have relatively frequent female sexuality (as do many of our close primate relatives), do not show much aggression over females. Third, why couldn't sexual competition, even if it existed, be regulated by cultural rules other than marriage? For instance, society might have adopted a rule whereby men and women circulated among all the opposite-sex members

of the group, each person staying a specified length of time with each partner. Such a system presumably would solve the problem of sexual competition. On the other hand, such a system might not work particularly well if individuals came to prefer certain other individuals. Jealousies attending those attachments might give rise to even more competition.

Other Mammals and Birds: Postpartum Requirements

None of the theories we have discussed explains convincingly why marriage is the only or the best solution to a particular problem. Also, we now have some comparative evidence on mammals and birds that casts doubt on those theories.[13] How can evidence from other animals help us evaluate theories about human marriage? If we look at the animals that, like humans, have some sort of stable female-male mating, as compared with those that are completely promiscuous, we can perhaps see what sorts of factors may predict male-female bonding in the warm-blooded animal species. Most species of birds, and some mammals such as wolves and beavers, have "marriage." Among 40 mammal and bird species, none of the three factors discussed previously—division of labor, prolonged infant dependency, and greater female sexuality—predicts or is correlated strongly with male-female bonding. With respect to division of labor by sex, most other animals have nothing comparable to a humanlike division of labor, but many have stable female-male matings anyway. The two other supposed factors—prolonged infant dependency and female sexuality—predict just the opposite of what we might expect. Mammal and bird species that have longer dependency periods or more female sexuality are less likely to have stable matings.

Does anything predict male-female bonding? One factor does among mammals and birds, and it may also help explain human marriage. Animal species in which females can simultaneously feed themselves and their babies after birth (*postpartum*) tend not to have stable matings; species in which postpartum mothers cannot feed themselves and their babies at the same time tend to have stable matings. Among the typical bird species, a mother would have difficulty feeding herself and her babies simultaneously. Because the young cannot fly for a while and must be protected in a nest, the mother risks losing them to other animals if she goes off to obtain food. But if she has a male bonded to her (as most bird species do), he can bring back food or take a turn watching the nest. Among animal species that have no postpartum feeding problem, babies are able to travel with the mother almost immediately after birth as she moves about to eat (as do grazers such as horses), or the mother can transport the babies as she moves about to eat (as do baboons and kangaroos). We think the human female has a postpartum feeding problem. When humans lost most of their body hair, babies could not readily travel with the mother by clinging to her fur. And when humans began to depend on certain kinds of food-getting that could be dangerous (such as hunting), mothers could not engage in such work with their infants along.[14]

© Punch/Rothco

"I do love you. But, to be perfectly honest, I would have loved any other lovebird who happened to turn up."
(Rothco Cartoons)

Recent research on the Hadza foragers of Tanzania appears to support this view. Frank Marlowe found that the caloric contribution of mothers and fathers depends on whether or not they have a nursing infant. Women may generally contribute more calories than men to the diet, but married women who are nursing contribute substantially less than other married women. The lower contribution of nursing mothers appears to be made up by the father. Fathers with nursing children contribute significantly more food to the household than fathers with older children.[15]

Even if we assume that human mothers have a postpartum feeding problem, we still have to ask if marriage is the most likely solution to the problem. We think so, because other conceivable solutions probably would not work as well. For example, if a mother took turns babysitting with another mother, neither might be able to collect enough food for both mothers and the two sets of children dependent on them. But a mother and father share the same set of children, and therefore it would be easier for them to feed themselves and their children adequately. Another possible solution is no pair bonding at all, just a promiscuous group of males and females. But in that kind of arrangement, we think, a particular mother probably would not always be able to count on some male to watch her baby when she had to go out for food or to bring her food when she had to watch her baby. Thus, it seems to us that the problem of postpartum feeding by itself helps to explain why some animals, including humans, have relatively stable male-female bonds.[16] Of course, there is still the question of whether research on other animals can be applied to human beings. We think it can, but not everybody will agree.

HOW DOES ONE MARRY?

When we say that marriage is a socially approved sexual and economic union, we mean that all societies have some way of marking the onset of a marriage, but the ways of doing so vary considerably. For reasons that we don't fully understand, some cultures mark marriages by elaborate rites and celebrations; others mark marriages in much more informal ways. And most societies have economic transactions before, during, or even after the onset of the marriages.

Marking the Onset of Marriage

Many societies have ceremonies marking the beginning of marriage. But others, such as the Taramiut Inuit, the Trobriand Islanders of the South Pacific, and the Kwoma of New Guinea, use different social signals to indicate that a marriage has taken place. Among the Taramiut Inuit, the betrothal is considered extremely important and is arranged between the parents at or before the time their children reach puberty. Later, when the youth is ready, he moves in with his betrothed's family for a trial period. If all goes well—that is, if the girl gives birth to a baby within a year or so—the couple are considered married. At this time, the wife goes with her husband to his camp.[17]

In keeping with the general openness of their society's attitudes toward sexual matters, a Trobriand couple advertise their desire to marry "by sleeping together regularly, by showing themselves together in public, and by remaining with each other for long periods at a time."[18] When a girl accepts a small gift from a boy, she demonstrates that her parents favor the match. Before long, she moves to the boy's house, takes her meals there, and accompanies her husband all day. Then the word goes around that the two are married.[19]

The Kwoma of New Guinea practice a trial marriage followed by a ceremony that makes the couple husband and wife. The girl lives for a while in the boy's home. When the boy's mother is satisfied with the match and knows that her son is too, she waits for a day when he is away from the house. Until that time, the girl has been cooking only for herself, and the boy's food has been prepared by his womenfolk. Now the mother has the girl prepare his meal. The young man returns and begins to eat his soup. When the first bowl is nearly finished, his mother tells him that his betrothed cooked the meal, and his eating it means that he is now married. At this news, the boy customarily rushes out of the house, spits out the soup, and shouts, "Faugh! It tastes bad! It is cooked terribly!" A ceremony then makes the marriage official.[20]

Just in the last three decades, "living together" has become more of an option in the United States and other Western countries. For most, living together is a prelude to marriage or kind of a trial marriage. For some, living together has become an alternative to marriage. Statistics in the United States suggest that a third of married women under age 45 have lived together with a man for at least some time period.[21]

Among those societies that have ceremonies marking the onset of marriage, feasting is a common element. It expresses publicly the unification of the two families by marriage. The Reindeer Tungus of Siberia set a wedding date after protracted negotiations between the two families and their larger kin groups. Go-betweens assume most of the responsibility for the negotiating. The wedding day opens with the two kin groups, probably numbering as many as 150 people, pitching their lodges in separate areas and offering a great feast. After the groom's gifts have been presented, the bride's dowry is loaded onto reindeer and carried to the groom's lodge. There, the climax of the ceremony takes place. The bride takes the wife's place—that is, at the right side of the entrance of the lodge—and members of both families sit in a circle. The groom enters and follows the bride around the circle, greeting each guest, while the guests, in their turn, kiss the bride on the mouth and hands. Finally, the go-betweens spit three times on the bride's hands, and the couple are formally husband and wife. More feasting and revelry bring the day to a close.[22]

In many cultures, marriage includes ceremonial expressions of hostility. Mock fights are staged in many societies. On occasion, hostility can have genuinely aggressive overtones, as among the Gusii of Kenya:

> Five young clansmen of the groom come to take the bride and two immediately find the girl and post

A young Iraqi couple in 2008 look at gold jewelry that will be part of her dowry. It is considered to be hers no matter what happens to the marriage.

themselves at her side to prevent her escape, while the others receive the final permission of her parents. When it has been granted the bride holds onto the house posts and must be dragged outside by the young men. Finally she goes along with them, crying and with her hands on her head.[23]

But the battle is not yet over. Mutual antagonism continues right onto the marriage bed, even up to and beyond coitus. The groom is determined to display his virility; the bride is equally determined to test it. "Brides," Robert and Barbara LeVine remarked, "are said to take pride in the length of time they can hold off their mates." Men can also win acclaim. If the bride is unable to walk the following day, the groom is considered a "real man."[24] Such expressions of hostility usually occur in societies in which the two sets of kin are actual or potential rivals or enemies. In many societies, it is common to marry women from "enemy" villages.

As this example suggests, marriage ceremonies often symbolize important elements of the culture. Whereas the Gusii ceremony may symbolize hostility between the two families, the ceremony may promote harmony between the families in other societies. For example, on the Polynesian island of Rotuma, a female clown is an important part of the ceremony. She is responsible for creating an enjoyable, joking atmosphere that facilitates interaction between the two sides.[25]

Economic Aspects of Marriage

"It's not man that marries maid, but field marries field, vineyard marries vineyard, cattle marry cattle." In its down-to-earth way, this German peasant saying indicates that, in many societies, marriage involves economic considerations. In our culture, economic considerations may or may not be explicit. However, in about 75 percent of the societies known to anthropology,[26] one or more explicit economic transactions take place before or after the marriage. The economic transaction may take several forms: bride price, bride service, exchange of females, gift exchange, dowry, or indirect dowry. The distribution of those forms among societies that have economic marriage transactions is shown in Figure 1.

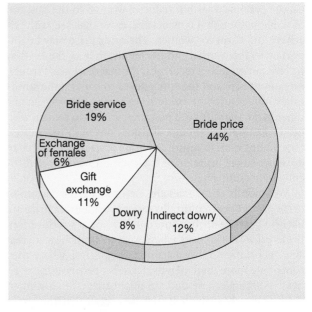

FIGURE 1 Distribution of Economic Marriage Transactions Among Societies That Have Them
Note that there are societies in the ethnographic record (25 percent) that lack any substantial economic transactions at marriage.

Source: Based on data from Schlegel and Eloul 1988, 291–309. Based on data from Alice Schlegel and RohnEloul, "Marriage Transactions: Labor, Property, and Status," *American Anthropologist* 90 (1988): 291–309.

Bride Price **Bride price** or **bride wealth** is a gift of money or goods from the groom or his kin to the bride's kin. The gift usually grants the groom the right to marry the bride and the right to her children. Of all the forms of economic transaction involved in marriage, bride price is the most common. In one cross-cultural sample, 44 percent of the societies with economic transactions at marriage practiced bride price; in almost all of those societies, the bride price was substantial.[27] Bride price occurs all over the world but is especially common in Africa and Oceania. Payment can be made in different currencies; livestock and food are two of the more common. With the increased importance of commercial exchange, money has increasingly become part of the bride price payments. Among the Nandi, the bride price consists of about five to seven cattle, one or two sheep and goats, cowrie shells, and money equivalent to the value of one cow. Even in unusual female-female marriages, the female "husband" must pay a bride price to arrange the marriage and be considered the "father."[28]

The Subanun of the Philippines have an expensive bride price—several times the annual income of the groom plus three to five years of bride service (described in the next section).[29] Among the Manus of the Admiralty Islands off New Guinea, a groom requires an economic backer, usually an older brother or an uncle, if he is to marry, but it will be years before he can pay off his debts. Depending on the final bride price, payments may be concluded at the time of the marriage, or they may continue for years afterward.[30]

Despite the connotations that bride price may have for us, the practice does not reduce a woman to the position of slave—although it is associated, as we shall see, with relatively low status for women. The bride price may be important to the woman and her family. Indeed, the fee they receive can serve as a security. If the marriage fails through no fault of hers and the wife returns to her kin, the family might not return the bride price to the groom. On the other hand, the wife's kin may pressure her to remain with her husband, even though she does not wish to, because they do not want to return the bride price or are unable to do so. A larger bride price is associated with more difficulty in obtaining a divorce.[31]

What kinds of societies are likely to have the custom of bride price? Cross-culturally, societies with bride price are likely to practice horticulture and lack social stratification. Bride price is also likely where women contribute a great deal to primary subsistence activities[32] and where they contribute more than men to all kinds of economic activities.[33] Although these findings might suggest that women are highly valued in such societies, recall that the status of women relative to men is not higher in societies in which women contribute a lot to primary subsistence activities. Indeed, bride price is likely to occur in societies in which men make most of the decisions in the household,[34] and decision making by men is one indicator of lower status for women.

Bride Service

Bride service, which is the next most common type of economic transaction at marriage—occurring in about 19 percent of the societies with economic transactions—requires the groom to work for the bride's family, sometimes before the marriage begins, sometimes after. Bride service varies in duration. In some societies, it lasts for only a few months; in others, as long as several years. Among the North Alaskan Eskimo, for example, the boy works for his in-laws after the marriage is arranged. To fulfill his obligation, he may simply catch a seal for them. The marriage may be consummated at any time while he is in service.[35] In some societies, bride service sometimes substitutes for bride price. An individual might give bride service to reduce the amount of bride price required. Native North and South American societies were likely to practice bride service, particularly if they were egalitarian food collectors.[36]

Exchange of Females

Of the societies that have economic transactions at marriage, 6 percent have the custom whereby a sister or female relative of the groom is exchanged for the bride. Among these societies are the Tiv of West Africa and the Yanomamö of Venezuela and Brazil. These societies tend to be horticultural, egalitarian, and to have a relatively high contribution of women to primary subsistence.[37]

Gift Exchange

Gift exchange, which involves the exchange of gifts of about equal value by the two kin groups about to be linked by marriage, occurs somewhat more often than the exchange of females (about 11 percent of those with economic transactions).[38] For example, among the Andaman Islanders, as soon as a boy and girl indicate their intention to marry, their respective sets of parents cease all communication and begin sending gifts of food and other objects to each other through a third party. This arrangement continues until the marriage is completed and the two kin groups are united.[39]

Dowry

A **dowry** is usually a substantial transfer of goods or money from the bride's family to the bride, the groom, or the couple.[40] Unlike the types of transactions we have discussed so far, the dowry, which occurs in about 8 percent of the societies with economic transactions, is usually not a transaction between the kin of the bride and the kin of the groom. A family has to have wealth to give a dowry, but because the goods go to the new household, no wealth comes back to the family that gave the dowry. Payment of dowries was common in medieval and Renaissance Europe, where the size of the dowry often determined the desirability of the daughter. The custom is still practiced in parts of eastern Europe and in sections of southern Italy and France, where land is often the major item the bride's family provides. Parts of India also practice the dowry.

In contrast to societies with bride price, societies with dowry tend to be those in which women contribute relatively little to primary subsistence activities, there is a high degree of social stratification, and a man is not allowed to be married to more than one woman simultaneously.[41] Why does dowry tend to occur in these types of societies? One theory suggests that the dowry is intended to guarantee future support for a woman and her children, even though she will not do much primary subsistence work. Another theory is that the dowry is intended to attract the best bridegroom for a daughter in monogamous societies with a high degree of social inequality. The dowry strategy is presumed to increase the likelihood that the daughter and her children will do well reproductively. Both theories are supported by recent cross-cultural research, with the second predicting dowry better.[42] But many stratified societies in which women and men have only one spouse at a time (including our own) do not practice dowry. Why this is so still needs to be explained.

Indirect Dowry

The dowry is provided by the bride's family to the bride, the groom, or the couple. But sometimes the payments to the bride originate from the groom's family. Because the goods are sometimes first given to the bride's father, who passes most if not all of them to her, this kind of transaction is called **indirect dowry.**[43] Indirect dowry occurs in about 12 percent of the societies in which marriage involves an economic transaction. For example, among the Basseri of southern Iran, the groom's father assumes the expense of setting up the couple's new household. He gives cash to the bride's father, who uses at least some of the money to buy his daughter household utensils, blankets, and rugs.[44]

RESTRICTIONS ON MARRIAGE: THE UNIVERSAL INCEST TABOO

Hollywood and its press agents notwithstanding, marriage is not always based solely on mutual love, independently discovered and expressed by the two life-partners-to-be. Nor is it based on sex or wealth alone. Even when love, sex, and economics are contributing factors, regulations specify whom one may or may not marry. Perhaps the most rigid regulation, found in *all* cultures, is the **incest taboo,** which prohibits sexual intercourse or marriage between some categories of kin.

The most universal aspect of the incest taboo is the prohibition of sexual intercourse or marriage between mother and son, father and daughter, and brother and sister. No society in recent times has permitted either sexual intercourse or marriage between those pairs. A few societies in the past, however, did permit incest, mostly within the royal and aristocratic families, though generally it was forbidden to the rest of the population. For example, the Incan and Hawaiian royal families allowed marriage within the family. Probably the best-known example of allowed incest involved Cleopatra of Egypt.

It seems clear that the Egyptian aristocracy and royalty indulged in father-daughter and brother-sister marriages. Cleopatra was married to two of her younger brothers at different times.[45] The reasons seem to have been partly religious—a member of the family of the pharaoh, who was considered a god, could not marry any "ordinary" human—and partly economic, for marriage within the family kept the royal property undivided. In Egypt, between 30 B.C. and A.D. 324, incest was allowed not just in the royal family; an estimated 8 percent of commoner marriages were brother-sister marriages.[46]

But, despite these exceptions, the fact remains that no culture we know of today permits or accepts incest within the nuclear family. Why is the familial incest taboo universal? Several explanations have been suggested.

Childhood-Familiarity Theory

The childhood-familiarity theory, suggested by Edward Westermarck, was given a wide hearing in the early 1920s. Westermarck argued that people who have been closely associated with each other since earliest childhood, such as siblings, are not sexually attracted to each other and therefore would avoid marriage with each other.[47] This theory was subsequently rejected because of evidence

Children eating in the Children's House's kitchen on an Israeli kibbutz.

that some children were sexually interested in their parents and siblings. Studies have suggested, however, that there might be something to Westermarck's theory.

Yonina Talmon investigated marriage patterns among the second generation of three well-established collective communities (*kibbutzim*) in Israel. In these collectives, children live with many members of their peer group in quarters separate from their families. They are in constant interaction with their peers, from birth to maturity. The study revealed that, among 125 couples, there was "not one instance in which both mates were reared from birth in the same peer group,"[48] despite parental encouragement of marriage within the peer group. Children reared in common not only avoided marriage, they also avoided any sexual relations among themselves.

Talmon stated that the people reared together firmly believed that overfamiliarity breeds sexual disinterest. As one of them told her, "We are like an open book to each other. We have read the story in the book over and over again and know all about it."[49] Talmon's evidence reveals not only the onset of disinterest and even sexual antipathy among children reared together, but a correspondingly heightened fascination with newcomers or outsiders, particularly for their "mystery."

Arthur Wolf's study of the Chinese in northern Taiwan also supports the idea that something about being reared together produces sexual disinterest. Wolf focused on a community still practicing the Chinese custom of *t'ung-yang-hsi,* or "daughter-in-law raised from childhood":

When a girl is born in a poor family . . . she is often given away or sold when but a few weeks or months old, or one or two years old, to be the future wife of a son in the family of a friend or relative which has a little son not betrothed in marriage. . . . The girl is called a "little bride" and taken home and brought up in the family together with her future husband.[50]

Wolf's evidence indicates that this arrangement is associated with sexual difficulties when the childhood "couple" later marry. Informants implied that familiarity results in disinterest and lack of stimulation. As an indication of their disinterest, these couples produce fewer offspring than spouses not raised together, they are more likely to seek extramarital sexual relationships, and they are more likely to get divorced.[51]

The Talmon and Wolf studies suggest, then, that children raised together are not likely to be sexually interested in each other when they grow up. Such disinterest is consistent with Westermarck's notion that the incest taboo may be more an avoidance of certain matings than a prohibition of them. There is one other piece of evidence consistent with this explanation of the incest taboo. Hilda and Seymour Parker compared two samples of fathers: those who had sexually abused their daughters and those who supposedly had not.[52] To maximize their similarities otherwise, the Parkers selected the two samples of fathers from the same prisons and psychiatric facilities. The Parkers found that the fathers who had committed incest with their daughters were much more likely than the other sample of fathers to have had little to do with bringing up their daughters, because they were not at home or hardly at home during the daughters' first three years of life. In other words, the fathers who avoided incest had been more closely associated with their daughters in childhood. That finding is consistent with Westermarck's suggestion that the incest taboo is a result of familiarity in childhood.

Although Westermarck was talking about the development of sexual aversion during early childhood, some researchers have asked how the childhood familiarity theory could explain the extension of incest taboos to first cousins. The familiarity argument implies that first-cousin marriage should be prohibited in societies in which first cousins grow up together in the same community. But that is not the case. Such societies are not more likely to prohibit first-cousin marriage.[53]

Even if there is something about familiarity in childhood that normally leads to sexual disinterest,[54] we still are left with the question of why societies have to prohibit marriages that would voluntarily be avoided because of disinterest. And why do many couples remain actively interested in each other sexually after years of marriage?

Freud's Psychoanalytic Theory

Sigmund Freud proposed that the incest taboo is a reaction against unconscious, unacceptable desires.[55] He suggested that the son is attracted to his mother (as the daughter is to her father) and as a result feels jealousy and hostility toward his father. But the son knows that these feelings cannot continue, for they might lead the father to retaliate against him; therefore, they must be renounced or repressed. Usually the feelings are repressed and retreat into the unconscious. But the desire to possess the mother continues to exist in the unconscious, and, according to

Freud, the horror of incest is a reaction to, or a defense against, the forbidden unconscious impulse.

Although Freud's theory may account for the aversion felt toward incest, or at least the aversion toward parent-child incest, it does not explain why society needs an explicit taboo, particularly on brother-sister incest. Nor does it account for the findings of sexual disinterest we discussed in connection with the Westermarck hypothesis.

Family-Disruption Theory

The family-disruption theory, often associated with Bronislaw Malinowski,[56] can best be summed up as follows: Sexual competition among family members would create so much rivalry and tension that the family could not function as an effective unit. Because the family must function effectively for society to survive, society has to curtail competition within the family. The familial incest taboo is thus imposed to keep the family intact.

But there are inconsistencies in this approach. Society could have shaped other rules about the sexual access of one member of the family to another that would also eliminate potentially disruptive competition. Also, why would brother-sister incest be so disruptive? As we noted, such marriages did exist in ancient Egypt. Brother-sister incest would not disrupt the authority of the parents if the children were allowed to marry when mature. The family-disruption theory, then, does not explain the origin of the incest taboo.

Cooperation Theory

The cooperation theory was proposed by the early anthropologist Edward B. Tylor and was elaborated by Leslie A. White and Claude Lévi-Strauss. It emphasizes the value of the incest taboo in promoting cooperation among family groups and thus helping communities to survive. As Tylor saw it, certain operations necessary for the welfare of the community can be accomplished only by large numbers of people working together. To break down suspicion and hostility between family groups and make such cooperation possible, early humans developed the incest taboo to ensure that individuals would marry members of other families. The ties created by intermarriage would serve to hold the community together. Thus, Tylor explained the incest taboo as an answer to the choice "between marrying out and being killed out."[57]

The idea that marriage with other groups promotes cooperation sounds plausible, but is there evidence to support it? After all, there are societies such as the Gusii in which marriage is often between hostile groups. But is that society an exception? Does marriage promote cooperation? Because people in all recent societies marry outside the family, we cannot test the idea that such marriages promote cooperation more than marriages within the family. We can, however, ask whether other kinds of out-marriage, such as marriage with other communities, promote cooperation with those communities. The evidence on that question does not support the cooperation theory. There is no greater peacefulness between communities when marriages are forbidden within the community and always arranged with other communities than when they are not.[58]

But even if marriage outside the family promoted cooperation with other groups, why would it be necessary to prohibit all marriages within the family? Couldn't families have required some of their members to marry outside the family if they thought it necessary for survival but permitted incestuous marriages when such alliances were not needed? Although the incest taboo might enhance cooperation between families, the need for cooperation does not adequately explain the existence of the incest taboo in all societies; other customs might also promote alliances. Furthermore, the cooperation theory does not explain the sexual aspect of the incest taboo. Societies could conceivably allow incestuous sex and still insist that children marry outside the family.

Inbreeding Theory

One of the oldest explanations for the incest taboo is inbreeding theory. It focuses on the potentially damaging consequences of inbreeding or marrying within the family. People within the same family are likely to carry the same harmful recessive genes. Inbreeding, then, will tend to produce offspring who are more likely to die early of genetic disorders than are the offspring of unrelated spouses. Recent evidence also suggests that inbreeding tends to increase the likelihood of diseases that affect people later in life, such as heart disease and diabetes.[59] For many years, inbreeding theory was rejected because, on the basis of dog-breeding practices, it was thought that inbreeding need not be harmful. The inbreeding practiced to produce prize-winning dogs, however, is not a good guide to whether inbreeding is harmful; dog breeders don't count the runts they cull when they try to breed for success in dog shows. We now have a good deal of evidence, from humans as well as other animals, that the closer the degree of inbreeding, the more harmful the genetic effects.[60]

Genetic mutations occur frequently. Although many pose no harm to the individuals who carry a single recessive gene, matings between two people who carry the same gene often produce offspring with a harmful or lethal condition. Close blood relatives are much more likely than unrelated individuals to carry the same harmful recessive gene. So, if close relatives mate, their offspring have a higher probability than the offspring of nonrelatives of inheriting the harmful trait.

One study compared children produced by familial incest with children of the same mothers produced by non-incestuous unions. About 40 percent of the incestuously produced children had serious abnormalities, compared with about 5 percent of the other children.[61] Matings between other kinds of relatives not as closely related also show harmful, but not as harmful, effects of inbreeding. These results are consistent with inbreeding theory. The likelihood that a child will inherit a double dose of a harmful recessive gene is lower the more distantly the child's parents are related. Also consistent with inbreeding theory is the fact that rates of abnormality are consistently higher in the offspring of uncle-niece marriages (which are allowed in some societies) than in the offspring of cousin marriages; for the offspring of uncle-niece marriages, the likelihood of inheriting a double dose of a harmful recessive is twice that for the offspring of first cousins.[62]

Although most scholars acknowledge the harmful effects of inbreeding, some question whether people in former days would have deliberately invented or borrowed the incest taboo because they knew that inbreeding was biologically harmful. William Durham's cross-cultural survey suggests that they did. Ethnographers do not always report the perceived consequences of incest, but in 50 percent of the reports Durham found, biological harm to the offspring was mentioned.[63] For example, Raymond Firth reported on the Tikopia, who live on an island in the South Pacific:

> The idea is firmly held that unions of close kin bear with them their own doom, their *mara*. . . . The idea [*mara*] essentially concerns barrenness. . . . The peculiar barrenness of an incestuous union consists not in the absence of children, but in their illness or death, or some other mishap. . . . The idea that the offspring of a marriage between near kin are weakly and likely to die young is stoutly held by these natives and examples are adduced to prove it.[64]

So, if the harm of inbreeding was widely recognized, people may have deliberately invented or borrowed the incest taboo.[65] But whether or not people actually recognized the harmfulness of inbreeding, the demographic consequences of the incest taboo would account for its universality, because reproductive and hence competitive advantages probably accrued to groups practicing the taboo. Thus, although cultural solutions other than the incest taboo might provide the desired effects assumed by the family-disruption theory and the cooperation theory, the incest taboo is the only possible solution to the problem of inbreeding.

As is discussed toward the end of the next section, a society may or may not extend the incest taboo to first cousins. That variation is also predictable from inbreeding theory, which provides additional support for the idea that the incest taboo was invented or borrowed to avoid the harmful consequences of inbreeding.

WHOM SHOULD ONE MARRY?

Probably every child in our society knows the story of Cinderella—the poor, downtrodden, but lovely girl who accidentally meets, falls in love with, and eventually marries a prince. It is a charming tale, but it is misleading as a guide to mate choice in our society. The majority of marriages simply do not occur in so free and coincidental a way in any society. In addition to the incest taboo, societies often have rules restricting marriage with other people, as well as preferences about which other people are the most desirable mates.

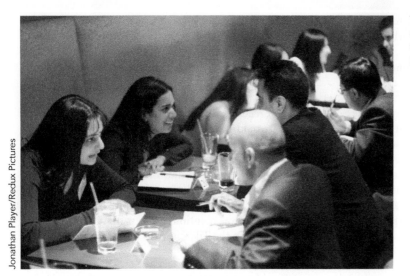

These young South Asian Hindus in Great Britain are "speed dating." They talk with potential spouses for three minutes each. Traditionally, parents arrange marriages.

Jonathan Player/Redux Pictures

Even in a modern, urbanized society such as ours, where theoretically mate choice is free, people tend to marry within their own class and geographic area. For example, studies in the United States consistently indicate that a person is likely to marry someone who lives close by.[66] Neighborhoods are frequently made up of people from similar class backgrounds, so it is unlikely that many of these alliances are Cinderella stories.

Arranged Marriages

In an appreciable number of societies, marriages are arranged; immediate families or go-betweens handle the negotiations. Sometimes betrothals are completed while the future partners are still children. This was formerly the custom in much of Hindu India, China, Japan, and eastern and southern Europe. Implicit in the arranged marriage is the conviction that the joining together of two kin groups to form new social and economic ties is too important to be left to free choice and romantic love.

An example of a marriage arranged for reasons of prestige comes from Clellan Ford's study of the Kwakiutl of British Columbia. Ford's informant described his marriage as follows:

When I was old enough to get a wife—I was about 25—my brothers looked for a girl in the same position that I and my brothers had. Without my consent, they picked a wife for me—Lagius' daughter. The one I wanted was prettier than the one they chose for me, but she was in a lower position than me, so they wouldn't let me marry her.[67]

Arranged marriages are becoming less common in many places, and couples are beginning to have more say about their marriage partners. But in 1960, marriages were still arranged on the Pacific island of Rotuma, and sometimes the bride and groom did not meet until the wedding day. Today, weddings are much the same, but couples are allowed to "go out" and have a say about whom they wish

to marry.[68] In a small Moroccan town, arranged marriages are still the norm, although a young man may ask his mother to make a marriage offer to a particular girl's parents, who may ask her whether she wants to accept the marriage offer. But dating is still not acceptable, so getting acquainted is hard to arrange.[69]

Exogamy and Endogamy

Marriage partners often must be chosen from outside one's own kin group or community; this is known as a rule of **exogamy.** Exogamy can take many forms. It may mean marrying outside a particular group of kin or outside a particular village or group of villages. Often, then, spouses come from a distance. For example, in Rani Khera, a village in India, 266 married women had come from about 200 different villages, averaging between 12 and 24 miles away; 220 local women had gone to 200 other villages to marry. As a result of these exogamous marriages, Rani Khera, a village of 150 households, was linked to 400 other nearby villages.[70] When there are rules of exogamy, violations are often believed to cause harm. On the islands of Yap in Micronesia, people who are related through women are referred to as "people of one belly." The elders say that, if two people from the same kinship group married, they would not have any female children and the group would die out.[71]

People in societies with very low population densities often have to travel considerable distances to meet mates. A study of foragers and horticulturalists found a clear relationship between population density and the distance between the communities of the husband and wife—the lower the density, the greater the marriage distance. Because foragers generally have lower densities than horticulturalists, they generally have further to go to find mates. Among the !Kung, for instance, the average husband and wife had lived 40 miles (65 kilometers) from each other before they were married.[72]

A rule of **endogamy** obliges a person to marry within some group. The caste groups of India traditionally have

migrants and immigrants

Arranging Marriages in the Diaspora

What happens when people move from a place with arranged marriage to a place where marriage is based on free choice and romantic love? Many people around the world or their parents are from places that reject love marriage because it could fizzle out. Love was not considered a sufficient basis for marriage. So parents and other kin, or hired go-betweens, would select your marriage partner, preferably someone from the same socioeconomic background. For example, in many parts of South Asia, one was supposed to marry someone from the same caste and class until recently. Many immigrant parents still insist that their children's marriages be arranged. But this is changing. Consider how some young South Asians in England are "arranging" their own marriages.

Go-betweens are replaced by Web sites, chat rooms, and personal advertisements on the Internet. A couple who "meet" first electronically might arrange a face-to-face meeting, in what's called "South Asian speed dating"; they agree to meet and talk—for just three minutes—at a restaurant or bar, and then they move on. The participants, who are in their 20s and middle class, consider themselves hip. They are quite comfortable blending behaviors from West and East. But many marriages are still arranged by relatives or go-betweens. Is it because there is discrimination against South Asians and therefore it is difficult to meet and marry other kinds of people? Is the same true for South Asians in the United States?

The United States has had a long history of discrimination against people of color, and South Asians generally have darker skins. So they may also encounter social barriers. Most immigrant groups in the past and present have had restricted opportunities to meet and marry people from different ethnic and class backgrounds. Poor people didn't belong to country clubs. Certain ethnic groups were not admitted, or only admitted sparingly, to Ivy League colleges. To be sure, some people were able to "move up" economically, and this provided more opportunities to meet people from other backgrounds. But marriages were generally restricted to your own class, religion, and locality. And this is still true for the most part. We might expect then that immigrants who come from South Asia would continue to practice arranged marriage. And many do. Young people may say that they would prefer to have a love marriage. But they wouldn't dream of marrying someone who was not like them. And so their parents hire a matchmaker to find them a spouse.

Rakhi is a lawyer in New York City. She is the daughter of Sikh immigrants from Punjab, India. (The Sikhs are a religious group.) As a young girl, Rakhi had built a shrine to an American movie star in her bedroom. But at the age of 27, she decided to marry someone like herself. But she was focused on her career and didn't have time to date. So her mother enlisted the help of a Sikh matchmaker who had been instructed by the mother of a man named Ranjeet to find a wife for him. Ranjeet also had thought he would marry for love. "But seeing how different cultures treated their families, I realized the importance of making the right match." When the matchmaker organized a party to which she invited Rakhi and Ranjeet (and their mothers), Rakhi's mother whispered: "I think he's the one." After the two young people dated secretly for two months, the matchmaker was once again summoned, this time to negotiate the marital arrangements. Some time later, Rakhi and Ranjeet were married in a Sikh temple in a New York suburb.

Sources: Alvarez 2003, Section 1, p. 3; Henderson 2002, Section 9, p. 2.

---

been endogamous. The higher castes believed that marriage with lower castes would "pollute" them, and such unions were forbidden. Caste endogamy is also found in some parts of Africa. In East Africa, a Masai warrior would never stoop to marry the daughter of an ironworker, nor would a former ruling caste Tutsi in Rwanda, in central Africa, think of marrying a person from the hunting caste Twa.

Cousin Marriages

Kinship terminology for most people in the United States does not differentiate between types of cousins. In some other societies, such distinctions may be important, particularly with regard to first cousins; the terms for the different kinds of first cousins may indicate which cousins are suitable marriage partners (sometimes even preferred mates) and which are not. Although most societies prohibit marriage with all types of first cousins,[73] some societies allow and even prefer particular kinds of cousin marriage.

Cross-cousins are children of siblings of the opposite sex; that is, a person's cross-cousins are the father's sisters' children and the mother's brothers' children. **Parallel cousins** are children of siblings of the same sex; a person's parallel cousins, then, are the father's brothers' children and the mother's sisters' children. The Chippewa Indians used to practice cross-cousin marriage, as well as cross-cousin joking. With his female cross-cousins, a Chippewa man was expected to exchange broad, risqué jokes, but he would not do so with his parallel cousins, with whom severe propriety was the rule. In general, in any society in which cross-cousin marriage is allowed but parallel cousin is not, there is a joking relationship between a man and his female cross-cousins. This attitude contrasts with the formal and very respectful relationship the man maintains with female parallel cousins. Apparently, the joking relationship signifies the possibility of marriage, whereas the respectful relationship signifies the extension of the incest taboo to parallel cousins.

When first-cousin marriage is allowed or preferred, it is usually with some kind of cross-cousin. Parallel-cousin marriage is fairly rare, but Muslim societies usually prefer such marriages, allowing other cousin marriages as well. The Kurds, who are mostly Sunni Muslims, prefer a young man to marry his father's brother's daughter (for the young woman, this would be her father's brother's son). The father and his brother usually live near each other, so the woman will stay close to home in such a marriage. The bride and groom are also in the same kin group, so marriage in this case also entails kin group endogamy.[74]

What kinds of societies allow or prefer first-cousin marriage? There is evidence from cross-cultural research that cousin marriages are most apt to be permitted in relatively large and densely populated societies. Perhaps this is because the likelihood of such marriages, and therefore the risks of inbreeding, are minimal in those societies. Many small, sparsely populated societies, however, permit or even sometimes prefer cousin marriage. How can these cases be explained? They seem to cast doubt on the interpretation that cousin marriage should be prohibited in sparsely populated societies, in which marriages between close relatives are more likely just by chance and the risks of inbreeding should be greatest. It turns out that most of the small societies that permit cousin marriage have lost a lot of people to epidemics. Many peoples around the world, particularly in the Pacific and in North and South America, suffered severe depopulation in the first generation or two after contact with Europeans, who introduced diseases (such as measles, pneumonia, and smallpox) to which the native populations had little or no resistance. Such societies may have had to permit cousin marriage to provide enough mating possibilities among the reduced population of eligible mates.[75]

Levirate and Sororate

In many societies, cultural rules oblige individuals to marry the spouse of deceased relatives. **Levirate** is a custom whereby a man is obliged to marry his brother's widow. **Sororate** obliges a woman to marry her deceased sister's husband. Both customs are exceedingly common, being the obligatory form of second marriage in a majority of societies known to anthropology.[76]

Among the Chukchee of Siberia, levirate obliges the next oldest brother to become the successor husband. He cares for the widow and children, assumes the sexual privileges of the husband, and unites the deceased's reindeer herd with his own, keeping it in the name of his brother's children. If there are no brothers, the widow is married to a cousin of her first husband. The Chukchee regard the custom more as a duty than as a right. The nearest relative is obliged to care for a woman left with children and a herd.[77]

HOW MANY DOES ONE MARRY?

We are accustomed to thinking of marriage as involving just one man and one woman at a time—**monogamy**—but most societies known to anthropology have allowed a man to be married to more than one woman at the same time—**polygyny.** At any given time, however, the majority of men in societies permitting polygyny are married monogamously; few or no societies have enough women to permit most men to have at least two wives. Polygyny's mirror image—one woman being married to more than one man at the same time, called **polyandry**—is practiced in very few societies. Polygyny and polyandry are the two types of **polygamy,** or plural spouse marriage. **Group marriage,** in which more than one man is married to more than one woman at the same time, sometimes occurs but is not customary in any known society.

Polygyny

The Old Testament has many references to men with more than one wife simultaneously: King David and King Solomon are just two examples of men polygynously married. Just as in the society described in the Old Testament, polygyny in many societies is a mark of a man's great wealth or high status. In such societies, only the very wealthy can, and are expected to, support more than one wife. Some Muslim societies, especially Arabic-speaking ones, still view polygyny in this light. But a man does not always have to be wealthy to be polygynous; indeed, in some societies in which women are important contributors to the economy, it seems that men try to have more than one wife to become wealthier.

Among the Siwai, a society in the South Pacific, status is achieved through feast giving. Pork is the main dish at these feasts, so the Siwai associate pig raising with prestige. This great interest in pigs sparks an interest in wives, because in Siwai society, women raise the food needed to raise pigs. Thus, although having many wives does not in itself confer status among the Siwai, the increase in pig herds that may result from polygyny is a source of prestige for the owner.[78]

Polygynously married Siwai men do seem to have greater prestige, but they complain that a household with multiple wives is difficult. Sinu, a Siwai, described his plight:

There is never peace for a long time in a polygynous family. If the husband sleeps in the house of one wife, the other one sulks all the next day. If the man is so stupid as to sleep two consecutive nights in the house of one wife, the other one will refuse to cook for him, saying, "So-and-so is your wife; go to her for food. Since I am not good enough for you to sleep with, then my food is not good enough for you to eat." Frequently the co-wives will quarrel and fight. My uncle formerly had five wives at one time and the youngest one was always raging and fighting the others. Once she knocked an older wife senseless and then ran away and had to be forcibly returned.[79]

Polygyny is practiced by some in this country, even though it is prohibited by law.

Co-wife conflict seems not to be present in some societies. For example, Margaret Mead reported that married life among the Arapesh of New Guinea, even in the polygynous marriages, was "so even and contented that there is nothing to relate of it at all."[80] Why might there be little or no obvious jealousy between co-wives in a society? One possible reason is that a man is married to two or more sisters—**sororal polygyny;** it seems that sisters, having grown up together, are more likely to get along and cooperate as co-wives than are co-wives who are not also sisters—**nonsororal polygyny.** Indeed, a recent cross-cultural study confirms that endemic conflict and persistent resentment were virtually ubiquitous in societies with nonsororal polygyny.[81] The most commonly reported reason for the conflict and resentment was insufficient access to the husband for sex and emotional support.

Perhaps because conflict is so common, polygynous societies have invented customs to try to lessen conflict and jealousy in co-wives:

1. Co-wives who are not sisters tend to have separate living quarters; sororal co-wives almost always live together. Among the Plateau Tonga in Africa, who practice nonsororal polygyny, the husband shares his personal goods and his favors among his wives, who live in separate dwellings, according to principles of strict equality. The Crow Indians practiced sororal polygyny, and co-wives usually shared a tepee.

2. Co-wives have clearly defined equal rights in matters of sex, economics, and personal possessions. For example, the Tanala of Madagascar require the husband to spend a day with each co-wife in succession. Failure to do so constitutes adultery and entitles the slighted wife to sue for divorce and alimony of up to one-third of the husband's property. Furthermore, the land is shared equally among all the women, who expect the husband to help with its cultivation when he visits them.

3. Senior wives often have special prestige. The Tonga of Polynesia, for example, grant to the first wife the status of "chief wife." Her house is to the right of her husband's and is called the "house of the father." The other wives are called "small wives," and their houses are to the left of the husband's. The chief wife has the right to be consulted before the small wives, and her husband is expected to sleep under her roof before and after a journey. Although this rule might seem to enhance the jealousy of the secondary wives, later wives are usually favored somewhat because they tend to be younger and more attractive. By this custom, then, the first wife may be compensated for her loss of physical attractiveness by increased prestige.[82]

We must remember that, although jealousy and conflict are commonly mentioned in polygynous marriages, they are not always present. People who practice polygyny may think it has considerable advantages. In a study conducted by Philip and Janet Kilbride in Kenya, female as well as male married people agreed that polygyny had economic and political advantages. Because they tend to be large, polygynous families provide plenty of farm labor and extra food that can be marketed. They also tend to be influential in their communities and are likely to produce individuals who become government officials.[83] And in South Africa, Connie Anderson found that women choose to be married to a man with other wives because the other wives could help with child care and household work, provide companionship, and allow more freedom to come and go. Some women said they chose polygynous marriages because there was a shortage of marriageable males.[84]

How can we account for the fact that polygyny is allowed and often preferred in most of the societies known to anthropology? Ralph Linton suggested that polygyny derives from a general male primate urge to collect females.[85] But if that were so, then why wouldn't all societies allow polygyny? Other explanations of polygyny have been suggested. We restrict our discussion here to those that statistically and strongly predict polygyny in worldwide samples of societies.

One theory is that polygyny will be permitted in societies that have a long **postpartum sex taboo.**[86] In these societies, a couple must abstain from intercourse until their child is at least a year old. John Whiting suggested that couples abstain from sexual intercourse for a long time after their child is born for health reasons. A Hausa woman reported:

A mother should not go to her husband while she has a child she is suckling. If she does, the child gets thin; he dries up, he won't be strong, he won't be healthy. If she goes after two years it is nothing, he is already strong before that, it does not matter if she conceives again after two years.[87]

The symptoms the woman described seem to be those of *kwashiorkor.* Common in tropical areas, kwashiorkor is a protein-deficiency disease that occurs particularly in children suffering from intestinal parasites or diarrhea. By observing a long postpartum sex taboo, and thereby ensuring that her children are widely spaced, a woman can nurse each child longer. If a child gets protein from

current research and issues

The Husband-Wife Relationship: Variation in Love, Intimacy, and Sexual Jealousy

Americans believe that love should be a basis of marriage. Does this ideal characterize most societies? We know the answer to that question: No. In fact, in many places, romantic love is believed to be a poor basis for marriage and is strongly discouraged. However, even though romantic love may not be a basis for marriage everywhere, it does occur almost everywhere. A recent cross-cultural survey suggests that about 88 percent of the world's societies show signs of romantic love—accounts of personal longing, love songs or love depicted in folklore, elopement because of affection, and passionate love described by informants quoted in ethnographies. So if love is nearly universal, why is it often discouraged as a basis for marriage?

Three conditions appear to predict such discouragement. One is that the husband and wife live in an extended family. In this situation, the family seems more concerned with how the in-marrying person gets along with others, and less concerned with whether the husband and wife love each other. A second condition predicting the discouragement of romantic love as a basis for marriage is that one of the spouses does most of the primary subsistence work or earns most of the couple's income. Third, romantic love is unlikely when men have more sexual freedom than women. In general, then, romantic love is discouraged as a basis for marriage under conditions of inequality—if one of the spouses is highly dependent on the other or the other's kin or the woman has fewer sexual rights than the man.

Intimacy is different from romantic love. It refers to how close the mar-

The valentine, as in this 19th-century British card, symbolizes romantic love.

ried couple are to each other—eating together, sleeping in the same bed, spending their leisure time together, as well as having frequent sex. In some societies, couples are together a lot; in others, they spend very little time together. Foraging societies seem on average to have more marital intimacy than more complex herding and agricultural societies, but the reasons are not entirely clear. Also, a high involvement in war seems to detract from intimacy.

When it comes to sexual jealousy, men are far more likely to be violent than women. Incidentally, infidelity is the most frequently reported reason for a husband to divorce a wife. Anthropologists with a biological orientation point out that fathers always have some uncertainty about whether their children are theirs, so males are much more likely for that reason alone to try to guard against rival males. But how can we account for the considerable

variation in jealousy from one society to another? It does seem that the more a society emphasizes the importance of getting married, the more it limits sex to the marriage relationship, the more it emphasizes property, and the more its males appear to exhibit sexual jealousy.

How are these various aspects of marriage related to each other? Does romantic love as a basis for marriage increase or decrease sexual jealousy? Does romantic love predict intimacy, or is romantic love more likely with less frequent contact between the spouses? We are still far from understanding how these different aspects are related. All we know is that an emphasis on love and intimacy does not preclude marital violence or marital dissolution.

Sources: Hendrix 2009; Betzig 1989; Jankowiak and Fischer 1992; de Munck and Korotayev 1999. 〰〰

mother's milk during its first few years, the likelihood of contracting kwashiorkor may be greatly reduced. Consistent with Whiting's interpretation is the fact that societies with low-protein staples (those whose principal foods are root and tree crops such as taro, sweet potatoes, bananas, and breadfruit) tend to have a long postpartum sex taboo. Societies with long postpartum sex taboos also tend to be

polygynous. Perhaps, then, a man's having more than one wife is a cultural adjustment to the taboo. As a Yoruba woman said,

When we abstain from having sexual intercourse with our husband for the two years we nurse our babies, we know he will seek some other woman. We would rather have her under our control as a co-wife so he is not spending money outside the family.[88]

Even if we agree that men will seek other sexual relationships during the period of a long postpartum sex taboo, it is not clear why polygyny is the only possible solution to the problem. After all, it is conceivable that all of a man's wives might be subject to the postpartum sex taboo at the same time. Furthermore, there may be sexual outlets outside marriage.

Another explanation of polygyny is that it is a response to an excess of women over men. Such an imbalanced sex ratio may occur because of the prevalence of warfare in a society. Because men and not women are generally the warriors, warfare almost always takes a greater toll of men's lives. Given that almost all adults in noncommercial societies are married, polygyny may be a way of providing spouses for surplus women. Indeed, there is evidence that societies with imbalanced sex ratios in favor of women tend to have both polygyny and high male mortality in warfare. Conversely, societies with balanced sex ratios tend to have both monogamy and low male mortality in warfare.[89]

A third explanation is that a society will allow polygyny when men marry at an older age than women. The argument is similar to the sex ratio interpretation. Delaying the age of marriage for men would produce an artificial, though not an actual, excess of marriageable women. Why marriage for men is delayed is not clear, but the delay does predict polygyny.[90]

Is one of these explanations better than the others, or are all three factors—long postpartum sex taboo, an imbalanced sex ratio in favor of women, and delayed age of marriage for men—important in explaining polygyny? One way of trying to decide among alternative explanations is to do what is called a *statistical-control analysis,* which allows us to see if a particular factor still predicts when the effects of other possible factors are removed. In this case, when the possible effect of sex ratio is removed, a long postpartum sex taboo no longer predicts polygyny and hence is probably not a cause of polygyny.[91] But both an actual excess of women and a late age of marriage for men seem to be strong predictors of polygyny. Added together, these two factors predict even more strongly.[92]

Behavioral ecologists have also suggested ecological reasons why both men and women might prefer polygynous marriages. If there are enough resources, men might prefer polygyny because they can have more children if they have more than one wife. If resources are highly variable and men control resources, women might find it advantageous to marry a man with many resources even if she is a second wife. A recent study of foragers suggests that foraging societies in which men control hunting or fishing territories are more likely to be polygynous. This finding is consistent with the theory, but the authors were surprised that control of gathering sites by men did not predict polygyny.[93] The main problem with the theory of variable resources and their marital consequences is that many societies, particularly in the "modern" world, have great variability in wealth, but

little polygyny. So behavioral ecologists have had to argue that polygyny is lacking because of socially imposed constraints. But why are those constraints imposed? The sex-ratio interpretation can explain the absence of polygyny in most commercialized modern societies. First, very complex societies have standing armies and male mortality in warfare is rarely as high *proportionately* as in simpler societies. Second, with commercialization, there are more possibilities for individuals to support themselves without being married. Degree of disease in the environment may also be a factor.

Bobbi Low has suggested that a high incidence of disease may reduce the prevalence of "healthy" men. In such cases, it may be to a woman's advantage to marry a "healthy" man even if he is already married, and it may be to a man's advantage to marry several unrelated women to maximize genetic variation (and disease resistance) among his children. Indeed, societies with many pathogens are more likely to have polygyny.[94] A recent cross-cultural study compared the degree of disease explanation of polygyny with the imbalanced sex-ratio explanation. Both were supported. The number of pathogens predicted particularly well in more densely populated complex societies, where pathogen load is presumably greater. The sex-ratio explanation predicted particularly well in sparser, nonstate societies.[95] Nigel Barber used data from modern nations to test these ideas. He found that sex-ratio and pathogen stress predicted polygyny in modern nations too.[96]

Polyandry

George Peter Murdock's "World Ethnographic Sample" included only four societies (less than 1 percent of the total) in which polyandry, or the marriage of several men to one woman, was practiced.[97] When the husbands are brothers we call it **fraternal polyandry;** if they are not brothers, it is **nonfraternal polyandry.** Some Tibetans, the Toda of India, and the Sinhalese of Sri Lanka have practiced fraternal polyandry. Among some Tibetans who practice fraternal polyandry, biological paternity seems to be of no particular concern; there is no attempt to link children biologically to a particular brother, and all children are treated the same.[98]

One possible explanation for the practice of polyandry is a shortage of women. The Toda practiced female infanticide;[99] the Sinhalese had a shortage of women but denied the practice of female infanticide.[100] A correlation between shortage of women and polyandry would account for why polyandry is so rare in the ethnographic record; an excess of men is rare cross-culturally.

Another possible explanation is that polyandry is an adaptive response to severely limited resources. Melvyn Goldstein studied Tibetans who live in the northwestern corner of Nepal, above 12,000 feet in elevation. Cultivable land is extremely scarce there, with most families having less than an acre. The people say they practice fraternal polyandry to prevent the division of a family's farm and animals. Instead of dividing up their land among them and each taking a wife, brothers preserve the family farm by sharing a wife. Although not recognized by the

Tibetans, their practice of polyandry minimizes population growth. There are as many women as men of marriageable age. But about 30 percent of the women do not marry, and, although these women do have some children, they have far fewer than married women. Thus, the practice of polyandry minimizes the number of mouths to feed and therefore maximizes the standard of living of the polyandrous family. In contrast, if the Tibetans practiced monogamy and almost all women married, the birth rate would be much higher and there would be more mouths to feed with the severely limited resources.[101]

Polyandry is still customary in some Tibetan communities although monogamous marriages actually outnumber polyandrous marriages. This is because a set of brothers may start off being married to one woman, younger brothers may later opt to marry separately and form their own households. Also, some households have only one son or daughter and polyandrous marriages are not possible. Wealth increases the likelihood of a young brother leaving, but mostly when the polyandrous household lacks agricultural fields, herds, and opportunities for trade.[102] Actually, in polygynous societies, monogamous marriages also outnumber polygynous marriages at any given time. But the reasons are different. Most polygynous societies practice nonsororal marriages and, when a man first marries, he is married monogamously. It usually requires significant resources to marry again (a bride price is common) and so subsequent marriages occur later in life.

THE FAMILY

Although family form varies from one society to another and even within societies, all societies have families. A **family** is a social and economic unit consisting minimally of one or more parents (or parent substitute) and their children. Members of a family always have certain reciprocal rights and obligations, particularly economic ones. Family members usually live in one household, but common residence is not a defining feature of families. In our society, children may live away while they go to college. Some members of a family may deliberately set up separate households to manage multiple business enterprises while maintaining economic unity.[103] In simpler societies, the family and the household tend to be indistinguishable; only in more complex societies, and in societies becoming dependent on commercial exchange, may some members of a family live elsewhere.[104]

Adoption

In many societies, the family does not have enough kin in the nuclear or extended family. They need to add new members to perform all of the necessary chores or to inherit access to family property. They may have a shortage because introduced diseases or natural disasters such as hurricanes have killed members (particularly young children) or because the adults don't get along and can't cooperate in the traditional ways. Many societies adopt children to deal with one or another of these problems. Or

they adopt one or more related children to relieve the pressure on resources in the family that adopts the child "out." This last one was the motive in the family Melvin Ember lived with at the beginning of his fieldwork in the Pacific islands of American Samoa.

The family already had six children. The oldest (Tavita), 11 at the time, was in school most of the day, as were three of the other children. Tavita was adopted informally. His natural mother, who lived in the same village, was a sister of Tavita's adoptive mother. By adopting Tavita "out," his natural family was relieved of the responsibility to feed and care for him; they already had nine children. The need to reduce the number of mouths to feed was a common motive for adoption in Samoan villages then, as it was elsewhere in the far Pacific islands because of depopulation and hurricanes.[105] In American Samoa, the availability of more jobs (teaching in the village, working for the central government and the canneries on the main island), and improved medical care (there was a medical dispensary in every village and a hospital on the main island) had generated unusual population growth. Many had already moved to Hawaii and the mainland United States to seek jobs. American Samoans can move to the United States without difficulty; all you need is the money to pay for an airline ticket. Remittances from living and working abroad constitute a major source of income for the family members still in American Samoa.[106]

Adoption does not just occur in developing societies. It occurs in industrial societies too. As of the 1990s (the latest figures available), there were more than 100,000 formal (legally recognized) adoptions in the United States per year. About 50 percent of the adoptions are of children who are relatives, usually close relatives; a large number of these adoptions may be solutions to resource problems for the natural mothers. Then more than 10,000 children from abroad who are not usually relatives are adopted each year. Most of the known adoptions, foreign and domestic, are arranged by middle-class or wealthier people. A sizeable amount of money may have to be spent, particularly with the foreign adoptions. Most of the adopted children, domestic and foreign, turn out as well as natural children.[107]

Variation in Family Form

The minimal family has one parent (or parent substitute). Single-parent families, usually headed by the mother, are common in some societies, but most societies typically have larger families. These larger family units usually include at least one **nuclear family** (a married couple and their children), but there is often polygamy, so there may be more than one spouse with more than one set of children. If a single-parent family, nuclear family, polygynous, or polyandrous family lives alone, each is an **independent family.** However, the **extended family** is the prevailing form of family in more than half the societies known to anthropology.[108] It may consist of two or more single-parent, monogamous, polygynous, or polyandrous families linked by a blood tie. Most commonly, the extended family consists of a

current research and issues

One-Parent Families: Why the Recent Increase?

Not only is the custom of marriage almost universal, but in most societies known to anthropology, most people marry. And they usually remarry if they divorce. This means that, except for the death of a spouse or temporarily during times of divorce or separation, one-parent families are relatively uncommon in most societies.

In many Western countries, however, there has been a dramatic increase recently in the percentage of one-parent families, most of which (about 90 percent) are female-headed families. For example, in the 1960s, about 9 percent of families in the United States were one-parent families, but in the mid-1980s, the figure jumped to about 24 percent. In 2004, the figure was 28 percent. Whereas Sweden once led the Western countries in percentage of one-parent families—about 13 percent in the 1970s—the United States now has the highest percentage.

Before we examine the reasons for the increase, we need to consider that there are a variety of ways to become a one-parent family. First, many one-parent families result from the divorce or separation of two-parent families. Second, many one-parent families result from births out of wedlock. In addition, some result from the death of a spouse, and others from the decision by a single person to have a child.

Many researchers suggest that the ease of divorce is largely responsible for the increase in one-parent families. On the face of it, this explanation seems plausible. But it is flawed. In many countries during the late 1960s and early 1970s, changes in the law made getting a divorce much easier, and the percentage of one-parent families did rise after that. But why did so many countries ease divorce restrictions at the same time? Did attitudes about marriage change first? A high divorce rate by itself will make for a higher percentage of one-parent households only if individuals do not remarry quickly. In the United States, for example, remarriage rates did decline sharply in the mid-1960s, particularly among younger, better-educated women, and so the

percentage of one-parent households may have risen for that reason. In many other countries, divorce rates stabilized in the 1980s, but the percentage of one-parent families still increased. Thus, easier divorce does not fully explain the increase in number of one-parent families.

Although some parents are clearly choosing to stay single, many might prefer to marry if they could find an appropriate spouse. In some countries, and among some ethnic groups within some countries, there are many fewer males than females, and sometimes a high proportion of the males have poor economic prospects. In the former Soviet Union, there are many more women than men because males are more likely to have died from war, alcoholism, and accidents. The United States does not have such a skewed sex ratio, but in some neighborhoods, particularly poor neighborhoods, there are very high mortality rates for young males. And many males in such neighborhoods do not have work. One study by Daniel Lichter and his colleagues estimated that for every 100 African American women between the ages of 21 and 28, there were fewer than 80 available African American men. If we count only men who are employed full- or part-time, the number of available men per 100 women drops below 50. And a recent comparison of 85 countries finds that single parenthood is much more likely when there is higher male unemployment as well as when there are fewer men than women of a comparable age. So there may be considerable merit to the argument that one-parent families (usually headed by women) will be likely when a spouse (particularly an employed one) is hard to find.

Another popular explanation for the rise in number of one-parent families is that, in contrast to the past, women can manage without husbands because of support from the state. This scenario seems to fit Sweden, where unmarried and divorced mothers receive many social supports and allowances for maternity

and educational leave. But Iceland has few social supports from the government and yet has the highest rate of out-of-wedlock births of all the Scandinavian countries. In the United States, the welfare argument fails to predict changes over time. The program called Aid to Families with Dependent Children provided aid largely to single mothers. If the theory about government help was correct, increases in such aid would generally predict increases in the percentage of mother-headed households. But, in fact, during the 1970s, the percentage of families receiving aid and the value of aid decreased, whereas the percentage of mother-headed households increased. In the 1980s, it was more difficult to go "on welfare," but the percentage of mother-headed households increased anyway.

Women might be more able to manage alone if they have high-paying employment, and therefore we might expect more one-parent families by choice, as more women enter the job market. But, although this may explain the choices of some women, recent research finds that employed women generally are *more* rather than less likely to marry.

In any case, there seems to be a general association between commercial economies and the possibility of one-parent families. Is there something about subsistence economies that promotes marriage and something about commercial economies that detracts from it? Although marriage is not universally based on love or companionship, it entails a great deal of economic and other kinds of interdependence, particularly in not-so-commercial economies. Market economies allow other possibilities; goods and services can be bought and sold, and governments may take over functions that kin and family normally handle. So the one-parent family is likely to remain an option—either a choice or a necessity—for some people.

Sources: Burns and Scott 1994; Lichter et al. 1992; Whitehead and Popenoe 2005; Barber 2003.

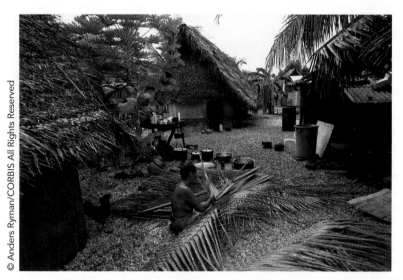

The traditional houses of an extended family on Satawal Island in the Carolines, Micronesia.

married couple and one or more of the married children, all living in the same house or household. The constituent nuclear families are normally linked through the parent-child tie. An extended family, however, is sometimes composed of families linked through a sibling tie. Such a family might consist of two married brothers, their wives, and their children. Extended families may be very large, containing many relatives and including three or four generations. A diagram of these different types of family can be found in Figure 2.

Extended-Family Households

In a society composed of extended-family households, marriage does not bring as pronounced a change in lifestyle as it does in our culture, where the couple typically moves to a new residence and forms a new, and basically independent, family unit. In extended families, the newlyweds are assimilated into an existing family unit. Margaret Mead described such a situation in Samoa:

In most marriages there is no sense of setting up a new and separate establishment. The change is felt in the change of residence for either husband or wife and in the reciprocal relations which spring up between the two families. But the young couple live in the main household, simply receiving a bamboo pillow, a mosquito net and a pile of mats for their bed. . . . The wife works with all the women of the household and waits on all the men. The husband

FIGURE 2 Anthropologists commonly use diagrams to represent family structures. At the top are four types of independent family assuming only two children (one male, one female) and only two spouses where multiple spouses are allowed. At the bottom are two types of extended family. These diagrams show only small extended families, but extended families can have many constituent family units if there are many children as well as plural marriages.

applied anthropology

Extended Families and Social Security: The Japanese Model in the 1950s and 1960s

For many years now, people in the United States (in and out of government) have warned that the Social Security system is in trouble, that it will be forced to reduce payments in the near future. There are two general ways to solve the problem, given the growing population to be served. The government could reduce payments, by extending the retirement age, for instance. Or it could increase funding for Social Security, by requiring taxpayers to pay more into the system while they are still working. But there is enormous resistance to changing the system. People don't want their Medicare and Medicaid payments to be reduced, and they are afraid of losing their medical insurance if they lose their jobs. In addition, many people don't want to wait to retire. So what else could be done? Have we explored all of the possible ways to repair the Social Security system?

One way is suggested by what the Japanese did in the 1950s and 1960s. Japan was industrializing. People were leaving the rural farming areas and moving to the cities to take jobs in industry. But there still were extended family households, particularly on the farm; many still lived with parents and children, sharing income and expenses. The extended families continued to exist because the economy was still lacking certain features common in the industrialized societies of the West. (The boom in Japanese exports, in cameras, automobiles, etc., was yet to develop.) First, geographic mobility (moving to "chase the job") occurred less often than in Western industrial economies; workers and even professionals changed jobs only rarely. Second, the government had not taken over many of the health and welfare functions of the extended family; indeed, the government still enforced the obligation of relatives to care for the aged and infirm. And third, ascribed or inherited status was still an important basis for economic advancement, and perhaps as useful as marks of achievement (e.g., a university degree) in obtaining the first job. The key to understanding the persistence of the extended family in Japan may lie in the fact that the country had a surplus of employable labor throughout its industrial history. In the presence of the unemployment and competitiveness that characterize a tight labor market, the extended family may survive because no other agencies are available to provide economic and social security.

An industrial economy in severe recession may persuade some young adults to consider living with their parents. When the U.S. economy collapsed between 2008 and 2009, many young people lost their jobs and couldn't find new ones. They had to abandon their independence in favor of extended family living. If you can't afford an apartment, even one you share with others, what can you do? You can move back home. At least that will limit your expenses. And it might also help relieve the pressure on the Social Security system, if the tax code were changed to provide additional deductions for older people who partially support children who have returned home. By moving back home, the younger generation could save money to buy an apartment or house later. And if the older people get a new tax deduction, there could be less need to revamp the Social Security system. Many young people have delayed marriage anyway. (More people are delaying marriage until their late 20s and early 30s.) The Congress could adjust the tax code to allow at least some people to choose to live in extended family households, which would allow the older people to receive lower Social Security payments. We might have to change the way we socialize our children—we may have to reduce the pressure to live independently. But it could be done. After all, necessity is the mother of invention. The tax code could favor the option of extended family living, and we might thereby relieve some of the financial pressure on the Social Security system.

Sources: M. Ember 1983; Long 2000.

shares the enterprises of the other men and boys. Neither in personal service given or received are the two marked off as a unit.[109]

A young couple in Samoa, as in other societies with extended families, generally has little decision-making power over the governing of the household. Often the responsibility of running the household rests with the senior male. Nor can the new family accumulate its own property and become independent; it is a part of the larger corporate structure:

So the young people bide their time. Eventually, when the old man dies or retires, they will own the homestead, they will run things. When their son grows up and marries, he will create a new subsidiary family, to live with them, work for the greater glory of *their* extended family homestead, and wait for them to die.[110]

The extended family is more likely than the independent nuclear family to perpetuate itself as a social unit. In contrast with the independent nuclear family, which by definition disintegrates with the death of the senior members (the parents), the extended family is always adding junior families (monogamous, polygamous, or both), whose members eventually become the senior members when their elders die.

Possible Reasons for Extended-Family Households

Why do most societies known to anthropology commonly have extended-family households? Extended-family households are found most frequently in societies with sedentary agricultural economies, so economic factors may play a role in determining household type. M. F. Nimkoff and Russell Middleton suggested how agricultural life, as opposed to a hunter-gatherer life, may favor extended families. The extended family may be a social mechanism that prevents the economically ruinous division of family property in societies in which property such as cultivated land is important. Conversely, the need for mobility in hunter-gatherer societies may make it difficult to maintain extended-family households. During certain seasons, the hunter-gatherers may be obliged to divide into nuclear families that scatter into other areas.[111]

But agriculture is only a weak predictor of extended-family households. Many agriculturalists lack them, and many nonagricultural societies have them. A different theory is that extended-family households come to prevail in societies that have incompatible activity requirements—that is, requirements that cannot be met by a mother or a father in a one-family household. In other words, extended-family households are generally favored when the work a mother has to do outside the home (cultivating fields or gathering foods far away) makes it difficult for her to also care for her children and do other household tasks. Similarly, extended families may be favored when the required outside activities of a father (warfare, trading trips, or wage labor far away) make it difficult for him to do the subsistence work required of males. There is cross-cultural evidence that societies with such incompatible activity requirements are more likely to have extended-family households than societies with compatible activity requirements, regardless of whether or not the society is agricultural. Even though they have incompatible activity requirements, however, societies with commercial or monetary exchange may not have extended-family households. In commercial societies, a family may be able to obtain the necessary help by "buying" the required services.[112]

Of course, even in societies with money economies, not everyone can buy required services. Those who are poor may need to live in extended families, and extended-family living may become more common even in the middle class when the economy is depressed. As a popular magazine noted,

> Whatever happened to the all-American nuclear family—Mom, Pop, two kids and a cuddly dog, nestled under one cozy, mortgaged roof? What happened was an economic squeeze: layoffs, fewer jobs for young people, more working mothers, a shortage of affordable housing and a high cost of living. Those factors, along with a rising divorce rate, a trend toward later marriages and an increase in the over-65 population, all hitting at once, are forcing thousands

of Americans into living in multigenerational families.[113]

In many societies, there are kin groups even larger than extended families.

SUMMARY ● ○ ○

1. All societies known today have the custom of marriage. Marriage is a socially approved sexual and economic union usually between a man and a woman that is presumed to be more or less permanent and that subsumes reciprocal rights and obligations between the two spouses and between the spouses and their children.

2. The way marriage is socially recognized varies greatly; it may involve an elaborate ceremony or none at all. Variations include childhood betrothals, trial marriage periods, feasting, and the birth of a baby.

3. Marriage arrangements often include an economic element. The most common form is the bride price, in which the groom or his family gives an agreed-upon amount of money or goods to the bride's family. Bride service exists when the groom works for the bride's family for a specified period. In some societies, a female from the groom's family is exchanged for the bride; in others, gifts are exchanged between the two families. A dowry is a payment of goods or money by the bride's family, usually to the bride. Indirect dowry is provided by the groom's family to the bride, sometimes through the bride's father.

4. No society in recent times has allowed sex or marriage between brothers and sisters, mothers and sons, or fathers and daughters.

5. Every society tells people whom they cannot marry, whom they can marry, and sometimes even whom they should marry. In quite a few societies, marriages are arranged by the couple's kin groups. Implicit in arranged marriages is the conviction that the joining of two kin groups to form new social and economic ties is too important to be left to free choice and romantic love. Some societies have rules of exogamy, which require marriage outside one's own kin group or community; others have rules of endogamy, requiring marriage within one's group. Although most societies prohibit all first-cousin marriages, some permit or prefer marriage with cross-cousins (children of siblings of the opposite sex) and parallel cousins (children of siblings of the same sex). Many societies have customs providing for the remarriage of widowed people. Levirate is a custom whereby a man marries his brother's widow. Sororate is the practice whereby a woman marries her deceased sister's husband.

6. We think of marriage as involving just one man and one woman at a time (monogamy), but most societies allow a man to be married to more than one woman at a time (polygyny). Polyandry, the marriage of one woman to several husbands, is rare.

7. The prevailing form of family in most societies is the extended family. It consists of two or more single-parent, monogamous (nuclear), polygynous, or polyandrous families linked by blood ties.

GLOSSARY TERMS ○ ● ○

bride price (or bride
   wealth)
bride service
cross-cousins
dowry
endogamy
exogamy
extended family
family
fraternal polyandry
group marriage
incest taboo
independent
   family
indirect dowry

levirate
marriage
monogamy
nonfraternal
   polyandry
nonsororal polygyny
nuclear family
parallel cousins
polyandry
polygamy
polygyny
postpartum sex
   taboo
sororal polygyny
sororate

CRITICAL QUESTIONS ○ ○ ●

1. Will it remain customary in our society to marry? Why do you think it will or will not?

2. Do you think extended-family households will become more common in our society? Why?

3. Why is polyandry so much less common than polygyny?

PEARSON
myanthrolab

Read Alan Howard and Jan Rensel's "Rotuma: Interpreting a Wedding" on MyAnthroLab and answer the following questions:

1. Howard and Rensel suggest that weddings among the Rotuma express their core values. What core values are expressed in their weddings?

2. How has courtship and marriage changed?

3. Compare the essential features of weddings in your culture (make sure to mention the name of your culture) with those described for the Rotuma.

NOTES ● ○ ○

1. W. N. Stephens 1963, 5.
2. Murdock 1949, 8.
3. Stephens 1963, 170–71.
4. Hua 2001.
5. Gough 1959; Unnithan 2009.
6. Hoebel 1960, 77.
7. Evans-Pritchard 1970, 1428–34.
8. D. O'Brien 1977; Oboler 1980.
9. Oboler 2009.
10. Murdock 1949, 7–8.
11. Ibid., 9–10.
12. See, for example, Linton 1936, 135–36.
13. M. Ember and C. R. Ember 1979.
14. Ibid.
15. Marlowe 2003, 221–223.
16. M. Ember and C. R. Ember 1979.
17. Graburn 1969, 188–200.
18. Malinowski 1932, 77.
19. Ibid., 88.
20. J. W. M. Whiting 1941, 125.
21. Doyle 2004.
22. Service 1978.
23. LeVine and LeVine 1963, 65.
24. Ibid.
25. For an extensive discussion of the symbolism of Rotuman weddings, see A. Howard and Rensel 2009.
26. Schlegel and Eloul 1987, 119.
27. Schlegel and Eloul 1988, 295, Table 1. We used the data to calculate the frequency of various types of economic transaction in a worldwide sample of 186 societies.
28. Oboler 2009.
29. Frake 1960.
30. Mead 1931, 206–208.
31. Borgerhoff Mulder et al. 2001.
32. Schlegel and Eloul 1988, 298–99.
33. Pryor 1977, 363–64.
34. Ibid.
35. Spencer 1968, 136.
36. Schlegel and Eloul 1988, 296–97.
37. Ibid.
38. Ibid.
39. Radcliffe-Brown 1922, 73.
40. Murdock 1967; Goody 1973, 17–21.
41. Pryor 1977, 363–65; Schlegel and Eloul 1988, 296–99.
42. Research is reported in Gaulin and Boster 1990, 994–1005. The first theory discussed herein is associated with Boserup 1970. The second is put forward by Gaulin and Boster.
43. Schlegel and Eloul 1988, following Goody 1973, 20.
44. Barth 1965, 18–19; as reported in (and coded as indirect dowry by) Schlegel and Eloul 1987, 131.
45. Middleton 1962, 606.
46. Durham 1991, 293–94, citing research by Hopkins 1980.
47. Westermarck 1894.
48. Talmon 1964, 492.
49. Ibid., 504.
50. A. Wolf 1968, 864.
51. A. Wolf and Chieh-shan Huang 1980, 159, 170, 185.
52. H. Parker and S. Parker 1986.
53. M. Ember 1975; Durham 1991, 341–57.
54. For a discussion of mechanisms that might lead to sexual aversion, see S. Parker 1976; 1984.
55. Freud 1943.
56. Malinowski 1927.
57. Quoted in L. A. White 1949, 313.
58. Kang 1979, 85–99.
59. Rudan and Campbell 2004.
60. Stern 1973, 494–95, as cited in M. Ember 1975, 256. For a review of the theory and evidence, see Durham 1991.
61. Seemanova 1971, 108–28, as cited in Durham 1991, 305–09.
62. Durham 1991, 305–09.
63. Ibid., 346–52.
64. Firth 1957, 287–88, cited (somewhat differently) in Durham 1991, 349–50.

65. A mathematical model of early mating systems suggests that people may have noticed the harmful effects of inbreeding once populations began to expand as a result of agriculture; people therefore may have deliberately adopted the incest taboo to solve the problem of inbreeding. See M. Ember 1975. For a similar subsequent suggestion, see Durham 1991, 331–39.
66. Goode 1982, 61–62.
67. C. S. Ford 1941, 149.
68. A. Howard and Rensel 2004.
69. S. S. Davis 2009.
70. Goode 1970, 210.
71. Lingenfelter 2009.
72. MacDonald and Hewlett 1999, 504–06.
73. M. Ember 1975, 262, Table 3.
74. Busby 2009.
75. M. Ember 1975, 260–69; see also Durham 1991, 341–57.
76. Murdock 1949, 29.
77. Bogoras 1909, cited in W. Stephens 1963, 195.
78. Oliver 1955, 352–53.
79. Ibid., 223–24, quoted in W. Stephens 1963, 58.
80. Mead 1950, 101.
81. Jankowiak et al. 2005.
82. The discussion of these customs is based on W. Stephens 1963, 63–67.
83. Kilbride and Kilbride 1990, 202–06.
84. C. Anderson 2000, 102–03.
85. Linton 1936, 183.
86. J. W. M. Whiting 1964.
87. Ibid., 518.
88. Ibid., 516–17.
89. M. Ember 1974b.
90. M. Ember 1984–1985. The statistical relationship between late age of marriage for men and polygyny was first reported by Witkowski 1975.
91. M. Ember 1974b, 202–205.
92. M. Ember 1984–1985. For other predictors of polygyny, see D. R. White and Burton 1988.
93. Sellen and Hruschka 2004.
94. Low 1990b.
95. M. Ember et al. 2007.
96. Barber 2008.
97. Coult and Habenstein 1965; Murdock 1957.
98. M. C. Goldstein 1987, 39.
99. Stephens 1963, 45.
100. Hiatt 1980.
101. M. Goldstein 1987. Formerly, in feudal Tibet, a class of serfs who owned small parcels of land also practiced polyandry. Goldstein suggests that a shortage of land would explain their polyandry too. See M. C. Goldstein 1971.
102. Haddix 2001.
103. For example, see M. L. Cohen 1976.
104. Pasternak 1976, 96.
105. Silk 1980; Damas 1983.
106. Melvin Ember, pers. comm.
107. K. Gibson 2009.
108. Coult and Habenstein 1965.
109. Mead 1961/1928, quoted in Stephens 1963, 134–35.
110. Ibid., 135.
111. Nimkoff and Middleton 1960.
112. Pasternak et al. 1976, 109–23.
113. Block 1983.

Marital Residence and Kinship

From Chapter 22 of *Anthropology*, 13/e. Carol R. Ember. Melvin Ember. Peter N. Peregrine. Copyright © 2011 by Pearson Education. Published by Prentice Hall. All rights reserved.

Marital Residence and Kinship

I n the United States and Canada, as well as in many other industrial societies, a young man and woman usually establish a place of residence apart from their parents or other relatives when they marry, if they have not already moved away before that. Our society is so oriented toward this pattern of marital residence—*neolocal (new-place) residence*—that it seems to be the obvious and natural one to follow. Some upper-income families begin earlier than others to train their children to live away from home by sending them to boarding schools at age 13 or 14 or to sleep-away summer camps. Young adults of all income levels learn to live away from home most of the year if they join the army or attend an out-of-town college. In any case, when young people marry, they generally live apart from family.

So familiar is neolocal residence to us that we tend to assume that all societies must practice the same pattern. On the contrary, of the 565 societies in George Peter Murdock's "World Ethnographic Sample," only about 5 percent followed this practice.[1] About 95 percent of the world's societies have had some other pattern of residence whereby a new couple settles within, or very close to, the household of the parents or some other close relative of either the groom or the bride. When married couples live near kin, it stands to reason that kinship relationships will figure prominently in the social life of the society. Marital residence largely predicts the types of kin groups found in a society, as well as how people refer to and classify their various relatives.

As we will see, kin groups that include several or many families and hundreds or even thousands of people are found in many societies and structure many areas of social life. Kin groups may have important economic, social, political, and religious functions.

● ○ ●

PATTERNS OF MARITAL RESIDENCE

In societies in which newly married couples customarily live with or close to their kin, the pattern of residence varies. Children in all societies are required to marry outside the nuclear family because of the incest taboo, and with few exceptions, couples in almost all societies live together after they are married. Therefore, some children have to leave home when they marry. But which married children remain at home and which reside elsewhere? Societies vary in the way they deal with this question, but there are not many different patterns. The prevailing one could be one of the following (the percentages of each in the ethnographic record do not sum to 100 because of rounding):

1. **Patrilocal residence.** The son stays and the daughter leaves, so that the married couple lives with or near the husband's parents (67 percent of all societies).

2. **Matrilocal residence.** The daughter stays and the son leaves, so that the married couple lives with or near the wife's parents (15 percent of all societies).

Dean Conger/CORBIS- NY

An Iban family at mealtime in their longhouse apartment, Borneo, Malaysia.

3. **Bilocal residence.** Either the son or the daughter leaves, so that the married couple lives with or near either the wife's or the husband's parents (7 percent of all societies).

4. **Avunculocal residence.** Both son and daughter normally leave, but the son and his wife settle with or near his mother's brother (4 percent of all societies).[2]

In these definitions, we use the phrase "the married couple lives *with or near*" a particular set of in-laws. When couples live with or near the kin of a spouse, the couple may live in the same household with those kin, creating an *extended-family* household, or they may live separately in an *independent-family* household, but nearby. (Because matrilocal, patrilocal, and avunculocal residence specify just one pattern, they are often called nonoptional or **unilocal residence** patterns.)

A fifth pattern of residence is neolocal, in which the newly married couple does not live with or near kin.

5. **Neolocal residence.** Both son and daughter leave; married couples live apart from the relatives of both spouses (5 percent of all societies).

Figure 1 graphically shows the percentage of societies in the ethnographic record that practice each of the five marital residence patterns.

How does place of residence affect the social life of the couple? Because the pattern of residence governs with or near whom individuals live, it largely determines which people those individuals interact with and have to depend on. If the kin of the husband surrounds a married couple, for example, the chances are that those relatives will figure importantly in the couple's future. Whether the couple lives with or near the

In many societies known to anthropology, the bride goes to live with or near the husband's family. In a reenactment of a traditional Korean wedding ceremony, a bride is carried to the home of the groom.

husband's or the wife's kin can also be expected to have important consequences for the status of the husband or wife. If married couples live patrilocally, as occurs in most societies, the wife may be far from her own kin. In any case, she will be an outsider among a group of male relatives who have grown up together. The feeling of being an outsider is particularly strong when the wife has moved into a patrilocal extended-family household.

Among the Tiv of central Nigeria,[3] the patrilocal extended family consists of the "great father," who is the head of the household, and his younger brothers, his sons, and his younger brothers' sons. Also included are the in-marrying wives and all unmarried children. (The sisters and daughters of the household head who have married would have gone to live where their husbands lived.)

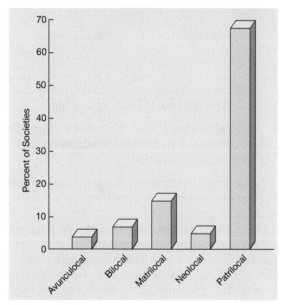

FIGURE 1 Percentage of Societies in the Ethnographic Record with Various Marital Residence Patterns

Source: Calculated from Allan D. Coult and Robert W. Habenstein 1965.

Authority is strongly vested in the male line, particularly the oldest of the household, who has authority over bride price, disputes, punishment, and plans for new buildings.

A somewhat different situation exists if the husband comes to live with or near his wife's parents. In this case, the wife and her kin take on somewhat greater importance, and the husband is the outsider. As we shall see, however, the matrilocal situation is not quite the mirror image of the patrilocal, because the husband's kin in matrilocal societies often are not far away. Moreover, even though residence is matrilocal, women often do not have as much to say in decision-making as their brothers do.

If the married couple does not live with or near the parents or close kin of either spouse, the situation is again quite different. It should not be surprising that relatives and kinship connections do not figure very largely in everyday life in neolocal residence situations.

Marital residence determines which kin will live, or not live, in the immediate vicinity of the married couple. Toward the end of this chapter, we consider the factors that may explain residential variation; these same factors may also help explain the types of kinship groups that develop.

THE STRUCTURE OF KINSHIP

In noncommercial societies, kinship connections structure many areas of social life—from the kind of access an individual has to productive resources to the kind of political alliances formed between communities and larger territorial groups. In some societies, in fact, kinship connections have an important bearing on matters of life and death.

Recall the social system described in Shakespeare's *Romeo and Juliet*. The Capulets and the Montagues were groups of kin engaged in lethal competition with each other, and the fatal outcome of Romeo and Juliet's romance was related to that competition. Although Romeo and Juliet's society had a commercial economy (but not, of course, an industrialized one), the political system of the city they lived in was a reflection of the way kinship was structured. Sets of kin of common descent lived together, and the various kin groups competed, and sometimes fought, for a prominent, or at least secure, place in the political hierarchy of the city-state.

If a preindustrial commercial society could be so structured by kinship, we can imagine how much more important kinship connections and kin groups are in many noncommercial societies that lack political mechanisms such as princes and councils of lords who try to keep the peace and initiate other activities on behalf of the community. It is no wonder that anthropologists often speak of the web of kinship as providing the main structure of social action in noncommercial societies.

If kinship is important, there is still the question of which set of kin a person affiliates with and depends on. After all, if every single relative were counted as equally important, there would be an unmanageably large number of people in each person's kinship network. Consequently, in most societies in which kinship connections are important, rules allocate each person to a particular and definable set of kin.

current research and issues

Neolocality and Adolescent Rebellion: Are They Related?

In our society, it is taken for granted that adolescence means turmoil and parent-child conflict. Teenagers, parents, and educators worry about how to reduce the conflict. But few in our society ask why the conflict occurs in the first place. Is it "natural" for adolescents to be rebellious? Are they rebellious in all cultures? If not, why do we have conflict in our society?

Margaret Mead first raised this issue. In her best-selling *Coming of Age in Samoa* (originally published in 1928), she said that conflict during adolescence was minimal in Samoa. Some researchers have recently criticized her analysis, but many field and comparative studies by anthropologists have since found that adolescence is not experienced in the same way in all societies. For example, in their systematic cross-cultural study of adolescence, Alice Schlegel and Herbert Barry concluded that relations between adolescents and their families were generally harmonious around the world. They suggested that, when family members need each other throughout their lives, independence, as expressed in adolescent rebelliousness, would be foolhardy. Indeed, Schlegel and Barry found that adolescents are likely to be rebellious only in societies, like our own, that have neolocal residence and considerable job and geographic mobility.

Why should this be? We might speculate that adolescent rebellion is an elaborate psychodrama that both parents and children play out to prepare themselves for separation. Children spend a considerable part of their lives being dependent on their parents. But they know they must move away, and that prospect may arouse anxiety. Children want to be independent, but independence is scary. Dependence is nice in some ways—at least it can make life easier (someone else cooks for you and so on)—but it is also less grown-up than independence. So what pushes a child to leave? Perhaps the conflict itself propels the departure. Teenagers ask for things they want, but they may know, at least unconsciously,

that their parents will say no. And parents often do say no, so the teenagers get angry and can't wait to be on their own. Parents are also ambivalent. They want their children to grow up, but they miss them when they leave. After a period of conflict, it may be a relief for all concerned when parents and children go their separate ways.

What if our social structure was different? What if parents and children knew that some of the children were going to spend the rest of their lives with or near the parents? And even those children who moved away, as some would have to in societies practicing matrilocal, patrilocal, avunculocal, or bilocal residence, would know they were going to spend the rest of their lives with or near their in-laws. Could teenagers in non-neolocal societies afford to have serious conflict with their parents? Could the parents afford to have serious conflict with the teenagers who will be staying put after their marriages? We think not. We suggest that adolescent conflict would be very disadvantageous in a non-neolocal society, and therefore we would expect its minimization or suppression when the residence pattern is other than neolocal.

There is another reason why rebelliousness might be associated with neolocality; it has to do with the fact that neolocality is predicted by commercial exchange. In the modern world, commercial societies are likely to have a great deal of occupational specialization and people with many different values. Thus, children are presented with a great many choices in a rapidly changing culture. Let us consider the effect of a rapidly changing technology. If children have to know and do things that the parents do not know about, how can we expect the children to want to follow in their parents' footsteps?

But a rapidly changing culture is not necessarily accompanied by parent-child conflict. Other conditions are probably also necessary to generate the conflict, if the situation in a Moroccan town is any guide. As part of a comparative research project on adolescence, Susan and Douglas Davis

interviewed young people in a small town in Morocco. The culture had changed a lot recently. Parents mostly worked at jobs in and related to agriculture; children aspired to white-collar jobs. Grandparents rarely saw a car; teenagers took trains to the capital. Only a few parents had gone to school; most teenagers did. Yet the Davises reported little serious parent-child conflict, despite the cultural changes. For example, 40 percent of the teenagers said that they had never disagreed with their mothers. Perhaps we need to consider other facets of the culture. For one thing, Morocco has an authoritarian political structure with a monarchy and a clear pyramid of offices; perhaps parent-child conflict is unlikely in such a political system because it emphasizes and requires obedience. A second possible consideration is that group life is more important than the individual. The family is the most important social group, and as such, cannot tolerate adolescent rebelliousness. A third possible consideration is that adults are supposed to avoid open conflict. The study by the Davises implies that adolescent rebelliousness is likely only in societies like the United States that emphasize individuality, personal autonomy, and individual achievement.

What we need is research that tries to untangle the various causal possibilities. To discover the possible effect of neolocality, rapid change, cultural emphasis on individual autonomy, or an authoritarian political system, we need to study samples of cultures that have different combinations of those traits. It is possible that they all are influential, or that some are more important than others, or that some cause the others. Whatever we discover in the future about the causality, we know now that adolescent rebelliousness is not inevitable or natural, that it is probably linked to some other aspects of cultural variation—as Margaret Mead suggested many years ago.

Sources: Mead 1961/1928; Schlegel and Barry 1991; M. Ember 1967; S. S. Davis 1993; 2009.

© Harvey Lloyd/ Taxi/Getty Images, Inc.

Totem poles often symbolize the history of a descent group. A totem pole in Ketchikan, Alaska.

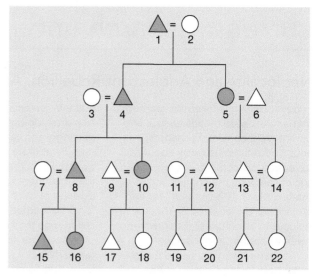

FIGURE 2 Patrilineal Descent
Individuals 4 and 5, who are the children of 1 and 2, affiliate with their father's patrilineal kin group, represented by the color red. In the next generation, the children of 3 and 4 also belong to the red kin group, because they take their descent from their father, who is a member of that group. However, the children of 5 and 6 do not belong to this patrilineal group, because they take their descent from their father, who is a member of a different group. That is, although the mother of 12 and 14 belongs to the red patrilineal group, she cannot pass on her descent affiliation to her children, and because her husband (6) does not belong to her patrilineage, her children (12 and 14) belong to their father's group. In the fourth generation, only 15 and 16 belong to the red patrilineal group, because their father is the only male member of the preceding generation who belongs to the red patrilineal group. In this diagram, then, 1, 4, 5, 8, 10, 15, and 16 are affiliated by the patrilineal descent; all the other individuals belong to other patrilineal groups.

Types of Affiliation with Kin

We distinguish three main types of affiliation with kin: *unilineal descent, ambilineal descent,* and *bilateral kinship.* The first two types (unilineal descent and ambilineal descent) are based on **rules of descent,** which are rules that connect individuals with particular sets of kin because of known or presumed common ancestry. By the particular rule of descent operating in their society, individuals can know more or less immediately which set of kin to turn to for support and help. As we shall see, bilateral kinship is not based on rules of descent or ancestry and does not create clear and unambiguous groups.

Unilineal descent refers to the fact that a person is affiliated with a group of kin through descent links of one sex only—either males only or females only. Thus, unilineal descent can be either patrilineal or matrilineal.

1. **Patrilineal descent** affiliates individuals with kin of both sexes related to them *through men only.* As Figure 2 indicates, the children in patrilineal systems in each generation belong to the kin group of their father; their father, in turn, belongs to the group of his father; and so on. Although a man's sons and daughters are all members of the same descent group, affiliation with that group is transmitted only by the sons to their children. Just as patrilocal residence is much more common than matrilocal residence, patrilineal descent is more common than matrilineal descent.

2. **Matrilineal descent** affiliates individuals with kin of both sexes related to them *through women only.* In each generation, then, children belong to the kin

group of their mother (see Figure 3). Although a woman's sons and daughters are all members of the same descent group, only her daughters can pass on their descent affiliation to their children.

Some have questioned the existence of unilineal descent and descent groups, suggesting that theorists have only imagined them. Reality could not possibly have been like that. But recent ethnohistorical analyses confirm that Native North American societies, like the Omaha, really did have patrilineal descent groups in the 19th century,[4] and the Chuuk (in the Pacific) still have functioning matrilineal groups, despite many years of Western contact.[5]

Unilineal rules of descent affiliate an individual with a line of kin extending back in time and into the future. By virtue of this line of descent, whether it extends through males or females, some very close relatives are excluded. For example, in a patrilineal system, your mother and your mother's parents do not belong to your patrilineal group, but your father and his father (and their sisters) do. In your own generation in a matrilineal or patrilineal system, some cousins are excluded, and in your children's generation, some of your nieces and nephews are excluded.

However, although unilineal rules of descent exclude certain relatives from membership in one's kin group, the excluded relatives are not necessarily ignored or forgotten, just as practical considerations restrict the effective size of

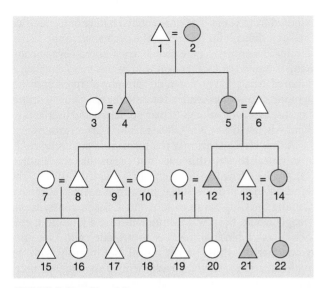

FIGURE 3 Matrilineal Descent
Individuals 4 and 5, who are the children of 1 and 2, affiliate with their mother's kin group, represented by the color green. In the next generation, the children of 5 and 6 also belong to the green kin group, because they take their descent from their mother, who is a member of that group. However, the children of 3 and 4 do not belong to this matrilineal group, because they take their descent from their mother, who is a member of a different group; their father, although a member of the green matrilineal group, cannot pass his affiliation on to them under the rule of matrilineal descent. In the fourth generation, only 21 and 22 belong to the green matrilineal group, because their mother is the only female member of the preceding generation who belongs. Thus, individuals 2, 4, 5, 12, 14, 21, and 22 belong to the same matrilineal group.

kinship networks in our own society. Indeed, in many unilineal societies, they may be entrusted with important responsibilities. For example, when a person dies in a patrilineal society, some members of the mother's patrilineal descent group may customarily be accorded the right to perform certain rituals at the funeral.

Unilineal rules of descent can form clear-cut, and hence unambiguous, groups of kin, which can act as separate units even after the death of individual members. Referring again to Figures 2 and 3, we can see that the individuals in the highlight color belong to the same patrilineal or matrilineal descent group without ambiguity; individuals in the fourth generation belong to the group just as much as those in the first generation. Say the patrilineal group has a name, the Hawks. Individuals know whether or not they are Hawks. If not, they belong to some other group, for each person belongs to only one line of descent. This fact is important if kin groups are to act as separate, nonoverlapping units. It is difficult for people to act together unless they know exactly who should get together. And it is easier for individuals to act together as a group if each one belongs to only one such group or line.

In contrast to unilineal descent, **ambilineal descent** affiliates individuals with kin related to them through men *or* women. In other words, some people in the society affiliate with a group of kin through their fathers; others affiliate through their mothers. Consequently, the descent groups show both female and male genealogical links, as illustrated in Figure 4.

These three rules of descent (patrilineal, matrilineal, and ambilineal) are usually, but not always, mutually exclusive. Most societies can be characterized as having only one rule of descent, but two principles are sometimes used to affiliate individuals with different sets of kin for different purposes. Some societies have, then, what is called **double descent or double unilineal descent,** whereby individuals affiliate for some purposes with a group of matrilineal kin and for other purposes with a group of patrilineal kin. Thus, two rules of descent, each traced through links of one sex only, are operative at the same time. For example, if there is a patrilineal system and a matrilineal one, individuals would belong to two groups at birth: the matrilineal group of the mother and the patrilineal group of the father. Imagine combining Figures 2 and 3. Individuals 4 and 5 would belong to both the patrilineal group (red in Figure 2) to which their father belongs and the matrilineal group (green in Figure 3) to which their mother belongs.

The way a society assigns names does not necessarily convey any information about a rule of descent. It is customary in North American society for children to have a last, or "family," name—usually their father's last name. All the people with the same last name do not conceive of themselves as descended from the same common ancestor; all Smiths do not consider themselves related. Nor do such people act together for any particular purpose. And many societies, even with rules of descent, do not give individuals the name of their kin group or of their father or mother. For example, among the patrilineal Luo of Kenya, babies were traditionally given names that described the circumstances of their birth (such as "born-in-the-morning"); their names did not include their father's or kin group's name. Only after the British established a colony in Kenya, and continuing after independence, did children get their father's personal name as a family name.

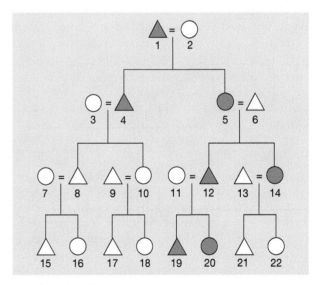

FIGURE 4 Ambilineal Descent
A hypothetical ambilineal group of kin is indicated by the color blue. Members 4 and 5 belong to this group because of a male link, their father (1); members 12 and 14 belong because of a female link, their mother (5); and members 19 and 20 belong because of a male link, their father (12). This is a hypothetical example because any combination of lineal links is possible in an ambilineal descent group.

Many societies, including our own, do not have lineal (matrilineal, patrilineal, or ambilineal) descent groups—sets of kin who believe they descend from a common ancestor. These are societies with **bilateral kinship.** *Bilateral* means "two-sided," and in this case, it refers to the fact that one's relatives on both the mother's and father's sides are equal in importance or, more usually, in unimportance. Kinship reckoning in bilateral societies does not refer to common descent but rather is horizontal, moving outward from close to more distant relatives rather than upward to common ancestors (see Figure 5).

The term **kindred** describes a person's bilateral set of relatives who may be called upon for some purpose. Most bilateral societies have kindreds that overlap in membership. In North America, we think of the kindred as including the people we might invite to weddings, funerals, or some other ceremonial occasion; a kindred, however, is not usually a definite group. As anyone who has been involved in creating a wedding invitation list knows, a great deal of time may be spent deciding which relatives ought to be invited and which ones can legitimately be excluded. Societies with bilateral kinship differ in precisely how distant relatives have to be before they are lost track of or before they are not included in ceremonial activities. In societies such as our own, in which kinship is relatively unimportant, fewer relatives are included in the kindred. In other bilateral societies, however, where kinship connections are somewhat more important, more would be included.

The distinctive feature of bilateral kinship is that, aside from brothers and sisters, no two people belong to exactly the same kin group. Your kindred contains close relatives spreading out on both your mother's and father's sides, but the members of your kindred are affiliated only by way of their connection to you (**ego,** or the focus). Thus, the kindred is an *ego-centered* group of kin. Because different people (except for brothers and sisters) have different mothers and fathers, your first cousins will have different kindreds, and even your own children will have different kindred from yours. The ego-centered nature of the kindred makes it difficult for it to serve as a permanent or persistent group. The only thing the people in a kindred have in common is the ego or focal person who brings them together. A kindred usually has no name, no common purpose, and only temporary meetings centered around the ego.[6] Furthermore, because everyone belongs to many different and overlapping kindreds, the society is not divided into clear-cut groups.

Although kindreds may not form clear-cut groups as in a unilineal society, this does not mean that the kindred cannot be turned to for help. In a bilateral society, the kindred may provide social insurance against adversity. Among the Chipewyan of subarctic Canada, for example, people would borrow a fishing net from a kindred member, or ask a kindred member to provide child care for a young person whose parent was ill. But recently, with the national and provincial governments providing resources such as housing and medical assistance, and with the increase in opportunities for wage labor, the kindred has ceased to be the main source of help for people in need. Aid from the state is making kinship less useful.[7]

VARIATION IN UNILINEAL DESCENT SYSTEMS

In a society with unilineal descent, people usually refer to themselves as belonging to a particular unilineal group or set of groups because they believe they share common descent in either the male (patrilineal) or female (matrilineal) line. Anthropologists distinguish several types of unilineal descent groups: lineages, clans, phratries, and moieties.

Lineages A **lineage** is a set of kin whose members trace descent from a common ancestor through known links. There may be **patrilineages** or **matrilineages,** depending on whether the links are traced through males only or through females only. Lineages are often designated

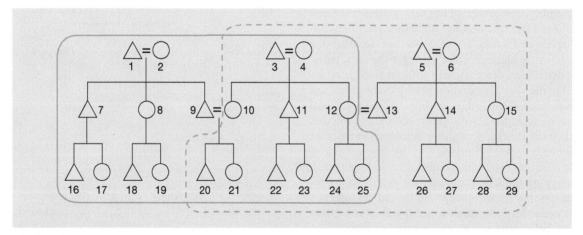

FIGURE 5 Bilateral Kinship
In a bilateral system, the kindred is ego-centered; hence, it varies with different points of reference (except for brothers and sisters). In any bilateral society, the kindred minimally includes parents, grandparents, aunts, uncles, and first cousins. So, if we look at the close kindred of the brother and sister 20 and 21 (enclosed by the solid line), it would include their parents (9 and 10), their aunts and uncles (7, 8, 11, 12), their grandparents (1, 2, 3, 4), and their first cousins (16–19, 22–25). But the kindred of the brother and sister 24 and 25 (shown by the dashed line) includes only some of the same people (3, 4, 10–12, 20–23); in addition, the kindred of 24 and 25 includes people not in the kindred of 20 and 21 (5, 6, 13–15, 26–29).

migrants and immigrants

Blood Is Thicker Than Water

With the spread of money economies, many societies no longer have kin groups like lineages, clans, phratries, and moieties—kin groups larger than families, sometimes much larger (possibly with hundreds and sometimes thousands of members). But if large kin groups are disappearing in the modern world, that doesn't mean they are completely gone. Lineages continue to be important for many Chinese, and for people in various parts of Africa and on islands in the Pacific. Lineages and clans in some places still "own" the cultivable land and other valuable property. Kinship may be particularly useful when it comes time to migrate to other countries. When that time comes, and it comes for millions of people every year, "blood is thicker than water," as the old saying goes. Migrants generally look to settle, at least at first, near or with relatives. The relatives may be genealogically close (siblings, uncles, aunts). Or they may be more distantly related, members of one's lineage or clan. Probably the most common reason migrants use kinship connections is that they need help, at least for a while, to make a living in the new country.

When looking for help from lineage mates or clansmen, you may not know exactly how you are related to them. All you might be able to say is that they belong to your lineage or clan. You know because they say they are "Li," "Park," or "Bear" like you. (Clans in some societies are believed to have animal ancestors.) It's like having an automatic friend in the new place, which can be very useful, particularly if you don't have close relatives there. Indeed, if you come from a region that has lineages, the first

person you might look up (even before you leave home) might be a lineage mate.

This is often what happens when Chinese from the Hong Kong area go abroad to seek their fortune. Consider the lineage known as the "Man," one of the five major lineages that dominated political life until the 1960s in the Hong Kong New Territories. Anthropologist James L. Watson has studied this group for more than 35 years, in the area around Hong Kong and in other parts of the world to which they have migrated. He has particularly tracked people from the village of San Tin, located on what used to be one of the front lines of the Cold War, 400 yards south of the border between British-controlled Hong Kong and Communist-controlled China.

People involved in the San Tin diaspora began to move away in the late 1950s. They had little money or assets. By the mid-1970s, they had managed to establish a chain of Chinese restaurants in England and other parts of Europe. Today, most of the grandchildren of the original migrants are wealthy professionals, and some are multimillionaires. Many in the current generation cannot speak or read Cantonese, the Chinese language of their ancestors. They now speak English, Dutch, or German.

The people who consider themselves members of the Man lineage trace their descent from Man Sai-go, the ancestor who settled near San Tin in the 14th century. Today, about 4,000 people living in more than 20 countries claim descent from Man Sai-go. The exact number is known only to the lineage master (zushang) and elders who manage the ancestral

estates (properties in land and other assets). For nearly 600 years, the Man survived on a kind of rice grown in the salty paddies along the Shenzhen River, which became the border between British Hong Kong and China in 1898. San Tin's farmers faced a crisis in the early 1950s. The markets for their rice were located on the Chinese side of the river, which was no longer regularly accessible. Unlike other lineages in the area, the Man could not convert to growing vegetables or white rice (which could not be grown in their salty paddies). They had two choices: go to Hong Kong to work in its booming factories or migrate to England to work in Chinese restaurants. Just before the British authorities banned migration to England in 1962, 85 percent to 90 percent of San Tin's able-bodied men left for Britain, lineage mates following lineage mates, to work in factories and hotels, as well as restaurants.

The village of San Tin became a remittance economy, with wives, children, and elders left behind, supported by the money sent home by the migrants who returned to San Tin for a visit every few years and then went back to Europe to work. Many of the migrants, when they retired, decided to join their children's families in the diaspora, and never again returned to San Tin.

The history of San Tin and its people illustrates how a supposedly premodern form of kinship, the Chinese lineage, is still very much alive in the modern world.

Sources: Brettell 1996, 793–97; McKeown 2005, 65–76; J. L. Watson 2004, 893–910.

by the name of the common male or female ancestor. In some societies, people belong to a hierarchy of lineages. That is, they first trace their descent back to the ancestor of a minor lineage, then to the ancestor of a larger and more inclusive major lineage, and so on.

Clans A **clan** (also sometimes called a **sib**) is a set of kin whose members believe themselves to be descended from

a common ancestor, but the links back to that ancestor are not specified. In fact, the common ancestor may not even be known. Clans with patrilineal descent are called **patriclans**; clans with matrilineal descent are called **matriclans.** Clans often are designated by an animal name (Bear, Wolf), called a **totem,** which may have some special significance for the group and, at the very least, is a means of group identification. The word *totem* comes from the

Ojibwa Indian word *ototeman,* "a relative of mine." In some societies, people have to observe taboos relating to their clan totem animal. For example, clan members may be forbidden to kill or eat their totem.

Although it may seem strange that an animal or plant should be a symbol of a kin group, animals as symbols of groups are familiar in our own culture. Football and baseball teams, for example, are often named for animals (Detroit Tigers, Baltimore Ravens, Philadelphia Eagles, Chicago Bears). Voluntary associations, such as men's clubs, are sometimes called by the name of an animal (Elks, Moose, Lions). Entire nations may be represented by an animal; we speak, for instance, of the American eagle and the British lion.[8] Why humans so often choose animal names to represent groups is an intriguing question for which we have no tested answer as yet.

Phratries   A **phratry** is a unilineal descent group composed of supposedly related clans or sibs. As with clans, the descent links in phratries are unspecified.

Moieties   When a whole society is divided into two unilineal descent groups, we call each group a **moiety.** (The word *moiety* comes from a French word meaning "half.") The people in each moiety believe themselves to be descended from a common ancestor, although they cannot specify how. Societies with moiety systems usually have relatively small populations (fewer than 9,000 people). Societies with phratries and clans tend to be larger.[9]

Combinations   Although we have distinguished several different types of unilineal descent groups, we do not wish to imply that all unilineal societies have only one type of descent group. Many societies have two or more types in various combinations. For example, some societies have lineages and clans; others may have clans and phratries but no lineages; and still others may have clans and moieties but neither phratries nor lineages. Aside from the fact that a society that has phratries must also have clans (because phratries are combinations of clans), all combinations of descent groups are possible. Even if societies have more than one type of unilineal kin group—for example, lineages and clans—there is no ambiguity about membership. Small groups are simply subsets of larger units; the larger units include people who say they are unilineally related further back in time.

Patrilineal Organization

Patrilineal organization is the most frequent type of descent system. The Kapauku Papuans, a people living in the central highlands of western New Guinea, are an example of a patrilineal society with various types of descent groups.[10] The hierarchy of groups to which the Kapauku are affiliated by virtue of the patrilineal descent system plays an extremely important part in their lives. All Kapauku belong to a patrilineage, to a patriclan that includes their lineage, and to a patriphratry that includes their clan.

The male members of a patrilineage—all the living males who can trace their actual relationship through males to a common ancestor—constitute the male population of a single village or, more likely, a series of adjoining villages. In other words, the lineage is a *territorial unit.* The male members of the lineage live together by virtue of a patrilocal rule of residence and a fairly stable settlement pattern. A son stays near his parents and brings his wife to live in or near his father's house; the daughters leave home and go to live with their husbands. If the group lives in one place over a long period, the male descendants of one man will live in the same territory. If the lineage is large, it may be divided into sublineages composed of people who trace their descent from one of the sons of the lineage ancestor. The male members of a sublineage live in a contiguous block within the larger lineage territory.

The members of the same patrilineage address each other affectionately, and within this group, a headman maintains law and order. Killing within the lineage is considered a serious offense, and any fighting that takes place is done with sticks rather than lethal weapons such as spears. The sublineage headman tries to settle grievances within the sublineage as quickly and as peacefully as possible. If a sublineage mate commits a crime against outsiders, all members of the sublineage may be considered responsible and their property seized, or a member of the sublineage may be killed in revenge by the victim's kin.

The Kapauku also belong to larger and more inclusive patrilineal descent groups—clans and phratries. All the people of the same clan believe they are related to each other in the father's line, but they are unable to say how they are related. If a member of the patriclan eats the clan's plant or animal totem, it is believed that the person will become deaf. Kapauku are also forbidden to marry anyone from their clan. In other words, the clan is exogamous.

Unlike the members of the patrilineage, the male members of the patriclan do not all live together. Thus, the lineage is the largest group of patrilineal kinsmen that is localized. The lineage is also the largest group of kinsmen that acts together politically. Among clan members, there is no mechanism for resolving disputes, and members of the same patriclan (who belong to different lineages) may even go to war with one another.

The most inclusive patrilineal descent group among the Kapauku is the phratry, each of which is composed of two or more clans. The Kapauku believe that the phratry was originally one clan, but that, in a conflict between brothers of the founding family, the younger brother was expelled and he formed a new clan. The two resulting clans are viewed as patrilineally related, because their founders are said to have been brothers. The members of a phratry observe all the totemic taboos of the clans that belong to that phratry. Intermarriage of members of the same clan is forbidden, but members of the same phratry, if they belong to different clans, may marry.

The Kapauku, then, have lineages with demonstrated kinship links and two kinds of descent groups with unknown descent links (clans and phratries).

Matrilineal Organization

Although societies with matrilineal descent seem in many respects like mirror images of their patrilineal counterparts, they differ in one important way. That difference

new perspectives on gender

Variation in Residence and Kinship: What Difference Does It Make to Women?

When we say that residence and kinship have profound effects on people's lives, what exactly do we mean? We may imagine that it is hard for a woman in a patrilocal society to move at marriage into another village where her husband has plenty of relatives and she has few. But do we have evidence of that? Most ethnographies usually do not give details about people's feelings, but some do. For example, Leigh Minturn gives us the text of a letter that one new Rajput bride (who grew up in the village of Khalapur, India) sent to her mother shortly after she married into her husband's village. The letter was written when the bride had been gone six weeks, but she repeatedly asked if her mother, her father, and her aunts had forgotten her. She begged to be called home and said her bags were packed. She described herself as "a parrot in a cage" and complained about her in-laws. The bride's mother was not alarmed; she knew that such complaints were normal, reflections of her daughter's separation anxiety. Seven years later, when Minturn returned to India, the mother reported the daughter to be happy. Still, a few other brides did have more serious symptoms: ghost possession, 24- to 36-hour comas, serious depression, or suicide. What research has not told us is whether these serious symptoms are present more often in patrilocal, patrilineal societies than in other societies, particularly matrilocal, matrilineal societies. Conversely, do men have some symptoms in matrilocal, matrilineal societies that they do not have in patrilocal societies? We do not know.

What about the status of women? Some research suggests that matrilocality and matrilineality enhance some aspects of women's status, but perhaps not as much as we might think. Even in matrilineal societies, men are usually the political leaders. The main effect of matrilocality and matrilineality appears to be that women control property, but they also tend to have more domestic authority in the home, more equal sexual restrictions, and more value placed on their lives. Alice Schlegel pointed out that women's status is not always relatively high in matrilineal societies, because they can be dominated by the husband or by brothers (because brothers play important roles in their kin groups). Only when neither the husband nor the brother dominates may women have considerable control over their own lives. Certainly the combination of matrilocality and matrilineality is better for women's status than patrilocality and patrilineality. Matrilocality and matrilineality might not enhance women's status because of the dominance of male matrilineal kin, but patrilocality and patrilineality are very likely to detract from women's status. Norma Diamond stated that, even after the Chinese Communist revolution, which abolished the landholding estates of patrilineages and gave women access to education as well as jobs outside the home, male dominance continued. The mode of production and labor changed, but patrilocality did not. Women were still usually the in-marrying strangers, and members of the patrilineage became a work team on the collective farm. Diamond pointed out that those few women who became local leaders were likely to have atypical marriages that allowed them to live in the villages of their birth.

Residence and descent also predict societal attempts to control reproduction. According to Suzanne Frayser, patrilineal societies have several sexual and reproductive dilemmas. One dilemma is the contradiction between the importance of males in kinship and the women's role in reproduction. If patrilineal societies denigrate women too much, women may try to decrease their reproduction. If patrilineal societies exalt women too much, that exaltation may detract from the value of men. A second dilemma has to do with paternity, which is essential for patrilineal descent but harder than maternity to be certain of. Frayser argued that, because kin group links are traced through males in patrilineal societies, they will do more to ensure that the man a woman marries is the father. Frayser suggested that patrilineal societies therefore will be more restrictive about a woman's sexuality. Indeed, the results of her cross-cultural study indicate that patrilineal societies are more likely than other societies to prohibit premarital and extramarital sex for women, and they are more likely to make it very difficult for a woman to divorce her husband.

Of course, we have to remember that there is considerable variation within patrilocal/patrilineal societies and matrilocal/matrilineal societies. In the patrilineal society that Audrey Smedley studied—the Birom of the Jos Plateau in Nigeria—women were formally barred from owning property, from holding political offices, and from major decision making. Yet, her fieldwork revealed that they had considerable autonomy in their personal lives in everyday life, including the legal right to take on lovers. Indeed, they had considerable indirect influence on decision making and were strong supporters of the patrilineal system. Smedley speculates that women support patrilineality in some environmental circumstances because it serves their interests and those of their children too. For example, male crops are highly valued, but such crops are grown on the more dangerous plains where men risked death at the hands of raiders from other groups. Food was scarce, so it may have been adaptive for everyone, including women, to give special status to men for growing crops in dangerous places.

Sources: Minturn 1993, 54–71; M. K. Whyte 1978b, 132–34; Schlegel 2009; N. Diamond 1975; Smedley 2004; Frayser 1985, 338–47.

has to do with who exercises authority. In patrilineal systems, descent affiliation is transmitted through males, and it is also the males who exercise authority. Consequently, in the patrilineal system, lines of descent and of authority converge. In a matrilineal system, however, although the line of descent passes through females, females rarely exercise authority in their kin groups. Usually males do. Thus, the lines of authority and descent do not converge.[11] Anthropologists do not completely understand why this is so, but it is an ethnographic fact. In any case, because males exercise authority in the kin group, an individual's mother's brother becomes an important authority figure, because he is the individual's closest male matrilineal relative in the parental generation. The individual's father does not belong to the individual's own matrilineal kin group and thus has no say in kin group matters.

The divergence of authority and descent in a matrilineal system has some effect on community organization and marriage. Most matrilineal societies practice matrilocal residence. Daughters stay at home after marriage and bring their husbands to live with them; sons leave home to join their wives. But the sons who are required to leave will be the ones who eventually exercise authority in their kin groups. This situation presents a problem. The solution that seems to have been realized in most matrilineal societies is that, although the males move away to live with their wives, they usually do not move too far away; indeed, they often marry women who live in the same village. Thus, matrilineal societies tend not to be locally exogamous—that is, members often marry people from inside the village—whereas patrilineal societies are often locally exogamous.[12]

The matrilineal organization on Chuuk, a group of small islands in the Pacific, illustrates the general pattern of authority in matrilineal systems.[13] The Chuukese have both matrilineages and matriclans. The matrilineage is a property-owning group whose members trace descent from a known common ancestor in the female line. The female lineage members and their husbands occupy a cluster of houses on the matrilineage's land. The property of the lineage group is administered by the oldest brother of the group, who allocates the productive property of his matrilineage and directs the work of the members. He also represents the group in dealings with the district chief and all outsiders, and he must be consulted on any matter that affects the group. There is also a senior woman of the lineage who exercises some authority, but only insofar as the activities of the women are concerned. She may supervise the women's cooperative work (they usually work separately from the men) and manage the household.

Within the nuclear family, the father and mother have the primary responsibility for raising and disciplining their children. When a child reaches puberty, however, the father's right to discipline or exercise authority over the child ceases. The mother continues to exercise her right of discipline, but her brother may interfere. A woman's brother rarely interferes with his sister's child before puberty, but he may exercise some authority after puberty, especially because he is an elder in the child's own matrilineage. On Chuuk, men rarely move far from their birthplace. As Ward Goodenough pointed out, "Since matrilocal residence takes the men away from their home lineages, most of them marry women whose lineage houses are within a few minutes' walk of their own."[14]

Although there are some differences between patrilineal and matrilineal systems, there are many similarities. In both types of systems there may be lineages, clans, phratries, and moieties, alone or in any combination. These kin groups, in either matrilineal or patrilineal societies, may perform any number of functions. They may regulate marriage, they may come to each other's aid economically or politically, and they may perform rituals together.

FUNCTIONS OF UNILINEAL DESCENT GROUPS

Unilineal descent groups exist in societies at all levels of cultural complexity.[15] Apparently, however, they are most common in noncommercial food-producing, as opposed to food-collecting, societies.[16] Unilineal descent groups often have important functions in the social, economic, political, and religious realms of life.

Regulating Marriage

In unilineal societies, individuals are not usually permitted to marry within their own unilineal descent groups. In some, however, marriage may be permitted within more inclusive kin groups but prohibited within smaller kin groups. In a few societies, marriage within the kin group is actually preferred.

But, in general, the incest taboo in unilineal societies is extended to all presumed unilineal relatives. For example, on Chuuk, which has matriclans and matrilineages, people are forbidden to marry anyone from their matriclan by the rule of descent group exogamy. The matrilineage is included within the matriclan, so the rule of descent group exogamy also applies to the matrilineage. Among the Kapauku, who have patriphratries, patriclans, and patrilineages, the largest descent group that is exogamous is the patriclan. The phratry may once have been exogamous, but the exogamy rule no longer applies to it. Some anthropologists have suggested that rules of exogamy for descent groups may have developed because the alliances between descent groups generated by such rules may be selectively favored under the conditions of life most unilineal societies face.

Economic Functions

Members of a person's lineage or clan are often required to side with that person in any quarrel or lawsuit, to help him or her get established economically, to contribute to a bride price or fine, and to support the person in life crises. Mutual aid often extends to economic cooperation on a regular basis. The unilineal descent group may act as a corporate unit in landownership. For example, among the Chuukese and the Kapauku, a lineage owns house sites and farmland. Descent group members may also support one another in such enterprises as clearing virgin bush or forest for farmland and providing food and other items for feasts, potlatches, curing rites, and ceremonial occasions, such as births, initiations, marriages, and funerals.

The descent group sometimes views money earned—either by harvesting a cash crop or by leaving the community for a time to work for cash wages—as belonging to all. In recent times, however, young people in some places have shown an unwillingness to part with their money, viewing it as different from other kinds of economic assistance.

Political Functions

The word *political*, as used by members of an industrialized society, generally does not apply to the vague powers that may be entrusted to a headman or the elders of a lineage or clan. But these people may have the right to assign land for use by a lineage member or a clan member. Headmen or elders may also have the right to settle disputes between two members within a lineage, although they generally lack power to force a settlement. And they may act as intermediaries in disputes between a member of their own clan and a member of an opposing kin group.

Certainly one of the most important political functions of unilineal descent groups is their role in warfare—the attempt to resolve disputes within and outside the society by violent action. In societies without towns or cities, the organization of such fighting is often in the hands of descent groups. The Tiv of central Nigeria, for instance, know very well at any given moment which lineages they will fight against, which lineages they will join as allies in case of a fight, which they will fight against using only sticks, and which must be attacked using bows and arrows.

Religious Functions

A clan or lineage may have its own religious beliefs and practices, worshiping its own gods or goddesses and ancestral spirits. The Tallensi of West Africa revere and try to pacify their ancestors. They view life as we know it as only a part of human existence; for them, life existed before birth and will continue after death. The Tallensi believe that the ancestors of their descent groups have changed their form but have retained their interest in what goes on within their society. They can show their displeasure by bringing sudden disaster or minor mishap and their pleasure by bringing unexpected good fortune. But people can never tell what will please them; ancestral spirits are, above all, unpredictable. Thus, the Tallensi try to account for unexplainable happenings by attributing them to the ever-watchful ancestors. Belief in the presence of ancestors also provides security; if their ancestors have survived death, so will they. The Tallensi religion is thus a religion of that descent group. The Tallensi are not concerned with other people's ancestors; they believe only one's own ancestors can plague or protect one.[17]

In some cultures, people worship or give gifts to ancestral spirits, as is common in China.

Reed Kaestner/CORBIS- NY

AMBILINEAL SYSTEMS

Societies with ambilineal descent groups are far less numerous than unilineal or even bilateral societies. Ambilineal societies, however, resemble unilineal ones in many ways. For instance, the members of an ambilineal descent group believe that they are descended from a common ancestor, although frequently they cannot specify all the genealogical links. The descent group is commonly named and may have an identifying emblem or even a totem; the descent group may own land and other productive resources; and myths and religious practices are often associated with the group. Marriage is often regulated by group membership, just as in unilineal systems, although kin group exogamy is not nearly as common as in unilineal systems. Moreover, ambilineal societies resemble unilineal ones in having various levels or types of descent groups. They may have lineages and higher orders of descent groups, distinguished (as in unilineal systems) by whether or not all the genealogical links to the supposed common ancestors are specified.[18]

The Samoans of the South Pacific are an example of an ambilineal society.[19] Samoa has two types of ambilineal descent groups, corresponding to what would be called clans and subclans in a unilineal society. Both groups are exogamous. Associated with each ambilineal clan are one or more chiefs. A group takes its name from the senior chief; subclans, of which there are always at least two, may take their names from junior chiefs.

The distinctiveness of the Samoan ambilineal system, compared with unilineal systems, is that individuals could belong to a number of ambilineal groups because people may be affiliated with an ambilineal group through their father or mother (and the parents, in turn, could be affiliated with any of their parents' groups). Affiliation with a Samoan descent group is optional, and people may theoretically affiliate with any or all of the ambilineal groups to which they are related. In practice, however, people are primarily associated with one group—the ambilineal group whose land they actually live on and cultivate—although they may participate in the activities (e.g., house building) of several groups. Because a person may belong to more than one ambilineal group, the society is not divided into separate kin groups, in contrast with unilineal societies. Consequently, the core members of each ambilineal group cannot all live together, as they could in unilineal societies, because each person belongs to more than one group and cannot live in several places at once.

Not all ambilineal societies have the multiple descent group membership that occurs in Samoa. In some ambilineal societies, a person may belong to only one group at any one time. In such cases, the society can be divided into separate, nonoverlapping groups of kin.

EXPLAINING VARIATION IN RESIDENCE

Questions can be raised as to why different societies have different patterns of residence. If married couples in most societies live with or near kin, as in patrilocal, matrilocal, bilocal, and avunculocal patterns of residence, then why do couples in some societies, such as our own, typically live apart from kin? And, among the societies in which couples live with or near kin, why do most choose the husband's side (patrilocal residence), but some the wife's side (matrilocal residence)? Why do some non-neolocal societies allow a married couple to go to either the wife's or the husband's kin (bilocal residence), whereas most others do not allow a choice?

Neolocal Residence

Many anthropologists have suggested that neolocal residence is related to the presence of a money or commercial economy. They argue that, when people can sell their labor or their products for money, they can buy what they need to live, without having to depend on kin. Because money is not perishable, unlike crops and other foods in a world largely lacking refrigeration, it can be stored for exchange at a later time. Thus, a money-earning family can resort to its own savings during periods of unemployment or disability, or it might be able to rely on monetary aid from the government, as in our own society. This strategy is impossible in nonmonetary economies, where people must depend on relatives for food and other necessities if they cannot provide their own for some reason.

There is cross-cultural evidence to support this interpretation. Neolocal residence tends to occur in societies with monetary or commercial exchange, whereas societies without money tend to have patterns of residence that locate a couple near or with kin.[20] The presence of money, then, partially accounts for neolocal residence: Money seems to allow couples to live on their own. Still, this fact does not quite explain why they choose to do so.

One reason may be that couples in commercial societies do better on their own because the jobs available require physical or social mobility. Or perhaps couples prefer to live apart from kin because they want to avoid some of the interpersonal tensions and demands that may be generated by living with or near kin. But why couples, when given money, should *prefer* to live on their own is not completely understood.

Matrilocal versus Patrilocal Residence

It is traditionally assumed that, in societies in which married children live near or with kin, the pattern of residence will tend to be patrilocal if males contribute more to the economy and matrilocal if women contribute more. However plausible that assumption may seem, the cross-cultural evidence does not support it. Where men do most of the primary subsistence work, residence is patrilocal no more often than would be expected by chance. Conversely, where women do an equal amount or more of the subsistence work, residence is no more likely to be matrilocal than patrilocal.[21] And if we counted all work inside and outside the home, most societies should be matrilocal because women usually do more. But that is not true either; most societies are not matrilocal.

applied anthropology

From Cross-Cultural Research to Archaeology: Reconstructing Marital Residence in the Prehistoric U.S. Southwest

Applied anthropology uses anthropological knowledge to solve problems. Usually, the problem is a practical problem outside anthropology. For example, forensic anthropology applies biological anthropology to help solve murders and other crimes. But sometimes the application is from one subfield of anthropology to another.

Cross-cultural studies using ethnographic data indicate that sisters are very likely to live in the same household if marital residence is matrilocal. The family unit is likely to be larger therefore with matrilocal residence, and the living (nonstorage) floor area of the house is also likely to be larger. In contrast to patrilocal societies, where the average living floor area is less than 72 square yards (60 square meters), the living floor area in matrilocal societies tends to be larger than 120 square yards (100 square meters). Apparently, sisters have less trouble living together than non-sisters, perhaps because they have grown up together.

Most anthropologists would assume that a relationship derived from comparative ethnography on preindustrial societies would apply also to human behavior in the prehistoric past. If that's true, and there is no good reason to doubt it, archaeological sites with living floor areas totaling more than 120 square yards (100 square meters) are likely to have had matrilocal marital residence. This prediction has been applied to the transition from pit houses to great houses in the U.S. Southwest. The pit houses between A.D. 500 and A.D. 700 averaged 18 square yards (15 square meters) in floor area, in contrast to the multiroom households from A.D. 900 to A.D. 1100 (as in Pueblo Bonito in New Mexico's Chaco Canyon) that ranged in size from 84 square yards to more than 360 square yards (70 square meters to 300 square meters). The latter households were probably matrilocal. Archaeologists know that the households had multiple rooms because there are double walls between adjacent households.

Years ago, some archaeologists suggested that a descent line of matrilineally related women, who would have occupied a site over time if couples lived matrilocally, should exhibit distinctive pottery design elements when compared with the pottery from other sites. After all, mothers would have taught daughters who would have taught their daughters. Perhaps because their calculations and measures were not simple counts such as number of potsherds found, the work by these pioneering archaeologists was ignored if not rejected. The study of kinship in archaeology, following the findings of cross-cultural research, is still wide open, particularly to investigators who are trained in statistical methods.

Sources: Peregrine 2001; M. Ember 1973; Divale 1977; Hill 1970; Longacre 1970.

We can predict whether residence will be matrilocal or patrilocal, however, from the type of warfare practiced in the society. In most societies known to anthropology, neighboring communities or districts are enemies. The type of warfare that breaks out periodically between such groups is called *internal,* because the fighting occurs between groups that speak the same language. In other societies, the warfare is never within the same society but only with other language groups. This pattern of warfare is referred to as purely *external.* Cross-cultural evidence suggests that, in societies where warfare is at least sometimes internal, residence is almost always patrilocal rather than matrilocal. In contrast, residence is usually matrilocal when warfare is purely external.[22]

How can we explain this relationship between type of warfare and matrilocal versus patrilocal residence? One theory is that patrilocal residence tends to occur with internal warfare because there may be concern over keeping sons close to home to help with defense. Because women do not usually constitute the fighting force in any society, having sons reside at home after marriage might be favored as a means of maintaining a loyal and quickly mobilized fighting force in case of surprise attack from nearby. If warfare is purely external, however, people may not be so concerned about keeping their sons at home because families need not fear attack from neighboring communities or districts.

With purely external warfare, then, the pattern of residence may be determined by other considerations, especially economic ones. If the women do most of the primary subsistence work in societies with purely external warfare, families might want their daughters to remain at home after marriage, so the pattern of residence might become matrilocal. If warfare is purely external but men still do more of the primary subsistence work, residence should still be patrilocal. Thus, the need to keep sons at home after marriage when there is internal warfare may take precedence over any considerations based on division of labor. Perhaps only when internal warfare is nonexistent may a female-dominant division of labor give rise to matrilocal residence.[23]

The frequent absence of men because of long-distance trade or wage labor in distant places may also provide an impetus for matrilocal residence even after warfare ceases. For example, among the Miskito of eastern Central America, matrilocality allowed domestic and village life to continue without interruption when men were away from home for long periods of time, working as lumberers,

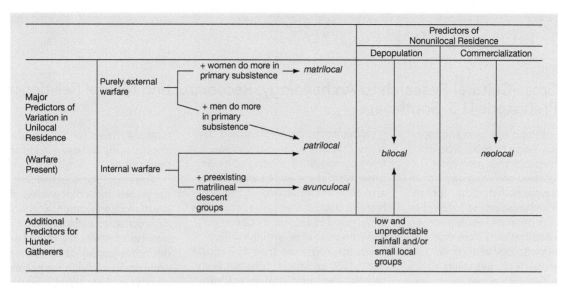

| | | | | Predictors of Nonunilocal Residence | |
				Depopulation	Commercialization
Major Predictors of Variation in Unilocal Residence	Purely external warfare	+ women do more in primary subsistence → *matrilocal*			
		+ men do more in primary subsistence			
(Warfare Present)			*patrilocal*	*bilocal*	*neolocal*
	Internal warfare				
		+ preexisting matrilineal descent groups → *avunculocal*			
Additional Predictors for Hunter-Gatherers				low and unpredictable rainfall and/or small local groups	

FIGURE 6 The Main Predictors of Marital Residence Patterns
An arrow indicates the suggested causal direction.

Source: Adapted from M. Ember and C. R. Ember 1983.
Adapted from Melvin Ember and Carol R. Ember, *Marriage, Family, and Kinship: Comparative Studies of Social Organization* (New Haven, CT: HRAF Press, 1983).

miners, and river transporters. More recently, men have worked away from home as deep-sea divers for lobster, for which there is a lot of demand in the international economy. These jobs were not always available, but when they were, the men went away to work at them to earn money. Even though some men would always be away from home, the Miskito continued to get food in their traditional ways, from farming (done mostly by the women) and from hunting and fishing (which was mostly men's work).[24]

Bilocal Residence

In societies that practice bilocal residence, a married couple goes to live with or near either the husband's or the wife's parents. Although this pattern seems to involve a choice for the married couple, theory and research suggest that bilocal residence may occur out of necessity instead. Elman Service suggested that bilocal residence is likely to occur in societies that have recently suffered a severe and drastic loss of population because of the introduction of new infectious diseases.[25] Over the last 400 years, contact with Europeans in many parts of the world has resulted in severe population losses among non-European societies that lacked resistance to the Europeans' diseases. If couples need to live with some set of kin to make a living in noncommercial societies, it seems likely that couples in depopulated, noncommercial societies might have to live with whichever spouse's parents and other relatives are still alive. This interpretation is supported by the cross-cultural evidence. Recently depopulated societies tend to have bilocal residence or frequent departures from unilocality, whereas societies that are not recently depopulated tend to have one pattern or another of unilocal residence.[26]

In hunter-gatherer societies, a few other circumstances may also favor bilocal residence. Bilocality tends to be found among those hunter-gatherers who have very small bands or unpredictable and low rainfall. Residential

"choice" in these cases may be a question of adjusting marital residence to where the couple will have the best chance to survive or to find close relatives with whom to live and work.[27] Figure 6 illustrates the main predictors of the various marital residence patterns.

Avunculocal Residence

Now that we have learned about matrilineal systems, the avunculocal pattern of residence, whereby married couples live with or near the husband's mother's brother, may become clearer. Although avunculocal residence is relatively rare, just about all avunculocal societies are matrilineal. As we have seen, the mother's brother plays an important role in decision making in most matrilineal societies. Aside from his brothers, who is a boy's closest male matrilineal relative? His mother's brother. Going to live with the mother's brother, then, provides a way of localizing

Trobriand Islanders have avunculocal residence and matrilineal descent groups.

male *matrilineal* relatives. But why should some matrilineal societies practice that form of residence? The answer may involve the prevailing type of warfare.

Avunculocal societies, in contrast with matrilocal societies, fight internally. Just as patrilocality may be a response to keep patrilineally related men home after marriage, avunculocality may also be a way of keeping related—in this case, matrilineally related—men together after marriage to provide for quick mobilization in case of surprise attack from nearby. Societies that already have strong, functioning matrilineal descent groups may choose initially, when faced with the emergence of fighting close to home, to switch to avunculocality rather than patrilocality. This is assuming that the close warfare results in high male mortality, which might make it more difficult to trace descent patrilineally than matrilineally. So such a society might begin to practice avunculocality rather than switch to patrilocality. Avunculocal residence would keep a higher number of related men together after marriage, compared with patrilocality, because there would be more possible links through women than through men if many men were dying relatively young in warfare.[28]

THE EMERGENCE OF UNILINEAL SYSTEMS

Unilineal kin groups play very important roles in the organization of many societies. But not all societies have such groups. In societies that have complex systems of political organization, officials and agencies take over many of the functions that kin groups might perform, such as organizing work and warfare and allocating land. But not all societies that lack complex political organization have unilineal descent systems. Why, then, do some societies have unilineal descent systems, but others do not?

It is generally assumed that unilocal residence, patrilocal or matrilocal, is necessary for the development of unilineal descent. Patrilocal residence, if practiced for some time in a society, will generate a set of patrilineally related males who live in the same territory. Matrilocal residence over time will similarly generate a localized set of matrilineally related females. It is no wonder, then, that matrilocal and patrilocal residence are cross-culturally associated with matrilineal and patrilineal descent, respectively.[29]

But, although unilocal residence might be necessary for the formation of unilineal descent groups, it is apparently not the only condition required. For one thing, many societies with unilocal residence lack unilineal descent groups. For another, merely because related males or related females live together by virtue of a patrilocal or matrilocal rule of residence, it does not necessarily follow that the related people will actually view themselves as a descent group and function as such. Thus, it appears that other conditions are needed to supply the impetus for the formation of unilineal descent groups.

There is evidence that unilocal societies that engage in warfare are more apt to have unilineal descent groups than unilocal societies without warfare.[30] It may be, then, that the presence of fighting in societies lacking complex systems of political organization provides an impetus to the formation of unilineal descent groups. Unilineal descent groups provide individuals with unambiguous groups of people who can fight or form alliances as discrete units.[31] There is no ambiguity about an individual's membership. It is perfectly clear whether someone belongs to a particular clan, phratry, or moiety. This feature of unilineal descent groups enables them to act as separate and distinct units—mostly, perhaps, in warfare.

EXPLAINING AMBILINEAL AND BILATERAL SYSTEMS

Why do some societies have ambilineal descent groups? Although the evidence is not clear-cut, it may be that societies with unilineal descent groups are transformed into ambilineal ones under special conditions, particularly in the presence of depopulation. We have already noted that depopulation may transform a previously unilocal society into a bilocal society. If that previously unilocal society also had unilineal descent groups, the descent groups may become transformed into ambilineal groups. If a society used to be patrilocal and patrilineal, for example, but some couples began to live matrilocally, then their children would be associated through their mother with a previously patrilineal descent group on whose land they may be living. Once this situation happens regularly, the unilineal principle may become transformed into an ambilineal principle.[32] Thus, ambilineal descent systems may have developed recently as a result of depopulation caused by the introduction of European diseases.

The conditions that favor bilateral systems are in large part opposite to those favoring unilineal descent. As we discussed, unilineal descent seems to develop in a nonstate society with unilocal residence that has warfare. If one needs an unambigious set of allies, bilateral systems are unlikely to provide them. Recall that bilateral systems are ego-centered; and every person, other than siblings, has a slightly different set of kin to rely on. Consequently, in bilateral societies, it is often not clear to whom one can turn and which person has responsibility for aiding another. Such ambiguity, however, might not be a liability in societies without warfare. In complex political systems that organize fighting on behalf of large populations, a standing army usually provides the fighting force, and mobilization of kin is not so important. Perhaps because warfare is somewhat less likely in foraging societies,[33] bilateral systems may often develop in foraging societies, just like bilaterality is likely in more complex societies because they don't need to rely on descent groups for war. Neolocal residence, which becomes more common with commercialization and market exchange, also works against unilineal descent, and therefore also makes a bilateral system more likely.

KINSHIP TERMINOLOGY

Our society, like all others, refers to a number of different kin by the same **classificatory terms.** Most of us probably never stop to think about why we name relatives the way we do. For example, we call our mother's brother and father's brother (and often mother's sister's husband and father's sister's husband) by the same term—*uncle*. It is not that we are unable to distinguish between our mother's or father's brother or that we do not know the difference between **consanguineal kin** (blood kin) and **affinal kin** (kin by marriage, or what we call *in-laws*). Instead, it seems that we do not usually find it necessary to distinguish between various types of uncles in our society.

However natural our system of classification may seem to us, countless field studies by anthropologists have revealed that societies differ markedly in how they group or distinguish relatives. The kinship terminology used in a society may reflect its prevailing kind of family, its rule of residence, its rule of descent, and other aspects of its social organization. Kin terms may also give clues to prior features of the society's social system, if, as many anthropologists believe,[34] the kin terms of a society are very resistant to change. The major systems of kinship terminology are the Omaha system, the Crow system, the Iroquois system, the Sudanese system, the Hawaiian system, and the Inuit (Eskimo) system.

Because it is the most familiar to us, let us first consider the kinship terminology system employed in our own and many other commercial societies. But it is by no means confined to commercial societies. In fact, this system is found in many Inuit societies.

Inuit, or Eskimo, System

The distinguishing features of the Inuit, or Eskimo, system (see Figure 7) are that all cousins are lumped together under the same term but are distinguished from brothers and sisters; all aunts are lumped under the same term and distinguished from the mother; and all uncles are lumped under the same term and distinguished from the father. In Figure 7 and in subsequent figures, the kin types that are referred to by the same term are colored and marked in the same way; for example, in the Inuit system, kin types 2 (father's brother) and 6 (mother's brother) are referred to by the same term (*uncle* in English). Note that, in this system—in contrast to the others we will examine—no other relatives are generally referred to by the same terms used for members of the nuclear family—mother, father, brother, and sister.

The Inuit type of kinship terminology is not generally found where there are unilineal or ambilineal descent groups; the only kin group that appears to be present is the

bilateral kindred.[35] Remember that the kindred in a bilateral kinship system is an ego-centered group. Although relatives on both my mother's and my father's sides are equally important, my most important relatives are generally those closest to me. This is particularly true in our society, where the nuclear family generally lives alone, separated from and not particularly involved with other relatives except on ceremonial occasions. Because the nuclear family is most important, we would expect to find that the terminology for kin types in the nuclear family is different from the terminology for all other relatives. And the mother's and father's sides are equally important (or unimportant), so it makes sense that we use the same terms (*aunt, uncle,* and *cousin*) for both sides of the family.

Omaha System

The Omaha system of kin terminology is named after the Omaha of North America, but the system is found in many societies around the world, usually those with patrilineal descent.[36] Referring to Figure 8, we can see immediately which types of kin are lumped together in an Omaha system. First, father and father's brother (numbers 2 and 3) are both referred to by the same term. This way of classifying relatives contrasts markedly with ours, in which no term that applies to a member of the nuclear family (father, mother, brother, sister) is applied to any other relative. What could account for the Omaha system of lumping? One interpretation is that father and father's brother are lumped in this system because most societies in which this system is found have patrilineal kin groups. Both father and father's brother are in the parental generation of my patrilineal kin group and may behave toward me similarly. My father's brother also probably lived near me as a child, because patrilineal societies usually have patrilocal residence. The term for father and father's brother, then, might be translated "male member of my patrilineal kin group in my father's generation."

A second lumping, which at first glance appears similar to the lumping of father and father's brother, is that of mother and mother's sister (4 and 5), both of whom are called by the same term. But more surprisingly, mother's brother's daughter (16) is also referred to by this term. Why? If we think of the term as meaning "female member of my mother's patrilineage of *any* generation," then the term makes sense. Consistent with this view, all the male members of my mother's patrilineage of any generation

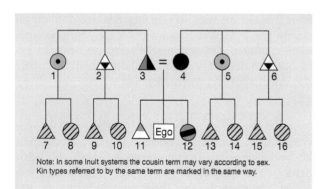

Note: In some Inuit systems the cousin term may vary according to sex.
Kin types referred to by the same term are marked in the same way.

FIGURE 7 Inuit (Eskimo) Terminology System

FIGURE 8 Omaha Kinship Terminology System

(mother's brother, 6; mother's brother's son, 15) are also referred to by one term.

It is apparent, then, that relatives on the father's and the mother's sides are grouped differently in this system. For members of my mother's patrilineal kin group, I lump all male members together and all female members together regardless of their generation. Yet, for members of my father's patrilineal kin group, I have different terms for the male and female members of different generations. George Peter Murdock suggested that a society lumps kin types when there are more similarities than differences among them.[37]

Using this principle, and recognizing that societies with an Omaha system usually are patrilineal, I realize that my father's patrilineal kin group is the one to which I belong and in which I have a great many rights and obligations. Consequently, people of my father's generation are likely to behave quite differently toward me than are people of my own generation. Members of my patrilineal group in my father's generation are likely to exercise authority over me, and I am required to show them respect. Members of my patrilineal group in my own generation are those I am likely to play with as a child and to be friends with. Thus, in a patrilineal system, people on my father's side belonging to different generations are likely to be distinguished. On the other hand, my mother's patrilineage is relatively unimportant to me (because I take my descent from my father). And because my residence is probably patrilocal, my mother's relatives will probably not even live near me. Thus, inasmuch as my mother's patrilineal relatives are comparatively unimportant in such a system, they become similar enough to be lumped together.

Finally, in the Omaha system, I refer to my male parallel cousins (my father's brother's son, 9; and my mother's sister's son, 13) in the same way I refer to my brother (12). I refer to my female parallel cousins (my father's brother's daughter, 10; and my mother's sister's daughter, 14) in the same way I refer to my sister (12). Considering that my father's brother and mother's sister are referred to by the same terms I use for my father and mother, this lumping of parallel cousins with **siblings** (brothers and sisters) is not surprising. If I call my own mother's and father's children (other than myself) "brother" and "sister," then the children of anyone whom I also call "mother" and "father" ought to be called "brother" and "sister" as well.

Crow System

The Crow system, named after another North American culture, has been called the mirror image of the Omaha system. The same principles of lumping kin types are employed, except that the Crow system is associated with matrilineal descent,[38] so the individuals in my mother's matrilineal group (which is my own) are not lumped across generations, whereas the individuals in my father's matrilineal group are. Comparing Figure 9 with Figure 8, we find that the lumping and separating of kin types are much the same in both, except that the lumping across generations in the Crow system appears on the father's side rather than on the mother's side. In other words, I call both

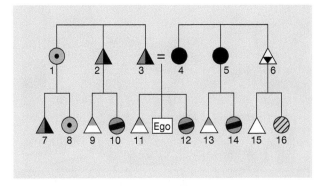

FIGURE 9 Crow Kinship Terminology System

my mother and my mother's sister by the same term (because both are female members of my matrilineal descent group in my mother's generation). I call my father, my father's brother, and my father's sister's son by the same term (all male members of my father's matrilineal group in any generation). I call my father's sister and my father's sister's daughter by the same term (both female members of my father's matrilineal group). And I refer to my parallel cousins in the same way I refer to my brother and sister.

Iroquois System

The Iroquois system, named after the Iroquois of North America, is similar to both the Omaha and Crow systems in the way in which I refer to relatives in my parents' generation (see Figure 10). That is, my father and my father's brother (2 and 3) are referred to by the same term, and my mother and my mother's sister (4 and 5) are referred to by the same term. However, the Iroquois system differs from the Omaha and Crow systems regarding my own generation. In the Omaha and Crow systems, one set of cross-cousins was lumped in the kinship terminology with the generation above. In the Iroquois system, both sets of cross-cousins (mother's brother's children, 15 and 16; and father's sister's children, 7 and 8) are referred to by the same terms, distinguished by sex. That is, mother's brother's daughter and father's sister's daughter are both referred to by the same term. Also, mother's brother's son and father's sister's son are referred to by the same term.

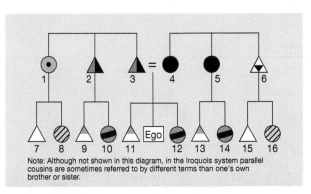

Note: Although not shown in this diagram, in the Iroquois system parallel cousins are sometimes referred to by different terms than one's own brother or sister.

FIGURE 10 Iroquois Terminology System

The Iroquois longhouses could house over 80 people. The female members of a matrilineage with their in-marrying husbands traditionally lived in one longhouse.

Parallel cousins always have terms different from those for cross-cousins and are sometimes, but not always, referred to by the same terms as one's brother and sister.

Like the Omaha and Crow systems, the Iroquois system has different terms for relatives on the father's and mother's sides. Such differentiation tends to be associated with unilineal descent, which is not surprising because unilineal descent involves affiliation with either mother's or father's kin. Why Iroquois, rather than Omaha or Crow, terminology occurs in a unilineal society requires explanation. One possible explanation is that Omaha or Crow is likely to occur in a developed, as opposed to a developing or decaying, unilineal system.[39] Another possibility is that Iroquois terminology emerges in societies that prefer marriage with both cross-cousins,[40] who are differentiated from other relatives in an Iroquois system.

Sudanese System

Unlike the Omaha, Crow, and Iroquois systems, the Sudanese system usually does not lump any relatives in the parents' and ego's generations. That is, the Sudanese system is usually a *descriptive system,* in which a different **descriptive term** is used for *each* of the relatives, as shown in Figure 11. What kinds of societies are likely to have such a system? Although societies with Sudanese terminology are likely to be patrilineal, they probably are different from most patrilineal societies that have Omaha or Iroquois terms. Sudanese terminology is associated with relatively great political complexity, class stratification, and occupational specialization. It has been suggested that, under such conditions, a kinship system may reflect the need to make fine distinctions among members of descent groups who have different opportunities and privileges in the occupational or class system.[41]

FIGURE 11 Sudanese Kinship Terminology System

FIGURE 12 Hawaiian Kinship Terminology System

The Omaha, Crow, Iroquois, and Sudanese systems, although different from one another and associated with somewhat different predictors, share one important feature: The terms used for the mother's and father's side of the family are not the same. If you imagine folding the kinship terminology diagrams in half, the two sides would not be the same. As we have seen in the Inuit system, however, the terms on the mother's and father's side of the family are *exactly* the same. This feature suggests that the two sides of the family are equally important or equally unimportant. The Hawaiian system discussed next also has the same terms on both sides, but kinship outside the nuclear family is more important.

Hawaiian System

The Hawaiian system of kinship terminology is the least complex in that it uses the smallest number of terms. In this system, all relatives of the same sex in the same generation are referred to by the same term (see Figure 12). Thus, all my female cousins are referred to by the same term as my sister; all male cousins are referred to by the same term as my brother. Everyone known to be related to me in my parents' generation is referred to by one term if female (including my mother) and by another term if male (including my father).

The fact that societies with Hawaiian kin terminology tend not to have unilineal descent groups[42] helps explain why kinship terms are the same on both sides of the family. Why are the terms for mother, father, sister, and brother used for other relatives? Perhaps because societies with Hawaiian terminology are likely to have large extended families[43] to which every type of relative in Figure 12 may belong because of alternative (bilocal) residence patterns.[44] So, in contrast to our own society, many kin are very important, a fact that seems to be reflected in the practice of referring to other relatives with the same terms that are used for nuclear family members.

SUMMARY ● ○ ○

1. In our society, and in many other industrial societies, a newly married couple usually establishes a place of residence apart from parents or relatives (neolocal residence). But about 95 percent of the world's societies have some pattern of residence whereby the new couple settles within or very close to the household of the parents or some other close relative of the groom or bride.

2. The four major patterns in which married couples live with or near kinsmen are the following:

   a. Patrilocal residence: The couple lives with or near the husband's parents (67 percent of all societies).

   b. Matrilocal residence: The couple lives with or near the wife's parents (15 percent of all societies).

   c. Bilocal residence: The couple lives with or near either the husband's parents or the wife's parents (7 percent of all societies).

   d. Avunculocal residence: The son and his wife settle with or near his mother's brother (4 percent of all societies).

3. In most societies where kinship is important, rules of affiliation allocate each person to a particular and definable set of kin. The three main types of affiliation with kin are: *unilineal descent, ambilineal descent,* and *bilateral kinship.*

4. Unilineal descent and ambilineal descent are based on rules of descent, which are rules that connect individuals with particular sets of kin because of known or presumed common ancestry. Unilineal descent refers to the fact that a person is affiliated with a group of kin through descent links of one sex only—either males only or females only. Thus, unilineal descent can be either patrilineal or matrilineal.

   a. Patrilineal descent affiliates individuals with kin of both sexes related to them through men only. In each generation, then, children belong to the kin group of their father.

   b. Matrilineal descent affiliates individuals with kin related to them through women only. In each generation, then, children belong to the kin group of their mother.

5. Ambilineal descent affiliates individuals with kin related to them through either men or women. Consequently, the descent groups show both female and male genealogical links.

6. Societies without lineal descent rules are bilateral societies. Relatives on both the mother's and father's sides of the family are of equal importance or, more usually, unimportance. Kindreds are ego-centered sets of kin who may be called together temporarily for some purpose.

7. With unilineal descent, people usually refer to themselves as belonging to a particular unilineal group or set of groups because they believe they share common descent in either the male or the female line. These people form what is called a unilineal descent group. There are several types, and a society may have more than one type:

   a. Lineages are sets of kin whose members trace descent from a common ancestor through known links.

   b. Clans are sets of kin who believe they are descended from a common ancestor but cannot specify the genealogical links.

   c. Phratries are groups of supposedly related clans.

   d. Moieties are said to exist when the whole society is divided into two unilineal descent groups without

specified links to the supposed common ancestor of each.

8. Unilineal descent groups are most common in societies in the middle range of cultural complexity—that is, in noncommercial food-producing, as opposed to food-collecting, societies. In such societies, unilineal descent groups often have important functions in the social, economic, political, and religious realms of life.

9. Societies differ markedly in how they group or distinguish relatives under the same or different kinship terms. The major systems of terminology are the Inuit (Eskimo), Omaha, Crow, Iroquois, Sudanese, and Hawaiian systems.

GLOSSARY TERMS ○ ● ○

affinal kin	matrilineage
ambilineal descent	matrilineal descent
avunculocal	matrilocal residence
residence	moiety
bilateral kinship	neolocal residence
bilocal residence	patriclans
clan or sib	patrilineage
classificatory term	patrilineal descent
consanguineal kin	patrilocal residence
descriptive term	phratry
double descent or double	rules of descent
unilineal descent	siblings
ego	totem
kindred	unilineal descent
lineage	unilocal residence
matriclans	

CRITICAL QUESTIONS ○ ○ ●

1. What other things about our society would change if we practiced other than neolocal residence?

2. Why does kinship provide the main structure of social action in noncommercial societies?

3. Why might it be important for unilineal descent groups to be nonoverlapping in membership?

PEARSON
myanthrolab

Read William L. Anderson's "Cherokee: The European Impact on the Cherokee Culture" on MyAnthroLab. Answer the following questions.

1. Describe the patterns of marital residence and descent practiced by the Cherokee.

2. What functions did the kin groups have?

3. How did European contact affect patterns of residence and descent?

NOTES ● ○ ○

1. Coult and Habenstein 1965; Murdock 1957.
2. Percentages calculated from Coult and Habenstein 1965.
3. L. Bohannan and P. Bohannan 1953.
4. J. H. Moore and Campbell 2002; Ensor 2003.
5. Lowe 2002.
6. J. D. Freeman 1961.
7. Jarvenpa 2004.
8. Murdock 1949, 49–50.
9. C. R. Ember et al. 1974, 84–89.
10. Pospisil 1963.
11. Schneider 1961a.
12. M. Ember and Ember 1971, 581.
13. Schneider 1961b.
14. Goodenough 1951, 145.
15. Coult and Habenstein 1965.
16. Data from Textor 1967.
17. Fortes 1949.
18. Davenport 1959.
19. The description of the Samoan descent system is based on M. Ember's 1955 to 1956 fieldwork. See also M. Ember 1959, 573–77; and Davenport 1959.
20. M. Ember 1967.
21. M. Ember and C. R. Ember 1971. See also Divale 1974.
22. M. Ember and Ember 1971, 583–85; Divale 1974.
23. M. Ember and Ember 1971. For a different theory—that matrilocal residence precedes, rather than follows, the development of purely external warfare—see Divale 1974.
24. Helms 2009; Herlihy 2007; see also M. Ember and Ember 1971
25. Service 1962, 137.
26. C. R. Ember and M. Ember 1972.
27. C. R. Ember 1975.
28. M. Ember 1974a.
29. Data from Textor 1967.
30. C. R. Ember et al. 1974.
31. The importance of warfare and competition as factors in the formation of unilineal descent groups is also suggested by Service 1962 and Sahlins 1961, 332–45.
32. C. R. Ember and Ember 1972.
33. C. R. Ember and Ember 1997.
34. See, for example, Murdock 1949, 199–222.
35. Reported in Textor 1967.
36. Ibid.
37. Murdock 1949, 125.
38. Textor 1967.
39. L. A. White 1939.
40. Goody 1970.
41. Pasternak 1976, 142.
42. Textor 1967.
43. Ibid.
44. This conjecture is based on unpublished cross-cultural research by the Embers.

Political Life: Social Order and Disorder

From Chapter 24 of *Anthropology*, 13/e. Carol R. Ember. Melvin Ember. Peter N. Peregrine. Copyright © 2011 by Pearson Education.
Published by Prentice Hall.

Political Life: Social Order and Disorder

or people in the United States, the phrase *political life* has many connotations. It may call to mind the various branches of government: the executive branch, from the president on the national level to governors on the state level to mayors on the local level; legislative institutions, from Congress to state legislatures to city councils; and administrative bureaus, from federal government departments to local agencies.

Political life may also evoke thoughts of political parties, interest groups, lobbying, campaigning, and voting. In other words, when people living in the United States think of political life, they may think first of "politics," the activities (not always apparent) that influence who is elected or appointed to political office, what public policies are established, how they get established, and who benefits from those policies.

But in the United States and in many other countries, *political life* involves even more than government and politics. Political life also involves ways of preventing or resolving troubles and disputes both within and outside the society. Internally, a complex society such as ours may employ mediation or arbitration to resolve industrial disputes, a police force to prevent crimes or track down criminals, and courts and a penal system to deal with lawbreakers as well as with social conflict in general. Externally, such a society may establish embassies in other nations and develop and utilize its armed forces both to maintain security and to support domestic and foreign interests.

By means of all these informal and formal political mechanisms, complex societies establish social order and minimize, or at least deal with, social disorder.

Formal governments have become more widespread around the world over the last 100 years, as powerful colonizing countries have imposed political systems upon others or as people less formally organized realized that they needed governmental mechanisms to deal with the larger world. But many societies known to anthropology did not have political officials, political parties, courts, or armies. Indeed, the band or village was the largest autonomous political unit in 50 percent of the societies in the ethnographic record, as of the times they were first described. And those units were only informally organized; that is, they did not have individuals or agencies formally authorized to make and implement policy or resolve disputes. Does this mean they did not have political life? If we mean political life as we know it in our own society, then the answer has to be that they did not. But if we look beyond our formal institutions and mechanisms—if we ask what functions these institutions and mechanisms perform—we find that all societies have had political activities and beliefs to create and maintain social order and cope with social disorder.

Many kinds of groups, families, descent groups, and associations, have political functions. But

NORMAN JOHN II

when anthropologists talk about *political organization* or *political life*, they are particularly focusing on activities and beliefs pertaining to *territorial groups*. Territorial groups, on whose behalf political activities may be organized, range from small communities, such as bands and villages, to large communities, such as towns and cities, to multilocal groups, such as districts or regions, entire nations, or even groups of nations.

As we shall see, the different types of political organization, as well as how people participate in politics and how they cope with conflict, are often strongly linked to variation in food-getting, economy, and social stratification.

● ○ ●

VARIATION IN TYPES OF POLITICAL ORGANIZATION

Societies in the ethnographic record vary in *level of political integration*—that is, the largest territorial group on whose behalf political activities are organized—and in the degree to which political authority is centralized or concentrated in the integrated group. When we describe the political integration of particular societies, we focus on their traditional political systems. In many societies known to anthropology, the small community (band or village) was traditionally the largest territorial group on whose behalf political activities were organized. The authority structure in such societies did not involve any centralization; there was no political authority whose jurisdiction included more than one community. In other societies, political activities were traditionally organized sometimes on behalf of a multilocal group, but there was no permanent authority at the top. And in still other societies, political activities were often traditionally organized on behalf of multilocal territorial groups, and there was a centralized or supreme political authority at the top. In the modern world, however, every society has been incorporated into some larger, centralized political system.

Elman Service suggested that most societies can be classified into four principal types of political organization: bands, tribes, chiefdoms, and states.[1] Although Service's classification does not fit all societies, it is a useful way to show how societies vary in trying to create and maintain social order. We often use the present tense in our discussion, because that is the convention in ethnographic writing, but readers should remember that most societies that used to be organized at the band, tribe, or chiefdom level are now incorporated into larger political entities. With a handful of exceptions, there are no politically autonomous bands or tribes or chiefdoms in the world anymore.

Band Organization

Some societies were composed of fairly small and usually nomadic groups of people. Each of these groups is conventionally called a **band** and is politically autonomous. That is, in **band organization,** the local group or community is the largest group that acts as a political unit. Because most recent foragers had band organization, some anthropologists contend that this type of political organization characterized nearly all societies before the development of

agriculture, or until about 10,000 years ago. But we have to remember that almost all of the described food-collecting societies are or were located in marginal environments; and almost all were affected by more dominant societies nearby.[2] So it is possible that what we call "band organization" may not have been typical of foragers in the distant or prehistoric past.

Bands are typically small, with less than 100 people usually, often considerably less. Each small band occupies a large territory, so population density is low. Band size often varies by season, with the band breaking up or recombining according to the food resources available at a given time and place. Inuit bands, for example, are smaller in the winter, when food is hard to find, and larger in the summer, when there is sufficient food to feed a larger group.

Political decision making within the band is generally informal. The "modest informal authority"[3] that does exist can be seen in the way decisions affecting the group are made. Because the formal, permanent office of leader typically does not exist, decisions such as when camp has to be moved or how a hunt is to be arranged are either agreed upon by the community as a whole or made by the best qualified member. Leadership, when an individual exercises it, is not the consequence of bossing or throwing one's weight about. Each band may have its informal **headman,** or its most proficient hunter, or a person most accomplished in rituals. There may be one person with all these qualities, or several people, but such a person or people will have gained status through the community's recognition of skill, good sense, and humility. Leadership, in other words, stems not from power but from influence, not from office but from admired personal qualities.

In Inuit bands, each settlement may have its headman, who acquires his influence because the other members of the community recognize his good judgment and superior skills. The headman's advice concerning the movement of the band and other community matters is generally heeded, but he possesses no permanent authority and has no power to impose sanctions of any kind. Inuit leaders are male, but men often consult their wives in private, and women who hunt seem to have more influence than those who do not.[4] In any case, leadership exists only in a very restricted sense, as among the Iglulik Inuit, for example:

> Within each settlement . . . there is as a rule an older man who enjoys the respect of the others and who decides when a move is to be made to another

TABLE 1	Suggested Trends in Political Organization and Other Social Characteristics					
Type of Organization	Highest Level of Political Integration	Specialization of Political Officials	Predominant Mode of Subsistence	Community Size and Population Density	Social Differentiation	Major Form of Distribution
Band	Local group or band	Little or none; informal leadership	Foraging or food collecting	Very small communities; very low density	Egalitarian	Mostly reciprocity
Tribe	Sometimes multilocal group	Little or none; informal leadership	Extensive (shifting) agriculture and/or herding	Small communities; low density	Egalitarian	Mostly reciprocity
Chiefdom	Multilocal group	Some	Extensive or intensive agriculture and/or herding	Large communities; medium density	Rank	Reciprocity and redistribution
State	Multilocal group; often entire language group	Much	Intensive agriculture and herding	Cities and towns; high density	Class and caste	Mostly market exchange

hunting center, when a hunt is to be started, how the spoils are to be divided, when the dogs are to be fed. . . . He is called *isumaitoq*, "he who thinks." It is not always the oldest man, but as a rule an elderly man who is a clever hunter or, as head of a large family, exercises great authority. He cannot be called a chief; there is no obligation to follow his counsel; but they do so in most cases, partly because they rely on his experience, partly because it pays to be on good terms with this man.[5]

A summary of the general features of band organization can be found in Table 1. Note, however, that there are exceptions to these generalizations. For example, not all known foragers are organized at the band level or have all the features of a band type of society. Classic exceptions are the Native American societies of the Northwest Pacific coast, who had enormous resources of salmon and other fish, relatively large and permanent villages, and political organization beyond the level of the typical band societies in the ethnographic record.

Tribal Organization

When local communities mostly act autonomously but there are kinship groups (such as clans or lineages) or associations (such as age-sets) that can potentially integrate several local groups into a larger unit (**tribe**), we say that the society has **tribal organization.** Unfortunately, the term *tribe* is sometimes used to refer to an entire society; that is, an entire language group may be called a tribe. But a tribal type of political system does not usually permit the entire society to act as a unit; all the communities in a tribal society may be linked only occasionally for some political (usually military) purpose. Thus, what distinguishes tribal from band political organization is the presence in the former of

some multilocal, but not usually societywide, integration. The multilocal integration, however, is *not permanent,* and it is *informal* in the sense that political officials do not head it. Frequently, the integration is called into play only when an outside threat arises; when the threat disappears, the local groups revert to self-sufficiency.[6] Tribal organization may seem fragile—and, of course, it usually is—but the fact that there are social ways to integrate local groups into larger political entities means that societies with tribal organization are militarily a good deal more formidable than societies with band organization.

In tribal societies, as among the Kayapo of Brazil, leadership tends not to be hereditary, but based on leadership qualities. There are no permanent chiefs of more than one community. Shown here is a Kayapo leader smoking a pipe.

337

Societies with tribal political organization are similar to band societies in their tendency to be egalitarian (see Table 1). At the local level, informal leadership is also characteristic. In those tribal societies where kinship provides the basic framework of social organization, the elders of the local kin groups tend to have considerable influence; where age-sets are important, a particular age-set is looked to for leadership. But, in contrast to band societies, societies with tribal organization generally are food producers. And because cultivation and animal husbandry are generally more productive than hunting and gathering, the population density of tribal societies is generally higher, local groups are larger, and the way of life is more sedentary than in hunter-gatherer bands.

Kinship Bonds Frequently communities are linked to each other by virtue of belonging to the same kin group, usually a unilineal group such as a lineage or clan. A **segmentary lineage system** is one type of tribal integration based on kinship. A society with such a system is composed of segments, or parts, each similar to the others in structure and function. Every local segment belongs to a hierarchy of lineages stretching farther and farther back genealogically. The hierarchy of lineages, then, unites the segments into larger and larger genealogical groups. The closer two groups are genealogically, the greater their general closeness. In the event of a dispute between members of different segments, people related more closely to one contestant than to another take the side of their nearest kinsman.

The Tiv of northern Nigeria offer a classic example of a segmentary lineage system, one that happens to link all the Tiv into a single genealogical structure or tribe. The Tiv are a large society, numbering more than 800,000. Figure 1 is a representation of the Tiv lineage structure as described by Paul Bohannan. In the figure, there are four levels of lineages. Each of the smallest lineages, symbolized by *a* through *h,* is in turn embedded in more inclusive lineages. So minimal lineages *a* and *b* are together in lineage *1.* Lineages *1* and *2* are embedded in lineage *A.* Territorial organization follows lineage hierarchy. As shown in the bottom of the figure, the most closely related lineages have territories near each other. Minimal lineages *a* and *b* live next to each other; their combined territory is the territory of their higher-order lineage, *1.* Lineage *A* in turn has a territory that is differentiated from lineage *B.* All of Tivland is said to descend from one ancestor, represented by *I.*[7]

Tiv lineage organization is the foundation of Tiv political organization. A look at Figure 1 helps to explain how. A dispute between lineages (and territories) *a* and *b* remains minor, because no more than "brother" segments are involved. But a dispute between *a* and *c* involves lineages *1* and *2* as well, with the requirement that *b* assist *a* and *d* support *c.* This process of mutual support, called **complementary opposition,** means that segments will unite only in a confrontation with some other group. Groups that will fight with each other in a minor dispute might coalesce at some later time against a larger group.

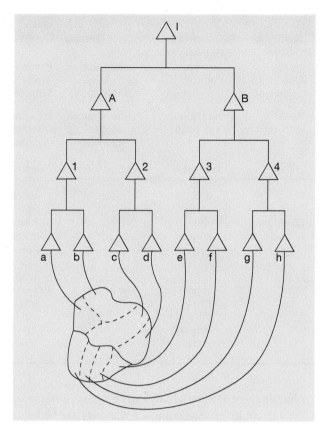

Figure 1 Tiv Lineage Segments and Their Territories

Source: Adapted from P. Bohannan 1954.
Adapted from Paul Bohannan, "The Migration and Expansion of the Tiv," *Africa,* 24 (1954): 3

The segmentary lineage system was presumably very effective in allowing the Tiv to intrude into new territory and take land from other tribal societies with smaller descent groups. Individual Tiv lineage segments could call on support from related lineages when faced with border troubles. Conflicts within the society—that is, between segments—especially in border areas, were often turned outward, "releasing internal pressure in an explosive blast against other peoples."[8]

Segmentary lineage systems may have military advantages even when they do not unite the entire society. A classic example is the Nuer of the Upper Nile region, who had tribal, but not societywide, organization because of their segmentary lineages. In the early 1800s, the Nuer had a territory of about 8,700 square miles, and the neighboring Dinka had ten times that much. But by 1890, the Nuer had cut a 100-mile swath through Dinka territory, increasing Nuer territory to 35,000 square miles. Even though the Nuer and Dinka were culturally very similar, the segmentary lineage organization of the Nuer seems to have given them a significant military advantage in their incursions into Dinka territory.[9]

A segmentary lineage system may generate a formidable military force, but the combinations of manpower it produces are temporary, forming and dissolving as the occasion demands.[10] Tribal political organization does not make for a political system that more or less permanently integrates a number of communities.

Age-Set Systems Age-sets can function as the basis of a tribal type of political organization, as among the Karimojong of northeastern Uganda.[11]

The Karimojong age-set system has an important bearing on day-to-day tribal life. As herders, Karimojong adults are often separated from their usual settlements. Herders will meet, mingle for a while, then go their separate ways, but each may call upon other members of his age-set wherever he goes. The age-set system is important among the Karimojong because it immediately allocates to each individual a place in the system and thereby establishes for him an appropriate pattern of response. A quarrel in camp will be settled by the representatives of the senior age-set who are present, regardless of which section of the tribe they may belong to.

Among the Karimojong, political leaders are not elected from among the elders of a particular age-set, nor are they appointed; they acquire their positions informally. Usually a man's background, and the ability he has demonstrated in public debates over a period of time, will result in his being considered by the men of his neighborhood to be their spokesman. His function is to announce what course of action seems required in a particular situation, to initiate that action, and then to coordinate it after it has begun.

Most political leaders exercise their authority within the local sphere because the pastoral nature of the Karimojong economy, with its dispersed groups and movement from one feeding ground to another, offers no alternative. From time to time, an elder may acquire the status of a prophet and be awarded respect and obedience on a tribal scale. He will be called upon to lead sacrifices (to avert misfortune), to undertake rainmaking (to bring prosperity), and so on. Yet even a prophet's prestige and authority do not warrant him a position of overlord or chief.[12]

Chiefdom Organization

Whereas a tribe has some informal mechanism that can integrate more than one community, a **chiefdom** has some *formal* structure that integrates more than one community into a political unit. The formal structure could consist of a council with or without a chief, but most commonly there is a person—the **chief**—who has higher rank or authority than others. Most societies at the chiefdom level of organization contain more than one multicommunity political unit or chiefdom, each headed by a district chief or a council. There may also be more than one level of chief beyond the community, such as district chiefs and higher-level chiefs. Compared with tribal societies, societies with chiefdoms are more densely populated and their communities more permanent, partly as a consequence of their generally greater economic productivity (see Table 1).

The position of chief, which is sometimes hereditary and generally permanent, bestows high status on its holder. Most chiefdoms have social ranking and accord the chief and his family greater access to prestige. The chief may redistribute goods, plan and direct the use of public labor, supervise religious ceremonies, and direct military activities on behalf of the chiefdom. In South Pacific chiefdoms, the chiefs carried out most of these duties. In Fijian chiefdoms, for example, the chief was responsible for the redistribution of goods and the coordination of labor:

> [The chief] could summon the community's labor on his own behalf, or on behalf of someone else who requested it, or for general purposes. . . . Besides his right to summon labor he accumulated the greater proportion of the first fruits of the yam crop . . . and he benefited from other forms of food presentation, or by the acquisition of special shares in ordinary village distribution. . . . Thus, the paramount [chief] would collect a significant part of the surplus production of the community and redistribute it in the general welfare.[13]

In contrast to leaders in tribal societies, who generally have to earn their privileges by their personal qualities, hereditary chiefs are said to have those qualities in their "blood." A high-ranking chief in Polynesia, a huge triangular area of islands in the South Pacific, inherited special religious power called *mana*. *Mana* sanctified his rule and protected him.[14] Chiefs in Polynesia had so much religious power that missionaries could convert people to Christianity only after their chiefs had been converted.[15]

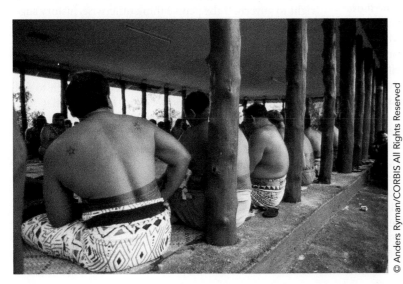

Samoan chiefs gather at an open meeting house for a *saofa'i*, or entitlement ceremony, during which a new chief gains his position.

In most chiefdoms, the chiefs did not have the power to compel people to obey them; people would act in accordance with the chief's wishes because the chief was respected and often had religious authority. But in the most complex paramount chiefdoms, such as those of Hawaii and Tahiti, the chiefs seemed to have more compelling sanctions than the "power" of respect or *mana*. Substantial amounts of goods and services collected by the chiefs were used to support subordinates, including specialists such as high priests, political envoys, and warriors who could be sent to quell rebellious factions.[16] When redistributions do not go to everybody—when chiefs are allowed to keep items for their own purposes—and when a chief begins to use armed force, the political system is on the way to becoming what we call a state.

State Organization

A state, according to one more or less standard definition, is "an autonomous political unit, encompassing many communities within its territory and having a centralized government with the power to collect taxes, draft men for work or war, and decree and enforce laws."[17] States, then, have a complex, centralized political structure that includes a wide range of permanent institutions with legislative, executive, and judicial functions and a large bureaucracy. Central to this definition is the concept of legitimate force used to implement policies both internally and externally. In states, the government tries to maintain a monopoly on the use of physical force.[18] This monopoly can be seen in the development of formal and specialized instruments of social control: a police force, a militia, or a standing army.

Just as a particular society may contain more than one band, tribe, or chiefdom, so may it contain more than one state. The contiguously distributed population speaking a single language may or may not be politically unified in a single state. Ancient Greece was composed of many city-states; so, too, was Italy until the 1870s. German speakers are also not politically unified; Austria and Germany are separate states, and Germany itself was not politically unified until the 1870s. We say that a society has **state organization** when it is composed of one or more political units that are states.

A state may include more than one society. Multisociety states are often the result of conquest or colonial control when the dominant political authority, itself a state, imposes a centralized government over a territory with many different societies and cultures, as the British did in Nigeria and Kenya.

Colonialism is a common feature of state societies. But not all colonialisms are alike. Archaeology and history tell us about various kinds of colonialism. The expanding state society may send people to build a new imperial settlement in some other place to trade or protect trade routes, like the British, Spanish, and others did. Or the colonial power may displace and move parts of the original population, as the Inka empire did.[19] Most of the expanding state societies we know about are usually called

empires. They incorporated other societies and states. The extension of U.S. power in modern times, for example, by persuading other countries to let the U.S. build military bases, has led some commentators to refer to an American empire, even though the United States did not always establish colonies where they had economic and political control.[20]

Nearly all of the multisociety states that emerged after World War II were the results of successful independence movements against colonial powers.[21] Most have retained their political unity despite the fact that they still contain many different societies. For example, Nigeria remains unified despite a civil war; the eastern section called Biafra (mostly populated by people of Ibo culture) tried unsuccessfully 30 years ago to secede, and subsequently there has been serious conflict among some of the constituent societies.

Multisociety or multiethnic states may also form voluntarily, in reaction to external threat. Switzerland comprises cantons, each of which speaks mainly French, German, Italian, or Romansch; the various cantons confederated originally to shake off control by the Holy Roman Empire. But some states have lost their unity recently, including the former Union of Soviet Socialist Republics (USSR) and much of Yugoslavia.

In addition to their strictly political features, intensive agriculture generally supports state-organized societies. The high productivity of the agriculture allows for the emergence of cities, a high degree of economic and other kinds of specialization, and market or commercial exchange. In addition, state societies usually have class stratification (see Table 1). Cities have grown tremendously in the last 100 years, largely as a result of migration and immigration. (See the Migrants and Immigrants box on the growth of cities.)

When states come into existence, people's access to scarce resources is radically altered. So, too, is their ability not to listen to leaders: You usually cannot refuse to pay taxes or avoid labor or military conscription and go unpunished. Of course, the rulers of a state do not maintain the social order by force alone. The people must believe, at least to some extent, that those in power have a legitimate right to govern. If the people think otherwise, history suggests that those in power may eventually lose their ability to control. Witness the recent downfall of Communist parties throughout most of eastern Europe and the former Soviet Union.

So force and the threat of force are not enough to explain the legitimacy of power, and the inequities that occur commonly, in state societies. But then what does? There are various theories. The rulers of early states often claimed divine descent to buttress their legitimacy, but this claim is rare nowadays. Another theory is that, if parents teach their children to accept all authority, such lessons may generalize to the acceptance of political authority. Some analysts think that people accept state authority for no good reason; the rulers are just able to fool them. Finally, some theorists think that states must provide people with real or rational advantages; otherwise,

migrants and immigrants

The Growth of Cities

Humans are a social bunch. They generally live in groups or communities. These groups range in size from bands to villages to town and cities. Each may function as a political entity; headmen, mayors, councils, and other political "officials" and groups organize activities on their behalf. Nearly half of the world's human population now lives in cities, which are usually defined as communities where few are directly involved in food getting. An even larger proportion of humanity will be urban dwellers 30 years from now.

The explosive growth of cities over the past century or so is not due to more births than deaths in the cities. Rather, cities have grown mostly because of migration from rural areas of the country, and from rural areas in other countries. Recall the exodus of the Irish to Britain and the United States because of the "potato famine," the massive migrations from the villages of Germany, Italy, and Greece in the 19th and 20th centuries, and the huge migrations particularly in the last 50 years from rural Mexico and China. It is probably safe to say that many millions of people in many parts of the world would move to the United States, Canada, and Western Europe tomorrow, if they could. Poverty is one "push" factor. Flight from persecution is another. Many parts of the world are not safe, particularly for poor people. Or other places look more promising. Think of the state of California in the United States. The vast majority of its inhabitants were born elsewhere. True, in the modern world, it is possible for some people to go "home" for a visit, even halfway around the world. But,

for many migrants now and in the recent past, the move was one way. Because you may have run away from poverty, persecution, and war, you couldn't (or wouldn't) go home again.

An increasing number of anthropologists call themselves "urban anthropologists." They study why people move, and how they adjust to new places. They do so because so many people are moving now. There are villages in rural Spain and France that are mostly empty during the week. The owners live and work in Barcelona or Paris, and they hardly ever go "home." Indeed, their village houses may not even be available to them much, because they are usually rented to tourists—from across the Atlantic, no less.

Cities everywhere have problems, even in the most developed countries. Providing water, power, sanitation, and other services to perhaps millions of city dwellers is difficult and expensive. Yet in every country, people are leaving rural areas and going to cities for a variety of reasons. Some are political refugees, like the Hmong from Laos who now live in St. Paul, Minnesota. Then there are the people from Congo and Sudan, from Kosovo and Northern Ireland, who have fled civil wars. There are other reasons to leave too. Technological improvements may have reduced the need for rural labor, which happened in the U.S. South after the 1930s. Or the rural opportunities cannot support the increased number of mouths to be fed. Where do they go? Usually not to other rural areas but rather to cities, often in other countries, where jobs are available. In the more urban-

ized countries, the cities have acquired "suburbs," where many of the people in a metropolitan area may actually live. But hardly anyone is left on the farm—only just a few percent of the population in the more developed countries.

In the last half of the 20th century, with the building of suburbs, there seems to have been a turning away from cities in many countries. Cities lost population as people moved to the suburbs to have more living space, a garden, "better" schools for their children, or to escape from the threat of violence. But recently, the flow has started to reverse in North America and elsewhere. The suburbanites are coming back to the cities, perhaps because people are getting tired of commuting longer distances to jobs and recreation. This is particularly so with wealthier people whose children have grown up and moved away, and with more people living until older ages, many want to move closer to the places where they mostly spend their time. Despite the social inequality and violence, cities have always been the places to go for jobs and other activities. Concerts, theaters, restaurants, museums, amusement parks, hospitals, and professional sports stadiums have always been located in cities or nearby.

The "push" out of the rural areas and the "pull" of the cities are hard to resist, despite the enormous political problems of urban living. As the old song laments, "Howya goin' keep 'em down on the farm after they've seen Paree?"

Source: M. Ember and Ember 2002.
Based on Ember and Ember 2002.

---

people would not think that the rulers deserve to exercise authority. Legitimacy is not an all-or-none phenomenon; it varies in degree.[22]

A state society can retain its legitimacy, or at least its power, for a long time. For example, the Roman Empire was a complex state society that dominated the Mediterranean and Near East for hundreds of years. It began as a

city-state that waged war to acquire additional territory. At its height, the Roman Empire embraced more than 55 million people;[23] the capital city of Rome had a population of well over a million.[24] The empire included parts of what are now Great Britain, France, Spain, Portugal, Germany, Rumania, Turkey, Greece, Armenia, Egypt, Israel, and Syria.

Popular will can change governments. Massive protest in the Ukraine led a newly elected president to resign.

Another example of a state society was the kingdom of Nupe in West Africa, now part of the nation-state of Nigeria. Nupe society was rigidly stratified. At the top of the social system was the king, or *etsu*. Beneath the king, members of the royal family formed the highest aristocratic class. Next in order were two other classes of nobility, the local chiefs and the military leaders. At the bottom were the commoners, who had neither prestige nor power and no share in political authority.

The Nupe king possessed ultimate authority in many judicial matters. Local village councils handled minor disputes and civil cases, but serious criminal cases were the prerogative of the king. Such cases, referred to as "crimes for the king," were brought before the royal court by the king's local representatives. The king and his counselors judged the cases and determined suitable punishments.

The most powerful influence of the state over the Nupe people was in the area of taxation. The king was given the power to impose taxes and collect them from every household. Payment was made either in money (cowrie shells originally and, later, British currency) or certain gifts, such as cloth, mats, and slaves. The king kept much of the revenue collected, and his local representatives and lords shared the remainder. In return for the taxes they paid, the people received security—protection against invasion and domestic disorder.[25]

Although all state societies employ coercion or the threat of it, some states are more autocratic than others. This is not just today, or in the recent past, but also in the distant past. The less autocratic states are characterized by more "collective action." They produce more public goods, such as transportation systems and redistribution systems, in times of need. The rulers do not aggrandize themselves as much or live that luxuriously. And, the rulers must rule within limits and must respond to grievances. They are accountable. The Lozi state of central southern Africa had more collective action than the Nupe state described. The Lozi built an extensive system of drainage canals that also facilitated transportation. In hungry times, royal herds and the "state" gardens were used to feed distressed villages. And rulers were not that much more elevated in standard of living. In contrast, the Nupe state financed very little in the way of public works, had little redistribution, and the rulers lived in elaborate palaces.[26] Collective action is a continuum; states at the higher end of that continuum have not been limited to a few world regions or particular time periods. Collection action theorists suggest that, when the state relies more heavily on resources from taxpayers, the rulers must give the public more in return or else face noncompliance and rebellion. Richard Blanton and Lane Fargher's comparative study of premodern states supports collection action theory.[27]

Factors Associated with Variation in Political Organization

The kinds of political organization we call band, tribal, chiefdom, and state are points on a continuum of levels of political integration or unification, from small-scale local autonomy to large-scale regional unification. There also is variation in political authority, from a few temporary and informal political leaders to large numbers of permanent, specialized political officials, from the absence of coercive political power to the monopoly of public force by a central authority. These aspects of variation in political organization are generally associated with shifts from foraging to more intensive food production, from small to large communities, from low to high population densities, from an emphasis on reciprocity to redistribution to market exchange, and from egalitarian to rank to fully stratified class societies.

The associations just outlined, which seem to be confirmed by the available cross-cultural evidence, are summarized in Table 1. With regard to the relation between level of subsistence technology and political complexity, one cross-cultural study employing a small random sample of societies found that the greater the importance of agriculture in a society, the larger the population that is politically unified and the greater the number and types of political officials.[28] A massive cross-cultural survey reported a similar trend: The more intensive the agriculture, the greater the likelihood of state organization; conversely, societies with no more than local political institutions are likely to depend on hunting, gathering, and fishing.[29]

With regard to community size, the first of these studies also suggested that the larger the leading community, the wider the range of political officials in the society.[30] Robert Textor presented a similar finding: Societies with state organization tend to have cities and towns, whereas those with only local political organization are more likely to have communities with an average population of fewer than 200 people.[31] Cross-cultural research also tends to confirm that societies with higher levels of political integration are more likely to exhibit social differentiation, especially in the form of class distinctions.[32]

Does this evidence provide us with an explanation for why political organization varies? Clearly, the data indicate that several factors are associated with political development, but exactly why changes in organization occur is not yet understood. Although economic development may be a necessary condition for political development,[33] that relation does not fully explain why political organization should become more complex just because the economy can support it. Some theorists have suggested that competition between groups may be a more important reason for political consolidation. For example, Elman Service suggested competition as a reason why a society might change from a band level of political organization to a tribal level. Band societies are generally hunter-gatherers. With a changeover to agriculture, population density and competition between groups may increase. Service believed that such competition would foster the development of some informal organization beyond the community—namely, tribal organization—for offense and defense.[34] Indeed, both unilineal kinship groups and age-set systems seem to be associated with warfare.

Among agriculturalists, defensive needs might also be the main reason for switching from informal multivillage political organization to more formal chiefdom organization. Formally organized districts are probably more likely to defeat autonomous villages or even segmentary lineage systems.[35] In addition, there may be economic reasons for political development. With regard to chiefdoms, Service suggested that chiefdoms will emerge when redistribution between communities becomes important or when large-scale coordinated work groups are required. The more important these activities are, the more important—and hence more "chiefly"—the organizer and his family presumably become.[36] But redistribution is far from a universal activity of chiefs.[37]

Theory and research on the anthropology of political development have focused mostly on the high end of the scale of political complexity, and particularly on the origins of the first state societies. Those earliest states apparently rose independently of one another, after about 3500 B.C., in what are now southern Iraq, Egypt, northwestern India, northern China, and central Mexico. Several theories have been proposed to explain the rise of the earliest states, but no one theory seems to fit all the known archaeological sequences culminating in early state formation. The reason may be that different conditions in different places favored the emergence of centralized government. The state, by definition, implies the power to organize large populations for collective purposes. In some areas, the impetus may have been the need to organize necessary local or long-distance trade or both. In other areas, the state may have emerged as a way to control defeated populations that could not flee. In still other instances, other factors or a combination of factors may have fostered the development of states. It is still not clear what the specific conditions were that led to the emergence of the state in each of the early centers.[38]

THE SPREAD OF STATE SOCIETIES

The state level of political development has come to dominate the world. Societies with states have larger communities and higher population densities than do band, tribal, and chiefdom societies. They also have armies that are ready to fight at almost any time. State systems that have waged war against chiefdoms and tribes have almost always won, and the result has usually been the political incorporation of the losers. For example, the British and, later, the U.S. colonization of much of North America led to the defeat and incorporation of many Native American societies.

A meeting of European Union heads of state and government in Rome. The EU is an organization encompassing many nation-states.

The defeat and incorporation of the Native Americans was at least partly due to the catastrophic depopulations they suffered because of epidemic diseases, such as smallpox and measles, that European colonists introduced. Catastrophic depopulation was commonly the outcome of the first contacts between European Americans and the natives of North and South America, as well as the natives of the far islands in the Pacific. People in the New World and the Pacific had not been exposed, and therefore were not resistant to the diseases the European Americans carried with them when they began to colonize the world. Before the expansion of Europeans, the people of the New World and the Pacific had been separated for a long time from the people and diseases on the geographically continuous landmass we separate into Europe, Africa, and Asia. Smallpox, measles, and the other former scourges of Europe had largely become childhood diseases that most individuals of European ancestry survived.[39]

Whether by depopulation, conquest, or intimidation, the number of independent political units in the world has decreased strikingly in the last 3,000 years, and especially in the last 200 years. Robert Carneiro estimated that in 1000 B.C., there may have been between 100,000 and 1 million separate political units in the world; today, there are fewer than 200.[40] In the ethnographic record, about 50 percent of the 2,000 or so societies described within the last 150 years had only local political integration. That is, the highest level of political integration in one out of two recent societies was the local community.[41] Thus, most of the decrease in the number of independent political units has occurred fairly recently.

But the recent secessions from the former Soviet Union and Yugoslavia and other separatist movements around the world suggest that ethnic rivalries may make for departures from the trend toward larger and larger political units. Ethnic groups that have been dominated by others in multinational states may opt for political autonomy, at least for a while. On the other hand, the separate nations of western Europe are becoming more unified every day, both politically and economically. So the trend toward larger political units may be continuing, even if there are departures from it now and then.

Extrapolating from past history, a number of investigators have suggested that the entire world will eventually come to be politically integrated, perhaps as soon as the 23rd century and no later than A.D. 4850.[42] Only the future will tell if this prediction will come true. And only the future will tell if further political integration in the world will occur peacefully—with all parties agreeing—or by force or the threat of force, as has happened so often in the past.

VARIATION IN POLITICAL PROCESS

Anthropologists are increasingly interested in the politics, or political processes, of the societies they study: who acquires influence or power, how they acquire it, and how

political decisions are made. But even though we have descriptive accounts of politics in many societies, there is still little comparative or cross-cultural research on what may explain variation in politics.[43]

Getting to Be a Leader

In those societies that have hereditary leadership, which is common in rank societies and in state societies with monarchies, rules of succession usually establish how leadership is inherited. Such leaders are often identifiable in some obviously visible way; they may be permanently marked or tattooed, as in chiefdoms in Polynesia, or they may wear elaborate dress and insignia, as in class-stratified societies. But for societies whose leaders are *chosen,* either as informal leaders or as political officials, we need a lot more research to understand why some kinds of people are chosen over others.

A few studies have investigated the personal qualities of leaders in tribal societies. One study, conducted among the Mekranoti-Kayapo of central Brazil, found that leaders, in contrast to followers, tend to be rated by their peers as higher in intelligence, generosity, knowledgeability, ambitiousness, and aggressiveness. Leaders also tend to be older and taller. And despite the egalitarian nature of Mekranoti society (at least with respect to sharing resources), sons of leaders are more likely than others to become leaders.[44]

Research in another Brazilian society, the Kagwahiv of the Amazon region, suggests another personal quality of leaders: They seem to have positive feelings about their fathers and mothers.[45] In many respects, studies of leaders in the United States show them to be not that different from their counterparts in Brazil. But there is one major difference: Mekranoti and Kagwahiv leaders are not wealthier than others; in fact, they give their wealth away. U.S. leaders are generally wealthier than others.[46]

"Big Men" In some egalitarian tribal societies, the quest for leadership seems quite competitive. In parts of New Guinea and South America, "big men" compete with other ambitious men to attract followers. Men who want to compete must show that they have magical powers, success in gardening, and bravery in war. But, most important, they have to collect enough goods to throw big parties at which the goods are given away. Big men have to work very hard to attract and keep their followings, for dissatisfied followers can always join other aspiring men.[47] The wives of big men are often leaders too. Among the Kagwahiv, for example, a headman's wife is usually the leader of the women in the community; she is responsible for much of the planning for feasts and often distributes the meat at them.[48]

Although the phenomenon of big men leaders is common throughout New Guinea, researchers are beginning to see variation in the type and extent of "bigmanship" in different areas of New Guinea. For example, in the southern Highlands, groups of men (not just big men) may engage in large-scale giveaways, so big men are not so different from ordinary men. In the northwestern Highlands, on the other hand, big men stand out from other men in striking ways. They make policy for groups of people and organize collective events, they have substantial access to pigs or to valuables acquired in exchanges, and they have control over a substantial amount of labor (more than one wife and fellow kin).[49]

We know that some big men are "bigger" than others, but how does a man get to be a big man? Among the Kumdi-Engamoi, a central Highlands group, a man who wants to be considered a *wua nium* (literally, a "great-important-wealthy man") needs to have many wives and daughters, because the amount of land controlled by a man and how much can be produced on that land depend on the number of women in his family. The more wives he has, the more land he is given to cultivate. He must also be a good speaker. Everyone has the right to speak and give speeches, but to get to be known as a big man requires speaking well and forcefully and knowing when to sum up a consensus. It usually takes a man until his thirties or forties to acquire more than one wife and to make his name through exchanges. When a man wants to inaugurate an exchange, he needs to get shells and pigs from his family and relatives. Once he has achieved a reputation as a *wua nium,* he can keep it only if he continues to perform well—that is, if he continues to distribute fairly, make wise decisions, speak well, and conduct exchanges.[50]

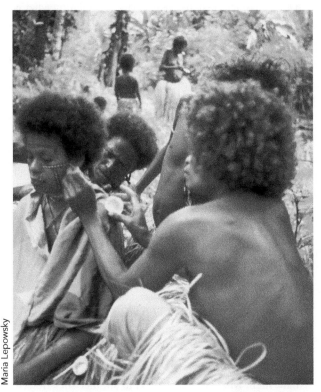

In many egalitarian societies, leadership shifts informally from one person to another. In much of New Guinea, there is more competition for achieving "big" status. On Vanatinai, the women compete as well as the men, so there are "big women" as well as "big men." Here a "big woman" paints the face of her cousin's widow for a feast honoring the dead man.

"Big Women" In contrast to most of mainland New Guinea, the islands off the southeastern coast are characterized by matrilineal descent. But, like the rest of New Guinea, the islands also have a shifting system of leadership in which people compete for "big" status. Here, though, the people competing are women as well as men, and so there are "big women" as well as "big men." On the island of Vanatinai, for example, women and men compete with each other to exchange valuables. Women lead canoe expeditions to distant islands to visit male as well as female exchange partners, women mobilize relatives and exchange partners to mount large feasts, and the women get to keep the ceremonial valuables exchanged, at least for a while.[51]

The prominence of women on Vanatinai may be linked to the disappearance of warfare—the colonial powers imposed peace; we call this "pacification." Inter-island exchanges became frequent when war became rarer in the early 20th century, giving women and men more freedom to travel. For men, but not women, war provided a path to leadership; champion warriors would acquire great renown and influence. It is not that women did not participate in war; they did, which is unusual cross-culturally, but a woman could not become a war leader. Now, in the absence of war, women have an opportunity through exchanges to become leaders, or "big women."

In one respect, however, women have less of an opportunity to acquire influence now. There are local government councils now, but all the councillors are male. Why? Some women were nominated for the posts, but they withdrew in embarrassment because they could not speak English. Big men or big women do not automatically have a path to these new positions; mostly young males who know English become the councillors. But this situation may change. With the opening of a government primary school in 1984, both girls and boys are learning English, so women in the future may be more likely to achieve leadership by becoming councillors.

Researchers continue to explore other features that may enhance a person's ability to become leaders where leadership is not hereditary. One fascinating new finding is that in the United States, after controlling for age and perceived attractiveness, individuals who are judged prior to the election to be more "competent" from photographs of their faces are more likely to win in congressional elections.[52] What makes a face look more "competent"? It has fewer "babyish" features—it is less round, has a bigger chin, smaller eyes, and a smaller forehead.[53] Whether these facial features also predict leadership cross-culturally is not yet known.

Political Participation

Political scientist Marc Ross conducted cross-cultural research on variation in degree of political participation. Ross phrased the research question: "Why is it that in some polities there are relatively large numbers of persons involved in political life, while in others political action is the province of very few?"[54]

Political participation in preindustrial societies ranges from widespread to low or nonexistent. In 16 percent of the societies examined, there is widespread participation; decision-making forums are open to all adults. The forums may be formal (councils and other governing bodies) or informal. Next in degree of political participation are societies (37 percent) that have widespread participation by some but not all adults (men but not women, certain classes but not others). Next are societies (29 percent) that have some but not much input by the community. Finally, 18 percent of the societies have low or nonexistent participation, which means that leaders make most decisions, and involvement of the average person is very limited.

Degree of political participation seems to be high in small-scale societies, as well as in modern democratic nation-states, but not in between (feudal states and preindustrial empires). Why? In small-scale societies, leaders do not have the power to force people to act; thus, a high degree of political participation may be the only way to get people to go along with decisions. In modern democracies, which have many powerful groups outside the government—corporations, unions, and other associations are examples—the central authorities may only theoretically have the power to force people to go along; in reality, they rely mostly on voluntary compliance. For example, the U.S. government failed when it tried with force (Prohibition, 1920–1933) to stop the manufacture, transport, and sale of alcoholic beverages.

Another factor may be early family experiences. Some scholars recently have suggested that the type of family people are raised in predicts the degree of political participation in a society. A large extended family with multiple generations tends to be hierarchical, with the older generations having more authority. Children may learn that they have to obey and subordinate their wishes to their elders. Societies with polygyny also seem to have less political participation. The ways of interacting in the family may carry over to the political sphere.[55]

A high degree of political participation seems to have an important consequence. In the modern world, democratically governed states rarely go to war with each other.[56] So, for example, the United States invaded three countries—Grenada, Panama, and Iraq—between 1980 and 1993, but no democracies. Similarly, it appears that more participatory, that is, more "democratic," political units in the ethnographic record fight with each other significantly less often than do less participatory political units, just as seems to be the case among modern nation-states.[57] Does this mean that democracies are more peaceful in general? Here there is more controversy. Judging by the frequency of war, modern democratic states do not look very different from autocratic states in their tendency to go to war. However, if you look at the severity of war as measured by casualty rates, democratic societies do look less warlike.[58] Exactly why more participation or more democracy is likely to lead to peace remains to be established. But there are policy implications

of the relationship, which we explore in the chapter on global problems.

RESOLUTION OF CONFLICT

The resolution of conflict may be accomplished peacefully by avoidance, community action, mediation or the negotiation of compromises, apology, appeal to supernatural forces, or adjudication by a third party. As we shall see, the procedures used usually vary with degree of social complexity; decisions by third parties are more likely in hierarchical societies.[59] But peaceful solutions are not always possible, and disputes may erupt into violent conflict. When violence occurs within a political unit in which disputes are usually settled peacefully, we call such violence crime, particularly when committed by an individual. When the violence occurs between groups of people from separate political units—groups between which there is no procedure for settling disputes—we usually call such violence *warfare*. When violence occurs between subunits of a population that had been politically unified, we call it *civil war*.

Peaceful Resolution of Conflict

Most modern industrialized states have formal institutions and offices, such as police, district attorneys, courts, and penal systems, to deal with minor disputes and more serious conflicts that may arise in society. All these institutions generally operate according to **codified laws**—that is, a set of explicit, usually written rules stipulating what is permissible and what is not. Transgression of the law by individuals gives the state the right to take action against them. The state has a monopoly on the legitimate use of force in the society, for it alone has the right to coerce subjects into agreement with regulations, customs, political edicts, and procedures.

Many societies lack such specialized offices and institutions for dealing with conflict. Yet, because all societies have peaceful, regularized ways of handling at least certain disputes, some anthropologists speak of the *universality of law*. E. Adamson Hoebel, for example, stated the principle as follows:

> Each people has its system of social control. And all but a few of the poorest of them have as a part of the control system a complex of behavior patterns and institutional mechanisms that we may properly treat as law. For, "anthropologically considered, law is merely one aspect of our culture—the aspect which employs the force of organized society to regulate individual and group conduct and to prevent redress or punish deviations from prescribed social norms."[60]

Law, then, whether informal as in simpler societies, or formal as in more complex societies, provides a means of dealing peacefully with whatever conflicts develop. That does not mean that conflicts are always resolved peacefully. But that also does not mean that people cannot learn

applied anthropology

Democracy and Economic Development

The subsistence economies that anthropologists traditionally study are becoming more commercialized as people increasingly produce goods and services for a market. And the pace of economic development is quickening, particularly in places that lacked industrial wage labor until recently, as their economies are increasingly integrated into the world system. What effect, if any, does economic development have on political participation? Can we speculate about the future on the basis of comparative research?

Most of the comparative research on the relationship between economic development and political participation has been cross-national, comparing data on different countries. Some countries are more democratic than others, with characteristics such as contested elections, an elected head of state, an elected powerful legislature, and the protection of civil liberties. In capitalist countries, more democracy is generally associated with higher levels of economic development, as measured by indicators such as per capita output; in countries that are not very industrialized, there is little democracy at the national level. Why should more democracy be associated with more economic development? The prevailing opinion is that economic development increases the degree of social equality in the country; and the more equality among interest groups, the more they demand participation in the political process, and hence the more democracy. Or, to put this theory another

way, as the economy develops, the more what we might call the middle and working classes can demand rewards and power, and therefore the less power the elite can retain.

What about the societies usually studied by anthropologists, the ones in what we call the cross-cultural or ethnographic record? We know that some of the highest levels of political participation occur in the least complex societies, such as foraging societies. Many adults in such societies have a say in decisions, and leadership is informal; leaders can retain their roles only if people voluntarily go along with them. Concentrated power and less political participation are more likely in chiefdoms and states than in band and tribal societies. The more hierarchical chiefdoms and states usually depend on agriculture, particularly intensive agriculture, which can produce more goods and services per capita than foraging economies can. So the relationship between economic development and political participation in the ethnographic record is *opposite* to what we find cross-nationally. That is, the more economic development, the less political participation in the societies studied by anthropologists. Why should this be so? It seems that social equality *decreases* as economic development increases in the ethnographic record (which does not include many industrialized societies). In that record, an economically developed society is likely to have features such as plowing, fertilizers, and irrigation, which make permanent cultiva-

tion of the fields and permanent communities possible. Such intensive agricultural activity is more conducive to concentrated wealth than is hunter-gatherer subsistence or shifting cultivation (horticulture). Thus, in the ethnographic record, the more economically developed societies have more social inequality and therefore less democracy.

The two sets of findings, the cross-national and the cross-cultural, are not that hard to reconcile. Social and economic inequality appears to work against democracy and extensive political participation. Social inequality increases with the switch from foraging to agriculture. But social inequality decreases with the switch from preindustrial agriculture to high (industrial) levels of economic development. Political participation decreases with the first switch and increases with the second, because social inequality first increases and then decreases.

So what does comparative research suggest about the future? If the middle and working classes feel they are not getting a fair return on their labor, their demands should increase. The elite may be willing to satisfy those increased demands; if they do, their power will be reduced. In either case, unless the elite try to retain their power at any cost, there should be more political participation and more democracy, at least in the long run.

Sources: Bollen 1993; Muller 1997; M. Ember, Ember, and Russett 1997; Ross 2009b.

---

to resolve their conflicts peacefully. The fact that there are societies with little or no violent conflict means that it may be possible to learn from them; it may be possible to discover how to avoid violent outcomes of conflicts. How come South Africa could move relatively peacefully from a society dominated by people from Europe to one with government and civil rights shared by all groups? On the other hand, Bosnia had very violent conflict between

ethnic groups and needed intervention by outside parties to keep the warring sides apart.[61]

Avoidance   Violence can often be avoided if the parties to a dispute voluntarily avoid each other or are separated until emotions cool down. Anthropologists have frequently remarked that foragers are particularly likely to make use of this technique. People may move to other bands or move their dwellings to opposite ends of camp. Shifting horticulturalists may also split up when conflicts get too intense. Avoidance is obviously easier in societies, such as band societies, that are nomadic or seminomadic and in which people have temporary dwellings. And avoidance is more feasible when people live independently and self-sufficiently (e.g., in cities and suburbs).[62] But even if conditions in such societies may make avoidance easier, we still need to know why some societies use avoidance more than confrontation as a way of resolving conflict.

Community Action Societies have found various ways of resolving disputes peacefully. One such way involves action by a group or the community as a whole; collective action is common in simpler societies that lack powerful authoritarian leaders.[63] Many Inuit societies, for example, frequently resolve disputes through community action. An individual's failure to heed a taboo or to follow the suggestions of a shaman leads to expulsion from the group, because the community cannot accept a risk to its livelihood. People who fail to share goods voluntarily will find them confiscated and distributed to the community, and they may be executed in the process. A single case of murder, as an act of vengeance (usually because of the abduction of a wife or as part of a blood feud), does not concern the community, but repeated murders do. Franz Boas gave a typical example:

> There was a native of Padli by the name Padlu. He had induced the wife of a native of Cumberland Sound to desert her husband and follow him. The deserted husband, meditating revenge . . . visited his friends in Padli, but before he could accomplish his intention of killing Padlu, the latter shot him. . . . A brother of the murdered man went to Padli to avenge the death . . . but he also was killed by Padlu. A third native of Cumberland Sound, who wished to avenge the death of his relatives, was also murdered by him.
>
> On account of these outrages the natives wanted to get rid of Padlu, but yet they did not dare to attack him. When the *pimain* (headman) of the Akudmurmuit learned of these events he started southward and *asked every man in Padli whether Padlu should be killed. All agreed;* so he went with the latter deer hunting . . . and . . . shot Padlu in the back.[64]

The killing of an individual is the most extreme action a community can take—we call it *capital punishment.* The community as a whole or a political official or a court may decide to administer such punishment, but capital punishment seems to exist in nearly all societies, from the simplest to the most complex.[65] It is often assumed that capital punishment deters crime. If it did, we would expect the abolition of capital punishment to be followed by an increase in homicide rates. But that does not seem to happen. A cross-national study indicates that the abolition of capital punishment tends to be followed by a decrease in homicide rates.[66]

Negotiation and Mediation In many conflicts, the parties to a dispute may come to a settlement themselves by **negotiation.** There aren't necessarily any rules for how they will do so, but any solution is "good" if it restores peace.[67] Sometimes an outside or third party is used to help bring about a settlement between the disputants. We call it **mediation** when the outside party tries to help bring about a settlement, but that third party does not have the formal authority to force a settlement. Both negotiation and mediation are likely when the society is relatively egalitarian and it is important for people to get along.[68]

Among the Nuer of East Africa, a pastoral and horticultural people, disputes within the community can be settled with the help of an informal mediator called the "leopard-skin chief." His position is hereditary, and makes its holder responsible for the social well-being of the district. Matters such as cattle stealing rarely come to the attention of the leopard-skin chief. But if, for example, a murder has been committed, the culprit will go at once to the house of the leopard-skin chief. Immediately the chief cuts the culprit's arm so that blood flows; until the cut has been made, the murderer may not eat or drink. If the murderer is afraid of vengeance by the slain man's family, he will remain at the house of the leopard-skin chief, which is considered sanctuary. Then, within the next few months, the chief attempts to mediate between the parties to the crime. He tries to arrange compensation by the slayer's kin to avoid a feud, and he persuades the dead man's kin that they ought to accept the compensation, usually in the form of cattle. The chief then collects the cattle—40 to 50—and takes them

Although mediation is commonly used in relatively egalitarian societies, it is also used in societies with courts and other formal adjudication procedures for minor conflicts. A teacher in the United States tries to mediate a dispute between two boys.

to the dead man's home, where he performs various sacrifices of cleansing and atonement.[69] Throughout the process, the chief acts as a go-between. He has no authority to force either party to negotiate, and he has no power to enforce a solution once it has been arrived at. However, he is able to take advantage of the fact that both disputants are anxious to avoid a blood feud.

Ritual Reconciliation—Apology   The desire to restore a harmonious relationship may also explain ceremonial apologies. An apology is based on deference—the guilty party shows obeisance and asks for forgiveness. Such ceremonies tend to occur in recent chiefdoms.[70] For example, among the Fijians of the South Pacific, when a person offends someone of higher status, the offended person and other villagers begin to avoid, and gossip about, the offender. If offenders are sensitive to village opinion, they will perform a ceremony of apology called *i soro*. One of the meanings of *soro* is "surrender." In the ceremony, the offender bows the head and remains silent while an intermediary speaks, presents a token gift, and asks the offended person for forgiveness. The apology is rarely rejected.[71]

Oaths and Ordeals   Still another way of peacefully resolving disputes is through oaths and ordeals, both of which involve appeals to supernatural power. An **oath** is the act of calling upon a deity to bear witness to the truth of what one says. An **ordeal** is a means used to determine guilt or innocence by submitting the accused to dangerous or painful tests believed to be under supernatural control.[72]

A common kind of ordeal, found in almost every part of the world, is scalding. Among the Tanala of Madagascar, the accused person, having first had his hand carefully examined for protective covering, has to reach his hand into a cauldron of boiling water and grasp, from underneath, a rock suspended there. He then plunges his hand into cold water, has it bandaged, and is led off to spend the night under guard. In the morning, his hand is unbandaged and examined. If there are blisters, he is guilty.

Oaths and ordeals have also been practiced in Western societies. Both were common in medieval Europe. Even today, in our own society, vestiges of oaths can be found. Children can be heard to say, "Cross my heart and hope to die," and witnesses in courts of law are obliged to swear to tell the truth.

Why do some societies use oaths and ordeals? John Roberts suggested that their use tends to be found in fairly complex societies in which political officials lack sufficient power to make and enforce judicial decisions or would make themselves unnecessarily vulnerable were they to attempt to do so. So the officials may use oaths and ordeals to let the gods decide guilt or innocence.[73] In contrast, smaller and less complex societies probably have no need for elaborate mechanisms such as courts, oaths, and ordeals to ascertain guilt. In such societies, everyone is aware of what crimes have been committed and who the guilty parties probably are.

Adjudication, Courts, and Codified Law   We call it **adjudication** when a third party acting as judge makes a decision that the disputing parties have to accept. Judgment may be rendered by one person (a judge), a panel of judges, a jury, or a political agent or agency (a chief, a royal personage, a council). Judges and courts may rely on codified law and stipulated punishments, but codified law is not necessary for decisions to be made. Codified laws and courts are not limited to Western societies. From the late 17th century to the early 20th century, for example, the Ashanti of West Africa had a complex political system with elaborate legal arrangements. The Ashanti state was a military-based empire possessing legal codes that resembled those of many ancient civilizations.[74] Ashanti law was based on a concept of natural law, a belief that there is an order of the universe whose principles lawmakers should follow in the decisions they make and in the regulations they design. In Ashanti court procedure, elders examined and cross-examined witnesses as well as parties to the dispute. There were also quasi-professional advocates, and appeals against a verdict could be made directly to a chief. Particularly noteworthy was the emphasis on intent when assessing guilt. Drunkenness constituted a valid defense for all crimes except murder and cursing a chief, and a plea of insanity, if proved, was upheld for all offenses. Ashanti punishments could be severe. Physical mutilation, such as slicing off the nose or an ear—even castration in sexual offenses—was often employed. Fines were more frequent, however, and death sentences could often be commuted to banishment and confiscation of goods.

Why do some societies have codified systems and others do not? One explanation, advanced by E. Adamson Hoebel, A. R. Radcliffe-Brown, and others, is that there is little need for formal legal guidelines in small, closely knit communities because competing interests are minimal. Hence, simple societies need little codified law. There are relatively few matters to quarrel about, and the general will of the group is sufficiently well known and demonstrated frequently enough to deter transgressors.

This point of view is echoed in Richard Schwartz's study of two Israeli settlements. In one communal kibbutz, a young man aroused a good deal of community resentment because he had accepted an electric teakettle as a gift. The general opinion was that he had overstepped the code about not having personal possessions, and he was so informed. Accordingly, he gave the kettle to the communal infirmary. Schwartz observed that "no organized enforcement of the decision was threatened, but had he disregarded the expressed will of the community, his life . . . would have been made intolerable by the antagonism of public opinion."[75]

In this community, where people worked and ate together, not only did everyone know about transgressions, but a wrongdoer could not escape public censure. Thus,

349

public opinion was an effective sanction. In another Israeli community, however, where individuals lived in widely separated houses and worked and ate separately, public opinion did not work as well. Not only were community members less aware of problems, but they had no quick way of making their feelings known. As a result, they established a judicial body to handle trouble cases.

Larger, more heterogeneous and stratified societies are likely to have more frequent disputes, which at the same time are less visible to the public. Individuals in stratified societies are generally not so dependent on community members for their well-being and hence are less likely to know of, or care about, others' opinions. In such societies, codified laws and formal authorities for resolving disputes develop—in order, perhaps, that disputes may be settled impersonally enough so that the parties can accept the decision and social order can be restored.

A good example of how more formal systems of law develop is the experience of towns in the American West during the gold rush period. These communities were literally swamped by total strangers. The townsfolk, having no control (authority) over these intruders because the strangers had no local ties, looked for ways to deal with the trouble cases that were continually flaring up. A first attempt at a solution was to hire gunslingers, who were also strangers, to act as peace officers or sheriffs, but this strategy usually failed. Eventually, towns succeeded in having federal authorities send in marshals backed by federal power.

Is there some evidence to support the theory that codified law is necessary only in larger, more complex societies? Data from a large, worldwide sample of societies suggest that codified law is associated with political integration beyond the local level. Murder cases, for example, are dealt with informally in societies that have only local political organization. In societies with multilocal political units, specialized political authorities tend to judge or adjudicate murder cases.[76] There is also some cross-cultural evidence that violence within a society tends to be less frequent when there are formal authorities (chiefs, courts) who have the power to punish murderers.[77] In general, adjudication or enforced decisions by outside authorities tend to occur in hierarchical societies with social classes and centralized power.[78]

Violent Resolution of Conflict

People often resort to violence when regular, effective alternative means of resolving a conflict are not available. Violence between individuals that is not considered legitimate is generally called **crime.** What is considered legitimate varies considerably from society to society. Researchers who study crime usually focus on the observed behaviors such as assault and homicide. When violence occurs between territorial entities such as communities, districts, or nations, we call it **warfare.** The type of warfare varies in scope and complexity from society to society. Sometimes a

distinction is made among feuding, raiding, and large-scale confrontations.[79]

Some scholars talk about a cultural pattern of violence. More often than not, societies with one type of violence have others. Societies with more war tend to have warlike sports, malevolent magic, severe punishment for crimes, high murder rates, feuding, and family violence.[80]

There are more peaceful societies. These societies are not conflict-free, but they try more to resolve conflict nonviolently. And like the Semai, they discourage aggression in their children without providing an aggressive model. What explains these more peaceful cultural patterns? Cross-cultural evidence supports the view that frequent warfare is the key to understanding all kinds of violence. Not only is war correlated with other kinds of aggression, but societies that are forced to stop fighting by more powerful societies appear to encourage aggression in their children less. It seems that, if war is frequent, the society encourages boys to be aggressive, so that they will grow up to be effective warriors. But socializing for aggression can spill over into other areas of life; high rates of crime and other violence may be inadvertent or unintended consequences of the encouragement of aggressiveness.[81] And societies with a lot of war commonly bestow high status on their warriors. Warriors are generally proud of their accomplishments, considering it an honor to be a brave and fierce warrior.[82]

Individual Violence   Although it may seem paradoxical at first, violent behavior itself is often used to try to control behavior. In some societies, it is considered necessary for parents to beat children who misbehave. They don't consider this criminal behavior or child abuse; they consider it punishment. Similar views may attach to interpersonal behavior between adults. If a person trespasses on your property or hurts someone in your family, some societies consider it appropriate or justified to kill or maim the trespasser. Is this social control, or is it just lack of control?

Systems of individual self-help are characteristic of egalitarian societies.[83] How is this different from "community action," which earlier we classified under peaceful resolution of conflict? Because community action is explicitly based on obtaining a consensus, it is likely to lead to the ending of a particular dispute. Individual action, or self-help, particularly if it involves violence, is not.

Feuding   Feuding is an example of how individual self-help may not lead to a peaceful resolution of conflict. **Feuding** is a state of recurring hostilities between families or groups of kin, usually motivated by a desire to avenge an offense—whether insult, injury, deprivation, or death—against a member of the group. The most common characteristic of the feud is that all members of the kin group carry the responsibility to avenge. The killing of any member of the offender's group is considered appropriate revenge, because the kin group as a whole is regarded as

new perspectives on gender

New Courts Allow Women to Address Grievances in Papua New Guinea

In most societies in New Guinea, women did not traditionally participate in the resolution of disputes. And they could not bring actions against men. But when village courts were introduced, women began to go to court to redress offenses against them.

In colonial times, the introduced Western-style courts followed Western law, primarily Australian and British common law, not native customary law. After Papua New Guinea became an independent country, those courts remained in place. The lowest of the courts, called local courts, were located in town centers, often far from villages, so villagers rarely brought cases to them. But, in 1973, a new kind of court was created. Called village courts, they were designed to settle local disputes in the villages, using a blend of customary law (relying on compromise) and Western law. In contrast to the local courts, magistrates in the village courts were not outsiders but were selected from the pool of traditional and local leaders who knew the local people.

When Richard Scaglion studied changes in village courts among the Abelam from 1977 to 1987, he noticed a shift toward the increased use of these courts by women. In 1977, most of the complainants were male, but most of them were female by 1987. In a wider study of court cases over many regions of Papua New Guinea, Scaglion and Rose Whittingham found that most of the cases in which women were the plaintiffs were attempts to redress sex-related offenses (sexual jealousy, rape, incest, domestic disputes) committed by males. Most disputes in New Guinea villages are settled informally by self-help or by appeal to a "big man"; the courts are appealed to only as a last resort. Serious sex-related cases are unlikely to be settled informally but, rather, in the village court. Apparently women do not believe that they can get satisfaction informally. So they go to the village court, where they win some sort of punishment for the defendant in about 60 percent of the cases, just about the same rate that men achieve when they bring a case seeking punishment.

Culture change introduced from the outside often works against native peoples. But Papuan New Guinea women have benefited from the new village court system, particularly in redressing grievances against males. The traditional system for resolving disputes was largely male-dominated (women could not be plaintiffs), and so the possibility of taking disputes to the new courts has given women some measure of legal equality with men.

Sources: Scaglion 1990; Scaglion and Whittingham 1985.

responsible. Nicholas Gubser told of a feud within a Nunamiut Inuit community, caused by a husband killing his wife's lover, that lasted for decades. The Nunamiut take feuds seriously, as do many societies, especially when murder has been committed. Closely related members of the murdered man recruit as many relatives as they can and try to kill the murderer or one of his close kin. Then the members of the murderer's kindred are brought into the feud. The two kindreds may snipe at each other for years.[84]

Feuds are by no means limited to small-scale societies; they occur as frequently in societies with high levels of political organization.[85]

© Yasuyoshi Chiba/AFP/Getty Images, Inc.

Large-scale confrontations occur in societies with armies, but they also occur in nonstate societies. The Masai of Kenya (shown here) battled with Kalenjin (not shown) over a land dispute following the 2008 disputed election.

Raiding Raiding is a short-term use of force, planned and organized, to realize a limited objective. This objective is usually the acquisition of goods, animals, or other forms of wealth belonging to another, often neighboring community.

Raiding is especially prevalent in pastoral societies, in which cattle, horses, camels, or other animals are prized and an individual's own herd can be augmented by theft. Raids are often organized by temporary leaders or coordinators whose authority may not last beyond the planning and execution of the venture. Raiding may also be organized for the purpose of capturing people. Sometimes people are taken to marry—the capture of women to be wives or concubines is fairly common[86]—or to be slaves. Slavery has been practiced in about 33 percent of the world's known societies, and war has been one way of obtaining slaves either to keep or to trade for other goods.[87] Raiding, like feuding, is often self-perpetuating: The victim of a raid today becomes the raider tomorrow.[88]

Large-Scale Confrontations Individual episodes of feuds and raids usually involve relatively small numbers of people and almost always an element of surprise. Because they are generally attacked without warning, the victims are often unable to muster an immediate defense. Large-scale confrontations, in contrast, involve a large number of people and planning of strategies of attack and defense by both sides. Large-scale warfare is usually practiced among societies with intensive agriculture or industrialization. Only these societies possess a technology sufficiently advanced to support specialized armies, military leaders, strategists, and so on. But large-scale confrontations are not limited to state societies; they occur, for example, among the horticultural Dugum Dani of central New Guinea.

The military history of the Dani, with its shifting alliances and confederations, is reminiscent of that of Europe, although Dani battles involve far fewer fighters and less sophisticated weaponry. Among the Dani, long periods of ritual warfare are characterized by formal battles announced through a challenge sent by one side to the opposing side. If the challenge is accepted, the protagonists meet at the agreed-upon battle site to set up their lines. Fighting with spears, sticks, and bows and arrows begins at midmorning and continues either until nightfall or until rain intervenes. There may also be a rest period during the midday heat during which the two sides shout insults at each other or talk and rest among themselves.

The front line of battle is composed of about a dozen active warriors and a few leaders. Behind them is a second line, still within arrow range, composed of those who have just left the forward line or are preparing to join it. The third line, outside arrow range, is composed of noncombatants—males too old or too young to participate and those recovering from wounds. This third line merely watches the battle taking place on the grassy plain. On the hillsides far back from the front line, some of the old men help to direct ancestral ghosts to the battle by gouging a line in the ground that points in the direction of the battlefield.[89]

Yet, as total as large-scale confrontations may be, even such warfare has cultural rules. Among the Dani, for instance, no fighting occurs at night, and weapons are limited to simple spears and bows and arrows. Similarly, in state societies, governments will sign "self-denying" pacts restricting the use of poison gas, germ warfare, and so forth. Unofficially, private arrangements are common. One has only to glance through the memoirs of national leaders of the two world wars to become aware of locally arranged truces, visits to one another's front positions, exchanges of prisoners of war, and so on.

Explaining Warfare

Most societies in the anthropological record have had warfare between communities or larger territorial groups. The vast majority of the societies in a recent cross-cultural study had at least occasional wars when they were first described, unless they had been pacified or incorporated by more dominant societies.[90] Yet, relatively little research has been done on the possible causes of war and why it varies in type and frequency. For instance, why have some people fought a great deal, and others only infrequently? Why in some societies does warfare occur internally, within the society or language group?

We have answers, based on cross-cultural studies, to some of those questions. There is evidence that people in preindustrial societies go to war mostly out of fear, particularly a fear of expectable but unpredictable natural disasters that will destroy food resources (e.g., droughts, floods, locust infestations). People may think they can protect themselves against such disasters ahead of time by taking things from defeated enemies. In any case, preindustrial societies with higher frequencies of war are very likely to have had a history of expectable but unpredictable disasters. The fact that chronic (annually recurring and therefore predictable) food shortages do not predict higher frequencies of war suggests that people go to war in an attempt to cushion the impact of the disasters they expect to occur in the future but cannot predict. Consistent with this tentative conclusion is the fact that the victors in war almost always take land or other resources from the defeated. And this is true for simpler as well as more complex preindustrial societies.[91] Might similar motives affect decisions about war and peace in the modern world?

We know that complex or politically centralized societies are likely to have professional armies, hierarchies of military authority, and sophisticated weapons.[92] But surprisingly, the frequency of warfare seems to be not much greater in complex societies than in simple band or tribal societies.[93] We have some evidence that warfare is unlikely to occur internally (within a society or territory) if it is small in population (21,000 or fewer people); in a larger society, there is a high likelihood of warfare within the society, between communities or larger territorial divisions.[94] In fact, complex societies, even if they are politically unified, are not less likely than simpler societies to have internal warfare.[95]

Oil is a valuable resource in the world today. Iraq has more oil in the ground than most other countries.

What about the idea that men in band and tribal societies may mostly go to war over women?[96] If this were true, those band and tribal societies with the most frequent wars should have shortages of women, and those with little or no war—less often than once in 10 years—should have more equal numbers of women and men. But the cross-cultural evidence clearly contradicts this theory. Band and tribal societies with more wars do not have fewer women.[97]

What, if anything, do we know about recent warfare between nation-states? Although many people think that military alliances lessen the chance of war, it turns out that nations formally allied with other nations do not necessarily go to war less often than nations lacking formal alliances. Countries that are allies are, of course, less likely to go to war with each other; however, alliances can drag dependent allies into wars they don't want.[98] Countries that are economically interdependent, that trade with each other for necessities, are less likely to go to war with each other.[99] Finally, military equality between nations, particularly when preceded by a rapid military buildup, seems to increase rather than lessen the chance of war between those nations.[100]

Clearly, these findings contradict some traditional beliefs about how to prevent war. Military buildups do not make war less likely, but trade does. What else may? We have already noted that participatory ("democratic") political systems are less likely to go to war with each other than are authoritarian political systems. The results of cross-cultural and cross-national studies may translate into policies that could minimize the risk of war in the world. Although war may be common in the world, it is not inevitable. Societies change over time. The Vikings were extremely militaristic, but Norway today is now a peaceful society. A comparative study of Polynesian societies shows that, although all derive from a common cultural heritage, the size of the islands people settled on strongly influenced their patterns of interpersonal violence and warfare. The smallest islands had the lowest lev-

els of violence and the least warfare. It appears that cooperation and harmony were more likely than violence in small "face-to face" societies.[101]

Political and Social Change

In addition to commercialization and religious change brought about by the expansion of Western and other countries, political changes have often occurred when a foreign system of government has been imposed. But, as recent events in the former Soviet Union and South Africa indicate, dramatic changes in a political system can also occur more or less voluntarily. Perhaps the most striking type of political change in recent years is the spread of participatory forms of government—"democracy."

To political scientists, democracy is usually defined in terms of voting by a substantial proportion of the citizenry, governments brought to power by periodic contested elections, a chief executive either popularly elected or responsible to an elected legislature, and often also civil liberties such as free speech. Depending on which criteria are used, only 12 to 15 countries qualified as democracies as of the beginning of the 20th century. The number decreased after World War I, as emerging dictatorships in Russia, Italy, Germany, central Europe, Japan, and elsewhere replaced democratic institutions. After World War II, despite all the rhetoric associated with the founding of the United Nations, the picture was not much different. Some members of the new North Atlantic Treaty Organization (NATO) were not democracies, and neither were many members of the wider Western alliance system, in Latin America, the Middle East, and Asia.

Not until the 1970s and 1980s did people, not just political scientists, start noticing that democracy was becoming more common in the world. By the early 1990s, President George H. W. Bush and then-candidate Bill Clinton were talking about the spread of the "democratic peace." As of 1992, about half of the countries in the world had more or less democratic governments, and others were in transition to democracy.[102] Social scientists do not yet understand why this change is happening. But it is possible that the global communication of ideas has a lot to do with it. Authoritarian governments can censor their own newspapers and prevent group meetings, and sophisticated technology can block Internet use and cell phone connections, but ultimately authoritarian governments really cannot stop the movement of ideas. The movement of ideas, of course, does not explain the acceptance of those ideas. Why democracy has recently diffused to more countries than ever before still requires explanation, as does why some countries do not find it appealing.

SUMMARY ● ○ ○

1. All societies have customs or procedures that, organized on behalf of territorial groups, result in decision making and the resolution of disputes. These ways of creating and maintaining social order and coping with social disorder vary from society to society.

2. Societies with a band type of political organization are composed of fairly small, usually nomadic groups. Each of these bands is politically autonomous, the band being the largest group that acts as a political unit. Authority within the band is usually informal. Societies with band organization generally are egalitarian hunter-gatherers. But band organization may not have been typical of foragers in the distant past.

3. Societies with tribal organization are similar to those with band organization in being egalitarian. But, in contrast with band societies, they generally are food producers, have a higher population density, and are more sedentary. Tribal organization is defined by the presence of groupings, such as clans and age-sets, that can integrate more than one local group into a larger whole.

4. The personal qualities of leaders in tribal societies seem to be similar to the qualities of leaders in the United States, with one major difference: U.S. leaders are generally wealthier than others in their society.

5. Chiefdom organization differs from tribal organization in having formal authority structures that integrate multicommunity political units. Compared with societies with tribal organization, societies with chiefdoms are more densely populated and their communities are more permanent. In contrast to "big men" in tribal societies, who generally have to earn their privileges by their personal qualities, chiefs generally hold their positions permanently. Most chiefdom societies have social ranking.

6. A state has been defined as a political unit composed of many communities and having a centralized government with the authority to make and enforce laws, collect taxes, and draft men for military service. In state societies, the government tries to maintain a monopoly on the use of physical force. In addition, states are generally characterized by class stratification, intensive agriculture (the high productivity of which presumably allows the emergence of cities), commercial exchange, a high degree of economic and other specialization, and extensive foreign trade. The rulers of a state cannot depend forever on the use or threat of force to maintain their power; the people must believe that the rulers are legitimate or have the right to govern.

7. Degree of political participation varies in the societies that anthropologists study, just as among modern nation-states. Degree of political participation seems to be high in small-scale societies, as well as in modern democratic nation-states, but not in those in between, such as feudal states and preindustrial empires.

8. Many societies lack specialized offices and institutions for dealing with conflict. Yet all societies have peaceful, regularized ways of handling at least certain disputes. Avoidance, community action, and negotiation and mediation are more common in simpler societies. Ritual apology occurs frequently in chiefdoms. Oaths and ordeals tend to occur in complex societies in which political officials lack power to enforce judicial decisions. Adjudication is more likely in stratified, more complex societies. Capital punishment seems to exist in nearly all societies, from the simplest to the most complex.

9. People are likely to resort to violence when regular, effective alternative means of resolving a conflict are not available. Violence can occur between individuals, within communities, and between communities. Violence that occurs between political entities such as communities, districts, or nations is generally referred to as warfare. The type of warfare varies in scope and complexity from society to society. Preindustrial societies with higher warfare frequencies are likely to have had a history of unpredictable disasters that destroyed food supplies. More often than not, societies with one type of violence have others.

10. One of the most striking types of political change in recent years is the spread of participatory forms of government—"democracy."

GLOSSARY TERMS ○ ● ○

adjudication	mediation
band	negotiation
band organization	oath
chief	ordeal
chiefdom	raiding
codified laws	segmentary lineage
complementary	system
opposition	state organization
crime	tribal organization
feuding	tribe
headman	warfare

CRITICAL QUESTIONS ○ ○ ●

1. When, if ever, do you think the world will be politically unified? Why do you think so?

2. Why don't informal methods of social control work well in societies like our own? Why don't formal methods work better than they do?

3. What does research on war and violence suggest about how to reduce their likelihood?

PEARSON
myanthrolab

Read the chapter by Thomas Abler, "Iroquois: The Tree of Peace and the War Kettle" on MyAnthroLab and answer the following questions:

1. What was the Iroquois Confederacy? What kind of political organization was it?

2. What role did men and women play in making war and making peace?

3. What kinds of impacts did the Europeans have on the Iroquois?

NOTES ● ○ ○

1. Service 1962.
2. Schrire 1984b; see also Leacock and Lee 1982, 8.
3. Service 1962, 109.
4. Briggs 1974.
5. Mathiassen 1928, 213.
6. Service 1962, 114–15.
7. Bohannan 1954, 3.
8. Sahlins 1961, 342.
9. R. C. Kelly 1985, 1.
10. Sahlins 1961, 345.
11. N. Dyson-Hudson 1966, Chapters 5 and 6.
12. Ibid.
13. Sahlins 1962, 293–94.
14. Sahlins 1963, 295.
15. Sahlins 1983, 519.
16. Sahlins 1963, 297.
17. Carneiro 1970, 733.
18. Weber 1947, 154.
19. Lightfoot 2005.
20. Ferguson 2004.
21. Wiberg 1983.
22. For an extensive review of the various theories about legitimacy, see R. Cohen 1988, 1–3.
23. Finley 1983.
24. Carcopino 1940, 18–20.
25. Our discussion of Nupe is based on S. F. Nadel 1935, 257–303.
26. Blanton and Fargher 2008.
27. Ibid.
28. M. Ember 1963.
29. Textor 1967.
30. M. Ember 1963.
31. Textor 1967.
32. Naroll 1961. See also Ross 1981.
33. M. Ember 1963, 244–46.
34. Service 1962; see also Braun and Plog 1982; Haas 1990.
35. A. Johnson and Earle 1987, 158; Carneiro 1990.
36. Service 1962, 112, 145.
37. Feinman and Nietzel 1984.
38. For a more detailed description and evaluation of the available theories, see Chapter 12 in C. Ember et al. 2007. See also Cohen and Service 1978. For more details, see chapter on the origin of the state.
39. McNeill 1976.
40. Carneiro 1978, 215.
41. Textor 1967.
42. Carneiro 1978; Hart 1948; Naroll 1967; Marano 1973, 35–40 (cf. Peregrine, Ember, and Ember 2004 and other articles in Graber 2004).
43. For a review of the descriptive literature until the late 1970s, see Vincent 1978.
44. D. Werner 1982.
45. Kracke 1979, 232.
46. D. Werner 1982.
47. Sahlins 1963.
48. Kracke 1979, 41.
49. Lederman 1990.
50. Brandewie 1991.
51. Lepowsky 1990.
52. Todorov et al. 2005.
53. Zebrowitz and Montepare 2005.
54. Ross 1988, 73. The discussion in this section draws mostly from Zebrowitz and Montepare 2005, 73–89, and from Ross 2009b.
55. Bondarenko and Korotayev 2000; Korotayev and Bondarenko 2000.
56. For studies of international relations that support these conclusions, see footnotes 2 and 3 in C. R. Ember, Ember, and Russett 1992; see also Chapter 3 in Russett and Oneal 2001.
57. C. R. Ember, Ember, and Russett 1992.
58. Rummel 2002b.
59. Scaglion 2009b.
60. Hoebel 1968/1954, 4, quoting S. P. Simpson and Field 1946, 858.
61. Fry and Björkqvist 1997.
62. D. Black 1993, 79–83.
63. Ross 1988.
64. Boas 1888, 668.
65. Otterbein 1986, 107.
66. Archer and Gartner 1984, 118–39.
67. Scaglion 2004b; D. Black 1993, 83–86.
68. Ibid.
69. Evans-Pritchard 1940, 291. The discussion of the Nuer follows this source.
70. Hickson 1986.
71. Ibid.; and Koch et al. 1977, 279.
72. J. M. Roberts 1967, 169.
73. Ibid., 192.
74. Hoebel 1968/1954, Chapter 9.
75. Schwartz 1954, 475.
76. Textor 1967.
77. Masumura 1977, 388–99.
78. Scaglion 2009b; Black 1993; Newman 1983, 131.
79. Otterbein and Otterbein 1965 and Fry 2006, 88 do not consider feuding to be warfare.
80. See summaries of the evidence in C. R. Ember and Ember 1994; see also Fry 2006.
81. C. R. Ember and Ember 1994.

82. Chacon and Mendoza 2007.
83. Newman 1983, 131; Ericksen and Horton 1992.
84. Gubser 1965, 151.
85. Otterbein and Otterbein 1965, 1476.
86. D. R. White 1988.
87. Patterson 1982, 345–52.
88. Gat 1999, 373, as referred to in Wadley 2003.
89. Heider 1970, 105–11; Heider 1979, 88–99.
90. M. Ember and Ember 1992, 188–89.
91. C. R. Ember and Ember 1992; M. Ember 1982. For a discussion of how Dani warfare seems to be motivated mainly by economic considerations, see Shankman 1991. B. W. Kang (2000, 878–79) finds a strong correlation between environmental stress and warfare frequency in Korean history.
92. Otterbein 1970.
93. C. R. Ember and Ember 1992; see also Otterbein 1970 and Loftin 1971.
94. C. R. Ember 1974.
95. Otterbein 1968, 283; Ross 1985.
96. Divale and Harris 1976, 521–38; see also Gibbons 1993.
97. C. R. Ember and Ember 1992, 251–52.
98. Singer 1980.
99. Russett and Oneal 2001, 89.
100. Ibid., 145–48.
101. Younger 2008.
102. Russett 1993, 10–11, 14, 138.

Religion and Magic

From Chapter 25 of *Anthropology*, 13/e. Carol R. Ember. Melvin Ember. Peter N. Peregrine. Copyright © 2011 by Pearson Education.
Published by Prentice Hall. All rights reserved.

Religion and Magic

s far as we know, all societies have possessed beliefs that can be grouped under the term *religion*. These beliefs vary from culture to culture and from time to time. Yet, despite their variety, we shall define **religion** as any set of attitudes, beliefs, and practices pertaining to *supernatural power*, whether that power be forces, gods, spirits, ghosts, or demons.

In our society, we divide phenomena into the natural and the supernatural, but not all languages or cultures make such a neat distinction. Moreover, what is considered **supernatural**—powers believed to be not human or not subject to the laws of nature—varies from society to society. Some of the variation is determined by what a society regards as natural. For example, some illnesses commonly found in our society are believed to result from the natural action of bacteria and viruses. In other societies, and even among some people in our own society, illness is thought to result from supernatural forces, and thus it forms a part of religious belief.

Beliefs about what is, or is not, a supernatural occurrence also vary within a society at a given time or over time. In Judeo-Christian traditions, for example, floods, earthquakes, volcanic eruptions, comets, and epidemics were once considered evidence of supernatural powers intervening in human affairs. It is now generally agreed that they are simply natural occurrences—even though many still believe that supernatural forces may be involved. Thus, the line between the natural and the supernatural varies in a society according to what people believe about the causes of things and events in the observable world. Similarly, what is considered sacred in one society may not be so considered in another.

In many cultures, what we would consider religious is embedded in other aspects of everyday life. That is, it is often difficult to separate the religious, economic, or political from other aspects of the culture. Such cultures have little or no specialization of any kind; there are no full-time priests, no purely religious activities. So the various aspects of culture we distinguish are not separate and easily recognized in many societies, as they are in complex societies such as our own. However, it is sometimes difficult even for us to agree whether or not a particular custom of ours is religious. After all, the categorizing of beliefs as religious, political, or social is a relatively new custom. The ancient Greeks, for instance, did not have a word for religion, but they did have many concepts concerning the behavior of their gods and their own expected duties to the gods.

When people's duties to their gods are linked with duty to their princes, it is difficult to separate religious from political ideas. As an example of our own difficulty in labeling a particular class of actions or beliefs as religious or social, consider our attitudes about wearing clothes. Is our belief that it is necessary to wear clothing, at least in the company of nonlovers, a religious principle, or is it something else? Recall that, in Genesis, the wearing of clothes or fig leaves is distinctly associated with the loss of innocence: Adam and Eve, after eating the apple, covered their nakedness. Accordingly,

when Christian missionaries first visited islands in the Pacific in the 19th century, they forced the native women to wear more clothes, particularly to cover their sexual parts. Were the missionaries' ideas about sex religious or social, or perhaps both?

● ○ ●

THE UNIVERSALITY OF RELIGION

Religious beliefs and practices are found in all known contemporary societies, and archaeologists think they have found signs of religious belief associated with *Homo sapiens* who lived at least 60,000 years ago. People then deliberately buried their dead, and many graves contain the remains of food, tools, and other objects that were probably thought to be needed in an afterlife. Some of the artistic productions of modern humans after about 30,000 years ago may have been used for religious purposes. For example, sculptures of females with ample secondary sex characteristics may have been fertility charms. Cave paintings in which the predominant images are animals of the hunt may reflect a belief that the image had some power over events. Perhaps early humans thought that their hunting would be more successful if they drew images depicting good fortune in hunting. The details of religions practiced in the distant past cannot be recovered. Yet evidence of ritual treatment of the dead suggests that early people believed in the existence of supernatural spirits and tried to communicate with, and perhaps influence, them.

We may reasonably assume the existence of prehistoric religion and we have evidence of the universality of religion in historic times, so we can understand why the subject of religion has been the focus of much speculation, research, and theorizing. As long ago as the 5th century B.C., Herodotus made fairly objective comparisons among the religions of the 50 or so societies he traveled to from his home in Greece. He noted many similarities among their gods and pointed out evidence of diffusion of religious worship. Since Herodotus's time some 2,500 years ago, scholars, theologians, historians, and philosophers have speculated about religion. Some have claimed superiority for their own forms of religion; others have derided the naive simplicity of others' beliefs; and some have expressed skepticism concerning all beliefs.

Speculation about which religion is superior is not an anthropological concern. What is of interest to anthropologists is why religion is found in all societies and how and why it varies from society to society. Many social scientists—particularly anthropologists, sociologists, and psychologists—have offered theories to account for the universality of religion. Most think that religions are created by humans in response to certain universal needs or conditions. We consider four such needs or conditions here: (1) a need for intellectual understanding, (2) reversion to childhood feelings, (3) anxiety and uncertainty, and (4) a need for community.

The Need to Understand

One of the earliest social scientists to propose a major theory of the origin of religion was Edward Tylor. In Tylor's view, religion originated in people's speculation about dreams, trances, and death. The dead, the distant, those in the next house, animals—all seem real in dreams and trances. Tylor thought that the lifelike appearances of these imagined people and animals suggest a dual existence for all things—a physical, visible body and a psychic, invisible soul. In sleep, the soul can leave the body and appear to other people; at death, the soul permanently leaves the body. Because the dead appear in dreams, people come to believe that the souls of the dead are still around.

Tylor thought that the belief in souls was the earliest form of religion; **animism** is the term he used to refer to belief in souls.[1] But many scholars criticized Tylor's theory for being too intellectual and not dealing with the emotional component of religion. One of Tylor's students, R. R. Marett, felt that Tylor's animism was too sophisticated an idea to be the origin of religion. Marett suggested that **animatism**—a belief in impersonal supernatural forces (e.g., the power of a rabbit's foot)—preceded the creation of spirits.[2] A similar idea is that, when people believe in gods, they are *anthropomorphizing*—attributing human characteristics and motivations to nonhuman, particularly supernatural, events.[3] Anthropomorphizing may be an attempt to understand what is otherwise incomprehensible and disturbing.

Reversion to Childhood Feelings

Sigmund Freud believed that early humans lived in groups, each of which was dominated by a tyrannical man who kept all the women for himself.[4] Freud postulated that, on maturing, the sons were driven out of the group. Later, they joined together to kill and eat the hated father. But then the sons felt enormous guilt and remorse, which they expressed (projected) by prohibiting the killing of a totem animal (the father substitute). Subsequently, on ritual occasions, the cannibalistic scene was repeated in the form of a totem meal. Freud believed that these early practices gradually became transformed into the worship of deities or gods modeled after the father.

Most social scientists today do not accept Freud's interpretation of the origin of religion. But there is widespread agreement with his idea that events in infancy can have long-lasting and powerful effects on beliefs and practices in adult life. Helpless and dependent on parents for many years, infants and children inevitably and unconsciously view their parents as all-knowing and all-powerful. When adults feel out of control or in need, they may unconsciously revert to their infantile and childhood feelings. They may then look to gods or magic to do what they cannot do for themselves, just as they looked to their parents to take care of their needs. As we shall see, there is evidence that feelings about the supernatural world parallel feelings in everyday life.

Anxiety and Uncertainty

Freud thought that humans would turn to religion during times of uncertainty, but he did not view religion positively, believing that humans would eventually outgrow the need for religion. Others viewed religion more positively. Bronislaw Malinowski noted that people in all societies are faced with anxiety and uncertainty. They may have skills and knowledge to take care of many of their needs, but knowledge is not sufficient to prevent illness, accidents, and natural disasters. The most frightening prospect is death itself. Consequently, there is an intense desire for immortality. As Malinowski saw it, religion is born from the universal need to find comfort in inevitable times of stress. Through religious belief, people affirm their convictions that death is neither real nor final, that people are endowed with a personality that persists even after death. In religious ceremony, humans can commemorate and communicate with those who have died, and achieve some measure of comfort in these ways.[5]

Theorists such as William James, Carl Jung, Erich Fromm, and Abraham Maslow have viewed religion even more positively: Religion is not just a way of relieving anxiety; it is thought to be therapeutic. James suggested that religion provides a feeling of union with something larger than oneself,[6] and Jung suggested that it helps people resolve their inner conflicts and attain maturity.[7] Fromm proposed that religion gives people a framework of values,[8] and Maslow argued that it provides a transcendental understanding of the world.[9]

The idea that religion relieves anxiety in times of greater stress is supported by a comparative study of fishermen. John Poggie and Richard Pollnac interviewed commercial fishermen from three New England ports about their ritual beliefs and practices. Most frequently mentioned were taboos such as "Don't turn a hatch cover upside down," "Don't whistle on a boat," and "Don't mention the word *pig* on board." When the fishermen were asked what these taboos meant, they talked about personal safety and preventing bad luck. Those fishermen who stay out for only a day at a time, fish closer to shore, or collect shellfish close to shore, report fewer taboos, consistent with the fact that they are less at risk from rough seas, storms, and inability to repair their boats if they break down.[10]

The Need for Community

All those theories of religion agree on one thing: Whatever the beliefs or rituals, religion may satisfy psychological needs common to all people. But some social scientists believe that religion springs from society and serves social, rather than psychological, needs. Émile Durkheim, a French sociologist, pointed out that living in society makes humans feel pushed and pulled by powerful forces. These forces direct their behavior, pushing them to resist what is considered wrong, pulling them to do what is considered right. These are the forces of public opinion, custom, and law. Because they are largely invisible and unexplained, people would feel them as mysterious forces and therefore come to believe in gods and spirits. Durkheim suggested that religion arises out of the experience of living in social groups; religious belief and practice affirm a person's place in society, enhance feelings of community, and give people confidence. He proposed that society is really the object of worship in religion.

Consider how Durkheim explained totemism, so often discussed by early religious theorists. He thought that nothing inherent in a lizard, rat, or frog—animal totems for some Australian aboriginal groups—would be sufficient to make them *sacred*. The totem animal therefore must be a symbol. But a symbol of what? Durkheim noted that the people are organized into clans, and each clan has its own totem animal; the totem distinguishes one clan

Fishermen working on a boat deck in choppy seas. The more danger involved in fishing, the more taboos fisherman seem to have.

from another. So the totem is the focus of the clan's religious rituals and symbolizes both the clan and the clan's spirits. It is the clan that is affirmed in ritual.[11]

Guy Swanson accepted Durkheim's belief that certain aspects or conditions of society generate the responses we call religious, but he thought that Durkheim was too vague about exactly what in society would generate the belief in spirits or gods. So what might? Swanson suggested that the belief in spirits derives from the existence of *sovereign groups* in a society. These are the groups that have independent jurisdiction (decision-making powers) over some sphere of life—the family, the clan, the village, the state. Such groups are not mortal; they persist beyond the lifetimes of their individual members. According to Swanson, then, the spirits or gods that people invent personify or represent the powerful decision-making groups in their society. Just like sovereign groups in a society, the spirits or gods are immortal and have purposes and goals that supersede those of individuals.[12]

VARIATION IN RELIGIOUS BELIEFS

There is no general agreement among scholars as to why people need religion, or how spirits, gods, and other supernatural beings and forces come into existence. (Any or all of the needs we have discussed, psychological or social, may give rise to religious belief and practice.) Yet there is general recognition of the enormous variation in the details of religious beliefs and practices. Societies differ in the kinds of supernatural beings or forces they believe in and the character of those beings. They also differ in the structure or hierarchy of those beings, in what the beings actually do, and in what happens to people after death. Variation exists also in the ways in which the supernatural is believed to interact with humans.

Types of Supernatural Forces and Beings

Supernatural Forces   Some supernatural forces have no personlike character. As we discussed earlier, Marett referred to such religious beliefs as animatism. For example, a supernatural, impersonal force called **mana,** after its Malayo-Polynesian name, is thought to inhabit some objects but not others, some people but not others. A farmer in Polynesia places stones around a field; the crops are bountiful; the stones have mana. During a subsequent year, the stones may lose their mana and the crops will be poor. People may also possess mana, as, for example, the chiefs in Polynesia were said to do. However, such power is not necessarily possessed permanently; chiefs who were unsuccessful in war or other activities were said to have lost their mana.

The word *mana* may be Malayo-Polynesian, but a similar concept is also found in our own society. We can compare mana to the power that golfers may attribute to some but, unhappily not all, of their clubs. A ballplayer might think a certain sweatshirt or pair of pants has supernatural power or force, and that more runs or points will be scored when they are worn. A four-leaf clover has mana; a three-leaf clover does not.

Objects, people, or places can be considered **taboo.** Anthony Wallace distinguished mana from taboo by pointing out that things containing mana are to be touched, whereas taboo things are not to be touched, for their power can cause harm.[13] Thus, those who touch them may themselves become taboo. Taboos surround food not to be eaten, places not to be entered, animals not to be killed, people not to be touched sexually, people not to be touched at all, and so on. An Australian aborigine could not normally kill and eat the animal that was his totem; Hebrew tribesmen were forbidden to touch a woman during menstruation or for seven days afterward.

Supernatural Beings   Supernatural beings fall within two broad categories: those of nonhuman origin, such as gods and spirits, and those of human origin, such as ghosts and ancestral spirits. Chief among the beings of nonhuman origin, **gods** are named personalities. They are often *anthropomorphic*—that is, conceived in the image of a person—although they are sometimes given the shapes of other animals or of celestial bodies, such as the sun or moon. Essentially, the gods are believed to have created themselves, but some of them then created, or gave birth to, other gods. Although some are seen as creator gods, not all peoples include the creation of the world as one of the acts of gods.

After their efforts at creation, many creator gods retire. Having set the world in motion, they are not interested in its day-to-day operation. Other creator gods remain interested in the ordinary affairs of human beings, especially the affairs of one small, chosen segment of humanity. Whether or not a society has a creator god, the job of running the creation is often left to lesser gods. The Maori of New Zealand, for example, recognize three important gods: a god of the sea, a god of the forest, and a god of agriculture. They call upon each in turn for help and try to get all three to share their knowledge of how the universe runs. The gods of the ancient Romans, on the other hand, specialized to a high degree. There were three gods of the plow, one god to help with the sowing, one for weeding, one for reaping, one for storing grain, one for manuring, and so on.[14]

Beneath the gods in prestige, and often closer to people, are multitudes of unnamed **spirits.** Some may be guardian spirits for people. Some, who become known for particularly efficacious work, may be promoted to the rank of named gods. Some spirits who are known to the people but are never invoked by them are of the hobgoblin type. Hobgoblins delight in mischief and can be blamed for any number of small mishaps; still other spirits take pleasure in deliberately working evil on behalf of people.

Many Native American groups believed in guardian spirits that had to be sought out, usually in childhood. For example, among the Sanpoil of northeastern Washington, boys and sometimes girls would be sent out on overnight vigils to acquire their guardians. Most commonly the spirits were animals, but they could also be uniquely shaped

A Guatemalan Maya family visits a cemetery on the Day of the Dead. It is believed that the spirits of the dead return for a visit on that day.

rocks, lakes, mountains, whirlwinds, or clouds. The vigil was not always successful. When it was, the guardian spirit appeared in a vision or dream, and always at first in human form. Conversation with the spirit would reveal its true identity.[15]

Ghosts are supernatural beings who were once human, and **ancestor spirits** are ghosts of dead relatives. The belief that ghosts or their actions can be perceived by the living is almost universal.[16] The near-universality of the belief in ghosts may not be difficult to explain. There are many cues in everyday experience that are associated with a loved one, and even after the death, those cues might arouse the feeling that the dead person is still somehow present. The opening of a door or the smell of tobacco or cologne in a room may evoke the idea that the person is still present, if only for a moment. Then, too, loved ones live on in dreams. Small wonder, then, that most societies believe in ghosts. If the idea of ghosts is generated by these familiar associations, we might expect that ghosts in most societies would be close relatives and friends, not strangers—and they are.[17]

Although the belief in ghosts is nearly universal, the spirits of the dead do not play an active role in the life of the living in all societies. In his cross-cultural study of 50 societies, Swanson found that people are likely to believe in active ancestral spirits where descent groups are important decision-making units. The descent group is an entity that exists over time, back into the past as well as forward into the future, despite the deaths of individual members.[18] The dead feel concern for the fortunes, the prestige, and the continuity of their descent group as strongly as the living. As a Lugbara elder (in northern Uganda in Africa) put it, "Are our ancestors not people of our lineage? They are our fathers and we are their children whom they have begotten. Those that have died stay near us in our homes and we feed and respect them. Does not a man help his father when he is old?"[19]

The Character of Supernatural Beings

Whatever type they may be, the gods or spirits venerated in a given culture tend to have certain personality or character traits. They may be unpredictable or predictable, aloof from or interested in human affairs, helpful or punishing. Why do the gods and spirits in a particular culture exhibit certain character traits rather than others?

We have some evidence from cross-cultural studies that the character of supernatural beings may be related to the nature of child training. Melford Spiro and Roy D'Andrade suggested that the god-human relationship is a projection of the parent-child relationship, in which case child-training practices might well be relived in dealings with the supernatural.[20] For example, if a child was nurtured immediately by her parents when she cried or waved her arms about or kicked, she might grow up expecting to be nurtured by the gods when she attracted their attention by performing a ritual. On the other hand, if her parents often punished her, she would grow up expecting the gods to punish her if she disobeyed them. William Lambert, Leigh Minturn Triandis, and Margery Wolf, in another cross-cultural study, found that societies with hurtful or punitive child-training practices are likely to believe that their gods are aggressive and malevolent; societies with less punitive child training are more likely to believe that the gods are benevolent.[21] These results are consistent with the Freudian notion that the supernatural world should parallel the natural. It is worth noting in this context that some peoples refer to the god as their father and to themselves as his children.

Structure or Hierarchy of Supernatural Beings

The range of social structures in human societies from egalitarian to highly stratified has its counterpart in the supernatural world. Some societies have gods or spirits that are not ranked; one god has about as much power as another. Other societies have gods or spirits that are ranked in prestige and power. For example, on the Pacific islands of Palau, which was a rank society, gods were ranked as people were. Each clan worshiped a god and a goddess that had names or titles similar to clan titles. Although a clan god was generally important only to the members of that clan, the gods of the various clans in a village were believed to be ranked in the same order that the clans were. Thus, the god of the highest-ranking clan was respected by all the clans of the village. Its shrine was given the place of honor in the center of the village and was larger and more elaborately decorated than other shrines.[22]

Although the Palauans did not believe in a high god or supreme being who outranked all the other gods, some societies do. Consider Judaism, Christianity, and Islam, which we call **monotheistic** religions. Although *monotheism* means "one god," most monotheistic religions actually include more than one supernatural being (e.g., demons, angels, the Devil). But the supreme being or high god, as the creator of the universe or the director of events (or both), is believed to be ultimately responsible for all events.[23] A **polytheistic** religion recognizes many important gods, no one of which is supreme.

Why do some societies have a belief in a high god and others do not? Recall Swanson's suggestion that people invent gods who personify the important decision-making groups in their society. He therefore hypothesized that societies with hierarchical political systems should be more likely to believe in a high god. In his cross-cultural study of 50 societies (none of which practiced any of the major world religions), he found that belief in a high god is strongly associated with three or more levels of "sovereign" (decision-making) groups. Of the 20 sample societies that had a hierarchy of three or more sovereign groups—for instance, family, clan, and chiefdom—17 possessed the idea of a high god. Of the 19 societies that had fewer than three levels of decision-making groups, only two had a high god.[24] Consistent with Swanson's findings, societies dependent on food production are more likely to have a belief in a high god than are food-collecting societies.[25] These results strongly suggest, then, that the realm of the gods parallels and may reflect the everyday social and political worlds. In the past, many state societies had state religions in which the political officials were also the officials of the temples (e.g., the pharaohs in Egypt). In recent times, most state societies have separated church and state, as in the United States and Canada.

Intervention of the Gods in Human Affairs

According to Clifford Geertz, when people face ignorance, pain, and the unjustness of life, they explain the events by the intervention of the gods.[26] Thus, in Greek religion, the direct intervention of Poseidon as ruler of the seas prevented Odysseus from getting home for 10 years. In the Old Testament, the direct intervention of Yahweh caused the great flood that killed most of the people in the time of Noah. In other societies, people may search their memories for a violated taboo that has brought punishment through supernatural intervention.

In addition to unasked-for divine interference, there are numerous examples of requests for divine intervention, either for good for oneself and friends or for evil for others. Gods are asked to intervene in the weather and to make the crops grow, to send fish to the fisherman and game to the hunter, to find lost things, and to accompany travelers and prevent accidents. They are asked to stop the flow of lava down the side of a volcano, to stop a war, or to cure an illness.

The gods do not intervene in all societies. In some, they intervene in human affairs; in others, they are not the slightest bit interested; and in still others, they interfere only occasionally. We have little research on why gods are believed to interfere in some societies and not in others. We do, however, have some evidence suggesting when the gods will take an interest in the morality or immorality of human behavior. Swanson's study suggests that the gods are likely to punish people for immoral behavior when there are considerable differences in wealth in the society.[27] His interpretation is that supernatural support of moral behavior is particularly useful where inequalities tax the ability of the political system to maintain social order and minimize social disorder. Envy of others' privileges may motivate some people to behave immorally; the belief that the gods will punish such behavior might deter it. More generally, the concern of gods with moral behavior is more likely in large, complex societies (see the box "Religion: A Force for Harmony and Cooperation?").

Life after Death

In many societies, ideas about an afterlife are vague and seemingly unimportant, but many other peoples have very definite and elaborate ideas of what happens after death. The Lugbara of Uganda see the dead as joining the ancestors of the living and staying near the family homesite. They retain an interest in the behavior of the living, both rewarding and punishing them. The Zuni of the southwestern United States think the dead join the past dead, known as the *katcinas*, in a katcina village at the bottom of a nearby lake. There they lead a life of singing and dancing and bring rain to the living Zuni. Just as they are swift to punish the priest who fails in his duty, they also punish the people in masks who ineffectively impersonate the katcinas during the dance ceremonies.[28]

The Chamulas have merged the ancient Mayan worship of the sun and moon with the Spanish conquerors' Jesus and Mary. Their vision of life after death contains a blending of the two cultures. All souls go to the underworld, where they live a humanlike life except that they are incapable of sexual intercourse. After the sun travels over the world, it travels under the underworld, so that the dead have sunlight. Only murderers and suicides are punished, being burned by the Christ-sun on their journey.[29]

Many Christians believe that the dead are divided into two groups: The unsaved are sent to everlasting

applied anthropology

Religion: A Force for Cooperation and Harmony?

Most social science theories about religion suggest that religious beliefs and rituals promote social cohesion and cooperation within the group that shares them. Some religions, including the major religions in the modern world (Buddhism, Christianity, Islam, Hinduism, Judaism), are more explicit than others in their direct concern with moral behavior. Moralizing religions believe that the gods will reward moral behavior and punish immoral behavior, and are generally found in large and complex societies. Such societies are likely to have towns or cities and less reliance on kinship and reciprocity to encourage moral behavior. Neighbors may not know each other well and although there may be codified law and courts, these mechanisms may not be sufficient to promote social order. Complex societies are also likely to have a large amount of social inequality, which increases the likelihood of property-related crime. The cross-cultural evidence is consistent with the theory that morality-based religions and collective rituals minimize antisocial behavior in groups of unrelated individuals. Perhaps to promote solidarity among unrelated people, religions in complex societies often extend kin terms to members of the religious communities, calling each other "brothers" and "sisters" or sometimes "God's children." Experimental evidence suggests individuals are more generous toward strangers if their religious feelings have been aroused. Religious communes are also four times as likely to survive compared with secular communes.

These studies raise important questions about exactly why and when moralizing religions came into existence and whether the spread of these religions had to do with their adaptive consequences. But there are also questions raised about mechanisms. For example, religious communes, as compared with secular communes, usually impose more requirements from members, such as food taboos, fasts, constraints on sex and possessions, and so on. A comparative study of communes suggests that the religious elements are more important than the commitments themselves. However, in experimental research, there are some hints that nonreligious conditions could also make people more cooperative. Experimental reminders of secular morality had as much effect as reminders of God. Also, there are examples of modern societies, especially in northern Europe, that are very cooperative, but not very religious.

But, even if religious belief and ritual promote greater in-group trust and cooperation, there is a dark side to strongly held religious belief—the potential for greater out-group conflict. History is replete with examples of people hurting others in the name of religion. Christianity and Islam are the two largest religions, possibly because of their zeal to convert others. Some of the biggest conflicts have occurred where the two largest religions meet. The Christian Crusades of the 11th century through 13th century were attempts to "liberate" sites in the Holy Land controlled by Muslims. Osama bin Laden cited the establishment of U.S. bases in Saudi Arabia, which "defiled" sacred lands in his view, as justification for the September 11, 2001, attacks on the United States. Religions, or, more precisely, religious groups, do not necessarily promote violence. After all, some of the founders of various religions preached nonviolence and harmony. Exactly what persuades a religious group to commit violence is not well understood. There are five warning signs. One is when leaders act as if only they know the truth. A second is a call to blind obedience to a religious leader. A third is when the people believe it is possible to establish an "ideal world." A fourth is acting as if "the end justifies the means." Lastly, and perhaps the clearest, is a call for "a holy war."

In the globalized world today, there is more admixture of all types—heterogeneous cities full of people of different colors, dress, ethnicities, and religions. This situation has two potential outcomes—the potential for different groups to live together peacefully, or a greater potential for violence. Whether the major religions will adapt to create a new morality for the new global circumstances remains to be seen. Research has not told us enough yet about how to achieve more harmony across different religions or across different ethnicities. We can hope that simply learning more about other individuals and groups—their hopes, dreams, and expectations, how they have adapted to their environments—may enhance tolerance.

Sources: Winkelman and Baker 2010, 259–65; 314-318; Norenzayan and Shariff 2008; Sosis and Bressler 2003; Stark 2001; Roes and Raymond 2003.

punishment and the saved to everlasting reward. Accounts differ, but hell is often associated with torture by fire, heaven with mansions. Several societies see the dead as returning to earth to be reborn. The Hindus use this pattern of reincarnation to justify one's caste in this life and to promise eventual release from the pain of life through the attainment of *nirvana*, or inclusion into the One.

A recent cross-cultural study asks why some societies judge where you will go after death and others do not. Support was found for the idea that judgmental beliefs parallel the society's economic practices. Some societies have considerable delay between labor inputs and return of food. For example, intensive agriculturalists need considerable labor input to plow, fertilize, or create irrigation systems, and many months go by until crops can be

A ghost festival in Thailand. The belief in ghosts is practically a cross-cultural universal.

© Peter Arnold, Inc.

harvested. Not planning ahead has dire long-term consequences. In contrast, mistakes by hunter-gatherers are realized more quickly and can be corrected more quickly. Religions that foster the idea that actions in the present will be judged after death reinforce the need for long-term planning. Consistent with this idea, societies with intensive agriculture are the most likely to believe that their actions in life affect where their souls will go after death.[30] This finding is consistent with Swanson's conclusion discussed previously that the gods are generally likely to punish people for immoral behavior when there are considerable differences in wealth in the society. Intensive agricultural societies tend to have considerable differences in wealth.

In many respects, the afterworld in many religions may resemble the everyday world, but we still have only a few comparative studies that show exactly how.

VARIATION IN RELIGIOUS PRACTICES

Beliefs are not the only elements of religion that vary from society to society. Societies vary in the kinds of religious practitioners they have. There is also variation in how people interact with the supernatural. The manner of approach to the supernatural varies from supplication—requests, prayers, and so on—to manipulation. Many of these interactions are highly *ritualized*. **Rituals** are repetitive sets of behaviors that occur in essentially the same patterns every time they occur. Religious rituals involve the supernatural in some way. They are generally collective, follow customary patterns, and are thought to strengthen faith.[31]

Ways to Interact with the Supernatural

How to get in touch with the supernatural has proved to be a universal problem. Wallace identified a number of

ways people the world over use, though not necessarily all together, including, but not limited to, prayer (asking for supernatural help), physiological experience (doing things to the body and mind), simulation (manipulating imitations of things), feasts, and sacrifices.[32] Prayer can be spontaneous or memorized, private or public, silent or spoken. The Lugbara do not say the words of a prayer aloud, for doing so would be too powerful; they simply think about the things that are bothering them. The gods know all languages.

Doing things to the body or mind may involve drugs (hallucinogenics such as peyote or opiates) or alcohol; social isolation or sensory deprivation; dancing or running until exhausted; being deprived of food, water, and sleep; and listening to repetitive sounds such as drumming. Such behaviors may induce trances or altered states of consciousness.[33] Erika Bourguignon found that achieving these altered states, which she generally referred to as *trances,* is part of religious practice in 90 percent of the world's societies.[34] In some societies, trances are thought to involve the presence of a spirit or power inside a person that changes or displaces that person's personality or soul. These types are referred to as possession trances. Other types of trances may involve the journey of a person's soul, experiencing visions, or transmitting messages from spirits. Possession trances are especially likely in societies that depend on agriculture and have social stratification, slavery, and more complex political hierarchies. Nonpossession trances are most likely to occur in food-collecting societies. Societies with moderate levels of social complexity have both possession and nonpossession trances.[35]

One puzzle is why there is a preponderance of women thought to be possessed. Alice Kehoe and Dody Giletti suggested that women are more likely than men to suffer from nutritional deficiencies because of pregnancy, lactation, and men's priority in gaining access to food. Calcium deficiency in particular can cause muscular spasms, convulsive seizures, and disorientation, all of which may foster the belief that an individual is possessed.[36] Douglas

Raybeck and his colleagues suggest that women's physiology makes them more susceptible to calcium deficiency even with an equivalent diet. In addition, women are subject to more stress because they are usually less able to control their lives. Higher levels of stress, they suggest, lower the body's reserves of calcium.[37] Erika Bourguignon suggests a more psychological explanation of women's preponderance in possession trances. In many societies, women are brought up to be submissive. But when possessed, women are taken over by spirits and they are not responsible for what they do or say—therefore, they can unconsciously do what they are not able to do consciously.[38] Although intriguing, these suggestions need to be tested on individuals in field situations.

Voodoo employs simulation, or the imitation of things. Dolls are made in the likeness of an enemy and then are maltreated in hopes that the original enemy will experience pain and even death.

Divination seeks practical answers from the supernatural about anything that is troublesome—decisions to be made, interpersonal problems, or illness. Diviners use a variety of methods, including altered states of consciousness and simulation through the use of objects such as Ouija boards or tarot cards.[39]

Omar Moore suggested that, among the Naskapi hunters of Labrador, divination is an adaptive strategy for successful hunting. The Naskapi consult the diviner every three or four days when they have no luck in hunting. The diviner holds a caribou bone over the fire, as if the bone were a map, and the burns and cracks that appear in it indicate where the group should hunt. Moore, unlike the Naskapi, did not believe that the diviner really can find out where the animals will be; the cracks in the bones merely provide a way of randomly choosing where to hunt. Because humans are likely to develop customary patterns of action, they might be likely to look for game according to some plan. But game might learn to avoid hunters who operate according to a plan. Thus, any method of ensuring against patterning or predictable plans—any random strategy—may be advantageous. Divination by "reading" the bones would seem to be a random strategy. It also relieves any individual of the responsibility of deciding where to hunt, a decision that might arouse anger if the hunt failed.[40]

The eating of a sacred meal is found in many religions. For instance, Holy Communion is a simulation of the Last Supper. Australian aborigines, normally forbidden to eat their totem animal, have one totem feast a year at which they eat the totem. Feasts are often part of marriage and funeral ceremonies, as well as a fringe benefit of the sacrifice of food to the gods.

Some societies make sacrifices to a god in order to influence the god's action, either to divert anger or to attract goodwill. Characteristic of all sacrifices is that something of value is given up to the gods, whether it be food, drink, sex, household goods, or the life of an animal or person. Some societies feel that the god is obligated to act on their behalf if they make the appropriate sacrifice.

© Reinhard Dirscherl/WaterFrame.de/Peter Arnold

A woman with offerings at a Hindu temple in Bali.

Others use the sacrifice in an attempt to persuade the god, realizing there is no guarantee that the attempt will be successful.

Of all types of sacrifice, we probably think that the taking of human life is the ultimate. Nevertheless, human sacrifice is not rare in the ethnographic and historical records. Why have some societies practiced it? One cross-cultural study found that, among preindustrial societies, those with full-time craft specialists, slavery, and the corvée are most likely to practice human sacrifice. The suggested explanation is that the sacrifice mirrors what is socially important: Societies that depend mainly on human labor for energy (rather than animals or machines) may think of a human life as an appropriate offering to the gods when people want something very important.[41] Later studies found that societies with human sacrifice were at a mid-range level of political complexity, having alliances and confederacies with other polities, but only weak political integration. Such societies also seemed to be subject to population pressure and frequently carried out warfare for land and other resources. Human sacrifice, with humans from the outside groups, may have been an attempt to terrorize people from the other polities.[42]

Magic

All these modes of interacting with the supernatural can be categorized in various ways. One dimension of variation is how much people in society rely on pleading, asking, or trying to persuade the supernatural to act on their behalf, as opposed to whether they believe they can compel the supernatural to help by performing certain acts. For example, prayer is asking; performing voodoo is presumably compelling. When people believe their action can compel the supernatural to act in some particular and intended way, anthropologists often refer to the belief and related practice as **magic.**

Magic may involve manipulation of the supernatural for good or for evil. Many societies have magical rituals designed to ensure good crops, the replenishment of game, the fertility of domestic animals, and the avoidance and cure of illness in humans. We tend to associate the belief in magic with societies simpler than our own, but some people in complex societies take magic seriously and many follow some magical practices.

People who engage in risky activities may try to ensure their safety by carrying or wearing lucky charms. They believe the charms protect them by invoking the help of supernatural beings or forces. We might also believe we can protect ourselves by not doing some things. For example, baseball players on a hitting streak may choose not to change their socks or sweatshirt for the next game (to continue their luck). Why magic appeals to some individuals but not others in our own society may help us explain why magic is an important part of religious behavior in many societies.

As we will see, the witch doctor and the shaman often employ magic to effect a cure. But the use of magic to bring about harm has evoked perhaps the most interest.

Sorcery and Witchcraft   Sorcery and witchcraft are attempts to invoke the spirits to work harm against people. Although the words *sorcery* and *witchcraft* are often used interchangeably, they are also often distinguished. **Sorcery** may include the use of materials, objects, and medicines to invoke supernatural malevolence. **Witchcraft** may be said to accomplish the same ills by means of thought and emotion alone. Evidence of witchcraft can never be found. This lack of visible evidence makes an accusation of witchcraft both harder to prove and harder to disprove.

To the Azande of Zaire, in central Africa, witchcraft was part of everyday living. It was not used to explain events for which the cause was known, such as carelessness or violation of a taboo, but to explain the otherwise unexplainable. A man is gored by an elephant. He must have been bewitched, because he had not been gored on other elephant hunts. A man goes to his beer hut at night, lights some straw, and holds it aloft to look at his beer. The thatch catches fire and the hut burns down. The man has been bewitched, for huts did not catch fire on hundreds of other nights when he and others did the same thing. Some of the pots of a skilled potter break; some of the bowls of a skilled carver crack. Witchcraft. Other pots, other bowls treated exactly the same have not broken.[43]

The witch craze in Europe during the 16th and 17th centuries and the witch trials in 1692 in Salem, Massachusetts, remind us that the fear of others, which the belief in witchcraft presumably represents, can increase and decrease in a society within a relatively short period of time. Many scholars have tried to explain these witch hunts. One factor often suggested is political turmoil, which may give rise to widespread distrust and a search for scapegoats. In the case of Europe during the 16th and 17th cen-

turies, small regional political units were being incorporated into national states, and political allegiances were in flux. In addition, as Swanson noted, the commercial revolution and related changes were producing a new social class, the middle class, and "were promoting the growth of Protestantism and other heresies from Roman Catholicism."[44] In the case of Salem, the government of Massachusetts colony was unstable and there was much internal dissension. In 1692, the year of the witchcraft hysteria, Massachusetts was left without an English governor, and judicial practices broke down. These extraordinary conditions saw the accusation of a single person for witchcraft become the accusation of hundreds and the execution of 20 people. Swanson suggested that the undermining of legitimate political procedures may have generated the widespread fear of witches.[45]

It is also possible that epidemics of witchcraft accusation, like in Salem as well as other New England and European communities, may be the result of real epidemics—epidemics of disease. The disease implicated in Salem and elsewhere is the fungus disease called ergot, which can grow on rye plants. (The rye flour that went into the bread that the Salem people ate may have been contaminated by ergot.) It is now known that people who eat grain products contaminated by ergot suffer from convulsions, hallucinations, and other symptoms, such as crawling sensations in the skin. We also now know that ergot contains LSD, the drug that produces hallucinations and other delusions that resemble those occurring in severe mental disorders.

The presumed victims of bewitchment in Salem and other places had symptoms similar to victims of ergot poisoning today. They suffered from convulsions and the sensations of being pricked, pinched, or bitten. They had visions and felt as if they were flying through the air. We cannot know for sure that ergot poisoning occurred during those times when witchcraft accusations flourished. There is no direct evidence, of course, because the "bewitched" were not medically tested. But we do have some evidence that seems to be consistent with the ergot theory. Ergot is known to flourish on rye plants under certain climatic conditions—particularly a very cold winter followed by a cool, moist spring and summer. Tree-ring growth indicates that the early 1690s were particularly cold in eastern New England, and the outbreaks of witchcraft accusation in Europe seem to have peaked with colder winter temperatures.[46] Interestingly, too, when witchcraft hysteria was greatest in Europe, Europeans were using an ointment containing a skin-penetrating substance that we now know produces hallucinations and a vivid sensation of flying.[47] It may not be cause for wonder, then, that our popular image of witches is of people flying through the air on broomsticks.

But whether or not epidemics of witchcraft hysteria are due to epidemics of ergot poisoning or episodes of political turmoil or both, we still have to understand why so many societies in the ethnographic record believe in witchcraft and sorcery in the first place. Why do so many societies believe that there are ways to invoke the spirits to work harm against people? One possible explanation, suggested by Beatrice Whiting, is that sorcery or witchcraft will be found in societies that lack procedures or judicial authorities to deal with crime and other offenses. Her theory is that all societies need some form of social control—some way of deterring most would-be offenders and of dealing with actual offenders. In the absence of judicial officials who, if present, might deter and deal with antisocial behavior, sorcery may be a very effective mechanism for social control. If you misbehave, the person you mistreated might cause you to become ill or even die. The cross-cultural evidence seems to support this theory. Sorcery is more important in societies that lack judicial authorities than in those that have them.[48]

Types of Practitioners

Individuals may believe that they can directly contact the supernatural, but almost all societies also have part-time or full-time religious or magical practitioners. Research suggests there are four major types of practitioners: shamans, sorcerers or witches, mediums, and priests. As we shall see, the number of types of practitioners in a society seems to vary with degree of cultural complexity.[49]

The Shaman The word *shaman* may come from a language that was spoken in eastern Siberia. The **shaman** is usually a part-time male specialist who has fairly high status in his community and is often involved in healing.[50] More generally, the shaman deals with the spirit world to try to get their help or to keep them from causing harm.[51] Here we focus on the methods shamans use to help others.

The shaman enters into a trance, or some other altered state of consciousness, and then journeys to other worlds to get help from guardians or other spirits. Dreams may be used to provide insight or as a way for shamans to commune with spirits. People may seek help

for practical matters, such as where to get food resources or whether to relocate, but solving a health problem is most often the goal of the shaman.[52] Shamans may also bring news from spirits, such as a warning about an impending disaster.[53]

Someone may receive a "call" to the role of shaman in recovering from an illness, through a vision quest, or in a dream. Shamans-in-training may enhance the vividness of their imagery by using hallucinogens, sleep or food deprivation, or engaging in extensive physical activity such as dancing. An important part of the process of being a shaman is learning to control the imagery and the spirit powers. Shamanistic training can take several years under the guidance of a master shaman.[54]

Sorcerers and Witches In contrast with shamans, who have fairly high status, sorcerers and witches of both sexes tend to have very low social and economic status in their societies.[55] Suspected sorcerers and witches are usually feared because they are thought to know how to invoke the supernatural to cause illness, injury, and death. Because sorcerers use materials for their magic, evidence of sorcery can be found, and suspected sorcerers are often killed for their malevolent activities. Because witchcraft supposedly is accomplished by thought and emotion alone, it may be harder to prove that someone is a witch, but the difficulty of proving witchcraft has not prevented people from accusing and killing others for being witches.

Mediums **Mediums** tend to be females. These part-time practitioners are asked to heal and divine while in possession trances—that is, when they are thought to be possessed by spirits. Mediums are described as having tremors, convulsions, seizures, and temporary amnesia.

Priests **Priests** are generally full-time male specialists who officiate at public events. They have very high status

Shamans are usually male. Here, female shamans in Korea perform a healing ritual.

and are thought to be able to relate to superior or high gods who are beyond the ordinary person's control. In most societies with priests, the people who get to be priests obtain their offices through inheritance or political appointment.[56] Priests are sometimes distinguished from other people by special clothing or a different hairstyle. The training of a priest can be vigorous and long, including fasting, praying, and physical labor, as well as learning the dogma and the ritual of his religion. Priests in the United States complete four years of theological school and sometimes serve first as apprentices under established priests. Priests do not receive a fee for their services but are supported by donations from parishioners or followers. Priests often have some political power as a result of their office—the chief priest is sometimes also the head of state or is a close adviser to the chief of state—and their material well-being is a direct reflection of their position in the priestly hierarchy.

The dependence on memorized ritual both marks and protects the priest. If a shaman repeatedly fails to effect a cure, he will probably lose his following, for he has obviously lost the support of the spirits. But if a priest performs his ritual perfectly and the gods choose not to respond, the priest will usually retain his position and the ritual will preserve its assumed effectiveness. The nonresponse of the gods will be explained in terms of the people's unworthiness of supernatural favor.

Practitioners and Social Complexity More complex societies tend to have more types of religious or magical practitioners. If a society has only one type of practitioner, it is almost always a shaman; such societies tend to be nomadic or seminomadic food collectors. Societies with two types of practitioners (usually shaman healers and priests) have agriculture. Those with three types of practitioners are agriculturalists or pastoralists with political integration beyond the community (the additional practitioner type tends to be either a sorcerer or witch or a medium). Finally, societies with all four types of practitioners have agriculture, political integration beyond the community, and social classes.[57]

RELIGION AND ADAPTATION

Following Malinowski, many anthropologists take the view that religions are adaptive because they reduce the anxieties and uncertainties that afflict all peoples. We do not really know that religion is the only means of reducing anxiety and uncertainty, or even that individuals or societies *have* to reduce their anxiety and uncertainty. Still, it seems likely that certain religious beliefs and practices have directly adaptive consequences. For example, the Hindu belief in the sacred cow has seemed to many to be the very opposite of a useful or adaptive custom. Their religion does not permit Hindus to slaughter cows. Why do the Hindus retain such a belief? Why do they allow all those cows to wander around freely, defecating all over the place, and not slaughter any of them? The contrast with our own use of cows could hardly be greater.

Marvin Harris suggested that the Hindu use of cows may have beneficial consequences that some other use of cows would not have. Harris pointed out that there may be a sound economic reason for not slaughtering cattle in India. The cows, and the males they produce, provide resources that could not easily be gotten otherwise. At the same time, their wandering around to forage is no strain on the food-producing economy.

The resources provided by the cows are varied. First, a team of oxen and a plow are essential for the many small farms in India. The Indians could produce oxen with fewer cows, but to do so, they would have to devote some of their food production to feeding those cows. In the present system, they do not feed the cows, and even though poor nutrition makes the cows relatively infertile, males, which are castrated to make oxen, are still produced at no cost to the economy. Second, cow dung is essential as a cooking fuel and fertilizer. The National Council of Applied Economic Research estimated that an amount of dung equivalent to 45 million tons of coal is burned annually. Moreover, it is delivered practically to the door each day at no cost. Alternative sources of fuel, such as wood, are scarce or costly. In addition, about 340 million tons of dung are used as manure—essential in a country obliged to derive three harvests a year from its intensively cultivated land. Third, although Hindus do not eat beef, cattle that die naturally or are butchered by non-Hindus are eaten by the lower castes, who, without the upper-caste taboo against eating beef, might not get this needed protein. Fourth, the hides and horns of the cattle that die are used in India's enormous leather industry. Therefore, because the cows do not themselves consume resources needed by people and it would be impossible to provide traction, fuel, and fertilizer as cheaply by other means, the taboo against slaughtering cattle may be very adaptive.[58]

RELIGIOUS CHANGE

In any society, religious beliefs and practices change over time, but some types of change are quite dramatic. Perhaps the most dramatic is religious conversion, particularly when large numbers of people switch to a completely new religion presented by missionaries or other proselytizers. Changing religion so drastically is perplexing to many scholars of religion who believe that religious beliefs are deeply connected to one's sense of identity, one's family, one's community, and ideas about the world.[59] Within the last few centuries, conversion has sometimes followed Western expansion and exploration. Contact with Westerners and other outsiders has also produced religious change in more indirect ways. In some native societies, contact has led to a breakdown of social structure and the growth of feelings of helplessness and spiritual demoralization. *Revitalization movements* have arisen as apparent attempts to restore such societies to their former confidence and prosperity. In recent times, religious *fundamentalist* movements have flourished. Some scholars have argued that such movements are also responses to the stress of rapid social change.

A Catholic mass under open skies conducted by missionaries among the Karamojong of Uganda.

As we will see, religious change, particularly of the dramatic kind, usually does not occur in a vacuum, but is often associated with other dramatic changes—economic, political, and demographic.

Religious Conversion

The two world religions with the greatest interest now in obtaining converts have been Christianity and Islam. Christian missionaries, supported by their churches back home, have been some of the earliest Western settlers in interior regions and out-of-the-way places. Traders have been the main proselytizers of Islam. Conversion to one of the world religions has often been associated with colonization and the expansion of state societies (see the box on colonialism and religious affiliation). The presence of people from other religions does not necessarily mean that people convert to the new religion. For example, missionaries have not met with equal success in all parts of the world. In some places, large portions of the native population have converted to the new religion with great zeal. In others, missionaries have been ignored, forced to flee, or even killed. We do not fully understand why missionaries have been successful in some societies and not in others.

We now examine the process of conversion on the island of Tikopia, as an example of religious change brought about by direct contact with missionaries.

Christianity on Tikopia Tikopia was one of the few Polynesian societies to retain its traditional religious system into the first decades of the 20th century. An Anglican mission was first established on the island in 1911. With it came a deacon and the founding of two schools for about

200 pupils. By 1929, approximately half the population had converted, and in the early 1960s, almost all of Tikopia gave at least nominal allegiance to Christianity.[60]

Traditional Tikopian belief embraced a great number of gods and spirits of various ranks who inhabited the sky, the water, and the land. One god in particular—the original creator and shaper of the culture—was given a place of special importance, but he was in no way comparable to the all-powerful God of Christianity. Unlike Christianity, Tikopian religion made no claim to universality. The Tikopian gods did not rule over all creation, only over Tikopia. It was thought that if one left Tikopia, one left the gods behind.

The people of Tikopia interacted with their gods and spirits primarily through religious leaders who were also the heads of descent groups. Clan chiefs presided over rituals associated with the everyday aspects of island life, such as house construction, fishing, planting, and harvesting. The chief was expected to intercede with the gods on the people's behalf, to persuade them to bring happiness and prosperity to the group. Indeed, when conditions were good, it was assumed that the chief was doing his job well. When disaster struck, the prestige of the chief often fell in proportion. Why did the Tikopia convert to Christianity? Firth suggested several contributing factors.

First, the mission offered the people the prospect of acquiring new tools and consumer goods. Although conversion alone did not provide such benefits, attachment to the mission made them more attainable. Later, it became apparent that education, particularly in reading and writing English, was helpful in getting ahead in the outside world. Mission schooling became valued and provided a further incentive for adopting Christianity.

Second, conversion may have been facilitated by the ability of chiefs, as religious and political leaders, to bring over entire descent groups to Christianity. Should a chief decide to transfer his allegiance to Christianity, the members of his kin group usually followed him. In 1923, when Tafua, chief of the Faea district of Tikopia, converted to the new religion, he brought with him his entire group— nearly half the population of the island. The ability of the chiefs to influence their kin groups, however, was both an asset and a hindrance to missionary efforts, because some chiefs steadfastly resisted conversion.

A final blow to traditional Tikopian religion came in 1955, when a severe epidemic killed at least 200 people in a population of about 1,700. According to Firth, "the epidemic was largely interpreted as a sign of divine discrimination," because three of the outstanding non-Christian religious leaders died.[61] Subsequently, the remaining non-Christian chiefs voluntarily converted to Christianity, and so did their followers. By 1966, all Tikopia, with the exception of one old woman, had converted to the new faith.

Although many Tikopians feel their conversion to Christianity has been a unifying, revitalizing force, the changeover from one religion to another has not been without problems. Christian missionaries on Tikopia have succeeded in eliminating the traditional Tikopian population-control devices of abortion, infanticide, and male

migrants and immigrants

Colonialism and Religious Affiliation

Many of us might like to think that we belong to a particular religious group because we prefer its beliefs and practices. And that may be true for people who have chosen to switch their religious affiliation. But many religious people affiliate with the religion they grew up with, or one very much like it.

Clearly, religious affiliation is a complex issue. But one thing stands out. You are not likely to choose an affiliation you have never been exposed to. This goes for people who believe in religion and also for people who don't. Most North Americans say they are Christians. But how come?

Would so many in North America be Christians if Europeans (mostly Christian) hadn't established colonies here and elsewhere in the last 500 years? Would there be Muslims in Indonesia, the Philippines, and North Africa if Arab kingdoms hadn't established colonies in those places after the 7th century? Would there have been Hindus in Sumatra if South Asians hadn't migrated and established the Srivijayan kingdom in Sumatra before the time of Christ? Would there have been Jews in

Yemen (until their emigration to Israel 50 years ago) if King Solomon's state had not colonized in the land of the Queen of Sheba more than 2,000 years ago? An expanding state society can directly or indirectly force a change in people's religious affiliation. It is not coincidental that the new religious affiliation usually matches the dominant society's.

Religion in some form may be a cultural universal. People may worship the supernatural, pray to it for help and guidance, and even try to control it (with "lucky charms" and other magic). But religion is not the same everywhere, as is evident in this chapter. Why people convert to a major religion carried by an expanding state society is still not completely understood. Sometimes the people do not convert, or do not convert right away. Anthropologist Elizabeth Brusco has written that one primary motivation for conversion, long recognized by scholars, is the desire to maximize advantages. In recent times, missionaries have offered new beliefs and practices that may be appealing, but they have also offered what

Brusco calls "protection, access to food and other desirable goods, medical care, literacy, technology, status, and, at times, political power." Was the same true, at least somewhat, in the past? Was adopting the new religion the best way to survive colonialism and its consequences?

Even if people adopt a religion, they often change important parts of it. For example, the Lahu of southwest China became Buddhist but the Buddha became a male-female couple rather than just a male. The Lahu were a stateless society (prior to the expansion of the Han Chinese) with a strong emphasis on gender equality. By identifying Buddha with their indigenous god, Xeul Sha, the image of the Buddha was changed. According to Lahu origin myths, Xeul Sha is a male-female pair of twins. They marry and propagate humanity. The identification of Xeul Sha with Buddha means that Buddha is considered a pair of male-female gods by most Lahu Buddhist villagers.

Sources: Brusco 1996; Stevens 1996; Du 2003.

---

celibacy. It is very possible that the absence of these controls will continue to intensify population pressure. The island, with its limited capacity to support life, can ill afford this outcome. Firth summed up the situation Tikopian society faced:

> In the history of Tikopia complete conversion of the people to Christianity was formerly regarded as a solution to their problems; it is now coming to be realized that the adoption and practice of Christianity itself represents another set of problems. As the Tikopia themselves are beginning to see, to be Christian Polynesians in the modern technologically and industrially dominated world, even in the Solomon Islands, poses as many questions as it supplies answers.[62]

Unfortunately, not all native peoples have made the transition to Christianity as painlessly as the Tikopia. In fact, the record is dismal in most cases. All too frequently, missionary activity tends to destroy a society's culture

and self-respect. It offers nothing in return but an alien, repressive system of values ill suited to the people's real needs and aspirations. Phillip Mason, a critic of European evangelists in Africa, pointed out some of the psychological damage inflicted by missionary activity.[63] The missionaries repeatedly stressed sin and guilt; they used the color black to represent evil and the color white to signify good; and they showed hostility toward pagan culture. Most damaging of all was their promise that Africans, provided they adopted the European's ways, would gain access both to the European's heaven and to European society. But no matter how diligently Africans attempted to follow missionary precepts or climb the socioeconomic ladder, they were soon blocked from entry into European homes, clubs, and even churches and seminaries.

Explaining Conversion Anthropologists have just begun to try to understand religious conversion. As the box on colonialism and religious affiliation and the Tikopia case suggest, some of the motivation for switching to a new religion may have to do with economic and political advantages associated with converting to the new religion. With regard to the recent spread of Islam in Africa, Jean Ensminger suggests that Islam provided opportunities for those who wanted to engage in trade— "Islam brought a common language of trade (Arabic), a monetary system, an accounting system, and a legal code to adjudicate financial contracts and disputes."[64] These institutions were shared across ethnic groups, making it possible to engage in long-distance trade. But what increased the attractiveness of Islamic trade? Ensminger's study of the Orma, a pastoralist group in Kenya, is instructive, for despite the presence of Islam for 300 years, it did not appear to be of interest to them. The Orma chiefs did trade, but the Orma were mostly self-sufficient and the need for trade appeared to be relatively low. However, the Orma were in serious trouble after successful attacks by the Masai and Somali in the late 1800s, which almost decimated them and depleted their cattle. After 1920, as they began to recover their population somewhat and their cattle began to be replenished, there was rapid conversion to Islam, mostly led by the young, who perhaps were attracted by the economic opportunities.[65]

Loss of population and the demoralization that it brings may also have played a significant role in conversion. Daniel Reff, comparing widespread conversion to Christianity in the Roman Empire after A.D. 150 and in northern Mexico after A.D. 1593, notes the parallels in both. In both situations, there were ravaging epidemics along with the presence of Christian personnel ready to help heal the sick. In Europe, about 8 percent of the population died before smallpox epidemics subsided in A.D. 190, and population continued to decline into the Middle Ages, perhaps to half of what it was. Population losses might have been more extreme in Mexico. In northern Mexico, an estimated 75 percent of the native populations died from disease. In Europe, Christians provided charity, food, and shelter for the ill, without regard to their status. The Jesuit missions in Mexico did not have that many personnel, but they did what they could to provide food, water, and "medicine."[66] Do epidemics play a role in other places? An exploratory cross-cultural study suggests that rapid population loss, usually from introduced diseases, predicts religious conversion, particularly when people believe that their traditional gods could help them.[67] If gods could have helped but didn't and people are dying in unusual numbers, people may think that the "gods have failed." In such circumstances, it is not surprising that people would be receptive to a new religion, particularly if it is preached by missionaries who are not dying.

Revitalization

The long history of religion includes periods of strong resistance to change as well as periods of radical change. Anthropologists have been especially interested in the founding of new religions or sects. The appearance of new religions is one of the things that may happen when cultures are disrupted by contact with dominant societies. Various terms have been suggested for these religious movements— cargo cults, nativistic movements, messianic movements, millenarian cults. Wallace suggested that they are all examples of **revitalization movements,** efforts to save a culture by infusing it with a new purpose and new life.[68] We turn to examples of such movements from North America and Melanesia.

The Seneca and the Religion of Handsome Lake The Seneca reservation of the Iroquois on the Allegheny River in New York State was a place of "poverty and humiliation" by 1799.[69] Demoralized by whiskey and dispossessed from their traditional lands, unable to compete with the new technology because of illiteracy and lack of training, the Seneca were at an impasse. In this setting, Handsome Lake, the 50-year-old brother of a chief, had the first of a number of visions. In them, he met with emissaries of the Creator who showed him heaven and hell and commissioned him to revitalize Seneca religion and society. This he set out to do for the next decade and a half. As his principal text, he used the *Gaiwiio,* or "Good Word," a gospel that contains statements about the nature of religion and eternity and a code of conduct for the righteous. The *Gaiwiio* is interesting both for the influence of Quaker Christianity it clearly reveals,[70] and for the way the new material was merged with traditional Iroquois religious concepts.

The first part of the "Good Word" has three main themes, one of which is the concept of an apocalypse. Handsome Lake offered many signs by which the faithful could recognize impending, cosmic doom. Great drops of fire would rain from the skies and a veil would be cast over the earth. False prophets would appear, witch women would openly cast spells, and poisonous creatures from the underworld would seize and kill those who had rejected the *Gaiwiio.* Second, the *Gaiwiio* emphasized sin. The great sins were disbelief in the "good way," drunkenness, witchcraft, and abortion. Sins had to be confessed and repented. Finally, the *Gaiwiio* offered salvation. Salvation could be won by following a code of conduct, attending certain important traditional rites, and performing public confession.

The second part of the *Gaiwiio* sets out the code of conduct. This code seems to orient the Seneca toward advantageous European American practices without separating them from their culture. The code has five main sections:

1. **Temperance.** All Seneca leaders were fully aware of the social disorders arising out of abuse of liquor. Handsome Lake went to great lengths to illustrate and explain the harmfulness of alcohol.

2. **Peace and social unity.** Seneca leaders were to cease their futile bickering, and all were to be united in their approach to the larger society.

3. **Preservation of tribal lands.** Handsome Lake, fearing the piecemeal alienation of Seneca lands, was far ahead of his contemporaries in demanding a halt in land sales to non-Seneca.

Ogallala Sioux performing the Ghost Dance at the Pine Ridge Indian Agency, South Dakota. Illustration by Frederic Remington, 1890. The Granger Collection.

A revitalization movement that became known as the Ghost Dance spread eastward from the Northwest from the 1870s to the 1890s. It was generally believed that, if people did the dance correctly, ghosts would come to life with sufficient resources to allow the people to return to their old ways, and, as a result of some cataclysm, the whites would disappear.

Source: Ogallala Sioux performing the Ghost Dance at the Pine Ridge Indian Agency, South Dakota. Illustration by Frederic Remington, 1890.

4. **Proacculturation (favoring external culture traits).** Though individual property and trading for profit were prohibited, the acquisition of literacy in English was encouraged so that people would be able to read and understand treaties and to avoid being cheated.

5. **Domestic morality.** Sons were to obey their fathers, mothers should avoid interfering with daughters' marriages, and husbands and wives should respect the sanctity of their marriage vows.

Handsome Lake's teaching seems to have led to a renaissance among the Seneca. Temperance was widely accepted, as were schooling and new farming methods. By 1801, corn yields had been increased tenfold, new crops (oats, potatoes, flax) had been introduced, and public health and hygiene had improved considerably. Handsome Lake himself acquired great power among his people. He spent the remainder of his life fulfilling administrative duties, acting as a representative of the Iroquois in Washington, and preaching his gospel to neighboring tribes. By the time of Handsome Lake's death in 1815, the Seneca clearly had undergone a dramatic rebirth, attributable at least in part to the new religion. Later in the century, some of Handsome Lake's disciples founded a church in his name that, despite occasional setbacks and political disputes, survives to this day.

Although many scholars believe cultural stress gives rise to these new religious movements, it is still important to understand exactly what the stresses are and how strong they have to become before a new movement emerges. Do different kinds of stresses produce different kinds of movements? And does the nature of the movement depend on the cultural elements already present? Let us consider some theory and research on the causes of the millenarian cargo cults that began to appear in Melanesia from about 1885 on.

Cargo Cults The *cargo cults* can be thought of as religious movements "in which there is an expectation of, and preparation for, the coming of a period of supernatural bliss."[71] Thus, an explicit belief of the cargo cults was the notion that some liberating power would bring all the Western goods (cargo in pidgin English) the people might want. For example, around 1932, on Buka in the Solomon Islands, the leaders of a cult prophesied that a tidal wave would sweep away the villages and a ship would arrive

current research and issues

One Appeal of Religion May Be the Wish for a Better World

There are many religions in the United States today, and new sects, often derisively called cults, emerge regularly. Few of us realize that nearly all of the major churches or religions in the world began as minority sects or cults. Indeed, some of the most established and prestigious Protestant churches were considered radical social movements at first. For example, what we now know as the United Church of Christ, which includes the Congregational Church, was founded by radicals in England who wanted church governance to be in the hands of the local congregation. Many of these radicals became the people we call Pilgrims, who had to flee to the New World. But they were very fundamentalist in their beliefs; for example, as late as the 1820s, Congregationalist-dominated towns in Connecticut prohibited celebrations of Christmas outside of church because such celebrations were not mentioned in the Bible. Nowadays, Congregationalists are among the most liberal Protestants.

We should not be surprised to learn that most of the various Protestant churches today, including some considered very conservative, began as militant sects that set out to achieve a better world. After all, that's why we call them "Protestant." At first, the rebellion was against Rome and the Catholic Church. Later, sects developed in opposition to church and government hierarchies. And remember that Christianity itself began as a radical group in the hinterland of the Roman Empire. So new sects or cults were probably always political and social, as well as religious, movements. Recall that the word *millennium*, as used in discussions of religious movements, refers to a wished-for or expected future time when human life and society will be perfect and free of troubles; the world will then be prosperous, happy, and peaceful. Nowadays, the wish for a better world may or may not be religiously inspired. Some people who seek a more perfect world believe that humans alone must achieve it.

How should we categorize this wish for a better world? Should we call it "conservative" because the imagined world may have existed in the past? If the imagined world does not yet exist, is it "radical" to believe it can be achieved? Maybe the wish for a more perfect world is neither conservative nor radical. Maybe it is just that people who are not satisfied with the world as it is think that something can be done to improve things, with or without divine assistance. However it will come, the "millennium" will be different from now, and better.

Ideas about the millennium, and the origins of new cults and religions, might best be viewed then as human hopes: Which ones do people have? Do they vary from culture to culture, and why? Are some hopes universal? And how might they be achieved?

Sources: Stark 1985; Trompf 1990.

---

with iron, axes, food, tobacco, cars, and arms. Work in the gardens ceased, and wharves and docks were built for the expected cargo.[72]

What may explain such cults? Peter Worsley suggested that an important factor in the rise of cargo cults and millenarian movements in general is the existence of oppression—in the case of Melanesia, colonial oppression. He suggested that the reactions in Melanesia took religious rather than political forms because they were a way of pulling together people who previously had no political unity and who lived in small, isolated social groups.[73] Other scholars, such as David Aberle, suggested that *relative deprivation* is more important than oppression in explaining the origins of cults; when people feel that they could have more, and they have less than what they used to have or less than others, they may be attracted to new cults.[74] Consistent with Aberle's general interpretation, Bruce Knauft's comparative study of cargo cults found that such cults were more important in Melanesian societies that had had decreasing cultural contact with the West, and presumably *decreasing* contact with valued goods, within the year prior to the cult's emergence.[75]

Fundamentalism For some scholars, one of the main attributes of fundamentalism is the literal interpretation of a sacred scripture. But recent scholars have suggested that fundamentalist movements need to be understood more broadly as religious or political movements that appear in response to the rapidly changing environment of the modern world. In this broader view, fundamentalism occurs in many religions, including those of Christians, Jews, Islamics, Sikhs, Buddhists, and Hindus. Although each movement is different in content, Richard Antoun suggests that fundamentalist movements have the following elements in common: the selective use of scripture to inspire and assert proof of particular certainties; the quest for purity and traditional values in what is viewed as an impure world; active opposition to what is viewed as a permissive secular society and a nation-state that separates religion from the state; and an incorporation of selected modern elements such as television to promote the movements' aims.[76]

Fundamentalist religious movements do appear to be linked to the anxieties and uncertainties associated with culture change in general and globalization in particular. Many people in many countries are repelled by new behaviors and attitudes, and react in a way that celebrates the old. As Judith Nagata puts it, fundamentalism is a "quest for certainty in an uncertain world."[77] Protestant fundamentalism flourished at the end of the 19th century in the United States as immigrant groups came into the country in great numbers and the country became industrialized and increasingly urbanized. The fundamentalists denounced foreign influences, the decline of the Bible as a guide to moral behavior, the teaching of evolution, and they succeeded in getting the country to prohibit the sale of alcoholic beverages. Recent Islamic fundamentalist movements seem to be responses to a different kind of challenge to the social order—increasing Westernization. Westernization may have first arrived in conjunction with colonial rule. Later, it may have been promoted by Western-educated native elites.[78] Antoun suggests that fundamentalist movements deliberately push certain practices because the leaders know they will outrage the secular opposition. Examples in recent Islamic fundamentalist movements are the extreme punishment of cutting off a hand for theft and requiring women to be covered by veils or head-to-toe covering in public.[79] Unfortunately, in present-day discourse, fundamentalism tends to be equated by Westerners with Islam itself. But, in historical perspective, all major religions have had fundamentalist movements in times of rapid culture change.

If the recent as well as distant past is any guide, we can expect religious belief and practice to be revitalized periodically, particularly during times of stress. Change associated with globalization appears to be accompanied by the rise of fundamentalist religious movements. Paradoxically, globalization has increased the spread of world religions but it has also increased the worldwide interest in shamanism and other features of religion that are different from the dominant religions. Thus, we can expect the world to continue to have religious variation.

SUMMARY ● ○ ○

1. Religion is any set of attitudes, beliefs, and practices pertaining to supernatural power. Such beliefs may vary within a culture as well as among societies, and they may change over time.

2. Religious beliefs are evident in all known cultures and are inferred from artifacts associated with *Homo sapiens* since at least 60,000 years ago.

3. Theories to account for the universality of religion suggest that humans create religion in response to certain universal needs or conditions, including a need for understanding, reversion to childhood feelings, anxiety or uncertainty, and a need for community.

4. There are wide variations in religious beliefs. Societies vary in the number and kinds of supernatural entities in which they believe. There may be impersonal supernatural forces (e.g., mana and taboo), supernatural beings of nonhuman origin (gods and spirits), and supernatural beings of human origin (ghosts and ancestor spirits). The religious belief system of a society may include any or all such entities.

5. Gods and spirits may be unpredictable or predictable, aloof from or interested in human affairs, helpful or punishing. In some societies, all gods are equal in rank; in others, there is a hierarchy of prestige and power among gods and spirits, just as among the humans in those societies.

6. A monotheistic religion is one in which there is one high god, as the creator of the universe or the director of events (or both); all other supernatural beings are either subordinate to, or function as alternative manifestations of, this god. A high god is generally found in societies with a high level of political development.

7. Faced with ignorance, pain, and injustice, people frequently explain events by claiming intervention by the gods. Such intervention has also been sought by people who hope it will help them achieve their own ends. The gods are likely to punish the immoral behavior of people in societies that have considerable differences in wealth.

8. Various methods have been used to attempt communication with the supernatural. Among them are prayer, taking drugs or otherwise affecting the body and mind, simulation, feasts, and sacrifices.

9. When people believe that their actions can compel the supernatural to act in a particular and intended way, anthropologists refer to the belief and related practice as magic. Sorcery and witchcraft are attempts to make the spirits work harm against people.

10. Almost all societies have part-time or full-time religious or magical practitioners. Recent cross-cultural research suggests that there are four major types of practitioners: shamans, sorcerers or witches, mediums, and priests. The number of types of practitioners seems to vary with degree of cultural complexity: The more complex the society, the more types of practitioners.

11. The history of religion includes periods of strong resistance to change and periods of radical change. Perhaps the most dramatic is religious conversion, particularly when large numbers of people switch to a completely new religion presented by missionaries or other proselytizers. In some native societies, contact has led to a breakdown of social structure and the growth of feelings of helplessness and spiritual demoralization. *Revitalization movements* have arisen as apparent attempts to restore such societies to their former confidence and prosperity. In recent times, religious *fundamentalist* movements have flourished. Religious change, particularly of the dramatic kind, usually does not occur in a vacuum, but is often associated with other dramatic changes—economic, political, and demographic.

GLOSSARY TERMS ○ ● ○

ancestor spirits	priests
animatism	religion
animism	revitalization
divination	movements
ghosts	rituals
gods	shaman
magic	sorcery
mana	spirits
mediums	supernatural
monotheistic	taboo
polytheistic	witchcraft

CRITICAL QUESTIONS ○ ○ ●

1. How does your conception of God compare with beliefs about supernatural beings in other religious systems?

2. What do you think is the future of religion? Explain your answer.

3. Could any of the religious practices you know about be classified as magic? Are they associated with anxiety-arousing situations?

PEARSON
myanthrolab

Read the chapter by Debra Picchi titled "Bakairí: The Death of an Indian" on MyAnthroLab, and answer the following questions:

1. How come the Bakairí did not ask whether Western medicine works, but Westerners asked whether shamanism works?

2. Why would a shaman be able to settle disputes?

NOTES ● ○ ○

1. Tylor 1979.
2. Marett 1909.
3. Guthrie 1993.
4. Freud 1967/1939; Badcock 1988, 126–27, 133–36.
5. Malinowski 1939, 959; Malinowski 1954, 50–51.
6. W. James 1902.
7. Jung 1938.
8. Fromm 1950.
9. Maslow 1964.
10. Poggie et al. 1976; Poggie and Pollnac 1988.
11. Durkheim 1961/1912.
12. Swanson 1969, 1–31.
13. A. Wallace 1966, 60–61.
14. Malefijt 1968, 153.
15. Ray 1954, 172–89.
16. Rosenblatt et al. 1976, 51.
17. Ibid., 55.
18. Swanson 1969, 97–108; see also Sheils 1975.
19. Middleton 1971, 488.
20. Spiro and D'Andrade 1958.
21. Lambert et al. 1959; Rohner 1975, 108.
22. H. G. Barnett 1960, 79–85.
23. Swanson 1969, 56.
24. Ibid., 55–81; see also W. D. Davis 1971. Peregrine (1996, 84–112) replicated Swanson's finding for North American societies.
25. Textor 1967; R. Underhill 1975.
26. Geertz 1966.
27. Swanson 1969, 153–74.
28. Bunzel 1971.
29. Gossen 1979.
30. Dickson et al. 2005.
31. Stark and Finke 2000, 107–08.
32. A. Wallace 1966, 52–67.
33. Winkelman 1986b, 178–83.
34. Bourguignon 1973.
35. Bourguignon and Evascu 1977; Winkelman 1986b, 196–98.
36. Kehoe and Giletti 1981.
37. Raybeck 1998, referring to Raybeck et al. 1989.
38. Bourguignon 2004, 572.
39. Winkleman and Peck 2004.
40. O. K. Moore 1957.
41. Sheils 1980.
42. Winkelman and Baker 2010, 293–96 and references therein.
43. Evans-Pritchard 1979, 362–66.
44. Swanson 1969, 150; see also H. R. Trevor-Roper 1971, 444–49.
45. Swanson 1969, 150–51.
46. Caporael 1976; Matossian 1982; and Matossian 1989, 70–80. For possible reasons to dismiss the ergot theory, see Spanos 1983.
47. Harner 1972.
48. B. B. Whiting 1950, 36–37; see also Swanson 1969, 137–52, 240–41.
49. Winkelman 1986a.
50. Ibid., 28–29.
51. Knecht 2003, 11.
52. Harner and Doore 1987, 3, 8–9; Noll 1987, 49; Krippner 1987, 128.
53. De Laguna 1972, 701C.
54. See Krippner 1987, 126-27; Noll 1987, 49–50.
55. Winkelman 1986a, 27–28.
56. Ibid., 27.
57. Ibid., 35–37.
58. M. Harris 1966.
59. Buckser and Glazier 2003; Rambo 2003.
60. Discussion is based on Firth 1970.
61. Ibid., 387.
62. Ibid., 418.
63. Mason 1962.
64. Ensminger 1997, 7.
65. Ibid.
66. Reff 2005; see also McNeill 1998 and Stark 1996.
67. C. R. Ember 1982.
68. A. Wallace 1966, 30.
69. A. Wallace 1970, 239.
70. The Quakers, long-time neighbors and trusted advisers of the Seneca, took pains not to interfere with Seneca religion, principles, and attitudes.
71. Worsley 1957, 12.
72. Ibid., 11, 115.
73. Ibid., 122.
74. Aberle 1971.
75. Knauft 1978.
76. Antoun 2001.
77. Nagata 2001.
78. Antoun 2001, 17–18.
79. Ibid., 45.

Applied, Practicing,
and Medical Anthropology

Applied, Practicing, and Medical Anthropology

nthropology is no longer a merely academic subject. A large number of anthropologists in the United States are applied and practicing anthropologists. Some estimates suggest that more than half of those with graduate degrees in anthropology are now employed outside of colleges and universities.[1] The fact that so many organizations hire anthropologists suggests an increasing realization that anthropology, what it has discovered and can discover about humans, is useful. Anthropologists who call themselves applied or practicing anthropologists work for a large variety of organizations, government agencies, international development agencies, private consulting firms, public health organizations, medical schools, public interest law firms, community development agencies, charitable foundations, and profit-seeking corporations (see the box on anthropology and business).

● ○ ●

Applied or **practicing anthropology** as a profession is explicitly concerned with making anthropological knowledge useful. Applied or practicing anthropologists may be involved in one or more phases of a project: assembling relevant knowledge, developing plans and policies, assessing the likely social and environmental impacts, implementation, and evaluating the project and its effects.[2] Anthropologists are most often involved in gathering information, rather than constructing policy or initiating action.[3] The organizations that hire the applied anthropologists usually set policy and have staff to execute projects. However, anthropologists are increasingly finding themselves involved in policy making and action. The field of applied or practicing anthropology is very diverse. In this chapter, we first focus on general issues: ethics; evaluating the effects of planned change; and the difficulties of implementing change. In the course of this discussion, we cover a variety of projects, mostly development projects. We then turn to several other kinds of applications: *cultural resource management*, the "social impact" studies required in connection with many government or private programs, and *forensic anthropology*—the use of physical anthropology to help identify human remains and assist in solving crimes. The chapter concludes with an extensive discussion of the application of anthropological knowledge to the study of health and illness.

ETHICS OF APPLIED ANTHROPOLOGY

Anthropologists have usually studied people who are disadvantaged—by imperialism, colonialism, and other forms of exploitation—and so it is no wonder that we care about the people's lives we have shared. But caring is not enough to improve others' lives. We may need basic research that allows us to understand how a condition might be successfully treated. A particular proposed "improvement" might actually not be an improvement; well-meaning efforts have sometimes produced harmful consequences. And even if we know that a change would be an improvement, there is still the problem of how to make

As part of a study funded by USAID, a multidisciplinary team consisting of anthropologists, engineers and agricultural experts from the United States met with villagers in Senegal to assess how the Manantali Dam might affect them.

Michael Horowitz

that change happen. The people to be affected may not want to change. Is it ethical to try to persuade them? And, conversely, is it ethical *not* to try? Applied anthropologists must take all of these matters into consideration in determining whether and how to act in response to a perceived need.

Anthropology as a profession has adopted certain principles of responsibility. Above all, an anthropologist's first responsibility is to those who are being studied; everything should be done to ensure that their welfare and dignity will be protected. Anthropologists also have a responsibility to those who will read about their research; research findings should be reported openly and truthfully.[4] But because applied anthropology often deals with planning and implementing changes in some population, ethical responsibilities can become complicated. Perhaps the most important ethical question is: Will the change truly benefit the potentially affected population?

In May 1946, the Society for Applied Anthropology established a committee to draw up a specific code of ethics for professional applied anthropologists. After many meetings and revisions, a statement on ethical responsibilities was finally adopted in 1948, and in 1983, the statement was revised.[5] According to the code, the targeted community should be included as much as possible in the formulation of policy,

so that people in the community may know in advance how the program will affect them. Perhaps the most important aspect of the code is the pledge not to recommend or take any action that is harmful to the interests of the community. The National Association for the Practice of Anthropology goes further: If the work the employer expects of the employee violates the ethical principles of the profession, the practicing anthropologist has the obligation to try to change those practices or, if change cannot be brought about, to withdraw from the work.[6]

Ethical issues are often complicated. Thayer Scudder described the situation of Gwembe Tonga villagers who were relocated after a large dam was built in the Zambezi Valley of central Africa. Economic conditions improved during the 1960s and early 1970s, as the people increasingly produced goods and services for sale. But then conditions deteriorated. By 1980, the villagers were in a miserable state; rates of mortality, alcoholism, theft, assault, and murder were up. Why? One reason was that they had cut back on producing their own food in favor of producing for the world market. Such a strategy works well when world market prices are high; however, when prices fall, so does the standard of living.[7] The situation described by Scudder illustrates the ethical dilemma for many

applied anthropology

Anthropology and Business

Only relatively recently have business-people come to realize that anthropologists have useful knowledge to contribute, particularly with regard to the globalization of trade, the increase in international investments and joint ventures, and the spread of multinational corporations. What can anthropology offer? One of the most important contributions of anthropology is the understanding of how much culture can influence relationships between people of different cultures. For example, anthropologists know that communication is much more than the formal understanding of another language. People in some countries, such as the United States, expect explicit, straightforward verbal messages, but people in other countries are more indirect in their verbal messages. In Japan and China, for example, negative messages are less likely than messages expressing politeness and harmony. Many Eastern cultures have ways of saying no without saying the word.

It is also important to understand that different cultures may have different values. People in the United States place a high value on the individual, but the importance of relationships with others may take precedence over individual needs in other places. People in the United States emphasize the future, youth, informality, and competitiveness, but the emphases in other societies are often the opposite. In any business arrangement, perhaps no difference is as salient as the value a culture places on time. As we say, "Time is money." If a meeting is arranged and the other person is late, say, 45 minutes, people from the United States consider it rude; but such a delay is well within the range of acceptable behavior in many South American countries.

Anthropologists have helped businesses become aware of their own "cultures" (sometimes referred to as *organizational cultures*). The organizational culture of a business may interfere with the acceptance of new kinds of workers, or it may interfere with changing business needs. If parts of that culture need to be changed, it is necessary first to identify what the culture involves and to understand how and why it developed the way it did. Anthropologists know how to identify cultural patterns on the basis of systematic observation and interviewing individuals.

Anthropologist Jill Kleinberg studied six Japanese-owned firms in the United States to understand the impact of both the larger culture and the organizational culture of the workplace. All six firms employed both Japanese and Americans, although the Japanese dominated the managerial positions. The main goal of the study was to discover why there was considerable tension in the six firms. Kleinberg's first order of business was to interview people about their views of work and their jobs. She found clear differences between the Japanese and the American employees that seemed to reflect broader cultural differences. Americans wanted a clear definition of the job and its attached responsibilities, and they also wanted their job titles, authority, rights, and pay to match closely. The Japanese, on the other hand, emphasized the need to be flexible in their responsibilities as well as their tasks. They also felt that part of their responsibility was to help their co-workers. Americans were uncomfortable because the Japanese managers did not indicate exactly what the workers were supposed to do; even if there was a job description, the manager did not appear to pay attention to it. Americans were given little information, were left out of decision making, and were frustrated by the lack of opportunity to advance. The Japanese thought that the Americans were too hard to manage, too concerned with money and authority, and too concerned with their own interests.

Dissatisfaction is a problem in any business. Absenteeism, high turnover, and lack of incentive on the job all detract from job performance and business capability. Kleinberg recommended giving all employees more information about the company as well as conducting training sessions about cross-cultural differences in business cultures. She also recommended making the Japanese philosophy of management more explicit during the hiring process so that the company would be able to find Americans who were comfortable with that philosophy. But she also suggested that the managerial structure be somewhat "Americanized" so that American employees could feel at ease. Finally, she recommended that Americans be given more managerial positions and contact with their Japanese counterparts overseas. These suggestions might not eliminate all problems, but they would increase mutual understanding and trust.

In a way, then, as Andrew Miracle notes, the work of the practicing anthropologist is similar to the shaman's in traditional societies. The people who call on shamans for help believe in their abilities to help, and the shaman tries to find ways to empower the client to think positively. To be sure, there are profound differences between shamans and applied anthropologists. Perhaps the most important is that applied anthropologists use research, not trance or magic, to effect an organizational cure. Like shamans, however, applied anthropologists must make an understandable diagnosis and help clients see the way to health and restored power.

Sources: Ferraro 2002; Kleinberg 1994; Miracle 2009.

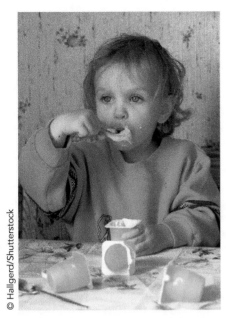

Businesses and consulting companies are doing more ethnographic research. Such research in the United States among families during the morning suggests that "breakfast" has become an intermittent series of snacks throughout the morning as families struggle with their time schedules and finding the right foods for their children.

applied anthropologists. As he said: "So how is it that I can still justify working for the agencies that fund such projects?" He points out that large-scale projects are almost impossible to stop. The anthropologist can choose to stand on the sidelines and complain or try to influence the project to benefit the affected population as much as possible.[8]

The problem described by Scudder comes about in part because the anthropologist is not often involved until after a decision is made to go ahead with a change program. This situation has begun to change as applied anthropologists are increasingly asked to participate in earlier stages of the planning process. Anthropologists are also increasingly asked to help in projects initiated by the affected party. Such requests may range from help in solving problems in corporate organizations to helping Native Americans with land claims. Because the project is consistent with the wishes of the affected population, the results are not likely to put the anthropologist into an ethical dilemma.

When physical anthropologists and archaeologists work with skeletal and even fossil materials, the ethical complications can become extremely complex. Consider the case of "Kennewick Man," a 9,200-year-old skeleton found in July 1996, along the Columbia River in Washington State. Before anthropologists could study the skeleton, the U.S. Army Corps of Engineers decided to turn the remains over to the Umatilla Indians, as the remains were found on Corps land within their reservation. The physical anthropologists and archaeologists who wanted to study this very old skeleton faced an ethical quandary: A group claiming to be related to the individual did not

want the study to be undertaken, but, without the study, the group's claim of relationship could not be firmly established.[9] The physical anthropologists and archaeologists filed a lawsuit under the Native American Graves Protection and Repatriation Act of 1900, which provides absolute protection to Native American graves on federal land, and which makes it a felony to collect, possess, or transfer human remains of known affinity to an existing Native American culture, except if approved by the members of that culture.[10]

At the core of the legal case was this question: To whom does this skeleton belong? If this is an individual who is related to contemporary Native Americans, then do the Umatilla get to speak for all Native American groups, even though 9,000 years separate them? Or should other Native American groups, who may also be descended from this individual or his group, also have a say in what happens? If this is an individual who appears not to be related to contemporary Native Americans, then should the U.S. government decide what happens to his remains? Underlying these questions was a deeper struggle between anthropologists and Native Americans over historic preservation and whose wishes and ideas carry the most weight. Archaeologists and physical anthropologists feel ethical responsibilities that can be in conflict when dealing with human remains. As part of the archaeological record, archaeologists and physical anthropologists have an ethical responsibility to protect and preserve human remains. As anthropologists, they have the ethical responsibility to consult with and follow the wishes of local groups with whom they are working. The "Kennewick Man" case highlights this ethical conflict, for which there seems no easy answer.

EVALUATING THE EFFECTS OF PLANNED CHANGE

The decision as to whether a proposed change would benefit the affected population is not always easy to make. In certain cases, as when improved medical care is involved, the benefits offered to the target group would seem to be unquestionable—we all feel sure that health is better than illness. However, what about the long-term effects? Consider a public health innovation such as inoculation against disease. Once the inoculation program was begun, the number of children surviving would probably increase. But will there be enough food for the additional population? Given the level of technology, capital, and land resources possessed by the population, there might not be enough resources to feed more people. Thus, the death rate, because of starvation, might rise to its previous level and perhaps even exceed it. Without additional changes to increase the food supply, the inoculation program in the long term might merely change the causes of death. This example shows that, even if a program of planned change has beneficial consequences in the short run, a great deal of thought and investigation has to be given to its long-term effects.

383

Debra Picchi raised questions about the long-term effects on the Bakairí Indians of a program by the Brazilian National Indian Foundation (FUNAI) to produce rice with machine technology.[11] The Bakairí of the Mato Grosso region largely practice slash-and-burn horticulture in gallery forests along rivers, with supplementary cattle raising, fishing, and hunting. In the early part of the 20th century, their population had declined to 150 people and they were given a relatively small reserve, much of it parched and infertile (*cerrado*). When the Bakairí population began to increase, FUNAI introduced a scheme to plant rice on formerly unused *cerrado* land, using machinery, insecticides, and fertilizer. FUNAI paid the costs for the first year and expected that the scheme would be self-supporting by the third year. The project did not go so well because FUNAI did not deliver all the equipment needed and did not provide adequate advice. Only half the expected rice was produced. Still, it was more food than the Bakairí had previously, so the program should have been beneficial to them.

But there were unanticipated negative side effects. Using *cerrado* land for agriculture reduced the area on which cattle could be grazed; cattle are an important source of high-quality protein. Mechanization also makes the Bakairí more dependent on cash for fuel, insecticides, fertilizer, and repairs. But cash is hard to come by. Only some individuals can be hired—usually men with outside experience who have the required knowledge of machinery. So the cash earned in the now-mechanized agriculture goes mainly to a relatively small number of people, creating new inequalities of income.

The benefits of programs or applied efforts are sometimes obvious. For example, Haiti has experienced serious deforestation. The process began in colonial times when the Spanish exported wood and the French cleared forests to grow sugarcane, coffee, and indigo. After Haiti's independence, foreign lumber companies continued to cut and sell hardwood. Wood is needed by the local population for fuel and for construction, but rapid population increases have increased the demand for fuel and wood, and the trees were rapidly diminishing. The loss of tree cover also speeds up erosion of topsoil. Forestry experts, environmentalists, and anthropologists all agree about the need to stop this trend. How to bring about the appropriate change is not so easy. The poorer people become, the more likely they are to cut down trees to sell.[12]

These failures were not the fault of anthropologists—indeed, most instances of planned change by governments and other agencies usually have begun without the input of anthropologists at all. Applied anthropologists have played an important role in pointing out the problems with programs like these that fail to evaluate long-term consequences. Such evaluations are an important part of convincing governments and other agencies to ask for anthropological help in the first place. Ironically, failure experiences are learning experiences: Applied anthropologists who study previous examples of planned change can often learn a great deal about what is likely or not likely to be beneficial in the long run.

DIFFICULTIES IN INSTITUTING PLANNED CHANGE

After numerous reforestation projects failed in Haiti, an anthropologist, Gerald Murray, was asked to help design a program that would work.[13] Understanding why previous projects failed was the first step in helping Murray design an effective project. One problem seems to have been that previous projects were run through the government's Ministry of Agriculture. The seedling trees that were given away were referred to as "the state's trees." So, when project workers told farmers not to cut the new trees down so as to protect the environment, farmers took this statement to mean that the land on which the trees were planted might be considered government land, which the farmers could not care less about. In the project proposed by Murray, private voluntary organizations rather than the Haitian government were used to distribute trees and the farmers were told that they were the tree owners. Ownership included the right to cut the trees and sell the wood, just as they could sell crops. In previous projects, farmers were given heavy, hard-to-transport seedlings that took a long time to mature. They were told to plant in a large communal woodlot, an idea inconsistent with the more individualistic Haitian land tenure arrangements. In the new plan, the tree seedlings given away were fast-growing species that matured in as little as four years. In addition, the new seedlings were very small and could be planted quickly. Perhaps most important of all, the new trees could be planted in borders or interspersed with other crops, interfering little with traditional crop patterns. To Murray's great surprise, by the end of two years, 2,500 Haitian households had planted 3 million seedlings. Over 20 years, the estimate is that over a 100 million trees were planted and over 350,000 farm families were involved in the project, more than 40 percent of rural households.[14] Also, farmers were not rushing to cut down trees. Because growing trees do not spoil, farmers were postponing their cutting and sales until they needed cash. So even though farmers were told that it was all right to cut down trees, a statement contrary to the message of previous reforestation projects, the landscape was filling up with trees.

People cut down trees in Haiti for firewood and to clear fields, resulting in severe deforestation. The need for reforestation is clear, but how to bring about change was not so clear.

Murray's lengthy participant observation and interviewing had helped him predict what might overcome the previous implementation difficulties and fit in with the Haitian farmers' needs. The idea that wood could be an important marketable cash crop was much more consistent with farmers' existing behavior—they already sold crops for cash when they needed it. The difference now was that, instead of cutting down naturally grown wood, they were raising wood just as they raised other crops.

Whether a program of planned change can be successfully implemented depends largely on whether the people want the proposed change and like the proposed program. Before an attempt can be made at cultural innovation, the innovators must determine whether the population is aware of the benefits of the proposed change. Lack of awareness can be a temporary barrier to solving the problem at hand. For example, health workers have often had difficulty convincing people that they were becoming ill because something was wrong with their water supply. Many people do not believe that disease can be transmitted by water. At other times, the population is perfectly aware of the problem. A case in point involved Taiwanese women who were introduced to family-planning methods beginning in the 1960s. The women knew they were having more children than they wanted or could easily afford, and they wanted to control their birth rate. They offered no resistance—they merely had to be given the proper devices and instructions, and the birth rate quickly fell to a more desirable, and more manageable, level.[15]

Overcoming Resistance

Many change projects experience resistance, and most of the time the change agents try to figure out how to overcome the resistance. But not all proposed change programs are beneficial to the recipients. Sometimes resistance is rational. Applied anthropologists have pointed to cases where the judgment of the affected population has been better than that of the agents of change. One such example occurred during a Venezuelan government–sponsored program to give infants powdered milk. The mothers rejected the milk, even though it was free, on the grounds that it implied that the mothers' milk was no good.[16] But who is to say that the resistance was not in fact intuitively smart, reflecting an awareness that such a milk program would not benefit the children? Medical research now indicates quite clearly that mothers' milk is far superior to powdered milk or formula. First, human milk best supplies the nutrients needed for human development. Second, it is now known that the mother, through her milk, is able to transmit antibodies (disease resistances) to the baby. And third, nursing delays ovulation and usually increases the spacing between births.[17]

The switchover to powdered milk and formula in many underdeveloped areas has been nothing short of a disaster, resulting in increased malnutrition and misery. For one thing, powdered milk must be mixed with water, but if the water and the bottles are not sterilized, more sickness is introduced. Then, too, if powdered milk has to be purchased, mothers without cash are forced to dilute the milk to stretch it. And if a mother feeds her baby formula or powder for even a short time, the process is tragically irreversible, for her own milk dries up and she cannot return to breast-feeding even if she wants to.

As the Venezuelan example suggests, individuals may be able to resist proposed medical or health projects because acceptance is ultimately a personal matter. Large development projects planned by powerful governments or agencies rarely are stoppable, but even they can be resisted successfully. The Kayapo of the Xingu River region of Brazil were able to cancel a plan by the Brazilian government to build dams along the river for hydroelectric power. The Kayapo gained international attention when some of their leaders appeared on North American and European television and then successfully organized a protest in 1989, by members of several tribal groups. Their success seemed to come in part from their ability to present themselves to the international community as guardians of the rain forest—an image that resonated with international environmental organizations that supported their cause. Although to outsiders it might seem that the Kayapo want their way of life to remain as it was, the Kayapo are not opposed to all change. In fact, they want greater access to medical care, other government services, and manufactured goods from outside.[18]

Even if a project is beneficial to a population, it may still meet with resistance, as the tree reforestation project in Haiti illustrated. Factors that may hinder acceptance can be divided roughly into three, sometimes overlapping, categories: *cultural, social,* and *psychological* barriers.

Cultural barriers are shared behaviors, attitudes, and beliefs that tend to impede the acceptance of an innovation. For example, members of different societies may view gift giving in different ways. Particularly in commercialized societies, things received for nothing are often believed to be worthless. When the government of Colombia instituted a program of giving seedling orchard trees to

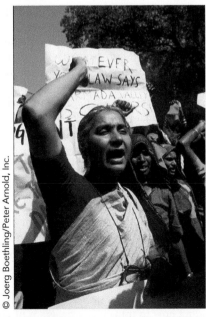

Medha Patkar leading a protest rally in New Delhi against Narmada dams.

farmers to increase fruit production, the farmers showed virtually no interest in the seedlings, many of which proceeded to die of neglect. When the government realized that the experiment had apparently failed, it began to charge each farmer a nominal fee for the seedlings. Soon the seedlings became immensely popular and fruit production increased.[19] Other examples of cultural resistance to change, which we discuss more when we discuss medical anthropology, are beliefs about sex that make it difficult for people to follow medical guidelines for safer sex.

It is very important for agents of change to understand what the shared beliefs and attitudes are. First, indigenous cultural concepts or knowledge can sometimes be used effectively to enhance educational programs. For instance, in a program in Haiti to prevent child mortality from diarrhea, change agents used the terminology for traditional native herbal tea remedies (*rafrechi*, or cool refreshment) to identify the new oral rehydration therapy, which is a very successful medical treatment. In native belief, diarrhea is a "hot" illness and appropriate remedies have to have cooling properties.[20] Second, even if indigenous beliefs are not helpful to the campaign, not paying attention to contrary beliefs can undermine the campaign. But uncovering contrary beliefs is not easy, particularly when they do not emerge in ordinary conversation.

The acceptance of planned change may also depend on social factors. Research suggests that acceptance is more likely if the change agent and the target or potential adopter are similar socially. But change agents may have higher social status and more education than the people they are trying to influence. So change agents may work more with higher-status individuals because they are more likely to accept new ideas. If lower-status individuals also have to be reached, change agents of lower status may have to be employed.[21]

Finally, acceptance may depend on psychological factors—that is, how the individuals perceive both the innovation and the agents of change. In the course of trying to encourage women in the southeastern United States to breast-feed rather than bottle-feed their infants, researchers discovered a number of reasons why women were reluctant to breast-feed their infants, even though they heard it was healthier. Many women did not have confidence that they would produce enough milk for their babies; they were embarrassed about breast-feeding in public; and their family and friends had negative attitudes.[22] In designing an educational program, change agents may have to address such psychological concerns directly.

Discovering and Utilizing Local Channels of Influence

In planning a project involving cultural change, the administrator of the project should find out what the normal channels of influence are in the population. In most communities, there are preestablished networks for communication, as well as people of high prestige or influence who are looked to for guidance and direction. An understanding of such channels of influence is extremely valuable when deciding how to introduce a program of change. In addition, it is useful to know at what times, and in what sorts of situations, one channel is likely to be more effective in spreading information and approval than another.

An example of the effective use of local channels of influence occurred when an epidemic of smallpox broke out in the Kalahandi district of the state of Orissa in India. The efforts of health workers to vaccinate villagers against the disease were consistently resisted. The villagers, naturally suspicious and fearful of these strange men with their equally strange medical equipment, were unwilling to offer themselves, and particularly their babies, to the peculiar experiments the strangers wished to perform. Afraid of the epidemic, the villagers appealed for help to their local priest, whose opinions on such matters they trusted. The priest went into a trance, explaining that the illness was the result of the goddess Thalerani's anger with the people. She could be appeased, he continued, only by massive feasts, offerings, and other demonstrations of the villagers' worship of her. Realizing that the priest was the village's major opinion leader, at least in medical matters, the frustrated health workers tried to get the priest to convince his people to undergo vaccination. At first, the priest refused to cooperate with the strange men, but when his favorite nephew fell ill, he decided to try any means available to cure the boy. He thereupon went into another trance, telling the villagers that the goddess wished all her worshipers to be vaccinated. Fortunately, the people agreed, and the epidemic was largely controlled.[23]

If channels of influence are not stable, using influential people in a campaign can sometimes backfire. In the educational campaign in Haiti to promote the use of oral rehydration therapy to treat diarrhea in children, Madame Duvalier, the first lady of Haiti at the time, lent her name to the project. Because there were no serious social or cultural barriers to the treatment and mothers reported that children took to the solutions well, success was expected. But in the middle of the campaign, Haiti became embroiled in political turmoil and the first lady's husband was overthrown. Some of the public thought that the oral rehydration project was a plot by the Duvaliers to sterilize children, and this suspicion fueled resistance.[24] As the earlier discussion of Haiti deforestation shows, people in Haiti were suspicious of any government-sponsored program.

Applied anthropologists often advocate integrating indigenous healers into medical change programs. This idea may encounter considerable resistance by the medical profession and by government officials who view such healers negatively. But this strategy may be quite effective in more isolated areas where indigenous healers are the only sources of health care. If they are involved in medical change programs, indigenous healers are likely to refer patients to hospitals when they feel unable to cope with an illness, and the hospitals choose sometimes to refer patients to the healers.[25]

Need for More Collaborative Applied Anthropology

Most large-scale programs of planned change originate with governments, international aid organizations, or other agencies. Even if the programs are well intentioned and even if the appropriate evaluations are made to ensure that the population will not be harmed, the population targeted for the change is usually not involved in the decision making. Some anthropologists, like Wayne Warry, think that applied anthropology should be more collaborative. Warry explains that he was asked by a Native Canadian elder whether he (Warry) would tolerate his own methods and interpretations if he were the native.[26] This question prompted him to involve himself in a project with Native Canadian collaborators, directed by the Mamaweswen Tribal Council. The project assesses health care needs and develops plans to improve local community health care. Funding is provided by the Canadian government as part of a program to transfer health care to the First Nations. Native researchers are conducting the surveys and workshops to keep the community informed about the project. The tribal council also reviews any publications and shares in any profits resulting from those publications.

Applied anthropologists may be increasingly asked to work on behalf of indigenous grassroots organizations. As we saw in the chapter on associations, the developing world has seen a proliferation of such groups. In some cases, these small groups and networks of such groups are starting to hire their own technical assistance.[27] When such organizations do the hiring, they control the decision making. There is increasing evidence that grassroots organizations are the key to effective development. For example, Kenyan farmers who belong to grassroots organizations produce higher farm yields than those farmers who do not belong, even though the latter group is exposed to more agricultural extension agents.[28] Grassroots organizations can succeed where government or outside projects fail. We have plenty of instances of people effectively resisting projects. Their willingness to change, and their participation in crucial decision making, may be mostly responsible for the success of a change project.

There is another kind of collaboration that is becoming increasingly important. Many projects require team efforts, working with people from other disciplines. Anthropologists increasingly have to be conversant with the theory and methods in other fields to understand and negotiate with other members of their team. Earlier anthropologists might have been more likely to work alone. Now that is less likely.[29]

Commuters look at 4th century ruins uncovered as part of a large scale CRM project associated with construction of the Athens metro system.

CULTURAL RESOURCE MANAGEMENT

Large-scale programs of planned change like those discussed earlier in this chapter have an impact not only on living people. They can also have an impact on the archaeological record left by the ancestors of living people. Recovering and preserving the archaeological record before programs of planned change disturb or destroy it is called **cultural resource management (CRM).** CRM work is carried out by archaeologists who are often called "contract archaeologists" because they typically work under contract to a government agency, a private developer, or a native group.

What kinds of impact can programs of planned change have on the archaeological record? In the 1960s, a large number of hydroelectric dam projects were initiated to provide flood control and to bring a stable source of electrical power to developing nations. In Egypt, a dam was built on the Nile River at a site called Aswan. Archaeologists realized that once the dam was in place a huge lake would form behind it, submerging thousands of archaeological sites, including the massive temple of Rameses II. Something needed to be done; the archaeological record had to be salvaged or protected. In the language of CRM, there needed to be a *mitigation plan* put into action. And there was. As the Aswan dam was being built, archaeologists went to work excavating sites that would be flooded. Archaeologists and engineers designed a way to take apart the temple of Rameses II and rebuild it, piece by piece, on higher ground where it would not be flooded. By the time the dam was completed in 1965, hundreds of sites had been investigated and two entire temple complexes moved.

Large-scale development projects are not the only projects that involve CRM archaeologists. In many nations, including the United States and Canada, historic preservation laws require any project receiving federal funds to ensure that archaeological resources are protected or their damage mitigated. Highway construction projects in the United States are common places to find CRM archaeologists at work. Virtually all highway projects rely on federal funding, and before a highway can be built, a complete archaeological survey of the proposed right-of-way has to be made. If archaeological sites are found, potential damage to them must be mitigated. A CRM archaeologist will work with the construction company, the state archaeologist, and perhaps a federal archaeologist to decide on the best course of action. In some cases, the archaeological site will be excavated. In others, the right-of-way may be moved. In still others, the decision is to allow the archaeological site to be destroyed, because it would be too costly to excavate or the site may not be significant enough to warrant excavation. Regardless of the decision, the CRM archaeologist plays a crucial role in assessing and protecting the archaeological record.

CRM archaeologists do not work only for state or federal agencies. In many nations today, CRM archaeologists are also working with native peoples to protect, preserve, and manage archaeological materials for them. Indeed, archaeologist John Ravesloot recently stated that "the future of American archaeology is with Indian communities functioning as active, not passive, participants in the

A forensic anthropologist digs out a body, apparently a victim of state-sponsored violence in Argentina between 1976 and 1983.

interpretation, management, and preservation of their rich cultural heritage."[30] One example of such a working relationship is the Zuni Heritage and Historic Preservation Office. During the 1970s, the Pueblo of Zuni decided it needed to train tribal members in archaeology to ensure that Zuni cultural resources and properties were managed properly. It hired three professional archaeologists and, with additional assistance from the National Park Service and the Arizona State Museum, initiated a program to train and employ tribal members in cultural resource management. Working with these non-Zuni archaeologists, the Pueblo of Zuni were able to establish their own historic preservation office that today manages and coordinates all historic preservation on the Zuni reservation, a task that the federal government managed until 1992. The Pueblo also established the Zuni Cultural Resource Enterprise, a Zuni-owned CRM business that employs both Zuni and non-Zuni archaeologists and carries out contract archaeology projects both on and off the Zuni reservation.[31]

Cultural resource management accounts for the majority of archaeology jobs in the United States.[32] As development and construction projects continue to affect the archaeological record, the need for well-trained CRM archaeologists is likely to persist.

FORENSIC ANTHROPOLOGY

Many of us are fascinated by detective stories. We are interested in crimes and why they occur, and we like to read about them, fictional or not. **Forensic anthropology** is the specialty in anthropology that is devoted to helping solve crimes and identifying human remains, usually by applying knowledge of physical anthropology.[33] It is attracting increasing attention by the public, and an increasing number of practitioners. One forensic anthropologist says she is called "the bone lady" by law enforcement personnel.[34] Like others in her line of work, she is asked to dig up or

examine human bones to help solve crimes. Narrowing down identification is one of the first priorities, but it is not as simple as on television shows. Are these the bones of a man or woman? How old was the person? How well the forensic anthropologist can answer these seemingly simple questions depends upon whether the remains include most bones of the skeleton. Identification of an adult's sex from remains is easier if the pelvis is present, but establishing sex in nonadult remains is not reliable from skeletal remains.[35] With regard to estimating age, only a wide age range can be estimated for adults, but a much narrower range can be estimated for nonadult remains. Forensic anthropologists are often asked for "race" as well. "Race" is not a useful biological category when applied to humans, but it is a significant social category. Forensic anthropologists can estimate with fairly high accuracy whether a person's ancestors came from Asia, Europe, or Africa, but they cannot detect skin color.[36] The police files may suggest that an adult male with Asian ancestry disappeared five years ago. The forensic anthropologist could say with a high probability that the remains were of an Asian male adult. Dental, surgical, or hospital records from that individual might lead to unique features that could be matched for more precise identification. Sometimes the forensic anthropologist can suggest the cause of death when the law enforcement people are stumped.

Some cultural anthropologists have also done forensic work, often in connection with legal cases involving Native Americans. For example, in 1978, Barbara Joans was asked to advise the defense in a trial of six older Bannock-Shoshoni women from the Fort Hall reservation who were accused of fraud. They had received "supplemental security income (SSI)," which the social service agency claimed they had no right to receive because they had not reported receiving rent money on land that they owned. Joans presented evidence that the women, although they spoke some English, did not have enough proficiency to understand the nuances of what the SSI people told them. The judge agreed with the defense and ruled that the SSI would have to use a Bannock-Shoshoni interpreter in the future when they went to the reservation to describe the requirements of the program.[37]

In recent years, Clyde Snow and other forensic anthropologists have been called on to confirm horrendous abuses of human rights. Governments have been responsible for the systematic killing of their citizens, and forensic anthropologists have helped to bring the perpetrators to justice. For example, Snow and other forensic anthropologists helped to confirm that the military dictatorship in Argentina in the 1980s was responsible for the deaths of many Argentine civilians who had "disappeared." The forensic anthropologists were also able to determine the location of mass graves and the identity of victims of state-organized brutality in Guatemala. In addition to bringing the perpetrators to justice, confirming the massacres and identifying the victims help the families of the "disappeared" put their anguish behind them. A special session (called "Uncovering the 'Disappeared': Clyde Snow and Forensic Anthropologists Work for Justice"[38]) at the annual meeting of the American Anthropological Association in November 2000 honored Snow and other forensic anthropologists.

© Horacio Villalobos/Corbis

MEDICAL ANTHROPOLOGY

Illness and death are significant events for people everywhere. No one is spared. So it should not be surprising that how people understand the causes of illness and death, how they behave, and what resources they marshal to cope with these events are extremely important parts of culture. Some argue that we will never completely understand how to treat illness effectively until we understand the cultural behaviors, attitudes, values, and the larger social and political milieu in which people live. Others argue that society and culture have little to do with the outcome of illness—the reason that people die needlessly is that they do not get the appropriate medical treatment.

But anthropologists, particularly those in **medical anthropology,** who are actively engaged in studying health and illness, are increasingly realizing that biological *and* social factors need to be considered if we are to reduce human suffering. For instance, some populations have an appalling incidence of infant deaths due to diarrhea. The origin of this situation is mostly biological, in the sense that the deaths are caused by bacterial infection. But why are so many infants exposed to those bacteria? Usually, the main reason is social. The affected infants are likely to be poor. Because they are poor, they are likely to live with infected drinking water. Similarly, malnutrition may be the biological result of a diet poor in protein, but such a diet is usually also a cultural phenomenon, reflecting a society with classes of people with very unequal access to the necessities of life. In many ways, therefore, medical anthropology, and anthropology in general, are developing in the direction of a "biocultural synthesis."[39]

Medical anthropology is part of this developing synthesis. Indeed, the growth of jobs in medical anthropology is one of the more striking developments in contemporary anthropology. Medical anthropology has developed into a very popular specialty, and the Society for Medical Anthropology is now the second largest unit in the American Anthropological Association.[40]

The medical profession's ways of treating illness may be able to treat some conditions well, but by itself the medical profession cannot tell us why some groups are more affected than others, or why the effectiveness of treatment varies from group to group. This section discusses cultural variation in conceptions of health and illness, cultural universals and variables in how illness is treated, the political and social forces that affect health, and contributions of medical anthropology to the study and treatment of some diseases and health conditions.

CULTURAL UNDERSTANDINGS OF HEALTH AND ILLNESS

Medical researchers and medical practitioners in the United States and other Western societies do not exist in a social vacuum. Many of their ideas and practices are influenced by the culture in which they live. We may think of medicine as purely based on "fact," but it is clear on reflection that many ideas stem from the culture in which the researchers reside. Consider the recent shift in attitudes toward birth. Not so long ago in the United States, fathers were excluded from

In China and elsewhere, tai chi exercises are believed to bring harmony and balance.

© Tibor Bognar/Alamy

the birth, hospitals whisked the baby away from the mother and only brought the baby to her infrequently, and visitors (but not attending nurses and doctors) had to wear masks when holding the baby. Rationalizations were given for those practices, but looking back at them, they do not appear to be based on scientific evidence. Many medical anthropologists now argue that the *biomedical paradigm* (the system in which physicians are trained) itself needs to be understood as part of the culture.

Discovering the health-related beliefs, knowledge, and practices of a cultural group—its **ethnomedicine**—is one of the goals of medical anthropology. How do cultures view health and illness? What are their theories about the causes of illness? Do those theories impact on how illnesses are treated? What is the therapeutic process? Are there specialized medical practitioners, and how do they heal? Are there special medicines, and how are they administered? These are just some of the questions asked by the anthropological study of ethnomedicine.

Concepts of Balance or Equilibrium

Many cultures have the view that the body should be kept in equilibrium or balance. The balance may be between hot and cold, or wet and dry, as in many cultures of Latin America and the Caribbean.[41] The notion of balance is not limited to opposites. For example, the ancient Greek system of medicine, stemming from Hippocrates, assumed that there were four "humors"—blood, phlegm, yellow bile, and black bile—that must be kept in balance. These humors have hot and cold as well as wet and dry properties. The Greek medical system was widely diffused in Europe and spread to parts of the Islamic world. In Europe, the humoral medical system was dominant until the germ theory replaced it in the 1900s.[42] In the Ayurvedic system, whose practice dates back 4,000 years in North India, Pakistan, Bangladesh, Sri Lanka, and in the Arab world, there are three humors (phlegm, bile, and flatulence), and a balance between hot and cold is also important.[43] The Chinese medical system, which dates back about 3,500 years, initially stressed the balance between the contrasting forces of *yin* and *yang* and later added the concept of humors, which were six in number in Chinese medicine.[44]

The concepts of hot and cold and *yin* and *yang* are illustrated in Emily Ahern's ethnographic description of the medical system of the Taiwanese Hokkien.[45] The body requires both hot and cold substances; when the body is out of balance, a lack of one substance can be restored by eating or drinking the missing substance. So, for example, when Ahern was faint with heat, she was told to drink some bamboo shoot soup because it was "cold." In the winter, you need more hot substances; in the summer, you want fewer. Some people can tolerate more imbalance than others; people who are older, for instance, can tolerate less imbalance than those who are young. A loss of blood means a loss of heat. So, for a month after childbirth, women eat mostly a soup made of chicken, wine, and sesame oil—all "hot" ingredients. Hot things to eat are generally oily, sticky, or come from animals; cold things tend to be soupy, watery, or made from plants.

The body also has *yin* and *yang* parts. The *yang* part is visible to the living. The *yin* part exists in the underworld in the shape of a house and tree. The roof of the house corresponds to a person's head, the walls to the skin, a woman's reproductive organs correspond to the flowers on the woman's tree, the roots of the tree to the legs, and so on. A shaman can enable villagers to go into a trance to look around in the underworld where the dead live. If a person has a health problem, a traveler may be sent to the underworld to see what is wrong with the person's *yin* house or tree. Fixing the *yin* house or tree should restore health to the *yang* part of the body. The *yin* world is also where ghosts reside; they sometimes may cause illness. In that case, people may ask for help from powerful gods who reside in the *yang* world.

Supernatural Forces

The Taiwanese Hokkien believe that most illnesses have natural or physiological causes, but around the world, it is more common to believe that illnesses are caused by supernatural forces. In fact, in a cross-cultural study of 139 societies, George P. Murdock found that only two societies did not have the belief that gods or spirits could cause illness, making such a belief a near universal. And 56 percent of those sample societies thought that gods or spirits were the major causes of illness.[46] Sorcery and witchcraft are common in the world's societies. Although humans practice both sorcery and witchcraft for good or evil, making people ill is one of their major uses. Illness can also be thought of as caused by the loss of one's soul, fate, retribution for violation of a taboo, or contact with a polluting or tabooed substance or object. Sorcery is believed to be a cause of illness by most societies on all continents; retribution because of violation of a taboo is also very frequent in all but one region of the world. The belief that soul loss can cause illness is absent in the area around the Mediterranean, uncommon in Africa, infrequent in the New World and the Pacific, and has its highest frequency in Eurasia.[47]

On Chuuk (Truk), an atoll in the central Pacific, serious illnesses and death are mainly believed to be the work of spirits. Occasionally, the spirits of relatives are to blame, although they usually do not cause serious damage. More often, illness is caused by the spirit of a particular locality or a ghost on a path at night.[48] Nowadays, one of two therapeutic options or their combination is often chosen—hospital medicine or Chuuk medicine. Chuuk medical treatment requires a careful evaluation of symptoms by the patient and the patient's relatives, because different spirits inflict different symptoms. If the symptom match is clear, the patient may choose an appropriate Chuuk medical formula to cure the illness. The patient may also ask whether he or she has done something wrong, and if so, what might point to the appropriate spirit and countervailing formula. For example, there is a taboo on having sexual relations before going to sea. If a person who violated this prohibition becomes ill, the reef spirits will be suspected. The Chuuk medical formula is supposed to cure illness quickly and dramatically. For this reason, Chuuk patients ask for a discharge from a hospital if their condition does not improve quickly. If treatment fails, the Chuukese believe that they need to reevaluate the diagnosis, sometimes with the aid of a diviner.[49] In contrasting their theories of illness to the American germ theory, the people of Chuuk point out that, although they have seen ghosts, they have never seen the germs that Americans talk about. Using both methods, some people recover and some do not, so the ultimate cause is a matter of faith.[50]

Among the Ojibwa, the most serious illnesses, the ones resistant to ordinary treatment, are thought to be due to retribution for doing wrong to another person, an animal, or a spirit. To cure such an illness, to yourself or to your children, you must reflect on your own conduct to see what you did wrong. Bad conduct cannot be withheld from the doctor or from the other people in the *wigwam*. On the contrary, only after confessing can medicine help.[51] The Hopi similarly believed that patients were responsible for their own illness, but the cause might be not just improper actions but also bad thoughts and anxiety. Witches could also cause illness, but the action of witches was most effective against people who were depressed or worried; so good thoughts ward off illness.[52]

The Biomedical Paradigm

In most societies, people simply think that their ideas about health and illness are true. Often people are not aware that there may be another way of viewing things until they confront another medical system. Western medical practice has spread widely. People with other medical systems have had to recognize that Western practitioners may consider their ideas about health and illness to be deficient, so they often need to decide which course (Western or non-Western) to follow in dealing with illness. Change, however, is not entirely one-way. For example, for a long time, the Western medical profession disparaged the Chinese practice of acupuncture, but now more medical practitioners are recognizing that acupuncture may provide effective treatment of certain conditions.

Most medical anthropologists use the term **biomedicine** to refer to the dominant medical paradigm in Western cultures today, with the *bio* part of the word emphasizing the biological emphasis of this medical system.

applied anthropology

Exploring Why an Applied Project Didn't Work

When applied projects do not succeed, it is important for researchers to try to figure out why. Part of the problem may be that the intended recipients' ideas about how things work may be very different from the researchers' ideas. Consider the following example.

In Guatemala, village health care workers were not only testing people for malaria but they were also offering free antimalarial drugs. Yet, surprisingly, a community survey found that only 20 percent of people with malaria symptoms took advantage of the free treatment. More surprisingly, most people with symptoms spent the equivalent of a day's wages to buy an injection that was not strong enough to be effective! Why? What was going on?

Finding the answer was not easy. First, researchers designed interviews to elicit folk concepts about illness. What kinds of illnesses are there? What are their causes? What are their symptoms, and how are different illnesses to be treated? They conducted interviews with a random sample of households to find out what illnesses people had and what they did about them. Then they asked people to consider different hypothetical scenarios (vignettes), with different types of people and different degrees of severity of illness, to find out what treatment they would choose. All of these methods were well thought out, but the answers still did not predict what people actually did when they thought they had malaria. Finally, the researchers devised precise comparisons of the kinds of pills the health care workers passed out and the pills and ampoules for in-

jections that the drugstore sold. They compared them two at a time, varying dosages and brands. People did think that more pills were more effective, as indeed they were. But they thought that the colorfully wrapped store-bought pill was more effective than the equivalent white unwrapped free pill, even though it was not. They also thought that one store-bought ampoule used for injections, for which they would pay a day's wages, was more effective than four pills of any kind! In fact, one ampoule was equivalent to only one pill.

Applied researchers often use such trial-and-error methods to find out how to get the information they need. Methods that work in one field setting don't always work in others. To get the information needed, researchers must sometimes let the subjects structure their own answers. At other times, as in this case, they may have to make very specific comparisons to get predictive answers. The people in the Guatemala study didn't believe that the free pills were strong enough to work, so they didn't use them. More research would be needed to uncover why they did not believe the free pills were effective. Was it because they were free? Was it because the store-bought drugs were attractively packaged? Or was there a belief that injections work better than pills? That's what the research process is like; it always leads to new questions, particularly more general questions requiring more extensive or more comparative research.

For example, the Guatemala project revealed why a particular program

was not successful in a particular area. But how widespread are the interfering beliefs? Are they found throughout Guatemala? Do they interfere with the introduction of other medicines? Are we dealing with problems that exist in other areas of Central and South America? Although we don't yet have answers to these more extensive questions, anthropologists have developed efficient methods for assessing variation in beliefs within and between cultures.

We now know that, if we ask one or two informants, we cannot assume that the answer is cultural. But that doesn't mean that we need to ask hundreds of people. If a belief is cultural and therefore commonly held, asking 10 to 20 individuals the same question is sufficient to provide the researcher with a high probability that an answer is correct. (The agreement among respondents is called *cultural consensus*.) So, for example, Guatemalan respondents mostly agreed about which illnesses were contagious. But they disagreed a lot about whether a particular disease should be treated with a "hot" or a "cold" remedy. Using cultural consensus methods, researchers can compare rural and urban residents, and they can also compare informants in different cultures. When we have more of these systematic comparisons, medical anthropologists and health practitioners may have a better understanding of how to implement medical care.

Sources: Weller 2009; Romney et al. 1986.

As Robert Hahn points out, biomedicine appears to focus on specific diseases and cures for those diseases. Health is not the focus, as it is thought to be the *absence* of disease. Diseases are considered to be purely natural, and there is relatively little interest in the person or the larger social and cultural systems. Doctors generally do not treat the whole body but tend to specialize, with the human body partitioned into zones that belong to different specialties. Death is seen as a failure, and biomedical practitioners do everything they can to prolong life, regardless of the circumstances under which the patient would live life.[53]

One of the most important discoveries that profoundly changed the course of Western medicine was Louis Pasteur's isolation of the organisms responsible for some major infectious diseases. Pasteur's discoveries stimulated the search for other disease-causing germs using scientific methods. But the *germ theory* of disease, although powerful, may have led researchers to pay less attention to the patient and the patient's social and cultural milieu.[54] For an example of how anthropologists try to redress the balance, see the box "Exploring Why an Applied Project Didn't Work."

TREATMENT OF ILLNESS

Anthropologists who study diseases in this and other cultures can be roughly classified into two camps. First, there are those (the more relativistic) who think that the culture so influences disease symptoms, incidence, and treatment that there are few if any cultural universals about any illness. If each culture is unique, we should expect its conception and treatment of an illness to be unique too, not like beliefs and practices in other cultures. Second, there are those (the more universalistic) who see cross-cultural similarities in the conception and treatment of illness, despite the unique qualities (particularly in the belief system) of each culture. For example, native remedies may contain chemicals that are the same as, or similar in effect to, chemicals used in remedies by Western biomedicine.[55] Readers should note that our classification here of medical anthropologists is a crude one; many medical anthropologists do not fall unambiguously into one or the other group. And the reality might be that a given culture is very much like other cultures in some respects but unique in other respects.

In their extensive research on Maya ethnomedicine, Elois Ann Berlin and Brent Berlin make a strong case that, although studies of the Maya have emphasized beliefs about illness that are based on supernatural causes, a good deal of Maya ethnomedicine is about natural conditions, their signs and symptoms, and the remedies used to deal with those conditions. In regard to gastrointestinal diseases, the Berlins found that the Maya have a wide-ranging and accurate understanding of anatomy, physiology, and symptoms. Furthermore, the remedies they use, including recommendations for food, drink, and herbal medicines, have properties that are not that different from those of the biomedical profession.[56]

Carole Browner also suggests that the emphasis on "hot-cold" theories of illness in Latin America has been overemphasized, to the neglect of other factors that influence choices about reproductive health and female health problems. In a study of the medical system in a highland Oaxacan community, Browner finds that certain plants are used to expel substances from the uterus—to facilitate labor at full term, to produce an abortion, or to induce menstrual flow. Other plants are used to retain things in

the uterus—to prevent excess blood loss during menstruation, to help healing after delivery, and to prevent miscarriage. Most of these plant remedies appear to work.[57]

The biomedical establishment has become increasingly aware of the value of studying the "traditional" medicinal remedies discovered or invented by people around the world. In studying the indigenous medicines of the Hausa of Nigeria, Nina Etkin and Paul Ross asked individuals to describe the physical attributes of more than 600 plants and their possible medicinal uses, more than 800 diseases and symptoms, and more than 5,000 prepared medicines. Although many medicines were used for treating sorcery, spirit aggression, or witchcraft, most medicines were used for illnesses regarded by the Hausa as having natural causes. Malaria is a serious endemic medical problem in the Hausa region, as in many areas of Africa. The Hausa use approximately 72 plant remedies for conditions connected with malaria—among them anemia, intermittent fever, and jaundice. Experimental treatment of malaria in laboratory animals supports the efficacy of many of the Hausa remedies. But perhaps the most important part of the Etkin and Ross findings is the role of diet. Although most medical research does not consider the possible medical efficacy of the *foods* that people eat in combating illness, food is, of course, consumed in much larger quantities and more often than medicine. It is noteworthy, therefore, that the Hausa eat many plants with antimalarial properties; in fact, dietary consumption of these plants appears to be greatest during the time of year when the risk of malarial infection is at its highest. Recent research has also discovered that foods and spices like garlic, onions, cinnamon, ginger, and pepper have antiviral or antibacterial properties.[58]

Medical Practitioners

In our society, we may be so used to consulting a full-time medical specialist (if we do not feel better quickly) that we tend to assume that biomedical treatment is the only effective medical treatment. If we are given a medicine, we expect it to have the appropriate medical effect and make us feel better. So, many in the biomedical system, practitioners and patients alike, are perplexed by the seeming effectiveness of other medical systems that are based in part on symbolic or ritual healing. As we noted earlier, many native plants have been shown to be medically effective, but their use is often accompanied by singing, dancing, noise making, or rituals. Our difficulty in understanding the healing in such practices probably stems from the assumption in biomedicine that the mind is fundamentally different from the body. Yet, there is increasing evidence that the *form* of treatment may be just as important as the *content* of treatment.[59]

The practitioners who deal with more than the body are sometimes referred to as *personalistic* practitioners. In a personalistic view, illness may be viewed as being due to something in one's social life being out of order. The cause could be retribution for one's own bad behavior or thoughts, or the work of an angry individual practicing sorcery or witchcraft. Or a bad social situation or a bad

A Dayak woman in Malaysia collects herbal medicine.

© Nigel Dickinson/Peter Arnold, Inc.

relationship may be thought of as provoking physical symptoms because of anxiety or stress. In societies with occupational specialization, priests, who are formally trained full-time religious practitioners, may be asked to convey messages or requests for healing to higher powers.[60] Societies with beliefs in sorcery and witchcraft as causes of illness typically have practitioners who are believed to be able to use magic in reverse—that is, to undo the harm invoked by sorcerers and witches. Sometimes sorcerers or witches themselves may be asked to reverse illnesses caused by others. However, they may not be sought out because they are often feared and have relatively low status.[61] Shamans are perhaps the most important medical practitioners in societies lacking full-time occupational specialization.

The Shaman The *shaman,* usually a male part-time specialist, is often involved in healing.[62] Westerners often call shamans "witch doctors" because they don't believe that shamans can effectively cure people. Do shamans effectively cure people? Actually, Westerners are not the only skeptics. A Native American named Quesalid from the Kwakiutl of the Pacific Northwest didn't believe that shamanism was effective either. So he began to associate with the shamans to spy on them and was taken into their group. In his first lessons, he learned

> a curious mixture of pantomime, prestidigitation, and empirical knowledge, including the art of simulating fainting and nervous fits, . . . sacred song, the technique for inducing vomiting, rather precise notions of auscultation or listening to sounds within the body to detect disorders and obstetrics, and the use of "dreamers," that is, spies who listen to private conversations and secretly convey to the shaman bits of information concerning the origins and symptoms of the ills suffered by different people. Above all, he learned the *ars magna.* . . . The shaman hides a little tuft of down in the corner of his mouth, and he throws it up, covered with blood at the proper moment—after having bitten his tongue or made his gums bleed—and solemnly presents it to his patient and the onlookers as the pathological foreign body extracted as a result of his sucking and manipulations.[63]

His suspicions were confirmed, but his first curing was a success. The patient had heard that Quesalid had joined the shamans and believed that only he could heal him. Quesalid remained with the shamans for the four-year apprenticeship, during which he could take no fee, and he became increasingly aware that his methods worked. He visited other villages, competed with other shamans in curing hopeless cases and won, and finally seemed convinced that his curing system was more valid than those of other shamans. Instead of denouncing the trickery of shamans, he continued to practice as a renowned shaman.[64]

After working with shamans in Africa, E. Fuller Torrey, a psychiatrist and anthropologist, concluded that they use the same mechanisms and techniques to cure patients as

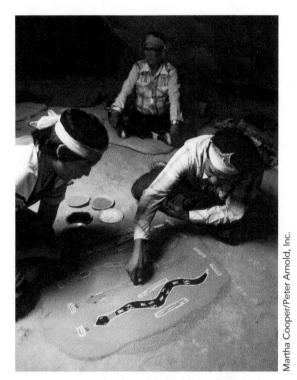

A Navajo medicine man performs a healing ceremony involving a snake painted on the ground.

psychiatrists and achieve about the same results. He isolated four categories used by healers the world over:

1. **The naming process.** If a disease has a name—"neurasthenia" or "phobia" or "possession by an ancestral spirit" will do—then it is curable; the patient realizes that the doctor understands his case.

2. **The personality of the doctor.** Those who demonstrate some empathy, nonpossessive warmth, and genuine interest in the patient get results.

3. **The patient's expectations.** One way of raising the patient's expectations of being cured is the trip to the doctor; the longer the trip—to the Mayo Clinic, Menninger Clinic, Delphi, or Lourdes—the easier the cure. An impressive setting (the medical center) and impressive paraphernalia (the stethoscope, the couch, attendants in uniform, the rattle, the whistle, the drum, the mask) also raise the patient's expectations. The healer's training is important. And high fees also help to raise a patient's expectations. (The Paiute doctors always collect their fees before starting a cure; if they don't, it is believed that they will fall ill.)

4. **Curing techniques.** Drugs, shock treatment, conditioning techniques, and so on have long been used in many different parts of the world.[65]

Biomedical research is not unaware of the effect of the mind on healing. In fact, considerable evidence has accumulated that psychological factors can be very important in illness. Patients who believe that medicine will help them often recover quickly even if the medicine is only a sugar pill or a medicine not particularly relevant to their condition. Such effects are called *placebo* effects.[66]

Placebos do not just have psychological effects. Although the mechanisms are not well understood, they may also alter body chemistry and bolster the immune system.[67]

Shamans may coexist with medical doctors. Don Antonio, a respected Otomi Indian shaman in central Mexico, has many patients, perhaps not as many as before modern medicine, but still plenty. In his view, when he was born, God gave him his powers to cure, but his powers are reserved for removing "evil" illnesses (those caused by sorcerers). "Good" illnesses can be cured by herbs and medicine, and he refers patients with those illnesses to medical doctors; he believes that doctors are more effective than he could be in those cases. The doctors, however, do not seem to refer any patients to Don Antonio or other shamans.[68]

Physicians The most important full-time medical practitioner in the biomedical system is the physician, and the patient-physician relationship is central. In the ideal scheme of things, the physician is viewed as having the ability, with some limits, of being able to treat illness, alleviate suffering, and prolong the life of the patient, as well as offering promises of patient confidentiality and privacy. The patient relies on the physician's knowledge, skill, and ethics. Consistent with the biomedical paradigm, doctors tend to treat patients as having "conditions" rather than as complete people. Physicians presumably rely on science for authoritative knowledge, but they place a good deal of importance on the value of their own clinical experience. Often, physicians consider their own observations of the patient to be more valuable than the reports by the patient. Because patients commonly go to physicians to solve a particular condition or sickness, physicians tend to try to do something about it even in the face of uncertainty. Physicians tend to rely on technology for diagnoses and treatment and place relatively low value on talking with patients. In fact, physicians tend to give patients relatively little information, and they may not listen very well.[69]

Despite the importance of physicians in biomedicine, patients do not always seek physician care. In fact, one-third of the population of the United States regularly consults with alternative practitioners, such as acupuncturists or chiropractors, often unbeknownst to the physician. Somewhat surprisingly, individuals with more education are more likely to seek alternative care.[70]

POLITICAL AND ECONOMIC INFLUENCES ON HEALTH

People with more social, economic, and political power in a society are generally healthier.[71] Inequality in health in socially stratified societies is not surprising. The poor usually have more exposure to disease because they live in more crowded conditions. And the poor are more likely to lack the resources to get quality care. For many diseases, health problems, and death rates, incidence or relative frequency varies directly with social class. In the United Kingdom, for example, people in the higher social classes are less likely to have headaches, bronchitis, pneumonia, heart disease, arthritis, injuries, and mental disorders, to name just a few of the differences.[72] Ethnic differences also predict health

inequities. In South Africa under apartheid, the 14 percent minority population, referred to as "white," controlled most of the income of the country and most of the high-quality land. "Blacks" were restricted to areas with shortages of housing, inadequate housing, and little employment. To get a job, families often had to be disrupted; usually the husband would have to migrate to find work. "Blacks" lived, on average, about nine years less than "whites" in 1985, and "black" infants died at about seven times the rate of "white" infants. In the United States recently, the differences between African Americans and European Americans in health are not as stark as in South Africa, but those favoring European Americans are still substantial. As of 1987, the difference in life expectancy was seven years, and African American infant mortality was about twice the rate for European American infants. Robert Hahn has estimated that poverty accounts for about 19 percent of the overall mortality in the United States.[73]

Inequities, because of class and ethnicity, are not limited to within-society differences. Power and economic differentials *between* societies also have profound health consequences. Over the course of European exploration and expansion, indigenous peoples died in enormous numbers from introduced diseases, wars, and conquests; they had their lands expropriated and diminished in size and quality. When incorporated into colonial territories or into countries, indigenous people usually become minorities and they are almost always very poor. These conditions of life not only affect the incidence of disease, they also tend to lead to greater substance abuse, violence, depression, and other mental pathologies.[74]

HEALTH CONDITIONS AND DISEASES

Medical anthropologists have studied an enormous variety of conditions. What follows is only a small sampling.

AIDS

Epidemics of infectious disease have killed millions of people within short periods of time throughout recorded history. The Black Death—bubonic plague—killed between 25 percent and 50 percent of the population of Europe, perhaps 75 million people, during the 14th century; an epidemic during the 6th century killed an estimated 100 million people in the Middle East, Asia, and Europe. Less noted in our history books, but also devastating, was the enormous depopulation that accompanied the expansion of Europeans into the New World and the Pacific from the 1500s on. Not only were people killed directly by European conquerors, millions also died from introduced diseases to which the natives had little or no resistance, diseases such as smallpox and measles that the Europeans brought with them but were no longer dying from.

The current state of medical science and technology may lull us into thinking that epidemics are a thing of the past. But the recent and sudden emergence of the disease we call **AIDS (acquired immune deficiency syndrome)** reminds us that new diseases, or new varieties of

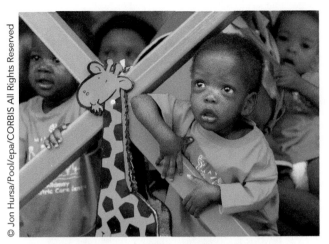

Millions of children in sub-Saharan Africa are orphaned because of AIDS. These orphaned children in Uganda look on during a visit by Britain's Queen Elizabeth to their center.

old diseases, can appear at any time. Like all other organisms, disease-causing organisms also evolve. The human immunodeficiency virus (HIV) that causes AIDS emerged only recently. Viruses and bacteria are always mutating, and new strains emerge that are initially a plague on our genetic resistance and on medical efforts to contain them.

Millions of people around the world already have the symptoms of AIDS, and millions more are infected with HIV but do not know they are infected. As of December 2007, 33 million adults and children in the world were living with HIV/AIDS.[75] There are a few signs of improvement since 2001. The percentage of people infected globally is now stable; some countries have improved with prevention efforts, and the number of new cases each year has gone down. However, AIDS is the major cause of death in sub-Saharan Africa and is still a leading cause of death worldwide.[76] There is still no cure. AIDS is a frightening epidemic not only because of its death toll. It is also frightening because it takes a long time (on average, four years) after exposure for symptoms to appear. This means that many people who have been infected by HIV but do not know they are infected may continue, unknowingly, to transmit the virus to others.[77]

Transmission occurs mostly via sexual encounters, through semen and blood. Drug users may also transmit HIV by way of contaminated needles. Transmission by blood transfusion has been virtually eliminated in this and other societies by medical screening of blood supplies. In many countries, however, there is still no routine screening of blood prior to transfusions. HIV may be passed from a pregnant woman to her offspring through the placenta and after birth through her breast milk. The rate of transmission between a mother and her baby is 20 percent to 40 percent. Children are also at great risk because they are likely to be orphaned by a parent's death from AIDS. At the turn of the 21st century, approximately 14 million children were parentless because of AIDS.[78]

Many people think of AIDS as only a medical problem that requires only a medical solution, without realizing that behavioral, cultural, and political issues need to be addressed as well. It is true that developing a vaccine or a drug to prevent people from getting AIDS and finding a permanent cure for those who have it will finally solve the problem. But, for a variety of reasons, we can expect that the medical solution alone will not be sufficient, at least not for a while. First, to be effective worldwide, or even within a country, a vaccine has to be inexpensive and relatively easy to produce in large quantities; the same is true of any medical treatment. Second, governments around the world have to be willing and able to spend the money and hire the personnel necessary to manage an effective program.[79] Third, future vaccination and treatment will require the people at risk to be willing to get vaccinated and treated, which is not always the case. Witness the fact that the incidence of measles is on the rise in the United States because many people are not having their children vaccinated.

There are now expensive drug treatments that significantly reduce the degree of HIV infection, but we do not know if an effective and inexpensive vaccine or treatment will be developed soon. In the meantime, the risk of HIV infection can be reduced only by changes in social, particularly sexual, behavior. But to persuade people to change their sexual behavior, it is necessary to find out exactly what they do sexually, and why they do what they do.

Research so far suggests that different sexual patterns are responsible for HIV transmission in different parts of the world. In the United States, England, northern Europe, Australia, and Latin America, the recipients of anal intercourse, particularly men, are the most likely individuals to acquire HIV infection; vaginal intercourse can also transmit the infection, usually from the man to the woman. Needle sharing can transmit the infection, too. In Africa, the most common mode of transmission is vaginal intercourse, and so women get infected more commonly in Africa than elsewhere.[80] In fact, in Africa there are slightly more cases of HIV in women as compared with men.[81]

Some researchers are arguing that, although the immediate cause of HIV infection may be mostly related to sexual practice, larger political and social issues, such as poverty and gender inequality, increase the likelihood of such infection. For example, sexually transmitted diseases increase the risk of HIV infection three to five times, but those who are poor are less likely to get adequate treatment. And, in the developing world, rural and poorer areas are also more likely to get tainted blood transfusions. Gender inequality is likely to increase the likelihood that women have to submit to unsafe sex, and women are even less likely than men to have access to adequate medical care.[82]

As of now, there are only two known ways to reduce the likelihood of sexual HIV transmission. One way is to abstain from sexual intercourse; the other is to use condoms. Male circumcision now appears to decrease the risk of HIV infection, but studies have not yet evaluated long-term effects.[83] Educational programs that teach how AIDS spreads and what one can do about it may reduce the spread somewhat, but such programs may fail where people have incompatible beliefs and attitudes about sexuality. For example, people in some central African societies believe that deposits of semen after conception are necessary for a successful pregnancy and generally enhance a woman's health and ability to reproduce. It might be expected then that people who have these beliefs about semen would choose not to use condoms; after all, condoms in their view are a threat to public health.[84] Educational programs may also emphasize the wrong message. Promiscuity may increase the risk of HIV transmission, so hardly anyone would question the wisdom of advertising to reduce the number of sexual partners. And, at least in the homosexual community in the United States, individuals report fewer sexual partners than in the past. What was not anticipated, however, was that individuals in monogamous relationships, who may feel safe, are less likely to use condoms or to avoid the riskiest sexual practices. Needless to say, sex with a regular partner who is infected is not safe![85] In what may seem like something of a paradox, the United Nations observed that, for most women in the world today, the major risk factor for being infected with HIV is being married.[86] It is not marriage, *per se*, that heightens the risk of HIV infection; rather, the proximate cause may be the lower likelihood of condom use or less abstinence by a married couple.

The stigmas associated with AIDS also hinder efforts to reduce its spread. In some societies, there is the widespread belief that homosexual men are particularly likely to get infected.[87] In other societies, AIDS may be thought to be due to promiscuity. If a woman asks a man to use a condom, she may be assumed to be a prostitute. In addition, many people mistakenly fear even proximity to AIDS victims, as if any kind of contact could result in infection.

To solve the problem of AIDS, we may hope that medical science will develop an effective and inexpensive vaccination or treatment that all can afford. There is a vaccine that seems to reduce HIV infection in monkeys to hardly detectable levels.[88] Perhaps soon there will be a similar vaccine for humans. In the meantime, we can try to understand why people engage in certain risky sexual practices. Such understanding may allow us to design educational and other programs that would help inhibit the spread of AIDS.

Mental and Emotional Disorders

Diagnosing mental or emotional disorders in one culture is difficult enough; diagnosing them in others poses much greater difficulty. Many researchers start with Western categories of mental illness and try to apply them elsewhere, without first trying to understand native conceptions of mental disorder. In addition, "mental" and "physical" disorders are rarely separate. For example, a host of illnesses can produce a loss of energy that some may see as depression; and fear or anger can produce physical symptoms such as a heart attack.[89]

When Western anthropologists first started describing mental illness in non-Western societies, there seemed to be unique illnesses in different cultures. These are referred to as *culture-bound syndromes*. For example, a mental disorder called *pibloktoq* occurred among some Eskimo adults of Greenland, usually women, who became oblivious to their surroundings and acted in agitated, eccentric

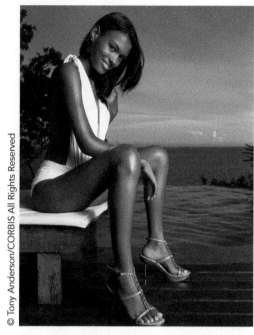

Cultures vary in their ideals of beauty, and ideals change over time. In the United States in the 1950s, "somewhat plump" was idealized. Beginning in the 1960s, thinness became idealized.

ways. They might strip themselves naked and wander across the ice and over hills until they collapsed of exhaustion. Another disorder, *amok*, occurred in Malaya, Indonesia, and New Guinea, usually among males. John Honigmann characterized it as a "destructive maddened excitement . . . beginning with depression and followed by a period of brooding and withdrawal [culminating in] the final mobilization of tremendous energy during which the 'wild man' runs destructively berserk."[90] *Anorexia nervosa*, the disorder involving aversion to food, may be unique to the relatively few societies that idealize slimness.[91] (See the box "Eating Disorders, Biology, and the Cultural Construction of Beauty.")

Some scholars think that each society's views of personality and concepts of mental illness have to be understood in their own terms. Western understandings and concepts cannot be applied to other cultures. For example, Catherine Lutz suggested that the Western concept of depression cannot be applied to the Pacific island of Ifaluk. The people there have many words for thinking or feeling about "loss and helplessness," but all their words are related to a specific need for someone, such as when someone dies or leaves the island. Such thoughts and feelings of loss are considered perfectly normal, and there is no word in their language for general hopelessness or "depression."[92] Therefore, Lutz questioned the applicability of the Western concept of depression as well as other Western psychiatric categories.

Other researchers are not so quick to dismiss the possible universality of psychiatric categories. Some think they have found a considerable degree of cross-cultural uniformity in conceptions of mental illness. Jane Murphy studied descriptions by the Inuit and the Yoruba, in Nigeria, of severely disturbed people. She found that their

applied anthropology

Eating Disorders, Biology, and the Cultural Construction of Beauty

Cultures differ about what they consider beautiful, including people. In many cultures, fat people are considered more beautiful than thin people. Melvin Ember did fieldwork years ago on the islands of American Samoa. When he returned to the main island after three months on a distant island, he ran into a Samoan acquaintance, a prominent chief. The chief said: "You look good. You gained weight." In reality, he had lost 30 pounds! The chief may not have remembered how heavy the anthropologist had been, but he clearly thought that fat was better than thin. Among the Azawagh Arabs of Niger, fatness was not merely valued and considered beautiful; great care was taken to ensure that young girls became fat by insisting and sometimes forcing them to drink large quantities of milk-based porridge.

Around the world, fatness is generally considered more desirable than thinness, particularly for women. Fatness is widely valued in these cultures not only because it is considered more beautiful, but also because it is thought to be a marker of health, fertility, and higher status in societies with social stratification. This view is in strong contrast to the ideal in the United States and many other Western societies, where fatness is thought to be unattractive, and to reflect laziness, a lack of self-control, and poor health. Thinness, particularly in the upper classes, is considered beautiful. How can we explain these differences in what is considered beautiful?

Recent cross-cultural research suggests that the picture is more complicated. It appears that societies with unpredictable resources actually value thinness, particularly in societies that have no way of storing food. At first glance, this seems puzzling. Shouldn't an individual who stores calories on the body be better off than an individual who is thin when facing starvation, particularly if there is no food storage? Perhaps. But 10 thin individuals will generally consume less than 10 heavier people, so perhaps there is a group advantage to being thin. Indeed, many societies with frequent episodes of famine encourage fasting or eating very light meals, as among the Gurage of Ethiopia. The strongest cross-cultural predictor of valuing fatness in women is what is often referred to as "machismo" or "protest masculinity." Societies with a strong emphasis on male aggression, strength, and sexuality are the most likely to value fatness in women; those with little machismo value thinness. Why machismo is associated with valuing fatness in women is far from clear. One suggestion is that machismo actually reflects male insecurity and fear of women. Such men may not be looking for closeness or intimacy with their wives, but they may want to show how potent they are by having lots of children. If fatness suggests fertility, men may look for wives who are fatter. Consistent with this idea, the ideal of thinness in women became more common in North America with the rise of women's movements in the 1920s and late 1960s. Consider that Marilyn Monroe epitomized beauty in the 1950s; she was well-rounded, not thin. Thin became more popular only when women began to question early marriage and having many children.

Behaviors associated with machismo became less acceptable at those times.

Cultural beliefs about what is considered a beautiful body can impose enormous pressures on females to achieve the ideal body type—whether it be fat or thin. In the United States and other Western countries, the effort to be thin can be carried to an extreme, resulting in the eating disorders anorexia and bulimia. If you suffer from these often fatal illnesses, you may regularly eat little and you may regularly force yourself to throw up, thus depriving your body of nutrients in your quest to be thinner and thinner. The irony of "thinness" being idealized in the United States and other Western countries is that obesity is becoming more common in those societies. In 2001, the incidence of obesity increased in the United States to 31 percent, and medical researchers worried about the increase in heart disease and diabetes resulting from obesity. Whether or not obesity is a result of an eating disorder (in the psychological sense) is more debatable. Researchers are finding biological causes of obesity, such as resistance to the hormone leptin, which regulates appetite, suggesting that much of the obesity "epidemic" has biological causes. Still, fast food, increasing sedentariness, and extremely large portion sizes are probably contributing factors also.

Sources: P. J. Brown 1997, 100; Loustaunau and Sobo 1997, 85; N. Wolf 1991; R. Popenoe 2004; C. R. Ember et al. 2005: J. L. Anderson et al. 1992; J. M. Friedman 2003.

descriptions not only were similar to each other but also corresponded to North American descriptions of schizophrenia. The Inuit word for "crazy" is *nuthkavihak*. They use this word when something inside a person seems to be out of order. *Nuthkavihak* people are described as talking to themselves, believing themselves to be animals, making strange faces, becoming violent, and so on. The Yoruba have a word, *were*, for people who are "insane." People described as *were* sometimes hear voices, laugh when there is nothing to laugh at, and take up weapons and suddenly hit people.[93]

Robert Edgerton found similarities in conceptions of mental illness in four East African societies. He noted not only that the four groups essentially agreed on the symptoms of psychosis but also that the symptoms they described were the same ones that are considered psychotic here.[94] Edgerton believed that the lack of exact translation in different cultures, such as the one pointed out by Lutz regarding Ifaluk, does not make comparison impossible. If researchers can come to understand another culture's views of personality and if the researchers can manage to communicate these views to people of other cultures, we can compare the described cases and try to discover what may be universal and what may be found only in some cultures.[95]

Some mental illnesses, such as schizophrenia and depression, seem so widespread that many researchers think they are probably universal. Consistent with this idea is the fact that schizophrenic individuals in different cultures seem to share the same patterns of distinctive eye movements.[96] Still, cultural factors may influence the risk of developing such diseases, the specific symptoms that are expressed, and the effectiveness of different kinds of treatment.[97] There may be some truly culture-bound (nearly unique) syndromes, but others thought at one time to be unique may be culturally varying expressions of conditions that occur widely. *Pibloktoq,* for example, may be a kind of hysteria.[98]

Biological but not necessarily genetic factors may be very important in the etiology of some of the widespread disorders such as schizophrenia.[99] With regard to hysteria, Anthony Wallace theorized that nutritional factors such as calcium deficiency may cause hysteria and that dietary improvement may account for the decline of this illness in the Western world since the 19th century.[100] By the early 20th century, the discovery of the value of good nutrition, coupled with changes in social conditions, had led many people to drink milk, eat vitamin-rich foods, and spend time in the sun (although spending a lot of time in the sun is no longer recommended because of the risk of skin cancer). These changes in diet and activity increased the intake of vitamin D and helped people to maintain a proper calcium level. Consequently, the number of cases of hysteria declined.

Regarding *pibloktoq,* Wallace suggested that a complex set of related variables may cause the disease. The Inuit live in an environment that supplies only a minimum amount of calcium. A diet low in calcium could result in two different conditions. One condition, rickets, would produce physical deformities potentially fatal in the Inuit hunting economy. People whose genetic makeup made them prone to rickets would be eliminated from the population through natural selection. A low level of calcium in the blood could also cause muscular spasms known as tetany. Tetany, in turn, may cause emotional and mental disorientation similar to the symptoms of *pibloktoq.* Such attacks last for only a relatively short time and are not fatal, so people who developed *pibloktoq* would have a far greater chance of surviving in the Arctic environment with a calcium-deficient diet than would people who had rickets.

Although researchers disagree about the comparability of mental illnesses among cultures, most agree that effective treatment requires understanding a culture's ideas about a mental illness—why people think it occurs, what treatments are believed to be effective, and how families and others respond to those afflicted.[101]

Susto *Susto* is often described as a "folk illness" or a culture-bound syndrome because there doesn't seem to be any direct counterpart in biomedical terms. In many areas of Latin America, it is believed that a person suffers susto, or becomes *astudado,* when a nonmaterial essence from the body becomes detached during sleep, or after suffering a fright. This essence is either held captive by supernatural forces or wanders freely outside the body.[102] Susto patients are described as restless during sleep, and listless, depressed, debilitated, and indifferent to food and hygiene during the day. Some researchers have suggested that people labeled as suffering from susto may in fact be suffering from mental illness. Believing that such conclusions were incomplete or premature, Arthur Rubel, Carl O'Nell, and Rolando Collado-Ardón designed a three-culture comparative study to evaluate whether susto victims were suffering from social, psychological, or organic problems. They compared individuals suffering from susto to other individuals matched by culture, age, and sex who defined themselves as "sick" when they came to health clinics (but who did not claim susto as their illness). The three cultures were Chichimec, Zapotec, and a Spanish-speaking mestizo community.[103]

From previous study of susto victims, Rubel and his colleagues hypothesized that susto was likely to strike people in socially stressful situations where they may think they are inadequate in required roles. For example, two cases of susto occurred among women who desperately wanted more children, but each had had a number of miscarriages (one had seven, the other two). In addition to measuring social stress, the researchers also had physicians evaluate organic problems with reference to the World Health Organization's *International Classification of Diseases.* Degree of psychiatric impairment was judged in an interview based on questions other researchers had previously developed. And seven years after the study, the researchers found out which, if any, of the studied individuals had died.

The research results supported the social stress hypothesis: Susto victims were significantly more likely to feel inadequate about social roles. The researchers did not expect to find evidence that susto victims had more psychiatric impairment or more organic disease. However, to their surprise, susto victims were also more likely to have had serious physical health problems. In fact, susto victims were more likely to have died in the seven years after the study. It is hard to say whether the susto victims had more disease because they were debilitated by susto or they were more prone to susto because they were physically sicker. The researchers guess that, because many of the conditions that created social role impairment were of long duration (such as many miscarriages), it seemed likely that susto itself put its victims at risk for biological diseases.[104]

Depression Just as one kind of stress seems to be involved in the folk illness susto, researchers have considered the role of other kinds of stress in producing various other forms of mental illness. One of the most important stressors may be economic deprivation. Many studies have found that the lower classes in socially stratified societies have much higher proportions of all kinds of mental illness. Acute stressors like death of a loved one, divorce, loss of a job, or a natural disaster predict higher rates of mental illness for all social classes; however, these events take more of a toll in lower-class families.[105]

In a study designed to evaluate the effect of these and other stressors on the prevalence of depression in an African American community in a southern city, William Dressler combined fieldwork methods and hypothesis testing to try to better understand depression.[106] Although many studies rely on treatment or hospitalization rates, Dressler decided that such rates drastically underestimate the incidence of depression, inasmuch as many people do not seek treatment. He decided to rely on a symptom checklist, which asked such questions as how often in the last week a person felt like crying, felt lonely, or felt hopeless about the future. Although such checklists do not provide clear divisions for characterizing someone as mildly depressed or seriously depressed, they do allow researchers to compare people along a continuum.

Dressler measured a variety of different possible stressors, including life crises, economic worries, perceived racial inequality, and problems in social roles, and found that some of the objective stressors, like life crises and unemployment, predict depression in the expected direction only in the lower classes. That is, for lower-class African Americans, unemployment and other life crises predicted more depression, but that result was not found among middle- and upper-class individuals. These results are consistent with previous findings that many stressors take more of a toll among poorer individuals. On the other hand, more subjective economic stressors, such as feeling you are not making enough money, predict depression across all class lines. So does "social role" stress, such as thinking you are missing promotions because you are African American or thinking that your spouse expects too much.[107]

Undernutrition

What people eat is intrinsically connected to their survival and the ability of a population to reproduce itself, so we would expect that the ways people obtain, distribute, and consume food have been generally adaptive.[108] For example, the human body cannot synthesize eight amino acids. Meat can provide all of these amino acids, and combinations of particular plants can also provide them for a complete complement of protein. The combination of maize and beans in many traditional Native American diets, or *tortillas* and *frijoles* in Mexico, can provide all the needed amino acids. In places where wheat (often made into bread) is the staple, dairy products combined with wheat also provide complete protein.[109] Even the way that people have prepared for scarcity, such as breaking up into mobile bands, cultivating crops that can better withstand drought, and preserving food in case of famine, are probably adaptive practices in unpredictable environments. Geneticists have proposed that populations in famine-prone areas may have had genetic selection for "thrifty genes"—genes

A sisal plant in Bahia, Brazil. The switch to sisal production led to undernutrition in children.

Michael J. Balick/Peter Arnold, Inc.

that allow individuals to need a minimum of food and store the extra in fatty tissue to get them past serious scarcity.[110] Customary diets and genetic changes may have been selected over a long stretch of time, but many serious nutritional problems observed today are due to rapid culture change. For instance, although "thrifty genes" may be adaptive during famine, they may become maladaptive when food is readily available. The high prevalence of diabetes and obesity in many populations today may be linked to such genes.

Often the switch to commercial or cash crops has harmful effects in another direction—creating undernutrition. For example, when the farmer-herders of the arid region in northeastern Brazil started growing sisal, a drought-resistant plant used for making twine and rope, many of them abandoned subsistence agriculture. The small landholders used most of their land for sisal growing and, when the price of sisal fell, they had to work as laborers for others to try to make ends meet. Food then had to be mostly bought, but if a laborer or sisal grower didn't earn enough, there was not enough food for the whole family.

Analysis of allocation of food in some households by Daniel Gross and Barbara Underwood suggests that the laborer and his wife received adequate nutrition, but the children often received much less than required. Lack of adequate nutrition usually results in retarded weight and height in children. As is commonly the case when there is substantial social inequality, the children from lower-income groups weigh substantially less than those from higher-income groups. But even though there were some economic differences before sisal production, the effects on nutrition appeared negligible before, judging from the fact that there was little or no difference in weight among

399

adults from higher and lower socioeconomic positions who grew up prior to sisal production. But more recently, 45 percent of the children from lower economic groups were undernourished as compared with 23 percent of those children from the higher economic groups.[111]

This is not to say that commercialization is always deleterious to adequate nutrition. For example, in the Highlands of New Guinea, there is evidence that the nutrition of children improved when families started growing coffee for sale. However, in this case, the families still had land to grow some crops for consumption. The extra money earned from coffee enabled them to buy canned fish and rice, which provided children with higher amounts of protein than the usual staple of sweet potatoes.[112]

Nutritional imbalances for females have a far-reaching impact on reproduction and the health of the infants they bear. In some cultures, the lower status of women has a direct bearing on their access to food. Although the custom of feeding males first is well known, it is less often realized that females end up with less nutrient-dense food such as meat. Deprivation of food sometimes starts in infancy where girl babies, as in India, are weaned earlier than boy babies.[113] Parents may be unaware that their differential weaning practice has the effect of reducing the amount of high-quality protein that girl infants receive. Indeed, in Ecuador, Lauris McKee found that parents thought that earlier weaning of girls was helpful to them. They believed that mothers' milk transmitted sexuality and aggression, both ideal male traits, to their infants and so it was important that girl babies be weaned early. Mothers weaned their girls at about 11 months and their boys at about 20 months, a 9-month difference. McKee found that girl infants had a significantly higher mortality than boy infants in their second year of life, suggesting that the earlier weaning time for girls and their probable undernutrition may have been responsible.[114]

Malnutrition and AIDS are biological and social problems.

SUMMARY ●○○

1. Applied or practicing anthropology as a profession is explicitly concerned with making anthropological knowledge useful. Applied or practicing anthropologists may be involved in one or more phases of programs that are designed to change peoples' lives: assembling relevant knowledge, constructing alternative plans, assessing the likely social and environmental impact of particular plans, implementing the programs, and monitoring the programs and their effects.

2. Applied or practicing anthropologists work for a large variety of organizations, government agencies, international development agencies, private consulting firms, public health organizations, medical schools, public interest law firms, community development agencies, charitable foundations, and profit-seeking corporations.

3. The code of ethics for those who work professionally as applied anthropologists specifies that the target population should be included as much as possible in the formulation of policy, so that people in the community may know in advance how the program may affect them. But perhaps the most important aspect of the code is the pledge not to be involved in any plan whose effect will not be beneficial. It is often difficult to evaluate the effects of planned changes. Long-term consequences may be detrimental even if the changes are beneficial in the short run.

4. Even if a planned change will prove beneficial to the targeted population, the people may not accept it. And if the proposed innovation is not utilized by the intended population, the project cannot be considered a success. Affected populations may reject or resist a proposed innovation for cultural, social, or psychological reasons. It is important to understand what the reasons are. The population may also resist the proposed change because they unconsciously or consciously know it is not good for them.

5. To be effective, change agents may have to discover and use the traditional channels of influence in introducing their projects.

6. Cultural resource management usually takes the form of "contract archaeology" to record and/or conserve the archaeology of a building site.

7. Forensic anthropology is the specialty in anthropology that is devoted to helping solve crimes and identifying human remains, usually by applying knowledge of physical anthropology.

8. Medical anthropologists suggest that biological and social factors need to be considered if we are to understand how to treat illness effectively and reduce the suffering in human life.

9. Many of the ideas and practices of medical practitioners are influenced by the culture in which they reside. Understanding ethnomedicine—the medical beliefs and practices of a society or cultural group—is one of the goals of medical anthropology.

10. Many cultures have the view that the body should be kept in equilibrium or balance. The balance may be between hot and cold, or wet and dry, or there may be other properties that need to be balanced.

11. The belief that gods or spirits can cause illness is a near universal. The belief in sorcery or witchcraft as a cause of illness is also very common.

12. Some anthropologists think that there are few cultural universals about conceptions of illness or its treatment, but some researchers are finding evidence that many of the plant remedies that indigenous peoples use contain chemicals that are the same as, or similar in effect to, chemicals used in Western biomedicine remedies.

13. In the biomedical system, medical practitioners emphasize disease and cures, focusing on the body of the patient, not the mind or the social circumstances of the patient. In some societies, healers are more

"personalistic," and illness may be viewed as something out of order in one's social life. Shamans are perhaps the most important medical practitioners in societies lacking full-time specialization. Biomedical practitioners are becoming more aware of the psychological factors involved in healing.

14. People with more social, economic, and political power in a society are generally healthier. In socially stratified societies, the poor usually have increased exposure to disease because they are more likely to live in crowded and unsafe conditions and they are less likely to get access to quality care. Power and economic differentials between societies also have had profound health consequences.

15. The enormous death toll of AIDS, the leading cause of adult death in many countries today, will be reduced when medical science develops effective and inexpensive medicines to treat victims of HIV or AIDS and a vaccine to prevent individuals from getting HIV. In the meantime, if the death toll from AIDS is to be reduced, changes in attitudes, beliefs, and practices regarding sexual activity are needed.

16. Anthropologists debate the extent to which mental and emotional disorders are comparable across cultures. Some illnesses such as schizophrenia and depression seem so widespread as to be probably universal. Others, such as susto or anorexia nervosa, appear to be culture-bound syndromes.

17. The ways that people obtain, distribute, and consume food have been generally adaptive. Geneticists have proposed that populations in famine-prone areas may have had genetic selection for "thrifty genes." Now these populations with regular food supplies may be prone to diabetes and obesity. Many of the serious nutritional problems of today are due to rapid culture change, particularly those making for an increasing degree of social inequality.

GLOSSARY TERMS ○ ● ○

AIDS (acquired immune deficiency syndrome)
applied or practicing anthropology
biomedicine
cultural resource management (CRM)
ethnomedicine
forensic anthropology
medical anthropology

CRITICAL QUESTIONS ○ ○ ●

1. What particular advantages do anthropologists have in trying to solve practical problems?

2. Is it ethical to try to influence people's lives when they have not asked for help? Explain your answer.

3. Why do native remedies often contain chemicals that are the same as, or similar in effect to, chemicals used in Western biomedicine remedies?

4. Why might people engage in sexual practices that increase their likelihood of contracting AIDS?

PEARSON
myanthrolab

Read the chapter by Andrew W. Miracle titled "A Shaman for Organizations" on MyAnthroLab. Answer the following questions:

1. Why does Miracle call himself a "shaman"?

2. According to Miracle, what skills are useful to an applied anthropologist? Why does he think so?

Read the chapter by Ruthbeth Finerman titled "Saraguro: Medical Choices, Medical Changes" on MyAnthroLab. Answer the following questions:

1. Why do the Saraguros continue mostly to rely on mothers to treat illness in the household?

2. How are Saraguro herbal treatments like your use of medicines? How are they unlike yours?

NOTES ● ○ ○

1. Nolan 2003, 2.
2. Kushner 1991.
3. Van Willigen 2002, 10.
4. "Appendix C: Statements on Ethics . . ." 2002; and "Appendix I: Revised Principles . . ." 2002.
5. Appendix A: Report of the Committee on Ethics . . . 2002; and Appendix F: Professional and Ethical Responsibilities . . . 2002.
6. Appendix H: National Association of Practicing Anthropologists' Ethical Guidelines . . . 2002.
7. Scudder 1978.
8. Ibid., 204ff.
9. A good summary of this extraordinary case was put together by Slayman 1997.
10. Public Law 101–601 (25 U.S.C. 3001–3013).
11. Picchi 1991, 26–38; for a more general description of the Bakairí, see Picchi 2009.
12. Murray 1997, 131.
13. Wulff and Fiste 1987; Murray and Bannister 2004.
14. Ibid.
15. Niehoff 1966, 255–67.
16. G. M. Foster 1969, 8–9.
17. Jelliffe and Jelliffe 1975.
18. W. H. Fisher 1994.
19. G. M. Foster 1969, 122–23.
20. Coreil 1989, 149–50.
21. Rogers 1983, 321–31.
22. Bryant and Bailey 1990.
23. Niehoff 1966, 219–24.
24. Coreil 1989, 155.
25. Warren 1989.
26. Warry 1990, 61–62; see also Lassiter 2008.
27. J. Fisher 1996, 57.
28. Ibid., 91; data from Kenya referred to in Oxby 1983.
29. Kedia 2008.
30. Ravesloot 1997, 174.
31. Anyon and Ferguson 1995.
32. Society for American Archaeology 2009.
33. Komar and Buikstra 2008, 11–12.
34. Manhein 1999.
35. Komar and Buikstra 2008, 126–145.

36. Brace 1995.
37. Joans 1997.
38. "Association Business: Clyde Snow . . ." 2000.
39. A. H. Goodman and Leatherman 1998; Kleinman et al. 1997.
40. Baer et al. 1997, viii.
41. Rubel and Haas 1996, 120; Loustaunau and Sobo 1997, 80–81.
42. Loustaunau and Sobo 1997, 82–83, referring to Magner 1992, 93.
43. Loustaunau and Sobo 1997, referring to Gesler 1991, 16.
44. Loustaunau and Sobo 1997, referring to C. Leslie 1976, 4; and G. Foster 1994, 11.
45. Ahern 1975, 92–97, as appearing in eHRAF World Cultures, 2000.
46. Murdock 1980, 20.
47. C. C. Moore 1988.
48. T. Gladwin and Sarason 1953, 64–66.
49. Mahony 1971, 34–38, as seen in eHRAF World Cultures, 2000.
50. Gladwin and Sarason 1953, 65.
51. Hallowell 1976.
52. J. E. Levy 1994, 318.
53. Hahn 1995, 133–39.
54. Loustaunau and Sobo 1997, 115.
55. For an exhaustively documented presentation of the more universalistic approach, see E. A. Berlin and Berlin 1996; see also Browner 1985, 13–32; and Rubel et al. 1984.
56. E. A. Berlin 1996.
57. Browner 1985; Ortiz de Montellano and Browner 1985.
58. Etkin and Ross 1997.
59. Moerman 1997, 240–41.
60. Loustaunau and Sobo 1997, 98–101.
61. Winkelman 1986a.
62. Ibid., 28–29.
63. Levi-Strauss 1963a, 169.
64. Boas 1930, 1–41, reported in Lévi-Strauss 1963b, 169–73.
65. Torrey 1972.
66. Loustaunau and Sobo 1997, 101–102; and Moerman 1997.
67. Loustaunau and Sobo 1997, 102.
68. Dow 1986, 6–9, 125.
69. Hahn 1995, 131–72.
70. Ibid., 165.
71. For a discussion of some of the relevant research, see Hahn 1995, 80–82.
72. Mascie-Taylor 1990, 118–21.
73. See references in Hahn 1995, 82–87.
74. A. Cohen 1999.
75. UNAIDS 2007, 1.
76. Ibid., 4–6.
77. Bolton 1989.
78. Reported in Carey et al. 2004, 462.
79. Bolton 1989.
80. Carrier and Bolton 1991; Schoepf 1988, 625, cited in Carrier and Bolton 1991.
81. Simmons et al. 1996, 64.
82. Ibid., 39–57.
83. L. K. Altman 2008.
84. Schoepf 1988, 637–38.
85. Bolton 1992.
86. Farmer 1997, 414. Married men in Thailand are gradually turning away from commercial sex and having affairs with married women who are believed to be safe; see Lyttleton 2000, 299.
87. Feldman and Johnson 1986, 2.
88. Shen and Siliciano 2000.
89. A. Cohen 2004.
90. Honigmann 1967, 406.
91. Kleinman 1988, 3.
92. Lutz 1985, 63–100.
93. J. Murphy 1981, 813.
94. Edgerton 1966.
95. Edgerton 1992, 16–45.
96. J. S. Allen et al. 1996.
97. Kleinman 1988, 34–52; Berry et al. 1992, 357–64.
98. Honigmann 1967, 401.
99. Kleinman 1988, 19.
100. A. Wallace 1972.
101. Kleinman 1988, 167–85.
102. Rubel et al. 1984, 8–9.
103. Ibid., 15–29, 49–69.
104. Ibid., 71–111.
105. Dressler 1991, 11–16.
106. Ibid., 66–94.
107. Ibid., 165–208.
108. Quandt 1996, 272–89.
109. McElroy and Townsend 2002.
110. See discussion in Leslie Lieberman 2004.
111. Gross and Underwood 1971.
112. McElroy and Townsend 2002, 187, referring to Harvey and Heywood 1983, 27–35.
113. Quandt 1996, 277.
114. McKee 1984, 96.

glossary

glossary

Absolute dating   A method of dating fossils in which the actual age of a deposit or specimen is measured. Also known as **chronometric dating.**

Accent   Differences in pronunciation characteristic of a group.

Acclimatization   Impermanent physiological changes that people make when they encounter a new environment.

Acculturation   The process of extensive borrowing of aspects of culture in the context of superordinate-subordinate relations between societies; usually occurs as the result of external pressure.

Acheulian   A stone toolmaking tradition dating from 1.5 million years ago. Compared with the Oldowan tradition, Acheulian assemblages have more large tools created according to standardized designs or shapes. One of the most characteristic and prevalent tools in the Acheulian tool kit is the so-called hand axe, which is a teardrop-shaped bifacially flaked tool with a thinned sharp tip. Other large tools might have been cleavers and picks.

Achieved qualities   Those qualities people acquire during their lifetime.

Adapid   A type of prosimian with many lemurlike features; appeared in the early Eocene.

Adaptation   Refers to genetic changes that allow an organism to survive and reproduce in a specific environment.

Adaptive customs   Cultural traits that enhance survival and reproductive success in a particular environment.

Adjudication   The process by which a third party acting as judge makes a decision that the parties to a dispute have to accept.

Aegyptopithecus   An Oligocene anthropoid and probably the best-known propliopithecid.

Affinal kin   One's relatives by marriage.

Age-grade   A category of people who happen to fall within a particular, culturally distinguished age range.

Age-set   A group of people of similar age and the same sex who move together through some or all of life's stages.

Agriculture   The practice of raising domesticated crops.

AIDS (Acquired Immune Deficiency Syndrome)   A disease caused by the HIV virus.

Allele   One member of a pair of genes.

Allen's rule   The rule that protruding body parts (particularly arms and legs) are relatively shorter in the cooler areas of a species' range than in the warmer areas.

Ambilineal descent   The rule of descent that affiliates individuals with groups of kin related to them through men or women.

Ancestor spirits   Supernatural beings who are the ghosts of dead relatives.

Animatism   A belief in supernatural forces.

Animism   A belief in a dual existence for all things—a physical, visible body and a psychic, invisible soul.

Anthropoids   One of the two suborders of primates; includes monkeys, apes, and humans.

Anthropological linguistics   The anthropological study of languages.

Anthropology   A discipline that studies humans, focusing on the study of differences and similarities, both biological and cultural, in human populations. Anthropology is concerned with typical biological and cultural characteristics of human populations in all periods and in all parts of the world.

Anthropometry   Refers to the study of variation in the size and shape of the human body.

Applied (practicing) anthropology   The branch of anthropology that concerns itself with applying anthropological knowledge to achieve practical goals, usually in the service of an agency outside the traditional academic setting.

^{40}Ar–^{39}Ar dating   Used in conjunction with potassium-argon dating, this method gets around the problem of needing different rock samples to estimate potassium and argon. A nuclear reactor is used to convert the ^{39}Ar to ^{39}K, on the basis of which the amount of ^{40}K can be estimated. In this way, both argon and potassium can be estimated from the same rock sample.

Arboreal   Adapted to living in trees.

Archaeology   The branch of anthropology that seeks to reconstruct the daily life and customs of peoples who lived in the past and to trace and explain cultural changes. Often lacking written records for study, archaeologists must try to reconstruct history from the material remains of human cultures. See also **Historical archaeology.**

Archaic   Time period in the New World during which food production first developed.

Ardipithecus ramidus   Perhaps the first hominid, dating to about 4.5 million years ago. Its dentition combines apelike and australopithecine-like features, and its skeleton suggests it was bipedal.

Artifact   Any object made by a human.

Ascribed qualities   Those qualities that are determined for people at birth.

Association   An organized group not based exclusively on kinship or territory.

Atlatl   Aztec word for "spear thrower."

Australopithecus   Genus of Pliocene and Pleistocene hominids.

Australopithecus aethiopicus   An early robust australopithecine.

Australopithecus afarensis   A species of *Australopithecus* that lived 4 million to 3 million years ago in East Africa and was definitely bipedal.

Australopithecus africanus   A species of *Australopithecus* that lived between about 3 million and 2 million years ago.

Australopithecus anamensis   A species of *Australopithecus* that lived perhaps 4.2 million years ago.

Australopithecus bahrelghazali   An early gracile australopithecine, dating to about 3 million years ago, and currently represented by only a single jaw. It is an interesting species because it is found in western Chad, distant from the East African Rift Valley where all other early australopithecines have been found.

Australopithecus boisei An East African robust australo-pithecine species dating from 2.2 million to 1.3 million years ago with somewhat larger cranial capacity than *A. africanus.* No longer thought to be larger than other aus-tralopithecines, it is robust primarily in the skull and jaw, most strikingly in the teeth. Compared with *A. robustus,* *A. boisei* has even more features that reflect a huge chewing apparatus.

Australopithecus garhi A gracile australopithecine, dating to about 2.5 million years ago.

Australopithecus robustus A robust australopithecine species found in South African caves dating from about 1.8 million to 1 million years ago. Not as large in the teeth and jaws as *A. boisei.*

Avunculocal residence A pattern of residence in which a married couple settles with or near the husband's mother's brother.

Balanced reciprocity Giving with the expectation of a straightforward immediate or limited-time trade.

Balancing selection A type of selection that occurs when a heterozygous combination of alleles is positively favored even though a homozygous combination is disfavored.

Band A fairly small, usually nomadic local group that is politically autonomous.

Band organization The kind of political organization where the local group or band is the largest territorial group in the society that acts as a unit. The local group in band societies is politically autonomous.

Behavioral ecology Typically tries to understand con-temporary human behavior using evolutionary principles. In addition to the principle of individual selection, behav-ioral ecologists point to the importance of analyzing eco-nomic tradeoffs because individuals have limited time and resources.

Bergmann's rule The rule that smaller-sized subpopula-tions of a species inhabit the warmer parts of its geographic range and larger-sized subpopulations the cooler areas.

Bifacial tool A tool worked or flaked on two sides.

Bilateral kinship The type of kinship system in which indi-viduals affiliate more or less equally with their mother's and father's relatives; descent groups are absent.

Bilocal residence A pattern of residence in which a married couple lives with or near either the husband's parents or the wife's parents.

Bilophodont Having four cusps on the molars that form two parallel ridges. This is the common molar pattern of Old World monkeys.

Biological (physical) anthropology The study of humans as biological organisms, dealing with the emergence and evo-lution of humans and with contemporary biological varia-tions among human populations.

Biomedicine The dominant medical paradigm in Western societies today.

Bipedalism Locomotion in which an animal walks on its two hind legs.

Blade A thin flake whose length is usually more than twice its width. In the blade technique of toolmaking, a core is pre-pared by shaping a piece of flint with hammerstones into a pyramidal or cylindrical form. Blades are then struck off until the core is used up.

Brachiators Animals that move through the trees by swing-ing hand over hand from branch to branch. They usually have long arms and fingers.

Bride price A substantial gift of goods or money given to the bride's kin by the groom or his kin at or before the mar-riage. Also called **bride wealth.**

Bride service Work performed by the groom for his bride's family for a variable length of time either before or after the marriage.

Burin A chisel-like stone tool used for carving and for mak-ing such artifacts as bone and antler needles, awls, and projec-tile points.

Canines The cone-shaped teeth immediately behind the incisors; used by most primates to seize food and in fighting and display.

Carpolestes A mouse-sized arboreal creature living about 56 million years ago; a strong candidate for the common primate ancestor.

Cash crop A cultivated commodity raised for sale rather than for personal consumption by the cultivator.

Caste A ranked group, often associated with a certain occu-pation, in which membership is determined at birth and marriage is restricted to members of one's own caste.

Catarrhines The group of anthropoids with narrow noses and nostrils that face downward. Catarrhines include mon-keys of the Old World (Africa, Asia, and Europe), as well as apes and humans.

Ceramics Objects shaped from clay and baked at high tem-perature (fired) to make them hard. Containers such as pots and jars are typical ceramics, though they can take on many forms and uses.

Cercopithecoids Old World monkeys.

Cerebral cortex The "gray matter" of the brain; the center of speech and other higher mental activities.

Chief A person who exercises authority, usually on behalf of a multicommunity political unit. This role is generally found in rank societies and is usually permanent and often hereditary.

Chiefdom A political unit, with a chief at its head, integrat-ing more than one community but not necessarily the whole society or language group.

Chromosomes Paired rod-shaped structures within a cell nucleus containing the genes that transmit traits from one generation to the next.

Chronometric dating See **Absolute dating.**

Civilization Urban society, from the Latin word for "city-state."

Clan A set of kin whose members believe themselves to be descended from a common ancestor or ancestress but cannot specify the links back to that founder; often designated by a totem. Also called a **sib.**

Class A category of people who have about the same op-portunity to obtain economic resources, power, and prestige.

Classificatory terms Kinship terms that merge or equate relatives who are genealogically distinct from one another; the same term is used for a number of different kin.

Class societies Societies containing social groups that have unequal access to economic resources, power, and prestige.

Cline The gradually increasing (or decreasing) frequency of a gene from one end of a region to another.

Code-switching Using more than one language in the course of conversing.

Codified laws Formal principles for resolving disputes in heterogeneous and stratified societies.

Cognates Words or morphs that belong to different languages but have similar sounds and meanings.

Commercial exchange See **Market (or commercial) exchange.**

Commercialization The increasing dependence on buying and selling, with money usually as the medium of exchange.

Complementary opposition The occasional uniting of various segments of a segmentary lineage system in opposition to similar segments.

Consanguineal kin One's biological relatives; relatives by birth.

Context The relationships between and among artifacts, ecofacts, fossils, and features.

Continental drift The movement of the continents over the past 135 million years. In the early Cretaceous (circa 135 million years ago), there were two "supercontinents": *Laurasia,* which included North America and Eurasia; and *Gondwanaland,* which included Africa, South America, India, Australia, and Antarctica. By the beginning of the Paleocene (circa 65 million years ago), Gondwanaland had broken apart, with South America drifting west away from Africa, India drifting east, and Australia and Antarctica drifting south.

Core vocabulary Nonspecialist vocabulary.

Corvée A system of required labor.

Cretaceous Geological epoch 135 million to 65 million years ago, during which dinosaurs and other reptiles ceased to be the dominant land vertebrates, and mammals and birds began to become important.

Crime Violence not considered legitimate that occurs within a political unit.

Cro-Magnons Humans who lived in western Europe about 35,000 years ago, they were once thought to be the earliest specimens of modern-looking humans, or *Homo sapiens sapiens.* But it is now known that modern-looking humans appeared earlier outside of Europe; the earliest so far found lived in Africa.

Cross-cousins Children of siblings of the opposite sex. One's cross-cousins are the father's sisters' children and mother's brothers' children.

Cross-cultural researcher An ethnologist who uses ethnographic data about many societies to test possible explanations of cultural variation to discover general patterns about cultural traits—what is universal, what is variable, why traits vary, and what the consequences of the variability might be.

Crossing-over Exchanges of sections of chromosomes from one chromosome to another.

Cultural anthropology The study of cultural variation and universals in the past and present.

Cultural ecology The analysis of the relationship between a culture and its environment.

Cultural relativism The attitude that a society's customs and ideas should be viewed within the context of that society's problems and opportunities.

Cultural resource management (CRM) The branch of applied anthropology that seeks to recover and preserve the archaeological record before programs of planned change disturb or destroy it.

Culture The set of learned behaviors, beliefs, attitudes, values, and ideals that are characteristic of a particular society or other social group.

Culture history A history of the cultures that lived in a given area over time. Until the 1950s, building such culture histories was a primary goal of archaeological research.

Cuneiform Wedge-shaped writing invented by the Sumerians around 3000 B.C.

Descriptive (structural) linguistics The study of how languages are constructed.

Dialect A variety of a language spoken in a particular area or by a particular social group.

Diastema A gap between the canine and first premolar found in apes.

Diffusion The borrowing by one society of a cultural trait belonging to another society as the result of contact between the two societies.

Directional selection A type of natural selection that increases the frequency of a trait (the trait is said to be positively favored, or adaptive).

Diurnal Active during the day.

Divination Getting the supernatural to provide guidance.

DNA Deoxyribonucleic acid; a long, two-stranded molecule in the genes that directs the makeup of an organism according to the instructions in its genetic code.

Domestication Modification or adaptation of plants and animals for use by humans. When people plant crops, we refer to the process as cultivation. It is only when the crops cultivated and the animals raised have been modified—are different from wild varieties—that we speak of plant and animal domestication.

Dominant The allele of a gene pair that is always phenotypically expressed in the heterozygous form.

Double descent or double unilineal descent A system that affiliates individuals with a group of matrilineal kin for some purposes and with a group of patrilineal kin for other purposes.

Dowry A substantial transfer of goods or money from the bride's family to the bride.

Dryopithecus Genus of ape from the later Miocene found primarily in Europe. It had thin tooth enamel and pointed molar cusps very similar to those of the fruit-eating chimpanzees of today.

Dual-inheritance theory In contrast to other evolutionary ecological perspectives, this theory gives much more importance to culture as part of the evolutionary process. Dual inheritance refers to both genes and culture playing different, but nonetheless important and interactive roles in transmitting traits to future generations.

Ecofacts Natural items that humans have used; things such as the remains of animals eaten by humans or plant pollens found on archaeological sites are examples of ecofacts.

Economic resources Things that have value in a culture, including land, tools and other technology, goods, and money.

Egalitarian societies Societies in which all people of a given age-sex category have equal access to economic resources, power, and prestige.

Ego In the reckoning of kinship, the reference point or focal person.

Enculturation See **Socialization.**

Endogamy The rule specifying marriage to a person within one's own group (kin, caste, community).

Eocene   A geological epoch 55 million to 34 million years ago during which the first definite primates appeared.

Epipaleolithic   Time period during which food production first developed in the Near East.

Ethnicity   The process of defining ethnicity usually involves a group of people emphasizing common origins and language, shared history, and selected aspects of cultural difference such as a difference in religion. Because different groups are doing the perceiving, ethnic identities often vary with whether one is inside or outside the group.

Ethnocentric   Refers to judgment of other cultures solely in terms of one's own culture.

Ethnocentrism   The attitude that other societies' customs and ideas can be judged in the context of one's own culture.

Ethnogenesis   Creation of a new culture.

Ethnographer   A person who spends some time living with, interviewing, and observing a group of people to describe their customs.

Ethnographic analogy   Method of comparative cultural study that extrapolates to the past from recent or current societies.

Ethnography   A description of a society's customary behaviors and ideas.

Ethnohistorian   An ethnologist who uses historical documents to study how a particular culture has changed over time.

Ethnology   The study of how and why recent cultures differ and are similar.

Ethnomedicine   The health-related beliefs, knowledge, and practices of a cultural group.

Ethnoscience   An approach that attempts to derive rules of thought from the logical analysis of ethnographic data.

Eugenics   Selectively breeding humans with desirable characteristics and preventing those with undesirable ones from having offspring.

Evolutionary psychology   A type of evolutionary ecological approach that is particularly interested in universal human psychology. It is argued that human psychology was primarily adapted to the environment that characterized most of human history—the hunting-gathering way of life.

Excavation   The careful removal of the archaeological deposits; the recovery of artifacts, ecofacts, fossils, and features from the soil in which those deposits have been buried.

Exogamy   The rule specifying marriage to a person from outside one's own group (kin or community).

Explanation   An answer to a *why* question. In science, there are two kinds of explanation that researchers try to achieve: associations and theories.

Extended family   A family consisting of two or more single-parent, monogamous, polygynous, or polyandrous families linked by a blood tie.

Extensive cultivation   A type of horticulture in which the land is worked for short periods and then left to regenerate for some years before being used again. Also called **shifting cultivation.**

Falsification   Showing that a theory seems to be wrong by finding that implications or predictions derivable from it are not consistent with objectively collected data.

Family   A social and economic unit consisting minimally of a parent and a child.

Fayum   A site southwest of Cairo, Egypt, where the world's best record of Oligocene primate fossils has been found.

Features   Artifacts of human manufacture that cannot be removed from an archaeological site. Hearths, storage pits, and buildings are examples of features.

Feuding   A state of recurring hostility between families or groups of kin, usually motivated by a desire to avenge an offense against a member of the group.

Fieldwork   Firsthand experience with the people being studied and the usual means by which anthropological information is obtained. Regardless of other methods that anthropologists may use (e.g., censuses, surveys), fieldwork usually involves participant-observation for an extended period of time, often a year or more. See **Participant-observation.**

Folklore   Includes all the myths, legends, folktales, ballads, riddles, proverbs, and superstitions of a cultural group. Generally, folklore is transmitted orally, but it may also be written.

Food production   The form of subsistence technology in which food-getting is dependent on the cultivation and domestication of plants and animals.

Foragers   People who subsist on the collection of naturally occurring plants and animals. Also referred to as **hunter-gatherers** or *food collectors.*

Foraging   May be generally defined as a food-getting strategy that obtains wild plant and animal resources through gathering, hunting, scavenging, or fishing; also known as food collection.

Foramen magnum   Opening in the base of the skull through which the spinal cord passes en route to the brain.

Forensic anthropology   The application of anthropology, usually physical anthropology, to help identify human remains and assist in solving crimes.

Fossils   The hardened remains or impressions of plants and animals that lived in the past.

Fraternal polyandry   The marriage of a woman to two or more brothers at the same time.

Functionalism   The theoretical orientation that looks for the part (function) that some aspect of culture or social life plays in maintaining a cultural system.

Gender differences   Differences between females and males that reflect cultural expectations and experiences.

Gender roles   Roles that are culturally assigned to genders.

Gender stratification   The degree of unequal access by the different genders to prestige, authority, power, rights, and economic resources.

Gene   Chemical unit of heredity.

Gene flow   The process by which genes pass from the gene pool of one population to that of another through mating and reproduction.

General evolution   The notion that higher forms of culture arise from and generally supersede lower forms.

Generalized reciprocity   Gift giving without any immediate or planned return.

General-purpose money   A universally accepted medium of exchange.

Genetic drift   The various random processes that affect gene frequencies in small, relatively isolated populations.

Genotype   The total complement of inherited traits or genes of an organism.

Genus   A group of related species; pl., genera.

Ghosts   Supernatural beings who were once human; the souls of dead people.

Globalization   The ongoing spread of goods, people, information, and capital around the world.

Gloger's rule The rule that populations of birds and mammals living in warm, humid climates have more melanin (and therefore darker skin, fur, or feathers) than populations of the same species living in cooler, drier areas.

Gods Supernatural beings of nonhuman origin who are named personalities; often anthropomorphic.

Gracile australopithecines The earliest group of australopithecines, usually differentiated from the robust australopithecines by their lighter dentition and smaller faces.

Group marriage Marriage in which more than one man is married to more than one woman at the same time; not customary in any known human society.

Group selection Natural selection of group characteristics.

Half-life The time it takes for half of the atoms of a radioactive substance to decay into atoms of a different substance.

Hand axe A teardrop-shaped stone tool characteristic of Acheulian assemblages.

Hard hammer A technique of stone tool manufacture where one stone is used to knock flakes from another stone. Flakes produced through hard hammer percussion are usually large and crude.

Headman A person who holds a powerless but symbolically unifying position in a community within an egalitarian society; may exercise influence but has no power to impose sanctions.

Hermeneutics The study of meaning.

Heterozygous Possessing differing genes or alleles in corresponding locations on a pair of chromosomes.

Hieroglyphics "Picture writing," as in ancient Egypt and in Mayan sites in Mesoamerica (Mexico and Central America).

Historical archaeology A specialty within archaeology that studies the material remains of recent peoples who left written records.

Historical linguistics The study of how languages change over time.

Holistic Refers to an approach that studies many aspects of a multifaceted system.

Hominids The group of hominoids consisting of humans and their direct ancestors. It contains at least two genera: *Homo* and *Australopithecus*.

Hominoids The group of catarrhines that includes both apes and humans.

Homo Genus to which modern humans and their ancestors belong.

Homo antecessor Refers to a group of hominid fossils found in the Atapuerca region of Spain that appear to be transitional between Neandertals and modern humans. They are closely related to *Homo heidelbergensis*, and many scholars believe they are the same species.

Homo erectus The first hominid species to be widely distributed in the Old World. The earliest finds are possibly 1.8 million years old. The brain (averaging 895–1,040 cc) was larger than that found in any of the australopithecines or *H. habilis* but smaller than the average brain of a modern human.

Homo floresiensis A dwarf species of hominid that lived on the Indonesian island of Flores until about 12,000 years ago and probably descended from an isolated *Homo erectus* population.

Homo habilis Dating from about 2 million years ago, an early species belonging to our genus, *Homo*, with cranial capacities averaging about 630–640 cc, about 50 percent of the brain capacity of modern humans.

Homo heidelbergensis A transitional species between *Homo erectus* and *Homo sapiens*.

Homo neandertalensis The technical name for the Neandertals, a group of robust and otherwise anatomically distinct hominids that are close relatives of modern humans—so close that some believe they should be classified as *Homo sapiens neandertalensis*.

Homo rudolfensis Early species belonging to our genus, *Homo*. Similar enough to *Homo habilis* that some paleoanthropologists make no distinction between the two.

Homo sapiens All living people belong to one biological species, *Homo sapiens*, which means that all human populations on earth can successfully interbreed. The first *Homo sapiens* may have emerged about 200,000 years ago.

Homo sapiens sapiens Modern-looking humans, undisputed examples of which appeared about 50,000 years ago; may have appeared earlier.

Homozygous Possessing two identical genes or alleles in corresponding locations on a pair of chromosomes.

Horticulture Plant cultivation carried out with relatively simple tools and methods; nature is allowed to replace nutrients in the soil, in the absence of permanently cultivated fields.

Human paleontology The study of the emergence of humans and their later physical evolution. Also called **paleoanthropology.**

Human variation The study of how and why contemporary human populations vary biologically.

Hunter-gatherers People who collect food from naturally occurring resources, that is, wild plants, animals, and fish. The term *hunter-gatherers* minimizes sometimes heavy dependence on fishing. Also referred to as **foragers** or *food collectors*.

Hybridization The creation of a viable offspring from the mating of two different species.

Hylobates The family of hominoids that includes gibbons and siamangs; often referred to as the lesser apes (as compared with the great apes such as gorillas and chimpanzees).

Hypotheses Predictions, which may be derived from theories, about how variables are related.

Hypoxia A condition of oxygen deficiency that often occurs at high altitudes. The percentage of oxygen in the air is the same as at lower altitudes, but because the barometric pressure is lower, less oxygen is taken in with each breath. Often, breathing becomes more rapid, the heart beats faster, and activity is more difficult.

Incest taboo Prohibition of sexual intercourse or marriage between mother and son, father and daughter, and brother and sister; often extends to other relatives.

Incisors The front teeth; used for holding or seizing food and preparing it for chewing by the other teeth.

Independent family A family unit consisting of one monogamous (nuclear) family, or one polygynous or one polyandrous family.

Indirect dowry Goods given by the groom's kin to the bride (or her father, who passes most of them to her) at or before her marriage.

Indicator artifacts and ecofacts Items that changed relatively rapidly and which, thus, can be used to indicate the relative age of associated items.

Indirect percussion A toolmaking technique common in the Upper Paleolithic. After shaping a core into a pyramidal or cylindrical form, the toolmaker can put a punch of antler or wood or another hard material into position and strike it with a hammer. Using a hammer-struck punch enabled toolmakers to strike off consistently shaped blades.

Individual selection Natural selection of individual characteristics.

Insectivore The order or major grouping of mammals, including modern shrews and moles, that is adapted to feeding on insects.

Intensive agriculture Food production characterized by the permanent cultivation of fields and made possible by the use of the plow, draft animals or machines, fertilizers, irrigation, water-storage techniques, and other complex agricultural techniques.

Kenyanthropus platyops A nearly complete 3.5 million year old skull found in western Kenya. It is thought by some scholars to be a species of gracile australopithecine (and hence should not be regarded as a separate genus).

Kenyapithecus An apelike primate from the middle Miocene found in East Africa. It had very thickly enameled teeth and robust jaws, suggesting a diet of hard, tough foods. Probably somewhat terrestrial.

Kindred A bilateral set of close relatives.

Kinesics The study of communication by nonvocal means, including posture, mannerisms, body movement, facial expressions, and signs and gestures.

Knuckle walking A locomotor pattern of primates such as the chimpanzee and gorilla in which the weight of the upper part of the body is supported on the thickly padded knuckles of the hands.

Laws (scientific) Associations or relationships that almost all scientists accept.

Levalloisian method A method that allowed flake tools of a predetermined size to be produced from a shaped core. The toolmakers first shaped the core and prepared a "striking platform" at one end. Flakes of predetermined and standard sizes could then be knocked off. Although some Levallois flakes date from as far back as 400,000 years ago, they are found more frequently in Mousterian tool kits.

Levirate A custom whereby a man is obliged to marry his brother's widow.

Lexical content Vocabulary or lexicon.

Lexicon The words and morphs, and their meanings, of a language; approximated by a dictionary.

Lineage A set of kin whose members trace descent from a common ancestor through known links.

Lithics The technical name for tools made from stone.

Lower Paleolithic The period of the Oldowan and Acheulian stone tool traditions.

Magic The performance of certain rituals that are believed to compel the supernatural powers to act in particular ways.

Maladaptive customs Cultural traits that diminish the chances of survival and reproduction in a particular environment.

Mana A supernatural, impersonal force that inhabits certain objects or people and is believed to confer success and/or strength.

Manumission The granting of freedom to a slave.

Market (or commercial) exchange Transactions in which the "prices" are subject to supply and demand, whether or not the transactions occur in a marketplace.

Marriage A socially approved sexual and economic union, usually between a man and a woman, that is presumed, both by the couple and by others, to be more or less permanent, and that subsumes reciprocal rights and obligations between the two spouses and their future children.

Matriclan A clan tracing descent through the female line.

Matrilineage A kin group whose members trace descent through known links in the female line from a common female ancestor.

Matrilineal descent The rule of descent that affiliates individuals with kin of both sexes related to them through women only.

Matrilocal residence A pattern of residence in which a married couple lives with or near the wife's parents.

Measure To describe how something compares with other things on some scale of variation.

Mediation The process by which a third party tries to bring about a settlement in the absence of formal authority to force a settlement.

Mediums Part-time religious practitioners who are asked to heal and divine while in a trance.

Meiosis The process by which reproductive cells are formed. In this process of division, the number of chromosomes in the newly formed cells is reduced by half, so that when fertilization occurs the resulting organism has the normal number of chromosomes appropriate to its species, rather than double that number.

Mesolithic The archaeological period in the Old World beginning about 12,000 B.C. Humans were starting to settle down in semipermanent camps and villages, as people began to depend less on big game (which they used to have to follow over long distances) and more on relatively stationary food resources such as fish, shellfish, small game, and wild plants rich in carbohydrates, proteins, and oils.

Messenger RNA A type of ribonucleic acid that is used in the cell to copy the DNA code for use in protein synthesis.

Microlith A small, razorlike blade fragment that was probably attached in a series to a wooden or bone handle to form a cutting edge.

Middle Paleolithic The time period of the Mousterian stone tool tradition.

Miocene The geological epoch from 24 million to 5.2 million years ago.

Mitosis Cellular reproduction or growth involving the duplication of chromosome pairs.

Moiety A unilineal descent group in a society that is divided into two such maximal groups; there may be smaller unilineal descent groups as well.

Molars The large teeth behind the premolars at the back of the jaw; used for chewing and grinding food.

Monogamy Marriage between only one man and only one woman at a time.

Monotheistic Believing that there is only one high god and that all other supernatural beings are subordinate to, or are alternative manifestations of, this supreme being.

Morph The smallest unit of a language that has a meaning.

Morpheme One or more morphs with the same meaning.

Morphology The study of how sound sequences convey meaning.

Mousterian tool assemblage Named after the tool assemblage found in a rock shelter at Le Moustier in the Dordogne region of southwestern France. Compared with an Acheulian assemblage, the Middle Paleolithic (40,000–300,000 years ago) Mousterian has a smaller proportion of large core tools such as hand axes and cleavers and a bigger proportion of small flake tools such as scrapers. Flakes were often altered or "retouched" by striking small flakes or chips from one or more edges.

Mutation A change in the DNA sequence, producing an altered gene.

Natural selection The outcome of processes that affect the frequencies of traits in a particular environment. Traits that enhance survival and reproductive success increase in frequency over time.

Neandertal The common name for the species *Homo neandertalensis.*

Negotiation The process by which the parties to a dispute try to resolve it themselves.

Neolithic Originally meaning "the new stone age," now meaning the presence of domesticated plants and animals. The earliest evidence of domestication comes from the Near East about 8000 B.C.

Neolocal residence A pattern of residence whereby a married couple lives separately, and usually at some distance, from the kin of both spouses.

Nocturnal Active during the night.

Nonfraternal polyandry Marriage of a woman to two or more men who are not brothers.

Nonsororal polygyny Marriage of a man to two or more women who are not sisters.

Normalizing selection The type of natural selection that removes harmful genes that arose by mutation.

Nuclear family A family consisting of a married couple and their young children.

Oath The act of calling upon a deity to bear witness to the truth of what one says.

Obsidian A volcanic glass that can be used to make mirrors or sharp-edged tools.

Occipital torus A ridge of bone running horizontally across the back of the skull in apes and some hominids.

Oldowan The earliest stone toolmaking tradition, named after the tools found in Bed I at Olduvai Gorge, Tanzania, from about 2.5 million years ago. The stone artifacts include core tools and sharp-edged flakes made by striking one stone against another. Flake tools predominate. Among the core tools, so-called choppers are common.

Oligocene The geological epoch 34 million to 24 million years ago during which definite anthropoids emerged.

Omnivorous Eating both meat and vegetation.

Omomyid A type of prosimian with many tarsierlike features that appeared in the early Eocene.

Operational definition A description of the procedure that is followed in measuring a variable.

Opposable thumb A thumb that can touch the tips of all the other fingers.

Optimal foraging theory The theory that individuals seek to maximize the returns (in calories and nutrients) on their labor in deciding which animals and plants they will go after.

Ordeal A means of determining guilt or innocence by submitting the accused to dangerous or painful tests believed to be under supernatural control.

Orrorin tugenensis An apparently bipedal primate dating to between 5.8 and 6 million years, making it possibly the earliest known hominid.

Osteology Refers to the study of bones.

Paleoanthropology See **Human paleontology.**

Paleocene The geological epoch 65 million to 55 million years ago.

Paralanguage Refers to all the optional vocal features or silences apart from the language itself that communicate meaning.

Parallel cousins Children of siblings of the same sex. One's parallel cousins are the father's brothers' children and the mother's sisters' children.

Parapithecids Small monkeylike Oligocene primates found in the Fayum area of Egypt.

Participant-observation Living among the people being studied—observing, questioning, and (when possible) taking part in the important events of the group. Writing or otherwise recording notes on observations, questions asked and answered, and things to check out later are parts of participant-observation.

Pastoralism A form of subsistence technology in which food-getting is based directly or indirectly on the maintenance of domesticated animals.

Patriclan A clan tracing descent through the male line.

Patrilineage A kin group whose members trace descent through known links in the male line from a common male ancestor.

Patrilineal descent The rule of descent that affiliates individuals with kin of both sexes related to them through men only.

Patrilocal residence A pattern of residence in which a married couple lives with or near the husband's parents.

Peasants Rural people who produce food for their own subsistence but who must also contribute or sell their surpluses to others (in towns and cities) who do not produce their own food.

Percussion flaking A toolmaking technique in which one stone is struck with another to remove a flake.

Personality integration of culture The theory that personality or psychological processes may account for connections between certain aspects of culture.

Pierolapithecus A middle Miocene ape that has wrists and vertebrae that would have made it capable of brachiation, but also has relatively short fingers like modern monkeys.

Phenotype The observable physical appearance of an organism, which may or may not reflect its genotype or total genetic constitution.

Phone A speech sound in a language.

Phoneme A sound or set of sounds that makes a difference in meaning to the speakers of the language.

Phonology The study of the sounds in a language and how they are used.

Phratry A unilineal descent group composed of a number of supposedly related clans (sibs).

Physical (biological) anthropology See **Biological (physical) anthropology.**

Platyrrhines The group of anthropoids that have broad, flat-bridged noses, with nostrils facing outward; these monkeys are currently found only in the New World (Central and South America).

Pleistocene A geological epoch that started 1.6 million years ago and, according to some, continues into the present. During this period, glaciers have often covered much of the earth's surface and humans became the dominant life form.

Plesiadipis   The most well known of the plesiadipiforms, possibly an archaic primate.

Pliocene   The geological epoch 5.2 million to 1.6 million years ago during which the earliest definite hominids appeared.

Political economy   The study of how external forces, particularly powerful state societies, explain the way a society changes and adapts.

Polyandry   The marriage of one woman to more than one man at a time.

Polygamy   Plural marriage; one individual is married to more than one spouse simultaneously. **Polygyny** and **polyandry** are types of polygamy.

Polygyny   The marriage of one man to more than one woman at a time.

Polyphony   Two or more melodies sung simultaneously.

Polytheistic   Recognizing many gods, none of whom is believed to be superordinate.

Pongids   Hominoids whose members include both the living and extinct apes.

Potassium-argon (K-Ar) dating   A chronometric dating method that uses the rate of decay of a radioactive form of potassium (^{40}K) into argon (^{40}Ar) to date samples from 5,000 years to 3 billion years old. The K-Ar method dates the minerals and rocks in a deposit, not the fossils themselves.

Postpartum sex taboo   Prohibition of sexual intercourse between a couple for a period of time after the birth of their child.

Potlatch   A feast among Pacific Northwest Native Americans at which great quantities of food and goods are given to the guests in order to gain prestige for the host(s).

Power   The ability to make others do what they do not want to do or influence based on the threat of force.

Practicing anthropology   See **Applied anthropology.**

Prairie   Grassland with a high grass cover.

Prehensile   Adapted for grasping objects.

Prehistory   The time before written records.

Premolars   The teeth immediately behind the canines; used in chewing, grinding, and shearing food.

Pressure flaking   Toolmaking technique whereby small flakes are struck off by pressing against the core with a bone, antler, or wooden tool.

Prestige   Being accorded particular respect or honor.

Priests   Generally full-time specialists, with very high status, who are thought to be able to relate to superior or high gods beyond the ordinary person's access or control.

Primary institutions   The sources of early experiences, such as family organization and subsistence techniques, that presumably help form the basic, or typical, personality found in a society.

Primary subsistence activities   The food-getting activities: gathering, hunting, fishing, herding, and agriculture.

Primate   A member of the mammalian order Primates, divided into the two suborders of prosimians and anthropoids.

Primatologists   People who study primates.

Primatology   The study of primates.

Probability value (*p*-value)   The likelihood that an observed result could have occurred by chance.

Proconsul   The best-known genus of proto-apes from the early Miocene.

Prognathic   A physical feature that is sticking out or pushed forward, such as the faces in apes and some hominid species.

Projective tests   Tests that utilize ambiguous stimuli; test subjects must project their own personality traits in order to structure the ambiguous stimuli.

Propliopithecids   Apelike anthropoids dating from the early Oligocene, found in the Fayum area of Egypt.

Prosimians   Literally "pre-monkeys," one of the two suborders of primates; includes lemurs, lorises, and tarsiers.

Protolanguage   A hypothesized ancestral language from which two or more languages seem to have derived.

Quadrupeds   Animals that walk on all fours.

Race   In biology, race refers to a subpopulation or variety of a species that differs somewhat in gene frequencies from other varieties of the species. All members of a species can interbreed and produce viable offspring. Many anthropologists do not think that the concept of race is usefully applied to humans because humans do not fall into geographic populations that can be easily distinguished in terms of different sets of biological or physical traits. Thus, race in humans is largely a culturally assigned category.

Rachis   The seed-bearing part of a plant. In the wild variety of grain, the rachis shatters easily, releasing the seeds. Domesticated grains have a tough rachis, which does not shatter easily.

Racism   The belief, without scientific basis, that some "races" are inferior to others.

Radiocarbon (or carbon-14, ^{14}C) dating   A dating method uses the decay of carbon-14 to date organic remains. It is reliable for dating once-living matter up to 50,000 years old.

Raiding   A short-term use of force, generally planned and organized, to realize a limited objective.

Random sample   A sample in which all cases selected have had an equal chance to be included.

Rank societies   Societies that do not have any unequal access to economic resources or power, but with social groups that have unequal access to status positions and prestige.

Recessive   An allele phenotypically suppressed in the heterozygous form and expressed only in the homozygous form.

Reciprocity   Giving and taking (not politically arranged) without the use of money.

Redistribution   The accumulation of goods (or labor) by a particular person or in a particular place and their subsequent distribution.

Relative dating   A method of dating fossils that determines the age of a specimen or deposit relative to a known specimen or deposit.

Religion   Any set of attitudes, beliefs, and practices pertaining to supernatural power, whether that power rests in forces, gods, spirits, ghosts, or demons.

Revitalization movements   New religious movements intended to save a culture by infusing it with a new purpose and life.

Revolution   A usually violent replacement of a society's rulers.

Ribosome   A structure in the cell used in making proteins.

Rituals   Repetitive sets of behaviors that occur in essentially the same patterns every time they occur. Religious rituals involve the supernatural in some way.

Robust australopithecines   A later group of australopithecines usually differentiated from the gracile australopithecines by their heavier dentition and larger faces.

411

Rules of descent Rules that connect individuals with particular sets of kin because of known or presumed common ancestry.

Sagittal crest A ridge of bone running along the top of the skull in apes and early hominids.

Sagittal keel An inverted V-shaped ridge running along the top of the skull in *Homo erectus.*

Sahelanthropus tchadensis A hominoid found in Chad dating to around 7 million years ago.

Sampling universe The list of cases to be sampled from.

Savanna Tropical grassland.

Secondary institutions Aspects of culture, such as religion, music, art, folklore, and games, which presumably reflect or are projections of the basic, or typical, personality in a society.

Secondary subsistence activities Activities that involve the preparation and processing of food either to make it edible or to store it.

Sedentarism Settled life.

Segmentary lineage system A hierarchy of more inclusive lineages; usually functions only in conflict situations.

Segregation The random sorting of chromosomes in meiosis.

Sex differences The typical differences between females and males that are most likely due to biological differences.

Sexually dimorphic A marked difference in size and appearance between males and females of a species.

Shaman A religious intermediary, usually part-time, whose primary function is to cure people through sacred songs, pantomime, and other means; sometimes called witch doctor by Westerners.

Shifting cultivation See **Extensive cultivation.**

Sib See **Clan.**

Siblings A person's brothers and sisters.

Sickle-cell anemia (sicklemia) A condition in which red blood cells assume a crescent (sickle) shape when deprived of oxygen, instead of the normal (disk) shape. The sickle-shaped red blood cells do not move through the body as readily as normal cells, and thus cause damage to the heart, lungs, brain, and other vital organs.

Sites Locations where the material remains of human activity have been preserved in a way that archaeologists or paleoanthropologists can recover them.

Sivapithecus A genus of ape from the later Miocene known for its thickly enameled teeth, suggesting a diet of hard, tough, or gritty items. Found primarily in western and southern Asia and now thought to be ancestral to orangutans.

Slash-and-burn A form of shifting cultivation in which the natural vegetation is cut down and burned off. The cleared ground is used for a short time and then left to regenerate.

Slaves A class of people who do not own their own labor or the products thereof.

Socialization A term anthropologists and psychologists use to describe the development, through the direct and indirect influence of parents and others, of children's patterns of behavior (and attitudes and values) that conform to cultural expectations. Also called **enculturation.**

Society A group of people who occupy a particular territory and speak a common language not generally understood by neighboring peoples. By this definition, societies do not necessarily correspond to nations.

Sociobiology Systematic study of the biological causes of human behavior. Compare with **behavioral ecology, evolutionary psychology,** and **dual-inheritance theory.**

Sociolinguistics The study of cultural and subcultural patterns of speaking in different social contexts.

Soft hammer A technique of stone tool manufacture in which a bone or wood hammer is used to strike flakes from a stone.

Sorcery The use of certain materials to invoke supernatural powers to harm people.

Sororal polygyny The marriage of a man to two or more sisters at the same time.

Sororate A custom whereby a woman is obliged to marry her deceased sister's husband.

Special-purpose money Objects of value for which only some goods and services can be exchanged.

Speciation The development of a new species.

Species A population that consists of organisms able to interbreed and produce viable and fertile offspring.

Specific evolution The particular sequence of change and adaptation of a society in a given environment.

Spirits Unnamed supernatural beings of nonhuman origin who are beneath the gods in prestige and often closer to the people; may be helpful, mischievous, or evil.

State An autonomous political unit with centralized decision making over many communities with power to govern by force (e.g., to collect taxes, draft people for work and war, and make and enforce laws). Most states have cities with public buildings; full-time craft and religious specialists; an "official" art style; a hierarchical social structure topped by an elite class; and a governmental monopoly on the legitimate use of force to implement policies.

State organization A society is described as having state organization when it includes one or more states.

Statistical association A relationship or correlation between two or more variables that is unlikely to be due to chance.

Statistically significant Refers to a result that would occur very rarely by chance. The result (and stronger ones) would occur fewer than 5 times out of 100 by chance.

Steppe Grassland with a dry, low grass cover.

Stratified An archaeological deposit that contains successive layers or strata.

Stratigraphy The study of how different rock formations and fossils are laid down in successive layers or strata. Older layers are generally deeper or lower than more recent layers.

Structuralism The theoretical orientation that human culture is a surface representation of the underlying structure of the human mind.

Structural linguistics See **Descriptive (structural) linguistics.**

Subculture The shared customs of a subgroup within a society.

Subsistence economies Economies in which almost all able-bodied adults are largely engaged in getting food for themselves and their families.

Supernatural Believed to be not human or not subject to the laws of nature.

Symbolic communication An arbitrary (not obviously meaningful) gesture, call, word, or sentence that has meaning even when its *referent* is not present.

Syntax The ways in which words are arranged to form phrases and sentences.

Taboo   A prohibition that, if violated, is believed to bring supernatural punishment.

Taphonomy   The study of how natural processes form and disturb archaeological sites.

Taurodontism   Having teeth with an enlarged pulp cavity.

Taxonomy   The classification of extinct and living organisms.

Terrestrial   Adapted to living on the ground.

Terrorism   The use or threat of violence to create terror in others, usually for political purposes.

Theoretical construct   Something that cannot be observed or verified directly.

Theoretical orientation   A general attitude about how phenomena are to be explained.

Theories   Explanations of associations or laws.

Totem   A plant or animal associated with a clan (sib) as a means of group identification; may have other special significance for the group.

Tribal organization   The kind of political organization in which local communities mostly act autonomously but there are kin groups (such as clans) or associations (such as age-sets) that can temporarily integrate a number of local groups into a larger unit.

Tribe   A territorial population in which there are kin or nonkin groups with representatives in a number of local groups.

Typology   A way of organizing artifacts in categories based on their particular characteristics.

Unifacial tool   A tool worked or flaked on one side only.

Unilineal descent   Affiliation with a group of kin through descent links of one sex only.

Unilocal residence   A pattern of residence (patrilocal, matrilocal, or avunculocal) that specifies just one set of relatives that the married couple lives with or near.

Unisex association   An association that restricts its membership to one sex, usually male.

Universally ascribed qualities   Those ascribed qualities (age, sex) that are found in all societies.

Upper Paleolithic   The time period associated with the emergence of modern humans and their spread around the world.

Variable   A thing or quantity that varies.

Variably ascribed qualities   Those ascribed qualities (such as ethnic, religious, or social class differences) that are found only in some societies.

Vertical clinging and leaping   A locomotor pattern characteristic of several primates, including tarsiers and galagos. The animal normally rests by clinging to a branch in a vertical position and uses its hind limbs alone to push off from one vertical position to another.

Warfare   Violence between political entities such as communities, districts, or nations.

Witchcraft   The practice of attempting to harm people by supernatural means, but through emotions and thought alone, not through the use of tangible objects.

"Y-5" pattern   Refers to the pattern of cusps on human molars. When looked at from the top, the cusps of the molars form a Y opening toward the cheek.

bibliography

'Abd Allah, Mahmud M. 1917. Siwan customs. *Harvard African Studies* 1:1–28.

Aberle, David. 1971. A note on relative deprivation theory as applied to millenarian and other cult movements. In *Reader in comparative religion*. 3rd ed., eds. W. A. Lessa and E. Z. Vogt. New York: Harper & Row.

Abler, Thomas S. 2009. Iroquois: The tree of peace and the war kettle. In MyAnthroLibrary, eds. C. R. Ember, M. Ember, and P. N. Peregrine. MyAnthroLibrary.com. Pearson.

Academic American Encyclopedia. 1980. Paper. Princeton, NJ: Areté.

Acheson, James M. 2006. Lobster and groundfish management in the Gulf of Maine: A rational choice perspective. *Human Organization* 65:240–52.

Adams, David B. 1983. Why there are so few women warriors. *Behavior Science Research* 18:196–212.

Adams, Robert McCormick. 1960. The origin of cities. *Scientific American* (September):153–68.

Adams, Robert McCormick. 1981. *Heartland of cities: Surveys of ancient settlement and land use on the central floodplain of the Euphrates.* Chicago: University of Chicago Press.

Ahern, Emily M. 1975. Sacred and secular medicine in a Taiwan village: A study of cosmological disorders. In *Medicine in Chinese cultures: Comparative studies of health care in Chinese and other societies,* eds. A. Kleinman et al. Washington, DC: U.S. Department of Health, Education, and Welfare, National Institutes of Health.

Aiello, Leslie C. 1992. Body size and energy requirements. In *The Cambridge encyclopedia of human evolution,* eds. S. Jones, R. Martin, and D. Pilbeam. New York: Cambridge University Press.

Aiello, Leslie C. 1993. The origin of the New World monkeys. In *The Africa-South America connection,* eds. W. George and R. Lavocat, 100–18. Oxford: Clarendon Press.

Aiello, Leslie C., and Mark Collard, 2001. Our newest oldest ancestor? *Nature* 410 (November 29):526–27.

Aiello, Leslie C., and Christopher Dean. 1990. *An introduction to human evolutionary anatomy,* 268–74. London: Academic Press.

Akmajian, Adrian, Richard A. Demers, Ann K. Farmer, and Robert M. Harnish. 2001. *Linguistics: An introduction to language and communication.* Cambridge, MA: The MIT Press.

Akmajian, Adrian, Richard A. Demers, and Robert M. Harnish. 1984. *Linguistics: An introduction to language and communication.* 2nd ed. Cambridge, MA: MIT Press.

Albert, Steven M., and Maria G. Cattell. 1994. *Old age in global perspective: Cross-cultural and cross-national views.* New York: G. K. Hall/Macmillan.

Alberts, Bruce, president of the National Academy of Sciences, November 9, 2000. "Setting the record straight regarding *Darkness in El Dorado,*" which can be found at the Web address: http://www4.nationalacademies.org/nas/nashome.nsf.

Alexander, John P. 1992. Alas, poor *Notharctus. Natural History* (August):55–59.

Algaze, Guillermo. 1993. *The Uruk world system: The dynamics of expansion of early Mesopotamian civilization.* Chicago: University of Chicago Press.

Allen, John S., and Susan M. Cheer. 1996. The non-thrifty genotype. *Current Anthropology* 37:831–42.

Allen, John S., A. J. Lambert, F. Y. Attah Johnson, K. Schmidt, and K. L. Nero. 1996. Antisaccadic eye movements and attentional asymmetry in schizophrenia in three Pacific populations. *Acta Psychiatrica Scandinavia* 94:258–65.

Alroy, John. 2001. A multispecies overkill simulation of the End-Pleistocene megafaunal mass extinction. *Science* 292 (June 8):1893–96.

Altman, Lawrence K. 2008. Protective effects of circumcision are shown to continue after trials' end. *New York Times,* August 12. http://www.nytimes.com.

Alvarez, Lizette. 2003. Arranged marriages get a little rearranging. *The New York Times,* June 22, p. 1.3.

Ambient Corporation. 2000. Energy: Investing for a new century. *New York Times,* October 30, EN1–EN8. A special advertisement produced by energy companies.

American Anthropological Association. 1991. Revised principles of professional responsibility, 1990. In *Ethics and the profession of anthropology: Dialogue for a new era,* ed. Carolyn Fluehr-Lobban, 274–79. Philadelphia: University of Pennsylvania Press.

Anderson, Connie M. 2000. The persistence of polygyny as an adaptive response to poverty and oppression in apartheid South Africa. *Cross-Cultural Research* 34:99–112.

Anderson, Craig A., and Brad J. Bushman. 2002. The effects of media violence on society. *Science* 295 (March 29): 2377–79.

Anderson, J. L., C. B. Crawford, J. Nadeau, and T. Lindberg. 1992. Was the Duchess of Windsor right? A cross-cultural review of the socioecology of ideal female body shape. *Ethnology and Sociobiology* 13:197–227.

Anderson, Richard L. 1989. *Art in small-scale societies.* 2nd ed. Englewood Cliffs, NJ: Prentice Hall.

Anderson, Richard L. 1990. *Calliope's sisters: A comparative study of philosophies of art.* Upper Saddle River, NJ: Prentice Hall.

Anderson, Richard L. 1992. Do other cultures have "art"? *American Anthropologist* 94:926–29.

Anderson, Sean K., and Stephen Sloan. 2002. *Historical dictionary of terrorism.* 2nd ed. Lanham, MD: Scarecrow Press.

Andrefsky, William. 1998. *Lithics: Macroscopic approaches to analysis.* New York : Cambridge University Press.

Andrews, Elizabeth. 1994. Territoriality and land use among the Akulmiut of western Alaska. In *Key issues in hunter-gatherer research,* eds. E. S. Burch Jr., and L. J. Ellanna. Oxford: Berg.

Andrews, Peter. 2000a. *Propliopithecidae.* In *Encyclopedia of human evolution and prehistory,* eds. I. Tattersall, E. Delson, and J. van Couvering. New York, Garland.

Andrews, Peter. 2000b. Proconsul. In *Encyclopedia of human evolution and prehistory,* eds. I. Tattersall, E. Delson, and J. van Couvering. New York: Garland.

Angier, Natalie. 2002. Why we're so nice: We're wired to cooperate. *New York Times,* Science Times, July 23, pp. F1, F8.

Anthony, David, Dimitri Y. Telegin, and Dorcas Brown. 1991. The origin of horseback riding. *Scientific American* (December): 94–100.

Antoun, Richard T. 2001. *Understanding fundamentalism: Christian, Islamic, and Jewish movements*. Walnut Creek, CA: AltaMira Press.

Anyon, Roger, and T. J. Ferguson. 1995. Cultural resources management at the Pueblo of Zuni, New Mexico, USA. *Antiquity* 69:913–30.

Aporta, Claudio, and Eric Higgs. 2005. Satellite culture: Global positioning systems, Inuit wayfinding, and the need for a new account of technology. *Current Anthropology* 46: 729–46.

Appendix A: Report of the Committee on Ethics, Society for Applied Anthropology. 2002. In *Ethics and the profession of anthropology*, ed. C. Fluehr-Lobban. Philadelphia: University of Pennsylvania Press.

Appendix C: Statements on Ethics: Principles of Professional Responsibility, Adopted by the Council of the American Anthropological Association, May 1971. 1991. In *Ethics and the profession of anthropology*, ed. C. Fluehr-Lobban. Philadelphia: University of Pennsylvania Press.

Appendix F: Professional and Ethical Responsibilities, SfAA. 2002. In *Ethics and the profession of anthropology*, ed. C. Fluehr-Lobban. Philadelphia: University of Pennsylvania Press.

Appendix H: National Association of Practicing Anthropologists' Ethical Guidelines for Practitioners, 1988. 1991. In *Ethics and the profession of anthropology*, ed. C. Fluehr-Lobban. Philadelphia: University of Pennsylvania Press.

Appendix I: Revised Principles of Professional Responsibility, 1990. 1991. In *Ethics and the profession of anthropology*, ed. C. Fluehr-Lobban. Philadelphia: University of Pennsylvania Press.

Aptekar, Lewis. 1988. *Street children of Cali*. Durham, NC: Duke University Press.

Aptekar, Lewis. 1991. Are Colombian street children neglected? The contributions of ethnographic and ethnohistorical approaches to the study of children. *Anthropology and Education Quarterly* 22:326–49.

Aptekar, Lewis. 1994. *Environmental disasters in global perspective*. New York: G. K. Hall/Macmillan.

Archer, Dane, and Rosemary Gartner. 1984. *Violence and crime in cross-national perspective*. New Haven, CT: Yale University Press.

Ardener, Shirley. 1995a/1964. The comparative study of rotating credit associations. In *Money-go-rounds*, eds. S. Ardener and S. Burman. Oxford: Berg.

Ardener, Shirley. 1995b/1964. Women making money go round: ROSCAs revisited." In *Money-go-rounds* eds. S. Ardener and S. Burman. Oxford: Berg.

Ardener, Shirley, and Sandra Burman, eds. 1995/1964. *Money-go-rounds: The importance of rotating savings and credit associations for women*. Oxford: Berg.

Argyle, Michael. 1994. *The psychology of social class*. New York: Routledge.

Armelagos, George J., and Alan H. Goodman. 1998. Race, racism, and anthropology. In *Building a new biocultural synthesis: Political-economic perspectives on human biology*, eds. A. H. Goodman and T. L. Leatherman. Ann Arbor: University of Michigan Press.

Armstrong, Robert P. 1981. *The powers of presence*. Philadelphia: University of Pennsylvania Press.

Aronoff, Joel, Andrew M. Barclay, and Linda A. Stevenson. 1988. The recognition of threatening facial stimuli. *Journal of Personality and Social Psychology* 54:647–55.

Aronoff, Joel, Barbara A. Woike, and Lester M. Hyman. 1992. Which are the stimuli in facial displays of anger and happiness? Configurational bases of emotion recognition. *Journal of Personality and Social Psychology* 62:1050–66.

Aronson, Joshua. 2002. Stereotype threat: Contending and coping with unnerving expectations. In *Improving academic performance*, ed. Joshua Aronson, 279–96. San Francisco: Academic Press.

Asch, Nancy B., and David L. Asch. 1978. The economic potential of *Iva annua* and its prehistoric importance in the Lower Illinois Valley. In *The nature and status of ethnobotany*, ed. R. Ford. Anthropological Papers No 67, Museum of Anthropology. Ann Arbor: University of Michigan.

Asch, Solomon. 1956. Studies of independence and conformity: A minority of one against a unanimous majority. *Psychological Monographs* 70:1–70.

Ascher, Robert. 1961. Analogy in archaeological interpretation. *Southwestern Journal of Anthropology* 17:317–25.

Asfaw, Berhane, Tim White, Owen Lovejoy, Bruce Latimer, Scott Simpson, and Glen Suwa. 1999. *Australopithecus garhi*: A new species of early hominid from Ethiopia. *Science* 284 (April 23):629–36.

Association business: Clyde Snow, forensic anthropologist, works for justice. *Anthropology News* (October 2000):12.

Ayala, Francisco J. 1995. The myth of Eve: Molecular biology and human origins. *Science* 270 (December 22):1930–36.

Ayala, Francisco J. 1996. Communication. *Science* 274 (November 29):1354.

Ayres, Barbara C. 1968. Effects of infantile stimulation on musical behavior. In *Folk song style and culture*, ed. A. Lomax. Washington, DC.

Ayres, Barbara C. 1973. Effects of infant carrying practices on rhythm in music. *Ethos* 1:387–404.

Bachnik, Jane M. 1992. The two "faces" of self and society in Japan. *Ethos* 20:3–32.

Bacon, Margaret, Irvin L. Child, and Herbert Barry III. 1963. A cross-cultural study of correlates of crime. *Journal of Abnormal and Social Psychology* 66:291–300.

Badcock, Christopher. 1988. *Essential Freud*. Oxford: Blackwell.

Badcock, C. R. 2000. *Evolutionary psychology: A critical introduction*. Cambridge: Blackwell.

Baer, Hans A., and Merrill Singer. 2009. *Global warming and the political ecology of health: Emerging crises and systemic solutions*. Walnut Creek, CA: Left Coast Press.

Baer, Hans A., Merrill Singer, and Ida Susser. 1997. *Medical anthropology and the world system: A critical perspective*. Westport, CT: Bergin & Garvey.

Bahn, Paul. 1998. Neanderthals emancipated. *Nature* 394 (August 20):719–20.

Bailey, Robert C., Genevieve Head, Mark Jenike, Bruce Owen, Robert Rectman, and Elzbieta Zechenter. 1989. Hunting and gathering in tropical rain forest: Is it possible? *American Anthropologist* 91:59–82.

Baldi, Philip. 1983. *An introduction to the Indo-European languages*. Carbondale: Southern Illinois University Press.

Balikci, Asen. 1970. *The Netsilik Eskimo*. Garden City, NY: Natural History Press.

Balter, Michael. 2001. In search of the first Europeans. *Science* 291 (March 2):1722–25.

Balter, Michael. 2007. Seeking agriculture's ancient roots. *Science* 316 (June 29):1830–35.

Balter, Michael, and Ann Gibbons. 2000. A glimpse of humans' first journey out of Africa. *Science* 288 (May 12):948–50.

Barak, Gregg. 1991. *Gimme shelter: A social history of homelessness in contemporary America*. New York: Praeger.

Barash, David P. 1977. *Sociobiology and behavior*. New York: Elsevier.

Barber, Nigel. 2000. The sex ratio as a predictor of cross-national variation in violent crime. *Cross-Cultural Research* 34:264–82.

Barber, Nigel. 2003. Paternal investment prospects and cross-national differences in single parenthood. *Cross-Cultural Research* 37:163–77.

Barber, Nigel. 2008. Explaining cross-national differences in polygyny intensity: Resource-defense, sex-ratio, and infectious diseases. *Cross-Cultural Research* 42:103–17.

Barinaga, Maria. 1992. Priming the brain's language pump. *Science* 255 (January 31):535.

Barlett, Peggy F. 1989. Industrial agriculture. In *Economic anthropology*, ed. S. Plattner. Stanford, CA: Stanford University Press.

Barnett, H. G. 1960. *Being a Palauan*. New York: Holt, Rinehart & Winston.

Barnosky, Anthony, Paul Koch, Robert Feranec, Scott Wing, and Alan Shabel. 2004. Assessing the causes of Late Pleistocene extinctions on the continents. *Science* 306 (October 1):70–75.

Barrett, D. E. 1984. Malnutrition and child behavior: Conceptualization, assessment and an empirical study of social-emotional functioning. In *Malnutrition and behavior: Critical assessment of key issues*, eds. J. Brozek and B. Schürch, 280–306. Lausanne, Switzerland: Nestlé Foundation.

Barrett, Stanley R. 1994. *Paradise: Class, commuters, and ethnicity in rural Ontario*. Toronto: University of Toronto Press.

Barry, Herbert III. 2007. Wealth concentration associated with frequent violent crime in diverse communities. *Social Evolution & History* 6:29–38.

Barry, Herbert III, Irvin L. Child, and Margaret K. Bacon. 1959. Relation of child training to subsistence economy. *American Anthropologist* 61:51–63.

Barth, Fredrik. 1965. *Nomads of South Persia*. New York: Humanities Press.

Barth, Fredrik. 1994. Enduring and emerging issues in the analysis of ethnicity. In *The anthropology of ethnicity*, eds. H. Vermeulen and C. Govers. Amsterdam: Het Spinhuis.

Bates, Daniel G., and Susan H. Lees, eds. 1996. *Case studies in human ecology*. New York: Plenum Press.

Bates, E. and V. A. Marchman, 1988. What is and is not universal in language acquisition. In *Language, communication, and the brain*, ed. F. Plum, 19–38. New York: Raven Press.

Bauman, Richard. 1992. Folklore. In *Folklore, cultural performances, and popular entertainments*, ed. R. Bauman. New York: Oxford University Press.

Baxter, Ellen, and Kim Hopper. 1981. *Private lives/public spaces: Homeless adults on the streets of New York City*. New York: Community Service Society of New York.

Beadle, George, and Muriel Beadle. 1966. *The language of life*. Garden City, NY: Doubleday.

Bearder, Simon K. 1987. Lorises, bushbabies, and tarsiers: Diverse societies in solitary foragers. In *Primate societies*, eds. B. Smuts et al. Chicago: University of Chicago Press.

Beattie, John. 1960. *Bunyoro: An African kingdom*. New York: Holt, Rinehart & Winston.

Begler, Elsie B. 1978. Sex, status, and authority in egalitarian society. *American Anthropologist* 80:571–88.

Begun, David. 2002. Miocene apes. In *Physical anthropology: Original readings in method and practice*, eds. P. N. Peregrine, C. R. Ember, and M. Ember. Upper Saddle River, NJ: Prentice Hall.

Behar, Ruth, and Deborah Gordon, eds. 1995. *Women writing culture*. Berkeley: University of California Press.

Behrman, Jere R., Alejandro Gaviria, and Miguel Székely. 2001. Intergenerational mobility in Latin America. Inter-American Development Bank, Working Paper #45. http://www.iadb.org/res/publications/pubfiles/pubWP-452.pdf (accessed June 2009).

Bellman, Beryl L. 1984. *The language of secrecy: Symbols and metaphors in Poro ritual*. New Brunswick, NJ: Rutgers University Press.

Benjamin, Lois. 1991. *The black elite: Facing the color line in the twilight of the twentieth century*. Chicago: Nelson-Hall.

Berggren, William A., Dennis V. Kent, John D. Obradovich, and Carl C. Swisher III. 1992. Toward a revised paleogene geochronology. In *Eocene-Oliocene climatic and biotic evolution*, eds. D. R. Prothero and W. A. Berggren. Princeton, NJ: Princeton University Press.

Berlin, Brent. 1992. *Ethnobiological classification: Principles of categorization of plants and animals in traditional societies*. Princeton, NJ: Princeton University Press.

Berlin, Brent, and Paul Kay. 1969. *Basic color terms: Their universality and evolution*. Berkeley: University of California Press.

Berlin, E. A. 1996. General overview of Maya ethnomedicine. In *Medical ethnobiology of the highland Maya of Chiapas, Mexico*, eds. E. A. Berlin and B. Berlin, 52–53. Princeton, NJ: Princeton University Press.

Berlin, Elois Ann, and Brent Berlin. 1996. *Medical ethnobiology of the highland Maya of Chiapas, Mexico: The gastrointestinal diseases*. Princeton, NJ: Princeton University Press.

Bernard, H. Russell. 2001. *Research methods in cultural anthropology: Qualitative and quantitative approaches*. 3rd ed. Walnut Creek, CA: AltaMira Press.

Bernardi, B. 1952. The age-system of the Nilo-Hamitic peoples. *Africa* 22:316–32.

Berns, G., J. Chappelow, C. Zink, G. Pagnoni, M. Martin-Skurski, and J. Richards. 2005. Neurobiological correlates of social conformity and independence during mental rotation. *Biological Psychiatry* 58: 245–53.

Berreman, Gerald D. 1960. Caste in India and the United States. *American Journal of Sociology* 66:120–27.

Berreman, Gerald D. 1972. Race, caste and other invidious distinctions in social stratification. *Race* 13:403–14.

Berreman, Gerald D. 1973. *Caste in the modern world*. Morristown, NJ: General Learning Press.

Berry, John W. 1971. Ecological and cultural factors in spatial perceptual development. *Canadian Journal of Behavioural Science* 3:324–36.

Berry, John W. 1976. *Human ecology and cognitive style*. New York: Wiley.

Berry, John W., and J. Bennett. 1989. Syllabic literacy and cognitive performance among the Cree. *International Journal of Psychology* 24:429–50.

417

Berry, John W., Ype H. Poortinga, Marshall H. Segall, and Pierre R. Dasen. 1992. *Cross-cultural psychology: Research and applications.* New York: Cambridge University Press.

Bestor, Theodore C. 2001. Supply-side sushi: Commodity, market, and the global city. *American Anthropologist* 103:76–95.

Betts, Richard A., Yadvinder Malhi, and J. Timmons Roberts. 2008. The future of the Amazon: New perspectives from climate, ecosystem, and social sciences. *Philosophical Transactions of the Royal Society* B, 363:1729–35.

Betzig, Laura. 1988. Redistribution: Equity or exploitation? In *Human reproductive behavior*, eds. L. Betzig, M. B. Mulder, and P. Turke, 49–63. Cambridge: Cambridge University Press.

Betzig, Laura. 1989. Causes of conjugal dissolution: A cross-cultural study. *Current Anthropology* 30:654–676.

Bickerton, Derek. 1983. Creole languages. *Scientific American* (July):116–22.

Bilby, Kenneth. 1996. Ethnogenesis in the Guianas and Jamaica: Two Maroon cases. In *Ethnogenesis in the Americas*, ed. J. D. Hill, 119–41. Iowa City: University of Iowa Press.

Bilsborough, Alan. 1992. *Human evolution.* New York: Blackie Academic & Professional.

Bindon, James R., and Douglas E. Crews. 1993. Changes in some health status characteristics of American Samoan men: Preliminary observations from a 12-year follow-up study. *American Journal of Human Biology* 5:31–37.

Bindon, James R., Amy Knight, William W. Dressler, and Douglas E. Crews. 1997. Social context and psychosocial influences on blood pressure among American Samoans. *American Journal of Physical Anthropology* 103:7–18.

Binford, Lewis R. 1971. Post-Pleistocene adaptations. In *Prehistoric agriculture*, ed. S. Struever. Garden City, NY: Natural History Press.

Binford, Lewis R. 1973. Interassemblage variability: The Mousterian and the "functional" argument. In *The explanation of culture change*, ed. C. Renfrew. Pittsburgh: University of Pittsburgh Press.

Binford, Lewis R. 1984. *Faunal remains from Klasies River mouth.* Orlando, FL: Academic Press.

Binford, Lewis R. 1987. Were there elephant hunters at Torralba? In *The evolution of human hunting*, eds. M. Nitecki and D. Nitecki. New York: Plenum.

Binford, Lewis R. 1990. Mobility, housing, and environment: A comparative study. *Journal of Anthropological Research* 46:119–52.

Binford, Lewis R., and Chuan Kun Ho. 1985. Taphonomy at a distance: Zhoukoudian, 'The cave home of Beijing Man'?" *Current Anthropology* 26:413–42.

Binford, Sally R., and Lewis R. Binford. 1969. Stone tools and human behavior. *Scientific American* (April):70–84.

Bishop, Ryan. 1996. Postmodernism. In *Encyclopedia of cultural anthropology*, eds. David Levinson and Melvin Ember, vol 3, 993–98. New York: Henry Holt.

Black, Donald. 1993. *The social structure of right and wrong.* San Diego: Academic Press.

Black, Francis L. 1992. Why did they die? *Science* 258 (December 11): 1739–40.

Blackwood, Evelyn. 1984a. *Cross-cultural dimensions of lesbian relations.* Master's Thesis. San Francisco State University. As referred to in Blackwood and Wieringa 1999.

Blackwood, Evelyn. 1984b. Sexuality and gender in certain Native American tribes: The case of cross-gender females. *Signs* 10:27–42.

Blackwood, Evelyn, and Saskia E. Wieringa. 1999. Sapphic shadows: Challenging the silence in the study of sexuality. In *Female desires: Same-sex relations and transgender practices across cultures*, eds. Evelyn Blackwood and Saskia E. Weiringa, 39–63. New York: Columbia University Press.

Blalock, Hubert M. 1972. *Social statistics.* 2nd ed. New York: McGraw-Hill.

Blanton, Richard E. 1976. The origins of Monte Albán. In *Cultural continuity and change*, ed. C.E. Cleland. New York: Academic Press.

Blanton, Richard E. 1978. *Monte Albán: Settlement patterns at the ancient Zapotec capital.* New York: Academic Press.

Blanton, Richard E. 1981. The rise of cities. In *Supplement to the handbook of Middle American Indians*, vol. 1., ed. J. Sabloff. Austin: University of Texas Press.

Blanton, Richard E. 2009. Variation in economy. In MyAnthroLibrary, eds. C. R. Ember, M. Ember, and P. N. Peregrine. MyAnthroLibrary.com. Pearson.

Blanton, Richard E., and Lane Fargher. 2008. *Collective action in the formation of pre-modern states.* New York: Springer.

Blanton, Richard E., Stephen A. Kowalewski, Gary Feinman, and Jill Appel. 1981. *Ancient Mesoamerica: A comparison of change in three regions.* New York: Cambridge University Press.

Bledsoe, Caroline H. 1980. *Women and marriage in Kpelle society.* Stanford, CA: Stanford University Press.

Block, Jean L. 1983. Help! They've all moved back home! *Woman's Day* (April 26):72–76.

Block, Jonathan I., and Doug M. Boyer. 2002. Grasping primate origins. *Science* 298 (November 22):1606–10.

Blount, Ben G. 1981. The development of language in children. In *Handbook of cross-cultural human development*, eds. R. H. Munroe, R. L. Munroe, and B. B. Whiting. New York: Garland.

Bluebond-Langner, Myra. 2007. Challenges and opportunities in the anthropology of childhoods: An introduction to "children, childhoods, and childhood studies." *American Anthropologist* 109:241–46.

Blumenschine, Robert J., Charles R. Peters, Fidelis T. Masao, Ronald J. Clarke, Alan L. Deino, Richard L. Hay, Carl C. Swisher, Ian G. Stanistreet, Gail M. Ashley, Lindsay J. McHenry, Nancy E. Sikes, Nikolaas J. van der Merwe, Joanne C. Tactikos, Amy E. Cushing, Daniel M. Deocampo, Jackson K. Njau, and James I. Ebert. 2003. Late Pliocene *Homo* and hominid land use from western Olduvai Gorge, Tanzania. *Science* 299 (February 21): 1217–21.

Blumler, Mark A., and Roger Byrne. 1991. The ecological genetics of domestication and the origins of agriculture. *Current Anthropology* 32:23–35.

Boas, Franz. 1888. *Central Eskimos.* Bureau of American Ethnology Annual Report No. 6. Washington, DC.

Boas, Franz. 1930. The religion of the Kwakiutl. *Columbia University contributions to Anthropology*, vol. 10, pt. 2. New York: Columbia University.

Boas, Franz. 1940. *Race, language, and culture.* New York: Macmillan.

Boas, Franz. 1964/1911. On grammatical categories. In *Language in culture and society*, ed. D. Hymes. New York: Harper & Row.

Boaz, Noel T., and Alan J. Almquist. 1997. *Biological anthropology: A synthetic approach to human evolution.* Upper Saddle River, NJ: Prentice Hall.

Boaz, Noel T., and Alan J. Almquist. 1999. *Essentials of biological anthropology*. Upper Saddle River, NJ: Prentice Hall.

Boaz, Noel T., and Alan J. Almquist. 2002. *Biological Anthropology: A Synthetic Approach to Human Evolution*. 2nd ed. Upper Saddle River, NJ: Prentice Hall.

Bock, Philip K. 1980. *Continuities in psychological anthropology: A historical introduction*. San Francisco: W. H. Freeman and Company.

Bock, Philip K. 1996. Psychological anthropology. In *Encyclopedia of cultural anthropology*, eds. David Levinson and Melvin Ember, vol 3, 1042–45. New York: Henry Holt.

Bodley, John H. 2008. *Victims of progress*. 5th ed. Lanham, MD: AltaMira Press.

Boehm, Christopher. 1993. Egalitarian behavior and reverse dominance hierarchy. *Current Anthropology* 34:230–31.

Boehm, Christopher. 1999. *Hierarchy in the forest: The evolution of egalitarian behavior*. Cambridge, MA: Harvard University Press.

Boesche, C., P. Marchesi, N. Marchesi, B. Fruth, and F. Joulian.1994. Is nut cracking in wild chimpanzees a cultural behavior? *Journal of Human Evolution* 26:325–38.

Bogin, Barry. 1988. *Patterns of human growth*. Cambridge: Cambridge University Press.

Bogoras, Waldemar. 1909. The Chukchee. Part 3. *Memoirs of the American Museum of Natural History*, 2.

Bohannan, Laura, and Paul Bohannan. 1953. *The Tiv of central Nigeria*. London: International African Institute.

Bohannan, Paul. 1954. The migration and expansion of the Tiv. *Africa* 24:2–16.

Bollen, Kenneth A. 1993. Liberal democracy: Validity and method factors in cross-national measures. *American Journal of Political Science* 37:1207–30.

Bolton, Ralph. 1973. Aggression and hypoglycemia among the Qolla: A Study in psychobiological anthropology. *Ethnology* 12:227–57.

Bolton, Ralph. 1989. Introduction: The AIDS pandemic, a global emergency. *Medical Anthropology* 10:93–104.

Bolton, Ralph. 1992. AIDS and promiscuity: Muddled in the models of HIV prevention. *Medical Anthropology* 14: 145–223.

Bond, Rod, and Peter B. Smith. 1996. Culture and conformity: A meta-analysis of studies using Asch's (1952b, 1956) line judgment task. *Psychological Bulletin* 11:111–37.

Bondarenko, Dmitri, and Andrey Korotayev. 2000. Family size and community organization: A cross-cultural comparison. *Cross-Cultural Research* 34:152–89.

Bordaz, Jacques. 1970. *Tools of the Old and New Stone Age*. Garden City, NY: Natural History Press.

Bordes, François. 1961. Mousterian cultures in France. *Science* 134 (September 22):803–10.

Bordes, François. 1968. *The Old Stone Age*. New York: McGraw-Hill, 51–97.

Borgerhoff Mulder, Monique, Margaret George-Cramer, Jason Eshleman, and Alessia Ortolani. 2001. A study of East African kinship and marriage using a phylogenetically based comparative method. *American Anthropologist* 103:1059–82.

Bornstein, Marc H. 1973. The psychophysiological component of cultural difference in color naming and illusion susceptibility. *Behavior Science Notes* 8:41–101.

Bortei-Doku, Ellen, and Ernest Aryeetey. 1995/1964. Mobilizing cash for business: Women in rotating Susu clubs in Ghana. In *Money-go-rounds*, eds. S. Ardener and S. Burman, 77–94. Oxford: Berg.

Boserup, Ester. 1970. *Woman's role in economic development*. New York: St. Martin's Press.

Boserup, Ester. 1993/1965. *The conditions of agricultural growth: The economics of agrarian change under population pressure*. Toronto: Earthscan Publishers.

Bossen, Laurel. 2000. Women farmers, small plots, and changing markets in China. In *Women farmers and commercial ventures: Increasing food security in developing countries*, ed. Anita Spring, 171–89. Boulder, CO: Lynne Rienner Press.

Bourguignon, Erika. 1973. Introduction: A framework for the comparative study of altered states of consciousness. In *Religion, altered states of consciousness, and social change*, ed. E. Bourguignon. Columbus: Ohio State University Press.

Bourguignon, Erika. 2004. Suffering and healing, subordination and power: Women and possession trance. *Ethos* 32:557–74.

Bourguignon, Erika, and Thomas L. Evascu. 1977. Altered states of consciousness within a general evolutionary perspective: A holocultural analysis. *Behavior Science Research* 12:197–216.

Bowen, Gabriel J., et al. 2002. Mammalian dispersal at the Paleocene/Eocene boundary. *Science* 295 (March 15): 2062–64.

Bowie, Katherine A. 2006. Of corvée and slavery: Historical intricacies of the division of labor and state power in northern Thailand. In *Labor in cross-cultural perspective*, eds. E. Paul Durrenberger and Judith E. Martí, 245–64. Lanham: Roman & Littlefield.

Bowles, S., H. Gintis, and M. Osborne. 2001. The determinants of earnings: A behavioral approach. *Journal of Economic Literature* 39:1137–76, as referred to in Godoy et al. 2004.

Boyd, Robert, and Peter J. Richerson. 1996/1985. *Culture and the evolutionary process*. Chicago: University of Chicago Press.

Boyd, Robert, and Peter J. Richerson. 2005. *The origin and evolution of cultures*. New York: Oxford University Press.

Boyd, Robert, and Joan Silk. 2000. *How humans evolved*. 2nd ed. New York: Norton.

Brace, C. Loring. 1995. Region does not mean 'race'—reality versus convention in forensic anthropology. *Journal of Forensic Sciences* 40:171–75.

Brace, C. Loring. 1996. A four-letter word called race. In *Race and other misadventures: Essays in honor of Ashley Montague in his ninetieth year*, eds. Larry T. Reynolds and Leonard Lieberman. New York: General Hall.

Brace, C. Loring. 2005. *"Race" is a four-letter word*. New York: Oxford University Press.

Brace, C. Loring, David P. Tracer, Lucia Allen Yaroch, John Robb, Kari Brandt, and A. Russell Nelson. 1993. Clines and clusters versus 'race': A test in ancient Egypt and the case of a death on the Nile. *Yearbook of Physical Anthropology* 36: 1–31.

Bradley, Candice. 1984–1985. The sexual division of labor and the value of children. *Behavior Science Research* 19:159–85.

Bradley, Candice. 1995. Keeping the soil in good heart: Weeding, women and ecofeminism. In *Ecofeminism*, ed. K. Warren. Bloomington: Indiana University Press.

Bradsher, Keith. 2002. Pakistanis fume as clothing sales to U.S. tumble. *New York Times*, June 23, p. 3.

Braidwood, Robert J. 1960. The agricultural revolution. *Scientific American* (September):130–48.

Braidwood, Robert J., and Gordon R. Willey. 1962. Conclusions and afterthoughts. In *Courses toward urban life*, eds. R. Braidwood and G. Willey. Chicago: Aldine.

Brain, C. K., and A. Sillen. 1988. Evidence from the Swartkrans Cave for the earliest use of fire. *Nature*, 336 (December 1):464–66.

Branda, Richard F., and John W. Eaton. 1978. Skin color and nutrient photolysis: An evolutionary hypothesis. *Science* 201 (August 18): 625–26.

Brandewie, Ernest. 1991. The place of the big man in traditional Hagen society in the central highlands of New Guinea. In *Anthropological approaches to political behavior*, eds. F. McGlynn and A. Tuden. Pittsburgh, PA: University of Pittsburgh Press.

Brandon, Robert N. 1990. *Adaptation and environment*. Princeton, NJ: Princeton University Press.

Bräuer, Günter. 1984. A craniological approach to the origin of anatomically modern *Homo sapiens* in Africa and implications for the appearance of modern Europeans. In *The origins of modern humans*, eds. F. Smith and F Spencer. New York: Alan R. Liss.

Braun, David P., and Stephen Plog. 1982. Evolution of "tribal" social networks: Theory and prehistoric North American evidence. *American Antiquity* 47:504–25.

Brettell, Caroline B. 1996. Migration. In *Encyclopedia of cultural anthropology*, vol. 3, 4 vols., eds. D. Levinson and M. Ember, 793–97. New York: Henry Holt.

Brettell, Caroline, and Robert V. Kemper. 2002. Migration and cities. In *Encyclopedia of urban cultures: Cities and cultures around the world*, vol. 1, 4 vols., eds. M. Ember and C. R. Ember, 30–38. Danbury, CT: Grolier/Scholastic.

Briggs, Jean L. 1974. Eskimo women: Makers of men. In *Many sisters: Women in cross-cultural perspective*, ed. C. J. Matthiasson. New York: Free Press.

Bringa, Tone. 1995. *Being Muslim the Bosnian way: Identity and community in a central Bosnian village*. Princeton, NJ: Princeton University Press, as examined in the eHRAF Collection of Ethnography on the Web.

Brinton, Crane. 1938. *The anatomy of revolution*. Upper Saddle River, NJ: Prentice Hall.

Brittain, John A. 1978. *Inheritance and the inequality of material wealth*. Washington, DC: Brookings Institution.

Britannica Online. 1995. Book of the year (1995): World affairs: Rwanda; and Book of the year (1995): Race and ethnic relations: Rwanda's complex ethnic history. *Britannica Online*, December.

Britannica Online. 1998 (February). Printing, typography, and photoengraving; History of prints: Origins in China: Transmission of paper to Europe (12th century).

Brodey, Jane E. 1971. Effects of milk on blacks noted. *New York Times* October 15, p. 15.

Brodwin, Paul E. 1996. Disease and culture. In *Encyclopedia of cultural anthropology*, vol. 1, eds. D. Levinson and M. Ember, 355–59. New York: Henry Holt.

Bromage, Timothy G., and M. Christopher Dean. 1985. Reevaluation of the age at death of immature fossil hominids. *Nature* 317(October 10):525–27.

Brooks, Alison S., Fatimah Linda Collier Jackson, and R. Richard Grinker. 1993. Race and ethnicity in America. *Anthro Notes* (National Museum of Natural History Bulletin for Teachers), 15, no. 3 (Fall): 1–3, 11–15.

Broom, Robert. 1950. *Finding the missing link*. London: Watts.

Broude, Gwen J. 1976. Cross-cultural patterning of some sexual attitudes and practices. *Behavior Science Research* 11:227–62.

Broude, Gwen J. 1980. Extramarital sex norms in cross-cultural perspective. *Behavior Science Research* 15: 181–218.

Broude, Gwen J. 2004. Sexual attitudes and practices. In *Encyclopedia of sex and gender: Men and women in the world's cultures*, vol. 1, eds. C. Ember and M. Ember, 177–86. New York: Kluwer Academic/Plenum Publishers.

Broude, Gwen J. 2009. Variations in sexual attitudes, norms, and practices. In MyAnthroLibrary, eds. C. R. Ember, M. Ember, and P. N. Peregrine. MyAnthroLibrary.com. Pearson

Broude, Gwen J., and Sarah J. Greene. 1976. Cross-cultural codes on twenty sexual attitudes and practices. *Ethnology* 15:409–29.

Brown, Cecil H. 1977. Folk botanical life-forms: Their universality and growth. *American Anthropologist* 79:317–42.

Brown, Cecil H. 1979. Folk zoological life-forms: Their universality and growth. *American Anthropologist* 81: 791–817.

Brown, Cecil H. 1984. World view and lexical uniformities. *Reviews in Anthropology* 11:99–112.

Brown, Cecil H., and Stanley R. Witkowski. 1980. Language universals. In *Toward explaining human culture*, eds. D. Levinson and M. J. Malone, Appendix B. New Haven, CT: HRAF Press.

Brown, Donald E. 1991. *Human universals*. Philadelphia: Temple University Press.

Brown, Frank H. 1992. Methods of dating. In *The Cambridge encyclopedia of human evolution*, eds. S. Jones, R. Martin, and D. Pilbeam. New York: Cambridge University Press.

Brown, Frank H. 2000. Geochronometry. In *Encyclopedia of human evolution and prehistory*, eds. I. Tattersall, G. Delson, and J. van Couvering. New York: Garland.

Brown, James A. 1983. Summary. In *Archaic hunters and gatherers in the American Midwest*, eds. J. L. Phillips and J. A. Brown, 5–10. New York: Academic Press.

Brown, James A. 1985. Long-term trends to sedentism and the emergence of complexity in the American Midwest. In *Prehistoric hunter-gatherers*, eds. T. Price and J. Brown, 201–31. Orlando, FL: Academic Press.

Brown, James A., and T. Douglas Price. 1985. Complex hunter-gatherers: Retrospect and prospect. In *Prehistoric hunter-gatherers*, eds. T. Price and J. Brown. Orlando, FL: Academic Press.

Brown, Judith K. 1970a. Economic organization and the position of women among the Iroquois. *Ethnohistory* 17:151–67.

Brown, Judith K. 1970b. A note on the division of labor by sex. *American Anthropologist* 72:1073–78.

Brown, Michael F. 2008. Cultural relativism 2.0. *Current Anthropology* 49:363–83.

Brown, Peter J. 1997. Culture and the evolution of obesity. In *Applying cultural anthropology*, eds. A. Podolefsky and P. J. Brown. Mountain View, CA: Mayfield.

Brown, Roger. 1965. *Social psychology*. New York: Free Press.

Brown, Roger. 1980. The first sentence of child and chimpanzee. In *Speaking of apes*, eds. T. A. Sebeok and J. Umiker-Sebeok. New York: Plenum Press.

Brown, Roger, and Marguerite Ford. 1961. Address in American English. *Journal of Abnormal and Social Psychology* 62:375–85.

Browner, C. H. 1985. Criteria for selecting herbal remedies. *Ethnology* 24:13–32.

Brues, Alice. 1992. Forensic diagnosis of race—General race versus specific populations. *Social Science and Medicine* 34:125–28.

Brumbach, Hetty Jo, and Robert Jarvenpa. 2006a. Chipewyan society and gender relations. In *Circumpolar lives and livelihood: A comparative ethnoarchaeology of gender and subsistence*, eds. R. Jarvenpa and H. J. Brumbach, 24–53. Lincoln, Nebraska: University of Nebraska Press.

Brumbach, Hetty Jo, and Robert Jarvenpa. 2006b. Conclusion: Toward a comparative ethnoarchaeology of gender. In *Circumpolar lives and livelihood: A comparative ethnoarchaeology of gender and subsistence*, ed. R. Jarvenpa and H. J. Brumbach, 287–323. Lincoln, Nebraska: University of Nebraska Press.

Brumfiel, Elizabeth M. 1976. Regional growth in the eastern Valley of Mexico: A test of the "population pressure" hypothesis. In *The early Mesoamerican village*, ed. K. Flannery. New York: Academic Press.

Brumfiel, Elizabeth M. 1983. Aztec state making: Ecology, structure, and the origin of the state. *American Anthropologist* 85:261–84.

Brumfiel, Elizabeth M. 1992. Distinguished lecture in archeology: Breaking and entering the ecosystem—gender, class, and faction steal the show. *American Anthropologist* 94: 551–67.

Brumfiel, Elizabeth M. 2009. Origins of social inequality. In MyAnthroLibrary, eds. C. R. Ember, M. Ember, and P. N. Peregrine. MyAnthroLibrary.com. Pearson.

Brunet, Michel, Alain Beauvilain, Yves Coppens, Elile Heintz, Aladji H. E. Moutaye, and David Pilbeam. 1995. The first australopithecine 2,500 kilometers west of the Rift Valley (Chad). *Nature* 378:273–75.

Brunet, Michel, Franck Guy, David Pilbeam, Hassane Taisso Mackaye, Andossa Likius, Djimdoumalbaye Ahounta, Alain Beauvilain, Cécile Blondel, Hervé Bocherens, Jean-Renaud Boisserie, Louis De Bonis, Yves Coppens, Jean Dejax, Christiane Denys, Philippe Duringer, Véra Eisenmann, Gongdibé Fanone, Pierre Fronty, Denis Geraads, Thomas Lehmann, Fabrice Lihoreau, Antoine Louchart, Adoum Mahamat, Gildas Merceron, Guy Mouchelin, Olga Otero, Pablo Pelaez Campomanes, Marcia Ponce De Leon, Jean-Claude Rage, Michel Sapanet, Mathieu Schuster, Jean Sudre, Pascal Tassy, Xavier Valentin, Patrick Vignaud, Laurent Viriot, Antoine Zazzo and Christoph Zollikofer. 2002. A new hominid from the upper Miocene of Chad, Central Africa. *Nature* 418 (July 11):145–51.

Brunvand, Jan Harold. 1993. *The baby train: And other lusty urban legends*. New York: Norton.

Brusco, Elizabeth E. 1996. Religious conversion. In *Encyclopedia of cultural anthropology*, vol. 3, eds. D. Levinson and M. Ember, 1100–04. New York: Henry Holt.

Bryant, Carol A., and Doraine F. C. Bailey. 1990. The use of focus group research in program development. In *Soundings*, eds. J. van Willigen and T. L. Finan. NAPA Bulletin No. 10. Washington, DC: American Anthropological Association.

Buckser, Andrew, and Stephen D. Glazier, eds. 2003. Preface. In *The anthropology of religious conversion*, eds. Andrew Buckser and Stephen D. Glazier. Lanham, MD: Roman & Littlefield.

Budiansky, Stephen. 1992. *The covenant of the wild: Why animals chose domestication*. New York: Morrow.

Buettner-Janusch, John. 1973. *Physical anthropology: A perspective*. New York: Wiley.

Bunzel, Ruth. 1971. The nature of katcinas. In *Reader in comparative religion*, 3rd ed., eds. W. A. Lessa and E. Z. Vogt. New York: Harper & Row.

Burbank, Victoria K. 1994. *Fighting women: Anger and aggression in aboriginal Australia*. Berkeley: University of California Press.

Burbank, Victoria K. 2009a. Adolescent socialization and initiation ceremonies. In MyAnthroLibrary, eds. C. R. Ember, M. Ember, and P. N. Peregrine. MyAnthroLibrary.com. Pearson.

Burbank, Victoria K. 2009b. Australian Aborigines: An adolescent mother and her family. In MyAnthroLibrary, eds. C. R. Ember, M. Ember, and P. N. Peregrine. MyAnthroLibrary.com. Pearson.

Burch, Ernest S., Jr. 2009. North Alaskan Eskimos: A changing way of life. In MyAnthroLibrary, eds. C. R. Ember, M. Ember, and P. N. Peregrine. MyAnthroLibrary.com. Pearson.

Burch, Ernest S., Jr. 1988. *The Eskimos*. Norman: University of Oklahoma Press.

Burkhalter, S. Brian, and Robert F. Murphy. 1989. Tappers and sappers: Rubber, gold and money among the Mundurucú. *American Ethnologist* 16:100–16.

Burns, Alisa, and Cath Scott. 1994. *Mother-headed families and why they have increased*. Hillsdale, NJ: Lawrence Erlbaum Associates.

Burton, Roger V., and John W. M. Whiting. 1961. The absent father and cross-sex identity. *Merrill-Palmer Quarterly Of Behavior And Development* 7(2):85–95.

Busby, Annette. 2009. Kurds: A culture straddling national borders. In MyAnthroLibrary, eds. C. R. Ember, M. Ember, and P. N. Peregrine. MyAnthroLibrary.com. Pearson.

Butzer, Karl W. 1982. Geomorphology and sediment stratigraphy. In *The Middle Stone Age at Klasies River Mouth in South Africa*, eds. R. Singer and J. Wymer. Chicago: University of Chicago Press.

Byrne, Bryan. 1994. Access to subsistence resources and the sexual division of labor among potters. *Cross-Cultural Research* 28:225–50.

Byrne, Roger. 1987. Climatic change and the origins of agriculture. In *Studies in the Neolithic and urban revolutions*, ed. L. Manzanilla. British Archaeological Reports International Series 349. Oxford.

Calvin, William H. 1983. *The throwing Madonna: Essays on the brain*. New York: McGraw-Hill.

Campbell, Donald T. 1965. Variation and selective retention in socio-cultural evolution. In *Social change in developing areas*, eds. H. Barringer, G. Blankstein, and R. Mack. Cambridge, MA: Schenkman.

Campbell, Joseph. 1949. *The hero with a thousand faces*. New York: Pantheon.

Cancian, Frank. 1980. Risk and uncertainty in agricultural decision making. In *Agricultural decision making*, ed. P. F. Barlett. New York: Academic Press.

Cann, Rebecca. 1988. DNA and human origins. *Annual Review of Anthropology* 17:127–43.

Cann, Rebecca, M. Stoneking, and A. C. Wilson. 1987. Mitochondrial DNA and human evolution. *Nature* 325 (January 1):31–36.

Caporael, Linnda R. 1976. Ergotism: The Satan loosed in Salem? *Science* (April 2):21–26.

Carbonell, Eudald, José M. Bermúdez de Castro, Josep M. Parés, Alfredo Pérez-González, Gloria Cuenca-Bescós, Andreu Ollé, Marina Mosquera, Rosa Huguet, Jan van der Made, Antonio Rosas, Robert Sala, Josep Vallverdú, Nuria García, Darryl E. Granger, María Martinón-Torres, Xosé P. Rodríguez, Greg M. Stock, Josep M. Vergès, Ethel Allué, Francesc Burjachs, Isabel Cáceres, Antoni Canals, Alfonso Benito, Carlos Díez, Marina Lozano, Ana Mateos, Marta Navazo, Jesús Rodríguez, Jordi Rosell, Juan L. Arsuaga. 2008. The first hominin of Europe. *Nature* 452 (March 27): 465–69.

Cardoso, Fernando Luis and Dennis Werner. 2004. Homosexuality. In *Encyclopedia of sex and gender: Men and women in the world's cultures*, vol 1., eds. C. Ember and M. Ember, 204–15. New York: Kluwer Academic/Plenum Publishers.

Carey, James W., Erin Picone-DeCaro, Mary Spink Neumann, Devorah Schwartz, Delia Easton, and Daphne Cobb St. John. 2004. HIV/AIDS research and prevention. In *Encyclopedia of medical anthropology: Health and illness in the world's cultures*, vol. 1, eds. C. R. Ember and M. Ember, 462–79. New York: Kluwer Academic/ Plenum.

Carcopino, Jerome. 1940. *Daily life in ancient Rome: The people and the city at the height of the empire*. Edited with bibliography and notes by Henry T. Rowell. Translated from the French by E. O. Lorimer. New Haven, CT: Yale University Press.

Carneiro, Robert L. 1968. Slash-and-burn cultivation among the Kuikuru and its implications for settlement patterns. In *Man in adaptation*, ed. Y. Cohen. Chicago, Aldine.

Carneiro, Robert L. 1970. A theory of the origin of the state. *Science* 169 (August 21):733–38.

Carneiro, Robert L. 1978. Political expansion as an expression of the principle of competitive exclusion. In *Origins of the state*, eds. R. Cohen and E. R. Service. Philadelphia: Institute for the Study of Human Issues.

Carneiro, Robert L. 1988. The circumscription theory: Challenge and response. *American Behavioral Scientist* 31: 497–511.

Carneiro, Robert L. 1990. Chiefdom-level warfare as exemplified in Fiji and the Cauca Valley. In *The anthropology of war*, ed. J. Haas. New York: Cambridge University Press.

Carpenter, C. R. 1940. A field study in Siam of the behavior and social relations of the gibbon (*Hylobates lar*). *Comparative Psychology Monographs* 16(5): 1–212.

Carpenter, Sandra. 2000. Effects of cultural tightness and collectivism on self-concept and causal attributions. *Cross-Cultural Research* 34:38–56.

Carrasco, Pedro. 1961. The civil-religious hierarchy in Mesoamerican communities: Pre-Spanish background and colonial development. *American Anthropologist* 63: 483–97.

Carrier, Joseph, and Ralph Bolton. 1991. Anthropological perspectives on sexuality and HIV prevention. *Annual Review of Sex Research* 2:49–75.

Carroll, John B., ed. 1956. *Language, thought, and reality: Selected writings of Benjamin Lee Whorf*. New York: Wiley.

Carroll, Michael. 1979. A new look at Freud on myth. *Ethos* 7:189–205.

Cartmill, Matt. 1974. Rethinking primate origins. *Science* (April 26):436–37.

Cartmill, Matt. 1992a. New views on primate origins. *Evolutionary Anthropology* 1: 105–11.

Cartmill, Matt. 1992b. Non-human primates. In *The Cambridge encyclopedia of human evolution*, eds. S. Jones, R. Martin, and D. Pilbeam. New York: Cambridge University Press.

Cartmill, Matt. 2009. Explaining primate origins. In MyAnthroLibrary, eds. C. R. Ember, M. Ember, and P. N. Peregrine. MyAnthroLibrary.com. Pearson.

Cashdan, Elizabeth A. 1980. Egalitarianism among hunters and gatherers. *American Anthropologist* 82:116–20.

Cashdan, Elizabeth. 2001. Ethnic diversity and its environmental determinants: Effects of climate, pathogens, and habitat diversity. *American Anthropologist* 103:968–91.

Caulkins, D. Douglas. 1997. Welsh. In *American immigrant cultures: Builders of a nation*, vol. 2, eds. D. Levinson and M. Ember, 935–41. New York: Macmillan Reference.

Caulkins, D. Douglas. 2009. Norwegians: Cooperative individualists. In MyAnthroLibrary, eds. C. R. Ember, M. Ember, and P. N. Peregrine. MyAnthroLibrary.com. Pearson.

Cavalli-Sforza, L. Luca, and Marcus W. Feldman. 1981. *Cultural transmission and evolution: A quantitative approach*. Princeton, NJ: Princeton University Press.

Cavalli-Sforza, L. Luca, and Marcus W. Feldman. 2003. The application of molecular genetic approaches to the study of human evolution. *Nature Genetics Supplement* 33: 266–75.

Caws, Peter. 1969. The structure of discovery. *Science* 166 (December 12): 1375–80.

Ceci, Stephen, and Wendy M. Williams. 2009. YES: The scientific truth must be pursued. *Nature* 457 (February 12): 788–789.

Center for Renewal of Science and Culture. 2001. The wedge strategy, cited in Barbara Forrest, "The wedge at work." In *Intelligent design creationism and its critics*. ed. Robert Pennock, 16. Boston, IT Press.

Cernea, Michael M., ed. 1991. *Putting people first: Sociological variables in development*. 2nd ed. New York: Oxford University Press.

Chacon, Richard J., and Rubén G. Mendoza. 2007. Ethical considerations and conclusions regarding indigenous warfare and ritual violence in Latin America. In *Latin American indigenous warfare and ritual violence*, eds. Richard J. Chacon and Rubén G. Mendoza. Tucson: University of Arizona Press.

Chafetz, Janet Saltzman. 1990. *Gender equity: An integrated theory of stability and change*. Sage Library of Social Research No. 176. Newbury Park, CA: Sage.

Chagnon, Napoleon. 1983. *Yanomamö: The fierce people*. 3rd ed. New York: Holt, Rinehardt, and Winston.

Chambers, J. K. 2002. Patterns of variation including change. In *The handbook of language variation and change*, eds. J. K. Chambers, Peter Trudgill, and Natalie Schilling-Estes. Malden, MA: Blackwell Publishers.

Chang, Kwang-Chih. 1968. *The archaeology of ancient China*. New Haven, CT: Yale University Press.

Chang, Kwang-Chih. 1970. The beginnings of agriculture in the Far East. *Antiquity* 44:175–85.

Chang, Kwang-Chih. 1981. In search of China's beginnings: New light on an old civilization. *American Scientist* 69:148–60.

Chang, Kwang-Chih. 1986. *Archaeology of ancient China*. 4th ed. New Haven, CT: Yale University Press, 234–94.

Chapais, Bernard. 2008. *Primeval kinship: How pair-bonding gave birth to human society*. Cambridge, MA: Harvard University Press.

Chard, Chester S. 1969. *Man in prehistory*. New York: McGraw-Hill.

Charles-Dominique, Pierre. 1977. *Ecology and behaviour of nocturnal primates*, trans. R. D. Martin. New York: Columbia University Press.

Charanis, Peter. 1953. Economic factors in the decline of the Roman Empire. *Journal of Economic History* 13: 412–24.

Chase, Philip, and Harold Dibble. 1987. Middle Paleolithic symbolism: A review of current evidence and interpretations. *Journal of Anthropological Archaeology* 6:263–69.

Chatterjee, Sankar. 1997. *The rise of birds: 225 million years of evolution.* Baltimore: Johns Hopkins.

Chatty, Dawn. 1996. *Mobile pastoralists: Development planning and social change in Oman.* New York: Columbia University Press.

Chaucer, Geoffrey. 1926. *The prologue to the Canterbury Tales, the Knights Tale, the Nonnes Prestes Tale*, ed. Mark H. Liddell. New York: Macmillan.

Chayanov, Alexander V. 1966. *The theory of peasant economy*, eds. Daniel Thorner, Basile Kerblay, and R. E. F. Smith. Homewood, IL: Richard D. Irwin.

Cheney, Dorothy, L., and Richard W. Wrangham. 1987. Predation. In *Primate societies*, eds. B. Smuts et al. Chicago: University of Chicago Press.

Chessa, Bernardo, Filipe Pereira, Frederick Arnaud, Antonio Amorim, Félix Goyache, Ingrid Mainland, Rowland R. Kao, Josephine M. Pemberton, Dario Beraldi, Michael J. Stear, Alberto Alberti, Marco Pittau, Leopoldo Iannuzzi, Mohammad H. Banabazi, Rudovick R. Kazwala, Ya-ping Zhang, Juan J. Arranz, Bahy A. Ali, Zhiliang Wang, Metehan Uzun, Michel M. Dione, Ingrid Olsaker, Lars-Erik Holm, Urmas Saarma, Sohail Ahmad, Nurbiy Marzanov, Emma Eythorsdottir, Martin J. Holland, Paolo Ajmone-Marsan, Michael W. Bruford, Juha Kantanen, Thomas E. Spencer, and Massimo Palmarini. 2009. Revealing the history of sheep domestication using retrovirus integrations. *Science* 324 (April 24):532–36.

Chibnik, Michael. 1980. The statistical behavior approach: The choice between wage labor and cash cropping in rural Belize. In *Agricultural decision making*, ed. P. F. Barlett. New York: Academic Press.

Chibnik, Michael. 1981. The evolution of cultural rules. *Journal of Anthropological Research* 37:256–68.

Chibnik, Michael. 1987. The economic effects of household demography: A cross-cultural assessment of Chayanov's theory. In *Household economies and their transformations*, ed. M. D. MacLachlan. Monographs in Economic Anthropology, No 3. Lanham, MD: University Press of America.

Chick, Garry. 1998. Games in culture revisited: A replication and extension of Roberts, Arth, and Bush [1959]. *Cross-Cultural Research* 32:185–206.

Childe, V. Gordon. 1950. The urban revolution. *Town Planning Review* 21:3–17.

Chimpanzee Sequencing and Analysis Consortium. 2005. Initial sequence of the chimpanzee genome and comparison with the human genome. *Nature* 437 (Sept. 1):69–87.

Chivers, David J. 1974. *The siamang in Malaya.* Basel, Switzerland: Karger.

Chomsky, Noam. 1975. *Reflections on language.* New York: Pantheon.

Christensen, Pia, Jenny Hockey, and Allison James, 2001. Talk, silence and the material world: Patterns of indirect communication among agricultural farmers in northern England. In *An anthropology of indirect communication*, eds. J. Hendry and C. W. Watson, 68–82. London: Routledge.

Ciochon, Russell L., and Dennis A. Etler. 1994. Reinterpreting past primate diversity. In *Integrative paths to the past*, eds. R. Corruccini and R. Ciochon. Upper Saddle River, NJ: Prentice Hall.

Ciochon, Russell L., and John G. Fleagle, eds. 1993. *The human evolution source book.* Upper Saddle River, NJ: Prentice Hall.

Ciochon, Russell, John Olsen, and Jamie James. 1990. *Other origins: The search for the giant ape in human prehistory.* New York: Bantam.

Claassen, Cheryl. 1991. Gender, shellfishing, and the Shell Mound Archaic. In *Engendering Archaeology*, eds. J. Gero and M. Conkey. Oxford: Blackwell.

Claassen, Cheryl. 2009. Gender and archaeology. In MyAnthroLibrary, eds. C. R. Ember, M. Ember, and P. N. Peregrine. MyAnthroLibrary.com. Pearson.

Clark, J. Desmond. 1970. *The prehistory of Africa.* New York: Praeger.

Clark, J. Desmond. 1977. Interpretations of prehistoric technology from ancient Egyptian and other sources. Pt. II: Prehistoric arrow forms in Africa as shown by surviving examples of the traditional arrows of the San Bushmen. *Paleorient* 3:127–50.

Clark, Gracia. 2000. Small-scale traders' key role in stabilizing and diversifying Ghana's rural communities and livelihoods. In *Women farmers and commercial ventures: Increasing food security in developing countries*, ed. Anita Spring, 253–70. Boulder, CO: Lynne Rienner Publishers, Inc.

Clark, Grahame. 1975. *The Earlier Stone Age settlement of Scandinavia.* Cambridge: Cambridge University Press.

Clark, Grahame, and Stuart Piggott. 1965. *Prehistoric societies.* New York: Knopf.

Clark, W. E. Le Gros. 1964. *The fossil evidence for human evolution*, 184. Chicago: University of Chicago Press.

Clarke, Ronald J., and P. V. Tobias. 1995. Sterkfontein member 2 foot bones of the oldest South African hominid. *Science* 269(July 28):521–24.

Clayman, Charles B., ed. 1989. *American Medical Association encyclopedia of medicine.* New York: Random House, 857–58.

Clifford, James. 1986. Introduction: Partial truths." In *Writing culture: The poetics and politics of ethnography*, eds. J. Clifford and G. E. Marcus. Berkeley: University of California Press.

Clottes, Jean. 2008. Rock art: An endangered heritage worldwide. *Journal of Anthropological Research* 64:1–18.

Clutton-Brock, Juliet. 1984. Dog. In *Evolution of domesticated animals*, ed. I. Mason. New York: Longman.

Clutton-Brock, Juliet. 1992. Domestication of animals. In *The Cambridge encyclopedia of human evolution*, eds. S. Jones, R. Martin, and D. Pilbeam. New York: Cambridge University Press.

Clutton-Brock, T. H., and Paul H. Harvey. 1977. Primate ecology and social organization. *Journal of Zoology* 183: 1–39.

Clutton-Brock, T. H., and Paul H. Harvey. 1980. Primates, brains and ecology. *Journal of Zoology* 190: 309–23.

Coale, Ansley J. 1974. The history of the human population. *Scientific American* (September):41–51.

Coe, Michael D. 1966. *The Maya.* New York: Praeger.

Cohen, Alex. 1990. A cross-cultural study of the effects of environmental unpredictability on aggression in folktales. *American Anthropologist* 92:474–79.

Cohen, Alex. 1999. *The mental health of indigenous peoples: An international overview.* Geneva: Department of Mental Health, World Health Organization.

Cohen, Alex. 2004. Mental disorders. In *Encyclopedia of medical anthropology: Health and illness in the world's cultures,* vol. 1, eds. C. R. Ember and M. Ember, 486–93. New York: Kluwer Academic/Plenum.

Cohen, Alex, and Paul Koegel. 2009. Homelessness. In MyAnthroLibrary, eds. C. R. Ember, M. Ember, and P. N. Peregrine. MyAnthroLibrary.com. Pearson.

Cohen, Mark N. 1977a. *The food crisis in prehistory: Overpopulation and the origins of agriculture.* New Haven, CT: Yale University Press.

Cohen, Mark N. 1977b. Population pressure and the origins of agriculture. In *Origins of agriculture,* ed. C. A. Reed. The Hague: Monton.

Cohen, Mark N. 1987. The significance of long-term changes in human diet and food economy. In *Food and evolution,* eds. M. Harris and E Ross. Philadelphia: Temple University Press.

Cohen, Mark. 1989. *Health and the rise of civilization.* New Haven, CT: Yale University Press.

Cohen, Mark N. 2009. Were early agriculturalists less healthy than food collectors? In MyAnthroLibrary, eds. C. R. Ember, M. Ember, and P. N. Peregrine. MyAnthroLibrary.com. Pearson.

Cohen, Mark Nathan, and George J. Armelagos. 1984b. Paleopathology at the origins of agriculture: Editors' summation. In *Paleopathology at the origins of agriculture,* eds. M. N. Cohen and G. J. Armelagos. Orlando, FL: Academic Press.

Cohen, Myron L. 1976. *House united, house divided: The Chinese family in Taiwan.* New York: Columbia University Press.

Cohen, Ronald. 1988. Introduction. In *State formation and political legitimacy,* vol. 6: *Political anthropology,* eds. R. Cohen and J. D. Toland. New Brunswick, NJ: Transaction Books.

Cohen, Ronald, and Elman R. Service, eds. 1978. *Origins of the state: The anthropology of political evolution.* Philadelphia: Institute for the Study of Human Issues.

Cohen, Wesley. 1995. Empirical studies of innovative activity. In *Handbook of the economics of innovation and technological change,* ed. P. Stoneman. Oxford: Blackwell.

COHMAP (Cooperative Holocene Mapping Project) Personnel. 1988. Climatic changes of the last 18,000 years. *Science* 241 (August 26):1043–52.

Colby, Benjamin N. 1996. Cognitive anthropology. In *Encyclopedia of cultural anthropology,* eds. David Levinson and Melvin Ember, vol. 1, 209–15. New York: Henry Holt.

Collier, Stephen, and J. Peter White. 1976. Get them young? Age and sex inferences on animal domestication in archaeology. *American Antiquity* 41:96–102.

Collins, Desmond. 1976. Later hunters in Europe. In *The origins of Europe,* ed. D. Collins. New York: Thomas Y. Crowell.

Collins, James, and Richard Blot. 2003. *Literacy and literacies.* Cambridge: Cambridge University Press.

Conklin, Beth A. 2002. Shamans versus pirates in the Amazonian treasure chest. *American Anthropologist* 104:1050–61.

Connah, Graham. 1987. *African civilizations: Precolonial cities and states in tropical Africa.* Cambridge: Cambridge University Press.

Conroy, Glenn C. 1990. *Primate evolution.* New York: Norton.

Cooper, Richard S., Charles N. Rotimi, and Ryk Ward. 1999. The puzzle of hypertension in African Americans. *Scientific American* (February):56–63.

Coreil, Jeannine. 1989. Lessons from a community study of oral rehydration therapy in Haiti. In *Making our research useful,* eds. J. van Willigen, B. Rylko-Bauer, and A. McElroy. Boulder, CO: Westview.

Coreil, Jeannine. 2004. Malaria and other major insect vector diseases. In *Encyclopedia of medical anthropology: Health and illness in the world's cultures,* vol. 1, eds. C. R. Ember and M. Ember, 479–85. New York: Kluwer Academic/Plenum.

Costin, Cathy Lynne. 2009. Cloth production and gender relations in the Inka Empire. In MyAnthroLibrary, eds. C. R. Ember, M. Ember, and P. N. Peregrine. MyAnthroLibrary.com. Pearson.

Coult, Allan D., and Robert W. Habenstein. 1965. *Cross tabulations of Murdock's "World ethnographic sample."* Columbia: University of Missouri Press.

Crawford, Gary W. 1992. Prehistoric plant domestication in East Asia. In *The origins of agriculture,* eds. C. Cowan and P. Watson. Washington, DC: Smithsonian Institution Press.

Crawford, R. D. 1984. Turkey. In *Evolution of domesticated animals,* ed. I. Mason. New York: Longman.

Creed, Gerald W. 2009. Bulgaria: Anthropological corrections to Cold War stereotypes. In MyAnthroLibrary, eds. C. R. Ember, M. Ember, and P. N. Peregrine. MyAnthroLibrary.com. Pearson.

Crockett, Carolyn, and John F. Eisenberg. 1987. Howlers: Variations in group size and demography. In *Primate societies.* eds. B. Smuts et al. Chicago: University of Chicago Press.

Crystal, David. 1971. *Linguistics.* Middlesex, UK: Penguin.

Crystal, David. 2000. *Language death.* Cambridge: Cambridge University Press.

Culotta, Elizabeth. 1995. New hominid crowds the field. *Science* 269 (August 18):918.

Culotta, Elizabeth. 2005. Calorie count reveals Neandertals out-ate hardiest modern humans. *Science* 307 (February 11):840.

Curtin, Philip D. 1984. *Cross-cultural trade in world history.* Cambridge: Cambridge University Press.

Cutright, Phillips. 1967. Inequality: A cross-national analysis. *American Sociological Review* 32:562–78.

Daiger, Stephen. 2005. Was the human genome project worth the effort? *Science* 308 (April 15):362–64.

Daly, Martin, and Margo Wilson. 1988. *Homicide.* New York: Aldine.

Damas, David. 1983. Demography and kinship as variables of adoption in the Carolines. *American Ethnologist* 10:328–44.

Daniel, I. Randolph. 2001. Early Eastern Archaic. In *Encyclopedia of prehistory,* vol. 6: North America, eds. P. N. Peregrine and M. Ember. Kluwer: Academic/Plenum.

Dart, Raymond. 1925. *Australopithecus africanus:* The man-ape of South Africa. *Nature* 115:195.

Darwin, Charles. 1970/1859. The origin of species. In *Evolution of man,* ed. L. B. Young. New York: Oxford University Press.

Dasen, Pierre R., John W. Berry, and N. Sartorius, eds. 1988. *Health and cross-cultural psychology: Toward applications.* Newbury Park, CA: Sage.

Dasen, Pierre R., and Alastair Heron. 1981. Cross-cultural tests of Piaget's theory. In *Handbook of cross-cultural psychology*, vol. 4: *Developmental psychology*, eds. H. C. Triandis and A. Heron. Boston: Allyn & Bacon.

Davenport, William. 1959. Nonunilinear descent and descent groups. *American Anthropologist* 61:557–72.

Davis, Deborah, and Stevan Harrell, eds. 1993. *Chinese families in the post-Mao era.* Berkeley: University of California Press.

Davis, Susan Schaefer. 1993. Rebellious teens? A Moroccan instance. Paper presented at MESA, November.

Davis, Susan Schaefer. 2009. Morocco: Adolescents in a small town. In MyAnthroLibrary, eds. C. R. Ember, M. Ember, and P. N. Peregrine. MyAnthroLibrary.com. Pearson

Davis, William D. 1971. Societal complexity and the nature of primitive man's conception of the supernatural. Ph.D. dissertation; University of North Carolina, Chapel Hill.

Dawson, Alistair. 1992. *Ice age earth.* London: Routledge: 24–71.

Dawson, J. L. M. 1967. Cultural and physiological influences upon spatial-perceptual processes in West Africa. *International Journal of Psychology* 2:115–28, 171–85.

Day, Michael. 1986. *Guide to fossil man.* 4th ed. Chicago: University of Chicago Press.

De Laguna, Frederica. 1972. *Under Mount Saint Elias: The history and culture of the Yakutat Tlingit.* Washington, DC: Smithsonian Institution Press, as seen in the eHRAF Collection of Ethnography on the Web, 2000.

De Lumley, Henry. 1969. A Paleolithic camp at Nice. *Scientific American* (May):42–50.

DeMenocal, Peter. 2001. Cultural responses to climate change during the late Holocene. *Science* 292 (April 27):667–73.

de Munck, Victor. 2000. *Culture, self, and meaning.* Prospect Heights, IL: Waveland Press.

De Munck, Victor C., and Andrey Korotayev. 1999. Sexual equality and romantic love: A reanalysis of Rosenblatt's study on the function of romantic love. *Cross-Cultural Research* 33:265–273.

De Villiers, Peter A., and Jill G. De Villiers. 1979. *Early language.* Cambridge, MA: Harvard University Press.

De Waal, Frans. 2001. *The ape and the sushi master: Cultural reflections of a primatologist.* New York: Basic Books.

De Waal, Frans, and Frans Lanting. 1997. *Bonobo: The forgotten ape.* Berkeley: University of California Press.

Deacon, Terrence. 1992. Primate brains and senses. In *The Cambridge encyclopedia of human evolution*, eds. S. Jones, R. Martin, and D. Pilbeam. New York: Cambridge University Press.

Denham, T. P., S. G. Haberle, C. Lentfer, R. Fullagar, J. Field, M. Therin, N. Porch, and B. Winsborough. 2003. Origins of agriculture at Kuk Swamp in the highlands of New Guinea. *Science* 301 (July 11):189–93.

Denny, J. Peter. 1979. The "extendedness" variable in classifier semantics: Universal features and cultural variation. In *Ethnolinguistics*, ed. M. Mathiot. The Hague: Mouton.

Dentan, Robert K. 1968. *The Semai: A nonviolent people of Malaya.* New York: Holt, Rinehart & Winston.

Devillers, Charles, and Jean Chaline. 1993. *Evolution: An evolving theory.* New York: Springer Verlag.

DeVore, Irven, and Melvin J. Konner. 1974. Infancy in hunter-gatherer life: An ethological perspective. In *Ethology and psychiatry*, ed. N. F. White. Toronto: Ontario Mental Health Foundation and University of Toronto Press.

Diament, Michelle. 2005. Diversifying their crops: Agriculture schools, focusing on job prospects, reach out to potential students from cities and suburbs. *The Chronicle of Higher Education* May 6, pp. A32–34.

Diamond, Jared. 1989. The accidental conqueror. *Discover* (December):71–76.

Diamond, Jared. 1991. The saltshaker's curse—Physiological adaptations that helped American Blacks survive slavery may now be predisposing their descendants to hypertension. *Natural History* (October):20–27.

Diamond, Jared. 1993. Who are the Jews? *Natural History* (November): 12–9.

Diamond, Jared. 1997a. *Guns, germs, and steel.* New York: Norton: 205–07.

Diamond, Jared. 1997b. Location, location, location: The first farmers. *Science* 278 (November 14):1243–44.

Diamond, Jared. 2004. The astonishing micropygmies. *Science* 306 (December 17):2047–48.

Diamond, Norma. 1975. Collectivization, kinship, and the status of women in rural China. In R. R. Reiter, *Toward an anthropology of women.* New York: Monthly Review Press.

Diamond, Stanley. 1974. *In search of the primitive: A critique of civilization.* New Brunswick, NJ: Transaction Books.

Dickson, D. Bruce. 1990. *The dawn of belief.* Tucson: University of Arizona Press, 42–44.

Dickson, D. Bruce, Jeffrey Olsen, P. Fred Dahm, and Mitchell S. Wachtel. 2005. Where do you go when you die? A cross-cultural test of the hypothesis that infrastructure predicts individual eschatology. *Journal of Anthropological Research* 1:53–79.

Dillehay, Thomas. 2000. *The settlement of the Americas.* New York: Basic Books.

Dirks, Robert. 1993. Starvation and famine. *Cross-Cultural Research* 27:28–69.

Dirks, Robert. 2009. Hunger and famine. In MyAnthroLibrary, eds. C. R. Ember, M. Ember, and P. N. Peregrine. MyAnthroLibrary.com. Pearson.

Divale, William T. 1974. Migration, external warfare, and matrilocal residence. *Behavior Science Research* 9:75–133.

Divale, William T. 1977. Living floor area and marital residence: A replication. *Behavior Science Research* 2:109–15.

Divale, William T., and Marvin Harris. 1976. Population, warfare, and the male supremacist complex. *American Anthropologist* 78:521–38.

Dobres, Marcia-Anne. 1998. Venus figurines. In *Oxford companion to archaeology*, ed. B. Fagan, 740–41. Oxford: Oxford University Press.

Dobzhansky, Theodosius. 1962. *Mankind evolving: The evolution of the human species.* New Haven, CT: Yale University Press.

Dobzhansky, Theodosius, 1973. *Genetic diversity and human equality.* New York: Basic Books.

Dohlinow, Phyllis Jay, and Naomi Bishop. 1972. The development of motor skills and social relationships among primates through play. In *Primate patterns*, ed. Phyllis Jay Dohlinow. New York: Holt, Rinehart & Winston.

Douglas, Mary. 1975. *Implicit meanings: Essays in anthropology.* London: Routledge and Kegan Paul.

Dow, James. 1986. *The shaman's touch: Otomi Indian symbolic healing.* Salt Lake City: University of Utah Press.

Dowling, John H. 1975. Property relations and productive strategies in pastoral societies. *American Ethnologist* 2: 419–26.

Doyle, Rodger. 2004. Living together: In the U.S. cohabitation is here to stay. *Scientific American* (January):28.

Doyle, Rodger. 2005. Leveling the playing field: Economic development helps women pull even with men. *Scientific American* (June):32.

Doyle, G. A., and R. D. Martin, eds. 1979. *The study of prosimian behavior.* New York: Academic Press.

Draper, Patricia. 1975. !Kung women: Contrasts in sexual egalitarianism in foraging and sedentary contexts. In *Toward an anthropology of women,* ed. R. R. Reiter. New York: Monthly Review Press.

Draper, Patricia, and Elizabeth Cashdan. 1988. Technological change and child behavior among the !Kung. *Ethnology* 27:339–65.

Dressler, William W. 1991. *Stress and adaptation in the context of culture.* Albany: State University of New York Press.

Dressler, William W. 1993. Health in the African American community: Accounting for health inequalities. *Medical Anthropology Quarterly* 7:325–45.

Dressler, William W., and Michael C. Robbins. 1975. Art styles, social stratification, and cognition: An analysis of Greek vase painting. *American Ethnologist* 2:427–34.

Driscoll, Carlos A., Juliet Clutton-Brock, Andrew Kitchener, and Stephen O'Brien. 2009. The taming of the cat. *Scientific American* (June):68–75.

Driscoll, Carlos A., Marilyn Menotti-Raymond, Alfred L. Roca, Karsten Hupe, Warren E. Johnson, Eli Geffen, Eric H. Harley, Miguel Delibes, Dominique Pontier, Andrew C. Kitchener, Nobuyuki Yamaguchi, Stephen J. O'Brien, and David W. Macdonald. 2007. The Near Eastern origin of cat domestication. *Science* (July 27):519–23.

Drucker, Philip. 1965. *Cultures of the north Pacific Coast.* San Francisco: Chandler.

Drucker, Philip. 1967. The potlatch. In *Tribal and peasant economies,* ed. G. Dalton. Garden City, NY: Natural History Press.

Duane, Daniel. 2003. Turning garbage into oil. *New York Times Magazine,* December 14, p. 100.

Du, Shanshan. 2003. Is Buddha a couple: Gender-Unitary perspectives from the Lahu of southwest China. *Ethnology* 42:253–71.

Duarte, Cidalia, J. Mauricio, P. B. Pettitt, P. Souto, E. Trinkaus, H. van der Plicht, and J. Zilhao. 1999. The early Upper Paleolithic human skeleton from the Abrigo do Lagar Velho (Portugal) and modern human emergence in Iberia. *Proceedings of the National Academy of Sciences of the United States* 96:7604–09.

Duhard, Jean-Pierre. 1993. Upper Paleolithic figures as a reflection of human morphology and social organization. *Antiquity* 67:83–91.

Dunbar, Robin, and Susanne Shultz. 2007. Evolution of the social brain. *Science* 317 (September 7):1344–47.

Dundes, Alan. 1965. Structural typology in North American Indian folktales. In *The study of folklore,* ed. A. Dundes. Upper Saddle River, NJ: Prentice Hall.

Dundes, Alan. 1989. *Folklore matters.* Knoxville: University of Tennessee Press.

Durham, William H. 1991. *Coevolution: Genes, culture and human diversity.* Stanford, CA: Stanford University Press.

Durkheim, Émile. 1938/1895. *The rules of sociological method.* 8th ed. Trans. Sarah A. Soloway and John H. Mueller. Ed. George E. Catlin. New York: Free Press.

Durkheim, Émile. 1961/1912. *The elementary forms of the religious life.* Trans. Joseph W. Swain. New York: Collier Books.

Durrenberger, E. Paul. 1980. Chayanov's economic analysis in anthropology. *Journal of Anthropological Research* 36: 133–48.

Durrenberger, E. Paul. 2001a. Anthropology and globalization. *American Anthropologist* 103:531–35.

Durrenberger, E. Paul. 2001b. Explorations of class and consciousness in the U.S. *Journal of Anthropological Research* 57:41–60.

Durrenberger, E. Paul, and Nicola Tannenbaum. 2002. Chayanov and theory in economic anthropology. In *Theory in economic anthropology,* ed. Jean Ensminger, 137–53. Walnut Creek, CA: AltaMira Press.

Dyson-Hudson, Neville. 1966. *Karimojong politics.* Oxford: Clarendon Press.

Dyson-Hudson, Rada, and Eric Alden Smith. 1978. Human territoriality: An ecological reassessment. *American Anthropologist* 80:21–41.

Eckhardt, William. 1975. Primitive militarism. *Journal of Peace Research* 12:55–62.

Eddy, Elizabeth M., and William L. Partridge, eds. 1987. *Applied anthropology in America.* 2nd ed. New York: Columbia University Press.

Edgerton, Robert B. 1966. Conceptions of psychosis in four East African societies. *American Anthropologist* 68:408–25.

Edgerton, Robert B. 1971. *The individual in cultural adaptation: A study of four East African peoples.* Berkeley: University of California Press.

Edgerton, Robert B. 1992. *Sick societies: Challenging the myth of primitive harmony.* New York: Free Press.

Eiseley, Loren C. 1958. The dawn of evolutionary theory. In *Darwin's century: Evolution and the men who discovered it,* ed. L. C. Eiseley, Garden City, NY: Doubleday.

Eisenberg, John F. 1977. Comparative ecology and reproduction of New World monkeys. In *The biology and conservation of the Callitrichidae.* ed. Devra Kleinman. Washington, DC: Smithsonian Institution.

Eisenstadt, S. N. 1954. African age groups. *Africa* 24:100–111.

Ekman, Paul, and Dachner Keltner. 1997. Universal facial expressions of emotion: An old controversy and new findings. In *Nonverbal communication: Where nature meets culture,* eds. U. Segerstrale and P. Molnar. Mahwah, NJ: Lawrence Erlbaum.

Eldredge, Niles, and Ian Tattersall. 1982. *The myths of human evolution.* New York: Columbia University Press.

Eliot, T. S. 1963. The love song of J. Alfred Prufrock. In *Collected poems, 1909–1962.* New York: Harcourt, Brace & World.

Ellis, Lee. 1986. Evidence of neuroandrogenic etiology of sex roles from a combined analysis of human, nonhuman primate and nonprimate mammalian studies. *Personality and Individual Differences* 7:519–52.

Ember, Carol R. 1973. Feminine task assignment and the social behavior of boys. *Ethos* 1:424–39.

Ember, Carol R. 1974. An evaluation of alternative theories of matrilocal versus patrilocal residence. *Behavior Science Research* 9:135–49.

Ember, Carol R. 1975. Residential variation among hunter-gatherers. *Behavior Science Research* 9:135–49.

Ember, Carol R. 1977. Cross-cultural cognitive studies. *Annual Review of Anthropology* 6:33–56.

Ember, Carol R. 1978a. Men's fear of sex with women: A cross-cultural study. *Sex Roles* 4:657–78.

Ember, Carol R. 1978b. Myths about hunter-gatherers. *Ethnology* 17:439–48.

Ember, Carol R. 1981. A cross-cultural perspective on sex differences. In *Handbook of cross-cultural human development*, eds. R. H. Munroe, R. L. Munroe, and B. B. Whiting. New York, Garland.

Ember, Carol R. 1982. The conditions favoring religious conversion. Paper presented at the annual meeting of the Society for Cross-Cultural Research, February. Minneapolis, Minnesota.

Ember, Carol R. 1983. The relative decline in women's contribution to agriculture with intensification. *American Anthropologist* 85:285–304.

Ember, Carol R. 2009. Universal and variable patterns of gender difference. In MyAnthroLibrary, eds. C. R. Ember, M. Ember, and P. N. Peregrine. MyAnthroLibrary.com. Pearson.

Ember, Carol R., and Melvin Ember. 1972. The conditions favoring multilocal residence. *Southwestern Journal of Anthropology* 28:382–400.

Ember, Carol R., and Melvin Ember. 1984. The evolution of human female sexuality: A cross-species perspective. *Journal of Anthropological Research* 40:202–10.

Ember, Carol R., and Melvin Ember. 1992. Resource unpredictability, mistrust, and war: A cross-cultural study. *Journal of Conflict Resolution* 36:242–62.

Ember, Carol R., and Melvin Ember. 1993. Issues in cross-cultural studies of interpersonal violence. *Violence and Victims* 8:217–33.

Ember, Carol R., and Melvin Ember. 1994. War, socialization, and interpersonal violence: A cross-cultural study. *Journal of Conflict Resolution* 38:620–46.

Ember, Carol R., and Melvin Ember. 1997. Violence in the ethnographic record: Results of cross-cultural research on war and aggression. In *Troubled times*, eds. D. Martin and D. Frayer. Langhorn, PA: Gordon and Breach.

Ember, Carol R., and Melvin Ember. 2005. Explaining corporal punishment of children: A cross-cultural study. *American Anthropologist* 107:609–619.

Ember, Carol R., and Melvin Ember. 2009. *Cross-cultural research methods.* 2nd ed. Lanham, CA: AltaMira Press.

Ember, Carol R., Melvin Ember, Andrey Korotayev, Victor de Munck. 2005. Valuing thinness or fatness in women: Reevaluating the effect of resource scarcity. *Evolution and Human Behavior* 26:257–70.

Ember, Carol R., Melvin Ember, and Burton Pasternak. 1974. On the development of unilineal descent. *Journal of Anthropological Research* 30:69–94.

Ember, Carol R., Melvin Ember, and Peter N. Peregrine. 2007. *Anthropology.* 13th ed. Upper Saddle River, NJ: Prentice Hall.

Ember, Carol R., Melvin Ember, and Bruce Russett. 1992. Peace between participatory polities: A cross-cultural test of the "democracies rarely fight each other" hypothesis. *World Politics* 44:573–99.

Ember, Carol R., and David Levinson. 1991. The substantive contributions of worldwide cross-cultural studies using secondary data. *Behavior Science Research* (special issue, Cross-cultural and comparative research: Theory and method), 25:79–140.

Ember, Melvin. 1959. The nonunilinear descent groups of Samoa. *American Anthropologist* 61:573–77.

Ember, Melvin. 1963. The relationship between economic and political development in nonindustrialized societies. *Ethnology* 2:228–48.

Ember, Melvin. 1967. The emergence of neolocal residence. *Transactions of the New York Academy of Sciences* 30: 291–302.

Ember, Melvin. 1970. Taxonomy in comparative studies. In *A handbook of method in cultural anthropology*, eds. R. Naroll and R. Cohen. Garden City, NY: Natural History Press.

Ember, Melvin. 1973. An archaelogical indicator of matrilocal versus patrilocal residence. *American Antiquity* 38: 177–82.

Ember, Melvin. 1974a. The conditions that may favor avunculocal residence. *Behavior Science Research* 9:203–9.

Ember, Melvin. 1974b. Warfare, sex ratio, and polygyny. *Ethnology* 13:197–206.

Ember, Melvin. 1975. On the origin and extension of the incest taboo. *Behavior Science Research* 10:249–81.

Ember, Melvin. 1978. Size of color lexicon: Interaction of cultural and biological factors. *American Anthropologist* 80:364–67.

Ember, Melvin. 1982. Statistical evidence for an ecological explanation of warfare. *American Anthropologist* 84:645–49.

Ember, Melvin 1983. The emergence of neolocal residence. In *Marriage, family, and kinship: Comparative studies of social organization*, eds. Melvin Ember and Carol R. Ember, 333–57. New Haven, CT: HRAF Press.

Ember, Melvin. 1984–1985. Alternative predictors of polygyny. *Behavior Science Research* 19:1–23.

Ember, Melvin. 1985. Evidence and science in ethnography: Reflections on the Freeman-Mead controversy. *American Anthropologist* 87:906–9.

Ember, Melvin, and Carol R. Ember. 1971. The conditions favoring matrilocal versus patrilocal residence. *American Anthropologist* 73:571–94.

Ember, Melvin, and Carol R. Ember. 1979. Male-Female bonding: A cross-species study of mammals and birds. *Behavior Science Research* 14:37–56.

Ember, Melvin, and Carol R. Ember. 1983. *Marriage, family, and kinship: Comparative studies of social organization.* New Haven, CT: HRAF Press.

Ember, Melvin, and Carol R. Ember. 1992. Cross-cultural studies of war and peace: Recent achievements and future possibilities. In *Studying war*, eds. S. P. Reyna and R. E. Downs. New York: Gordon and Breach.

Ember, Melvin, and Carol R. Ember. 1999. Cross-language predictors of consonant-vowel syllables. *American Anthropologist* 101:730–42.

Ember, Melvin, and Carol R. Ember, eds. 2002. *Encyclopedia of urban cultures: Cities and cultures around the world*, 4 vols. Danbury, CT: Grolier/Scholastic.

Ember, Melvin, Carol R. Ember, and Bobbi S. Low. 2007. Comparing explanations of polygyny. *Cross-Cultural Research* 41:428–40.

Ember, Melvin, Carol R. Ember, and Bruce Russett. 1997. Inequality and democracy in the anthropological record. In *Inequality, democracy, and economic development*, ed. M. I. Midlarsky. Cambridge: Cambridge University Press.

Ember, Melvin, Carol R. Ember, and Ian Skoggard, eds. 2005. *Encyclopedia of diasporas: Immigrant and refugee cultures around the world*, 2 vols. New York: Kluwer Academic/ Plenum.

Ensminger, Jean. 1997. Transaction costs and Islam: Explaining conversion in Africa. *Journal of Institutional and Theoretical Economics* 153:4–29.

Ensminger, Jean. 2002. Experimental economics: A powerful new method for theory testing in anthropology. In *Theory in economic anthropology*, ed. J. Ensminger, 59–78. Walnut Creek, CA: AltaMira Press.

Ensor, Bradley E. 2003. Kinship and marriage among the Omaha, 1886–1902. *Ethnology* 42:1–14.

Epstein, Cynthia Fuchs. 1988. *Deceptive distinctions: Sex, gender, and the social order.* New York: Russell Sage Foundation.

Erchak, Gerald M. 2009. Family violence. In MyAnthroLibrary, eds. C. R. Ember, M. Ember, and P. N. Peregrine. MyAnthroLibrary.com. Pearson.

Ericksen, Karen Paige. 1989. Male and female age organizations and secret societies in Africa. *Behavior Science Research* 23:234–64.

Ericksen, Karen Paige, and Heather Horton. 1992. "Blood feuds": Cross-cultural variations in kin group vengeance. *Behavior Science Research* 26:57–85.

Erickson, Clark. 1988. Raised field agriculture in the Lake Titicaca basin. *Expedition* 30(1):8–16.

Erickson, Clark. 1989. Raised fields and sustainable agriculture in the Lake Titicaca basin of Peru. In *Fragile lands of Latin America*, ed. John Browder, 230–48. Boulder: Westview.

Erickson, Clark. 1998. Applied archaeology and rural development. In *Crossing currents: Continuity and change in Latin America*, eds. Michael Whiteford and Scott Whiteford, 34–45. Upper Saddle River, NJ: Prentice Hall.

Erickson, Edwin. 1968. Self-assertion, sex role, and vocal rasp. In *Folk song style and culture*, ed. A. Lomax. Washington, DC.

Errington, J. Joseph. 1985. On the nature of the sociolinguistic sign: Describing the Javanese speech levels. In *Semiotic mediation*, eds. E. Mertz and R. J. Parmentier. Orlando, FL: Academic Press.

Ervin, Alexander M. 1987. Styles and strategies of leadership during the Alaskan Native land claims movement: 1959–71. *Anthropologica* 29:21–38.

Eswaran, Vinayak. 2002. A diffusion wave out of Africa. *Current Anthropology* 43:749–74.

Etienne, Mona, and Eleanor Leacock, eds. 1980. *Women and colonization: Anthropological perspectives.* New York: Praeger.

Etienne, Robert. 1992. *Pompeii: The day a city died.* New York: Abrams.

Etkin, Nina L., and Paul J. Ross. 1997. Malaria, medicine, and meals: A biobehavioral perspective. In *The anthropology of medicine*, eds. L. Romanucci-Ross, D. E. Moerman, and L. R. Tancredi, 169–209. Westport, CT: Bergin & Garvey.

Euripides. 1937. The Trojan women. In *Three Greek plays*, trans. E. Hamilton, 52. New York: Norton.

Evans-Pritchard, E. E. 1940. The Nuer of the Southern Sudan. In *African political systems*, eds. M. Fortes and E. E. Evans-Pritchard. New York: Oxford University Press.

Evans-Pritchard, E. E. 1970. Sexual inversion among the Azande. *American Anthropologist* 72:1428–34.

Evans-Pritchard, E. E. 1979. Witchcraft explains unfortunate events. In *Reader in comparative religion*, 3rd ed., eds. W. A. Lessa and E. Z. Vogt. New York: Harper & Row.

Eveleth, Phyllis B., and James M. Tanner. 1990. *Worldwide variation in human growth.* 2nd ed. Cambridge: Cambridge University Press.

Everett, Margaret. 2007. The "I" in gene: Divided property, fragmented personhood, and the making of a genetic privacy law. *American Ethnologist* 34(2): 375–86.

Eversole, Robyn. 2005. "Direct to the poor": Revisited: Migrant remittances and development assistance. In *Migration and economy: Global and local dynamics*, ed. Lillian Trager, 289–322. Walnut Creek, CA: AltaMira Press.

Fagan, Brian M. 1972. *In the beginning.* Boston: Little, Brown.

Fagan, Brian M. 1989. *People of the earth: An introduction to world prehistory.* 6th ed. Glenview, IL: Scott, Foresman.

Fagan, Brian M. 1991. *Ancient North America: The archaeology of a continent.* London: Thames and Hudson.

Falk, Dean. 1987. Hominid paleoneurology. *Annual Review of Anthropology* 16:13–30.

Falk, Dean. 1988. Enlarged occipital/marginal sinuses and emissary foramina: Their significance in hominid evolution. In *Evolutionary history of the "robust" australopithecines*, ed. F. E. Grine. New York: Aldine.

Falk, Dean, C. Hildebolt, K. Smith, M. J. Morwood, T. Sutikna, P. Brown, Jatmiko, E. W. Saptomo, B. Brunsden, F. Prior. 2005. The brain of LBI, *Homo floresiensis. Science* 308 (April 8):242–45.

Farley, Reynolds. 1996. *The new American reality: Who we are, how we got here, where we are going.* New York: Russell Sage Foundation.

Farmer, Paul. 1997. Ethnography, social analysis, and the prevention of sexually transmitted HIV infection among poor women in Haiti. In *The anthropology of infectious disease*, eds. M. C. Inhorn and P. J. Brown, 413–38. Amsterdam: Gordon and Breach.

Featherman, David L., and Robert M. Hauser. 1978. *Opportunity and change.* New York: Academic Press.

Feder, Kenneth. 2000. *Past in perspective.* 2d ed. Mountain View, CA: Mayfield Publishing Company.

Fedigan, Linda Marie. 1982. *Primate paradigms: Sex roles and social bonds.* Montreal: Eden Press.

Fedoroff, Nina. 2003. Prehistoric GM corn. *Science* 302 (November 14):1158–59.

Fehr, Ernst and Urs Fischbacher. 2003. The nature of human altruism. *Nature* (October 23):785–91.

Feibel, Craig S., and Francis H. Brown. 1993. Microstratigraphy and paleoenvironments. In *The Nariokotome* Homo erectus *Skeleton*, eds. A. Walker and R. Leakey. Cambridge, MA: Harvard University Press.

Feinman, Gary, and Jill Neitzel. 1984. Too many types: An overview of sedentary prestate societies in the Americas. In *Advances in archaeological methods and theory*, ed. M. B. Schiffer, vol. 7. Orlando, FL: Academic Press.

Feinman, Gary M., Stephen A. Kowalewski, Laura Finsten, Richard E. Blanton, and Linda Nicholas. 1985. Long-term demographic change: A perspective from the Valley of Oaxaca, Mexico. *Journal of Field Archaeology* 12:333–62.

Feldman, Douglas A., and Thomas M. Johnson. 1986. Introduction. In *The social dimensions of AIDS*, eds. D. A. Feldman and T. M. Johnson. New York: Praeger.

Ferguson, R. Brian, and Neil L. Whitehead. 1992. Violent edge of empire. In *War in the tribal zone*, eds. R. B. Ferguson and N. Whitehead, 1–30. Santa Fe, NM: School of American Research Press.

Ferguson, Niall. 2004. *Colossus: The price of America's empire.* New York: Penguin Press.

Fernea, Elizabeth, and Robert Fernea, as reported in M. Kay Martin and Barbara Voorhies, 1975. *Female of the species.* New York: Columbia University Press.

Ferraro, Gary P. 2002. *The cultural dimension of international business.* 4th ed. Upper Saddle River, NJ: Prentice Hall.

Fessler, Daniel M. T. 2002. Windfall and socially distributed willpower: The psychocultural dynamics of rotating savings and credit associations in a Bengkulu village. *Ethos* 30:25–48.

Finley, M. I. 1983. *Politics in the ancient world.* Cambridge: Cambridge University Press.

Finnis, Elizabeth. 2006. Why grow cash crops? Subsistence farming and crop commercialization in the Kolli Hills, South India. *American Anthropologist* 108:363–69.

Firth, Raymond. 1957. *We, the Tikopia.* Boston: Beacon Press.

Firth, Raymond. 1959. *Social change in Tikopia.* New York: Macmillan.

Firth, Raymond. 1970. *Rank and religion in Tikopia.* Boston: Beacon Press.

Fischer, John L. 1958. Social influences on the choice of a linguistic variant. *Word* 14:47–56.

Fischer, John. 1961. Art styles as cultural cognitive maps. *American Anthropologist* 63:80–83.

Fish, Paul R. 1981. Beyond tools: Middle Paleolithic debitage analysis and cultural inference. *Journal of Anthropological Research* 37:374–86.

Fisher, Julie. 1996. Grassroots organizations and grassroots support organizations: Patterns of interaction. In *Transforming societies, transforming anthropology,* ed. E. F. Moran. Ann Arbor: University of Michigan Press.

Fisher, William F. 1997. Doing good? The politics and antipolitics of NGO practices. *Annual Review of Anthropology* 26:439–64.

Fisher, William H. 1994. Megadevelopment, environmentalism, and resistance: The institutional context of Kayapo indigenous politics in central Brazil." *Human Organization* 53:220–32.

Flannery, Kent V. 1965. The ecology of early food production in Mesopotamia. *Science* 147 (March 12):1247–56.

Flannery, Kent V. 1971. The origins and ecological effects of early domestication in Iran and the Near East. In *Prehistoric agriculture,* ed. S. Struever. Garden City, NY: Natural History Press.

Flannery, Kent V. 1972. The cultural evolution of civilizations. *Annual Review of Ecology and Systematics* 3:399–426.

Flannery, Kent V. 1973a. The origins of agriculture. *Annual Review of Anthropology* 2:271–310.

Flannery, Kent V. 1973b. The origins of the village as a settlement type in Mesoamerica and the Near East: A comparative study. In *Territoriality and proxemics,* ed. R. Tringham. Andover, MA: Warner.

Flannery, Kent V., ed. 1986. *Guila Naquitz: Archaic foraging and early agriculture in Oaxaca, Mexico.* Orlando, FL: Academic Press.

Fleagle, John G. 1994. Anthropoid origins. In *Integrative paths to the past,* eds. R. Corruccini and R. Ciochon. Upper Saddle River, NJ: Prentice Hall.

Fleagle, John G. 1999. *Primate adaptation and evolution.* 2nd ed. San Diego: Academic Press.

Fleagle, John G., and Richard F. Kay. 1983. New interpretations of the phyletic position of Oligocene hominoids. In *New interpretations of ape and human ancestry,* eds. R. Ciochon and R. Corruccini. New York: Plenum.

Fleagle, John G., and Richard F. Kay. 1985. The paleobiology of catarrhines. In *Ancestors,* ed. E. Delson. New York: Alan R. Liss.

Fleagle, John G., and Richard F. Kay, 1987. The phyletic position of the *Parapithecidae. Journal of Human Evolution* 16:483–531.

Fluehr-Lobban, Carolyn. 2006. *Race and racism: An introduction.* Lanham,: AltaMira Press.

Ford, Clellan S. 1941. *Smoke from their fires.* New Haven, CT: Yale University Press.

Ford, Clellan S., and Frank A. Beach. 1951. *Patterns of sexual behavior.* New York: Harper.

Forrest, Barbara, 2001. The wedge at work. In *Intelligent design creationism and its critics.* ed. Robert Pennock. Boston: MIT Press.

Fortes, Meyer. 1949. *The web of kinship among the Tallensi.* New York: Oxford University Press.

Fossey, Dian. 1983. *Gorillas in the mist.* Boston: Houghton Mifflin.

Foster, Brian L. 1974. Ethnicity and commerce. *American Ethnologist* 1:437–47.

Foster, George M. 1962. *Traditional cultures and the impact of technological change.* New York: Harper & Row.

Foster, George M. 1969. *Applied anthropology.* Boston: Little, Brown.

Foster, George M. 1994. *Hippocrates' Latin American legacy: Humoral medicine in the New World.* Amsterdam: Gordon and Breach.

Foucault, Michel. 1970. *The order of things: An archaeology of the human sciences.* New York: Random House.

Fowler, Melvin L. 1975. A pre-Columbian urban center on the Mississippi. *Scientific American* (August):92–101.

Frake, Charles O. 1960. The Eastern Subanun of Mindanao. In *Social Structure in Southeast Asia,* ed. G. P. Murdock. Chicago: Quadrangle.

Franciscus, Robert G., and Erik Trinkaus. 1988. Nasal morphology and the emergence of *Homo erectus. American Journal of Physical Anthropology* 75:517–27.

Frank, André Gunder. 1967. *Capitalism and underdevelopment in Latin America: Historical studies of Chile and Brazil.* New York: Monthly Review Press.

Fratkin, Elliot. 2008. Pastures lost: The decline of mobile pastoralism among Maasai and Rendille in Kenya, East Africa. In *Economies and the transformation of landscape,* eds. Lisa Cliggett and Christopher A. Pool, 149–68. Lanham, AltaMira Press.

Frayer, David W. 1981. Body size, weapon use, and natural selection in the European Upper Paleolithic and Mesolithic. *American Anthropologist* 83:57–73.

Frayer, David W., and Milford H. Wolpoff. 1985. Sexual dimorphism. *Annual Review of Anthropology* 14:429–73.

Frayer, David W., M. Wolpoff, A. Thorne, F. Smith, and G. Pope. 1993. Theories of modern human origins: The paleontological test. *American Anthropologist* 95:24–27.

Frayser, Suzanne G. 1985. *Varieties of sexual experience.* New Haven, CT: HRAF Press.

Freedman, Daniel G. 1979. Ethnic differences in babies. *Human Nature* (January):36–43.

Freeman, Derek. 1983. *Margaret Mead and Samoa: The making and unmaking of an anthropological myth.* Cambridge, MA: Harvard University Press.

Freeman, J. D. 1961. On the concept of the kindred. *Journal of the Royal Anthropological Institute* 91:192–220.

Freeman, Leslie G. 1994 Torralba and Ambrona: A review of discoveries. In *Integrative paths to the past*, eds. R. Coruccini and R. Ciochon. Upper Saddle River, NJ: Prentice Hall.

Freud, Sigmund. 1943/1917. *A general introduction to psychoanalysis*. Garden City, NY: Garden City Publishing. (Originally published in German)

Freud, Sigmund. 1967/1939. *Moses and monotheism*. Katherine Jones, trans. New York: Vintage Books.

Freyman, R. 1987. The first technology. *Scientific American* (April): 112.

Fried, Morton H. 1967. *The evolution of political society: An essay in political anthropology*. New York: Random House.

Friedl, Ernestine. 1962. *Vasilika: A village in modern Greece*. New York: Holt, Rinehart & Winston.

Friedman, Jeffrey M. 2003. A war on obesity, not the obese. *Science* 299 (February 7):856–58.

Friedrich, Paul. 1970. *Proto-Indo-European trees: The arboreal system of a prehistoric people*. Chicago: University of Chicago Press.

Friedrich, Paul. 1986. *The language parallax*. Austin: University of Texas Press.

Friedman, Saul S. 1980. Holocaust. In *Academic American* [now Grolier] *Encyclopedia*, vol. 10. Princeton, NJ: Areté.

Frisancho, A. Roberto, and Lawrence P. Greksa. 1989. Development responses in the acquisition of functional adaptation to high altitude. In *Human population biology*, eds. M. Little and J. Haas. New York: Oxford University Press.

Frisch, Rose. E. 1980. Fatness, puberty, and fertility. *Natural History* (October):16–27.

Fromm, Erich. 1950. *Psychoanalysis and religion*. New Haven, CT: Yale University Press.

Fry, Douglas P. 2006. *The human potential for peace: An anthropological challenge to assumptions about war and violence*. New York: Oxford University Press.

Fry, Douglas P., and Kaj Björkqvist, eds. 1997. *Cultural variation in conflict resolution: Alternatives to violence*. Mahwah, NJ: Lawrence Erlbaum Associates.

Futuyma, Douglas. 1982. *Science on trial*. New York: Pantheon.

Gabunia, Leo, A. Vekua, D. Lordkipanidze, et al. 2000. Earliest Pleistocene hominid cranial remains from Dmanisi, Republic of Georgia: Taxonomy, geological setting, and age. *Science* 288 (May 12):1019–25.

Gal, Susan. 1988. The political economy of code choice. In *Codeswitching*, ed. M. Heller. Berlin: Mouton de Gruyter, 245–64.

Galdikas, Biruté M. F. 1979. Orangutan adaptation at Tanjung Puting Reserve: Mating and ecology." In *The great apes*. eds. D. Hamburg and E. McCown. Menlo Park, CA: Benjamin/Cummings.

Gardner, Beatrice T., and R. Allen Gardner. 1980. Two comparative psychologists look at language acquisition. In *Children's language*, vol. 2, ed. K. Nelson. New York: Halsted Press.

Gardner, R. Allen, and Beatrice T. Gardner. 1969. Teaching sign language to a chimpanzee. *Science* 165 (August 15): 664–72.

Garn, Stanley M. 1971. *Human races*. 3rd ed. Springfield, IL: Charles C Thomas.

Gartner, Rosemary. 2009. Crime variations across cultures and nations. In MyAnthroLibrary, eds. C. R. Ember, M. Ember, and P. N. Peregrine. MyAnthroLibrary.com. Pearson.

Gat, Azar. 1999. The pattern of fighting in simple, small-scale, prestate societies. *Journal of Anthropological Research* 55:563–83.

Gaulin, Steven J. C., and James S. Boster. 1990. Dowry as female competition. *American Anthropologist* 92:994–1005.

Gay, Kathlyn. 1986. *Ergonomics: Making products and places fit people*. Hillside, New Jersey: Enslow.

Geertz, Clifford. 1960. *The religion of Java*. New York: Free Press.

Geertz, Clifford. 1966. Religion as a cultural system. In *Anthropological approaches to the study of religion*, ed. M. Banton. New York: Praeger.

Geertz, Clifford. 1973a. "Deep play: Notes on the Balinese cockfight." In *The interpretation of cultures*, ed. C. Geertz. New York: Basic Books.

Geertz, Clifford. 1973b. Thick description: Toward an interpretative theory of culture. In *The interpretation of cultures*, ed. C. Geertz. New York: Basic Books.

Geertz, Clifford. 1984. "From the native's point of view": On the nature of anthropological understanding. In *Culture theory*, eds. R. A. Shweder and R. A. LeVine. New York: Cambridge University Press.

Geiger, H. Jack. 2003. Racial and ethnic disparities in diagnosis and treatment: A review of the evidence and a consideration of causes. In *Unequal treatment: confronting racial and ethnic disparities in health care*, eds. Brian D. Smedley, Adrienne Y. Stith, and Alan R. Nelson, 417–54. Washington, DC: National Academy Press.

Gelles, Richard J., and Murray A. Straus. 1988. *Intimate violence*. New York: Simon & Schuster.

Gentner, W., and H. J. Lippolt. 1963. The potassium-argon dating of upper tertiary and Pleistocene deposits. In *Science in archaeology*, eds. D. Brothwell and E. Higgs. New York: Basic Books.

Gero, Joan M., and Margaret W. Conkey, eds. 1991. *Engendering archaeology: An introduction to women and prehistory*. Oxford: Blackwell.

Gesler, W. 1991. *The cultural geography of health care*. Pittsburgh, PA: University of Pittsburgh Press.

Gibbons, Ann. 1993. Warring over women. *Science* 261 (August 20):987–88.

Gibbons, Ann. 1995. First Americans: Not mammoth hunters, but forest dwellers? *Science* 268 (April 19): 346–47.

Gibbons, Ann. 2001. The riddle of co-existence. *Science* 291(March 2):1725–29.

Gibbons, Ann. 2002. One scientist's quest for the origin of our species. *Science* 298 (November 29):1708–11.

Gibbons, Ann. 2003. Oldest members of *Homo sapiens* discovered in Africa. *Science* 300 (June 13):1641.

Gibbons, Ann. 2008. The birth of childhood. *Science* 322 (November 14): 1040–43.

Gibbs, James L., Jr. 1965. The Kpelle of Liberia. In *Peoples of Africa*, ed. J. L. Gibbs, Jr. New York: Holt, Rinehart & Wintson.

Gibson, Kathleen R., and Stephen Jessee. 1999. Language evolution and expansions of multiple neurological processing areas. In *The origins of language*, ed. B. J. King, 189–227. Santa Fe, NM: School of American Research Press.

Gibson, Kyle. 2009. Differential parental investment in families with both adopted and genetic children. *Evolution and Human Behavior* 30:184–89.

Gilbert, M. Thomas P., Dennis L. Jenkins, Anders Götherstrom, Nuria Naveran, Juan J. Sanchez, Michael Hofreiter, Philip Francis Thomsen, Jonas Binladen, Thomas F. G. Higham, Robert M. Yohe, II, Robert Parr, Linda Scott Cummings, and Eske Willerslev. 2008. DNA from pre-Clovis human coprolites in Oregon, North America. *Science* 320 (May 9):786–89.

Gilligan, Carol. 1982. *In a different voice: Psychological theory and women's development.* Cambridge, MA: Harvard University Press.

Gilligan, Carol, and Jane Attanucci. 1988. Two moral orientations. In *Mapping the moral domain*, eds. C. Gilligan, J. V. Ward, and J. M. Taylor. Cambridge, MA: Harvard University Press.

Gilliland, Mary Kay. 1995. Nationalism and ethnogenesis in the former Yugoslavia. In *Ethnic identity: Creation, conflict, and accommodation*, 3rd ed., eds. L. Romanucci-Ross and G. A. De Vos, 197–221. Walnut Creek, CA: Alta Mira Press.

Gilman, Antonio. 1990. The development of social stratification in Bronze Age Europe. *Current Anthropology* 22:1–23.

Gimbutas, Marija. 1974. An archaeologist's view of PIE* in 1975. *Journal of Indo-European Studies* 2:289–307.

Gingerich, P. D. 1986. *Pleisiadipis* and the delineation of the order primates. In *Major topics in primate evolution*, eds. B. Wood, L. Martin, and P. Andrews, 32–46. Cambridge: Cambridge University Press.

Gladwin, Christina H. 1980. A theory of real-life choice: Applications to agricultural decisions. In *Agricultural decision making*, ed. P. F. Barlett. New York: Academic Press.

Gladwin, Thomas, and Seymour B. Sarason. 1953. *Truk: Man in paradise.* New York: Wenner-Gren Foundation for Anthropological Research.

Gleitman, Lila R., and Eric Wanner. 1982. Language acquisition: The state of the state of the art. In *Language acquisition*, eds. E. Wanner and L. R. Gleitman. Cambridge: Cambridge University Press.

Godoy, Ricardo, Elizabeth Byron, Victoria Reyes-Garcia, William R. Leonard, Karishma Patel, Lilian Apaza, Eddy Pérez, Vincent Vadez, and David Wilke. 2004. Patience in a foraging-horticultural society: A test of competing hypotheses. *Journal of Anthropological Research* 60:179–202.

Goebel, Ted, Michael Waters, and Dennis O'Rourke. 2008. The late Pleistocene dispersal of modern humans in the Americas. *Science* 319 (March 14):1479–1502.

Golden, Frederic, Michael Lemonick, and Dick Thompson. 2000. The race is over. *Time* (July 3): 18–23.

Goldizen, Anne Wilson. 1987. Tamarins and marmosets: Communal care of offspring. In *Primate Societies*, eds. B. Smuts et al. Chicago: University of Chicago Press.

Goldschmidt, Walter. 1999. Dynamics and status in America. *Anthropology Newsletter* 40(5):62, 64.

Goldstein, Donna. 1998. Nothing bad intended: Child discipline, punishment, and survival in a shantytown in Rio de Janeiro. In *Small wars: The cultural politics of childhood*, eds. Nancy Scheper-Hughes and Carolyn Sargeant, 389–415. Berkeley: University of California-Berkeley Press.

Goldstein, Joshua S. 2001. *War and gender: How gender shapes the war system and vice versa.* New York: Cambridge University Press.

Goldstein, Joshua S. 2004. War and gender. In *Encyclopedia of sex and gender: Men and women in the world's cultures*, vol. 1, eds. C. R. Ember and M. Ember, 107–116. New York: Kluwer Academic/Plenum Publishers.

Goldstein, Melvyn C. 1971. Stratification, polyandry, and family structure in central Tibet. *Southwestern Journal of Anthropology* 27:65–74.

Goldstein, Melvyn C. 1987. When brothers share a wife. *Natural History* (March):39–48.

Goodall, Jane. 1963. My life among wild chimpanzees. *National Geographic* (August): 272–308.

Goode, William J. 1970. *World revolution and family patterns.* New York: Free Press.

Goode, William J. 1982. *The family.* 2nd ed. Upper Saddle River, NJ: Prentice Hall.

Goodenough, Ward H. 1951. *Property, kin, and community on Truk.* New Haven, CT: Yale University Press.

Goodman, Alan H., and George J. Armelagos. 1985. Disease and death at Dr. Dickson's Mounds. *Natural History* (September):12–19.

Goodman, Alan H., John Lallo, George J. Armelagos, and Jerome C. Rose. 1984. Health changes at Dickson Mounds, Illinois (A.D. 950–1300). In *Paleopathology at the origins of agriculture*, eds. M. N. Cohen and G. J. Armelagos. Orlando, FL: Academic Press.

Goodman, Alan H., and Thomas L. Leatherman, eds. 1998. *Building a new biocultural synthesis: Political-economic perspectives on human biology.* Ann Arbor: University of Michigan Press.

Goodman, Madeleine J., P. Bion Griffin, Agnes A. Estioko-Griffin, and John S. Grove. 1985. The compatibility of hunting and mothering among the Agta hunter-gatherers of the Philippines. *Sex Roles* 12:1199–209.

Goodman, Morris. 1992. Reconstructing human evolution from proteins. In *The Cambridge encyclopedia of human evolution.* eds. S. Jones, R. Martin, and D. Pilbeam. New York: Cambridge University Press.

Goodrich, L. Carrington. 1959. *A short history of the Chinese people.* 3rd ed. New York: Harper & Row.

Goody, Jack. 1970. Cousin terms. *Southwestern Journal of Anthropology* 26:125–42.

Goody, Jack. 1973. Bridewealth and dowry in Africa and Eurasia. In *Bridewealth and dowry*, eds. J. Goody and S. H. Tambiah. Cambridge: Cambridge University Press.

Gordon, C. G., and K. E. Friedl. 1994. Anthropometry in the U.S. armed forces. In *Anthropometry: The individual and the population*, eds. S. J. Ulijaszek and C. G. N. Mascie-Taylor, 178–210. Cambridge, Cambridge University Press.

Gore, Rick. 2002. The first pioneer? *National Geographic* (August).

Goren-Inbar, Naama, N. Alperson, M. Kislev, O. Simchoni, Y. Melamed, A. Ben-Nun, and E. Werker. 2004. Evidence of hominid control of fire at Gesher Benot Ya'aqov, Israel. *Science* 304 (April 30):725–27.

Gorman, Chester. 1970. The Hoabinhian and after: Subsistence patterns in Southeast Asia during the Late Pleistocene and early recent periods. *World Archaeology* 2:315–19.

Gossen, Gary H. 1979. Temporal and spatial equivalents in Chamula ritual symbolism. In *Reader in comparative religion*, 4th ed., eds. W. A. Lessa and E. Z. Vogt. New York: Harper & Row.

Gough, Kathleen. 1959. The Nayars and the definition of marriage. *Journal of the Royal Anthropological Institute* 89:23–34.

Gould, Richard A. 1969. *Yiwara: Foragers of the Australian desert.* New York: Scribner's.

Gowlett, John A. J. 2008. Deep roots of kin: Developing the evolutionary perspective from prehistory. In *Early human kinship: From sex to social reproduction*, eds. Nicholas Allen, Hilary Callan, Robin Dunbar, and Wendy James, 41–57. Oxford: Blackwell.

Graber, Robert, ed. 2004. Special issue. The future state of the world: An anthropological symposium. *Cross-Cultural Research* 38:95–207.

Graburn, Nelson H. 1969. *Eskimos without igloos*. Boston: Little, Brown.

Graham, Susan Brandt. 1979. Biology and human social behavior: A response to van den Berghe and Barash. *American Anthropologist* 81:357–60.

Grant, Bruce S. 2002. Sour grapes of wrath. *Science* 297 (August 9): 940–41.

Grant, Peter R. 1991. Natural selection and Darwin's finches. *Scientific American* (October): 82–87.

Grant, Peter R., and Rosemary Grant. 2002. Unpredictable evolution in a 30-year study of Darwin's finches. *Science* 296 (April 26):707–11.

Gravlee, Clarence C., H. R. Bernard, and W. R. Leonard. 2003. Heredity, environment, and cranial form: A reanalysis of Boas's immigrant data. *American Anthropologist* 105: 125–38.

Gray, J. Patrick. 1996. Sociobiology. In *Encyclopedia of cultural anthropology*, eds. David Levinson and Melvin Ember, vol. 4, 1212–19. New York: Henry Holt.

Gray, J. Patrick. 1985. *Primate sociobiology*. New Haven, CT: HRAF Press.

Gray, J. Patrick, and Linda D. Wolfe. 1980. Height and sexual dimorphism of stature among human societies. *American Journal of Physical Anthropology* 53: 446–52.

Gray, J. Patrick, and Linda Wolfe. 2009. What accounts for population variation in height? In MyAnthroLibrary, eds. C. R. Ember, M. Ember, and P. N. Peregrine. MyAnthroLibrary.com. Pearson.

Grayson, Donald K. 1977. Pleistocene avifaunas and the overkill hypothesis. *Science* 195 (February 18):691–92.

Grayson, Donald K. 1984. Explaining Pleistocene extinctions: Thoughts on the structure of a debate. In *Quaternary extinctions*, eds. P. S. Martin and R. Klein. Tucson: University of Arizona Press.

Green, Richard E., Anna-Sapfo Malaspinas, Johannes Krause, Adrian W. Briggs, Philip L.F. Johnson, Caroline Uhler, Matthias Meyer, Jeffrey M. Good, Tomislav Maricic, Udo Stenzel, Kay Prüfer, Michael Siebauer, Hernán A. Burbano, Michael Ronan, Jonathan M. Rothberg, Michael Egholm, Pavao Rudan, Dejana Brajković, Željko Kućan, Ivan Gušić, Mårten Wikström, Liisa Laakkonen, Janet Kelso, Montgomery Slatkin, and Svante Pääbo. 2008. A complete Neandertal mitochondrial genome sequence determined by high-throughput sequencing. *Cell* 134: 416–26.

Greenberg, Joseph H. 1972. Linguistic evidence regarding Bantu origins. *Journal of African History* 13:189–216.

Greenberg, Joseph H., and Merritt Ruhlen. 1992. Linguistic origins of Native Americans. *Scientific American* (November):94–99.

Greenfield, Patricia M., Ashley E. Maynard, and Carla P. Childs. 2000. History, culture, learning, and development. *Cross-Cultural Research* 34:351–74.

Greenfield, Patricia Marks, and E. Sue Savage-Rumbaugh. 1990. Grammatical combination in *Pan paniscus*: Processes of learning and invention in the evolution and development of language. In *"Language" and intelligence in monkeys and apes*, eds. S. Parker and K. Gibson. New York: Cambridge University Press.

Gregor, Thomas A., Daniel R. Gross., 2004. Guilt by association: The culture of accusation and the American Anthropological Association's investigation of *Darkness in El Dorado*. *American Anthropologist* 106: 687–98.

Gregory, C. A. 1982. *Gifts and commodities*. New York: Academic Press.

Greksa, Lawrence P., and Cynthia M. Beall. 1989. Development of chest size and lung function at high altitude. In *Human population biology*, eds. M. Little and J. Haas. New York: Oxford University Press.

Grenoble, Lenore A., and Lindsay J. Whaley. 2006. *Saving languages: An introduction to language revitalization*. Cambridge: Cambridge University Press.

Grine, Frederick E. 1988a. Evolutionary history of the 'robust' australopithecines: A summary and historical perspective. In *Evolutionary history of the "robust" australopithecines*, ed. F. E. Grine. New York: Aldine.

Grine, Frederick E., ed. 1988b. *Evolutionary history of the "robust" australopithecines*. New York: Aldine.

Grine, Frederick E. 1993. Australopithecine taxonomy and phylogeny: Historical background and recent interpretation. In *The Human evolution source book*, eds. R. Ciochon and J. Fleagle. Upper Saddle River, NJ: Prentice Hall.

Gröger, B. Lisa. 1981. Of men and machines: Cooperation among French family farmers. *Ethnology* 20:163–75.

Gross, Daniel R., George Eiten, Nancy M. Flowers, Francisca M. Leoi, Madeline Latiman Ritter, and Dennis W. Werner. 1979. Ecology and acculturation among native peoples of central Brazil. *Science* 206 (November 30):1043–50.

Gross, Daniel R., and Barbara A. Underwood. 1971. Technological change and caloric costs: Sisal agriculture in northeastern Brazil. *American Anthropologist* 73:725–40.

Grossman, Daniel. 2002. Parched turf battle. *Scientific American* (December):32–33.

Grubb, Henry J. 1987. Intelligence at the low end of the curve: Where are the racial differences? *Journal of Black Psychology* 14: 25–34.

Gubser, Nicholas J. 1965. *The Nunamiut Eskimos: Hunters of caribou*. New Haven, CT: Yale University Press.

Guest, Greg, and Eric C. Jones. 2005. Globalization, health, and the environment: An introduction. In *Globalization, health, and the environment: An integrated perspective*, ed. Greg Guest, 3–26. Lanham, MD: Roman & Littlefield.

Guiora, Alexander Z., Benjamin Beit-Hallahmi, Risto Fried, and Cecelia Yoder. 1982. Language environment and gender identity attainment. *Language Learning* 32:289–304.

Gumperz, John J. 1961. Speech variation and the study of Indian civilization. *American Anthropologist* 63:976–88.

Gumperz, John J. 1971. Dialect differences and social stratification in a North Indian village. In *Language in social groups: Essays by John J. Gumperz*, selected and introduced by Anwar S. Dil. Stanford, CA: Stanford University Press.

Gunders, S., and J. W. M. Whiting. 1968. Mother-infant separation and physical growth. *Ethnology* 7: 196–206.

Gurr, Ted Robert. 1989a. Historical trends in violent crime: Europe and the United States. In *Violence in America*, vol. 1: *The history of crime*, ed. T. R. Gurr. Newbury Park, CA: Sage.

Gurr, Ted Robert. 1989b. The history of violent crime in America: An overview. In *Violence in America*, vol. 1: *The history of crime*, ed. T. R. Gurr. Newbury Park, CA: Sage.

Gurven, Michael, Kim Hill, and Hillard Kaplan. 2002. From forest to reservation: Transitions in food-sharing behavior among the Ache of Paraguay. *Journal of Anthropological Research* 58:93–120.

Guthrie, Dale R., 1984. Mosaics, allelochemics, and nutrients: An ecological theory of Late Pleistocene megafaunal extinctions. In *Quaternary extinctions*, eds. P. S. Martin and R. Klein. Tucson: University of Arizona Press.

Guthrie, Stewart Elliott. 1993. *Faces in the clouds: A new theory of religion*. New York: Oxford University Press.

Haas, Jonathan. 1990. Warfare and the evolution of tribal polities in the prehistoric Southwest. In *The anthropology of war*, ed. J. Haas. New York: Cambridge University Press.

Haas, Jonathan, Winifred Creamer, and Alvaro Ruiz. 2004. Dating the late Archaic occupation of the Norte Chico region in Peru. *Nature* 432 (December 23):1020–23.

Haas, Mary R. 1944. Men's and women's speech in Koasati. *Language* 20:142–49.

Habicht, J. K. A. 1979. *Paleoclimate, paleomagnetism, and continental drift*. Tulsa, OK: American Association of Petroleum Geologists.

Haddix, Kimber A. 2001. Leaving your wife and your brothers: When polyandrous marriages fall apart. *Evolution and Human Behavior* 22:47–60.

Hage, Jerald, and Charles H. Powers. 1992. *Post-industrial lives: Roles and relationships in the 21st century*. Newbury Park, CA: Sage.

Hahn, Robert A. 1995. *Sickness and healing: An anthropological perspective*. New Haven, CT: Yale University Press.

Hailie-Selassie, Yohannes. 2001. Late Miocene hominids from the Middle Awash, Ethiopia. *Nature* 412 (July 12):178–81.

Haldane, J. B. S. 1963. Human evolution: Past and future. In *Genetics, paleontology, and evolution*, eds. G. Jepsen, E. Mayr, and G. Simpson. New York: Atheneum.

Hall, Edward T. 1966. *The hidden dimension*. Garden City, NY: Doubleday.

Hallowell, A. Irving. 1976. Ojibwa world view and disease. In *Contributions to anthropology: Selected papers of A. Irving Hallowell*. Chicago: University of Chicago Press, 410–13.

Halpern, Diane F. 2000. *Sex differences in cognitive abilities*. 3rd ed. Mahwah, NJ: Lawrence Erlbaum Associates.

Hames, Raymond. 1990. Sharing among the Yanomamö. Part I. The effects of risk. In *Risk and uncertainty in tribal and peasant economies*, ed. E. Cashdan. Boulder, CO: Westview.

Hames, Raymond. 2009. Yanomamö: Varying adaptations of foraging horticulturalists. In MyAnthroLibrary, eds. C. R. Ember, M. Ember, and P. N. Peregrine. MyAnthroLibrary.com. Pearson.

Hammer, Michael F., and Stephen L. Zegura. 1996. The role of the Y chromosome in human evolutionary studies. *Evolutionary Anthropology* 5:116–34.

Hammer, Michael F., and Stephen L. Zegura. 2002. The human Y chromosome haplogroup tree. *Annual Review of Anthropology* 31:303–21.

Handwerker, W. Penn, and Paul V. Crosbie. 1982. Sex and dominance. *American Anthropologist* 84:97–104.

Hanna, Joel M., Michael A. Little, and Donald M. Austin. 1989. Climatic physiology. In *Human population biology*, eds. M. Little and J. Haas. New York: Oxford University Press.

Hannah, Alison C., and W. C. McGrew. 1987. Chimpanzees using stones to crack open oil palm nuts in Liberia. *Primates* 28: 31–46.

Hannerz, Ulf. 1996. *Transnational connections: Culture, people, places*. London: Routledge.

Hanotte, Olivier, et al. 2002. African pastoralism: Genetic imprints of origins and migrations. *Science* 296 (April 12): 336–43.

Hanson, Jeffery R. 1988. Age-set theory and Plains Indian age-grading: A critical review and revision. *American Ethnologist* 15:349–64.

Harcourt, A. H. 1979. The social relations and group structure of wild mountain gorillas. In *The great apes*. eds. D. Hamburg and E. McCown. Menlo Park, CA: Benjamin/Cummings.

Hardin, Garrett. 1968. The tragedy of the commons. *Science* 162 (December 13):1243–48.

Hardoy, Jorge, and David Satterthwaite. 1987. The legal and the illegal city. In *Shelter, settlement, and development*, ed. L. Rodwin. Boston: Allen & Unwin.

Hare, Brian, Michelle Brown, Christina Williamson, and Michael Tomasello. 2002. The domestication of social cognition in dogs. *Science*, 298 (November 22): 1634–36.

Harkness, Sara, and Charles M. Super. 1997. An infant's three Rs. A box in M. Small, Our babies, ourselves, *Natural History* (October):45.

Harlan, Jack R. 1967. A wild wheat harvest in Turkey. *Archaeology* 20:197–201.

Harlow, Harry F., et al. 1966. Maternal behavior of rhesus monkeys deprived of mothering and peer association in infancy. *Proceedings of the American Philosophical Society* 110: 58–66.

Harner, Michael. 1972. The role of hallucinogenic plants in European witchcraft. In *Hallucinogens and shamanism*, ed. M. Harner. New York: Oxford University Press.

Harner, Michael J. 1975. Scarcity, the factors of production, and social evolution. In *Population, ecology, and social evolution*, ed. S. Polgar. The Hague: Mouton.

Harner, Michael, and Gary Doore. 1987. The ancient wisdom in shamanic cultures. In *Shamanism*, comp. S. Nicholson. Wheaton, IL: Theosophical Publishing House.

Harper, Douglas. 2003. Slavery in the North. http://www.slavenorth.com/ (accessed June, 2009).

Harrell-Bond, Barbara. 1996. Refugees. In *Encyclopedia of cultural anthropology*, vol. 3, eds. D. Levinson and M. Ember, 1076–81. New York: Henry Holt.

Harris, David R. 1977. Settling down: An evolutionary model for the transformation of mobile bands into sedentary communities. In *The evolution of social systems*, eds. J. Friedman and M. Rowlands. London: Duckworth.

Harris, Marvin. 1964. *Patterns of race in the Americas*. New York: Walker.

Harris, Marvin. 1966. The cultural ecology of India's sacred cattle. *Current Anthropology* 7:51–63.

Harris, Marvin. 1968. *The rise of anthropological theory: A history of theories of culture*. New York: Thomas Y. Crowell.

Harris, Marvin. 1975. *Cows, pigs, wars and witches: The riddles of culture*. New York: Random House, Vintage.

Harris, Marvin. 1979. *Cultural materialism: The struggle for a science of culture*. New York: Random House.

Harrison, G. A., James M. Tanner, David R. Pilbeam, and P. T. Baker. 1988. *Human biology: An introduction to human evolution, variation, growth, and adaptability.* 3rd ed. Oxford: Oxford University Press.

Harrison, Gail G. 1975. Primary adult lactase deficiency: A problem in anthropological genetics. *American Anthropologist* 77: 812–35.

Harrison, Peter D., and B. L. Turner, II, eds. 1978. *Pre-Hispanic Maya agriculture.* Albuquerque: University of New Mexico Press.

Harrison, T. 1986. A reassessment of the phylogenetic relationships of *Oreopithecus bamboli. Journal of Human Evolution* 15:541–84.

Harrison, T., and L. Rook. 1997. Enigmatic anthropoid or misunderstood ape? The phylogenetic status of *Oreopithecus bamboli* reconsidered. In *Function, phylogeny and fossils: Miocene hominoid evolution and adaptation,* eds. D. R. Begun, C. V. Ward, and M. D. Rose, 327–62. New York: Plenum.

Hart, Hornell. 1948. The logistic growth of political areas. *Social Forces* 26:396–408.

Hartwig, W. C. 1994. Pattern, puzzles and perspectives on platyrrhine origins. In *Integrative paths to the past,* eds. R. Corruccini and R. Ciochon, 69–93. Upper Saddle River, NJ: Prentice Hall.

Harvey, Philip W., and Peter F. Heywood. 1983. Twenty-five years of dietary change in Simbu Province, Papua New Guinea. *Ecology of Food and Nutrition* 13:27–35.

Hassan, Fekri A. 1981. *Demographic archaeology.* New York: Academic Press.

Hatch, Elvin. 1997. The good side of relativism. *Journal of Anthropological Research* 53:371–81.

Haug, Gerald, et al. 2003. Climate and the collapse of Maya civilization. *Science* 299 (March 14):1731–35.

Hausfater, Glenn, Jeanne Altmann, and Stuart Altmann. 1982. Long-term consistency of dominance relations among female baboons. *Science* 217 (August 20): 752–54.

Hawkins, Alicia, and M. Kleindienst. 2001. Aterian. In *Encyclopedia of prehistory,* vol. 1: *Africa,* eds. P. N. Peregrine and M. Ember. New York: Kluwer Academic/ Plenum, 23–45.

Hayden, Thomas. 2000. A genome milestone. *Newsweek* (July 3):51–52.

Haynes, Vance. 1973. The Calico site: Artifacts or geofacts? *Science* 181 (July 27):305–10.

Hays, Terence E. 1994. Sound symbolism, onomatopoeia, and New Guinea frog names. *Journal of Linguistic Anthropology* 4:153–74.

Hays, Terence E. 2009. From ethnographer to comparativist and back again. In MyAnthroLibrary, eds. C. R. Ember, M. Ember, and P. N. Peregrine. MyAnthroLibrary.com. Pearson.

Heider, Karl. 1970. *The Dugum Dani.* Chicago: Aldine.

Heider, Karl. 1979. *Grand Valley Dani: Peaceful warriors.* New York: Holt, Rinehart & Winston.

Heise, David R. 1967. Cultural patterning of sexual socialization. *American Sociological Review* 32:726–39.

Heller, Monica, ed. 1988. *Codeswitching: Anthropological and sociolinguistic perspectives.* Berlin: Mouton de Gruyter.

Helms, Mary W. 1975. *Middle America.* Upper Saddle River, NJ: Prentice Hall.

Helms, Mary W. 2009. Miskito: Adaptations to colonial empires, past and present. In MyAnthroLibrary, eds. C. R. Ember, M. Ember, and P. N. Peregrine. MyAnthroLibrary. com. Pearson.

Henderson, Harry. 2001. *Global terrorism: The complete reference guide.* New York: Checkmark Books.

Henderson, Stephen. 2002. Weddings: Vows; Rakhi Dhanoa and Ranjeet Purewal. *The New York Times,* August 18, p. 9.2.

Hendrix, Llewellyn. 1985. Economy and child training reexamined. *Ethos* 13:246–61.

Hendrix, Llewellyn. 2009. Varieties of marital relationships. In MyAnthroLibrary, eds. C. R. Ember, M. Ember, and P. N. Peregrine. MyAnthroLibrary.com. Pearson.

Henrich, Joseph, Robert Boyd, Samuel Bowles, Colin Camerer, Ernst Fehr, and Herbert Gintis, eds. 2004. *Foundations of human sociality: Economic experiments and ethnographic evidence from fifteen small-scale societies.* Oxford: Oxford University Press.

Henry, Donald O. 1989. *From foraging to agriculture: The Levant at the end of the ice age.* Philadelphia: University of Pennsylvania Press.

Henry, Donald O. 1991. Foraging, sedentism, and adaptive vigor in the Natufian: Rethinking the linkages. In *Perspectives on the past,* ed. G. A. Clark. Philadelphia: University of Pennsylvania Press.

Henry, Edward O. 1976. The variety of music in a North Indian village: Reassessing cantometrics. *Ethnomusicology* 20:49–66.

Henshilwood, Christopher, et al. 2002. Emergence of modern human behavior: Middle Stone Age engravings from South Africa. *Science.* 295 (February 15):1278–80.

Herlihy, Laura Hobson. 2007. Matrifocality and women's power on the Miskito Coast. *Ethnology* 46:133–49.

Herrmann, Esther, Joseph Call, Maria Victoria Herandez-Lloreda, Brain Hare, and Michael Tomasello. 2007. Humans have evolved specialized skills in social cognition: The cultural intelligence hypothesis. *Science* 317 (September 7): 1360–65.

Herrman, Helen. 1990. A survey of homeless mentally ill people in Melbourne, Australia. *Hospital and Community Psychiatry* 41:1291–92.

Herrnstein, Richard J., and Charles Murray. 1994. *The bell curve: Intelligence and class structure in American life.* New York: Free Press.

Hewes, Gordon W. 1961. Food transport and the origin of hominid bipedalism. *American Anthropologist* 63: 687–710.

Hewlett, Barry. 2004. Diverse contexts of human infancy. In MyAnthroLibrary, eds. C. R. Ember, M. Ember, and P. N. Peregrine. MyAnthroLibrary.com. Pearson.

Hewlett, Barry S., and L. L. Cavalli-Sforza. 1986. Cultural transmission among Aka Pygmies. *American Anthropologist* 88:922–34.

Hiatt, L. R. 1980. Polyandry in Sri Lanka: A test case for parental investment theory. *Man* 15:583–98.

Hickey, Gerald Cannon. 1964. *Village in Vietnam.* New Haven, CT: Yale University Press.

Hickson, Letitia. 1986. The social contexts of apology in dispute settlement: A cross-cultural study. *Ethnology* 25: 283–94.

Higley, Stephen Richard. 1995. *Privilege, power, and place: The geography of the American upper class,* 1–47. Lanham, MD: Rowman & Littlefield.

Hill, Carole. 2000. Strategic issues for rebuilding a theory and practice synthesis, *NAPA Bulletin* 18:1–16.

Hill, Donald R. 2005. Music of the African diaspora in the Americas. In *Encyclopedia of diasporas: Immigrant and refugee cultures around the world,* eds. M. Ember, C. R.

434

Ember, and I. Skoggard, 363–73. New York: Kluwer Academic/Plenum.

Hill, James N. 1970. *Broken K Pueblo: Prehistoric social organization in the American Southwest. Anthropological Papers of the University of Arizona*, Number 18. Tucson: University of Arizona Press.

Hill, Jane H. 1978. Apes and language. *Annual Review of Anthropology* 7:89–112.

Hill, Jane H. 2009. Do apes have language? In MyAnthroLibrary, eds. C. R. Ember, M. Ember, and P. N. Peregrine. MyAnthroLibrary.com. Pearson.

Hill, Jonathan D. 1996. Introduction: Ethnogenesis in the Americas. 1492–1992. In *Ethnogenesis in the Americas*, ed. J. D. Hill, 1–19. Iowa City: University of Iowa Press.

Hill, Kim, and A. Magdalena Hurtado. 2004. The ethics of anthropological research with remote tribal populations. In *Lost paradises and the ethics of research and publication*, eds. F. M. Salzano and A. M. Hurtado, 193–210. Oxford: Oxford University Press.

Hill, Kim, Hillard Kaplan, Kristen Hawkes, and A. Magdalena Hurtado. 1987. Foraging decisions among Aché hunter-gatherers: New data and implications for optimal foraging models. *Ethology and Sociobiology* 8:1–36.

Hill, Susan T. 2001. *Science and engineering doctorate awards: 2000*, NSF 02-305. National Science Foundation, Division of Science Resources Statistics. VA: Arlington.

Hillel, Daniel. 2000. *Salinity management for sustainable irrigation: Integrating science, environment, and economics.* Washington, DC. The World Bank.

Himmelgreen, David A., and Deborah L. Crooks. 2005. Nutritional anthropology and its application to nutritional issues and problems. In *Applied anthropology: Domains of application*, eds. Satish Kedia and John van Willigen, 149–88. Westport, CT: Praeger. Hinkes, Madeleine. 1993. Race, ethnicity, and forensic anthropology. *National Association for Applied Anthropology Bulletin* 13:48–54.

Hitchcock, Robert K. and Megan Beisele. 2000. Introduction. In *Hunters and gatherers in the modern world: Conflict, resistance, and self-determinations*, eds. P. P. Schweitzer, M. Biesele, and R. K. Hitchcock, 1–27. New York: Berghahn Books.

Hobsbawm, E. J. 1970. *Age of revolution.* New York: Praeger.

Hockett, C. F., and R. Ascher. 1964. The human revolution. *Current Anthropology* 5:135–68.

Hodgson, Jason, and Todd Driscoll. 2008. No evidence of a Neandertal contribution to modern human diversity. *Genome Biology* 9:206.1–206.7.

Hoebel, E. Adamson. 1960. *The Cheyennes: Indians of the Great Plains.* New York: Holt, Rinehart & Winston.

Hoebel, E. Adamson. 1968/1954. *The law of primitive man.* New York: Atheneum.

Hoffecker, John F., W. Roger Powers, and Ted Goebel. 1993. The colonization of Beringia and the peopling of the New World. *Science* 259 (January 1):46–53.

Hoffman, Lois Wladis. 1988. Cross-cultural differences in child-rearing goals. In *Parental behavior in diverse societies*, eds. R. A. LeVine, P. M. Miller, and M. M. West. San Francisco: Jossey-Bass.

Hoijer, Harry. 1964. Cultural implications of some Navaho linguistic categories. In *Language in culture and society*, ed. D. Hymes. New York: Harper & Row.

Holdaway, R. N., and C. Jacomb. 2000. Rapid extinction of the moas (*Aves: Dinornithiformes*): Model, test, and implications. *Science* 287 (March 24):2250–57.

Holden, Constance. 2000. Selective power of UV. *Science* 289 (September 1): 1461.

Hole, Frank. 1992. Origins of agriculture. In *The Cambridge encyclopedia of human evolution*, eds. S. Jones, R. Martin, and D. Pilbeam. New York: Cambridge University Press.

Hole, Frank. 1994. Environmental shock and urban origins. In *Chiefdoms and early states in the Near East*, eds. G. Stein and M. Rothman. Madison, WI: Prehistory Press.

Hole, Frank, Kent V. Flannery, and James A. Neely. 1969. *Prehistory and human ecology of the Deh Luran Plain. Memoirs of the Museum of Anthropology*, No. 1. Ann Arbor: University of Michigan.

Hollan, Douglas. 1992. Cross-cultural differences in the self. *Journal of Anthropological Research* 48:289–90.

Holloway, Marguerite. 1993. Sustaining the Amazon. *Scientific American* (July):91–99.

Holloway, Ralph L. 1974. The casts of fossil hominid brains. *Scientific American* (July):106–15.

Holmes, Janet. 2001. *An introduction to sociolinguistics.* 2nd ed. London: Longman.

Honigmann, John J. 1967. *Personality in culture.* New York: Harper & Row.

Hoogbergen, Wim. 1990. *The Boni Maroon Wars in Suriname.* Leiden: E. J. Brill.

Hooper, Judith. 2002. *Of moths and men: The untold story of science and the peppered moth.* New York: W. W. Norton.

Hopkins, K. 1980. Brother-sister marriage in Roman Egypt. *Comparative Studies in Society and History* 22:303–54.

Houston, Stephen D. 1988. The phonetic decipherment of Mayan glyphs. *Antiquity* 62:126–35.

Howard, Alan, and Jan Rensel. 2009. Rotuma: Interpreting a wedding. In MyAnthroLibrary, eds. C. R. Ember, M. Ember, and P. N. Peregrine. MyAnthroLibrary.com. Pearson.

Howell, F. Clark. 1966. Observations on the earlier phases of the European Lower Paleolithic. In *Recent studies in paleoanthropology. American anthropologist.* Special publication, April, 88–200.

Howell, Nancy. 1979. *Demography of the Dobe !Kung.* New York: Academic Press.

Howrigan, Gail A. 1988. Fertility, infant feeding, and change in Yucatan. *New Directions for Child Development* 40:37–50.

Hrdy, Sarah Blaffer. 1977. *The langurs of Abu: Female and male strategies of reproduction.* Cambridge, MA: Harvard University Press.

Hua, Cai. 2001. *A society without fathers or husbands: the Na of China*, trans. Asti Hustvedt. New York: Zone Books.

Huang, H. T. 2002. Hypolactasia and the Chinese diet. *Current Anthropology* 43: 809–19.

Human Development Report 1993. 1993. Published for the United Nations Development Programme. New York: Oxford University Press, 9–25.

Human Development Report 2001. 2001. Published for the United Nations Development Programme. New York: Oxford University Press, 9–25.

Humphrey, Caroline, and Stephen Hugh-Jones. 1992. Introduction: Barter, exchange and value. In *Barter, exchange and value*, eds. C. Humphrey and S. Hugh-Jones. New York: Cambridge University Press.

Hunt, Morton. 1974. *Sexual behavior in the 1970s.* Chicago: Playboy Press.

Hunt, Robert C. 2000. Labor productivity and agricultural development: Boserup revisited. *Human Ecology* 28: 251–77.

Hurtado, Ana M., Kristen Hawkes, Kim Hill, and Hillard Kaplan. 1985. Female subsistence strategies among the Aché hunter-gatherers of eastern Paraguay. *Human Ecology* 13:1–28.

Huss-Ashmore, Rebecca, and Francis E. Johnston. 1985. Bioanthropological research in developing countries. *Annual Review of Anthropology* 14:475–527.

Huxley, Thomas H. 1970. Man's place in nature. In *Evolution of man*, ed. L. Young. New York: Oxford University Press.

Hymes, Dell. 1974. *Foundations in sociolinguistics: An ethnographic approach.* Philadelphia: University of Pennsylvania Press.

Irons, William. 1979. Natural selection, adaptation, and human social behavior. In *Evolutionary Biology and Human Social Behavior*, eds. N. Chagnon and W. Irons. North Scituate, MA: Duxbury.

Irwin, Marc H., Gary N. Schafer, and Cynthia P. Feiden. 1974. Emic and unfamiliar category sorting of Mano farmers and U.S. undergraduates. *Journal of Cross-Cultural Psychology* 5:407–23.

Isaac, Glynn. 1971. The diet of early man: Aspects of archaeological evidence from Lower and Middle Pleistocene sites in Africa. *World Archaeology* 2:277–99.

Isaac, Glynn. 1984. The archaeology of human origins: Studies of the Lower Pleistocene in East Africa, 1971–1981. In *Advances in world archaeology*, eds. F. Wendorf and A. Close. Orlando, FL: Academic Press.

Isaac, Glynn, ed., assisted by Barbara Isaac. 1997. *Plio-Pleistocene archaeology.* Oxford: Clarendon Press.

Itkonen, T. I. 1951. The Lapps of Finland. *Southwestern Journal of Anthropology* 7:32–68.

Jablonski, Nina G., and George Chaplin. 2000. The evolution of human skin color. *Journal of Human Evolution* 39:57–106.

Jacobs, Sue-Ellen, and Christine Roberts. 1989. Sex, sexuality, gender and gender variance. In *Gender and anthropology*, ed. S. Morgen. Washington, DC: American Anthropological Association.

Jaeger, J., T. Thein, M. Benammi, Y. Chaimanee, A. N. Soe, T. Lwin, T. Tun, S. Wai, and S. Ducrocq. 1999. A new primate from the middle Eocene of Myanmar and the Asian early origins of anthropoids. *Science* 286 (October 15):528–30.

James, Allison. 2007. Giving voice to children's voices: Practices and problems, pitfalls and potentials. *American Anthropologist* 109:261–72.

James, William. 1902. *The varieties of religious experience: A study in human nature.* New York: Modern Library.

Jankowiak, William R. 2009. Urban Mongols: Ethnicity in communist China. In MyAnthroLibrary, eds. C. R. Ember, M. Ember, and P. N. Peregrine. MyAnthroLibrary.com. Pearson.

Jankowiak, William R., and Edward F. Fischer. 1992. A cross-cultural perspective on romantic love. *Ethnology* 31:149–55.

Jankowiak, William, M. Diane Nell, and Ann Buckmaster. 2002. Managing infidelity: A cross-cultural perspective. *Ethnology* 41:85–101.

Jankowiak, William, Monica Sudakov, and Benjamin C. Wilreker. 2005. Co-wife conflict and co-operation. *Ethnology* 44:81–98.

Janzen, Daniel H. 1973. Tropical agroecosystems. *Science* 182 (December 21):1212–19.

Jarvenpa, Robert. 2004. *Silot'ine:* An insurance perspective on Northern Dene kinship networks in recent history. *Journal of Anthropological Research* 60:153–78.

Jarvenpa, Robert, and Hetty Jo Brumbach. 2006. Chipewyan hunters: A task differentiation analysis. In *Circumpolar lives and livelihood: A comparative ethnoarchaeology of gender and subsistence*, eds. Robert Jarvenpa and Hetty Jo Brumbach, 54–78. Lincoln, Nebraska: University of Nebraska Press.

Jayaswal, Vidula. 2002. South Asian Upper Paleolithic. In *Encyclopedia of prehistory*, vol. 8: *South and Southwest Asia*, eds. P. N. Peregrine and M. Ember. New York: Kluwer Academic/Plenum.

Jelliffe, Derrick B., and E. F. Patrice Jelliffe. 1975. Human milk, nutrition, and the world resource crisis. *Science* 188 (May 9):557–61.

Jennings, J. D. 1968. *Prehistory of North America.* New York: McGraw-Hill.

Jensen, Arthur. 1969. How much can we boost IQ and scholastic achievement? *Harvard Educational Review* 29:1–123.

Joans, Barbara. 1997. Problems in Pocatello: A study in linguistic misunderstanding. In *Applying cultural anthropology: An introductory reader*, 3rd ed., eds. A. Podolefsky and P. J. Brown, 51–54. Mountain View: CA: Mayfield.

Johannes, R. E. 1981. *Words of the lagoon: Fishing and marine lore in the Palau District of Micronesia.* Berkeley: University of California Press.

Johanson, Donald C., and Maitland Edey. 1981. *Lucy: The beginnings of humankind.* New York: Simon & Schuster.

Johanson, Donald C., and Tim D. White. 1979. A systematic assessment of early African hominids. *Science* 203 (January 26):321–30.

Johnson, Allen, and Timothy Earle. 1987. *The evolution of human societies: From foraging group to agrarian state.* Stanford, CA: Stanford University Press.

Johnson, Amber Lynn. 2002. Cross-cultural analysis of pastoral adaptations and organizational states: A preliminary study. *Cross-Cultural Research* 36:151–80.

Johnson, Gregory A. 1977. Aspects of regional analysis in archaeology. *Annual Review of Anthropology* 6:479–508.

Johnson, Gregory A. 1987. The changing organization of Uruk administration on the Susiana Plain. In *Archaeology of western Iran*, ed. F. Hole. Washington, DC: Smithsonian Institution Press.

Johnson-Hanks, Jennifer. 2006. *Uncertain honor: Modern motherhood in an African crisis.* Chicago: University of Chicago Press.

Johnson, Jeffrey G., Patricia Cohen, Elizabeth M. Smailies, Stephanie Kasen, and Judith S. Brook. 2002. Television viewing and aggressive behavior during adolescence and adulthood. *Science* 295 (March 29):2468–70.

Johnston, David Cay. 1999. Gap between rich and poor found substantially wider. *New York Times*, National, September 5, p. 16.

Jolly, Alison. 1985. *The evolution of primate behavior.* 2nd ed. New York: Macmillan.

Jolly, Clifford. 1970. The seed-eaters: A new model of hominid differentiation based on a baboon analogy. *Man* 5:5–28.

Jones, Martin, and Xinyi Liu. 2009. Origins of agriculture in East Asia. *Science* 324 (May 8):730–31.

Jones, Nicholas Blurton, Kristen Hawkes, and James F. O'Connell. 1996. The global process and local ecology: How should we explain differences between the Hadza and the !Kung? In *Cultural diversity among twentieth-century foragers*, ed. S. Kent. Cambridge: Cambridge University Press.

Jones, Steve, Robert Martin, and David Pilbeam, eds. 1992. *The Cambridge encyclopedia of human evolution.* New York: Cambridge University Press.

Judge, W. James, and Jerry Dawson. 1972. Paleo-Indian settlement technology in New Mexico. *Science* 176 (June 16): 1210–16.

Jung, Carl G. 1938. *Psychology and religion.* New Haven, CT: Yale University Press.

Jungers, William L. 1988a. Relative joint size and hominoid locomotor adaptations with implications for the evolution of hominid bipedalism. *Journal of Human Evolution* 17:247–65.

Jungers, William L. 1988b. New estimates of body size in australopithecines. In *Evolutionary history of the "robust" australopithecines*, ed. F. Grine. New York: Aldine.

Jungers, William L., W. E. H. Harcourt-Smith, R. E. Wunderlich, M. W. Tocheri, S. G. Larson, T. Sutikna, Rokus Awe Due, and M. J. Morwood. 2009. The foot of *Homo floresiensis. Nature* 459 (May 7):81–84.

Kamin, Leon J. 1995. Behind the curve. *Scientific American* (February): 99–103.

Kang, Bong W. 2000. A reconsideration of population pressure and warfare: A protohistoric Korean case. *Current Anthropology* 41:873–81.

Kang, Gay Elizabeth. 1979. Exogamy and peace relations of social units: A cross-cultural test. *Ethnology* 18:85–99.

Kaplan, Hillard, and Kim Hill. 1985. Food sharing among Aché foragers: Tests of explanatory hypotheses. *Current Anthropology* 26:223–46.

Kaplan, Hillard, Kim Hill, and A. Magdalena Hurtado. 1990. Risk, foraging and food sharing among the Aché. In *Risk and uncertainty in tribal and peasant economies*, ed. E. Cashdan. Boulder, CO: Westview.

Kaplan, Hillard, Kim Hill, Jane Lancaster, and A. Magdalena Hurtado. 2000. A theory of human life history evolution, diet, intelligence, and longevity. *Evolutionary Anthropology* 9:156–84.

Kardiner, Abram, with Ralph Linton. 1946/1939. *The individual and his society.* New York: Golden Press. (Originally published 1939 by Columbia University Press.)

Kasarda, John D. 1971. Economic structure and fertility: A comparative analysis. *Demography* 8, no. 3 (August): 307–18.

Katzner, Kenneth. 2002. *Languages of the world.* Routledge.

Kay, Richard F. 2000a. *Parapithecidae.* In *Encyclopedia of human evolution and prehistory*, eds. I. Tattersall, E. Delson, and J. van Couvering. New York: Garland.

Kay, Richard F. 2000b. Teeth. In *Encyclopedia of human evolution and prehistory*, eds. I. Tattersall, E. Delson, and J. van Couvering. New York: Garland.

Kay, Richard F., C. Ross, and B. A. Williams. 1997. Anthropoid origins. *Science* 275 (February 7):797–804.

Kedia, Satish. 2008. Recent changes and trends in the practice of anthropology. *NAPA Bulletin* 29:14–28.

Kedia, Satish, and John van Willigen, eds. 2005. Applied anthropology: Domains of application. Wesport, CT: Praeger.

Keeley, Lawrence H. 1980. *Experimental determination of stone tool uses: A microwear analysis.* Chicago: University of Chicago Press.

Keeley, Lawrence H. 1991. Ethnographic models for late glacial hunter-gatherers. In *The late glacial in north-west Europe: Human adaptation and environmental change at the end of the Pleistocene*, eds. N. Barton, A. J. Roberts, and D. A. Roe. London: Council for British Archaeology. *CBA Research Report* 77:179–90.

Keenan, Elinor. 1989. Norm-makers, norm-breakers: Uses of speech by men and women in a Malagasy community. In *Explorations in the ethnography of speaking*, 2nd ed., eds. R. Bauman and J. Sherzer. New York: Cambridge University Press.

Kehoe, Alice B., and Dody H. Giletti. 1981. Women's preponderance in possession cults: The calcium-deficiency hypothesis extended. *American Anthropologist* 83:549–61.

Keller, Helen. 1974/1902. *The story of my life.* New York: Dell.

Kelley, Jay. 1992. The evolution of apes. In *The Cambridge encyclopedia of human evolution*, eds. S. Jones, R. Martin, and D. Pilbeam. New York: Cambridge University Press.

Kelly, Raymond C. 1974. Witchcraft and sexual relations: An exploration in the social and semantic implications of the structure of belief. Paper presented at the annual meeting of the American Anthropological Association, Mexico City.

Kelly, Raymond C. 1985. *The Nuer conquest: The structure and development of an expansionist system.* Ann Arbor: University of Michigan Press.

Kelly, Robert L. 1995. *The foraging spectrum: Diversity in hunter-gatherer lifeways.* Washington, DC: Smithsonian Institution Press.

Kent, Susan, ed. 1996. *Cultural diversity among twentieth-century foragers: An African perspective.* Cambridge: Cambridge University Press.

Kerr, Richard A. 1998. Sea-floor dust shows drought felled Akkadian empire. *Science* 299 (January 16):325–26.

Khosroshashi, Fatemeh. 1989. Penguins don't care, but women do: A social identity analysis of a Whorfian problem. *Language in Society* 18:505–25.

Kilbride, Philip L., and Janet C. Kilbride. 1990. Polygyny: A modern contradiction? In P. L. Kilbride and J. C. Kilbride, *Changing family life in East Africa: Women and children at risk.* University Park: Pennsylvania State University Press.

Kimbel, William H., T. D. White, and D. C. Johansen. 1984. Cranial morphology of *Australopithecus afarensis*: A comparative study based on composite reconstruction of the adult skull. *American Journal of Physical Anthropology* 64:337–88.

King, Barbara J. 1999a. Introduction. In *The origins of language*, ed. B. J. King, 3–19. Santa Fe, NM: School of American Research Press.

King, Barbara. 1999b. *The origins of language: What nonhuman primates can tell us.* Santa Fe: School of American Research Press.

King, J. C. H. 1986. Tradition in Native American art. In *The arts of the North American Indian*, ed. E. L. Wade. New York: Hudson Hills Press.

King, Marie-Claire, and Arno Motulsky. 2002. Mapping human history. *Science* 298 (December 20): 2,342–43.

King, Seth S. 1979. Some farm machinery seems less than human. *New York Times* April 8, p. E9.

Kingston, John D., Bruno D. Marino, and Andrew Hill. 1994. Isotopic evidence for Neogene hominid paleoenvironments in the Kenya Rift Valley. *Science* 264 (May 13):955–59.

Kitchen, Andrew, Michael Miyamoto, and Connie Mulligan. 2008. A three-stage colonization model for the peopling of the Americas. *PLoS ONE* 3(2):e1596.

437

Klass, Morton. 2009. Is there "caste" outside of India? In MyAnthroLibrary, eds. C. R. Ember, M. Ember, and P. N. Peregrine. MyAnthroLibrary.com. Pearson.

Klein, Richard G. 1974. Ice-Age hunters of the Ukraine. *Scientific American* (June):96–105.

Klein, Richard G. 1977. The ecology of early man in Southern Africa. *Science* 197 (July 8):115–26.

Klein, Richard G. 1983. The Stone Age prehistory of Southern Africa. *Annual Review of Anthropology* 12:25–48.

Klein, Richard G. 1987. Reconstructing how early people exploited animals: Problems and prospects. In *The evolution of human hunting*, eds. M. Nitecki and D. Nitecki. New York: Plenum.

Klein, Richard G. 1989. *The human career: Human biological and cultural origins.* Chicago: University of Chicago Press.

Klein, Richard G. 1994. Southern Africa before the ice age. In *Integrative paths to the past*, eds. R. Corruccini and R. Ciochon. Upper Saddle River, NJ: Prentice Hall.

Klein, Richard G. 2003. Whither the Neanderthals. *Science* 299 (March 7):1525–28.

Klein, Richard, and Blake Edgar. 2002. *The dawn of human culture.* New York: John Wiley and Sons.

Kleinberg, Jill. 1994. Practical implications of organizational culture where Americans and Japanese work together. In *Practicing anthropology in corporate America*, ed. A. T. Jordan. Arlington, VA: American Anthropological Association.

Kleinman, Arthur. 1988. *Rethinking psychiatry: From cultural category to personal experience.* New York: Macmillan.

Kleinman, Arthur, Veena Das, and Margaret Lock, eds. 1997. *Social suffering.* Berkeley: University of California Press.

Klima, Bohuslav. 1962. The first ground-plan of an Upper Paleolithic loess settlement in Middle Europe and its meaning. In *Courses toward urban life*, eds. R. Braidwood and G. Willey. Chicago: Aldine.

Klineberg, Otto. 1935. *Negro intelligence and selective migration.* New York: Columbia University Press.

Klineberg, Otto, ed. 1944. *Characteristics of the American Negro.* New York: Harper & Brothers.

Klineberg, Otto. 1979. Foreword. In M. H. Segall, *Cross-cultural psychology.* Monterey, CA: Brooks/Cole.

Kluckhohn, Clyde. 1948. As an anthropologist views it. In *Sex habits of American men*, ed. A. Deutsch. Upper Saddle River, NJ: Prentice Hall.

Kluckhohn, Clyde. 1965. Recurrent themes in myths and mythmaking. In *The study of folklore*, ed. A. Dundes. Upper Saddle River, NJ: Prentice Hall.

Knauft, Bruce M. 1978. Cargo cults and relational separation. *Behavior Science Research* 13:185–240.

Knecht, Peter. 2003. Aspects of shamanism: An introduction. In *Shamans in Asia*, eds. C. Chilson and P. Knecht, 1–30. London: RoutledgeCurzon.

Koch, Klaus-Friedrich, Soraya Altorki, Andrew Arno, and Letitia Hickson. 1977. Ritual reconciliation and the obviation of grievances: A comparative study in the ethnography of law. *Ethnology* 16:269–84.

Kolbert, Elizabeth. 2005. Last words. *The New Yorker* (June 6):46–59.

Komar, Debra A., and Jane E. Buikstra. 2008. *Forensic anthropology: Contemporary theory and practice.* New York: Oxford University Press.

Konner, Melvin, and Carol Worthman. 1980. Nursing frequency, gonadal function, and birth spacing among !Kung hunter-gatherers. *Science* 267 (February 15):788–91.

Korbin, Jill E. 1981. Introduction. In *Child abuse and neglect*, ed. J. E. Korbin. Berkeley: University of California Press.

Korotayev, Andrey and Dmitri Bondarenko. 2000. Polygyny and democracy: A cross-cultural comparison. *Cross-Cultural Research* 34:190–208.

Kottak, Conrad Phillip. 1996. The media, development, and social change. In *Transforming societies, transforming anthropology*, ed. E. F. Moran. Ann Arbor: University of Michigan Press.

Kottak, Conrad P. 1999. The new ecological anthropology. *Current Anthropology* 101: 23–35.

Kracke, Waud H. 1979. *Force and persuasion: Leadership in an Amazonian society.* Chicago: University of Chicago Press.

Krahn, H., T. F. Hartnagel, and J. W. Gartrell. 1986. Income inequality and homicide rates: Cross-national data and criminological theories. *Criminology* 24:269–95.

Kramer, Andrew. 2009. The natural history and evolutionary fate of *Homo erectus*. In MyAnthroLibrary, eds. C. R. Ember, M. Ember, and P. N. Peregrine. MyAnthroLibrary.com. Pearson.

Kramer, Samuel Noel. 1963. *The Sumerians: Their history, culture, and character.* Chicago: University of Chicago Press.

Krause, Johannes, Carles Lalueza-Fox, Ludovic Orlando, Wolfgang Enard, Richard E. Green, Hernán A. Burbano, Jean-Jacques Hublin, Catherine Hänni, Javier Fortea, Marco de la Rasilla, Jaume Bertranpetit, Antonio Rosas, and Svante Pääbo. 2007. The derived FOXP2 variant of modern humans was shared with Neandertals. *Current Biology* 17(21):1908–12.

Krebs, J. R., and N. B. Davies, eds. 1984. *Behavioural ecology: An evolutionary approach.* 2nd ed. Sunderland, MA: Sinauer.

Krebs, J. R., and N. B. Davies. 1987. *An introduction to behavioural ecology.* 2nd ed. Sunderland, MA: Sinauer.

Krings, Matthias, A. Stone, R. W. Schmitz, H. Krainitzki, M. Stoneking, and S. Paabo. 1997. Neandertal DNA sequences and the origin of modern humans. *Cell* 90:19–30.

Krippner, Stanley. 1987. Dreams and shamanism. In *Shamanism*, comp. S. Nicholson, 125–32. Wheaton, IL: Theosophical Publishing House.

Kristof, Nicholas D. 1997. Japan's invisible minority: Burakumin. *Britannica Online*, December.

Kristof, Nicholas D. 1995. Japan's invisible minority: Better off than in past, but still outcasts. *New York Times*, International, November 30, A18.

Kroeber, Theodora. 1967. *Ishi in two worlds.* Berkeley: University of California Press.

Kuehn, Steven. 1998. New evidence for Late Paleoindian-early Archaic subsistence behavior in the western Great Lakes. *American Antiquity* 63:457–76.

Kulick, Don. 1992. *Language shift and cultural reproduction.* Cambridge: Cambridge University Press.

Kushner, Gilbert. 1991. Applied anthropology. In *Career explorations in human services*, eds. W. G. Emener and M. Darrow. Springfield, IL: Charles C Thomas.

Lakoff, Robin. 1973. Language and woman's place. *Language in Society* 2:45–80.

Lakoff, Robin. 1990. Why can't a woman be less like a man? In *Talking power*, ed. R. Lakoff. New York: Basic Books.

Lalueza-Fox, Carles, Holger Römpler, David Caramelli, Claudia Stäubert, Giulio Catalano, David Hughes, Nadin Rohland, Elena Pilli, Laura Longo, Silvana Condemi, Marco de la Rasilla, Javier Fortea, Antonio Rosas, Mark Stoneking, Torsten Schöneberg, Jaume Bertranpetit, and Michael

Hofreiter. 2007. A Melanocortin 1 Receptor Allele suggests varying pigmentation among Neanderthals. *Science* 318 (November 30):1453–55.

Lambert, Helen. 2001. Not talking about sex in India: Indirection and the communication of bodily intention. In *An anthropology of indirect communication*, eds. J. Hendry and C. W. Watson, 51–67. London: Routledge.

Lambert, Patricia M., Banks L. Leonard, Brian R. Billman, Richard A. Marlar, Margaret E. Newman, and Karl J. Reinhard. 2000. Response to critique of the claim of cannibalism at Cowboy Wash. *American Antiquity* 65(2):397–406.

Lambert, William W., Leigh Minturn Triandis, and Margery Wolf. 1959. Some correlates of beliefs in the malevolence and benevolence of supernatural beings: A cross-societal study. *Journal of Abnormal and Social Psychology* 58: 162–69.

Lamphere, Louise. 2006. Foreward: Taking stock—The transformation of feminist theorizing in anthropology. In *Feminist anthropology: Past, present, and future*, eds. Pamela L. Geller and Miranda K. Stockett, ix–xvi. Philadelphia: University of Pennsylvania Press.

Lancy, David F. 2007. Accounting for variability in mother-child play. *American Anthropologist* 109:273–84.

Lancy, David F. 2008. *The anthropology of childhood: Cherubs, chattel, changelings.* Cambridge: Cambridge University Press.

Landauer, Thomas K. 1973. Infantile vaccination and the secular trend in stature. *Ethos* 1: 499–503.

Landauer, Thomas K., and John W. M. Whiting. 1964. Infantile stimulation and adult stature of human males. *American Anthropologist* 66:1007–28.

Landauer, Thomas K., and John W. M. Whiting. 1981. Correlates and consequences of stress in infancy. In *Handbook of cross-cultural human development.* eds. R. H. Munroe, R. Munroe, and B. Whiting. New York: Garland.

Landecker, Hannah. 2000. Immortality, in vitro: A history of the HeLa Cell Line. In *Biotechnology and culture: Bodies, anxieties, ethics*, ed. Paul Brodwin, 53–74. Bloomington: Indiana University Press.

Lang, Sabine. 1999. Lesbians, men-women and two-spirits: Homosexuality and gender in Native American cultures. In *Female desires: Same-sex relations and transgender practices across cultures*, eds. Evelyn Blackwood and Saskia E. Weiringa, 91–116. New York: Columbia University Press.

Langness, Lewis L. 1974. *The study of culture.* San Francisco: Chandler and Sharp.

Lareau, Annette. 2003. *Unequal childhoods: Class, race, and family life.* Berkeley, CA: University of California Press.

Larsen, Clark Spenser. 2009. Bare bones anthropology: The bioarchaeology of human remains. In MyAnthroLibrary, eds. C. R. Ember, M. Ember, and P. N. Peregrine. MyAnthroLibrary.com. Pearson.

Larsen, Clark Spenser. 1997. *Bioarchaeology: Interpreting behavior from the human skeleton.* Cambridge, Cambridge University Press.

Larson, C. L., J. Aronoff, I. C. Sarinopoulos, and D. C. Zhu. 2009. Recognizing threat: A simple geometric shape activates neural circuitry for threat detection. *Journal of Cognitive Neuroscience* 21:1523–35.

Larson, C. L., J. Aronoff, and J. Stearns. 2007. The shape of threat: Simple geometric forms evoke rapid and sustained capture of attention. *Emotion* 7:526–34.

Lassiter, Luke. 2008. Moving past public anthropology and doing collaborative research. *NAPA Bulletin* 29:70–86.

Lassiter, Luke Eric, Hurley Goodall, Elizabeth Campbell, and Michelle Natasya Johnson, eds., 2004. *The other side of Middletown: Exploring Muncie's African American community.* Walnut Creek, CA: AltaMira Press.

Lawless, Robert, Vinson H. Sutlive, Jr., and Mario D. Zamora, eds. 1983. *Fieldwork: The human experience.* New York: Gordon and Breach.

Layton, Robert. 1992. *Australian rock art: A new synthesis.* Cambridge: Cambridge University Press.

Le, Huynh-Nhu. 2000. Never leave your little one alone: Raising an Ifaluk child. In *A world of babies: Imagined child care guides for seven societies*, eds. Judy DeLoache and Alma Gottlieb, 199–220. Cambridge: Cambridge University Press.

Leach, Jerry W. 1983. Introduction. In *The kula*, eds. J. W. Leach and E. Leach. Cambridge: Cambridge University Press.

Leacock, Eleanor. 1954. The Montagnais 'hunting territory' and the fur trade. *American Anthropological Association Memoir* 78:1–59.

Leacock, Eleanor, and Richard Lee. 1982. Introduction. In *Politics and history in band societies*, eds. E. Leacock and R. Lee. Cambridge: Cambridge University Press.

Leakey, Louis S. B. 1960. Finding the world's earliest man. *National Geographic* (September): 420–35.

Leakey, Louis S. B. 1965. *Olduvai Gorge, 1951–1961*, vol. I: *A preliminary report on the geology and fauna.* Cambridge: Cambridge University Press.

Leakey, Maeve, C. S. Feibel, I. McDougall, and A. Walker. 1995. New four-million-year-old hominid species from Kanapoi and Allia Bay, Kenya. *Nature* 376 (August 17):565–71.

Leakey, Maeve, Fred Spoor, Frank Brown, Patrick Gathogo, Christopher Kiarie, Louise Leakey, Ian McDougall. 2001. New Hominin genus from Eastern Africa shows diverse middle Pliocene lineages. *Nature* 410 (March 22):433–51.

Leakey, Mary. 1971. *Olduvai Gorge: Excavations in Beds I and II.* Cambridge: Cambridge University Press.

Leakey, Mary. 1979. *Olduvai Gorge: My search for early man.* London: Collins.

Lederman, Rena. 1990. Big men, large and small? Towards a comparative perspective. *Ethnology* 29:3–15.

Lee, Phyllis C. 1983. Home range, territory and intergroup encounters. In *Primate social relationship: An integrated approach.* ed. R. A. Hinde. Sunderland, MA: Sinauer.

Lee, Richard B. 1968. What hunters do for a living, or, how to make out on scarce resources. In *Man the hunter*, eds. R. B. Lee and I. DeVore. Chicago: Aldine.

Lee, Richard B. 1972. Population growth and the beginnings of sedentary life among the !Kung bushmen. In *Population growth*, ed. B. Spooner. Cambridge, MA: MIT Press.

Lee, Richard B. 1979. *The !Kung San: Men, women, and work in a foraging society.* Cambridge: Cambridge University Press.

Lees, Susan H., and Daniel G. Bates. 1974. The origins of specialized nomadic pastoralism: A systemic model. *American Antiquity* 39:187–93.

Leibowitz, Lila. 1978. *Females, males, families: A biosocial approach.* North Scituate, MA: Duxbury.

Leis, Nancy B. 1974. Women in groups: Ijaw women's associations. In *Woman, culture, and society*, eds. M. Z. Rosaldo and L. Lamphere. Stanford, CA: Stanford University Press.

Lenski, Gerhard. 1984/1966. *Power and privilege: A theory of social stratification.* Chapel Hill: University of North Carolina Press.

Leonard, William R. 2002. Food for thought: Dietary change was a driving force in human evolution. *Scientific American* (December): 108–15.

Leonhardt, David, and Geraldine Fabrikant. 2009. Rise of the super-rich hits a sobering wall. *New York Times*, August 20, p. A1 of the New York Edition.

Lepowsky, Maria. 1990. Big men, big women and cultural autonomy. *Ethnology* 29:35–50.

Leslie, C. 1976. Introduction. In *Asian medical systems: A comparative study*, ed. C. Leslie. Los Angeles: University of California Press.

Levine, James A., Robert Weisell, Simon Chevassus, Claudio D. Martinez, and Barbara Burlingame. 2002. The distribution of work tasks for male and female children and adults separated by gender. In *Science* 296 (May 10):1025.

Levine, Nancy E. 1988. Women's work and infant feeding: A case from rural Nepal. *Ethnology* 27:231–51.

LeVine, Robert A. 1966. *Dreams and deeds: Achievement motivation in Nigeria.* Chicago: University of Chicago Press.

LeVine, Robert A. 1988. Human parental care: Universal goals, cultural strategies, individual behavior. In *Parental behavior in diverse societies*, eds. R. A. LeVine, P. M. Miller, and M. M. West. San Francisco: Jossey-Bass.

LeVine, Robert A. 2007. Ethnographic studies of childhood: A historical overview. *American Anthropologist* 109: 247–60.

LeVine, Robert A., and Barbara B. LeVine. 1963. Nyansongo: A Gusii Community in Kenya. In *Six cultures*, ed. B. B. Whiting. New York: Wiley.

Levinson, David. 1989. *Family violence in cross-cultural perspective.* Newbury Park, CA: Sage.

Levinson, David, and Melvin Ember, eds., 1997. *American immigrant cultures: Builders of a nation*, 2 vols. New York: Macmillan Reference.

Lévi-Strauss, Claude. 1963a. The sorcerer and his magic. In C. Lévi-Strauss, *Structural anthropology*. New York: Basic Books.

Lévi-Strauss, Claude. 1963b. *Structural anthropology.* Trans. Claire Jacobson and Brooke Grundfest Schoepf. New York: Basic Books.

Lévi-Strauss, Claude. 1966. *The savage mind*, trans. George Weidenfeld and Nicolson, Ltd. Chicago: University of Chicago Press. [First published in French 1962.]

Lévi-Strauss, Claude. 1969a. *The elementary structures of kinship*, rev. ed., trans. James H. Bell and J. R. von Sturmer, ed. Rodney Needham. Boston: Beacon Press. [First published in French 1949.]

Lévi-Strauss, Claude. 1969b. *The raw and the cooked*, trans. John Weightman and Doreen Weightman. New York: Harper & Row [First published in French 1964.]

Levy, Jerrold E. 1994. Hopi shamanism: A reappraisal. In *North American Indian anthropology: Essays on society and culture*, eds. R. J. DeMallie and A. Ortiz, 307–27. Norman: University of Oklahoma Press.

Lewontin, Richard. 1972. The apportionment of human diversity. *Evolutionary Biology* 6(1):381–98.

Lewin, Roger. 1983a. Is the orangutan a living fossil? *Science* 222 (December 16):1222–23.

Lewin, Roger. 1983b. Fossil Lucy grows younger, again. *Science* 219(January 7):43–44.

Lewin, Tamar. 1994. Sex in America: Faithfulness in marriage is overwhelming. *New York Times*, National, October 7, A1, A18.

Lewis, Oscar. 1951. *Life in a Mexican village: Tepoztlan revisited.* Urbana: University of Illinois Press.

Lewis, Oscar (with the assistance of Victor Barnouw). 1958. *Village life in northern India.* Urbana: University of Illinois Press.

Lichter, Daniel T., Diane K. McLaughlin, George Kephart, and David J. Landry. 1992. Race and the retreat from marriage: A shortage of marriageable men? *American Sociological Review* 57:781–99.

Lieberman, Daniel E. 1995. Testing hypotheses about recent human evolution from skulls: Integrating morphology, function, development, and phylogeny. *Current Anthropology* 36:159–97.

Lieberman, Leonard. 1999. Scientific insignificance. *Anthropology Newsletter* 40: 11–12.

Lieberman, Leonard, Rodney Kirk, and Alice Littlefield. 2003. Perishing paradigm: Race 1931–99. *American Anthropologist* 105: 110–13.

Lieberman, Leslie Sue. 2004. Diabetes mellitus and medical anthropology. In *Encyclopedia of medical anthropology: Health and illness in the world's cultures*, vol. I, eds. Carol R. Ember and Melvin Ember, 335–53. New York: Kluwer Academic Press/Plenum Publishers.

Light, Ivan, and Zhong Deng. 1995/1964. Gender differences in ROSCA participation within Korean business households in Los Angeles. In *Money-go-rounds: The importance of rotating savings and credit associations for women*, eds. S. Ardener and S. Burman, 217–40. Oxford: Berg.

Lightfoot, Kent G. 2005. The archaeology of colonialism: California in cross-cultural perspective. In *The archaeology of colonial encounters: Comparative perspectives*, ed. G. J. Stein, 207–35. Santa Fe, NM: School of American Research.

Lingenfelter, Sherwood G. 2009. Yap: Changing roles of men and women. In MyAnthroLibrary, eds. C. R. Ember, M. Ember, and P. N. Peregrine. MyAnthroLibrary.com. Pearson.

Linton, Ralph. 1936. *The study of man.* New York: Appleton-Century-Crofts.

Linton, Ralph. 1945. *The cultural background of personality.* New York: Appleton-Century-Crofts.

Little, Kenneth. 1965/1966. The political function of the Poro. *Africa* 35:349–65; 36: 62–71.

Little, Kenneth. 1957. The role of voluntary associations in West African urbanization. *American Anthropologist* 59:582–93.

Little, Kenneth. 1965. *West African urbanization.* New York: Cambridge University Press.

Lock, Margaret. 2009. Japan: Glimpses of everyday life. In MyAnthroLibrary, eds. C. R. Ember, M. Ember, and P. N. Peregrine. MyAnthroLibrary.com. Pearson.

Loftin, Colin K. 1971. *Warfare and societal complexity: A cross-cultural study of organized fighting in preindustrial societies.* PhD dissertation, University of North Carolina at Chapel Hill.

Loftin, Colin, David McDowall, and James Boudouris. 1989. Economic change and homicide in Detroit, 1926–1979. In *Violence in America*, vol. 1: *The history of crime*, ed. T. R. Gurr. Newbury Park, CA: Sage.

Lomax, Alan, ed. 1968. *Folk song style and culture.* American Association for the Advancement of Science Publication No. 88. Washington, DC.

Long, Susan Orpett. 2000. Introduction. In *Caring for the elderly in Japan and the U.S.*, ed. Susan Orpett Long, 6–7. London: Routledge.

Longacre, William. 1970. *Archaeology as anthropology: A case study.* Anthropological papers of the University of Arizona, Number 17. Tucson: University of Arizona Press.

Loomis, W. Farnsworth. 1967. Skin-pigment regulation of vitamin-D biosynthesis in man. *Science* 157 (August 4): 501–06.

Los Angeles Times 1994. Plundering earth is nothing new. News Service, as reported in the *New Haven Register*, June 12, pp. A18–A19.

Loustaunau, Martha O., and Elisa J. Sobo. 1997. *The cultural context of health, illness, and medicine.* Westport, CT: Bergin & Garvey.

Lovejoy, Arthur O. 1964. *The great chain of being: A study of the history of an idea.* Cambridge, MA: Harvard University Press.

Lovejoy, C. Owen. 1981. The origin of man. *Science* 211 (January 23):341–50.

Lovejoy, C. Owen. 1988. Evolution of human walking. *Scientific American* (November):118–25.

Low, Bobbi. 1990a. Human responses to environmental extremeness and uncertainty. In *Risk and uncertainty in tribal and peasant economies*, ed. E. Cashdan. Boulder, CO: Westview.

Low, Bobbi. 1990b. Marriage systems and pathogen stress in human societies. *American Zoologist* 30:325–39.

Low, Bobbi S. 2009. Behavioral ecology, "sociobiology" and human behavior. In MyAnthroLibrary, eds. C. R. Ember, M. Ember, and P. N. Peregrine. MyAnthroLibrary.com. Pearson.

Lowe, Edward D. 2002. A widow, a child, and two lineages: Exploring kinship and attachment in Chuuk. *American Anthropologist* 104:123–37.

Lucy, John A. 1992. *Grammatical categories and cognition: A case study of the linguistic relativity hypothesis.* Cambridge: Cambridge University Press.

Lumbreras, Luis. 1974. *The peoples and cultures of ancient Peru.* Washington, DC: Smithsonian Institution Press.

Luria, A. R. 1976. *Cognitive development: Its cultural and social foundations.* Cambridge, MA: Harvard University Press.

Lutz, Catherine. 1985. Depression and the translations of emotional worlds. In *Culture and depression*, eds. A. Kleinman and B. Good. Berkeley: University of California Press.

Lynd, Robert S., and Helen Merrell Lynd. 1929. *Middletown.* New York: Harcourt, Brace.

Lynd, Robert S., and Helen Merrell Lynd. 1937. *Middletown in transition.* New York: Harcourt, Brace.

Lyons, Nona Plessner. 1988. Two perspectives: On self, relationships, and morality. In *Mapping the moral domain*, eds. C. Gilligan, J. V. Ward, and J. M. Taylor. Cambridge, MA: Harvard University Press.

Lyttleton, Chris. 2000. *Endangered relations: Negotiating sex and AIDS in Thailand.* Bangkok: White Lotus Press.

MacArthur, R. H., and E. O. Wilson. 1967. *Theory of island biogeography.* Princeton, NJ: Princeton University Press.

Maccoby, Eleanor E., and Carol N. Jacklin. 1974. *The psychology of sex differences.* Stanford, CA: Stanford University Press.

Macdonald, Douglas H., and Barry S. Hewlett. 1999. Reproductive interests and forager mobility. *Current Anthropology* 40:501–23.

MacKinnon, John, and Kathy MacKinnon. 1980. The behavior of wild spectral tarsiers. *International Journal of Primatology* 1: 361–79.

MacNeish, Richard S. 1991. *The origins of agriculture and settled life.* Norman: University of Oklahoma Press.

Madrigal, Lorena. 1989. Hemoglobin genotype, fertility, and the malaria hypothesis. *Human Biology* 61:311–25.

Magner, L. 1992. *A history of medicine.* New York: Marcel Dekker.

Mahony, Frank Joseph. 1971. *A Trukese theory of medicine.* Ann Arbor, MI: University Microfilms.

Malefijt, Annemarie De Waal. 1968. *Religion and culture: An introduction to anthropology of religion.* New York: Macmillan.

Malin, Edward. 1986. *Totem poles of the Pacific Northwest coast.* Portland, OR: Timber Press.

Malinowski, Bronislaw. 1920. Kula: The circulating exchange of valuables in the Archipelagoes of eastern New Guinea. *Man* 51(2):97–105.

Malinowski, Bronislaw. 1927. *Sex and repression in savage society.* London: Kegan Paul, Trench, Trubner.

Malinowski, Bronislaw. 1932. *The sexual life of savages in northwestern Melanesia.* New York: Halcyon House.

Malinowski, Bronislaw. 1939. The group and the individual in functional analysis. *American Journal of Sociology* 44:938–64.

Malinowski, Bronislaw. 1954. Magic, science, and religion. In B. Malinowski, *Magic, science, and religion and other essays.* Garden City, NY: Doubleday.

Mangin, William P. 1965. The role of regional associations in the adaptation of rural migrants to cities in Peru. In *Contemporary cultures and societies of Latin America*, eds. D. B. Health and R. N. Adams. New York: Random House.

Mangin, William. 1967. Latin American squatter settlements: A problem and a solution. *Latin American Research Review* 2:65–98.

Manhein, Mary H. 1999. *The bone lady: Life as a forensic anthropologist.* Baton Rouge: Louisiana State University Press.

Maquet, Jacques. 1986. *The aesthetic experience: An anthropologist looks at the visual arts.* New Haven, CT: Yale University Press.

Marano, Louis A. 1973. A macrohistoric trend toward world government. *Behavior Science Notes* 8:35–40.

Marcus, George E., and Michael M. J. Fischer. 1986. *Anthropology as cultural critique: An experimental moment in the human sciences.* Chicago: University of Chicago Press.

Marcus, Joyce. 1983. On the nature of the Mesoamerican city. In *Prehistoric settlement patterns*, eds. E. Vogt and R. Leventhal. Albuquerque: University of New Mexico Press.

Marcus, Joyce. 2009. Maya hieroglyphs: History or propaganda?" In MyAnthroLibrary, eds. C. R. Ember, M. Ember, and P. N. Peregrine. MyAnthroLibrary.com. Pearson.

Marcus, Joyce, and Kent V. Flannery. 1996. *Zapotec civilization.* London: Thames and Hudson.

Marett, R. R. 1909. *The thresholds of religion.* London: Methuen.

Marks, Jonathan. 1994. Black, white, other: Racial categories are cultural constructs masquerading as biology. *Natural History* (December): 32–35.

Marks, Jonathan. 2002. Genes, bodies, and species. In *Physical anthropology: Original reading in method and practice*, eds. P. N. Peregrine, C. R. Ember, and M. Ember. Upper Saddle River, NJ: Prentice Hall.

Marks, Jonathan. 2009. Genes, bodies, and species. In MyAnthroLibrary, eds. C. R. Ember, M. Ember, and P. N. Peregrine. MyAnthroLibrary.com. Pearson.

Marlowe, Frank W. 2003. A critical period for provisioning by Hadza men: Implications for pair bonding. *Evolution and Human Behavior* 24:217–29.

Marshack, Alexander. 1972. *The roots of civilization.* New York: McGraw-Hill.

Marshall, Eliot. 2000. Rival genome sequencers celebrate a milestone together. *Science* 288 (June 30):2294–95.

Marshall, Larry G. 1984. Who killed cock robin? An investigation of the extinction controversy. In *Quaternary extinctions,* eds. P. Martin and R. Klein. Tucson: University of Arizona Press.

Marshall, Lorna. 1961. Sharing, talking and giving: Relief of social tensions among !Kung Bushmen. *Africa* 31:239–42.

Martin, M. Kay, and Barbara Voorhies. 1975. *Female of the species.* New York: Columbia University Press.

Martin, Paul S. 1973. The discovery of America. *Science* 179 (March 9):969–74.

Martin, Paul S., and H. E. Wright, eds. 1967. *Pleistocene extinctions: The search for a cause.* New Haven, CT: Yale University Press.

Martin, Robert D. 1975. Strategies of reproduction. *Natural History* (November): 48–57.

Martin, Robert D. 1990. *Primate origins and evolution: A phylogenetic reconstruction.* Princeton, NJ: Princeton University Press.

Martin, Robert D. 1992. Classification and evolutionary relationships. In *The Cambridge encyclopedia of human evolution.* eds. S. Jones, R. Martin, and D. Pilbeam. New York: Cambridge University Press.

Martin, Robert D., and Simon K. Bearder. 1979. Radio bush baby. *Natural History* (October): 77–81.

Martorell, Reynaldo. 1980. Interrelationships between diet, infectious disease and nutritional status. In *Social and biological predictors of nutritional status, physical growth and neurological development,* eds. L. Greene and F. Johnston. New York: Academic Press.

Martorell, Reynaldo, Juan Rivera, Haley Kaplowitz, and Ernesto Pollitt. 1991. Long-term consequences of growth retardation during early childhood. Paper presented at the Sixth International Congress of Auxology, September 15–19, Madrid.

Mascie-Taylor, C. G. Nicholas. 1990. The biology of social class. In *Biosocial aspects of social class,* ed. C. G. N. Mascie-Taylor, 117–42. Oxford: Oxford University Press.

Maslow, Abraham H. 1964. *Religions, values, and peak-experiences.* Columbus: Ohio State University Press.

Mason, Philip. 1962. *Prospero's magic.* London: Oxford University Press.

Masumura, Wilfred T. 1977. Law and violence: A cross-cultural study. *Journal of Anthropological Research* 33: 388–99.

Mathiassen, Therkel. 1928. *Material culture of Iglulik Eskimos.* Copenhagen: Glydendalske.

Matossian, Mary K. 1982. Ergot and the Salem witchcraft affair. *American Scientist* 70:355–57.

Matossian, Mary K. 1989. *Poisons of the past: Molds, epidemics, and history.* New Haven, CT: Yale University Press.

Maybury-Lewis, David. 1967. *Akwe-Shavante society.* Oxford: Clarendon Press.

Mayer, Philip, and Iona Mayer. 1970. Socialization by peers: The youth organization of the Red Xhosa. In *Socialization: The approach from social anthropology,* ed. Philip Mayer, 159–89. London: Tavistock.

Mayr, Ernst. 1982. *The growth of biological thought: Diversity, evolution, and inheritance.* Cambridge, MA: Belknap Press of Harvard University Press.

Mazess, Richard B. 1975. Human adaptation to high altitude. In *Physiological Anthropology,* ed. A. Damon. New York: Oxford University Press.

McCain, Garvin, and Erwin M. Segal. 1988. *The game of science.* 5th ed. Monterey, CA: Brooks/Cole.

McCarthy, Frederick D., and Margaret McArthur. 1960. The food quest and the time factor in Aboriginal economic life. In *Records of the Australian-American scientific expedition to Arnhem Land,* ed. C. P. Mountford, vol. 2: *Anthropology and Nutrition.* Melbourne: Melbourne University Press.

McClelland, David C. 1961 *The achieving society.* New York: Van Nostrand.

McCorriston, Joy, and Frank Hole. 1991. The ecology of seasonal stress and the origins of agriculture in the Near East. *American Anthropologist* 93:46–69.

McCracken, Robert D. 1971. Lactase deficiency: An example of dietary evolution. *Current Anthropology* 12: 479–500.

McDermott, LeRoy. 1996. Self-representation in female figurines. *Current Anthropology* 37:227–75.

McDonald, Kim A. 1998. New evidence challenges traditional model of how the New World was settled. *Chronicle of Higher Education* (March 13):A22.

McElreath, Richard, and Pontus Strimling. 2008. When natural selection favors imitation of parents. *Current Anthropology* 49:307–16.

McElroy, Ann, and Patricia Townsend. 2002. *Medical anthropology in ecological perspective.* 3rd ed. Boulder, CO: Westview.

McHenry, Henry M. 1982. The pattern of human evolution: Studies on bipedalism, mastication, and encephalization. *Annual Review of Anthropology* 11:151–73.

McHenry, Henry M. 1988. New estimates of body weight in early hominids and their significance to encephalization and megadontia in "robust" australopithecines. In *Evolutionary history of the "robust" australopithecines,* ed. F. E. Grine. New York: Aldine.

McHenry, Henry M. 2009. Robust australopithecines. Our family tree, and homoplasy. In MyAnthroLibrary, eds. C. R. Ember, M. Ember, and P. N. Peregrine. MyAnthroLibrary.com. Pearson.

McKee, Lauris. 1984. Sex differentials in survivorship and the customary treatment of infants and children. *Medical Anthropology* 8:91–108.

McKeown, Adam. 2005. Chinese diaspora. In *Encyclopedia of diasporas: Immigrant and refugee cultures around the world,* vol. 1, eds. M. Ember, C. R. Ember, and I. Skoggard, 65–76. New York: Kluwer Academic/Plenum.

McMullin, Ernan. 2001. Plantinga's defense of special creation. In *Intelligent design creationism and its critics,* ed. R. Pennock, 174. Boston: MIT Press.

McNeill, William H. 1967. *A world history.* New York: Oxford University Press.

McNeill, William H. 1976. *Plagues and peoples.* Garden City, NY: Doubleday/Anchor.

McNeill, William H. 1998. *Plagues and peoples.* New York: Anchor Books/Doubleday.

Mead, Margaret. 1931. *Growing up in New Guinea.* London: Routledge & Kegan Paul.

Mead, Margaret. 1950/1935. *Sex and temperament in three primitive societies.* New York: Mentor.

Mead, Margaret. 1961/1928. *Coming of age in Samoa.* 3rd ed. New York: Morrow.

Meek, C. K. 1940. *Land law and custom in the colonies.* London: Oxford University Press.

Meggitt, Mervyn J. 1964. Male-female relationships in the highlands of Australian New Guinea. *American Anthropologist* 66:204–24.

Meggitt, Mervyn J. 1977. *Blood is their argument: Warfare among the Mae Enga tribesmen of the New Guinea highlands.* Palo Alto, CA: Mayfield.

Meillassoux, Claude. 1968. *Urbanization of an African community.* Seattle: University of Washington Press.

Mellaart, James. 1961. Roots in the soil. In *The dawn of civilization,* ed. S. Piggott. London: Thomas & Hudson.

Mellaart, James. 1964. A Neolithic city in Turkey. *Scientific American* (April):94–104.

Mellars, Paul. 1994. The Upper Paleolithic revolution. In *The Oxford illustrated prehistory of Europe,* ed. B. Cunliffe, 42–78. Oxford: Oxford University Press.

Mellars, Paul. 1996. *The Neanderthal legacy.* Princeton, NJ: Princeton University Press, 405–19.

Mellars, Paul. 1998. The fate of the Neaderthals. *Nature* 395(October 8):539–40.

Mellor, John W., and Sarah Gavian. 1987. Famine: Causes, prevention, and relief. *Science* 235 (January 30):539–44.

Meltzer, David J. 1993. Pleistocene peopling of the Americas. *Evolutionary Anthropology* 1 (1):157–69.

Merbs, Charles F. 1992. A new world of infectious disease. *Yearbook of Physical Anthropology* 35:3–42.

Merrill, Elizabeth Bryant. 1987. Art styles as reflections of sociopolitical complexity. *Ethnology* 26:221–30.

Messer, Ellen. 1996. Hunger vulnerability from an anthropologist's food system perspective. In *Transforming societies, transforming anthropology,* ed. E. F. Moran. Ann Arbor: University of Michigan Press.

Middleton, John. 1971. The cult of the dead: Ancestors and ghosts. In *Reader in comparative religion,* 3rd ed., eds. W. A. Lessa and E. Z. Vogt. New York: Harper & Row.

Middleton, Russell. 1962. Brother-sister and father-daughter marriage in ancient Egypt. *American Sociological Review* 27:603–11.

Milanovic, Branko. 2005. *World's apart: Measuring international and global inequality.* Princeton: Princeton University Press.

Miller, Bruce G. 1992. Women and politics: Comparative evidence from the Northwest Coast. *Ethnology* 31:367–82.

Miller, Greg. 2004. Listen, baby. *Science* 306 (November 12): 1127.

Miller, Joan G. 1994. Cultural diversity in the morality of caring: Individually oriented versus duty-based interpersonal moral codes. *Cross-Cultural Research* 28:3–39.

Millon, René. 1967. Teotihuacán. *Scientific American* (June):38–48.

Millon, René. 1976. Social relations in ancient Teotihuacán. In *The valley of Mexico,* ed. E. Wolf. Albuquerque: University of New Mexico Press.

Milton, Katharine. 1981. Distribution patterns of tropical plant foods as an evolutionary stimulus to primate mental development. *American Anthropologist* 83: 534–48.

Milton, Katharine. 1988. Foraging behaviour and the evolution of primate intelligence. In *Machiavellian intelligence:*

Social expertise and the evolution of intellect in monkeys, apes, and humans, eds. Richard W. Bryne and Andrew Whiten, 285–305. Oxford: Clarendon Press.

Milton, Katharine. 2009. The evolution of a physical anthropologist. In MyAnthroLibrary, eds. C. R. Ember, M. Ember, and P. N. Peregrine. MyAnthroLibrary.com. Pearson.

Miner, Horace. 1956. Body rituals among the Nacirema. *American Anthropologist* 58:504–05.

Minturn, Leigh. 1993. *Sita's daughters: Coming out of Purdah: The Rajput women of Khalapur revisited.* New York: Oxford University Press.

Minturn, Leigh, and Jerry Stashak. 1982. Infanticide as a terminal abortion procedure. *Behavior Science Research* 17:70–85.

Mintz, Sidney W. 1956. Canamelar: The subculture of a rural sugar plantation proletariat. In *The people of Puerto Rico,* J. H. Steward et al. Urbana: University of Illinois Press.

Minugh-Purvis, Nancy. 2009. Neandertal growth: Examining developmental adaptations in earlier *Homo sapiens.* In MyAnthroLibrary, eds. C. R. Ember, M. Ember, and P. N. Peregrine. MyAnthroLibrary.com. Pearson.

Miracle, Andrew W. 2009. A shaman to organizations. In MyAnthroLibrary, eds. C. R. Ember, M. Ember, and P. N. Peregrine. MyAnthroLibrary.com. Pearson.

Mitchell, Donald. 2009. Nimpkish: Complex foragers on the northwest coast of North America. In MyAnthroLibrary, eds. C. R. Ember, M. Ember, and P. N. Peregrine. MyAnthroLibrary.com. Pearson.

Mittermeier, Russell A., and Eleanor J. Sterling. 1992. Conservation of primates. In *The Cambridge encyclopedia of human evolution.* eds. S. Jones, R. Martin, and D. Pilbeam. New York: Cambridge University Press.

Moerman, Daniel E. 1997. Physiology and symbols: The anthropological implications of the placebo effect. In *The anthropology of medicine,* 3rd ed., eds. L. Romanucci-Ross, D. E. Moerman, and L. R. Tancredi, 240–53. Westport, CT: Bergin & Garvey.

Molnar, Stephen. 1998. *Human variation: Races, types, and ethnic groups.* 4th ed. Upper Saddle River, NJ: Prentice Hall.

Monot, Marc, et al. 2005. On the origin of leprosy. *Science* 308 (May 13):1040–42.

Monsutti, Alessandro. 2004. Cooperation, remittances, and kinship among the Hazaras. *Iranian Studies* 37:219–40.

Mooney, Kathleen A. 1978. The effects of rank and wealth on exchange among the coast Salish. *Ethnology* 17:391–406.

Moore, Carmella Caracci. 1988. An optimal scaling of Murdock's theories of illness data—An approach to the problem of interdependence. *Behavior Science Research* 22:161–79.

Moore, Carmella C. 1997. Is love always love? *Anthropology Newsletter* (November):8–9.

Moore, Carmella C., A. Kimball Romney, Ti-Lien Hsia, Craig D. Rusch. 1999. The universality of the semantic structure of emotion terms: Methods for the study of inter- and intracultural variability. *American Anthropologist* 101:529–46.

Moore, John H., and Janis E. Campbell. 2002. Confirming unilocal residence in Native North America. *Ethnology* 41:175–88.

Moore, Omar Khayyam. 1957. Divination: A new perspective. *American Anthropologist* 59:69–74.

Moran, Emilio F. 1993. *Through Amazon eyes: The human ecology of Amazonian populations.* Iowa City: University of Iowa Press.

Moran, Emilio F., ed. 1996. *Transforming societies, transforming anthropology*. Ann Arbor: University of Michigan Press.

Moran, Emilio F. 2000. *Human adaptability: An introduction to ecological anthropology*. 2nd ed. Boulder, CO: Westview.

Morell, Virginia. 1995. The Earliest Art Becomes Older—And More Common." *Science*, 267 (March 31): 1908–09.

Morgan, Lewis H. 1964/1877. *Ancient society*. Cambridge, MA: Harvard University Press.

Morris, John. 1938. *Living with Lepchas: A book about the Sikkim Himalayas*. London: Heinemann.

Morrison, Kathleen D., and Laura L. Junker. 2002. *Forager-traders in South and Southeast Asia: Long-term histories*. Cambridge: Cambridge University Press.

Morwood, M. J., R. Soejono, R. Roberts, T. Sutikna, C. Turney, K. Westaway, W. Rink, J. Zhao, G. van den Bergh, R. Due, D. Hobbs, M. Moore, M. Bird, and L. Fiffeld. 2004. Archaeology and age of a new hominin from Flores in Eastern Indonesia. *Nature* 431 (October 28):1087–91.

Moser, Stephanie. 1998. *Ancestral images: The iconography of human origins*. Ithaca, NY: Cornell University Press.

Motulsky, Arno. 1971. Metabolic polymorphisms and the role of infectious diseases in human evolution. In *Human populations, genetic variation, and evolution*, ed. L. N. Morris. San Francisco: Chandler.

Moyá-solá, Salvador, et al. 2004. *Pierolapithecus catalaunicus*. A new middle Miocene great ape from Spain. *Science* 306 (November 19):1339–44.

Mukerjee, Madhusree. 1996. Field notes: Interview with a parrot. *Scientific American* (April):28.

Mukhopadhyay, Carol C., and Patricia J. Higgins. 1988. Anthropological studies of women's status revisited: 1977–1987. *Annual Review of Anthropology* 17:461–95.

Muller, Edward N. 1997. Economic determinants of democracy. In *Inequality, democracy, and economic development*, ed. M. Midlarsky, 133–55. Cambridge: Cambridge University Press.

Müller-Haye, B. 1984. Guinea pig or cuy. In *Evolution of domesticated animals*, ed. I. Mason. New York: Longman.

Munroe, Robert L., Robert Hulefeld, James M. Rodgers, Damon L. Tomeo, Steven K. Yamazaki. 2000. Aggression among children in four cultures. *Cross-Cultural Research* 34:3–25.

Munroe, Robert L., and Ruth H. Munroe. 1969. A cross-cultural study of sex, gender, and social structure. *Ethnology* 8:206–11.

Munroe, Robert L., Ruth H. Munroe, and John W. M. Whiting. 1981. Male sex-role resolutions. In *Handbook of cross-cultural human development*, eds. R. H. Munroe, R. L. Munroe, and B. B. Whiting. New York: Garland.

Munroe, Robert L., Ruth H. Munroe, and Stephen Winters. 1996. Cross-cultural correlates of the consonant-vowel (cv) syllable. *Cross-Cultural Research* 30:60–83.

Munroe, Ruth H., and Robert L. Munroe. 1980. Infant experience and childhood affect among the Logoli: A longitudinal study. *Ethos* 8:295–315.

Munroe, Ruth H., Robert L. Munroe, and Harold S. Shimmin. 1984. Children's work in four cultures: Determinants and consequences. *American Anthropologist* 86:369–79.

Murdock, George P. 1949. *Social structure*. New York: Macmillan.

Murdock, George P. 1957. World ethnographic sample. *American Anthropologist* 59:664–87.

Murdock, George P. 1967. Ethnographic atlas: A summary. *Ethnology* 6:109–236.

Murdock, George P. 1980. *Theories of illness: A world survey*. Pittsburgh: University of Pittsburgh Press.

Murdock, George P., and Caterina Provost. 1973. Factors in the division of labor by sex: A cross-cultural analysis. *Ethnology* 12:203–25.

Murdock, George P., and Douglas R. White. 1969. Standard cross-cultural sample. *Ethnology* 8:329–69.

Murphy, Jane. 1981. Abnormal behavior in traditional societies: Labels, explanations, and social reactions. In *Handbook of cross-cultural human development*, eds. R. H. Munroe, R. L. Munroe, and B. B. Whiting. New York: Garland.

Murphy, Robert F. 1960. *Headhunter's heritage: Social and economic change among the Mundurucú*. Berkeley: University of California Press.

Murphy, Robert F., and Julian H. Steward. 1956. Tappers and trappers: Parallel process in acculturation. *Economic Development and Cultural Change* 4 (July):335–55.

Murray, Gerald F. 1997. The domestication of wood in Haiti: A case study in applied evolution. In *Applying cultural anthropology: An introductory reader*, eds. A. Podolefsky and P. J. Brown. Mountain View CA: Mayfield.

Murray, G. F., and M. E. Bannister. 2004. Peasants, agroforesters, and anthropologists: A 20-year venture in income-generating trees and hedgerows in Haiti. *Agroforestry Systems* 61:383–97.

Musgrave, Jonathan H., R. A. H. Neave, and A. J. N. W. Prag. 1984. The skull from Tomb II at Vergina: King Philip II of Macedon. *Journal of Hellenistic Studies* 104:60–78.

Myers, Fred R. 1988. Critical trends in the study of hunter-gatherers. *Annual Review of Anthropology* 17:261–82.

Nadel, S. F. 1935. Nupe state and community. *Africa* 8:257–303.

Nadel, S. F. 1942. *A black Byzantium: The kingdom of Nupe in Nigeria*. London: Oxford University Press.

Nag, Moni, Benjamin N. F. White, and R. Creighton Peet. 1978. An anthropological approach to the study of the economic value of children in Java and Nepal. *Current Anthropology* 19:293–301.

Nagata, Judith. 2001. Beyond theology: Toward an anthropology of "fundamentalism." *American Anthropologist* 103:481–98.

Nagel, Ernest. 1961. *The structure of science: Problems in the logic of scientific explanation*. New York: Harcourt, Brace & World.

Napier, J. R. 1970. Paleoecology and catarrhine evolution. In *Old World monkeys: Evolution, systematics, and behavior*. eds. J. R. Napier and P. H. Napier. New York: Academic Press.

Napier, J. R., and P. H. Napier. 1967. *A handbook of living primates*. New York: Academic Press.

Naroll, Raoul. 1961. Two solutions for Galton's problem. In *Readings in cross-cultural methodology*, ed. Frank Moore, 221–45. New Haven, CT: HRAF Press.

Naroll, Raoul. 1967. Imperial cycles and world order. *Peace Research Society: Papers* 7:83–101.

Naroll, Raoul. 1983. *The moral order: An introduction to the human situation*. Beverly Hills, CA: Sage.

Nash, Manning. 1989. *The cauldron of ethnicity in the modern world*. Chicago: University of Chicago Press.

National Coalition for the Homeless. 2008 (June). How many people experience homelessness? NCH Fact Sheet #2.

http://www.nationalhomeless.org/factsheets/How_Many. html (accessed September 3, 2009).

National Science Foundation, Division of Science Resources Statistics. 2008. *Science and engineering doctorate awards: 2006.* Detailed Statistical Tables NSF 09-311. Arlington, VA. Available at http://www.nsf.gov/statistics/nsf09311/ (accessed August 14, 2009).

Neel, James V., Willard R. Centerwall, Napoleon A. Chagnon, and Helen L. Casey. 1970. Notes on the effect of measles and measles vaccine in a virgin-soil population of South American Indians. *American Journal of Epidemiology* 91:418–29.

Nelson, Nici. 1995/1964. The Kiambu group: A successful women's ROSCA in Mathare Valley, Nairobi (1971 to 1990). In *Money-go-rounds: The importance of rotating savings and credit associations for women,* eds. S. Ardener and S. Burman, 49–69. Oxford: Berg.

Nepstead, Daniel C., Claudia M. Stickler, Britaldo Soares-Filho, and Frank Merry. 2008. Interactions among Amazon land use, forests, and climate: Prospects for a near-term forest tipping point. *Philosophical Transactions of the Royal Society* B, 363:1737–46.

Nerlove, Sara B. 1974. Women's workload and infant feeding practices: A relationship with demographic implications. *Ethnology* 13:207–14.

Neumann, Katharina. 2003. New Guinea: A cradle of agriculture. *Science* 301 (July 11):180–81.

Nevins, Allan. 1927. *The American states during and after the revolution.* New York: Macmillan.

Newbury, Catherine. 1988. *The cohesion of oppression: Clientship and ethnicity in Rwanda, 1860–1960.* New York: Columbia University.

Newman, Katherine S. 1983. *Law and economic organization: A Comparative study of preindustrial societies.* Cambridge, MA: Cambridge University Press.

Newman, K. S. 1988. *Falling from grace: The experience of downward mobility in the American middle class.* New York: The Free Press.

Newman, K. S. 1993. *Declining fortunes: The withering of the American dream.* New York: Basic Books.

Newsweek. 1973. The first dentist. *Newsweek,* March 5, 73.

Nicholls, David, ed. 1998. *The Cambridge history of American music.* Cambridge. Cambridge University Press.

Nicolson, Nancy A. 1987. Infants, mothers, and other females. In *Primate Societies,* eds. B. Smuts et al. Chicago: University of Chicago Press.

Niehoff, Arthur H. 1966. *A casebook of social change.* Chicago: Aldine.

Nimkoff, M. F., and Russell Middleton. 1960. Types of family and types of economy. *American Journal of Sociology* 66:215–25.

Nisbett, Richard E. 2009. Education is all in your mind. *New York Times.* Sunday Opinion, February 8, p. 12.

Nishida, Toshisada. 1992. Introduction to the conservation symposium. In Naosuke Itoigawa, Yukimaru Sugiyama, Gene P. Sackett, and Roger K. R. Thompson, *Topics in primatology,* vol. 2. Tokyo: University of Tokyo Press.

Nissen, Henry W. 1958. Axes of behavioral comparison. In *Behavior and evolution,* eds. A. Roe and G. G. Simpson. New Haven, CT: Yale University Press.

Nolan, Riall W. 2003. Anthropology in practice: Building a career outside the academy. Boulder: Lynne Rienner Publishers.

Noll, Richard. 1987. The presence of spirits in magic and madness. In *Shamanism,* comp. S. Nicholson, 47–61. Wheaton, IL: Theosophical Publishing House.

Norenzayan, Ara, and Azim F. Shariff. 2008. The origin and evolution of religious prosociality. *Science* 322 (October 3): 58–62.

Normile, Dennis. 1998. Habitat seen playing larger role in shaping behavior. *Science* 279 (March 6): 1454–55.

Noss, Andrew J., and Barry S. Hewlett. 2001. The contexts of female hunting in central Africa. *American Anthropologist* 103:1024–40.

Nussbaum, Martha C. 1995. Introduction. In M. C. Nussbaum and J. Glover, *Women, culture, and development: A study of human capabilities.* Oxford: Clarendon Press.

Oakley, Kenneth. 1964. On man's use of fire, with comments on tool-making and hunting. In *Social life of early man,* ed. S. L. Washburn. Chicago: Aldine.

Oboler, Regina Smith. 1980. Is the female husband a man? Woman/woman marriage among the Nandi of Kenya. *Ethnology* 19:69–88.

Oboler, Regina Smith. 2009. Nandi: From cattle-keepers to cash-crop farmers. In MyAnthroLibrary, eds. C. R. Ember, M. Ember, and P. N. Peregrine. MyAnthroLibrary.com. Pearson.

O'Brian, Robin. 1999. Who weaves and why? Weaving, loom complexity, and trade. *Cross-Cultural Research* 33:30–42.

O'Brien, Denise. 1977. Female husbands in southern Bantu societies. In *Sexual stratification,* ed. A. Schlegel. New York: Columbia University Press.

Oerlemans, J. 2005. Extracting a climate signal from 169 glacial records. *Science* 38 (April 28):675–77.

Ogburn, William F. 1922. *Social change.* New York: Huebsch.

Okamura, Jonathan Y. 1983. Filipino hometown associations in Hawaii. *Ethnology* 22:341–53.

Oliver, Douglas L. 1955. *A Solomon Island society.* Cambridge, MA: Harvard University Press.

Oliver, Douglas L. 1974. *Ancient Tahitian society,* vol. 1: *Ethnography.* Honolulu: University of Hawaii Press.

Olsen, Steve. 2002. Seeking the signs of selection. *Science* 298 (November 15): 1324–25.

Olszewski, Deborah I. 1991. Social complexity in the Natufian? Assessing the relationship of ideas and data. In *Perspectives on the past,* ed. G. Clark. Philadelphia: University of Pennsylvania Press.

Orlove, Benjamin, and Stephen Brush. 1996. Anthropology and the conservation of biodiversity. *Annual Review of Anthropology* 25:329–52.

Ortiz de Montellano, B. R., and C. H. Browner. 1985. Chemical bases for medicinal plant use in Oaxaca, Mexico. *Journal of Ethnopharmacology* 13:57–88.

Ortner, Sherry B. 1984. Theory in anthropology since the sixties. *Comparative Studies in Society and History* 26:126–66.

Osti, Roberto. 1994. The eloquent bones of Abu Hureyra. *Scientific American* (August):1.

Otterbein, Keith. 1968. Internal war: A cross-cultural study. *American Anthropologist* 70:277–89.

Otterbein, Keith. 1970. *The evolution of war.* New Haven, CT: HRAF Press.

Otterbein, Keith. 1986. *The ultimate coercive sanction: A cross-cultural study of capital punishment.* New Haven, CT: HRAF Press.

Otterbein, Keith, and Charlotte Swanson Otterbein. 1965. An eye for an eye, a tooth for a tooth: A cross-cultural study of feuding. *American Anthropologist* 67:1470–82.

445

Ovchinnikov, Igor V., et al. 2000. Molecular analysis of Neanderthal DNA from the Northern Caucasus. *Nature* 404 (March 30):490–94.

Oxby, Clare. 1983. Farmer groups in rural areas of the third world. *Community Development Journal* 18:50–59.

Paige, Jeffery M. 1975. *Agrarian revolution: Social movements and export agriculture in the underdeveloped world.* New York: Free Press.

Paine, Robert. 1994. *Herds of the tundra.* Washington, DC: Smithsonian Institution Press.

Paley, William. 1810. *Natural theology.* Boston: Joshua Belcher.

Palsson, Gisli. 1988. Hunters and gatherers of the sea. In *Hunters and gatherers. 1. History, evolution and social change,* eds. T. Ingold, D. Riches, and J. Woodburn. New York: St. Martin's Press.

Parfit, Michael. 2000. Who were the first Americans? *National Geographic* (December): 41–67.

Parker, Seymour. 1976. The precultural basis of the incest taboo: Toward a biosocial theory. *American Anthropologist* 78:285–305.

Parker, Seymour. 1984. Cultural rules, rituals, and behavior regulation. *American Anthropologist* 86:584–600.

Parker, Hilda, and Seymour Parker. 1986. Father-daughter sexual abuse: An emerging perspective. *American Journal of Orthopsychiatry* 56:531–49.

Parker, Sue Taylor. 1990. Why big brains are so rare. In *"Language" and intelligence in monkeys and apes,* eds. S. Parker and K. Gibson. New York: Cambridge University Press.

Pasternak, Burton. 1976. *Introduction to kinship and social organization.* Upper Saddle River, NJ: Prentice Hall.

Pasternak, Burton. 2009. Han: Pastoralists and farmers on a Chinese frontier. In MyAnthroLibrary, eds. C. R. Ember, M. Ember, and P. N. Peregrine. MyAnthroLibrary.com. Pearson.

Pasternak, Burton, Carol R. Ember, and Melvin Ember. 1976. On the conditions favoring extended family households. *Journal of Anthropological Research* 32:109–23.

Patterson, Leland. 1983. Criteria for determining the attributes of man-made lithics. *Journal of Field Archaeology* 10:297–307.

Patterson, Orlando. 1982. *Slavery and social death: A comparative study.* Cambridge, MA: Harvard University Press.

Patterson, Orlando. 2000. Review of *One drop of blood: The American misadventure of race,* by Scott L. Malcomson. *New York Times Book Review,* October 22, pp. 15–16.

Patterson, Thomas C. 1971. Central Peru: Its population and economy. *Archaeology* 24:316–21.

Patterson, Thomas C. 1981. *The evolution of ancient societies: A world archaeology.* Upper Saddle River, NJ: Prentice Hall.

Peacock, James L. 1986. *The anthropological lens: Harsh light, soft focus.* Cambridge: Cambridge University Press.

Peacock, Nadine, and Robert Bailey. 2009. Efe: Investigating food and fertility in the Ituri rain forest." In MyAnthroLibrary, eds. C. R. Ember, M. Ember, and P. N. Peregrine. MyAnthroLibrary.com. Pearson.

Peak, Lois. 1991. *Learning to go to school in Japan: The transition from home to preschool.* Berkeley: University of California Press.

Pearsall, Deborah. 1992. The origins of plant cultivation in South America. In *The origins of agriculture,* eds. C.

Cowan and P. Watson. Washington, DC: Smithsonian Institution Press.

Pelto, Gretel H., Alan H. Goodman, and Darna L. Dufour. 2000. The biocultural perspective in nutritional anthropology. In *Nutritional anthropology: Biocultural perspectives on food and nutrition,* eds. Alan H. Goodman, Darna L. Dufour, and Gretel H. Pelto, 1–9. Mountain View, CA: Mayfield Publishing.

Pelto, Pertti J., and Ludger Müller-Wille. 1987. Snowmobiles: Technological revolution in the Arctic. In *Technology and social change,* 2nd ed., eds. H. R. Bernard and P. J. Pelto. Prospect Heights, IL: Waveland Press.

Pelto, Pertti J., and Gretel H. Pelto. 1975. Intra-cultural diversity: Some theoretical issues. *American Ethnologist* 2:1–18.

Pennisi, Elizabeth. 2000. Finally, the book of life and instructions for navigating it. *Science* 288 (June 30):2304–07.

Pennisi, Elizabeth. 2001a. Malaria's beginnings: On the heels of hoes? *Science* 293 (July 20):416–17.

Pennisi, Elizabeth. 2001b. Genetic change wards off malaria. *Science* 294 (November 16):1,439.

Pennisi, Elizabeth. 2007. Genomicists tackle the primate tree. *Science* 316 (April 13):218–21.

Pennisi, Elizabeth. 2009. Tales of a prehistoric human genome. *Science* 323 (February 13):866–71.

Pepperberg, Irene Maxine. 1999. *The Alex studies: Cognitive and communicative abilities of grey parrots.* Cambridge, MA: Harvard University Press.

Peregrine, Peter N. 1996. The birth of the gods revisited: A partial replication of Guy Swanson's (1960) cross-cultural study of religion. *Cross-Cultural Research* 30:84–112.

Peregrine, Peter N. 2001a. Southern and Eastern Africa Later Stone Age. In *Encyclopedia of prehistory,* vol. 1, *Africa,* eds. P. N. Peregrine and M. Ember, 272–73. New York: Kluwer Academic/Plenum.

Peregrine, Peter N. 2001b. Cross-cultural approaches in archaeology. *Annual Review of Anthropology* 30:1–18.

Peregrine, Peter N. 2007a. Racial hierarchy: I. Overview. In *Encyclopedia of race and racism,* ed. John H. Moore, 461–62. New York, Macmillian Reference.

Peregrine, Peter N. 2007b. Cultural correlates of ceramic styles. *Cross-Cultural Research* 41:223–35.

Peregrine, Peter N., and Peter Bellwood. 2001. Southeast Asia Upper Paleolithic. In *Encyclopedia of prehistory,* vol. 3: *East Asia and Oceania,* eds. P. N. Peregrine and M. Ember, 307–09. New York: Kluwer Academic/Plenum.

Peregrine, Peter N., Carol R. Ember, and Melvin Ember. 2000. Teaching critical evaluation of Rushton. *Anthropology Newsletter* 41 (February): 29–30.

Peregrine, Peter N., Carol R. Ember, and Melvin Ember. 2003. Cross-cultural evaluation of predicted associations between race and behavior. *Evolution and Human Behavior* 24: 357–64.

Peregrine, Peter N., Melvin Ember, and Carol R. Ember. 2004. Predicting the future state of the world using archaeological data: An exercise in archaeomancy. *Cross-Cultural Research* 38:133–46.

Perry, Donna L. 2005. Wolof women, economic liberalization, and the crisis of masculinity in rural Senegal. *Ethnology* 44:207–26.

Petersen, Erik B. 1973. A survey of the Late Paleolithic and the Mesolithic of Denmark. In *The Mesolithic in Europe,* ed. S. K. Kozlowski. Warsaw: Warsaw University Press.

Petersen, L. R., G. R. Lee, and G. J. Ellis. 1982. Social structure, socialization values, and disciplinary techniques: A cross-cultural analysis. *Journal of Marriage and the Family* 44:131–42.

Pfaff, C. 1979. Constraints on language mixing. *Language* 55:291–318, as cited in *An introduction to sociolinguistics*, 2nd ed., ed. R. Wardhaugh. Oxford: Blackwell.

Pfeiffer, John E. 1978. *The emergence of man*. 3rd ed. New York: Harper & Row.

Phillips, Kevin. 1990. *The politics of rich and poor: Wealth and the American electorate in the Reagan aftermath*. New York: Random House.

Phillipson, D. W. 1976. Archaeology and Bantu linguistics. *World Archaeology* 8:65–82.

Phillipson, David W. 1993. *African archaeology*. 2nd ed. New York: Cambridge University Press.

Piaget, Jean. 1970. Piaget's theory. In *Carmichael's manual of child psychology*, vol. 1, 3rd ed., ed. P. Mussen. New York: Wiley.

Picchi, Debra. 1991. The impact of an industrial agricultural project on the Bakairí Indians of central Brazil. *Human Organization* 50:26–38.

Picchi, Debra. 2009. Bakairí: The death of an Indian. In MyAnthroLibrary, eds. C. R. Ember, M. Ember, and P. N. Peregrine. MyAnthroLibrary.com. Pearson.

Pickford, Martin, Brigette Senut, Dominique Gommercy, and Jacques Treil. 2002. Bipedalism in *Orrorin tugenensis* revealed by its femora. *Comptes Rendu de l'Académie des Science des Paris*, Palevol 1, 1–13.

Pilbeam, David. 1972. *The ascent of man*. New York: Macmillan.

Pilbeam, David, and Stephen Jay Gould. 1974. Size and Scaling in Human Evolution. *Science* 186 (December 6): 892–900.

Piperno, Dolores, and Karen Stothert. 2003. Phytolith evidence for early holocene cucurbita domestication in southwest Ecuador. *Science* 299 (February, 14):1054–57.

Plattner, Stuart, ed. 1985. *Markets and marketing*. Monographs in Economic Anthropology, No. 4. Lanham, MD: University Press of America.

Plattner, Stuart. 1989. Marxism. In *Economic anthropology*, ed. S. Plattner. Stanford, CA: Stanford University Press.

Poggie, John J., Jr., and Richard B. Pollnac. 1988. Danger and rituals of avoidance among New England fishermen. *MAST: Maritime Anthropological Studies* 1:66–78.

Poggie, John J., Jr., Richard B. Pollnac, and Carl Gersuny. 1976. Risk as a basis for taboos among fishermen in southern New England. *Journal for the Scientific Study of Religion* 15:257–62.

Polanyi, Karl. 1957. The economy as instituted process. In *Trade and market in the early empires*, eds. K. Polanyi, C. M. Arensberg, and H. W. Pearson. New York: Free Press.

Polanyi, Karl, Conrad M. Arensberg, and Harry W. Pearson, eds. 1957. *Trade and market in the early empires*. New York: Free Press.

Polednak, Anthony P. 1974. Connective tissue responses in negroes in relation to disease. *American Journal of Physical Anthropology* 41:49–57.

Pollier, Nicole. 2000. Commoditization, cash, and kinship in postcolonial Papua New Guinea. In *Commodities and globalization: Anthropological perspectives*, eds. Angelique Haugerud, M. Priscilla Stone, and Peter D. Little, 197–217. Lanham, MD: Rowman & Littlefield.

Pope, Geoffrey G. 1989. Bamboo and human evolution. *Natural History* (October):49–57.

Popenoe, Rebecca. 2004. *Feeding desire: Fatness, beauty, and sexuality among a Saharan people*. London: Routledge.

Pospisil, Leopold. 1963. *The Kapauku Papuans of West New Guinea*. New York: Holt, Rinehart & Winston.

Post, Peter W., Farrington Daniels, Jr., and Robert T. Binford, Jr. 1975. Cold injury and the evolution of "white" skin. *Human Biology* 47:65–80.

Potts, Richard. 1984. Home bases and early hominids. *American Scientist* 72:338–47.

Potts, Richard. 1988. *Early hominid activities at Olduvai*. New York: Aldine.

Powell, Joseph. 2005. *The first Americans*. New York: Cambridge University Press.

Powers, William K., and Marla N. Powers. 2009. Lakota: A study in cultural continuity. In MyAnthroLibrary, eds. C. R. Ember, M. Ember, and P. N. Peregrine. MyAnthroLibrary.com. Pearson.

Poyatos, Fernando. 2002. *Nonverbal communication across disciplines*, vol. 1. Philadelphia: John Benjamins Publishing Company.

Prag, A. J. N. W. 1990. Reconstructing Phillip II of Macedon: The "nice" version. *American Journal of Archaeology* 94:237–47.

Prag, John, and Richard Neave. 1997. *Making faces: Using forensic and archaeological evidence*. College Station: Texas A&M University Press.

Preuschoft, Holger, David J. Chivers, Warren Y. Brockelman, and Norman Creel, eds. 1984. *The lesser apes: Evolutionary and behavioural biology*. Edinburgh: Edinburgh University Press.

Price, Sally. 1989. *Primitive art in civilized places*. Chicago: University of Chicago Press.

Price-Williams, Douglass. 1961. A study concerning concepts of conservation of quantities among primitive children. *Acta Psychologica* 18:297–305.

Pringle, Heather. 1998. The slow birth of agriculture. *Science* 282 (November 20):1446–50.

Pryor, Frederic L. 1977. *The origins of the economy: A comparative study of distribution in primitive and peasant economies*. New York: Academic Press.

Pryor, Frederic L. 2005. *Economic systems of foraging, agricultural, and industrial societies*. Cambridge: Cambridge University Press.

Public Law 101-601 (25 U.S.C. 3001–3013).

Quandt, Sara A. 1996. Nutrition in anthropology. In *Handbook of medical anthropology*, rev. ed., eds. C. F. Sargent and T. M. Johnson, 272–89. Westport, CT: Greenwood Press.

Quinn, Naomi. 1977. Anthropological studies on women's status. *Annual Review of Anthropology* 6:181–225.

Radcliffe-Brown, A. R. 1922. *The Andaman Islanders: A study in social anthropology*. Cambridge: Cambridge University Press.

Radcliffe-Brown, A. R. 1952. *Structure and function in primitive society*. London: Cohen & West.

Radinsky, Leonard. 1967. The oldest primate endocast. *American Journal of Physical Anthropology* 27:358–88.

Rambo, Lewis R. 2003. Anthropology and the study of conversion. In *The anthropology of religious conversion*, eds. Andrew Buckser and Stephen D. Glazier, 211–22. Lanham, MD: Roman & Littlefield.

Rappaport, Roy A. 1967. Ritual regulation of environmental relations among a New Guinea people. *Ethnology* 6: 17–30.

Rasmussen, D. Tab. 1990. Primate origins: Lessons from a neotropical marsupial. *American Journal of Primatology* 22:263–77.

Rathje, William L. 1971. The origin and development of lowland classic Maya civilization. *American Antiquity* 36:275–85.

Ravesloot, John. 1997. Changing Native American perceptions of archaeology and archaeologists. In *Native Americans and archaeologists*, eds. N. Swidler et al. Walnut Creek, CA: AltaMira Press.

Ray, Verne F. 1954. *The Sanpoil and Nespelem: Salishan peoples of northeastern Washington.* New Haven, CT: Human Relations Area Files.

Raybeck, Douglas. 1998. Toward more holistic explanations: Cross-cultural research and cross-level analysis. *Cross-Cultural Research* 32:123–42.

Raybeck, Douglas, J. Shoobe, and J. Grauberger. 1989. Women, stress and participation in possession cults: A reexamination of the calcium deficiency hypothesis. *Medical Anthropology Quarterly* 3:139–61.

Redman, Charles L. 1978. *The rise of civilization: From early farmers to urban society in the ancient Near East.* San Francisco: W. H. Freeman.

Redman, Charles. 1999. *Human impact on ancient environments.* Tucson: University of Arizona Press.

Reed, David, V. Smith, S. Hammond, A. Rogers, and D. Clayton. 2004. Genetic analysis of lice supports direct contact between modern and archaic humans. *PLoS Biology* 2 (November):1972–83.

Reff, Daniel T. 2005. *Plagues, priests, and demons: Sacred narratives and the rise of Christianity in the Old World and the New.* Cambridge: Cambridge University Press.

Reisner, Marc. 1993. *Cadillac desert: The American West and its disappearing water.* Rev. ed. New York: Penguin.

Relethford, John. 1990. *The human species: An introduction to biological anthropology.* Mountain View, CA: Mayfield.

Renfrew, Colin. 1969. Trade and culture process in European history. *Current Anthropology* 10:156–69.

Renfrew, Colin. 1987. *Archaeology and language: The puzzle of Indo-European origins.* London: Jonathan Cape.

Rennie, John. 2002. 15 answers to creationist nonsense. *Scientific American* (July): 78–85.

Revkin, Andrew C. 2005. Tracking the imperiled bluefin from ocean to sushi platter. *The New York Times*, May 3, pp. F1, F4.

Rhine, Stanley. 1993. Skeletal criteria for racial attribution. *National Association for Applied Anthropology Bulletin* 13:54–67.

Rice, Patricia C. 1981. Prehistoric Venuses: Symbols of motherhood or womanhood? *Journal of Anthropological Research* 37:402–14.

Rice, Patricia C., and Ann L. Paterson. 1986. Validating the cave art—Archeofaunal relationship in Cantabrian Spain. *American Anthropologist* 88:658–67.

Rice, Patricia C., and Ann L. Paterson. 1985. Cave art and bones: Exploring the interrelationships. *American Anthropologist* 87:94–100.

Richard, Alison F. 1985. *Primates in nature.* New York: W. H. Freeman.

Richard, Alison F. 1987. Malagasy prosimians: Female dominance. In *Primate societies*, eds. B. Smuts et al. Chicago: University of Chicago Press.

Richardson, Curtis J., Peter Reiss, Najah A. Hussain, Azzam J. Alwash, and Douglas J. Pool. 2005. The restoration potential of the Mesopotamian marshes of Iraq. *Science* 307(February 25):1307–11.

Richerson, Peter J., and Robert Boyd. 2005. *Not by genes alone: How culture transformed human evolution.* Chicago: University of Chicago Press.

Richmond, Brian G., and William L. Jungers. *Orrorin tugenensis* femoral morphology and the evolution of human bipedalism. *Science* 319 (21, March 2008):1662–65.

Riesenfeld, Alphonse. 1973. The effect of extreme temperatures and starvation on the body proportions of the rat. *American Journal of Physical Anthropology* 39:427–59.

Rightmire, G. Philip. 1984. *Homo sapiens* in sub-Saharan Africa. In *The origins of modern humans*, eds. F. H. Smith and F. Spencer. New York: Alan R. Liss.

Rightmire, G. Philip. 1990. *The evolution of* Homo erectus: *Comparative anatomical studies of an extinct human species.* Cambridge: Cambridge University Press.

Rightmire, G. Philip. 1997. Human evolution in the Middle Pleistocene: The role of *Homo heidelbergensis. Evolutionary Anthropology* 6:218–27.

Rightmire, G. Philip. 2000. *Homo erectus.* In *Encyclopedia of human evolution and prehistory*, eds. I. Tattersall, E. Delson, and J. van Couvering. New York: Garland.

Rijksen, H. D. 1978. *A field study on Sumatran Orang Utans* (Pongo Pygmaeus Abelii Lesson 1827): *Ecology, Behaviour and Conservation.* Wageningen, The Netherlands: H. Veenman and Zonen.

Ritter, Madeline Lattman. 1980. The conditions favoring age-set organization. *Journal of Anthropological Research* 36:87–104.

Rivers, W. H. R. 1967/1906. *The Todas.* Oosterhout, N.B., The Netherlands: Anthropological Publications.

Roberts, D. F. 1953. Body weight, race, and climate. *American Journal of Physical Anthropology*, 533–58.

Roberts, D. F. 1978. *Climate and human variability.* 2nd ed. Menlo Park, CA: Cummings.

Roberts, John M. 1967. Oaths, autonomic ordeals, and power. In *Cross-cultural approaches*, ed. C. S. Ford. New Haven, CT: HRAF Press.

Roberts, John M., and Brian Sutton-Smith. 1962. Child training and game involvement. *Ethnology* 1:166–85.

Roberts, John M., Malcolm J. Arth, and Robert R. Bush. 1959. Games in culture. *American Anthropologist* 61:597–605.

Robins, Ashley H. 1991. *Biological perspectives on human pigmentation.* New York: Cambridge University Press.

Robinson, John G., and Charles H. Janson. 1987. Capuchins, squirrel monkeys, and atelines: Socioecological convergence with Old World primates. In *Primate societies*. eds. B. Smuts et al. Chicago: University of Chicago Press.

Robinson, John G., Patricia C. Wright, and Warren G. Kinzey. 1987. Monogamous cebids and their relatives: Intergroup calls and spacing. In *Primate societies*, eds. B. Smuts et al. Chicago: University of Chicago Press.

Robinson, Roy. 1984. Cat. In *Evolution of domesticated animals*, ed. I. Mason. New York: Longman.

Rodwin, Lloyd, and Bishwapriya Sanyal. 1987. Shelter, settlement, and development: An overview. In *Shelter, settlement, and development*, ed. L. Rodwin. Boston: Allen & Unwin.

Roes, Frans L., and Michel Raymond. 2003. Belief in moralizing gods. *Evolution and Human Behavior* 24:126–35.

Rogers, Alan, D. Iltis, and S. Wooding. 2004. Genetic variation at the MCIR locus and the time since loss of human body hair. *Current Anthropology* 45:105–08.

Rogers, Everett M. 1983. *Diffusion of innovations.* 3rd ed. New York: Free Press.

Rogoff, Barbara. 1990. *Apprenticeship in thinking: Cognitive development in social context.* New York: Oxford University Press.

Rogoff, Barbara. 1981. Schooling and the development of cognitive skills. In *Handbook of cross-cultural psychology*, vol. 4: *Developmental psychology*, eds. H. C. Triandis and A. Heron. Boston: Allyn & Bacon.

Rohner, Ronald P. 1975. *They love me, they love me not: A worldwide study of the effects of parental acceptance and rejection.* New Haven, CT: HRAF Press.

Rohner, Ronald P. 1976. Sex differences in aggression: Phylogenetic and enculturation perspectives. *Ethos* 4:57–72.

Rohner, Ronald P., and Preston A. Britner. 2002. Worldwide mental health correlates of parental acceptance-rejection: Review of cross-cultural research and intracultural evidence. *Cross-Cultural Research* 36:16–47.

Romaine, Suzanne. 1994. *Language in society: An introduction to sociolinguistics.* Oxford: Oxford University Press.

Romanucci-Ross, Lola, and George A. De Vos, eds. 1995. *Ethnic identity: Creation, conflict, and accommodation.* 3rd ed. Walnut Creek, CA: AltaMira Press.

Romanucci-Ross, Lola, Daniel E. Moerman, and Laurence R. Tancredi, eds. 1997. *The anthropology of medicine: From culture to method.* 3rd ed. Westport, CT: Bergin & Garvey.

Romney, A. Kimball, Carmella C. Moore, and Craig D. Rusch. 1997. Cultural universals: Measuring the semantic structure of emotion terms in English and Japanese. *Proceedings of the National Academy of Sciences, U.S.A.,* 94:5489–94.

Romney, A. Kimball, Susan C. Weller, and William H. Batchelder. 1986. Culture as consensus: A theory of culture and informant accuracy. *American Anthropologist* 88:313–38.

Roosens, Eugeen E. 1989. *Creating ethnicity: The process of ethnogenesis.* Newbury Park, CA: Sage Publications.

Roosevelt, Anna Curtenius. 1984. Population, health, and the evolution of subsistence: Conclusions from the conference. In *Paleopathology at the origins of agriculture*, eds. M. Cohen and G. Armelagos. Orlando, FL: Academic Press.

Roosevelt, Anna Curtenius. 1992. Secrets of the forest. *The Sciences* (November/December):22–28.

Roosevelt, Anna Curtenius, et al. 1996. Paleoindian cave dwellers in the Amazon: The peopling of the Americas. *Science* 272 (April 19):373–84.

Roscoe, Paul. 2002. The hunters and gatherers of New Guinea. *Current Anthropology* 43:153–62.

Rose, M. D. 1984. Food acquisition and the evolution of positional behaviour: The case of bipedalism. In *Food acquisition and processing in primates*, eds. D. Chivers, B. Wood, and A. Bilsborough. New York: Plenum.

Roseberry, William. 1988. Political economy. *Annual Review of Anthropology* 17:161–259.

Rosenberger, A. L. 1979. Cranial anatomy and implications of *Dolichocebus*, a late Oligocene ceboid primate. *Nature* 279 (May 31):416–18.

Rosenblatt, Paul C. 2009. Human rights violations. In MyAnthroLibrary, eds. C. R. Ember, M. Ember, and P. N. Peregrine. MyAnthroLibrary.com. Pearson.

Rosenblatt, Paul C., R. Patricia Walsh, and Douglas A. Jackson. 1976. *Grief and mourning in cross-cultural perspective.* New Haven, CT: HRAF Press.

Ross, Marc Howard. 1981. Socioeconomic complexity, socialization, and political differentiation: A cross-cultural study. *Ethos* 9:217–47.

Ross, Marc Howard. 1985. Internal and external conflict and violence. *Journal of Conflict Resolution* 29:547–79.

Ross, Marc Howard. 1986. Female political participation: A cross-cultural explanation. *American Anthropologist* 88:843–58.

Ross, Marc Howard. 1988. Political organization and political participation: Exit, voice, and loyalty in preindustrial societies. *Comparative Politics* 21:73–89.

Ross, Marc Howard. 2009a. Ethnocentrism and ethnic conflict. In MyAnthroLibrary, eds. C. R. Ember, M. Ember, and P. N. Peregrine. MyAnthroLibrary.com. Pearson.

Ross, Marc Howard. 2009b. Political participation. In MyAnthroLibrary, eds. C. R. Ember, M. Ember, and P. N. Peregrine. MyAnthroLibrary.com. Pearson.

Roth, Eric Abella. 2001. Demise of the sepaade tradition: Cultural and biological explanations. *American Anthropologist* 103:1014–23.

Rubel, Arthur J., and Michael R. Hass. 1996. Ethnomedicine. In *Medical anthropology*, rev. ed., eds. C. F. Sargent and T. M. Johnson. Westport, CT: Praeger.

Rubel, Arthur J., Carl O'Nell, and Rolando Collado-Ardón (with the assistance of John Krejci and Jean Krejci). 1984. *Susto: A folk illness.* Berkeley: University of California Press.

Rubel, Paula, and Abraham Rosman. 1996. Structuralism and poststructuralism. In *Encyclopedia of cultural anthropology*, eds. David Levinson and Melvin Ember, vol. 4, 1263–72. New York: Henry Holt.

Rubin, J. Z., F. J. Provenzano, and R. F. Haskett. 1974. The eye of the beholder: Parents' views on the sex of new borns. *American Journal of Orthopsychiatry* 44:512–19.

Rudan, Igor, and Harry Campbell. 2004. Five reasons why inbreeding may have considerable effect on post-reproductive human health. *Collegium Antropologicum* 28:943–50.

Rudmin, Floyd Webster. 1988. Dominance, social control, and ownership: A history and a cross-cultural study of motivations for private property. *Behavior Science Research* 22:130–60.

Ruff, Christopher B., and Alan Walker. 1993. Body size and body shape. In *The Nariokotome* Homo erectus *skeleton*, eds. A. Walker and R. Leakey. Cambridge, MA: Harvard University Press.

Rumbaugh, Duane M. 1970. Learning skills of anthropoids. In *Primate behavior*, vol. 1., ed. L. Rosenblum. New York: Academic Press.

Rummel, R. J. 2002a. "Death by Government." Chapter 1. Accessed at http://www.hawaii.edu/powerkills/DBG.CHAP1.HTM.

Rummel, R. J. 2002b. Democracies are less warlike than other regimes. Accessed at http://www.hawaii.edu/powerkills/DP95.htm.

Rummel, R. J. 2002c. Statistics of democide. Chapter 17. Accessed at http://www.hawaii.edu/powerkills/SOD.CHAP17.HTM.

Rummel, R. J. 2002d. Statistics of democide. Chapter 21. Accessed at http://www.hawaii.edu/powerkills/SOD.CHAP21.HTM.

Rummel. R. J. 2009. 20th century democide. http://www.hawaii.edu/powerkills/20th.htm (accessed September 5, 2009).

Ruskin, John. 1963. Of king's treasures. In *The genius of John Ruskin*, ed. J. D. Rosenberg. New York: Braziller.

Russell, Elbert W. 1972. Factors of human aggression. *Behavior Science Notes* 7:275–312.

Russett, Bruce (with the collaboration of William Antholis, Carol R. Ember, Melvin Ember, and Zeev Maoz). 1993. *Grasping the democratic peace: Principles for a post–cold war world*. Princeton, NJ: Princeton University Press.

Russett, Bruce, and John R. Oneal. 2001. *Triangulating peace: Democracy, interdependence, and international organizations*. New York: Norton.

Russon, Anne E. 1990. The development of peer social interaction in infant chimpanzees: Comparative social, Piagetian, and brain perspectives. In *"Language" and intelligence in monkeys and apes*, eds. S. Parker and K. Gibson. New York: Cambridge University Press.

Ruvolo, Maryellen. 1997. Genetic diversity in Hominoid primates. *Annual Review of Anthropology* 26: 515–40.

Sade, D. S. 1965. Some aspects of parent-offspring and sibling relationships in a group of rhesus monkeys, with a discussion of grooming. *American Journal of Physical Anthropology* 23:1–17.

Sagan, Carl. 1975. A cosmic calendar. *Natural History* (December): 70–73.

Sahlins, Marshall D. 1958. *Social stratification in Polynesia*. Seattle: University of Washington Press.

Sahlins, Marshall D. 1961. The segmentary lineage: An organization of predatory expansion. *American Anthropologist* 63:332–45.

Sahlins, Marshall D. 1962. *Moala: Culture and nature on a Fijian island*. Ann Arbor: University of Michigan Press.

Sahlins, Marshall D. 1963. Poor man, rich man, big-man, chief: Political types in Melanesia and Polynesia. *Comparative Studies in Society and History* 5:285–303.

Sahlins, Marshall D. 1972. *Stone Age economics*. Chicago: Aldine.

Sahlins, Marshall. 1983. Other times, other customs: The anthropology of history. *American Anthropologist* 85:517–44.

Sahlins, Marshall, and Elman Service. 1960. *Evolution and culture*. Ann Arbor: University of Michigan Press.

Salzman, Philip Carl. 1996. Pastoralism. In *Encyclopedia of cultural anthropology*, vol. 3., eds. D. Levinson and M. Ember, 899–905. New York: Henry Holt.

Salzman, Philip Carl. 1999. Is inequality universal? *Current Anthropology* 40:31–61.

Salzman, Philip Carl. 2001. *Understanding culture: An introduction to anthropological theory*, 135. Long Grove, IL: Waveland.

Salzman, Philip Carl. 2002. Pastoral nomads: Some general observations based on research in Iran. *Journal of Anthropological Research* 58:245–64.

Sanday, Peggy R. 1973. Toward a theory of the status of women. *American Anthropologist* 75:1682–700.

Sanday, Peggy R. 1974. Female status in the public domain. In *Woman, culture, and society*, eds. M. Z. Rosaldo and L. Lamphere. Stanford, CA: Stanford University Press.

Sanders, William T. 1968. Hydraulic agriculture, economic symbiosis, and the evolution of states in central Mexico. In *Anthropological archaeology in the Americas*, ed. B. Meggers. Washington, DC: Anthropological Society of Washington.

Sanders, William T., and Barbara J. Price. 1968. *Mesoamerica*. New York: Random House.

Sanders, William T., Jeffrey R. Parsons, and Robert S. Santley. 1979. *The basin of Mexico: Ecological processes in the evolution of a civilization*. New York: Academic Press.

Sanderson, Stephen K. 1995. Expanding world commercialization: The link between world-systems and civilizations. In *Civilizations and world systems: Studying world-historical change*, ed. S. K. Sanderson. Walnut Creek, CA: AltaMira Press.

Sapir, Edward. 1931. Conceptual categories in primitive languages. Paper presented at the autumn meeting of the National Academy of Sciences, New Haven, CT. Published in *Science* 74.

Sapir, Edward. 1938. Why cultural anthropology needs the psychiatrist. *Psychiatry* 1:7–12.

Sapir, Edward, and M. Swadesh. 1964. American Indian grammatical categories. In *Language in culture and society*, ed. D. Hymes. New York: Harper & Row.

Sarich, Vincent M. 1968. The origin of hominids: An immunological approach. In *Perspectives on human evolution*, vol. 1., eds. S. L. Washburn and P. C. Jay. New York: Holt, Rinehart & Winston.

Sarich, Vincent M., and Allan C. Wilson. 1966. Quantitative immunochemistry and the evolution of primate albumins: Micro-component fixations. *Science* 154 (December 23):1563–66.

Sassaman, Kenneth. 1996. Early Archaic settlement in the South Carolina coastal plain. In *The Paleoindian and early Archaic Southeast*, eds. D. G. Anderson and K. E. Sassaman, 58–83. Tuscaloosa: University of Alabama Press.

Sattler, Richard A. 1996. Remnants, renegades, and runaways: Seminole ethnogenesis reconsidered. In *Ethnogenesis in the Americas*, ed. J. D. Hill, 36–69. Iowa City: University of Iowa Press.

Savage-Rumbaugh, E. S. 1992. Language training of apes. In *The Cambridge encyclopedia of human evolution*, eds. S. Jones, R. Martin, and D. Pilbeam. New York: Cambridge University Press.

Savage-Rumbaugh, E. S. 1994. Hominid evolution: Looking to modern apes for clues. In *Hominid culture in primate perspective*, eds. D. Quiatt and J. Itani. Niwot: University Press of Colorado.

Savolainen, Peter, J. Luo, J. Lunderberg, and T. Leitner. 2002. Genetic evidence for an East Asian origin of domestic dogs. *Science* 296 (November 22):1610–14.

Scaglion, Richard. 1990. Legal adaptation in a Papua New Guinea village court. *Ethnology* 29:17–33.

Scaglion, Richard. 2009a. Abelam: Giant yams and cycles of sex, warfare and ritual. In MyAnthroLibrary, eds. C. R. Ember, M. Ember, and P. N. Peregrine. MyAnthroLibrary. com. Pearson.

Scaglion, Richard. 2009b. Law and society. In MyAnthroLibrary, eds. C. R. Ember, M. Ember, and P. N. Peregrine. MyAnthroLibrary.com. Pearson.

Scaglion, Richard, and Rose Whittingham. 1985. Female plaintiffs and sex-related disputes in rural Papua New Guinea. In *Domestic violence in Papua New Guinea*, ed. S. Toft. New Guinea; Law Reform Commission.

Scarr, Sandra, and Kathleen McCartney. 1983. How people make their own environments: A theory of genotype–environment effects. *Child Development*, 54:424–35.

Schaller, George. 1963. *The mountain gorilla: Ecology and behavior*. Chicago: University of Chicago Press.

Schaller, George. 1964. *The year of the gorilla.* Chicago: University of Chicago Press.

Schaller, George. 1972. *The Serengeti lion: A study of predator-prey relations.* Chicago: University of Chicago Press.

Schick, Kathy D., and Nicholas Toth. 1993. *Making silent stones speak.* New York: Simon & Schuster.

Schlegel, Alice. 1989. Gender issues and cross-cultural research. *Behavior Science Research* 23:265–80.

Schlegel, Alice. 1991. Status, property, and the value on virginity. *American Ethnologist* 18:719–34.

Schlegel, Alice. 2009. The status of women. In MyAnthroLibrary, eds. C. R. Ember, M. Ember, and P. N. Peregrine. MyAnthroLibrary.com. Pearson.

Schlegel, Alice, and Herbert Barry, III. 1986. The cultural consequences of female contribution to subsistence. *American Anthropologist* 88:142–50.

Schlegel, Alice, and Herbert Barry III. 1991. *Adolescence: An anthropological inquiry.* New York: Free Press.

Schlegel, Alice, and Rohn Eloul. 1987. A new coding of marriage transactions. *Behavior Science Research* 21:118–40.

Schlegel, Alice, and Rohn Eloul. 1988. Marriage transactions: Labor, property, and status. *American Anthropologist* 90:291–309.

Schneider, David M. 1961a. Introduction: The distinctive features of matrilineal descent groups. In *Matrilineal kinship*, eds. D. M. Schneider and K. Gough, 1–29. Berkeley: University of California Press.

Schneider, David M. 1961b. Truk. In *Matrilineal kinship*, eds. D. M. Schneider and K. Gough, 202–33. Berkeley: University of California Press.

Schoepf, B. 1988. Women, AIDS and economic crisis in central Africa. *Canadian Journal of African Studies* 22:625–44.

Schrauf, Robert W. 1999. Mother tongue maintenance among North American ethnic groups. *Cross-Cultural Research* 33:175–92.

Schrire, Carmel, ed. 1984a. *Past and present in hunter-gatherer studies.* Orlando, FL: Academic Press.

Schrire, Carmel. 1984b. Wild surmises on savage thoughts. In *Past and present in hunter-gatherer studies*, ed. C. Schrire. Orlando, FL: Academic Press.

Schwartz, Richard D. 1954. Social factors in the development of legal control: A case study of two Israeli settlements. *Yale Law Journal* 63 (February):471–91.

Scientific American. 2005. Crossroads for Planet Earth. *Scientific American.* Special Issue, September.

Scott, Janny, and David Leonhardt. 2005. Class in America: Shadowy lines that still divide. *New York Times*, National, May 15, pp. 1, 26.

Scribner, Sylvia, and Michael Cole. 1981. *The psychology of literacy.* Cambridge, MA: Harvard University Press.

Scudder, Thayer. 1978. Opportunities, issues and achievements in development anthropology since the mid-1960s: A personal view. In *Applied anthropology in America*, 2nd ed., eds. E. M. Eddy and W. L. Partridge. New York: Columbia University Press.

Seemanová, Eva. 1971. A study of children of incestuous matings. *Human Heredity* 21:108–28.

Segal, Edwin S. 2004. Cultural constructions of gender. In *Encyclopedia of sex and gender: Men and women in the world's cultures*, vol. 1, eds. C. Ember and M. Ember, 3–10. New York: Kluwer Academic/Plenum Publishers.

Segal, Robert A. 1987. *Joseph Campbell: An introduction.* New York: Garland.

Segall, Marshall H. 1979. *Cross-cultural psychology: Human behavior in global perspective.* Monterey, CA: Brooks/Cole.

Segall, Marshall, Pierre R. Dasen, John W. Berry, and Ype H. Poortinga. 1990. *Human behavior in global perspective: An introduction to cross-cultural psychology.* New York: Pergamon.

Sellen, Daniel W., and Daniel J. Hruschka. 2004. Extracted-food resource-defense polygyny in Native Western North American societies at contact. *Current Anthropology* 45:707–14.

Semenov, S. A. 1970. *Prehistoric technology.* Trans. M. W. Thompson. Bath, England: Adams & Dart.

Sengupta, Somini. 2002. Money from kin abroad helps Bengalis get by. *New York Times*, June 24, A3.

Senner, Wayne M. 1989. Theories and myths on the origins of writing: A historical overview. In *The origins of writing*, ed. W. M. Senner. Lincoln: University of Nebraska Press.

Serre, David, André Langaney, Mario Chech, Maria Teschler-Nicola, Maja Paunovic, Philippe Mennecier, Michael Hofreiter, Göran Possnert, and Svante Pääbo. 2004. No evidence of Neandertal mtDNA contribution to early modern humans. *PLoS Biology* 2:313–17.

Service, Elman R. 1962. *Primitive social organization: An evolutionary perspective.* New York: Random House.

Service, Elman R. 1975. *Origins of the state and civilization: The process of cultural evolution.* New York: Norton.

Service, Elman R. 1978. *Profiles in ethnology.* 3rd ed. New York: Harper & Row.

Service, Elman R. 1979. *The hunters.* 2nd ed. Upper Saddle River, NJ: Prentice Hall.

Seyfarth, Robert M., and Dorothy L. Cheney., 1982. How monkeys see the world: A review of recent research on East African vervet monkeys. In *Primate communication*, eds. C. T. Snowdon, C. H. Brown, and M. R. Petersen. New York: Cambridge University Press.

Seyfarth, Robert M., Dorothy L. Cheney, and Peter Marler. 1980. Monkey response to three different alarm calls: Evidence of predator classification and semantic communication. *Science* 210 (November 14):801–03.

Shanklin, Eugenia. 1993. *Anthropology and race.* Belmont, CA: Wadsworth.

Shankman, Paul. 1991. Culture contact, cultural ecology, and Dani warfare. *Man* 26:299–321.

Shankman, Paul. 2009. Sex, lies, and anthropologists: Margaret Mead, Derek Freeman, and Samoa. In MyAnthroLibrary, eds. C. R. Ember, M. Ember, and P. N. Peregrine. MyAnthroLibrary.com. Pearson.

Sheils, Dean. 1975. Toward a unified theory of ancestor worship: A cross-cultural study. *Social Forces* 54:427–40.

Sheils, Dean. 1980. A comparative study of human sacrifice. *Behavior Science Research* 15:245–62.

Shen, Xuefei, and Robert F. Siliciano. 2000. Preventing AIDS but not HIV-1 infection with a DNA vaccine. *Science* 290 (October 20):463–65.

Shibamoto, Janet S. 1987. The womanly woman: Japanese female speech. In *Language, gender, and sex in comparative perspective*, eds. S. U. Philips, S. Steele, and C. Tanz. Cambridge: Cambridge University Press.

Shipman, Pat. 1986. Scavenging or hunting in early hominids: Theoretical framework and tests. *American Anthropologist* 88:27–43.

Shulman, Seth. 1993. Nurturing native tongues. *Technology Review* (May/June):16.

Shuy, Roger. 1960. Sociolinguistic research at the Center for Applied Linguistics: The correlation of language and sex. *Giornata Internazionale di Sociolinguistica*. Rome: Palazzo Baldassini.

Sih, Andrew, and Katharine A. Milton. 1985. Optimal diet theory: Should the !Kung eat mongongos? *American Anthropologist* 87:395–401.

Silk, Joan. 1980. Adoption and kinship in Oceania. *American Anthropologist* 82:799–820.

Silk, Joan. 2007. Social components of fitness in primate groups. *Science* 317 (September 7):1347–51.

Silver, Harry R. 1981. Calculating risks: The socioeconomic foundations of aesthetic innovation in an Ashanti carving community. *Ethnology* 20:101–14.

Simcha Lev-Yadun, Avi Gopher, and Shahal Abbo, 2000. The cradle of agriculture. *Science* 288 (June 2):1602–03.

Simmons, Alan H., Ilse Köhler-Rollefson, Gary O. Rollefson, Rolfe Mandel, and Zeidan Kafafi. 1988. Ain Ghazal: A major Neolithic settlement in central Jordan. *Science* 240 (April 1):35–39.

Simmons, Janie, Paul Farmer, and Brooke G. Schoepf. 1996. A global perspective. In *Women, poverty, and AIDS: Sex, drugs, and structural violence*, eds. P. Farmer, M. Connors, and J. Simmons, 39–90. Monroe, ME: Common Courage Press.

Simons, Elwyn L. 1992. The primate fossil record. In *The Cambridge encyclopedia of human evolution*, eds. S. Jones, R. Martin, and D. Pilbeam. New York: Cambridge University Press.

Simons, Elwyn L. 1995. Skulls and anterior teeth of *Catopithecus* (Primates: Anthropoidea) from the Eocene shed light on anthropoidean origins. *Science* 268 (June 30):1885–88.

Simons, Elwyn L., and D. T. Rassmussen. 1996. Skull of *Catopithecus browni*, an early tertiary catarrhine. *American Journal of Physical Anthropology* 100:261–92.

Simpson, George Gaylord. 1971. *The meaning of evolution*. New York: Bantam.

Simpson, S. P., and Ruth Field. 1946. Law and the social sciences. *Virginia Law Review* 32:858.

Simpson, Scott W. 2009. *Australopithecus afarensis* and human evolution. In MyAnthroLibrary, eds. C. R. Ember, M. Ember, and P. N. Peregrine. MyAnthroLibrary.com. Pearson.

Simpson, Scott W., Jay Quade, Naomi Levin, Robert Butler, Guillaume Dupont-Nivet, Melanie Everett, Sileshi Semaw. 2008. A female *Homo erectus* pelvis from Gona, Ethiopia. *Science* 322 (November 14):1089–91.

Singer, J. David. 1980. Accounting for international war: The state of the discipline. *Annual Review of Sociology* 6:349–67.

Singer, Ronald, and John Wymer. 1982. *The Middle Stone Age at Klasies River mouth in South Africa*. Chicago: University of Chicago Press.

Sipes, Richard G. 1973. War, sports, and aggression: An Empirical test of two rival theories. *American Anthropologist* 75:64–86.

Skomal, Susan N., and Edgar C. Polomé, eds. 1987. *Proto-Indo-European: The archaeology of a linguistic problem*. Washington, DC: Washington Institute for the Study of Man.

Slayman, Andrew. 1997. A battle over old bones. *Archaeology* 50:16–23.

Slocum, Sally. 1975. Woman the gatherer: Male bias in anthropology. In *Toward an anthropology of women*, ed. Rayna Reiter. New York: Monthly Review Press.

Small, Meredith. 1997. Our babies, ourselves. *Natural History* (October):42–51.

Smay, Diana, and George Armelagos. 2000. Galileo wept: A critical assessment of the use of race in forensic anthropology. *Transforming Anthropology* 9 (2):19–29.

Smedley, Audrey. 2004. *Women creating patrilyny*. Walnut Creek, CA: AltaMira.

Smedley, Brian D., Adrienne Y. Stith, and Alan R. Nelson, eds. 2003. *Unequal treatment: confronting racial and ethnic disparities in health care*. Washington, DC: National Academy Press.

Smith, B. Holly. 1986. Dental development in *Australopithecus* and early *Homo*. *Nature* 323 (September 25):327–30.

Smith, Bruce D. 1992a. Prehistoric plant husbandry in eastern North America. In *The origins of agriculture*, eds. C. Cowan and P. Watson. Washington, DC: Smithsonian Institution Press.

Smith, Bruce D. 1992b. *Rivers of change*. Washington, DC: Smithsonian Institution Press.

Smith, Eric A. 1983. Anthropological applications of optimal foraging theory: A critical review. *Current Anthropology* 24:625–40.

Smith, Fred H. 1984. Fossil hominids from the Upper Pleistocene of central Europe and the origin of modern humans. In *The origins of modern humans*, eds. F. H. Smith and F. Spencer. New York: Alan R. Liss.

Smith, Fred H., and Frank Spencer, eds. 1984. *The origins of modern humans: A world survey of the fossil evidence*. New York: Alan R. Liss.

Smith, John Maynard. 1989. *Evolutionary genetics*. New York: Oxford University Press.

Smith, Michael G. 1966. Preindustrial stratification systems. In *Social structure and mobility in economic development*, eds. N. J. Smelser and S. M. Lipset. Chicago: Aldine.

Smith, M. W. 1974. Alfred Binet's remarkable questions: A cross-national and cross-temporal analysis of the cultural biases built into the Stanford-Binet Intelligence Scale and other Binet Tests. *Genetic Psychology Monographs* 89:307–34.

Smith, Waldemar R. 1977. *The fiesta system and economic change*. New York: Columbia University Press.

Smuts, Barbara B., Dorothy L. Cheney, Robert M. Seyfarth, Richard W. Wrangham, and Thomas T. Struhsaker, eds. 1987. *Primate societies*. Chicago: University of Chicago Press.

Snowdon, Charles T. 1999. An empiricist view of language evolution and development. In *The origins of language*, ed. B. J. King, 79–114. Santa Fe, NM: School of American Research Press.

Society for American Archaeology. 2009. FAQs for students. http://www.saa.org/ForthePublic/FAQs/ForStudents/tabid/101/Default.aspx (accessed August 26, 2009).

Soffer, Olga. 1993. Upper Paleolithic adaptations in central and eastern Europe and man-mammoth interactions. In *From Kostenki to Clovis*, eds. O. Soffer and N. D. Praslov. New York: Plenum.

Soffer, Olga, J. M. Adovasio, and D. C. Hyland. 2000. The "Venus" figurines: Textiles, basketry, gender, and status in the Upper Paleolithic. *Current Anthropology* 41:511–37.

Solis, Ruth Shady, Jonathan Haas, and Winifred Creamer. 2001. Dating Caral, a preceramic site in the Supe Valley of the central coast of Peru. *Science* 292 (April 27):723–26.

Solon, Gary. 2002. Cross-country differences in intergenerational earnings mobility. *Journal of Economic Perspectives* 16:59–66.

Sosis, Richard. 2002. Patch choice decisions among Ifaluk fishers. *American Anthropologist* 104:583–98.

Sosis, Richard, and Eric R. Bressler. 2003. Cooperation and commune longevity: A test of the costly signaling theory of religion. *Cross-Cultural Research* 37:211–39.

Southworth, Franklin C., and Chandler J. Daswani. 1974. *Foundations of linguistics.* New York: Free Press.

Spanos, Nicholas P. 1983. Ergotism and the Salem witch panic: A critical analysis and an alternative conceptualization. *Journal of the History of the Behavioral Sciences* 19:358–69.

Sparks, Corey, and R. L. Jantz. 2003. Changing times, changing faces: Franz Boas's immigrant study in modern perspective. *American Anthropologist* 105: 333–37.

Spencer, Frank. 1984. The Neandertals and their evolutionary significance: A brief historical survey. In *The origins of modern humans,* eds. F. H. Smith and F. Spencer. New York: Alan R. Liss.

Spencer, Robert F. 1968. Spouse-exchange among the North Alaskan Eskimo. In *Marriage, family and residence,* eds. P. Bohannan and J. Middleton. Garden City, NY: Natural History Press.

Sperber, Dan. 1985. *On Anthropological Knowledge: Three Essays.* Cambridge: Cambridge University Press.

Speth, John D. 2009. Were our ancestors hunters or scavengers? In MyAnthroLibrary, eds. C. R. Ember, M. Ember, and P. N. Peregrine. MyAnthroLibrary.com. Pearson.

Speth, John D., and Dave D. Davis. 1976. Seasonal variability in early hominid predation. *Science* 192 (April 30): 441–45.

Speth, John D., and Katherine A. Spielmann. 1983. Energy source, protein metabolism, and hunter-gatherer subsistence strategies. *Journal of Anthropological Archaeology* 2:1–31.

Spiro, Melford E. 1982. *Oedipus in the Trobriands.* Chicago: University of Chicago Press.

Spiro, Melford. 1993. Is the Western conception of the self "peculiar" within the context of the world cultures?" *Ethos* 21:107–53.

Spiro, Melford E., and Roy G. D'Andrade. 1958. A cross-cultural study of some supernatural beliefs. *American Anthropologist* 60:456–66.

Spring, Anita. 1995. *Agricultural development and gender issues in Malawi.* Lanham, MD: University Press of America.

Spring, Anita. 2000a. Agricultural commercialization and women farmers in Kenya. In *Women farmers and commercial ventures: Increasing food security in developing countries,* ed. Anita Spring, 317–41. Boulder, CO: Lynne Rienner Publishers.

Spring, Anita. 2000b. Commercialization and women farmers: Old paradigms and new themes. In *Women farmers and commercial ventures: Increasing food security in developing countries,* ed. Anita Spring, 1–37. Boulder, CO: Lynne Rienner Publishers.

Spring, Anita, ed., 2000c. *Women farmers and commercial ventures: Increasing food security in developing countries.* Boulder, CO, Lynne Rienner Publishers.

Stairs, Arlene. 1992. Self-image, world-image: Speculations on identity from experiences with Inuit. *Ethos* 20:116–26.

Stanford, Craig. 2009. Chimpanzee hunting behavior and human evolution. In MyAnthroLibrary, eds. C. R. Ember, M. Ember, and P. N. Peregrine. MyAnthroLibrary.com. Pearson.

Stark, Rodney. 1985. *The future of religion: Secularization, revival and cult formation.* Berkeley: University of California Press.

Stark, Rodney. 1996. *The rise of Christianity: A sociologist reconsiders history.* Princeton, NJ: Princeton University Press.

Stark, Rodney. 2001. Gods, rituals and the moral order. *Journal for the Scientific Study of Religion* 40:619–36.

Stark, Rodney, and Roger Finke. 2000. *Acts of faith: explaining the human side of religion.* Berkeley: University of California Press.

Starling, Anne, and Jay Stock. 2007. Dental indicators of health and stress in early Egyptian and Nubian agriculturalists: A difficult transition and gradual recovery. *American Journal of Physical Anthropology* 134(4):520–28.

Stedman, Hansell, B. Kozyak, A. Nelson, D. Thesier, L. Su, D. Low, C. Bridges, J. Shrager, N. Minugh-Purvis, and M. Mitchell. 2004. Myosin gene mutation correlates with anatomical changes in the human lineage. *Nature* 428 (March 25):415–18.

Steegman, A. T., Jr. 1975. Human adaptation to cold. In *Physiological anthropology,* ed. A. Damon. New York: Oxford University Press.

Stein, P., and B. Rowe. 2000. *Physical anthropology.* 7th ed. Boston: McGraw Hill.

Steiner, Christopher B. 1990. Body personal and body politic: Adornment and leadership in cross-cultural perspective. *Anthropos* 85:431–45.

Stephens, William N. 1963. *The family in cross-cultural perspective.* New York: Holt, Rinehart & Winston.

Stephens, William N. 1972. A cross-cultural study of modesty. *Behavior Science Research* 7:1–28.

Stern, Curt. 1973. *Principles of human genetics.* 3rd ed. San Francisco: W. H. Freeman.

Stevens, Phillips, Jr. 1996. Religion. In *Encyclopedia of cultural anthropology,* vol. 3, eds. D. Levinson and M. Ember, 1088–100. New York: Henry Holt.

Steward, Julian H. 1955a. The concept and method of cultural ecology. In *Theory of Culture Change,* ed. J. H. Steward. Urbana: University of Illinois Press.

Steward, Julian H. 1955b. *Theory of culture change.* Urbana: University of Illinois Press.

Steward, Julian H., and Louis C. Faron. 1959. *Native peoples of South America.* New York: McGraw-Hill.

Stewart, T. D. 1950. Deformity, trephanating, and mutilation in South American Indian skeletal remains. In *Handbook of South American Indians,* vol. 6, ed. J. A. Steward, *Physical Anthropology, Linguistics, and Cultural Geography.* Bureau of American Ethnology Bulletin 143. Washington, DC: Smithsonian Institution.

Stimpson, David, Larry Jensen, and Wayne Neff. 1992. Cross-cultural gender differences in preference for a caring morality. *Journal of Social Psychology* 132:317–22.

Stini, William A. 1971. Evolutionary implications of changing nutritional patterns in human populations. *American Anthropologist* 73:1019–30.

Stini, William A. 1975. *Ecology and human adaptation.* Dubuque, IA: Wm. C. Brown.

Stockett, Miranda K., and Pamela L. Geller. 2006. Introduction. In *Feminist anthropology: Past, present, and future*, eds. Pamela L. Geller and Miranda K. Stockett, 1–19. Philadelphia: University of Pennsylvania Press.

Stodder, James. 1995. The evolution of complexity in primitive exchange. *Journal of Comparative Economics* 20:205.

Stogdill, Ralph M. 1974. *Handbook of leadership: A survey of theory and research.* New York: Macmillan.

Stokstad, Erik. 2008. Privatization prevents collapse of fish stocks, global analysis shows. *Science* 321:1619.

Stoneking, Mark. 1997. Recent African origin of human mitochondrial DNA. In *Progress in population genetics and human evolution*, eds. P. Donnelly and S. Tavaré, 1–13. New York: Springer.

Straus, Murray A. 1991. Physical violence in American families: Incidence rates, causes, and trends. In *Abused and battered*, eds. D. D. Knudsen and J. L. Miller. New York: Aldine.

Straus, Murray A. 1995. Trends in cultural norms and rates of partner violence: An update to 1992. In *Understanding partner violence: Prevalence, causes, consequences, and solutions*, eds. S. M. Stith and M. A. Straus, 30–33. Minneapolis, MN: National Council on Family Relations. http://pubpages.unh.edu/~mas2/v56.pdf/ (accessed August 2002).

Straus, Murray A. 2001. Physical aggression in the family: Prevalence rates, links to non-family violence, and implications for primary prevention of societal violence. In *Prevention and control of aggression and the impact on its victims*, ed. M. Martinez, 181–200. New York: Kluwer Academic/Plenum.

Straus, Murray A. 2009. Prevalence and social causes of corporal punishment by parents in world perspective. Paper presented at the annual meeting of the Society for Cross-Cultural Research, Las Vegas, Nevada, February 20, 2009.

Straus, Murray A., and Carrie L. Yodanis. 1996. Corporal punishment in adolescence and physical assaults on spouses in later life: What accounts for the link? *Journal of Marriage and the Family* 58:825–41.

Straus, Murray A., and Glenda Kaufman Kantor. 1994 (July). Change in Spouse assault rates from 1975 to 1992: A comparison of three national surveys in the United States. Paper presented at the 13th World Congress of Sociology, Bielefeld, Germany. http://pubpages.unh.edu/~mas2/v55.pdf/ (accessed August 2002).

Straus, Murray A., and Glenda Kaufman Kantor. 1995. Trends in physical abuse by parents from 1975 to 1992: A comparison of three national surveys. Paper presented at the annual meeting of the American Society of Criminology, Boston, November 18. http://pubpages.unh.edu/~mas2/V57.pdf/ (accessed August 2002).

Strauss, Lawrence Guy. 1982. Comment on White. *Current Anthropology* 23:185–86.

Strauss, Lawrence Guy. 1989. On early hominid use of fire. *Current Anthropology* 30:488–91.

Stringer, Christopher B. 1985. Evolution of a species. *Geographical Magazine* 57:601–07.

Stringer, Christopher B. 2000. Neandertals. In *Encyclopedia of human evolution and prehistory*, eds. I. Tattersall, E. Delson, and J. van Couvering. New York: Garland.

Stringer, Christopher. B. 2003. Out of Ethiopia. *Nature* 423 (June 12):692–95.

Stringer, Christopher B, and Clive Gamble. 1993. *In search of the Neandertals.* New York: Thames and Hudson.

Stringer, Christopher B., J. J. Hublin, and B. Vandermeersch. 1984. The origin of anatomically modern humans in western Europe. In *The origins of modern humans*, eds. F. H. Smith and F. Spencer. New York: Alan R. Liss.

Suárez-Orozco, Marcelo. 1992. A grammar of terror: Psychocultural responses to state terrorism in dirty war and post-dirty war Argentina. In *The paths to domination, resistance, and terror*, eds. C. Nordstrom and J. Martin, 219–59. Berkeley, CA: University of California Press.

Super, Charles M., and Sara Harkness. 1997. The cultural structuring of child development. In *Handbook of cross-cultural psychology*, vol. 2, 2nd ed., eds. J. W. Berry, P. R. Dasen, and T. S. Saraswathi, 1–39. Boston: Allyn & Bacon.

Susman, Randall L., ed. 1984. *The pygmy chimpanzee: Evolutionary biology and behavior.* New York: Plenum.

Susman, Randall L. 1994. Fossil evidence for early hominid tool use. *Science* 265(September 9):1570–73.

Susman, Randall L., Jack T. Stern, Jr., and William L. Jungers. 1985. Locomotor adaptations in the Hadar hominids. In *Ancestors: The hard evidence*, ed. E. Delson, 184–92. New York: Alan R. Liss.

Sussman, Robert W. 1972. Child transport, family size, and the increase in human population size during the Neolithic. *Current Anthropology* 13:258–67.

Sussman, Robert W. 1991. Primate origins and the evolution of angiosperms. *American Journal of Primatology* 23: 209–23.

Sussman, Robert W., and W. G. Kinzey. 1984. The ecological role of the callitrichidae: A review. *American Journal of Physical Anthropology* 64:419–49.

Sussman, Robert W., and Peter H. Raven. 1978. Pollination by lemurs and marsupials: An archaic coevolutionary system. *Science* 200 (May 19):734–35.

Swanson, Guy E. 1969. *The birth of the gods: The origin of primitive beliefs.* Ann Arbor: University of Michigan Press.

Sweeney, James J. 1952. African negro culture. In *African folktales and sculpture*, ed. P. Radin. New York: Pantheon.

Swisher, C. C., III, G. H. Curtis, T. Jacob, A. G. Getty, A. Suprijo, and Widiasmoro. 1994. Age of the earliest known hominids in Java, Indonesia. *Science* 263 (February 25): 1118–21.

Szalay, Frederick S. 1968. The beginnings of primates. *Evolution* 22:32–33.

Szalay, Frederick S. 1972. Paleobiology of the earliest primates. In *The functional and evolutionary biology of the primates*, ed. R. Tuttle, 3–35. Chicago: University of Chicago Press.

Szalay, Frederick S. 1975. Hunting-scavenging protohominids: A model for hominid origins. *Man* 10:420–29.

Szalay, Frederick S., and Eric Delson. 1979. *Evolutionary history of the primates.* New York: Academic Press.

Szalay, Frederick S., I. Tattersall, and R. Decker. 1975. Phylogenetic relationships of *Plesiadipis*—Postcranial evidence. *Contributions to Primatology* 5:136–66.

Szklut, Jay, and Reed, Robert Roy. 1991. Community anonymity in anthropological research: A reassessment. In *Ethics and the profession of anthropology: Dialogue for a new era*, ed. Carolyn Fluehr-Lobban, 97–116. Philadelphia: University of Pennsylvania Press.

Tainter, Joseph. 1988. *The collapse of complex societies.* Cambridge: Cambridge University Press, 128–52.

Takahata, Naoyuki, and Yoko Satta. 1997. Evolution of the primate lineage leading to modern humans: Phylogenetic and demographic inferences from DNA sequences. *Publications of the National Academy of Sciences* 94 (April 29):4811–15.

Takezawa, Yasuko. 2006. Race should be discussed and understood across the globe. *Anthropology News* (February/March).

Talmon, Yonina. 1964. Mate selection in collective settlements. *American Sociological Review* 29:491–508.

Tamari, Tal. 1991. The development of caste systems in West Africa. *Journal of African History* 32:221–50.

Tamari, Tal. 2005. Kingship and caste in Africa: History, diffusion and evolution. In *The character of kingship*, ed. Declan Quigley, 141–70. Oxford: Berg Publishers.

Tannenbaum, Nicola. 1984. The misuse of Chayanov: 'Chayanov's Rule' and empiricist bias in anthropology. *American Anthropologist* 86:927–42.

Tannen, Deborah. 1990. *You just don't understand: Women and men in conversation*. New York: William Morrow and Company.

Tattersall, Ian. 1982. *The primates of Madagascar*. New York: Columbia University Press.

Tattersall, Ian. 1997 (April). Out of Africa again . . . and again? *Scientific American* 276:60–68.

Tattersall, Ian. 1999. *The Last Neanderthal*. Boulder, CO: Westview, 115–16.

Tattersall, Ian. 2002. Paleoanthropology and evolutionary theory. In *Physical anthropology: Original readings in method and practice*, eds. P. N. Peregrine, C. R. Ember, and M. Ember. Upper Saddle River, NJ: Prentice Hall.

Tattersall, Ian. 2009. Paleoanthropology and evolutionary theory. In MyAnthroLibrary, eds. C. R. Ember, M. Ember, and P. N. Peregrine. MyAnthroLibrary.com. Pearson.

Tattersall, Ian, and Jeffrey Schwartz. 2000. *Extinct humans*. Boulder, CO: Westview.

Tattersall, Ian, Eric Delson, and John Van Couvering, eds. 2000. *Encyclopedia of Human Evolution and Prehistory*. New York: Garland.

Taylor, Christopher C. 2005. Mutton, mud, and runny noses: A hierarchy of distaste in early Rwanda. *Social Analysis* 49:213–30.

Taylor, R. E., and M. J. Aitken, eds. 1997. *Chronometric Dating in Archaeology*. New York: Plenum.

Teleki, Geza. 1973. The omnivorous chimpanzee. *Scientific American* (January): 32–42.

Templeton, Alan R. 1993. The "Eve" hypotheses: A genetic critique and reanalysis. *American Anthropologist* 95:51–72.

Templeton, Alan R. 1996. Gene lineages and human evolution. *Science* 272 (May 31):1363.

Terborgh, John. 1983. *Five new world primates: A study in comparative ecology*. Princeton, NJ: Princeton University Press.

Textor, Robert B., comp. 1967. *A cross-cultural summary*. New Haven, CT: HRAF Press.

Thomas, David Hurst. 1986. *Refiguring anthropology: First principles of probability and statistics*. Prospect Heights, IL: Waveland.

Thomas, David Hurst. 2000. *Skull wars*. New York: Basic Books.

Thomas, Elizabeth Marshall. 1959. *The harmless people*. New York: Knopf.

Thomas, Wesley. 1993. *A traditional Navajo's perspectives on the cultural construction of gender in the Navajo world*. Paper presented at the University of Frankfurt, Germany. As referred to in Lang 1999.

Thomason, Sarah Grey, and Terrence Kaufman. 1988. *Language contact, creolization, and genetic linguistics*. Berkeley: University of California Press.

Thompson, Elizabeth Bartlett. 1966. *Africa, past and present*. Boston: Houghton Mifflin.

Thompson, Ginger. 2002. Mexico is attracting a better class of factory in its south. *New York Times*, June 29, p. A3.

Thompson, Richard H. 2009. Chinatowns: Immigrant communities in transition. In MyAnthroLibrary, eds. C. R. Ember, M. Ember, and P. N. Peregrine. MyAnthroLibrary.com. Pearson.

Thompson, Richard H. 1996. Assimilation. In *Encyclopedia of cultural anthropology*, vol. 1, 4 vols., eds. D. Levinson and M. Ember, 112–16. New York: Henry Holt.

Thompson, Stith. 1965. Star Husband Tale. In *The study of folklore*, ed. A. Dundes. Upper Saddle River, NJ: Prentice Hall.

Thompson-Handler, Nancy, Richard K. Malenky, and Noel Badrian. 1984. Sexual behavior of *Pan paniscus* under natural conditions in the Lomako Forest, Equateur, Zaire." In *The pygmy chimpanzee*, ed. R. Susman. New York: Plenum.

Thorpe, S. K. S, R. L. Holder, and R. H. Compton. Origin of human bipedalism as an adaptation for locomotion on flexible branches. *Science* 316 (June 2007):1328–31.

Thurnwald, R. C. 1934. Pigs and currency in Buin: Observations about primitive standards of value and economics. *Oceania* 5:119–41.

Tierney, Patrick. 2000. *Darkness in El Dorado*. New York: Norton.

Tishkoff, Sarah A., et al. 2009. The genetic structure and history of Africans and African Americans. *Science Express* 22 (May 2009), 324(5930):1035–44.

Tobias, Philip V. 1994. The craniocerebral interface in early hominids: Cerebral impressions, cranial thickening, paleoneurobiology, and a new hypothesis on encephalization. In *Integrative paths to the past*, eds. R. Corruccini and R. Ciochon. Upper Saddle River, NJ: Prentice Hall.

Tobin, Joseph J., David Y. H. Wu, and Dana H. Davidson. 1989. *Preschool in three cultures: Japan, China, and the United States*. New Haven, CT: Yale University Press.

Tocheri, Matthew, Caley Orr, Susan Larson, Thomas Sutikna, Jatmiko, E. Wahyu Saptomo, Rokus Awe Due, Tony Djubiantono, Michael J. Morwood, William L. Jungers. 2007. The primitive wrist of *Homo floresiensis* and its implications for hominin evolution. *Science* 317 (September 21):1743–45.

Todorov, Alexander, Anesu N. Mandisodza, Amir Goren, and Crystal C. Hall. 2005. Inference of competence from faces predict election outcomes. *Science* 308 (June 10):1623–26.

Tollefson, Kenneth D. 2009. Tlingit: Chiefs past and present. In MyAnthroLibrary, eds. C. R. Ember, M. Ember, and P. N. Peregrine. MyAnthroLibrary.com. Pearson.

Tomasello, Michael. 1990. Cultural transmission in the tool use and communicatory signaling of chimpanzees. In *"Language" and intelligence in monkeys and apes*, eds. S. Parker and K. Gibson. New York: Cambridge University Press.

Torrey, E. Fuller. 1972. *The mind game: Witchdoctors and psychiatrists*. New York: Emerson Hall.

Torry, William I. 1986. Morality and harm: Hindu peasant adjustments to famines. *Social Science Information* 25:125–60.

Traphagan, John W., and L. Keith Brown. 2002. Fast food and intergenerational commensality in Japan: New styles and old patterns. *Ethnology* 41:119–34.

Travis, John. 2000. Human genome work reaches milestone. *Science News* (July 1): 4–5.

Treiman, Donald J., and Harry B. G. Ganzeboom. 1990. Cross-national comparative status-attainment research. *Research in Social Stratification and Mobility* 9:117.

Trevor-Roper, H. R. 1971. The European witch-craze of the sixteenth and seventeenth centuries. In *Reader in comparative religion*, 3rd ed., eds. W. A. Lessa and E. Z. Vogt. New York: Harper & Row.

Triandis, Harry C. 1995. *Individualism and collectivism*. Boulder, CO: Westview.

Trigger, Bruce G. 1989. *A history of archaeological thought.* Cambridge: Cambridge University Press.

Trinkaus, Erik. 1984. Western Asia. In *The origins of modern humans*, eds. F. H. Smith and F. Spencer. New York: Alan R. Liss.

Trinkaus, Erik. 1985. Pathology and the posture of the La Chapelle-aux-Saints Neandertal. *American Journal of Physical Anthropology* 67:19–41.

Trinkaus, Erik. 1986. The Neandertals and modern human origins. *Annual Review of Anthropology* 15:193–218.

Trinkaus, Erik. 1987a. Bodies, brawn, brains and noses: Human ancestors and human predation. In *The evolution of human hunting*, eds. M. Nitecki and D. Nitecki. New York: Plenum.

Trinkaus, Erik. 1987b. "The Neandertal Face: Evolutionary and Functional Perspectives on a Recent Hominid Face." *Journal of Human Evolution*, 16: 429–43.

Trinkaus, Erik, and William W. Howells. 1979. The Neanderthals. *Scientific American* (December):118–33.

Trinkaus, Erik, and Pat Shipman. 1993a. *The Neandertals: Changing the image of mankind.* New York: Knopf.

Trinkaus, Erik, and Pat Shipman. 1993b. Neandertals: Images of ourselves. *Evolutionary Anthropology* 1:194–201.

Trompf, G. W., ed. 1990. *Cargo cults and millenarian movements: Transoceanic comparisons of new religious movements.* Berlin: Mouton de Gruyter.

Trouillot, Michel-Rolph. 2001. The anthropology of the state in the age of globalization: Close encounters of the deceptive kind. *Current Anthropology* 42:125–38.

Trudgill, Peter. 1983. *Sociolinguistics: An introduction to language and society.* Rev. ed. New York: Penguin.

Turner, B. L. 1970. Population density in the classic Maya lowlands: New evidence for old approaches. *Geographical Review* 66 (January):72–82.

Turner, Christy G., II. 1987. Telltale teeth. *Natural History* (January):6–9.

Turner, Christy G., II. 1989. Teeth and prehistory in Asia. *Scientific American* (February):88–95.

Turner, C. G. 2005. A synoptic history of physical anthropological studies on the peopling of Alaska and the Americas. *Alaska Journal of Anthropology* 3:157–70.

Turner, Terence. 1993. The role of indigenous peoples in the environmental crisis: The example of the Kayapo of the Brazilian Amazon. *Perspectives in Biology and Medicine* 36(3):526–45.

Turner, Terence. 1995. An indigenous people's struggle for socially equitable and ecologically sustainable production: The Kayapo revolt against extractivism. *Journal of Latin American Anthropology* 1:98–121.

Tuttle, Russell H. 1986. *Apes of the world: Their social behavior, communication, mentality, and ecology.* Park Ridge, NJ: Noyes.

Tylor, Edward B. 1971/1958. *Primitive culture.* New York: Harper Torchbooks.

Tylor, Edward B. 1979. Animism. In *Reader in comparative religion*, 4th ed., eds. W. A. Lessa and E. Z. Vogt. New York: Harper & Row.

Uberoi, J. P. Singh. 1962. *The politics of the Kula Ring: An analysis of the findings of Bronislaw Malinowski.* Manchester, UK: University of Manchester Press.

Ucko, Peter J., and Andrée Rosenfeld. 1967. *Paleolithic cave art.* New York: McGraw-Hill.

Udy, Stanley H., Jr. 1970. *Work in traditional and modern society.* Upper Saddle River, NJ: Prentice Hall.

UNAIDS. 2007 (December). *AIDS epidemic update.* Retrieved from http://data.unaids.org/pub/EPISlides/2007/2007_epiupdate_en.pdf

UN News Centre. 2005. Norway at top, Niger at bottom of UN's 2005 human development index. http://www.un.org/apps/news/story.asp?NewsID=15707&Cr=human&Cr1=development (accessed June, 20, 2009).

UN Works. n.d. Retrieved from http://www.un.org/works/goingon/mongolia/lessonplan_homelessness.html.

Underhill, Ralph. 1975. Economic and political antecedents of monotheism: A cross-cultural study. *American Journal of Sociology* 80:841–61.

Underhill, Ruth M. 1938. *Social organization of the Papago Indians.* New York: Columbia University Press.

United Nation's Development Programme. 2007. *Human Development Report 2007/2008: Fighting climate change: Human solidarity in a divided world.* http://hdr.undp.org/en/media/HDR_20072008_EN_Complete.pdf (accessed June, 20, 2009).

United Nations Human Settlements Programme. 2003. The challenge of slums: global report on human settlements, 2003. Nairobi, Kenya.

Unnithan, N. Prabha. 2009. Nayars: Tradition and change in marriage and family. In MyAnthroLibrary, eds. C. R. Ember, M. Ember, and P. N. Peregrine. MyAnthroLibrary.com. Pearson.

U.S. Census Bureau. 2002. The big payoff: Educational entertainment and synthetic estimates of work-life earnings. *Statistical abstract of the United States: 1993.* 113th ed. Washington, DC: U.S. Government Printing Office.

U.S. Department of Justice. 1988 (November). Prevalence, incidence, and consequences of violence against women: Findings from the National Violence against Women Survey. Washington, DC.

U.S. Department of Justice. 1994 (April). Violent crime. NCJ-147486. Washington, DC.

U.S. Department of Justice. 2000. Children as victims. *Juvenile Justice Bulletin 1999.* National Report Series. Washington, DC.

U.S. Department of Justice. n.d. Bureau of Justice statistics homicide trends in the U.S: Long-term trends and patterns. http://www.ojp.gov/bjs/homicide/hmrt.htm (accessed Sept. 5, 2009).

U.S. Environmental Protection Agency. 2009. http://epa.gov/oecaagct/ag101/demographics.html (accessed October 15, 2009).

Vadez, Vincent, Victoria Reyes-Garcia, Tomás Huanca, William R. Leonard. 2008. Cash cropping, farm technologies, and deforestation: What are the connections? A model with empirical data from the Bolivian Amazon. *Human Organization* 67:384–96.

Valente, Thomas W. 1995. *Network models of the diffusion of innovations*. Cresskill, NJ: Hampton Press.

Valladas, H., J. L. Joron, G. Valladas, O. Bar-Yosef, and B. Vandermeersch. 1988. Thermoluminescence dating of Mousterian "Proto-Cro-Magnon" remains from Israel and the origin of modern man. *Nature* 337 (February 18):614–16.

Van der Leeuw, Sander. 1999. *The Archaeomedes Project: Understanding the natural and anthropogenic causes of desertification and land degradation*. Luxembourg: European Union.

Van der Leeuw, Sander, François Favory, and Jean Jacques Girardot. 2002. The archaeological study of environmental degradation: An example from southeastern France. In *The archaeology of global change*, eds. C. Redman, S. R. James, P. Fish, and J. D. Rogers, 112–29. Washington, DC: Smithsonian.

Van der Merwe, N. J. 1992. Reconstructing prehistoric diet. In *The Cambridge encyclopedia of human evolution*, eds. S. Jones, R. Martin, and D. Pilbeam. New York: Cambridge University Press.

Van Hear, Nicholas. 2004. Refugee diasporas or refugees in diaspora. In *Encyclopedia of diasporas: Immigrant and refugee cultures around the world*, vol. 1, eds. M. Ember, C. R. Ember, and I. Skoggard, 580–89. New York: Kluwer Academic/Plenum.

Van Lawick-Goodall, Jane. 1971. *In the shadow of man*. Boston: Houghton Mifflin.

Van Schaik, C. P. M. Ancrenaz, G. Borgen, B. Galdikas, C. D. Knott, I. Singleton, A. Suzuki, S. S. Utami, and M. Merrill. 2003. Orangutan cultures and the evolution of material culture. *Science* 299 (January 3):102–05.

Van Willigen, John. 2002. *Applied anthropology: An introduction*. 3rd ed. Westport, CT: Bergin and Garvey.

Vayda, Andrew P., and Roy A. Rappaport. 1968. Ecology: Cultural and noncultural." In *Introduction to cultural anthropology*, ed. J. H. Clifton. Boston: Houghton Mifflin.

Vayda, Andrew P., Anthony Leeds, and David B. Smith. 1962. The place of pigs in Melanesian subsistence. In *Symposium*, ed. V. E. Garfield. Seattle: University of Washington Press.

Vekua, Abesalom, David Lordkipanidze, G. Philip Rightmire, Jordi Agusti, Reid Ferring, Givi Maisuradze, Alexander Mouskhelishvili, Medea Nioradze, Marcia Ponce de Leon, Martha Tappen, Merab Tvalchrelidze, and Christoph Zollikofer. 2002. A new skull of early *Homo* from Dmanisi, Georgia. *Science* 297 (July 5):85–89.

Vigil, James Diego. 1988. Group processes and street identity: Adolescent Chicano gang members. *Ethos* 16:421–45.

Vigil, James Diego. 2009. Mexican Americans: Growing up on the streets of Los Angeles. In MyAnthroLibrary, eds. C. R. Ember, M. Ember, and P. N. Peregrine. MyAnthroLibrary. com. Pearson.

Vigilant, Linda, Mark Stoneking, Henry Harpending, Kristen Hawkes, and Allan C. Wilson. 1991. African populations and the evolution of human mitochrondrial DNA. *Science* 253 (September 27):1503–07.

Vincent, Joan. 1978. Political anthropology: Manipulative strategies. *Annual Review of Anthropology* 7:175–94.

Visaberghi, Elisabetta, and Dorothy Munkenbeck Fragaszy. 1990. Do monkeys ape? In *"Language" and intelligence in monkeys and apes*, eds. S. Parker and K. Gibson. New York: Cambridge University Press.

Vogel, Joseph O. 2009. De-mystifying the past: Great Zimbabwe, King Solomon's mines, and other tales of Old Africa. In MyAnthroLibrary, eds. C. R. Ember, M. Ember, and P. N. Peregrine. MyAnthroLibrary.com. Pearson.

Vohs, Kathleen D., Nicole L. Mead, and Miranda R. Goode. 2006. The psychological consequences of money. *Science* 314 (November 17):1154–56.

von Frisch, Karl. 1962. Dialects in the language of the bees. *Scientific American* (August):78–87.

Vrba, Elizabeth S. 1995. On the connection between paleoclimate and evolution. In *Paleoclimate and evolution*, eds. E. S. Vrba, G. H. Denton, T. C. Partridge, and L. H. Burckle, 24–45. New Haven, CT: Yale University Press.

Wadley, Reed L. 2003. Lethal treachery and the imbalance of power in warfare and feuding. *Journal of Anthropological Research* 59:531–54.

Wagley, Charles. 1974. Cultural influences on population: A comparison of two Tupi tribes. In *Native South Americans*, ed. P. J. Lyon. Boston: Little, Brown.

Wald, Matthew L. 2000. Hybrid cars show up in M.I.T.'s crystal ball. *New York Times* November 3, F1.

Waldbaum, Jane C. 2005. Helping hand for China. *Archaeology* 58:6.

Waldman, Amy. 2005. Sri Lankan maids' high price for foreign jobs. *The New York Times*, May 8, pp. 1, 20.

Walker, Alan, and R. Leakey. 1988. The evolution of *Australopithecus boisei*. In *Evolutionary history of the "robust" australopithecines*, ed. F. Grine, 247–58. New York: Aldine.

Wallace, Alfred Russell. 1970/1858. On the tendency of varieties to depart indefinitely from the original type. (Originally published in 1858.) In *Evolution of Man*, ed. L. B. Young. New York: Oxford University Press.

Wallace, Anthony. 1966. *Religion: An anthropological view*. New York: Random House.

Wallace, Anthony. 1972. Mental illness, biology and culture. In *Psychological anthropology*, 2nd ed., ed. F. L. K. Hsu. Cambridge, MA: Schenkman.

Wallerstein, Immanuel. 1974. *The modern world-system*. New York: Academic Press.

Wanner, Eric, and Lila R. Gleitman, eds. 1982. *Language acquisition: The state of the art*. Cambridge: Cambridge University Press.

Ward, Peter M. 1982. Introduction and purpose. In *Self-help housing*, ed. P. M. Ward. London: Mansell.

Ward, Steve. 1997. The taxonomy and phylogenetic relationships of *Sivapithecus* revisited. In *Function, phylogeny and fossils: Miocene hominoid evolution and adaptation*, eds. D. R. Begun, C. V. Ward, and M. D. Rose, 269–90. New York: Plenum.

Ward, Steve, B. Brown, A. Hill, J. Kelley, and W. Downs. 1999. *Equatorius*: A new hominoid genus from the middle Miocene of Kenya. *Science* 285 (August 27):1382–86.

Wardhaugh, Ronald. 2002. *An introduction to sociolinguistics*. 4th ed. Oxford: Blackwell.

Warner, John Anson. 1986. The individual in Native American art: A sociological view. In *The arts of the North American Indian*, ed. E. L. Wade. New York: Hudson Hills Press.

Warner, W. Lloyd, and Paul S. Lunt. 1941. *The social life of a modern community*. New Haven, CT: Yale University Press.

Warren, Dennis M. 1989. Utilizing indigenous healers in national health delivery systems: The Ghanaian experiment.

In *Making our research useful,* eds. J. van Willigen, B. Rylko-Bauer, and A. McElroy. Boulder, CO: Westview.

Warry, Wayne. 1986. Kafaina: Female wealth and power in Chuave, Papua New Guinea. *Oceania* 57:4–21.

Warry, Wayne. 1990. Doing unto others: Applied anthropology, collaborative research and native self-determination. *Culture* 10:61–62.

Washburn, Sherwood. 1960. Tools and human evolution. *Scientific American* (September):62–75.

Watson, James L. 2004. Presidential address: Virtual kinship, real estate, and diaspora formation—the Man lineage revisited. *Journal of Asian Studies* 63:893–910.

Weaver, Muriel Porter. 1993. *The Aztecs, Maya, and their predecessors.* 3rd ed. San Diego: Academic Press.

Webb, Karen E. 1977. An evolutionary aspect of social structure and a verb "have." *American Anthropologist* 79:42–49.

Weber, Max. 1947. *The theory of social and economic organization.* Trans. A. M. Henderson and Talcott Parsons. New York: Oxford University Press.

Weiner, Annette B. 1976. *Women of value, men of renown: New perspectives in Trobriand exchange.* Austin: University of Texas Press.

Weiner, Annette B. 1987. *The Trobrianders of Papua New Guinea.* New York: Holt, Rinehart and Winston.

Weiner, J. S. 1954. Nose shape and climate. *Journal of Physical Anthropology* 4:615–18.

Weiner, Jonathan. 1994. *Beak of the finch.* New York: Vintage.

Weiner, Steve, Q. Xi, P. Goldberg, J. Liu, and O. Bar-Yousef. 1998. Evidence for the use of fire at Zhoukoudian, China. *Science,* 281 (July 10):251–53.

Weinreich, Uriel. 1968. *Languages in contact.* The Hague: Mouton.

Weisner, Thomas S. 2004. The American dependency conflict. *Ethos* 29:271–95.

Weisner, Thomas S., and Ronald Gallimore. 1977. My brother's keeper: Child and sibling caretaking. *Current Anthropology* 18:169–90.

Weisner, Thomas S., Mary Bausano, and Madeleine Kornfein. 1983. Putting family ideals into practice: Pronaturalism in conventional and nonconventional California families. *Ethos* 11:278–304.

Weiss, Harvey, and Raymond S. Bradley. 2001. What drives societal collapse? *Science* 291 (January 26):609–10.

Weiss, Harvey, M. A. Courty, W. Wetterstrom, F. Guichard, L. Senior, R. Meadow, and A. Curnow. 1993. The genesis and collapse of third millennium north Mesopotamian civilization. *Science* 261 (August 20):995–1004.

Weller, Susan C. 2009. The research process. In MyAnthroLibrary, eds. C. R. Ember, M. Ember, and P. N. Peregrine. MyAnthroLibrary.com. Pearson.

Wenke, Robert J. 1984. *Patterns in prehistory: Humankind's first three million years.* 2nd ed. New York: Oxford University Press.

Wenke, Robert. 1990. *Patterns in prehistory: Humankind's first three million years.* 3rd ed. New York: Oxford University Press.

Werner, Dennis. 1975. *On the societal acceptance or rejection of male homosexuality.* Master's thesis, Hunter College of the City University of New York.

Werner, Dennis. 1978. Trekking in the Amazon forest. *Natural History* (November):42–54.

Werner, Dennis. 1979. A cross-cultural perspective on theory and research on male homosexuality. *Journal of Homosexuality* 4:345–62.

Werner, Dennis. 1982. Chiefs and presidents: A comparison of leadership traits in the United States and among the Mekranoti-Kayapo of central Brazil. *Ethos* 10:136–48.

Werner, Dennis. 1984. Child care and influence among the Mekranoti of central Brazil. *Sex Roles* 10:395–404.

Westermarck, Edward. 1894. *The history of human marriage.* London: Macmillan.

Weston, Eleanor, and Adrian Lister. 2009. Insular dwarfism in hippos and a model for brain size reduction in *Homo floresiensis. Nature* 459 (May 7):85–88.

Wheat, Joe B. 1967. A Paleo-Indian bison kill. *Scientific American* (January):44–52.

Wheatley, Paul. 1971. *The pivot of the four quarters.* Chicago: Aldine.

Wheeler, Peter. 1984. The evolution of bipedality and loss of functional body hair in hominids. *Journal of Human Evolution* 13:91–98.

Wheeler, Peter. 1991. The influence of bipedalism in the energy and water budgets of early hominids. *Journal of Human Evolution* 23:379–88.

Whitaker, Ian. 1955. *Social relations in a nomadic Lappish community.* Oslo: Utgitt av Norsk Folksmuseum.

White, Benjamin. 1973. Demand for labor and population growth in colonial Java. *Human Ecology* 1, no. 3 (March): 217–36.

White, Douglas R. 1988. Rethinking polygyny: Co-wives, codes, and cultural systems. *Current Anthropology* 29:529–88.

White, Douglas R., and Michael L. Burton. 1988. Causes of polygyny: Ecology, economy, kinship, and warfare. *American Anthropologist* 90:871–87.

White, Douglas R., Michael L. Burton, and Lilyan A. Brudner. 1977. Entailment theory and method: A cross-cultural analysis of the sexual division of labor. *Behavior Science Research* 12:1–24.

White, Frances. J. 1996. *Pan paniscus* 1973 to 1996: Twenty-three years of field research. *Evolutionary Anthropology* 5: 11–17.

White, Leslie A. 1939. A problem in kinship terminology. *American Anthropologist* 41:569–70.

White, Leslie A. 1949. *The science of culture: A study of man and civilization.* New York: Farrar, Straus & Cudahy.

White, Leslie A. 1968. The expansion of the scope of science. In *Readings in anthropology,* ed. M. H. Fried, vol. 1, 2nd ed. New York: Thomas Y. Crowell.

White, Randall. 1982. Rethinking the Middle/Upper Paleolithic transition. *Current Anthropology* 23:169–75.

White, Tim D. 2003. Early hominids—Diversity or distortion? *Science* 299 (March 28):1994–97.

White, Tim D., and Pieter Arend Folkens. 2000. *Human osteology.* 2nd ed. San Diego: Academic Press.

White, Tim D., Donald C. Johanson, and William H. Kimbel. 1981. *Australopithecus africanus:* Its phyletic position reconsidered. *South African Journal of Science* 77:445–70.

White, Timothy D., G. Suwa, and B. Asfaw. 1994. *Australopithecus ramidus,* a new species of early hominid from Aramis, Ethiopia. *Nature* 371 (September 22): 306–33.

White, Timothy D., G. Suwa, and B. Asfaw. 1995. Corrigendum: *Australopithecus ramidus,* a new species of early hominid from Aramis, Ethiopia. *Nature* 375 (May 4):88

Whitehead, Barbara Defoe, and David Popenoe. 2005. *The state of our unions: Marriage and family: What does the*

Scandinavian experience tell us? National Marriage Project: Rutgers University.

Whiten, A., J. Goodall, W. McGrew, T. Nishida, V. Reynolds, Y. Yugiyama, Yugiyama, C. Yugiyama, R. Wrangham, and C. Boesch. 1999. Cultures in chimpanzees. *Nature* 399 (June 17): 682–85.

Whiting, Beatrice Blyth. 1950. *Paiute sorcery*. Viking Fund Publications in Anthropology No. 15. New York: Wenner-Gren Foundation.

Whiting, Beatrice B. 1965. Sex identity conflict and physical violence. *American Anthropologist* 67:123–40.

Whiting, Beatrice B., and Carolyn Pope Edwards. 1973. A cross-cultural analysis of sex differences in the behavior of children aged three through eleven. *Journal of Social Psychology* 91:171–88.

Whiting, Beatrice Blyth, and Carolyn Pope Edwards (in collaboration with Carol R. Ember, Gerald M. Erchak, Sara Harkness, Robert L. Munroe, Ruth H. Munroe, Sara B. Nerlove, Susan Seymour, Charles M. Super, Thomas S. Weisner, and Martha Wenger). 1988. *Children of different worlds: The formation of social behavior*. Cambridge, MA: Harvard University Press.

Whiting, Beatrice B., and John W. M. Whiting (in collaboration with Richard Longabaugh). 1975. *Children of six cultures: A psycho-cultural analysis*. Cambridge, MA: Harvard University Press.

Whiting, John W. M. 1941. *Becoming a Kwoma*. New Haven, CT: Yale University Press.

Whiting, John W. M. 1964. Effects of climate on certain cultural practices. In *Explorations in cultural anthropology*, ed. W. Goodenough. New York: McGraw-Hill.

Whiting, John W. M., and Irvin L. Child. 1953. *Child training and personality: A cross-cultural study*. New Haven, CT: Yale University Press.

Whittaker, John C. 1994. *Flintknapping: Making and understanding stone tools*. Austin: University of Texas Press.

Whyte, Martin K. 1978a. Cross-cultural codes dealing with the relative status of women. *Ethnology* 17:211–37.

Whyte, Martin K. 1978b. *The status of women in preindustrial societies*. Princeton, NJ: Princeton University Press.

Wiberg, Hakan. 1983. Self-determination as an international issue. In *Nationalism and self-determination in the Horn of Africa*, ed. I. M. Lewis. London: Ithaca Press.

Wilden, Anthony. 1987. *The rules are no game: The strategy of communication*. London: Routledge and Kegan Paul.

Wikan, Unni. 1982. *Beyond the veil in Arabia*. Baltimore: The Johns Hopkins University Press.

Wilford, John Noble. 1995. The transforming leap, from 4 legs to 2. *New York Times* September 5, p. C1ff.

Wilford, John Noble. 1997. Ancient German spears tell of mighty hunters of Stone Age. *New York Times*, March 4, p. C6.

Wilkinson, Robert L. 1995. Yellow fever: Ecology, epidemiology, and role in the collapse of the classic lowland Maya civilization. *Medical Anthropology* 16:269–94.

Williams, George C. 1992. *Natural selection: Domains, levels, and challenges*. New York: Oxford University Press.

Williams, Melvin D. 2009. Racism: The production, reproduction, and obsolescence of social inferiority. In MyAnthroLibrary, eds. C. R. Ember, M. Ember, and P. N. Peregrine. MyAnthroLibrary.com. Pearson.

Williams, Walter L. 1992. *The spirit and the flesh*. Boston: Beacon Press.

Wilmsen, Edwin N., ed. 1989. *We are here: Politics of Aboriginal land tenure*. Berkeley: University of California Press.

Wilson, Edward O. 1975. *Sociobiology: The new synthesis*. Cambridge, MA: Belknap Press of Harvard University Press.

Wilson, Monica. 1963/1951. *Good company: A study of Nyakyusa age villages*. Boston: Beacon Press.

Winkelman, Michael 1986a. Magico-religious practitioner types and socioeconomic conditions. *Behavior Science Research* 20:17–46.

Winkelman, Michael. 1986b. Trance states: A theoretical model and cross-cultural analysis. *Ethos* 14:174–203.

Winkelman, Michael, and John R. Baker. 2010. *Supernatural as natural: A biocultural approach to religion*. Upper Saddle River, NJ: Pearson Prentice Hall.

Winkleman, Michael, and Philip M. Peck, eds. 2004. *Divination and healing: Potent vision*. Tucson: University of Arizona Press.

Winterbottom, Robert. 1995. The tropical forestry plan: Is it working? In *Global ecosystems: Creating options through anthropological perspectives*, ed. P. J. Puntenney. *NAPA Bulletin* 15.

Winterhalder, Bruce. 1990. Open field, common pot: Harvest variability and risk avoidance in agricultural and foraging societies. In *Risk and uncertainty in tribal and peasant economies*, ed. E. Cashdan. Boulder, CO: Westview.

Witkin, Herman A. 1967. A cognitive style approach to cross-cultural research. *International Journal of Psychology* 2:233–50.

Witkowski, Stanley R. 1975. *Polygyny, age of marriage, and female status*. Paper presented at the annual meeting of the American Anthropological Association, San Francisco.

Witkowski, Stanley R., and Cecil H. Brown. 1978. Lexical universals. *Annual Review of Anthropology* 7:427–51.

Witkowski, Stanley R., and Harold W. Burris. 1981. Societal complexity and lexical growth. *Behavior Science Research* 16:143–59.

Wittfogel, Karl. 1957. *Oriental despotism: A comparative study of total power*. New Haven, CT: Yale University Press.

Wolf, Arthur. 1968. Adopt a daughter-in-law, marry a sister: A Chinese solution to the problem of the incest taboo. *American Anthropologist* 70:864–74.

Wolf, Arthur P., and Chieh-Shan Huang. 1980. *Marriage and adoption in China, 1845–1945*. Stanford, CA: Stanford University Press.

Wolf, Eric. 1955. Types of Latin American peasantry: A preliminary discussion. *American Anthropologist* 57:452–71.

Wolf, Eric R. 1956. San José: Subcultures of a "traditional" coffee municipality. In *The people of Puerto Rico*, J. H. Steward et al. Urbana: University of Illinois Press.

Wolf, Eric. 1966. *Peasants*. Upper Saddle River, NJ: Prentice Hall.

Wolf, Eric. 1984. Culture: Panacea or problem. *American Antiquity* 49:393–400.

Wolf, Naomi. 1991. *The beauty myth: How images of beauty are used against women*. New York: Morrow.

Wolff, Ronald G. 1991. *Functional chordate anatomy*. Lexington, MA: D. C. Heath.

Wolpoff, Milford H. 1971. Competitive exclusion among lower Pleistocene hominids: The single species hypothesis. *Man* 6:601–13.

Wolpoff, Milford H. 1983. *Ramapithecus* and human origins: An anthropologist's perspective of changing interpretations.

In *New interpretations of ape and human ancestry*, eds. R. Ciochon and R. Corruccini. New York: Plenum.

Wolpoff, Milford H. 1999. *Paleoanthropology*. 2nd ed. Boston: McGraw-Hill, 501–04, 727–31.

Wolpoff, Milford H., and Abel Nkini. 1985. Early and Early Middle Pleistocene hominids from Asia and Africa. In *Ancestors*, ed. E. Delson. New York: Alan R. Liss.

Wolpoff, Milford H. A. G. Thorne, J. Jelinek, and Zhang Yinyun. 1993. The case for sinking *Homo erectus*: 100 years of *Pithecanthropus* is enough! In *100 years of* Pithecanthropus: *The* Homo Erectus *problem*, ed. J. L. Franzen. *Courier Forshungsinstitut Senckenberg* 171:341–61.

Women in science '93: Gender and the culture of science. 1993. *Science* 260 (April 16):383–430.

Wong, Kate. 2003. An ancestor to call our own. *Scientific American* (January):54–63.

Wong, Kate, 2005. The littlest human. *Scientific American* (February): 56–65.

Wood, Bernard A. 1992. Evolution of australopithecines. In *The Cambridge encyclopedia of human evolution*, eds. S. Jones, R. Martin, and D. Pilbeam. New York: Cambridge University Press.

Wood, Bernard A. 1994. Hominid paleobiology: Recent achievements and challenges. In *Integrative paths to the past*, eds. R. Corruccini and R. Ciochon. Upper Saddle River, NJ: Prentice Hall.

Wood, Gordon S. 1992. *The radicalism of the American Revolution*. New York: Knopf.

Wood, James W., George R. Milner, Henry C. Harpending, and Kenneth M. Weiss. 1992. The osteological paradox: Problems of inferring prehistoric health from skeletal samples. *Current Anthropology* 33:343–70.

Wood, Wendy, and Alice H. Eagly. 2002. A cross-cultural analysis of the behavior of women and men: Implications for the origins of sex differences. *Psychological Bulletin* 128:699–727.

Woodburn, James. 1968. An introduction to Hadza ecology. In *Man the hunter*, eds. R. B. Lee and I. DeVore. Chicago: Aldine.

World Bank. 2004. *World development indicators 2004*. Washington, DC: World Bank Publications.

Worsley, Peter. 1957. *The trumpet shall sound: A study of "cargo" cults in Melanesia*. London: MacGibbon & Kee,

Wrangham, Richard W. 1980. An ecological model of female-bonded primate groups. *Behaviour* 75:262–300.

Wright, Gary A. 1971. Origins of food production in Southwestern Asia: A survey of ideas. *Current Anthropology* 12:447–78.

Wright, George O. 1954. Projection and displacement: A cross-cultural study of folktale aggression. *Journal of Abnormal and Social Psychology* 49:523–28.

Wright, Henry T. 1986. The evolution of civilizations. In *American archaeology past and future*, ed. D. Meltzer, D. Fowler, and J. Sabloff. Washington, DC: Smithsonian Institution Press.

Wright, Henry T., and Gregory A. Johnson. 1975. Population, exchange, and early state formation in southwestern Iran. *American Anthropologist* 77:267–77.

Wulff, Robert, and Shirley Fiste. 1987. The domestication of wood in Haiti. In R. M. Wulff and S. J. Fiste, *Anthropological praxis*. Boulder, CO: Westview.

Yamei, Hou, R. Potts, Y. Baoyin, et al. 2000. Mid-Pleistocene Acheulean-like stone technology of the Bose Basin, South China. *Science* 287 (March 3):1622–26.

Yan, Yunxiang. 2006. Girl power: Young women and the waning of patriarchy in rural North China. *Ethnology* 45:105–23.

Yergin, Daniel. 2002. Giving aid to world trade. *New York Times*, June 27, p. A29.

Yinger, J. Milton. 1994. *Ethnicity: Source of strength? Source of conflict?* Albany: State University Press.

Young, Frank W. 1970. A fifth analysis of the Star Husband Tale. *Ethnology* 9:389–413.

Young, T. Cuyler, Jr. 1972. Population densities and early Mesopotamian urbanism. In *Man, settlement and urbanism*, eds. P. J. Ucko, R. Tringham, and G. W. Dimbley. Cambridge, MA: Scherkmn.

Younger, Stephen M. 2008. Conditions and mechanisms for peace in precontact Polynesia. *Current Anthropology* 49:927–34.

Zebrowitz, Leslie A., and Joann M. Montepare. 2005. Appearance *does* matter. *Science* 308 (June 10):1565–66.

Zechenter, Elizabeth M. 1997. In the name of culture: Cultural relativism and the abuse of the individual. *Journal of Anthropological Research* 53:319–47.

Zeder, Melinda A. 1991. *Feeding cities: Specialized animal economy in the ancient Near East*. Washington, DC: Smithsonian Institution Press.

Zeder, Melinda A. 1994. After the revolution: Post-Neolithic subsistence in northern Mesopotamia." *American Anthropologist* 96:97–126.

Zihlman, Adrienne L. 1992. The emergence of human locomotion: The evolutionary background and environmental context. In *Topics in primatology*, vol. 1, eds. T. Nishida, et al.

Zimmer, Carl. 1999. Kenyan skeleton shakes ape family tree. *Science* 285 (August 27):1335–37.

Zimmer, Carl. 2004. Faster than a hyena? Running may make humans special. *Science* 306 (November 19):1283.

Zohary, Daniel. 1969. The progenitors of wheat and barley in relation to domestication and agriculture dispersal in the Old World. In *The domestication and exploitation of plants and animals*, eds. P. J. Ucko and G. W. Dimbleby. Chicago: Aldine.

ndex